REEDS

PRACTICAL Boat Ow

BRITAIN'S BIGGEST SELLING YACHTING MAGAZIN

SMALL C
ALMAN
2011

GW00725440

EDITORS

Andy Du Port & Rob Buttress

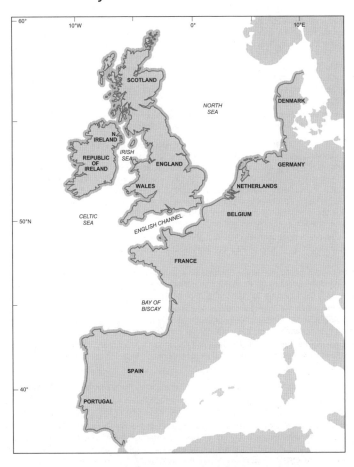

THE UNITED KINGDOM AND IRELAND
PLUS DENMARK TO GIBRALTAR

PLEASE SEE IMPORTANT SAFETY NOTE ON PAGE 2

2011

Editors: Andy Du Port & Rob Buttress

The Editors would like to thank the many official bodies who have kindly provided essential information in the preparation of this Almanac. They include the UK Hydrographic Office, Trinity House, Northern Lighthouse Board, Irish Lights, HM Nautical Almanac Office, HM Stationery Office, HM Customs, Meteorological Office and the Maritime and Coastguard Agency.

Information from the Admiralty List of Lights, Admiralty Tide Tables and the Admiralty List of Radio Signals is reproduced with the permission of the UK Hydrographic Office and the Controller of HMSO. Extracts from the following are published by permission of the Controller of HM Stationery Office: International Code of Signals, 1969. Meteorological Office Weather Services for Shipping. Phases of the Moon and Sun/Moon rising and setting times are derived from the current editions of the Channel and Eastern Almanacs, and are included by permission of HM Nautical Almanac Office. UK and Foreign tidal predictions are supplied by the UK Hydrographic Office, Taunton, TA1 2DN. Acknowledgment is also made to the following authorities for permission to use tidal predictions stated: Danish Safety Administration, Farvandsvæsnet: Esbjerg. SHOM, France: Dunkerque, Dieppe, Le Havre, Cherbourg, St Malo, Brest, Pointe de Grave, Authorisation (No 165/2010). Rijkswaterstaat, The Netherlands: Vlissingen, and Hoek van Holland. BSH, Hamburg and Rostock: Helgoland, Wilhelmshaven and Cuxhaven (BSH 11123/2008-07). Vlaamse Hydrografie, Belgium: Zeebrugge. Instituto Hidrográfico de la Marina, Spain: La Coruña, Authorisation (No 03/10). Marinho Instituto Hidrográfico, Portugal: Lisboa, Authorisation (No 3/2010). **Warning**: The UK Hydrographic Office has not verified the reproduced data and does not accept any liability for the accuracy of reproduction or any modifications made thereafter.

Corrections Any necessary corrections will be published on the website www.reedsalmanacs.co.uk. Data in this almanac is corrected up to Edition 26/2010 of the *Admiralty Notices to Mariners*.

IMPORTANT SAFETY NOTE AND LEGAL DISCLAIMER

This Almanac is intended as a navigational aid only and to assist with basic planning for your passage. The information, charts, maps and diagrams in this Almanac should not be relied on for navigational purposes and should always be used in conjunction with current official hydrographic data. Whilst every care has been taken in its compilation, this Almanac may contain inaccuracies and is no substitute for the relevant official hydrographic charts and data, which should always be consulted in advance of, and whilst, navigating in the relevant area. Before setting out you should also check local conditions with the harbourmaster or other appropriate office responsible for your intended area of navigation.

Before using any waypoint or coordinate listed in this Almanac it must first be plotted on an appropriate official hydrographic chart to check its usefulness, accuracy and appropriateness for the prevailing weather and tidal conditions.

To the extent that the editors or publishers become aware that corrections are required, these will be published on the website www.reedsalmanacs.co.uk. Readers should therefore regularly check the website for any such corrections. Data in this Almanac is corrected up to Edition 26/2010 of the Admiralty Notices to Mariners.

The publishers, editors and their agents accept no responsibility for any errors or omissions, or for any accident, loss or damage (including without limitation any indirect, consequential, special or exemplary damages) arising from the use or misuse of, or reliance upon, the information contained in this Almanac.

The decision to use and rely on any of the data in this Almanac is entirely at the discretion of, and is the sole responsibility of, the Skipper or other individual in control of the vessel in connection with which it is being used or relied upon.

Correspondence Letters on nautical matters should be addressed to editors@reedsalmanacs.co.uk

Practical Boat Owner is published monthly by IPC Magazines Ltd, Blue Fin Building, 110 Southwark Street, London SE1 0SU. For subscription enquiries and overseas orders call 0845 676 7778 (fax: 01444 445599).

Almanac manager: Chris Stevens
Cartography & production: Chris Stevens

Adlard Coles Nautical
36 Soho Square, London W1D 3QY
Tel: +44 (0)207 758 0200 Fax: +44 (0)207 758 0222
www.reedsalmanacs.co.uk

Foreword

Welcome to the 2011 Small Craft Almanac brought to you by Practical Boat Owner magazine and the editors at Reeds.

For a volume so small (it's designed to be light to carry and easy to stow) the Almanac contains a huge amount of information. Most people buy their copy each year for the tide tables, essential even if you're just going out for the afternoon. If you're planning a longer cruise, the tide times and our famous stream atlases and tidal gate information are invaluable.

With this book onboard, you have instant reminders of ships' lights, code flags, buoys and chart symbols, weather sources, communications, safety procedures and much more.

We hope you find it a useful companion through 2011.

Sarah Norbury
Editor
Practical Boat Owner
Britain's biggest-selling yachting magazine

Contents

ABBREVIATIONS

AC, ACA	Admiralty chart, chart agent
AC	Shore power (electrical)
ACN	Adlard Coles Nautical
Al	Alternating lt
ALL	Admiralty list of lights
ALRS	Admiralty list of radio signals
ASD	Admiralty sailing directions (Pilot)
ATT	Admiralty tide tables
ATT	Atterisage (landfall/SWM) buoy
Bcn, Bn	Beacon
Bkwtr	Breakwater
BST	British summer time (DST)
CD	Chart datum
Cf	Compare, cross-refer to
CG	Coastguard
Ch	Channel (VHF)
chan.	Channel (navigational)
COG	Course over the ground
CROSS	Centre régional opérationnel de surveillance et sauvetage (MRCC)
CRS	Coast radio station(s)
DF	Direction finding
Dia	Diaphone (fog signal)
Dir Lt	Directional light
DSC	Digital selective calling
DST	Daylight saving time
DZ	Danger zone (buoy)
E	East
ECM	East cardinal mark (buoy/beacon)
ED	Existence doubtful, European datum
EPIRB	Emergency pos'n indicating radio bn
F	Fixed light. Beaufort wind force
FFL	Fixed and flashing lt
Fl	Flashing light
FM	Frequency modulation
FV	Fishing vessel
G	Green. Gravel
GMDSS	Global maritime distress & safety system
H, Hrs, h	Hour(s)
H24	Continuous
HAT	Highest astronomical tide
Hbr	Harbour
Hd	Head, headland
HF	High frequency
HJ	Day service, sunrise to sunset
HO	Office hours, Hydrographic office
ht	Height
HW	High water
HX	No fixed hours
Hz	Hertz
IALA	Int'l association of lt ho authorities
IDM	Isolated danger mark (buoy/bcn)
IMO	Int'l maritime organisation
Inmarsat	Int'l maritime satellite system
IPTS	Int'l port traffic signals
Is, I	Island, Islet
Iso	Isophase light
ITZ	Inshore traffic zone
Kn	Knot(s)
Lanby	Large automatic navigational buoy
Lat	Latitude
LB	Lifeboat
Ldg	Leading (lt)
LF	Low frequency
Long	Longitude
LT	Local time
Lt(s)	Light(s)
Lt F	Light float
Lt Ho	Lighthouse
Lt V	Light vessel
LW	Low water
M	Sea mile(s)
m	Metre(s)
MCA	Maritime & Coastguard Agency
Météo	Météorologie/weather
MF	Medium frequency
MHWN	Mean HW neaps
MHWS	Mean HW springs
MHz	Megahertz
MLWN	Mean LW neaps
MLWS	Mean LW springs
MMSI	Maritime mobile service identity
Mo	Morse
MRCC	Maritime rescue co-ordination centre
MRSC	Maritime rescue sub-centre (not in UK)
MSI	Maritime safety information
N	North
NCM	North cardinal mark (buoy/bcn)
Oc	Occulting light
PHM	Port-hand mark (buoy/bcn)
Pt(e), (a)	Point(e), Punta
Q	Quick flashing
R	Red. River
Ra	Coast radar station
Racon	Radar transponder beacon
RG	Emergency RDF station
R/T	Radiotelephony
S	South
s	second(s) of time
SAR	Search and rescue
SCM	South cardinal mark (buoy/bcn)
SHM	Starboard-hand mark (buoy/bcn)
Sig Stn	Signal station
SMS	Short message service (texting)
SNSM	Société nationale de sauvetage en mer (French LB service)
SOG	Speed over the ground
SOLAS	Safety of life at sea (Convention)
SPM	Special mark (buoy/bcn)
SRR	SAR Region
SSB	Single sideband (radio)
Stn	Station
SWM	Safe water mark, landfall buoy
Tfc	Traffic
TSS	Traffic separation scheme
UQ	Ultra quick flashing lt
UT	Universal time
VHF	Very high frequency
VNF	Voie navigable de France (canals)
VQ	Very quick flashing lt
VTS	Vessel traffic service
W	West, White
WCM	West cardinal mark (buoy/bcn)
WGS	World geodetic system (datum)
WIP	Work in progress
WPT	Waypoint
Y	Yellow, orange, amber

GENERAL VOCABULARY. See also weather vocabulary on page 82

ENGLISH	GERMAN	FRENCH	SPANISH	DUTCH
ASHORE				
Ashore	An Land	A terre	A tierra	Aan land
Airport	Flughafen	Aéroport	Aeropuerto	Vliegveld
Bank	Bank	Banque	Banco	Bank
Boathoist	Bootskran	Travelift	Travelift	Botenlift
Boatyard	Bootswerft	Chantier naval	Astilleros	Jachtwerf
Bureau de change	Wechselstelle	Bureau de change	Cambio	Geldwisselkantoor
Bus	Bus	Autobus	Autobús	Bus
Chandlery	Yachtausrüster	Shipchandler	Efectos navales	Scheepswinkel
Chemist	Apotheke	Pharmacie	Farmacia	Apotheek
Dentist	Zahnarzt	Dentiste	Dentista	Tandarts
Doctor	Arzt	Médecin	Médico	Dokter
Engineer	Motorenservice	Ingénieur/mécanique	Mecánico	Ingenieur
Ferry	Fähre	Ferry/transbordeur	Ferry	Veer/Pont
Garage	Autowerkstatt	Station service	Garage	Garage
Harbour	Hafen	Port	Puerto	Haven
Hospital	Krankenhaus	Hôpital	Hospital	Ziekenhuis
Mast crane	Mastenkran	Grue	Grúa	Masten kraan
Post office	Postamt	Bureau de poste/PTT	Correos	Postkantoor
Railway station	Bahnhof	Gare de chemin de fer	Estación de ferrocanil	Station
Sailmaker	Segelmacher	Voilier	Velero	Zeilmaker
Shops	Geschäfte	Boutiques	Tiendas	Winkels
Slip	Slip	Cale	Varadero	Helling
Supermarket	Supermarkt	Supermarché	Supermercado	Supermarkt
Taxi	Taxi	Taxi	Taxis	Taxi
Village	Ort	Village	Pueblo	Dorp
Yacht club	Yachtclub	Club nautique	Club náutico	Jacht club
NAVIGATION				
Abeam	Querab	A côté	Por el través	Naast
Ahead	Voraus	Avant	Avante	Voor
Astern	Achteraus	Arrière	Atrás	Achter
Bearing	Peilung	Cap	Maración	Peiling
Buoy	Tonne	Bouée	Boya	Boei
Binoculars	Fernglas	Jumelles	Prismáticos	Verrekijker
Channel	Kanal	Chenal	Canal	Kanaal
Chart	Seekarte	Carte	Carta náutica	Zeekaart
Compass	Kompass	Compas	Compás	Kompas
Compass course	Kompass Kurs	Cap du compas	Rumbo de aguja	Kompas koers
Current	Strömung	Courant	Coriente	Stroom
Dead reckoning	Koppelnavigation	Estime	Estimación	Gegist bestek
Degree	Grad	Degré	Grado	Graden
Deviation	Deviation	Déviation	Desvio	Deviatie
Distance	Entfernung	Distance	Distancia	Afstand
Downstream	Flußabwärts	En aval	Río abajo	Stroom afwaards
East	Ost	Est	Este	Oost
Ebb	Ebbe	Jusant	Marea menguante	Eb
Echosounder	Echolot	Sondeur	Sonda	Dieptemeter
Estimated position	Gegißte Position	Point estimé	Posición estimado	Gegiste positie
Fathom	Faden	Une brasse	Braza	Vadem
Feet	Fuß	Pieds	Pie	Voet
Flood	Flut	Flot	Flujo de marea	Vloed
Handbearing compass	Handpeilkompass	Compas de relèvement	Compás de marcaciones	Handpeil kompas

ENGLISH	GERMAN	FRENCH	SPANISH	DUTCH
Harbour guide	Hafenhandbuch	Guide du port	Guia del Puerto	Havengids
High water	Hochwasser	Peine mer	Altamer	Hoog water
Latitude	Geographische Breite	Latitude	Latitud	Breedte
Leading lights	Feuer in Linie	Alignement	Luz de enfilación	Geleide lichten
Leeway	Abdrift	Dérive	Hacia sotavento	Drift
Lighthouse	Leuchtturm	Phare	Faro	Vuurtoren
List of lights	Leuchtfeuer Verzeichnis	Liste des feux	Listude de Luces	Lichtenlijst
Log	Logge	Loch	Corredera	Log
Longitude	Geographische Länge	Longitude	Longitud	Lengte
Low water	Niedrigwasser	Basse mer	Bajamar	Laag water
Metre	Meter	Mètre	Metro	Meter
Minute	Minute	Minute	Minuto	Minuut
Nautical almanac	Nautischer Almanach	Almanach nautique	Almanaque náutico	Almanak
Nautical mile	Seemeile	Mille nautique	Milla marina	Zeemijl
Neap tide	Nipptide	Morte-eau	Marea muerta	Dood tij
North	Nord	Nord	Norte	Noord
Pilot	Lotse	Pilote	Práctico	Loods/Gids
Pilotage book	Handbuch	Instructions nautiques	Derrotero	Vaarwijzer
RDF	Funkpeiler	Radio gonio	Radio-gonió	Radio richtingzoeker
Radar	Radar	Radar	Radar	Radar
Radio receiver	Radio, Empfänger	Réceptor radio	Receptor de radio	Radio ontvanger
Radio transmitter	Sender	Emetteur radio	Radio-transmisor	Radio zender
River outlet	Flußmündung	Embouchure	Embocadura	Riviermond
South	Süd	Sud	Sud, Sur	Zuid
Spring tide	Springtide	Vive-eau	Marea viva	Springtij/ springvloed
Tide	Tide, Gezeit	Marée	Marea	Getijde
Tide tables	Tidenkalender	Annuaire des marées	Anuario de mareas	Getijdetafel
True course	Wahrer Kurs	Vrai cap	Rumbo	Ware Koers
Upstream	Flußaufwärts	En amont	Río arriba	Stroom opwaards
VHF	UKW	VHF	VHF	Marifoon
Variation	Mißweisung	Variation	Variación	Variatie
Waypoint	Wegpunkt	Point de rapport	Waypoint	Waypoint/Route punt
West	West	Ouest	Oeste	West

OFFICIALDOM

Certificate of registry	Schiffszertifikat	Acte de franchisation	Doc de matrícuia	Zeebrief
Check in	Einklarieren	Enregistrement	Registrar	Check-in
Customs	Zoll	Douanes	Aduana	Douane
Declare	Verzollen	Déclarer	Declarar	Aangeven
Harbour master	Hafenmeister	Capitaine du port	Capitán del puerto	Havenmeester
Insurance	Versicherung	Assurance	Seguro	Verzekering
Insurance certificate	Versicherungspolice	Certificat d'assurance	Certificado deseguro	Verzekeringsbewijs
Passport	Paß	Passeport	Pasaporte	Paspoort
Police	Polizei	Police	Policía	Politie
Pratique	Verkehrserlaubnis	Pratique	Prático	Verlof tot ontscheping
Prohibited area	Sperrgebiet	Zone interdite	Zona de prohibida	Verboden gebied
Register	Register	Liste de passagers	Lista de tripulantes/rol	Register
Ship's log	Logbuch	Livre de bord	Cuaderno de bitácora	Logboek
Ship's papers	Schiffspapiere	Papiers de bateau	Documentos del barco	Scheepspapieren
Surveyor	Gutachter	Expert maritime	Inspector	Opzichter

Chapter 1 - Navigation

PASSAGE PLANNING FORM

DATE:........................ FROM: .... TO:.. DIST: ....nm

ALTERNATIVE DESTINATION(S): ....

WEATHER FORECAST: ....

....

FORECASTS AVAILABLE DURING PASSAGE: ....

....

TIDES

DATE:...	DATE:...	DATE:...
PLACE:.......................................	PLACE:.......................................	PLACE:.......................................
HW	HW	HW ....
LW	LW	LW ....
HW	HW	HW ....
LW	LW	LW ....

COEFFICIENT: ....

HEIGHT OF TIDE AT: ....

.... hrs .... m .... hrs .... m .... hrs .... m

DEPTH CONSTRAINTS: ....

TIDAL STREAMS AT: ....

TURNS .... AT .... TOTAL SET (FM .... TO ....): ....° .... nm

TURNS .... AT .... TOTAL SET (FM .... TO ....): ....° .... nm

NET TIDAL STREAM FOR PASSAGE: ....° ....NM

ESTIMATED TIME: ....hrs ETD: .... ETA: ....

SUN/MOON SUNRISE: .... SUNSET: ....

MOONRISE: .... MOONSET: .... PHASE: ....

WAYPOINTS	NO	NAME	TRACK/DISTANCE (TO NEXT WAYPOINT)
	....	....	.... / ....
	....	....	.... / ....
	....	....	.... / ....
	....	....	.... / ....
	....	....	.... / ....

DANGERS CLEARING BEARINGS/RANGES/DEPTHS

....

....

LIGHTS/MARKS EXPECTED ....

....

COMMUNICATIONS PORT/MARINA .... VHF .... ☎ ....

PORT/MARINA .... VHF .... ☎ ....

NOTES (CHARTS PREPARED & PAGE NUMBERS OF RELEVANT PILOTS/ALMANACS/ETC): ....

....

....

PASSAGE PLANNING AND SOLAS V

Before you start to navigate you need to plan: where you are going, how to get there and what factors may influence the plan. To most people this is commonsense, but is also the law; see Regulation 34 in chapter V of the International Convention for Safety of Life at Sea (SOLAS).

Regulation 34 **Safe Navigation and avoidance of dangerous situations** is quite short and bland. The MCA have provided extra guidance for small craft skippers at www.mcga.gov.uk.

Legally all voyages/passages by any vessel that goes to sea must be pre-planned. 'Going to sea' is defined as proceeding beyond sheltered waters. Even in very familiar waters every passage, however short, must be pre-planned, but for small craft the degree of planning may be less than for big ships.

The passage plan need not be in writing, which makes it hard to consult. However a written plan, in the event of legal action, is clear proof that planning has been done. A passage planning form is therefore included on the previous page; it may be photocopied and enlarged to suit individual needs.

The MCA states that Regulation 34 does not herald a regime of pre-departure or spot checks on small craft. But obviously it might apply to an incident or accident involving a pleasure craft where it can be proved that the skipper did not carry out any form of passage planning; in which case the MCA would have clear authority to take action under the Merchant Shipping Act. For small craft skippers the emphasis on passage planning has shifted from good practice to a legal requirement.

SOLAS V, Regulation 34 (as paraphrased)

All passage plans, however short, should consider or better still answer the following questions:

- **Limitations of the vessel:** Is your craft suitable for the intended passage? Is proper safety equipment and enough fuel, water and stores onboard?
- **Crew:** Is the crew sufficiently experienced and physically capable? Cold, tiredness and seasickness can soon render crew incapable of performing their tasks properly, thus overburdening the skipper both physically and mentally.
- **Navigational dangers:** Are you aware of navigational dangers which may affect the passage? If not, check up-to-date charts, pilot books and the current PBO Almanac.
- **Tides:** Do you know times/heights of HW & LW at departure, destination and alternate ports? Are you aware of tidal streams and races expected on passage? Does your passage plan make best use of all tidal data?
- **Weather:** Before leaving, is the forecast suitable for the likely duration of the passage? Whilst at sea what updates can be obtained for destination and alternate?
- **Contingency plan:** Have you an alternative plan to cope with weather deterioration, gear failure, accident or injury? Which ports of refuge or bolt-holes are available?
- **GPS:** Do not become over-reliant on it. It *can* fail, usually at the most awkward moment. Can you navigate safely without it? Do you have a back-up set?
- **Information ashore:** Does someone ashore know your plans and what to do should he/she become concerned? If you get into difficulties the CG Voluntary Identification Scheme (CG66) helps the Coastguard to help you more quickly. It is easy to join – and free.

Passage planning form

Before reaching this stage, much thought and study must go into drafting the plan. Any plan for any project goes through some or all of the following phases:

- Deciding the aim – not always obvious.
- Gathering the facts – time consuming but essential.
- Assessing the information now available.
- Formulating the plan. Think laterally.

A form ensures that the plan has been methodically prepared and minimises the risk of errors or omissions. Use a form in which you must actively tick off items and/or insert data into boxes – rather than passively glancing at a screed and saying 'Yes, done all that'. That may well not be the case.

The following notes amplify some of the passage planning form items:

- Tidal streams around headlands tend to form gates, especially on a coastal passage. Note when the tides are fair or foul and the times of slack water.
- Times of entry/exit at a harbour may be affected by bars, sills and locks.
- A detailed pilotage plan/sketch for any unfamiliar harbour always helps.
- Involve your crew with passage plans.

DISTANCES (M) ACROSS THE ENGLISH CHANNEL

ENGLAND / FRANCE/CI	Longships	Falmouth	Fowey	Plymouth bkwtr	Salcombe	Dartmouth	Torbay	Weymouth	Poole Hbr Ent	Needles Lt Ho	Nab Tower	Littlehampton	Shoreham	Brighton	Newhaven	Eastbourne	Folkestone	Dover
Le Conquet	112	112	123	125	125	137	144	172	188	194	212	230	240	245	249	261	295	301
L'Aberwrac'h	102	97	106	107	105	117	124	153	168	174	192	211	219	224	228	239	275	280
Roscoff	110	97	101	97	91	100	107	130	144	149	165	184	193	197	200	211	246	252
Trébeurden	120	105	106	102	94	102	109	129	142	147	164	181	190	194	197	208	244	249
Tréguier	132	112	110	101	94	98	102	116	128	132	147	162	170	174	177	188	224	229
Lézardrieux	142	121	118	107	94	100	105	115	126	130	140	157	165	169	172	184	219	224
St Q.-Portrieux	159	137	135	124	111	115	121	127	135	135	146	162	171	174	178	189	225	230
St Malo	172	149	146	133	118	120	124	125	130	130	143	157	166	170	173	184	220	225
St Helier	155	130	123	108	93	95	100	99	104	104	115	132	140	144	147	158	194	199
St Peter Port	139	113	104	89	73	70	75	71	79	83	97	112	120	124	127	135	174	179
Braye (Alderney)	146	116	106	89	72	69	71	54	60	62	73	91	100	103	106	114	153	159
Cherbourg	168	138	125	107	92	87	88	66	64	63	68	81	90	92	96	102	140	145
St Vaast	194	164	150	132	116	111	112	83	76	72	71	80	87	88	90	96	132	138
Ouistreham	229	198	185	167	151	146	147	117	107	100	86	91	92	91	90	92	125	130
Deauville	236	205	192	174	158	153	154	122	111	104	88	89	88	87	85	87	120	125
Le Havre	231	200	187	169	153	148	148	118	105	97	82	82	83	82	79	80	115	120
Fécamp	242	212	197	179	163	157	157	120	105	96	75	71	68	65	62	62	90	95
Dieppe	268	237	222	204	188	180	180	142	125	117	91	80	75	70	64	63	70	75
Boulogne	290	258	242	224	208	198	195	153	135	127	97	81	71	66	59	47	28	25
Calais	305	272	257	239	223	213	210	168	150	141	111	96	86	81	74	62	26	22

NOTES

1. This Table applies to Areas 1–3, and 14–16, each of which also contains its own internal Distance Table. Approximate distances in nautical miles are by the most direct route, while avoiding dangers and allowing for Traffic Separation Schemes.

2. For ports within the Solent, add the appropriate distances given in Area 2 to those shown above under either Needles Lighthouse or Nab Tower.

AREA 1 *South West England - Isles of Scilly to Anvil Point*

SELECTED LIGHTS, BUOYS & WAYPOINTS

Positions are referenced to WGS84

ISLES OF SCILLY TO THE LIZARD

ISLES OF SCILLY
Bishop Rock ☆ Fl (2) 15s 44m **20M**; part obsc 204°-211°, obsc 211°-233° and 236°-259°; Gy ○ twr with helo platform; **Racon T, 18M, 254°-215°**; 49°52'·37N 06°26'·74W.
Round Rock ⌿ 49°53'·10N 06°25'·19W.
Gunner ⌿ 49°53'·64N 06°25'·08W.
Old Wreck ⫞ VQ; 49°54'·26N 06°22'·81W.
Peninnis Hd ☆ Fl 20s 36m **17M**; 231°-117° but partially obsc 048°-083° within 5M; W ○ twr on B frame, B cupola; 49°54'·28N 06°18'·22W.
Spanish Ledge ⫞ Q (3) 10s; *Bell;* 49°53'·94N 06°18'·86W.
N Bartholomew ⬿ Fl R 5s; 49°54'·49N 06°19'·99W.
Bacon Ledge ⬿ Fl (4) R 5s; 49°55'·22N 06°19'·27W.
Tresco Flats, Hulman ⫞ Fl G 4s, 49°56'·29N 06°20'·31W.
Little Rag Ledge ⫞ Fl (2) R 5s, 49°56'·43N 06°20'·43W.
Bryher, Bar Quay ⫞ Q (3) 10s, 49°57'·35N 06°20'·85W.
Crow Rock ⫞ Fl (2) 10s; 49°56'·26N 06°18'·49W.
Hats ⫞ VQ (6) + L Fl 10s; 49°56'·21N 06°17'·14W.
Spencers Ledge ⫞ Q (6) + L Fl 15s; 49°54'·78N 06°22'·06W.
St Agnes, Porth Conger ⫞ QG, 49°53'·76N 06°20'·40W.
Steeple Rock ⫞ Q (9) 15s; 49°55'·46N 06°24'·24W.
Round Island ☆ Fl 10s 55m **18M**; 021°-288°; *Horn (4) 60s;* **Racon M, 10M;** 49°58'·74N 06°19'·40W.
St Martin's, Higher Town quay ⫞ Fl R 5s, 49°57'·45N 06°16'·84W.

SCILLY TO LAND'S END
Seven Stones ⬿ Fl (3) 30s 12m **25M**; H24; *Horn (3) 60s;* **Racon O, 15M;** 50°03'·62N 06°04'·34W.
Wolf Rock ☆ Fl 15s 34m **16M**; H24; *Horn 30s;* **Racon T, 10M;** 49°56'·72N 05°48'·57W.
Longships ☆ Fl (2) WR 10s 35m **W16M**, R11M; 189°-R-327°-W-189°; Gy ○ twr with helicopter platform; *Horn 10s;* 50°04'·01N 05°44'·81W.
Runnel Stone ⫞ Q (6) + L Fl 15s; *Bell;* 50°01'·19N 05°40'·36W.
Tater-du ☆ Fl (3) 15s 34m **20M**; 241°-074°; W ○ twr 50°03'·14N 05°34'·68W. Same twr FR 31m 13M, 060°-074° over Runnel Stone and in places 074°-077° (3°) within 4M; *Horn (2) 30s.*

NEWLYN and PENZANCE
S Pier ⫞ Fl 5s 10m 9M; W ○ twr; 253°-336°; 50°06'·19N 05°32'·57W.
N Pier ⫞ F WG 4m 2M; 238°-G-248°, W over hbr; 50°06'·19N 05°32'·62W.
Penzance S Pier ⫞ Fl WR 5s 11m **W17M**, R12M; 159°-R-268°-W-344·5°-R-shore; 50°07'·07N 05°31'·68W.
Lizard ☆ Fl 3s 70m **26M**; H24; 250°-120°, partly visible 235°-250°; W 8-sided twr; *Horn 30s;* 49°57'·61N 05°12'·13W.

FALMOUTH TO START POINT

FALMOUTH
St Anthony Head ☆ Iso WR 15s 22m, **W16M**, R14M, H24; 295°-W-004°-R-022°-W-172°; W 8-sided twr; *Horn 30s;* 50°08'·47N 05°00'·96W.
Black Rock ⬢ Fl (2) 10s 3M; 50°08'·72N 05°02'·00W.
St Mawes ⫞ Q (6) + L Fl 15s; 50°09'·10N 05°01'·42W.
Mylor chan ▲ Fl G 6s; 50°10'·79N 05°02'·70W.

MEVAGISSEY
Victoria Pier ⫞ Fl (2) 10s 9m 12M; *Dia 30s;* 50°16'·15N 04°46'·93W.

FOWEY
Cannis Rock ⫞ Q (6) + L Fl 15s; *Bell;* 50°18'·38N 04°39'·95W.
Fowey ⫞ L Fl WR 5s 28m W11M, R9M; 284°-R-295°-W-028°-R-054°; 50°19'·62N 04°38'·84W.
Whitehouse Pt ⫞ Iso WRG 3s 11m W11M, R/G8M; 017°-G-022°- W-032°-R-037°; R col; 50°19'·98N 04°38'·24W.

POLPERRO
Spy House Pt ⫞ Iso WR 6s 30m 7M; W288°-060°, R060°-288°; 50°19'·81N 04°30'·70W.

LOOE and EDDYSTONE
Banjo Pier ☆ Oc WR 3s 8m **W15M**, R12M; 207°-R267°- W-313°-R-332°; 50°21'·05N 04°27'·06W.
Eddystone ☆ Fl (2) 10s 41m **17M**; Gy twr, helicopter platform; *Horn 30s;* **Racon T, 10M,** 50°10'·85N 04°15'·94W. Same twr, Iso R 10s 28m 8M; 110·5°-130·5° over Hand Deeps.

PLYMOUTH
Draystone ⬿ Fl (2) R 5s; 50°18'·85N 04°11'·07W.
Plymouth W bkwtr ⫞ Fl WR 10s 19m W12M, R9M; 262°-W-208°-R-262°; W ○ twr. Same twr, Iso 4s 12m 10M; vis 033°-037°; *Horn 15s;* 50°20'·07N 04°09'·53W.
The Bridge Channel. No 1, ⫞ QG 4m; 50°21'·03N 04°09'·53W. No 2, ⫞ QR 4m.
E Bkwtr ⬢ L Fl WR 10s 9m W8M, R6M; 190°-R-353°-W-001°-R-018°-W-190°; 50°20'·01N 04°08'·25W.
Ldg lts 349°. Front, Mallard Shoal ⫞ Q WRG 5m W10M, R/G3M; 233°-G-043°- R-067°-G-087°-W-099°-R-108°; 50°21'·60N 04°08'·33W. Rear, Hoe ⫞ Oc G 1·3s 11m 3M, 310°-040°; W ▽, Or bands.
Queen Anne's Battery (QAB) ldg lts ⫞ 048·5°. Front, Oc R 8s; R/W bcn; 50°21'·84N 04°07'·84W. Rear, Oc R 8s 14m 3M; 50°21'·89N 04°07'·75W.
Fisher's Nose, Fl (3) R 10s 4M; 50°21'·80N 04°08'·01W.
Sutton Hbr lock; IPTS; 50°21'·98N 04°07'·96W.
Plymouth Yacht Haven (PYH), outer bkwtr, E end, 2 FG (vert); 50°21'·59N 04°07'·15W.
Mayflower marina, outer bkwtr, E end, 2 FR (vert).

RIVER YEALM

The Sand Bar ⚓ Fl R 5s; 50°18'·59N 04°04'·12W.

SALCOMBE

Sandhill Pt Dir ☆ 000°: Fl WRG 2s 27m W10M, R/G7M; 182·5°-G-357·5°-W-002·5°-R-182·5°; R/W ◊ on W mast; 50°13'·77N 03°46'·67W. 000° on with Pound Stone R/W ⚓, 230m S.

Start Pt ☆ Fl (3) 10s 62m **25M**; 184°-068°. Same twr: FR 55m 12M; 210°-255° over Skerries Bank; *Horn 60s;* 50°13'·33N 03°38'·54W.

START POINT TO ANVIL POINT

DARTMOUTH

Kingswear Dir ☆ 328°: Iso WRG 3s 9m 8M; 318°-G-325°-W-331°-R-340°; W ○ twr; 50°20'·81N 03°34'·10W.

Mewstone ⚓ VQ (6) + L Fl 10s; 50°19'·92N 03°31'·89W.

West Rock ⚓ Q (6) + L Fl 15s; 50°19'·86N 03°32'·47W.

Homestone ⚓ QR; 50°19'·61N 03°33'·55W.

Castle Ledge ⚓ Fl G 5s; 50°19'·99N 03°33'·12W.

BRIXHAM

Berry Head ☆ Fl (2) 15s 58m **19M**; vis 100°-023°; W twr; 50°23'·97N 03°29'·01W. R lts on radio mast 5·7M NW, inland of Paignton.

Victoria bkwtr ☆ Oc R 15s 9m 6M; W twr; 50°24'·33N 03°30'·78W.

Fairway Dir ☆ 159°: Iso WRG 5s 4m 6M; 145°-G-157°-W-161°-R-173°; 50°23'·83N 03°30'·57W.

TORQUAY

⚓ QG (May-Sep); 50°27'·42N 03°31'·80W.

TEIGNMOUTH

Outfall ⚓ Fl Y 5, 288°/1·3M to hbr ent.

Bar ⚓ Fl G 2s; 50°32'·44N 03°29'·25W.

The Point ⚓ Oc G 6s 3M & FG (vert); 50°32'·42N 03°30'·05W.

RIVER EXE

Exe ⚓ Mo (A) 10s; 50°35'·90N 03°23'·70W.

No. 1 ⚓ 50°36'·07N 03°23'·78W.

No. 2 ⚓ 50°36'·03N 03°23'·91W.

Ldg lts 305°. Front, Iso 2s 6m 7M, 50°36'·99N 03°25'·34W. Rear, Q 12m 7M, 57m from front.

No. 10 ⚓ Fl R 3s; 50°36'·73N 03°24'·77W.

No. 12 Warren Pt ⚓ 50°36'·91N 03°25'·40W.

LYME REGIS

Outfall ⚓ Q (6) + L Fl 15s; 50°43'·17N 02°55'·66W.

Ldg lts 284°: Front, Victoria Pier ☆ Oc WR 8s 6m, W9M, R7M; 296°-R-116°-W-296°; 50°43'·19N 02°56'·17W. Rear, FG 8m 9M, 240m from front.

WEST BAY (BRIDPORT)

W pier root, Dir ☆ F WRG 5m 4M; 165°-G-331°-W-341°-R-165°; 50°42'·62N 02°45'·89W.

W pier ☆ Iso R 2s 5m 4M; 50°42'·51N 02°45'·83W.

E pier ☆ Iso G 2s 5m 4M; 50°42'·53N 02°45'·80W.

PORTLAND

Portland Bill lt ho ☆ Fl (4) 20s 43m **25M**. vis 221°-244° (gradual change from 1 Fl to 4 Fl); 244°-117° (shows 4 Fl); 117°-141° (gradual change from 4 Fl to 1 Fl). W ○ twr; *Dia 30s;* 50°30'·85N 02°27'·38W. Same twr: FR 19m 13M; 271°-291° over Shambles.

W Shambles ⚓ Q (9) 15s; *Bell;* 50°29'·78N 02°24'·40W.

E Shambles ⚓ Q (3) 10s; *Bell;* 50°30'·78N 02°20'·08W.

Portland hbr, outer bkwtr (N end) ☆ QR 14m 5M; 013°-268°; 50°35'·11N 02°24'·87W.

NE Bkwtr (A Hd) ☆ Fl 2·5s 22m 10M; 50°35'·16N 02°25'·07W.

NE Bkwtr (B Hd) ☆ Oc R 15s 11m 5M; 50°35'·65N 02°25'·88W.

WEYMOUTH TO ANVIL POINT

Weymouth ldg lts 239·6°: both FR 5/7m 7M; Front 50°36'·46N 02°26'·87W, R ♦ on W post; rear 17m from front, R ♦ on W mast.

N Pier hd ☆ 2 FG (vert) 9m 6M; 50°36'·59N 02°26'·63W.

S Pier hd ☆ Q 10m 9M; 50°36'·57N 02°26'·49W. IPTS 190m SW.

Lulworth Cove, E point 50°37'·00N 02°14'·78W.

Anvil Pt ☆ Fl 10s 45m **19M**; vis 237°-076° (H24); W ○ twr and dwelling; 50°35'·51N 01°57'·60W.

		1	2	3	4	5	6	7	8	9	10	11	12	13	14	15	16	17
1	Longships	**1**																
2	Scilly (Crow Rock)	22	**2**															
3	Penzance	15	35	**3**														
4	Lizard Point	23	42	16	**4**													
5	Falmouth	39	60	32	16	**5**												
6	Mevagissey	52	69	46	28	17	**6**											
7	Fowey	57	76	49	34	22	7	**7**										
8	Looe	63	80	57	39	29	16	11	**8**									
9	Plymouth (bkwtr)	70	92	64	49	39	25	22	11	**9**								
10	River Yealm (ent)	72	89	66	49	39	28	23	16	4	**10**							
11	Salcombe	81	102	74	59	50	40	36	29	22	17	**11**						
12	Start Point	86	103	80	63	55	45	40	33	24	22	7	**12**					
13	Dartmouth	95	116	88	72	63	54	48	42	35	31	14	9	**13**				
14	Torbay	101	118	96	78	70	62	55	50	39	38	24	15	11	**14**			
15	Exmouth	113	131	107	90	82	73	67	61	51	49	33	27	24	12	**15**		
16	Lyme Regis	126	144	120	104	96	86	81	74	63	62	48	41	35	30	21	**16**	
17	Portland Bill	135	151	128	112	104	93	89	81	73	70	55	49	45	42	36	22	**17**

DISTANCE TABLES
Approx distances in nautical miles are by the most direct route allowing for dangers and TSS.

AREA 2 *South Central England – Anvil Point to Selsey Bill*

SELECTED LIGHTS, BUOYS & WAYPOINTS

Positions are referenced to WGS84

SWANAGE TO ISLE OF WIGHT

SWANAGE
Pier Hd ⚓ 2 FR (vert) 6m 3M; 50°36'·56N 01°56'·95W.
Peveril Ledge ⚓ QR; 50°36'·41N 01°56'·10W.

POOLE HARBOUR and APPROACHES
Poole Bar (No.1) ▲ QG; *Bell.*; 50°39·32N 01°55'·16W.

SWASH CHANNEL/EAST LOOE CHANNEL
South Hook *l*; 50°39'·70N 01°55'·20W.
No. 3 ▲ Fl G 3s; 50°39'·76N 01°55'·49W.
Training Bank ⚓ 2 FR (vert); 50°39'·84N 01°55'·92W.
Channel (No. 8) ⚓ Fl R 2s; 50°40'·45N 01°56'·26W.
Swash (No.9) *l* Q (9) 15s; 50°40'·88N 01°56'·70W.
East Looe 1 ▲ Fl G 5s; 50°41'·09N 01°55'·82W.
East Looe 4 (Limit 10 knots) ⚓ Fl R 2s; 50°41'·09N 01°56'·17W.
South Deep. Marked by lit and unlit Bns from ent South of Brownsea Castle to Furzey Is.

MIDDLE SHIP and NORTH CHANNELS
Bell (No. 15) *l* Q (6) + L Fl 15s; *Bell*; 50°41'·36N 01°57'·12W.
Marked by PHM and SHM Lt buoys.
Aunt Betty (No.22) *l* Q (3)10s; 50°41'·96N 01°57'·39W.
Diver (No. 25) *l* Q (9) 15s; 50°42'·28N 01°58'·34W.
Stakes (No. 29) *l* Q (6) + L Fl 15s; 50°42'·43N 01°59'·01W.

WAREHAM CHANNEL
Wareham Chan initially m'kd by ▲'s and ⚓'s and then by stakes.

WESTERN APPROACHES TO SOLENT

NEEDLES and NORTH CHANNELS
Needles Fairway *l* L Fl 10s; *Bell*; 50°38'·24N 01°38'·98W.
SW Shingles *l*Fl R 2·5s; 50°39'·35N 01°37'·45W.
Bridge *l* VQ (9) 10s; **Racon (T) 10M**; 50°39'·63N 01°36'·88W.
Needles 50°39'·73N 01°35'·50W; Oc (2) WRG 20s 24m **W17M**, R14M, R13M G14M; ○ Twr, R band and lantern; vis: shore-R-300°-W-083°-R (unintens)-212°-W-217°-G-224°. *Horn (2) 30s* H24. 01°33'·55W.
NE Shingles *l* Q (3) 10s; 50°41'·96N 01°33'·41W.
Hurst Point ☆ 50°42'·48N 01°33'·03W; Fl (4) WR 15s 23m W13M, R11M; W ○ Twr; vis:080°-W(unintens)-104°, 234°-W-244°-R-250°-W-053°. Same structure, Iso WRG 4s 19m **W21M, R18M, G17M**; vis: 038·8°-G-040·8°-W-041·8°-R- 043·8°; By day W7M, R5M, G5M.
N Head ▲ Fl (3) G 10s; 50°42'·69N 01°35'·52W.

YARMOUTH/LYMINGTON
Sconce *l* Q; *Bell*; 50°42'·53N 01°31'·43W.
Black Rock ▲ Fl G 5s; 50°42'·58N 01°30'·64W.
Y'mouth E F'wy ⚓ Fl R 2s. 50°42'·64N 01°29'·88W.
Pier Head, centre, ⚓ 2 FR (vert) 2M; G col. High intensity FW (occas); 50°42'·51N 01°29'·97W.
Jack in the Basket *l* Fl R 2s 9m; 50°44'·27N 01°30'·57W.
No. 1 *l* Fl G 2s 2m 3M; G △ on pile; 50°44'·41N 01°30'·48W.
Lymington Bank ⚓ Fl (2) R 5s. *Bell*; 50°43'·10N 01°30'·85W.
Solent Bank ⚓ Fl (3) R 10s; 50°44'·23N 01°27'·37W.
Hamstead Ledge ▲ Fl (2) G 5s; 50°43'·87N 01°26'18W.
Newtown River *l* Q(9)15s; 50°43'·75N 01°24'·96W.
W Lepe ⚓ Fl R 5s; 50°45'·24N 01°24'·09W.
Salt Mead ▲ Fl (3) G 10s; 50°44'·51N 01°23'·04W.
Gurnard Ledge ▲ Fl (4) G 15s; 50°45'·51N 01°20'·59W.
E Lepe ⚓ Fl (2) R 5s; *Bell*; 50°45'·93N 01°21'·07W.
Lepe Spit *l* Q (6) + L Fl 15s; 50°46'·78N 01°20'·64W.
Beaulieu Millenium Dir lt 334°. ⚓ Oc WRG 4s 13m W4M, R3M, G3M; vis: 318°-G-330°-W-337°-R-348°; 50°47'·12N 01°21'·90W.
NE Gurnard ▲ Fl (3) R 10s; 50°47'·06N 01°19'·42W.
W Bramble *l* VQ (9) 10s; *Bell*; **Racon (T) 3M.**; 50°47'·20N 01°18'·65W.
W Knoll ⚓ Fl Y 2·5s; 50°47'·43N 01°17'·84W.
Williams Ship'g ⚓ (or) Fl Y 4s; 50°47'·11N01°18'·08W.
S Bramble ▲ Fl G 2·5s; 50°46'·98N 01°17'·72W.

COWES
Gurnard *l* Q; 50°46'·22N 01°18'·84W.
Prince Consort *l* VQ; 50°46'·42N 01°17'·55W.
No. 1 ▲ Fl G 3s; 50°46'·07N 01°18'·03W.
No. 2 ⚓ QR; 50°46'·07N 01°17'·87W.

SOUTHAMPTON WATER/RIVER HAMBLE
CALSHOT SPIT ⚓ Fl 5s 5m 10M; R hull, Lt Twr amidships; *Horn (2) 60s*; 50°48'·35N 01°17'·64W.
Calshot *l* VQ; *Bell* ; 50°48'·44N 01°17'·03W.
Black Jack ⚓ Fl (2) R 4s; 50°49'·13N 01°18'·09W.
Hook *l* QG; *Horn (1) 15s*; 50°49'·52N 01°18'·30W.
Bald Head ▲ Fl G 2·5s; 50°49'·80N 01°18'·06W.
Hamble Pt *l* Q (6) + L Fl 15s; 50°50'·15N 01°18'·66W.
No. 1 *l* QG 2m 2M; 50°50'·34N 01°18'·65W.
No. 2 *l* Q (3) 10s 2m 2M; 50°50'·39N 01°18'·77W.
Greenland ▲ IQ G 10s; 50°51'·11N 01°20'·38W.
Weston Shelf ▲ Fl (3) G 15s; 50°52'·71N 01°23'·26W.
Hythe Pier Hd ⚓ 2 FR (vert) 12m 5M; 50°52'·49N 01°23'·61W.

SOUTHAMPTON/ITCHEN/TEST
Swinging Ground No. 1 ▲ Oc G 4s; 50°53'·00N 01°23'·44W.
Queen Elizabeth II Terminal, S end ⚓ 4 FG (vert) 16m 3M; 50°53'·00N 01°23'·71W.
Gymp ⚓ QR; 50°53'·17N 01°24'·30W.

THE EAST SOLENT

NORTH CHANNEL/HILLHEAD

Hillhead ⚲Fl R 2·5s; 50°48'·07N 01°16'·00W.
Hillhead ⚲ Or Bn; 50°49'·06N 01°14'·78W.
E Bramble ⚲ VQ (3) 5s; 50°47'·23N 01°13'·64W.

EASTERN SOLENT MARKS/WOOTTON

W Ryde Middle ⚲ Q (9) 15s; 50°46'·48N 01°15'·79W.
Norris ⚲ Fl (3) R 10s; 50°45'·97N 01°15'·51W.
N Ryde Middle ⚲ Fl (4) R 20s; 50°46'·61N 01°14'·31W.
S Ryde Middle ⚲ Fl G 5s; 50°46'·13N 01°14'·16W.
Peel Bank ⚲ Fl (2) R 5s; 50°45'·49N 01°13'·35W.
SE Ryde Middle ⚲ VQ (6)+L Fl 10s; 50°45'·93N 01°12'·10W.
NE Ryde Middle ⚲ Fl (2) R 10s; 50°46'·21N 01°11'·88W.
Wootton Bn ⚲ Q 1M; (NB); 50°44'·53N 01°12'·13W.
Mother Bank ⚲ Fl R 3s; 50°45'·49N 01°11'·21W.
Browndown ⚲ Fl G 15s; 50°46'·57N 01°10'·95W.

PORTSMOUTH and APPROACHES

Horse Sand Ft ⚲ Iso G 2s 21m 8M; 50°45'·01N 01°04'·34W.
Horse Sand ⚲ Fl G 2·5s; 50°45'·53N 01°05'·27W.
Outer Spit ⚲ Q (6) + L Fl 15s; 50°45'·58N 01°05'·50W.
Mary Rose ⚲ Fl Y 5s; 50°45'·80N 01°06'·20W.
No. 1 Bar (NB) ⚲ Fl (3) G 10s; 50°46'·77N 01°05'·81W.
No. 2 ⚲ Fl (3) R 10s; 50°46'·69N 01°05'·97W.
No. 4 (NB) ⚲ QR; 50°47'·01N 01°06'·36W.
BC Outer ⚲ Oc R 15s; 50°47'·32N 01°06'·68W.
Fort Blockhouse ⚲ Dir lt 320°; WRG 6m W13M, R5M, G5M; vis: 310°- Oc G-316°-Al WG(W phase incr with brg), 318·5°-Oc-321·5°-Al WR (R phase incr with brg), 324°-Oc R-330°. 2 FR (vert) 20m E; 50°47'·37N 01°06'·74W.
Ballast ⚲ Fl R 2·5s; 50°47'·62N 01°06'·83W.

EASTERN APPROACHES TO THE SOLENT

Outer Nab 1 ⚲ VQ (9) 10s; 50°38'·18N 00°56'·88W.
Outer Nab 2 ⚲ VQ (3) 5s; 50°38'·43N 00°57'·70W.

Nab Tower ☆ 50°40'·08N 00°57'·15W; Fl 10s 27m **16M**, *Horn (2) 30s*; **Racon (T) 10M.**
N 2 ⚲ Fl Y 2·5s. 6M; 50°41'·03N 00°56'·74W.
N 1 ⚲ Fl Y (4)10s; 50°41'·26N 00°56'·52W.
N 7 ⚲ Fl Y 2·5s; 50°42'·35N 00°57'·20W.
New Grounds ⚲ VQ (3) 5s; 50°41'·84N 00°58'·49W.
Nab End ⚲ Fl R 5s; *Whis*; 50°42'·63N 00°59'·49W.
Dean Tail ⚲ Fl G 5s; 50°42'·99N 00°59'·17W.
Dean Tail S ⚲ Q (6) + L Fl 10s; 50°43'·04N 00°59'·57W.
Dean Tail N ⚲ Q; 50°43'·13N 00°59'·57W.
St Helens ⚲ Fl (3) R 15s; 50°43'·36N 01°02'·41W.
Horse Elbow ⚲QG; 50°44'·26N 01°03'·88W.
Cambrian Wreck ⚲ 50°44'·43N 01°03'·43W.
Warner ⚲ QR; *Whis*; 50°43'·87N 01°03'·99W.
W Princessa ⚲ Q (9) 15s; 50°40'·16N 01°03'·65W.
Bembridge Ledge ⚲ Q (3) 10s; 50°41'·15N 01°02'·81W
St Helen's Fort ☆ (IOW) Fl (3) 10s 16m 8M; large ○ stone structure; 50°42'·30N 01°05'·05W.

SE COAST OF THE ISLE OF WIGHT

St Catherine's Point ☆ 50°34'·54N 01°17'·87W; Fl 5s 41m **27M**; vis: 257°-117°; FR 35m **17M** (same Twr) vis: 099°-116°.
Ventnor Haven W Bwtr ⚲ 2 FR (vert) 3M; 50°35'·50N 01°12'·30W.

LANGSTONE and APPROACHES

Winner ⚲; 50°45'·10N 01°00'·10W.
Langstone F'wy ⚲ L Fl 10s; 50°46'·32N 01°01'·36W.

CHICHESTER ENTRANCE

West Pole (tripod) ⚲ Fl R 5s 14m 7M; 50°45'·45N 00°56'·59W.
Bar ⚲ Fl(2) R 10s 10m 4M; 50°46'·02N 00°56'·38W.
Eastoke ⚲ QR; 50°46'·68N 00°56'·11W.
West Winner ⚲ QG; Tide gauge. 50°46'·88N 00°55'·98W.

		1																	
1	Portland Bill	1																	
2	Weymouth	8	2																
3	Swanage	22	22	3															
4	Poole Hbr ent	28	26	6	4														
5	Needles Lt Ho	35	34	14	14	5													
6	Lymington	42	40	20	24	6	6												
7	Yarmouth (IOW)	40	39	18	22	4	2	7											
8	Beaulieu River ent	46	45	25	29	11	7	7	8										
9	Cowes	49	46	28	27	14	10	9	2	9									
10	Southampton	55	54	34	34	20	16	16	9	9	10								
11	R. Hamble (ent)	53	51	32	34	18	12	13	6	6	5	11							
12	Portsmouth	58	57	37	35	23	19	19	12	10	18	13	12						
13	Langstone Hbr	61	59	39	39	25	21	21	14	12	21	18	5	13					
14	Chichester Bar	63	62	42	42	28	23	24	17	15	23	18	8	5	14				
15	Bembridge	59	58	38	39	24	18	19	13	10	18	15	5	6	8	15			
16	Nab Tower	64	63	43	44	29	23	24	18	15	24	19	10	7	6	6	16		
17	St Catherine's Pt	45	44	25	25	12	19	21	27	15	36	29	20	20	19	17	15	17	
18	Littlehampton	79	79	60	61	46	44	45	38	36	45	42	31	28	25	28	22	35	18

DISTANCE TABLES
Approx distances in nautical miles are by the most direct route allowing for dangers and TSS.

AREA 3 South East England – Selsey Bill to North Foreland

SELECTED LIGHTS, BUOYS & WAYPOINTS

Positions are referenced to WGS84

SELSEY BILL TO NORTH FORELAND

SELSEY BILL AND THE OWERS
S Pullar ⚓ VQ (6) + L Fl 10s; 50°38'·84N 00°49'·29W.
Boulder ⚓ Fl G 2·5s; 50°41'·56N 00°49'·09W.
Street ⚓ QR; 50°41'·69N 00°48'·89W.
Mixon ⚓ Fl R 5s; 50°42'·35N 00°46'·21W.
Owers ⚓ Q (6) + L Fl 15s; *Bell*; **Racon (O) 10M.**; 50°38'·59N 00°41'·09W.
E'Boro Hd ⚓ Q (3) 10s *Bell*; 50°41'·54N 00°39'·09W

LITTLEHAMPTON/SHOREHAM
Littlehampton W Pier Hd ⚓ QR 7m 6M; 50°47'·88N 00°32'·46W.
Shoreham E Bkwtr Hd ⚓ Fl G 5s 8M; *Siren 120s*; 50°49'·54N 00°14'·80W.

BRIGHTON MARINA
W Bkwtr Hd ⚓ QR 10m 7M; W ○ structure, R bands; *Horn (2) 30s*; 50°48'·50N 00°06'·38W.
E Bkwtr Hd ⚓ QG 8m 7M and Fl (4) WR 20s 16m W10M, R8M; W pillar, G bands; vis: 260°-R- 295°-W-100°; 50°48'·47N 00°06'·37W.

NEWHAVEN TO DUNGENESS
Newhaven Bkwtr Hd ⚓ Oc (2) 10s 17m 12M; 50°46'·56N 00°03'·50E.
GREENWICH ⚓ 50°24'·54N 00°00'·10E; Fl 5s 12m **15M**; Riding lt FW; R hull; **Racon (M) 10M**; *Horn 30s*.
Beachy Head ☆ 50°44'·03N 00°14'·49E; Fl (2) 20s 31m **20M**; W round twr, R band and lantern; vis: 248°-101°; (H24); *Horn 30s*.
Royal Sovereign ☆ Fl 20s 28m 12M; W ○ twr, R band on W cabin on col; *Horn (2) 30s*; 50°43'·45N 00°26'·09E.

SOVEREIGN HBR/RYE
Sovereign Hr Marina ⚓ Fl (3) 15s 12m 7M.; 50°47'·24N 00°19'·83E.
Rye Fairway , L Fl 10s; 50°54'·04N 00°48'·04E.

DUNGENESS - DOVER STRAIT
Dungeness ☆ 50°54'·81N 00°58'·56E; Fl 10s 40m **21M**; B ○ twr, W bands and lantern, floodlit; Part obsc 078°-shore; (H24). F RG 37m 10M (same twr); vis: 057°-R-073°-G-078°-196°-R-216°; *Horn (3) 60s*;FR Lts shown between 2·4M and 5·2M WNW when firing taking place. QR on radio mast 1·2M NW.
Folkestone Bkwtr Hd ⚓ 51°04'·56N 01°11'·69E; Fl (2) 10s 14m **22M**; *Dia (4) 60s*. In fog Fl 2s; vis: 246°-306°, intens 271·5°-280·5°.
VARNE ⚓ 51°01'·29N 01°23'·90E; Fl R 5s12m **15M**; **Racon (T)10M**; *Horn 30s*.

DOVER TO NORTH FORELAND
Dover Admiralty Pier Extension Hd ⚓ 51°06'·69N 01°19'·66E; Fl 7·5s 21m **20M**; W twr; vis: 096°-090°, obsc in The Downs by S Foreland inshore of 226°; *Horn 10s;* Int Port Tfc sigs.
Knuckle ☆ 51°07'·04N 01°20'·49E; Fl (4) WR 10s 15m **W15M**, R13M; W twr; vis: 059°-R-239°-W-059°.
SW Goodwin ⚓ Q (6) + L Fl 15s;51°08'·50N 01°28'·88E.
E GOODWIN ⚓ 51°13'·26N 01°36'·37E; Fl 15s 12m **23M**; R hull with lt twr amidships; **Racon (T) 10M;** *Horn 30s.*
NE Goodwin ⚓ Q (3) 10s; **Racon (M) 10M.** 51°20'·31N 01°34'·16E.
Goodwin Fork ⚓ Q (6) + L Fl 15s; *Bell;* 51°14'·33N 01°26'·86E.
NW Goodwin ⚓ Q (9) 15s; *Bell;* 51°16'·65N 01°28'·50E.
Gull Stream ⚓ QR; 51°18'·26N 01°29'·69E.

RAMSGATE/BROADSTAIRS
RA ⚓ Q(6) + L Fl 15s; 51°19'·60N 01°30'·13E.
E Brake ⚓ Fl R 5s; 51°19'·47N 01°29'·20E.
Broadstairs Knoll ⚓ Fl R 2·5s; 51°20'·88N 01°29'·48E.
North Foreland ☆ 51°22'·49N 01°26'·70E; Fl (5) WR 20s 57m **W19M, R16M, R15M**; W 8-sided twr; vis: shore-W-150°-R(**16M**)-181°-R(**15M**)-200°-W-011°; H24.

DISTANCE TABLES
Approx distances in nautical miles are by the most direct route allowing for dangers and TSS.

		1	2	3	4	5	6	7	8	9	10	11	12	13	14	15	16	17
1	Nab Tower	1																
2	Boulder Lt Buoy	5	2															
3	Owers Lt Buoy	11	8	3														
4	Littlehampton	19	13	12	4													
5	Shoreham	32	24	21	13	5												
6	Brighton	35	28	24	17	5	6											
7	Newhaven	40	34	29	24	12	7	7										
8	Beachy Head Lt	46	41	36	30	20	14	8	8									
9	Eastbourne	51	45	40	34	24	19	12	7	9								
10	Rye	72	67	62	56	46	41	34	25	23	10							
11	Dungeness Lt	76	71	66	60	50	44	38	30	26	9	11						
12	Folkestone	92	84	81	76	65	60	53	43	40	23	13	12					
13	Dover	97	89	86	81	70	65	58	48	45	28	18	5	13				
14	Ramsgate	112	104	101	96	85	80	73	63	60	43	33	20	15	14			
15	N Foreland Lt	115	107	104	99	88	83	76	66	63	46	36	23	18	3	15		
16	Sheerness	146	139	135	132	119	114	107	97	96	79	67	54	49	34	31	16	
17	London Bridge	188	184	177	177	161	156	149	139	141	124	109	96	91	76	73	45	17

AREA 4 East England – North Foreland to Berwick-upon-Tweed

SELECTED LIGHTS, BUOYS & WAYPOINTS

Positions are referenced to WGS84

THAMES ESTUARY – SOUTHERN

(Direction of buoyage generally East to West)

IMPORTANT NOTE. Regular changes are made to Thames Estuary buoyage. Check Notices to Mariners for the latest information.

OUTER APPROACHES

Foxtrot 3 ⌐ 51°24'·2N 02°00'·4E; Fl 10s 12m **15M**; **Racon (T) 10M**; *Horn 10s*.

Drill Stone ⌑ Q (3) 10s ; 51°25'·88N 01°42'·89E.

NE Spit ⌑ VQ (3) 5s; *Racon (T) 10M*; 51°27'·93N 01°29'·89E.

N KENT COAST/THE SWALE

East Margate ⌇ Fl R 2·5s; 51°27'·03N 01°26'·40E.

Foreness Pt O'fall ⌇ Fl R 5s; 51°24'·61N 01°26'·02E.

SE Margate ⌑ Q (3) 10s; 51°24'·05N 01°20'·40E.

Hook Spit ◣ QG; 51°24'·08N 01°12'·09E.

Spaniard ⌑ Q (3) 10s; 51°26'·23N 01°04'·00E.

Spile ◣ Fl G 2·5s; 51°26'·43N 00°55'·70E.

Whitstable Street ⌇ Fl R 2s; 51°24'·00N 01°01'·54E.

Pollard Spit ⌇ Q R; 51°22'·98N 00° 58'·57E.

Queenboro Spit ⌑ Q (3) 10s; 51°25'·81N 00°43'·93E.

PRINCES CHANNEL /MEDWAY/SEA REACH

Princes Outer ⌑ VQ (6) + L Fl 10s; 51°28'·89N 01°20'·43E.

Sea Reach 1 ⌑ Fl Y 2·5s; **Racon (T) 10M**; 51°29'·45N 00°52'·57E.

Medway ⌑ Mo (A) 6s; 51°28'·83N 00°52'·81E.

FOULGER'S - FISHERMAN'S GATS

Long Sand Inner ⌇ Mo 'A' 15s; 51°38'·80N 01°25'·60E.

Long Sand Outer ⌇ L Fl 10s; 51°35'·90N 01°26'·00E.

Outer Fisherman ⌑ Q (3) 10s; 51°33'·89N 01°25'·01E.

Inner Fisherman ⌇ Q R; 51°36'·07N 01°19'·87E.

THAMES ESTUARY – NORTHERN

KENTISH KNOCK

Kentish Knock ⌑ Q (3) 10s; *Whis*; 51°38'·08N 01°40·43E.

S Knock ⌑ Q (6) + L Fl 15s; *Bell*; 51°34'·13N 01°34'·29E.

BLACK DEEP

No. 9 ⌑ Q (6) + L Fl 15s; 51°35'·13N 01°15'·09E.

No. 2 ⌇ Fl (4) R 15s; 51°45'·63N 01°32'·20E.

Sunk Hd Tr ⌑ Q; *Whis*; 51°46'·63N 01°30'·51E.

Black Deep ⌇ QR. 51°47'·60N 01°35'·79E.

Long Sand Hd ⌑ VQ; *Whis*; 51°47'·90N 01°39'·42E.

BARROW DEEP

SW Barrow ⌑ Q(6) + L Fl 15s; *Bell*; 51°32'·29N 01°00'·31E.

Barrow No. 9 ⌑ VQ (3) 5s; 51°35'·34N 01°10'·30E.

Barrow No. 5 ◣ Fl G 10s; 51°40'·03N 01°16'·20E.

Barrow No. 3 ⌑ Q (3) 10s; **Racon (M)10M**; 51°42'·02N 01°20'·24E.

WEST SWIN AND MIDDLE DEEP

Blacktail Spit ◣ Fl (3) G 10s; 51°31'·47N 00°56'·74E.

Maplin ⌑ Q G; *Bell*; 51°33'·66N 01°01'·59E.

W Swin ⌇ QR; 51°33'·40N 01°01'·97E.

Maplin Edge ◣ 51°35'·33N 01°03'·64E.

Maplin Bank ⌇ Fl (3) R 10s; 51°35'·50N 01°04'·70E.

EAST SWIN (KING'S) CHANNEL

NE Maplin ◣ Fl G 5s; *Bell*; 51°37'·43N 01°04'·90E.

S Whitaker ◣ Fl (2) G 10s; 51°40'·17N 01°09'·11E.

W Sunk ⌑ Q (9) 15s; 51°44'·33N 01°25'·80E.

Gunfleet Spit ⌑ Q (6) + L Fl 15s; *Bell*; 51°45'·33N 01°21'·70E.

Gunfleet Old Lt Ho 51°46'·09N 01°20'·39E.

WHITAKER CHANNEL AND RIVER CROUCH

Whitaker ⌑ Q (3) 10s; *Bell*; 51°41'·43N 01°10'·51E.

Swin Spitway ⌑ Iso 10s; *Bell*; 51°41'·95N 01°08'·35E.

Whitaker ⅃ 51°39'·64N 01°06'·16E.

Ridge ⌇ Fl R 10s; 51°40'·13N 01°04'·87E.

Sunken Buxey ⌑ Q; 51°39'·54N 01°00'·59E.

Outer Crouch ⌑ Q(6)+LFl 15s; 51°38'·38N 00°58'·48E.

GOLDMER GAT/WALLET/COLNE BAR

NE Gunfleet ⌑ Q (3) 10s; 51°49'·93N 01°27'·79E.

Wallet No. 2 ⌇ Fl R 5s; 51°48'·88N 01°22'·99E.

Wallet No. 4 ⌇ Fl (4) R 10s; 51°46'·53N 01°17'·23E.

Wallet Spitway ⌇ L Fl 10s; *Bell*; 51°42'·86N 01°07'·30E.

Knoll ⌑ Q; 51°43'·88N 01°05'·07E.

N Eagle ⌑ Q; 51°44'·71N 01°04'·32E.

NW Knoll ⌇ Fl (2) R 5s; 51°44'·35N 01°02'·17E.

Colne Bar ◣ Fl (2) G 5s; 51°44'·61N 01°02'·57E.

Bench Head ◣ Fl (3) G 10s; 51°44'·69N 01°01'·10E.

Inner Bench Hd ⌇ Fl (2) R 5s; 51°45'·96N 01°01'·74E.

Brightlingsea Spit ⌑ Q (6) + L Fl 15s; 51°48'·08N 01°00'·70E.

RIVER BLACKWATER/WALTON BACKWATERS

The Nass ⅃ VQ (3) 5s 6m 2M; 51°45'·83N 00°54'·83E.

Thirslet ◣ Fl (3) G 10s; 51°43'·73N 00°50'·39E. 00°57'·10E.

Naze Tower; 51°51'·87N 01°17'·29E.

Pye End ⌇ L Fl 10s; 51°55'·03N 01°17'·90E.

Crab Knoll No. 3 ◣ Fl G 5s; 51°54'·41N 01°16'·41E.

Island Point ⌑ Q; 51°53'·36N 01°15'·36E.

HARWICH APPROACHES

(Direction of buoyage North to South)

MEDUSA CHAN/CORK SAND/ROUGHS

Medusa ◣ Fl G 5s; 51°51'·23N 01°20'·35E.

Stone Banks ⌇ FlR 5s; 51°53'·19N 01°19'·23E.

S Cork ⌑ Q (6) + L Fl 15s; 51°51'·33N 01°24'·09E.

Roughs Tr SE ⌑ Q (3) 10s; 51°53'·64N 01°28'·94E.

Cork Sand Yacht Bn ⟂ VQ ; 51°55'·21N 01°25'·20E.

HARWICH CHANNEL

Sunk Inner ⌐ Iso 3s 11m 12M, **Racon (T)**; *Horn 30s*; 51°51'·03N 01°34'·89E.

S Shipwash ⟂⟂ 2 By(s) Q (6) + L Fl 15s; 51°52'·71N 01°33'·97E.

Outer Tidal Bn ⟂ Mo (U) 15s 2m 3M; 51°52'·85N 01°32'·34E.

SW Shipwash ⟂ Q (9)15s; 51°54'·75N 01°34'·21E.

Haven ⟂ Mo (A) 5s; 51°55'·76N 01°35'·56E.

HA ⟂ Iso 5s; 51°56'·75N 01°30'·66E.

Harwich Chan No. 1 ⟂ Fl Y 2·5s; **Racon (T)10M**; 51°56'·13N 01°27'·06E.

S Bawdsey ⟂ Q (6) + L Fl 15s; *Whis*; 51°57'·23N 01°30'·19E.

Platters ⟂ Q (6) + L Fl 15s; 51°55'·64N 01°20'·97E.

Rolling Ground ⟂ QG; 51°55'·55N 01°19'·75E.

Inner Ridge ⌐ QR; 51°55'·38N 01°20'·20E.

Landguard ⟂ Q; 51°55'·45N 01°18'·84E.

HARWICH TO ORFORDNESS

OFFSHORE MARKS

E Shipwash ⟂ VQ (3) 5s; 51°57'·08N 01°37'·89E.

N Shipwash ⟂ Q 7M; **Racon (M) 10M**; *Whis*; 52°01'·73N 01°38'·27E.

S Galloper ⟂ Q(6) L Fl 15s; **Racon (T)10M**; 51°43'·98N 01°56'·43E.

Outer Gabbard ⟂ Q (3) 10s; **Racon (O)10M**; 51°57'·83N 02°04'·19E.

DEBEN/ORE/SUFFOLK COAST

Woodbridge Haven ⌐ Mo(A)15s; 51°58'·20N 01°23'·85E.

Cutler ⟂ QG; 51°58'·51N 01°27'·48E.

SW Whiting ⟂ Q (6) + L Fl 10s; 52°00'·96N 01°30'·69E.

Orford Haven ⌐ L Fl 10s; *Bell*. 52°01'·62N 01°28'·00E.

NE Whiting ⟂ Q (3) 10s; 52°03'·61N 01°33'·32E.

NE Bawdsey ⟂ Fl G 10s; 52°01'·73N 01°36'·09E.

ORFORDNESS TO GT YARMOUTH

(Direction of buoyage is South to North)

Orford Ness ☆ 52°05'·03N 01°34'·46E; Fl 5s 28m **20M**; W ○ twr, R bands. F WRG 14m **W17M**, R13M, **G15M** (same twr). vis: R shore-210°, 038°-R-047°-G-shore; **Racon (T) 18M**. FR 13m 12M vis: 026°- 038° over Whiting Bank.

Aldeburgh Ridge ⌐ QR; 52°06'·72N 01°36'·95E.

Southwold ☆ 52°19'·63N 01°40'·89E; Fl (4) WR 20s 37m **W16M, R12M**, R14M; vis 204°-R (intens)- 215°-W-001°.

LOWESTOFT/GT YARMOUTH APPROACHES

E Barnard ⟂ Q (3) 10s; 52°25'·14N 01°46'·38E .

Newcome Sand ⟂ QR; 52°26'·28N 01°46'·97E.

S Holm ⟂ VQ (6) + L Fl 10s; 52°27'·05N 01°47'·15E.

Kirkley ☆ Oc WRG 10s 17m, W8M, R6M, G6M, vis: 210°-G-224°-W-229°-R-313°; 52°27'·71N 01°44'·54E.

N Newcome ⌐ Fl (4) R 15s; 52°28'·39N 01°46'·37E.

Lowestoft ☆ 52°29'·22N 01°45'·35; Fl 15s 37m **23M**; W twr; part obscd 347°- shore;

E Newcome ⌐ Fl (2) R 5s; 52°28'·51N 01°49'·21E.

Corton ⟂ Q (3) 10s; *Whis*; 52°31'·13N 01°51'·39E.

E. Holm ⌐ Fl (3) R 10s; 52°30'·64N 01°49'·72E.

S Corton ⟂ Q (6) + L Fl 15s; *Bell*; 52°32'·70N 01°49'·50E.

Holm Sand ⟂ Q. 52°33'·36N 01°46'·85E.

W Corton ⟂ Q (9) 15s; 52°34'·59N 01°46'·62E.

Gorleston South Pier Hd ⟂ Fl R 3s 11m 11M; vis: 235°-340°; *Horn (3) 60s*; 52°34'·33N 01°44'·28E.

GREAT YARMOUTH TO THE WASH

(Direction of buoyage ⟳ South to North)

GT YARMOUTH/COCKLE GATWAY/OFFSHORE

SW Scroby ⟂ Fl G 2·5s; 52°35'·82N 01°46'·26E.

Scroby Sands Wind Farm, 30 turbines centred on 52°39'·00N 01°47'·00E. NW, NE, SW, SE extremities (F.R Lts) Fl Y 5s 5M Horn Mo (U) 30s.

N Scroby ⟂ VQ; 52°41'·39N 01°46'·47E.

Cockle ⟂ VQ (3) 5s; *Bell*; 52°44'·03N 01°43'·59E.

Winterton Church **Racon (T) 10M**; 52°42'·92N 01°41'·21E.

Cross Sand ⟂ L Fl 10s 6m 5M; **Racon (T)10M**; 52°37'·03N 01°59'·14E.

NE Cross Sand ⟂ VQ (3) 5s; 52°44'·22N 01° 58'·80E.

Smith's Knoll ⟂ Q (6) + L Fl 15s 7M; **Racon (T) 10M**; 52°43'·52N 02°17'·89E.

S Winterton Ridge ⟂ Q (6) + L Fl 15s; 52°47'·21N 02°03'·44E.

Newarp ⟂ L Fl 10s 7M; **Racon (O) 10M**; 52°48'·37N 01°55'·69E.

S Haisbro ⟂ Q (6) + L Fl 15s; *Bell*; 52°50'·82N 01°48'·29E.

N Haisbro ⟂ Q; **Racon (T) 10M**; 53°00'·22N 01°32'·29E.

Happisburgh ☆ Fl (3) 30s 41m 14M; 52°49'·21N 01°32'·18E.

N NORFOLK COAST/THE WASH

Cromer ☆ 52°55'·45N 01°19'·01E; Fl 5s 84m **21M**; 8-sided twr; vis: 102°-307° H24; **Racon (O) 25M**.

E Sheringham ⟂ Q (3) 10s; 53°02'·21N 01°14'·84E.

Blakeney O'falls ⌐ Fl (2) R 5s; *Bell*; 53°03'·01N 01°01'·37E.

Wells Leading Buoy ⌐ Fl (2) R 5s; 52°59'·64N 00°50'·74E.

S Race ⟂ Q (6) + L Fl 15s; *Bell*; 53°07'·81N 00°57'·34E.

S Inner Dowsing ⟂ Q (6) + L Fl 15s; 53°12'·12N 00°33'·69E.

Burnham Flats ⟂ Q (9) 15s; *Bell*; 53°07'·53N 00°34'·89E.

N Well ⟂ L Fl 10s; *Whis*; **Racon (T) 10M**; 53°03'·02N 00°27'·90E.

Roaring Middle ⟂ L Fl 10s 7m 8M; 52°58'·64N 00°21'·08E.

Sunk ⚲ Q (9) 15s; 52°56'·29N 00°23'·40E.
Boston Roads ⚲ L Fl 10s; 52°57'·66N 00°16'·04E.

THE WASH TO THE RIVER HUMBER

Dudgeon⚲Q (9) 15s 7M; **Racon (O) 10M**; 53°16'·62N 01°16'·90E.

E Dudgeon ⚲ Q (3) 10s; 53°19'·72N 00°58'·69E.

N Outer Dowsing ⚲ Q; 53°33'·52N 00°59'·59E, *Racon (T) 10M*.

B.1D Platform Dowsing ⚲ 53°33'·68N 00°52'·63E; Fl (2) 10s 28m **22M**; Morse (U) R 15s 28m 3M; *Horn (2) 60s*.

Inner Dowsing ⚲ Q (3) 10s 7M, **Racon (T) 10M**; *Horn 60s*; 53°19'·10N 00°34'·80E.

Protector ⚲ Fl R 2·5s; 53°24'·84N 00°25'·12E.

Humber ⚲ G lt float L Fl 10s 7M; *Horn (2) 30s*; **Racon (T) 7M**; 53°38'·70N 00°21'·24E.

SPURN ⚲ Q (3) 10s 10m 8M; *Horn 20s*; **Racon (M) 5M**; 53°33'·56N 00°14'·20E.

RIVER HUMBER TO RIVER TYNE
BRIDLINGTON/FILEY

SW Smithic ⚲ Q (9) 15s; 54°02'·41N 00°09'·21W.

Flamborough Hd ☆ 54°06'·98N 00°04'·96W; Fl (4) 15s 65m **24M**; W ○ twr; *Horn (2) 90s*.

Filey Brigg ⚲ Q (3) 10s; *Bell*; 54°12'·74N 00°14'·60W.

SCARBOROUGH/WHITBY

Scarborough Pier ⚲ Iso 5s 17m 9M; W○twr; vis: 219°-039° (tide sigs); *Dia 60s*; 54°16'·91N 00°23'·40W.

Whitby ⚲ Q; *Bell*; 54°30'·33N 00°36'·58W.

Whitby High ☆ 54°28'·67N 00°34'·10W; Ling Hill Fl WR 5s 73m **18M**, R16M; W 8-sided twr and dwellings; vis: 128°-R-143°-W- 319°.

Salt Scar ⚲ 54°38'·12N 01°00'·12W VQ; *Bell*.

TEES BAY/HARTLEPOOL/SUNDERLAND

Tees Fairway ⚲Iso 4s 8m 8M; **Racon (B) unknown range**; *Horn (1) 5s*; 54°40'·94N 01°06'·48W.

Bkwtr Hd S Gare ☆ 54°38'·85N 01°08'·27W; Fl WR 12s 16m **W20M, R17M**; W ○ twr; vis: 020°-W-274°-R-357°; *Sig Stn; Horn 30s*.

Longscar ⚲ Q (3) 10s; *Bell*; 54°40'·86N 01°09'·89W.

The Heugh ☆ 54°41'·79N 01°10'·56W; Fl (2) 10s 19m**19M** ; W twr.

Hartlepool Old Pier Hd ⚲ Fl WG 3s 13m 7M; vis: 317°-W-325°-G- 317°; 54°41'·60N 01°11'·09W.

Sunderland Roker Pier Hd ☆ 54°55'·28N 01°21'·15W; Fl 5s 25m **23M**; W □ twr, 3 R bands and cupola: vis: 211°- 357°; *Siren 20s*.

TYNE ENTRANCE/NORTH SHIELDS

Ent North Pier Hd ☆ 55°00'·88N 01°24'·18W; Fl (3) 10s 26m **26M**; Gy □ twr, W lantern; *Horn 10s*.

RIVER TYNE TO BERWICK-ON-TWEED
BLYTH/COQUET ISLAND/ AMBLE

Blyth F'w'y ⚲ Fl G 3s; *Bell*;55°06'·59N 01°28'·60W.

Blyth E Pier Hd ☆ 55°06'·98N 01°29'·37W; Fl (4) 10s 19m **21M**, W twr; same structure FR 13m 13M, vis:152°-249°; Horn (3) 30s.

Coquet ☆ 55°20'·03N 01°32'·39W; Fl (3) WR 20s 25m **W19M, R15M**; W □ twr, turreted parapet, lower half Gy; vis: 330°-R-140°-W-163°-R-180°-W-330°; sector boundaries are indeterminate and may appear as Alt WR; *Horn 30s*.

Amble N Pier Hd ⚲ Fl G 6s 12m 6M; 55°20'·39N 01°34'·25W.

BAMBURGH/FARNE ISLANDS

The Falls ⚲ Fl R 2·5s; 55°34'·61N 01°37'·12W.

Shoreston Outcars ⚲ QR; 55°35'·88N 01°39'·34W.

Bamburgh Black Rocks Point ☆ 55°36'·99N 01°43'·45W; Oc(2) WRG 8s 12m **W14M**, R11M, G11M; W bldg; vis: 122°-G-165°-W-175°-R-191°-W-238°-R- 275°-W- 289°-G-300°.

Inner Farne ⚲ Fl (2) WR 15s 27m W10M, R7M; W○twr; vis: 119°-R-280°-W-119°; 55°36'·92N 01°39'·35W.

Longstone ☆ **W side** 55°38'·62N 01°36'·65W; Fl 20s 23m **24M**; R twr, W band; *Horn (2) 60s*.

Swedman ⚲ Fl G 2·5s; 55°37'·65N 01°41'·63W.

HOLY ISLAND

Ridge ⚲ Q (3) 10s; 55°39'·70N 01°45'·97W.

Triton ⚲ QG; 55°39'·59N 01°46'·82W.

Plough Seat ⚲ QR; 55°40'·37N 01°44'·97W.

Goldstone ⚲ QG; 55°40'·25N 01°43'·64W.

BERWICK-ON-TWEED

Bkwtr Hd ⚲ Fl 5s 15m 6M; vis: 201°-009°, (obscured 155°-201°); W ○ twr, R cupola and base; FG (same twr) 8m 1M; vis 009°-G-155°; 55°45'·88N 01°59'·06W.

		1		11	31	61	78	91	107	126	189	205	205	232	Berwick-upon-Tweed	11
1	Ramsgate	1														
2	Sheerness	34	2		10	27	42	65	81	102	157	176	185	203	Amble	10
3	Gravesend	56	22	3		9	16	36	51	70	138	149	156	180	Sunderland	9
4	London Bridge	76	45	23	4		8	24	39	58	122	137	140	169	Hartlepool	8
5	Burnham-on-Crouch	44	34	53	76	5		7	16	35	88	114	121	143	Whitby	7
6	Brightlingsea	41	28	47	71	22	6		6	20	81	98	105	130	Scarborough	6
7	Harwich	40	50	65	83	31	20	7		5	58	83	87	114	Bridlington	5
8	River Deben (ent)	45	55	71	89	35	23	6	8		4	72	75	113	Hull	4
9	Southwold	62	80	95	113	58	46	30	23	9		3	34	83	Boston	3
10	Lowestoft	72	90	105	123	68	56	40	33	10	10		2	85	King's Lynn	2
11	Great Yarmouth	79	97	112	130	76	63	52	41	18	7	11		1	Great Yarmouth	1

AREA 5 *E Scotland – Berwick-upon-Tweed to C Wrath & N Isles*

SELECTED LIGHTS, BUOYS & WAYPOINTS

Positions are referenced to WGS84

BERWICK-UPON-TWEED TO BASS ROCK

EYEMOUTH/ST ABB'S/DUNBAR

Blind Buss ↙ Q; 55°52'·80N 02°05'·25E.

Eyemouth E Bkwtr Hd ≰ Iso R 2s 8m 8M; 55°52'·50N 02°05'·29W.

St Abb's Hd ☆ 55°54'·96N 02°08'·29W; Fl 10s 68m **26M**; W twr; **Racon (T) 18M**.

Bass Rock, S side, ☆ Fl (3) 20s 46m 10M; W twr; vis: 241°-107°; 56°04'·61N 02°38'·48W.

FIRTH OF FORTH - SOUTH SHORE

SOUTH SIDE TO LEITH/PORT EDGAR

Fidra ☆ 56°04'·39N 02°47'·13W; Fl (4) 30s 34m **24M**; W twr; obsc by Bass Rk, Craig Leith & Lamb Is.

Wreck ⩰ Fl (2) R 10s; 56°04'·39N 02°52'·39W.

Inchkeith F'wy ⩎ Iso 2s; **Racon (T) 5M**; 56°03'·49N 03°00'·10W.

Narrow Deep ⩰ Fl (2) R 10s; 56°01'·46N 03°04'·59W.

Craigh Waugh ↙ Fl (2) 10s;56°00'·26N 03°04'·47W.

Leith Approach ⩰ Fl R 3s; 55°59'·95N 03°11'·51W.

Inch Garvie, NW ≰ L Fl 5s 9m 11M; 56°00'·10N 03°23'·37W.

Forth Rail Br. Centres of spans have W Lts and ends of cantilevers R Lts, defining N and S chans. Centre Piers; 2 Aero FR 47m 5M; 56°00'·33N 03°21'·79W.

Forth Road Br. N susp twr Iso G 4s 7m 6M on E and W sides. S susp twr Iso R 4s 7m 6M on E and W sides.

Port Edgar W Bkwtr Hd ≰ Fl R 4s 4m 8M; 55°59'·86N 03°24'·78W. W blockhouse

NORTH CHANNEL/MIDDLE BANK

Inchkeith ☆ 56°02'·01N 03°08'·17W; Fl 15s 67m **22M**; stone twr.

No. 7 ▲ QG; *Bell;* **Racon (T) 5M**; 56°02'·80N 03°10'·97W.

Oxcars ☆ Fl (2) WR 7s 16m W13M, R12M; W twr, R band; vis: 072°-W-087°-R-196°-W-313°-R-072°; 56°01'·36N 03°16'·84W.

FIRTH OF FORTH - N SHORE; ELIE TO FIFE NESS/RIVER TAY/ARBROATH

Elie Ness ☆ 56°11'·04N 02°48'·77W; Fl 6s 15m **18M**; W twr.

St Monans Bkwtr Hd ≰ Oc WRG 6s 5m W7M, R4M, G4M; vis: 282°-G-355°-W-026°-R-038°; 56°12'·20N 02°45'·94W.

Anstruther, W Pier Hd ≰ 2 FR (vert) 5m 4M; Gy mast; *Horn (3) 60s (occas);* 56°13'·18N 02°41'·84W.

Isle of May ☆ 56°11'·12N 02°33'·46W(Summit); Fl (2) 15s 73m **22M**; ☐ twr on stone dwelling.

Fife Ness ☆ 56°16'·74N 02°35'·19W; Iso WR 10s 12m **W21M, R20M**; W bldg; vis: 143°-W-197°-R-217°-W-023°.

N Carr ↙ Q (3) 10s 3m 5M; 56°18'·05N 02°32'·94W.

Bell Rk ☆ 56°26'·08N 02°23'·21W; Fl 5s 28m **18M; Racon (M) 18M.**

Tay F'wy ⩎ L Fl 10s; 56°28'·30N 02°36'·60W.

Abertay N ↙ Q (3) 10s; **Racon (T) 8M**; 56°27'·39N 02°40'·36W.

Horse Shoe ↙ Q (6) + L Fl 15s; 56°27'·28N 02°50'·20W.

Tayport High Lt Ho ☆ 56°27'·17N 02°53'·96W; Dir lt 269°; Iso WRG3s 24m **W22M, R17M, G16M**; W twr; vis:267°-G-268°-W-270°-R-271°;56°27'·04N 02°56'·55W.

Arbroath E Pier S Elbow ≰ Fl G 3s 8m 5M; W twr; shows FR when hbr closed; *Siren (3) 60s* (occas) 56°33'·25N 02°34'·97W.

MONTROSE TO RATTRAY HEAD

MONTROSE/JOHNSHAVEN/GOURDON

Scurdie Ness ☆ 56°42'·10N 02°26'·24W; Fl (3) 20s 38m **23M**; W twr; **Racon (T) 14-16M.**

Montrose Ldg Lts 271·5°. Front, FR 11m 5M; W twin pillars, R bands; 56°42'·21N 02°27'·41W. Rear, 272m from front, FR 18m 5M; W twr, R cupola.

Johnshaven, Ldg Lts 316°. Front, FR 5m; 56°47'·62N 02°20'·26W . Rear, 85m from front, FG 20m; shows R when unsafe to enter hbr.

Gourdon Hbr, Ldg Lts 358°. Front, FR 5m 5M; W twr; shows G when unsafe to enter; *Siren (2) 60s* (occas); 56°49'·69N 02°17'·24W. Rear, 120m from front, FR 30m 5M; W twr.

STONEHAVEN/ABERDEEN/PETERHEAD

Stonehaven Outer Pier Hd ≰ Iso WRG 4s 7m 5M; vis: 214°-G-246°-W-268°-R-280°; 56°57'·59N 02°12'·00W.

Girdle Ness ☆ Fl (2) 20s 56m **22M**; obsc by Greg Ness when brg more than about 020°; **Racon (G) 25M**; 57°08'·34N 02°02'·91W.

Aberdeen F'wy ⩎ Mo (A) 5s; **Racon (T) 7M**; 57°09'·31N 02°01'·95W.

Torry Ldg lts 235·7°. Front, FR or FG 14m 5M; FR entry safe, FG when entry dangerous; vis: 195°-279°; 57°08'·37N 02°04'·51W. Rear, FR 19m 5M.

Buchan Ness ☆ Fl 5s 40m **28M**; W twr, R bands; **Racon (O) 14-16M**; 57°28'·23N 01°46'·51W.

Cruden Skares ⩰ Fl R 10s; 57°23'·17N 01°50'·36W.

Peterhead Marina N Bkwtr Hd ≰ QG 5m 2M; vis: 185°-300°; 57°29'·81N 01°47'·49W.

Rattray Hd ☆ 57°36'·61N 01°49'·03W; Fl (3) 30s 28m **24M**; W twr; **Racon (M) 15M.**

RATTRAY HEAD TO INVERNESS

Rattray Hd ☆ 57°36'·61N 01°49'·03W Fl (3) 30s 28m 24M; W twr; **Racon (M) 15M**; *Horn (2) 45s.*

FRASERBURGH/MACDUFF/BANFF

Fraserburgh, Balaclava Bkwtr Head ⚓ Fl (2) G 8s 26m 6M; dome on W twr; vis: 178°-326°; 57°41'·51N 01°59'·70W.

Kinnaird Hd ☆ 57°41'·87N 02°00'·26W Fl 5s 25m 22M; vis: 092°-297°.

Macduff Pier Hd ⚓ Fl (2) WRG 6s 12m W9M, R7M; W twr; vis: shore-G-115°-W-174°-R-210°; 57°40'·25N 02°30'·02W.

Banff N Pier Hd ⚓ Fl 4s; 57°40'·22N 02°31'·27W.

WHITEHILLS/PORTSOY/FINDOCHTY

Whitehills Pier Hd ⚓ 57°40'·80N 02°34'·88W Fl WR 3s 7m W9M, R6M; W twr; vis: 132°-R-212°-W-245°.

Portsoy Pier Ldg Lts 173°, Front Fl G 4s 20m 3M; post; 57°41'·09N 02°41'·40W. Rear Q G 22m 3M; R △ on BW post.

Findochty Middle Pier Ldg Lts 166°, Front FR 6m 3M; 57°41'·90N 02°54'·20W. Rear FR 10m 3M.

BUCKIE/LOSSIEMOUTH/HOPEMAN

West Muck ⚓ QR 5m 7M; tripod; 57°41'·06N 02°58'·01W.

N Pier 60m from Hd ☆ 57°40'·9N 02°57'·5W Oc R 10s 15m **15M** W twr.

BURGHEAD/FINDHORN/NAIRN

Lossiemouth S Pier Hd ⚓ Fl R 6s 11m 5M; *Siren 60s;* 57°43'·42N 03°16'·69W.

Covesea Skerries ☆ 57°43'·47N 03°20'·45W Fl WR 20s 49m **W24M, R20M**; W twr; vis: 076°-W-267°-R-282°.

Hopeman W Pier Hd ⚓ Oc G 4s 8m 4M; 57°42'·69N 03°26'·29W.

Burghead N Bkwtr Hd ⚓ Oc 8s 7m 5M; 57°42'·09N 03°30'·03W.

Findhorn Landfall ⚓ LF 10s; 57°40'·34N 03°38'·77W.

Nairn W Pier Hd ⚓ QG 5m 1M; Gy post; 57°35'·60N 03°51'·63W.

INVERNESS FIRTH/CALEDONIAN CANAL

Navity Bk ⚓ Fl (3) G 15s; 57°38'·16N 04°01'·18W.

Riff Bank S ⚓ Q (6) + L Fl 15s; 57°36'·73N 04°00'·97W.

Craigmee ⚓ Fl R 6s 3m 4M; 57°35'·30N 04°05'·04W.

Chanonry ☆ 57°34'·44N 04°05'·57W Oc 6s 12m **15M**; W twr; vis: 148°-073°.

Kessock Bridge Centre , Or △; **Racon (K) 6M**; 57°29'·97N 04°13'·79W.

Clachnaharry, S Tr'ng Wall Hd ⚓ Iso G 4s 5m 2M; tfc sigs; 57°29'·43N 04°15'·86W.

INVERNESS TO DUNCANSBY HEAD

CROMARTY FIRTH

Fairway ⚓ L Fl 10s; **Racon (M) 5M**; 57°39'·96N 03°54'·19W.

Cromarty Bank ⚓ Fl (2) G 10s; 57°40'·66N 03°56'·78W.

Buss Bank ⚓ Fl R 3s 57°40'·97N 03°59'·54W.

The Ness ☆ 57°40'·98N 04°02'·20W Oc WR 10s 18m **W15M**, R11M; W twr; vis: 079°-R-088°-W-275°, obsc by N Sutor when brg less than 253°.

Three Kings ⚓ Q (3) 10s; 57°43'·73N 03°54'·25W.

DORNOCH FIRTH/LYBSTER/WICK

Tarbat Ness ☆ 57°51'·88N 03°46'·76W Fl (4) 30s 53m 24M; W twr, R bands; **Racon (T) 14-16M.**

Lybster, S Pier Hd ⚓ Oc R 6s 10m 3M; 58°17'·79N 03°17'·41W.

Clyth Ness Lt Ho (unlit), W twr, R band; 58°18'·64N 03°12'·74W.

Wick S Pier Hd ⚓ Fl WRG 3s 12m W12M, R9M, G9M; W 8-sided twr; vis: 253°-G-270°-W-286°-R-329°; Bell (2) 10s (occas); 58°26'·34N 03°04'·73W.

Noss Hd ☆ 58°28'·71N 03°03'·09W Fl WR 20s 53m **W25M, R21M**; W twr; vis: shore-R-191°-W-shore.

DUNCANSBY HEAD TO CAPE WRATH

Duncansby Hd ☆ 58°38'·65N 03°01'·58W Fl 12s 67m 22M; W twr; **Racon (T).**

Pentland Skerries ☆ 58°41'·41N 02°55'·49W Fl (3) 30s 52m **23M**; W twr.

Lother Rock ⚓ Fl 2s 13m 6M; **Racon (M)10M**; 58°43'·79N 02°58'·69W.

Swona N Hd ⚓ Fl (3) 10s 16m 10M; 58°45'·11N 03°03'·10W.

Stroma ☆, Swilkie Point 58°41'·75N 03°07'·01W Fl (2) 20s 32m **26M**; W twr.

Dunnet Hd ☆ 58°40'·28N 03°22'·60W Fl (4) 30s 105m **23M**.

Scrabster Q. E. Pier Hd ⚓ Fl (2) 4s 8m 8M 58°36'·66N 03°32'·31W.

Strathy Pt ☆ 58°36'·04N 04°01'·12W Fl 20s 45m **26M**; W twr on W dwelling. F.R. on chy 100° 8·5M.

Sule Skerry ☆ 59°05'·09N 04°24'·38W Fl (2) 15s 34m **21M**; W twr; **Racon (T).**

North Rona ☆ 59°07'·27N 05°48'·91W Fl (3) 20s 114m **24M**.

Sula Sgeir ⚓ Fl 15s 74m 11M; □ structure; 59°05'·61N 06°09'·57W.

Loch Eriboll, White Hd ⚓ Fl WR10s 18m W13M, R12M; W twr and bldg; vis: 030°-W-172°-R-191°-W-212°; 58°31'·01N 04°38'·90W.

Cape Wrath ☆ 58°37'·54N 04°59'·94W Fl (4) 30s 122m **22M**; W twr.

ORKNEY ISLANDS

Tor Ness ☆ 58°46'·78N 03°17'·86W Fl 5s 21m **17M**; W twr.

Cantick Hd (S Walls, SE end) ☆ 58°47'·23N 03°07'·88W Fl 20s 35m 13M; W twr.

SCAPA FLOW AND APPROACHES
Ruff Reef, off Cantick Hd ⚡Fl 10s 10m 6M; 58°47'·43N 03°07'·80W.

Hoxa Hd ⚡ Fl WR 3s 15m W9M, R6M; W twr; vis: 026°-W-163°-R-201°-W-215°; 58°49'·31N 03°02'·09W.

Stanger Hd ⚡ Fl R 5s 25m 8M 58°48'·96N 03°04'·74W.

CLESTRAN SOUND/HOY SOUND
Peter Skerry ▲ Fl G 6s; 58°55'·25N 03°13'·51W.

Riddock Shoal ⚬ Fl (2) R 12s; 58°55'·89N 03°15'·00W.

Graemsay Is Hoy Sound Low ☆ Ldg Lts 104°. **Front**, 58°56'·42N 03°18'·60W Iso 3s 17m **15M**; W twr; vis: 070°-255°. **High Rear**, 1·2M from front, Oc WR 8s 35m **W20M, R16M**; W twr; vis: 097°-R-112°-W-163°-R-178°-W-332°; obsc on Ldg line within 0·5M.

STROMNESS
Stromness ⚬ QR; 58°57'·25N 03°17'·61W.

N Pier Hd ⚡ Fl R 3s 8m 5M; 58°57'·75N 03°17'·71W.

AUSKERRY/KIRKWALL
Copinsay ☆ 58°53'·77N 02°40'·35W Fl (5) 30s 79m **21M**; W twr.

Auskerry ☆ 59°01'·51N 02°34'·34W Fl 20s 34m **20M**; W twr.

Scargun Shoal v Q (3) 10s; 59°00'·69N 02°58'·58W.

Kirkwall Pier N end ☆ 58°59'·29N 02°57'·72W Iso WRG 5s 8m **W15M**, R13M, G13M; W twr; vis: 153°-G-183°-W-192°-R-210°.

WIDE FIRTH
Linga Skerry ⚐ Q (3) 10s; 59°02'·39N 02°57'·56W.

Boray Skerries ⚐ Q (6) + L Fl 15s; 59°03'·65N 02°57'·66W.

Skertours ⚐ Q; 59°04'·11N 02°56'·72W.

Galt Skerry ⚐ Q; 59°05'·21N 02°54'·20W.

Brough of Birsay ☆ 59°08'·19N 03°20'·41W Fl (3) 25s 52m **18M**.

Papa Stronsay NE end, The Ness Fl(4)20s 8m 9M; W twr; 59°09'·34N 02°34'·93W

STRONSAY, PAPA SOUND
Quiabow ▲ Fl (2) G 12s; 59°09'·82N 02°36'·30W.

No. 1 ▲ Fl G 5s; (off Jacks Reef) 59°09'·16N 02°36'·51W.

Whitehall Pier Hd ⚡ 2 FG (vert) 8m 4M; 50°08'·61N 02°35'·96W.

SANDAY ISLAND/NORTH RONALDSAY
Start Pt ☆ 59°16'·69N 02°22'·71W Fl (2) 20s 24m **18M**.

N Ronaldsay ☆ NE end, 59°23'·37N 02°23'·03W Fl 10s 43m **24M**; R twr, W bands; **Racon (T) 14-17M**.

WESTRAY/PIEROWALL
Noup Head ☆ 59°19'·86N 03°04'·23W Fl 30s 79m **20M**; W twr; vis: about 335°-282° but partially obsc 240°-275°.

Pierowall E Pier Head ⚡ Fl WRG 3s 7m W11M, R7M, G7M; vis: 254°-G-276°-W-291°-R-308°-G-215°; 59°19'·35N 02°58'·53W.

Papa Westray, Moclett Bay Pier Head ⚡ Fl WRG 5s 7m W5M, R3M,G3M; vis: 306°-G-341°-W-040°-R-074°; 59°19'·60N 02°53'·52W.

SHETLAND ISLES

FAIR ISLE
Skadan South ☆, 59°30'·84N 01°39'·16W Fl (4) 30s 32m **22M**; W twr; vis: 260°-146°, obsc inshore 260°-282°; **Horn (2) 60s**.

Skroo ☆ N end 59°33'·13N 01°36'·58W Fl (2) 30s 80m **22M**; W twr; vis: 086·7°-358°.

MAINLAND, SOUTH
Sumburgh Head ☆ 59°51'·21N 01°16'·58W Fl (3) 30s 91m **23M**.

Pool of Virkie, Marina E Bkwtr Head ⚡ 2 FG (vert) 6m 5M; 59°53'·01N 01°17'·16W.

BRESSAY/LERWICK
Bressay, Kirkabister Ness ☆ 60°07'·20N 01°07'·29W; Fl (2) 20s 32m **23M**.

Soldian Rock ⚐ Q (6) + L Fl 15s 60°12'·51N 01°04'·73W.

Gremista Marina S Hd ⚡ Iso R 4s 3m 2M; 60°10'·20N 01°09'·61W.

Rova Hd ⚡ 60°11'·46N 01°08'·60W Fl (3) WRG 18s 12m W12M, R9M, G9M; W twr; vis: 090°-R-182°-W-191°-G-213°-R-241°-W-261·5°-G-009°-R-040°. Same structure and synhcronised: Fl (3) WRG 18s 14m **W16M**, R13M, G13M; vis: 176·5°-R-182°-W-191°-G-196·5°.

The Brethren Rock ⚐ Q (9) 15s; 60°12'·35N 01°08'·24W.

The Unicorn Rock ⚐ VQ (3) 5s; 60°13'·51N 01°08'·48W.

Dales Voe ⚡ Fl (2) WRG 8s 5m W4M, R3M, G3M; vis: 220°-G-227°-W-233°-R-240°; 60°11'·79N 01°11'·23W.

Dales Voe Quay ⚡ 2 FR (vert) 9m 3M; 60°11'·60N 01°10'·48W.

1	Berwick-upon-Tweed	1			11	155	79	47	76	104	144	126	120	125	145		Cape Wrath	11
2	Eyemouth	10	2		10	95	124	120	148	190	170	162	156	160		Lerwick	10
3	Dunbar	26	17	3	9	50	46	74	114	104	90	95	115		Kirkwall	9
4	Port Edgar	58	50	34	4	8	31	59	99	89	75	80	100		Scrabster	8
5	Methil	45	36	20	20	5	7	29	69	58	44	50	72		Wick	7
6	Fife Ness	38	29	17	34	16	6	6	43	32	26	44	74		Helmsdale	6
7	Dundee	58	49	37	54	36	20	7	5	13	34	59	90		Inverness	5
8	Montrose	59	51	43	61	43	27	27	8	4	23	48	79		Nairn	4
9	Stonehaven	72	66	60	78	60	44	45	20	9	3	25	56		Lossiemouth	3
10	Aberdeen	82	78	73	90	72	56	57	32	13	10	2	33		Banff/Macduff	2
11	Peterhead	105	98	93	108	94	78	80	54	35	25	11		Peterhead	1

AREA 6 *NW Scotland – C Wrath to Oban including The Western Isles*

SELECTED LIGHTS, BUOYS & WAYPOINTS

Positions are referenced to WGS84

CAPE WRATH TO LOCH TORRIDON

Cape Wrath ☆ 58°37'·54N 04°59'·99W Fl (4) 30s 122m **22M**; W twr.

LOCH INCHARD/LOCH LAXFORD

Bodha Ceann na Saile ⚓ Q; 58°27'·24N 05°04'·01W.
Kinlochbervie Dir lt 327° ☆. 58°27'·49N 05°03'·08W WRG 15m **16M**; vis: 326°-FG-326·5°-Al GW-326·75°-FW-327·25°-Al RW-327·5°-FR-328°.
Stoer Head ☆ 58°14'·43N 05°24'·07W Fl 15s 59m **24M**; W twr.

LOCH INVER/SUMMER ISLES/ULLAPOOL

Soyea I ⚓ Fl (2) 10s 34m 6M; 58°08'·56N 05°19'·67W.
Glas Leac ⚓ Fl WRG 3s 7m 5M; 58°08'·68N 05°16'·36W.
Rubha Cadail ⚓ Fl WRG 6s 11m W9M, R6M, G6M; W twr; vis: 311°-G-320°-W-325°-R-103°-W-111°-G-118°-W-127°-R-157°-W-199°; 57°55'·51N 05°13'·40W.
Ullapool Pt ⚓ QR; 57°53'·70N 05°10'·68W.
Cailleach Head ⚓ Fl (2) 12s 60m 9M; W twr; vis: 015°-236°; 57°55'·81N 05°24'·23W.

LOCH EWE/LOCH GAIRLOCH

Fairway ⚓ L Fl 10s; 57°51'·98N 05°40'·09W.
Rubha Reidh ☆ 57°51'·52N 05°48'·72W Fl (4) 15s 37m **24M**.
Glas Eilean ⚓ Fl WRG 6s 9m W6M, R4M; vis: 080°-W-102°-R-296°-W-333°-G-080°; 57°42'·79N 05°42'·42W.
Gairloch Pier ⚓ 57°42'·59N 05°41'·03W QR 6m 2M.

OUTER HEBRIDES – EAST SIDE

LEWIS
Butt of Lewis ☆ 58°30'·89N 06°15'·84W Fl 5s 52m **25M**; R twr; vis: 056°-320°.
Tiumpan Head ☆ 58°15'·66N 06°08'·29W Fl (2) 15s 55m **25M**; W twr.
Reef Rock ⚓ QR; 58°11'·58N 06°21'·97W.
Arnish Point ☆ Fl WR 10s 17m W9M, R7M; W ○ twr; vis: 088°-W-198°-R-302°-W-013°; 58°11'·50N 06°22'·16W.
Rubh' Uisenis ⚓ Fl 5s 24m 11M; W twr; 57°56'·25N 06°28'·36W.
Shiants ⚓ QG; 57°54'·57N 06°25'·70W.
Sgeir Inoe ⚓ Fl G 6s; **Racon (M) 5M**; 57°50'·93N 06°33'·93W.
Scalpay, **Eilean Glas** ☆ 57°51'·41N 06°38'·55W Fl (3) 20s 43m **23M**; W twr, R bands; **Racon (T) 16-18M**.
Sgeir Bràigh Mor ⚓ Fl G 6s; 57°51'·51N 06°43'·84W.
Sgeir Graidach ⚓ Q (6) + L Fl 15s; 57°50'·36N 06°41'·37W.
Tarbert ⚓ Oc WRG 6s 10m 5M; 57°53'·82N 06°47'·93W

SOUND OF HARRIS/BERNERAY

Fairway ⚓ L Fl 10s; 57°40'·35N 07°02'·15W.
Cabbage ⚓ Fl (2) R 6s; **Racon (T) 5M (3cm)**; 57°42'·13N 07°03'·96W.
Bo Stainan ⚓ VQ(6) + LF 10s. 57°45'·76N 07°02'·40W
Trench ⚓ Q (3) G 10s; 57°41'·89N 07°09'·00W.

LOCH MADDY

Weaver's Pt ⚓ 57°36'·49N 07°06'·00W Fl 3s 24m 7M; W hut.
Glas Eilean Mòr ⚓ 57°35'·95N 07°06'·70W Fl (2) G 4s 8m 5M.

SOUTH UIST, LOCH CARNAN

Landfall ⚓ L Fl 10s; 57°22'·27N 07°11'·52W.
Ushenish ☆ (S Uist) 57°17'·89N 07°11'·58W Fl WR 20s 54m **W19M, R15M**; W twr; vis: 193°-W-356°-R-018°.

LOCH BOISDALE/BARRA/CASTLEBAY

MacKenzie Rk ⚓ Fl (3) R 15s 3m 4M; 57°08'·24N 07°13'·71W.
Calvay E End ⚓ Fl (2) WRG 10s 16m W7M, R4M, G4M; W twr; vis: 111°-W-190°-G-202°-W-286°-R-111°; 57°08'·53N 07°15'·38W.
Binch Rock ⚓ Q (6) + L Fl 15s; 57°01'·60N 07°17'·12W.
Bo Vich Chuan ⚓ Q (6) + L Fl 15s; **Racon (M) 5M**; 56°56'·15N 07°23'·31W.
Castle Bay S ⚓ Fl (2) R 8s; **Racon (T) 7M**; 56°56'·09N 07°27'·21W.
Barra Hd ☆ 56°47'·11N 07°39'·26W Fl 15s 208m **18M**; W twr; obsc by islands to NE.

OUTER HEBRIDES – WEST SIDE

Flannan I ☆, Eilean Mór 58°17'·32N 07°35'·23W Fl (2) 30s 101m **20M**; W twr; obsc in places by Is to W of Eilean Mór.
Haskeir I ☆ 57°41'·98N 07°41·36W Fl 20s 44m **23M**; W twr.
Monach Isles ☆ Fl (2) 15s 47m **18M**; R brick twr; 57°31'·55N 07°41·68W.

LOCH TORRIDON TO MULL

LITTLE MINCH/NORTH SKYE/RONA
Eugenie Rk ⚓ Q 6 + LF 15s; 57°46'·47N 06°27'·28W.
Eilean Trodday ⚓ Fl (2) WRG 10s 52m W12M, R9M, G9M; W Bn; vis: W062°-R088°-130°-W-322°-G-062°; 57°43'·64N 06°17'·89W.
Comet Rock ⚓ Fl R 6s; 57°44'·60N 06°20'·50W.
Rona NE Point £ 57°34'·68N 05°57'·56W Fl 12s 69m 19M; W twr; vis: 050°-358°.

CROWLIN ISLANDS/RAASAY

Sgeir Mhór ⚓ Fl G 5s; 57°24'·57N 06°10'·53W.
Eilean Beag ⚓ Fl 6s 32m 6M; W Bn; 57°21'·21N 05°51'·42W.
Eyre Pt ⚓ Fl WR 3s 6m W9M, R6M; W twr; vis: 215°-W-266°-R- 288°-W-063°; 57°20'·01N 06°01'·29W.

KYLE AKIN AND KYLE OF LOCH ALSH
Carragh Rk ⚓ Fl (2) G 12s; **Racon (T) 5M**; 57°17'·18N 05°45'·36W.
Skye Br Centre ⚓ Oc 6s; 57°16'·57N 05°44'·58W.
String Rock ⚓ Fl R 6s; 57°16'·50N 05°42'·89W.
Sgeir-na-Caillich ⚓ Fl (2) R 6s 3m 4M; 57°15'·59N 05°38'·90W.

SOUND OF SLEAT
Kyle Rhea ⚓ Fl WRG 3s 7m W8M, R5M, G5M; W Bn; vis: shore-R-219°-W-228°-G-338°-W-346°-R-shore.
Ornsay, SE end ☆ 57°08'·59N 05°46'·88W Oc 8s 18m **15M**; W twr; vis: 157°-030°.
Pt. of Sleat ⚓ Fl 3s 20m 9M; W twr; 57°01'·08N 06°01'·08W.

MALLAIG
Sgeir Dhearg ⚓ QG; 57°00'·74N 05°49'·50W.
N Pier, E end ⚓ Iso WRG 4s 6m W9M, R6M, G6M; Gy twr; vis: 181°-G-185°-W-197°-R-201°. Fl G 3s 14m 6M; same structure; 57°00'·47N 05°49'·50W.

NW SKYE
Neist Point ☆ 57°25'·41N 06°47'·30W Fl 5s 43m **16M**; W twr.

WEST OF MULL AND SMALL ISLES
Hyskeir ☆ 56°58'·14N 06°40'·87W Fl (3) 30s 41m **24M**; W twr. **Racon (T) 14-17M**.
Bogha Ruadh⚓ Fl G 5s 4m 3M; 56°49'·56N 06°13'·05W.
Bo Faskadale ⚓ Fl (3) G 18s; 56°48'·18N 06°06'·37W.
Ardnamurchan ☆ 56°43'·63N 06°13'·58W Fl (2) 20s 55m **24M**; Gy twr; vis: 002°-217°.

TIREE
Roan Bogha ⚓ Q (6) + L Fl 15s 3m 5M; 56°32'·23N 06°40'·18W.
Placaid Bogha ⚓ Fl G 4s; 56°33'·22N 06°44'·06W.
Scarinish ☆, S side of ent 56°30'·01N 06°48'·27W Fl 3s 11m **16M**; W ☐ twr; vis: 210°-030°.
Skerryvore ☆ 56°19'·36N 07°06'·88W Fl 10s 46m **23M**; Gy twr; **Racon (M) 18M**; *Horn 60s*.

Cairn na Burgh More (Treshnish Is), Fl (3) 15s 36m 8M; solar panels on framework tr; 56°31'·05N 06°22'·95W.

LOCH NA LÀTHAICH (LOCH LATHAICH)
Dubh Artach ☆ 56°07'·94N 06°38'·08W; Fl (2)30s 44m **20M**; Gy twr, R band.

SOUND OF MULL
LOCH SUNART/TOBERMORY/LOCH ALINE
Ardmore Pt ⚓ Fl (2) 10s 18m 13M; 56°39'·37N 06°07'·70W.
New Rks ⚓ Fl G 6s 56°39'·05N 06°03'·30W.
Rubha nan Gall ☆ 56°38'·33N 06°04'·00W Fl 3s 17m **15M**; W twr.
Avon Rock ⚓ Fl (4) R 12s; 56°30'·78N 05°46'·80W.
Yule Rocks ⚓ Fl R 15s; 56°30'·01N 05°43'·96W.
Glas Eileanan Gy Rks ⚓ Fl 3s 11m 6M; W ◯ twr on W base; 56°29'·77N 05°42'·83W.
Craignure Ldg Lts 240·9°. Front, FR 10m; 56°28'·26N 05°42'·28W. Rear, 150m from front, FR 12m; vis: 225·8°-255·8°.

MULL TO OBAN
Lismore ☆, SW end 56°27'·34N 05°36'·45W Fl 10s 31m **17M**; W twr; vis: 237°-208°.
Lady's Rk ⚓ Fl 6s 12m 5M; 56°26'·92N 05°37'·05W.
Duart Pt ⚓ Fl (3) WR 18s 14m W5M, R3M; vis: 162°-W-261°-R-275°-W-353°-R-shore; 56°26'·84N 05°38'·77W.

DUNSTAFFNAGE BAY
Pier Hd ⚓ NE end, 2 FG (vert) 4m 2M; 56°27'·21N 05°26'·18W.

OBAN
N spit of Kerrera ⚓ Fl R 3s 9m 5M; W col, R bands; 56°25'·49N 05°29'·56W.
Dunollie ⚓ Fl (2) WRG 6s 7m W8M, G6M, R6M; vis: 351°-G- 020°- W-047°-R-120°-W-138°-G-143°; 56°25'·37N 05°29'·05W.
Corran Ledge ⚓ VQ (9) 10s; 56°25'·19N 05°29'·11W.
Oban N Pier Mid ⚓ 2 FG (vert) 8m 5M; 56°24'·87N 05°28'·49W.

1	Cape Wrath	1															
2	Ullapool	54	2														
3	Stornoway	53	45	3													
4	East Loch Tarbert	75	56	33	4												
5	Portree	83	57	53	42	5											
6	Kyle of Lochalsh	91	63	62	63	21	6										
7	Mallaig	112	82	83	84	42	21	7									
8	Eigg	123	98	97	75	54	35	14	8								
9	Castlebay (Barra)	133	105	92	69	97	76	59	46	9							
10	Tobermory	144	114	115	87	74	53	32	20	53	10						
11	Loch Aline	157	127	128	100	87	66	45	33	66	13	11					
12	Fort William	198	161	162	134	121	98	75	63	96	43	34	12				
13	Oban	169	138	139	111	100	77	56	44	77	24	13	29	13			
14	Loch Melfort	184	154	155	117	114	93	69	61	92	40	27	45	18	14		
15	Craobh Haven	184	155	155	117	114	92	70	60	93	40	27	50	21	5	15	
16	Crinan	187	157	158	129	112	95	74	63	97	42	30	54	25	14	9	16
17	Mull of Kintyre	232	203	189	175	159	143	121	105	120	89	87	98	72	62	57	51	17

DISTANCE TABLES

Approx distances in nautical miles are by the most direct route allowing for dangers and TSS.

SELECTED LIGHTS, BUOYS & WAYPOINTS

Positions are referenced to WGS84

OBAN TO LOCH CRAIGNISH

Bogha Nuadh ⚓ Q (6) + LFl 15s; 56°21'·69N 05°37'·88W.

Fladda ⚡ Fl (2) WRG 9s 13m W11M, R9M, G9M; W twr; vis: 169°-R-186°-W-337°-G-344°-W-356°-R-026°; 56°14'·89N 05°40'·83W.

Dubh Sgeir (Luing) ⚡ Fl WRG 6s 9m W6M, R4M. G4M; W twr; vis: W000°- R010°- W025°- G199°-000°; **Racon (M) 5M**; 56°14'·76N 05°40'·20W.

The Garvellachs, Eileach an Naoimh, SW end ⚡ Fl 6s 21m 9M; W Bn; vis: 240°-215°; 56°13'·04N 05°49'·06W.

LOCH MELFORT/CRAOBH HAVEN

Melfort Pier ⚡ Dir FR 6m 3M; (Private shown 1/4 to 31/10); 56°16'·14N 05°30'·19W.

Craobh Marina Bkwtr Hd ⚡ Iso WRG 5s 10m, W5M, R3M, G3M; vis:114°-G-162°-W-183°-R-200°; 56°12'·78N 05°33'·52W.

COLONSAY TO ISLAY

COLONSAY/SOUND OF ISLAY/PORT ELLEN

Scalasaig, Rubha Dubh ⚡ Fl (2) WR 10s 8m W8M, R6M; W bldg; vis: shore-R- 230°-W-337°-R-354°; 56°04'·01N 06°10'·90W.

Rhubh' a Mháil (Ruvaal) ☆ 55°56'·18N 06°07'·46W Fl (3) 15s 45m **19M**; W twr.

Black Rocks ⚓ Fl G 6s; 55°47'·50N 06°04'·09W.

McArthur's Hd ⚡ Fl (2) WR 10s 39m W14M, R11M; W twr; W in Sound of Islay from NE coast,159°-R-244°-W-E coast of Islay; 55°45'·84N 06°02'·90W.

Eilean a Chùirn ⚡ Fl (3) 18s 26m 8M; W Bn; obsc when brg more than 040°; 55°40'·12N 06°01'·22W.

Gigha Rocks ⚓ Q (9) 15s; 55°39'·20N 05°43'·65W.

Otter Rk ⚓ Q (6) + L Fl 15s; 55°33'·86N 06°07'·92W.

Port Ellen ⚓ QG; 55°37'·00N 06°12'·27W.

Orsay Is, **Rhinns of Islay** ☆ 55°40'·40N 06°30'·84W Fl 5s 46m **24M**; W twr; vis: 256°-184°.

JURA TO MULL OF KINTYRE

SOUND OF JURA/CRAIGHOUSE/L SWEEN/GIGHA

Reisa an t-Struith, S end of Is ⚡ Fl (2) 12s 12m 7M; W col; 56°07'·77N 05°38'·91W.

Ruadh Sgeir ⚡ Fl 6s 15m 9M; W ○ twr; 56°04'·32N 05°39'·77W.

Skervuile ⚡ Fl 15s 22m 9M; W twr; 55°52'·46N 05°49'·85W.

Eilean nan Gabhar ⚡ Fl 5s 7m 8M; framework twr; vis: 225°-010°; 55°50'·04N 05°56'·25W.

Sgeir Gigalum ⚓ Fl G 6s 3m 4M; 55°39'·96N 05°42'·67W.

Cath Sgeir ⚓ Q (9) 15s; 55°39'·66N 05°47'·50W.

Gigalum Rks ⚓ Q (9) 15s; 55°39'·20N 05°43'·70W.

WEST LOCH TARBERT

Dunskeig Bay ⚡ Q (2) 10s 11m 8M; 55°45'·22N 05°35'·00W.

Eileen Tráighe (off S side) ⚓ Fl (2) R 5s 5m 3M; R post; 55°45'·37N 05°35'·75W.

Mull of Kintyre ☆ 55°18'·64N 05°48'·25W Fl (2) 20s 91m **24M**; W twr on W bldg; vis: 347°-178°.

CRINAN CANAL/ARDRISHAIG

Crinan, E of lock ent ⚡ Fl WG 3s 8m 4M; W twr, R band; vis: shore-W-146°-G-shore; 56°05'·48N 05°33'·37W.

Ardrishaig Bkwtr Hd ⚡ LFl WRG 6s 9m 4M; vis:287°-G-339°-W-350°-R-035°; 56°00'·76N 05°26'·59W.

Sgeir Sgalag No. 49 ⚓ Fl G 5s; 56°00'·36N 05°26'·30W.

LOCH FYNE TO SANDA ISLAND

EAST LOCH TARBERT

Madadh Maol ⚡ Fl R 2·5s 4m 3M; 55°52'·02N 05°24'·25W.

KILBRANNAN SOUND/CARRADALE BAY

Crubon Rk ⚓ Fl (2) R 12s; 55°34'·48N 05°27'·07W.

Otterard Rk ⚓ Q (3) 10s; 55°27'·07N 05°31'·11W.

CAMPBELTOWN LOCH

Davaar N Pt ☆ 55°25'·69N 05°32'·42W Fl (2) 10s 37m **23M**; W twr; vis: 073°-330°.

Methe Bk 'C' ⚓ Fl (2) 6s; 55°25'·30N 05°34'·42W.

Arranman's Barrels ⚓ Fl (2) R 12s; 55°19'·40N 05°32'·87W.

Sanda Island ☆ 55°16'·50N 05°35'·01W Fl 10s 50m **15M**; W twr; Vis: 242°-121°.

Patersons Rk ⚓ Fl (3) R 18s; 55°16'·90N 05°32'·48W.

KYLES OF BUTE TO RIVER CLYDE

KYLES OF BUTE/CALADH

Rubha Ban ⚓ Fl R 4s; 55°54'·95N 05°12'·40W.

Burnt I No. 42 ⚓ (S of Eilean Buidhe) Fl R 2s; 55°55'·76N 05°10'·39W.

Rubha á Bhodaich ⚓ Fl G; 55°55'·38N 05°09'·59W.

Ardmaleish Pt No. 41 ⚓ Q; 55°53'·02N 05°04'·70W.

FIRTH OF CLYDE

Ascog Patches No. 13 ⚓ Fl (2) 10s 5m 5M; 55°49'·71N 05°00'·25W.

Toward Pt ☆ 55°51'·73N 04°58'·79W Fl 10s 21m **22M**; W twr.

Skelmorlie ⚓ Iso 5s; 55°51'·65N 04°56'·34W.

WEMYSS/INVERKIP/HOLY LOCH

Kip ⚓ Fl G 5s; 55°54'·49N 04°52'·98W.

Warden Bank ⚓ Fl G 2s; 55°54'·77N 04°54'·54W.

Cowal ⚓ L Fl 10s; 55°56'·00N 04°54'·83W.

The Gantocks ⚡ Fl R 6s 12m 6M; ○ twr; 55°56'·45N 04°55'·08W.

Cloch Point ⚡ Fl 3s 24m 8M; W ○ twr, B band, W dwellings; 55°56'·55N 04°52'·74W.
Holy Loch Marina 2 FR (vert) 4m 1M; 55°59'·00N 04°56'·80W.

LOCH LONG/LOCH GOIL/GOUROCK

Loch Long ⚓ Oc 6s; 55°59'·15N 04°52'·42W.
Ashton ⚓ Iso 5s; 55°58'·10N 04°50'·65W.
Whiteforeland ⚓ L Fl 10s; 55°58'·11N 04°47'·28W.
Rosneath Patch ⚓ Fl (2) 10s 5m 10M; 55°58'·52N 04°47'·45W.

ROSNEATH/RHU NARROWS/GARELOCH

Ldg Lts 356°. **Front, No. 7N** ⚓ 56°00'·05N 04°45'·36W
Dir lt 356°. WRG 5m **W16M**, R13M, G13M; vis: 353°-Al WG- 355°- FW-357°-Al WR-000°-FR-002°.
Dir lt 115° WRG 5m **W16M**, R13M, G13M; vis: 111°-Al WG-114°-FW- 116°-Al WR-119°-FR-121°.
Row ⚓ Fl G 5s; 55°59'·84N 04°45'·13W.
Cairndhu ⚓ Fl G 2·5s; 56°00'·35N 04°46'·00W.
Rhu SE ⚓ Fl G 3s; 56°00'·64N 04°47'·17W.
Rhu NE ⚓ QG; 56°01'·02N 04°47'·58W.
Rhu Spit ⚓ Fl 3s 6m 6M; 56°00'·84N 04°47'·34W. 8m 8M. are Fl G and Lts on N bank are Fl R.

CLYDE TO LOCH RYAN

LARGS/FAIRLIE

Approach ⚓ L Fl 10s; 55°46'·40N 04°51'·85W.
Largs Marina S Bkwtr Hd ⚡ Oc G 10s 4m 4M; 55°46'·36N 04°51'·73W.
Fairlie Patch ⚓ Fl G 1·5s; 55°45'·38N 04°52'·34W.

MILLPORT, GREAT CUMBRAE

The Eileans, W end ⚡ QG 5m 2M; 55°44'·89N 04°55'·59W.
Mountstuart ⚓ L Fl 10s; 55°48'·00N 04°57'·57W.
Portachur ⚓ Fl G 3s; 55°44'·35N 04°58'·52W.
Little Cumbrae Is, Cumbrae Elbow ⚡ Fl 6s 28m 14M; W twr; vis: 334°-193°; 55°43'·22N 04°58'·06W.

ARDROSSAN/TROON

Ardrossan N Bkwtr Hd ⚡ Fl R 5s 7m 5M; R gantry; 55°38'·53N 04°49'·64W.
W Crinan Rk ⚓ Fl R 4s; 55°38'·47N 04°49'·89W.
Eagle Rock ⚓ 55°38'·21N 04°49'·69W Fl G 5s.
Troon ⚓ Fl G 4s; 55°33'·06N 04°41'·35W.
Lady I ⚓ Fl 2s 19m 8M; W Bn; 55°31'·63N 04°44'·04W.

ARRAN/RANZA/LAMLASH

Hamilton Rk ⚓ Fl R 6s; 55°32'·63N 05°04'·90W.
Pillar Rk Pt ☆ (Holy Island), 55°31'·04N 05°03'·67W Fl (2) 20s 38m **25M**; W □ twr.
Pladda ☆ 55°25'·50N 05°07'·12W Fl (3) 30s 40m **17M**; W twr.

AYR/GIRVAN/LOCH RYAN

S. Nicholas ⚓ 55°28'·12N 04°39'·44W Fl G 2s.
Turnberry Point ☆, near castle ruins 55°19'·56N 04°50'·71W Fl 15s 29m **24M**; W twr.
Ailsa Craig ☆ 55°15'·12N 05°06'·52W Fl 4s 18m **17M**; W twr; vis: 145°-028°.
Girvan S Pier Hd 2 FG (vert) 8m 4M; W twr; 55°14'·72N 04°51'·90W.
Milleur Point ⚓ Q; 55°01'·28N 05°05'·66W.
Cairn Pt ⚡ Fl (2) R 10s 14m 12M; W twr; 54°58'·46N 05°01'·85W.

LOCH RYAN TO KIRKUDBRIGHT

Corsewall Point ☆ 55°00'·41N 05°09'·58W Fl (5) 30s 34m **22M**; W twr; vis: 027°-257°.
Crammag Hd ☆ 54°39'·90N 04°57'·92W Fl 10s 35m **18M**; W twr.
Mull of Galloway ☆, SE end 54°38'·08N 04°51'·45W Fl 20s 99m **28M**; W twr; vis: 182°-105°.

KIRKCUDBRIGHT BAY

Hestan I, E end ⚡ Fl (2) 10s 42m 9M; 54°49'·95N 03°48'·53W.

#		1	2	3	4	5	6	7	8	9	10	11	12	13	14
1	Loch Craignish	**1**													
2	Crinan	5	**2**												
3	Ardrishaig	14	9	**3**											
6	East Loch Tarbert	24	19	10	**4**										
5	Campbeltown	55	50	39	31	**5**									
6	Lamlash	48	43	34	25	24	**6**								
7	Largs	48	43	34	24	39	17	**7**							
8	Kip Marina	53	48	39	28	50	25	10	**8**						
9	Greenock	59	54	45	36	53	31	16	6	**9**					
10	Rhu (Helensburgh)	62	57	48	37	59	33	19	9	4	**10**				
11	Troon	54	49	40	33	33	16	20	29	34	38	**11**			
12	Girvan	67	62	53	43	29	20	33	46	49	51	21	**12**		
13	Stranraer	89	84	75	65	34	39	56	69	65	74	44	23	**13**	
14	Kirkcudbright	136	131	122	114	88	92	110	116	124	125	97	94	71	**14**

DISTANCE TABLES
Approx distances in nautical miles are by the most direct route allowing for dangers and TSS.

AREA 8 NW England & Wales – Kirkcudbright & Isle of Man to Swansea

SELECTED LIGHTS, BUOYS & WAYPOINTS

Positions are referenced to WGS84

SOLWAY FIRTH TO BARROW-IN-FURNESS
SILLOTH/MARYPORT
Two Feet Bk ⎏ Q (9) 15s; 54°42'·90N 03°47'·10W.
Solway ⚓ Fl G 4s; 54°46'·80N 03°30'·14W.
Maryport S Pier Hd ⚡.Fl 1·5s 10m 6M;54°43'·07N 03°30'·64W.
S Workington ⎏ VQ (6) + L Fl 10s; 54°37'·01N 03°38'·58W.
Whitehaven W Pier Hd ⚡ Fl G 5s 16m 8M; W ○ twr; 54°33'·17N 03°35'·92W.

Saint Bees Hd ☆ 54°30'·81N 03°38'·23W Fl (2) 20s 102m **18M**; W○ twr; obsc shore-340°.
Selker ⚓ Fl (3) G 10s; *Bell;* 54°16'·14N 03°29'·58W.
Lightning Knoll ⚓ L Fl 10s; *Bell;* 53°59'·83N 03°14'·28W.
Isle of Walney ☆ 54°02'·92N 03°10'·64W Fl 15s 21m **23M**; stone twr; obsc 122°-127° within 3M of shore.

ISLE OF MAN
Whitestone Bk ⎏ Q (9) 15s; 54°24'·58N 04°20'·41W.
Point of Ayre ☆ 54°24'·94N 04°22'·13W Fl (4) 20s 32m **19M**; W twr, two R bands; **Racon (M) 13-15M.**
Low Lt Ho (unlit), RW twr, B base; 54°25'·03N 04°21'·86W.
Thousla Rk ⚡ Fl R 3s 9m 4M; 54°03'·73N 04°48'·05W.
Calf of Man Lighthouse (disused), white 8-sided tower.
Chicken Rk ⚡ Fl 5s 38m 21M; twr; 54°02'·26N 04°50'·32W.
Douglas Head ☆ 54°08'·60N 04°27'·95W Fl 10s 32m **24M**; W twr; obsc brg more than 037°. FR Lts on radio masts 1 and 3M West.
Maughold Head ☆ 54°17'·72N 04°18'·58W Fl (3) 30s 65m **21M.**
Bahama ⎏ VQ (6) + L Fl 10s; 54°20'·01N 04°08'·57W.
King William Bank ⎏ Q (3) 10s; 54°26'·01N 04°00'·08W.

BARROW TO RIVERS MERSEY AND DEE
MORECAMBE/FLEETWOOD/RIVER RIBBLE
Morecambe ⎏ Q (9) 15s; 53°52'·01N 03°24'·10W.
Lune Deep ⎏ Q (6) + L Fl 15s; **Racon (T);** 53°56'·07N 03°12'·9W.
R Lune ⎏ Q (9) 15s; 53°58'·63N 03°00'·03W.
53°58'·89N 02°52'·96W.
Gut ⚓ L Fl 10s; 53°41'·74N 03°08'·98W.
Jordan's Spit ⎏ Q (9) 15s; 53°35'·76N 03°19'·28W.

RIVER MERSEY APPROACHES
Bar ⊏ Fl 5s 12M; **Racon (T) 10M;** 53°32'·01N 03°20'·98W.
Q1 ⚓ VQ; 53°31'·00N 03°16'·72W.

Formby ⎏ Iso 4s; 53°31'·13N 03°13'·48W.
Crosby ⚓ Oc 5s 11m 8M; R hull, W stripes; 53°30'·72N 03°06'·29W.
Brazil ⚓ QG; 53°26'·84N 03°02'·24W.

RIVER DEE
HE1 ⎏ Q (9) 15s; 53°26'·33N 03°18'·08W.
Hilbre I ⚡ Fl R 3s 14m 5M; W twr; 53°22'·99N 03°13'·72W.
Salisbury Mid ⚓ Fl (3) R 10s; 53°21'·30N 03°16'·39W.
Dee ⎏ Q (6) + L Fl 15s; 53°21'·99N 03°18'·68W.

N AND NW WALES COAST
RIVER DEE TO CONWY
N Hoyle ⎏ VQ; 53°26'·68N 03°30'·58W.
S Hoyle Outer ⚓ Fl R 2·5s; 53°21'·47N 03°24'·70W.
Prestatyn ⚓ QG; 53°21'·51N 03°28'·51W.
N Hoyle Wind Farm (30 turbines) centred on 53°25'·00N 03°27'·00W. NW, NE, SW, SE extremities (F.R Lts) Fl Y 2.5s 5M Horn Mo (U) 30s.
W Constable ⎏ Q (9) 15s; **Racon (M) 10M;** 53°23'·14N 03°49'·26W.
N Constable ⎏ VQ; 53°23'·76N 03°41'·42W.
Conwy F'wy ⚓ L Fl 10s; 53°17'·95N 03°55'·58W.
C2 ⚓ Fl (2) R 10s; 53°17'·64N 03°54'·71W.

MENAI STRIAT - N APPROACHES
Trwyn-Du ⚡ Fl 5s 19m 12M; W ○ castellated twr, B bands; vis: 101°-023°; *Bell (1) 30s,* sounded continuously; 53°18'·77N 04°02'·44W.
Ten Feet Bank ⚓ QR; 53°19'·47N 04°02'·82W.

ANGLESEY
Point Lynas ☆ 53°24'·98N 04°17'·35W Oc 10s 39m **18M**; W castellated twr; vis: 109°-315°; *Horn 45s;* H24 in periods of reduced visibility.
Archdeacon Rock ⎏ Q; 53°26'·71N 04°30'·87W.
The Skerries ☆ 53°25'·27N 04°36'·55W Fl (2) 15s 36m **20M**; W ○ twr, R band; **Racon (T) 25M.** Iso R 4s 26m 10M; same twr; vis: 233°-253°; *Horn (2) 60s.* H24 in periods of reduced visibility.
Langdon ⎏ Q (9) 15s; 53°22'·74N 04°38'·74W.
Holyhead Bkwtr Hd ⚡ Fl (3) G 10s 21m 14M; W ☐ twr, B band; Fl Y vis: 174°-226°; 53°19'·86N 04°37'·16W.
Marina Bkwtr Hd ⚡ 2 FR (vert); 53°19'·31N 04°38'·63W.
South Stack ☆ 53°19'·31N 04°41'·98W Fl 10s 60m **24M**; (H24); W ○ twr; obsc to N by N Stack and part obsc in Penrhos bay; *Horn 30s.* Fog Det lt vis: 145°-325°.

MENAI STRAIT TO BARDSEY ISLAND
CAERNARFON APPROACHES
(Direction of buoyage ⇲ SW to NE)
C2 ⚓ Fl R 10s; 53°07'·07N 04°24'·52W.
Llanddwyn I ⚡Fl WR 2·5s 12m W7M, R4M; W twr;

vis: 280°-R- 015°-W-120°; 53°08'·05N 04°24'·79W.
Mussel Bank ⌀ Fl (2) R 5s; 53°07'·27N 04°20'·81W.

LLEYN PENINSULA/BARDSEY ISLAND

Porth Dinllaen, Careg y Chwislen ↨ 52°56'·99N 04°33'·51W.

Bardsey I ☆ 52°44'·97N 04°48'·02W Fl (5) 15s 39m **26M**; W ☐ twr, R bands; obsc by Bardsey Is 198°-250° and in Tremadoc B when brg less than 260°.

CARDIGAN BAY

St Tudwal's ⚲ Fl WR 15s 46m W14, R10M; vis: 349°-W-169°-R- 221°-W-243°-R-259°-W-293°-R-349°; obsc by East I 211°-231°; 52°47'·92N 04°28'·30W.

PWLLHELI/PORTHMADOG/BARMOUTH/ ABERDOVEY

Pwllheli App ⌀ Iso 2s; 52°53'·02N 04°23'·07W.
Porthmadog Fairway ⌀ L Fl 10s; 52°52'·97N 04°11'·18W.
Barmouth Outer ⌀ L Fl 10s; 52°42'·62N 04°04'·83W.
Sarn Badrig Causeway ⌀Q (9) 15s; *Bell;* 52°41'·19N 04°25'·36W .
Sarn-y-Bwch ⌀ VQ (9) 10s; 52°34'·81N 04°13'·58W.
Aberdovey Outer ⌀ Iso 4s; 52°32'·00N 04°05'·56W.
Patches ⌀ Q (9) 15s; 52°25'·83N 04°16'·41W.

ABERYSTWYTH/FISHGUARD

Aberystwyth S Bkwtr Hd ⚲ Fl (2) WG 10s 12m 10M; vis: 030°-G- 053°-W-210°; 52°24'·40N 04°05'·52W.
Fishguard N Bkwtr Hd ⚲ Fl G 4·5s 18m 13M; *Bell (1) 8s;* 52°00'·76N 04°58'·23W. 89m 5M.

Strumble Head ☆ 52°01'·79N 05°04'·43W Fl (4) 15s 45m **26M**;   vis: 038°-257°; (H24).

BISHOPS AND SMALLS

South Bishop ☆ 51°51'·14N 05°24'·74W Fl 5s 44m **16M**; W ◯ twr; *Horn (3) 45s;* **Racon (O)10M**; (H24).
The Smalls ☆ 51°43'·27N 05°40'·19W Fl (3) 15s 36m **18M**; **Racon (T)** ; *Horn (2) 60s.* Same twr, Iso R 4s 33m 13M; vis: 253°-285° over Hats & Barrels Rk; both Lts shown H24 in periods of reduced visibility.

Skokholm I ☆, 51°41'·64N 05°17'·22W Fl WR 10s 54m **W18M, R15M**;   vis: 301°-W-154°-R-301°; partially obsc 226°-258°.

W & S WALES - BRISTOL CHANNEL
MILFORD HAVEN

St Ann's Head ☆ 51°40'·87N 05°10'·42W Fl WR 5s 48m **W18M, R17M,** R14M; W 8-sided twr; vis: 233°-W-247°- R -285°- R(intens) -314°- R -332°-W131°, partially obscured between 124°-129°; *Horn (2) 60s.*
W Blockhouse Pt ↨ Ldg Lts 022·5°. Front, F 54m 13M; B stripe on W twr; vis: 004·5°-040·5°; intens on lead. By day 10M; vis: 004·5°-040·5°; **Racon (Q) range unknown;** 51°41'·31N 05°09'·56W.
Watwick Point Common Rear ☆, 0·5M from front, F 80m **15M**; vis: 013·5°-031·5°. By day 10M; vis: 013·5°-031·5°; **Racon (Y).**
St Ann's ⌀ Fl R 2·5s; 51°40'·25N 05°10'·51W.
Sheep ▲ QG; 51°40'·06N 05°08'·31W.
Dakotian ⌀ Q (3) 10s; 51°42'·15N 05°08'·29W.
Turbot Bk ⌀ VQ (9) 10s; 51°37'·41N 05°10'·08W.
St Gowan ⌀Q (6) + L Fl 15s, *Whis,* **Racon (T) 10M;** 51°31'·93N 04°59'·77W.

TENBY/CARMARTHEN BAY/BURRY INLET

Caldey I ⚲ Fl (3) WR 20s 65m W13M, R9M; vis: R173°-W212°- R088°-102°; 51°37'·90N 04°41'·08W.
Spaniel ⌀ Q (3) 10s; 51°38'·06N 04°39'·74W.
Tenby Pier Hd ⚲ FR 7m 7M; 51°40'·40N 04°41'·89W.
DZ7 ⌀ Fl Y 10s; 51°38'·09N 04°30'·12W.
DZ5 ⌀ Fl Y 2·5s; 51°36'·37N 04°24'·39W.
Burry Port ⚲ Fl 5s 7m **15M**.
W. Helwick (W HWK) ⌀ (9) 15s; **Racon (T) 10M;** *Whis;* 51°31'·40N 04°23'·65W Q.
E. Helwick ⌀ VQ (3) 5s; *Bell;* 51°31'·80N 04°12'·68W.

SWANSEA BAY

Ledge ⌀ VQ (6) + L Fl 10s; 51°29'·93N 03°58'·77W.
Mixon ⌀ Fl (2) R 5s; *Bell;* 51°33'·12N 03°58'·78W.

																		DISTANCE TABLES
1.	Portpatrick	**1**																Approx distances in nautical miles are by the most direct route allowing for dangers and TSS.
2.	Mull of Galloway	16	**2**															
3.	Kirkcudbright	48	32	**3**														
4.	Maryport	65	49	26	**4**													
5.	Workington	63	47	25	6	**5**												
6.	Ravenglass	70	54	40	30	23	**6**											
7.	Point of Ayre	38	22	28	37	31	34	**7**										
8.	Peel	41	26	46	55	49	52	18	**8**									
9.	Douglas	60	42	46	50	44	39	19	30	**9**								
10.	Glasson Dock	101	85	74	66	60	37	64	85	63	**10**							
11.	Fleetwood	95	79	68	59	53	30	58	80	57	10	**11**						
12.	Liverpool	118	102	97	89	83	60	80	86	70	52	46	**12**					
13.	Conwy	111	95	95	92	86	58	72	72	59	62	56	46	**13**				
14.	Beaumaris	109	93	94	95	89	72	71	73	58	66	60	49	12	**14**			
15.	Caernarfon	117	103	104	105	99	82	81	73	68	76	70	59	22	10	**15**		
16.	Holyhead	93	81	94	96	90	69	68	62	50	79	73	68	36	32	26	**16**	
17.	Fishguard	171	158	175	175	169	160	153	140	134	153	147	136	100	88	78	89	**17**

SELECTED LIGHTS, BUOYS & WAYPOINTS | Positions are referenced to WGS84

BRISTOL CHANNEL (NORTH SHORE)
SWANSEA BAY/PORT TALBOT/PORTHCAWL
Mixon ⚓ Fl (2) R 5s; *Bell;* 51°33'·12N 03°58'·78W.
Grounds ⚑ VQ (3) 5s; 51°32'·81N 03°53'·47W.
Mumbles ☆ 51°34'·01N 03°58'·27W Fl (4) 20s 35m
15M; W twr; *Horn (3) 60s.*
SW Inner Green Grounds ⚑ Q (6) + L Fl 15s; *Bell;*
51°34'·06N 03°57'·03W.
Cabenda ⚑ VQ (6) + L Fl 10s; **Racon (Q)**; 51°33'·36N
03°52'·23W.
P Talbot N Outer ⚓ Fl R 5s; 51°33'·78N 03°51'·38W.
Kenfig ⚑ VQ (3) 5s; 51°29'·44N 03°46'·06W.
W Scar ⚑ Q (9) 15s, *Bell,* **Racon (T) 10M;** 51°28'·31N
03°55'·57W.
S Scar ⚑ Q (6) + L Fl 15s; 51°27'·61N 03°51'·58W.
E Scar ⚑ Q (3) 10s; *Bell;* 51°27'·98N 03°46'·76W.
Fairy ⚑ Q (9) 15s; *Bell;* 51°27'·86N 03°42'·07W.
Tusker ⚓ Fl (2) R 5s *Bell;* 51°26'·85N 03°40'·74W
W Nash ⚑ VQ (9) 10s ; *Bell;* 51°25'·99N 03°45'·95W.
East Nash ⚑ Q (3) 10s; 51°24'·06N 03°34'·10W.
Nash ☆ 51°24'·03N 03°33'·06W Fl (2) WR 15s
56m **W21M, R16M**; vis: 280°-R-290°-W-100°-R-
120°-W-128°.

BARRY/CARDIFF/PENARTH/NEWPORT
Breaksea ⚑ L Fl 10s; **Racon (T) 10M;** 51°19'·88N
03°19'·08W.
Merkur ⚓ QR; 51°21'·88N 03°15'·95W.
Barry W Bkwtr Hd ⚞ Fl 2·5s 12m 10M; 51°23'·46N
03°15'·52W.
Lavernock Spit ⚑ VQ (6) + L Fl 10s; 51°23'·02N
03°10'·82W.
Mackenzie ⚓ QR; 51°21'·75N 03°08'·24W.
Wolves ⚑ VQ; 51°23'·13N 03°08'·88W.
Flat Holm ☆, SE Pt 51°22'·54N 03°07'·14W Fl (3) WR
10s 50m **W15M**, R12M; W ○ twr; vis: 106°-R-140°-
W-151°-R-203°-W-106°; (H24).
Weston ⚓ Fl (2) R 5s; 51°22'·60N 03°05'·75W.
Monkstone Rk ⚞ Fl 5s 13m 12M; 51°24'·89N
03°06'·02W.
Ranie ⚓ Fl (2) R 5s; 51°24'·23N 03°09'·39W.
S Cardiff ⚑ Q (6) + L Fl 15s; *Bell;* 51°24'·18N
03°08'·57W.
Outer Wrach ⚑ Q (9) 15s; 51°26'·20N 03°09'·46W.
N Cardiff ⚓ QG; 51°26'·52N 03°07'·19W.
EW Grounds ⚑ L Fl 10s 7M; *Bell;* **Racon (T) 7M;**
51°27'·12N 02°59'·95W.
Newport Deep ⚓ Fl (3) G 10s; *Bell;*51°29'·36N
02°59'·12W.
East Usk ☆ 51°32'·40N 02°58'·01W Fl (2) WRG
10s 11m W11M,R10M, G10M; vis: 284°-W-290°
-obscd shore-324°-R-017°-W-037°-G-115°-W-120°.

Also Oc WRG 10s 10m W11M, R9M, G9M; vis:
018°-G-022°-W- 024°-R-028°.

SEVERN ESTUARY
THE SHOOTS
Lower Shoots ⚑ Q (9) 15s 6m 7M; 51°33'·85N
02°42'·05W.
2nd Severn Crossing, Centre span ⚞ Q Bu 5M; **Racon
(O) (3cm) range unknown**; 51°34'·45N 02°42'·03W.
Old Man's Hd ⚑ VQ (9) W 10s 6m 7M; 51°34'·74N
02°41'·69W.
Lady Bench (Lts in line 234°) ⚑ QR 6m 6M; 51°34'·85N
02°42'·20W. Rear, Oc R 5s 38m 3M.
Charston Rk ⚞ Fl 3s 5m 8M; 51°35'·35N 02°41'·68W.
Chapel Rk ⚞ Fl WRG 2·6s 6m 8M, vis: W213°- G284°-
W049°-R051·5°-160°; 51°36'·44N 02°39'·21W.

SEVERN BRIDGE TO SHARPNESS
Aust ⚞ 2 QG (vert) 11m 6M; 51°36'·16N 02°38'·00W.
West Tower ⚞ 3 QR (hor) on upstream/downstream
sides; *Siren (3) 30s;* obscured 040°-065°; 51°36'·73N
02°38'·80W.
Centre of span ⚞ Q Bu, each side; 51°36'·59N
02°38'·43W.
Lyde Rock ⚞ Q WR 5m 5M; vis: 148°-R-237°-W-
336°-R-067°; 51°36'·89N 02°38'·67W.
COUNTS ⚓ Q; 51°39'·48N 02°35'·84W .
LEDGES ⚑ 51°39'·77N 02°34'·15W Fl (3) G 10s.
Bull Rock ⚞ Fl 3s 6m 8M; 51°41'·80N 02°29'·89W.
Sharpness S Pier Hd ⚞ 2 FG (vert) 6m 3M; *Siren 20s;*
51°42'·97N 02°29'·12W.

BRISTOL CHANNEL (SOUTH SHORE)
BRISTOL DEEP
N Elbow ⚓ QG; *Bell;* 51°26'·97N 02°58'·65W.
S Mid Grounds ⚑ VQ (6) + L Fl 10s; 51°27'·62N
02°58'·68W.
E Mid Grounds ⚓ Fl R 5s; 51°27'·75N 02°54'·98W.
Clevedon ⚑ VQ; 51°27'·39N 02°54'·93W.
Welsh Hook ⚑ Q (6) + L Fl 15s; 51°28'·53N
02°51'·86W.
Avon ⚓ Fl G 2·5s; 51°27'·92N 02°51'·73W.
Black Nore Pt ☆ 51°29'·09N 02°48'·05W Fl (2) 10s
11m **17M**; obsc by Sand Pt when brg less than 049°;
vis: 044°-243°.
Firefly ⚓ Fl (2) G 5s; 51°29'·96N 02°45'·35W.
Portishead Pt ☆ 51°29'·68N 02°46'·42W Q (3) 10s
9m **16M**; B twr, W base; vis: 060°-262°; *Horn 20s.*

AVONMOUTH/RIVER AVON
Royal Edward Dock N Pier Hd ⚞ Fl 4s 15m 10M; vis:
060°-228·5°; 51°30'·49N 02°43'·09W.
Avonmouth S Pier Hd ⚞ Oc RG 30s 9m 10M and
FBu 4m 1M; *Bell(1) 10s;* vis: 294°-R-036°-G-194°;
51°30'·37N 02°43'·10W.

BRISTOL CHANNEL (SOUTH SHORE)

E Culver ⚓ Q (3) 10s; 51°18'·00N 03°15'·44W.
W Culver ⚓ VQ (9) 10s; 51°17'·37N 03°18'·68W.
Gore ⚓ Iso 5s; *Bell;* 51°13'·94N 03°09'·79W.

BURNHAM-ON-SEA/RIVER PARRETT

Lower Lt Ent ⚡ Fl 7·5s 7m 12M; vis: 074°-164°; 51°14'·89N 03°00'·36W.Dir lt 076°. F WRG 4m W12M, R10M, G10M; vis: 071°-G- 075°-W-077°-R-081°.
Bridgewater Bar No. 1 ⚓ QR; 51°14'·53N 03°03'·75W.

WATCHET/MINEHEAD

Watchet W Bkwtr Hd ⚡ Oc G 3s 9m 9M; 51°11'·03N 03°19'·74W.
Minehead Bkwtr Hd ⚡ Fl (2) G 5s 4M; vis: 127°-262°; 51°12'·81N 03°28'·36W.
Lynmouth Foreland ☆ 51°14'·73N 03°47'·21W Fl (4) 15s 67m **18M**; W ○ twr; vis: 083°-275°; (H24).

LYNMOUTH/WATERMOUTH/ILFRACOMBE

Lynmouth Harbour Arm ⚡ 2 FG (vert) 6m 5M; 51°13'·92N 03°49'·84W.
Sand Ridge ▲ Q G; 51°15'·01N 03°49'·77W.
Copperas Rock ▲ Fl G 2·5s; 51°13'·78N 04°00'·60W.
Watermouth ⚡ Oc WRG 5s 1m 3M; W △; vis: 149·5°-G-151·5°-W- 154·5°-R-156·5°; 51°12'·93N 04°04'·60W.
Lantern Hill ⚡ Fl G 2·5s 39m 6M; 51°12'·66N 04°06'·78W.
Horseshoe ⚓ Q; 51°15'·02N 04°12'·96W.
Bull Point ☆ 51°11'·94N 04°12'·09W Fl (3) 10s 54m **20M**; W ○ twr, obscd shore-056°. Same twr; FR 48m 12M; vis: 058°-096°.
Morte Stone ▲ Fl G 5s; 51°11'·30N 04°14'·95W.
Baggy Leap ▲ Fl G 10s; 51°08'·92N 04°16'·97W.

BIDEFORD, RIVERS TAW AND TORRIDGE

Bideford F'wy ⚓ L Fl 10s; *Bell;* 51°05'·25N 04°16'·25W.
Bideford Bar ▲ Q G; 51°04'·89N 04°14'·62W.
Pulley ▲ Fl G 10s; 51°04'·08N 04°12'·70W.
Instow ☆ Ldg Lts 118°. **Front,** 51°03'·62N 04°10'·67W Oc 6s 22m **15M**; vis: 104·5°-131·5°. **Rear,** 427m from front, Oc 10s 38m **15M**; vis: 104°-132°; (H24).

Crow Pt ⚡ Fl WR 2. 5s 8m W6M R5M; vis: 225°-R-232°-W-237°-R-358°-W-015°-R-045°; 51°03'·96N 04°11'·39W.

CLOVELLY/HARTLAND/LUNDY

Clovelly Hbr Quay Hd ⚡ 50°59'·92N 04°23'·83W Fl G 5s 5m 5M.
Lundy Near North Pt ☆ 51°12'·10N 04°40'·65W Fl 15s 48m **17M**; vis: 009°-285°.
Lundy South East Pt ☆ 51°09'·72N 04°39'·37W Fl 5s 53m **15M**; vis: 170°-073°; *Horn 25s.*
Jetty Head ⚡ Fl R 3s 8m 3M; 51°09'·80N 04°39'·20W.
Hartland Point ☆ 51°01'·29N 04°31'·59W Fl (6) 15s 37m **25M**; (H24); *Horn 60s.*

NORTH CORNWALL

PADSTOW/NEWQUAY

Stepper Point ⚡ L Fl 10s 12m 4M; 50°34'·12N 04°56'·72W.
Greenaway ⚓ Fl (2) R 10s; 50°33'·78N 04°56'·06W.
Bar ▲ Fl G 5s; 50°33'·46N 04°56'·12W.
Padstow N Quay Hd ⚡ 2 FG (vert) 6m 2M; 50°32'·50N 04°56'·16W.
Trevose Head ☆ 50°32'·94N 05°02'·13W Fl 7·5s 62m **21M**; *Horn (2) 30s.*
Newquay N Pier Hd ⚡ 2 FG (vert) 5m 2M; 50°25'·07N 05°05'·19W..

HAYLE/ST IVES

The Stones ⚓ Q; 50°15'·64N 05°25'·51W.
Godrevy I ⚡ Fl WR 10s 37m W12M, R9M; vis: 022°-W-101°-R-145°-W-272°; 50°14'·54N 05°24'·04W.
Hayle App ⚓ QR; 50°12'·26N 05°26'·30W.
St Ives App ▲ 50°12'·85N 05°28'·42W
East Pier Hd ⚡ 2 FG (vert) 8m 5M; 50°12'·80N 05°28'·61W.
West Pier Hd ⚡ 2 FR (vert) 5m 3M; 50°12'·77N 05°28'·73W.
Pendeen ☆ 50°09'·90N 05°40'·32W Fl (4) 15s 59m **16M**; vis: 042°-240°; in bay between Gurnard Hd and Pendeen it shows to coast; *Horn 20s.*

For Lts further W see Area 1 SW England - *Isles of Scilly to Anvil Point.*

1	Aberystwyth	1		12	64	66	122	164	192	224	254	286	299	318	361	Kilrush	12
2	Fishguard	40	2		11	13	69	111	139	171	201	233	246	265	308	Dingle	11
3	Milford Haven	84	48	3		10	56	102	131	165	188	227	242	252	295	Valentia	10
4	Tenby	107	71	28	4		9	42	70	102	132	164	177	196	239	Baltimore	9
5	Swansea	130	94	55	36	5		8	35	69	95	135	150	168	202	Kinsale	8
6	Cardiff	161	125	86	66	46	6		7	34	65	100	115	133	172	Youghal	7
7	Sharpness	192	156	117	106	75	33	7		6	32	69	84	102	139	Dunmore East	6
8	Avonmouth	175	139	100	89	58	20	18	8		5	34	47	66	108	Rosslare	5
9	Burnham-on-Sea	169	133	94	70	48	53	50	33	9		4	15	36	75	Arklow	4
10	Ilfracombe	128	92	53	35	25	44	74	57	45	10		3	21	63	Wicklow	3
11	Padstow	142	106	70	70	76	97	127	110	98	55	11		2	48	Dun Laoghaire	2
12	Longships	169	133	105	110	120	139	169	152	140	95	50	12		1	Carlingford Lough	1

AREA 10 *Ireland – South and Westwards from Rockabill to Inisheer*

SELECTED LIGHTS, BUOYS & WAYPOINTS

| Positions are referenced to WGS84 |

LAMBAY ISLAND TO TUSKAR ROCK

MALAHIDE/LAMBAY ISLAND/HOWTH

Taylor Rks ⚓ Q; 53°30'·21N 06°01'·87W.

Rowan Rocks ⚓ Q (3) 10s; 53°23'·88N 06°03'·27W.

Howth E Pier Hd ⚓ Fl (2) WR 7·5s 13m W12M, R9M; W twr; vis: W256°-R295°-256°; 53°23'·66N 06°04'·03W.

Baily ☆ 53°21'·70N 06°03'·14W Fl 15s 41m **26M**; twr.

Rosbeg E ⚓ Q (3) 10s; 53°21'·02N 06°03'·45W.

Rosbeg S ⚓ Q (6) + L Fl 15s; 53°20'·22N 06°04'·17W.

S Burford ⚓ VQ (6) + L Fl 10s; *Whis;* 53°18'·07N 06°01'·27W.

PORT OF DUBLIN/DUN LAOGHAIRE

Dublin Bay ⚓ Mo (A) 10s; **Racon (M)**; 53°19'·92N 06°04'·64W.

Great S Wall Hd Poolbeg ☆ Fl R 4s 20m 10M*(synchro with N.Bull)*; R ○ twr; *Horn (2) 60s;* 53°20'·53N 06°09'·08W

Dublin N Bank ☆ 53°20'·69N 06°10'·59W Oc G 8s 10m **16M**; G ☐ twr.

Dun Laoghaire E Bkwtr Hd ⚓ 53°18'·15N 06°07'·62W Fl (2) R 8s 16m **17M**; twr, R lantern; *Horn 30s* (or *Bell (1) 6s)*; Fog Det Lt VQ.

Muglins ⚓Fl R 5s 14m 11M; 53°16'·55N 06°04'·58W.

Bennett Bk ⚓ Q (6) + L Fl 15s; 53°20'·17N 05°55'·11W.

Kish Bank ☆ 53°18'·64N 05°55'·48W Fl (2) 20s 29m **22M**; W twr, R band; **Racon (T) 15M**; *Horn (2) 30s.*

S Codling ⚓ VQ (6) + L Fl 10s; 53°04'·74N 05°49'·76W.

S India ⚓ Q (6) + L Fl 15s; 53°00'·36N 05°53'·31W.

CODLING LANBY ⚓ 53°03'·02N 05°40'·76W Fl 4s 12m **15M**; tubular structure on By; **Racon (G)10M**; *Horn 20s.*

WICKLOW/ARKLOW

Wicklow E Pier Hd ⚓ Fl WR 5s 11m 6M; W twr, R base and cupola; vis: 136°-R-293°-W-136°; 52°58'·99N 06°02'·07W.

Wicklow Head ☆ 52°57'·95N 05°59'·89W; Fl (3) 15s 37m **23M**; W twr.

N Arklow ⚓ Q; 52°53'·86N 05°55'·21W.

Arklow Bank Wind Farm from 52°48'·47N 05°56'·57W to 52°46'·47N 05°57'·11W, N and S Turbines Fl Y 5s14m 10M + Fl W Aero lts. AIS transmitters. Other turbines Fl Y 5s.

S Arklow ⚓ Q (6) + L Fl 15s; **Racon (O)10M**; 52°40'·20N 05°58'·89W.

No. 2 Glassgorman ⚓ Fl (4) R 10s; 52°44'·52N 06°05'·36W.

S Blackwater ⚓ Q (6) + L Fl 15s; 52°22'·76N 06°12'·86W.

WEXFORD/ROSSLARE

S Long ⚓ VQ (6) + L Fl 10s; 52°14'·84N 06°15'·64W.

Splaugh ⚓ Fl (2) R 6s; 52°14'·37N 06°16'·76W.

Tuskar ☆ 52°12'·17N 06°12'·42W Q (2) 7·5s 33m **24M**; W twr; *Horn (4) 45s,* **Racon (T)** 18M.

TUSKAR ROCK TO OLD HD OF KINSALE

S Rock ⚓ Q (6) + L Fl 15s; 52°10'·80N 06°12'·84W.

Barrels ⚓ Q (3) 10s; 52°08'·32N 06°22'·05W.

KILMORE/WATERFORD

St Patrick's Bridge ⚓ Fl R 6s; (Apr-Sep); 52°09'·30N 06°34'·71W.

Kilmore Quay SWM ⚓ Iso 10s; (Apr-Sep); 52°09'·20N 06°35'·30W.

Coningbeg ⚓ Q(6)+LFl 15s, Racon, AIS; 52°03'·20N 06°38'·57W.

Hook Hd ☆ 52°07'·32N 06°55'·85W Fl 3s 46m **23M**; W twr, two B bands; **Racon (K) 10M** vis 237°-177°; *Horn (2) 45s.*

Waterford ⚓ Fl R 3s. Fl (3) R 10s; 52°08'·95N 06°57'·00W.

Dunmore East Pier Head ☆ 52°08'·93N 06°59'·37W Fl WR 8s 13m **W17M**, R13M; Gy twr, vis: W225°- R310°- 004°.

DUNGARVAN

Helvick ⚓ Q (3) 10s; 52°03'·61N 07°32'·25W.

Mine Head ☆ 51°59'·52N 07°35'·25W Fl (4) 30s 87m **20M**; W twr, B band; vis: 228°-052°.

YOUGHAL/BALLYCOTTON

Youghal W side of ent ☆ 51°56'·57N 07°50'·53W Fl WR 2·5s 24m **W17M**, R13M; W twr; vis: W183°- R273°- W295°- R307°- W351°-003°.

Ballycotton ☆ 51°49'·52N 07° 59'·09W Fl WR 10s 59m **W21M, R17M**; B twr, within W walls, B lantern; vis: W238°- R048°-238°; *Horn (4) 90s.*

CORK

Cork ⚓ L Fl 10s; **Racon (T) 7M**; 51°42'·92N 08°15'·60W.

Fort Davis Ldg lts 354·1°. Front, 51°48'·82N 08°15'·80W Dir WRG 29m **17M**; vis: FG351·5°- AlWG352·25°- FW353°-AlWG355°-FR355·75°-356·5°. Rear, Dognose Quay, 203m from front, Oc 5s 37m 10M; Or 3, synch with front.

Roche's Point ☆ 51°47'·59N 08°15'·29W Fl WR 3s 30m **W20M, R16M**; vis: Rshore- W292°- R016°- 033°, W(unintens) 033°- R159°- shore.

KINSALE/OYSTER HAVEN

Bulman ⚓ Q (6) + L Fl 15s; 51°40'·14N 08°29'·74W.

Charle's Fort ⚓ Fl WRG 5s 18m W9M, R6M, G7M; vis: G348°- W358°- R004°-168°; H24; 51°41'·74N 08°29'·97W.

OLD HEAD OF KINSALE TO MIZEN HEAD

Old Head of Kinsale ☆, S point 51°36'·28N 08°32'·03W Fl (2) 10s 72m **20M**; B twr, two W bands; *Horn (3) 45s.*

Galley Head ✩ summit 51°31'·80N 08°57'·19W Fl (5) 20s 53m **23M**; W twr; vis: 256°-065°.

Kowloon Br ⌊ Q (6) + L Fl 15s; 51°27'·58N 09°13'·75W.

BALTIMORE/SCHULL/CROOKHAVEN

Barrack Pt ⚡ Fl (2) WR 6s 40m W6M, R3M; vis: R168°-W294°-038°; 51°28'·33N 09°23'·65W.

Fastnet ✩, W end 51°23'·35N 09°36'·19W Fl 5s 49m **27M**; Gy twr, *Horn (4) 60s*, **Racon (G) 18M**.

Mizen Head ✩ 51°27'·00N 09°49'·24W Iso 4s 55m **15M**; vis: 313°-133°.

MIZEN HEAD TO DINGLE BAY

Sheep's Hd ✩ 51°32'·60N 09°50'·95W Fl (3) WR 15s 83m **W18M, R15M**; W bldg; vis: 007°-R-017°-W-212°.

BANTRY BAY/KENMARE RIVER

Roancarrigmore ✩ 51°39'·19N 09°44'·83W Fl WR 3s 18m **W18M**, R14M; W☐twr, B band; vis: 312°-W-050°-R-122°-R(unintens)-242°-R-312°. Reserve lt W8M, R6M obsc 140°-220°.

Ardnakinna Pt ✩ 51°37'·11N 09°55'·08W Fl (2) WR 10s 62m **W17M**, R14M; W ○ twr; vis: 319°-R- 348°-W- 066°-R-shore.

Bull Rock ✩ 51°35'·51N 10°18'·08W Fl 15s 83m **21M**; W twr; vis: 220°-186°.

Skelligs Rock ✩ 51°46'·12N 10°32'·51W Fl (3) 15s 53m **19M**; W twr; vis: 262°-115°; part obsc within 6M 110°-115°.

VALENTIA/PORTMAGEE

Fort (Cromwell) Point ✩ 51°56'·02N 10°19'·27W Fl WR 2s 16m **W17M, R15M**; W twr; vis: 304°-R-351°,102°-W-304°; obsc from seaward by Doulus Head when brg more than 180°.

DINGLE BAY TO LOOP HEAD
DINGLE BAY/VENTRY/DINGLE/FENIT

Inishtearaght ✩, W end Blasket Islands 52°04'·55N 10°39'·68W Fl (2) 20s 84m **19M**; W twr; vis: 318°-221°; **Racon (O)**.

Little Samphire Is ✩ 52°16'·26N 09°52'·91W Fl WRG 5s 17m **W16M**, R13M; G13M; Bu ○ twr; vis: 262°-R-275°, 280-R-090°-G-140°-W- 152°-R-172°.

SHANNON ESTUARY

Ballybunnion ⌊ VQ; **Racon (M) 6M**; 52°32'·52N 09°46'·93W.

Kilcredaune Hd ✩ Fl 6s 41m **15M**; W twr; 52°34'·79N 09°42'·58W; obsc 224°-247° by hill within 1M. twr; vis: 208°-092°; 52°36'·32N 09°31'·03W.

Loop Head ✩ 52°33'·68N 09°55'·96W Fl (4) 20s 84m **23M**.

Positions are referenced to WGS84

North and Westwards from Rockabill to Inisheer
LAMBAY ISLAND TO DONAGHADEE

Rockabill ✩ 53°35'·82N 06°00'·25W Fl WR 12s 45m **W22M, R18M**; W twr, B band; vis: 178°-W-329°-R-178°; H24.

DROGHEDA/DUNDALK

Drogheda Port Appr Dir lt 53°43'·30N 06°14'·73W WRG 10m **W19M, R15M**, G15M; vis: 268°-FG- 269°-AI WG-269·5°-FW-270·5°-AI WR-271°-FR-272°; H24.

Dundalk Pile Light ✩ 53°58'·56N 06°17'·70W Fl 15s 10m **21M**; W Ho; vis: 124°-W-151°-R-284°-W-313°-R-124°; *Horn (3) 60s*.

CARLINGFORD LOUGH

Hellyhunter ⌊ Q (6) + L Fl 15s; **Racon**; 54°00'·35N 06°02'·10W.

Haulbowline ✩ 54°01'·19N 06°04'·74W Fl (3) 10s 32m **17M**; Gy twr; reserve lt 15M.

DUNDRUM BAY

St John's Point ✩ 54°13'·61N 05°39'·30W Q (2) 7·5s 37m **25M**; B twr, Y bands; H24 when horn is operating. Auxiliary Light ✩ Fl WR 3s 14m **W15M**, R11M; same twr, vis: 064°-W-078°-R-shore; Fog Det lt VQ 14m vis: 270°; *Horn (2) 60s*.

STRANGFORD LOUGH/ARDS PENINSULA

Strangford ⍟ L Fl 10s; 54°18'·61N 05°28'·67W.
Bar Paddy ⌊ Q (6) + L Fl 15s; 54°19'·34N 05°30'·51W.
Butter Paddy ⌊ Q (3) 10s; 54°22'·45N 05°25'·74W.
South Rock ⍟ 54°24'·49N 05°22'·02W Fl (3) R 30s 7m

BALLYWATER/DONAGHADEE

Skulmartin ⍟ L Fl 10s; *Whis*; 54°31'·82N 05°24'·80W.
Donaghadee ✩, S Pier Hd 54°38'·70N 05°31'·86W Iso WR 4s 17m **W18M**, R14M; W twr; vis: shore-W-326°-R-shore; *Siren 12s*.

DONAGHADEE TO RATHLIN ISLAND
BELFAST LOUGH/BANGOR

Mew I ✩ NE end 54°41'·91N 05°30'·79W Fl (4) 30s 37m; B twr, W band; **Racon (O) 14M**.

S Briggs ⍟ 54°41'·19N 05°35'·72W Fl (2) R 10s.
Bangor N Pier Hd ⚡ Iso R 12s 9m 9M; 54°40'·03N 05°40'·34W.
Belfast Fairway ⌊ LFl 10s; *Horn (1) 16s*; **Racon (G)**; 54°41'·71N 05°46'·24W

CARRICKFERGUS/LARNE

Carrickfergus Marina E Bkwtr Hd ⚡ QG 8m 3M; 54°42'·58N 05°48'·69W.

Black Hd ✩ 54°45'·99N 05°41'·33W Fl 3s 45m **27M**; W 8-sided twr.

N Hunter Rock ⌊ Q; 54°53'·04N 05°45'·13W.

Larne Chaine Twr ☆ Iso WR 5s 23m **16M**; Gy twr; vis: 230°-W-240°-240°-R-shore; 54°51'·27N 05°47'·90W.

East Maiden ⚓ Fl (3) 20s 29m 24M; W twr, B band; **Racon (M) 11-21M.** Auxiliary lt Fl R 5s 15m 8M; 54°55'·74N 05°43'·65W; same twr; vis:142°-182° over Russel and Highland Rks.

RATHLIN ISLAND TO INISHTRAHULL
RATHLIN ISLAND
Altacarry Head Rathlin East ☆ 55°18'·06N 06°10'·30W Fl (4) 20s 74m **26M**; W twr, B band; vis: 110°-006° and 036°-058°; **Racon (G) 15-27M.**

Rathlin W 0·5M NE of Bull Pt ⚓ 55°18'·05N 06°16'·82W Fl R 5s 62m **22M**; W twr, lantern at base; vis: 015°-225°; H24.

LOUGH FOYLE
Foyle ⚓ L Fl 10s; 55°15'·32N 06°52'·60W.

Inishowen ☆ 55°13'·56N 06°55'·75W Fl (2) WRG 10s 28m **W18M**, R14M, G14M; W twr, 2 B bands; vis: 197°-G-211°-W-249°-R-000°; Horn (2) 30s. Fog Det lt VQ 16m vis: 270°.

Inishtrahull ☆ 55°25'·86N 07°14'·62W Fl (3) 15s 59m 19M; W twr; obscd 256°-261° within 3M; **Racon (T) 24M 060°-310°.**

INISHTRAHULL TO BLOODY FORELAND
L SWILLY/MULROY BAY/SHEEPHAVEN
Fanad Head ☆ 55°16'·57N 07°37'·91W Fl (5) WR 20s 39m **W18M**, R14M; W twr; vis 100°-R-110°-W-313°-R-345°-W-100°.

Limeburner ⚓ Q Fl; 55°18'·54N 07°48'·40W.

Tory Island ☆ 55°16'·36N 08°14'·97W Fl (4) 30s 40m 27M; B twr, W band; vis: 302°-277°; **Racon (M) 12-23M**; H24.

Bloody Foreland ⚓ Fl WG 7·5s 14m W6M, G4M; vis: 062°-W-232°-G-062°; 55°09'·51N 08°17'·03W.

BLOODY F'LD TO RATHLIN O'BIRNE
Aranmore, Rinrawros Pt ☆ 55°00'·90N 08°33'·66W Fl (2) 20s 71m **27M**; W twr; obsc by land about 234°-007° and about 013°. Auxiliary lt Fl R 3s 61m 13M, same twr; vis: 203°-234°.

Rathlin O'Birne, W side ☆ 54°39'·80N 08°49'·94W Fl WR 15s 35m **W18M**, R14M; W twr; vis: 195°-R-307°-W-195°; **Racon (O) 13M, vis 284°-203°.**

RATHLIN O'BIRNE TO EAGLE ISLAND
St John's Pt ⚓ Fl 6s 30m 14M; W twr; 54°34'·16N 08°27'·64W.

Rotten I ☆ 54°36'·97N 08°26'·41W; Fl WR 4s 20m **W15M**, R11M; W twr; vis: W255°-R008°- W039°-208°.

SLIGO
Wheat Rk ⚓ Q (6) + LFl 15s; 54°18'·84N 08°39'·10W.

EAGLE ISLAND TO SLYNE HEAD
Eagle Is, W end ☆ 54°17'·02N 10°05'·56W Fl (3) 15s 67m **19M**; W twr.

Black Rk ☆ 54°04'·03N 10°19'·25W Fl WR 12s 86m **W20M**, R16M; W twr; vis: 276°-W-212°-R-276°.

BROAD HAVEN/BLACKSOD/CLEW BAYS
Gubacashel Pt ⚓ Iso WR 4s 27m W17M, R12M; 110°-R-133°-W-355°-R-021° W twr; 54°16'·06N 09°53'·33W.

Blacksod ⚓ Q (3) 10s; 54°05'·89N 10°03'·01W.

Achillbeg I S Point ☆ 53°51'·51N 09°56'·85W Fl WR 5s 56m **W18M**, R18M, R15M; W ☐ twr on ☐ building; vis: 262°-R-281°-W-342°-R- 060°-W- 092°-R(intens)-099°-W-118°.

Inishgort S Point ⚓ L Fl 10s 11m 10M; W twr. Shown H24; 53°49'·61N 09°40'·25W.

Slyne Hd, North twr, Illaunamid ☆ 53°23'·99N 10°14'·06W; Fl (2) 15s 35m **19M**; B twr.

SLYNE HEAD TO BLACK HEAD
GALWAY BAY/INISHMORE
Eeragh, Rock Is ☆ 53°08'·10N 09°51'·39W Fl 15s 35m **23M**; W twr, two B bands; vis: 297°-262°.

Straw Is ☆ 53°07'·06N 09°37'·85W Fl (2) 5s 11m **15M**; W twr.

Black Hd ⚓ Fl WR 5s 20m W11M, R8M, W ☐ twr; vis: 045°- R268°-276°; 53°09'·26N 09°15'·83W.

Inisheer ☆ 53°02'·78N 09°31'·58W Iso WR 12s 34m **W20M**, R16M; vis: 225°-W(partially vis >7M)-231°, 231°-W-245°-R-269°-W-115°; **Racon (K) 13M.**

		1	2	3	4	5	6	7	8	9	10	11	12	13	14	15
1	Strangford Lough	1														
2	Bangor	34	2													
3	Carrickfergus	39	6	3												
4	Larne	45	16	16	4											
5	Carnlough	50	25	26	11	5										
6	Portrush	87	58	60	48	35	6									
7	Lough Foyle	92	72	73	55	47	11	7								
8	L Swilly (Fahan)	138	109	104	96	81	48	42	8							
9	Burtonport	153	130	130	116	108	74	68	49	9						
10	Killybegs	204	175	171	163	148	115	109	93	43	10					
11	Sligo	218	189	179	177	156	123	117	107	51	30	11				
12	Eagle Island	234	205	198	193	175	147	136	123	72	62	59	12			
13	Westport	295	266	249	240	226	193	187	168	120	108	100	57	13		
14	Galway	338	309	307	297	284	253	245	227	178	166	163	104	94	14	
15	Kilrush	364	335	332	323	309	276	270	251	203	191	183	142	119	76	15

See table on page 36 for distances anticlockwise between Kilrush and Carlingford Lough

DISTANCE TABLES
Approx distances in nautical miles are by the most direct route allowing for dangers and TSS.

33

AREA 11 *West Denmark – Skagen to Rømø*

SELECTED LIGHTS, BUOYS & WAYPOINTS

Positions are referenced to WGS84

SKAGEN
Skagen W ☆ Fl (3) WR 10s 31m **W17M/R12M**; 053°-W-248°-R-323°; W ○ twr; 57°44'·92N 10°35·66E.
Skagen ☆ Fl 4s 44m **23M**; Gy ○ twr; **Racon G, 20M**; 57°44'·11N 10°37'·76E.
Skagen No 1A ↙ L Fl 10s; **Racon N**; 57°43'·42N 10°53'·51E.

HIRTSHALS
Hirtshals ☆ F Fl 30s 57m **F 18M**; **Fl 25M**; W ○ twr, approx 1M SSW of hbr ent; 57°35'·07N 09°56'·45E.
Outer W mole ⚲ Fl G 3s 14m 6M; G mast; *Horn 15s*; 57°35'·97N 09°57'·36E.

HANSTHOLM
Hanstholm ☆ Fl (3) 20s 65m **26M**; shown by day in poor vis; W 8-sided twr; 57°06'·65N 08°35'·74E, approx 1M S of the hbr ent.
Hanstholm ↙ LFl 10s; 57°08'·10N 08°34'·94E.

THYBORØN
Landfall ↙ L Fl 10s; **Racon T, 10M**; 56°42'·55N 08°08'·70E.
Approach ☆ Fl (3) 10s 24m 12M; 56°42'·49N 08°12'·90E.
Bovbjerg ☆ L Fl (2) 15s 62m **16M**; 56°30'·74N 08°07'·13E.

THORSMINDE HAVN (Positions approx)
Lt ho ⚲ F 30m 13M; 56°22'·34N 08°06'·99E.
S mole ⚲ Iso G 2s 9m 4M; 56°22'·26N 08°06'·92E.

HVIDE SANDE
Lyngvig ☆ Fl 5s 53m **22M**; 56°02'·95N 08°06'·17E.
N outer bkwtr ⚲ Fl R 3s 7m 8M; 55°59'·94N 08°06'·55E.
Lt ho ⚲ F 27m 14M; 56°00'·00N 08°07'·35E.

HORNS REV
Blåvands Huk ☆ Fl (3) 20s 55m **23M**; W □ twr; 55°33'·46N 08°04'·95E.

Horns Rev is encircled clockwise by:
Tuxen ↙ Q; 55°34'·22N 07°41'·92E on the N side.
Vyl ↙ Q (6) + L Fl 15s; 55°26'·22N 07°49'·99E.
No. 2 ↙ L Fl 10s; 55°28'·74N 07°36'·49E, SW side.
Horns Rev W ↙ Q (9) 15s; 55°34'·47N 07°26'·05E.
Slugen Channel (crosses Horns Rev ESE/WNW)
▲ L Fl G 10s; 55°33'·99N 07°49'·38E.
⚲ Fl (3) R 10s; 55°29'·42N 08°02'·56E.
Wind farm in □ 2·7M x 2·5M, centred on 55°29'·22N 07°50'·21E: 80 turbines all R lts, the 12 perimeter turbines are lit Fl (3) Y 10s. NE and SW turbines, **Racon (U)**.

APPROACHES TO ESBJERG
Grådyb ↙ L Fl 10s; **Racon G, 10M**; 55°24'·63N 08°11'·59E.
Sædding Strand 053·8° triple ldg lts: to Nos 7/8 buoys; H24: **Front** Iso 2s 13m **21M**; 052°-056°; R bldg; 55°29'·74N 08°23'·87E.
Middle Iso 4s 26m **21M**; 051°-057°; R twr, W bands; 55°29'·94N 08°24'·33E, 630m from front.
Rear F 37m **18M**; 052°-056°; R twr; 55°30'·18N 08°24'·92E, 0·75M from front.
Ldg lts 067°, to Nos 9/10 buoys. Both FG 10/25m **16M**, H24. Front, Gy tripod; rear, Gy twr, 55°28'·76N 08°24'·70E.
Ldg lts 049°, to No 16 buoy/Jerg. Both FR 16/27m **16M**, H24. Front, W twr; rear, Gy twr, 55°29'·92N 08°23'·75E.

FANØ
Slunden outer ldg lts 242°, both Iso 2s 5/8m 3M; 227°-257°. Front, twr; 55°27'·20N 08°24'·53E. Rear, twr, 106m from front.
Nordby marina 55°26'·65N 08°24'·53E.

APPROACHES (Lister Tief) TO RØMØ
Rode Klit Sand ↙ Q (9) 15s, 55°11'·11N 08°04'·88E (130°/9M to Lister Tief ↙).
Lister Tief ↙ Iso 8s, *Whis;* 55°05'·32N 08°16'·80E.
Lister Landtief No 5 ♦ 55°03'·68N 08°24'·73E.
Rømø S mole ⚲ Fl R 3s 7m 2M; Gy twr; 55°05'·19N 08°34'·31E.

		1	2	3	4	5	6	7	8	9	10	11	12	13	14	15	16	17	18
1	Skagen	**1**																	
2	Hirtshals	33	**2**																
3	Hanstholm	85	52	**3**															
4	Thyborln	114	84	32	**4**														
5	Torsminde	141	108	56	24	**5**													
6	Hvide Sande	162	179	77	45	24	**6**												
7	Esbjerg	200	174	122	90	76	54	**7**											
8	Fanl	210	177	125	93	79	57	3	**8**										
9	Rlml	233	200	148	116	94	73	30	33	**9**									
10	H rnum	248	215	163	131	108	86	70	73	29	**10**								
11	Husum	275	247	195	163	152	131	95	98	68	45	**11**							
12	Kiel/Holtenau	261	233	281	249	232	208	180	183	189	126	129	**12**						
13	Bremerhaven	306	285	233	201	185	163	127	129	107	83	82	123	**13**					
14	Wilhelmshaven	414	296	242	310	184	162	125	128	106	82	82	123	45	**14**				
15	Helgoland	259	238	186	154	141	119	83	85	63	39	47	104	44	43	**15**			
16	Cuxhaven	304	284	232	200	162	138	110	113	85	56	66	70	58	56	38	**16**		
17	Wangerooge	283	262	210	178	168	147	109	112	94	68	52	108	38	27	24	42	**17**	
18	Hamburg	338	317	265	233	216	192	163	167	139	99	113	90	81	110	88	54	61	**18**

DISTANCE TABLES
Approx distances in nautical miles are by the most direct route allowing for dangers and TSS.

SELECTED LIGHTS, BUOYS & WAYPOINTS

Positions are referenced to WGS84

SYLT

Lister Tief ↙ Iso 8s; *Whis;* 55°05'·33N 08°16'·79E.

List West ⚓ Oc WRG 6s 19m W14M, R11M, G10M; 040°-R-133°-W-227°-R-266·4°-W-268°-G-285°-W-310°-W(unintens)-040°; W twr, R lantern; 55°03'·15N 08°24'·00E.

List Ost ⚓ Iso WRG 6s 22m W14M, R11M, G10M; 010·5°-W(unintens)-098°-W-262°-R-278°-W-296°-R-323·3°-W-324·5°-G-350°-W-010·5°; W twr, R band; 55°02'·93N 08°26'·58E.

List Hafen, N mole ⚓ FG 8m 4M; 218°-038°; G mast; 55°01'·03N 08°26'·52E.

Kampen, Rote Kliff ☆ L Fl WR 10s 62m W20M, R16M; 193°-W-260°- W (unintens)-339°-W-165°-R-193°; W twr, B band; 54°56'·76N 08°20'·38E.

Hörnum ☆ Fl (2) 9s 48m 20M; 54°45'·23N 08°17'·47E.

Hbr, N pier ⚓ FG 6m 4M, 024°-260°.

Vortrapptief ↙ Iso 4s; 54°34'·88N 08°13'·06E.

AMRUM ISLAND

Norddorf ☆ Oc WRG 6s 22m W15M, R12M, G11M; 031°-W-097°-R-176·5°-W-178·5°-G-188°; W ◯ twr, R lantern; 54°40'·13N 08°18'·46E.

Amrum ☆ Fl 7·5s 63m 23M; R twr, W bands; 54°37'·84N 08°21'·23E.

FÖHR ISLAND

Nieblum Dir lt ☆ Oc (2) WRG 10s 11m W19M, R/G15M; 028°-G-031°-W-032·5°-R-035·5°; R twr, W band; 54°41'·10N 08°29'·20E.

DAGEBÜLL

Dagebüll Iso WRG 8s 23m W18M, R/G15M; 042°-G-043°-W-044·5°- R-047°; G mast; 54°43'·82N 08°41'·43E. FW lts on N and S moles.

RIVER HEVER

Hever ↙ Iso 4s; *Whis;* 54°20'·41N 08°18'·82E.

Westerheversand ☆ Oc (3) WRG 15s 41m W21M, R17M, G16M; 012·2°-W-069°-G-079·5°-W-080·5°-R-107°-W-233°-R-248°; 54°22'·37N 08°38'·36E.

RIVER EIDER

Eider ↙ Iso 4s; 54°14'·54N 08°27'·61E.

St Peter ☆ L Fl (2) WR 15s 23m W15M, R12M; 271°-R-280·5°-W-035°-R-055°-W-068°-R-091°-W-120°; R twr, B lantern; 54°17'·24N 08°39'·10E.

BÜSUM

Süderpiep ↙ Iso 8s; *Whis;* 54°05'·82N 08°25'·70E.

Büsum ☆ Iso WR 6s 22m W19M, R12M; 248°-W-317°-R-024°-W-148°; 54°07'·60N 08°51'·48E.

GB Light V ⬳ Iso 8s 12m 17M; *Horn Mo (R) 30s;* Racon T, 8M; 54°10'·80N 07°27'·60E.

HELGOLAND

Helgoland ☆ Fl 5s 82m 28M; brown ☐ twr, B lantern, W balcony; 54°10'·91N 07°52'·93E.

Vorhafen. Ostmole, S elbow ⚓ Oc WG 6s 5m W6M, G3M; 203°-W-250°-G-109°; G post; fog det lt; 54°10'·31N 07°53'·94E.

Düne. Ldg lts 020°. Front ⚓ Iso 4s 11m 8M; 54°10'·87N 07°54'·80E. Rear, Iso WRG 4s 17m W11M, R/ G10M; synch; 010°-G-018·5°-W-021°-R-030; 106°-G-125°-W-130°-R-144°.

RIVER ELBE APPROACHES

Elbe ↙ Iso 10s; Racon T, 8M; 53°59'·95N 08°06'·49E. No.1 ↙ QG; 53°59'·21N 08°13'·20E.

Neuwerk ☆, S side, L Fl (3) WRG 20s 38m W16M, R12M, G11M; 165·3°-G-215·3°-W-238·8°-R-321°; 343°-R-100°; 53°54'·92N 08°29'·73E.

CUXHAVEN/OTTERNDORF

Marina, F WR & F WG ⚓; 53°52'·43N 08°42'·49E.

Medem ⚓ Fl (3) 12s 6m 5M; B △, on B col; 53°50'·15N 08°53'·85E.

BRUNSBÜTTEL

Ldg lts 065·5°: both Iso 3s 24/46m 16/21M; synch; R twrs, W bands. Front ☆ 53°53'·32N 09°08'·47E.

Alter Vorhafen ⚓ F WG 14m W10M, G6M; 266·3°-W-273·9°-G-088·8°; 53°53'·27N 09°08'·59E.

HAMBURG, WEDEL YACHT HAFEN

E ent ⚓ FG 5m 3M; 53°34'·25N 09°40'·79E.

City Sport Hafen ⚓ Iso Or 2s; 53°32'·52N 09°58'·81E.

RIVER WESER APPROACH CHANNELS

ALTE WESER

Schlüsseltonne ↙ Iso 8s; 53°56'·25N 07°54'·76E.

Alte Weser ☆ F WRG 33m W23M, R19M, G18M; 288°-W-352°-R-003°-W-017°- G-045°-W-074°-G-118°-W-123°- R-140°-G-175°-W-183°-R-196°-W-238°; *Horn Mo (AL) 60s;* 53°51'·79N 08°07'·65E.

NEUE WESER

3/Jade ⚓ Fl (2+1) G 15s; Racon T, 8M; 53°52'·40N 07°44'·00E.

Tegeler Plate ☆ Oc (3) WRG 12s 21m W21M, R17M, G16M; 329°-W-340°-R-014°-W-100°-G-116°-W-119°-R-123°-G-144°-W-147°-R-264°; 53°47'·87N 08°11'·45E.

BREMERHAVEN

No. 61 ↙ QG; 53°32'·26N 08°33'·93E (Km 66·0).

Vorhafen S pier hd ⚓ FG 15m 5M; 355°-265°; 53°32'·09N 08°34'·50E.

BREMEN
Hasenbüren Sporthafen ⚓ 2 FY (vert); 53°07'·51N 08°40'·03E.

RIVER JADE APPROACHES
Jade-Weser ⚓ Oc 4s; **Racon T, 8M;** 53°58'·33N 07°38'·83E.
Mellumplate ☆ FW 28m **24M;** 116·1°-116·4°; R ☐ twr, W band; 53°46'·28N 08°05'·51E.

HOOKSIEL
No. 37/Hooksiel 1 ⚓ IQ G 13s; 53°39'·37N 08°06'·58E.
Vorhafen ent ⚓ L Fl R 6s 9m 3M; 53°38'·63N 08°05'·25E.

WILHELMSHAVEN
Fluthafen N mole ⚓ F WG 9m,W6M, G3M; 216°-W-280°-G-010°-W-020°-G-130°; 53°30'·86N 08°09'·32E.

WANGEROOGE
Harle ⚓ Iso 8s; 53°49'·24N 07°48'·92E.
Buhne W bkwtr ⚓ FR 3m 4M; 53°46'·33N 07°51'·93E.

SPIEKEROOG
Otzumer Balje ⚓ Iso 4s; 53°48'·11N 07°37'·12E.
Spiekeroog ⚓ FR 6m 4M; 53°45'·0N 07°37'·7E.

LANGEOOG
Accumer Ee ⚓ Iso 8s; 53°46·96N 07°25·91E. (freq. moved)
W mole ⚓ Oc WRG 6s 8m W7M, R5M, G4M; 064°-G-070°-W-074°-R-326°-W-330°-G-335°-R-064°; *Horn Mo (L) 30s;* 53°43'·42N 07°30'·13E .

NORDERNEY
Norderney N ⚓ Q; 53°46'·06N 07°17'·12E.
Dovetief ⚓ Iso 4s; 53°45'·48N 07°12'·70E.
Schluchter ⚓Iso 8s; 53°44'·48N 07°02'·27E.
W mole ⚓ Oc (2) R 9s 13m 4M; 53°41'·9N 07°09'·9E.

Norderney ☆ Fl (3) 12s 59m **23M;** unintens 067°-077° and 270°-280°; R 8-sided twr; 53°42'·58N 07°13'·83E.

BENSERSIEL
E training wall head ⚓ Oc WRG 6s 6m W5M, R3M, G2M; 110°-G-119°-W-121°-R-110°; R post & platform; 53° 41'·80N 07°32'·84E.
Ldg lts 138°, both Iso 6s 12/18m 9M.
Inner hbr, W mole hd FG; E mole hd FR.

DORNUMER-ACCUMERSIEL
AB3 ⚓ IQ G 13s; 53°41'·50N 07°29'·34E.
W bkwtr head, approx 53°41'·04N 07°29'·30E.

NESSMERSIEL
N mole ⚓ Oc 4s 6m 5M; G mast; 53°41'·9N 07°21'·7E.

NORDDEICH
W trng wall head ⚓ FG 8m 4M, 021°-327°; G framework twr; 53°38'·7N 07°09'·0E.
Outer ldg lts 144°, both B masts. Front, Iso WR 6s 6m W6M, R5M; 078°-R-122°-W-150°. Rear, Iso 6s 9m 6M; synch, 140m from front.

RIVER EMS APPROACHES
GW/EMS ⚲ Iso 8s 12m **17M;** *Horn Mo (R) 30s (H24);* **Racon T, 8M;** 54°09'·96N 06°20'·72E.
Borkumriff ⚓ Oc 4s; **Racon T, 8M;** 53°47'·44N 06°22'·05E.
Osterems ⚓ Iso 4s; 53°41'·91N 06°36'·17E.
Riffgat ⚓ Iso 8s; 53°38'·96N 06°27'·10E.
Westerems ⚓ Iso 4s; **Racon T, 8M;** 53°36'·93N 06°19'·39E.
H1⚓ 53°34'·91N 06°17'·97E.

BORKUM
Borkum Grosser ☆ Fl (2) 12s 63m **24M;** 53°35'·32N 06°39'·64E. Same twr, ⚓ F WRG 46m **W19M, R/** **G15M;** 107·4°-G-109°-W-111·2°- R-112·6°.
Fischerbalje ☆ Oc (2) 16s 15m 3M; 260°-W-123°; Fog det lt; R/W twr on tripod; 53°33'·18N 06°42'·90E.

EMDEN
Outer hbr, W pier ⚓ FR 10m 4M; R 8-sided twr; *Horn Mo (ED) 30s;* 53°20'·06N 07°10'·49E.
E pier ⚓ FG 7m 5M; 53°20'·05N 07°10'·84E.

		1	2	3	4	5	6	7	8	9	10	11	12	13	14	15	16	17	18
1	Esbjerg	**1**																	
2	H rnum Lt (Sylt)	47	**2**																
3	Husum	95	48	**3**															
4	Hamburg	163	112	113	**4**														
5	Kiel/Holtenau	179	128	129	90	**5**													
6	Brunsb ttel	126	75	76	37	53	**6**												
7	Cuxhaven	110	63	66	54	70	17	**7**											
8	Bremerhaven	127	80	82	81	131	78	58	**8**										
9	Wilhelmshaven	125	78	82	110	123	70	56	45	**9**									
10	Hooksiel	116	69	73	101	117	64	47	36	9	**10**								
11	Helgoland	83	38	47	88	104	51	38	44	43	35	**11**							
12	Wangerooge	109	60	52	61	108	55	42	38	27	19	24	**12**						
13	Langeoog	119	72	77	114	130	77	60	47	43	34	35	21	**13**					
14	Norderney	123	77	85	81	137	84	69	62	53	44	44	29	18	**14**				
15	Emden	165	129	137	174	190	137	120	115	106	97	85	80	63	47	**15**			
16	Borkum	133	97	105	104	163	110	95	88	80	71	67	55	46	31	32	**16**		
17	Delfzijl	155	119	127	159	173	120	105	100	89	83	81	65	56	41	10	22	**17**	
18	Den Helder	187	192	198	229	245	192	175	180	159	150	153	148	130	115	125	95	115	**18**

DISTANCE TABLES
Approx distances in nautical miles are by the most direct route allowing for dangers and TSS.

SELECTED LIGHTS, BUOYS & WAYPOINTS

Positions are referenced to WGS84

DELFZIJL TO DEN HELDER

DELFZIJL
W mole ⚓ FG; 53°19'·01N 07°00'·26E.
Ldg lts 203° both Iso 4s. Front, 53°18'·62N 07°00'·16E.

LAUWERSOOG
W mole head ⚓ FG; *Horn (2) 30s;* 53°24'·68N 06°12'·00E.
Schiermonnikoog ☆ Fl (4) 20s 43m **28M**; dark R ○ twr; 53°29'·19N 06°08'·76E. Same twr: FWR 29m **W15M**, R12M; W210°-221°, R221°-230°.
WG (Westgat) ⚲ Iso 8s; **Racon N;** 53°32'·00N 05°58'·54E.

ZEEGAT VAN AMELAND
Ameland, W end ☆ Fl (3) 15s 57m **30M**; 53°26'·92N 05°37'·52E.

ZEEGAT VAN TERSCHELLING
ZS ⚲ Iso 4s; **Racon T;** 53°19'·71N 04°55'·86E.
SM1-ZS10 ⚲ Fl(2+1) G 10s; 53°18'·99N 05°03'·60E.

WEST TERSCHELLING
Brandaris Twr ☆ Fl 5s 54m **29M**, Y ☐ twr; 53°21'·61N 05°12'·85E.
W hbr mole ⚓ FR 5m 5M; R post, W bands; *Horn 15s;* 53°21'·25N 05°13'·09E.

VLIELAND
Vuurduin ☆ Iso 4s 54m **20M**; 53°17'·69N 05°03'·46E.
E mole hd ⚓ FG; 53°17'·68N 05°05'·51E.

HARLINGEN
P9/BO44 ⚲ VQ; 53°10'·59N 05°23'·88E.
Pollendam ldg lts 112°, both Iso 6s 8/19m 13M (H24); B masts, W bands. Front, 53°10'·51N 05°24'·18E. Rear, vis 104·5°-119·5°.
N mole hd ⚓ FR 9m 4M; R/W pedestal; 53°10'·59N 05°24'·32E.

KORNWERDERZAND SEALOCK
W mole ⚓ FG 9m 7M; *Horn Mo(N) 30s;* 53°04'·77N 05°20'·03E.

DEN OEVER SEALOCK
LW ⚲ L Fl 10s; 52°59'·51N 04°55'·90E,.
Ldg lts 131°, both Oc 10s 6m 7M; 127°-137°. Front, 52°56'·32N 05°02'·98E. Rear, 280m SE.

EIERLANDSCHE GAT
Eierland ☆ Fl (2) 10s 52m **29M**; R ○ twr; 53°10'·93N 04°51'·30E, N tip of Texel.

OUDESCHILD
Dir ⚓ Oc 6s; intens 291°; 53°02'·40N 04°50'·94E; leads 291° into hbr. N mole hd FG 6m. S mole hd ⚓ FR 6m; *Horn (2) 30s;* 53°02'·33N 04°51'·17E.
ZH ⚲ VQ (6) + L Fl 10s; 52°54'·65N 04°34'·71E.
TX1 ⚲ Fl G 5s; 52°48'·01N 04°15'·50E.
Vinca G ⚲ Q (9) 15s; **Racon D;** 52°45'·93N 04°12'·35E.

MOLENGAT (from the N)
MG ⚲ Mo (A) 8s; 53°03'·91N 04°39'·36E.
MG1 ⚲ Iso G 4s; 53°02'·89N 04°40'·84E.
S14-MG17 ⚲ VQ (6) + L Fl 10s; 52°58'·50N 04°43'·60E.

DEN HELDER
Ldg lts 191°, both Oc G 5s 15/24m 14M, synch. Front, vis 161°-221°; 52°57'·37N 04°47'·08E.
Marinehaven, W bkwtr head ⚓ QG 11m 8M; *Horn 20s;* 52°57'·95N 04°47'·07E (Harssens Is).
Ent W side, ⚓ Fl G 5s 9m 4M (H24); 180°-067°; 52°57'·78N 04°47'·08E. Marina ent FG and FR.

SCHULPENGAT (from the SSW)
Dir ☆ 026·5°, Dir WRG, Al WR, Al WG, **W22M R/G 18M**, church spire; 025·1°-FG-025·6°-Al WG-026·3°-FW-026·7-Al WR-027·4°-F R-027·9°; shown H24.
SG ⚲ Mo (A) 8s; **Racon Z;** 52°52'·90N 04°37'·90E.
Schilbolsnol ☆ F WRG 27m **W15M**, R12M, G11M; 338°-W-002°-G-035°-W(ldg sector)-038°-R-051°-W-068°; post; 53°00'·50N 04°45'·68E (on Texel).
Kijkduin ☆ Fl (4) 20s 56m **30M**; vis 360°; brown twr; 52°57'·33N 04°43'·58E.

IJMUIDEN TO STELLENDAM

IJMUIDEN
⚲ Mo (A) 8s; **Racon Y, 10M;** 52°28'·44N 04°23'·78E.
Ldg lts (FW 5M by day; 090·5°-100·5°). **Front** ☆ F WR 30m **W16M**, R13M; 050°-W-122°-R-145°-W-160°; tidal and traffic signals; dark R ○ twrs; 52°27'·70N 04°34'·47E. **Rear** ☆ Fl 5s 52m **29M**; 019°-199°. (FW 4M by day; 090·5°-110·5°); 560m from front.
S bkwtr hd ⚓ FG 14m 10M (in fog Fl 3s); *Horn (2) 30s;* W twr, G bands; 52°27'·82N 04°31'·94E.
N bkwtr hd ⚓ FR 15m 10M; 52°28'·05N 04°32'·55E.

AMSTERDAM
IJ8 ⚲ Iso R 8s (for Sixhaven);52°22'·86N 04°54'·37E.

SCHEVENINGEN
SCH ⚲ Iso 4s; 52°07'·75N 04°14'·14E. W mole ⚓ FG 12m 9M; G twr, W bands; 52°06'·22N 04°15'·16E.

APPROACHES to HOEK VAN HOLLAND
Noord Hinder ⚲ Fl (2) 10s; *Horn (2) 30s;* **Racon T, 12-15M;** 52°00'·04N 02° 51'·03E.
Goeree ☆ Fl (4) 20s 32m **28M**; *Horn (4) 30s;* **Racon T, 12-15M;** 51°55'·42N 03°40'·03E.
Indusbank N ⚲ VQ; 52°02'·88N 04°03'·55E.
MO ⚲ Mo (A) 8s; 52°00'97N 03°58'·06E.
MVN ⚲ VQ; 51°59'·59N 04°00'·19E.
MV ⚲ Q (9) 15s; 51°57'·44N 03°58'·40E.
SB-M ⚲ Fl(2)Y 10s; *Racon Z;* 52°00·08N 3°53·18E.
Westhoofd, Fl (3) 15s 55m **30M**; R ☐ tr. 51°48'·78N 03°51'·82E.

HOEK VAN HOLLAND
Nieuwe Waterweg ldg lts 107°: both Iso R 6s 29/43m 18M; 099.5°-114.5°; Front, 51°58'·55N 04°07'·53E.
Maasvlakte ☆ Fl (5) 20s 67m **28M**, H24; 340°-267°; 51°58'·20N 04°00'·85E.
Nieuwe Zuiderdam ⚓ FG 25m 10M; *Horn 10s*; G twr, W bands; 51°59'·13N 04°02'·47E.

SLIJKGAT and STELLENDAM
SG ⚓ Iso 4s; 51°51'·93N 03°51'·40E.
N mole ⚓ FG; *Horn (2) 15s*; 51°49'·87N 04°02'·01E.

ROOMPOTSLUIS TO TERNEUZEN
Schouwenbank ⚓ Mo (A) 8s; **Racon O, 10M**; 51°44'·94N 03°14'·32E.
West Schouwen ☆ Fl (2+1)15s 57m **30M**; Gy twr, R diagonals; 51°42'·53N 03°41'·48E
Westpit ⚓ Iso 8s; 51°33'·65N 03°09'·92E.

ROOMPOTSLUIS
N bkwtr ⚓ FR 7m; 51°37'·30N 03°40'·09E.
Kaloo ⚓ Iso 8s; 51°35'·56N 03°23'·23E.
Westkapelle ☆, Common rear, Fl 3s 49m **28M**; partially obsc'd; ☐ twr; 51°31'·75N 03°26'·80E.

OOSTGAT
Ldg lts 149·5°: Front, Noorderhoofd Oc WRG 10s 20m; W13M, R/G10M; 353°-R-008°-G-029°-W-169°; R ○ twr, W band; 51°32'·40N 03°26'·21E.
OG5 ▲ Iso G 8s; 51°33'·95N 03°25'·92E.

VLISSINGEN
Songa ▲ QG; 51°25'·16N 03°33'·66E.
Koopmanshaven, W mole root, ⚓ Iso WRG 3s 15m W12M, R10M, G9M; 253°-R-277°-W-284°-R-297°-W-306·5°-G-013°-W-024°-G-033°-W-035°-G-039°-W-055°-G-084·5°-R-092°-G-111°-W-114°; R pylon; 51°26'·37N 03°34'·52E.
E mole ⚓ FG 7m; W mast; 51°26'·32N 03°34'·66E.

BRESKENS
ARV-VH ⚓ Q; 51°24'·71N 03°33'·89E.
Yacht hbr, W mole ⚓ FG 7m; 51°24'·04N 03°34'·06E.

TERNEUZEN
W mole ⚓ Oc WRG 5s 15m W9M, R7M, G6M; 090°-R-115°-W-120°-G-130°-W-245°-G-249°-W-279°-R-004°; B & W post; 51°20'·54N 03°49'·58E.

BELGIUM

ANTWERPEN
Royerssluis, ldg lts 091°, both FR. FR/FG,ent to Willemdok ④. Linkeroever marina ent, FR/FG.

ZEEBRUGGE
A2 ⚓ Iso 8s; 51°22'·42N 03°07'·05E.
Ldg lts 136°, both Oc 5s 22/45m 8M; 131°-141°; H24, synch; W cols, R bands. Front, 51°20'·71N 03°13'·11E.
W outer mole ⚓ Oc G 7s 31m 7M; *Horn (3) 30s*; IPTS; 51°21'·73N 03°11'·17E.
Leopold II mole ☆ Oc WR 15s 22m, **W20M, R18M**; 068°-W-145°-R-212°-W-296°; IPTS; *Horn (3+1) 90s*; 51°20'·85N 03°12'·17E.

BLANKENBERGE
Lt ho ☆ Fl (2) 8s 30m **20M**; 065°-245°; W twr, B top; 51°18'·76N 03°06'·87E.
E pier ⚓ FR 12m 11M; 290°-245°; W ○ twr; *Bell (2) 15s*; 51°18'·91N 03°06'·56E.
W pier ⚓ FG 14m 11M; intens 065°-290°, unintens 290°-335°; W ○ twr; 51°18'·89N 03°06'·43E.

OOSTENDE
A1 ⚓ Iso 8s; 51°22'·37N 02°53'·34E.
Ldg lts 143°: both Iso 4s (triple vert) 36/46m 4M, 068°-218°. Front, 51°13'·80N 02°55'·89E.
Oostende lt ho ☆ Fl (3) 10s 65m **27M**; obsc 069·5°-071°; 51°14'·18N 02°55'·83E.
E pier ⚓ and *Horn* have been withdrawn. The E pier has been demolished (2008) and a new pier is being built further east; WIP until 2012 is marked by 1 NCM buoy Q; 2 SPM buoys QY; and 3 PHM buoys QR.

NIEUWPOORT
Lt ho ☆ Fl (2) R 14s 28m **16M**; R ○ twr, W bands; 51°09'·28N 02°43'·80E, 2 ca E of E pier root.
E pier ⚓ FR 11m 10M; vis 025°-250° & 307°-347°; 51°09'·40N 02°43'·08E.
W pier ⚓ FG 11m 9M; vis 025°-250° & 284°-324°; IPTS; *Bell (2) 10s*; 51°09'·35N 02°43'·00E.

1	Delfzijl	1																
2	Terschelling	85	2															
3	Harlingen	102	19	3														
4	Den Oever	110	34	21	4													
5	Den Helder	115	39	30	11	5												
6	Amsterdam	159	83	81	62	51	6											
7	IJmuiden	146	70	68	49	38	13	7										
8	Scheveningen	171	95	93	74	63	38	25	8									
9	Rotterdam	205	129	127	108	97	72	59	34	9								
10	Hook of Holland	185	109	107	88	77	52	39	14	20	10							
11	Stellendam	201	125	123	104	93	68	55	30	36	16	11						
12	Roompotsluis	233	157	155	136	125	100	87	50	68	48	32	12					
13	Vlissingen	228	152	150	131	120	99	86	61	67	47	45	24	13				
14	Zeebrugge	239	163	161	142	131	106	93	68	74	54	50	28	16	14			
15	Blankenberge	244	168	166	147	136	111	98	73	79	59	55	33	21	5	15		
16	Oostende	239	163	161	142	131	110	106	81	87	67	72	40	29	13	9	16	
17	Nieuwpoort	262	186	184	165	154	129	116	91	97	77	83	51	39	23	18	9	17

DISTANCE TABLES
Approx distances in nautical miles are by the most direct route allowing for dangers and TSS.

AREA 14 *North France – Dunkerque to Cap de la Hague*

SELECTED LIGHTS, BUOYS & WAYPOINTS

Positions are referenced to WGS84

BELGIAN BORDER TO CAP GRIS-NEZ
OFFSHORE MARKS
WH Zuid ⚓ Q (6) + L Fl 15s; 51°22'·78N 02°26'·25E.
Bergues N ⚓ Q; 51°19'·92N 02°24'·50E.
Oostdyck radar twr; ☆ Mo (U) 15s 15m 12M; *Horn Mo (U) 30s;* **Racon O;** 51°16'·49N 02°26'·83E.
Bergues ⚓ Fl G 4s; 51°17'·15N 02°18'·62E.
Ruytingen N ⚓ Fl (3) G 12s; 51°13'·10N 02°10'·28E, VQ.
Ruytingen SE ⚓ VQ (3) 15s; 51°09'·20N 02°08'·92E.
Sandettié SW ⚓ Q (9) 15s 5M; 51°09'·72N 01°45'·60E.
Sandettié ⌐ Fl 5s 12m **12M;** R hull; *Horn 30s;* **Racon T, 10M;** 51°09'·34N 01°47'·10E.

PASSE DE ZUYDCOOTE
E12 ⚓ VQ (6) + L Fl 10s; 51°07'·90N 02°30'·80E.
E11 ⚓ Fl G 4s; 51°06'·90N 02°30'·91E.
E9 ⚓ Fl (2) G 6s; 51°05'·66N 02°29'·68E.

PASSE DE L'EST
E6 ⚓ QR; 51°04'·86N 02°27'·08E.
E2 ⚓ Fl (2) R 6s; 51°04'·32N 02°22'·31E.
⚓ Q (6) + L Fl 15s; 51°04'·29N 02°21'·72E.

DUNKERQUE PORT EST
Jetée Est ☆ Fl (2) R 6s 12m **10M;** 51°03'·59N 02°21'·20E. **Jetée Ouest** ☆ Fl (2) G 6s 35m **10M.**
Dunkerque lt ho ☆ Fl (2) 10s 59m **26M;** 51°02'·93N 02°21'·86E. 137·5° ldg lts, both Oc (2) 6s 7/10m 12M.

GRAVELINES
W jetty ⚡ Fl (2) WG 6s 9m W8M, G6M; 317°-W-327°-G-085°-W-244°; 51°00'·94N 02°05'·48E.

DUNKERQUE, WEST APPROACH
DW29 ⚓ Q G; 51°03'·85N 02°20'·21E.
DW18 ⚓ Fl (3) R 12s; 51°03'·47N 02°10'·37E.
RCE ⚓ Iso G 4s; 51°02'·43N 01°53'·21E.
Dyck ⚓ Fl 3s; **Racon B;** 51°02'·99N 01°51'·78E.

CALAIS
Jetée Est ☆ Fl (2) R 6s 12m **17M;** Gy twr, R top; *Horn (2) 40s;* 50°58'·40N 01°50'·46E.
Jetée Ouest ⚡ Iso G 3s 12m 9M; W twr, G top; *Bell 5s;* 50°58'·24N 01°50'·40E.
Calais ☆ Fl (4) 15s 59m **22M;** vis 073°-260°; W 8-sided twr, B top; 50°57'·68N 01°51'·21E.

CALAIS, WESTERN APPROACH
Calais Approche ⚓ VQ (9) 10s; 50°58'·89N 01°45'·10E.
CA2 ⚓ Fl R 4s; 50°58'·15N 01°45'·68E.
CA1 ⚓ Fl G 4s; 50°57'·64N 01°46'·14E.
Sangatte ⚡ Oc WG 4s 13m W8M, G5M; 065°-G-089°-W-152°-G-245°; 50°57'·19N 01°46'·47E.
CA4 ⚓ Fl (2) R 6s; 50°58'·38N 01°48'·65E.
Cap Gris-Nez ☆ Fl 5s 72m **29M;** 005°-232°; W twr, B top; *Horn 60s;* 50°52'·09N 01°34'·94E.

CAP GRIS-NEZ TO LE HAVRE
DOVER STRAIT TSS, French side
Ruytingen SW ⚓ Fl (3) G 12s; 51°04'·98N 01°46'·83E.
ZC2 ⚓ Fl (2+1) Y 15s; 50°53'·53N 01°30'·88E.
ZC1 ⚓ Fl (4) Y 15s; 50°44'·99N 01°27'·21E.
Vergoyer N ⚓ VQ; **Racon C, 5-8M;** 50°39'·64N 01°22'·18E.
Vergoyer E ⚓ VQ (3) 5s; 50°35'·74N 01°19'·65E.
Bassurelle ⚓ Fl (4) R 15s 6M; **Racon B, 5-8m;** 50°32'·74N 00°57'·69E.
Vergoyer SW ⚓ VQ (9) 10s; 50°26'·98N 01°00'·00E.

BOULOGNE
Approche Boulogne ⚓ VQ (6) + L Fl 10s 8m 6M; 50°45'·31N 01°31'·07E.
Digue Carnot (S) ☆ Fl (2+1) 15s 25m **19M;** W twr, G top; *Horn (2+1) 60s;* 50°44'·44N 01°34'·05E.
Cap d'Alprech ☆ Fl (3) 15s 62m **23M;** W twr, B top; 50°41'·90N 01°33'·75E, 2·5M S of hbr ent.

LE TOUQUET and ÉTAPLES
Le Touquet ☆ Fl (2) 10s 54m **25M;** Or twr, brown band, W&G top; 50°31'·43N 01°35'·49E.
Pointe du Haut-Blanc ☆ Fl 5s 44m **23M;** W twr, R bands, G top; 50°23'·89N 01°33'·62E.

ST VALÉRY-SUR-SOMME
ATSO ⚓ Mo (A) 12s; 50°14'·00N 01°28'·08E.
Trng wall hd, ⚓ Fl G 2.5s 2m 1M; 50°12'·25N 01°35'·85E.
Cayeux-sur-Mer ☆ Fl R 5s 32m **22M;** W twr, R top; 50°11'·65N 01°30'·67E.

LE TRÉPORT
Ault ☆ Oc (3) WR 12s 95m **W15M,** R11M; 040°-W-175°-R-220°; W twr, R top; 50°06'·28N 01°27'·23E.
Jetée Ouest ☆ Fl (2) G 10s 15m **20M;** W twr, G top; *Horn (2) 30s;* 50°03'·87N 01°22'·13E.

DIEPPE
DI ⚓ VQ (3) 5s; 49°57'·05N 01°01'·25E.
Jetée Ouest ⚡ Iso G 4s 11m 8M; W twr, G top; *Horn 30s;* 49°56'·27N 01°04'·95E.
Pte d'Ailly ☆ Fl (3) 20s 95m **31M;** W ☐ twr, G top; *Horn (3) 60s;* 49°54'·96N 00°57'·49E.

SAINT VALÉRY-EN-CAUX
Jetée Est ⚡ Fl (2) R 6s 8m 4M; 49°52'·40N 00°42'·70E.

FÉCAMP
Jetée Nord ☆ Fl (2) 10s 15m **16M;** Gy twr, R top; 49°45'·93N 00°21'·78E.
Jetée Sud ⚡ QG 14m 9M; Gy twr, G top; 49°45'·88N 00°21'·80E.
Cap d'Antifer ☆ Fl 20s 128m **29M;** 021°-222°; Gy 8-sided twr, G top; 49°41'·01N 00°09'·90E.

LE HAVRE

Cap de la Hève ☆ Fl 5s 123m **24M**; 225°-196°; W 8-sided twr, R top; 49°30'·74N 00°04'·15E.

LHA ⌑ Mo (A) 12s 10m 6M; R&W; **Racon, 8-10M**; 49°31'·38N 00°09'·88W.

Digue Nord ☆ Fl R 5s 15m **21M**; IPTS; W ○ twr, R top; *Horn 15s;* 49°29'·19N 00°05'·44E.

LE HAVRE TO CAP DE LA HAGUE

CHENAL DE ROUEN/HONFLEUR

No. 2 ⧈ QR; **Racon T**; 49°27'·40N 00°01'·35E.

Ratier NW ⧈ Fl G 2·5s; 49°26'·85N 00°02'·50E.

No. 20 ⧈ QR; 49°25'·85N 00°13'·51E. Honfleur Digue Ouest ⚲ QG 10m 6M; 49°25'·68N 00°13'·81E.

DEAUVILLE/TROUVILLE

Ratelets ⧈ Q (9) 15s; 49°25'·29N 00°01'·71E.

E jetty ⚲ Fl (4) WR 12s 8m W7M, R4M; 131°-W-175°-R-131°; 49°22'·22N 00°04'·33E.

DIVES-SUR-MER

DI ⧈ L Fl 10s; 49°19'·18N 00°05'·84W.

No. 1 ⬥ 49°18'·50N 00°05'·67W.

Dir lt 159·5°, Oc (2+1) WRG 12s 6m, W12M, R/G9M; 125°-G-157°-W-162°-R-194°;49°17'·80N 00°05'·24W.

OUISTREHAM

Ldg lts 185°, both Dir Oc (3+1) R 12s 10/30m **17M**.

Front, 49°17'·09N 00°14'·80W.

Lt ho ☆ Oc WR 4s 37m **W17M**, R13M; 115°-R-151°-W-115°; 49°16'·85N 00°14'·80W.

COURSEULLES-SUR-MER

Courseulles ⧈ Iso 4s; 49°21'·28N 00°27'·69W.

W jetty ⚲ Iso WG 4s 7m; W9M, G6M; 135°-W-235°-G-135°; 49°20'·41N 00°27'·37W.

Ver ☆ Fl (3)15s 42m **26M**; 49°20'·39N 00°31'·15W.

Arromanches Ent buoys; ⬥ 49°21'·35N 00°37'·26W; ⚓ 49°21'·25N00°37'·30W.

PORT-EN-BESSIN

W mole ⚲ Fl WG 4s 14m, W10M, G7M; G065°-114·5°, W114·5°-065°; 49°21'·17N 00°45'·39W.

GRANDCAMP

Ldg lts 146°, both Dir Q 9/12m **15M**, 144·5°-147·5°.

Front ☆, 49°23'·42N 01°02'·92W.

Jetée Est ⚲ Oc (2) R 6s 9m 9M; 49°23'·52N 01°02'·98W.

CARENTAN

C-I ⧈ Iso 4s; 49°25'·44N 01°07'·08W.

Trng wall ⧈ Fl (4) G 15s; 49°21'·94N 01°09'·96W.

Iles St-Marcouf ⚲ VQ (3) 5s 18m 8M; □ Gy twr, G top; 49°29'·86N 01°08'·82W.

ST VAAST-LA-HOUGUE

Le Gavendest ⧈ Q (6) + L Fl 15s; *Whis;* 49°34'·36N 01°13'·89W.

Jetty ⚲ Dir Oc (2) WRG 6s 12m W10M, R/G7M; 219°-R-237°-G-310°-W-350°-R-040°; *Siren Mo (N) 30s;* 49°35'·17N 01°15'·41W.

BARFLEUR

Ldg lts 219·5°, both Oc (3) 12s 7/13m 10M; synch. Front, W □ twr;49°40'·18N 01°15'·61W.

W jetty ⚲ Fl G 4s 8m 6M; 49°40'·32N 01°15'·57W.

Pte de Barfleur ☆ Fl (2) 10s 72m **29M**; Gy twr, B top; *Horn (2) 60s;* 49°41'·78N 01°15'·96W.

Les Équets ⧈ Q 8m 3M; 49°43'·62N 01°18'·36W.

La Pierre Noire ⧈ Q (9) 15s 8m 4M;49°43'·53N 01°29'·09W.

CHERBOURG

La Truite ⧈ Fl (4) R 15s; 49°40'·33N 01°35'·50W.

Fort de l'Est ⚲ Iso G 4s 19m 9M; 49°40'·28N 01°35'·93W.

CH1 ⧈ L Fl 10s 8m 4M; *Whis;* 49°43'·24N 01°42'·09W.

Fort de l'Ouest ☆ Fl (3) WR 15s 19m **W24M, R20M**; 122°-W-355°-R-122°; Gy twr, R top; *Horn (3) 60s;* 49°40'·45N 01°38'·87W.

Digue de Querqueville ⚲ Fl (4) G 15s 8m 4M; W col, G top; 49°40'·30N 01°39'·80W.

Marina W mole ⚲ Fl (3) G 12s 7m 6M; 49°38'·87N 01°37'·15W. E side, ⚲ Fl (3) R 12s 6m 6M; W col, R lantern; 49°38'·91N 01°37'·08W.

OMONVILLE-LA-ROGUE

L'Étonnard ⬥ 49°42'·32N 01°49'·85W.

Cap de la Hague ☆ Fl 5s 48m **23M**; Gy twr, W top; *Horn 30s;* 49°43'·31N 01° 57'·28W.

		1	2	3	4	5	6	7	8	9	10	11	12	13	14	15	16	17	18	19
1.	Dunkerque-Est	**1**																		
2.	Calais	28	**2**																	
3.	Boulogne	49	21	**3**																
4.	St Valéry-sur-Somme	86	58	37	**4**															
5.	Le Tréport	90	62	41	16	**5**														
6.	Dieppe	100	74	53	30	15	**6**													
7.	St Valéry-en-Caux	109	81	62	42	28	16	**7**												
8.	Fécamp	121	93	76	57	44	32	17	**8**											
9.	Le Havre	148	121	103	84	71	61	47	27	**9**										
10.	Honfleur	157	129	108	92	80	67	51	35	13	**10**									
11.	Deauville/Trouville	152	125	108	91	79	61	53	34	9	13	**11**								
12.	Dives-sur-Mer	155	129	110	94	83	66	55	38	16	19	9	**12**							
13.	Ouistreham	160	138	115	97	85	73	59	41	20	24	15	9	**13**						
14.	Courseulles	162	136	115	100	87	75	60	44	24	30	23	18	14	**14**					
15.	Grandcamp	177	150	130	118	104	94	80	62	47	52	45	41	37	27	**15**				
16.	Carentan	187	159	139	126	112	100	85	09	56	61	55	50	45	36	13	**16**			
17.	St Vaast	179	151	131	120	107	96	80	65	54	61	54	50	46	35	16	20	**17**		
18.	Barfleur	175	147	128	118	105	94	78	64	56	62	57	53	48	39	21	26	10	**18**	
19.	Cherbourg	188	160	142	131	120	108	94	80	71	77	73	69	66	57	40	44	28	21	**19**

DISTANCE TABLES

Approx distances in nautical miles are by the most direct route allowing for dangers and TSS.

AREA 15 N Central France (Cap de la Hague to St Quay) & Channel Is

SELECTED LIGHTS, BUOYS & WAYPOINTS

Positions are referenced to WGS84

DIELETTE TO ST MALO

DIELETTE
W bkwtr Dir lt 140°, Iso WRG 4s 12m W10M, R/G7M;
070°-G-135°-W-145°-R-180°; 49°33'·18N 01°51'·81W.
E bkwtr ⚲ Fl R 4s 6m 2M; 49°33'·21N 01°51'·78W.

CARTERET
Cap de Carteret ☆ Fl (2+1) 15s 81m 26M; Gy twr, G
top; 49°22'·40N 01°48'·41W.
W bkwtr ⚲ Oc R 4s 7m 7M; W post, R top; 49°22'·17N
01°47'·30W.

PORTBAIL
PB ⌀ 49°18'·37N 01°44'·75W.
Ldg lts 042°: Front, Q 14m 10M, 49°19'·75N 01°42'·50W.
Rear, Oc 4s 20m 10M; stubby ch spire.

PASSAGE DE LA DÉROUTE
Les Trois-Grunes ⌀ Q (9) 15s, 49°21'·84N 01°55'·21W.
Le Sénéquet ⚲ Fl (3) WR 12s 18m W13M, R10M;
083·5°-R-116·5°-W-083·5°; 49°05'·48N 01°39'·73W.
NE Minquiers ⌀ VQ (3) 5s; *Bell;* 49°00'·85N
01°55'·30W.
S Minquiers ⌀ Q (6) + L Fl 15s; 48°53'·09N
02°10'·10W.

ÎLES CHAUSEY
L'Enseigne, W twr, B top; 48°53'·67N 01°50'·37W.
Grande Île ☆ Fl 5s 39m 23M; Gy ☐ twr, G top; *Horn
30s;* 48°52'·17N 01°49'·34W.
⌀ [SCM] Dir Oc(3)WRG 12s 5m, W9M, R/G6M;
079°-W-291°-G-329°-W-335°-R-079°; B beacon, Y
top; 48°52'·46N 01°49'·39W Le Pignon ⚲ Fl (2) WR 6s
10m, W9M, R6M; 005°-R- 150°-W-005°; B twr, W band;
48°53'·49N 01°43'·36 W.

GRANVILLE
Pte du Roc ☆ Fl (4) 15s 49m 23M; 48°50'·06N
01°36'·78W.
Le Loup ⌀ Fl (2) 6s 8m 11M; 48°49'·57N 01°36'·24W.
Marina S bkwtr ⚲ Fl (2) R 6s 12m 5M; W post, R top;
Horn (2) 40s; 48°49'·89N 01°35'·90W. Marina sill, E &
W sides: Oc (2) G 6s & Oc (2) R 6s.

CANCALE
Pierre-de-Herpin ☆ Iso 4s 20m 13M; 48°43'·77N
01°48'·92W.
Jetty ⚲ Fl (3) G 12s 3m 3M; 48°40'·10N 01°51'·11W.

ST MALO TO ST QUAY-PORTRIEUX

ST MALO, CHENAL DE LA PETITE PORTE
Outer ldg lts 129·7°: Front, Le Grand Jardin ☆ Fl (2) R
10s 24m 15M, 48°40'·20N 02°04'·97W. Rear, La Balue
☆ FG 20m 22M; 48°37'·60N 02°00'·24W.
St Malo Fairway ⌀ Iso 4s; 48°41'·39N 02°07'·28W.
Inner ldg lts 128·6°, both Dir FG 20/69m 22/25M; H24.
Front, Les Bas Sablons ☆; W ☐ twr, B top; 48°38'·16N
02°01'·30W. Rear, La Balue ☆, above.

CHENAL DE LA GRANDE PORTE
Outer ldg lts 089·1°: Front, Le Grand Jardin ☆ (as
above). Rear, Rochebonne ☆ Dir FR 40m 24M;
48°40'·26N 01°58'·71W.
Môle des Noires hd ⚲ VQ R 11m 6M; W twr, R top;
Horn (2) 20s; 48°38'·52N 02°01'·91W.
Bas-Sablons marina ⚲ Fl G 4s 7m 5M; 48°38'·42N
02°01'·70W.

LA RANCE BARRAGE
La Jument ⚲ Fl G 4s 6m 4M; G twr, 48°37'·44N
02°01'·76W. Barrage lock, NW wall ⚲ Fl (2) G 6s 6m
5M, 191°-291°; 48°37'·06N 02°01'·73W.

ST CAST
Môle ⚲ Iso WG 4s 12m, W9M, G6M; 180°-G-206°-W-
217°-G-235°-W-245°-G-340°; 48°38'·41N 02°14'·61W.
Cap Fréhel ☆ Fl (2) 10s 85m 29M; Gy ☐ twr, G lantern;
48°41'·05N 02°19'·13W. Reserve light range 15M.

ERQUY
S môle ⚲ Fl (2) WRG 6s 11m W10M, R/G7M;
081°-W-094°-G-111°-W-120°-R-081°; W twr;
48°38'·07N 02°28'·66W.

DAHOUET
La Petite Muette ⌀ Fl WRG 4s 10m W9M, R/G6M;
055°-G-114°-W-146°-R-196°; 48°34'·82N 02°34'·19W.

BAIE DE SAINT BRIEUC and LE LÉGUÉ
Grand Léjon ☆ Fl (5) WR 20s 17m W18M, R14M;
015°-R-058°-W-283°-R-350°-W-015°; R twr, W bands;
48°44'·91N 02°39'·87W.
Le Rohein ⌀ Q (9) WRG 15s 13m, W8M, R/G5M;
072°-R-105°-W-180°-G-193°-W-237°-G-282°-W-301°-G-
330°-W-072°; Y twr, B band; 48°38'·80N 02°37'·77W.
Le Légué ⌀ Mo (A) 10s; 48°34'·32N 02°41'·15W.
Pte à l'Aigle ⚲ VQ G 13m 8M; 48°32'·12N
02°43'·11W.

BINIC
N môle ⚲ Oc (3) 12s 12m 11M; unintens 020°-110°; W
twr, G lantern; 48°36'·07N 02°48'·92W.

SAINT QUAY-PORTRIEUX
La Roselière ⌀ VQ (6) + L Fl 10s; 48°37'·29N
02°46'·18W.
Herflux ⚲ Dir ⚲ 130°, Fl (2) WRG 6s 10m, W 8M,
R/G 6M; 115°-G-125°-W-135°-R-145°; 48°39'·07N
02°47'·95W.
Île Harbour ⚲ Fl WRG 4s 16m, W9M, R/G 6M;
011°-R-133°-G-270°-R-306°-G-358°-W-011°;
48°39'·99N 02°48'·49W.
Marina, NE mole elbow, Dir lt 318·2°: Iso WRG
4s 16m W15M, R/G11M; 159°-W-179°-G-316°-
W-320·5°-R-159°; 48°38'·99N 02°49'·09W.
NE môle hd ⚲ Fl (3) G 12s 10m 2M; 48°38'·84N
02°48'·91W.

CHANNEL ISLANDS
THE CASQUETS AND ALDERNEY
Casquets ☆ Fl (5) 30s 37m **24M**, H24; *Horn (2) 60s*; **Racon T, 25M**; 49°43'·32N 02°22'·63W.

Quenard Pt ☆ Fl (4) 15s 37m **23M**, H24; 085°-027°; *Horn 30s*; 49°43'·75N 02°09'·86W.

Braye, ldg lts 215°: both Q 8/17m 9/12M, synch; 210°-220°. Front, old pier, 49°43'·40N 02°11'·91W.

Admiralty bkwtr ⚓ L Fl 10s; 49°43'·82N 02°11'·67W.

GUERNSEY, LITTLE RUSSEL CHANNEL
Platte Fougère ☆ Fl WR 10s 15m **16M**; 155°-W-085°-R-155°; W 8-sided twr, B band; *Horn 45s*; **Racon P**; 49°30'·83N 02°29'·14W.

Petite Canupe ⚓ Q (6) + L Fl 15s; 49°30'·20N 02°29'·14W. ⚓ L Fl 10s 49°30'·15N 02°29'·66W.

Beaucette marina Ldg lts 276°, both FR. Front, 49°30'·19N 02°30'·23W.

Roustel ⚓ Q 8m 7M; 49°29'·23N 02°28'·79W.

Platte ⚓, Fl WR 3s 6m, W7M, R5M; 024°-R-219°-W-024°; G conical twr; 49°29'·08N 02°29'·57W.

Brehon ⚓ Iso 4s 19m 9M, 49°28'·28N 02°29'·28W.

BIG RUSSEL
Noire Pute ⚓ Fl (2) WR 15s 8m 6M; 220°-W-040°-R-220°; on 2m high rock; 49°28'·21N 02°25'·02W.

Lower Heads ⚓ Q (6) + L Fl 15s; *Bell*; 49°25'·85N 02°28'·55W.

ST PETER PORT
Outer ldg lts 220°: **Front**, Castle bkwtr, Al WR 10s 14m **16M**; 187°-007°; *Horn 15s*; 49°27'·31N 02°31'·45W. Rear, Oc 10s 61m 14M; 179°-269°.

White Rock pier ⚓ Oc G 5s 11m 14M; tfc sigs; 49°27'·38N 02°31'·59W.

S Fairway ⚓ QG; 49°27'·30N 02°31'·76W.

HAVELET BAY
Oyster Rock ⚓ QG; 49°27'·04N 02°31'·47W.

Moulinet ⚓ QR; 49°26'·97N 02°31'·54W. Two inner buoys are also ⚓ QG and ⚓ QR.

HERM Hbr ldg lts 078° ⚓ 2F occas; W drums; 49°28'·25N 02°27'·11W.

SARK
Corbée du Nez ⚓ Fl (4) WR 15s 14m 8M; 057°-W-230°-R-057°; W structure; 49°27'·09N 02°22'·17W.

Point Robert ☆ Fl 15s 65m **20M**; W 8-sided twr; *Horn (2) 30s*; 49°26'·19N 02°20'·75W.

LES ÉCREHOU
Écrevière ⚓ Q (6) + L Fl 15s; 49°15'·26N 01°52'·15W.

JERSEY (North coast)
Sorel Point ☆ L Fl WR 7·5s 50m **15M**; 095°-W-112°-R-173°-W-230°-R-269°-W-273°; 49°15'·60N 02°09'·54W.

JERSEY (West and South coasts)
Grosnez Point ☆ Fl (2) WR 15s 50m **W19M, R17M**; 081°-W-188°-R-241°; 49°15'·50N 02°14'·80W.

La Corbière ☆ Iso WR 10s 36m **W18M, R16M**; shore-W-294°-R-328°-W-148°-R-shore; W ○ twr; *Horn Mo (C) 60s*; 49°10'·79N 02°15'·01W.

WESTERN PASSAGE
Ldg lts 082°. Front Oc 5s 23m 14M; 034°-129°; 49°10'·16N 02°05'·09W. Rear, Oc R 5s 46m 12M.

Noirmont Pt ⚓ Fl (4) 12s 18m 10M; B twr, W band; 49°09'·91N 02°10'·08W.

ST HELIER
Elizabeth marina: Dir ⚓ 106°: FWRG 4m 1M; 096°-G-104°-W-108°-R-119°; 49°10'·76N 02°07'·12W.

Marina ent ⚓ Oc G 4s 2M; 49°10'·83N 02°07'·13W.

Red & Green Passage, ldg lts 022·7° on dayglo R dolphins: Front, ⚓ Oc G 5s 10m 11M; 49°10'·63N 02°06'·94W. Rear, ⚓ Oc R 5s 18m 12M.

East Rock ⚓ QG; 49°09'·95N 02°07'·29W.

Victoria pier hd, Port control twr; IPTS; 49°10'·57N 02°06'·88W.

JERSEY (South-East coast)
Demie de Pas ⚓ Mo (D) WR 12s 11m, W14M, R10M; 130°-R-303°-W-130°; *Horn (3) 60s*; **Racon T, 10M**; B bn twr, Y top; 49°09'·01N 02°06'·15W.

Violet ⚓ L Fl 10s; 49°07'·81N 01°57'·14W.

GOREY
Pier Hd Dir lt 298°, ⚓ WRG, 6m 8M; 293·5°-G-296·5°-W-299·5°-R-302·5°; ⚓ OcRG 5s 8m 12M; 304°-R-353°-G-304°; W twr on pierhead; 49°11'·80N 02°01'·34W.

ST CATHERINE BAY
Verclut bkwtr ⚓ Fl 1·5s 18m 13M; 49°13'·34N 02°00'·64W.

		1	2	3	4	5	6	7	8	9	10	11	12	13	14	15	16	17
1	Cherbourg	1																
2	Omonville	10	2															
3	Braye (Alderney)	25	15	3														
4	St Peter Port	44	34	23	4													
5	Creux (Sark)	37	29	22	10	5												
6	St Helier	64	51	46	29	24	6											
7	Carteret	41	29	28	31	23	26	7										
8	Portbail	49	33	32	35	27	25	5	8									
9	Iles Chausey	69	61	58	48	43	25	33	30	9								
10	Granville	75	67	66	55	50	30	38	35	9	10							
11	Dinan	102	91	85	66	64	50	62	59	29	35	11						
12	St Malo	90	79	73	54	52	38	50	47	17	23	12	12					
13	Dahouet	88	80	72	54	52	41	60	59	37	45	41	29	13				
14	Le Légué/St Brieuc	96	86	76	57	56	46	69	69	41	49	45	33	8	14			
15	Binic	95	84	75	56	55	46	70	70	43	51	45	33	10	8	15		
16	St Quay-Portrieux	88	80	73	56	51	46	64	64	47	54	47	35	11	7	4	16	
17	Lézardrieux	88	80	68	48	38	47	68	71	53	54	61	49	33	32	30	21	17

DISTANCE TABLES

Approx distances in nautical miles are by the most direct route allowing for dangers and TSS.

SELECTED LIGHTS, BUOYS & WAYPOINTS

Positions are referenced to WGS84

PAIMPOL TO L'ABERWRAC'H

OFFSHORE MARKS
Roches Douvres ☆ Fl 5s 60m **28M**; 49°06'·28N 02°48'·89W.

PAIMPOL
L'Ost Pic ⨳ Fl(4) WR 15s 20m, W9M, R6M; 105°-W-116°-R-221°-W-253°-R-291°-W-329°; 48°46'·76N 02°56'·44W.
La Jument ⬚ 48°47'·34N 02°57'·97W.
Ldg lts 262·2°, both QR 5/12m 7/14M. Front, Kernoa jetty; W & R hut; 48°47'·09N 03°02'·44W.

ÎLE DE BRÉHAT
Rosédo ☆ Fl 5s 29m **20M**; 48°51'·45N 03°00'·30W.
Le Paon ⨳ Oc WRG 4s 22m W11M, R/G8M; 033°-W-078°-G-181°-W-196°-R-307°-W-316°-R-348°; Y twr; 48°51'·93N 02°59'·17W.

LÉZARDRIEUX
Ldg lts 224·7°: Front, **La Croix** ☆ Q 15m **18M**; 48°50'·22N 03°03'·24W. Rear **Bodic** ☆ Dir Q 55m **22M**.
Coatmer ldg lts 218·7°: Front, Q RG 16m R/G7M; 200°-R-250°-G-053°; 48°48'·26N 03°05'·75W. Rear, QR 50m 7M; vis 197°-242°.

JAUDY (TRÉGUIER) RIVER
Les Héaux de Bréhat ☆ Fl (4) WRG 15s 48m, **W15M**, R/G11M; 227°-R-247°-W-270°-R-302°-W-227°; Gy ○ twr; 48°54'·50N 03°05'·18W.
Ldg lts 137°: Front, Oc 4s 12m 11M; 042°-232°; 48°51'·55N 03°07'·90W. Rear, Dir Oc R 4s 34m **15M**.
La Corne ⨳ Fl (3) WRG 12s 14m W8M, R/G6M; 052°-W-059°-R-173°-G-213°-W-220°-R-052°; W twr, R base; 48°51'·34N 03°10'·63W.

PERROS-GUIREC
Passe de l'Est, ldg lts 224·5°. Front ☆ Dir Oc (4) 12s 28m **15M**; 48°47'·87N 03°26'·66W. Rear ☆, Dir Q 79m **21M**; intens 221°-228°.

PLOUMANAC'H
Men-Ruz ⨳ Oc WR 4s 26m W12M, R9M; 226°-W- 242°-R-226°; pink ☐ twr; 48°50'·26N 03°29'·03W.

TRÉBEURDEN
Ar Gouredec ⎨ VQ (6) + L Fl 10s; 48°46'·41N 03°36'·60W. NW bkwtr ⨳ Fl G 2·5s 8m 2M; IPTS; 48°46'·34N 03°35'·20W.

PRIMEL-TRÉGASTEL
Ldg lts 152°, both ⨳ QR 35/56m 7M, R vert stripe on W ☐. Front, 48°42'·45N 03°49'·20W.

BAIE DE MORLAIX
Chenal du Tréguier ldg lts 190·5°: Front, ⨳ Île Noire Oc (2) WRG 6s 15m, W11M, R/G8M; 051°-G-135°-R-211°-W-051°; 48°40'·34N 03°52'·56W. **La Lande** ☆ Fl 5s 85m **23M**; 48°38'·19N 03°53'·16W. Common rear for both channels.

Grande Chenal ldg lts 176·4°: Front, **Île Louet** ☆ Oc (3) WG 12s 17m **W15M,** G10M; 305°-W-244°-G-305°; W ☐ twr, B top; 48°40'·40N 03°53'·34W.

CANAL DE L'ÎLE DE BATZ

Ar-Chaden ⌇ Q (6) + L Fl WR 15s 14m, W8M, R6M; 262°-R-289·5°-W-293°-R-326°- W-110°; YB twr; 48°43'·93N 03°58'·26W.
Men-Guen-Bras ⌇ Q WRG 14m, W9M, R/ G6M; 068°-W-073°-R-197°-W-257°-G-068°; BY twr; 48°43'·76N 03°58'·07W.
Lt ho ☆ Fl (4) 25s 69m **23M**; 48°44'·71N 04°01'·63W.

L'ABER WRAC'H

Île-Vierge ☆ Fl 5s 77m **27M**; 337°-325°; Gy twr; 48°38'·33N 04°34'·06W.
Libenter ⎨ Q (9) 15s 6M; 48°37'·45N 04°38'·46W.
Outer ldg lts 100·1°: Front ⨳ QR 20m 7M; 48°36'·88N 04°34'·56W. Rear ⨳ Dir Q 55m 12M.

CHENAL DU FOUR TO PORNICHET

Le Four ☆ Fl (5) 15s 28m **18M**; Gy ○ twr; *Horn (3+2) 60s*; 48°31'·38N 04°48'·32W.
Ldg lts 158·5°. Front, **Kermorvan** ☆ Fl 5s 20m **22M**; W ☐ twr; *Horn 60s*; 48°21'·72N 04°47'·42W.
Rear, **Pte de St Mathieu** ☆ Fl 15s 56m **29M**; W twr, R top; 48°19'·79N 04°46'·27W.
Grande Vinotière ⌇ L Fl R 10s; 48°21'·93N 04°48'·43W.
Les Vieux-Moines ⌇ Fl R 4s 16m 5M; 280°-133°; R 8-sided twr; 48°19'·33N 04°46'·63W.
Pte du Toulinguet ☆ Oc (3) WR 12s **W15M,** R11M; shore-W-028°-R-090°-W-shore; 48°16'·82N 04°37'·73W.

BREST

Moulin Blanc ⎨ Fl (3) R 12s; 48°22'·79N 04°25'·99W.

CAMARET

N môle ⨳ Iso WG 4s 7m W12M, G9M; 135°-W-182°-G-027°; 48°16'·85N 04°35'·32W.

MORGAT

Pte de Morgat ☆ Oc (4) WRG 12s 77m **W15M**, R11M, G10M; Shore-W-281°-G-301°-W-021°-R-043°; 48°13'·17N 04°29'·81W.

DOUARNENEZ

Île Tristan ⨳ Oc (3) WR 12s 35m, W13M, R10M; shore-W-138°-R-153°-W-shore; 48°06'·14N 04°20'·25W.

RAZ DE SEIN

Tévennec ⨳ Q WR 28m W9M R6M; 090°-W-345°-R-090°; 48°04'·28N 04°47'·73W. Same twr, Dir ⨳ Fl 4s 24m 12M; intens 324°-332°.
La Vieille ☆ Oc (2+1) WRG 12s 33m **W18M**, R13M, G14M; 290°-W-298°-R-325°-W-355°-G-017°-W-035°-G-105°-W-123°-R-158°-W-205°; Gy ☐ twr; *Horn (2+1) 60s*; 48°02'·43N 04°45'·43W.
La Plate ⎨ VQ (9) 10s 8M; 48°02'·35N 04°45'·61W.

AUDIERNE

Kergadec Dir ⚡006°: Q WRG 43m 12/9M; 000°-G-005·3°-W-006·7°-R-017°; 48°00'·95N 04°32'·78W.

LOCTUDY

Pte de Langoz ☆ Fl (4) WRG 12s 12m, **W15M**, R/G11M; 115°-W-257°-G-284°-W-295°-R-318°-W-328°-R-025°; 47°49'·87N 04°09'·59W.

BENODET

Ldg lts 345·5°: Front Dir Oc (2+1) G 12s 11m **17M**; W ○ twr, G stripe; 47°52'·31N 04°06'·70W. Rear ⚡ Oc (2+1) 12s 48m 11M; 338°-016°, synch.

PORT-LA-FORÊT

Cap Coz ⚡ Fl (2) WRG 6s 5m, 7/5M; shore-R-335°-G-340°-W-346°-R-shore; 47°53'·48N 03°58'·28W.

ÎLES DE GLÉNAN

Penfret ☆ Fl R 5s 36m **21M**; W ☐ twr, R top; 47°43'·26N 03°57'·17W.

CONCARNEAU

Ldg lts 028·5°: Front, ⚡ Q 14m 13M; 006·5°-093°; 47°52'·15N 03°55'·08W. **Rear** ☆ Dir Q 87m **23M**; intens 026·5°-030·5°; spire, 1·34M from front.
Marina ⚡ Fl (4) R 15s 3m 1M; 47°52'·20N 03°54'·72W.

ÎLE DE GROIX

Pen Men ☆ Fl (4) 25s 60m **29M**; 309°-275°; W ☐ twr, B top; 47°38'·86N 03°30'·54W.
Port Tudy, ⚡ Iso G 4s 12m 6M; 47°38'·70N 03°26'·74W.

LORIENT

Passe de l'Ouest ldg lts 057°: both Dir Q 11/22m 13/18M. Front, 47°42'·13N 03°21'·83W

BELLE ÎLE

Pte des Poulains ☆ Fl 5s 34m **23M**; 023°-291°; W ☐ twr and dwelling; 47°23'·28N 03°15'·17W.
Sauzon, ⚡ Fl G 4s 8m 8M; 47°22'·51N 03°13'·10W.
Le Palais, N jetty ⚡ QG 11m 7M; obsc 298°-170°; W twr, G top; 47°20'·84N 03°09'·04W. S jetty QR.
La Teignouse ☆ Fl WR 4s 20m **W15M**, R11M; 033°-W-039°-R-033°; 47°27'·45N 03°02'·79W.

ÎLE DE HOUAT

Port St-Gildas N môle ⚡ Fl (2) WG 6s 8m W9M, G6M; 168°-W-198°-G-210°-W-240°-G-168°; W twr, G top; 47°23'·57N 02°57'·34W.

ÎLE DE HOËDIC

Port de l'Argol bkwtr ⚡ Fl WG 4s 10m W9M, G6M; 143°-W-163°-G-183°-W-194°-G-143°; W twr, G top; 47°20'·69N 02°52'·56W.

PORT HALIGUEN

E bkwtr hd ⚡ Oc (2) WR 6s 10m, W11M, R8M; 233°-W-240·5°-R-299°-W-306°-R-233°; W twr, R top; 47°29'·30N 03°05'·99W.

LA TRINITÉ-SUR-MER

Ldg lts 347°: Front, ⚡ Q WRG 11m W10M, R/G7M; 321°-G-345°-W-013·5°-R-080°; 47°34'·08N 03°00'·37W.
Rear, Dir Q 21m **15M**; synch.
Marina ⚡ Iso R 4s 8m 5M; 47°35'·27N 03°01'·47W.

CROUESTY

Ldg lts 058°, Dir Q 10/27m **19M**: Front; 47°32'·54N 02°53'·94W. Rear ☆, grey lt ho.

VILAINE RIVER

Pte de Penlan ☆ Oc (2) WRG 6s 26m, **W15M**, R/G11M; 292·5°-R-025°-G-052°-W-060°-R-138°-G-180°; W twr, R bands; 47°30'·98N 02°30'·13W.

PIRIAC-SUR-MER

Inner mole ⚡ Oc (2) WRG 6s 8m, W10M, R/G7M; 066°-R-148°-G-194°-W-201°-R-221°; *Siren 120s (occas)*; 47°22'·93N 02°32'·72W.

LA TURBALLE

Ldg lts 006·5°, both Dir Iso R 4s 11/19m 3M; intens 004°-009°; Front, 47°20'·80N 02°30'·87W.
Jetée de Garlahy ⚡ Fl (4) WR 12s 13m, W10M, R7M; 060°-R-315°-W-060°; W pylon, R top; 47°20'·70N 02°30'·93W.

PORNICHET (La Baule)

S bkwtr ⚡ Iso WRG 4s 11m, W10M, R/G7M; 303°-G-081°-W-084°-R-180°; 47°15'·49N 02°21'·15W.

DISTANCE TABLES

Approx distances in nautical miles are by the most direct route allowing for dangers and TSS.

1	Lézardrieux	1	12	16	18	24	42	43	45	72	97	100	105	124	Pornic	12
2	Tréguier	22	2	11	12	24	39	40	41	66	87	90	95	113	St Nazaire	11
3	Perros-Guirec	28	21	3	10	13	30	30	34	55	78	80	85	106	La Baule/Pornichet	10
4	Trébeurden	40	32	17	4	9	18	22	27	48	73	75	79	100	Le Croisic	9
5	Morlaix	60	46	36	23	5	8	28	36	57	78	80	84	105	Arzal/Camoël	8
6	Roscoff	54	41	28	17	12	6	7	16	37	58	60	64	85	Crouesty	7
7	L'Aberwrac'h	84	72	60	49	48	32	7	6	26	47	48	54	74	Le Palais (Belle Isle)	6
8	Le Conquet	106	98	83	72	68	55	29	8	5	32	33	38	61	Lorient	5
9	Brest (marina)	114	107	92	83	79	67	42	18	9	4	4	12	37	Concarneau	4
10	Morgat	126	118	103	92	88	75	49	20	24	10	3	12	36	Port-la-Forêt	3
11	Douarnenez	131	123	108	97	93	80	54	25	29	11	11	2	30	Loctudy	2
12	Audierne	135	128	113	102	98	86	55	30	34	27	30	12	1	Audierne	1

SELECTED LIGHTS, BUOYS & WAYPOINTS

Positions are referenced to WGS84

RIVER LOIRE TO ÎLE D'OLÉRON

Pte de Saint-Gildas ⚲ Q WRG 20m, W14M, R/G10M; 264°-R-308°-G-078°-W-088°-R-174°-W-180°-G-264°; col on W house; 47°08'·02N 02°14'·76W.

PORNIC
Appr buoy ⚲ L Fl 10s; 47°06'·45N 02°06'·64W.
Pte de Noëveillard ⚲ Oc (4) WRG 12s 22m W13M, R/G9M; Shore-G-051°-W-079°-R-shore; W ☐ twr, G top, W dwelling; 47°06'·62N 02°06'·92W.

ÎLE DE NOIRMOUTIER

Île du Pilier ☆ Fl (3) 20s 33m **29M**; Gy twr; 47°02'·55N 02°21'·61W. Same twr, ⚲ QR 10m 11M, 321°-034°.
Les Boeufs ⚲ VQ (9) 10s; 46°55'·04N 02°28'·02W.
L'Herbaudière, ldg lts 187·5°, both Q 5/21m 7M, Gy masts. Front, 47°01'·59N 02°17'·85W.
Martroger ⚲, Q WRG 11m W9M, R/G6M; 033°-G-055°-W-060°-R-095°-G-124°-W-153°-R-201°-W-240°-R-033°; 47°02'·60N 02°17'·12W.
W jetty ⚲ Oc (2+1) WG 12s 9m W10M, G7M; 187·5°-W-190°-G-187·5°; 47°01'·63N 02°17'·86W.
Noirmoutier-en-L'Île jetty ⚲ Oc (2) R 6s 6m 6M; W col, R top; 46°59'·27N 02°13'·14W.

ÎLE D'YEU

Petite Foule (main lt) ☆ Fl 5s 56m **24M**; W ☐ twr, G lantern; 46°43'·05N 02°22'·96W.

Port Joinville ldg lts 219°, both QR 11/16m 6M, 169°-269°: Front 46°43'·61N 02°20'·95W.
NW jetty ⚲ Oc (3) WG 12s 7m, W11M, G8M; Shore-G-150°-W-232°-G-279°-W-285°-G-shore; W 8-sided twr, G top; 46°43'·77N 02°20'·82W.

Pte des Corbeaux ☆ Fl (2+1) R 15s 25m **20M**; 083°-143° obsc by Île d'Yeu; 46°41'·42N 02°17'·11W.
Port de la Meule ⚲ Oc WRG 4s 9m, W9M, R/G6M; 007·5°-G-018°-W-027·5°-R-041·5°; Gy twr, R top; 46°41'·66N 02°20'·75W.

SAINT GILLES-CROIX-DE-VIE

Pte de Grosse Terre ☆ Fl (4) WR 12s 25m, **W18M, R15M**; 290°- R-339°-W-125°-R-145°; W truncated twr; 46°41'·54N 01°57'·92W.
Ldg lts 043·7°,Q 7/28m **15M**; 033·5°-053·5°: Front, 46°41'·85N 01°56'·67W
Pilours ⚲ Q (6) + L Fl 15s;   *Bell;* 46°40'·98N 01°58'·10W.
Jetée de la Garenne ⚲ Fl G 4s 8m 6M; 46°41'·45N 01°57'·26W.

LES SABLES D'OLONNE

Les Barges ⚲ Fl (2) R 10s 25m 13M; Gy twr; 46°29'·70N 01°50'·50W.
L'Armandèche ☆ Fl (2+1) 15s 42m **24M**; 295°-130°; W 6-sided twr, R top; 46°29'·40N 01°48'·29W.
Nouch Sud ⚲ Q (6) + L Fl 15s; 46°28'·55N 01°47'·42W.

SW Pass, ldg lts 032·5°, Iso 4s 12/33m **16M**, H24: Front ☆, 46°29'·42N 01°46'·37W.
SE Pass, ldg lts 320°: Front ⚲ QG 11m 8M; 46°29'·44N 01°47'·51W. Rear ⚲ Q 33m 13M.
Jetée St Nicolas (W jetty) ⚲ QR 16m 8M; 143°-094°; W twr, R top; 46°29'·23N 01°47'·52W.

BOURGENAY

Ldg lts 040°, QG 9/19m 7M. Front; 46°26'·37N 01°40'·61W. Rear, 010°-070°; 162m from front.
Landfall ⚲ L Fl 10s; 46°25'·28N 01°41'·91W.
Ent ⚲ Fl R 4s & ⚲ Iso G 4s; 46°26'·29N 01°40'·75W.

ÎLE-DE-RÉ

Les Baleineaux ⚲ VQ 23m 7M; pink twr, R top; 46°15'·81N 01°35'·22W.
Les Baleines ☆ Fl (4) 15s 53m **27M**; conspic Gy 8-sided twr, R lantern; 46°14'·64N 01°33'·69W.
Chanchardon ⚲ Fl WR 4s 15m W11M, R8M; 118°-R-290°-W-118°; 46°09'·73N 01°28'·44W.
Chauveau ☆ Oc (3) WR 12s 27m **W15M**, R11M; 057°-W-094°-R-104°-W-342°-R-057°; W ○ twr, R top; 46°08'·03N 01°16'·42W.

ARS-EN-RÉ

Les Islattes ⚲ Q 13m 3M; BY bcn twr; 46°14'·03N 01°23'·33W.
Dir ⚲ 268° Oc WRG 4s, W10M, R/G 7M; 275·5°-G-267·5°-W-268·5°-R-274·5°; 46°14'·05N 01°28'·60W.
Le Fier d'Ars, inner ldg lts 232·5°: ⚲ Q 5/13m 9/11M; 46°12'·76N 01°30'·60W. Rear ⚲ Q 11M.

ST MARTIN DE RÉ

Rocha ⚲ Q; 46°14'·74N 01°20'·64W.
Lt ho, E of ent ⚲ Oc (2) WR 6s 18m W10M, R7M; Shore-W-245°-R-281°-W-shore; W twr, R top; 46°12'·44N 01°21'·89W.
W mole ⚲ Fl G 2·5s 10m 6M; 46°12'·49N 01°21'·89W.

LA ROCHELLE

Ldg lts 059°, both Dir Q 15/25m 13/14M; synch; by day Fl 4s; Front; 46°09'·35N 01°09'·16W.
Pte des Minimes ⚲ Fl (3) WG 12s 8m; W8M, G5M; 059°-W-213°; 313°-G-059°; 46°08'·33N 01°10'·68W.
Tour Richelieu ⚲ Fl R 4s 10m 9M; 46°08'·90N 01°10'·34W.
Marina ⚲ Fl (2)G 6s 9m 7M; 46°08'·82N 01°10'·15W.

LA CHARENTE

Ldg lts 115°, Dir QR 8/21m **19/20M**: Front ☆, 45°57'·96N 01°04'·38W.
Fort Boyard ⚲ Q (9) 15s; 45°59'·96N 01°12'·87W.
Île d'Aix ☆ Fl WR 5s 24m **W24M, R20M**; 103°-R-118°-W-103°; 46°00'·60N 01°10'·67W.

ÎLE D'OLÉRON

Chassiron ☆ Fl 10s **28M**; 46°02'·80N 01°24'·61W.
Antioche ⚲ Q 20m 11M; 46°03'·94N 01°23'·71W.

ST DENIS

Dir ⚡205°, IsoWRG 4s 14m, W11M, R/G8M; 190°-G-204°-W-206°-R-220°;46°01'·61N 01°21'·91W.
E jetty ⚡ Fl (2) WG 6s 6m, W9M, G6M; 205°-G-277°-W-292°-G-165°; 46°02'·10N 01°22'·06W.

R GIRONDE TO THE SPANISH BORDER

GIRONDE, PASSE DE L'OUEST

Pte de la Coubre ☆ Fl (2) 10s 64m **28M**; 45°41'·78N 01°13'·99W. Also, F RG 42m, R12M, G10M; 030°-R-043°-G-060°-R-110°.
BXA ⓛ Iso 4s 8m 7M; **Racon** ; 45°37'·53N 01°28'·69W.
Ldg lts 081·5° (not valid E of Nos 4 & 5 buoys). **Front** ☆, Dir Iso 4s 21m **20M**; 45°39'·56N 01°08'·76W. Same structure, Q (2) 5s 10m 3M.
La Palmyre, common rear ☆ Dir Q 57m **27M**; 45°39'·71N 01°07'·24W. Same twr, Dir FR **17M**.

Cordouan ☆ Oc (2+1) WRG 12s 60m, **W22M**, R/G18M; 014°-W-126°-G-178·5°-W-267°-R   -294·5°-R-014°; 45°35'·16N 01°10'·39W.

PASSE SUD (or DE GRAVE)

Ldg lts 063°: **Front**, Dir QG 22m **16M**; 45°33'·72N 01°05'·03W. **Rear**, Oc WRG 4s 26m, **W17M**, R/G13M; 033°-W-233·5°-R-303°-W-312°-G-330°-W-341°-025°.
G ⓛ 45°30'·32N 01°15'·56W.
G3 ⓛ 45°32'·78N 01°07'·72W.
Ldg lts 041°, both Dir QR 33/61m **18M**. **Front, Le Chay** ☆ intens 039·5°-042·5°; W twr, R top; 45°37'·30N 01°02'·40W. **Rear, St Pierre** ☆, intens 039°-043°; R water twr, 0·97M from front.
G5 ⓛ 45°33'·97N 01°06'·39W.
G4 ⓛ 45°34'·70N 01°05'·79W.
G6 ⓛ 45°34'·88N 01°04'·81W.

ROYAN

R1 ⓛ Iso G 4s; 45°36'·56N 01°01'·96W.
NE jetty ⚡ Fl (3) G 12s 2m 5M; 45°37'·23N 01°01'·49W.

PORT-MÉDOC

N bkwtr ⚡ QG 4M; 45°33'·42N 01°03'·48W.
S bkwtr ⚡ QR 4M; 45°33'·37N 01°03'·44W.

PAUILLAC

Pauillac, NE elbow ⚡ Fl G 4s 7m 5M; 45°11'·96N 00°44'·61W.
Ent E side ⚡ QG 7m 4M; 45°11'·86N 00°44'·60W.

BORDEAUX

Lock into Bassins Nos 1 & 2, 44°51'·74N 00°32'·94W.

ARCACHON, PASSE NORD

Cap Ferret ☆ Fl R 5s 53m **27M**; W ◯ twr, R top; 44°34'·05N 01°18'·71W. Same twr, ⚡ Oc (3) 12s.
ATT-ARC ⓛ L Fl 10s 8m 5M; 44°33'·80N 01°18'·69W.
Note: Buoys are moved as the channel shifts.

1N	ⓛ	44°33'·74N 01°17'·78W.
3N	ⓛ	44°34'·49N 01°16'·43W.
5N	ⓛ	44°34'·78N 01°15'·92W.
7N	ⓛ	44°35'·44N 01°14'·76W.
9N	ⓛ	44°36'·96N 01°14'·34W.
11	ⓛ	44°37'·35N 01°14'·10W.
15	▲	44°39'·85N 01°12'·04W.

Marina ⚡ QG 6m 6M; 44°39'·77N 01°09'·15W.

CAPBRETON

Digue Nord ⚡ Fl (2) R 6s 13m 12M; W ◯ twr, R top; *Horn 30s*; 43°39'·38N 01°27'·01W.
Estacade Sud ⚡ Fl (2) G 6s 9m 8M; 43°39'·25N 01°26'·89W.
Marina ent, Fl G 4s and Fl R 4s.

ANGLET/BAYONNE

BA ⓛ L Fl 10s; 43°32'·59N 01°32'·76W.
Outer ldg lts 090°, both Q 9/15m 19M.
Outer S bkwtr ⓛ Q (9) 15s 15m 6M; 43°31'·60N 01°31'·68W. Anglet marina ent ⚡ Fl G 2·5s 6m 2M; 43°31'·57N 01°30'·51W.

ST JEAN DE LUZ

Inner ldg lts 150·7°, both Dir QG 18/27m **16M**; intens 149·5°-152·2°. **Front, E jetty** ☆ W ☐ twr, R stripe; 43°23'·25N 01°40'·15W. **Rear** ☆, W ☐ twr, G stripe; at S corner of marina.

HENDAYE

Cabo Higuer ☆ Fl (2) 10s 63m **23M**; 43°23'·51N 01°47'·53W (in Spain).
W trng wall ⚡ Fl (3) G 9s 9m 5M; 43°22'·82N 01°47'·36W.
E trng wall ⚡ L Fl R 10s 7m 5M.
Marina ent, E side ⚡ Fl Y 4s 5m 3M.

1	Port Joinville	1														
2	St Gilles-C-de-Vie	18	2													
3	Sables d'Olonne	31	16	3												
4	Bourgenay	40	25	9	4											
5	St Martin (I de Ré)	55	44	27	20	5										
6	La Rochelle	66	51	36	29	12	6									
7	Rochefort	84	75	61	54	36	26	7								
8	R La Seudre	89	71	58	52	33	24	30	8							
9	Port St Denis	59	48	33	30	21	13	26	22	9						
10	Port Bloc/Royan	97	85	71	60	56	52	68	27	42	10					
11	Bordeaux	152	140	126	115	111	107	123	82	97	55	11				
12	Cap Ferret	138	130	113	110	102	98	114	75	88	68	123	12			
13	Capbreton	192	186	169	166	165	156	172	131	145	124	179	58	13		
14	Anglet/Bayonne	200	195	181	178	177	168	184	143	157	132	187	70	12	14	
15	Santander	212	210	204	204	206	202	218	184	192	180	235	133	106	103	15
16	Cabo Finisterre	377	395	393	394	406	407	423	399	397	401	456	376	370	373	274	16

DISTANCE TABLES
Approx distances in nautical miles are by the most direct route allowing for dangers and TSS.

AREA 18 N & NW Spain – French border to Portuguese border

SELECTED LIGHTS, BUOYS & WAYPOINTS

Positions are referenced to WGS84

FRENCH BORDER TO BAYONA

FUENTERRABIA (See Hendaye, previous page)
Marina ent, ☆ Fl (4) G 11s 9m 3m; 43°22'·59N 01°47'·51W. ☆ Fl (4) R 11s 9m 1M, close SW.

PASAJES
☖ Mo (A) 6s 11M; 43°21'·19N 01°56'·12W.
Senocozulúa Dir ☆ 155·75°; Oc (2) WRG 12s 50m W6M, R/G3M; 129·5°-G-154·5°-W-157°-R-190°; W twr; **Racon M**; 43°19'·90N 01°55'·61W.

SAN SEBASTIÁN
Ldg lts 158°: Front ☆ QR 10m 7M; 143°-173°; 43°18'·89N 01°59'·47W. Rear ☆ Oc R 4s 16m 7M.
Igueldo ☆ Fl (2+1) 15s 132m **26M**; 43°19'·35N 02°00'·64W.

GUETARIA
I. de San Antón ☆ Fl (4) 15s 91m **21M**; 43°18'·62N 02°12'·09W.
N mole ☆ Fl (3) G 9s 11m 5M; 43°18'·26N 02°11'·91W.

ZUMAYA
Lt ho ☆ Oc (1+3) 12s 39m 12M; Port sigs; 43°18'·14N 02°15'·07W. Marina ent, ☆ Fl (3) R 9s 6m 1M and ☆ Fl (2+1) G 10s 6m 1M.

LEQUEITIO
P Amandarri ☆ Fl G 4s 8m 5M; 43°21'·99N 02°29'·94W.
Cabo de Santa Catalina ☆ Fl (1+3) 20s 44m **17M**; *Horn Mo (L) 20s;* 43°22'·67N 02°30'·69W.

ELANCHOVE
Digue N ☆ Fl G 3s 8m 4M. **Cabo Machichaco** ☆ Fl 7s 120m **24M**; *Siren Mo (M) 60s;* 43°27'·30N 02°45'·19W.

BILBAO
Punta Galea ☆ Fl (3) 8s 82m **19M**; 011°-227°; *Siren Mo (G) 30s;* 43°22'·30N 03°02'·14W.
Pta Lucero bkwtr head ☆ Fl G 5s 21m 10M; *Racon X, 20M;* 43°22'·67N 03°05'·04W.
Getxo marina bkwtr ☆QR 5m 1M, R col; 43°20'·23N 03°01'·02W.
Las Arenas marina (RCMA) ☆ Oc G 4s 1m 1M; 43°19'·83N 03°00'·98W; and Oc R 4s 2m 1M.

CASTRO URDIALES
Castillo de Santa Ana ☆ Fl (4) 24s 47m **20M**; W twr; *Siren Mo (C) 60s;* 43°23'·06N 03°12'·89W.
N bkwtr ☆ Fl G 3s 12m 6M; 43°22'·86N 03°12'·54W.

LAREDO and RIA DE SANTOÑA
Santoña ldg lts 283·5°: Front, ☆ Fl 2s 5m 8M; 43°26'·33N 03°27'·62W. Rear, ☆ Oc (2) 5s 12m 11M.
C. Ajo ☆ Oc (3) 16s 69m **17M**; 43°30'·70N 03°35'·72W.

SANTANDER
Cabo Mayor ☆ Fl (2) 10s 89m **21M**; *Horn Mo (M) 40s;* 43°29'·37N 03°47'·51W.
Marina de Santander, ldg lts 235·6°: Front ☆ Iso 2s 9m 2M; 43°25'·75N 03°48'·83W. Rear ☆ Oc 5s.
Marina ent QR and QG.

Pta del Torco de Afuera ☆ Fl (1+2) 24s 33m **22M**; W twr; 43°26'·51N 04°02'·61W.

RIBADESELLA
Pta del Caballo ☆ Fl (4) R 11s 10m 5M; 278·4°-212·9°; ○ twr; 43°28'·08N 05°03'·98W.
Marina trng wall ☖ Q; approx 43°27'·83N 05°03'·70W.
Somos ☆ Fl (2+1) 12s 113m **25M**; twr; 43°28'·08N 05°03'·98W.
C. Lastres ☆ Fl (5) 25s 116m **23M**. W ○ twr; 43°32'·03N 05°18'·07W.

GIJÓN
Piedra Sacramento ☆ Fl (2) G 6s 9m 5M; 8-sided twr; 43°32'·90N 05°40'·21W.
Marina, N bkwtr ☆ Fl (2) R 6s 7m 3M; 43°32'·85N 05°40'·08W.
C. de Torres ☆ Fl (2) 10s 80m **18M**; 43°34'·29N 05°41'·97W.
C. Peñas ☆ Fl (3) 15s 115m **35M**; Gy 8-sided twr; *Siren Mo (P) 60s;* 43°39'·31N 05°50'·90W.

CUDILLERO
Pta Rebollera ☆ Oc (4) 16s 42m **16M**; W 8-sided twr; *Siren Mo (D) 30s;* 43°33'·96N 06°08'·68W.
Ent, N bkwtr ☆ Fl (3) G 9s 3m 2M.
C. Vidio ☆ Fl 5s 99m **25M**; *Siren Mo (V) 60s;* 43°35'·60N 06°14'·79W.
C. Busto ☆ Fl (4) 20s 84m **25M**; 43°34'·13N 06°28'·23W.

LUARCA
Punta Altaya ☆ Oc (3) 15s 63m 14M; W ☐ twr; *Siren Mo (L) 30s;* 43°33'·03N 06°31'·85W.
Ldg lts 170°, W cols, R bands: Front ☆ Fl 5s 18m 2M; 43°32'·78N 06°32'·11W. Rear ☆ Oc 4s 25m 2M.

RÍA DE RIBADEO
Pta de la Cruz ☆ Fl (4) R 11s 16m 7M; 43°33'·40N 07°01'·75W.
Isla Pancha ☆ Fl (3+1) 20s 26m **21M**; *Siren Mo (R) 30s;* 43°33'·39N 07°02'·53W, W side of entrance.
1st ldg lts 140°, both R ◇s, W twrs. Front ☆ Iso R 18m 5M; 43°32'·83N 07°01'·53W. Rear ☆ Oc R 4s.
2nd ldg lts 205°. Front, ☆ VQ R 8m 3M; R ◇, W twr; 43°32'·49N 07°02'·24W. Rear ☆ Oc R 2s 18m 3M.
Yacht hbr, ☆ Fl G 5s 9m 3M; 43°32'·45N 07°02'·16W.

RÍA DE VIVERO
Pta de Faro ☆ Fl R 5s 18m 7M; 43°42'·74N 07°35'·03W.
Pta Socastro ☆ Fl G 5s 18m 7M; 43°43'·08N 07°36'·42W.
Cillero, outer bkwtr ☆ Fl (2) R 7s 8m 5M; 43°40'·93N 07°36'·16W.
Marina ent ☆ Fl (2+1) G 15s 7m 1M; 43°40'·22N 07°35'·62W.
Pta de la Estaca de Bares ☆ Fl (2) 7·5s 99m **25M**; *Siren Mo (B) 60s;* 43°47'·21N 07°41'·14W.
Cabo Ortegal ☆ Fl (2+1) 15s 122m **18M**; W ○ twr, R band; 43°46'·30N 07°52'·20W.

RÍA DE CEDEIRA

Piedras de Media Mar ⚓ Fl (2) 7s 12m 4M; BRB twr; 43°39'·37N 08°04'·79W.

Bkwtr ⚡ Fl (2) R 7s 10m 4M; 43°39'·30N 08°04'·20W.

Cabo Prior ☆ Fl (1+2) 15s 105m **22M**; 055·5°-310°; 6-sided twr; 43°34'·05N 08°18'·87W.

Punta del Castro ⚡ Fl (2) 7s 42m 8M; W 6-sided twr; 43°30'·47N 08°19'·73W.

RÍA DE FERROL

Cabo Prioriño Chico ☆ Fl 5s 34m **23M**; 225°-129·5°; W 8-sided twr; 43°27'·52N 08°20'·40W.

RÍAs DE ARES & DE BETANZOS

Ares bkwtr ⚡ Fl (3) R 9s; 43°25'·35N 08°14'·27W.

Sada marina ⚡ Fl (4) G 11s; 43°21'·76N 08°14'·54W.

LA CORUÑA

Torre de Hércules ☆ Fl (4) 20s 104m **23M**; *Siren Mo (L) 30s;* 43°23'·15N 08°24'·39W.

Ldg Its 108·5°: Front ⚡ Oc WR 4s 54m, W8M R3M; 000°-R-023°; 100·5°-R-105·5°-W-114·5°-R-153°; **Racon M, 18M; 020°-196°;** 43°23'·00N 08°21'·28W. Rear ⚡ Fl 4s 79m 8M; 357·5°-177·5°.

Ldg Its 182°: Front, ⚡ Iso WRG 2s 27m, W10M, R/ G7M; 146·4°-G-180°-W-184°-R-217·6°; **Racon X, 11-21M;** 43°20'·59N 08°22'·25W. Rear ⚡ Oc R 4s.

Darsena de la Marina ⚡ Fl (3) G 9s 8m 3M; 43°21'·01N 08°23'·66W.

RÍA DE CORME Y LAGE

Pt Lage ☆ Fl (5) 20s 64m **20M**; 43°13'·84N 09°00'·65W.

Lage, N mole ⚡ Fl G 3s 15m 4M; 43°13'·34N 08°59'·96W.

Corme, mole ⚡ Fl (2) R 5s 12m 3M; 43°15'·64N 08°57'·83W.

C. Villano ☆ Fl (2) 15s 102m **28M**; *Siren Mo (V) 60s;* **Racon M, 35M;** 43°09'·60N 09°12'·70W

RÍA DE CAMARIÑAS

Ldg Its 081°: Front ⚡ Fl 5s 13m 9M; 43°07'·37N 09°11'·56W. Rear ⚡ Iso 4s 25m 11M.

Outer bkwtr ⚡ Fl R 5s 7m 3M; 43°07'·45N 09°10'·70W.

Cabo Toriñana ☆ Fl (2+1) 15s 63m **24M; Racon T, 35M** *(1.7M SE of ☆);* 43°03'·17N 09°18'·01W.

Cabo Finisterre ☆ Fl 5s 141m **23M; Racon O, 35M;** 42°52'·93N 09°16'·29W.

RÍA DE MUROS

Pta Queixal ⚡ Fl (2+1) 12s; 42°44'·36N 09°04'·75W.

Muros ⚡ Fl (4) G 11s 9m 3M; 42°46'·54N 09°03'·14W.

Portosin ⚡ Fl (3) G 9s 8m 5M; 42°45'·94N 08°56'·93W.

Pta Cabeiro ⚡ Oc WR 3s 35m 9/6M; 050°-R-054·5°-W-058·5°-R-099·5°-W-189·5°; 42°44'·37N 08°59'·44W.

RÍA DE AROUSA (Selected lights only)

Isla Sálvora ☆ Fl (3+1) 20s 38m **21M**; 42°27'·82N 09°00'·80W. Same twr, ⚡ Fl (3) 20s; 126°-160°.

Santa Uxia ⚡ Fl (2) R 7s 7m 4M; 42°33'·58N 08°59'·24W. 50m SE, ⚡ Fl R 5s 8m 5M.

Isla Rúa ⚡ Fl (2) WR 7s 25m 12M; 121·5°-R-211·5°-W-21·5°; **Racon K, 211°-121°, 10-20M;** 42°32'·95N 08°56'·38W.

Pobra do Caramiñal E bkwtr ⚡ Fl (3) G 9s 9m 5M; ○ twr, G band; 42°36'·28N 08°55'·87W.

Villagarcia, N mole ⚡ Iso 2s 2m 10M; 42°36'·11N 08°46'·33W. Marina ent, QG & QR, both 6m 3M.

Piedras Negras marina ⚡ Fl (4) WR 11s 5m, W4M R3M; 305°-W-315°-R-305; 42°27'·49N 08°55'·11W.

RÍA DE PONTEVEDRA

Isla Ons ☆ Fl (4) 24s 125m **25M**; 8-sided twr; 42°22'·94N 08°56'·17W.

Sangenjo ⚡ QR 5m 4M; 42°23'·81N 08°48'·06W.

Combarro ⚡ Fl (2) R 8s 7m 3M; 42°25'·78N 08°42'·23W.

Aguete ⚓ Fl (4) G 11s 3M, 42°22'·66N 08°44'·21W.

RÍA DE VIGO

Ldg Its 129°: Front, ⚡ Fl 3s 36m 9M; 42°15'·15N 08°52'·37W. Rear ⚡ Oc 6s 53m 11M.

S Chan ldg Its 069·3°: **Front** ☆ Iso 2s 16m **18M;** *Horn Mo (V) 60s;* **Racon B, 22M;** 42°11'·12N 08°48'·89W. **Rear** Oc 4s 48m **18M.**

Marina, QG/ QR, 10m 5M, 42°14'·56N 08°43'·41W.

BAYONA

Las Serralleiras ⚓ Q (9) 15s 4M; 42°09'·23N 08°53'·35W.

Ldg Its 084°: Front ⚡ Fl 6s 8m 10M; 42°08'·24N 08°50'·09W.

Rear, **Panjón Dir** ⚡ 084°, Oc WRG 4s **W18M, R15M,** G14M; 079°-G-083°-W-085°-R-088°; 42°08'·34N 08°48'·84W.

C. Silleiro ☆ Fl (2+1) 15s 84m **24M**; W 8-sided twr; R bands; 42°06'·27N 08°53'·80W.

⚓ Q; 42°07'·29N 08°54'·73W, 9ca NW of C. Silleiro.

		1	2	3	4	5	6	7	8	9	10	11	12	13	14	15	16	17	18	19	20
1.	Le Conquet	**1**																			
2.	Fuenterrabia	330	**2**																		
3.	San Sebastian	326	13	**3**																	
4.	Zumaya	322	23	13	**4**																
5.	Cabo Machichaco	308	44	34	20	**5**															
6.	Bilbao (ent)	311	63	58	39	19	**6**														
7.	Santander	300	92	82	63	48	39	**7**													
8.	San Vicente de la B	300	116	108	93	77	63	38	**8**												
9.	Gijon	293	171	160	147	128	115	90	56	**9**											
10.	Cabo Penas	286	179	168	154	135	123	97	63	12	**10**										
11.	Ribadeo	306	224	213	199	180	176	150	128	65	53	**11**									
12.	Vivero	308	250	239	225	206	202	176	143	92	80	33	**12**								
13.	Cabo Ortegal	305	267	256	242	215	211	185	151	100	88	41	18	**13**							
14.	La Coruña	340	305	294	280	253	249	223	189	138	126	79	56	38	**14**						
15.	Cabo Villano	380	342	337	317	290	286	260	226	213	163	116	93	75	45	**15**					
16.	Muros	402	380	369	355	328	324	298	264	251	201	154	131	113	83	38	**16**				
17.	Vilagarcia	442	420	409	395	368	364	338	304	291	241	194	171	153	123	78	40	**17**			
18.	Sanxenxo	449	427	416	402	375	371	345	311	298	248	201	178	160	130	85	42	26	**18**		
19.	Vigo	453	434	423	409	382	378	352	318	305	255	208	185	167	137	92	35	35	18	**19**	
20.	Bayona	453	434	423	409	382	378	352	318	305	255	208	185	167	137	92	35	36	19	11	**20**

DISTANCE TABLES

Approx distances in nautical miles are by the most direct route allowing for dangers and TSS.

SELECTED LIGHTS, BUOYS & WAYPOINTS

Positions are referenced to WGS84

SPANISH BORDER TO CASCAIS

Montedor ☆ Fl (2) 9·5s 102m 22M; R twr; *Horn Mo (S) 25s;* 41°45'·09N 08°52'·49W.

VIANA DO CASTELO

Dir lt Oc WRG 4s 15m 8/6M; 350°-G-005°-W-010°-R-025°; 41°41'·12N 08°50'·21W.
Outer mole ≰ Fl R 3s 9M; *Horn 30s;* 41°40'·46N 08°50'·66W.
No. 2 ⌔ Fl R 3s; 41°40'·53N 08°50'·48W.
E mole ≰ Fl G 3s 9M; 41°40'·67N 08°50'·25W.
No. 1 ▲ Fl G 3s; 41°40'·68N 08°50'·29W.
No. 3 ▲ Fl (2) G 3s; 41°40'·86N 08°50'·24W.
No. 4 ⌔ Fl (2+1) R 5s; 41°40'·89N 08°50'·36W.
Nos. 5-13 ▲s are Fl G 3s. Nos. 6-14 ⌔s are Fl R 3s.
No. 13 ▲ Fl G 3s; 41°41'·49N 08°49'·27W, SSE of marina ent at 41°41'·59N 08°49'·33W.

PÓVOA DE VARZIM

Molhe N ≰ Fl R 3s 14m 12M; *Siren 40s;* 41°22'·29N 08°46'·23W. Molhe S ≰ L Fl G 6s 4M.

LEIXÕES

Tanker mooring ⌑ Fl (3) 15s 6M; *Horn (U) 30s;* 41°12'·10N 08°45'·07W.
Leça ☆ Fl (3) 14s 56m **28M**; W twr, B bands; 41°12'·08N 08°42'·73W.
Outer N mole ≰ Fl WR 5s 23m W12M, R9M; 001°-R-180°-W-001°; *Horn 20s;* 41°10'·37N 08°42'·49W.
S mole ≰ Fl G 4s 16m 7M; 328°-285°; *Horn 30s;* 41°10'·68N 08°42'·35W.
Marina ≰ L Fl (2) R 12s 4m 2M; 41°11'·08N 08°42'·27W.

AVEIRO

Lt ho Aero ☆ Fl (4) 13s 65m **23M**; R/W twr; 40°38'·57N 08°44'·88W. Same twr ≰ Fl G 4s 53m 9M, rear 085·4° ldg lt. Front 085·4° ldg lt Fl G 3s 16m 9M; 40°38'·54N 08°45'·48W.
Ldg lts 065·6°: Front ≰ Oc R 3s 7m 9M; 40°38'·82N 08°44'·99W. Rear ≰ Oc R 6s 15m 9M, 440m fm frnt Molhe ≰ Fl R 3s 11m 8M; W col, R bands; 40°38'·61N 08°45'·81W.
Molhe S ≰ Fl G 3s 16m 9M; front 085·4° ldg lt. Molhe Central ≰ L Fl G 5s; 40°38'·64N 08°44'·95W.
Baia de São Jacinto, S bkwtr Fl R 3s; 40°39'·21N 08°43'·96W. N bkwtr Fl G 4s, 40°38'·39N 08°43'·77W.

FIGUEIRA DA FOZ

Cabo Mondego ☆ Fl 5s 96m **28M**; W twr and house; *Horn 30s;* 40°11'·43N 08°54'·32W.
Ldg lts 081·5°, W cols, R bands: Front ≰ Iso R 5s 6m 8M; 40°08'·83N 08°51'·23W. Rear, ≰ Oc R 6s.
Molhe N ≰ Fl R 6s 14m 9M; *Horn 35s;* 40°08'·74N 08°52'·50W. Marina ent Fl (2) R 8s and Fl (2) G 8s.
Molhe S ≰ Fl G 6s 13m 7M; 40°08'·59N 08°52'·41W.

Penedo da Saudade ☆ Fl (2) 15s 54m **30M**; ☐ twr, and house; 39°45'·84N 09°01'·89W.

NAZARÉ

Pontal da Nazaré ≰ Oc 3s 49m 14M; twr & bldg; *Siren 35s;* 39°36'·25N 09°05'·18W.
Molhe S ≰ L Fl G 5s 14m 8M; 39°35'·34N 09°04'·76W.
Molhe N ≰ L Fl R 5s 14m 9M.

FARILHÃO and ILHA DA BERLENGA

Farilhão Grande ≰ Fl (2) 5s 99m 13M; 39°28'·73N 09°32'·72W.
Ilha da Berlenga ☆ Fl 10s 120m **16M**; W ☐ twr and houses; *Horn 28s;* 39°24'·90N 09°30'·63W.
Cabo Carvoeiro ☆ Fl (3) R 15s 56m **15M**; W ☐ twr; *Horn 35s;* 39°21'·61N 09°24'·51W.

PENICHE

Molhe W ≰ Fl R 3s 13m 9M; W twr, R bands; *Siren 120s;* 39°20'·85N 09°22'·56W.
C. da Roca ☆ Fl (4) 17s 164m **26M**; W twr and bldgs; 38°46'·88N 09°29'·90W.
Cabo Raso ☆ Fl (3) 9s 22m **15M**; 324°-189°; R twr; *Horn Mo (I) 60s;* 38°42'·56N 09°29'·15W.

CASCAIS TO CAPE ST VINCENT

CASCAIS

Ldg lts 284·7°: Front, ☆ Oc WR 6s 24m **W18M**, R14M; 233°-R-334°-W-098°; *Horn 10s;* 38°41'·42N 09°25'·27W. Rear, ☆ Iso WR 2s **W19M, R16M**; 326°-W-092°; 278°-R-292°; W twr. Marina S mole ≰ Fl (3) R 4s 8m 6M; 38°41'·58N 09°24'·84W.

LISBOA

Triple ldg lts 047·1°: Front, ☆ Oc R 3s 30m **21M**; 38°41'·94N 09°15'·97W. Middle, ☆ Oc R 6s 81m **21M**; **Racon Q, 15M**. Rear, ☆ Iso 6s 153m **21M**; 38°43'·65N 09°13'·63W.
No. 1 ⌀ Fl G 2s; 38°39'·55N 09°18'·79W.
Forte Bugio ≰ Fl G 5s 27m 9M; ○ twr on fortress; *Horn Mo (B) 30s;* 38°39'·62N 09°17'·93W.
No. 5 ⌀ Fl G 4s; 38°40'·43N 09°17'·66W.
No. 7 ⌀ Fl G 5s; 38°40'·64N 09°16'·90W.
No. 9 ⌀ Fl G 6s; 38°40'·63N 09°14'·49W.
Ponte 25 de Abril: Fl (3) G 9s and Fl (3) R 9s on the N (38°41'·64N 09°10'·69W) and S pillars.
Cabo Espichel ☆ Fl 4s 167m **26M**; W 6-sided twr; *Horn 31s;* 38°24'·94N 09°13'·05W.

SESIMBRA

Ldg lts 003·5°, L Fl R 5s 9/21m 7/6M: Front, 38°26'·56N 09°06'·16W. Rear 34m from front.

SETÚBAL

Ldg lts 039·7°, both Iso Y 6s 12/60m **22M**. Front, R structure, W stripes; 38°31'·08N 08°54'·01W.

NAVIGATION

No. 1 ⚓ Fl G 3s 5M; 38°26'·98N 08°58'·18W.
No. 2 ⚓ Fl (2) R 10s 13m 9M; **Racon B, 15M;**
38°27'·21N 08°58'·45W.
Forte de Outão ⚓ Oc R 6s 33m 12M; 38°29'·31N
08°56'·06W.
Pinheiro da Cruz ⚓ Fl 3s; 38°15'·46N 08°46'·34W.

SINES
Cabo de Sines ☆ Fl (2) 15s 55m **26M;** 37°57'·56N
08°52'·83W.
W mole ⚓ Fl 3s 20m 12M; 37°56'·48N 08°53'·33W.
Sines W ⚓ Fl R 3s 6M; 37°56'·12N 08°53'·25W.
Marina mole ⚓ Fl G 4s 4M; W twr, G bands;
37°57'·03N 08°52'·03W.
C. Sardão ☆ Fl (3) 15s 67m **23M;** 37°35'·94N
08°49'·02W.

CAPE ST VINCENT/SAGRES
Cabo de São Vicente ☆ Fl 5s 84m **32M;** *Horn Mo (I)*
30s; 37°01'·36N 08°59'·78W.
Ponta de Sagres ⚓ Iso R 2s 52m 11M; 36°59'·66N
08°56'·94W.
Baleeira mole ⚓ Fl WR 4s 12m, W14M, R11M;
254°-W-355°-R-254°; 37°00'·67N 08°55'·46W.

CAPE ST VINCENT TO SPANISH BORDER

LAGOS
Pta da Piedade ☆ Fl 7s 50m **20M;** 37°04'·81N
08°40'·20W.
W mole ⚓ Fl (2) R 6s 5M; W col, R bands; 37°05'·85N
08°40'·02W.
E mole ⚓ Fl (2) G 6s 6M; W col, G bands; 37°05'·96N
08°39'·96W.
Alvor ent, ⚓ Fl R/G 4s; W twrs, R/G bands; 37°07'·13N
08°37'·14W.

PORTIMÃO
Ponta do Altar ☆ L Fl 5s 31m **16M;** 290°-170°; W twr
and bldg; 37°06'·34N 08°31'·17W.
Ldg lts 019·1°: Both ⚓ Iso R 6s 18/30m 6M; W cols,
R bands. Front 37°07'·35N 08°31'·31W. Rear 54m
from front.
E mole ⚓ Fl G 5s 9m 7M; 37°06'·50N 08°31'·59W.
W mole ⚓ Fl R 5s 9m 7M; 37°06'·52N 08°31'·77W.
No. 2 ⚓ Fl R 4s; 37°07'·04N 08°31'·46W.
Marina ent, S side ⚓ Fl R 6s 3M; 37°07'·10N
08°31'·58W.
N side ⚓ Fl G 6s 3M; 37°07'·14N 08°31'·58W.

N Mole ⚓ Iso R 4s 8m 3M; 37°07'·33N 08°31'·59W.
Pta de Alfanzina ☆ Fl (2) 15s 62m **29M;** 37°05'·22N
08°26'·59W.

ALBUFEIRA
Ponta da Baleeira ⚓ Oc 6s 30m 11M; 37°04'·84N
08°15'·85W.
N bkwtr ⚓, Fl (2) G 5s 9m 4M, approx 37°04'·90N
08°15'·52W.
S bkwtr ⚓, Fl (2) R 5s 9m 4M.
Praia da Albufeira, E end of bay, Olhos de Água ⚓
L Fl 5s 29m 7M; 37°05'·47N 08°11'·40W.

VILAMOURA
Vilamoura ☆, Fl 5s 17m **19M;** 37°04'·50N
08°07'·42W.
Marina, W mole ⚓ Fl R 4s 13m 5M; 37°04'·19N
08°07'·49W.
E mole ⚓ Fl G 4s 13m 5M; 37°04'·22N 08°07'·42W.

FARO, OLHÃO and TAVIRA
Ent from sea: E mole ⚓ Fl G 4s 9m 6M; 36°57'·79N
07°52'·14W.
W mole ⚓ Fl R 4s 9m 6M; 37°57'·84N 08°52'·26W,
appr on 352°.
Access ldg lts 020·9°: Front, Barra Nova ⚓ Oc 4s 8m
6M; 37°58'·22N 07°52'·00W. Rear, **Cabo de Santa**
Maria ☆ Fl (4) 17s 49m **25M;** W ○ twr; 36°58'·48N
07°51'·88W.
No. 6 ⚓ Fl R 6s; 36°58'·49N 07°52'·12W (NW to Faro;
NE to Olhão).
No. 20 ⚓ Fl R 6s, 37°00'·13N 07°55'·11W (edge of
AC 83 approx 2M before **Faro** proper).
No. 8 ⚓ Fl R 3s; 36°59'·90N 07°51'·07W, thence N
& E to **Olhão.**
Tavira ldg lts 325·9°: Front, ⚓ Fl R 3s 6m 4M. Rear, Iso
⚓ R 6s 9m 5M. W mole ⚓ Fl R 2·5s 7m 7M; 37°06'·79N
07°37'·10W.

VILA REAL DE SANTO ANTONIO
Lt ho ☆ Fl 6·5s 51m **26M;** W twr, B bands; 37°11'·23N
07°25'·00W.
R. Guadiano, Bar buoys ⚓ Q (3) G 6s; 37°08'·90N
07°23'·44W.
No. 2 ⚓ Fl R 4s; 37°08'·83N 07°23'·74W.
W bkwtr ⚓ Fl R 5s 4M; 37°09'·75N 07°24'·03W.
Marina, Fl R 3s at S corner; Fl R 3s/Fl G 3s at ent; Fl
R 3s at N corner.

See also Area 20 Distance Table

		1										
1	Longships	1										
2	Ushant (Créac'h)	100	2									
3	La Coruña	418	338	3								
4	Cabo Villano	439	365	43	4							
5	Bayona	510	436	114	71	5						
6	Viana do Castelo	537	468	141	98	32	6					
7	Leixões (Pôrto)	565	491	169	126	63	33	7				
8	Nazaré	659	585	263	220	156	127	97	8			
9	Cabo Carvoeiro	670	596	274	231	171	143	114	22	9		
10	Cabo Raso	710	636	314	271	211	183	154	62	40	10	
11	Lisboa (bridge)	686	652	330	287	227	199	170	78	56	16	11
12	Cabo Espichel	692	658	336	293	233	205	176	84	62	22	23	12

DISTANCE TABLES
Approx distances in nautical
miles are by the most direct
route allowing for dangers
and TSS.

AZORES – SELECTED LIGHTS

Positions are referenced to WGS 84

ILHA DAS FLORES

Ponta do Albarnaz ⚡, Fl 5s 103m 22M, 035°-258°; W twr, R cupola. 39°31'·20N 31°14'·12W.

Ponta das Lajes ☆, Fl (3) 28s 98m **26M**, 263°-054°; W twr, R cupola. 39°22'·56N 31°10'·59W.

PORTO DAS LAJES, ldg lts 250·8°: Front, L Fl G 7s 17m 2M, 39°22'·74N 31°10'·24W; rear Oc G 4s. Bkwtr hd ⚡ Fl (2) R 10s 2M; 39°22'·75N 31°09'·94W.

ILHA DO FAIAL

Ponta dos Cedros ⚡, Fl 7s 144m 12M; 38°38'·29N 28°43'·36W.

Ponta da Ribeirinha ⚡, Fl (3) 20s 131m 12M; post; 38°35'·73N 28°36'·15W, E end of island.-

HORTA
Boa Viagem ⚡ Iso G 1·5s 12m 9M; appr brg 285°; B column on R cupola; 38°32'·28N 28°37'·49W.

Bkwtr hd ⚡ Fl R 3s 20m 11M; W structure. 38°32'·03N 28°37'·27W.

Ldg lts 195·8°: both Iso G 2s 13/15m 2M; Red X on W posts, R bands. Front 38°31'·67N 28°37'·51W.

ILHA DO PICO (Pico mountain 38°28'·11N 28°23'·92W) Ponta de São Mateus ⚡ Fl 5s 33m 13M, 284°-118°; W twr, R cupola. 38°25'·35N 28°26'·93W, SW side of island. **Ponta da Ilha** ☆ Fl (3) 15s 28m **24M**, 166°-070°; W twr, R cupola and bldg; 38°24'·84N 28°01'·83W, E tip of island.

ILHA DE SÃO JORGE

Ponta dos Rosais ⚡ Fl (2) 10s 259m 8M. 38°45'·24N 28°18'·71W, WNW tip of island.

Ponta da Topo ☆ Fl (3) 20s 57m **20M**, 133°-033°; W twr, R bldg. 38°32'·92N 27°45'·24W, E tip of island.

ILHA TERCEIRA

Ponta da Sereta ☆ Fl (3) 15s 95m **21M**; W col, R top; 38°45'·97N 27°22'·45W, NW end of island.

Lajes ☆ Aero Al Fl WG 10s 132m **W28M, G23M**.

Praia da Vitoria, N mole Fl 5s 11m 10M; G lantern; W post Bk bands; 38°43'·59N 27°03'·06W. S mole Fl R 3s 8M; W twr, R bands; 38°43'·24N 27°02'·92W.

NAVIGATION

Ponta das Contendas ☆ Fl (4) WR 15s 53m **W23M, R20M**; 220°-W-020°-R-044°-W-072°-R-093°; W twr, R top; 38°38'·62N 27°05'·07W.

Monte Brasil, Oc WR 10s 21m 12M; 191°-R-295°-W-057°; W col, R bands; 38°38'·60N 27°13'·04W.

ANGRA DO HEROISMO

Ldg lts 340·9°: front, Fl R 4s 29m 7M, R mast; 38°39'·25N 27°13'·09W. Rear, Oc R 6s 54m 7M.

Marina ent, S side (Porto Pipas) ⚡ Fl G 3s 14m 6M; N mole, ⚡ Fl (2) R 6s 8m 3M; 38°39'·12N 27°12'·95W.

ILHA DE SAO MIGUEL

Ponta da Ferraria ☆ Fl (3) 20s 106m **27M**; 339°-174°; W twr, R cupola. 37°51'·21N 25°51'·02W.

Airport ☆ Aero Al Fl WG 10s 83m **W28M, G23M**; 282°-124°; control twr; 37°44'·64N 25°42'·46W.

Santa Clara ☆ L Fl 5s 26m **15M**; 282°-102°; R lantern; 37°43'·99N 25°41'·15W.

Ponta Garça ☆ L Fl WR 5s 100m **W16M**, R13M; 240°-W-080-R-100°; 37°42'·85N 25°22'·18W.-

Ponta do Arnel ☆ Aeromarine Fl 5s 65m **25M**; 157°-355°; W twr on ho; 37°49'·43N 25°08'·12W.

PONTA DELGADA

Terminal pier E hd ⚡ Fl(2)R 5s 3M; W twr, R bands; 37°44'·35N 25°39'·61W.

Terminal pier W hd ⚡ Fl(3)G 15s 3M; W twr, G bands; 37°44'·24N 25°39'·83W.

Quebra fl oating bkwtr S end ⚡ Q(6)+LFl W 15s 3M; 2 ▼ (vert) on Bk bcn, Y top; 37°44'·26N 25°39'·97W.

Bkwtr head ⚡ L Fl R 6s 16m 10M; W twr, R bands; 37°44'·18N 25°39'·40W.

Naval Club Dir lt 309°: Fl (2) WRG 5s 24m 10M H24; 306°-G-308°-W-310°-R-312°; 37°44'·39N 25°39'·42W.

Marina mole hd ⚡ Fl G 3s 12m 10M; W twr, G bands; 37°44'·32N 25°39'·57W.

Forte S. Bras Dir lt 262°: Fl (4) WRG 8s 13m 10M H24; 259°-G-261°-W-263°-R-265°; 37°44'·08N 25°40'·39W.

Ilhéus das Formigas ⚡ Fl (2) 12s 21m 12M; W twr. 37°16'·29N 24°46'·87W (20M NE of Santa Maria).

ILHA DE SANTA MARIA

Ponta do Castelo ☆ Aeromarine Fl (3) 13·5s 113m **25M**; 181°-089°; W □ twr and bldg. 36°55'·75N 25°00'·97W, SE corner of island.

1	Falmouth	1										
2	Brest	136	2									
3	La Coruña	440	350	3								
4	Bayona	554	456	114	4							
5	Leixões (Pôrto)	617	526	176	63	5						
6	HORTA	1235	1202	966	927	937	6					
7	PONTA DELGADA	1183	1145	862	813	815	151	7				
8	Lisboa	780	658	327	227	163	904	771	8			
9	Cabo São Vicente	888	757	426	318	263	934	794	102	9		
10	Cádiz	1022	901	560	452	397	1068	928	236	134	10	
11	Europa Point	1087	960	618	506	455	1125	984	294	192	72	11
12	Casablanca	1114	978	637	525	474	1065	918	313	211	187	188	12

1	131	152	190	282	320	Flores	1
2	48	69	152	191		Horta	2
3	44	138	185			Graciosa	3
4	94	143				Terceira	4
5	54					Ponta Delgada	5
6						Sta Maria	6

DISTANCE TABLES

Approx distances in nautical miles are by the most direct route allowing for dangers and TSS.

51

AREA 20 *SW Spain & Gibraltar – Ayamonte to Gibraltar and Ceuta*
SELECTED LIGHTS, BUOYS & WAYPOINTS | Positions are referenced to WGS84 |

PORTUGUESE BORDER TO CADIZ
AYAMONTE (E side of Rio Guadiana)
Bar buoys ↟ Q (3) G 6s; 37°08'·90N 07°23'·44W.
⬧ Fl R 4s; 37°09'·14N 07°23'·82W.
W trng wall ⚡ Fl R 5s 4M; 37°09'·75N 07°24'·03W.
E trng wall ⚡ Fl G 3s 4M; 37°09'·93N 07°23'·63W.
Vila Real de Santo Antònio ☆ Fl 6·5s 51m **26M**;
W twr, B bands; 37°11'·23N 07°25'·00W (Portugal).
Marina ent, ⚡ QR & ⚡ QG; 37°12'·61N 07°24'·43W.

ISLA CANELA and ISLA CRISTINA
Appr ⬧ Fl 10s; 37°10'·51N 07°19'·49W.
W mole ⚡ VQ (2) R 5s 9m 4M; 37°10'·83N 07°19'·58W.
Ldg lts 313°: Front ⚡ Q 8m 5M; 37°11'·50N
07°20'·40W approx. Rear ⚡ Fl 4s 13m 5M.
Both marina entrances are QR and QG.

RIO DE LAS PIEDRAS
No 1 Bar ⬧ L Fl 10s; 37°11'·64N 07°03'·00W. The
shifting chan is marked by lateral lt buoys.
El Rompido ☆ Fl (2) 10s 41m **24M**; W twr, B bands;
37°13'·12N 07°07'·69W.

RIA DE HUELVA
Punta Umbria, ⬧ L Fl 10s; 37°08'·78N 06°56'·74W.
No. 1 ⬧ Fl (2) G 10s; No. 2 ⬧ Fl (2) R 10s; 37°09'·14N
06°56'·60W.
Bkwtr hd ⚡ VQ (6) + L Fl 10s 8m 5M; 37°09'·85N
06°56'·93W.
Marina wavebreak, S hd, Fl (2) R 10s 1M; 37°10'·40N
06°56'·38W.
N head, Fl (3) R 15s 1M; 37°10'·40N 06°56'·48W.
Dir ⚡ 339·2°, WRG 59m 8M; 337·5°- Fl G-338°-
FG-338·6°-OcG-339·1°-FW-339·3°-OcR-339·8°-FR-
340·4°-Fl R-340·9°; W twr; 37°08'·57N 06°50'·66W.
No. 1 ⬧ Fl G 5s; 37°06'·26N 06°49'·46W.
No. 2 ⬧ Fl R 5s; 37°06'·33N 06°49'·72W.
Bkwtr hd ⚡ Fl (3+1) WR 20s 29m, W12M, R9M;
165°-W-100°-R-125°; **Racon K, 12M**; 37°06'·47N
06°49'·93W.
No. 3 ⬧ Fl (2) G 10s; 37°06'·87N 06°49'·77W.
No. 5 ⬧ Fl (3) G 15s; 37°07'·38N 06°50'·03W.
No. 7 ⬧ Fl (4) G 20s; 37°07'·77N 06°50'·29W.

MAZAGÓN
Picacho lt ho ☆ Fl (2+4) 30s 52m **25M**; 37°08'·10N
06°49'·56W.
Marina, S pier ⚡ QG 7m 2M; 37°07'·91N 06°50'·03W.
⬧ Fl (2) 10s; 37°04'·22N 06°43'·67W.
La Higuera ☆ Fl (3) 20s 45m **20M** 37°00'·47N
06°34'·16W.

CHIPIONA
Bajo Salmedina ⚡ Q (9) 15s 9m 5M; 36°44'·27N
06°28'·64W.

Pta de Chipiona ☆ Fl 10s 67m **25M**; 36°44'·26N
06°26'·53W.
Marina, No. 2 ⬧ Fl (2) R 7s; 36°45'·14N 06°25'·59W.
N bkwtr ⚡ Fl (2) G 10s 6m 5M; 36°44'·96N
06°25'·70W.

RÍO GUADALQUIVIR
No. 1 ⬧ L Fl 10s; **Racon M, 10M**; 36°45'·74N
06°27'·03W.
Ldg lts 068·9°: Front ⚡ Q 28m 10M; 36°47'·84N
06°20'·24W. Rear, ⚡ Iso 4s 60m 10M.
No. 3 ⬧ Fl G 5s; 36°46'·16N 06°25'·36W.
Selected buoys in sequence as far as Bonanza:
No. 7 ⬧ Fl (3) G 10s; 36°46'·61N 06°24'·02W.
No. 8 ⬧ Fl (3) R 10s; 36°46'·67N 06°24'·12W.
No. 11 ⬧ Fl G 5s; 36°46'·96N 06°22'·90W.
No. 12 ⬧ Fl R 5s; 36°47'·05N 06°22'·94W.
No. 14 ⬧ Fl (2) R 6s; 36°47'·21N 06°22'·39W.
No.13 ⬧ Fl (2) G 6s; 36°47'·12N 06°22'·36W.
No.17 ⬧ Fl (4) G 12s; 36°47'·46N 06°21'·23W.
No. 20 ⬧ Fl R 5s; 36°47'·81N 06°20'·70W.
Bonanza lt ho Fl 5s 22m 6M; 36°48'·17N 06°20'·15W.

SEVILLA
No. 52 bcn ⚡ Fl (2+1) R 21s 9m 5M; 37°18'·97N
06°00'·83W. Gelves marina Fl R 5s; 37°20'·42N
06°01'·39W; and Fl G 3s.
Lock, 37°19'·86N 05°59'·74W, for city centre.
CN Sevilla pontoons, 37°22'·20N 05°59'·59W.

BAY OF CADIZ
Rota Aero ☆ Alt Fl WG 9s 79m **17M**; R/W chequered
water twr, conspic; 36°38'·13N 06°20'·84W.
Rota ⚡ Oc 4s 33m 13M; W lt ho, R band; 36°36'·96N
06°21'·44W.
Marina, S pier ⚡ Fl (3) R 10s 8m 9M; 36°36'·96N
06°21'·44W.

P'TO SHERRY/P'TO DE SANTA MARIA
Puerto Sherry marina, S bkwtr ⚡ Oc R 4s 4M;
36°34'·64N 06°15'·25W. N bkwtr ⚡ Oc G 5s 3M.
Santa María ldg lts 040°: Front ⚡ QG 16m 4M;
36°35'·77N 06°13'·36W. Rear ⚡ Iso G 4s 20m 4M.
W trng wall ⚡ Fl R 5s 10m 3M; 36°34'·34N
06°14'·96W.

CÁDIZ CITY and PUERTO AMERICA
⬧ L Fl 10s; 36°33'·84N 06°19'·90W.
No. 1 ⬧ Fl G 3s; 36°33'·12N 06°19'·07W.
No. 3 ⬧ Fl (2) G 4s; 36°33'·15N 06°18'·31W.
No. 5 ⬧ Fl (3) G 13s; 36°33'·08N 06°17'·31W.
San Felipe mole ⚡ Fl G 3s 10m 5M; G twr; 36°32'·56N
06°16'·77W.
P'to America marina, NE bkwtr, ⚡ Fl (4) G 16s 1M.
RCN pier ⚡ FG; 36°32'·34N 06°17'·13W.

International Free Zone hbr: No. 1 ⨼ Fl (3) G 9s; 36°30'·66N 06°15'·45W.

Puerto Elcano marina 36°30'·08N 06°15'·45W.

Castillo de San Sebastián ☆ Fl (2) 10s 38m **25M**; *Horn Mo (N) 20s;* 36°31'·70N 06°18'·97W.

CADIZ TO GIBRALTAR
SANCTI PETRI
Punta del Arrecife ⚡ Q (9) 15s 7m 3M; 36°23'·71N 06°13'·58W.

Castle ⚡ Fl 3s 18m 9M; 36°22'·75N 06°13'·33W.

Outer ldg lts 050°: Front ⚡ Fl 5s 12m 6M. Rear ⚡ Oc (2) 6s 16m 6M.

No. 1 ⨼ Fl (3) G 9s; 36°22'·50N 06°12'·93W.

No. 2 ⨼ Fl (3) R 9s; 36°22'·46N 06°12'·81W.

No. 3 ⨼ Fl (4) G 11s; 36°22'·64N 06°12'·65W.

No. 4 ⨼ Fl (4) R 11s; 36°22'·66N 06°12'·71W.

Inner ldg lts 346·5°: Front ⚡ Fl 5s 11m 6M. Rear ⚡ Oc (2) 6s 21m.

⨼ Fl G 5s 8m 2M & ⨼ Fl R 5s; 36°23'·10N 06°12'·65W.

Cabo Roche ☆ Fl (4) 24s 44m **20M**; 36°17'·75N 06°08'·59W.

Cabo Trafalgar ☆ Fl (2+1) 15s 50m **22M**; 36°10'·95N 06°02'·12W.

BARBATE
Ltho⚡Fl(2)WR7s22m,W10M,R7M;281°-W-015°-R-095°; W twr, R bands; 36°11'·21N 05°55'·43W.

SW mole ⚡ Fl R 4s 11m 5M; 36°10'·78N 05°55'·56W.

Marina ent, Fl (4) Y 20s 1M (anti-oil boom) and Fl R 4s 2M.

⨼ Q; 36°10'·75N 05°55'·40W (1ca E of hbr ent) marks N end of a roughly △-shaped tunny net.

Torre de Gracia ⚡ Oc (2) 5s 74m 13M; 36°05'·38N 05°48'·69W.

TARIFA
Tarifa ☆ Fl (3) WR 10s 40m **W26M**, **R18M**; 113°-W-089°-R-113°; W twr; *Siren Mo (O) 60s;* **Racon C, 20M;** 36°00'·06N 05°36'·60W.

Outer SE mole ⚡ Fl G 5s 11m 5M; vis 249°-045°; G twr with statue; 36°00'·38N 05°36'·24W.

ALGECIRAS
Pta Carnero ☆ Fl (4) WR 20s 42m, **W16M**, R13M; 018°-W-325°-R-018°; *Siren Mo (K) 30s;* 36°04'·61N 05°25'·57W.

⨼ Q (3) 10s; 36°06'·73N 05°24'·76W.

Marina, outer S jetty ⚡ Fl (3) R 9s 7m 3M; 36°07'·10N 05°26'·13W.

LA LÍNEA
⨼ Fl (3) G 6s; 36°09'·53N 05°22'·03W.

Dique de Abrigo ⚡ Fl (2) G 7s 8m 4M; 36°09'·51N 05°22'·05W.

GIBRALTAR
Aero ⚡ Mo (GB) R 10s 405m **30M**; 36°08'·57N 05°20'·60W.

Europa Pt ☆ Iso 10s 49m **19/15M**; vis 197°-042° & 067°-125°; W twr, R band; 36°06'·58N 05°20'·69W.

Also ⚡ FR 44m **15M**; 042°-067°; *Horn 20s.*

Same twr ⚡ Oc R 10s 49m **15M**; 042°-067°.

'A' Head ☆ Fl 2s 18m **15M**; *Horn 10s;* 36°08'·03N 05°21'·85W.

'B' head ⚡ QR 9m 5M; 36°08'·14N 05°21'·84W.

Queensway Quay marina, N ent ⚡ FR/FG, 36°08'·16N 05°21'·39W.

Yacht fuelling station; 36°08'·90N 05°21'·37W.

MOROCCO (WEST TO EAST)
Cap Spartel ☆ Fl (4) 20s 94m **30M**; Y ☐ twr; *Dia (4) 90s;* 35°47'·47N 05°55'·43W.

TANGIER
Navaids are reported unreliable. They may be missing, unlit, off station or not as charted.

Monte Dirección (Le Charf) ☆ Oc (3) WRG 12s 88m **W16M**, R12M, G11M; 140°-G-174·5°-W-200°-R-225°; 35°45'·98N 05°47'·35W.

⨼ L Fl 10s; 35°47'·66N 05°47'·03W.

N pier ⚡ Fl (3) 12s 20m 14M; 35°47'·47N 05°47'·60W.

Jetée des Yachts ⚡ Iso G 4s 6m 6M; 35°47'·23N 05°48'·14W.

Pta Malabata ☆ Fl 5s 77m **22M**. W ☐ twr; 35°48'·99N 05°44'·92W.

Pte Círes ⚡ Fl (3) 12s 44m **18M**; 060°-330°; 35°54'·51N 05°28'·92W.

CEUTA (Spanish enclave)
Punta Almina ⚡ Fl (2) 10s 148m 22M; 35°53'·90N 05°16'·85W.

W pier ⚡ Fl G 5s 13m 15M; *Siren 15s;* **Racon O, 12M;** 35°53'·75N 05°18'·68W.

E pier ⚡ Fl R 5s 13m 5M; vis 245°-210°; 35°53'·73N 05°18'·47W.

Marina ent, N bkwtr ⚡ Fl (4) R 11s 8m 1M; 35°53'·45N 05°18'·90W.

		1	2	3	4	5	6	7	8	9	10	11	12	13
1	Nazaré	1												
2	Cabo Carvoeiro	22	2											
3	Cabo Raso	62	40	3										
4	Lisboa (bridge)	78	56	16	4									
5	Cabo Espichel	84	62	22	23	5								
6	Sines	118	96	54	57	34	6							
7	Cabo São Vicente	169	147	104	108	85	57	7						
8	Lagos	189	167	124	128	105	77	20	8					
9	Vilamoura	212	190	147	151	128	100	43	27	9				
10	Cádiz	303	281	238	242	219	191	134	120	95	10			
11	Cabo Trafalgar	320	298	255	259	236	208	151	139	115	28	11		
12	Tarifa	344	322	279	283	260	232	175	163	139	52	24	12	
13	Gibraltar	360	338	295	299	276	248	191	179	155	68	40	16	13

DISTANCE TABLES

Approx distances in nautical miles are by the most direct route allowing for dangers and TSS.

Times are UT - add 1 hour in non-shaded months to convert to Summer Time

SUN RISE/SET LATITUDE 56°N – 2011

	Rise Set JANUARY	Rise Set FEBRUARY	Rise Set MARCH	Rise Set APRIL	Rise Set MAY	Rise Set JUNE
1	0831 1536	0756 1632	0653 1733	0532 1837	0417 1939	0322 2034
4	0830 1540	0750 1639	0645 1740	0524 1844	0410 1945	0319 2038
7	0829 1544	0744 1645	0637 1746	0516 1850	0404 1951	0317 2041
10	0827 1549	0737 1652	0630 1752	0508 1856	0358 1956	0315 2044
13	0824 1554	0731 1659	0622 1759	0501 1902	0352 2002	0314 2047
16	0820 1559	0724 1705	0614 1805	0453 1908	0346 2008	0313 2049
19	0817 1605	0717 1712	0606 1811	0446 1914	0341 2013	0313 2050
22	0813 1611	0710 1718	0558 1817	0438 1920	0336 2019	0313 2051
25	0808 1617	0702 1725	0550 1823	0431 1926	0331 2024	0314 2051
28	0803 1624	0655 1731	0542 1829	0424 1933	0327 2028	0316 2050
31	0757 1630		0534 1835		0324 2033	

	JULY	AUGUST	SEPTEMBER	OCTOBER	NOVEMBER	DECEMBER
1	0318 2049	0403 2008	0503 1856	0602 1736	0706 1620	0806 1531
4	0321 2047	0409 2002	0509 1848	0608 1729	0712 1614	0811 1529
7	0324 2045	0415 1956	0515 1840	0614 1721	0719 1608	0815 1527
10	0327 2042	0420 1949	0521 1832	0620 1713	0725 1602	0819 1526
13	0331 2039	0426 1942	0527 1824	0626 1705	0732 1556	0823 1525
16	0336 2035	0432 1935	0533 1816	0632 1658	0738 1551	0826 1525
19	0340 2031	0438 1928	0538 1808	0639 1650	0744 1546	0828 1526
22	0345 2026	0444 1921	0544 1800	0645 1643	0750 1542	0830 1527
25	0350 2021	0450 1913	0550 1752	0651 1636	0755 1538	0831 1529
28	0356 2016	0456 1906	0556 1744	0658 1629	0801 1534	0832 1531
31	0401 2010	0501 1858		0704 1623		0832 1534

SUN RISE/SET LATITUDE 48°N – 2011

	Rise Set JANUARY	Rise Set FEBRUARY	Rise Set MARCH	Rise Set APRIL	Rise Set MAY	Rise Set JUNE
1	0750 1617	0728 1659	0642 1744	0539 1830	0443 1913	0405 1951
4	0750 1620	0724 1704	0636 1748	0533 1834	0438 1917	0403 1954
7	0749 1624	0720 1709	0630 1753	0527 1838	0433 1921	0402 1956
10	0748 1627	0715 1714	0624 1757	0521 1843	0429 1925	0401 1958
13	0746 1631	0711 1719	0618 1802	0515 1847	0425 1929	0400 2000
16	0745 1635	0706 1723	0612 1806	0510 1851	0421 1933	0400 2002
19	0742 1639	0700 1728	0606 1811	0504 1855	0417 1937	0400 2003
22	0740 1644	0655 1733	0600 1815	0458 1900	0414 1940	0401 2003
25	0737 1648	0649 1738	0554 1819	0453 1904	0411 1944	0401 2004
28	0733 1653	0644 1742	0548 1824	0448 1908	0408 1947	0403 2004
31	0730 1658		0541 1828		0406 1950	

	JULY	AUGUST	SEPTEMBER	OCTOBER	NOVEMBER	DECEMBER
1	0404 2003	0436 1936	0517 1842	0558 1740	0644 1642	0728 1609
4	0406 2002	0439 1932	0521 1836	0603 1734	0649 1638	0732 1608
7	0408 2001	0443 1927	0526 1830	0607 1728	0653 1633	0735 1607
10	0411 1959	0447 1923	0530 1824	0611 1722	0658 1629	0738 1607
13	0414 1957	0451 1917	0534 1818	0616 1716	0703 1625	0741 1607
16	0417 1955	0456 1912	0538 1811	0620 1710	0707 1622	0744 1607
19	0420 1952	0500 1907	0542 1805	0624 1705	0712 1619	0746 1608
22	0423 1949	0504 1901	0546 1759	0629 1659	0716 1616	0747 1610
25	0427 1945	0508 1856	0550 1753	0634 1654	0720 1613	0749 1611
28	0431 1942	0512 1850	0554 1746	0638 1649	0724 1611	0749 1613
31	0434 1938	0516 1844		0643 1644		0750 1616

Times are UT - add 1 hour in non-shaded months to convert to Summer Time

SUN RISE/SET LATITUDE 40°N – 2011

NAVIGATION

	Rise Set JANUARY	Rise Set FEBRUARY	Rise Set MARCH	Rise Set APRIL	Rise Set MAY	Rise Set JUNE
1	0722 1645	0709 1719	0634 1751	0545 1824	0501 1854	0433 1922
4	0722 1648	0706 1722	0630 1755	0540 1827	0457 1857	0432 1925
7	0722 1651	0703 1726	0625 1758	0535 1830	0454 1900	0431 1926
10	0722 1653	0700 1729	0620 1801	0531 1833	0450 1903	0431 1928
13	0721 1657	0656 1733	0616 1804	0526 1836	0447 1906	0431 1930
16	0720 1700	0652 1737	0611 1807	0521 1839	0444 1909	0431 1931
19	0718 1703	0648 1740	0606 1811	0517 1842	0442 1912	0431 1932
22	0717 1707	0644 1743	0601 1814	0513 1845	0439 1914	0431 1932
25	0715 1710	0640 1747	0556 1817	0509 1848	0437 1917	0432 1933
28	0712 1714	0636 1750	0551 1820	0505 1851	0435 1919	0433 1933
31	0710 1717		0546 1823		0434 1922	

	JULY	AUGUST	SEPTEMBER	OCTOBER	NOVEMBER	DECEMBER
1	0435 1933	0458 1914	0527 1832	0556 1743	0629 1658	0702 1635
4	0436 1932	0501 1911	0530 1827	0559 1738	0632 1655	0705 1635
7	0438 1932	0504 1908	0533 1823	0602 1734	0635 1651	0708 1635
10	0440 1931	0506 1904	0536 1818	0605 1729	0639 1648	0710 1635
13	0442 1929	0509 1900	0539 1813	0608 1724	0642 1646	0713 1635
16	0444 1928	0512 1856	0541 1808	0611 1720	0646 1643	0715 1636
19	0447 1926	0515 1852	0544 1803	0614 1715	0649 1641	0717 1637
22	0449 1923	0518 1847	0547 1758	0617 1711	0653 1639	0719 1638
25	0452 1921	0521 1843	0550 1753	0621 1707	0656 1638	0720 1640
28	0454 1918	0524 1838	0553 1748	0624 1703	0659 1636	0721 1642
31	0457 1915	0526 1834		0627 1659		0722 1644

MOON RISE/SET LATITUDE 56°N – 2011

	Rise Set JANUARY	Rise Set FEBRUARY	Rise Set MARCH	Rise Set APRIL	Rise Set MAY	Rise Set JUNE
1	0558 1250	0659 1500	0526 1404	0429 1645	0313 1808	0249 2033
4	0830 1559	0749 1844	0609 1744	0506 2019	0415 2140	0540 2241
7	0929 1947	0822 2219	0644 2118	0612 2348	0639 ****	0945 2341
10	1002 2323	0908 0045	0737 ****	0845 0132	1033 0100	1403 0011
13	1042 0149	1057 0411	0947 0252	1249 0255	1453 0149	1826 0114
16	1216 0528	1451 0611	1347 0433	1723 0345	1927 0246	2125 0341
19	1556 0748	1932 0707	1827 0526	2200 0448	2252 0454	2236 0733
22	2032 0847	**** 0757	2307 0623	0017 0714	**** 0838	2314 1115
25	**** 0932	0247 0935	0136 0824	0154 1057	0043 1221	2357 1449
28	0347 1050	0503 1249	0330 1155	0237 1434	0120 1554	0047 1820
31	0631 1345		0417 1534		0217 1929	

	JULY	AUGUST	SEPTEMBER	OCTOBER	NOVEMBER	DECEMBER
1	0324 2043	0635 2012	1008 1929	1159 1914	1258 2135	1200 2304
4	0730 2149	1101 2102	1415 2118	1430 2233	1354 0006	1241 0128
7	1149 2235	1515 2230	1629 ****	1533 0104	1434 0340	1334 0459
10	1609 2348	1757 0023	1726 0313	1613 0440	1531 0711	1523 0810
13	1920 0126	1904 0410	1805 0651	1702 0812	1729 1016	1844 1007
16	2041 0510	1943 0753	1856 1023	1840 1127	2055 1203	2245 1107
19	2122 0857	2028 1127	2042 1335	2150 1333	**** 1300	0133 1157
22	2203 1232	2158 1450	**** 1534	0031 1438	0355 1353	0552 1326
25	2320 1603	**** 1708	0300 1636	0457 1531	0819 1539	0851 1642
28	0105 1840	0404 1816	0736 1731	0931 1704	1056 1912	1005 2043
31	0506 1955	0837 1908		1228 2017		1048 ****

55

Times are UT - add 1 hour in non-shaded months to convert to Summer Time

MOON RISE/SET LATITUDE 48°N – 2011

	Rise Set JANUARY	Rise Set FEBRUARY	Rise Set MARCH	Rise Set APRIL	Rise Set MAY	Rise Set JUNE
1	0511 1337	0623 1534	0455 1433	0427 1643	0330 1745	0332 1947
4	0748 1639	0737 1853	0602 1748	0526 1954	0454 2057	0620 2207
7	0912 2001	0832 2205	0658 2059	0653 2303	0723 2329	0959 2332
10	1008 2313	0941 0014	0815 ****	0928 0048	1054 0036	1349 0019
13	1111 0123	1145 0323	1033 0205	1308 0234	1446 0151	1744 0149
16	1304 0440	1520 0540	1411 0407	1711 0351	1850 0316	2044 0427
19	1630 0711	1930 0704	1820 0527	2118 0523	2208 0541	2218 0756
22	2035 0840	2335 0823	2229 0653	**** 0800	2353 0906	2319 1114
25	**** 0952	0159 1023	0048 0912	0126 1122	0036 1224	0000 1425
28	0302 1136	0424 1326	0257 1225	0232 1435	0134 1534	0128 1736
31	0547 1427		0408 1540		0254 1847	

	JULY	AUGUST	SEPTEMBER	OCTOBER	NOVEMBER	DECEMBER
1	0407 2006	0647 2005	0946 1955	1115 1958	1227 2204	1148 2312
4	0747 2137	1044 2122	1329 2204	1354 2307	1345 0019	1251 0121
7	1139 2250	1432 2313	1554 0007	1519 0122	1446 0331	1405 0429
10	1530 ****	1717 0108	1714 0330	1620 0436	1604 0639	1607 0727
13	1837 0213	1847 0432	1815 0644	1731 0745	1812 0932	1914 0936
16	2020 0537	1949 0751	1927 0953	1924 1044	2122 1134	2249 1059
19	2124 0900	2055 1101	2127 1251	2222 1259	**** 1254	0119 1214
22	2226 1211	2243 1406	**** 1502	0047 1428	0338 1414	0512 1407
25	**** 1521	0037 1632	0312 1630	0444 1547	0736 1622	0813 1719
28	0150 1800	0421 1806	0718 1752	0851 1745	1022 1944	0950 2054
31	0528 1940	0824 1924		1150 2054		1055 ****

MOON RISE/SET LATITUDE 40°N – 2011

	Rise Set JANUARY	Rise Set FEBRUARY	Rise Set MARCH	Rise Set APRIL	Rise Set MAY	Rise Set JUNE
1	0440 1409	0558 1558	0434 1453	0425 1642	0343 1730	0401 1917
4	0720 1706	0728 1900	0557 1751	0540 1937	0521 2028	0647 2143
7	0859 2012	0839 2154	0709 2045	0721 2233	0752 2302	1010 2326
10	1012 2306	1004 ****	0840 2342	0957 0018	1109 0019	1340 0025
13	1131 0104	1217 0251	1104 0134	1320 0219	1441 0153	1716 0213
16	1336 0408	1540 0517	1428 0348	1702 0355	1825 0337	2015 0457
19	1653 0646	1928 0702	1815 0528	2050 0547	2138 0613	2205 0812
22	2037 0834	2312 0841	2204 0714	2350 0831	2337 0926	2322 1114
25	**** 1007	0128 1055	0017 0944	0107 1139	0031 1227	0013 1408
28	0232 1206	0358 1351	0235 1247	0229 1436	0145 1520	0155 1706
31	0517 1456		0401 1545		0319 1819	

	JULY	AUGUST	SEPTEMBER	OCTOBER	NOVEMBER	DECEMBER
1	0435 1940	0655 2001	0930 2013	1047 2027	1205 2224	1140 2318
4	0800 2129	1032 2136	1259 2234	1329 2331	1339 0029	1258 0116
7	1131 2300	1403 2343	1530 0034	1509 0135	1455 0324	1427 0409
10	1504 0011	1650 0137	1706 0341	1626 0432	1627 0617	1636 0658
13	1807 0244	1835 0448	1822 0639	1751 0726	1841 0903	1934 0914
16	2005 0556	1953 0749	1949 0933	1953 1015	2141 1113	2252 1054
19	2125 0901	2115 1044	2157 1221	2245 1235	**** 1251	0109 1226
22	2243 1156	2313 1337	**** 1440	0058 1420	0325 1429	0445 1435
25	**** 1452	0105 1607	0320 1625	0436 1559	0708 1651	0746 1744
28	0219 1732	0433 1758	0705 1808	0824 1813	0958 2007	0939 2103
31	0543 1929	0815 1936		1123 2119		1100 ****

SPEED, TIME AND DISTANCE (NAUTICAL MILES)

Speed in knots

Time in minutes	1	2	3	4	5	6	7	8	9	10	15	20
1	0·0	0·0	0·1	0·1	0·1	0·1	0·1	0·1	0·2	0·2	0·3	0·3
2	0·0	0·1	0·1	0·1	0·2	0·2	0·2	0·3	0·3	0·3	0·5	0·7
3	0·1	0·1	0·2	0·2	0·3	0·3	0·4	0·4	0·5	0·5	0·8	1·0
4	0·1	0·1	0·2	0·3	0·3	0·4	0·5	0·5	0·6	0·7	1·0	1·3
5	0·1	0·2	0·3	0·3	0·4	0·5	0·6	0·7	0·8	0·8	1·3	1·7
6	0·1	0·2	0·3	0·4	0·5	0·6	0·7	0·8	0·9	1·0	1·5	2·0
7	0·1	0·2	0·4	0·5	0·6	0·7	0·8	0·9	1·1	1·2	1·8	2·3
8	0·1	0·3	0·4	0·5	0·7	0·8	0·9	1·1	1·2	1·3	2·0	2·7
9	0·2	0·3	0·5	0·6	0·8	0·9	1·1	1·2	1·4	1·5	2·3	3·0
10	0·2	0·3	0·5	0·7	0·8	1·0	1·2	1·3	1·5	1·7	2·5	3·3
11	0·2	0·4	0·6	0·7	0·9	1·1	1·3	1·5	1·7	1·8	2·8	3·7
12	0·2	0·4	0·6	0·8	1·0	1·2	1·4	1·6	1·8	2·0	3·0	4·0
13	0·2	0·4	0·7	0·9	1·1	1·3	1·5	1·7	2·0	2·2	3·3	4·3
14	0·2	0·5	0·7	0·9	1·2	1·4	1·6	1·9	2·1	2·3	3·5	4·7
15	0·3	0·5	0·8	1·0	1·3	1·5	1·8	2·0	2·3	2·5	3·8	5·0
16	0·3	0·5	0·8	1·1	1·3	1·6	1·9	2·1	2·4	2·7	4·0	5·3
17	0·3	0·6	0·9	1·1	1·4	1·7	2·0	2·3	2·6	2·8	4·3	5·7
18	0·3	0·6	0·9	1·2	1·5	1·8	2·1	2·4	2·7	3·0	4·5	6·0
19	0·3	0·6	1·0	1·3	1·6	1·9	2·2	2·5	2·9	3·2	4·8	6·3
20	0·3	0·7	1·0	1·3	1·7	2·0	2·3	2·7	3·0	3·3	5·0	6·7
21	0·4	0·7	1·1	1·4	1·8	2·1	2·5	2·8	3·2	3·5	5·3	7·0
22	0·4	0·7	1·1	1·5	1·8	2·2	2·6	2·9	3·3	3·7	5·5	7·3
23	0·4	0·8	1·2	1·5	1·9	2·3	2·7	3·1	3·5	3·8	5·8	7·7
24	0·4	0·8	1·2	1·6	2·0	2·4	2·8	3·2	3·6	4·0	6·0	8·0
25	0·4	0·8	1·3	1·7	2·1	2·5	2·9	3·3	3·8	4·2	6·3	8·3
30	0·5	1·0	1·5	2·0	2·5	3·0	3·5	4·0	4·5	5·0	7·5	10·0
35	0·6	1·2	1·8	2·3	2·9	3·5	4·1	4·7	5·3	5·8	8·8	11·7
40	0·7	1·3	2·0	2·7	3·3	4·0	4·7	5·3	6·0	6·7	10·0	13·3
45	0·8	1·5	2·3	3·0	3·8	4·5	5·3	6·0	6·8	7·5	11·3	15·0
50	0·8	1·7	2·5	3·3	4·2	5·0	5·8	6·7	7·5	8·3	12·5	16·7

DISTANCE (NAUTICAL MILES) OFF RISING/DIPPING LIGHTS

Height of eye in feet

Height of light in metres	2	3	4	5	6	7	8	9	10	20	30	40	50
2	4·6	4·9	5·2	5·5	5·7	6·0	6·2	6·4	6·6	8·1	9·2	10·2	11·0
3	5·2	5·6	5·9	6·2	6·4	6·6	6·8	7·0	7·2	8·7	9·9	10·8	11·7
4	5·8	6·1	6·4	6·7	6·9	7·2	7·4	7·6	7·8	9·3	10·4	11·4	12·2
5	6·3	6·6	6·9	7·2	7·4	7·7	7·9	8·1	8·3	9·8	10·9	11·9	12·7
6	6·7	7·1	7·4	7·6	7·9	8·1	8·3	8·5	8·7	10·2	11·3	12·3	13·2
7	7·1	7·5	7·8	8·0	8·3	8·5	8·7	8·9	9·1	10·6	11·8	12·7	13·6
8	7·5	7·8	8·2	8·4	8·7	8·9	9·1	9·3	9·5	11·0	12·1	13·1	14·0
9	7·8	8·2	8·5	8·8	9·0	9·2	9·5	9·7	9·8	11·3	12·5	13·5	14·3
10	8·2	8·5	8·8	9·1	9·4	9·6	9·8	10·0	10·2	11·7	12·8	13·8	14·6
11	8·5	8·9	9·2	9·4	9·7	9·9	10·1	10·3	10·5	12·0	13·1	14·1	15·0
12	8·8	9·2	9·5	9·7	10·0	10·2	10·4	10·6	10·8	12·3	13·4	14·4	15·3
13	9·1	9·5	9·8	10·0	10·3	10·5	10·7	10·9	11·1	12·6	13·7	14·7	15·6
14	9·4	9·7	10·0	10·3	10·6	10·8	11·0	11·2	11·4	12·9	14·0	15·0	15·8
15	9·6	10·0	10·3	10·6	10·8	11·1	11·3	11·5	11·6	13·1	14·3	15·3	16·1
16	9·9	10·3	10·6	10·8	11·1	11·3	11·5	11·7	11·9	13·4	14·6	15·5	16·4
17	10·2	10·5	10·8	11·1	11·3	11·6	11·8	12·0	12·2	13·7	14·8	15·8	16·6
18	10·4	10·8	11·1	11·4	11·6	11·8	12·0	12·2	12·4	13·9	15·1	16·0	16·9
19	10·7	11·0	11·3	11·6	11·8	12·1	12·3	12·5	12·7	14·2	15·3	16·3	17·1
20	10·9	11·3	11·6	11·8	12·1	12·3	12·5	12·7	12·9	14·4	15·5	16·5	17·3
25	12·0	12·3	12·6	12·9	13·2	13·4	13·6	13·8	14·0	15·5	16·6	17·6	18·4
30	13·0	13·3	13·6	13·9	14·1	14·4	14·6	14·8	15·0	16·5	17·6	18·6	19·4
40	14·7	15·1	15·4	15·7	15·9	16·1	16·3	16·5	16·7	18·2	19·4	20·3	21·2
50	16·3	16·6	16·9	17·2	17·4	17·7	17·9	18·1	18·3	19·8	20·9	21·9	22·7
60	17·7	18·0	18·3	18·6	18·8	19·1	19·3	19·5	19·7	21·2	22·3	23·3	24·1

CONVERSION TABLE

Sq inches to sq millimetres *multiply by* **645.20**	**Sq millimetres to sq inches** *multiply by* **0.0016**
Inches to millimetres *multiply by* **25.40**	**Millimetres to inches** *multiply by* **0.0394**
Sq feet to square metres *multiply by* **0.093**	**Sq metres to sq feet** *multiply by* **10.7640**
Inches to centimetres *multiply by* **2.54**	**Centimetres to inches** *multiply by* **0.3937**
Feet to metres *multiply by* **0.305**	**Metres to feet** *multiply by* **3.2810**
Nautical miles to kilometres *multiply by* **1.852**	**Kilometres to nautical miles** *multiply by* **0.5400**
Statute miles to kilometres *multiply by* **1.609**	**Kilometres to statute miles** *multiply by* **0.6214**
Statute miles to nautical miles *multiply by* **0.8684**	**Nautical miles to statute miles** *multiply by* **1.1515**
HP to metric HP *multiply by* **1.014**	**Metric HP to HP** *multiply by* **0.9862**
Pounds per sq inch to kg per sq centimetre *multiply by* **0.0703**	**Kg per sq centimetre to pounds per sq inch** *multiply by* **14.2200**
HP to kilowatts *multiply by* **0.746**	**Kilowatts to HP** *multiply by* **1.341**
Cu inches to cu centimetres *multiply by* **16.39**	**Cu centimetres to cu inches** *multiply by* **0.0610**
Imperial gallons to litres *multiply by* **4.540**	**Litres to imperial gallons** *multiply by* **0.2200**
Pints to litres *multiply by* **0.5680**	**Litres to pints** *multiply by* **1.7600**
Pounds to kilogrammes *multiply by* **0.4536**	**Kilogrammes to pounds** *multiply by* **2.2050**

LIGHT CHARACTERISTICS

CLASS OF LIGHT	International abbreviations	National abbreviations	Illustration Period shown ⊢————⊣
FIXED	F		
OCCULTING (total duration of light longer than dark)			
Single-occulting		Oc Occ	
Group-occulting eg	Oc(2)	Gp Occ(2)	
Composite group-occulting eg	Oc(2+3)	Gp Occ(2+3)	
ISOPHASE (light and dark equal)		Iso	
FLASHING (total duration of light shorter than dark)			
Single-flashing	Fl		
Long-flashing (flash 2s or longer)	L Fl		
Group-flashing eg	Fl(3)	Gp Fl(3)	
Composite group-flashing eg	Fl(2+1)	Gp Fl(2+1)	
QUICK (50 to 79, usually either 50 or 60, flashes per min.)			
Continuous quick	Q	Qk Fl	
Group quick eg	Q(3)	Qk Fl(3)	
Interrupted quick	IQ	Int Qk Fl	
VERY QUICK (80 to 159, usually either 100 or 120, flashes per min.)			
Continuous very quick	VQ	V Qk Fl	
Group very quick eg	VQ(3)	V Qk Fl(3)	
Interrupted very quick	IVQ	Int V Qk Fl	
ULTRA QUICK (160 or more, usually 240 to 300, flashes per min.)			
Continuous ultra quick	UQ		
Interrupted ultra quick	IUQ		
MORSE CODE eg	Mo(K)		
FIXED AND FLASHING	F Fl		
ALTERNATING eg	Al. WR	Alt. WR	

COLOUR	International abbreviations	NOMINAL RANGE in miles	International abbreviations
White	W (may be omitted)	Light with single range	eg 15M
Red	R	Light with two different ranges	eg 15/10M
Green	G	Light with three or more ranges	eg 15-7M
Blue	Bu		
Violet	Vi	**PERIOD** is given in seconds	eg 90s
Yellow	Y	**DISPOSITION** horizontally disposed	(hor)
Orange	Y		
Amber	Y	**ELEVATION** is given in metres (m) or feet (ft) above MHWS	

Chapter 2 - Weather

Beaufort scale

Force	Wind speed (knots)	(km/h)	(m/sec)	Description	State of sea	Probable wave ht(m)
0	0–1	0–2	0–0·5	Calm	Like a mirror	0
1	1–3	2–6	0·5–1·5	Light airs	Ripples like scales are formed	0
2	4–6	7–11	2–3	Light breeze	Small wavelets, still short but more pronounced, not breaking	0·1
3	7–10	13–19	4–5	Gentle breeze	Large wavelets, crests begin to break; a few white horses	0·4
4	11–16	20–30	6–8	Moderate breeze	Small waves growing longer; fairly frequent white horses	1
5	17–21	31–39	8–11	Fresh breeze	Moderate waves, taking more pronounced form; many white horses, perhaps some spray	2
6	22–27	41–50	11–14	Strong breeze	Large waves forming; white foam crests more extensive; probably some spray	3
7	28–33	52–61	14–17	Near gale	Sea heaps up; white foam from breaking waves begins to blow in streaks	4
8	34–40	63–74	17–21	Gale	Moderately high waves of greater length; edge of crests break into spindrift; foam blown in well-marked streaks	5·5

Terminology used in forecasts

Pressure systems' speed of movement

Slowly	< 15 knots
Steadily	15–25 knots
Rather quickly	25–35 knots
Rapidly	35–45 knots
Very rapidly	> 45 knots

Visibility

Good	> 5 miles
Moderate	2–5 miles
Poor	1000 metres–2 miles
Fog	< 1000 metres

Barometric pressure tendency

Rising/falling slowly: Change of 0·1 to 1·5 hPa/mb in the preceding 3 hours.

Rising/falling: Change of 1·6 to 3·5 hPa/mb in the preceding 3 hours.

Rising/falling quickly: Change of 3·6 to 6 hPa/mb in the preceding 3 hours.

Rising/falling very rapidly: Change of > 6 hPa/mb in the preceding 3 hours.

Now rising/falling: Pressure has been falling (rising) or steady in the preceding 3 hours, but was definitely rising (falling) at the time of observation.

Gale warnings

A *Gale* warning means that winds of at least F8 (34-40kn) or gusts up to 43-51kn are expected somewhere within the area, but not necessarily over the whole area

Severe Gale means winds of at least F9 (41-47kn) or gusts reaching 52-60kn

Storm means winds of F10 (48-55kn) or gusts of 61-68kn

Violent Storm means winds of F11 (56-63kn) or gusts of 69+ kn

Hurricane Force means winds of F12 (64+ kn)

Gale warnings remain in force until amended or cancelled. If a gale persists for >24 hours the warning is re-issued.

Timing of gale warnings from time of issue

Imminent	<6 hrs
Soon	6–12 hrs
Later	>12 hrs

Strong wind warnings

Issued, if possible 6 hrs in advance, when winds F6 or more are expected up to 5M offshore; valid for 12 hrs.

MAP OF UK SHIPPING FORECAST AREAS

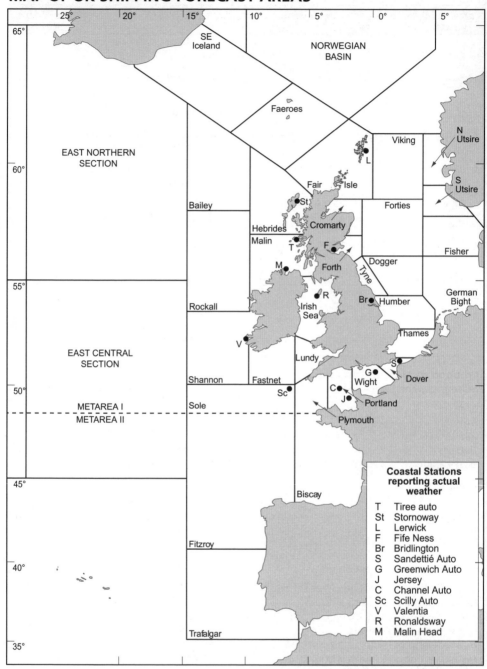

Coastal Stations reporting actual weather

T	Tiree auto
St	Stornoway
L	Lerwick
F	Fife Ness
Br	Bridlington
S	Sandettié Auto
G	Greenwich Auto
J	Jersey
C	Channel Auto
Sc	Scilly Auto
V	Valentia
R	Ronaldsway
M	Malin Head

SHIPPING FORECAST RECORD Time/Day/Date ....

GENERAL SYNOPSIS

at .... UT/BST

System position	Present position at	Movement	Forecast

Gales	SEA AREA FORECAST	Wind (At first)	(Later)	Weather	Visibility
	VIKING				
	NORTH UTSIRE				
	SOUTH UTSIRE				
	FORTIES				
	CROMARTY				
	FORTH				
	TYNE				
	DOGGER				
	FISHER				
	GERMAN BIGHT				
	HUMBER				
	THAMES				
	DOVER				
	WIGHT				
	PORTLAND				
	PLYMOUTH				
	BISCAY				
	FITZROY				
	TRAFALGAR				
	SOLE				
	LUNDY				
	FASTNET				
	IRISH SEA				
	SHANNON				
	ROCKALL				
	MALIN				
	HEBRIDES				
	BAILEY				
	FAIR ISLE				
	FAEROES				
	S E ICELAND				

COASTAL REPORTS BST at .... UTC	Wind Direction	Force	Weather	Visibility	Pressure	Change	COASTAL REPORTS	Wind Direction	Force	Weather	Visibility	Pressure	Change
Tiree Auto (T)							Greenwich Lt V (G)						
Stornoway (St)							Jersey (J)						
Lerwick (L)							Channel Auto (C)						
Fife Ness (F)							Scilly Auto (Sc)						
Bridlington (Br)							Valentia (V)						
Sandettie Auto (S)							Ronaldsway (R)						
							Malin Head (M)						

SOURCES OF WEATHER INFORMATION IN THE UK

BBC Radio 4 Shipping forecasts
are broadcast at:

0048 LT[1]	LW, MW, FM
0520 LT[1]	LW, MW, FM
1201 LT	LW only
1754 LT	LW, FM (Sat/Sun)

[1] Includes weather reports from coastal stations

Frequencies

LW		198 kHz
MW	Tyneside	603 kHz
	London & N Ireland	720 kHz
	Redruth	756 kHz
	Plymouth & Enniskillen	774 kHz
	Aberdeen	1449 kHz
	Carlisle	1485 kHz
FM	England	92·4–94·6 MHz
	Scotland	91·3–96·1 MHz
		103·5–104·9 MHz
	Wales	92·8–96·1 MHz
		103·5–104·9 MHz
	N Ireland	93·2–96·0 MHz
		103·5–104·6 MHz
	Channel Islands	94·8 MHz

The Shipping forecast contains:
Time of issue; summary of gale warnings in force at that time; a general synopsis of weather systems and their expected development and movement over the next 24 hours; sea area forecasts for the same 24 hours, including wind direction/force, weather and visibility in each; and an outlook for the following 24 hours.

Gale warnings for all affected areas are broadcast at the earliest break in Radio 4 programmes after receipt, as well as after the next news bulletin.

Shipping forecasts cover large sea areas, and rarely include the detailed variations that may occur near land. The inshore waters forecast can be more helpful on coastal passages.

Weather reports from coastal stations follow the 0048 and 0520 shipping forecasts. They include wind direction and force, present weather, visibility, and sea-level pressure and tendency, if available. The stations are shown on the previous page.

BBC Radio 4 Inshore waters forecast
A forecast for inshore waters (up to 12M offshore) in 17 areas around the UK and N Ireland, valid for 24 hrs, is broadcast after the 0048 and 0520 coastal station reports. It includes forecasts of wind direction and force, weather, visibility, sea state and an outlook for a further 24 hrs. It ends with a national inshore outlook for the next 3 days. The 17 inshore areas are defined by the following well-known places and headlands, clockwise around the UK: Cape Wrath, Orkney, Rattray Hd, Berwick-upon-Tweed, Whitby, Gibraltar Point, N Foreland, Selsey Bill, Lyme Regis, Land's End, St David's Head, Great Ormes Head, Isle of Man, Mull of Galloway, Carlingford Lough, Lough Foyle, Mull of Kintyre, Ardnamurchan Pt and Shetland.

Strong wind warnings are issued by the Met Office whenever winds of Force 6 or more are expected over coastal waters up to 5M offshore.

Reports of actual weather. The 0048 broadcast includes a set of coastal station reports. These include: Boulmer, *Bridlington*, Sheerness, St Catherine's Point*, *Scilly*, Milford Haven, Aberporth, Valley, Liverpool (Crosby), *Ronaldsway*, Larne, Machrihanish*, Greenock, *Stornoway*, *Lerwick*, Wick*, Aberdeen and Leuchars. Asterisk* denotes an automatic station. Stations in italics also feature in the 0520 coastal reports.

BBC general (land) forecasts
Land area forecasts may include an outlook up to 48 hours beyond the shipping forecast, plus more details of frontal systems and weather along the coasts. The most comprehensive land area forecasts are broadcast by Radio 4 on the frequencies above.

Land area forecasts – Wind strength
Wind descriptions used in land forecasts, with their Beaufort scale equivalents, are:

Calm	0	Fresh	5
Light	1–3	Strong	6–7
Moderate	4	Gale	8

Land area forecasts – Visibility
The following visibility definitions are used in land forecasts:

Mist	2000m–1000m
Fog	<1000m
Dense fog	< 50m

NAVTEX

Navtex is the prime method of disseminating MSI, with typical coverage out to 270 miles offshore. A dedicated aerial, receiver and LCD screen (or integrated printer) are required but receipt is free and no contract is required. The user selects which stations and categories are recorded for automatic display or printing.

Two frequencies are used: 518 kHz and *490 kHz*. 518 kHz messages are in English (occas. in the national language as well), with excellent coverage of Europe. Interference between stations is avoided by time sharing and by limiting the range of transmitters to about 300M. Navtex information applies only to the geographic area for which each station is responsible.

490 kHz (for clarity shown in italics throughout this chapter) is used abroad for transmissions in the national language. In the UK it is used for inshore waters forecasts in English. Identification letters for 490 kHz stations differ from 518 kHz stations.

Weather information accounts for about 75% of all messages and Navtex is particularly valuable when out of range of other sources, otherwise occupied or if there is a language problem.

Messages

Each message is prefixed by a four-character group:

The first character is the code letter of the transmitting station (eg **E** for Niton).

The second character is the message category, see below.

The third and fourth are message serial numbers, running from 01 to 99 and then re-starting at 01.

The serial number 00 denotes urgent messages which are always printed.

Messages which are corrupt or have already been printed are rejected.

Weather messages, and certain other message types, are dated and timed.

Message categories

A*	Navigational warnings
B*	Meteorological warnings
C	Ice reports
D*	SAR info and piracy warnings
E	Weather forecasts
F	Pilot service
H	Loran-C
J	Satellite navigation
K	Other electronic navaids
L	Subfacts and Gunfacts (UK)
V	Amplifies Navwarnings initially sent under A; plus weekly oil/gas rig moves.
W-Y	Special service, trials
Z	No messages on hand at scheduled time

Missing category letters are unallocated.

*The receiver cannot reject these categories.

Navtex stations/areas – UK & W Europe

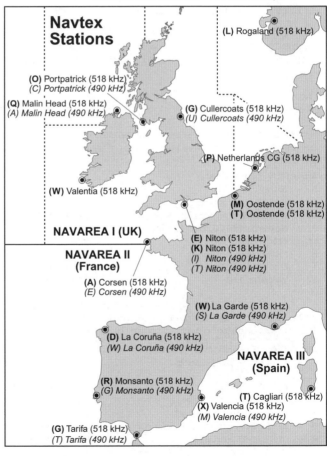

Navtex Stations

(L) Rogaland (518 kHz)

(O) Portpatrick (518 kHz)
(C) Portpatrick (490 kHz)

(Q) Malin Head (518 kHz)
(A) Malin Head (490 kHz)

(G) Cullercoats (518 kHz)
(U) Cullercoats (490 kHz)

(P) Netherlands CG (518 kHz)

(W) Valentia (518 kHz)

(M) Oostende (518 kHz)
(T) Oostende (518 kHz)

NAVAREA I (UK)

NAVAREA II (France)

(E) Niton (518 kHz)
(K) Niton (518 kHz)
(I) Niton (490 kHz)
(T) Niton (490 kHz)

(A) Corsen (518 kHz)
(E) Corsen (490 kHz)

(W) La Garde (518 kHz)
(S) La Garde (490 kHz)

(D) La Coruña (518 kHz)
(W) La Coruña (490 kHz)

NAVAREA III (Spain)

(R) Monsanto (518 kHz)
(G) Monsanto (490 kHz)

(T) Cagliari (518 kHz)
(X) Valencia (518 kHz)
(M) Valencia (490 kHz)

(G) Tarifa (518 kHz)
(T) Tarifa (490 kHz)

UK 518 kHz stations

The times (UT) of weather messages are in bold; the times of an extended outlook (a further 2 or 3 days beyond the shipping forecast period) are in italics.

G – Cullercoats   *0100*   0500   **0900**   1300   1700   **2100**
Fair Isle clockwise to Thames, excluding N & S Utsire, Fisher and German Bight.

O – Portpatrick   *0220*   **0620**   1020   1420   **1820**   2220
Lundy clockwise to SE Iceland.

E – Niton   *0040*   0440   **0840**   1240   1640   **2040**
Thames clockwise to Fastnet, excluding Trafalgar.

UK 490 kHz stations (in yellow) provide forecasts for UK inshore waters, a national 3 day outlook for inshore waters and, at times in bold, reports of actual weather at some or all of the places listed below. To receive these reports select message category 'V' on the receiver. Times (UT) are listed in chronological order. Reports include some or all of: Sea level pressure (hPa/mb), wind direction and speed (kn), weather, visibility (M), air and sea temperatures (°C), dewpoint temperature (°C) and mean wave height (m).

A – Malin Head   **0000**   **0400**   0800   **1200**   **1600**   2000
Lough Foyle to Carlingford Lough, Mull of Galloway to Cape Wrath, the Minch.
Note times of forecasts and actuals not known at time of going to press.

C – Portpatrick Land's End to Shetland   **0020**   **0420**   0820   **1220**   **1620**   2020
N Rona, Stornoway, S Uist, Lusa (Skye), Tiree, Macrihanish, Belfast, Malin Hd, Belmullet, St Bees Hd, Ronaldsway, Crosby, Valley, Aberporth, Roches Pt, Valentia, St Mawgan.

I – Niton The Wash to St David's Head   **0120**   0520   **0920**   1320   1720   **2120**
Sandettie Lt V, Greenwich Lt V, Solent, Hurn airport, Guernsey airport, Jersey airport, Portland, Channel Lt V, Plymouth, Culdrose, Seven Stones Lt V, St Mawgan & Roches Pt.

U – Cullercoats Cape Wrath to N Foreland   **0320**   0720   **1120**   **1520**   1920   **2320**
Sandettie Lt V, Manston, Shoeburyness, Weybourne, Donna Nook, Boulmer, Leuchars, Aberdeen, Lossiemouth, Wick, Kirkwall, Lerwick, Foula, K7 Met buoy, Sule Skerry.

Navtex coverage abroad: Selected Navtex stations in Metareas I and II, with identity codes and transmission times, are listed below. Times of weather messages are shown in **bold**. Gale warnings are usually transmitted 4 hourly.

METAREA I (Co-ordinator – UK)   Transmission times (UT)

K – Niton (Note 1)	0140	0540	0940	1340	1740	2140
L – Pinneberg, Hamburg	*0150*	*0550*	*0950*	*1350*	*1750*	*2150*
M – Oostende, Belgium (Note 2)	0200	0600	1000	1400	1800	2200
P – Netherlands CG, Den Helder	**0230**	0630	1030	**1430**	1830	2230
Q – Malin Head, Eire	0240	**0640**	1040	1440	**1840**	2240
S – Pinneberg, Hamburg	**0300**	**0700**	1100	**1500**	**1900**	**2300**
T – Oostende, Belgium (Note 3)	0310	**0710**	1110	1510	**1910**	2310
W – Valentia, Eire	0340	**0740**	**1140**	1540	**1940**	**2340**

Notes:
1 In English, no weather; only Nav warnings for waters from Cap Gris Nez to Île de Bréhat.
2 No weather information, only Nav warnings for NavArea Juliett.
3 Forecasts and strong wind warnings for Thames and Dover, plus Nav info for Belgium.

METAREA II (Co-ordinator – France)

A – Corsen, Le Stiff, France	**0000**	0400	0800	**1200**	1600	2000
E – Corsen, Le Stiff, France (In French)	*0040*	*0440*	*0840*	*1240*	*1640*	*2040*
D – Coruña, Spain	0030	0430	**0830**	1230	1630	**2030**
W – Coruña, Spain (in Spanish)	*0340*	*0740*	*1140*	*1540*	*1940*	*2340*
F – Horta, Açores, Portugal	**0050**	**0450**	**0850**	**1250**	**1650**	**2050**
G – Tarifa, Spain (English & Spanish)	0100	0500	**0900**	1300	1700	**2100**
R – Monsanto, Portugal	**0250**	**0650**	**1050**	**1450**	**1850**	**2250**

MARINECALL WEATHER BY TELEPHONE & FAX

Marinecall is a private company providing a wide range of inshore and offshore telephone and fax weather services, quality controlled by Met Office forecasters.

> For further information contact:
> Marinecall Customer Services
> Buongiorno UK Ltd
> Avalon House, 57-63 Scrutton Street
> London EC2A 4PF
> ☎ 0845 610 1800 (M-F 0900-1700)
> www.marinecall.co.uk
> marinecall@itouch.co.uk

Inshore and Offshore forecasts start with a 48 hour inshore waters forecast for the coastal area and up to 12 miles offshore. This is followed by a 5-day sea area forecast based upon data from the Met Office Atmospheric Weather model relating to the lat/long for the area you have selected. Forecasts are updated three times daily at 0700/1200/1800 LT.

Operation

Dial the telephone or fax number shown for the required inshore, offshore or European weather forecast areas.

Listen to the spoken menu and select a location, or for faster (cheaper) operation, enter one of the 4-digit location codes (a full list of these is at www.marinecall.co.uk).

Inshore Areas

Cape Wrath to Rattray Head
  ☎ 09068 969 641   📠 09065 222 341
Rattray Head to Berwick
  ☎ 09068 969 642   📠 09065 222 342
Berwick to Whitby
  ☎ 09068 969 643   📠 09065 222 343
Whitby to Gibraltar Point
  ☎ 09068 969 644   📠 09065 222 344
Gibraltar Point to North Foreland
  ☎ 09068 969 645   📠 09065 222 345
North Foreland to Selsey Bill
  ☎ 09068 969 646   📠 09065 222 346
Selsey Bill to Lyme Regis
  ☎ 09068 969 647   📠 09065 222 347
Lyme Regis to Hartland Point
  ☎ 09068 969 648   📠 09065 222 348
Hartland Point to St David's Head
  ☎ 09068 969 649   📠 09065 222 349
St David's Head to Great Ormes Head
  ☎ 09068 969 650   📠 09065 222 350
Great Ormes Head to Mull of Galloway
  ☎ 09068 969 651   📠 09065 222 351

Mull of Galloway to Mull of Kintyre
  ☎ 09068 969 652   📠 09065 222 352
Mull of Kintyre to Ardnamurchan
  ☎ 09068 969 653   📠 09065 222 353
Ardnamurchan to Cape Wrath
  ☎ 09068 969 654   📠 09065 222 354
Lough Foyle to Carlingford Lough
  ☎ 09068 969 655   📠 09065 222 355

Offshore Areas

English Channel
  ☎ 09068 969 657   📠 09065 222 357
Southern North Sea
  ☎ 09068 969 658   📠 09065 222 358
Irish Sea
  ☎ 09068 969 659   📠 09065 222 359
Bay of Biscay
  ☎ 09068 969 660   📠 09065 222 360
North West Scotland
  ☎ 09068 969 661   📠 09065 222 361
Northern North Sea
  ☎ 09068 969 662   📠 09065 222 362

European Areas

North East France
  ☎ 09064 700 421   📠 09065 501 611
North France
  ☎ 09064 700 422   📠 09065 501 612
North Brittany
  ☎ 09064 700 423   📠 09065 501 613
South Brittany
  ☎ 09064 700 424   📠 09065 501 614
South Biscay
  ☎ 09064 700 425   📠 09065 501 615

Marinecall Online

You may buy all weather forecasts online at www.marinecall.co.uk. Buying online gives unlimited access to all areas during the subscribed period. Subscriptions available for 24 hrs, 1 week, 1 month, 3 months, 6 months and 12 months.

Pricing

> 09068 / 09064 calls cost £0·60 / minute.
> 090655 calls cost £1 / minute.
> 090652 calls cost £1·50 / minute
> Note: costs are from a UK landline and calls from mobile phones may be subject to network operator charges.

You can only access Marinecall from within the UK (including Channel Islands) from a landline or mobile network which receives a UK operator signal.

For information on how to use Marinecall from overseas, visit www.marinecall.co.uk and look up Marinecall Club.

WEATHER

INTERNET WEATHER SOURCES

The Internet provides a useful back-up for GMDSS services as well as information not available by conventional means.

www.metoffice.gov.uk/weather/marine/ has texts of all high seas, shipping and inshore waters forecasts, warnings, weather actuals from coastal stations, light vessels and data buoys. www.bbc.co.uk/weather/coast/ has texts of Navtex broadcasts.

National meteorological services provide the best forecasts for their own waters.

Other useful websites include:
www.franksweather.co.uk/
www.weatheronline.com/www.saildocs.com/
www.mailasail.com/www.grib.us/
www.passageweather.com/
www.windfinder.com/www.xcweather.co.uk/
www.windguru.com/www.theyr.com /
www.wetterzentrale.de/topkarten/tknf.html

Broadcasts of shipping and inshore waters forecasts by HM Coastguard

HM CG Centres routinely broadcast MSI every 3 hours at the local times below.

Each broadcast contains one of 3 different Groups of MSI:

Group A, the full broadcast, contains the Shipping forecast, a new Inshore waters forecast and 24 hrs outlook, Gale warnings, a 3 day forecast for Fishermen in the winter months*, Navigational (WZ) warnings and Subfacts & Gunfacts where relevant ‡. 'A' broadcast times are in bold type.

Group B contains a new Inshore waters forecast, plus the previous outlook, and Gale warnings. 'B' broadcast times are in plain type.

Group C is a repeat of the Inshore forecast and Gale warnings (as per the previous Group A or B) plus new Strong wind warnings. 'C' broadcast times are italicised.

Notes
*Fisherman's 3 day forecast (1 Oct-31 Mar).
‡ Subfacts & Gunfacts.

Coastguard	Shipping forecast areas	Inshore areas		Broadcast times, Local time							
South Coast				B	C	A	C	B	C	A	C
Falmouth‡	Portland, Plymouth, Sole, Shannon, Fastnet	8, 9		0110	*0410*	**0710**	*1010*	1310	*1610*	**1910**	*2210*
Brixham‡	Same as Falmouth CG	8, 9		0110	*0410*	**0710**	*1010*	1310	*1610*	**1910**	*2210*
Portland	Plymouth, Portland, Wight	6–8		0130	*0430*	**0730**	*1030*	1330	*1630*	**1930**	*2230*
Solent	Plymouth, Portland, Wight	6–8		0130	*0430*	**0730**	*1030*	1330	*1630*	**1930**	*2230*
Dover	Dover, Wight, Thames, Humber	5, 6		0110	*0410*	**0710**	*1010*	1310	*1610*	**1910**	*2210*
East Coast				B	C	A	C	B	C	A	C
Thames	Dover, Wight, Thames, Humber	5, 6		0110	*0410*	**0710**	*1010*	1310	*1610*	**1910**	*2210*
Yarmouth	Humber, German Bight, Dogger, Tyne	3–5		0150	*0450*	**0750**	*1050*	1350	*1650*	**1950**	*2250*
Humber	Same as Yarmouth CG	3–5		0150	*0450*	**0750**	*1050*	1350	*1650*	**1950**	*2250*
Forth	Tyne, Forth, Cromarty, Forties, Fair Isle	1, 2		0130	*0430*	**0730**	*1030*	1330	*1630*	**1930**	*2230*
Aberdeen‡	Same as Forth CG	1, 2		0130	*0430*	**0730**	*1030*	1330	*1630*	**1930**	*2230*
Shetland	Cromarty, Viking, Fair Isle, Faeroes	1, 16		0110	*0410*	**0710**	*1010*	1310	*1610*	**1910**	*2210*
West Coast				B	C	A	C	B	C	A	C
Stornoway‡	Rockall, Malin, Hebrides, Bailey, Fair Is, Faeroes, SE Iceland	16		0110	*0410*	**0710**	*1010*	1310	*1610*	**1910**	*2210*
Clyde‡	Rockall, Malin, Hebrides, Bailey	14, 15		0210	*0510*	**0810**	*1110*	1410	*1710*	**2010**	*2310*
Belfast‡	Irish Sea, Malin	12–14		0110	*0410*	**0710**	*1010*	1310	*1610*	**1910**	*2210*
Liverpool	Irish Sea	11, 12		0130	*0430*	**0730**	*1030*	1330	*1630*	**1930**	*2230*
Holyhead	Irish Sea	10, 11		0150	*0450*	**0750**	*1050*	1350	*1650*	**1950**	*2250*
Milford Hvn	Lundy, Fastnet, Irish Sea	9, 10		0150	*0450*	**0750**	*1050*	1350	*1650*	**1950**	*2250*
Swansea	Lundy, Fastnet, Irish Sea	9, 10		0150	*0450*	**0750**	*1050*	1350	*1650*	**1950**	*2250*

MSI broadcasts are transmitted via remote aerial sites geographically selected to give optimum coverage. The table below lists their positions and the VHF broadcast channel to be used. It will be one of channels 10, 23, 84 or 86 and is also specified in a prior announcement on Ch 16.

To minimise the risk of missing a broadcast, pre-select Ch 16 on Dual watch with the relevant (clearest) channel; and/or monitor the prior announcement to verify the working channel. **MF frequencies** (*kHz*), as quoted below, are also used for the broadcasts, primarily for fishermen.

Falmouth CG

Trevose Head	84	50°33'N 05°02'W
St Mary's (Scilly)	86	49°56'N 06°18'W
Lizard*	*2226kHz*, 23	49°58'N 05°12'W
Falmouth	84	50°09'N 05°03'W

Brixham CG

Fowey	10	50°20'N 04°38'W
Rame Head	86	50°19'N 04°13'W
East Prawle	84	50°13'N 03°42'W
Dartmouth	10	50°21'N 03°35'W
Berry Head	23	50°24'N 03°29'W

Portland CG

Beer Head	86	50°41'N 03°05'W
Grove Pt (Portland Bill)	84	50°33'N 02°25'W

Solent CG

Needles	86	50°39'N 01°35'W
Boniface (Ventnor, IoW)	23	50°36'N 01°12'W
Newhaven	86	50°47'N 00°03'E

Dover CG

Fairlight (Hastings)	84	50°52'N 00°39'E
Langdon (Dover)	86	51°08'N 01°21'E

Thames CG

Shoeburyness	23	51°31'N 00°47'E
Bradwell (R Blackwater)	86	51°44'N 00°53'E
Walton-on-the-Naze	23	51°51'N 01°17'E
Bawdsey (R Deben)	84	52°00'N 01°25'E

Yarmouth CG

Lowestoft	23	52°29'N 01°46'E
Great Yarmouth	86	52°36'N 01°43'E
Trimingham (Cromer)	23	52°54'N 01°21'E
Langham (Blakeney)	86	52°57'N 00°58'E
Guy's Head (Wisbech)	23	52°48'N 00°13'E

Humber CG

Easington (Spurn Hd)	86	53°39'N 00°06'E
Flamborough*	*2226kHz*, 23	54°07'N 00°05'W
Ravenscar	86	54°24'N 00°30'W
Hartlepool	23	54°42'N 01°10'W
Cullercoats (Blyth)	86	55°04'N 01°28'W
Newton	23	55°31'N 01°37'W

Forth CG

St Abbs/Cross Law	86	55°54'N 02°12'W
Craigkelly (Burntisland)	23	56°04'N 03°14'W
Fife Ness	84	56°17'N 02°35'W
Inverbervie	23	56°51'N 02°16'W

Aberdeen CG

Greg Ness*	*2226kHz*, 86	57°08'N 02°03'W

Windyheads Hill	23	57°39'N 02°14'W
Rosemarkie (Cromarty)	86	57°38'N 04°05'W
Noss Head (Wick)	84	58°29'N 03°03'W
Durness (Loch Eriboll)	23	58°34'N 04°44'W

Shetland CG

Wideford Hill (Kirkwall)	86	58°59'N 03°01'W
Fitful Head (Sumburgh)	23	59°54'N 01°23'W
Lerwick (Shetland)	84	60°10'N 01°08'W
Collafirth*	*2226kHz*, 86	60°32'N 01°23'W
Saxa Vord (Unst)	23	60°42'N 00°51'W

Stornoway CG

Butt of Lewis	*1743kHz*, 86	58°28'N 06°14'W
Portnaguran (Stornoway)	84	58°15'N 06°10'W
Forsnaval (W Lewis)	23	58°13'N 07°00'W
Melvaig (Loch Ewe)	23	57°50'N 05°47'W
Rodel (S Harris)	86	57°45'N 06°57'W
Clettreval (N Uist)	84	57°37'N 07°26'W
Skriag (Portree, Skye)	84	57°23'N 06°15'W
Drumfearn (SE Skye)	86	57°12'N 05°48'W
Barra	10	57°01'N 07°30'W
Arisaig (S of Mallaig)	23	56°55'N 06°50'W

Clyde CG

Glengorm (N Mull)	23	56°38'N 06°08'W
Tiree	*1883kHz*, 86	56°31'N 06°57'W
Torosay (E Mull)	10	56°27'N 05°43'W
Clyde CG (Greenock)	84	55°58'N 04°48'W
South Knapdale (Loch Fyne)	23	55°55'N 05°28'W
Kilchiaran (W Islay)	84	55°46'N 06°27'W
Lawhill (Ardrossan)	86	55°42'N 04°50'W
Rhu Staffnish (Kintyre)	10	55°22'N 05°32'W

Belfast CG

Navar (Lower L Erne)	86	54°28'N 07°54'W
Limvady (Lough Foyle)	84	55°06'N 06°53'W
West Torr (Fair Head)	86	55°12'N 06°06'W
Black Mountain (Belfast)	23	54°35'N 06°01'W
Orlock Point (Bangor)	84	54°40'N 05°35'W
Slievemartin (Rostrevor)	86	54°06'N 06°10'W

Liverpool CG

Caldbeck (Carlisle)	23	54°46'N 03°07'W
Snaefell (Isle of Man)	86	54°16'N 04°28'W
Langthwaite (Lancaster)	84	54°02'N 02°46'W
Moel-y-Parc (Anglesey)	23	53°13'N 04°28'W

Holyhead CG

Great Ormes Head	86	53°20'N 03°51'W
South Stack (Holyhead)	23	53°19'N 04°41'W

Continued overleaf

WEATHER

WEATHER

Milford Haven CG			Swansea CG		
Blaenplwyf			Mumbles	86	51°34'N 03°59'W
(Aberystwyth)	84	52°22'N 04°06'W	St Hilary (Barry)	23	51°27'N 03°25'W
Dinas Hd (Fishguard)	86	52°00'N 04°54'W	Severn Bridges	86	51°36'N 02°38'W
St Ann's Head	84	51°40'N 05°11'W	Combe Martin	23	51°12'N 04°03'W
Monkstone (Tenby)	84	51°42'N 04°41'W	Hartland Point	86	51°01'N 04°31'W

Inshore waters forecasts: Area boundaries used by the Coastguard

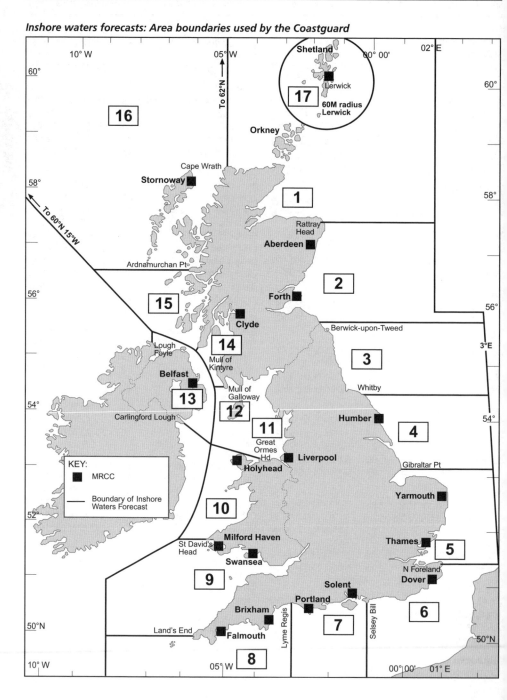

CHANNEL ISLANDS

Jersey Meteorological department

From the CI and UK call ☎ 0900 665 0022 for the Channel Islands recorded shipping forecast. From France call ☎ +44 1534 448787. For Guernsey only, call ☎ 06969 8800; it is chargeable. For more detailed info call ☎ +44 1534 448770, 🖷 448778.

Forecasts include: general situation, 24hr forecast for wind, weather, vis, sea state, swell, sea temperature, plus 2 & 4 day outlooks and St Helier tide times/heights. The area is bounded by 50°N, 03°W and the mainland from Cap de la Hague to Ile de Bréhat.

Weather broadcasts and bulletins

BBC Radio Guernsey 93·2 MHz, 1116 kHz
Bulletins for the waters around Guernsey, Herm and Sark are broadcast Mon-Fri at 0630, 0730 and 0830 LT; Sat/Sun at 0730 and 0830 LT. They contain forecast, synopsis, coastal forecast, storm warnings and wind strength. In the summer coastal reports are included from: Portland, Chan lt V, Alderney, Guernsey, Jersey, Cherbourg, Cap de la Hague and Dinard. ☎ 01481 200600

BBC Radio Jersey 1026 kHz, 88·8 MHz.
Storm warnings on receipt. Wind info for Jersey waters: Mon-Fri 0725, 0825, 1325, 1725 LT; Sat/Sun 0725, 0825. ☎ 01534 870000
Shipping forecast for local waters: Mon-Fri @ H+00 (0600-1900, after the news) and 0625 & 1625 LT; Sat/Sun @ H+00 (0700-1300, after the news) and 0725 LT.

Jersey Coastguard Ch 25, 82. Gale warnings at 0307, 0907, 1507, 2107UT. Gale warnings, synopsis, 24h forecast, outlook for next 24 hrs, plus reports from observation stations, are broadcast on request and at 0645*, 0745*, 0845*, 1245, 1845, 2245 UT; *broadcast 1 hr earlier when DST in force. ☎ 01534 447705.

IRELAND

Met Éireann (Irish Met Office) is at Glasnevin Hill, Dublin 9, Ireland. ☎ 1 806 4200, 🖷 1 806 4247, www.met.ie. General forecasting division: ☎ 1 806 4255, 🖷 1 806 4275 (H24, charges may apply).

Coast radio stations

CRS and their VHF channels are listed below (anti-clockwise from Malin Head) and shown overleaf. Weather bulletins for 30M offshore and the Irish Sea are broadcast on VHF at 0103, 0403, 0703, 1003, 1303, 1603, 1903 and 2203UT after an announcement on Ch 16. Broadcasts are made 1 hour earlier when DST is in force. Bulletins include gale warnings, synopsis and a 24-hour forecast.

Malin Head	23	Bantry	23
Glen Head	24	Mizen Head	04
Donegal Bay	02	Cork	26
Belmullet	83	Mine Head	83
Clifden	26	Rosslare	23
Galway	04	Wicklow Head	02
Shannon	28	Dublin	83
Valentia	24	Carlingford	04

Gale warnings are broadcast on these VHF channels on receipt and at 0033, 0633, 1233 and 1833 UT, after an announcement Ch 16.

MF Valentia Radio broadcasts forecasts for sea areas Shannon and Fastnet on 1752 kHz at 0833 & 2033 UT, and on request.

Gale warnings are broadcast on 1752 kHz on receipt and at 0303, 0903, 1503 and 2103 (UT) after an announcement on 2182 kHz.

Malin Head does not broadcast weather information on 1677 kHz. At Dublin there is no MF transmitter.

Radio Telefís Éireann (RTE) Radio 1

RTE Radio 1 broadcasts weather bulletins daily at 0602, 1253 & 2355LT on 252kHz (LW) Summerhill (15M W ofDublin airport) and FM (88·2-95·2MHz).

Bulletins contain a situation, forecast and coastal reports. Forecasts include: wind, weather, vis, swell (if higher than 4m) and a 24 hrs outlook.

Gale warnings are included in hourly news bulletins on FM & MF.

Coastal reports include wind, weather, visibility, pressure and pressure tendency. The change over the last 3 hrs is described as:

Steady	=	0–0·4hPa
Rising/falling slowly	=	0·5–1·9
Rising/falling	=	2·0–3·4
Rising/falling rapidly	=	3·5–5·9
Rising/falling very rapidly	=	> 6·0

Weather by telephone

The latest sea area forecast and gale warnings are available as recorded messages H24 from Weatherdial.

WEATHER

Dial ☎ 1550 123 plus the suffixes below:

850	Munster
851	Leinster
852	Connaught
853	Ulster
854	Dublin (plus winds in Dublin Bay and HW times)
855	Coastal waters and Irish Sea.

Weather by fax

Similar information, plus isobaric, swell and wave charts and any small craft warnings (>F6 up to 10M offshore; Apr-Sep inc) is available H24 by Weatherdial Fax.

Dial 📠 1550 131 838 (from within ROI only). From the menu below select the required 4-digit product code (see 0400 for full listing):

0015: Latest analysis chart
0016: Forecast valid for next 24 hrs

0017: Forecast valid for next 36 hrs
0018: Forecast valid for next 48 hrs
0021: Forecasts for coastal waters and Irish Sea
0031, 0032, 0033, 0034: Forecast (days 1-4) for sea/swell wave hts/periods

5-day forecasts (plain language, farming/ national) 0001: Munster. 0002: Leinster. 0003: Connaught. 0004: Ulster. 0005: Dublin.

Sea Planners provide graphic forecasts for up to 5 days (updated at 0430 daily) of expected winds and waves at the following seven offshore positions:

0041:	53°N 05°30'W
0042:	51°N 06°W
0043:	51°N 10°30'W
0044:	53°N 11°W
0045:	54°N 11°W
0046:	55°N 10°W
0047:	56°N 08°W

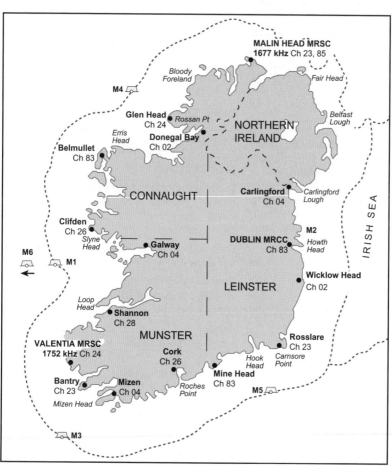

Provinces, headlands, sea areas and coastal stations referred to in weather broadcasts are shown here. Forecasts for coastal waters cover areas within 30M of the shore.

DENMARK

Gale warnings and forecasts are broadcast on receipt, on request and at 0133, 0533, 0933, 1333, 1733, 2133 UT in Danish/English by remote CRS, callsign *Lyngby Radio:*

Areas	VHF Channels
2 South Baltic	02, 04,
3 West Baltic	01, 02, 03, 04, 07, 28
4 The Belts & Sound	01, 02, 03, 04, 05, 07, 28, 65, 83
5 Kattegat	03, 04, 05, 07, 64, 65, 66, 83
6 Skagerrack	01, 02, 04, 64, 66
8 Fisher	01, 02, 23, 26
9 German Bight	02, 23

Forecast areas: see above. Skagen and Blåvand CRS broadcast on MF gale warnings for all areas on receipt.

Areas 2–5 are north of the Kiel Canal and east of 10°E.

MF: Blåvand 1734 kHz, Skagen 1758 kHz, Skamlebæk 1704 kHz and Rønne 2586 kHz broadcast gale warnings for all areas in Danish/**English** on receipt.

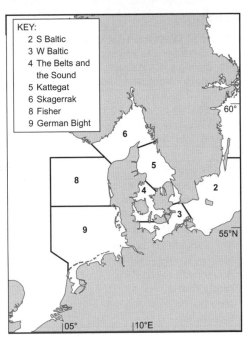

KEY:
2 S Baltic
3 W Baltic
4 The Belts and the Sound
5 Kattegat
6 Skagerrak
8 Fisher
9 German Bight

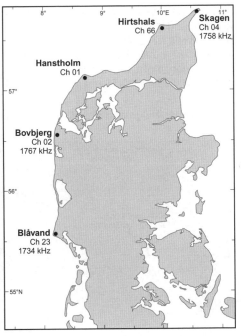

Danmarks Radio, Programme 1

Kalundborg (55°44′N 11°E) broadcasts on MW 1062 kHz:

- Gale warnings, weather reports and forecast for areas 2-6, 8, 9 at 0545, 0845, 1145, 1745LT.
- A 5 day forecast for areas 2-6, 8 and 9 at 1145 & 1745LT.

Danmarks Meteorologiske Institut (DM)

provides marine forecasts in Danish, **English** and German on www.dmi.dk/dmi/index/

GERMANY

Deutsche Wetterdienst (DWD)

DWD (German weather service) provides Met info through a databank which is updated twice daily; more often for weather reports and text forecasts.

DWD ☎ + 49 (0) 40 6690 1851. 📠 + 49 (0) 40 6690 1946. www.dwd.de seeschifffahrt@dwd.de.

Traffic Centres

Traffic Centres, below, broadcast local storm warnings, weather bulletins, visibility (and when appropriate ice reports) in German or **English** on request.

Traffic Centre	VHF Ch	Every
German Bight Traffic	80	H+00
Cuxhaven-Elbe Traffic	71 (outer Elbe)	H+35
Brunsbüttel-Elbe Traffic	68 (lower Elbe)	H+05
Kiel Kanal II (E-bound)	02	H+15 & H+45
Kiel Kanal III (W-bound)	03	H+20 & H+50
Bremerhaven-Weser Traffic	02, 04, 05, 07, 21, 22, 82	H+20
Bremen-Weser Traffic	19, 78, 81	H+30
Hunte Traffic	63	H+30
Jade Traffic	20, 63	H+10
Ems Traffic	15, 18, 20, 21	H+50

Coast Radio Stations

DP07 (Seefunk) has commercial CRS, below, at:

Nordfriesland (Sylt) Ch 26. **Elbe-Weser** Ch 01, 24. **Hamburg** (Control centre) Ch 83. **Bremen** Ch 25. **Borkum** Ch 28.

DP07 broadcasts (only in German): gale and strong wind warnings on receipt. At 0745Ⓐ, 0945, 1245, 1645 and 1945Ⓐ UT for Fisher, German Bight and Humber, DP07 broadcasts: a synopsis, 12hr forecast, 24hrs outlook and coastal station reports. Ⓐsummer only. Also a 4–5 day outlook for the North Sea (and Baltic) at 0945 and 1645.

Radio broadcasting: Nord Deutscher Rundfunk (NDR)

NDR 1 Welle Nord (FM)

A summary, outlook and wind forecast for the German Bight are broadcast after the news at H (0600-2200LT) and at H +30 (0530-17300LT) by:

Sylt 90·9 MHz; **Helgoland** 88·9 MHz; **Hamburg**

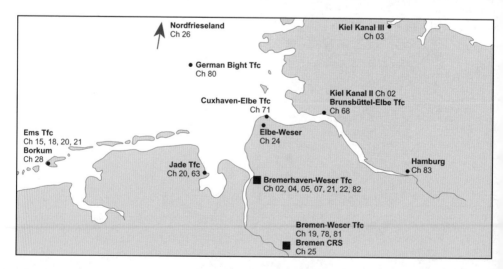

89·5 MHz; **Flensburg** 89·6 MHz; **Heide** 90·5 MHz; **Kiel** 91·3 MHz.

NDR Info (AM)
Synopsis, forecast and coastal station reports for the North Sea (and Baltic) are broadcast at 0005, 0830 and 2205 UT on 972 (Hamburg) & 702 (Flensburg) kHz.

Radio Bremen (MW and FM)
Warnings of extreme weather conditions in German Bight, with associated hazards, are broadcast after the news by: **Bremerhaven** 936 kHz; 89·3, 92·1, 95·4 & 100·8 MHz; and by **Bremen** 88·3, 93·8, 96·7 & 101·2 MHz.

Telephone forecasts (Marineweather)
For wind forecast and outlook (1 April – 30 Sept) call 0190 1160 (only within Germany) plus two digits for the following areas:

45	North Frisian Islands and Helgoland
46	R Elbe, Cuxhaven to Hamburg
47	Weser , Jade Bay and Helgoland
48	East Frisians and Ems Estuary
53	For pleasure craft

For year-round weather synopsis, forecast and outlook, call 0190 1169 plus two digits:

20	General information
21	North Sea and Baltic
22	German Bight, Fisher and SW North Sea
31	Reports for North Sea and Baltic

For the latest wind warnings (greater than F6) and storm warnings for individual areas of the North Sea coasts, call +49 40 66901209 (H24). If no warning is in force, a wind forecast for the German Bight, west and southern Baltic is given.

WEATHER

NETHERLANDS
VHF MSI broadcasts
Forecasts for 7 areas to 30M offshore and 3 inland waterways (IJsselmeer, Marken and Zierikzee) are broadcast in **English** and Dutch at 0805, 1305, 1905, 2305 LT on VHF as shown below, **without** prior announcement on Ch 16 or 70.

VHF Ch 23: Schiermonnikoog, Kornwerderzand, Wezep, Huisduinen (Den Helder), IJmuiden, Renesse, Woensdrecht.

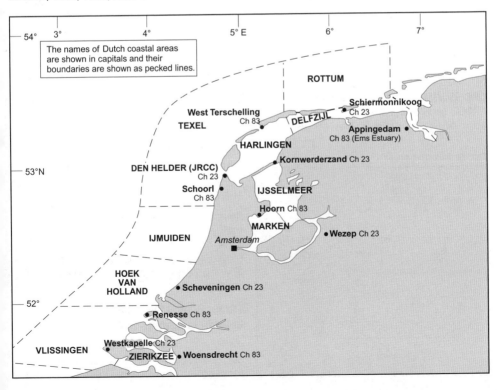

The names of Dutch coastal areas are shown in capitals and their boundaries are shown as pecked lines.

VHF Ch 83:
Appingedam, West Terschelling, Hoorn, Schoorl, Scheveningen, Westkapelle. All stations monitor Ch 16.

MF weather broadcasts
Forecasts for areas Dover, Thames, Humber, German Bight, Dogger, Fisher, Forties and Viking are broadcast by Scheveningen in **English** at 0940 & 2140 UT on 3673 kHz. Gale warnings for these areas are broadcast in **English** on receipt and at 0333, 0733, 1133, 1533, 1933 and 2333 UT.

Radio Noord-Holland (FM)
Coastal forecasts for northern areas, gale warnings and wind strength are broadcast in Dutch, Mon-Fri at 0730, 0838, 1005, 1230 and 1705LT; Sat/Sun 1005, by: **Haarlem** 97.6 MHz and **Wieringermeer** 93.9 MHz.

Omroep Zeeland (FM)
Coastal forecasts for southern areas, synopsis, gale warnings and wind strength are broadcast in Dutch, Mon-Fri at 0715, 0915, 1215 and 1715LT; Sat/Sun 1015, by:

Philippine 97.8 MHz and **Goes** 101.9 MHz.

BELGIUM, Coast radio stations
Oostende Radio, after prior notice on VHF 16, DSC 70 and 2182kHz, broadcasts in **English** and Dutch on VHF 27, MF 2256, 2376 and 2761 kHz: Strong wind warnings on receipt and after the next 2 silent periods. Forecasts for Thames, Dover and the Belgian coast at 0720 LT and 0820, 1720 UT.

Antwerpen Radio broadcasts in **English** and Dutch on VHF Ch 24 for the Schelde estuary: Gale warnings on receipt and at every H+55. Also strong wind warnings (F6+) on receipt and at every H+55.

FRANCE
Le Guide Marine is a useful, free annual booklet which summarises the various means by which weather forecasts and warnings are broadcast or otherwise disseminated. It is available from marinas or Météo-France, 1 quai Branly, 75340 Paris. ☎ 01.45.56.74.36; ▨ 01.45.56.71.70. marine@meteo.fr www.meteo.fr

CROSS VHF and MF broadcasts
CROSS broadcasts Met bulletins in French, after an announcement on Ch 16. In the English Channel broadcasts can be given in English, on request Ch 16. Broadcasts include: Any gale warnings, general situation, 24 hrs forecast (actual weather, wind, sea state and vis) and further trends for coastal waters, which extend 20M offshore. VHF channels, remote stations and local times are shown below.

Gale warnings feature in Special Met Bulletins (*Bulletins Météorologique Spéciaux* or BMS). They are broadcast in French by all CROSS on VHF at H+03 and at other times on MF frequencies as shown below.

CROSS GRIS-NEZ Ch 79
Belgian border to Baie de la Somme

Dunkerque	0720, 1603, 1920
St Frieux	0710, 1545, 1910

Baie de la Somme to Cap de la Hague
L'Ailly
0703, 1533, 1903
Gale warnings for areas 12-13 are broadcast in French on MF 1650 & 2677 kHz at 0833 & 2033LT

CROSS JOBOURG Ch 80
Baie de la Somme to Cap de la Hague

Antifer	0803, 1633, 2003
Port-en-Bessin	0745, 1615, 1945
Jobourg	0733, 1603, 1933

French forecast areas

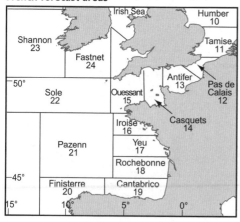

Cap de la Hague to Pointe de Penmarc'h

Jobourg	0715, 1545, 1915
Granville	0703, 1533, 1903

Gale warnings for areas 13-14 in **English** on receipt and at H+20 and H+50. No gale warnings on MF.

CROSS CORSEN Ch 79

Cap de la Hague to Pte de Penmarc'h (Times in bold = 1 May to 30 Sep only).

Cap Fréhel	0545, 0803, **1203**, 1633, 2003
Bodic	0533, 0745, **1145**, 1615, 1945
Ile de Batz	0515, 0733, **1133**, 1603, 1933
Le Stiff	0503, 0715, **1115**, 1545, 1915

WEATHER

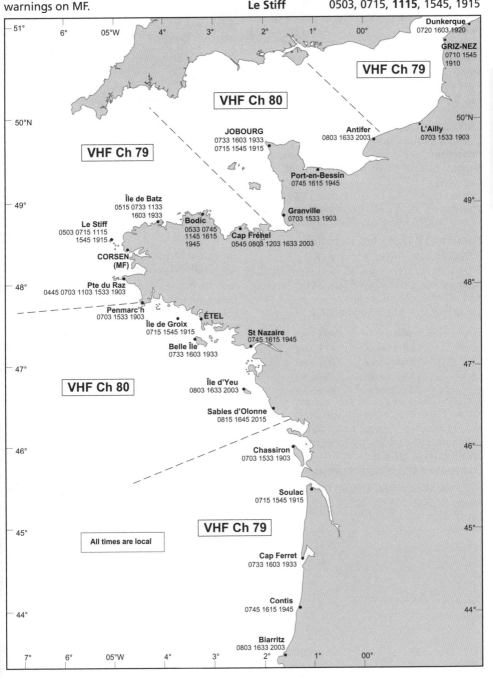

51°   6°   05°W   4°   3°   2°   1°   00°

Dunkerque
0720 1603 1920

GRIZ-NEZ
0710 1545
1910

VHF Ch 79

VHF Ch 80

50°N   50°N

JOBOURG
0733 1603 1933
0715 1545 1915

Antifer
0803 1633 2003

L'Ailly
0703 1533 1903

VHF Ch 79

Port-en-Bessin
0745 1615 1945

49°   49°

Île de Batz
0515 0733 1133
1603 1933

Bodic
0533 0745
1145 1615
1945

Granville
0703 1533 1903

Le Stiff
0503 0715 1115
1545 1915

Cap Fréhel
0545 0803 1203 1633 2003

CORSEN
(MF)

48°   **Pte du Raz**   48°
0445 0703 1103 1533 1903

Penmarc'h
0703 1533 1903

ÉTEL

Île de Groix
0715 1545 1915

St Nazaire
0745 1615 1945

Belle Île
0733 1603 1933

47°   47°

VHF Ch 80

Île d'Yeu
0803 1633 2003

Sables d'Olonne
0815 1645 2015

46°   **Chassiron**   46°
0703 1533 1903

Soulac
0715 1545 1915

VHF Ch 79

45°   45°

All times are local

Cap Ferret
0733 1603 1933

Contis
0745 1615 1945

44°   44°

Biarritz
0803 1633 2003

7°   6°   05°W   4°   3°   2°   1°   00°

Pte du Raz 0445, 0703, **1103**, 1533, 1903

Corsen broadcasts gale warnings for areas 13-22 in French at 0815 and 2015LT on MF 1650 & 2677 kHz.

CROSS ÉTEL Ch 80

Pte de Penmarc'h to l'Anse de l'Aiguillon
(46° 15'N 01°10'W). Étel has no MF freqs

Penmarc'h	0703, 1533, 1903
Ile de Groix	0715, 1545, 1915
Belle Ile	0733, 1603, 1933
Saint-Nazaire	0745, 1615, 1945
Ile d'Yeu	0803, 1633, 2003
Les Sables d'Olonne	0815, 1645, 2015

CROSS ÉTEL Ch 79

L'Anse de l'Aiguillon to Spanish border

Chassiron	0703, 1533, 1903
Soulac	0715, 1545, 1915
Cap Ferret	0733, 1603, 1933
Contis	0745, 1615, 1945
Biarritz	0803, 1633, 2003

Commercial radio broadcasting

Radio France (Inter-Service-Mer)
Broadcasts in French on LW 162 kHz at 2003LT daily: gale warnings, synopsis, 24 hrs forecast and outlook for all areas.
MF broadcasts are made at 0640LT by:

Brest	1404 kHz
Rennes	711 kHz
Bordeaux	1206 kHz
Bayonne	1494 kHz
Toulouse	945 kHz

Radio France Internationale (RFI)

RFI broadcasts gale warnings, synopsis, development and 24 hrs forecasts in French on HF at 1130 UT daily.
Frequencies and reception areas are:

6175 kHz: North Sea, English Channel, Bay of Biscay. 15300, 15515, 17570 and 21645 kHz: North Atlantic, E of 50°W.

See opposite for the High Seas forecast areas in the Eastern Atlantic.

Engineering bulletins giving any changes in frequency are transmitted between H+53 and H+00.

Local radio (FM)

Radio France Cherbourg broadcasts daily at 0829 LT:

Coastal forecast, gale warnings, visibility, wind strength, tidal information, small craft warnings, in French, for the Cherbourg peninsula on the following frequencies:

St Vaast-la-Hougue	85·0 MHz
Cherbourg	100·7 MHz
Cap de la Hague	99·8 MHz
Carteret	99·9 MHz

Forecasts by telephone

For recorded Inshore and Coastal forecasts. Dial 08·92·68·02·dd (dd is the number, as given, for the *département*); press the * key then 1 to access the main menu. Follow instructions:

For Inshore (*rivage*) or Coastal (*côte*) bulletins, say 'STOP' as your choice is spoken.

Inshore bulletins contain 7 day forecasts, tide times, actual reports, sea temperature, surf conditions, etc.

Coastal bulletins contain strong wind/gale warnings, general synopsis, 24 hrs forecast and outlook. Five bulletins cover the N & W coasts, out to 20M offshore.

For Offshore bulletins (*large*), out to 200M offshore, dial ☎ 08·92·68·08·77. Select one of three offshore areas (English Channel & southern North Sea, Bay of Biscay or the N part of the western Mediterranean) by saying 'STOP' as it is named. Offshore bulletins contain strong wind/gale warnings, the general synopsis and forecast, and the outlook for up to 7 days.

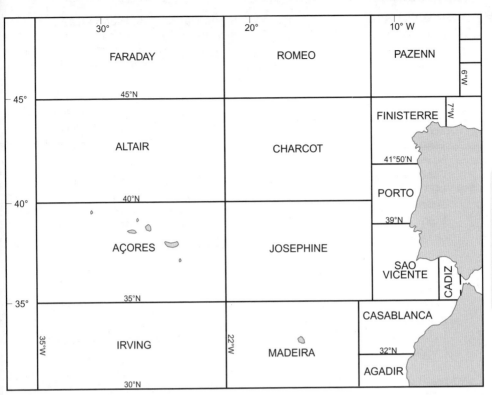

Forecast areas for the Eastern Atlantic and Coastal/Offshore Areas off France, Spain, Portugal and North West Africa

NOTES

NORTH WEST SPAIN
Coast radio stations

VHF weather warnings and 48h coastal forecasts are broadcast in Spanish at 0840, 1240 and 2010 UT by:

Pasajes	Ch 27
Bilbao	Ch 26
Santander	Ch 24
Cabo Peñas	Ch 26
Navia	Ch 60
Cabo Ortegal	Ch 02
La Coruña	Ch 26
Finisterre	Ch 22
Vigo	Ch 65
La Guardia	Ch 21

Gale warnings, synopsis and 24h/48h forecasts for Atlantic areas are broadcast on MF at 0703, 1303 and 1903 UT by:

Machichaco	1707 kHz
Cabo Peñas	1677 kHz
La Coruña	1698 kHz
Finisterre	1764 kHz

Coastguard weather broadcasts

Gale warnings and coastal forecasts are broadcast in Spanish and English on receipt and as listed below:

Bilbao*	Ch 10	4 hrly from 0033, except 0633
Santander	Ch 74	0245, 0445, 0645, 0845, 1045, 1445, 1845, 2245
Gijón	Ch 10	2 hrly (0215-2215)
Coruña	Ch 10	4 hrly from 0005
Finisterre	Ch 11	4 hrly from 0233
Vigo	Ch 10	4 hrly from 0015

*Bilbao also broadcasts High Seas gale warnings and forecasts 4 hourly from 0233.

Navtex

Coruna Navtex (D) transmits on 518 kHz at 0830 and 2030 UT: gale warnings, synopsis and the forecast for the following 24 hrs, valid out to 450M offshore.
Coruna Navtex (W) transmits in Spanish on 490 kHz at 1140 & 1940 UT: the same weather information as above.

Radio Nacional de España (MW)

Broadcasts storm warnings, synopsis and 12h or 18h forecasts for Cantábrico and Galicia at 1100, 1400, 1800 & 2200 LT in Spanish. Stations/frequencies are:

San Sebastián	774 kHz
Bilbao	639 kHz
Santander	855 kHz
Oviedo	729 kHz
La Coruña	639 kHz

Recorded telephone forecasts

This service is only available within Spain and for vessels equipped with Autolink. For a recorded weather bulletin in Spanish, call:

☎ 906 365 372 for the coasts of Cantábrico and Galicia.

☎ 906 365 374 for High Seas bulletins.

PORTUGAL AND THE AZORES
Broadcasts by Radionaval Portugal

Broadcasts in Portuguese and **English** are on Ch 11 at the times (UT) below. They contain: Storm, gale and poor visibility warnings; synopsis and 24 hrs forecasts for three coastal zones out to 20M offshore; see opposite:

Leixões   0705, 1905
Coastal waters of N and Central zones.

Alges (also on MF 2657 kHz)   0905, 2105
Coastal waters of all 3 zones.

Faro   0805, 2005
Coastal waters of Central and S Zones.

Horta (Azores, LT)   0900, 2100
Waters off Faial, Pico, Graciosa, São Jorge and Terceira

Waters off Corvo and Flores   1000, 1900

Radiofusão Portuguesa

Broadcasts weather bulletins for coastal waters in Portuguese at 1100 UT. Stations (N-S) and frequencies are:

Porto	720 kHz
Viseu	666 kHz
Montemer (Coimbra)	630 kHz
Lisboa 1	666 kHz
Miranda do Douro	630 kHz
Elvas	720 kHz
Faro	97·6 MHz, 720 kHz

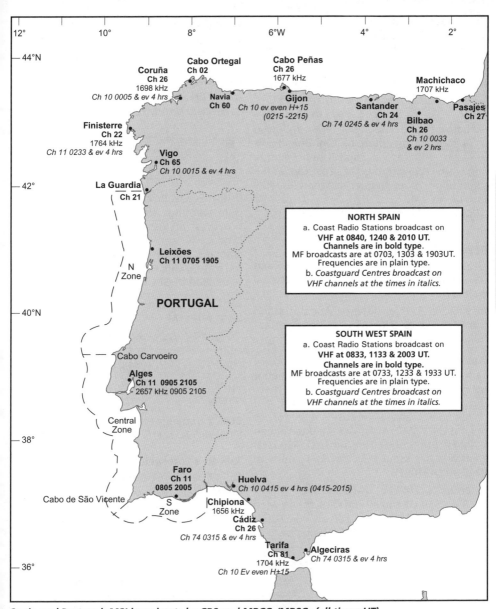

Spain and Portugal: MSI broadcasts by CRS and MRCCs/MRSCs (all times UT)

SOUTH WEST SPAIN

Coast radio stations

CRS broadcast gale warnings, synopsis, 24h and 48h forecasts for Atlantic and Mediterranean areas, in Spanish, at the times (UT) and on the VHF and MF frequencies shown below:

Chipiona	1656 kHz	0733	1233	1933
Cadiz	Ch 26	0833	1133	2003
Tarifa	Ch 81	0833	1133	2003
	1704 kHz	0733	1233	1933
Malaga	Ch 26	0833	1133	2003
Cabo Gata	Ch 27	0833	1133	2003

Coastguard broadcasts

Weather bulletins are broadcast in Spanish and **English** on the VHF channels and times (UT) below:

Huelva	Ch 10	4 hrly (0415-2015)
Cadiz	Ch 74	4 hrly from 0315
Tarifa	Ch 10, 67	Every even H+15.

Actual wind and visibility at Tarifa, followed by a forecast for Strait of Gibraltar, Cádiz Bay and Alborán, in **English** and Spanish. Fog (visibility) warnings are broadcast at the same times, more frequently when visibility falls below 2M.

Algeciras	Ch 74	4 hrly from 0315 and at 0515.

Recorded telephone forecasts

The service is only available within Spain and for Autolink-equipped vessels. For a coastal waters bulletin in Spanish call:

☎ 906 365 373 for Atlantic Andalucia and the Canaries. ☎ 906 365 374 for High Seas bulletin for Atlantic areas.

Navtex

Tarifa (G, 518 kHz) transmits weather bulletins in English at 0900 and 2100 UT. These include: Gale warnings, general synopsis and development and a forecast, valid for 24 hrs, for the N Atlantic and W Mediterranean within 450M of the coast. Tarifa (T, 490 kHz) transmits the same bulletins in Spanish at 0710 and 1910 UT.

Valencia (X, 518 kHz) transmits in English at 0750 & 1950 UT similar data for the W Med within 450M of the coast. Ditto Valencia (M, 490 kHz) in Spanish at 1000 & 1800UT.

GIBRALTAR

Gibraltar Broadcasting Corporation (GBC)

Gibraltar Radio broadcasts in English: General synopsis, situation, wind direction and force, visibility and sea state, radius 5M from Gibraltar. Frequencies are 1458 kHz, 91·3 MHz, 92·6 MHz and 100·5 MHz. Times (UT):

Mon-Fri:	0530, 0630, 0730, 1030, 1230
Sat:	0530, 0630, 0730, 1030
Sun:	0630, 0730, 1030

British Forces Broadcasting Service (BFBS)

Gale warnings for the Gibraltar area are broadcast on receipt by BFBS 1 and 2. All broadcasts are in English and comprise: Shipping forecast, wind, weather, visbility, sea state, swell, HW and LW times for waters within 5M of Gibraltar.

BFBS 1 frequencies and times (Local): 93·5, 97·8* MHz FM.

Mon-Fri:	0745, 0845, 1005, 1605
Sat:	0845, 0945, 1202
Sun:	0845, 0945, 1202, 1602

* This frequency is reported to have greater range.

BFBS 2 frequencies and time:
89·4, 99·5 MHz FM. Mon-Fri: 1200 Local time

Talk to a forecaster

Call ☎ 08700 767 818 to talk to a forecaster in Gibraltar about local weather in the Med or Canaries. Pay a flat rate of £17·00 by credit card, for a typical 5–10 mins briefing.

WEATHER VOCABULARY

English	German	French	Spanish	Dutch
Air mass	Luftmasse	Masse d'air	Massa de aire	Luchtmassa
Anticyclone	Antizyklonisch	Anticyclone	Anticiclón	Hogedrukgebied
Area	Gebiet	Zone	Zona	Gebied
Backing wind	Rückdrehender Wind	Vent reculant	Rolar el viento	Krimpende wind
Barometer	Barometer	Baromètre	Barómetro	Barometer
Breeze	Brise	Brise	Brisa	Bries
Calm	Flaute	Calme	Calma	Kalmte
Centre	Zentrum	Centre	Centro	Centum
Clouds	Wolken	Nuages	Nube	Wolken
Cold	Kalt	Froid	Frio	Koud
Cold front	Kaltfront	Front froid	Frente frio	Kou front
Cyclonic	Zyklonisch	Cyclonique	Ciclonica	Cycloonachtig
Decrease	Abnahme	Affaiblissement	Disminución	Afnemen
Deep	Tief	Profond	Profundo	Diep
Deepening	Vertiefend	Approfondissant	Ahondamiento	Verdiepend
Depression	Sturmtief	Dépression	Depresión	Depressie

English	German	French	Spanish	Dutch
Direction	Richtung	Direction	Direción	Richting
Dispersing	Auflösend	Se dispersant	Disipación	Oplossend
Disturbance	Störung	Perturbation	Perturbación	Verstoving
Drizzle	Niesel	Bruine	Lioviena	Motregen
East	Ost	Est	Este	Oosten
Extending	Ausdehnung	S'étendant	Extension	Uitstrekkend
Extensive	Ausgedehnt	Etendu	General	Uitgebreid
Falling	Fallend	Descendant	Bajando	Dalen
Filling	Auffüllend	Secomblant	Relleno	Vullend
Fog	Nebel	Brouillard	Niebla	Nevel
Fog bank	Nebelbank	Ligne de brouillard	Banco de niebla	Mist bank
Forecast	Vorhersage	Prévision	Previsión	Vooruitzicht
Frequent	Häufig	Fréquent	Frecuenta	Veelvuldig
Fresh	Frisch	Frais	Fresco	Fris
Front	Front	Front	Frente	Front
Gale	Sturm	Coup de vent	Temporal	Storm
Gale warning	Sturmwarnung	Avis de coup de vent	Aviso de temporal	Stormwaarschuwing
Good	Gut	Bon	Bueno	Goed
Gradient	Druckunterschied	Gradient	Gradiente	Gradiatie
Gust, squall	Bö	Rafalle	Ráfaga	Windvlaag
Hail	Hagel	Grêle	Granizo	Hagel
Haze	Diesig	Brume	Calina	Nevel
Heavy	Schwer	Abondant	Abunante	Zwaar
High	Hoch	Anticyclone	Alta presión	Hoog
Increasing	Zunehmend	Augmentant	Aumentar	Toenemend
Isobar	Isobar	Isobare	Isobara	Isobar
Isolated	Vereinzelt	Isolé	Aislado	Verspreid
Lightning	Blitze	Eclair de foudre	Relampago	Bliksem
Local	Örtlich	Locale	Local	Plaatselijk
Low	Tief	Dépression	Baja presión	Laag
Mist	Dunst	Brume légere	Nablina	Mist
Moderate	Mäßig	Modéré	Moderado	Matig
Moderating	Abnehmend	Se modérant	Medianente	Matigend
Moving	Bewegend	Se déplacant	Movimiento	Bewegend
North	Nord	Nord	Septentrional	Noorden
Occluded	Okklusion	Couvert	Okklusie	Bewolkt
Poor	Schlecht	Mauvais	Mal	Slecht
Precipitation	Niederschlag	Précipitation	Precipitación	Neerslag
Pressure	Druck	Pression	Presión	Druk
Rain	Regen	Pluie	Iluvia	Regen
Ridge	Hochdruckbrücke	Crête	Cresta	Rug
Rising	Ansteigend	Montant	Subiendo	Stijgen
Rough	Rauh	Agitée	Bravo o alborotado	Ruw
Sea	See	Mer	Mar	Zee
Seaway	Seegang	Haute mer	Alta mar	Zee
Scattered	Vereinzelt	Sporadiques	Difuso	Verspreid
Shower	Schauer	Averse	Aguacero	Bui
Slight	Leicht	Un peu	Leicht	Licht
Slow	Langsam	Lent	Lent	Langzaam
Snow	Schnee	Neige	Nieve	Sneeuw
South	Süd	Sud	Sur	Zuiden
Storm	Sturm	Tempête	Temporal	Storm
Sun	Sonne	Soleil	Sol	Zon
Swell	Schwell	Houle	Mar de fondo	Deining
Thunder	Donner	Tonnerre	Tormenta	Donder
Thunderstorm	Gewitter	Orage	Tronada	Onweer
Trough	Trog, Tiefausläufer	Creux	Seno	Trog
Variable	Umlaufend	Variable	Variable	Veranderlijk
Veering	Rechtdrehend	Virement de vent	Dextrogiro	Ruimende wind
Warm front	Warmfront	Front chaud	Frente calido	Warm front
Weather	Wetter	Temps	Tiempo	Weer
Wind	Wind	Vent	Viento	Wind
Weather report	Wetterbericht	Météo	Previsión	Weer bericht meteorologica

WEATHER

Chapter 3 - Communications

RADIO OPERATION

Avoiding interference

Before transmitting, first listen on the VHF channel. If occupied, wait for a break before transmitting, or choose another channel. If you cause interference you must comply immediately with any request from a Coastguard or Coast radio station to stop transmitting.

Control of communications

Ship-to-Shore: Communications between ship and shore stations are controlled by the latter, except in distress, urgency or safety cases.

Intership: The ship *called* controls communication. If you call another ship, then it has control. If you are called by a ship, you assume control. If a shore-based station breaks in, both ships must comply with instructions given.

Radio confidentiality

Private conversations heard on the radio must not be reproduced, passed on or otherwise used.

Making yourself understood

Clear R/T speech is vital. If a message cannot be understood by the receiver it is useless. Messages which have to be written down at the receiving station should be spoken slowly. This gives time for it to be written down by the receiving operator. If the transmitting operator himself writes it down all should be well. The average reading speed is 250 words a minute, whilst average writing speed is only 20.

When speaking, consider the following:

- **What** to say, ie *voice Procedure*
- **How** to say it, ie *voice Technique*

Voice Procedure is discussed below and overleaf. It includes procedural words, callsigns, making contact etc.

Voice Technique depends on a few simple rules:

Hold the microphone a few inches in front of the mouth and speak directly into it at a normal level. Speak clearly so that there can be no confusion. The voice should be pitched up at a higher level than normal. Do not drop the voice pitch at the end of a phrase or sentence. Emphasise words with weak syllables; 'Tower', if badly pronounced, could sound like 'tar'. Non Anglophones, or people with strong regional accents must try to pronounce words as clearly as possible.

Difficult words may be spelled phonetically, preceded with 'I spell'. If the word can be pronounced, include it before and after it has been spelt. For example, the message 'I will berth on the yacht *Coila*' would be sent as: 'I will berth on the yacht *Coila* – I spell – Charlie Oscar India Lima Alfa – *Coila*'.

The phonetic alphabet

The syllables to emphasise are underlined

Letter	Morse	Phonetic	Spoken as
A	• –	Alfa	AL-fah
B	– • • •	Bravo	BRAH-voh
C	– • – •	Charlie	CHAR-lee
D	– • •	Delta	DELL-tah
E	•	Echo	ECK-oh
F	• • – •	Foxtrot	FOKS-trot
G	– – •	Golf	GOLF
H	• • • •	Hotel	hoh-TELL
I	• •	India	IN-dee-ah
J	• – – –	Juliett	JEW-lee-ett
K	– • –	Kilo	KEY-loh
L	• – • •	Lima	LEE-mah
M	– –	Mike	MIKE
N	– •	November	no-VEM-ber
O	– – –	Oscar	OSS-car
P	• – – •	Papa	pa-PAH
Q	– – • –	Quebec	keh-BECK
R	• – •	Romeo	ROW-me-oh
S	• • •	Sierra	see-AIR-rah
T	–	Tango	TANG-go
U	• • –	Uniform	OO-nee-form
V	• • • –	Victor	VIK-tah
W	• – –	Whiskey	WISS-key
X	– • • –	X-Ray	ECKS-ray
Y	– • – –	Yankee	YANG-key
Z	– – • •	Zulu	ZOO-loo

Phonetic numerals

When numerals are transmitted, the following pronunciations make them easier to understand.

No	Morse	Spoken	No	Morse	Spoken
1	• – – – –	WUN	6	– • • • •	SIX
2	• • – – –	TOO	7	– – • • •	SEV-EN
3	• • • – –	TREE	8	– – – • •	AIT
4	• • • • –	FOW-ER	9	– – – – •	NIN-ER
5	• • • • •	FIFE	0	– – – – –	ZERO

Numerals are transmitted digit by digit except that multiples of thousands may be spoken as follows:

Numeral	Spoken as
44	FOW-ER FOW-ER
90	NIN-ER ZERO
136	WUN TREE SIX
500	FIFE ZERO ZERO
1478	WUN FOW-ER SEV-EN AIT
7000	SEV-EN THOU-SAND

COMMUNICATIONS

COMMUNICATIONS

Punctuation
Punctuation marks should be used only where their omission would cause confusion.

Mark	Word	Spoken as
.	Decimal	DAY-SEE-MAL
,	Comma	COMMA
.	Stop	STOP

Procedural words or 'prowords'
These are used to shorten transmissions

All after and **All before.** Used after proword 'say again' to request repetition of a part of a message

Correct Reply to repeat of message that was preceded by prowords 'read back for check' when it has been correctly repeated. Often said twice

Correction Cancel the last word or group of words. The correct word or group follows. Spoken when an error has been made in a transmission.

I say again I repeat the transmission or the part indicated (see 'All after' and 'All before').

I spell I shall spell the next word or group of letters phonetically

Out This is the end of working to you

Over Invitation to reply

Read back If the receiver is doubtful about accuracy of all or part of message he may repeat it back to the sending station, preceding the repetition with prowords 'I read back'

Station calling Used when a station is uncertain of the calling station's identification/callsign

This is This transmission is from the station whose callsign or name immediately follows

Wait If a called station cannot accept traffic immediately, it will reply '**WAIT.......MINUTES**', with reason if delay may exceed 10 minutes

Word after or Word before Used after the proword 'say again' to request repetition

Wrong Reply to repetition of message preceded by prowords 'read back' when it has been incorrectly repeated

Calls, calling and callsigns
Shore stations normally use a callsign of their geographic name followed by Coastguard or Radio, eg Solent Coastguard, Dublin Radio etc. Vessels usually identify themselves by the ship's name but the International callsign may be used in certain cases. If two yachts have the same or confusingly similar names, give your International callsign when starting communications, and thereafter use your ship's name as callsign.

'All ships' broadcast
Address used by Coastguard Radio where broadcast information is to be received or used by all who intercept it, eg gale warnings etc. No reply is needed.

Communicating with a coast radio station
Call initially on a working channel or very briefly on channel 16 to establish a working channel.

- Pause to check the working channel is clear before transmitting
- Use low power (1 watt) if close enough , ie up to 10 miles away. High power (25 watts) drains more from the battery
- The callsign of calling station up to three times only, and prowords 'This is'
- Say how many R/T calls you have to make
- Proword 'Over'

Using high power decreases battery state and the range your VHF will achieve. Continued calling also clutters up the channel and denies access to other users.

Aerial faults commonly reduce your transmitting range. Possibly the station aerial for the channel chosen is directionally orientated and you are on the wrong side. Try another channel or station. Call again when closer.

RADIO DATA

SHORT, MEDIUM and LONG RANGE RADIO COMMUNICATIONS
A suitable radio receiver on board will provide weather forecasts and time signals at scheduled times on a number of frequencies in various wavebands. With a maritime receiver you are not limited to the familiar BBC and commercial broadcasts. HM Coastguard transmit navigation warnings, storm warnings and weather messages for shipping in their respective sea areas.

Short range radiotelephony (RT) transmits and receives on VHF channels in the marine VHF (Very High Frequency) band. The equipment and procedures are simple, but range is normally limited to about 20 miles from ship to shore, rather less from ship to ship. Interconnection with national telephone systems is possible on certain VHF/RT channels when a yacht is within range of a Coast Radio Station, although there are now no such stations on the mainland of the UK, France or the Netherlands. Mobile telephones are now by far the most common form of ship to shore communication.

Medium range two-way communication operate in the marine MF (medium frequency) RT band, the 2MHz 'trawler band'. Single sideband techniques are employed on these medium frequencies and SSB equipment is essential. The effective range depends on the power of the transmitter and the sensitivity of the associated receiver; in general this might be up to 200 miles from certain (but not all) Coast Radio Stations.

THE MARINE VHF BAND

VHF is used by most vessels, Coast Radio Stations, CG centres and other rescue services. Its range is slightly better than the line of sight between the transmitting and receiving aerials. A good aerial, as high as possible, is most important.

In the Marine VHF band (156·00–174·00 MHz) the individual frequencies are separated from their neighbours by exactly 25kHz 'elbow-room' to eliminate mutual interference. Each frequency is given a channel number, not necessarily consecutive. Thus 55 channels are available, plus some with special purposes (see below).

VHF Channel Grouping

Channels are grouped for three main purposes, but some can be used for more than one purpose. They are listed below in their preferred order of usage:

• **Public correspondence** (ie link calls via CRS into the shore telephone system): Ch 26, 27, 25, 24, 23, 28, 04, 01, 03, 02, 07, 05, 84, 87, 86, 83, 85, 88, 61, 64, 65, 62, 66, 63, 60, 82, 78, 81.

• **Inter-ship:** Ch 06, 08, 10, 13, 09, 72, 73, 67, 69, 77, 15, 17. Remember these, so that if another vessel calls you, you can swiftly nominate a working channel from within this group.

• **Port Operations:**
Ch 12, 14, 11, 13, 09, 68, 71, 74, 69, 73, 17, 15, 20, 22, 18, 19, 21, 05, 07, 02, 03, 01, 04, 78, 82, 79, 81, 80, 60, 63, 66, 62, 65, 64, 61, 84.

Special purposes. The following channels have one specific purpose only:

Ch 0 (156·00 MHz): SAR ops, not available to yachts.

Ch's 10 (156·500 MHz), **23** (161·750 MHz) **84** (161·825 MHz) and **86** (161·925 MHz): for MSI broadcasts by HMCG.

Ch 13 (156·650 MHz): Intership safety of navigation (sometimes referred to as bridge-to-bridge); a possible channel for calling a merchant ship if no contact on Ch 16.

Ch 16 (156·80 MHz): Distress, Safety and calling. *See Chapter 4 for Distress and Safety.* Ch 16 will be monitored by ships, CG centres (and, in some areas, any remaining Coast Radio Stations) for Distress and Safety until at least 2005, in parallel with DSC Ch 70. Yachts should monitor Ch 16. After an initial call, the stations concerned **must** switch to a working channel, except for Safety matters.

Ch 67 (156·375 MHz): the Small Craft Safety channel in the UK, accessed via Ch 16.

Ch 70 (156·525 MHz): exclusively for digital selective calling for Distress and Safety purposes.

Ch 80 (157·025 MHz): the primary working channel between yachts and UK marinas.

Ch M (157·85 MHz): the secondary working channel between yachts and UK marinas; previously known as Ch 37.

Ch M2 (161·425 MHz): for race control, with Ch M as stand-by. YCs may apply to use Ch M2.

SILENCE PERIODS

The periods are the 3 minutes immediately after the whole and half hours, ie H to H+03 and H+30 to H+33, when no transmissions should be made.

MEDIUM RANGE MF RADIO

Single sideband MF/RT provides communications in the offshore waters of the UK and Western Europe where small craft may be out of VHF contact. A receiver alone gives the ability to hear weather bulletins, storm and navigation warnings for local sea areas broadcast from CRS in the 1.6 to 4.0MHz maritime band, ie on frequencies from 1605 to 4200 kHz.

MF transmissions tend to follow the curvature of the earth, which makes them suitable for direction-finding. For this reason, and because of their good range, the marine Distress R/T frequency (2182 kHz) is in the MF band.

TRAFFIC LISTS

If a Coast Radio station has messages for a vessel, but is unable to contact her, that vessel's name will be added to the Traffic List broadcast at (usually) two hour intervals. This is not a system much used by yachts and small craft.

LONG RANGE HF RADIO

HF radios use short wave frequencies in the 4, 8, 12, 16 and 22 MHz bands, as chosen to suit propagation conditions. HF is more expensive than MF and requires more power, but can provide worldwide coverage. A good installation and skilled operating techniques are essential for satisfactory results.

COMMUNICATIONS

GLOBAL COMMUNICATIONS

Once out of range of VHF/MF or wireless telephony/broadband service, the yachtsman's communications options are limited to MF/HF radio and satellite systems (Satcoms).

A yachtsman embarking on an extended offshore venture would usually choose a mix of equipment for sensible reasons of redundancy, this will allow a choice of listening and transmitting, via terrestrial and satellite radio systems, to meet his needs at various times and in different circumstances. A typical setup might include a fixed or handheld satcoms transceiver, a HF SSB transceiver and receiver. For data capability, these would be interfaced to an on-board PC.

HF/single sideband radio (HF-SSB)

HF SSB radios use frequencies in the 4, 8, 12, 16 and 22 MHz bands (short wave), provide worldwide coverage and usually include MF frequencies as well.

Despite rapid growth in marine satellite communications, HF SSB remains a popular choice amongst long-distance cruisers, providing a cost-free voice (and limited email) capability for cruisers, sometimes operating over vast distances. Operators have the Long Range Certificate (LRC) or General Operators Certificate (GOC). To use Amateur (ham) bands (giving more frequencies and higher power, therefore range) operators must take the ham examination.

Using HF SSB radio for email requires a radio modem, often proprietary to the supplier. Though slow and requiring some skill to operate effectively, the almost-nil operating costs appeal to many and SSB radio has a strong following amongst blue-water cruisers. Established suppliers include Sailmail and Globe Wireless.

HF SSB radio is also extensively used for receipt of weatherfax images, although a receive-only SSB radio (with an adequate, grounded antenna installation) may be used rather than a full transceiver. Though declining in popularity, several useful weatherfax transmitting stations remain, including Northwood, UK and Offenbach, Germany.

Satellite Communications (Satcoms)

Satellite communications systems operate over **Ultra High Frequency (UHF)** radio using digital technology that makes them simpler-to-operate and more reliable for voice (and

data) communications than HF SSB radio; they operate with either a dedicated ship installation or a standalone handheld terminal. Apart from the equipment purchase (and installation if necessary), ongoing costs usually include a monthly service fee and usage charges that will be related to either the amount of satellite time used, or the volume of data transmitted and received.

For two-way voice communications, the 'Ship Station' (aka 'Mobile Earth Station') transmits to a visible satellite that is simultaneously in sight of a 'Land Earth Station', eg Goonhilly, Cornwall. From there, the call is routed to its destination through the normal terrestrial telephone network.

The satellite 'constellations' have different architectures. Inmarsat for example has four geostationary (GEO) satellites, one each positioned over the Pacific and Indian oceans and two over the Atlantic. Because they are comparatively high up 19,400M (36,000km), each satellite has a large signal 'footprint', overlapping the next one and thus world-wide coverage is provided (although not in the polar regions above about 70°N and 70°S).

Other systems employ many more Low Earth Orbit (LEO) satellites orbiting the Earth about 540M (1,000km) above the surface.

The smaller, low-data rate, handheld voice terminals incorporate an omni-directional antenna that works best with an unobstructed view of the satellite. Fixed installations use an external gyro-stabilised antenna (to keep it pointing at the satellite as the boat moves); more powerful systems that support higher data rates employ antenna radomes that are really too large for installation aboard a 10–15m yacht.

The GMDSS provides automatic distress, urgency and safety communications, with some satcom systems (eg Inmarsat C) providing a red button that alerts a Maritime Rescue Coordination Centre (MRCC) when pressed.

There are several service providers, each offering an array of capabilities. The table opposite provides a useful summary of systems that might be used aboard a 10–20m yacht.

This is a fast moving market place and you should check with manufacturers/retailers for up-to-date specifications and prices.

COMMUNICATIONS

[1] typical, **if** in coverage area [2] using VOIP [3] Likely to be expensive	Wired Broadband	Wi-Fi	Cellular GSM	Cellular GPRS	Cellular 3G	Wi-Max
Range offshore[1] (NM)	0	0-1	0-15	0-15	0-15	0-30
Voice communication	Y[2]	Y[2]	Y	Y	Y	Y[2]
Text messages	Y	Y	Y	Y	Y	Y
Light email traffic	Y	Y	Y[3]	Y	Y	Y
Text weather forecasts	Y	Y	Y[3]	Y	Y	Y
Heavy email traffic	Y	Y	✕	Y[3]	Y	Y
Graphical weather forecasts	Y	Y	✕	Y[3]	Y	Y
Full web browsing	Y	Y	✕	Y[3]	Y	Y

SATELLITE COMMUNICATION SERVICES

System	Antenna	Satellites	Coverage	GMDSS	Phone (voice)	Fax	SMS text	Position tracking	Data rate
INMARSAT C	Omni-directional	4 GEO	Global excepting polar regions	Yes	No	Yes	Yes	Yes (GPS)	Very low, uneconomic for email
INMARSAT Mini-M	Gyro-stabilised 40cms diameter	4 GEO	Global excepting polar regions	No	Yes	Yes	No	No	2.4kbps
INMARSAT D+	Omni-directional	4 GEO	Global excepting polar regions	No	No	No	No	Yes (GPS)	Very low, uneconomic for email
Fleet 33	Gyro-stabilised 40cms diameter	4 GEO	Global excepting polar regions	No	Yes	Yes	Yes	No	9.6kbps uncompressed
Iridium	Omni-directional	66 LEO	Global	No	Yes	Out only	Yes	No	Data kit required 2.4kbps, higher with compression
Globalstar	Omni-directional	40 LEO	Global excepting polar regions	No	Yes	Yes	Yes	To 10km	9.6kbps uncompressed, 38.6kbps compressed, 56k with data kit
Thuraya	Omni-directional	1 GEO	Europe, N Africa & Middle East, India	No	Yes	Yes	Yes	Yes (GPS)	9.6kbps (144kbps possible with land *DSL receiver)

*DSL (Digital Subscriber Line) allows broadband Internet access via normal copper telephone lines. It is used in the wireless/Satcoms arena to denote broadband-like speeds over the wireless link. This usually means data transfer speeds of 5 to 24mbps which is fast for Satcoms.

PORT and/or MARINA VHF channels & telephone numbers

NOTES. **Ch 16** is almost universally guarded, so is omitted. *In larger ports it is sensible to monitor the VTS channel (if any) or the primary port channel (in bold) before changing to a marina channel.* Times are local, unless marked UT. Abbreviations are at the front of the book. Telephone codes are shown only once unless more than one applies.

ENGLAND – SOUTH COAST

ISLES OF SCILLY, St Mary's HM Ch 14 (0800-1700); ☎ 01720 422768. *Falmouth CG* covers Scilly and the TSS off Land's End on Ch 23. **Tresco** HM ☎ 07778 601237.

NEWLYN HM Ch 09, **12** (M-F: 0800-1700, Sat: 0800-1200). ☎ 01736 362523.

PENZANCE HM Ch 09, **12** (M-F: 0830-1730 and HW –2 to +1). ☎ 01736 366113.

FALMOUTH *Falmouth Hbr Radio* Ch 11, **12**, 14 (M-F 0800-1700). ☎ 01326 312285.
Ch 80: Falmouth ☎ 316620 and Port Pendennis marinas ☎ 311113. **Ch 12**: Visitors Yacht Haven ☎ 310991; St Mawes HM ☎ 270553. **Ch M** (HO): Mylor Yacht Hbr ☎ 372121.

TRURO HM *Carrick One* Ch 12. ☎ 01872 272130. **Ch M** (HO): Malpas Marine ☎ 271260.

MEVAGISSEY HM Ch 14 (Summer: 0900-2100, Winter: 0900-1700). ☎ 01726 843305.

CHARLESTOWN HM Ch 14, HW –2 to +1, only when a vessel is expected. ☎ 01726 70241.

FOWEY HM Ch 12 (0900-1700); also Hbr Patrol (0900-2000). ☎ 01726 832471. Water taxi: Ch 06.

LOOE. HM Ch 16, occas. ☎ 01503 262839.

PLYMOUTH *Long Room Port Control* Ch 14 H24, ☎ 01752 836528. **QAB** Ch 80, ☎ 671142. **Sutton Hbr lock**: Ch 12 H24, ☎ 204702. **Cattewater HM** Ch 14 (M-F 0900-1700), ☎ 836528. **Plymouth Yacht Haven**, Ch 80, M; ☎ 404231. **Mayflower marina**, Ch 80; ☎ 556633.

SALCOMBE HM & launch: Ch 14, May to mid-Sep: 7/7, 0600-2100; otherwise: M-F 0900-1600; ☎ 01548 843791. *Hbr Taxi* Ch 12. Fuel barge Ch 06, ☎ 07801 798862. *Egremont* (ICC) Ch M.

DARTMOUTH HM *Dartnav* Ch 11, 7/7 0730-dusk; ☎ 01803 832337. Darthaven marina Ch 80, ☎ 752545. Dart & Noss-on-Dart marinas Ch 80, ☎ 833351. Fuel barge Ch 06. Water taxi Ch 08.

TORBAY HBRS Brixham Marina Ch 80, ☎ 01803 882929; YC, ☎ 853332, & Water taxi *Shuttle* Ch M. Torquay Marina Ch 80, ☎ 200210. Fuel Ch M.

EXETER Exmouth Marina Ch 14, ☎ 01395 269314. **Retreat BY**: Ch M, ☎ 01392 874720. **Port of Exeter** HM Ch 12, M-F: 0730-1730 and when vessel due; ☎ 274306.

LYME REGIS HM Ch 14. Summer 0800-2000, winter 1000-1500. ☎ 01297 442137.

BRIDPORT HM Ch 11. ☎ 01308 423222.

PORTLAND PORT Port Control Ch 74 (H24). ☎ 01305 824044. **Sailing Academy** ☎ 866000.

WEYMOUTH HM & Town Bridge: Ch 12, M-F 0800-2000 summer & when vessel due; ☎ 01305 838423. **Marina** Ch 80, ☎ 767576. **Fuel** Ch 60.

POOLE
HM/bridge Ch 14 (H24); Code 01202 ☎ 440233. **Marinas Ch 80 M**: Salterns ☎ 709971. Parkstone YC ☎ 743610. Poole Quay ☎ 649488. Cobbs Quay ☎ 674299. **Poole Bay Fuels: Ch M** M-F: 0900-1730; Sat/Sun 0830-1800. ☎ 07768 71511.

YARMOUTH (IoW)
HM & Yar bridge **Ch 68** H24. ☎ 01983 760321. Water taxi **Ch 15**.

LYMINGTON
Marinas Ch 80, M: Yacht Haven ☎ 01590 677071. Berthon Marina ☎ 01590 673312.

COWES
Harbour Radio, Chain Ferry & Folly Inn Ch 69 Mon-Fri: 0800-1700. Marinas **Ch 80, M**. Tel code 01983: Yacht Haven ☎ 299975. Shepards ☎ 297821. East Cowes ☎ 293983. Island Hbr **Ch 80**, ☎ 822999. Water Taxi **Ch 06**.

NEWPORT HM & Yacht Hbr **Ch 69** 0800-1600. ☎ 01983 525994.

RYDE HM **Ch 80**. Summer 0900-2000, Winter HX. ☎ 01983 613879. Access HW±2.

BEMBRIDGE Marina **Ch 80**, ☎ 01983 872828. Hbr launch **Ch M**.

SOUTHAMPTON
Port Ops and VTS Ch 12 14. Marinas **Ch 80, M**. Tel code 02380: Hythe ☎ 207073. Ocean Village ☎ 229385. Shamrock Quay ☎ 229461. Kemp's ☎ 632323.

HAMBLE
Hbr Radio Ch 68 Apr-Sep daily 0600-2200; Oct-Mar 0700-1830. Marinas **Ch 80, M**. Tel code 02380: Hamble Pt ☎ 452464. Port Hamble ☎ 452741. Mercury ☎ 455994. Water Taxi **Ch 77**, ☎ 454512. Tel code 01489: Universal ☎ 574272. Swanwick ☎ 885000.

PORTSMOUTH
VTS **Ch 11** (& *QHM* if essential). Marinas **80**. Tel code 02392: Haslar ☎ 601201. Gosport ☎ 524811. Royal Clarence ☎ 523810. Port Solent ☎ 210765. THE CAMBER (Commercial Hbr): *Portsmouth Hbr Radio* **Ch 11** 14 (H24).

LANGSTONE HBR
HM **Ch 12**. Summer, daily 0830-1700; Winter, M-F 0830-1700; Sat/Sun 0830-1300. Southsea Marina **Ch 80, M, ☎** 02392 822719.

CHICHESTER
HM *Chichester Hbr Radio* **Ch 14**. 1 Apr-Sep: M-Fri: 0830-1700. Sat: 0900-1300. 1 Oct - 31 Mar: 0900-1300, 1400-1700. Marinas **Ch 80, M**. Sparkes ☎ 02392 463572. Tel code 01243: Northney ☎ 466321. Emsworth Yacht Hbr ☎ 377727. Thornham ☎ 375335. Birdham Pool ☎ 512310. Chichester ☎ 512731. Water taxi **Ch 08** 0900-1800, mobile 07970 378350

LITTLEHAMPTON HM/Bridge **Ch 71** 0900-1700. Marina **Ch 80, M**; ☎ 01903 241663.

SHOREHAM HM & lock *Shoreham Hbr Radio* **Ch 14** (H24). Marina ☎ 01273 593801.

BRIGHTON
Marina *Brighton Control* **Ch M 80**; ☎ 01273 819919.

NEWHAVEN HM & Bridge *Newhaven Radio* **Ch 12**. Marina **Ch 80, M**; ☎ 01273 513881.

EASTBOURNE
Sovereign Hbr, inc lock/berthing: **Ch 17**. ☎ 01323 470099.

RYE *Hbr Radio,* **Ch 14** 0900-1700 or when ship due. ☎ 01797 225225.

FOLKESTONE
Port Control **Ch 15** for entry; ☎ 01303 254597.

DOVER
Port Control **Ch 74** for entry. Marina Ch 80; ☎ 01304 241663.

RAMSGATE
Port Control **Ch 14**. Marina **Ch 80**; ☎ 01843 572110.

ENGLAND – EAST COAST

WHITSTABLE
Hbr Radio Ch 09 12, Mon-Fri: 0830-1700 and –3HW+1. ☎ 01227 274086.

MEDWAY
Medway VTS **Ch 74**. Kingsferry Bridge (W Swale) **Ch 10** H24. Marinas **Ch 80, M**. Tel code 01634: Gillingham ☎ 280022. Hoo ☎ 250311. Chatham ☎ 899200.

PORT OF LONDON
LONDON VTS: Ch 69 from sea to Sea Reach No 4 buoy. **Ch 68** Sea Reach No 4 to Crayford Ness. **Ch 14, 22,** W of Crayford Ness.
Thames Barrier Ch 14. ☎ 020 8855 0315.

RIVER THAMES
Patrol Launches *Thames Patrol* **Ch 06, 13, 14, 68** King George V Dock lock *KG Control* **Ch 13**. West India Dock lock **Ch 13** Greenwich Yacht Club **Ch M**

Thames lock (Brentford) **Ch 74** Summer 0800-1800; Winter 0800-1630.
Cadogan Pier **Ch 14** 0900-1700.
Marinas Ch 80, M; Tel code 0207: Gallions Point ☎ 4767054. Poplar Dock ☎ 5151046. South Dock ☎ 2522244. Limehouse Basin ☎ 3089930. St Katherine Haven ☎ 2645312. Chelsea Hbr ☎ 2259100. Brentford Dock ☎ 0208 2328941.

RIVER ROACH Havengore Bridge **Ch 72** *Shoe Bridge* HW±2. ☎ 01702 383436.

BURNHAM-ON-CROUCH
Ch 80: HM Launch 0900-1700. Yacht Hbr ☎ 01621 782150. Essex Marina ☎ 01702 258531.

RIVER BLACKWATER
Marinas **Ch 80, M**; Tel code 01621: Tollesbury ☎ 869202. Bradwell ☎ 776235. **Ch M:** Blackwater ☎ 740264. Heybridge Lock, **Ch 80** ☎ 853506.

RIVER COLNE
Brightlingsea Hbr Radio **Ch 68** 0800-2000. ☎ 01206 302200, mob 07952 734814.

WALTON BACKWATERS
Titchmarsh Marina **Ch 80,** ☎ 01255 672185.

RIVERS STOUR AND ORWELL
HARWICH VTS **Ch 71,** 11, 20, H24
SUNK VTS **Ch 14,** H24
Orwell Navigation Service **Ch 68,** H24
Marinas **Ch 80, M**. Tel code 01473: Shotley ☎ 788982. Suffolk Hbr ☎ 659240. Woolverstone ☎ 780206. Fox's ☎ 689111. Neptune ☎ 215204. Ipswich Haven ☎ 236644.

RIVER DEBEN HM *Odd Times* **Ch 08**. Tidemill Yacht Hbr ☎ 01394 385745.

SOUTHWOLD *Port Radio* **Ch 09 12**. HM ☎ 01502 724712.

LOWESTOFT
Hbr Control **Ch 11, 14**. HM ☎ 01502 572286.
Royal Norfolk & Suffolk YC **Ch 80**. ☎ 566726.
Haven Marina **Ch 80** ☎ 580300. **Mutford Bridge & Lock Ch 09, 14** ☎ 531778.

GREAT YARMOUTH
Yarmouth Radio **Ch 12**. HM ☎ 01493 335511.
Haven & Breydon bridges **Ch 12**.

WELLS-NEXT-THE-SEA
Wells Hbr **Ch 12**, HJ, HW±2 and when vessel expected. HM ☎ 01328 711646.

WISBECH Ch 09 HW–3 when vessel expected. HM 01945 588059. Sutton Bridge **Ch 09**

KING'S LYNN
Harbour Radio **Ch 14** 11 Mon-Fri: 0800-1700 and –3HW+1. HM ☎ 01553 773411.

BOSTON
Port Control **Ch 12** Mon-Fri 0800-1700 and HW HW -2½ to HW + 1½. HM ☎ 01205 362328.
Grand Sluice **Ch 74** only when lock operates. Marina ☎ 364420.

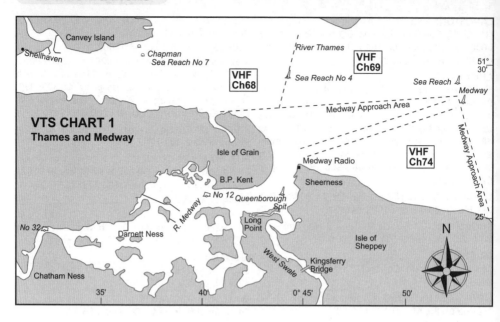

VTS CHART 1
Thames and Medway

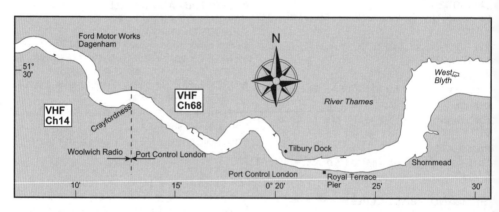

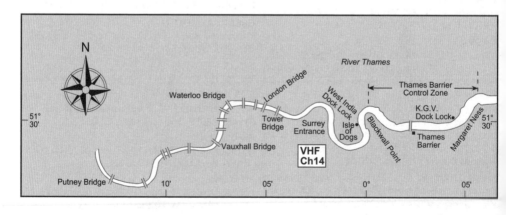

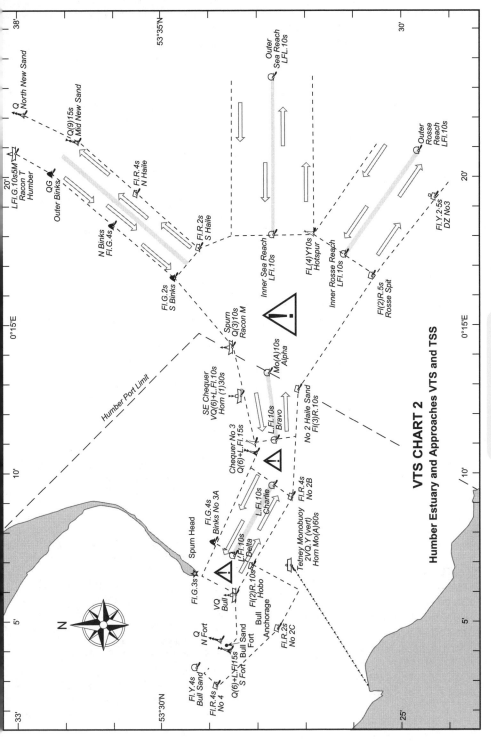

VTS CHART 2

Humber Estuary and Approaches VTS and TSS

RIVER HUMBER
VTS 1, Ch 14 to seaward of Clee Ness Lt F
VTS 2, Ch 12 Clee Ness–Gainsborough (R Trent) & Goole (R Ouse). MSI broadcasts Ch 12 & 14 every 2 hrs from 0103LT.
Grimsby Docks Radio **Ch 74**; 18 79 H24
Marinas: Grimsby, Meridian Quay **Ch 74**, ☎ 01472 268424. **Hull, Ch 80**, ☎ 01482 330508.
South Ferriby, Sluice **Ch 74**. **Brough**, Humber Yawl club ☎ 01482 667224. **Goole** Boathouse ☎ 01405 763985.

BRIDLINGTON
HM, call **Ch 16**; work **Ch 12**. ☎ 01262 670148.

SCARBOROUGH
HM *Scarborough Port Control* **Ch 12** H24. ☎ 01723 373530.

WHITBY
HM, Bridge & Marina **Ch 11, 12** H24. ☎ 01947 602354.

RIVER TEES and HARTLEPOOL
Monitor *Tees Port control* **Ch 14**, 08, 11, 12, 22. Hartlepool Marina **Ch 80, M** H24. ☎ 01429 865744.

SEAHAM
HM **Ch 12**, M-F 0800-1700. ☎ 0191 5161700.

SUNDERLAND
Hbr Radio **Ch 14** (H24). Marina **Ch 80, M**. ☎ 0191 5144721.

RIVER TYNE
Tyne VTS **Ch 12**, 08, 11, inc Info service.
Royal Quays Marina **Ch 80**. ☎ 0191 2728282.
St Peter's Marina **Ch 80**. ☎ 0191 2654472.

BLYTH
Port control **Ch 12**, 11. ☎ 01670 352066. Marina ☎ 01670 353636 (R Northumberland YC).

WARKWORTH HARBOUR (Amble)
HM Ch 16, work **Ch 14**. ☎ 01665 710306. Marina **Ch 80**, ☎ 01665 712168.

BERWICK-UPON-TWEED
HM **Ch 12**, M-F 0800-1700. ☎ 01289 307404.

SCOTLAND
EYEMOUTH HM **Ch 12**, 06 HO. ☎ 01890 750223.

FIRTH OF FORTH
Forth Navigation **Ch 71**; may work 12, 20.
PORT EDGAR Marina **Ch 80, M**. ☎ 0131 3313330.
GRANTON, Royal Forth YC, Call *Boswell* **Ch M**. ☎ 0131 5523006.
GRANGEMOUTH Docks **Ch 14**. ☎ 01324 498566.
FORTH & CLYDE CANAL *Carron Sea Lock* **Ch 74**. ☎ 01324 483034.
METHIL Docks **Ch 14**. ☎ 01324 498585.
ANSTRUTHER Ch 11. ☎ 01333 310836.
DUNDEE *Harbour Radio* **Ch 12**. ☎ 01382 224121.
Royal Tay YC Ch M. ☎ 01382 477516.

PERTH *Perth Harbour* **Ch 09**. ☎ 01738 624056.
ARBROATH *Port Control* **Ch 11**. ☎ 01241 872166.
MONTROSE *Port Control* **Ch 12**. ☎ 01674 672302.
STONEHAVEN HM **Ch 11**. ☎ 01569 762741.
ABERDEEN VTS **Ch 12**, ☎ 01224 597000.
PETERHEAD *Peterhead Hbrs* **Ch 14** for cl'nce to enter/exit. Marina ☎ 01779 477868.
FRASERBURGH Ch 12 H24, ☎ 01346 515858.
MACDUFF Ch 12 H24, ☎ 01261 832236.
BANFF Ch 12, ☎ 01261 815544.
WHITEHILLS *Whitehills Hbr Radio* **Ch 14**, ☎ 01261 861291.
BUCKIE Ch 12, 16 (H24), ☎ 01542 831700.

LOSSIEMOUTH
HM **Ch 12** 0700-1700. Marina, ☎ 01343 813066.

HOPEMAN and BURGHEAD
Same HM: *Burghead Radio* **Ch 14** HX, ☎ 01343 835337.

NAIRN HM/Marina ☎ 01667 454330. No VHF.

INVERNESS
HM **Ch 12**, M-Fri 0900-1700; Tel code 01463: ☎ 715715.
Clachnaharry Sealock **Ch 74**, ☎ 713896. HW ±4.
Inverness Marina **Ch 12**.
Seaport Marina ☎ 239745.
Caley Marina ☎ 236539.

HELMSDALE Ch 13, ☎ 01431 821692.
WICK Ch 14 HX, ☎ 01955 602030.

SCRABSTER
HM **Ch 12** H24. Call on arr/dep, ☎ 01847 892779.

ORKNEY HARBOURS NAVIGATION SERVICE
Orkney Harbour Radio **Ch 09 11 12**
Stromness HM **Ch 14** M-Fri 0900-1700; Tel code 01856: ☎ 850744. Marina, ☎ 465825.
Kirkwall *Hbr Radio* **Ch 14**, ☎ 872292. M-Fri, 0800-1700.
Westray Pier, *Pierowall Hbr* **Ch 14** when vessel expected. ☎ 01857 677216.

SHETLAND
Lerwick Hbr Radio **Ch 12** ☎ 01595 692991.
Scalloway Hbr Radio **Ch 09, 12**, M-F 0700-1800, Sat 0900-1230. Piermaster ☎ 01595 880574.
Sullom Voe VTS **Ch 14** for tfc info, weather & radar assistance on request. ☎ 01806 242551.
Balta Sound Harbour **Ch 16, 20** HO

OUTER HEBRIDES
STORNOWAY HM **Ch 12** H24, ☎ 01851 702688.
Loch Maddy, N Uist Ch 12, ☎ 01876 500337.
St Kilda, *Kilda Radio* **Ch 16**, ☎ 01870 604406.

MAINLAND
Kinlochbervie Ch 14 HX, ☎ 01971 521235.
Loch Inver Ch 09 HX, ☎ 01571 844247.

ULLAPOOL Ch 14, ☎ 01854 612724.

Loch Gairloch Hbr Ch 16, ☎ 01445 712140.

ISLE OF SKYE
Portree Ch 12 (occas), ☎ 01478 612926.

Kyle Akin Ch 11, ☎ 01599 534167.

KYLE OF LOCH ALSH Ch 11, ☎ 01599 534589.

Mallaig Ch 09 HO, ☎ 01687 462154.

Tiree, Gott Bay Pier, Ch 31, ☎ 01879 230337.

Coll, Arinagour Pier, Ch 31, ☎ 01879 230347.

L Sunart, Salen Bay, Ch 16, ☎ 01967 431333.

ISLAND OF MULL
Tobermory, Ch 12, M HJ, ☎ 01688 302017.

Loch Lathaich; Sound of Iona; Craignure Pier.

Corpach basin & lock/Caledonian Canal Ch 74, ☎ 01397 772249.

DUNSTAFFNAGE Marina, Ch M, ☎ 01631 566555.

Oban *North Bay* Ch 12. Marina, ☎ 01631 565333.

L Melfort, Kilmelford Haven, Ch M, ☎ 01852 200248.

L Shuna, Craobh Marina, Ch M, ☎ 01852 500222.

L Craignish, Ardfern Ch 80, M, ☎ 01852 500247.

CRINAN CANAL, Ch 74. BWB, ☎ 01546 603210.

Islay, Port Ellen, ☎ 01496 300301; no VHF.

Tarbert, Loch Fyne Ch 14, ☎ 01880 820344.

Portavadie Marina Ch 80, ☎ 01700 811075.

CAMPBELTOWN Ch 12, 13, ☎ 01586 552552.

ROTHESAY, Bute Ch 12, ☎ 01700 500630.

LARGS Yacht Haven Ch 80, M, ☎ 01475 675333.

KIP Marina Ch 80, M, ☎ 01475 521485.

HOLY LOCH Marina Ch 80, M, ☎ 01369 701800.

RHU Marina Ch 80, M, ☎ 01436 820238.

ARDROSSAN Marina Ch 80, M, ☎ 01294 607077.

IRVINE HM/Bridge Ch 12, ☎ 01292 487286.

TROON Ch 14. Marina Ch 80, M, ☎ 01294 315553.

GIRVAN HM Ch 12, ☎ 01465 713648.

KIRKCUDBRIGHT HM Ch 12, ☎ 01557 331135.

ENGLAND W COAST AND WALES

MARYPORT Marina Ch 80, ☎ 01900 814431.

WORKINGTON HM Ch 14, ☎ 01900 602301.

WHITEHAVEN Marina Ch 12, ☎ 01946 692435.

ISLE OF MAN (Tel code 01624) If unable to contact IoM hbrs below, call Douglas.

Douglas *Hbr Control* Ch 12 H24.

Port St Mary HM Ch 12 HJ, ☎ 833205.

Peel HM Ch 12 HJ, ☎ 842338.

Ramsey HM Ch 12 0800-1600. HO, ☎ 812245.

MAINLAND
GLASSON DOCK Marina Ch 69, ☎ 01524 751491.

FLEETWOOD *Fleetwood Dock Radio* (HW±2) Ch 12 for Marina, ☎ 01253 879062.

PRESTON Lock *Riversway* Ch 14. Marina Ch 80, ☎ 01772 733595.

LIVERPOOL *Mersey Radio* Ch 12. Info Ch 09. Radar Ch 18. Liverpool Marina (Brunswick Dock) Ch M, ☎ 0151 7076777. Albert Dock Ch M, ☎ 0151 7096558; access via Canning Dock lock.

CONWY HM Ch 14. Marinas, both Ch 80: Conwy, ☎ 01492 593000. Deganwy 576888.

MENAI STRAIT and ANGLESEY
Beaumaris/Menai HM Ch 69, ☎ 01248 712312.

Caernarfon, HM & Victoria Dock Ch 80, ☎ 01286 672118. Mon-Fri: 0900-1700 Sat: 0900-1200

HOLYHEAD *Port Control* Ch 14, ☎ 01407 606700. Marina 764242.

MAINLAND
PWLLHELI, HM Ch 12. Marina Ch 80, M, ☎ 01758 704081.

PORTHMADOG *Hbr* Ch 12, ☎ 01766 512927.

BARMOUTH HM *Barmouth Hbr* Ch 12, ☎ 01341 280671.

ABERDOVEY *Aberdovey Hbr* Ch 12, ☎ 01654 767626.

ABERYSTWYTH HM Ch 14. Marina Ch 80, ☎ 01970 611422.

FISHGUARD HM Ch 14, ☎ 01348 873369.

MILFORD HAVEN Monitor *Port Control* (and *Patrol launch*) Ch 12, whilst under way. Milford Docks Pierhead Ch 18. Milford Dock Marina Ch 14, ☎ 01646 696312. Neyland Yacht Haven Ch 80, M, ☎ 01646 601601.

Tenby Ch 80, ☎ 01834 842717.

Saundersfoot Ch 11

SWANSEA
Tawe Lock Ch 18. Marina Ch 80, ☎ 01792 470310.

BARRY *Barry Radio* Ch 11. HM ☎ 01446 732665.

CARDIFF *Cardiff Radio* Ch 14. Barrage control Ch 18. Penarth Marina Ch 80, ☎ 02920 705021.

NEWPORT HM Ch 71, ☎ 0870 6096699.

SHARPNESS *Sharpness Radio* Ch 13 for lock. Marina, ☎ 01453 811476. Canal Ch 74

BRISTOL *Bristol VTS* Ch 12 with intentions. *City Docks Radio* Ch 14 (low power) to confirm. *Bristol Floating Hbr* Ch 73. Bristol Marina Ch 80, ☎ 0117 9213198.

PORTISHEAD Marina Ch 80, ☎ 0198 4631264.

BURNHAM-ON-SEA HM Ch 08, ☎ 01938 822666.

WATCHET Marina **Marina Ch 80**, ☎ 01984 631264.

COMMUNICATIONS

ILFRACOMBE HM **Ch 80, ☎** 01271 862108.

APPLEDORE-BIDEFORD HM *Two Rivers* **Ch 12,** Appledore ☎ 01237 474569.

BUDE HM **Ch 12, ☎** 01288 353111.

PADSTOW HM **Ch 12, ☎** 01841 532239.

ST IVES HM **Ch 12, ☎** 01736 795018.

IRELAND

ROSSAVEEL Ch 12, ☎ 091 572108.

GALWAY, HM **Ch 12, ☎** 091 561874.

SHANNON ESTUARY *Shannon Ports Radio* **Ch 11** (HO), ☎ 087 2560427.

KILRUSH Marina Ch 80, ☎ 06590 52072.

LIMERICK HBR Ch 12 13, ☎ 061 315377.

MFENIT HM **Ch 14, M, ☎** 066 7136231.

DINGLE HM **Ch 14** (no calls req'd), ☎ 066 9151629.

CAHERSIVEEN (Valentia) Marina Ch 80, ☎ 066 9472777.

BANTRY BAY, Lawrence Cove Marina **Ch M, ☎** 027 75044.

CASTLETOWN BEARHAVEN ⚓, ☎ 027 70220.

CROOKHAVEN ⚓, ☎ 028 35319.

SCHULL ⚓, mobile ☎ 086 1039105.

BALTIMORE Ch 09, mobile 087 2351485.

GLANDORE HM **Ch 06, ☎** 028 34737.

COURTMACSHERRY HM ☎ 08610 40812.

KINSALE HM **Ch 14 ☎** 021 4772503. Marinas **Ch M:** KYC ☎ 4772196. Castlepark ☎ 4774959.

CORK *Cork Hbr Radio* **Ch 12,** 14 H24. HM ☎ 021 4273125. Marinas **Ch M:** Crosshaven ☎ 4831161. Salve ☎ 4831145. Royal Cork YC ☎ 4831023. East Ferry ☎ 4813390.

YOUGHAL HM/Pilots **Ch 14** Mon-Fri 0900-1700 and when ships expected. ☎ 024 92577.

DUNMORE EAST HM/Pilots **Ch 14 ☎** 051 383166.

WATERFORD & NEW ROSS Ch 12, 14. ☎ 051 873501.

KILMORE QUAY Ch 09. Marina, ☎ 053 29955.

ROSSLARE HM **Ch 12** H24, ☎ 053 33114.

WEXFORD Hbr Boat club. **Ch 16, ☎** 053 22039.

ARKLOW HM **Ch 12, ☎** 0402 32466. Marina 39901.

WICKLOW HM **Ch 14** 12, ☎ 0404 67455.

DUN LAOGHAIRE HM **Ch 14, ☎** 01 2801130. YCs & Marina **Ch M:** Marina 2020040. National 2805725. R. St George 2801811. R. Irish 2809452. DL Motor YC 2801371.

DUBLIN HM and VTS *Dublin VTS* **Ch 12,** 13. Poolbeg Marina **Ch M, ☎** 01 6689983. Lifting

bridge *Eastlink* **Ch 12, 13.** City moorings, ☎ 01 8183300.

HOWTH HM **Ch 11.** Marina Ch M, 80, ☎ 01 8392777.

MALAHIDE Marina **Ch 80, M, ☎** 01 8454129.

CARLINGFORDFORD LOUGH
Carlingford Marina Ch M, ☎ 042 93730739.

Warrenpoint Ch 12, ☎ 028 41752878.

Kilkeel Ch 12, ☎ 028 41762287.

ARDGLASS (Phennick Cove) Marina **Ch M, 80, ☎** 028 44842332.

STRANGFORD LOUGH
HM **Ch 12 14, ☎** 028 44881637.

Portaferry Marina Ch 80, M, ☎ 07703 209780.

Donaghadee Copelands Marina, ☎ 028 91882184.

BELFAST VTS *Belfast Hbr Radio* **Ch 12. Marinas Ch 80, M:** Carrickfergus, ☎ 028 93366666. Bangor, ☎ 028 91453217.

LARNE *Port Control* **Ch 14,** 11.

Glenarm HM/Marina, mobile ☎ 07703 606763.

Ballycastle HM/Marina, mob ☎ 07803 505084.

PORTRUSH HM **Ch 12, ☎** 028 70822307.

COLERAINE HM **Ch 12.** Marina, ☎ 028 70832086.

LONDONDERRY *Hbr radio* **Ch 14, ☎** 028 71860555.

L SWILLY Fahan Marina, ☎ 074 9360008.

KILLYBEGS HM **Ch 14, ☎** 07497 31032.

Burton Port HM **Ch 06, 12, 14, ☎** 075 42155.

SLIGO HM **Ch 12,** 14, ☎ 071 9153819.

DENMARK

Skagen HM **Ch 12** 13 HX, ☎ 98 941346.

Hirtshals HM **Ch 12** 13 HX, ☎ 98 941422.

Torup Strand HM **Ch 12** 13 HX.

Hanstholm HM **Ch 12** 13 HX, ☎ 97 961833.

THYBORØN HM **Ch 12** 13 H24, ☎ 97 831188.

Thisted (Limfjord) Ch 12 13 HX, ☎ 97 911400.

Torsminde HM **Ch 12** 13, ☎ 24 233345.

Hvide Sande HM **Ch 12** HX, ☎ 97 311633.

ESBJERG *Hbr Control* **Ch 12** 13 14 H24, ☎ 75 124000. Fanø HM, ☎ 75 163100.

Rømø HM **Ch 10, 12, 13** HX, ☎ 74 755245.

GERMANY

HELGOLAND HM **Ch 67, ☎** 04725 81593583.
May-Aug Mon-Thu 0700-1200, 1300-2000. Fri-Sun 0700-1200.
Sep-Apr Mon-Thu 0700-1200, 1300-1600. Fri 0700-1200.

List HM **Ch 11**, ☎ 046 51870374.
Hörnum HM **67**, ☎ 046 51881027.
Wyk HM **Ch 11**, ☎ 046 81500430.
Pellworm HM **Ch 11**, ☎ 048 44726.
Husum HM **Ch 11**, ☎ 048 16670.
R. Eider sealock **Ch 14**, ☎ 04833 4535211.
Büsum HM **Ch 11**, ☎ 048 413607.

INNER DEUTSCHE BUCHT (GERMAN BIGHT)
VTS, Eastern part **Ch 80**, ☎ 04421 489282.
VTS, Western part **Ch 79**

BRUNSBÜTTEL HM **Ch 06**, ☎ 04852 88418.

NORD-OSTSEE KANAL (KIEL CANAL)
VTS Canal I   **Ch 13**, ☎ 04852 885371.
VTS Canal II   **Ch 02**, ☎ 04852 885369.
VTS Canal III   **Ch 03**, ☎ 0431 3603456.
VTS Canal IV   **Ch 12**, ☎ 0431 3603465.
Brieholz, **Ch 73**
Ostermoor, **Ch 73**

RIVER ELBE
CUXHAVEN HM **Ch 69** HX, ☎ 04721 500150.
Cuxhaven Marina, ☎ 37363. YC Marina, ☎ 34111.
R. Stör Lock **Ch 09** Bridge opens on request.
Glückstadt HM **Ch 08**, ☎ 04124 913200.

HAMBURG Port HM **Ch 12**, ☎ 040 7411540.
VTS Hamburg Port Traffic **Ch 13, 14, 74**. Wedel
Yacht Hbr, ☎ 040 1034438. City Sporthafen, ☎
040 364297.

BREMERHAVEN Weser VTS **Ch 22**. Port **Ch 12**, ☎
0471 59613401. Locks **Ch 69, 70**. Marinas Weser YC,
☎ 23531. NYC, ☎ 77555. WVW, ☎ 73268.

BREMEN Port Radio **Ch 03**, ☎ 0421 3618504.

JADE VTS Jade Traffic **Ch 63, 20**.

WILHEMSHAVEN
Port **Ch 11**, ☎ 04421 154580. Sealock **Ch 13**.
Bridges **Ch 11**. Marinas Nassauhafen, ☎ 41439.
Wiking Sportsboothafen, ☎ 41301.

HOOKSIEL Ch 63. Alterhafen Marina.

WANGEROOGE HM **Ch 17**, ☎ 04469 1322. Marina,
☎ 942126.

SPIEKEROOG HM No VHF, ☎ 04976 9193133.

DORNUMER-ACCUMERSIEL HM No VHF, ☎ 04933
2510. YC ☎ 2240.

LANGEOOG HM **Ch 17**, ☎ 04972 301.

NORDERNEY HM **Ch 17**, ☎ 04932 82826.

NORDDEICH HM **Ch 17**, ☎ 04931 81317.

BORKUM HM **Ch 14**, ☎ 04922 81317.

EMS VTS Ems Traffic **Ch 15, 18, 20, 21**

EMDEN HM & locks **Ch 13**, ☎ 04921 897260.
YC Marina, ☎ 997147. Mariners' Club, ☎ 953795.
City Marina, ☎ 8907211.

NETHERLANDS
DELFZIJL/EEMSHAVEN VTS is not compulsory
for leisure craft. **Delfzijl Radar** Ch 03 gives radar
assistance when visibility falls below 2000m.
Eemshaven Radar Ch 01. **Port Control** Ch 66
broadcasts info every even H+10.

DELFZIJL HBR. HM Ch 14; ☎ 0596 640400. **Locks**
Ch 26, M-Sat H24, Sun & hols on request; ☎
693293. **Bridges:** Weiwerder Ch 11. Heemskes &
Handelshaven Ch 14. **Farmsumerhaven**, Ch 66,
☎ 640494.

EEMSHAVEN HM Ch 14; ☎ 516142. Radar Ch 19.

LAUWERSOOG. HM, Havendienst, Ch 09; ☎ 0519
39023. Mon 0000-1700; Tu-Wed 0800-1700; Th-Sat
0700-1500.

TERSCHELLING VTS Call/monitor Brandaris Ch 02;
☎ 0562 443100. **Marina**, Ch 31; ☎ 443337.

VLIELAND. HM Ch 12. **Marina**, Ch 31; ☎ 0562
451729.

HARLINGEN HM Ch 11 (not on Sun); ☎ 0517
413423. **Locks** Ch 22.

OUDESCHILD HM Ch 12; ☎ 0222 312710. **Marina**,
Ch 31; ☎ 0222 321227. See Den Helder VTS.

DEN HELDER VTS. Monitor Tfc Centre Ch 62, H24;
broadcasts info and gives radar surveillance. **PORT
CONTROL** Ch 14; ☎ 0223 62770. **Marina** ☎ 652645.
Bridge: Moormanbrug Ch 18. **Lock:** Koopvaarders
Ch 22.

IJSSELMEER Den Oever lock Ch 20, ☎ 0227
511383. **Port** Ch 11, ☎ 511303. Marina ☎ 511789.
Kornwerderzand lock Ch 18, ☎ 0517 57441.

ENKHUIZEN Naviduct (also Krabbersgat) Ch 22.

IJMUIDEN VTS. Traffic Centre Ch 07, Roads (W
of IJmuiden buoy). Thence **Port Control** Ch 61 to
Noordzeesluizen (locks).
Seaport Marina Ch 75, ☎ 0255 560300.

NORDZEEKANAAL VTS
Noordzeesluizen. Sluis IJmuiden Ch 22.
Noordzeekanaal. Ch 03, from locks to km 11·2.

AMSTERDAM
Port Control Ch 68 (Km 11·2 to Oranjesluisen).
Port Info Ch 14. Access to Standing Mast route:
Westerkeersluis Ch 22. **Haarlem hbr** Ch 18.
Marinas: Sixhaven, ☎ 020 6329429. **WV Aeolus**,
☎ 6360791. **Aquadam**, ☎ 6320616.
Access to Markermeer: **Oranjesluisen** Ch 18.

SCHEVENINGEN. Traffic Centre & Port Ch 21; ☎
070 3527711. **Marina** Ch 31; ☎ 070 3520017.

HOEK VAN HOLLAND ROADSTEAD
To cross the mouth of the Maas, call Maas Entrance
Ch 03, with vessel's name, position and course.
Follow a track close W of a line joining buoys MV,
MVN and Indusbank N. See VTS Chart No 4. Whilst
crossing, maintain continuous listening watch and
keep a very sharp lookout.

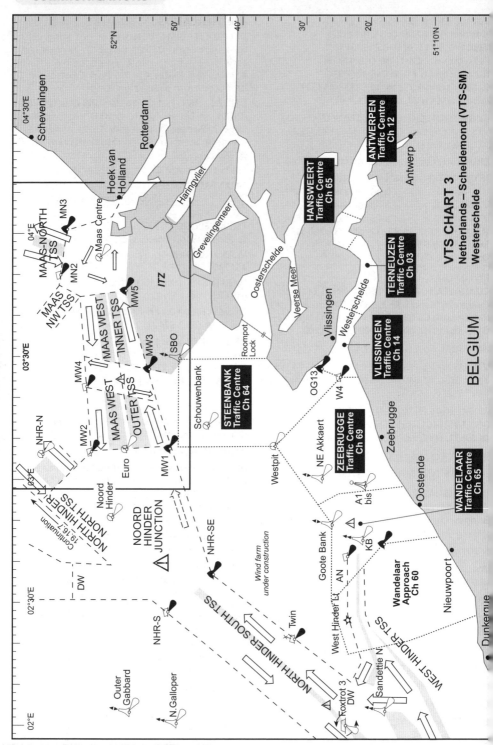

VTS CHART 4
Netherlands – Approaches to Nieuwe Waterweg

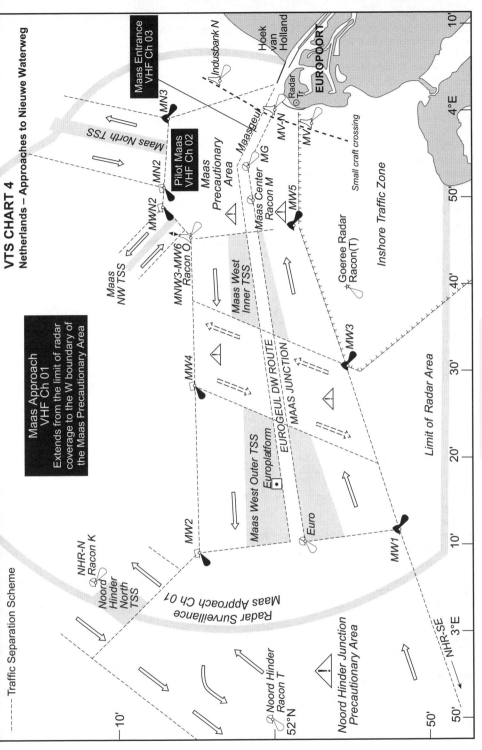

- - - - Traffic Separation Scheme

Maas Entrance
VHF Ch 03

Maas North TSS

Pilot Maas
VHF Ch 02

Maas
Precautionary
Area

Maas Approach
VHF Ch 01
Extends from the limit of radar
coverage to the W boundary of
the Maas Precautionary Area

Maas
NW TSS

MNW2

MN2

MN3

MWN2

MNW3-MW6
Racon O

Maas West
Inner TSS

Maas Center
Racon M   MG

MW5

MV-N

MV-L

Radar
Tr.

Hoek
van
Holland

Indusbank N

EUROPORT

Small craft crossing

Goeree Radar
Racon(T)

Inshore Traffic Zone

MW3

EUROGEUL DW ROUTE

MAAS JUNCTION

Maas West Outer TSS

Europlatform

MW4

MW2

Euro

MW1

Limit of Radar Area

NHR-N
Racon K

Noord
Hinder
North
TSS

Radar Surveillance
Maas Approach Ch 01

Noord Hinder
Racon T
52°N

Noord Hinder Junction
Precautionary Area

NHR-SE

3°E

4°E

10' — 50'

COMMUNICATIONS

99

COMMUNICATIONS

NIEUWE WATERWEG VTS.
Outer areas as shown on VTS Charts 3 & 4:
Maas Approach Ch 01. **Pilot Maas** Ch 02. **Maas Entrance** Ch 03.
HCC *Central Traffic Control* Ch 14 19.
Report to/monitor continuously the relevant Tfc Centre, as listed from seaward to City Marina:
Rozenburg Ch 65; Maassluis Ch 80; Botlek Ch 61; Eemhaven Ch 63; Waalhaven Ch 60; Maasbruggen Ch 81.

ROTTERDAM Rotterdam Tfc Centre Ch 11. **Hbr Coordination Centre** (HCC) Ch 19.
Marinas/Yacht hbrs: Vlaardingen ☎ 010 4344700; Lock Ch 20. **Spuihaven** ☎ 4667765. Coolhaven ☎ 4738614. Veerhaven ☎ 4365446. **City Marina** ☎ 0187 48540986, via Erasmus bridge Ch 18.

STELLENDAM Haringvliet lock & lifting bridge:
Goereese Sluis Ch 20, ☎ 0187 497350. Opening hrs: M-F 0000-2200. 1 Nov - 1 Apr: Sat 0800-2200; Sun 0800-1000, 1600-1800. 1 Apr - 1 Nov: Sat & Sun 0800-2000. **Marina** Ch 31, ☎ 493769.

OOSTERSCHELDE
Lock *Roompotsluis* Ch 18, ☎ 0111 659265. Opening hours: Mon & Thu, 0000-2200; Tue & Sun, 0600-0000; Wed H24; Fri & Sat: 0600-2200. **Roompot Marina** Ch 31.

WESTERSCHELDE VTS
See VTS Chart No 3. Reporting is not compulsory for leisure craft, but they should monitor the VHF channel for the appropriate Traffic Area. Each Traffic Area is controlled by a Traffic Centre and bounded by buoys. *In emergency call the relevant Traffic Centre: Ch 67.*
Tfc Centre Steenbank & Radar Ch 64.
Tfc Centre Vlissingen Ch 14. **Radar** Ch 21. **Info broadcast** Ch 14 H+55.
Tfc Centre Terneuzen & Radar Ch 03. **Info broadcast** Ch 11 H+00.
Tfc Centre Hansweert Ch 65.
Antwerpen, Zeebrugge and Wandelaar Traffic Areas are listed under Belgium.
VLISSINGEN De Ruyter Marina no VHF, ☎ 0118 414498, mobile 06 5353 7181. *Flushing Port Control* Ch 09. **Sealocks & canal bridge** Ch 22. **VVW Schelde Marina** Ch 14, ☎ 465912.
BRESKENS Marina, Ch 31, ☎ 0117 381902.
TERNEUZEN Port control Ch 11. **Marina**, ☎ 0115 697089. **Oostsluis** (E lock, small craft) Ch 18.

BELGIUM

ANTWERPEN, Tfc Centre Zandvliet Ch 12. **Info broadcast** Ch 12 H+35.

ANTWERPEN PORT Calling and safety Ch 74. **Royerssluis** Ch 22. **Siberia & Londen bridges** Ch 62. **Willemdok Marina** Ch 23, ☎ 03 2315066. **Linkeroever Marina** Ch 09, ☎ 03 2190895.

ZEEBRUGGE Tfc Centre Zeebrugge Ch 69. **Inf** broadcasts Ch 69 H+15.

ZEEBRUGGE Port Control Ch 71 H24, ☎ 05(546867. **Marina** ☎ 544903. **E lock** Ch 68.

BLANKENBERGE Marinas: VNZ, ☎ 050 429150, 8 **SYCB,** ☎ 411420, Ch 31. **VVW** ☎ 417536, Ch 23.

WANDELAAR Tfc Centre Wandelaar Ch 65 **Wandelaar Approach** Ch 60.

OOSTENDE Port Control Ch 09 H24, ☎ 059 566313 Mercator lock, ☎ 321669, & marina, ☎ 705762 Ch 14 H24. **Marinas: RNSYC,** ☎ 505912. RYCO ☎ 321452.

NIEUWPOORT Port HM Ch 09 H24, ☎ 058 233000 **Marinas: KYCN,** Ch 23, ☎ 234413. **WSKLM,** Ch 23 ☎ 5233641. **VVW-N,** Ch 08, ☎ 235232.

NORTH FRANCE

DUNKERQUE Port & VTS Ch 73, H24. The VTS doe: not affect leisure craft, but monitor Ch 73. **Marina:** Ch 09: Grande Large ☎ 03.28.63.23.00. YCMN ☎ 03.28.66.79.90. **Trystram lock** Ch 73.

GRAVELINES HM/Marina, Ch 09, ☎ 03.28.23.19.45.

CALAIS VTS, Port Control & Marina Ch 17 H24, ☎ 03.21.34.55.23.

BOULOGNE Boulogne Port, ☎ 03.21.31.52.43, Ch 12, H24. **Marina** Ch 09, ☎ 06.76.98.74.98.

LE TOUQUET/ÉTAPLES-SUR-MER Ch 09, 77. **Étaples Marina,** ☎ 03.21.84.54.03.

LE TRÉPORT Marina/lock Ch 12, 72, ☎ 02.35.50.63.06

DIEPPE Port HM Ch 12, HO. **Marina** Ch 09, ☎ 02.35.40.19.79.

ST VALÉRY-EN-CAUX Entry gate & marina Ch 09 ☎ 02.35.97.01.30.

FÉCAMP Port HM, Ch 10, **12,** ☎ 02.35.28.25.53 **Marina & Bérigny lock,** Ch 09, ☎ 02.35.28.13.58.

LE HAVRE Control Tower Ch **12,** 20. **Port Ops** Ch 67, 69. **Marina,** Ch 09, ☎ 02.35.21.23.95.

LA SEINE VTS Rouen Port Control Ch 73 (Estuary), 68 (River). **Honfleur radar** Ch 15, 19, **73.**

HONFLEUR HM Ch **17,** 73 HX, ☎ 02.31.14.61.09 **Lock,** ☎ 02.31.98.72.82, **& Bridge** Ch 17 H24.

ROUEN Port HM Ch **73,** 68 H24. **Halte Nautique,** ☎ 02.32.08.31.40.

ROUEN – PARIS, LOCKS Amfreville Ch 18. **Notre-Dame-de-la-Garenne** Ch 22. **Mericourt** Ch 18. **Andrésy** Ch 22. **Bougival** Ch 22. **Chatou** Ch 18. Suresnes Ch 22.

PARIS-ARSENAL Marina Ch 09, ☎ 01.43.41.39.32.

DEAUVILLE Port Deauville lock, ☎ 02.31.88.95.66; Marina ☎ 02.31.98.30.01, Ch 09 0800-1730. **Port Morny** gate ☎ 02.31.88.57.89; Marina, Ch 09, ☎ 02.31.98.50.40.

DIVES-SUR-MER. Marina Ch 09, ☎ 02.31.24.48.00.

OUISTREHAM Port 74; lock Ch 12, ☎ 02.31.36.22.00. Marina Ch 09, ☎ 02.31.96.91.37. Canal Ch 68. CAEN HM/Marina Ch 74, ☎ 02.31.95.24.47.

COURSEULLES-SUR-MER Marina Ch 09, ☎ 02.31.37.51.69.

PORT-EN-BESSIN HM, ☎ 02.31.21.70.49. Gate/bridge Ch 18, ☎ 02.31.21.71.77.

GRANDCAMP Marina Ch 09, ☎ 02.31.22.63.16.

CARENTAN Lock Ch 09, ☎ 02.33.71.10.85. Marina Ch 09, ☎ 02.33.42.24.44.

ST VAAST-LA-HOUGUE Marina Ch 09, ☎ 02.33.21.61.00.

BARFLEUR HM, ☎ 02.33.54.08.29. No VHF.

CHERBOURG VTS (yachts to monitor) Vigie du Homet Ch 12 H24. Marina Chantereyne Ch 09, ☎ 02.33.87.65.70. Gate (B du Commerce) Ch 06.

OMONVILLE-LA-ROGUE No VHF/Tel. 6 W ⚓s.

DIÉLETTE Marina Ch 09, ☎ 02.33.53.68.78.

CARTERET Marina Ch 09, ☎ 02.33.04.70.84.

PORTBAIL Yacht hbr Ch 09, ☎ 02.33.04.83.48.

GRANVILLE Port HM Ch 12. Marina Ch 09, ☎ 02.33.50.20.06.

ST MALO Port HM Ch 12 H24. Marinas Ch 09: Bas Sablons, ☎ 02.99.81.71.34. Bassin Vauban, ☎ 02.99.56.51.91. DINARD, ☎ 02.99.46.65.55.

R RANCE barrage lock Ch 13, ☎ 02.99.46.21.87. Chatelier lock Ch 14, ☎ 02.99.39.55.66.

ST CAST-LE-GUILDO Marina ☎ 02 96 81 04 43

DAHOUËT Marina Ch 09, ☎ 02.96.72.82.85.

LE LÉGUÉ HM/Marina Ch 12, ☎ 02.96.77.49.85.

BINIC Marina Ch 09, ☎ 02.96.73.61.86.

ST QUAY-PORTRIEUX Marina ☎ 02.96.70.81.30. Ch 09.

PAIMPOL Lock/Marina Ch 09, ☎ 02.96.20.47.65.

LÉZARDRIEUX Marina Ch 09, ☎ 02.96.20.14.22.

PONTRIEUX Lock/Marina Ch 12, ☎ 02.96.95.34.87.

TRÉGUIER Marina Ch 09, ☎ 02.96.92.42.37.

PERROS-GUIREC Marina Ch 09, ☎ 02.96.49.80.50.

PLOUMANAC'H Marina Ch 09, ☎ 02.96.91.44.31.

TRÉBEURDEN Marina Ch 09, ☎ 02.96.23.64.00.

MORLAIX Marina Ch 09, ☎ 02.98.62.13.14.

ROSCOFF HM/S Basin Ch 09, ☎ 02.98.69.76.37.

BLOSCON Ferry Port Ch 12, ☎ 02.98.61.27.84.

L'ABERWRAC'H Marina Ch 09, ☎ 02.98.04.91.62.

CHANNEL ISLANDS

ALDERNEY, Braye Hbr, Alderney Radio Ch 74, ☎ 01481 822620. If no contact, try St Peter Port Radio.

GUERNSEY Beaucette Marina, Ch 80, ☎ 01481 245000. St Sampson Ch 12 H24 via St Peter Port

Control Ch 12 H24, ☎ 720229.

Victoria Marina Ch M, 80 HO, ☎ 725987. St Peter Port Radio Ch 20 H24 (only for link calls).

JERSEY St Helier Port Control Ch 14 H24; 8M max range. St Helier Marina, ☎ 01534 885508, has no VHF; call Ch 14 only if essential.

Gorey Ch 74, ☎ 853616.

WEST FRANCE

BREST VTS Brest Port Ch 08 H24. Marina Ch 09, ☎ 02.98.02.20.02.

CAMARET Marina Ch 09, ☎ 02.98.27.95.99.

MORGAT Marina Ch 09, ☎ 02.98.27.01.97.

DOUARNENEZ HM Ch 12. Marinas Ch 09: Tréboul ☎ 02.98.74.02.56; Port Rhu ☎ 02.98.92.00.67.

AUDIERNE No VHF. Marina ☎ 02.98.74.04.93. Ste Evette ☎ 02.98.70.00.28.

LOCTUDY Marina Ch 09, ☎ 02.98.87.51.36.

BENODÉT Marinas Ch 09: Penfoul ☎ 02.98.57.05.78. Ste Marine ☎ 02.98.56.38.72.

PORT-LA-FORÊT Marina Ch 09, ☎ 02.98.56.98.45.

CONCARNEAU Marina Ch 09, ☎ 02.98.97.57.96.

LORIENT Port Ch 12. Marinas Ch 09: Ban-Gâvres ☎ 02.97.65.48.25. Kernével ☎ 02.97.65.48.25. Port Louis ☎ 02.97.83.59.55. Locmiquélic ☎ 02.97.33.59.51. Lorient ☎ 02.97.21.10.14.

PORT TUDY Marina Ch 09, ☎ 02.97.86.54.62.

RIVER ÉTEL Marina Ch 13, ☎ 02.97.55.46.62.

BELLE ILE Sauzon HM Ch 09, ☎ 02.97.31.63.40. Le Palais HM Ch 09, ☎ 02.97.31.42.90.

PORT HALIGUEN Marina Ch 09, ☎ 02.97.50.20.56.

LA TRINITÉ Marina Ch 09, ☎ 02.97.55.71.49.

VANNES Marina Ch 09, ☎ 02.97.54.16.08.

CROUESTY Marina Ch 09, ☎ 02.97.53.73.33.

LA VILAINE Arzal Marina Ch 09, ☎ 02.97.45.02.97.

PIRIAC Marina Ch 09, ☎ 02.40.23.52.32.

LA TURBALLE Marina Ch 09, ☎ 02.40.23.41.65.

LE CROISIC Marina Ch 09, ☎ 02.40.23.10.95.

LE POULIGUEN Marina Ch 09, ☎ 02.40.11.97.97.

PORNICHET Marina Ch 09, ☎ 02.40.61.03.20.

ST-NAZAIRE VTS Loire Ports Control Ch 14. Port HM Ch 14, ☎ 02.40.91.03.17.

PORNIC Marina Ch 09, ☎ 02.40.82.05.40.

L'HERBAUDIÈRE Marina Ch 09, ☎ 02.51.39.05.05.

PORT JOINVILLE Marina Ch 09, ☎ 02.51.58.38.11.

ST GILLES-CROIX-DE-VIE Marina Ch 09, ☎ 02.51.55.30.83.

LES SABLES D'OLONNE Port HM Ch 12, ☎ 02.51.95.11.79. Marina Ch 09, ☎ 02.51.32.51.16.

BOURGENAY Marina Ch 09, ☎ 02.51.22.20.36.

ILE DE RÉ Ars-en-Ré Ch 09, ☎ 05.46.29.08.52. St Martin Ch 09, ☎ 05.46.09.26.69.

COMMUNICATIONS

LA ROCHELLE Marinas Ch 09: **Port des Minimes** ☎ 05.46.44.41.20. **Vieux Port** ☎ 05.46.41.32.05.

ROCHEFORT Marina Ch 09, ☎ 05.46.83.99.06.

ILE D'OLÉRON St Denis Ch 09, ☎ 05.46.47.97.97. **Boyardville** Ch 09, ☎ 05.46.76.48.56.

LA GIRONDE VTS Ch 12 (yachts to monitor). Radar *Bordeaux Port Control* Ch 12 on request. Depths in Gironde broadcast Ch 17 every 5 mins.

ROYAN Marina Ch 09, ☎ 05.46.38.72.22.

PORT-MÉDOC Marina Ch 09, ☎ 05.56.09.69.75.

PAUILLAC Marina Ch 09, ☎ 05.56.59.12.16.

BORDEAUX HM *Bordeaux Traffic* Ch 12, ☎ 05.56.31.58.64. **Bassin 2**, ☎ 05.56.90.59.57.

ARCACHON Marina Ch 09, ☎ 05.56.22.36.75.

CAPBRETON Marina Ch 09, ☎ 05.58.72.21.23.

ANGLET Marina Ch 09, ☎ 05.59.63.05.45.

ST JEAN-DE-LUZ Marina Ch 09, ☎ 05.59.47.26.81.

HENDAYE Marina Ch 09, ☎ 05.59.48.06.10.

N AND NW SPAIN

FUENTERRABIA Marina Ch 09, ☎ 943 641711.

GUETARIA Marina Ch 09, ☎ 943 580959.

ZUMAYA Marina Ch 73, ☎ 943 860938.

BILBAO *Port Control* Ch 12. **Marinas** Ch 09: **Getxo** ☎ 944 912367. **Las Arenas** ☎ 944 637600.

SANTANDER Marina Ch 09, ☎ 942 369288.

GIJON Marina Ch 09, ☎ 985 344543.

CUDILLERO HM/Yacht hbr Ch 27, ☎ 985 591114.

RIBADEO Marina Ch 09, ☎ 982 131444.

VIVERO Marina Ch 09, ☎ 982 570610.

RÍA DE ARES Marina Ch 09, ☎ 981 468787.

RÍA DE BETANZOS Marina Ch 09, ☎ 981 619015.

LA CORUÑA Marina Ch 09, ☎ 981 914142.

RÍA DE CAMARIÑAS Marina Ch 09, ☎ 981 737130.

RÍA DE MUROS HM Muros, ☎ 981 826005. **CN Portosin Marina** Ch 09, ☎ 981 766598.

RÍA DE AROUSA Marinas Ch 09: **Caraminal**, ☎ 981 830970. **Sta Uxia**, ☎ 981 873801. **Vilagarcia**, ☎ 986 511175. **Piedras Negras**, ☎ 986 738430.

RÍA DE PONTEVEDRA Marinas Ch 09: **Sangenxo**, ☎ 986 720517. **Aguete**, ☎ 986 702373. **Combarro**, ☎ 986 778 415.

RÍA DE VIGO VTS *Vigo Traffic* Ch 10. **Marina** Ch 09, ☎ 986 449694.

BAYONA MRCY Ch 06, ☎ 986 385000. **Bayona Marina** Ch 09, ☎ 986 385107.

PORTUGAL

VIANA DO CASTELO Marina Ch 09, ☎ 258 359546.

PÓVOA DE VARZIM Marina Ch 09, ☎ 252 688121.

LEIXÕES Port Ch 11. **Marina** Ch 09, ☎ 229 964895.

AVEIRO Port HM Ch 11, 12, 13, ☎ 234 366250.

FIGUEIRA DA FOZ Marina Ch 09, ☎ 233 402910.

NAZARÉ Marina Ch 09, ☎ 262 561401.

PENICHE Marina Ch 09, ☎ 262 783331.

CASCAIS Marina Ch 09, ☎ 214 824800.

LISBOA VTS *Lisboa Port Control* Ch 74. **Marina Doca de Alcântara** Ch 05, 09, 12, ☎ 213 922048. **Marina Parque das Nações**, ☎ 213 949066.

SESIMBRA Port Ch 11. **Marina** Ch 09, ☎ 212 233451.

SETÚBAL VTS (applies to yachts >15m LOA) *Port Control* Ch 73. **Marina** Ch 09, ☎ 265 452076.

SINES Port Ch 11. **Marina** Ch 09, ☎ 269 860612.

LAGOS Port Ch 11. **Marina** Ch 09, ☎ 282 770210.

PORTIMÃO HM Ch 11. **Marina** Ch 09, ☎ 282 400680.

ALBUFEIRA. Marina Ch 09, ☎ 289 510180.

VILAMOURA. Marina Ch 09, ☎ 289 310560.

FARO ☎ 289 894990; **OLHÃO** ☎ 703160, Ch 11.

VILA REAL DE SANTO ANTÓNIO Port Ch 11. **Marina** Ch 09, ☎ 281 541571.

SW SPAIN

AYAMONTE Marina Ch 09, ☎ 959 321294.

IS CANELA, ☎ 959 479000; **CRISTINA**, ☎ 343501.

MAZAGON Marina Ch 09, ☎ 959 536251.

CHIPIONA Port Ch 12. **Marina** Ch 09, ☎ 956 373844.

SEVILLA Port Ch 12. **Marinas** Ch 09: **Gelves** ☎ 955 761212. **Marina Yachting** ☎ 954 230326. **CN Sevilla** ☎ 954 454777.

CÁDIZ Port *Cádiz Trafico* Ch 74. **Marinas** Ch 09: **Rota** ☎ 956 454777. **Pto Sherry** ☎ 870103. **Pto de Sta Maria** ☎ 852527. **Pto America** ☎ 223666.

SANCTI PETRI Marina Ch 09, ☎ 956 496169.

BARBATE Marina Ch 09, ☎ 956 431907.

TARIFA VTS *Tarifa Traffic* Ch 10, ☎ 956 684757. **Info** Ch 67 (on request) inc weather in TSS/ITZ.

ALGECIRAS Marina Ch 09, ☎ 956 572503.

GIBRALTAR AND MOROCCO

GIBRALTAR Port Ch 12, to be monitored whilst under way or at ⚓ in the Bay. **Marinas**, Ch 71: Queensway Quay, ☎ 350 44700; Marina Bay, ☎ 74322; Sheppards, ☎ 75148. **Customs** Ch 14. **Commercial Port** Ch 06.

TANGIER Port Ch 16, ☎ (00 2129) 3993 7495.

CEUTA (Spain) Marina Ch 09, ☎ 956 513753.

COAST RADIO STATIONS

Coast Radio Stations (CRS) deal with public correspondence (and a few other things). They enable a yachtsman to be linked by radio into the public telephone system in order to converse with a subscriber ashore, ie he can make or receive a Link call.

However the mobile 'phone has to a great extent rendered Link calls obsolescent. Thus there are no longer any CRS in the UK, France and Netherlands. In Germany a limited service is provided by a commercial company (see below).

CRS still operate in the Channel Islands, Ireland*, Denmark, Belgium, Spain and Portugal; see below. But they too may gradually be withdrawn. *In Ireland CRS no longer handle commercial link calls, but Medico link calls are still available on both VHF and MF.

The CG does **not** handle Link calls, except in Denmark and Belgium where the functions of CG and CRS have always been co-located.

CHANNEL ISLANDS

ST PETER PORT RADIO 49°27'·00N 02°32'00W
☎ 01481 720672 📠 01534 714177
Link calls on **Ch 62** only. Ch 20 is used for navigation, pilotage and ships' business

JERSEY COAST GUARD 49°10'·85N 02°14'30W
☎ 01534 447705 📠 01534 499089
Link calls on **Ch 25** only

REPUBLIC OF IRELAND

A Coast Radio service is provided by the Dept of the Marine, Leeson Lane, Dublin 2, Eire. ☎ +353 (0)1 662 0922; ext 670 for enquiries. Broadcasts are made on a working channel/frequency following a prior announcement on Ch 16 and 2182 kHz. Ch 67 is used for Safety messages only.
VHF calls to an Irish Coast Radio Station should be made on a working channel. Only use Ch 16 in case of difficulty or in emergency.

NW and SE Ireland

Weather broadcasts at 0103, 0403, 0703, 1003, 1303, 1603, 1903, 2203 UT and at 0033, 0633, 1233, 1833 UT on the VHF Channels below. Nav warnings are broadcast at 0033, 0433, 0833, 1233, 1633 and 2033 UT.

Clifden Radio	53°30'N 09°56'W	Ch 26
Belmullet Radio	54°16'N 10°03'W	Ch 83
Donegal Bay	54°22'N 08°31'W	Ch 02
Glen Head Radio	54°44'N 08°43'W	Ch 24
MALIN HD RADIO	55°22'N 07°21'W	Ch 23
MF 1677 kHz, ☎ +353 (0) 77 70103		
MMSI 002500100 DSC: 2187·5 kHz		

Carlingford Radio	54°05'N 06°19'W	Ch 04
DUBLIN RADIO	53°23'N 06°04'W	Ch 83
Wicklow Hd Radio	52°58'N 06°00'W	Ch 02
Rosslare Radio	52°15'N 06°20'W	Ch 23
Mine Hd Radio	52°00'N 07°35'W	Ch 83

SW Ireland

Weather is broadcast at 0103, 0403, 0703, 1003, 1303, 1603, 1903, 2203 and at 0033, 0633, 1233, 1833 UT on the VHF Channels listed. Navwarnings are broadcast every 4 hrs from 0233.

Cork Radio	51°51'N 08°29'W	Ch 26
Mizen Radio	51°34'N 09°33'W	Ch 04
Bantry Radio	51°38'N 10°00'W	Ch 23
VALENTIA RADIO	51°56'N 10°21'W	Ch 24
MF 1752 kHz, ☎ + 353 (0) 66947 6109		
MMSI 002500200, DSC: 2187·5 kHz		
Shannon Radio	52°31'N 09°36'W	Ch 28
Galway Bay Radio	53°18'N 09°07'W	Ch 04

DENMARK

All VHF/MF CRS are remotely controlled from Lyngby Radio (55°50N 11°25'E) (MMSI 002191000). The callsign for all stations is Lyngby Radio. Call on working frequencies to help keep Ch 16 clear. The stations listed below monitor Ch 16 H24 and Ch 70 DSC. Traffic lists are broadcast on all VHF channels every odd H+05. All MF stations, except Skagen, keep watch H24 on 2182 kHz. Blåvand, Skagen and Lyngby also monitor MF 2187·5 kHz DSC. MF DSC Public correspondence facilities are available from Blåvand and Skagen on 1624·5 and 2177 kHz.

VHF & MF CRS		
Skagen	57°44'N 10°35'E	Ch 04
MF: Tx 1758, Rx 2045, 2102		
Hirtshals	57°31'N 09°57'E	Ch 66
Hanstholm	57°07'N 08°39'E	Ch 01
Bovbjerg	56°32'N 08°10'E	Ch 02
MF: Tx 1767, Rx 2045, 2111		
Blåvand	55°33'N 08°07'E	Ch 23
MF: Tx 1734, Rx 2045, 2078		

GERMANY

CRS: **DPO7 – Seefunk (Hamburg)** *(MMSI 002113100)*. All stns monitor DSC Ch 70 and 16. Traffic lists are broadcast: 0745, 0945, 1245, 1645, 1945 and H & H+30 on request Ch 16.

Nordfriesland	54°31'N 08°41'E	Ch 26
Elbe-Weser	53°50'N 08°39'E	Ch 24
Hamburg	53°33'N 09°58'E	Ch 83
Bremen	53°05'N 08°48'E	Ch 25
Accumersiel	53°40'N 07°29'E	Ch 28
Borkum	53°35'N 06°40'E	Ch 61

COMMUNICATIONS

NORTH SPAIN

All stns guard DSC Ch 70 H24. Ch 16 is not continuously guarded. Call on working channel below; the callsign is the name of the station followed by Radio; all are remotely controlled by Bilbao Comms Centre. Navigation warnings on VHF at 0840 & 2010 after weather broadcast.

Pasajes	43°17'N 01°55'W	Ch 27
Machichaco MF 1707 kHz	43°27'N 02°45'W	No VHF
BILBAO	43°22'N 03°02'W	Ch 26
Santander	43°25'N 03°36'W	Ch 24
Cabo Peñas MF 1677 kHz	43°26'N 05°35'W	Ch 26
Navia	43°25'N 06°50'W	Ch 60

NORTH WEST SPAIN

Details as for N Spain. All stations are remotely controlled by Coruña Comms Centre.

Cabo Ortegal	43°35'N 07°47'W	Ch 02
CORUÑA MF 1698 kHz	43°22'N 08°27'W	Ch 26
Finisterre	42°54'N 09°16'W	Ch 22
Vigo	42°10'N 08°41'W	Ch 65
La Guardia	41°53'N 08°52'W	Ch 21

PORTUGAL

Stations are remotely controlled by Lisboa. All monitor Ch 16 H24. The callsign is the name of the station followed by Radio.

Arga	41°48'N 08°41'W	24, 25, 28, 83
Arestal	40°46'N 08°21'W	12, 24-26, 85
Montejunto	39°10'N 09°03'W	24, 25, 27, 86
LISBOA	38°33'N 09°11'W	12, 23, 25, 26, 83
	MF 2182 kHz.	
Atalaia	38°10'N 08°38'W	12, 23-25, 85
Foia	37°50'N 08°35'W	23, 24, 27, 28
Estoi	37°10'N 07°50'W	24, 27, 28, 86

AZORES

Stations are remotely controlled by Lisboa. All monitor Ch 16 H24. The callsign is the name of the station followed by Radio.

Flores	39°27'N 31°32'W	Ch 23-26
Faial	38°35'N 28°43'W	Ch 24-26, 28
Pico	38°24'N 28°44'W	Ch 23, 24, 26
Sao Miguel	37°45'N 25°40'W	Ch 23-27

SOUTH WEST SPAIN

Stations are remotely controlled from Malaga. Initially call Ch 16 H24 using station callsign, ie name + Radio. Navwarnings 0833 & 2033 after the weather.

Chipiona	36°42'N 06°25'W MF 1656kHz	No VHF
Cádiz	36°22'N 06°17'W	Ch 26
Tarifa	36°03'N 05°33'W MF 1704 kHz	Ch 81

SHAPES

◆	Towing vessel - length of tow > 200m	Rule 24
▼	Yacht under sail *and* power	Rule 25
⧗	Vessel fishing or trawling	Rule 26
⧗+▲	Vessel fishing with outlying gear >150m long	Rule 26
● ◆ ●	Vessel restricted in her ability to manoeuvre	Rule 27
● ●	Vessel not under command	Rule 27
▮	Vessel constrained by her draught	Rule 28
●	Vessel at anchor	Rule 30

SOUND SIGNALS

MANOEUVRING AND WARNING Rule 34

•	A short blast = about 1 second.	
—	A prolonged blast = 4 – 6 seconds.	
•	I am altering course to **Starboard**	
••	I am altering course to **Port**	
•••	My engines are going **Astern**	
•••••	I do not understand your intentions/ actions	

Note: The above sound signals may be supplemented by light signals flashed on an all-round white light with least range of 5 miles.

In a narrow channel

— — •	I intend to overtake on your starboard side.	
— — ••	I intend to overtake on your port side.	
— • — •	I agree with your overtaking signal	
—	Warning by vessel nearing a bend where other vessels may not be seen	
—	Approaching vessel acknowledges.	

VESSELS IN RESTRICTED VISIBILITY Rule 35

–	Power-driven vessel making way.
– –	Power-driven vessel underway, but stopped and not making way.
– ••	A **sailing vessel**; vessels not under command; restricted in ability to manoeuvre; constrained by draught; engaged in fishing, towing or pushing.
– •••	Vessel being towed or, if more than one vessel is towed, the last vessel in the tow.

Vessels at anchor

🔔	Bell, ring for 5 seconds every minute
🔔⟍	Vessel >100m: Bell forward, ring for 5 seconds every minute; plus
⊙	Gong aft, for 5 seconds every minute.
• – •	Optional extra to warn any approaching vessel

Sailing vessels < 12m at ⚓ do not have to sound the above fog signals. But if they do not, they *must* make an efficient noise every 2 minutes.

INTERNATIONAL PORT TRAFFIC SIGNALS (IPTS)

IPTS are widely used on the Continent, but less so around the UK. They may also be used to control traffic at locks and bridges.

- The main movement signal is always 3 lights in a vertical column, to which no extra light shall be added. Thus it is always recognisable as IPTS, as distinct from some kind of navigational lights.

- Red lights ® indicate *Do not proceed.*

- Green lights ⑥ indicate *Proceed, subject to the conditions stipulated*. To avoid confusion ® and ⑥ lights are never displayed together.

- Signals may be omni-directional ie seen by all vessels simultaneously; or directional, ie seen only from outside or from inside the harbour.

- Some ports may only use signals 2 and 4, or only Signal 1 when necessary

- Signal 1 *Serious Emergency* must show at least 60 flashes/minute.

- All other signals may be fixed or slow occulting, eg every 10s (helpful when background glare poses a problem), but never a mixture of both.

- Signal 5 assumes that VHF, signal lamp, loud-hailer, auxiliary signal or other means of communication will specifically inform a vessel that she may proceed.

- Exemption signals. A single Ⓨ light, shown to the left of signals 2 or 5 and level with the upper light, means *Vessels which can safely navigate outside the main channel need not comply with the main message.* This signal is obviously important to small craft, which nevertheless have a

No	Lights		Main message
1	☼®☼ ☼®☼ ☼®☼	Flashing	Serious emergency – all vessels to stop or divert according to instructions
2	® ® ®		Vessels shall not proceed (*Note:* Some ports may use an exemption signal, as in 2a below)
3	⑥ ⑥ ⑥	Fixed or Slow Occulting	Vessels may proceed. One-way traffic
4	⑥ ⑥ Ⓦ		Vessels may proceed. Two-way traffic
5	⑥ Ⓦ ⑥		A vessel may proceed only when she has received specific orders to do so. (*Note:* Some ports may use an exemption signal, as in 5a below)
Exemption signals and messages			
2a	Ⓨ ® ® ®	Fixed or Slow Occulting	Vessels shall not proceed, except that vessels which navigate outside the main channel need not comply with the main message
5a	Ⓨ ⑥ Ⓦ ⑥	Fixed or Slow Occulting	A vessel may proceed when she has received specific orders to do so, except that vessels which navigate outside the main channel need not comply with the main message
Auxiliary signals and messages			
White and/or yellow lights, displayed with the main lights			

clear duty to keep clear of manoeuvring vessels.

- Auxiliary signals (only Ⓦ and/or Ⓨ lights) may be locally authorised and displayed to the right of the main signal. Their meanings must be promulgated.

Chapter 4 - Safety

SAFETY EQUIPMENT

There are very few regulations about what safety equipment should be carried in non-commercial small craft (less than 13·7m LOA), but SOLAS V requires *all* vessels to carry, if practicable, a **radar reflector** and to have access to a **table of life-saving signals**. The latter can be found inside the front cover of this Almanac, or may be downloaded from: www.mcga.gov.uk/c4mca/signals.pdf. Radar reflectors vary in size, effectiveness and price. An active X- and S-band target enhancer is best, but a relatively inexpensive passive radar reflector may be suitable for inshore and coastal use.

Other safety equipment is a matter of judgement. What you carry will depend on the size of your craft and your crusing area. More equipment is required in an ocean-going yacht which regularly makes offshore passages than in a small weekend cruiser which rarely ventures outside sheltered waters. If you put to sea in anything larger than a dayboat or dinghy, you should consider the following as a minimum requirement. Some of the items – lifejackets, for example – apply to *all* craft. This is not a comprehensive list; further guidance is obtainable from the MCA, the RYA and in *Reeds Nautical Almanac*.

For the yacht, a good **anchor and ground tackle** (preferably all chain, but otherwise a rope/chain combination) is essential. If all else fails, at least you should be able to prevent being driven onto a lee shore while sorting out the problem or awaiting assistance. An **alternative means of propulsion** will get you out of trouble if the wind drops or, in a power boat, the main engine fails. A readily deployable outboard motor may suffice. Mechanical breakdowns are only too common, and you should have the knowledge to carry out basic maintenance and repairs. For this a **set of tools and spare parts** should be carried, not forgetting **ample fuel** for your planned passage.

Floods and fires, although rare, need serious consideration. A **hand bilge pump** and at least one **strong bucket** should deal with minor leaks. A set of **softwood bungs** may be used to seal a burst skin fitting or small hole in the hull. The number of **fire extinguishers** on board will depend on the size of vessel and the type of fuel used for propulsion and cooking. Be sure they are readily available and in date, and check them regularly.

For personal safety, a **lifejacket** should be available for every crew member, and everyone must know how to fit and inflate it. All lifejackets should be checked at least annually, particularly the condition and security of the gas cylinder. But a lifejacket on its own will not prevent a man overboard (MOB). In all but the smallest vessels, a **safety harness** which is secured to a strongpoint or jackstay, should be worn when there is any risk of falling over the side, by non-swimmers and at night. Recovering an MOB is far, far more difficult than it may seem. **Lifebelts, danbuoys, lights and other MOB equipment** all have their place, but remaining on board must be the top priority.

If you do need to call for help, a **VHF DSC radio** is now the primary means of letting others know you have a problem, but be sure to comply with the correct procedures to avoid delays and ambiguities. Do not rely on a mobile phone to summon assistance - coverage does not extend far offshore, and a call is not 'broadcast' to vesels which may be able to help. **Flares** are still recommended, the number and type depending on your sailing area.

Charts and navigational instruments are not strictly 'safety equipment' but if you don't know where you are, you will eventually get into trouble! GPS, radar and other electronic aids are susceptible to failure, so **paper charts for the area** must be carried and kept fully up to date. This Almanac and the associated monthly online updates will help you to do so.

Finally, there is no substitute for common sense, self-sufficiency and a healthy respect for the elements.

DISTRESS, URGENCY, SAFETY

Distress (MAYDAY): Must only be used if a ship or person is in *grave and imminent danger and requires immediate assistance*. It may be appropriate for a man overboard if not quickly recovered.

Urgency (PAN-PAN): *A very urgent message concerning the safety of a vessel or person.* May be used for urgent medical advice.

Safety (SÉCURITÉ): Used typically by coast stations to announce navigational or weather warnings. May be used by vessels to report a hazard; if you are becalmed in a shipping lane, for example.

HOW TO MAKE A DISTRESS CALL

- Switch on the VHF Radio
- Select **Channel 16**
- Make sure Dual Watch is disabled
- Select **HIGH POWER (25W)**
- Hold down the transmit button on the microphone; say slowly and clearly:
- **MAYDAY, MAYDAY, MAYDAY**
- This is....................................(Say your boat's name 3 times)
- MAYDAY...........(Repeat your boat's name once)
- My position is.................... (See below)
- *Tell them what is wrong*: For example, the boat is sinking; how many people (including you) on board; if you have fired flares; if you are abandoning ship etc. If there is time, repeat your position
- **I require immediate assistance. Over** - This means: please reply
- Release the microphone button and listen for an acknowledgement
- If you can't hear clearly, adjust the volume and/or squelch controls

If there is no reply, check the radio switches and repeat the message

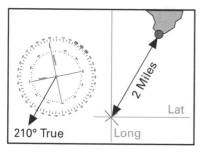

210° True | Lat | Long

Give your position as either:

Lat and Long (from the GPS); or

Bearing and distance <u>from</u> a known landmark or feature (see left for eg: 'My position is 210° True, 2 miles from Portland Bill'); or

General location if appropriate (eg: 'Aground on the Bramble Bank')

Say if you are not sure – do not guess!

MAYDAY RELAY

- **If you hear a MAYDAY call, write it down**
- If practicable to give assistance, acknowledge the call
- If you can't offer assistance and no acknowledgement is heard:
- Select VHF **Channel 16**
- Select **HIGH POWER (25W)**
- Make sure Dual Watch is disabled
- Hold down the transmit button on the microphone; say slowly and clearly:
- **MAYDAY RELAY, MAYDAY RELAY, MAYDAY RELAY**
- **This is......................(say your boat's name 3 times)**
- **State the MAYDAY message, exactly as you wrote it down**
- **Over** - This means: please reply
- Release the button and listen

HELICOPTER RESCUE

- **COMMUNICATE ON CHANNEL 16**
- Use flares or smoke when helicopter is seen or heard
- Helicopter may ask you to drop sails and motor on a specific course
- You may be asked to stream the casualty astern in the dinghy
- Brief yourcrew early (too noisy when helicopter is close)
- **HELM MUST KEEP ON COURSE** and not be distracted
- Weighted line lowered
- Let it touch boat or water first (to earth any static charge)
- Take in slack line only
- **PULL IN AS DIRECTED**
- **DO NOT SECURE IT TO THE BOAT**
- **DO AS YOU ARE TOLD**

  Note: The text and sketch relate to a Hi-line transfer, one of several techniques which may be used

MEDICAL HELP

- **CH 16, High power, Dual watch off**
- **PAN PAN** .... (repeat 3 times)
- **ALL STATIONS** .... (repeat 3 times)
- **This is** .... (repeat 3 times)
- **Over**
  Next message should contain:
  Yacht's name, callsign, nationality
  Yacht's position and nearest harbour
  Patient's details, symptoms and advice wanted
  The medication you have on board

FIRST AID

The objectives of First Aid at sea are to:

- **Preserve life** • **Prevent further damage**
- **Relieve pain and distress** • **Deliver a live casualty ashore**

With any casualty be calm, reassuring and methodical. But first ensure your own safety and that of the vessel. If in doubt call for advice and assistance.

MEDICAL ADVICE can be obtained almost anywhere in European waters by making an All-Stations 'PAN PAN' call or a DSC Urgency Alert to the Coastguard or to a Coast Radio Station. They will connect you to a doctor or to the nearest hospital.

The Urgency signal 'PAN PAN' is always advised, especially abroad, because it is internationally understood and eliminates most language problems; it is also free.

As a layman you are not qualified to judge how serious the casualty's condition is – so get the best possible advice and/or help as quickly as possible. **Urgent help needed** is shown below against the more serious medical problems.

Be ready to describe the patient's symptoms, eg consciousness, pulse rate, breathing rate, temperature, skin colour, site and type of injury, any pain, amount of blood lost etc. If a doctor needs to come aboard, or a casualty has to be landed, the Coastguard will arrange.

If non-urgent, wait until in harbour. Consider calling the port authority before arrival so that a doctor or paramedic can meet you on arrival.

MEDICAL CARE ABROAD It is sensible to carry the European Health Insurance Card (EHIC) which entitles you to medical treatment on a reciprocal basis, although it may not cover the full charge. See *www.dh.gov.uk* for full details.

EMERGENCY RESUSCITATION (ABC)

The immediate procedure for any collapsed or apparently unconscious person is: Assess whether or not the casualty is conscious. Carefully shake his/her shoulders and ask loudly 'What's happened?' or 'Are you all right?' or give a command such as 'Open your eyes'. An unconscious casualty will not respond.

A = Airway

Remove any visible obstruction from the casualty's mouth (leave well-fitting dentures in place). Listen at the mouth for breathing. Tilt the head backwards, using head tilt and chin lift to maintain a clear airway.

Check the area is clear of danger. Place casualty in recovery position if breathing.

B = Breathing

Keeping the airway open, check whether the casualty is breathing normally by **looking** for chest movement, **listening** at the mouth for breathing sounds and **feeling** for breath on your cheek. Look, listen and feel for 10 seconds before deciding that breathing is absent.

If the casualty is not breathing and the airway is clear, mouth to mouth ventilation can be started, in conjunction with 'External chest compression' below: kneel beside the casualty, maintain head tilt and chin lift, and pinch the nostrils. Take a deep breath and blow two full breaths into patient's mouth. Watch for rise and fall of chest.

C = Circulation

Assess the casualty for signs of circulation by looking, listening and feeling for normal breathing, coughing, any movement or improvement in colour. Check for signs of circulation for no more than 10 seconds. If circulation stops, the breathing will also stop.

If there are no signs of a circulation or you are at all unsure, assume that the heart has stopped. This is called **cardiac arrest**. The casualty will be unconscious and may appear very pale, grey or bluish in colour.

An artificial circulation will have to be provided by chest compression. Casualties with cardiac arrest will need both rescue breathing and chest compression, a combination known as Cardio Pulmonary Resuscitation (**CPR**).

External chest compression

To start external chest compression, lay the casualty face up on a hard, flat surface. Kneel beside casualty. The point at which pressure will be applied is the centre of the chest.

Place the heel of your hand on top of the other hand and interlock your fingers.

Depress breastbone 4–5cm (1½–2in) then release.

With either one or two operators give 30 chest compressions and continue cycles of 2 breaths to 30 compressions. Use a compression rate of 100 per minute. Chest compression must always be combined with rescue breathing so after every 30 compressions, give 2 effective rescue breaths. *Do not stop.*

Action plan for the resuscitation of adults
Casualty unconscious but is breathing normally:

- *Urgent help needed*
- Turn casualty into the recovery position
- Check for continued breathing

Casualty is unconscious and not breathing:
- **Urgent help needed**
- Give 2 effective rescue breaths
- Check for signs of circulation

If no sign of a circulation, give 30 chest compressions and continue cycles of 2 breaths to 30 compressions.

If breathing restarts, place casualty in the recovery position.

BITES AND STINGS Injected poison from bites and stings usually only causes local swelling and discomfort, but some people may react severely. For insect stings, resuscitate if collapse occurs; otherwise give rest, painkillers, antihistamines (eg chlorpheniramine).

BLEEDING – OPEN WOUND Bleeding is often very dramatic, but is virtually always controllable.
- Apply firm continuous direct pressure; bandage on a large pad. If bleeding continues, bandage more pads on top of initial pads; then press directly over wound for at least 10 minutes (blood takes this long to clot).
- Elevate if wound is on a limb.
- Do *not* apply a tourniquet. This practice is out of date due to the danger of losing a limb.

BLEEDING – INTERNAL (CLOSED INJURY)
Follows fractured bones, crush injuries, or rupture of organs such as the liver or spleen. Treat for shock which may appear rapidly. *Urgent help needed*.

BURNS AND SCALDS Move the victim into fresh air to avoid inhaling smoke.
ABC – Airway, Breathing, Circulation
- Stop further injury: dip the whole of the burnt part into cold water for 10–15 minutes. Seawater is excellent but may be very painful.
- Remove only loose clothing. Do not pull off clothing stuck to the skin.
- Cover with sterile dressing. If skin is broken or blistered, use sterile paraffin gauze beneath the dressing. Separate burnt fingers with paraffin gauze. Never use adhesive dressings.
- Do not prick blisters or apply ointments.
- Elevate burnt limb and immobilise.
- Give strong painkillers.
- Treat for shock: give frequent and copious drinks of water.
- Start giving antibiotics for major burns. If burns extensive or deep, *urgent help needed*.

CHOKING If blockage by some object (eg a peanut) is suspected, turn the casualty on his side and give up to 5 sharp back slaps with the flat of the hand between the shoulder blades. Check mouth and remove any obstruction.

If unsuccessful, wrap both arms around the victim's waist from behind, and give 5 sharp upward thrusts with both fists into the abdomen above the navel but below the ribs so as to cause coughing. Clear object from mouth.

CUTS AND WOUNDS Often dramatic but only potentially serious if nerves, tendons or blood vessels are severed.
Clean thoroughly with antiseptic. Remove dirt or other foreign bodies. Small clean cuts can be closed using as many Steristrips as necessary to keep the skin edges together. Skin must be dry. Leave for 5 days at least. Larger deep cuts may require stitches; apply a dressing and seek help. Do not try amateur surgery at sea.
Ragged lacerations or very dirty wounds – do not attempt to close these. Clean as well as possible, sprinkle antibiotic powder in wound and apply a dressing. Seek help. If in doubt a wound is best left open and lightly covered to keep it clean and dry.
Fingers and toes Blood may collect under the nail following an injury. Release the blood by piercing the nail with a red hot needle or paper clip. It will not hurt!

DENTAL PAIN seems worse at sea; prevention is better than cure. Dentanurse is an emergency treatment pack which enables an amateur to make temporary repairs, eg replacing crowns, lost fillings. It contains zinc oxide and Eugenol.
Throbbing toothache made worse by hot or cold or when bitten on. Clean out any cavity and apply temporary filling. Take painkiller.
Dull toothache tender to bite on; gum swollen or red with possible discharge. Treat as above but also take an antibiotic.
Broken tooth or filling Cover exposed surfaces with zinc oxide paste. Teeth knocked out should be put in a clean container with milk or moist gauze for a dentist to re-implant asap. This can be attempted onboard - ideally within 1 hour
Bleeding gums Clean teeth more thoroughly. Use regular hot salt water rinses and antibiotics.
Pain round wisdom tooth Clean area with toothbrush; use hot salt water rinses; take antibiotics and painkillers.
Mouth ulcers Hot salt water rinses.

DIARRHOEA Can become serious, especially in young children if much fluid is lost. Stop food, give plenty of fluid. Plain water is usually sufficient, or add salt (1 teaspoonful/litre) and sugar (4–5 teaspoons/litre). Lomotil or Imodium tablets are very effective in adults.

DROWNING ABC Clear seaweed, dentures. If not breathing start mouth to mouth ventilation as soon as possible and in the water if practicable. If no pulse, start chest compression as soon as on board. Keep the head low so that vomit is not inhaled and water can drain.

If stomach is bulging, turn casualty on to side to empty water and avoid inhaling it. Prevent cooling. Remove wet clothes; wrap casualty in blankets to warm him/her.

Continue resuscitation until the casualty revives or death is certain. Hypothermia may mimic death. Do not abandon resuscitation until the casualty has been warmed or signs of death persist despite attempts at warming.

Once revived, put in the recovery position.

Any person rescued from drowning may collapse in the next 24 hours as the lungs react to inhaled water. *Urgent help needed.*

EYE INJURIES are potentially serious. Never put old or previously opened ointment or drops into an eye; serious infection could result.

Foreign object Flush with clean water, pull the lower lid out to inspect, remove object with a clean tissue. For objects under upper eyelid, ask casualty to grasp lashes and pull the upper lid over the lower lid. An eye-bath is very effective. Blinking under water may help. After removal of object, insert sterile antibiotic ointment inside pulled out lower lid. Cover with pad.

Corrosive fluid Flush continuously with water for 15 minutes. Give painkillers and chloramphenicol ointment; cover with pad. *Seek help asap.*

Conjunctivitis Sticky, weeping eye with yellow discharge. Chloramphenicol 4 times a day.

FISH HOOKS Push the hook round until the point and barb can be cut off; withdraw the hook. Dress the holes and give an antibiotic.

FRACTURES AND DISLOCATIONS Fracture is a broken bone. Dislocation is a displaced joint. Both produce pain (aggravated by attempted movement), localised swelling, abnormal shape, and a grating feeling on movement (if it is a fracture). Blood vessels or nerves around the fracture or dislocation may also be damaged causing a cold, pale, or numb limb below the site of the injury.

Fractures of large bones such as the femur (upper leg) will result in major internal bleeding and may cause shock. When complications occur *urgent help is needed*.

Early application of a splint and raising the injured limb where possible will reduce pain and complications. Treat for shock and pain.

Specific fractures and dislocations
Cheek Caused by a direct blow. Rarely serious but requires specialist care.

Jaw Beware of associated brain or spinal injury. Remove blood and teeth fragments; leave loose teeth in place; protect broken teeth. Ensure airway is clear. Start regular antiseptic mouth washes and antibiotics. Support jaw with bandage over top of the head. Give only fluids by mouth.

Neck May result from a direct blow, a fall or a whiplash type injury. If conscious, casualty may complain of pain, tingling, numbness or weakness in limbs below the injury. *Mishandling may damage the spinal cord, causing paralysis or death.* Avoid movement and support the head. Immobilise by wrapping a folded towel around the neck. If movement is necessary then lift the victim as one rigid piece, never allowing the neck to bend. *Urgent help needed.*

Nose Control bleeding by pinching.

Ribs Very painful. Strapping is not advised.

Spine Fracture of the spine below the neck, may cause *paralysis or death*. Mishandling of the victim may greatly worsen the damage. Avoid movement if possible. Lift the casualty without allowing the spine to sag. *Urgent help needed.*

Collar bone Support arm in sling.

Dislocated shoulder If this has happened before, the casualty may remedy the dislocation himself; otherwise do not attempt to remedy it in case a fracture exists.

Upper arm Support the arm with a collar and cuff inside the shirt, ie tie a clove hitch around the wrist and loop the ends behind the neck.

Forearm and wrist Splint (eg with battens or wood). Do not bandage tightly. Elevate or support in a sling.

Fingers Elevate hand and, unless badly crushed, leave unbandaged; keep moving. If very wobbly, bandage to adjacent finger.

Lower limb
Thigh Shock may be considerable. Strap to other leg with padding between. Gently straighten the lower leg. If necessary apply traction at the ankle to help straighten the leg. Do not bandage too tightly.

Knee Twisting injuries or falls damage the ligaments and cartilages of the knee. Very painful and swollen. Treat as for fracture.

Lower leg Pad very well. Splint using oar, broom handle or similar pieces of wood.

Ankle Fracture or severe sprain may be indistinguishable. Immobilise in neutral position with foot at right angles. Raise the limb.

HEART ATTACK Severe 'crushing' chest pain; may spread to shoulders, neck or arms. Sweating, then bluish lips, then collapse.

Breathing and heart may stop. Give one 300mg aspirin tablet (to chew) **Urgent help needed**. Rest, reassure. If unconscious: recovery position; observe breathing and pulse. If breathing stops or no pulse, start mouth to mouth ventilation and chest compression immediately; do not stop.

STROKE Symptoms: sudden unconsciousness, paralysis or weakness on one side of the body, slurring of speech, or if the victim has any difficulty smiling, speaking, raising both arms, sticking out tongue. Place in recovery position and check airway. **Urgent help needed** – treatment within 3 hours can reverse the effects of a stroke.

HEAT STROKE Cool casualty by spraying with cold water or wrap the casualty in a cold wet sheet until their temperature under the tongue falls to 38°C. Encourage drinking (1 teaspoon of salt/half litre of water). If casualty stops sweating, has a rapid pounding pulse and is becoming unconscious: **Urgent help needed**.

HYPOTHERMIA Symptoms include: unreasonable behaviour, apathy and confusion; unsteady gait, stumbling; slurring of speech; pale, cold skin; slow, weak pulse; slow breathing; shivering. It leads to collapse, unconsciousness and ultimately death.

ABC Put in recovery position. If not breathing, start mouth to mouth ventilation. Be prepared to use chest compressions.

Remove wet clothing. Avoid wind chill. Dry and wrap in blankets or sleeping bag plus warm hat and cover, if available, in foil survival bag. **Urgent help needed**.

Give hot sweet drinks if conscious. Do not give alcohol, rub the skin, or place very hot objects against skin.

SEASICKNESS is aggravated by anxiety, fatigue and boredom. Symptoms: lethargy, dizziness, headache and nausea/vomiting. Help prevent by taking anti-seasickness pills, avoiding rich foods and alcohol. Take frequent small amounts of fluid and food. Keep warm; keep busy. Prolonged seasickness may cause serious loss of fluid – seek advice.

SHOCK can result from almost any accident or medical emergency; it can lead to collapse.

Signs and symptoms Thirst, apathy, nausea, restlessness. Pale, cold, clammy skin, sweating. Rapid, weak pulse. Rapid, shallow breathing. Dull, sunken eyes, bluish lips.

ABC Control any bleeding. Lay the casualty flat or in recovery position; raise legs 20°. Splint any fractures; avoid movement. Avoid chilling, keep warm. Give pain killers. Reassure

the casualty. Do not let the casualty eat, drink, smoke or move unnecessarily. If complaining of thirst, moisten the lips with a little water. Note: Fluids may be life saving in cases of dehydration (eg diarrhoea, vomiting, severe burns).

FIRST AID KIT

Stow the following items in a waterproof container, readily accessible and clearly marked:

Triangular bandage x 2 (doubles as a sling)
Crepe bandage 75mm x 2
Gauze bandage 50mm x 2
Elastoplast 75mm x 1
Band Aids (or similar) various shapes and sizes
Wound dressings, 1 large, 1 medium
Sterile non-adhesive dressing (Melolin) x 5
Steristrips x 5 packs
Cotton wool. Safety pins. Thermometer.
Scissors and forceps, good quality stainless steel
Disposable gloves
Antiseptic solution (eg Savlon)
Sunscreen with high protection factor
Antifungal powder or cream (athlete's foot)
Insect repellent (DEET, diethyltoluamide)
Individual choice of anti-seasick tablets
Antibiotic eye ointment (prescription only)

Additional items for extended cruising

Vaccinations – a course may need to start as much as 6 months before departure.
Syringes 2ml x 2 (if carrying injections)
Dental kit – see Dental pain.

DRUGS

*Prescriptions are needed for asterisked drugs. Out of date drugs are potentially dangerous – destroy them.

Drug, purpose and dose

Paracetamol, painkiller. 1-2 500mg tablets 4 hrly.

**Dihydrocodeine*, strong painkiller. 1-2 30mg tablets   4 hrly.

Chlorpheniramine, antihistamine. 1 x 4mg tablet 8 hrly.

Aludrox, indigestion. 1-2 before meals.

Loperamide, diarrhoea. 2 x 2mg capsules initially, then 1 after each loose stool; max 8 day.

Senokot, constipation. 2-4 tablets per day.

Tetracycline, antibiotic. 1 x 250mg capsule, 4 times per day.

**Amoxycillin*, antibiotic. 2 x 250 mg capsules 8 hrly. (Beware penicillin allergy)

**Erythromycin*, antibiotic for penicillin-allergic adults.   4 x 250mg tablets daily.

Cinnarizine, seasickness. 2 x 15mg tablets before sailing, then 1 every 8 hrs.

OBSERVATION FORM

The information recorded by you on this form will be invaluable in helping doctors and/or paramedics ashore to diagnose the problem and arrange the best possible treatment for your casualty.

This is particularly important if there may be a considerable time lapse between requesting medical help and the casualty reaching hospital.

- Keep photocopies of this form in your First Aid kit so as to preserve the original. Whilst awaiting help, record your careful observations by ticking or annotating the various boxes at 10 minute intervals. This will help doctors detect any improvement or deterioration in the casualty's condition.

- If within radio range of shore attempt to pass the observations via the Coastguard to a medical authority; or ask a ship to relay.

- Before the casualty is taken off the yacht ensure that this form and personal documents (money, passport, EHIC and mobile 'phone) are securely tied to him/her.

DATE ....   CASUALTY'S NAME .... AGE .... M/F ....

Times of observations @ 10 minute intervals:		10	20	30	40	50	60
EYES Observe for reactions whilst testing other responses	Open spontaneously						
	Open when spoken to						
	Open to painful stimulus						
	Nil response						
MOVEMENT Apply painful stimulus: Pinch ear lobe or skin on back of hand	Obeys commands						
	Responds						
	Nil response						
SPEECH Speak clearly and directly, close to the casualty's ear	Responds sensibly to queries						
	Seems confused						
	Uses inappropriate words						
	Incomprehensible sounds						
	Nil response						
PULSE (Beats per minute) Take adult's pulse at wrist or neck. Note rate and whether beats are: weak (w); strong (s); regular (reg) or irregular (irreg)	Over 110						
	101-110						
	91-100						
	81-90						
	71-80						
	61-70						
	Below 61						
BREATHING (Breaths per minute) Note rate and whether breathing is: quiet (q); noisy (n); easy (e); or difficult (d)	Over 40						
	31-40						
	21-30						
	11-20						
	Below 11						

GMDSS

The Global Maritime Distress and Safety System (GMDSS) is a sophisticated, but complex, semi-automatic, third-generation communications system. Although not compulsory for yachts, its potential for saving life, particularly when far offshore and out of VHF range, is so great that every yachtsman should seriously consider it. Equipment costs continue to fall. Training courses, leading to the award of the Short Range Certificate (SRC) of Competence, are widely available. The Long Range Certificate covers MF, HF, SatCom, EPIRBs and SART.

Recommended reading:

- *ALRS, Vol 5* (UK Hydrographic Office)
- *GMDSS: a User's Handbook* (Bréhaut/ACN)
- *GMDSS for small craft* (Clemmetsen/Fernhurst)
- *Reeds VHF/DSC Handbook* (Fletcher/ACN)

Purpose

GMDSS enables a coordinated SAR operation to be mounted rapidly and reliably anywhere at sea. To this end, terrestrial and satellite communications and navigation equipment is used to alert SAR authorities ashore and ships in the vicinity to a Distress incident or Urgency situation. GMDSS also promulgates Maritime Safety Information.

Sea areas

For the purposes of GMDSS, the world's sea areas are divided into 4 categories (A1-4), defined mainly by the range of radio communications. These are:

A1 An area within R/T coverage of at least one VHF Coastguard or Coast radio station in which continuous VHF alerting is available via DSC. Range: 20–50M from the CG/CRS.

A2 An area, excluding sea area A1, within R/T coverage of at least one MF CG/CRS in which continuous DSC alerting is available. Range: approx 50–250M from the CG/CRS.

A3 An area between 76°N and 76°S, excluding sea areas A1 and A2, within coverage of HF or an Inmarsat satellite in which continuous alerting is available.

A4 An area outside sea areas A1, A2 and A3, ie the polar regions, within coverage of HF.

In each category of sea area certain types of radio equipment must be carried by GMDSS vessels: in A1 areas VHF DSC; A2 areas VHF and MF DSC; A3 areas VHF, MF and HF or SatCom; A4 VHF, MF and HF.

Most UK yachtsmen will operate in A1 areas (the English Channel, for example, is an A1 area) where a simple VHF radio and a Navtex receiver will initially meet GMDSS requirements. As equipment becomes more affordable, yachtsmen may decide to fit GMDSS. This will become increasingly necessary as the present system for sending and receiving Distress calls is run down. The CG will continue a loudspeaker watch on VHF Ch 16 until further notice.

Functions

Regardless of the sea areas in which they operate, vessels complying with GMDSS must be able to perform certain functions:

- transmit ship-to-shore Distress alerts by two independent means
- receive shore-to-ship Distress alerts
- transmit & receive ship-to-ship Distress alerts
- transmit signals for locating incidents
- transmit and receive communications for SAR co-ordination
- transmit/receive maritime safety info, eg navigation and weather warnings

Distress alerts

A Distress alert is simply a Distress call using DSC. It is transmitted on Ch 70 and is automatically repeated five times. Whenever possible, a Distress alert should always include the last known position and time in UT. The position is normally entered automatically from an interfaced GPS, but can be entered manually if required. The nature of the distress can also be selected from the receiver's menu. The vessel's identity (MMSI number) is automatically included.

GMDSS requires participating ships to be able to send Distress alerts by two out of three independent means. These are:

- Digital Selective Calling (DSC) using terrestrial communications, ie VHF Ch 70,

SAFETY

115

MF 2187·5 kHz, or HF distress and alerting frequencies in the 4, 6, 8,12 and 16 MHz bands.

- Emergency Position Indicating Radio Beacons (EPIRBs). See below.
- Inmarsat, via ship terminals.

Digital Selective Calling

DSC is an essential component of GMDSS. It is so called because information is sent by a burst of digital code; selective because it can be addressed to a specific DSC-equipped vessel or to a selected group of vessels.

In all DSC messages every vessel and relevant shore station has a 9-digit identification number, or MMSI (Maritime Mobile Service Identity), which is in effect an automatic, electronic callsign.

DSC is used to transmit Distress alerts from ships, to receive Distress acknowledgements from ships or shore stations; to send Urgency and Safety alerts; to relay Distress alerts; and for routine calling & answering. A thorough working knowledge is needed.

Using the procedures and switches applicable to your particular VHF/DSC radio, a VHF/DSC Distress alert might be sent as follows:

- Briefly press the (red, guarded) Distress button. The set automatically switches to Ch 70 (DSC Distress chan). Press again for 5 seconds to transmit a basic Distress alert with position & time. It then reverts to Ch 16.

- If time permits, select the nature of distress from the menu, eg Collision, then press the Distress button for five seconds to send a full Distress alert.

A CG/CRS automatically sends a Distress acknowledgement on Ch 70, before replying on Ch 16. Ships in range should reply directly on Ch 16.

If a Distress acknowledgement is not received from a CG/CRS, the Distress alert will automatically be repeated every four minutes.

When a DSC Distress acknowledge-ment has been received, or after about 15 seconds, the vessel in distress should transmit a MAYDAY message by voice on Ch 16, adding its MMSI.

NB: If a Distress alert is inadvertently transmitted, an All stations DSC message cancelling the false alert (by date and time) must be sent at once.

Maritime Safety Information (MSI)

MSI consists of the vital navigational, weather and safety messages which traditionally were sent to vessels at sea by CRS in Morse, but by R/T on VHF and MF in more recent years – and now by GMDSS. For navigation and weather warnings see this and chapter 2 respectively.

GMDSS transmits MSI in English by two independent but complementary means, Navtex and SafetyNet.

- Navtex on MF (518 kHz and 490 kHz) which can be received out to about 300 miles offshore, see Chapter 2.

- SafetyNet uses Inmarsat-C satellites to cover beyond MF range, except Area A4. Enhanced Group Calling (EGC) is a part of SafetyNet which enables MSI to be sent to selected groups of users in any of the four oceans.

Emergency Position Indicating Radio Beacons (EPIRB) may be hand-held or float-free, they transmit on 406 MHz. (Note that 121·5 MHz, 243·0 MHz and L-band EPIRBS are no longer used.) Most EPIRBs have a built in GPS and about 48 hours of battery life. They communicate via the Cospas-Sarsat (C/S) network of geostationary and polar orbit satellites. Although C/S will relay an EPIRB signal to earth with no delay, the position of a non-GPS EPIRB may take several hours to determine. The cost of an EPIRB ranges from less than £300 to more than £1000 for float-free, GPS models.

An EPIRB transmits data which is uniquely coded to identify the individual beacon and, because it may be transmitting from anywhere in the world, it must be registered. The UK registration centre is:

The EPIRB Registry, The Maritime and Coastguard Agency, MRCC Falmouth, Pendennis Point, Castle Drive, Falmouth, Cornwall TR11 4WZ; n 01326 211569; email: epirb @mcga.gov.uk.

It is just as important that any changes are immediately notified. False alerts caused by inadvertent or incorrect use of EPIRBs put a significant burden on SAR Centres and may coincide with an actual distress situation.

All crew members should be aware of the proper use of the particular EPIRB onboard. Make sure that testing is adequately supervised; that the EPIRB is correctly installed and maintained; and that it is not activated if assistance is already available. If an EPIRB is activated accidentally, make every effort to advise the nearest MRCC of the false alert as soon as possible.

Personal Locator Beacons (PLB) operate on the same principle. They must also be registered but they do not have a vessel-specific MMSI. A PLB with GPS costs about £250.

Search And Rescue Transponders (SART) are radar transceivers which operate on 9 GHz and respond to 3 cm (X-band) radars, like a small portable Racon (see Chapter 3). They are primarily intended for use in liferafts to help searching ships and aircraft find survivors. The transmitted signal shows on a radar screen as 12 dots radiating out from the SART's position. A SART costs about £500.

SAFETY

UK EMERGENCY VHF DIRECTION FINDING SERVICE

VHF DF is for emergency use only, ie 'one stage down' from real distress. It is remotely controlled H24 by a CG Centre (MRCC) and is not a free navigational service. After contact on Ch 16, invariably Ch 67 is used for the DF procedure; this may be a count from 1-10. Note that the bearing obtained is in °True *from the station to the vessel*. VHF-DF stations are marked on charts by a dot and magenta circle, suffixed 'RG'.

STATION	CONTROLLED BY MRCC	POSITION	
St Mary's, Isles of Scilly	Falmouth	49°55'·73N	06°18'·25W
Lands End	Falmouth	50°08'·13N	05°38'·19W
Lizard	Falmouth	49°57'·60N	05°12'·06W
Rame Head	Brixham	50°19'·03N	04°13'·20W
East Prawle	Brixham	50°13'·10N	03°42'·50W
Berry Head	Brixham	50°23'·97N	03°29'·05W
Grove Point	Portland	50°32'·93N	02°25'·20W
Hengistbury Head	Portland	50°42'·95N	01°45'·64W
Boniface	Solent	50°36'·21N	01°12'·03W
Selsey	Solent	50°43'·80N	00°48'·22W
Newhaven	Solent	50°46'·93N	00°03'·01E
Fairlight	Dover	50°52'·19N	00°38'·74E
Langdon Battery	Dover	51°07'·97N	01°20'·59E
North Foreland	Dover	51°22'·53N	01°26'·72E
Shoeburyness	Thames	51°31'·38N	00°46'·50E
Bawdsey	Thames	51°59'·60N	01°25'·00E
Lowestoft	Yarmouth	52°28'·60N	01°42'·20E
Trimingham	Yarmouth	52°54'·57N	01°20'·60E
Skegness	Yarmouth	53°09'·00N	00°21'·00E
Easington	Humber	53°39'·13N	00°05'·90E
Flamborough	Humber	54°07'·06N	00°05'·07W
Ravenscar	Humber	54°23'·83N	00°30'·68W
Hartlepool	Humber	54°41'·79N	01°10'·57W
Tynemouth	Humber	55°01'·07N	01°24'·99W
Cullercoats	Humber	55°04'·00N	01°28'·00W
Newton	Humber	55°31'·01N	01°37'·10W
Crosslaw	Forth	55°54'·48N	02°12'·31W
Fife Ness	Forth	56°16'·70N	02°35'·30W
Inverbervie	Forth	56°51'·10N	02°15'·65W
Windyhead	Aberdeen	57°38'·90N	02°14'·50W
Noss Head	Aberdeen	58°28'·80N	03°03'·00W
Wideford Hill	Shetland	58°59'·29N	03°01'·40W
Compass Head	Shetland	59°52'·05N	01°16'·30W
Dunnet Head	Aberdeen	58°40'·31N	03°22'·52W
Sandwick	Stornoway	58°12'·65N	06°21'·27W
Rodel	Stornoway	57°44'·90N	06°57'·41W
Barra	Stornoway	57°00'·81N	07°30'·42W
Tiree	Clyde	56°30'·62N	06°57'·68W
Kilchiaran	Clyde	55°45'·90N	06°27'·19W
Law Hill	Clyde	55°41'·76N	04°50'·46W
Snaefell	Liverpool	54°15'·84N	04°27'·66W
Walney Island	Liverpool	54°06'·61N	03°16'·00W
Great Ormes Head	Holyhead	53°19'·96N	03°51'·25W
Rhiw	Holyhead	52°50'·00N	04°37'·82W
St Ann's Head	Milford Haven	51°40'·97N	05°10'·52W
Hartland Pt	Swansea	51°01'·22N	04°31'·40W
Trevose Head	Falmouth	50°32'·91N	05°01'·99W

NORTHERN IRELAND

Orlock Head	Belfast	54°40'·41N	05°34'·97W
West Torr	Belfast	55°11'·70N	06°05'·20W

CHANNEL ISLANDS

Guernsey	Ship transmits on Ch 16 (Distress only)	49°26'·27N	02°35'·77W
Jersey	or Ch 67 (Guernsey) or Ch 82 (Jersey)	49°10'·85N	02°14'·30W

VHF EMERGENCY DIRECTION FINDING SERVICES

Compass Head

N

Wideford Hill

Dunnett Head

Noss Head

Sandwick

Rodel

Windyhead

Barra

Inverbervie

Tiree

Fife Ness

Kilchiaran

Crosslaw

Law Hill

Newton

Cullercoats
Tynemouth

West Torr

Hartlepool

Orlock Head

Ravenscar

Snaefell
Walney Island

Flamborough

Easington

Great Ormes Head

Skegness

Rhiw

Trimingham

Lowestoft

Bawdsey

St Ann's Head

Shoeburyness

North Foreland

Langdon Battery
Fairlight

Dunkerque

Hartland

Selsey Bill

Hengistbury Head

Gris-Nez
Boulogne

Trevose Head

Grove Point

Boniface

Newhaven

Rame Head

Berry Head

Ault

Land's End

E Prawle

Levy

Dieppe

St Mary's

Lizard

Homet

Barfleur

Fécamp

Jobourg

Saint-Vaast

La Hève

La Hague

Guernsey

Carteret

Villerville

Roches-Douvres

Jersey

Port-en-Bessin

Ploumanach

Le Roc

Batz

Bréhat

Brignogan

Grouin

Créach

Saint-Cast

Saint-Mathieu

Toulinguet

S-Quay-Portrieux

Cap de la Chèvre

Pointe du Raz

Beg-Meil

Penmarc'h

Étel

Beg Melen

Saint-Julien

Port Louis

Piriac

Le Talut

Chemoulin

Taillefer

Saint-Sauveur

Les Baleines

Chassiron

La Coubre

Pointe de Grave

Cap Ferret

Messanges

Socoa

United Kingdom	Ch 16 (Distress only) Ch 67
Guernsey	Ch 16 (Distress) Ch 67
Jersey	Ch 16 (Distress) Ch 82
France	Ch 16 11 67

SAFETY

HM COASTGUARD - MRCC CONTACT DETAILS

EASTERN REGION

PORTLAND COASTGUARD
50°36'N 02°27'W. DSC MMSI 002320012
Custom House Quay, Weymouth DT4 8BE.
☎ 01305 760439. 🖷 01305 760451.
Area: Topsham to Chewton Bunney (50°44'N
01°42'W).

SOLENT COASTGUARD
50°48'N 01°12'W. DSC MMSI 002320011
44A Marine Parade West, Lee-on-Solent,
PO13 9NR. ☎ 02392 552100. 🖷 02392
554131. Area: Chewton Bunney to Beachy
Hd. Call on Ch 67 to keep Ch 16 clear.

DOVER COASTGUARD
50°08'N 01°20'E. DSC MMSI 002320010
Langdon Battery, Dover CT15 5NA.
☎ 01304 210008. 🖷 01304 225762.
Area: Beachy Head to Reculver Towers
(51°23'N 01°12'E). Operates Channel
Navigation Information Service.

THAMES COASTGUARD
51°51'N 01°17'E. MMSI 002320009
East Terrace, Walton-on-the-Naze CO14 8PY.
☎ 01255 675518. 🖷 01255 679415.
Area: Reculver Towers to Southwold.

LONDON COASTGUARD
51°30'N 00°03'E. MMSI 002320063
Thames Barrier Navigation Centre, Unit 28,
34 Bowater Rd, Woolwich, London SE18 5TF.
☎ 0208 312 7380. 🖷 0208 309 8196.
Area: River Thames from Shell Haven Pt
(N bank) & Egypt Bay (S bank) up-river to
Teddington Lock.

YARMOUTH COASTGUARD
52°37'N 01°43'E. MMSI 002320008
Haven Bridge House, North Quay, Great
Yarmouth NR30 1HZ.
☎ 01493 851338. 🖷 01493 331975.
Area: Southwold to Haile Sand Fort.

†HUMBER COASTGUARD
54°06'N 00°11'W. MMSI 002320007
Lime Kiln Lane, Bridlington, N Humberside
YO15 2LX.
☎ 01262 672317. 🖷 01262 400779.
Area: Haile Sand Fort to Scottish border.

SCOTLAND & NORTHERN IRELAND

FORTH COASTGUARD
56°17'N 02°35'W. MMSI 002320005

Fifeness, Crail, Fife KY10 3XN.
☎ 01333 450666. 🖷 01333 450703.
Area: English border to Doonies Pt (57°01'N
02°10'W).

†ABERDEEN COASTGUARD
57°08'N 02°05'W. MMSI 002320004
Marine House, Blaikies Quay, Aberdeen
AB11 5PB.
☎ 01224 592334. 🖷 01224 575920.
Area: Doonies Pt to Cape Wrath, incl
Pentland Firth.

†SHETLAND COASTGUARD
60°09'N 01°08'W. MMSI 002320001
Knab Road, Lerwick ZE1 0AX.
☎ 01595 692976. 🖷 01595 693634.
Area: Orkney, Fair Isle and Shetland.

†*STORNOWAY COASTGUARD
58°12'N 06°22'W. MMSI 002320024
Battery Pt, Stornoway, Isle of Lewis H51 2RT.
☎ 01851 702013. 🖷 01851 706796.
Area: Cape Wrath to Ardnamurchan Pt,
Western Isles and St Kilda.

†*CLYDE COASTGUARD
55°58'N 04°48'W. MMSI 002320022
Navy Bldgs, Eldon St, Greenock PA16 7QY.
☎ 01475 729988. 🖷 01475 888095.
Area: Ardnamurchan Pt to Mull of Galloway
inc islands.

*BELFAST COASTGUARD
54°40'N 05°40'W. MMSI 002320021
Bregenz House, Quay St, Bangor, Co Down
BT20 5ED.
☎ 02891 463933. 🖷 02891 469854.
Area: Carlingford Lough to Lough Foyle.

WESTERN REGION

LIVERPOOL COASTGUARD
53°30'N 03°03'W. MMSI 002320019
Hall Rd West, Crosby, Liverpool L23 8SY.
☎ 0151 9313341. 🖷 0151 9320978
Area: Mull of Galloway to Queensferry
(near Chester).

†HOLYHEAD COASTGUARD
53°19'N 04°38'W. MMSI 002320018
Prince of Wales Rd, Holyhead, Anglesey
LL65 1ET.
☎ 01407 762051. 🖷 01407 761613
Area: Queensferry to Friog (1·6M S of
Barmouth).

†MILFORD HAVEN COASTGUARD

51°42′N 05°03′W. MMSI 002320017
Gorsewood Drive, Hakin, Milford Haven, SA73 2HD.
☎ 01646 690909. 📠 01646 697287.
Area: Friog to River Towy (11M N of Worms Head).

SWANSEA COASTGUARD

51°34′N 03°58′W. MMSI 002320016
Tutt Head, Mumbles, Swansea SA3 4EX.
☎ 01792 366534. 📠 01792 368371.
Area: River Towy to Marsland Mouth (near Bude).

†*FALMOUTH COASTGUARD

50°09′N 05°03′W. MMSI 002320014
Pendennis Point, Castle Drive, Falmouth TR11 4WZ.
☎ 01326 317575. 📠 01326 315610.
Area: Marsland Mouth (near Bude) to Dodman Point.

*BRIXHAM COASTGUARD

50°24′N 03°31′W. DSC MMSI 002320013
King's Quay, Brixham TQ5 9TW.
☎ 01803 882704. 📠 01803 859562.
Area: Dodman Point to Topsham (R. Exe).

NOTES: †Monitors DSC MF 2187.5 kHz.
*Broadcasts Gunfacts/Subfacts.

NATIONAL COASTWATCH INSTITUTION

The NCI is a charity dedicated to the safety of all mariners in UK coastal waters. Since 1994 it has re-introduced visual watch stations, usually by re-opening abandoned CG lookouts. Over long stretches of coastline volunteer NCI watchkeepers alone provide the vitally important visual watch link with HM CG, the RNLI and other SAR services. Many lives have been saved as a direct result of their actions.

VHF Ch 16 is monitored to detect weak distress messages. All passing small boats are logged to assist in the search for missing craft. By day NCI reports actual weather and sea states to yachtsmen requesting local conditions; see ☎ below.

Most NCI stations can warn a yacht of an apparently dangerous course by light signal, ie 'U' ··− (You are standing into danger). In poor visibility some stations keep a radar watch to 20M offshore. Ⓡ = Radar equipped.

The 35 NCI stations below were/are operational in 2009/10. They are marked on the Area maps by ©, for Coastwatch.

Area 1

Gwennap Head Ⓡ	01736 871351
Penzance	01736 367063
Bass Point (Lizard) Ⓡ	01326 290212
Nare Point (Helford River)	01326 231113
Portscatho (w/ends only)	01872 580180
Charlestown Ⓡ	01726 817068
Polruan (Fowey) Ⓡ	01726 870291
Rame Head (Plymouth) Ⓡ	01752 823706
Prawle Point (Salcombe) Ⓡ	01548 511259
Froward Pt (Dartmouth) Ⓡ	07976 505649
Teignmouth	01626 772377
Exmouth	01395 222492
Portland Bill Ⓡ	01305 860178
St Alban's Head Ⓡ	01929 439220

Area 2

Peveril Pt (Swanage) Ⓡ	01929 422596
Lee on Solent	023 9255 6758
Gosport	023 9276 5194

Area 3

Shoreham	07530 041733
Newhaven	01273 516464
Folkestone (Copt Pt)	01303 227132

Area 4

Herne Bay (w/ends only)	01227 743208
Whitstable (w/ends only)	07932 968707
Holehaven (Canvey Is)	01268 696971
Southend (w/ends only)	07815 945210
Felixstowe	01394 670808
Great Yarmouth Ⓡ	01493 440384
Mundesley (Norfolk) Ⓡ	01263 722399
Wells-next-the-Sea Ⓡ	01328 710587
Skegness Ⓡ	01754 610900
Hartlepool Ⓡ	01429 274931
Sunderland Life Brigade Ⓡ	01915 672579
Berwick (w/e; limited hrs)	07950 149865

Area 8

Rossall Point (Fleetwood)	01253 681378
Wooltack Point	07817 871549
Worms Head (Gower)	01792 390167

Area 9

Nells Point (Barry)	01446 420746
Boscastle (N Cornwall) Ⓡ	01840 250965
Stepper Point (Padstow) Ⓡ	07810 898041
St Agnes Head	01872 552073
St Ives Ⓡ	01736 799398
Cape Cornwall Ⓡ	01736 787890

For full details visit: www.nci.org.uk

Royal National Lifeboat Institution

The RNLI is a registered charity which saves life at sea. It provides, on call H24, a lifeboat service up to 50M off the UK and Irish coasts.

There are 230+ lifeboat stations, 130 all-weather and 191 inshore LBs from 4·9 to 17·0m LOA, plus 3 hovercraft. There are 131 LBs in the reserve fleet. All new LBs are capable of at least 25 knots.

When launched on service, lifeboats >10m keep watch on VHF and MF DSC as well as VHF Ch 16. They can also use alternative frequencies to contact other vessels, SAR aircraft, HM CG, Coast radio stations or other SAR agencies. All lifeboats show a quick-flashing blue light when on operational service.

The RNLI also actively promotes safety at sea by providing a free comprehensive safety service to members and the general public including advice, publications and demonstrations. The RNLI aims to save lives and prevent accidents by helping people be prepared through water safety awareness.

A new and useful A5 size, ring-bound RNLI Handbook covers emergencies, first aid, seamanship, weather, navigation and engines – recommended.

For more details of how the RNLI can help you to be safer at sea, call the RNLI on 0800 328 0600, email seasafety@rnli.org.uk or visit www.rnli.org.uk.

To support the RNLI by becoming a member, contact: RNLI, West Quay Road, Poole, Dorset BH15 1HZ.
☎ 01202 663000. 📠 01202 663167.

THE CHANNEL ISLANDS

There is no CG as such in the Channel Islands. The HMs at St Peter Port and St Helier direct SAR operations within the Northern and Southern areas respectively.

Communications on VHF, MF and DSC are provided by St Peter Port Radio and Jersey Coastguard (Coast radio stations).

Close liaison is maintained with adjacent French SAR authorities. A distress situation may be controlled by the Channel Islands or France, whichever is more appropriate. For example a British yacht in difficulty in French waters may be handled by St Peter Port or Jersey so as to avoid language problems; and vice versa for a French yacht.

ST PETER PORT RADIO 49°27'·00N 02°32'00W. DSC MMSI 002320064. ☎ 01481 720672. 📠 714177. Area: Channel Islands North.

JERSEY CG 49°10'·85N 02°14'30W. DSC MMSI 002320060. ☎: 01534 741121. 📠: 499089. Area: Channel Islands South.

SEARCH AND RESCUE ABROAD
THE IRISH REPUBLIC

The Irish CG co-ordinates SAR operations around the coast of Ireland via Dublin MRCC, Malin Head and Valentia MRSCs and remote sites. It may liaise with the UK and France during any rescue operation within 100M of the Irish coast.

It is part of the Dept of Marine, Leeson Lane, Dublin 2. ☎ (01) 6620922; 📠 (01) 6620795. The Irish EPIRB Registry is co-located; ☎ (01) 6199280; 📠 (01) 6621571.

The MRCC/MRSCs are co-located with the Coast radio stations of the same name and manned by the same staff. All stations keep watch H24 on VHF Ch 16 and DSC Ch 70. If ashore dial 999 or 112 in an emergency and ask for Marine Rescue.

Details of the MRCC/MRSCs are as follows:

DUBLIN (MRCC)
53°20'N 06°15W. DSC MMSI 002500300 (+2187·5 kHz).

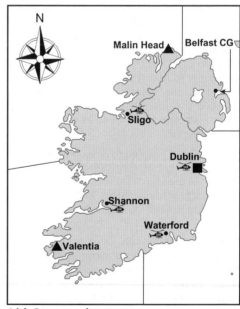

Irish Coastguard centres

☎ +353 1 662 0922/3; 🖷 +353 1 662 0795.
Area: Carlingford Lough to Youghal.

VALENTIA (MRSC)
51°56'N 10°21'W.DSC MMSI 002500200
(+2187·5 kHz).
☎ +353 669 476 109; 🖷 +353 669 476 289.
Area: Youghal to Slyne Head.

MALIN HEAD (MRSC)
55°22'N 07°20W. DSC MMSI 002500100
(+2187·5 kHz).
☎ +353 77 70103; 🖷 +353 77 70221.
Area: Slyne Head to Lough Foyle.

SAR resources
The Irish CG provides some 50 units around the coast and is on call H24. The RNLI maintains 4 stations around the coast and operates 42 lifeboats; six community-run inshore

rescue boats are also available.

Sikorsky S-61 helicopters, based at Dublin, Waterford, Shannon and Sligo, can respond within 15 to 45 minutes and operate to a radius of 200M. They are equipped with infrared search equipment and can uplift 30 survivors.

Military and civilian aircraft and vessels, together with the Garda and lighthouse service, can also be called upon.

Some stations provide specialist cliff climbing services. They are manned by volunteers, who are trained in first aid and equipped with inflatables, breeches buoys, cliff ladders, etc. Their ☎ numbers (the Leader's residence) are given, where appropriate, under each port.

DENMARK
The national SAR agency is: Ministry of Defence, 42 Holmens Kanal,DK-1060 København K, Denmark.
☎ +45 339 23320; 🖷 +45 333 20655.

The SAR coordinator for Denmark is MRCC Århus, ☎ +45 894 33099 ext 3203; 🖷 +45 894 33230; mrcc@sok.dk. Århus has no direct communications with vessels in distress, but operates via two MRSCs and several Coast radio stations (CRS). MRSC Kattegat, ☎ +45 992 22255; 🖷 +45 992 22838, deals with the W coast of Denmark.

Lyngby Radio
This is the main Danish CRS and is DSC VHF/MF/HF equipped (☎ +45 452 89800; 🖷 +45 458 82485, lyngby-radio@tdc.dk MMSI 002191000).

It operates through remote sites at Skagen, Hirtshals, Hantsholm, Bovbjerg and Blavand, all of which guard Ch 16 H24 and use callsign *Lyngby Radio*. Their VHF and MF frequencies are shown in the chartlet opposite.

There are at least 12 lifeboats stationed at the major harbours along the west coast. They are designed to double up as Pilot boats.

Firing practice areas
There are 4 such areas on the W coast as in the chartlet and listed below. Firing times are broadcast daily by Danmarks Radio 1 after the weather at 1645UT. Times can also be obtained from the Range office Ch 16 or ☎.

Ⓐ Tranum & Blokhus ☎ 982 35088 or call *Tranum*.
Ⓑ Nymindegab ☎ 752 89355 or call *Nymindegab*.
Ⓒ Oksbøl ☎ 765 41213 or call *Oksbøl*.
Ⓓ Rømø E ☎ 747 55219; Rømø W ☎ 745 41340 – or call *Fly Rømø*.

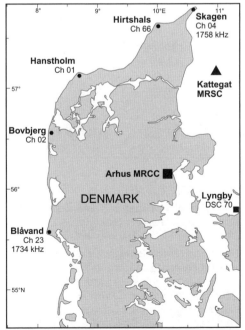

Danish Coastguard centres

GERMANY

The national SAR agency is: *Deutsche Gesellschaft zur Rettung Schiffbrüchiger* (DGzRS), the German Sea Rescue Service. Werderstrasse 2, Hermann-Helms-Haus, D-28199 Bremen. mail@mrcc-bremen.de. ☎ 421 537 070; 🖷 421 537 0714.

DGzRS is responsible for coordinating SAR operations, supported by ships and SAR helicopters of the German Navy.

Bremen MRCC (☎ 421 536870; 🖷 421 5368714; MMSI 002111240), using callsign *Bremen Rescue Radio,* maintains an H24 watch on Ch 16 and DSC Ch 70 via remote Coast radio stations at:

Blumenthal / Borkum / Cuxhaven / Helgoland / kampen / Norderney / Stade / Wangerooge / Westerhever.

There are 21 offshore lifeboats, LOA 23–44m,

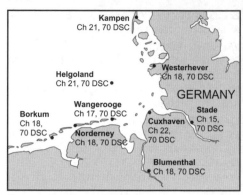

German Coastguard stations

and 21 smaller <10m lifeboats, based at List, Amrum, Helgoland, Cuxhaven, Bremerhaven, Wilhelmshaven, Langeoog, Norderney and Borkum. There are also many inshore lifeboats.

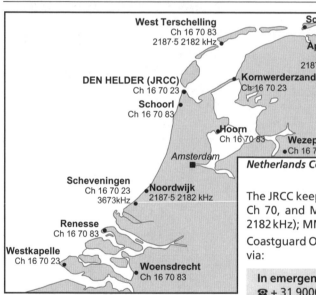

Netherlands Coastguard stations

The JRCC keeps a listening watch H24 on DSC Ch 70, and MF DSC 2187·5 kHz (but not on 2182 kHz); MMSI 002442000.

Coastguard Operations can be contacted H24 via:

In emergency:
☎ + 31 9000 111 or dial 112.

Operational telephone number:
☎ + 31 223 542300. 🖷 + 31 223 658358; ccc@kustwacht.nl If using a mobile phone, call 9000 111, especially if the International emergency number 112 is subject to delays.

Admin/info (HO)
☎+ 31 223 658300. 🖷+31 223 658303. info@kustwacht.nl PO Box 10000, 1780 CA Den Helder.

THE NETHERLANDS

The national SAR agency is: SAR Commission, Directorate Transport Safety (DGG), PO Box 20904, 2500 EX The Hague, Netherlands.

The Netherlands CG at Den Helder, co-located with the Navy HQ, coordinates SAR operations as the Dutch JRCC for A1 and A2 Sea Areas. (JRCC = Joint Rescue Coordination Centre – marine & aeronautical.) Callsign is *Netherlands Coastguard,* but *Den Helder Rescue* during SAR operations.

Remote CG stations are shown above. Working channels are VHF 23 and 83.

BELGIUM

The Belgian CG coordinates SAR operations from Oostende MRCC, callsign *Coastguard Oostende*. The MRCC and *Oostende Radio* (Coast radio rtation) both keep listening watch H24 on Ch 16, 2182 kHz and DSC Ch 70 and 2187·5 kHz.

Coastguard stations

MRCC OOSTENDE
☎ +32 59 701000; ✆ +32 59 703605. MMSI 002050480.

MRSC Nieuwpoort
☎ +32 58 230000; ✆ +32 58 231575.

MRSC Zeebrugge
☎ +32 50 550801; ✆ +32 50 547400.

RCC Brussels (COSPAS/SARSAT agency)
☎ +32 2 7200338; ✆ +32 2 7524201.

Coast Radio Stations

OOSTENDE Radio
☎ 59 702438; ✆ 59 701339.
Ch 16, DSC Ch 70 and MF DSC 2187·5 kHz.
MMSI 002050480.

Antwerpen Radio (remotely controlled by Oostende CRS) MMSI 002050485. Ch 16, DSC Ch 70.

Resources

Offshore and inshore lifeboats are based at Nieuwpoort, Oostende and Zeebrugge.

The Belgian Air Force provides helicopters from Koksijde near the French border. The Belgian Navy also participates in SAR operations as required.

FRANCE – CROSS

Four CROSS (Centres Régionaux Opérationnels de Surveillance et de Sauvetage, ie an MRCC) provide a permanent, H24, all weather operational presence along the N and W coasts and liaise with foreign CGs.

CROSS' main functions include:

- Co-ordinating SAR operations.
- Navigational surveillance.
- Broadcasting navigational warnings.
- Broadcasting weather information.
- Anti-pollution control.
- Marine and fishery surveillance.

CROSS locations and areas of responsibility

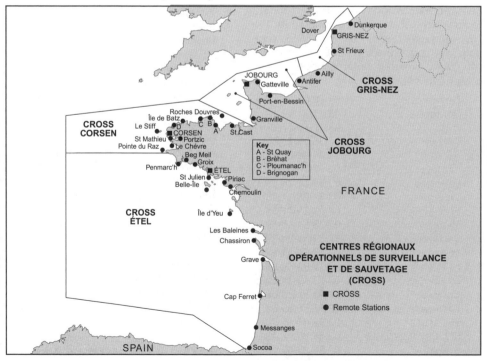

All centres keep watch on VHF Ch 16 as well as Ch 70 (DSC)and co-ordinate SAR on Ch 15, 67, 68, 73. They also broadcast gale warnings, weather forecasts and local navigational warnings.

CROSSA Étel specialises in medical advice and responds to alerts from Cospas/Sarsat satellites.

CROSS can be contacted by R/T, by ☎, through Coast Radio Stations, via the National Gendarmerie or Affaires Maritimes, or via a Semaphore station. Call *Semaphore* stations on Ch 16 (working Ch 10) or by ☎ as listed later in this section.

CROSS also monitor TSS in the Dover Strait, off Casquets and off Ouessant using, for example, the callsign *Corsen Traffic*.

For medical advice call CROSS which will contact a doctor or SAMU (Service d'Aide Médicale Urgente). In harbour/marina SAMU responds faster to a medical emergency than calling a doctor. Simply dial 15.

CROSS stations (Emergency ☎ 1616).

CROSS Gris-Nez
50°52'N 01°35'E   MMSI 002275100
☎ 03 21 87 21 87; ▨ 03 21 87 78 55
Belgian border to Cap d'Antifer.

NavWarnings Ch 79 at every H+10 via Dunkerque, Saint-Frieux and L'Ailly.

CROSS Jobourg
49°41'N 01°54'W   MMSI 002275200
☎ 02 33 52 72 13; ▨ 02 33 52 71 72
Cap de la Hague to Mont St Michel

NavWarnings Ch 80 every H+20 and H+50 via Antifer, Ver-sur-Mer, Gatteville, Jobourg, Granville and Roche Douvres.

CROSS Corsen
48°24'N 04°47'W   MMSI 002275300
☎ 02 98 89 31 31; ▨ 02 98 89 65 75
Mont St Michel to Pointe de Penmarc'h.

NavWarnings Ch 79 every H+10 and H+40 via Cap Fréhel, Bodic, Ile de Batz, Le Stiff and Pte du Raz.

CROSS Étel
47°39'N 03°12'W   MMSI 002275000
☎ 02 97 55 35 35; ▨ 02 97 55 49 34
Pte de Penmarc'h to the Spanish border

NavWarnings Ch 79 for Landes range activity via Chassiron 1903; Soulac 1915; Cap Ferret 1933; Contis 1945; and Biarritz 2003.

Semaphore stations keep visual, radar and radio watch (Ch 16); are equipped with VHF DF; relay emergency calls to CROSS; show gale warning signals, repeat forecasts and offer local weather reports. Hours sunrise-sunset, but * H24.

* Dunkerque	03·28·66·86·18	* Ploumanac'h	02·96·91·46·51
Boulogne	03·21·31·32·10	Batz	02·98·61·76·06
Ault	03·22·60·47·33	* Brignogan	02·98·83·50·84
Dieppe	02·35·84·23·82	* Ouessant Stiff	02·98·48·81·50
* Fécamp	02·35·28·00·91	* St-Mathieu	02·98·89·01·59
* La Hève	02·35·46·07·81	* Portzic (Ch 08)	02·98·22·21·47
* Le Havre	02·35·21·74·39	Toulinguet	02·98·27·90·02
Villerville	02·31·88·11·13	Cap-de-la-Chèvre	02·98·27·09·55
* Port-en-Bessin	02·31·21·81·51	* Pointe-du-Raz	02·98·70·66·57
St-Vaast	02·33·54·44·50	* Penmarc'h	02·98·58·61·00
* Barfleur	02·33·54·04·37	Beg Meil	02·98·94·98·92
Lévy	02·33·54·31·17	* Port-Louis	02·97·82·52·10
* Le Homet	02·33·92·60·08	Étel Mât Fenoux	02·97·55·35·35
La Hague	02·33·52·71·07	Beg Melen (Groix)	02·97·86·80·13
Carteret	02·33·53·85·08	Talut (Belle-Île)	02·97·31·85·07
Barneville Le Roc	02·33·50·05·85	St-Julien	02·97·50·09·35
St-Cast	02·96·41·85·30	Piriac-sur-Mer	02·40·23·59·87
* St Quay-Portrieux	02·96.70.42.18	* Chemoulin	02·40·91·99·00
Bréhat	02·96·20·00·12	St-Sauveur (Yeu)	02·51·58·31·01
		Les Baleines (Ré)	05·46·29·42·06
		Chassiron (Oléron)	05·46·47·85·43
		* Pointe-de-Grave	05·56·09·60·03
		Cap Ferret	05·56·60·60·03
		Messanges	05·58·48·94·10
		* Socoa	05·59·47·18·54

EMERGENCY VHF DF SERVICE

A yacht in emergency can call CROSS on VHF Ch 16, 11 or 67 to obtain a true bearing of the yacht *from* the DF station. These monitor Ch 16 and other continuously scanned frequencies, which include Ch 1-29, 36, 39, 48, 50, 52, 55, 56 and 60-88. The Semaphore stations overleaf are also equipped with VHF DF.

HJ = Day service only.

VHF DF stations, are listed below geographically from NE to W then S:

Station	Lat/Long	Hrs
Dunkerque	51°03'.40N 02°20'.40E	H24
*Gris-Nez	50°52'.20N 01°35'.01E	H24
Boulogne	50°44'.00N 01°36'.00E	HJ
Ault	50°06'.50N 01°27'.50E	HJ
Dieppe	49°56'.00N 01°05'.20E	HJ
Fécamp	49°46'.10N 00°22'.20E	H24
La Hève	49°30'.60N 00°04'.20E	H24
Villerville	49°23'.20N 00°06'.50E	HJ
Port-en-Bessin	49°21'.10N 00°46'.30W	H24
Saint-Vaast	49°34'.50N 01°16'.50W	HJ
Barfleur	49°41'.90N 01°15'.90W	H24
Levy	49°41'.70N 01°28'.20W	HJ
†Homet	49°39'.50N 01°37'.90W	H24
*Jobourg	49°41'.50N 01°54'.50W	H24
La Hague	49°43'.60N 01°56'.30W	HJ
Carteret	49°22'.40N 01°48'.30W	HJ
Le Roc	48°50'.10N 01°36'.90W	HJ
Grouin/Cancale	48°42'.60N 01°50'.60W	HJ
Saint-Cast	48°38'.60N 02°14'.70W	HJ
St-Quay-Port'x	48°39'.30N 02°49'.50W	H24
Bréhat	48°51'.30N 03°00'.10W	HJ
Ploumanac'h	48°49'.50N 03°28'.20W	H24
Batz	48°44'.80N 04°00'.60W	HJ
Brignogan	48°40'.60N 04°19'.70W	H24
Creac'h (Ushant)	48°27'.60N 05°07'.70W	HJ
*Creac'h	48°27'.60N 05°07'.80W	H24
†Saint-Mathieu	48°19'.80N 04°46'.20W	H24
Toulinguet	48°16'.80N 04°37'.50W	HJ
Cap de la Chèvre	48°10'.20N 04°33'.00W	HJ
Pointe du Raz	48°02'.30N 04°43'.80W	H24
Penmarc'h	47°47'.90N 04°22'.40W	H24
Beg-Meil	47°51'.30N 03°58'.40W	HJ
Beg Melen	47°39'.20N 03°30'.10W	HJ
†Port-Louis	47°42'.60N 03°21'.80W	H24
*Etel	47°39'.80N 03°12'.00W	H24
Saint-Julien	47°29'.70N 03°07'.50W	HJ
Taillefer	47°21'.80N 03°09'.00W	HJ
Le Talut	47°17'.70N 03°13'.00W	HJ
Piriac	47°22'.50N 02°33'.40W	HJ
Chemoulin	47°14'.10N 02°17'.80W	H24
Saint-Sauveur	46°41'.70N 02°18'.80W	HJ
Les Baleines	46°14'.60N 01°33'.70W	HJ
Chassiron	46°02'.80N 01°24'.50W	HJ
La Coubre	45°41'.90N 01°13'.40W	H24
Pointe de Grave	45°34'.30N 01°03'.90W	HJ
Cap Ferret	44°37'.50N 01°15'.00W	HJ
Messanges	43°48'.80N 01°23'.90W	HJ
Socoa	43°23'.30N 01°41'.10W	H24

Lifeboats

The lifeboat service Société National de Sauvetage en Mer (SNSM) comes under CROSS, but ashore it is best to contact local lifeboat stations direct. A hefty charge may be levied if a SNSM lifeboat attends a vessel not in distress.

Navigation warnings

Long-range warnings are broadcast by SafetyNet for Navarea II, which includes the W coast of France. The N coast is in Navarea I.

Avurnavs (AVis URgents aux NAVigateurs) are regional, coastal and local warnings issued by Cherbourg and Brest and broadcast by Niton and Brest Navtex and on MF. Warnings are prefixed by 'Sécurité Avurnav'.

SPAIN

The Society for Maritime Rescue and Safety (Sociedad de Salvamento y Seguridad Maritima – SASEMAR) is the national agency for SAR operations (and the prevention of pollution); akin to MCA in the UK.

MRCC Madrid coordinates SAR operations via 3 MRCCs (Bilbao, Gijon and Finisterre) on the N coast and Tarifa MRCC on the SW coast – as listed below.

All Centres monitor (H24) VHF Ch 16, MF 2182 kHz and DSC Ch 70, 2187·5 kHz. They also broadcast weather as shown in Chapter 2 and Nav warnings; but do *not* handle commercial link calls.

North and North West Spain

In N and NW Spain CG Centres do not keep continuous watch on Ch 16, so call on a working channel.

Spanish and Portuguese Coastguard Radio Stations

PORTUGAL

The Portuguese Navy coordinates SAR in two regions, Lisboa and Santa Maria (Azores) via MRCCs at Lisboa, Ponta Delgada (Azores) and one planned at Horta (Azores). A network of CRS maintains an H24 listening watch on all distress frequencies.

The Naval HQ (Estado Maior da Armada, 3 Divisao) is at: Praca do Comercio, 1188 Lisboa Codex, Portugal.

☎ 21 346 8965. 📠 21 347 9591.

MAINLAND

Lisboa MRCC
38°41'N 09°19'W   MMSI 002630100
☎ 21 4401919; 📠 21 4401954. mrcclisboa@netc.pt
Planned DSC Ch 70; 2187·5 kHz

Remotely controlled MF DSC stations are planned (2005) at:
Apulia 41°28'N 08°45'W. MMSI 002630200.
Sagres 37°00'N 08°56'W. MMSI 002630400.

AZORES

Ponta Delgada MRCC
37°44'N 25°40'W   MMSI 002040100
☎ 296 281777; 📠 296 281999
mrccdelgada@mail.telepac.pt
Planned DSC Ch 70; 2187·5 kHz.

SOUTH-WEST SPAIN

Tarifa MRCC coordinates SAR in SW Spain and the Gibraltar Strait.

Tarifa MRCC
36°01'N 05°35'W   MMSI 002240994
☎ 956 684740; 📠 956 680 606.

Huelva MRSC
37°13'N 07°07'W   MMSI 002241012
☎ 959 243000; 📠 959 242103.

Cadiz MRSC
36°32'N 06°18'W   MMSI 002241011
☎ 956 214253; 📠 956 226091.

Algeciras MRSC (controlled by Malaga MRCC)
36°08'N 05°26'W   MMSI 002241001
☎ 956 580930; 📠 956 585402.

MADRID MRCC
MMSI 002241008 ☎ 91 7559 132/3;
📠 9I 5261440.

Bilbao MRCC
43°21'N 03°02'W   MMSI 002240996
☎ 944 839411; 📠 944 83 9161.

Santander MRSC
43°28'N 03°43'W   MMSI 002241009
☎ 942 213 030; 📠 942 213 638.

Gijón MRCC
43°34'N 05°42'W   MMSI 002240997
☎ 985 326050; 📠 985 320908.

Finisterre MRCC
42°42'N 08°59'W   MMSI 002240993
☎ 981 767320; 📠 981 767740.

Coruña MRSC
43°22'N 08°23'W   MMSI 002241022
☎ 981 209541; 📠 981 209518.

Vigo MRSC
42°10'N 08°41'W   MMSI 002240998
☎ 986 222230; 📠 986 228957.

Chapter 5 – Tides

TIDES

2011 TIMES OF HW DOVER AND MEAN RANGES

JANUARY

Day	HW	Range	HW
1	0823	4.1	2059
2	0925	4.5	2152
3	1018	4.9	2238
4	1103	5.3	2319
5	1142	5.3	2357
6	1218	5.3	--
7	0034	5.3	1254
8	0111	5.1	1329
9	0144	4.8	1402
10	0214	4.6	1433
11	0244	4.2	1505
12	0319	3.7	1547
13	0408	3.2	1655
14	0522	2.9	1825
15	0644	3.0	1932
16	0751	3.5	2029
17	0846	4.1	2118
18	0936	4.8	2204
19	1022	5.3	2247
20	1106	5.7	2330
21	1149	6.1	--
22	0012	6.2	1232
23	0055	6.3	1315
24	0140	6.1	1400
25	0226	5.7	1448
26	0316	5.0	1542
27	0412	4.3	1647
28	0519	3.5	1806
29	0643	3.3	1933
30	0814	3.5	2049
31	0927	4.1	2146

FEBRUARY

Day	HW	Range	HW
1	1019	4.6	2230
2	1058	5.1	2307
3	1132	5.3	2342
4	1203	5.4	--
5	0016	5.4	1234
6	0048	5.3	1303
7	0115	5.2	1327
8	0136	5.0	1348
9	0159	4.7	1413
10	0230	4.3	1448
11	0311	3.7	1534
12	0405	2.9	1646
13	0553	2.8	1857
14	0726	3.2	2004
15	0829	3.9	2059
16	0922	4.8	2147
17	1009	5.5	2231
18	1053	6.0	2314
19	1134	6.5	2356
20	1215	6.7	--
21	0037	6.7	1257
22	0120	6.5	1339
23	0204	5.9	1425
24	0251	5.1	1516
25	0345	4.1	1617
26	0450	3.3	1733
27	0616	2.9	1906
28	0811	3.2	2035

MARCH

Day	HW	Range	HW
1	0921	3.9	2131
2	1007	4.5	2213
3	1042	5.1	2248
4	1112	5.3	2322
5	1140	5.4	2353
6	1208	5.4	--
7	0021	5.4	1234
8	0044	5.3	1254
9	0101	5.2	1313
10	0124	4.9	1339
11	0156	4.7	1415
12	0236	3.9	1500
13	0327	3.3	1603
14	0457	2.8	1824
15	0703	3.1	1938
16	0809	4.0	2036
17	0903	4.9	2126
18	0951	5.7	2211
19	1034	6.3	2254
20	1115	6.7	2336
21	1156	6.8	--
22	0017	6.8	1237
23	0100	6.4	1320
24	0143	5.9	1405
25	0230	5.0	1456
26	0324	4.0	1555
27	0428	3.2	1703
28	0547	2.8	1827
29	0749	3.1	2002
30	0856	3.7	2101
31	0939	4.3	2144

APRIL

Day	HW	Range	HW
1	1014	4.9	2221
2	1043	5.2	2254
3	1111	5.3	2324
4	1139	5.3	2351
5	1204	5.3	--
6	0012	5.3	1225
7	0033	5.3	1247
8	0059	5.1	1317
9	0132	4.8	1355
10	0214	4.2	1443
11	0308	3.5	1551
12	0440	3.2	1747
13	0636	3.4	1906
14	0744	4.1	2007
15	0839	4.9	2100
16	0928	5.7	2147
17	1012	6.1	2232
18	1055	6.4	2315
19	1137	6.6	2358
20	1219	6.4	--
21	0041	6.3	1303
22	0127	5.7	1349
23	0214	4.9	1439
24	0307	4.2	1534
25	0406	3.5	1634
26	0514	3.1	1744
27	0646	3.2	1906
28	0807	3.5	2015
29	0856	4.1	2104
30	0934	4.5	2144

MAY

Day	HW	Range	HW
1	1007	4.8	2219
2	1037	5.1	2250
3	1107	5.1	2318
4	1135	5.2	2344
5	1202	5.3	--
6	0012	5.2	1231
7	0044	5.0	1306
8	0121	4.8	1348
9	0207	4.4	1440
10	0305	4.0	1547
11	0425	3.8	1709
12	0600	3.9	1827
13	0711	4.3	1934
14	0811	4.8	2031
15	0903	5.3	2123
16	0951	5.7	2212
17	1037	6.0	2259
18	1122	6.1	2345
19	1206	6.0	--
20	0029	5.8	1250
21	0114	5.5	1335
22	0200	5.1	1422
23	0249	4.4	1510
24	0341	3.8	1602
25	0438	3.5	1700
26	0543	3.3	1805
27	0655	3.4	1913
28	0757	3.6	2011
29	0845	4.0	2058
30	0925	4.4	2137
31	1002	4.7	2213

JUNE

Day	HW	Range	HW
1	1036	4.9	2248
2	1111	5.2	2323
3	1145	5.2	2359
4	1222	5.2	--
5	0036	5.3	1302
6	0118	5.1	1346
7	0205	4.9	1436
8	0259	4.7	1532
9	0402	4.4	1636
10	0516	4.3	1746
11	0633	4.3	1858
12	0741	4.5	2004
13	0841	4.8	2105
14	0936	5.1	2201
15	1026	5.4	2252
16	1112	5.6	2338
17	1156	5.6	--
18	0021	5.6	1238
19	0103	5.4	1320
20	0144	5.2	1401
21	0226	4.8	1443
22	0310	4.3	1527
23	0358	3.9	1613
24	0452	3.5	1707
25	0553	3.3	1809
26	0656	3.2	1912
27	0755	3.5	2009
28	0845	3.9	2059
29	0930	4.4	2143
30	1011	4.8	2226

JULY

Day	HW	Range	HW
1	1050	5.2	2306
2	1130	5.3	2347
3	1210	5.6	--
4	0027	5.7	1251
5	0109	5.7	1335
6	0154	5.6	1421
7	0242	5.3	1511
8	0337	4.8	1607
9	0440	4.3	1711
10	0556	4.1	1826
11	0716	4.0	1946
12	0827	4.2	2058
13	0928	4.6	2200
14	1020	5.0	2251
15	1104	5.3	2333
16	1144	5.5	--
17	0010	5.6	1223
18	0047	5.5	1301
19	0122	5.3	1337
20	0158	5.0	1412
21	0232	4.6	1444
22	0307	4.2	1518
23	0347	3.6	1601
24	0448	3.2	1706
25	0604	2.9	1823
26	0714	3.0	1932
27	0813	3.6	2031
28	0904	4.2	2121
29	0949	4.8	2207
30	1031	5.4	2249
31	1112	5.7	2330

AUGUST

Day	HW	Range	HW
1	1152	6.0	--
2	0011	6.2	1234
3	0052	6.2	1316
4	0135	6.1	1401
5	0221	5.6	1448
6	0312	5.0	1542
7	0413	4.2	1645
8	0528	3.7	1803
9	0657	3.4	1938
10	0818	3.8	2101
11	0923	4.3	2200
12	1011	4.9	2244
13	1051	5.3	2320
14	1127	5.6	2352
15	1203	5.6	--
16	0024	5.5	1237
17	0055	5.3	1309
18	0124	5.2	1335
19	0148	4.8	1356
20	0209	4.5	1422
21	0238	4.0	1458
22	0320	3.3	1550
23	0445	2.7	1743
24	0639	2.8	1905
25	0745	3.3	2008
26	0839	4.1	2100
27	0926	5.0	2147
28	1009	5.6	2229
29	1050	6.1	2310
30	1131	6.4	2350
31	1212	6.5	--

SEPTEMBER

Day	HW	Range	HW
1	0030	6.5	1254
2	0113	6.3	1338
3	0158	5.6	1426
4	0250	4.9	1520
5	0351	4.0	1625
6	0505	3.2	1746
7	0635	3.1	1935
8	0806	3.5	2056
9	0908	4.3	2147
10	0953	5.0	2226
11	1030	5.3	2258
12	1104	5.3	2327
13	1138	5.5	2356
14	1209	5.4	--
15	0024	5.3	1237
16	0049	5.3	1257
17	0107	5.0	1315
18	0127	4.6	1341
19	0158	4.2	1418
20	0240	3.4	1506
21	0340	2.8	1648
22	0604	2.8	1840
23	0714	3.3	1944
24	0811	4.2	2037
25	0859	5.1	2123
26	0943	5.8	2206
27	1025	6.3	2246
28	1107	6.6	2327
29	1149	6.6	--
30	0008	6.5	1232

OCTOBER

Day	HW	Range	HW
1	0052	6.2	1317
2	0128	5.6	1405
3	0231	4.8	1501
4	0331	3.8	1607
5	0440	3.2	1724
6	0601	3.1	1915
7	0734	3.4	2032
8	0838	4.2	2120
9	0923	4.8	2157
10	1001	5.2	2228
11	1036	5.3	2256
12	1108	5.3	2325
13	1138	5.3	2353
14	1203	5.3	--
15	0016	5.2	1224
16	0036	5.1	1245
17	0101	4.8	1315
18	0134	4.3	1352
19	0218	3.7	1442
20	0318	3.2	1559
21	0516	3.1	1808
22	0637	3.4	1914
23	0738	4.2	2009
24	0829	5.1	2057
25	0916	5.7	2141
26	1000	6.2	2224
27	1044	6.4	2306
28	1128	6.5	2349
29	1213	6.3	--
30	0035	6.0	1259
31	0123	5.5	1349

NOVEMBER

Day	HW	Range	HW
1	0214	4.8	1444
2	0311	4.0	1545
3	0412	3.4	1654
4	0520	3.2	1820
5	0640	3.3	1944
6	0752	3.8	2037
7	0844	4.3	2118
8	0926	4.6	2153
9	1003	5.0	2224
10	1036	5.1	2255
11	1106	5.2	2324
12	1134	5.2	2351
13	1200	5.2	--
14	0017	5.1	1228
15	0047	4.9	1301
16	0124	4.6	1341
17	0209	4.2	1431
18	0307	3.8	1537
19	0423	3.5	1715
20	0548	3.7	1836
21	0659	4.2	1937
22	0757	4.8	2030
23	0850	5.3	2119
24	0940	5.7	2207
25	1028	6.0	2253
26	1115	6.2	2338
27	1201	6.1	--
28	0024	5.8	1248
29	0110	5.5	1336
30	0158	4.9	1426

DECEMBER

Day	HW	Range	HW
1	0247	4.4	1519
2	0340	3.8	1616
3	0437	3.5	1720
4	0541	3.3	1832
5	0651	3.3	1938
6	0753	3.6	2031
7	0844	4.1	2114
8	0927	4.4	2152
9	1003	4.8	2227
10	1037	5.0	2300
11	1111	5.1	2332
12	1144	5.2	--
13	0005	5.2	1218
14	0040	5.2	1254
15	0118	5.0	1334
16	0201	4.8	1420
17	0251	4.6	1515
18	0350	4.2	1621
19	0459	4.0	1743
20	0615	4.1	1902
21	0728	4.3	2008
22	0832	4.6	2106
23	0929	5.1	2159
24	1023	5.5	2248
25	1112	5.8	2332
26	1156	5.9	--
27	0015	5.8	1239
28	0057	5.6	1321
29	0139	5.3	1403
30	0221	4.8	1447
31	0305	4.4	1534

2011 TIDAL COEFFICIENTS

Date	Jan am	Jan pm	Feb am	Feb pm	Mar am	Mar pm	Apr am	Apr pm	May am	May pm	June am	June pm	July am	July pm	Aug am	Aug pm	Sept am	Sept pm	Oct am	Oct pm	Nov am	Nov pm	Dec am	Dec pm
1	60	64	69	74	54	60	72	76	71	74	74	76	78	81	99	101	108	105	98	91	65	58	59	53
2	68	72	78	81	66	71	79	81	76	78	78	80	84	86	102	102	99	92	82	73	51	46	48	45
3	75	79	84	86	76	80	83	85	80	81	81	81	88	89	101	98	85	76	64	56	42	41	42	41
4	81	83	87	88	83	86	86	86	82	82	81	80	90	89	94	89	67	59	48	43	41	42	41	41
5	85	85	87	86	87	88	86	85	81	80	79	78	88	86	83	77	51	45	43	40	44	47	42	44
6	85	84	85	83	89	88	84	81	79	76	76	73	84	81	70	63	45	42	40	43	51	55	47	51
7	83	81	80	76	87	86	79	75	74	70	71	68	77	73	56	50	42	45	47	53	59	63	54	58
8	78	75	73	68	84	81	72	67	67	63	65	63	68	64	51	48	49	55	58	63	67	70	62	65
9	72	68	64	58	78	74	62	57	59	55	61	60	64	61	47	49	61	67	68	72	73	75	68	71
10	64	59	53	48	69	64	52	47	53	51	60	60	58	56	53	58	72	77	76	79	77	78	74	76
11	55	50	43	38	59	53	43	40	51	52	61	63	57	58	63	69	81	84	81	83	79	79	78	79
12	46	41	34	32	47	42	40	40	52	55	65	69	61	65	74	78	86	88	84	84	79	79	80	80
13	38	35	32	33	37	34	43	48	59	65	72	76	69	73	82	85	88	88	84	83	78	76	80	79
14	34	34	37	43	34	34	55	63	70	77	80	83	77	81	87	89	88	86	82	81	74	72	78	76
15	35	38	50	59	37	43	71	80	82	88	86	88	84	86	89	89	84	82	78	76	69	66	74	71
16	43	48	68	77	51	60	88	95	92	96	90	91	88	88	88	86	79	75	72	69	62	58	69	66
17	55	61	85	93	69	79	101	106	99	100	90	89	88	87	84	81	71	67	64	60	54	51	63	60
18	68	75	100	106	88	97	110	112	101	100	88	85	86	83	77	73	61	56	54	50	49	47	58	56
19	81	88	111	114	104	110	112	110	98	95	82	79	80	77	68	64	51	45	45	41	47	49	56	56
20	93	97	115	115	114	117	107	103	91	86	75	71	73	68	58	53	40	35	38	37	49	52	57	59
21	101	103	113	109	118	117	97	90	81	75	66	62	64	59	47	42	32	30	37	38	57	63	62	66
22	105	105	104	97	114	109	83	75	70	64	57	53	54	49	37	33	31	34	43	49	69	76	71	76
23	103	100	89	80	103	95	67	60	59	53	48	45	44	40	33	31	39	46	56	64	82	88	81	85
24	96	91	71	61	87	78	53	46	49	45	42	40	37	35	31	34	55	63	73	81	93	97	89	93
25	85	78	53	45	68	59	42	42	43	44	40	39	35	34	40	46	73	81	89	96	100	102	95	96
26	70	63	40	41	51	43	39	38	41	41	39	41	36	39	54	62	90	97	102	106	102	102	96	95
27	56	50	38	39	43	38	40	43	42	44	44	47	44	49	70	78	104	109	109	111	100	97	94	91
28	46	46	43	48	36	37	47	51	47	50	51	56	56	62	86	93	112	114	111	109	93	88	87	83
29	45	46			40	45	55	59	54	57	60	65	68	75	99	104	115	113	105	101	82	77	79	74
30	49	53			51	57	64	67	61	64	70	74	81	86	108	111	110	105	95	88	70	65	68	63
31	59	64			62	67			68	71			91	95	112	111			80	73			57	51

Tidal coefficients indicate the magnitude of the tide on any particular day without having to look up and calculate the range, and thus determine whether it is springs, neaps or somewhere in between. This table is valid for all areas covered by this Almanac. Typical values are:

120	Very big spring tide
95	**Mean spring tide**
70	Average tide
45	**Mean neap tide**
20	Very small neap tide

TIDES

TIDAL CALCULATIONS

Find the height at a given time (STANDARD PORT)

1. On Standard Curve diagram, plot heights of HW and LW occuring either side of required time and join by sloping line.
2. Enter HW Time and sufficient others to bracket required time.
3. From required time, proceed vertically to curves, using heights plotted in (1) to help interpolation between Spring and Neaps. Do NOT extrapolate.
4. Proceed horizontally to sloping line, thence vertically to Height scale.
5. Read off height.

EXAMPLE:

Find the height of tide at ULLAPOOL at 1900 on 6th January

From tables	JANUARY	
ULLAPOOL	**6** 0420	4.6
	1033	1.6
	1641	4.6
	F 2308	1.2

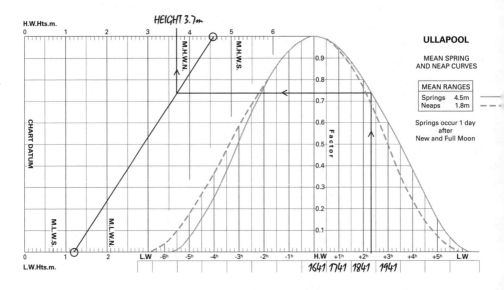

Find the time for a given height (STANDARD PORT)

1. On Standard Curve diagram, plot heights of HW and LW occurring either side of required event and join by sloping line.
2. Enter HW time and those for half-tidal cycle covering required event.
3. From required height, proceed vertically to sloping line, thence horizontally to curves, using heights plotted in (1) to assist interpolation between Spring and Neaps. Do NOT extrapolate.
4. Proceed vertically to Time scale.
5. Read off time.

EXAMPLE:
Find the time at which the afternoon tide at ULLAPOOL falls to 3.7m on 6 January

From tables	JANUARY	
ULLAPOOL	**6** 0420 1033 1641 F 2308	4.6 1.6 4.6 1.2

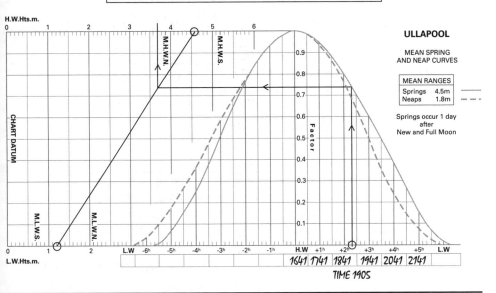

Find the time and height of HW and LW at a Secondary Port

EXAMPLE:
Find the time and height of the afternoon HW and LW at ST MARY's (Isles of Scilly) on 14th July (BST)

Note: *The data used in this example do not refer to the year of these tables.*

From tables	JULY	
PLYMOUTH (DEVONPORT)	**14** 0309 0927 1532 SA 2149	1.0 5.3 1.1 5.0

From tables

Location	Lat	Long	High Water		Low Water		MHWS	MHWN	MLWN	MLWS
DEVONPORT *Standard port*	50°22'N	4°11'W	0000 and 1200	0600 and 1800	0000 and 1200	0600 and 1800	5.5	4.4	2.2	0.8
St Mary's, *Scilly*	49° 55'N	6°19'W	–0035	–0100	–0040	–0025	+0.2	–0.1	–0.2	–0.1

TIDES

TIDAL PREDICTION FORM (NP 204)

STANDARD PORT ...Devonport... TIME/HEIGHT REQUIRED...pm...

SECONDARY PORT St Mary's ... DATE 14 July ... TIME ZONE B.S.T

	TIME		HEIGHT		
STANDARD PORT	HW	LW	HW	LW	RANGE
	1 2149	2 1532	3 5.0	4 1.1	5 3.9
Seasonal change	Standard Ports -		6 0.0	6 0.0	
DIFFERENCES	7* -0044	8 -0032	9 0.1	10 -0.1	
Seasonal change *	Secondary Ports +		11 0.0	11 0.0	
SECONDARY PORT	12 2105	13 1500	14 5.1	15 1.0	
Duration	16 0605		LW 1500 UT = 1600 BST		
			HW 2105 UT = 2205 BST		

* The seasonal changes are generally less than – 0.1m and for most purposes can be ignored. See Admiraly Tide Tables Vol 1. for details

CLEARANCE BELOW BRIDGES AND OVERHEAD POWER LINES

Vertical clearance heights are above the level of HAT (Highest Astronomical Tide) instead of MHWS as in the past. HAT is always a higher level than MHWS, as shown in the diagram on the back cover flap. It helps to draw such a diagram and insert the relevant dimensions when calculating overhead clearances. The Height of HAT above Chart Datum is stated at the foot of each page of Standard port tide tables. New editions of Admiralty charts are referenced to HAT; earlier editions to MHWS. Check the title block under **Height**s.

INTERMEDIATE TIMES/HEIGHTS (SECONDARY PORT)

These are the same as the appropriate calculations for a Standard Port except that the Standard Curve diagram for the Standard Port must be entered with HW and LW heights and times for the Secondary Port obtained on Form N.P. 204. When interpolating between the Spring and Neap curves the Range at the Standard Port must be used.

EXAMPLE:

Find the height of the tide at PADSTOW at 1100 on 28th February. Find the time at which the morning tide at PADSTOW falls to 4.9m on 28th February.

Note: The data in these examples do not refer to the year of these tables.

From tables	FEBRUARY	
MILFORD HAVEN		
	28 0315	1.1
	0922	6.6
	1538	1.3
	TU 2145	6.3

Location	Lat	Long	High Water		Low Water		MHWS	MHWN	MLWN	MLWS
			0100	0700	0100	0700				
MILFORD HAVEN	51°42′N	5°03′W	and	and	and	and	**7.0**	**5.2**	**2.5**	**0.7**
Standard port			1300	1900	1300	1900				
River Camel										
Padstow	50°33′N	4°56′W	−0055	−0050	−0040	−0050	+0.3	+0.4	+0.1	+0.1
Wadebridge	50°31′N	4°50′W	−0052	−0052	+0235	+0245	−3.8	−3.8	−2.5	−0.4

TIDAL PREDICTION FORM (NP 204)

STANDARD PORT ....*Milford Haven*.... TIME/HEIGHT REQUIRED.........*1100 : 4.9*

SECONDARY PORT ..*Padstow*..... DATE *28 Feb* .... TIME ZONE.... *UT*

	TIME		HEIGHT		
	HW	**LW**	**HW**	**LW**	**RANGE**
STANDARD PORT	¹ 0922	² 1538	³ 6·6	⁴ 1·3	⁵ 5·3
Seasonal change	Standard Ports +		⁶ 0·0	⁶ 0·0	
DIFFERENCES	⁷* -0052	⁸ –	⁹ +0·3	¹⁰ +0·1	
Seasonal change *	Secondary Ports -		¹¹ 0·0	¹¹ 0·0	
SECONDARY PORT	¹² 0830	¹³ –	¹⁴ 6·9	¹⁵ 1·4	
Duration	¹⁶ –				

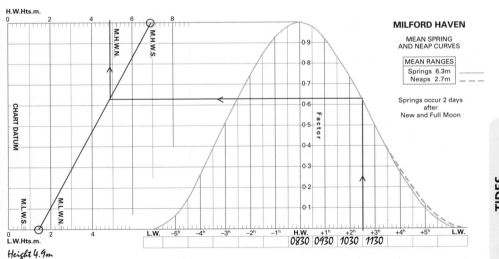

H.W.Hts.m.

MILFORD HAVEN

MEAN SPRING
AND NEAP CURVES

MEAN RANGES
Springs 6.3m
Neaps 2.7m

Springs occur 2 days
after
New and Full Moon

CHART DATUM

M.H.W.N. M.H.W.S. M.L.W.S. M.L.W.N.

Factor

L.W. −5ʰ −4ʰ −3ʰ −2ʰ −1ʰ H.W. +1ʰ +2ʰ +3ʰ +4ʰ +5ʰ L.W.

0830 0930 1030 1130

L.W.Hts.m.

Height 4.9m

TIDES

135

SPECIAL INSTRUCTIONS FOR PLACES BETWEEN BOURNEMOUTH AND SELSEY BILL

• Owing to the rapid change of tidal characteristics and distortion of the tidal curve in this area, curves are shown for individual ports. It is a characteristic of the tide here that Low Water is more sharply defined than High Water and these curves have therefore been drawn with their times relative to that of Low Water.

• Apart from differences caused by referring the times to Low Water the procedure for obtaining intermediate heights at places whose curves are shown is identical to that used for normal Secondary Ports.

• The **height** differences for ports between Bournemouth and Yarmouth always refer to the higher High Water, i.e. that which is shown as reaching a factor of 1.0 on the curves. Note that the **time** differences, which are not required for this calculation, also refer to the higher High Water.

• The tide at ports between Bournemouth and Christchurch shows considerable change of shape and duration between Springs and Neaps and it is not practical to define the tide with only two curves. A third curve has therefore been drawn for the range at Portsmouth at which the two High Waters are equal at the port concerned – this range being marked on the body of the graph. Interpolation here should be between this 'critical' curve and either the Spring or Neap curve as appropriate.

Note that while the critical curve extends throughout the tidal cycle the Spring and Neap curves stop at the higher High Water. Thus for a range at Portsmouth of 3.5m the factor for 7 hours after LW at Bournemouth should be referred to the following Low Water, whereas had the range at Portsmouth been 2.5, it should be referred to the preceding Low Water.

NOTES

1. NEWPORT. Owing to the constriction of the River Medina, Newport requires slightly different treatment since the harbour dries out at 1.4m. The calculation should be performed using the Low Water Time and Height Differences for Cowes and the High Water Height Differences for Newport. Any calculated heights which fall below 1.4m should be treated as 1.4m

2. CHRISTCHURCH (Tuckton). Low Waters do not fall below 0.7m except under very low river flow conditions.

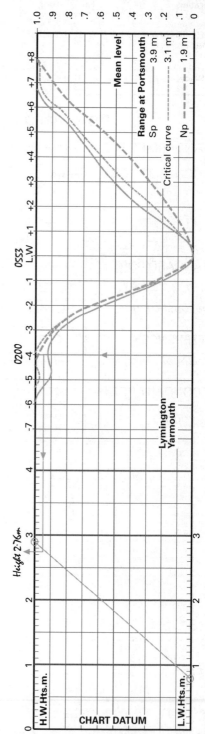

To find the Height of tide at a given time at any Secondary Port between Bournemouth and Selsey Bill

1. Complete top section of N.P. 204 (as below). Omit HW time column (Boxes 1,7,12)
2. On Standard Curve diagram (previous page), plot Secondary Port HW and LW heights and join by sloping line.
3. From the time required, using Secondary Port LW time, proceed vertically to curve, interpolating as necessary using Range at Portsmouth. Do NOT extrapolate.
4. Proceed horizontally to sloping line, thence vertically to Height Scale.
5. Read off height.

EXAMPLE:
Find the height of tide at LYMINGTON at 0200 UT on 18th November

From tables	NOVEMBER	
	0110	4.6
18 0613	1.1
PORTSMOUTH	1318	4.6
	SA 1833	1.0

From tables

Location	Lat	Long	High Water		Low Water		MHWS	MHWN	MLWN	MLWS
			0000	0600	0500	1100				
PORTSMOUTH	50°48'N	1°07'W	and	and	and	and	4.7	3.8	1.9	0.8
Standard port			1200	1800	1700	2300				
Lymington	50°46'N	1°32'W	−0110	+0005	−0020	−0020	−1.7	−1.2	−0.5	−0.1

STANDARD PORT _Portsmouth_   TIME/HEIGHT REQUIRED _0200_

SECONDARY PORT _Lymington_   DATE _18 Nov_   TIME ZONE _UT_

	TIME		HEIGHT		
	HW	LW	HW	LW	RANGE
STANDARD PORT	1 −	2 0613	3 4.6	4 1.1	5 3.5
Seasonal change	Standard Ports -		6 0.0	6 0.0	
DIFFERENCES	7* −	8 −0020	9 −1.7	10 −0.2	
Seasonal change *	Secondary Ports +		11 0.0	11 0.0	
SECONDARY PORT	12 −	13 0553	14 2.9	15 0.9	
Duration	16 −				

* The Seasonal changes are generally less than ± 0.1m and for most purposes can be ignored. See Admiralty Tide Tables Vol 1 for full details.

TIDAL CURVES - BOURNEMOUTH TO FRESHWATER

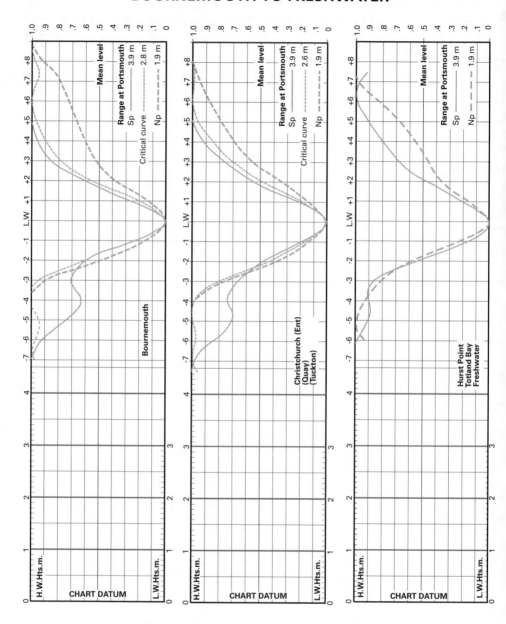

Note: The curves for Lymington and Yarmouth are on page 136, together with a worked example.

TIDAL CURVES -
BUCKLERS HARD TO SELSEY BILL

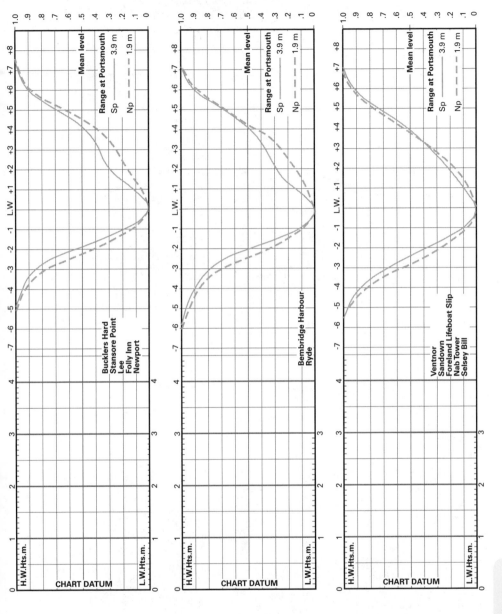

ENGLISH CHANNEL AND SOUTH BRITTANY

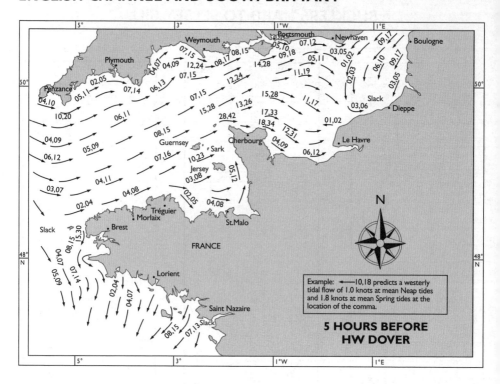

Example: ←10,18 predicts a westerly tidal flow of 1.0 knots at mean Neap tides and 1.8 knots at mean Spring tides at the location of the comma.

5 HOURS BEFORE HW DOVER

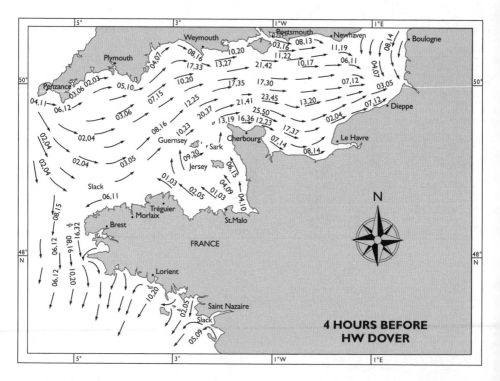

4 HOURS BEFORE HW DOVER

ENGLISH CHANNEL AND SOUTH BRITTANY

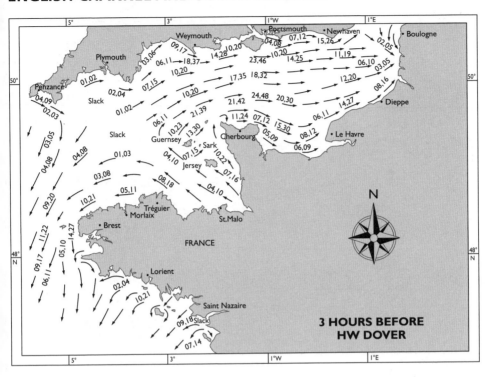

3 HOURS BEFORE HW DOVER

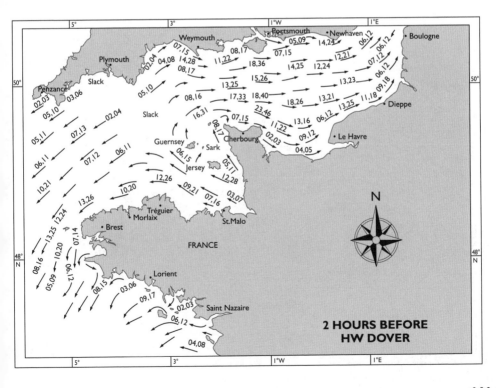

2 HOURS BEFORE HW DOVER

ENGLISH CHANNEL AND SOUTH BRITTANY

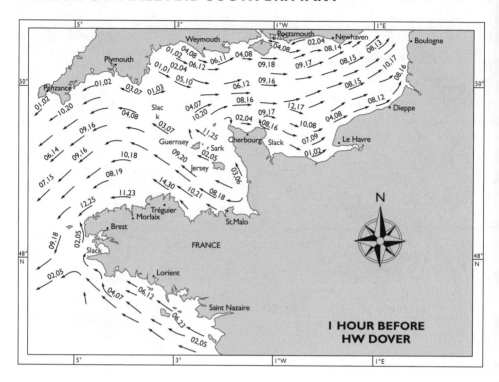

1 HOUR BEFORE HW DOVER

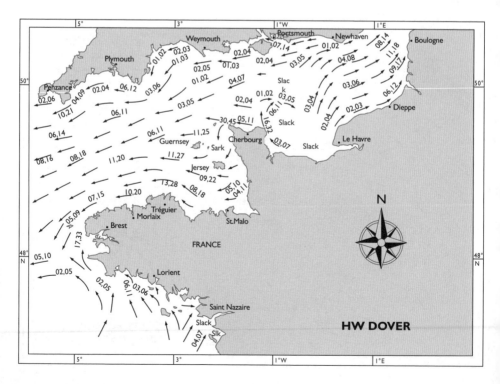

HW DOVER

ENGLISH CHANNEL AND SOUTH BRITTANY

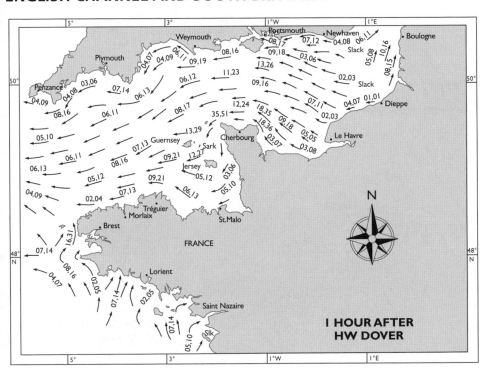

1 HOUR AFTER HW DOVER

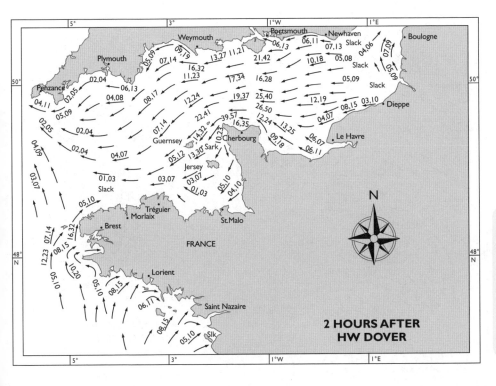

2 HOURS AFTER HW DOVER

ENGLISH CHANNEL AND SOUTH BRITTANY

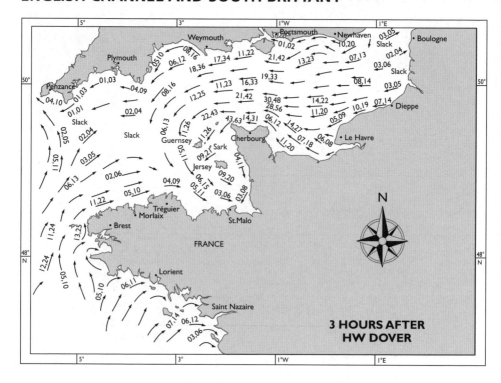

3 HOURS AFTER HW DOVER

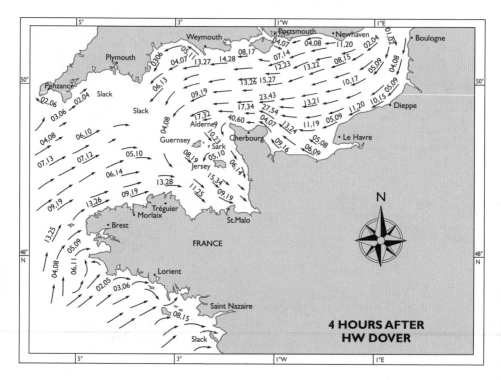

4 HOURS AFTER HW DOVER

ENGLISH CHANNEL AND SOUTH BRITTANY

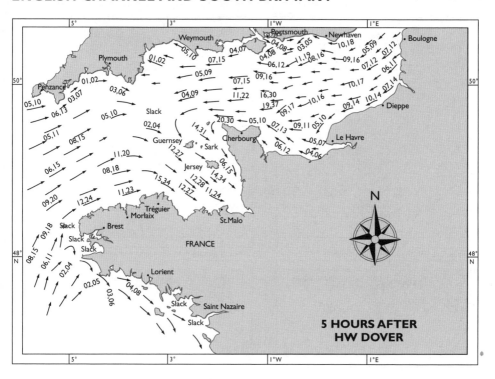

5 HOURS AFTER HW DOVER

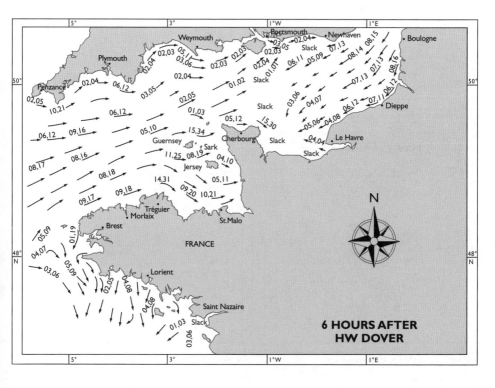

6 HOURS AFTER HW DOVER

PORTLAND

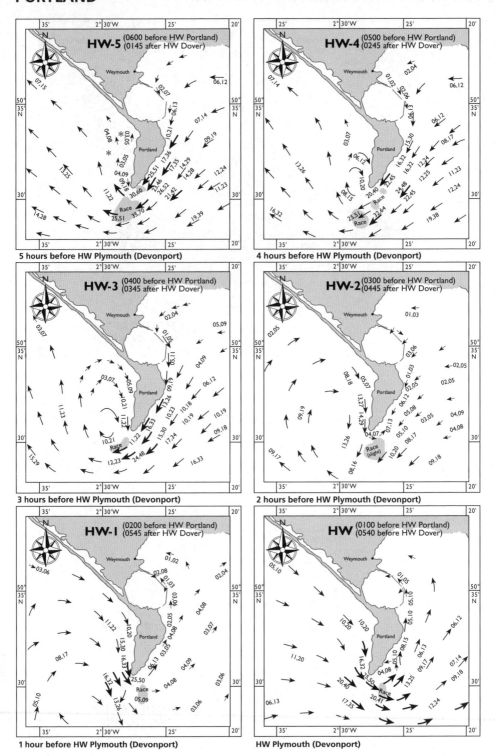

HW-5 (0600 before HW Portland) (0145 after HW Dover)

5 hours before HW Plymouth (Devonport)

HW-4 (0500 before HW Portland) (0245 after HW Dover)

4 hours before HW Plymouth (Devonport)

HW-3 (0400 before HW Portland) (0345 after HW Dover)

3 hours before HW Plymouth (Devonport)

HW-2 (0300 before HW Portland) (0445 after HW Dover)

2 hours before HW Plymouth (Devonport)

HW-1 (0200 before HW Portland) (0545 after HW Dover)

1 hour before HW Plymouth (Devonport)

HW (0100 before HW Portland) (0540 before HW Dover)

HW Plymouth (Devonport)

PORTLAND

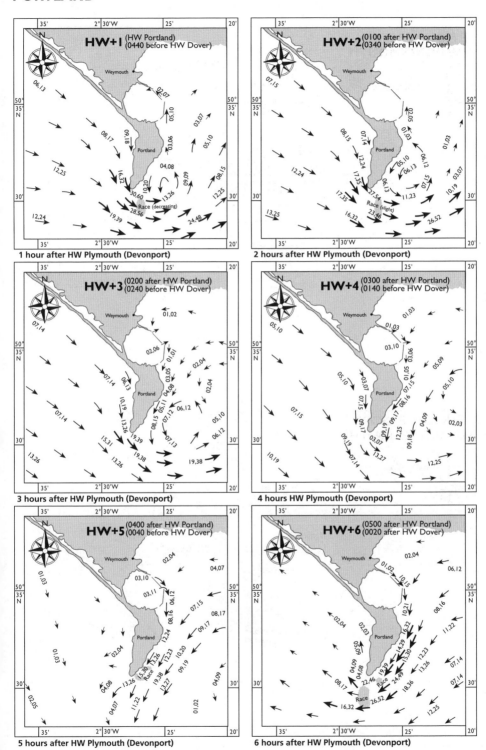

1 hour after HW Plymouth (Devonport)

2 hours after HW Plymouth (Devonport)

3 hours after HW Plymouth (Devonport)

4 hours HW Plymouth (Devonport)

5 hours after HW Plymouth (Devonport)

6 hours after HW Plymouth (Devonport)

ISLE OF WIGHT

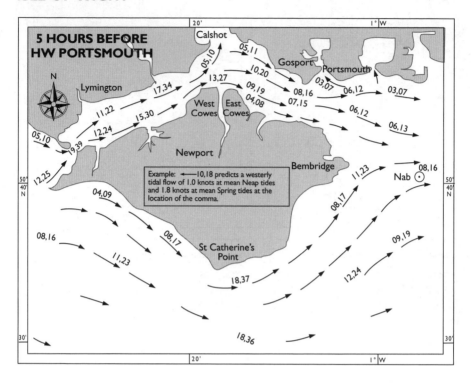

5 HOURS BEFORE HW PORTSMOUTH

Example: ◄—10,18 predicts a westerly tidal flow of 1.0 knots at mean Neap tides and 1.8 knots at mean Spring tides at the location of the comma.

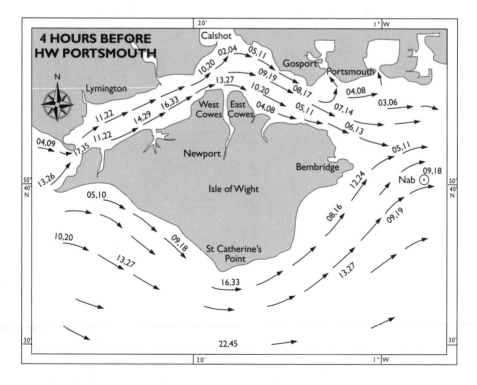

4 HOURS BEFORE HW PORTSMOUTH

ISLE OF WIGHT

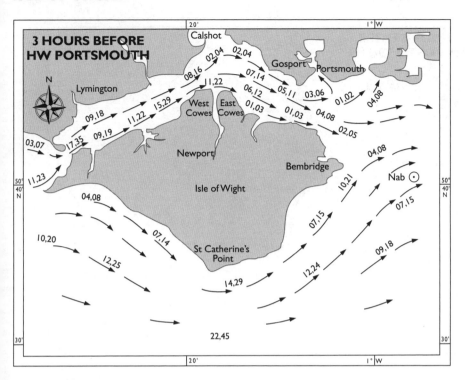

3 HOURS BEFORE HW PORTSMOUTH

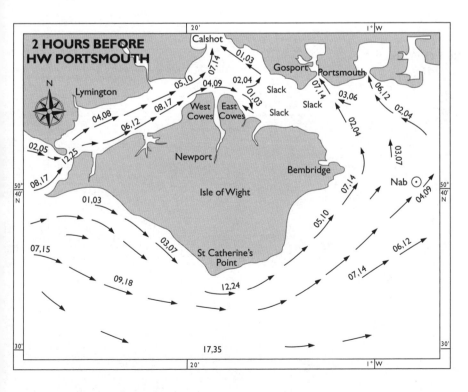

2 HOURS BEFORE HW PORTSMOUTH

ISLE OF WIGHT

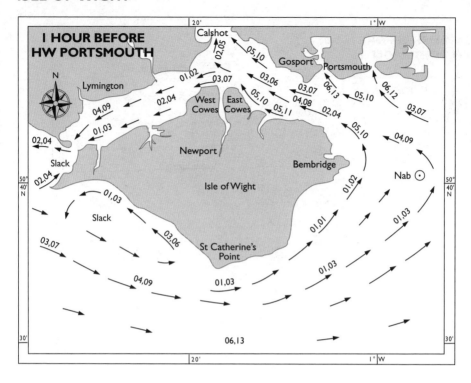

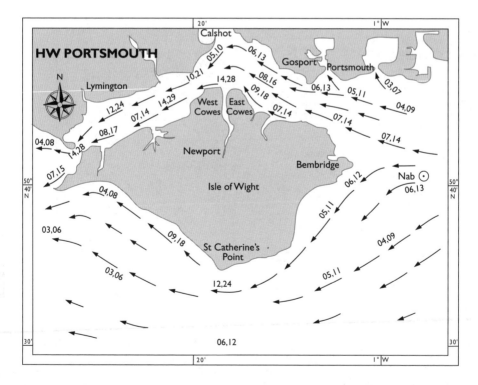

ISLE OF WIGHT

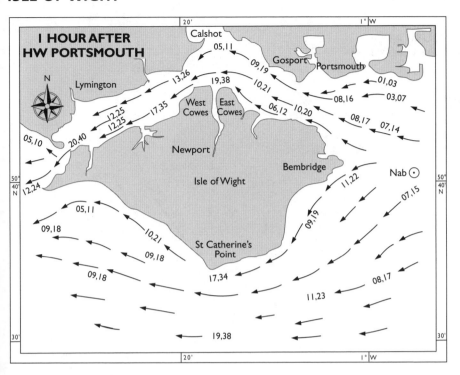

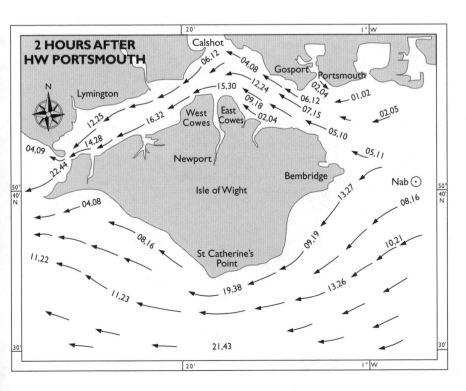

ISLE OF WIGHT

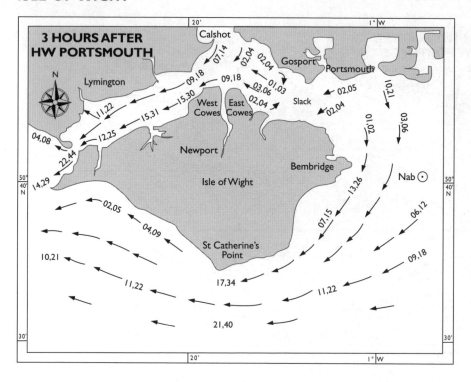

3 HOURS AFTER HW PORTSMOUTH

Calshot
Gosport
Portsmouth
Lymington
West Cowes
East Cowes
Newport
Bembridge
Isle of Wight
Nab ⊙
St Catherine's Point

07.14 · 02.04 · 02.04
09.18 · 09.18 · 01.03 · 03.06
11.22 · 15.30 · 03.06 · 02.05
15.31 · 02.04 · 02.04 · 10.21 · 03.06
12.25 · Slack · 01.02
04.08 · 02.04 · 13.26
22.44 · 07.15 · 06.12
14.29 · 09.18
02.05 · 04.09 · 11.22
10.21 · 17.34 · 11.22
11.22 · 21.40

50° 40' N
50° 40' N
30'
30'
20'
20'
1° W
1° W

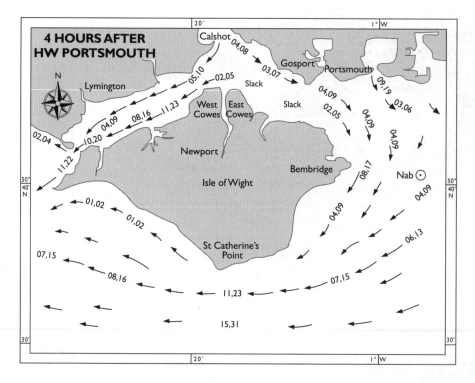

4 HOURS AFTER HW PORTSMOUTH

Calshot
Gosport
Portsmouth
Lymington
West Cowes
East Cowes
Newport
Bembridge
Isle of Wight
Nab ⊙
St Catherine's Point

04.08 · 03.07
05.10 · 02.05 · Slack · 08.19 · 03.06
04.09 · 08.16 · 11.23 · Slack · 04.09 · 04.09
02.04 · 10.20 · 02.05
11.22 · 04.09
08.17
01.02 · 01.02 · 04.09 · 04.09
07.15 · 06.13
08.16 · 07.15
11.23 · 07.15
15.31

50° 40' N
50° 40' N
30'
30'
20'
20'
1° W
1° W

ISLE OF WIGHT

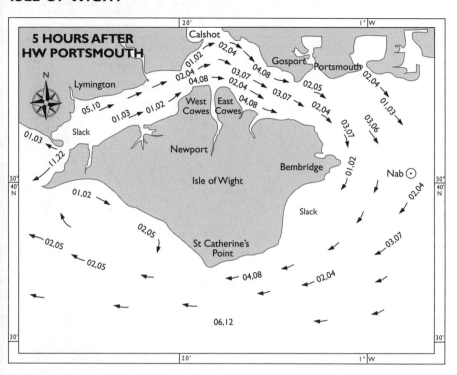

5 HOURS AFTER HW PORTSMOUTH

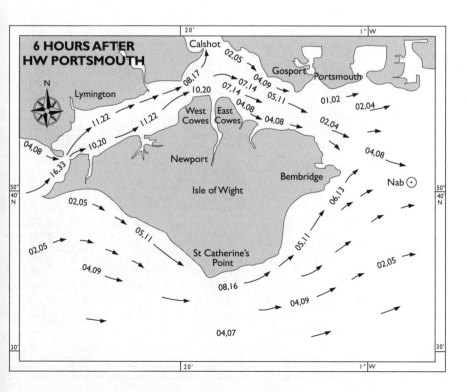

6 HOURS AFTER HW PORTSMOUTH

CHANNEL ISLANDS

Example: ←—10,18 predicts a westerly tidal flow of 1.0 knots at mean
Neap tides and 1.8 knots at mean Spring tides at the location of the comma.

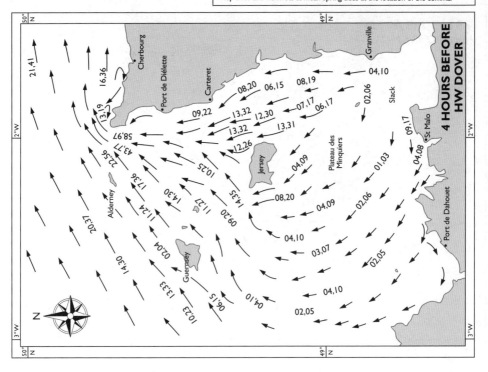

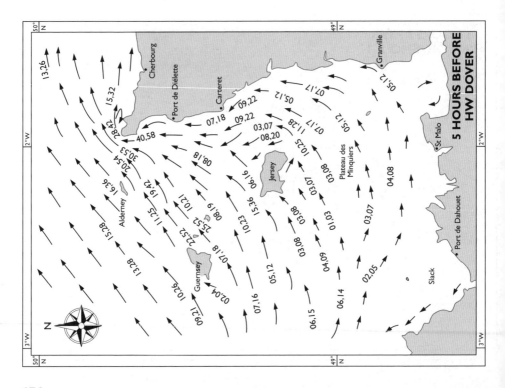

CHANNEL ISLANDS

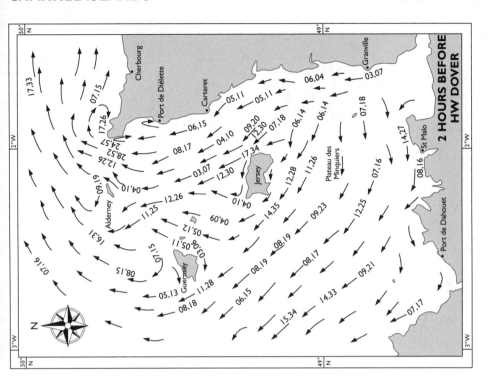

2 HOURS BEFORE HW DOVER

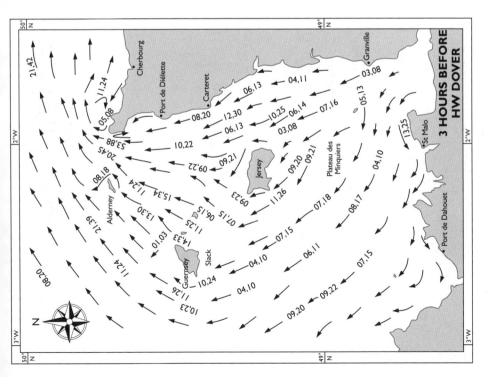

3 HOURS BEFORE HW DOVER

CHANNEL ISLANDS

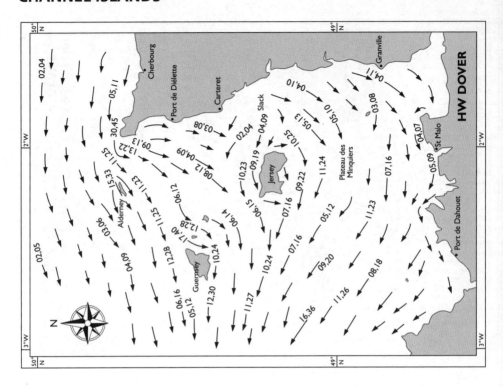

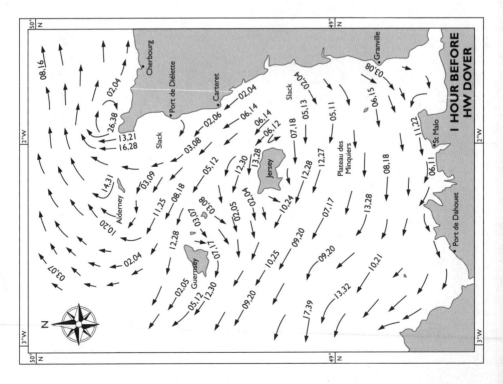

CHANNEL ISLANDS

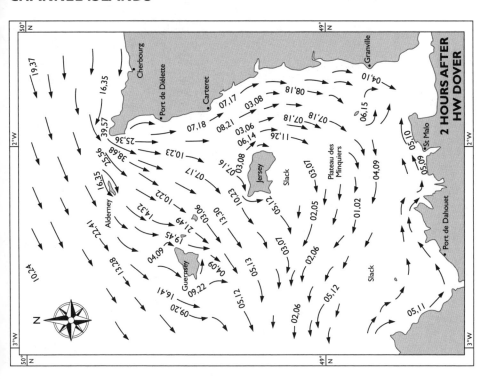

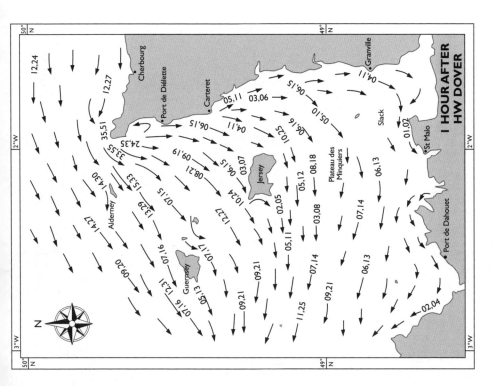

CHANNEL ISLANDS

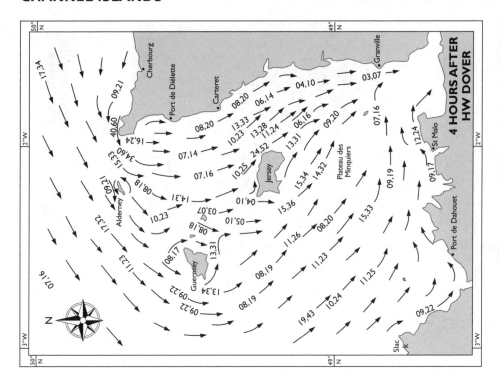

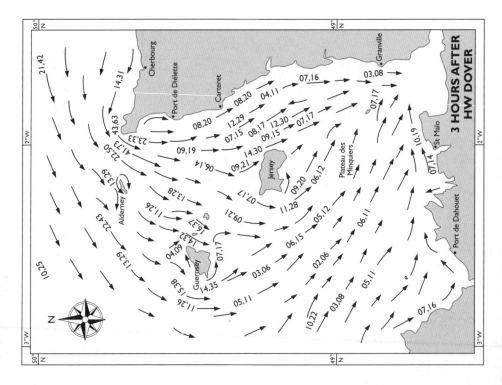

CHANNEL ISLANDS

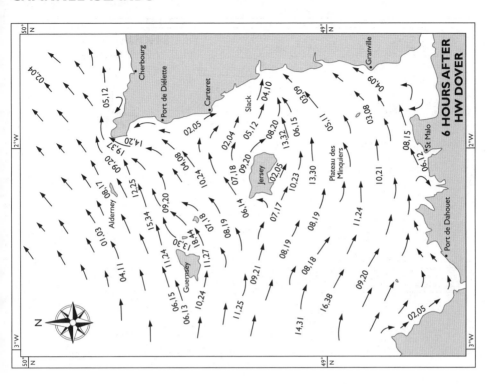

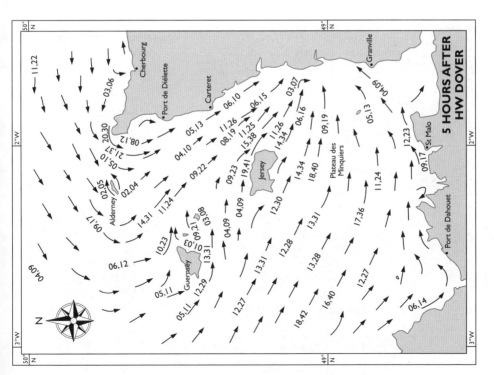

NORTH SEA

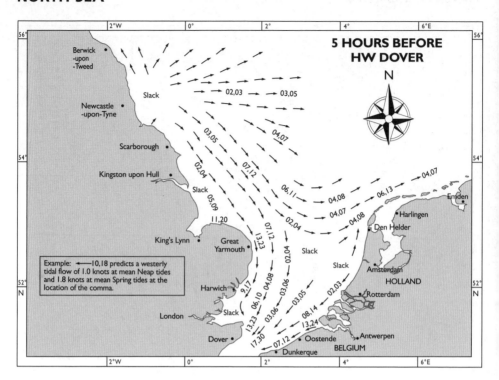

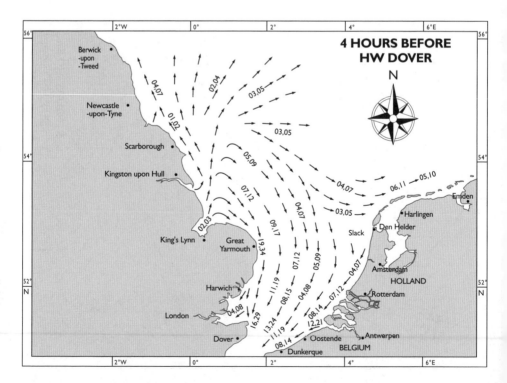

NORTH SEA

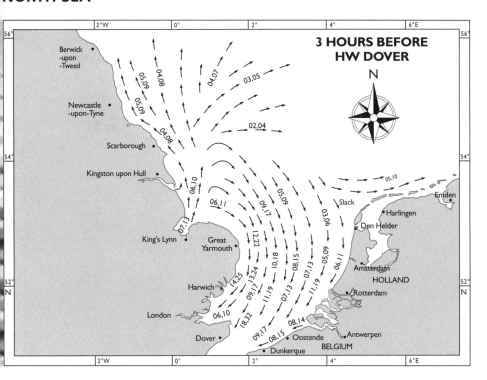

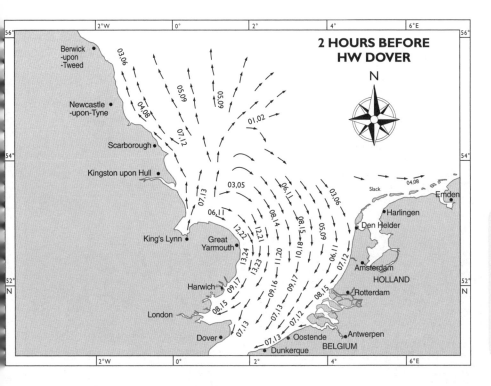

NORTH SEA

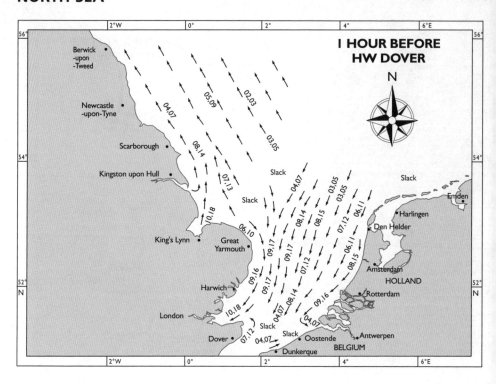

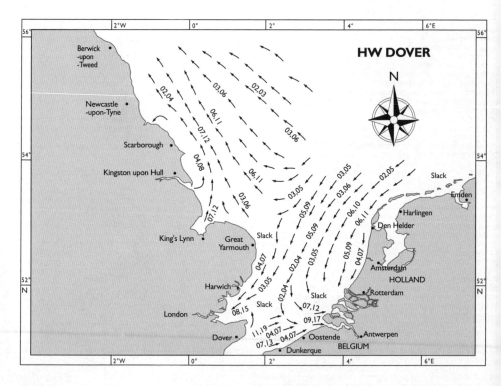

NORTH SEA

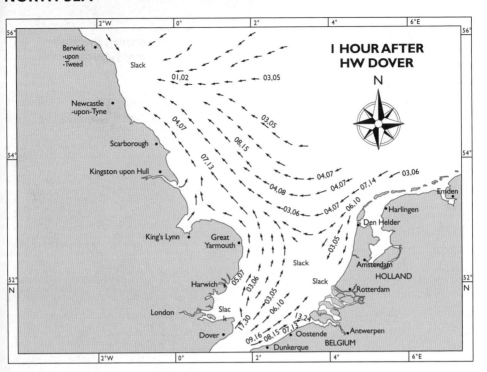

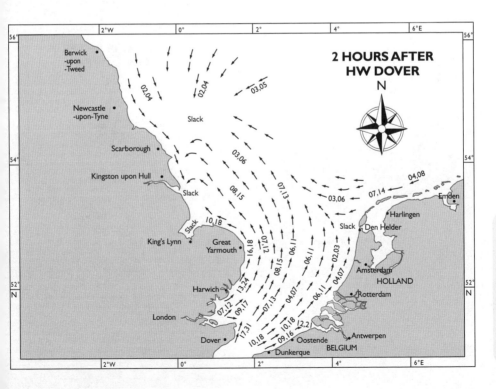

NORTH SEA

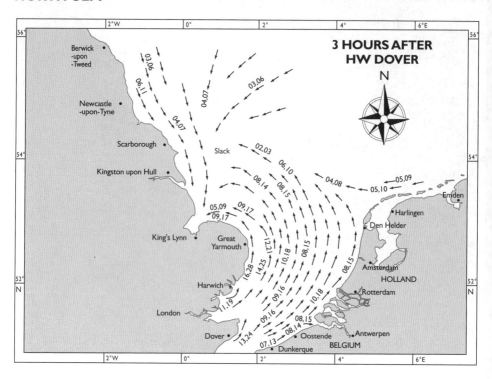

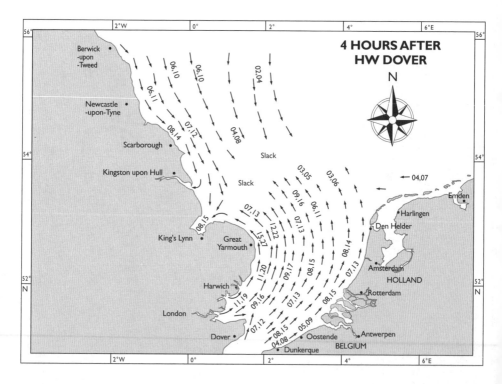

NORTH SEA

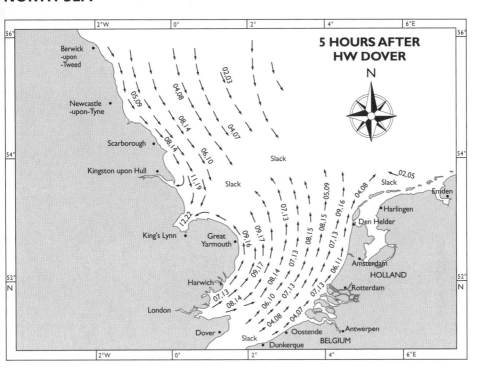

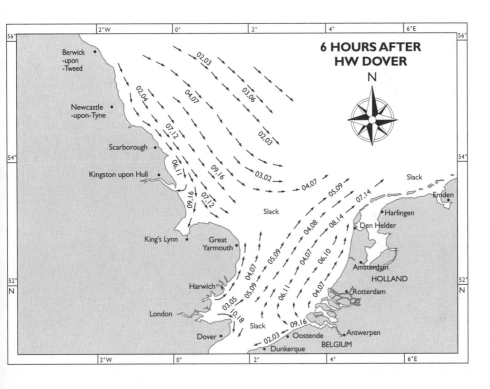

SCOTLAND

Example: ←—10,18 predicts a westerly tidal flow of 1.0 knots at mean Neap tides and 1.8 knots at mean Spring tides at the location of the comma.

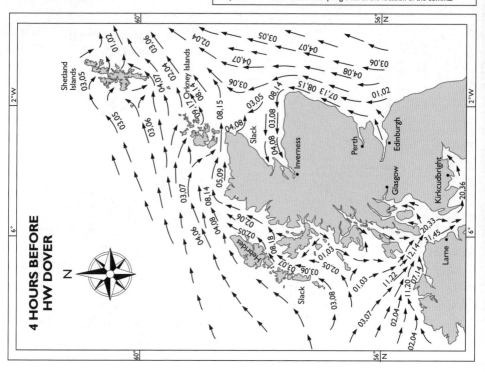

4 HOURS BEFORE HW DOVER

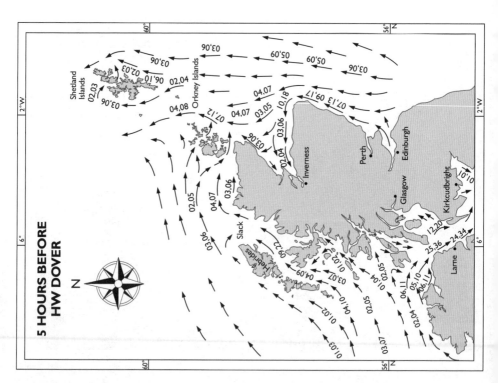

5 HOURS BEFORE HW DOVER

SCOTLAND

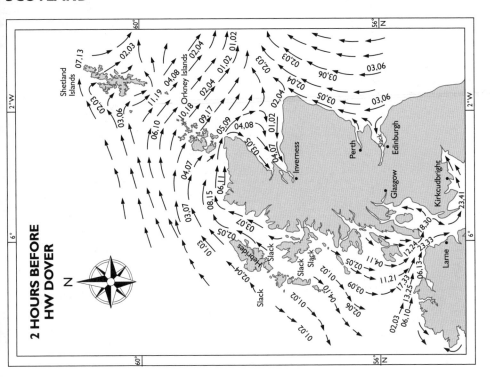

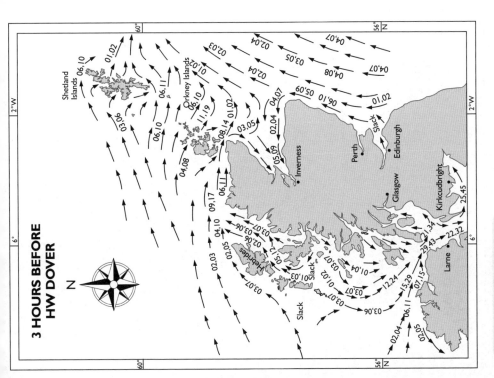

SCOTLAND

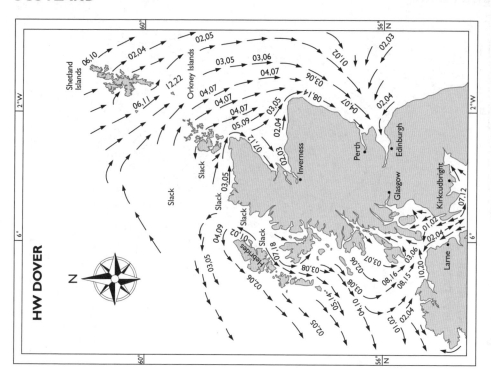

HW DOVER

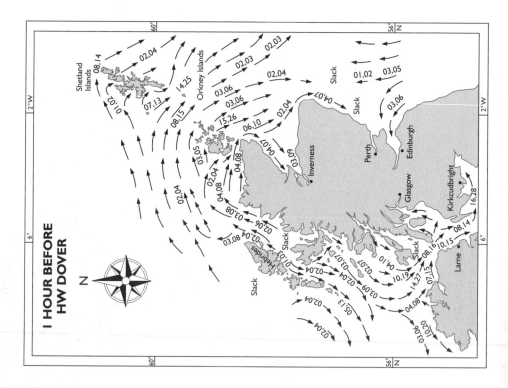

1 HOUR BEFORE HW DOVER

SCOTLAND

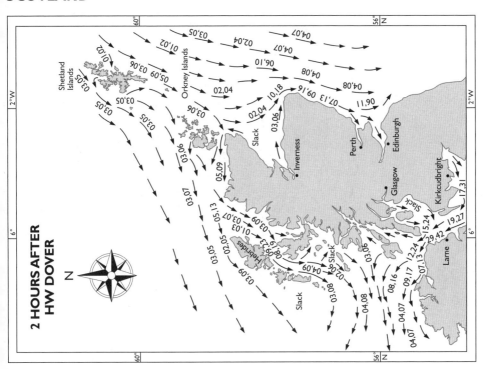

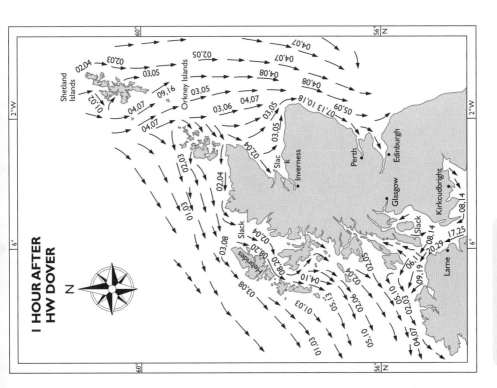

SCOTLAND

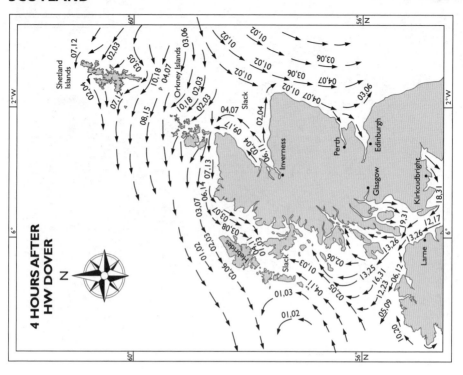

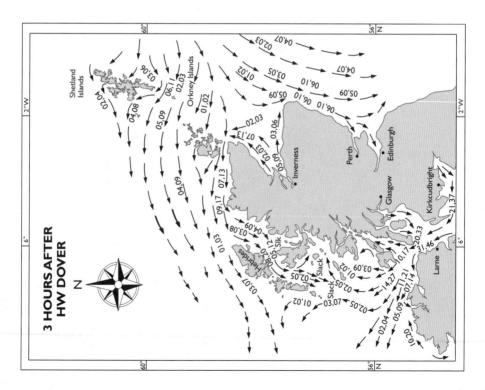

SCOTLAND

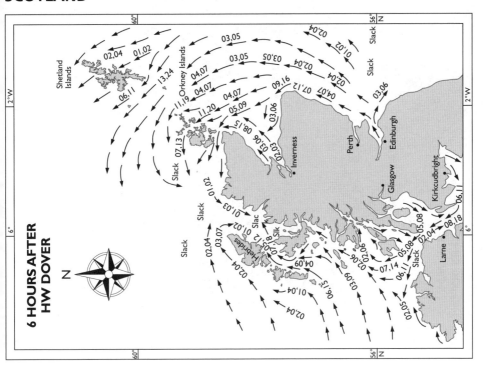

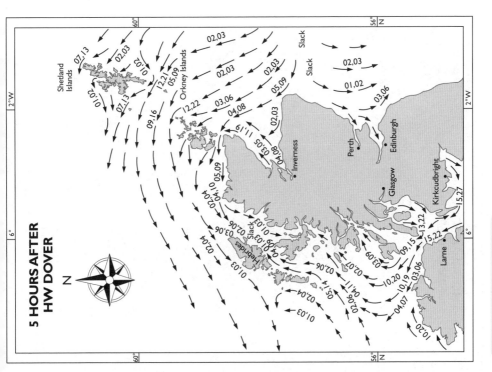

WEST UK AND IRELAND

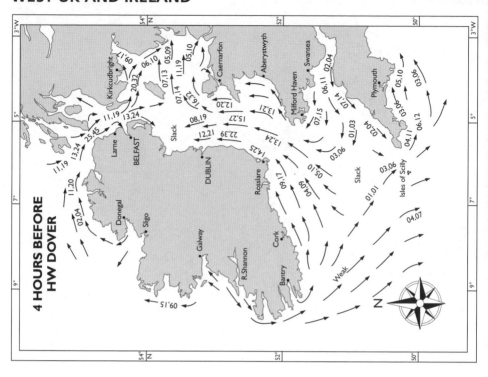

4 HOURS BEFORE HW DOVER

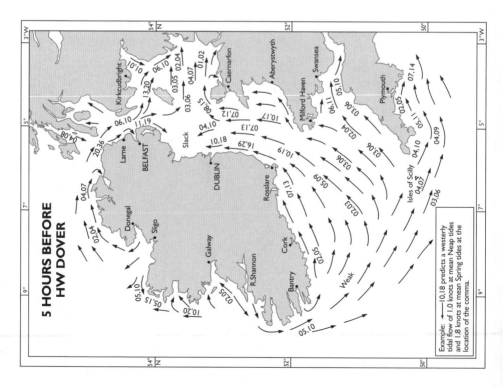

5 HOURS BEFORE HW DOVER

Example: → 10,18 predicts a westerly tidal flow of 1.0 knots at mean Neap tides and 1.8 knots at mean Spring tides at the location of the comma.

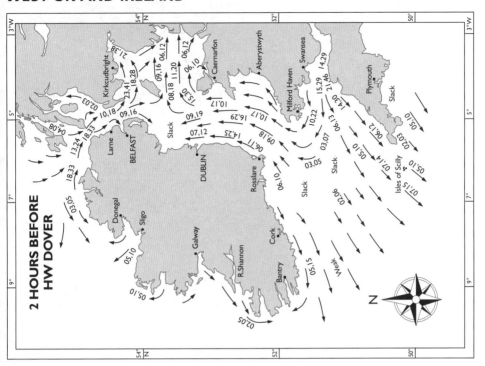

2 HOURS BEFORE HW DOVER

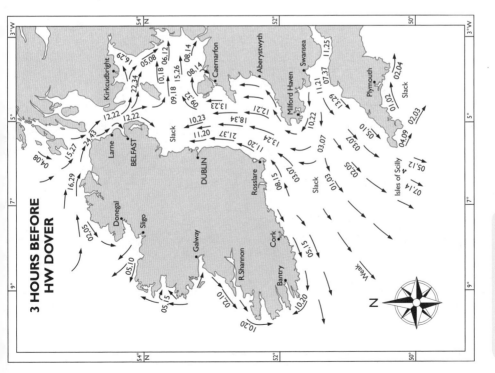

3 HOURS BEFORE HW DOVER

TIDES

WEST UK AND IRELAND

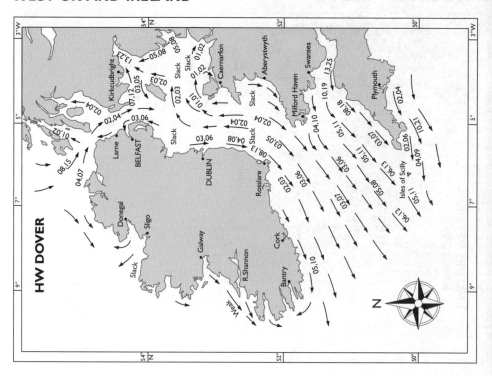

HW DOVER

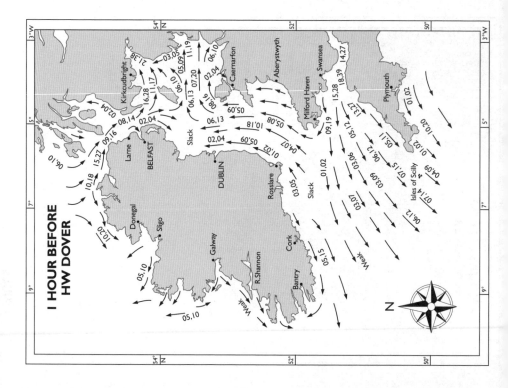

1 HOUR BEFORE HW DOVER

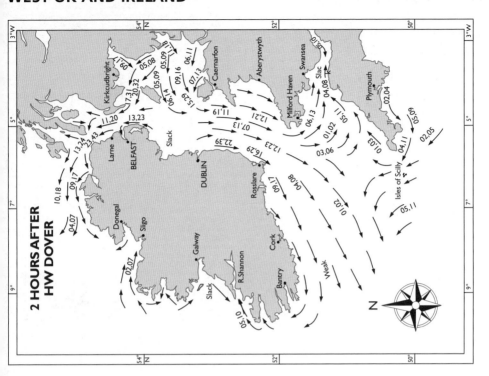

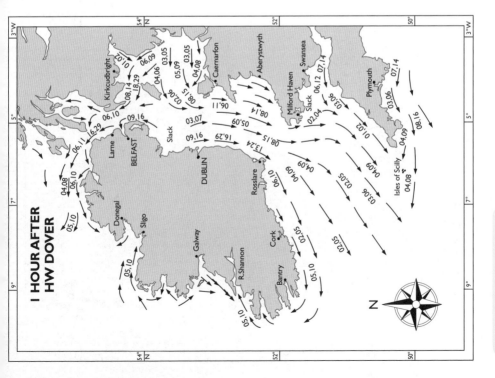

WEST UK AND IRELAND

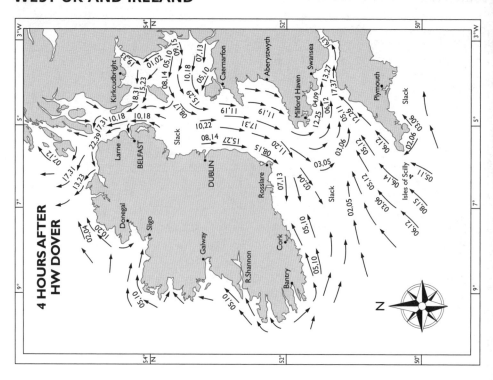

4 HOURS AFTER HW DOVER

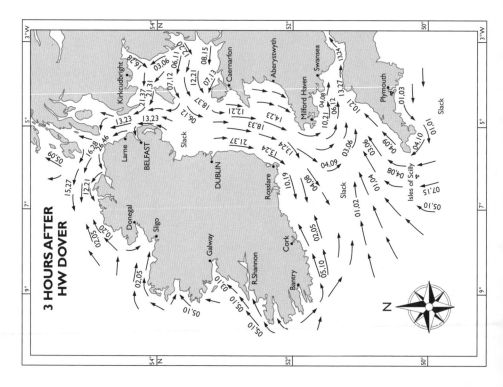

3 HOURS AFTER HW DOVER

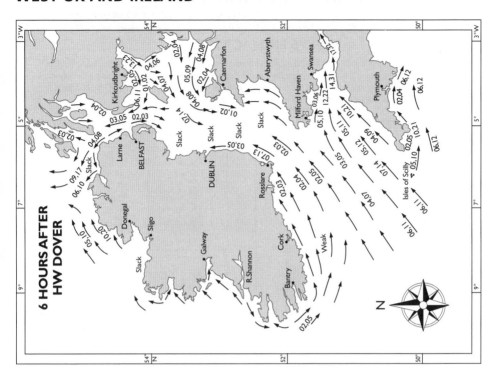

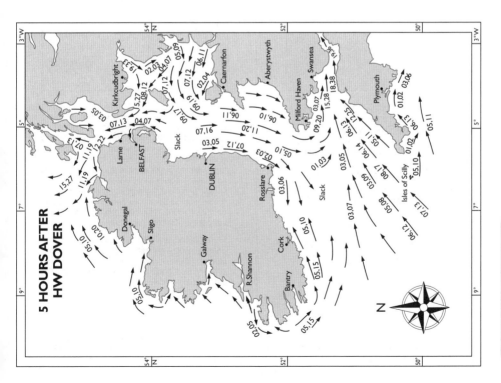

TIDAL GATES - SOUTHERN ENGLAND

A guide to the time of tide turn at tidal gates, the approximate maximum strength of the tidal flow (spring rates shown - neaps are approximately 60% of these), and the position and timing of races, counter tides, etc.

LAND'S END (AC 1148)

Tidal streams set hard north/south round Land's End, and east/west around Gwennap and Pendeen. But the inshore currents run counter to the tidal streams. By staying close inshore, this tidal gate favours a N-bound passage. With careful timing nearly 9½hrs of fair tide can be carried, from HWD−3 to HWD+5. The chartlets, referenced to HW Dover, depict both tidal streams and inshore currents.

FLOOD	EBB

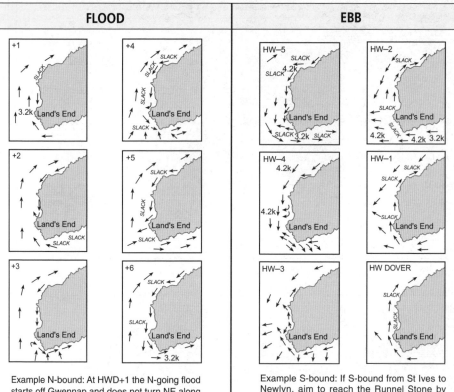

Example N-bound: At HWD+1 the N-going flood starts off Gwennap and does not turn NE along the N Cornish coast until HWD+3. But as early as HWD−3 an inshore current is beginning to set north. Utilise this by arriving off Runnel Stone at HWD−2 and then keeping within ¼M of the shore. If abeam the Brisons at HWD, the tide and current should serve for the next 6 or 7 hours to make good St Ives, or even Newquay and Padstow.

Example S-bound: If S-bound from St Ives to Newlyn, aim to reach the Runnel Stone by HWD+5, ie with 2hrs of E-going tide in hand for the remaining 9M to Newlyn. To achieve this 20M passage, leave St Ives 5 hours earlier, ie at HWD. Buck a foul tide for the first 3 hours, then use the S-going inshore current, keeping as close inshore as is prudent, only moving seaward to clear the Wra and the Brisons. This timing would also suit a passage from S Wales or the Bristol Channel, going inshore of Longships if conditions allow.

From Ireland, ie Cork or further W, the inshore passage would not benefit. But aim to be off the Runnel Stone at HWD+5 if bound for Newlyn; or at HWD+3 if bound for Helford/Falmouth, with the W-going stream slackening and 5hrs of fair tide to cover the remaining 20M past the Lizard.

With acknowledgements to the Royal Cruising Club Pilotage Foundation for their kind permission to use the tid. stream chartlets and text written by Hugh Davies, as first published in Yachting Monthly *magazine.*

TIDAL GATES - SOUTHERN ENGLAND

A guide to the time of tide turn at tidal gates, the approximate maximum strength of the tidal flow (spring rates shown - neaps are approximately 60% of these), and the position and timing of races, counter tides, etc.

FLOOD	EBB

THE LIZARD (AC 777, 2345)

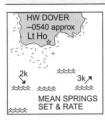

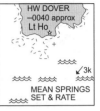

Drying rocks lie approx 5 cables S of the Lizard lt ho and extend westwards. 49°57'N is about as far N as yachts may safely pass inshore of the Race, which extends 2-3M to seaward of these rocks. Race conditions may also exist SE of the Lizard with short, heavy seas in westerlies. If passing S of the Race, route via 49°55'N 05°13'W to clear the worst of the Race.

Inshore the E-going Channel flood, 2kn max @ springs, begins at HW Dover +0145; and outside the Race at approx HWD +0300.	Inshore the W-going Channel ebb, 3kn max @ springs, begins at HW Dover –0345; and outside the Race at HWD –0240.

START POINT (AC 1634)

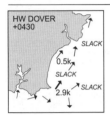

Start Pt, and to a lesser extent Prawle Pt (3.3M WSW), can be slow to round when W-bound with a fair tide against a W'ly wind raising a bad sea. Drying rocks extend 3 cables SSE of the lt ho and a Race may extend up to 1.7M ESE and 1.0M S of the lt ho. It is safe to pass between the Race and the rocks, but in bad weather wiser to go outside the Race. The Skerries Bank (least depth 2.1m) lies 8 cables NE of Start Pt. On both the flood and the ebb back eddies form between Start Pt and Hallsands, 1M NW.

The NE-going Channel flood, 3.1kn max @ springs, begins at HW Dover +0430.	The SW-going Channel ebb, 2.2kn max @ springs, begins at HW Dover –0140, but an hour earlier it is possible to round Start Pt close inshore using the back eddy.

PORTLAND (AC 2255)

Tidal streams off Portland Bill run very strongly. The notorious Portland Race is caused by the almost constant strong southerly flow down both sides of the Bill meeting the main E and W-going streams in the English Channel. The violence of the race is increased by the sudden decrease in depth on Portland Ledge. The tidal stream chartlets on Pages 158–159 show that the race shifts to the E on the flood, and to the W on the ebb. Even in calm weather the race can be dangerous for small craft; in heavy weather or with wind against tide the whole area should be given a wide berth. In such conditions, pass at least 3 miles S of the Bill and do not pass between Portland and The Shambles bank.

In settled weather, with winds <F4/5, but not at springs nor with wind against tide, passage may be made very close S of the Bill in the narrow stretch of relatively smooth water N of the race. Night passage should not be attempted due to numerous fishing floats which may be semi-submerged.

Seaward of the race the Channel flood sets east from HW Plymouth -1 to HW +5; the ebb sets west from HW Plymouth +5 to HW -1.

Inshore passage

E-bound across Lyme Bay timing is critical to be close inshore about 2M north of the Bill by HW Plymouth –2 to achieve passage around the Bill between HW Plymouth –2 to HW+1.	W-bound timing is easier if starting from Portland Hbr, Weymouth or Lulworth Cove. Aim to be close inshore about 2M north of the Bill at HW Plymouth +4, and make the passage between HW Plymouth +5 and HW–5.

When using the inshore passage be particularly wary of being set S into the race itself.

ST ALBAN'S HEAD (AC 2610)

A sometimes vicious Race forms over St Alban's Ledge, a rocky dorsal ridge (least depth 8.5m) which extends approx 4M SW from St Alban's Head. Three yellow naval target buoys (DZ A, B and C) straddle the middle and outer sections, but are only occasionally used. In settled weather and at neaps the Race may be barely perceptible in which case it can be crossed with impunity. Avoid it either by keeping to seaward via 50°31'.40N 02°07'.80W; or by using the narrow inshore passage at the foot of St Alban's Head.

Based on a position 1M S of St Alban's Head, the tidal stream windows are:

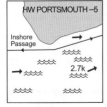

ESE-going stream starts at HW Portsmouth +0530. Spring rates are the same, max 4kn. Along the W side of St Alban's Head the stream runs almost continuously SE due to a back eddy.	WNW-going stream starts at HW Portsmouth. Overfalls extend 2.5M further SW than on the E-going stream and are more dangerous to small craft. Slack water lasts barely half an hour.

The inshore passage lies as close to the foot of St Alban's Head as feels comfortable. It may be hard to see the width of clear water in the inshore passage until committed to it, but except in onshore gales when it is better to stay offshore, the passage will be swiftly made with only a few, if any, overfalls. The NCI station on the Head (☎ 01929 439220) may advise on conditions.

TIDAL GATES - SOUTHERN ENGLAND

A guide to the time of tide turn at tidal gates, the approximate maximum strength of the tidal flow (spring rates shown - neaps are approximately 60% of these), and the position and timing of races, counter tides, etc.

FLOOD	EBB

THE NEEDLES CHANNEL (AC 2035)

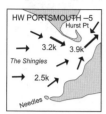

The Needles Channel lies between the SW Shingles PHM buoy and the Bridge WCM buoy. Once through this narrow section the channel widens with the Island shore to starboard and the long, drying 1.2m, Shingles bank to port. Abeam Hurst Castle the channel again narrows (assisted by The Trap, a shoal spit south of Hurst Castle) before opening out into the west Solent.

Study carefully the hourly tidal stream chartlets for the Isle of Wight on pp.186-191 and the values shown on AC 2035 at tidal diamonds B, C, D and E.

The ENE-going flood runs from HW Portsmouth +5 until HW P −1½, at springs reaching 3.1kn at The Bridge and 3.9kn at Hurst.

The WSW-going ebb runs from HW P −1 until HW P +4½, reaching 4.4kn at Hurst and 3.4kn at The Bridge, both spring rates. The ebb sets strongly WSW across the Shingles which with adequate rise is routinely crossed by racing yachts; but cruisers should stay clear even in calm conditions when any swell causes the sea to break heavily.

Prevailing W/SW winds, even if only F4, against the ebb raise dangerous breaking seas in the Needles Channel and at The Bridge, a shallow ridge extending 9 cables west from the Needles light. Worst conditions are often found just after LW slack. In such conditions it is safer to go via the North Channel to Hurst. In W/SW gales avoid the Needles altogether by sheltering at Poole or going east-about via Nab Tower.

ON PASSAGE UP CHANNEL

The following 3 tidal gates (Looe Channel, Beachy Head and Dungeness) are components in the tidal conveyor belt which, if stepped onto at the outset, can enable a fastish yacht to carry a fair tide for 88M from Selsey Bill to Dover. Go through the Looe at slackish water, HW Portsmouth +4½ (HW Dover +5). Based on a mean SOG of 7 knots, Beachy Head will be passed at HW D −1, Dungeness at HW D +3 and Dover at HW +5½, only bucking the first of the ebb in the last hour. A faster boat could make Ramsgate. The down-Channel passage is less rewarding and many yachts will pause at Brighton.

LOOE CHANNEL (AC 2045, 1652)

This channel is little shorter than the detour south of the Owers, but is much used by yachts on passage from/to points east of the Solent. Although adequately lit, it is best not attempted at night due to many lobster floats; nor in onshore gales as searoom is limited by extensive shoals on which the sea breaks.

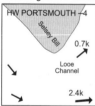

The E-going flood runs from HW Portsmouth +4½ (HW Dover +5) until HW P −1½ (HW D −1), at springs reaching 2.4kn near the Boulder and Street light buoys which mark its narrow western end; they may be hard to see in other than good visibility. Max neap rate is 1.2kn.

The W-going ebb runs from HW P −1½ (HW D −1) until HW P +4½ (HW D +5), at springs reaching 2.6kn near Boulder and Street. Max neap rate is 1.3kn.

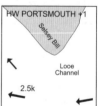

At the wider eastern end of the channel (near E Borough Head buoy) rates are greatly reduced.

BEACHY HEAD (AC 1652, 536)

Stay at least 5 cables to seaward of the towering chalk cliffs to avoid isolated boulders and rocky, part-drying ridges such as Head Ledge. The lt ho stands on a drying rock ledge. Close inshore many fishing floats are a trap for the unwary. In bad weather stay 2M offshore to avoid overfalls caused by a ridge of uneven ground which extends 1M SSE from Beachy Head.

2M south of Beachy Head the E-going flood starts at HW Dover +0530, max spring rate 2.6kn.

The W-going ebb starts at HW Dover +0030, max spring rate 2.0kn.

Between 5M and 7M east of Beachy Head avoid breakers and eddies caused by the Horse of Willingdon, Royal Sovereign and other shoals.

DUNGENESS (AC 536, 1892)

Tidal stream atlases: Dungeness is on the east and west edges respectively of NP 250 (English Channel) and NP 233 (Dover Strait). The nearest tidal stream diamond (2.2M SE of Dungeness) is 'H' on AC 536 and 'B' on AC 1892; their positions and values are the same.

The NE-going flood starts at HW Dover −0100, max spring rate 1.9kn.

The SW-going ebb starts at HW Dover +0430, max spring rate 2.1kn.

TIDAL GATES - NORTH EAST SCOTLAND

A guide to the time of tide turn at tidal gates, and in straits and estuaries, showing the approximate strength of the tidal flow (spring rates shown - neaps are approximately 60% of these), and the position and timing of races, counter tides etc.

FLOOD	EBB

FIRTHS of FORTH (AC 175) & TAY (AC 1481)

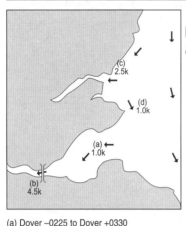

Tidal streams are quite weak in the outer part of the Firth, increasing as the narrows at islands and the bridges are approached.
Apart from the stream of the Tay, which attains 5 knots in most places, the coastwise tidal streams between Fife Ness and Arbroath are weak.

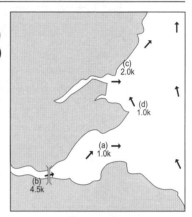

(a) Dover –0225 to Dover +0330
(b) Dover –0200 to Dover +0400
(c) Dover –0210 to Dover +0420
(d) Dover –0110 to Dover +0520

(a) Dover +0330 to Dover –0225
(b) Dover +0400 to Dover –0200
(c) Dover +0420 to Dover –0210
(d) Dover +0520 to Dover –0110

PASSAGES FROM FORTH & TAY

Northbound. Leave before HW (Dover +0400) to be at N Carr at Dover +0600. Bound from Forth to Tay aim to arrive at Abertay By at LW slack (Dover –0200).
Southbound. Leave before LW (Dover -0200) to be at Bass Rk at HW Dover. Similar timings if bound from Tay to Forth, leave late in ebb to pick up early flood off St Andrews to N Carr and into Forth.

INVERNESS & CROMARTY FIRTHS (AC 1077)

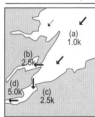

Tidal streams in the Inverness Firth and approaches are not strong, except in the Cromarty Firth Narrows, the Fort George Narrows and the Kessock Road, including off the entrance to the Caledonian Canal.

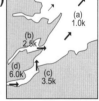

(a) Dover –0555 to Dover +0030
(b) Dover –0400 to Dover +0115
(c) Dover –0400 to Dover –0220
(d) Dover –0430 to Dover +0100

(a) Dover +0030 to Dover –0555
(b) Dover +0115 to Dover –0400
(c) Dover +0115 to Dover –0440
(d) Dover –0130 to Dover +0545

PENTLAND FIRTH & ORKNEYS (AC 1954)

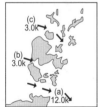

The tide flows strongly around and through the Orkney Islands. The Pentland Firth is a dangerous area for all craft, tidal flows reach 12 knots between Duncansby Head and S Ronaldsay. W of Dunnet Hd & Hoy is less violent. There is little tide within Scapa Flow.

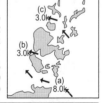

(a) Dover –0500 to Dover +0100
(b) Dover +0500 to Dover –0110
(c) Dover –0530 to Dover +0040

(a) Dover +0115 to Dover –0535
(b) Dover –0110 to Dover +0050
(c) Dover +0040 to Dover –0530

SHETLAND ISLANDS (AC 219)

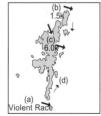

The tidal flow around the Shetland Islands rotates as the cycle progresses. When the flood begins, at –0400 HW Dover, the tidal flow is to the E, at HW Dover it is S, at Dover +0300 it is W, and at –0600 Dover it is N.

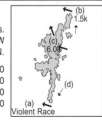

(a) Dover –0410 to Dover +0020
(b) Dover –0400 to Dover +0030
(c) Dover –0530 to Dover +0100
(d) Dover –0400 to Dover –0200

(a) Dover +0050 to Dover –0410
(b) Dover +0130 to Dover –0500
(c) Dover +0100 to Dover –0530
(d) Dover +0200 to Dover +0500

TIDES

TIDAL GATES - NORTH WEST SCOTLAND

A guide to the time of tide turn at tidal gates, the approximate maximum strength of the tidal flow (spring rates shown - neaps are approximately 60% of these), and the position and timing of races, counter tides, etc.

FLOOD	EBB

SOUND OF HARRIS (AC 2642)

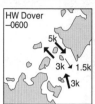

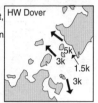

The behaviour of tidal streams in the Sd of Harris varies from day to night, springs to neaps, and winter to summer. The following data applies to daylight, in summer at spring tides in the Cope Channel. Further information can be sought in the Admiralty West of Scotland Pilot.
HW Dover - HW D +0200: SE stream.
HW D +0300 - HW D +0600: Incoming stream from both ends.
HW D −0600 - HW D −0500: NW stream.
HW D −0500 - HW Dover: Outgoing stream from both ends.
At neaps in summer the stream will run SE for most of the day.
Tide rates shown are the maxima likely to be encountered at any time.

THE LITTLE MINCH (AC 1795)

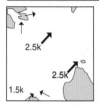

The N going stream on both shores begins at HW Dover +0430 (HW Ullapool -0345), with the strongest flow from mid channel to the Skye coast. There is a W going counter tide E of Vaternish Point.

The S going stream on both shores begins at HW Dover −0130 (HW Ullapool +0240), with the strongest flow from mid channel to the Skye coast. The E going stream in Sound of Scalpay runs at up to 2k.The E going flood and W going ebb in Sound of Scalpay run at up to 2k.

KYLE OF LOCHALSH & KYLERHEA (AC 2540)

NOTE: THESE STREAMS ARE SUBJECT TO VARIATION

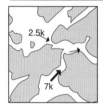

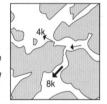

N going stream in Kyle Rhea begins HW Dover +0140 (HW Ullapool +0555) and runs for 6 hours. The E going stream in Kyle Akin begins (Sp) HW Dover +0350 (HW Ullapool −0415). (Nps) HW Dover −0415 (HW Ullapool).

S going stream in Kyle Rhea begins HW Dover -0415 (HW Ullapool) and runs for 6 hours. The W going stream in Kyle Akin begins (Sp) HW Dover −0015 (HW Ullapool +0400). (Nps) HW Dover +0140 (HW Ullapool +0555).

ARDNAMURCHAN POINT (AC 2171)

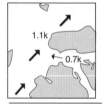

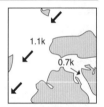

The N going stream off Ardnamurchan begins at HW Dover +0130 (HW Oban −0525). The E going stream in the Sound of Mull begins at HW Dover +0555 (HW Oban −0100).

The S going stream off Ardnamurchan begins at HW Dover −0430 (HW Oban +0100). The W going stream in the Sound of Mull begins at HW Dover −0130 (HW Oban +0400).

SOUND OF MULL - EAST (AC 2171)

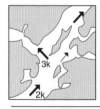

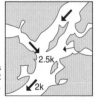

The N going stream in the Firth of Lorne begins at HW Dover −0100 (HW Oban −0430). The W going stream in the Sound of Mull begins at HW Dover +0105 (HW Oban −0550). The ingoing tides at Lochs Feochan, Etive and Creran begin at HW Dover +0300, −0100 & +0030.

The S going stream in the Firth of Lorne begins at HW Dover +0500 (HW Oban −0155). The E going stream in the Sound of Mull begins at HW Dover +0555 (HW Oban −0025). The outgoing tides at Lochs Feochan, Etive and Creran begin at HW Dover −0500, −0520 & −0505.

SOUND OF LUING & DORUS MOR (AC 2343)

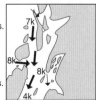

The N or W going stream begins as follows:
Dorus Mor: HW Dover −0200 (HW Oban +0330). Springs: 8 knots.
Corryvreckan: HW D −0120 (HW O +0410). Sp: 8.5 knots.
Cuan Sound: HW D −0110 (HW O +0420). Sp: 6 knots.
Sound of Jura: HW D −0130 (HW O +0400). Sp: 4 knots.
Sound of Luing: HW D −0100 (HW O +0430). Sp: 7 knots.
The S or E going stream begins as follows:
Dorus Mor: HW Dover +0440 (HW Oban −0215). Springs: 8 knots.
Corryvreckan: HW D +0445 (HW O −0210). Sp: 8.5 knots.
Cuan Sound: HW D +0455 (HW O −0200). Sp: 6 knots.
Sound of Jura: HW D +0450 (HW O −0205). Sp: 4 knots.
Sound of Luing: HW D +0500 (HW O −0155). Sp: 7 knots.

TIDAL GATES - SOUTH WEST SCOTLAND

A guide to the time of tide turn at tidal gates, the approximate maximum strength of the tidal flow (spring rates shown - neaps are approximately 60% of these), and the position and timing of races, counter tides, etc.

FLOOD	EBB

SOUNDS OF ISLAY AND GIGHA (AC 2168)

Main flood begins +0015 HW Dover (HW Oban +0545). Streams turn approx 1 hr earlier in Gigha Sd & at Kintyre & Jura shores. S going stream for 9hrs close inshore between Gigha and Machrihanish starting HW Dover (HW Oban –0530).

Main ebb begins HW Dover –0545 (HW Oban –0015). Streams turn 1 hr earlier in Gigha Sd, Kintyre & Jura shores. Overfalls off McArthur's Hd.

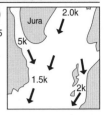

NORTH CHANNEL - NORTH (AC 2798)

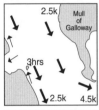

Main flood begins HW Dover –0600 (HW Greenock +0505). Races off Mull of Kintyre, Altacarry Hd & Fair Hd. Counter tides in bays of Antrim coast. W-going streams in Rathlin Sd, counter tide from Sanda Sd to Machrihanish last 1h30 - 2 hrs.

Main ebb begins HW Dover (HW Greenock –0120). Races off Mull of Kintyre & Altacarry Hd. Counter tides in bays of Antrim coast, counter tide from Macrihanish to Sanda Sd last 1h30 - 2 hrs.

NORTH CHANNEL - SOUTH (AC 2198)

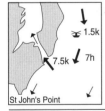

Irish coast - flood begins HW Dover +0610 (HW Belfast –0600). Scottish coast - HW Dover +0430 (HW Greenock +0310). Races off Copeland Is. & Mull of Galloway. Counter tide off Donaghadee and Island Magee last 3 hrs of flood.

Irish coast - ebb begins HW Dover –0015 (HW Belfast). Scottish coast - HW Dover –0130 (HW Greenock –0250). Races off Copeland Is. & Mull of Galloway. Flood begins 2 hrs early close inshore N of Mull of Galloway.

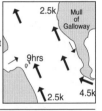

APPROACHES TO STRANGFORD LOUGH (AC 2156)

The tide cycle is approx 3 hours later than in the N Channel

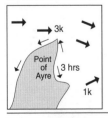

Flood runs for 6 hours from HW Dover –0345 (HW Belfast –0330), with a maximum rate of 7.5 knots at Rue Point. The strong flow flattens the sea in onshore winds and entrance can be made in strong winds.

Ebb runs for 6 hours from HW Dover +0215 (HW Belfast +0230), max rate 7.5k, E of Angus Rk. If entering against ebb use West Channel with care. Smoothest water near Bar Pladdy Buoy when leaving.

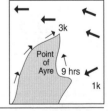

ISLE OF MAN - NORTH (AC 2094)

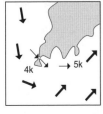

E going stream at Point of Ayre begins HW Dover –0545 (HW Liverpool –0600). Counter tide inside banks E of Point. In Ramsey Bay the S Going tide runs for 3h from +0530 Dover (+0515 Liverpool).

W going stream at Point of Ayre begins HW Dover +0015 (HW Liverpool). Counter tide inside banks W of Point. In Ramsey Bay the N going tide runs for 9h from –0330 Dover (–0345 Liverpool).

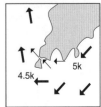

ISLE OF MAN - SOUTH (AC 2094)

E going stream begins –0600 Dover (Liverpool +0610). Overfalls and race E of Chicken Rock. Calf Sound: The E going stream begins earlier, at approximately Dover +0400 (Liverpool +0345).

W going stream begins +0015 Dover (HW Liverpool). Overfalls and race N of Chicken Rock. Calf Sound:The W going stream begins earlier, at approximately –0130 Dover (–0145 Liverpool). Note: all times may vary due to weather conditions.

TIDES

MENAI STRAIT (AC 1464) – TIDAL GATES

FLOOD

(T) : turning → : < 2k ➡ : 2-4k ⦀➡ : 4k +

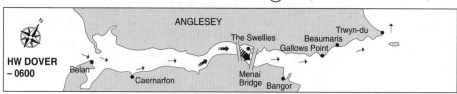

HW DOVER – 0600

LOCAL LW: Caernarfon: HW Dover –0555. Port Dinorwic: –0620. Menai: –0540. Beaumaris: –0605.

HW DOVER – 0500

HW DOVER – 0400

HW DOVER – 0300

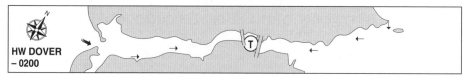

HW DOVER – 0200

SLACK WATER IN THE SWELLIES: HW Dover –0200 to –0230.

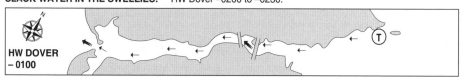

HW DOVER – 0100

LOCAL HW: Belan: HW Dover –0115. Caernarfon: –0105. Port Dinorwic: –0050.

THE SWELLIES

WESTBOUND: Leave or pass Beaumaris in time to arrive at the Swellies by HW Dover –0230 to –0200. If in doubt about passage speed, leave early; the adverse tide will check your progress. For a first time passage this is useful, as the yacht's speed over the ground is reduced. Late arrival will mean a faster passage, but with perhaps less control.

EASTBOUND: Leave or pass Port Dinorwic in time to arrive at Menai Bridge by HW Dover –0230 to –0200. Progress towards the Swellies should be closely monitored, as you are travelling with the last of the flood. Early arrival will mean a fast, perhaps dangerous passage, being late may make it impossible.

MENAI STRAIT (AC 1464) – TIDAL GATES *contd*

EBB

(T) : turning → : < 2k ⇒ : 2-4k ⫸ : 4k +

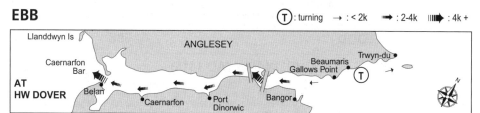

AT HW DOVER

LOCAL HW TIMES: Menai: Dover – 0005. Beaumaris: Dover – 0010

HW DOVER + 0100

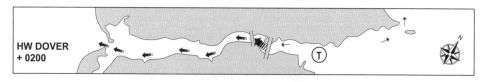

HW DOVER + 0200

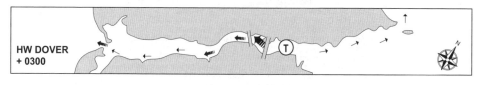

HW DOVER + 0300

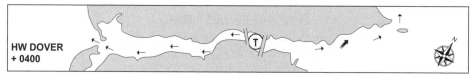

HW DOVER + 0400

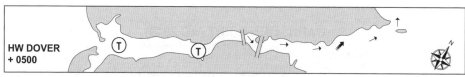

HW DOVER + 0500

LOCAL LW TIMES: Belan: Dover + 0520.

CAERNARFON BAR

CAERNARFON BAR is without question highly dangerous in certain conditions. Buoys are located to suit changing channel; positions obtainable from Caernarfon Port Radio - VHF Ch 16; 06, 12: 2h–HW, or when vessel expected. Beware cross track tides near high water. Bar impassable during or after fresh or strong onshore weather. Keep strictly in channel.

OUTWARD BOUND: Do not leave Belan Narrows after half tide, better as soon as possible after the ebb commences, which gives maximum depth and duration of fair tide if bound S & W.	INWARD BOUND: Locating the bar buoys may be difficult; head for Llanddwyn I. until they are located. Only cross after half tide (HW Dover –0400), which inevitably limits onward passage to max of 3 hours.

TIDES

TIDAL GATES - IRISH SEA

A guide to the time of tide turn at tidal gates, the approximate strength of the tidal flow (spring rates shown — neaps are approximately 60% of these), and the position and timing of races, counter tides, etc.

FLOOD	EBB

DUBLIN BAY (AC 1415)

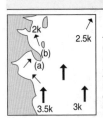
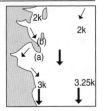

Tide between Rosbeg bank and Howth Hd (a) runs NE from HW Dublin +0300 for 9h30. In Howth Sd (b) the stream is NW going from +0430 to –0130.
New flood and ebb tides begin close to the S shore and N of Baily up to 1h before HW Dublin .

The tide between Rosbeg bank and Howth Hd (a) runs SW from HW Dublin for 3h. In Howth Sd (b) the stream is SE going from –0130 to +0430.
Strengths of streams increase S of Dublin Bay, and decrease N of it.

N W ANGLESEY (AC 1977)

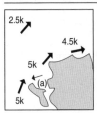
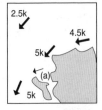

Flood tide close to the coast runs at over 5k springs, and at about 2.5k 7 miles offshore. The brief period of slack water offshore is 1h before HW Dover (1h15 before HW L'pool). Slack water lasts longer in Holyhead Bay.

Ebb tide close to the coast runs at over 5k springs, and at about 2.5k 7 miles offshore. Slack water is 5h after HW Dover (4h45 after HW L'pool). There is no significant counter tide in Holyhead Bay, but the ebb starts first there, giving about 9h W-going tide N of the harbour (a).

BARDSEY SOUND (AC 1971)

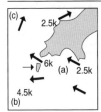
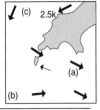

The tide turns to the NW or NE (flood) as follows:
at (a): HW Dover +0300;
at (b): HW D +0500;
at (c): –0545 HW D.
These times are approximate.
There is a strong eddy down tide of Bardsey Island and overfalls throughout the area.

The tide turns to the SW or SE (ebb) as follows:
at (a): HW Dover –0300;
at (b): HW D –0100 ;
at (c): at HW D –0030.
These times are approximate.
There is a strong eddy down tide of Bardsey Island and overfalls throughout the area.

S W WALES (AC 1478)

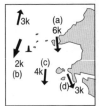
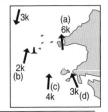

The tide turns to the S or SE (Bristol Channel flood) as follows:
at (a): HW Dover –0200;
at (b) & (c): HW D –0100 ;
at (d): –0300 HW D

The tide turns to the N or NW (Bristol Channel ebb) as follows:
at (a): HW Dover +0400;
at (b) & (c): HW D +0500 ;
at (d): +0300 HW D

CARNSORE POINT (AC 2049)

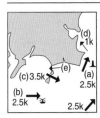
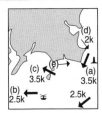

The tide turns to the NE or N (Irish Sea flood) as follows:
at (a): HW Dover +0500; at (b): HW D +0520; at (c): HW D +0600; at (d): –0600 HW D. NE going streams are shorter in duration and weaker than SE going - careful passage planning is essential.

The tide turns to the SW or S as follows:
at (a): –0200 HW D ; at (b): HW D –0020; at (c): –0015 HW D; at (d): –0300 HW Dover. Leaving Rosslare at –0300 HW D a yacht can carry a fair tide for about 8h until HW D +0515 off Hook Head.

NOTE: The tide turns on St Patrick's Bridge (e) up to 2 hours earlier than in Saltee Sound

CORK COAST (AC 2049)

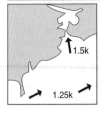
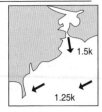

The tide, which flows coastwise, turns to the NE at HW Dover +0045. There is an eddy 5 miles ESE of Old Head of Kinsale at HW Dover +0400. The ingoing Cork Harbour tide begins at HW Dover +0055.

The tide turns SW at HW Dover +0500. The outgoing Cork Harbour tide begins at HW Dover –0540.

SECONDARY PORTS: TIME & HEIGHT DIFFERENCES
SOUTH COAST OF ENGLAND *Time zone UT*

Location	Lat	Long	High Water		Low Water		MHWS	MHWN	MLWN	MLWS
			0000	**0600**	**0000**	**0600**				
PLYMOUTH (DEVONPORT)	50 22N	4 11W	and	and	and	and	**5.5**	**4.4**	**2.2**	**0.8**
Standard port			**1200**	**1800**	**1200**	**1800**				
Isles of Scilly, St Mary's	49 55N	6 19W	–0035	–0100	–0040	–0025	+0.2	–0.1	–0.2	–0.1
Penzance & Newlyn	50 06N	5 33W	–0040	–0110	–0035	–0025	+0.1	0.0	–0.2	0.0
Porthleven	50 05N	5 19W	–0045	–0105	–0030	–0025	0.0	–0.1	–0.2	0.0
Lizard Point	49 57N	5 12W	–0045	–0100	–0030	–0030	–0.2	–0.2	–0.3	–0.2
Coverack	50 01N	5 05W	–0030	–0050	–0020	–0015	–0.2	–0.2	–0.3	–0.2
Helford River Entrance	50 05N	5 05W	–0030	–0035	–0015	–0010	–0.2	–0.2	–0.3	–0.2
FALMOUTH	50 09N	5 03W	*Standard port (no Secondaries)*							
River Fal, Truro	50 16N	5 03W	–0020	–0025	*Dries*	*Dries*	–2.0	–2.0	*Dries*	
Mevagissey	50 16N	4 47W	–0015	–0020	–0010	–0005	–0.1	–0.1	–0.2	–0.1
Par	50 21N	4 42W	–0010	–0015	–0010	–0005	–0.4	–0.4	–0.4	–0.1
River Fowey, Fowey	50 20N	4 38W	–0010	–0015	–0010	–0005	–0.1	–0.1	–0.2	–0.2
Lostwithiel	50 24N	4 40W	+0005	–0010	*Dries*	*Dries*	–4.1	–4.1	*Dries*	
Looe	50 21N	4 27W	–0010	–0010	–0005	–0005	–0.1	–0.2	–0.2	–0.2
Whitsand Bay	50 20N	4 15W	0000	0000	0000	0000	0.0	+0.1	–0.1	+0.2
River Tamar										
Saltash	50 24N	4 12W	0000	+0010	0000	–0005	+0.1	+0.1	+0.1	+0.1
Cargreen	50 26N	4 12W	0000	+0010	+0020	+0020	0.0	0.0	–0.1	0.0
Cotehele Quay	50 29N	4 13W	0000	+0020	+0045	+0045	–0.9	–0.9	–0.8	–0.4
River Tavy, Lopwell	50 28N	4 09W	*No data*	*No data*	*Dries*	*Dries*	–2.6	–2.7	*Dries*	
River Lynher, Jupiter Point	50 23N	4 14W	+0010	+0005	0000	–0005	0.0	0.0	+0.1	0.0
St Germans	50 23N	4 18W	0000	0000	+0020	+0020	–0.3	–0.1	0.0	+0.2
Turnchapel	50 22N	4 07W	0000	0000	+0010	–0015	0.0	+0.1	+0.2	+0.1
Bovisand Pier	50 20N	4 08W	0000	–0020	0000	–0010	–0.2	–0.1	0.0	+0.1
River Yealm, Entrance	50 18N	4 04W	+0006	+0006	+0002	+0002	–0.1	–0.1	–0.1	–0.1
			0100	**0600**	**0100**	**0600**				
PLYMOUTH (DEVONPORT)	50 22N	4 11W	and	and	and	and	**5.5**	**4.4**	**2.2**	**0.8**
Standard port			**1300**	**1800**	**1300**	**1800**				
Salcombe	50 13N	3 47W	0000	+0010	+0005	–0005	–0.2	–0.3	–0.1	–0.1
Start Point	50 13N	3 39W	+0015	+0015	+0005	+0010	–0.1	–0.2	+0.1	+0.2
River Dart										
DARTMOUTH	50 21N	3 34W	*Standard port (no Secondaries)*							
Greenway Quay	50 23N	3 35W	+0030	+0045	+0025	+0005	–0.6	–0.6	–0.2	–0.2
Totnes	50 26N	3 41W	+0030	+0040	+0115	+0030	–2.0	–2.1	*Dries*	
Torquay	50 28N	3 31W	+0025	+0045	+0010	0000	–0.6	–0.7	–0.2	–0.1
Teignmouth, Approaches	50 33N	3 29W	+0020	+0050	+0025	0000	–0.9	–0.8	–0.2	–0.1
Teignmouth, New Quay	50 33N	3 30W	+0025	+0055	+0040	+0005	–0.8	–0.8	–0.2	+0.1
Exmouth Approaches	50 36N	3 23W	+0030	+0050	+0015	+0005	–0.9	–1.0	–0.5	–0.3
River Exe										
Exmouth Dock	50 37N	3 25W	+0035	+0055	+0050	+0020	–1.5	–1.6	–0.9	–0.6
Starcross	50 38N	3 27W	+0040	+0100	+0055	+0025	–1.4	–1.5	–0.8	–0.1
Turf Lock	50 40N	3 28W	+0045	+0100	+0034	*No data*	– 1.6	–1.6	–1.2	*No data*
Topsham	50 41N	3 28W	+0045	+0105	*No data*	*No data*	– 1.5	–1.6	*No data*	
Lyme Regis	50 43N	2 56W	+0040	+0100	0000	+0005	–1.2	–1.3	–0.5	–0.2
Bridport (West Bay)	50 42N	2 45W	+0025	+0040	0000	0000	–1.4	–1.4	–0.6	–0.2
Chesil Beach	50 37N	2 33W	+0040	+0055	–0005	+0010	–1.6	–1.5	–0.5	0.0
Chesil Cove	50 34N	2 28W	+0035	+0050	–0010	+0005	–1.5	–1.6	–0.5	–0.2
			0100	**0700**	**0100**	**0700**				
PORTLAND	50 34N	2 26W	and	and	and	and	**2.1**	**1.4**	**0.8**	**0.1**
Standard port			**1300**	**1900**	**1300**	**1900**				
Lulworth Cove, Mupe Bay	50 37N	2 14W	+0005	+0015	–0005	0000	+0.1	+0.1	+0.2	+0.1
			—	—	**0500**	**1100**				
POOLE HARBOUR	50 42N	1 59W			and	and	**2.2**	**1.7**	**1.2**	**0.6**
Standard port			—	—	**1700**	**2300**				
Swanage	50 37N	1 57W	—	—	–0045	+0055	–0.2	–0.1	0.0	–0.1
Poole Harbour Entrance	50 41N	1 57W	—	—	–0025	–0010	0.0	0.0	0.0	0.0
Ro-Ro terminal	50 42N	1 59W	*Standard port*							
Pottery Pier	50 42N	1 59W	—	—	–0010	0000	–0.2	0.0	+0.1	+0.2
Wareham, River Frome	50 41N	2 06W	—	—	+0130	+0145	0.0	0.0	0.0	+0.3
Cleavel Point	50 40N	2 00W	—	—	–0005	–0005	–0.1	–0.2	0.0	*No data*
			0000	**0600**	**0500**	**1100**				
PORTSMOUTH	50 48N	1 07W	and	and	and	and	**4.7**	**3.8**	**1.9**	**0.8**
Standard port			**1200**	**1800**	**1700**	**2300**				
Bournemouth	50 43N	1 52W	–0240	+0055	–0050	–0030	–2.7	–2.2	–0.8	–0.3
Christchurch Entrance	50 43N	1 45W	–0230	+0030	–0035	–0035	–2.9	–2.4	–1.2	–0.2

Location	Lat	Long	High Water		Low Water		MHWS	MHWN	MLWN	MLWS
Christchurch Quay	50 44N	1 47W	−0210	+0100	+0105	+0055	−2.9	−2.4	−1.0	0.0
Christchurch, Tuckton	50 44N	1 47W	−0205	+0110	+0110	+0105	−3.0	−2.5	−1.0	+0.1
Hurst Point	50 42N	1 33W	−0115	−0005	−0030	−0025	−2.0	−1.5	−0.5	−0.1
Lymington	50 46N	1 32W	−0110	+0005	−0020	−0020	−1.7	−1.2	−0.5	−0.1
Bucklers Hard	50 48N	1 25W	−0040	−0010	+0010	−0010	−1.0	−0.8	−0.2	−0.3
Stansore Point	50 47N	1 20W	−0050	−0010	−0005	−0010	−0.8	−0.5	−0.3	−0.1
Isle of Wight										
Yarmouth	50 42N	1 30W	−0105	+0005	−0025	−0030	−1.7	−1.2	−0.3	0.0
Totland Bay	50 41N	1 33W	−0130	−0045	−0035	−0045	−2.2	−1.7	−0.4	−0.1
Freshwater	50 40N	1 31W	−0210	+0025	−0040	−0020	−2.1	−1.5	−0.4	0.0
Ventnor	50 36N	1 12W	−0025	−0030	−0025	−0030	−0.8	−0.6	−0.2	+0.2
Sandown	50 39N	1 09W	0000	+0005	+0010	+0025	−0.6	−0.5	−0.2	0.0
Foreland Lifeboat Slip	50 41N	1 04W	−0005	0000	+0005	+0010	+0.1	+0.1	0.0	+0.1
Bembridge Harbour	50 42N	1 07W	+0020	0000	+0100	+0020	−1.5	−1.4	−1.3	−1.0
Ryde	50 44N	1 10W	−0010	+0010	−0005	−0005	−0.1	0.0	0.0	0.0
Medina River										
Cowes	50 46N	1 18W	−0015	+0015	0000	−0020	−0.5	−0.3	−0.1	0.0
Folly Inn	50 44N	1 17W	−0015	+0015	0000	−0020	−0.6	−0.4	−0.1	+0.2
Newport	50 42N	1 17W	No data	No data	No data	No data	−0.6	−0.4	+0.1	+0.8
			0400	**1100**	**0000**	**0600**				
SOUTHAMPTON	50 53N	1 24W	and	and	and	and	4.5	3.7	1.8	0.5
Standard port			**1600**	**2300**	**1200**	**1800**				
Calshot Castle	50 49N	1 18W	0000	+0025	0000	0000	0.0	0.0	+0.2	+0.3
Redbridge	50 55N	1 28W	−0020	+0005	0000	−0005	−0.1	−0.1	−0.1	−0.1
River Hamble										
Warsash	50 51N	1 18W	+0020	+0010	+0010	0000	0.0	+0.1	+0.1	+0.3
Bursledon	50 53N	1 18W	+0020	+0020	+0010	+0010	+0.1	+0.2	+0.2	+0.2
			0500	**1000**	**0000**	**0600**				
PORTSMOUTH	50 48N	1 07W	and	and	and	and	4.7	3.8	1.9	0.8
Standard port			**1700**	**2200**	**1200**	**1800**				
Lee-on-the-Solent	50 48N	1 12W	−0005	+0005	−0015	−0010	−0.2	−0.1	+0.1	+0.2
Chichester Harbour Entrance	50 47N	0 56W	−0010	+0005	+0015	+0020	+0.2	+0.2	0.0	+0.1
Northney	50 50N	0 58W	+0010	+0015	+0015	+0025	+0.2	0.0	−0.2	−0.3
Bosham	50 50N	0 52W	0000	+0010	No data	No data	+0.2	+0.1	No data	
Itchenor	50 48N	0 52W	−0005	+0005	+0005	+0025	+0.1	0.0	−0.2	−0.2
Dell Quay	50 49N	0 49W	+0005	+0015	no data	No data	+0.2	+0.1	No data	
Selsey Bill	50 43N	0 47W	+0010	−0010	+0035	+0020	+0.5	+0.3	−0.1	−0.2
Nab Tower	50 40N	0 57W	+0015	0000	+0015	+0015	−0.2	0.0	+0.2	0.0
			0500	**1000**	**0000**	**0600**				
SHOREHAM	50 50N	0 15W	and	and	and	and	6.3	4.8	1.9	0.6
Standard port			**1700**	**2200**	**1200**	**1800**				
Pagham	50 46N	0 43W	+0015	0000	−0015	−0025	−0.7	−0.5	−0.1	−0.1
Bognor Regis	50 47N	0 40W	+0010	−0005	−0005	−0020	−0.6	−0.5	−0.2	−0.1
River Arun										
Littlehampton Entrance	50 48N	0 33W	+0010	0000	−0005	−0010	−0.4	−0.4	−0.2	−0.2
Littlehampton UMA wharf	50 49N	0 33W	+0015	+0005	0000	+0045	−0.7	−0.7	−0.3	+0.2
Arundel	50 51N	0 33W	No data	+0120	No data	No data	−3.1	−2.8	No data	
Worthing	50 48N	0 22W	+0010	0000	−0005	−0010	−0.1	−0.2	0.0	0.0
Brighton	50 49N	0 08W	0000	−0005	0000	0000	+0.3	+0.2	+0.1	0.0
Newhaven	50 47N	0 04E	−0015	−0010	0000	0000	+0.2	+0.1	−0.1	−0.2
Eastbourne	50 46N	0 17E	−0010	−0005	+0015	+0020	+1.1	+0.6	+0.2	+0.1
			0000	**0600**	**0100**	**0700**				
DOVER	51 07N	1 19E	and	and	and	and	6.8	5.3	2.1	0.8
Standard port			**1200**	**1800**	**1300**	**1900**				
Hastings	50 51N	0 36E	0000	−0010	−0030	−0030	+0.8	+0.5	+0.1	−0.1
Rye Approaches	50 55N	0 47E	+0005	−0010	No data	No data	+1.0	+0.7	No data	
Rye Harbour	50 56N	0 48E	+0005	−0010	Dries	Dries	−1.4	−1.7	Dries	
Dungeness	50 55N	0 58E	−0010	−0015	−0020	−0010	+1.0	+0.6	+0.4	+0.1
Folkestone	51 05N	1 12E	−0020	−0005	−0010	−0010	+0.4	+0.4	0.0	−0.1
Deal	51 13N	1 25E	+0010	+0020	+0010	+0005	−0.6	−0.3	0.0	0.0
Richborough	51 18N	1 21E	+0015	+0015	+0030	+0030	−3.4	−2.6	−1.7	−0.7
Ramsgate	51 20N	1 25E	+0030	+0030	+0017	+0007	−1.6	−1.3	−0.7	−0.2

EAST COAST ENGLAND *Time Zone UT*

Location	Lat	Long	High Water		Low Water		MHWS	MHWN	MLWN	MLWS
			0100	**0700**	**0100**	**0700**				
MARGATE	51 23N	1 23E	and	and	and	and	4.8	3.9	1.4	0.5
Standard port			**1300**	**1900**	**1300**	**1900**				
Herne Bay	51 23N	1 07E	+0034	+0022	+0015	+0032	+0.6	+0.4	+0.1	0.0
Whitstable approaches	51 22N	1 02E	+0042	+0029	+0025	+0050	+0.6	+0.6	+0.1	0.0

Location	Lat	Long	High Water		Low Water		MHWS	MHWN	MLWN	MLWS
SHEERNESS	51 27N	0 45E	0200 and 1400	0800 and 2000	0200 and 1400	0700 and 1900	5.8	4.7	1.5	0.6
Standard port										
River Swale										
Grovehurst Jetty	51 22N	0 46E	–0007	0000	0000	+0016	0.0	0.0	0.0	–0.1
Faversham	51 19N	0 54E	*No data*	*No data*	*No data*	*No data*	–0.2	–0.2	*No data*	
River Medway										
Bee Ness	51 25N	0 39E	+0002	+0002	0000	+0005	+0.2	+0.1	0.0	0.0
Bartlett Creek	51 23N	0 38E	+0016	+0008	*No data*	*No data*	+0.1	0.0	*No data*	
Darnett Ness	51 24N	0 36E	+0004	+0004	0000	+0010	+0.2	+0.1	0.0	–0.1
Chatham, Lock approaches	51 24N	0 33E	+0010	+0012	+0012	+0018	+0.3	+0.1	–0.1	–0.2
Upnor	51 25N	0 32E	+0015	+0015	+0015	+0025	+0.2	+0.2	–0.1	–0.1
Rochester, Strood Pier	51 24N	0 30E	+0018	+0018	+0018	+0028	+0.2	+0.2	–0.2	–0.3
Wouldham	51 21N	0 27E	+0030	+0025	+0035	+0120	–0.2	–0.3	–1.0	–0.3
New Hythe	51 19N	0 28E	+0035	+0035	+0220	+0240	–1.6	–1.7	–1.2	–0.3
Allington Lock	51 17N	0 30E	+0050	+0035	*No data*	*No data*	–2.1	–2.2	–1.3	–0.4
River Thames										
Southend–on–Sea	51 31N	0 43E	–0005	–0005	–0005	–0005	0.0	0.0	–0.1	–0.1
Coryton	51 30N	0 31E	+0005	+0010	+0010	+0010	+0.4	+0.3	0.0	0.0
LONDON BRIDGE	51 30N	0 05W	0300 and 1500	0900 and 2100	0400 and 1600	1100 and 2300	7.1	5.9	1.3	0.5
Standard port										
Tilbury	51 27N	0 22E	–0055	–0040	–0050	–0115	–0.7	–0.5	+0.1	0.0
North Woolwich	51 30N	0 05E	–0020	–0020	–0035	–0045	–0.1	0.0	+0.2	0.0
Albert bridge	51 29N	0 10W	+0025	+0020	+0105	+0110	–0.9	–0.8	–0.7	–0.4
Hammersmith bridge	51 29N	0 14W	+0040	+0035	+0205	+0155	–1.4	–1.3	–1.0	–0.5
Kew bridge	51 29N	0 17W	+0055	+0050	+0255	+0235	–1.8	–1.8	–1.2	–0.5
Richmond lock	51 28N	0 19W	+0105	+0055	+0325	+0305	–2.2	–2.2	–1.3	–0.5
SHEERNESS	51 27N	0 45E	0200 and 1400	0700 and 1900	0100 and 1300	0700 and 1900	5.8	4.7	1.5	0.6
Standard port										
Thames Estuary Shivering Sand	51 30N	1 05E	–0025	–0019	–0008	–0026	–0.6	–0.6	–0.1	–0.1
WALTON-ON-THE-NAZE	51 51N	1 17E	0000 and 1200	0600 and 1800	0500 and 1700	1100 and 2300	4.2	3.4	1.1	0.4
Standard port										
Whitaker Beacon	51 40N	1 06E	+0022	+0024	+0033	+0027	+0.6	+0.5	+0.2	+0.1
Holliwell Point	51 38N	0 56E	+0034	+0037	+0100	+0037	+1.1	+0.9	+0.3	+0.1
River Roach Rochford	51 35N	0 43E	+0050	+0040	*Dries*	*Dries*	–0.8	–1.1	*Dries*	
River Crouch										
Burnham-on-Crouch	51 37N	0 48E	+0050	+0035	+0115	+0050	+1.0	+0.8	–0.1	–0.2
North Fambridge	51 38N	0 41E	+0115	+0050	+0130	+0100	+1.1	+0.8	0.0	–0.1
Hullbridge	51 38N	0 38E	+0115	+0050	+0135	+0105	+1.1	+0.8	0.0	–0.1
Battlesbridge	51 37N	0 34E	+0120	+0110	*Dries*	*Dries*	–1.8	–2.0	*Dries*	
River Blackwater										
Bradwell Waterside	51 45N	0 54E	+0035	+0023	+0047	+0004	+1.0	+0.8	+0.2	0.0
Osea Island	51 43N	0 46E	+0057	+0045	+0050	+0007	+1.1	+0.9	+0.1	0.0
Maldon	51 44N	0 42E	+0107	+0055	*No data*	*No data*	–1.3	–1.1	*No data*	
West Mersea	51 47N	0 54E	+0035	+0015	+0055	+0010	+0.9	+0.4	+0.1	+0.1
River Colne										
Brightlingsea	51 48N	1 00E	+0025	+0021	+0046	+0004	+0.8	+0.4	+0.1	0.0
Colchester	51 53N	0 56E	+0035	+0025	*Dries*	*Dries*	0.0	–0.3	*Dries*	
Clacton-on-Sea	51 47N	1 10E	+0012	+0010	+0025	+0008	+0.3	+0.1	+0.1	+0.1
Bramble Creek	51 53N	1 14E	+0010	–0007	–0005	+0010	+0.3	+0.3	+0.3	+0.3
Sunk Head	51 47N	1 30E	0000	+0002	–0002	+0002	–0.3	–0.3	–0.1	–0.1
Harwich	51 57N	1 17E	+0007	+0002	–0010	–0012	–0.2	0.0	0.0	0.0
Mistley	51 57N	1 05E	+0032	+0027	–0010	–0012	0.0	0.0	–0.1	–0.1
Ipswich	52 03N	1 10E	+0022	+0027	0000	–0012	0.0	0.0	–0.1	–0.1
WALTON–ON–THE–NAZE	51 51N	1 17E	0100 and 1300	0700 and 1900	0100 and 1300	0700 and 1900	4.2	3.4	1.1	0.4
Standard port										
Felixstowe Pier	51 57N	1 21E	–0005	–0007	–0018	–0020	–0.5	–0.4	0.0	0.0
River Deben										
Woodbridge Haven	51 59N	1 24E	0000	–0005	–0020	–0025	–0.5	–0.5	–0.1	+0.1
Woodbridge	52 05N	1 19E	+0045	+0025	+0025	–0020	–0.2	–0.3	–0.2	0.0
Bawdsey	52 01N	1 26E	–0016	–0020	–0030	–0032	–0.8	–0.6	–0.1	–0.1
Orford Haven										
Bar	52 02N	1 28E	–0026	–0030	–0036	–0038	–1.0	–0.8	–0.1	0.0
Orford Quay	52 05N	1 32E	+0040	+0040	+0055	+0055	–1.4	–1.1	0.0	+0.2
Slaughden Quay	52 08N	1 36E	+0105	+0105	+0125	+0125	–1.3	–0.8	–0.1	+0.2
Iken Cliffs	52 09N	1 31E	+0130	+0130	+0155	+0155	–1.3	–1.0	0.0	+0.2

TIDES

TIDES

Location	Lat	Long	High Water		Low Water		MHWS	MHWN	MLWN	MLWS
			0300 and 1500	0900 and 2100	0200 and 1400	0800 and 2000				
LOWESTOFT	52 28N	1 45E	0300 and 1500	0900 and 2100	0200 and 1400	0800 and 2000	2.4	2.1	1.0	0.5
Standard port										
Orford Ness	52 05N	1 35E	+0135	+0135	+0135	+0125	+0.4	+0.6	−0.1	0.0
Aldeburgh	52 09N	1 36E	+0130	+0130	+0115	+0120	+0.3	+0.2	−0.1	−0.2
Minsmere Sluice	52 14N	1 38E	+0110	+0110	+0110	+0110	0.0	−0.1	−0.2	−0.2
Southwold	52 19N	1 40E	+0105	+0105	+0055	+0055	0.0	0.0	−0.1	0.0
Great Yarmouth										
Gorleston-on-Sea	52 34N	1 44E	−0035	−0035	−0030	−0030	0.0	0.0	0.0	0.0
Britannia Pier	52 36N	1 45E	−0105	−0100	−0040	−0055	+0.1	+0.1	0.0	0.0
Caister-on-Sea	52 39N	1 44E	−0120	−0120	−0100	−0100	0.0	−0.1	0.0	0.0
Winterton-on-Sea	52 43N	1 42E	−0225	−0215	−0135	−0135	+0.8	+0.5	+0.2	+0.1
IMMINGHAM	53 38N	0 11W	0100 and 1300	0700 and 1900	0100 and 1300	0700 and 1900	7.3	5.8	2.6	0.9
Standard port										
Cromer	52 56N	1 18E	+0050	+0030	+0050	+0130	−2.1	−1.7	−0.5	−0.1
Blakeney Bar	52 59N	0 59E	+0035	+0025	+0030	+0040	−1.6	−1.3	No data	
Blakeney	52 57N	1 01E	+0115	+0055	No data	No data	−3.9	−3.8	No data	
Wells Bar	52 59N	0 49E	+0020	+0020	+0020	+0020	−1.3	−1.0	No data	
Wells	52 57N	0 51E	+0035	+0045	+0340	+0310	−3.8	−3.8	Not below CD	
Burnham Overy Staithe	52 58N	0 48E	+0045	+0055	No data	No data	−5.0	−4.9	No data	
The Wash										
Hunstanton	52 56N	0 29E	+0010	+0020	+0105	+0025	+0.1	−0.2	−0.1	0.0
West Stones	52 50N	0 21E	+0025	+0025	+0115	+0040	−0.3	−0.4	−0.3	+0.2
King's Lynn	52 45N	0 24E	+0030	+0030	+0305	+0140	−0.5	−0.8	−0.8	+0.1
Outer Westmark Knock	52 53N	0 13E	+0010	+0015	+0040	+0020	−0.2	−0.5	−0.6	−0.4
Wisbech Cut	52 48N	0 13E	+0020	+0010	+0120	+0055	−0.3	−0.7	−0.4	No data
Port Sutton bridge	52 46N	0 12E	+0030	+0020	+0130	+0105	−0.3	−0.6	−0.6	+0.3
Wisbech	52 40N	0 09E	+0055	+0040	Dries	Dries	−0.2	−0.6	Dries	Dries
Lawyer's Creek	52 53N	0 05E	+0010	+0020	No data	No data	−0.3	−0.6	No data	
Tabs Head	52 56N	0 05E	0000	+0005	+0125	+0020	+0.2	−0.2	−0.2	−0.2
Boston	52 58N	0 01W	0000	+0010	+0140	+0050	−0.5	−1.0	−0.9	−0.5
Skegness	53 09N	0 21E	+0010	+0015	+0030	+0020	−0.4	−0.5	−0.1	0.0
Inner Dowsing Light Tower	53 19N	0 35E	0000	0000	+0010	+0010	−0.9	−0.7	−0.1	+0.3
River Humber										
Bull Sand Fort	53 34N	0 04E	−0020	−0030	−0035	−0015	−0.4	−0.3	+0.1	+0.2
Grimsby	53 35N	0 04W	−0012	−0012	−0015	−0015	−0.2	−0.1	0.0	+0.2
Hull, King George Dock	53 44N	0 16W	+0010	+0010	+0021	+0017	+0.3	+0.2	−0.1	−0.2
Hull, Albert Dock	53 44N	0 21W	+0019	+0019	+0033	+0027	+0.3	+0.1	−0.1	−0.2
Humber Bridge	53 43N	0 27W	+0027	+0022	+0049	+0039	−0.1	−0.4	−0.7	−0.6
River Trent										
Burton Stather	53 39N	0 42W	+0105	+0045	+0335	+0305	−2.1	−2.3	−2.3	Dries
Flixborough Wharf	53 37N	0 42W	+0120	+0100	+0400	+0340	−2.3	−2.6	Dries	
Keadby	53 36N	0 44W	+0135	+0120	+0425	+0410	−2.5	−2.8	Dries	
Owston Ferry	53 29N	0 46W	+0155	+0145	Dries	Dries	−3.5	−3.9	Dries	
River Ouse										
Blacktoft	53 42N	0 43W	+0100	+0055	+0325	+0255	−1.6	−1.8	−2.2	−1.1
Goole	53 42N	0 52W	+0130	+0115	+0355	+0350	−1.6	−2.1	−1.9	−0.6
R TEES ENTRANCE	54 38N	1 09W	0000 and 1200	0600 and 1800	0000 and 1200	0600 and 1800	5.5	4.3	2.0	0.9
Standard port										
Bridlington	54 05N	0 11W	+0100	+0050	+0055	+0050	+0.6	+0.4	+0.3	+0.2
Filey Bay	54 13N	0 16W	+0042	+0042	+0047	+0034	+0.3	+0.6	+0.4	+0.1
Scarborough	54 17N	0 23W	+0040	+0040	+0030	+0030	+0.2	+0.3	+0.3	0.0
Whitby	54 29N	0 37W	+0015	+0030	+0020	+0005	+0.1	0.0	−0.1	−0.1
Middlesborough Dock ent	54 35N	1 13W	+0000	+0002	+0000	−0003	+0.1	+0.2	+0.1	−0.1
Tees (Newport) Bridge	54 34N	1 16W	−0002	+0004	+0005	−0003	+0.1	+0.2	0.0	−0.1
Hartlepool	54 42N	1 12W	−0004	−0004	−0006	−0006	−0.1	−0.1	−0.2	−0.1
Seaham	54 50N	1 19W	−0015	−0015	−0015	−0015	−0.3	−0.2	0.0	−0.2
Sunderland	54 55N	1 22W	−0017	−0017	−0016	−0016	−0.2	−0.1	0.0	0.0
R TYNE, NORTH SHIELDS	55 00N	1 26W	0200 and 1400	0800 and 2000	0100 and 1300	0800 and 2000	5.0	3.9	1.8	0.7
Standard port										
Newcastle-upon-Tyne	54 58N	1 36W	+0003	+0003	+0008	+0008	+0.3	+0.2	+0.1	+0.1
Blyth	55 07N	1 29W	+0005	−0007	−0001	+0009	0.0	0.0	−0.1	+0.1
Coquet Island	55 20N	1 32W	−0010	−0010	−0020	−0020	+0.1	+0.1	0.0	+0.1
Amble	55 20N	1 34W	−0013	−0013	−0016	−0020	0.0	0.0	+0.1	+0.1

Location	Lat	Long	High Water		Low Water		MHWS	MHWN	MLWN	MLWS
North Sunderland	55 35N	1 39W	−0048	−0044	−0058	−0102	−0.2	−0.2	−0.2	0.0
Holy Island	55 40N	1 48W	−0043	−0039	−0105	−0110	−0.2	−0.2	−0.3	−0.1
Berwick	55 46N	1 59W	−0053	−0053	−0109	−0109	−0.3	−0.1	−0.5	−0.1

SCOTLAND *Time Zone UT*

Location	Lat	Long	High Water		Low Water		MHWS	MHWN	MLWN	MLWS
			0300	0900	0300	0900				
LEITH	55 59N	3 11W	and	and	and	and	5.6	4.4	2.0	0.8
Standard port			1500	2100	1500	2100				
Eyemouth	55 52N	2 05W	−0005	+0007	+0012	+0008	−0.4	−0.3	0.0	+0.1
Dunbar	56 00N	2 31W	−0005	+0003	+0003	−0003	−0.3	−0.3	0.0	+0.1
Fidra	56 04N	2 47W	−0001	0000	−0002	+0001	−0.2	−0.2	0.0	0.0
Cockenzie	55 58N	2 57W	−0007	−0015	−0013	−0005	−0.2	0.0	*No data*	
Granton	55 59N	3 13W	0000	0000	0000	0000	0.0	0.0	0.0	0.0
River Forth Grangemouth	56 02N	3 41W	+0015	+0010	−0050	−0045	0.0	−0.1	−0.2	−0.2
Kincardine	56 04N	3 43W	+0015	+0030	−0030	−0030	0.0	−0.2	−0.5	−0.3
Alloa	56 06N	3 48W	+0040	+0040	+0025	+0025	−0.2	−0.5	*No data*	−0.7
Stirling	56 07N	3 56W	+0100	+0100	*No data*		−2.9	−3.1	−2.3	−0.7
Firth of Forth										
Burntisland	56 03N	3 14W	+0013	+0004	−0002	+0007	+0.1	0.0	+0.1	+0.2
Kirkcaldy	56 09N	3 09W	+0005	0000	−0004	−0001	−0.3	−0.3	−0.2	−0.2
Methil	56 11N	3 00W	−0005	−0001	−0001	−0001	−0.1	−0.1	−0.1	−0.1
Anstruther Easter	56 13N	2 42W	−0018	−0012	−0006	−0008	−0.3	−0.2	0.0	0.0
			0000	0600	0100	0700				
ABERDEEN	57 09N	2 04W	and	and	and	and	4.3	3.4	1.6	0.6
Standard port			1200	1800	1300	1900				
River Tay										
Bar	56 28N	2 38W	+0100	+0100	+0050	+0110	+0.9	+0.8	+0.3	+0.1
Dundee	56 27N	2 58W	+0140	+0120	+0055	+0145	+1.3	+0.9	+0.4	+0.2
Newburgh	56 21N	3 14W	+0215	+0200	+0250	+0335	−0.2	−0.4	−1.1	−0.5
Perth	56 24N	3 25W	+0220	+0225	+0510	+0530	−0.9	−1.4	−1.2	−0.3
Arbroath	56 33N	2 35W	+0056	+0037	+0034	+0055	+1.0	+0.8	+0.4	+0.2
Montrose	56 42N	2 28W	+0055	+0055	+0030	+0040	+0.5	+0.4	+0.2	0.0
Stonehaven	56 58N	2 12W	+0013	+0008	+0013	+0009	+0.2	+0.2	+0.1	0.0
Peterhead	57 30N	1 46W	−0035	−0045	−0035	−0040	−0.4	−0.3	+0.1	+0.1
Fraserburgh	57 41N	2 00W	−0105	−0115	−0120	−0110	−0.6	−0.5	−0.2	0.0
			0200	0900	0400	0900				
ABERDEEN	57 09N	2 04W	and	and	and	and	4.3	3.4	1.6	0.6
Standard port			1400	2100	1600	2100				
Banff	57 40N	2 31W	−0100	−0150	−0150	−0050	−0.4	−0.2	−0.1	+0.2
Whitehills	57 41N	2 35W	−0122	−0137	−0117	−0127	−0.4	−0.3	+0.1	+0.1
Buckie	57 41N	2 57W	−0130	−0145	−0125	−0140	−0.2	−0.2	0.0	0.0
Lossiemouth	57 43N	3 18W	−0125	−0200	−0130	−0130	−0.2	−0.2	0.0	0.0
Burghead	57 42N	3 29W	−0120	−0150	−0135	−0120	−0.2	−0.2	0.0	0.0
Nairn	57 36N	3 52W	−0120	−0150	−0135	−0130	0.0	−0.1	0.0	+0.1
McDermott Base	57 36N	3 59W	−0110	−0140	−0120	−0115	−0.1	−0.1	+0.1	+0.3
			0300	1000	0000	0700				
ABERDEEN	57 09N	2 04W	and	and	and	and	4.3	3.4	1.6	0.6
Standard port			1500	2200	1200	1900				
Inverness Firth										
Fortrose	57 35N	4 08W	−0125	−0125	−0125	−0125	0.0	0.0	*No data*	
Inverness	57 30N	4 15W	−0050	−0150	−0200	−0150	+0.5	+0.3	+0.2	+0.1
Cromarty Firth										
Cromarty	57 42N	4 03W	−0120	−0155	−0155	−0120	0.0	0.0	+0.1	+0.2
Invergordon	57 41N	4 10W	−0105	−0200	−0200	−0110	+0.1	+0.1	+0.1	+0.1
Dingwall	57 36N	4 25W	−0045	−0145	*No data*	*No data*	+0.1	+0.2	*No data*	
			0300	0800	0200	0800				
ABERDEEN	57 09N	2 04W	and	and	and	and	4.3	3.4	1.6	0.6
Standard port			1500	2000	1400	2000				
Dornoch Firth										
Portmahomack	57 50N	3 50W	−0120	−0210	−0140	−0110	−0.2	−0.1	+0.1	+0.1
Meikle Ferry	57 51N	4 08W	−0100	−0140	−0120	−0055	+0.1	0.0	−0.1	0.0
Golspie	57 58N	3 59W	−0130	−0215	−0155	−0130	−0.3	−0.3	−0.1	0.0
			0000	0700	0200	0700				
WICK	58 26N	3 05W	and	and	and	and	3.5	2.8	1.4	0.7
Standard port			1200	1900	1400	1900				
Helmsdale	58 07N	3 39W	+0025	+0015	+0035	+0030	+0.4	+0.3	+0.1	0.0
Duncansby Head	58 39N	3 02W	−0115	−0115	−0110	−0110	−0.4	−0.4	*No data*	
Orkney Islands										
Muckle Skerry	58 41N	2 55W	−0025	−0025	−0020	−0020	−0.9	−0.8	−0.4	−0.3

TIDES

191

Location	Lat	Long	High Water		Low Water		MHWS	MHWN	MLWN	MLWS
Burray Ness	58 51N	2 52W	+0005	+0005	+0015	+0015	–0.2	–0.3	–0.1	–0.1
Deer Sound	58 58N	2 50W	–0040	–0040	–0035	–0035	–0.3	–0.3	–0.1	–0.1
Kirkwall	58 59N	2 58W	–0042	–0042	–0041	–0041	–0.5	–0.4	–0.1	–0.1
Egilsay	59 09N	2 57W	–0125	–0125	–0125	–0125	–0.1	0.0	+0.2	+0.1
Whitehall	58 09N	2 36W	–0030	–0030	–0025	–0030	–0.1	0.0	+0.2	+0.2
Loth	59 11N	2 42W	–0045	–0045	–00558	–0105	–0.4	–0.3	+0.1	+0.2
Kettletoft Pier	59 14N	2 36W	–0030	–0025	–0025	–0025	0.0	0.0	+0.2	+0.2
Rapness	59 15N	2 52W	–0205	–0205	–0205	–0205	+0.1	0.0	+0.2	0.0
Pierowall	59 19N	2 59W	–0150	–0150	–0145	–0145	+0.2	0.0	0.0	–0.1
Tingwall	59 05N	3 03W	–0200	–0125	–0145	–0125	–0.4	–0.4	–0.1	–0.1
Stromness	58 58N	3 18W	–0225	–0135	–0205	–0205	+0.1	–0.1	0.0	0.0
St Mary's	58 54N	2 55W	–0140	–0140	–0140	–0140	–0.2	–0.2	0.0	–0.1
Widewall Bay	58 49N	3 01W	–0155	–0155	–0150	–0150	+0.1	–0.1	–0.1	–0.3
Bur Wick	58 44N	2 58W	–0100	–0100	–0150	–0150	–0.1	–0.1	+0.2	+0.1
			0000	**0600**	**0100**	**0800**				
LERWICK	60 09N	1 08W	and	and	and	and	**2.1**	**1.7**	**0.9**	**0.5**
Standard port			**1200**	**1800**	**1300**	**2000**				
Fair Isle	59 32N	1 36W	–0006	–0015	–0031	–0037	+0.1	0.0	+0.1	+0.1
Shetland Islands										
Sumburgh (Grutness Voe)	59 53N	1 17W	+0006	+0008	+0004	–0002	–0.3	–0.3	–0.2	–0.1
Dury Voe	60 21N	1 10W	–0015	–0015	–0010	–0010	0.0	–0.1	0.0	–0.2
Out Skerries	60 25N	0 45W	–0025	–0025	–0010	–0010	+0.1	0.0	0.0	–0.1
Toft Pier	60 28N	1 12W	–0105	–0100	–0125	–0115	+0.2	+0.1	–0.1	–0.1
Burra Voe (Yell Sound)	60 30N	1 03W	–0025	–0025	–0025	–0025	+0.2	+0.1	0.0	–0.1
Mid Yell	60 36N	1 03W	–0030	–0020	–0035	–0025	+0.3	+0.2	+0.2	+0.1
Balta Sound	60 46N	0 50W	–0055	–0055	–0045	–0045	+0.2	+0.1	0.0	–0.1
Burra Firth	60 48N	0 52W	–0110	–0110	–0115	–0115	+0.4	+0.2	0.0	0.0
Bluemull Sound	60 42N	1 00W	–0135	–0135	–0155	–0155	+0.5	+0.2	+0.1	0.0
Sullom Voe	60 27N	1 18W	–0135	–0125	–0135	–0120	0.0	0.0	–0.2	–0.2
Hillswick	60 29N	1 29W	–0220	–0220	–0200	–0200	–0.1	–0.1	–0.1	–0.1
Scalloway	60 08N	1 16W	–0150	–0150	–0150	–0150	–0.5	–0.4	–0.3	0.0
Bay of Quendale	59 54N	1 21W	–0025	–0025	–0030	–0030	–0.4	–0.3	0.0	+0.1
Foula	60 07N	2 03W	–0140	–0130	–0140	–0120	–0.1	–0.1	0.0	0.0
			0200	**0700**	**0100**	**0700**				
WICK	58 26N	3 05W	and	and	and	and	**3.5**	**2.8**	**1.4**	**0.7**
Standard port			**1400**	**1900**	**1300**	**1900**				
Stroma	58 40N	3 08W	–0115	–0115	–0110	–0110	–0.4	–0.5	–0.1	–0.2
Gills Bay	58 38N	3 10W	–0150	–0150	–0202	–0202	+0.7	+0.7	+0.6	+0.3
Scrabster	58 37N	3 33W	–0255	–0225	–0240	–0230	+1.5	+1.2	+0.8	+0.3
Sule Skerry	59 05N	4 24W	–0320	–0255	–0315	–0250	+0.4	+0.3	+0.2	+0.1
Loch Eriboll Portnancon	58 30N	4 42W	–0340	–0255	–0315	–0255	+1.6	+1.3	+0.8	+0.4
Kyle of Durness	58 36N	4 47W	–0350	–0350	–0315	–0315	+1.1	+0.7	+0.4	–0.1
Rona	59 08N	5 49W	–0410	–0345	–0330	–0340	–0.1	–0.2	–0.2	–0.1
			0100	**0700**	**0300**	**0900**				
STORNOWAY	58 12N	6 23W	and	and	and	and	**4.8**	**3.7**	**2.0**	**0.7**
Standard port			**1300**	**1900**	**1500**	**2100**				
Outer Hebrides										
Loch Shell	58 00N	6 25W	–0013	0000	0000	–0017	0.0	–0.1	–0.1	0.0
E Loch Tarbert	57 54N	6 48W	–0025	–0010	–0010	–0020	+0.2	0.0	+0.1	+0.1
Leverburgh	57 46N	7 02W	–0041	–0020	–0015	–0025	–0.2	–0.2	–0.2	–0.1
Bays Loch	57 43N	7 10W	–0038	–0013	–0014	–0027	–0.1	–0.2	–0.2	–0.1
Loch Maddy	57 36N	7 09W	–0044	–0014	–0016	–0030	0.0	–0.1	–0.1	0.0
Loch Carnan	57 22N	7 16W	–0050	–0010	–0020	–0040	–0.3	–0.5	–0.1	–0.1
Loch Skiport	57 20N	7 16W	–0100	–0025	–0024	–0024	–0.2	–0.4	–0.3	–0.2
Loch Boisdale	57 09N	7 16W	–0055	–0030	–0020	–0040	–0.7	–0.7	–0.3	–0.2
Barra (North Bay)	57 00N	7 24W	–0103	–0031	–0034	–0048	–0.6	–0.5	–0.2	–0.1
Castle Bay	56 57N	7 29W	–0115	–0040	–0045	–0100	–0.5	–0.6	–0.3	–0.1
Barra Head	56 47N	7 38W	–0115	–0040	–0045	–0055	–0.8	–0.7	–0.2	+0.1
Shillay	57 32N	7 42W	–0103	–0043	–0047	–0107	–0.6	–0.7	–0.7	–0.3
Balivanich	57 29N	7 23W	–0103	–0017	–0031	–0045	–0.7	–0.6	–0.5	–0.2
Scolpaig	57 39N	7 29W	–0033	–0033	–0040	–0040	–1.0	–0.9	–0.5	0.0
W Loch Tarbert	57 55N	6 55W	–0015	–0015	–0046	–0046	–1.1	–0.9	–0.5	0.0
Little Bernera	58 16N	6 52W	–0021	–0011	–0017	–0027	–0.5	–0.6	–0.4	–0.2
Carloway	58 17N	6 47W	–0040	+0020	–0035	–0015	–0.6	–0.5	–0.4	–0.1
St Kilda Village Bay	57 48N	8 34W	–0040	–0040	–0045	–0045	–1.4	–1.2	–0.8	–0.3
Flannan Isles	58 17N	7 35W	–0026	–0016	–0016	–0026	–0.9	–0.7	–0.6	–0.2
Rockall	57 36N	13 41W	–0055	–0055	–0105	–0105	–1.8	–1.5	–0.9	–0.2

Location	Lat	Long	High Water		Low Water		MHWS	MHWN	MLWN	MLWS
			0000	0600	0300	0900				
ULLAPOOL	57 54N	5 09W	and	and	and	and	**5.2**	**3.9**	**2.1**	**0.7**
Standard port			1200	1800	1500	2100				
Loch Bervie	58 27N	5 03W	+0020	+0010	+0010	+0020	−0.4	−0.3	−0.2	−0.1
Loch Laxford	58 24N	5 05W	+0015	+0015	+0005	+0005	−0.3	−0.4	−0.2	0.0
Eddrachillis Bay										
Badcall Bay	58 19N	5 08W	+0005	+0005	+0005	+0005	−0.7	−0.5	−0.5	+0.2
Loch Nedd	58 14N	5 10W	0000	0000	0000	0000	−0.3	−0.2	−0.2	0.0
Loch Inver	58 09N	5 18W	−0005	−0005	−0005	−0005	−0.2	0.0	0.0	+0.1
Summer Isles Tanera Mor	58 01N	5 24W	−0005	−0005	−0010	−0010	−0.1	+0.1	0.0	+0.1
Loch Ewe Mellon Charles	57 51N	5 38W	−0010	−0010	−0010	−0010	−0.1	−0.1	−0.1	0.0
Loch Gairloch Gairloch	57 43N	5 41W	−0020	−0020	−0010	−0010	0.0	+0.1	−0.3	−0.1
Loch Torridon Shieldaig	57 31N	5 39W	−0020	−0020	−0015	−0015	+0.4	+0.3	+0.1	0.0
Inner Sound Applecross	57 26N	5 49W	−0010	−0015	−0010	−0010	0.0	0.0	0.0	+0.1
Loch Carron Plockton	57 21N	5 39W	+0005	−0025	−0005	−0010	+0.5	+0.5	+0.5	+0.2
Rona Loch a' Bhraige	57 35N	5 58W	−0020	0000	−0010	0000	−0.1	−0.1	−0.1	−0.2
Skye										
Broadford Bay	57 15N	5 54W	−0015	−0015	−0010	−0015	+0.2	+0.1	+0.1	0.0
Portree	57 24N	6 11W	−0025	−0025	−0025	−0025	+0.1	−0.2	−0.2	0.0
Loch Snizort (Uig Bay)	57 35N	6 22W	−0045	−0020	−0005	−0025	+0.1	−0.4	−0.2	0.0
Loch Dunvegan	57 27N	6 38W	−0105	−0030	−0020	−0040	0.0	−0.1	0.0	0.0
Loch Harport	57 20N	6 25W	−0115	−0035	−0020	−0100	−0.1	−0.1	0.0	+0.1
Soay Camus nan Gall	57 09N	6 13W	−0055	−0025	−0025	−0045	−0.4	−0.2	*No data*	
Loch Alsh										
Kyle of Lochalsh	57 17N	5 43W	−0040	−0020	−0005	−0025	+0.1	0.0	0.0	−0.1
Dornie Bridge	57 17N	5 31W	−0040	−0010	−0005	−0020	+0.1	−0.1	0.0	0.0
Kyle Rhea Glenelg Bay	57 13N	5 38W	−0105	−0035	−0035	−0055	−0.4	−0.4	−0.9	−0.1
Loch Hourn	57 06N	5 34W	−0125	−0050	−0040	−0110	−0.2	−0.1	−0.1	+0.1
			0000	0600	0100	0700				
OBAN	56 25N	5 29W	and	and	and	and	**4.0**	**2.9**	**1.8**	**0.7**
Standard port			1200	1800	1300	1900				
Loch Nevis										
Inverie Bay	57 02N	5 41W	+0030	+0020	+0035	+0020	+1.0	+0.9	+0.2	0.0
Mallaig	57 00N	5 50W	+0017	+0017	+0017	+0017	+1.0	+0.7	+0.3	+0.1
Eigg Bay of Laig	56 55N	6 10W	+0015	+0030	+0040	+0005	+0.7	+0.6	−0.2	− 0.2
Loch Moidart	56 47N	5 53W	+0015	+0015	+0040	+0020	+0.8	+0.6	− 0.2	−0.2
Coll Loch Eatharna	56 37N	6 31W	+0025	+0010	+0015	+0025	+0.4	+0.3	*No data*	
Tiree Gott Bay	56 31N	6 48W	0000	+0010	+0005	+0010	0.0	+0.1	0.0	0.0
			0100	0700	0100	0800				
OBAN	56 25N	5 29W	and	and	and	and	**4.0**	**2.9**	**1.8**	**0.7**
Standard port			1300	1900	1300	2000				
Mull										
Carsaig Bay	56 19N	5 58W	−0015	−0005	−0030	+0020	+0.1	+0.2	0.0	−0.1
Iona	56 20N	6 23W	−0010	−0005	−0020	+0015	0.0	+0.1	−0.3	−0.2
Bunessan	56 19N	6 14W	−0015	−0015	−0010	−0015	+0.3	+0.1	0.0	−0.1
Ulva Sound	56 29N	6 08W	−0010	−0015	0000	−0005	+0.4	+0.3	0.0	−0.1
Loch Sunart Salen	56 43N	5 47W	−0015	+0015	+0010	+0005	+0.6	+0.5	−0.1	−0.1
Sound of Mull										
Tobermory	56 37N	6 04W	+0025	+0010	+0015	+0025	+0.4	+0.4	0.0	0.0
Salen	56 31N	5 57W	+0045	+0015	+0020	+0030	+0.2	+0.2	−0.1	0.0
Loch Aline	56 32N	5 46W	+0012	+0012	*No data*	*No data*	+0.5	+0.3	*No data*	
Craignure	56 28N	5 42W	+0030	+0005	+0010	+0015	0.0	+0.1	−0.1	−0.1
Loch Linnhe										
Corran	56 43N	5 14W	+0007	+0007	+0004	+0004	+0.4	+0.4	−0.1	0.0
Corpach	56 51N	5 07W	0000	+0020	+0040	0000	0.0	0.0	−0.2	−0.2
Loch Eil Head	56 51N	5 20W	+0025	+0045	+0105	+0025	*No data*		*No data*	
Loch Leven Head	56 43N	5 00W	+0045	+0045	+0045	+0045	*No data*		*No data*	
Loch Linnhe Port Appin	56 33N	5 25W	−0005	−0005	−0030	0000	+0.2	+0.2	+0.1	+0.1
Loch Creran										
Barcaldine Pier	56 32N	5 19W	+0010	+0020	+0040	+0015	+0.1	+0.1	0.0	+0.1
Loch Creran Head	56 33N	5 16W	+0015	+0025	+0120	+0020	−0.3	−0.3	−0.4	−0.3
Loch Etive										
Dunstaffnage Bay	56 27N	5 26W	+0005	0000	0000	+0005	+0.1	+0.1	+0.1	+0.1
Connel	56 27N	5 24W	+0020	+0005	+0010	+0015	−0.3	−0.2	−0.1	+0.1
Bonawe	56 27N	5 13W	+0150	+0205	+0240	+0210	−2.0	−1.7	−1.3	−0.5
Seil Sound	56 18N	5 35W	−0035	−0015	−0040	−0015	−1.3	−0.9	−0.7	−0.3
Colonsay Scalasaig	56 04N	6 11W	−0020	−0005	−0015	+0005	−0.1	−0.2	−0.2	−0.2
Jura Glengarrisdale Bay	56 07N	5 47W	−0020	0000	−0010	0000	−0.4	−0.2	0.0	−0.2

TIDES

Location	Lat	Long	High Water		Low Water		MHWS	MHWN	MLWN	MLWS
Islay										
Rubha A'Mhail	55 56N	6 07W	−0020	0000	+0005	−0015	−0.3	−0.1	−0.3	−0.1
Ardnave Point	55 52N	6 20W	−0035	+0010	0000	−0025	−0.4	−0.2	−0.3	−0.1
Orsay	55 41N	6 31W	−0110	−0110	−0040	−0040	−1.4	−0.6	−0.5	−0.2
Bruichladdich	55 46N	6 22W	−0105	−0035	−0110	−0110	−1.8	−1.3	−0.4	+0.1
Port Ellen	55 38N	6 11W	−0530	−0050	−0045	−0530	−3.1	−2.1	−1.3	−0.4
Port Askaig	55 51N	6 06W	−0110	−0030	−0020	−0020	−1.9	−1.4	−0.8	−0.3
Sound of Jura										
Craighouse	55 50N	5 57W	−0230	−0250	−0150	−0230	−3.0	−2.4	−1.3	−0.6
Loch Melfort	56 15N	5 29W	−0055	−0025	−0040	−0035	−1.2	−0.8	−0.5	−0.1
Loch Beag	56 09N	5 36W	−0110	−0045	−0035	−0045	−1.6	−1.2	−0.8	−0.4
Carsaig Bay	56 02N	5 38W	−0105	−0040	−0050	−0050	−2.1	−1.6	−1.0	−0.4
Sound of Gigha	55 41N	5 44W	−0450	−0210	−0130	−0410	−2.5	−1.6	−1.0	−0.1
Machrihanish	55 25N	5 45W	−0520	−0350	−0340	−0540	Mean range 0.5 metres			
			0000	0600	0000	0600				
GREENOCK	55 57N	4 46W	and	and	and	and	3.4	2.8	1.0	0.3
Standard port			1200	1800	1200	1800				
Firth of Clyde										
Southend, Kintyre	55 19N	5 38W	−0030	−0010	+0005	+0035	−1.3	−1.2	−0.5	−0.2
Campbeltown	55 25N	5 36W	−0025	−0005	−0015	+0005	−0.5	−0.3	+0.1	+0.2
Carradale	55 36N	5 28W	−0015	−0005	−0005	+0005	−0.3	−0.2	+0.1	+0.1
Loch Ranza	55 43N	5 18W	−0015	−0005	−0010	−0005	−0.4	−0.3	−0.1	0.0
Loch Fyne										
East Loch Tarbert	55 52N	5 24W	−0005	−0005	0000	−0005	+0.2	+0.1	0.0	0.0
Inveraray	56 14N	5 04W	+0011	+0011	+0034	+0034	−0.1	+0.1	−0.5	−0.2
Kyles of Bute										
Rubha a'Bhodaich	55 55N	5 09W	−0020	−0010	−0007	−0007	−0.2	−0.1	+0.2	+0.2
Tighnabruich	55 55N	5 13W	+0007	−0010	−0002	−0015	0.0	+0.2	+0.4	+0.5
Firth of Clyde – continued										
Millport	55 45N	4 56W	−0005	−0025	−0025	−0005	0.0	−0.1	0.0	+0.1
Rothesay Bay	55 50N	5 03W	−0020	−0015	−0010	−0002	+0.2	+0.2	+0.2	+0.2
Wemyss Bay	55 53N	4 53W	−0005	−0005	−0005	−0005	0.0	0.0	+0.1	+0.1
Loch Long										
Coulport	56 03N	4 53W	−0011	−0011	−0008	−0008	0.0	0.0	0.0	0.0
Lochgoilhead	56 10N	4 54W	+0015	0000	−0005	−0005	−0.2	−0.3	−0.3	−0.3
Arrochar	56 12N	4 45W	−0005	−0005	−0005	−0005	0.0	0.0	−0.1	−0.1
Gare Loch										
Rhu Marina	56 01N	4 46W	−0007	−0007	−0007	−0007	−0.1	−0.1	−0.1	−0.2
Faslane	56 04N	4 49W	−0010	−0010	−0010	−0010	0.0	0.0	−0.1	−0.2
Garelochhead	56 05N	4 50W	0000	0000	0000	0000	0.0	0.0	0.0	−0.1
River Clyde										
Helensburgh	56 00N	4 44W	0000	0000	0000	0000	0.0	0.0	0.0	0.0
Port Glasgow	55 56N	4 41W	+0010	+0005	+0010	+0020	+0.2	+0.1	0.0	0.0
Bowling	55 56N	4 29W	+0020	+0010	+0030	+0055	+0.6	+0.5	+0.3	+0.1
Clydebank (Rothesay Dock)	55 54N	4 24W	+0025	+0015	+0035	+0100	+1.1	+0.9	+0.6	+0.3
Glasgow	55 51N	4 16W	+0025	+0015	+0035	+0105	+1.3	+1.1	+0.7	+0.4
Firth of Clyde – continued										
Brodick Bay	55 35N	5 08W	−0013	−0013	−0008	−0008	−0.2	−0.1	0.0	+0.1
Lamlash	55 32N	5 07W	−0016	−0036	−0024	−0004	−0.2	−0.2	No data	
Ardrossan	55 38N	4 49W	−0020	−0010	−0010	−0010	−0.2	−0.2	+0.1	+0.1
Irvine	55 36N	4 42W	−0020	−0020	−0030	−0010	−0.3	−0.3	−0.1	0.0
Troon	55 33N	4 41W	−0025	−0025	−0020	−0020	−0.2	−0.2	0.0	0.0
Ayr	55 28N	4 39W	−0025	−0025	−0030	−0015	−0.4	−0.3	+0.1	+0.1
Girvan	55 15N	4 52W	−0025	−0040	−0035	−0010	−0.3	−0.3	−0.1	0.0
Loch Ryan Stranraer	54 55N	5 02W	−0030	−0025	−0010	−0010	−0.2	−0.1	0.0	+0.1
			0000	0600	0200	0800				
LIVERPOOL	53 27N	3 01W	and	and	and	and	9.4	7.5	3.2	1.1
Standard port			1200	1800	1400	2000				
Portpatrick	54 51N	5 07W	+0022	+0030	−0003	−0032	−5.6	−4.5	−2.3	−0.8
Luce Bay										
Drummore	54 42N	4 53W	+0035	+0045	+0010	+0015	−3.5	−2.6	−1.2	−0.5
Port William	54 46N	4 35W	+0035	+0035	+0020	−0005	−3.0	−2.3	−1.1	No data
Wigtown Bay										
Isle of Whithorn	54 42N	4 22W	+0025	+0030	+0020	0000	−2.5	−2.1	−1.1	−0.4
Garlieston	54 47N	4 22W	+0030	+0040	+0025	0000	−2.4	−1.8	−0.8	No data
Solway Firth										
Kirkcudbright Bay	54 48N	4 04W	+0020	+0020	+0005	−0005	−1.9	−1.6	−0.8	0.3
Hestan Islet	54 50N	3 48W	+0030	+0030	+0015	+0020	−1.1	−1.2	−0.8	−0.2
Southerness Point	54 52N	3 36W	+0035	+0035	+0025	+0005	−0.8	−0.8	No data	

Location	Lat	Long	High Water		Low Water		MHWS	MHWN	MLWN	MLWS
Annan Waterfoot	54 58N	3 16W	+0055	+0110	+0215	+0305	−2.3	−2.7	−3.0	
Torduff Point	54 58N	3 09W	+0110	+0145	+0515	+0405	−4.2	−5.0		
Redkirk	54 59N	3 06W	+0115	+0220	+0710	+0440	−5.6	−6.3		
WEST COAST OF ENGLAND										
Silloth	54 52N	3 24W	+0035	+0045	+0040	+0050	−0.2	−0.4	−0.9	−0.3
Maryport	54 43N	3 30W	+0021	+0036	+0017	+0002	−0.8	−0.9	−0.7	−0.2
Workington	54 39N	3 34W	+0025	+0025	+0015	+0005	−1.3	−1.2	−0.6	−0.2
Whitehaven	54 33N	3 36W	+0010	+0020	+0005	0000	−1.4	−1.2	−0.8	−0.1
Tarn Point	54 17N	3 25W	+0010	+0010	+0005	−0005	−1.1	−1.1	−0.7	−0.2
Duddon Bar	54 09N	3 20W	+0007	+0007	+0005	−0001	−0.9	−0.9	−0.6	−0.2
LIVERPOOL *Standard port*	53 27N	3 01W	0000 and 1200	0600 and 1800	0200 and 1400	0700 and 1900	9.4	7.5	3.2	2.1
Barrow-in-Furness	54 06N	3 12W	+0020	+0020	+0010	+0010	+0.1	−0.2	−0.2	0.0
Ulverston	54 11N	3 04W	+0025	+0045	No data	no data	−0.1	−0.2	No data	
Arnside	54 12N	2 51W	+0105	+0140	No data	no data	+0.4	+0.1	No data	
Morecambe	54 04N	2 53W	+0010	+0015	+0025	+0010	+0.1	−0.1	−0.3	0.0
Heysham	54 02N	2 55W	+0010	+0010	+0010	−0005	+0.2	−0.1	−0.2	0.0
River Lune Glasson Dock	54 00N	2 51W	+0025	+0035	+0215	+0235	−2.8	−3.1	No data	
Lancaster	54 03N	2 49W	+0115	+0035	Dries	Dries	−5.1	−5.0	Dries	
River Wyre										
Wyre Lighthouse	53 57N	3 02W	−0005	−0005	0000	−0005	−0.2	−0.2	No data	
Fleetwood	53 56N	3 00W	−0004	−0004	−0006	−0006	−0.2	−0.2	−0.2	+0.1
Blackpool	53 49N	3 04W	−0010	0000	−0010	−0020	−0.5	−0.5	−0.4	−0.1
River Ribble Preston	53 45N	2 45W	+0015	+0015	+0330	+0305	−4.1	−4.2	−3.1	−1.0
Liverpool Bay										
Southport	53 39N	3 01W	−0015	−0005	No data	No data	−0.4	−0.4	No data	
Formby	53 32N	3 07W	−0010	−0005	−0025	−0025	−0.4	−0.2	−0.3	−0.1
River Mersey										
Alfred Dock	53 24N	3 01W	+0007	+0007	0000	0000	−0.1	−0.1	−0.3	−0.2
Eastham	53 19N	2 57W	+0014	+0014	+0006	+0006	+0.2	0.0	−0.4	−0.5
Hale Head	53 19N	2 48W	+0035	+0030	No data	No data	−2.5	−2.6	No data	
Widnes	53 21N	2 44W	+0045	+0050	+0355	+0340	−4.3	−4.5	−2.8	−0.6
Fiddler's Ferry	53 22N	2 40W	+0105	+0120	+0535	+0445	−6.0	−6.4	−2.7	−0.6
River Dee										
Hilbre Island	53 23N	3 14W	−0011	−0006	−0013	−0018	−0.4	−0.3	−0.1	+0.2
Chester	53 12N	2 54W	+0110	+0110	+0455	+0455	−5.4	−5.5	Dries	
Connah's Quay (Wales)	53 13N	3 03W	+0005	+0020	+0350	+0335	−4.7	−4.5	Dries	
Mostyn Docks (Wales)	53 19N	3 16W	−0015	−0010	−0025	−0025	−0.9	−0.8	No data	
Isle of Man Peel	54 14N	4 42W	+0010	+0010	−0020	−0030	−4.2	−3.2	−1.7	−0.7
Ramsey	54 19N	4 22W	+0010	+0020	−0010	−0020	−2.0	−1.6	−0.9	−0.4
Douglas	54 09N	4 28W	+0010	+0020	−0020	−0030	−2.5	−2.1	−0.6	−0.3
Port St Mary	54 04N	4 44W	+0010	+0020	−0015	−0035	−3.5	−2.7	−1.6	−0.6
Calf Sound	54 04N	4 48W	+0010	+0010	−0020	−0030	−3.3	−2.7	−1.2	−0.5
Port Erin	54 05N	4 46W	0000	+0020	−0015	−0055	−4.2	−3.3	−1.6	−0.7
WALES										
Colwyn Bay	53 18N	3 43W	−0020	−0020	No data	No data	−1.5	−1.3	No data	
Llandudno	53 20N	3 50W	−0020	−0020	−0035	−0040	−1.7	−1.4	−0.7	−0.3
HOLYHEAD *Standard port*	53 19N	4 37W	0000 and 1200	0600 and 1800	0500 and 1700	1100 and 2300	5.6	4.4	2.0	0.7
Conwy	53 17N	3 50W	+0025	+0035	+0120	+0105	+2.3	+1.8	+0.6	+0.4
Menai Strait										
Beaumaris	53 16N	4 05W	+0025	+0010	+0055	+0035	+2.0	+1.6	+0.5	+0.1
Menai Bridge	53 13N	4 10W	+0030	+0010	+0100	+0035	+1.7	+1.4	+0.3	0.0
Port Dinorwic	53 11N	4 13W	−0015	−0025	+0030	0000	0.0	0.0	0.0	+0.1
Caernarfon	53 09N	4 16W	−0030	−0030	+0015	−0005	−0.4	−0.4	−0.1	−0.1
Fort Belan	53 07N	4 20W	−0040	−0015	−0025	−0005	−1.0	−0.9	−0.2	−0.1
Trwyn Dinmor	53 19N	4 03W	+0025	+0015	+0050	+0035	+1.9	+1.5	+0.5	+0.2
Moelfre	53 20N	4 14W	+0025	+0020	+0050	+0035	+1.9	+1.4	+0.5	+0.2
Amlwch	53 25N	4 20W	+0020	+0010	+0035	+0025	+1.6	+ 1.3	+0.5	+0.2
Cemaes Bay	53 25N	4 27W	+0020	+0025	+0040	+0035	+1.0	+0.7	+0.3	+0.1
Trearddur Bay	53 16N	4 37W	−0045	−0025	−0015	−0015	−0.4	−0.4	0.0	+0.1
Porth Trecastell	53 12N	4 30W	−0045	−0025	−0005	−0015	−0.6	−0.6	0.0	0.0
Llanddwyn Island	53 08N	4 25W	−0115	−0055	−0030	−0020	−0.7	−0.5	−0.1	0.0
Trefor	53 00N	4 25W	−0115	−0100	−0030	−0020	−0.8	−0.9	−0.2	−0.1
Porth Dinllaen	52 57N	4 34W	−0120	−0105	−0035	−0025	−1.0	−1.0	−0.2	−0.2
Porth Ysgaden	52 54N	4 39W	−0125	−0110	−0040	−0035	−1.1	−1.0	−0.1	−0.1
Bardsey Island	52 46N	4 47W	−0220	−0240	−0145	−0140	−1.2	−1.2	−0.5	−0.1

TIDES

Location	Lat	Long	High Water		Low Water		MHWS	MHWN	MLWN	MLWS
			0100	0800	0100	0700				
MILFORD HAVEN	51 42N	5 03W	and	and	and	and	7.0	5.2	2.5	0.7
Standard port			1300	2000	1300	1900				
Cardigan Bay										
Aberdaron	52 48N	4 43W	+0210	+0200	+0240	+0310	−2.4	−1.9	−0.6	−0.2
St Tudwal's Roads	52 49N	4 29W	+0155	+0145	+0240	+0310	−2.2	−1.9	−0.7	−0.2
Pwllheli	52 53N	4 24W	+0210	+0150	+0245	+0320	−2.0	− 1.8	−0.6	−0.2
Criccieth	52 55N	4 14W	+0210	+0155	+0255	+0320	−2.0	−1.8	−0.7	−0.3
Porthmadog	52 55N	4 08W	+0235	+0210	*No data*	*No data*	−1.9	−1.8	*No data*	
Barmouth	52 43N	4 03W	+0215	+0205	+0310	+0320	−2.0	−1.7	−0.7	0.0
Aberdovey	52 33N	4 03W	+0215	+0200	+0230	+0305	−2.0	−1.7	−0.5	0.0
Aberystwyth	52 24N	4 05W	+0145	+0130	+0210	+0245	−2.0	−1.7	−0.7	0.0
New Quay	52 13N	4 21W	+0150	+0125	+0155	+0230	−2.1	−1.8	−0.6	−0.1
Aberporth	52 08N	4 33W	+0135	+0120	+0150	+0220	−2.1	−1.8	−0.6	−0.1
Port Cardigan	52 07N	4 41W	+0140	+0120	+0220	+0130	−2.3	−1.8	−0.5	0.0
Cardigan (Town)	52 05N	4 40W	+0220	+0150	*No data*	*No data*	−2.2	−1.6	*No data*	
Fishguard	52 01N	4 59W	+0115	+0100	+0110	+0135	−2.2	−1.8	−0.5	+0.1
Porthgain	51 57N	5 11W	+0055	+0045	+0045	+0100	−2.5	−1.8	−0.6	0.0
Ramsey Sound	51 53N	5 19W	+0030	+0030	+0030	+0030	−1.9	−1.3	−0.3	0.0
Solva	51 52N	5 12W	+0015	+0010	+0035	+0015	−1.5	−1.0	−0.2	0.0
Little Haven	51 46N	5 07W	+0010	+0010	+0025	+0015	−1.1	−0.8	−0.2	0.0
Martin's Haven	51 44N	5 15W	+0010	+0010	+0015	+0015	−0.8	−0.5	+0.1	+0.1
Skomer Island	51 44N	5 17W	−0005	−0005	+0005	+0005	−0.4	−0.1	0.0	0.0
Dale Roads	51 42N	5 09W	−0005	−0005	−0008	−0008	0.0	0.0	0.0	−0.1
Cleddau River										
Neyland	51 42N	4 57W	+0002	+0010	0000	0000	0.0	0.0	0.0	0.0
Black Tar	51 45N	4 54W	+0010	+0020	+0005	0000	+0.1	+0.1	0.0	−0.1
Haverfordwest	51 48N	4 58W	+0010	+0025	*Dries*	*Dries*	−4.8	−4.9	*Dries*	
Stackpole Quay	51 37N	4 54W	−0005	+0025	−0010	−0010	+0.9	+0.7	+0.2	+0.3
Tenby	51 40N	4 42W	−0015	−0010	−0015	−0020	+1.4	+1.1	+0.5	+0.2
Towy River										
Ferryside	51 46N	4 22W	0000	−0010	+0220	0000	−0.3	−0.7	−1.7	−0.6
Carmarthen	51 51N	4 18W	+0010	0000	*Dries*	*Dries*	−4.4	−4.8	*Dries*	
Burry Inlet										
Burry Port	51 41N	4 15W	+0003	+0003	+0007	+0007	+1.6	+1.4	+0.5	+0.4
Llanelli	51 40N	4 10W	−0003	−0003	+0150	+0020	+0.8	+0.6	*No data*	
Mumbles	51 34N	3 58W	+0005	+0010	−0020	−0015	+2.3	+1.7	+0.6	+0.2
River Neath Entrance	51 37N	3 51W	+0002	+0011	*Dries*	*Dries*	+2.7	+2.2	*Dries*	
Port Talbot	51 35N	3 49W	+0003	+0005	−0010	−0005	+2.8	+2.2	+1.0	+0.5
Porthcawl	51 28N	3 42W	+0005	+0010	−0010	−0005	+2.9	+2.3	+0.8	+0.3
			0600	1100	0300	0800				
BRISTOL, AVONMOUTH	51 30N	2 44W	and	and	and	and	13.2	9.8	3.8	1.0
Standard port			1800	2300	1500	2000				
Barry	51 23N	3 16W	−0025	−0025	−0130	−0045	−1.7	−1.0	−0.2	0.0
Flat Holm	51 23N	3 07W	−0015	−0015	−0035	−0035	−1.4	−1.0	−0.5	0.0
Steep Holm	51 20N	3 06W	−0020	−0020	−0040	−0040	−1.7	−1.1	−0.5	−0.4
Cardiff	51 27N	3 10W	−0015	−0015	−0100	−0030	−1.0	−0.5	0.0	0.0
Newport	51 33N	2 59W	−0020	−0010	0000	−0020	−1.1	−0.9	−0.6	−0.6
River Wye Chepstow	51 39N	2 40W	+0020	+0020	*No data*	*No data*		*No data*		*No data*
			0000	0600	0000	0700				
BRISTOL, AVONMOUTH	51 30N	2 44W	and	and	and	and	13.2	9.8	3.8	1.0
Standard port			1200	1800	1200	1900				

WEST COAST OF ENGLAND

Location	Lat	Long	High Water		Low Water		MHWS	MHWN	MLWN	MLWS
River Severn										
Sudbrook	51 35N	2 43W	+0010	+0010	+0025	+0015	+0.2	+0.1	−0.1	+0.1
Beachley (Aust)	51 36N	2 38W	+0010	+0015	+0040	+0025	−0.2	−0.2	−0.5	−0.3
Inward Rocks	51 39N	2 37W	+0020	+0020	+0105	+0045	−1.0	−1.1	−1.4	−0.6
Narlwood Rocks	51 39N	2 36W	+0025	+0025	+0120	+0100	−1.9	−2.0	−2.3	−0.8
White House	51 40N	2 33W	+0025	+0025	+0145	+0120	−3.0	−3.1	−3.6	−1.0
Berkeley	51 42N	2 30W	+0030	+0045	+0245	+0220	−3.8	−3.9	−3.4	−0.5
Sharpness Dock	51 43N	2 29W	+0035	+0050	+0305	+0245	−3.9	−4.2	−3.3	−0.4
Wellhouse Rock	51 44N	2 29W	+0040	+0055	+0320	+0305	−4.1	−4.4	−3.1	−0.2
Epney	51 42N	2 24W	+0130	*No data*	*No data*	*No data*	−9.4	*No data*	*No data*	
Minsterworth	51 50N	2 23W	+0140	*No data*	*No data*	*No data*	−10.1	*No data*	*No data*	
Llanthony	51 51N	2 21W	+0215	*No data*	*No data*	*No data*	−10.7	*No data*	*No data*	
			0200	0800	0300	0800				
BRISTOL, AVONMOUTH	51 30N	2 44W	and	and	and	and	13.2	9.8	3.8	1.0
Standard port			1400	2000	1500	2000				
River Avon										
Shirehampton	51 29N	2 41W	0000	0000	+0035	+0010	−0.7	−0.7	−0.8	0.0
Sea Mills	51 29N	2 39W	+0005	+0005	+0105	+0030	−1.4	−1.5	−1.7	−0.1
Cumberland Basin Entrance	51 27N	2 37W	+0010	+0010	*Dries*	*Dries*	−2.9	−3.0	*Dries*	

Location	Lat	Long	High Water		Low Water		MHWS	MHWN	MLWN	MLWS
Portishead	51 30N	2 45W	−0002	0000	No data	No data	−0.1	−0.1	No data	
Clevedon	51 27N	2 52W	−0010	−0020	−0025	−0015	−0.4	−0.2	+0.2	0.0
St Thomas Head	51 24N	2 56W	0000	0000	−0030	−0030	−0.4	−0.2	+0.1	+0.1
English & Welsh Grounds	51 28N	2 59W	−0008	−0008	−0030	−0030	−0.5	−0.8	−0.3	0.0
Weston-super-Mare	51 21N	2 59W	−0020	−0030	−0130	−0030	−1.2	−1.0	−0.8	−0.2
River Parrett										
Burnham-on-Sea	51 14N	3 00W	−0020	−0025	−0030	0000	−2.3	−1.9	−1.4	−1.1
Bridgwater	51 08N	3 00W	−0015	−0030	+0305	+0455	−8.6	−8.1	*Dries*	
Hinkley Point	51 13N	3 08W	−0020	−0025	−0100	−0040	−1.7	−1.4	−0.2	−0.2
Watchet	51 11N	3 20W	−0035	−0050	−0145	−0040	−1.9	−1.5	+0.1	+0.1
Minehead	51 13N	3 28W	−0037	−0052	−0155	−0045	−2.6	−1.9	−0.2	0.0
Porlock Bay	51 13N	3 38W	−0045	−0055	−0205	−0050	−3.0	−2.2	−0.1	−0.1
Lynmouth	51 14N	3 50W	−0055	−0115	No data	No data	−3.6	−2.7	No data	
			0100	**0700**	**0100**	**0700**				
MILFORD HAVEN	51 42N	5 03W	and	and	and	and	**7.0**	**5.2**	**2.5**	**0.7**
Standard port			**1300**	**1900**	**1300**	**1900**				
Ilfracombe	51 13N	4 07W	−0016	−0016	−0041	−0031	+2.3	+1.8	+0.6	+0.3
Rivers Taw & Torridge										
Appledore	51 03N	4 12W	−0020	−0025	+0015	−0045	+0.5	0.0	−0.9	−0.5
Yelland Marsh	51 04N	4 10W	−0010	−0015	+0100	−0015	+0.1	−0.4	−1.2	−0.6
Fremington	51 05N	4 07W	−0010	−0015	+0030	−0030	−1.1	−1.8	−2.2	−0.5
Barnstaple	51 05N	4 04W	0000	−0015	−0155	−0245	−2.9	−3.8	−2.2	−0.4
Bideford	51 01N	4 12W	−0020	−0025	0000	0000	−1.1	−1.6	−2.5	−0.7
Clovelly	51 00N	4 24W	−0030	−0030	−0020	−0040	+1.3	+1.1	+0.2	+0.2
Lundy	51 10N	4 39W	−0025	−0025	−0020	−0035	+0.9	+0.7	+0.3	+0.1
Bude	50 50N	4 33W	−0040	−0040	−0035	−0045	+0.7	+0.6	No data	
Boscastle	50 41N	4 42W	−0045	−0010	−0110	−0100	+0.3	+0.4	+0.2	+0.2
Port Isaac	50 35N	4 50W	−0100	−0100	−0100	−0100	+0.5	+0.6	0.0	+0.2
River Camel										
Padstow	50 33N	4 56W	−0055	−0050	−0040	−0050	+0.3	+0.4	+0.1	+0.1
Wadebridge	50 31N	4 50W	−0052	−0052	+0235	+0245	−3.8	−3.8	−2.5	−0.4
Newquay	50 25N	5 05W	−0100	−0110	−0105	−0050	0.0	+0.1	0.0	−0.1
Perranporth	50 21N	5 09W	−0100	−0110	−0110	−0050	−0.1	0.0	0.0	+0.1
St Ives	50 13N	5 29W	−0050	−0115	−0105	−0040	−0.4	−0.3	−0.1	+0.1
Cape Cornwall	50 08N	5 42 W	−0130	−0145	−0120	−0120	−1.0	−0.9	−0.5	−0.1
Sennen Cove	50 05N	5 42W	−0130	−0145	−0125	−0125	−0.9	−0.4	No data	
			0000	**0700**	**0000**	**0500**				
# IRELAND										
DUBLIN, NORTH WALL	53 21N	6 13W	and	and	and	and	**4.1**	**3.4**	**1.5**	**0.7**
Standard port			**1200**	**1900**	**1200**	**1700**				
Courtown	52 39N	6 13W	−0328	−0242	−0158	−0138	−2.8	−2.4	−0.5	0.0
Arklow	52 48N	6 08W	−0315	−0201	−0140	−0134	−2.7	−2.2	−0.6	−0.1
Wicklow	52 59N	6 02W	−0019	−0019	−0024	−0026	−1.4	−1.1	−0.4	0.0
Greystones	53 09N	6 04W	−0008	−0008	−0008	−0008	−0.5	−0.4	No data	
Dun Laoghaire	53 18N	6 08W	−0006	−0001	−0002	−0003	0.0	0.0	0.0	+0.1
Dublin Bar	53 21N	6 09W	−0006	−0001	−0002	−0003	0.0	0.0	0.0	+0.1
Howth	53 23N	6 04W	−0007	−0005	+0001	+0005	0.0	−0.1	−0.2	−0.2
Malahide	53 27N	6 09W	+0002	+0003	+0009	+0009	+0.1	−0.2	−0.4	−0.2
Balbriggan	53 37N	6 11W	−0021	−0015	+0010	+0002	+0.3	+0.2	No data	
River Boyne Bar	53 43N	6 14W	−0005	0000	+0020	+0030	+0.4	+0.3	−0.1	−0.2
Dunany Point	53 52N	6 14W	−0028	−0018	−0008	−0006	+0.7	+0.9	No data	
Dundalk Soldiers Point	54 00N	6 21W	−0010	−0010	0000	+0045	+1.0	+0.8	+0.1	−0.1
# NORTHERN IRELAND										
Carlingford Lough										
Cranfield Point	54 01N	6 04W	−0027	−0011	+0005	−0010	+0.7	+0.9	+0.3	+0.2
Warrenpoint	54 06N	6 15W	−0020	−0010	+0025	+0035	+1.0	+0.7	+0.2	+0.0
Newry (Victoria Lock)	54 09N	6 19W	+0005	+0015	+0045	*Dries*	+1.2	+0.9	+0.1	*Dries*
			0100	**0700**	**0000**	**0600**				
BELFAST	54 36N	5 55W	and	and	and	and	**3.5**	**3.0**	**1.1**	**0.4**
Standard port			**1300**	**1900**	**1200**	**1800**				
Kilkeel	54 03N	5 59W	+0040	+0030	+0010	+0010	+1.2	+1.1	+0.4	+0.4
Newcastle	54 12N	5 53W	+0025	+0035	+0020	+0040	+1.6	+1.1	+0.4	+0.1
Killough Harbour	54 15N	5 38W	0000	+0020	No data	No data	+1.8	+1.6	No data	
Ardglass	54 16N	5 36W	+0010	+0015	+0005	+0010	+1.7	+1.2	+0.6	+0.3
Strangford Lough										
Killard Point	54 19N	5 31W	+0011	+0021	+0005	+0025	+1.0	+0.8	+0.1	+0.1
Strangford	54 22N	5 33W	+0147	+0157	+0148	+0208	+0.1	+0.1	−0.2	0.0
Quoile Barrier	54 22N	5 41W	+0150	+0200	+0150	+0300	+0.2	+0.2	−0.3	−0.1
Killyleagh	54 24N	5 39W	+0157	+0207	+0211	+0231	+0.3	+0.3	No data	
South Rock	54 24N	5 25W	+0023	+0023	+0025	+0025	+1.0	+0.8	+0.1	+0.1
Portavogie	54 27N	5 26W	+0010	+0020	+0010	+0020	+1.2	+0.9	+0.3	+0.2

TIDES

Location	Lat	Long	High Water		Low Water		MHWS	MHWN	MLWN	MLWS
Donaghadee	54 39N	5 32W	+0020	+0020	+0023	+0023	+0.5	+0.4	0.0	+0.1
Carrickfergus	54 43N	5 48N	+0005	+0005	+0005	+0005	−0.3	−0.3	−0.2	−0.1
Larne	54 51N	5 48W	+0005	0000	+0010	−0005	−0.7	−0.5	−0.3	0.0
Red Bay	55 04N	6 03W	+0022	−0010	+0007	−0017	−1.9	−1.5	−0.8	−0.2
Cushendun	55 08N	6 02W	+0010	−0030	0000	−0025	−1.7	−1.5	−0.6	−0.2
Portrush	55 12N	6 40W	−0433	−0433	−0433	−0433	−1.6	−1.6	−0.3	0.0
Coleraine	55 08N	6 40W	−0403	−0403	−0403	−0403	−1.3	−1.2	−0.2	0.0
			0200	0900	0200	0800				
GALWAY	53 16N	9 03W	and	and	and	and	5.1	3.9	2.0	0.6
Standard port			1400	2100	1400	2000				
Londonderry	55 00N	7 19W	+0254	+0319	+0322	+0321	−2.4	−1.8	−0.8	−0.1

IRELAND

Location	Lat	Long	High Water		Low Water		MHWS	MHWN	MLWN	MLWS
Inishtrahull	55 26N	7 14W	+0100	+0100	+0115	+0200	−1.8	−1.4	−0.4	−0.2
Bulbinbeg	55 22N	7 20W	+0120	+0120	+0135	+0135	−1.3	−1.1	−0.4	−0.1
Trawbreaga Bay	55 19N	7 23W	+0115	+0059	+0109	+0125	−1.1	−0.8	No data	
Lough Swilly										
Rathmullan	55 06N	7 32W	+0125	+0050	+0126	+0118	−0.8	−0.7	−0.1	−0.1
Fanad Head	55 17N	7 38W	+0115	+0040	+0125	+0120	−1.1	−0.9	−0.5	−0.1
Mulroy Bay Bar	55 15N	7 46W	+0108	+0052	+0102	+0118	−1.2	−1.0	No data	
Fanny's Bay	55 12N	7 49W	+0145	+0129	+0151	+0207	−2.2	−1.7	No data	
Seamount Bay	55 11N	7 44W	+0210	+0154	+0226	+0242	−3.1	−2.3	No data	
Cranford Bay	55 09N	7 42W	+0329	+0313	+0351	+0407	−3.7	−2.8		
No data										
Sheephaven Downies Bay	55 11N	7 50W	+0057	+0043	+0053	+0107	−1.1	−0.9	No data	
Inishbofin Bay	55 10N	8 10W	+0040	+0026	+0032	+0046	−1.2	−0.9	No data	
			0600	1100	0000	0700				
GALWAY	53 16N	9 03W	and	and	and	and	5.1	3.9	2.0	0.6
Standard port			1800	2300	l200	1900				
Gweedore Harbour	55 04N	8 19W	+0048	+0100	+0055	+0107	−1.3	−1.0	−0.5	−0.1
Burtonport	54 59N	8 26W	+0042	+0055	+0115	+0055	−1.2	−1.0	−0.6	−0.1
Loughros More Bay	54 47N	8 30W	+0042	+0054	+0046	+0058	−1.1	−0.9	No data	
Donegal Bay										
Killybegs	54 38N	8 26W	+0040	+0050	+0055	+0035	−1.0	−0.9	−0.5	0.0
Donegal Hbr, Salt Hill Quay	54 38N	8 12W	+0038	+0050	+0052	+0104	−1.2	−0.9	No data	
Mullaghmore	54 28N	8 27W	+0036	+0048	+0047	+0059	−1.4	−1.0	−0.4	−0.2
Sligo Hbr (Oyster Island)	54 18N	8 34W	+0043	+0055	+0042	+0054	−1.0	−0.9	−0.5	−0.1
Ballysadare Bay, Culleenamore	54 16N	8 36W	+0059	+0111	+0111	+0123	−1.2	−0.9	No data	
Killala Bay (Inishcrone)	54 13N	9 06W	+0035	+0055	+0030	+0050	−1.3	−1.2	−0.7	−0.2
Broadhaven	54 16N	9 53W	+0040	+0050	+0040	+0050	−1.4	−1.1	−0.4	−0.1
Blacksod Bay										
Blacksod Quay	54 06N	10 04W	+0025	+0035	+0040	+0040	−1.2	−1.0	−0.6	−0.2
Inishbiggle	54 00N	9 53W	+0055	+0100	+0125	+0110	−1.3	− 0.9	−0.5	0.0
Clare Island	53 48N	9 57W	+0015	+0021	+0039	+0027	−0.6	−0.4	−0.1	+0.2
Clew Bay Inishgort	53 50N	9 40W	+0035	+0045	+0115	+0100	−0.7	−0.5	−0.2	+0.2
Killary Harbour	53 38N	9 53W	+0021	+0015	+0035	+0029	−1.0	−0.8	−0.4	−0.1
Inishbofin Bofin Harbour	53 37N	10 12W	+0013	+0009	+0021	+0017	−1.0	−0.8	−0.4	−0.1
Clifden Bay	53 29N	10 04W	+0005	+0005	+0016	+0016	−0.7	−0.5	No data	
Slyne Head	53 24N	10 14W	+0002	+0002	+0010	+0010	−0.7	−0.5	No data	
Roundstone Bay	53 23N	9 55W	+0003	+0003	+0008	+0008	−0.7	−0.5	−0.3	−0.1
Kilkieran Cove	53 19N	9 44W	+0005	+0005	+0016	+0016	−0.3	−0.2	−0.1	0.0
Aran Islands Killeany Bay	53 07N	9 40W	−0008	−0008	+0003	+0003	−0.4	−0.3	−0.2	−0.1
Liscannor	52 56N	9 23W	−0003	−0007	+0006	+0002	−0.4	−0.3	No data	
Seafield Point	52 48N	9 30W	−0006	−0014	+0004	−0004	−0.5	−0.4	No data	
Kilrush	52 38N	9 30W	−0006	+0027	+0057	−0016	−0.1	−0.2	−0.3	−0.1
Limerick Dock	52 40N	8 38W	+0135	+0141	+0141	+0219	+1.0	+0.7	−0.8	−0.2
			0500	1100	0500	1100				
COBH	51 51N	8 18 W	and	and	and	and	4.1	3.2	1.3	0.4
Standard port			1700	2300	1700	2300				
Tralee Bay Fenit Pier	52 16N	9 52W	−0057	−0017	−0029	−0109	+0.5	+0.2	+0.3	+0.1
Smerwick Harbour	52 12N	10 24W	−0107	−0027	−0041	−0121	−0.3	−0.4	No data	
Dingle Harbour	52 07N	10 15W	−0111	−0041	−0049	−0119	−0.1	0.0	+0.3	+0.4
Castlemaine Hbr Cromane Pt	52 08N	9 54W	−0026	−0006	−0017	−0037	+0.4	+0.2	+0.4	+0.2
Valentia Harbour										
Knights Town	51 56N	10 18W	−0118	−0038	−0056	−0136	−0.6	−0.4	−0.1	0.0
Ballinskelligs Bay Castle	51 49N	10 16W	−0119	−0039	−0054	−0134	−0.5	−0.5	−0.1	0.0
Kenmare River										
West Cove	51 46N	10 03W	−0113	−0033	−0049	−0129	−0.6	−0.5	−0.1	0.0
Dunkerron Harbour	51 52N	9 39W	−0117	−0027	−0050	−0140	−0.2	−0.3	+0.1	0.0

Location	Lat	Long	High Water		Low Water		MHWS	MHWN	MLWN	MLWS
Coulagh Bay										
Ballycrovane Hbr	51 43N	9 57W	−0116	−0036	−0053	−0133	−0.6	−0.5	−0.1	0.0
Black Ball Harbour	51 36N	10 02W	−0115	−0035	−0047	−0127	−0.7	−0.6	−0.1	+0.1
Bantry Bay										
Castletown Bearhaven	51 39N	9 54W	−0048	−0012	−0025	−0101	−0.9	−0.6	−0.1	0.0
Bantry	51 41N	9 28W	−0045	−0025	−0040	−0105	−0.7	−0.6	−0.2	+0.1
Dunmanus Bay										
Dunbeacon Harbour	51 37N	9 33W	−0057	−0025	−0032	−0104	−0.8	−0.7	−0.3	−0.1
Dunmanus Harbour	51 32N	9 40W	−0107	−0031	−0044	−0120	−0.7	−0.6	−0.2	0.0
Crookhaven	51 28N	9 44W	−0057	−0033	−0048	−0112	−0.8	−0.6	−0.4	−0.1
Skull	51 31N	9 32W	−0040	−0015	−0015	−0110	−0.9	−0.6	−0.2	0.0
Baltimore	51 29N	9 23W	−0025	−0005	−0010	−0050	−0.6	−0.3	+0.1	+0.2
Castletownshend	51 32N	9 10W	−0020	−0030	−0020	−0050	−0.4	−0.2	+0.1	+0.3
Clonakilty Bay	51 35N	8 50W	−0033	−0011	−0019	−0041	−0.3	−0.2	No data	
Courtmacsherry	51 38N	8 43W	−0025	−0008	−0008	−0015	−0.1	−0.1	−0.0	+0.1
Kinsale	51 42N	8 31W	−0019	−0005	−0009	−0023	−0.2	0.0	+0.1	+0.2
Roberts Cove	51 45N	8 19W	−0005	−0005	−0005	−0005	−0.1	0.0	0.0	+0.1
Cork Harbour										
Ringaskiddy	51 50N	8 19W	+0005	+0020	+0007	+0013	+0.1	+0.1	+0.1	+0.1
Marino Point	51 53N	8 20W	0000	+0010	0000	+0010	+0.1	+0.1	0.0	0.0
Cork City	51 54N	8 27W	+0005	+0010	+0020	+0010	+0.4	+0.4	+0.3	+0.2
Ballycotton	51 50N	8 01W	−0011	+0001	+0003	−0009	0.0	0.0	−0.1	0.0
Youghal	51 57N	7 51W	0000	+0010	+0010	0000	−0.2	−0.1	−0.1	−0.1
Dungarvan Harbour	52 05N	7 34W	+0004	+0012	+0007	−0001	0.0	+0.1	−0.2	0.0
Waterford Harbour										
Dunmore East	52 09N	6 59W	+0008	+0003	0000	0000	+0.1	0.0	+0.1	+0.2
Cheekpoint	52 16N	7 00W	+0022	+0020	+0020	+0020	+0.3	+0.2	+0.2	+0.1
Kilmokea Point	52 17N	7 00W	+0026	+0022	+0020	+0020	+0.2	+0.1	+0.1	+0.1
Waterford	52 16N	7 07W	+0057	+0057	+0046	+0046	+0.4	+0.3	−0.1	+0.1
New Ross	52 24N	6 57W	+0100	+0030	+0055	+0130	+0.3	+0.4	+0.3	+0.4
Baginbun Head	52 10N	6 50W	+0003	+0003	−0008	−0008	−0.2	−0.1	+0.2	+0.2
Great Saltee	52 07N	6 37W	+0019	+0009	−0004	+0006	−0.3	−0.4	No data	
Carnsore Point	52 10N	6 22W	+0029	+0019	−0002	+0008	−1.1	−1.0	No data	
Rosslare Europort	52 15N	6 21W	+0045	+0035	+0015	−0005	−2.2	−1.8	−0.5	−0.1
Wexford Harbour	52 20N	6 27W	+0126	+0126	+0118	+0108	−2.1	−1.7	−0.3	+0.1

DENMARK *Time zone −0100*

Location	Lat	Long	High Water		Low Water		MHWS	MHWN	MLWN	MLWS
			0300 and 1500	0700 and 1900	0100 and 1300	0800 and 2000				
ESBJERG	55 28N	8 27E					1.9	1.5	0.5	0.1
Standard port										
Hirtshals	57 36N	9 58E	+0055	+0320	+0340	+0100	−1.6	−1.3	−0.4	−0.1
Hanstholm	57 08N	8 36E	+0100	+0340	+0340	+0130	−1.6	−1.2	−0.4	−0.1
Thyborøn	56 42N	8 14E	+0120	+0230	+0410	+0210	−1.5	−1.2	−0.4	−0.1
Torsminde	56 22N	8 07E	+0045	+0050	+0040	+0010	−1.3	−1.0	−0.4	−0.1
Hvide Sande	56 00N	8 08E	0000	+0010	−0015	−0025	−1.1	−0.8	−0.3	−0.1
Blavands Huk	55 33N	8 05E	−0120	−0110	−0050	−0100	−0.1	−0.1	−0.2	−0.1
Esbjerg, Gradyb Bar	55 26N	8 15E	−0130	−0115	No data	No data	−0.4	−0.3	−0.2	−0.1
Havneby (Rømø)	55 05N	8 34E	−0040	−0005	0000	−0020	0.0	+0.1	−0.2	−0.2
Hojer	54 58N	8 40E	−0020	+0015	No data	No data	+0.5	+0.6	−0.1	−0.1

GERMANY *Time zone −0100*

Location	Lat	Long	High Water		Low Water		MHWS	MHWN	MLWN	MLWS
			0100 and 1300	0600 and 1800	0100 and 1300	0800 and 2000				
HELGOLAND	54 11N	7 53E					2.7	2.4	0.5	0.0
Standard port										
Lister Tief, List	55 01N	8 26E	+0252	+0240	+0201	+0210	−0.7	−0.6	−0.3	0.0
Hörnum	54 45N	8 18E	+0223	+0218	+0131	+0137	−0.4	−0.3	−0.2	0.0
Amrum - Hafen	54 38N	8 23E	+0138	+0137	+0128	+0134	+0.2	+0.2	−0.1	0.0
Dagebüll	54 44N	8 41E	+0226	+0217	+0211	+0225	+0.5	+0.5	−0.2	0.0
Suderoogsand	54 25N	8 30E	+0116	+0102	+0038	+0122	+0.5	+0.4	0.0	0.0
River Hever, Husum	54 28N	9 01E	+0205	+0152	+0118	+0200	+1.1	+1.0	−0.1	0.0
Suederhoeft	54 16N	8 42E	+0103	+0056	+0051	+0112	+0.7	+0.6	−0.2	0.0
Eidersperrwerk	54 16N	8 51E	+0120	+0115	+0130	+0155	+0.7	+0.6	−0.1	0.0
Linnenplate	54 13N	8 40E	+0047	+0046	+0034	+0046	+0.7	+0.6	−0.1	−0.1
Büsum	54 07N	8 52E	+0054	+0049	−0001	+0027	+0.9	+0.8	−0.1	0.0

Location	Lat	Long	High Water		Low Water		MHWS	MHWN	MLWN	MLWS
			0200 and 1400	0800 and 2000	0200 and 1400	0900 and 2100				
CUXHAVEN	53 52N	8 43E					3.8	3.4	0.9	0.5
Standard port										
River Elbe Großer Vogelsand	54 00N	8 29E	−0044	−0046	−0101	−0103	0.0	0.0	+0.1	−0.1
Scharhörn	53 58N	8 28E	−0045	−0047	−0101	−0103	0.0	0.0	0.0	−0.1
Otterndorf	53 50N	8 52E	+0029	+0029	+0027	+0027	−0.1	−0.1	−0.1	0.0

TIDES

TIDES

Location	Lat	Long	High Water		Low Water		MHWS	MHWN	MLWN	MLWS
Brunsbüttel	53 53N	9 08E	+0057	+0105	+0121	+0112	−0.3	−0.2	−0.1	0.0
Glückstadt	53 47N	9 25E	+0205	+0214	+0220	+0213	−0.2	−0.1	−0.1	0.0
Stadersand	53 38N	9 32E	+0241	+0245	+0300	+0254	−0.1	0.0	−0.2	0.0
Schulau	53 34N	9 42E	+0304	+0315	+0337	+0321	+0.1	+0.2	−0.3	−0.1
Seemannshoeft	53 32N	9 53E	+0324	+0332	+0403	+0347	+0.3	+0.3	−0.4	−0.2
Hamburg	53 33N	9 58E	+0338	+0346	+0422	+0406	+0.3	+0.4	−0.4	−0.3
			0200	0800	0200	0900				
WILHELMSHAVEN	53 31N	8 09E	and	and	and	and	**4.8**	**4.2**	**1.1**	**0.5**
Standard port			1400	2000	1400	2100				
River Weser										
Alter Weser lt ho	53 32N	8 08E	−0055	−0048	−0015	−0029	−1.0	−0.9	−0.1	0.0
Dwarsgat	53 43N	8 18E	−0015	+0002	−0006	−0001	−0.5	−0.4	−0.1	0.0
Bremerhaven	53 33N	8 34E	+0029	+0046	+0033	+0038	−0.1	0.0	−0.1	0.0
Nordenham	53 28N	8 29E	+0051	+0109	+0055	+0058	0.0	+0.1	−0.2	−0.1
Brake	53 19N	8 29E	+0120	+0119	+0143	+0155	−0.2	−0.1	−0.4	−0.2
Elsfleth	53 16N	8 29E	+0137	+0137	+0206	+0216	−0.2	−0.1	−0.3	0.0
Vegesack	53 10N	8 37E	+0208	+0204	+0250	+0254	−0.2	−0.1	−0.5	−0.2
Bremen	53 07N	8 43E	+0216	+0211	+0311	+0314	0.0	0.0	−0.6	−0.3
River Jade										
Wangerooge East	53 46N	7 59E	−0058	−0053	−0024	−0034	−1.0	−0.8	−0.1	0.0
Wangerooge West	53 47N	7 52E	−0101	−0058	−0035	−0045	−1.0	−0.9	−0.1	0.0
Schillig	53 42N	8 03E	−0031	−0025	−0006	−0014	−0.7	−0.6	−0.1	0.0
Hooksiel	53 39N	8 05E	−0023	−0022	−0008	−0012	−0.5	−0.4	−0.1	0.0
			0200	0700	0200	0800				
HELGOLAND	54 11N	7 53E	and	and	and	and	**2.7**	**2.4**	**0.5**	**0.0**
Standard port			1400	1900	1400	2000				
East Frisian Islands and coast										
Spiekeroog	53 45N	7 41E	+0003	−0003	−0031	−0012	+0.4	+0.3	−0.1	0.0
Neuharlingersiel	53 42N	7 42E	+0014	+0008	−0024	−0013	+0.5	+0.4	−0.1	−0.1
Langeoog	53 43N	7 30E	+0003	−0001	−0034	−0018	+0.3	+0.3	0.0	0.0
Norderney (Riffgat)	53 42N	7 09E	−0024	−0030	−0056	−0045	+0.1	+0.1	0.0	0.0
Norddeich Hafen	53 39N	7 09E	−0018	−0017	−0029	−0012	+0.1	+0.1	−0.1	−0.1
Juist	53 40N	7 00E	−0026	−0032	−0019	−0008	+0.6	+0.5	+0.4	+0.4
River Ems										
Memmert	53 38N	6 54E	−0032	−0038	−0114	−0103	+0.5	+0.5	+0.3	+0.4
Borkum (Fischerbalje)	53 33N	6 45E	−0048	−0052	−0124	−0105	+0.4	+0.4	+0.3	+0.4
Emshorn	53 30N	6 50E	−0037	−0041	−0108	−0047	+0.5	+0.5	+0.4	+0.4
Knock	53 20N	7 02E	+0018	+0005	−0028	+0004	+1.1	+1.0	+0.4	+0.5
Emden	53 20N	7 11E	+0041	+0028	−0011	+0022	+1.3	+1.2	+0.4	+0.4

NETHERLANDS *Time zone −0100*

Location	Lat	Long	High Water		Low Water		MHWS	MHWN	MLWN	MLWS
			0200	0700	0200	0800				
HELGOLAND	54 11N	7 53E	and	and	and	and	**2.7**	**2.4**	**0.5**	**0.0**
Standard port			1400	1900	1400	2000				
Delfzijl	53 20N	6 56E	+0020	−0005	−0040	0000	+1.0	+1.0	+0.3	+0.4
Eemshaven	53 26N	6 52E	−0025	−0045	−0115	−0045	+0.5	+0.5	+0.3	+0.4
Huibergat	53 35N	6 24E	−0150	−0150	−0210	−0210	0.0	0.0	+0.2	+0.3
Schiermonnikoog	53 28N	6 12E	−0120	−0130	−0240	−0220	+0.2	+0.1	+0.2	+0.3
Waddenzee										
Lauwersoog	53 25N	6 12E	−0130	−0145	−0235	−0220	+0.2	+0.2	+0.2	+0.5
Nes	53 26N	5 47E	−0135	−0150	−0245	−0225	+0.2	+0.2	+0.2	+0.5
West Terschelling	53 22N	5 13E	−0220	−0250	−0335	−0310	−0.3	−0.2	+0.1	+0.3
Vlieland-Haven	53 18N	5 06E	−0250	−0320	−0355	−0330	−0.3	−0.2	+0.1	+0.4
Harlingen	53 10N	5 25E	−0155	−0245	−0210	−0130	−0.3	−0.3	0.0	+0.4
Kornwerderzand	53 04N	5 20E	−0210	−0315	−0300	−0215	−0.5	−0.4	0.0	+0.3
Den Oever	52 56N	5 02E	−0245	−0410	−0400	−0305	−0.7	−0.6	−0.1	+0.3
Oudeschild	53 02N	4 51E	−0310	−0420	−0445	−0400	−0.8	−0.7	0.0	+0.3
Den Helder	52 58N	4 45E	−0410	−0520	−0520	−0430	−0.8	−0.7	+0.1	+0.2
Noordwinning (Platform K13–A)	53 13N	3 13E	−0420	−0430	−0520	−0530	−0.9	−0.9	+0.2	+0.3
			0300	0900	0400	1000				
VLISSINGEN	51 27N	3 36E	and	and	and	and	**5.0**	**4.1**	**1.1**	**0.5**
Standard port			1500	2100	1600	2200				
IJmuiden	52 28N	4 35E	+0145	+0140	+0305	+0325	−2.8	−2.3	−0.7	−0.2
Scheveningen	52 06N	4 16E	+0105	+0100	+0220	+0245	−2.7	−2.2	−0.7	−0.2
Europlatform	52 00N	3 17E	+0005	−0005	−0030	−0055	−2.7	−2.2	−0.6	−0.1
Nieuwe Waterweg										
HOEK VAN HOLLAND			*Standard port, no Secondaries*							
Maassluis	51 55N	4 15E	+0155	+0115	+0100	+0310	−2.9	−2.3	−0.8	−0.2
Nieuwe Maas, Vlaardingen	51 54N	4 21E	+0150	+0120	+0130	+0330	−2.9	−2.3	−0.8	−0.2
Haringvlietsluizen	51 50N	4 02E	+0015	+0015	+0015	−0020	−2.0	−1.9	−0.7	−0.2

Location	Lat	Long	High Water		Low Water		MHWS	MHWN	MLWN	MLWS
Ooster Schelde										
Roompot Buiten	51 37N	3 40E	−0015	+0005	+0005	−0020	−1.3	−1.1	−0.4	−0.1
Walcheren, Westkapelle	51 31N	3 27E	−0025	−0015	−0010	−0025	−0.6	−0.6	−0.2	−0.1
Westerschelde										
Terneuzen	51 20N	3 50E	+0020	+0020	+0020	+0030	+0.3	+0.4	0.0	+0.1
Hansweert	51 27N	4 00E	+0100	+0050	+0040	+0100	+0.6	+0.7	0.0	0.0
Bath	51 24N	4 13E	+0125	+0115	+0115	+0140	+1.1	+1.0	+0.1	+0.1

BELGIUM *Time zone −0100*

Location	Lat	Long	High Water		Low Water		MHWS	MHWN	MLWN	MLWS
Antwerpen	51 21N	4 14E	+0128	+0116	+0121	+0144	+1.2	+1.0	+0.1	+0.1
Blankenberge	51 19N	3 07E	−0040	−0040	−0040	−0040	−0.3	0.0	+0.3	+0.2
			0300	0900	0300	0900				
ZEEBRUGGE	51 21N	3 12E	and	and	and	and	4.8	4.0	1.1	0.5
Standard port			1500	2100	1500	2100				
Oostende	51 14N	2 56E	−0019	−0019	−0008	−0008	+0.4	+0.3	+0.2	+0.1
Nieuwpoort	51 09N	2 43E	−0031	−0031	−0010	−0010	+0.7	+0.5	+0.3	+0.1

FRANCE *Time zone −0100*

Location	Lat	Long	High Water		Low Water		MHWS	MHWN	MLWN	MLWS
			0200	0800	0200	0900				
DUNKERQUE	51 03N	2 22E	and	and	and	and	6.0	5.0	1.5	0.6
Standard port			1400	2000	1400	2100				
Gravelines	51 01N	2 06E	−0010	−0015	−0010	−0005	+0.5	+0.3	0.0	0.0
Sandettie Bank	51 09N	1 47E	−0015	−0025	−0020	−0005	+0.1	−0.1	−0.1	−0.1
Calais	51 58N	1 51E	−0020	−0030	−0015	−0005	+1.2	+0.9	+0.6	+0.3
Wissant	50 53N	1 40E	−0035	−0050	−0030	−0010	+1.9	+1.5	+0.8	+0.4

BOULOGNE		*Standard port, no Secondaries*								

Location	Lat	Long	High Water		Low Water		MHWS	MHWN	MLWN	MLWS
			0100	0600	0100	0700				
DIEPPE	49 56N	1 05E	and	and	and	and	9.3	7.4	2.5	0.8
Standard port			1300	1800	1300	1900				
Le Touquet, Étaples	50 31N	1 35E	+0005	+0015	+0030	+0030	+0.2	+0.3	+0.4	+0.4
Berck	50 24N	1 34E	+0005	+0015	+0030	+0030	+0.5	+0.5	+0.4	+0.4
La Somme										
Le Hourdel	50 13N	1 34E	+0020	+0020	No data	No data	+0.8	+0.6	No data	
St Valéry	50 11N	1 37E	+0035	+0035	No data	No data	+0.9	+0.7	No data	
Cayeux	50 11N	1 29E	0000	+0005	+0015	+0010	+0.5	+0.6	+0.4	+0.4
Le Tréport	50 04N	1 22E	+0005	0000	+0007	+0007	+0.1	+0.1	0.0	+0.1
St Valéry−en−Caux	49 52N	0 42E	−0005	−0005	−0015	−0020	−0.5	−0.4	−0.1	−0.1
Fécamp	49 46N	0 22E	−0015	−0010	−0030	−0040	−1.0	−0.6	+0.3	+0.4
Etretat	49 42N	0 12E	−0020	−0020	−0045	−0050	−1.2	−0.8	+0.3	+0.4
			0000	0500	0000	0700				
LE HAVRE	49 29N	0 07E	and	and	and	and	7.9	6.6	2.8	1.2
Standard port			1200	1700	1200	1900				
Antifer (Le Havre)	49 39N	0 09E	+0025	+0015	+0005	−0005	+0.1	0.0	0.0	0.0
La Seine										
Chenal du Rouen	49 26N	0 07E	0000	0000	0000	+0015	0.0	−0.1	0.0	−0.1
Honfleur	49 25N	0 14E	−0150	−0135	+0025	+0040	0.0	0.0	+0.1	+0.4
Tancarville	49 28N	0 28E	−0135	−0120	+0030	+0145	+0.1	+0.1	+0.1	+0.3
Quilleboeuf	49 28N	0 32E	−0055	−0110	+0105	+0210	+0.1	+0.1	+0.5	+1.4
Vatteville	49 29N	0 40E	+0015	−0040	+0205	+0240	−0.1	−0.1	+0.9	+2.2
Caudebec	49 32N	0 44E	−0005	−0030	+0220	+0300	−0.1	−0.1	+1.0	+2.3
Heurteauville	49 27N	0 49E	+0055	+0005	+0250	+0330	−0.2	−0.1	+1.2	+2.6
Duclair	49 29N	0 53E	+0210	+0125	+0350	+0410	−0.2	0.0	+1.5	+3.2
Rouen	49 27N	1 06E	+0305	+0240	+0505	+0515	−0.1	+0.2	+1.6	+3.3
Trouville	49 22N	0 05E	−0100	−0010	0000	+0005	+0.4	+0.3	+0.3	+0.1
Dives	49 18N	0 05W	−0100	−0010	0000	0000	+0.3	+0.2	+0.2	+0.1
Ouistreham	49 17N	0 15W	−0045	−0010	−0005	0000	−0.3	−0.3	−0.2	−0.3
Courseulles-sur-Mer	49 20N	0 27W	−0045	−0015	−0020	−0025	−0.5	−0.5	−0.1	−0.1
Arromanches	49 21N	0 37W	−0055	−0025	−0025	−0035	−0.6	−0.6	−0.2	−0.2
Port-en-Bessin	49 21N	0 45W	−0055	−0030	−0030	−0035	−0.7	−0.7	−0.2	−0.1
Alpha-Baie de Seine	49 49N	0 20W	+0030	+0020	−0005	−0020	−1.0	−0.9	−0.4	−0.2
			0300	1000	0400	1000				
CHERBOURG	49 39N	1 38W	and	and	and	and	6.4	5.0	2.5	1.1
Standard port			1500	2200	1600	2200				
Rade de la Capelle	49 25N	1 05W	+0115	+0050	+0130	+0115	+0.8	+0.9	+0.1	+0.1
Iles Saint Marcouf	49 30N	1 08W	+0115	+0050	+0125	+0110	+0.6	+0.7	+0.1	+0.1
St Vaast-la-Hougue	49 34N	1 16W	+0120	+0050	+0120	+0115	+0.3	+0.5	0.0	−0.1
Barfleur	49 40N	1 15W	+0110	+0055	+0050	+0050	+0.1	+0.3	0.0	0.0

TIDES

Location	Lat	Long	High Water		Low Water		MHWS	MHWN	MLWN	MLWS
Omonville	49 42N	1 50W	−0010	−0010	−0015	−0015	−0.1	−0.1	0.0	0.0
Goury	49 43N	1 57W	−0100	−0040	−0105	−0120	+1.7	+1.6	+1.0	+0.3

CHANNEL ISLANDS *Time zone UT*

Location	Lat	Long	High Water		Low Water		MHWS	MHWN	MLWN	MLWS
			0300	0900	0200	0900				
ST HELIER	49 11N	2 07W	and	and	and	and	11.0	8.1	4.0	1.4
Standard port			1500	2100	1400	2100				
Alderney, Braye	49 43N	2 12W	+0050	+0040	+0025	+0105	−4.8	−3.4	−1.5	−0.5
Sark, Maseline Pier	49 26N	2 21W	+0005	+0015	+0005	+0010	−2.1	−1.5	−0.6	−0.3
Guernsey, ST PETER PORT	49 27N	2 31W	*Standard port (no Secondaries)*							
Jersey										
St Catherine Bay	49 13N	2 01W	0000	+0010	+0010	+0010	0.0	−0.1	0.0	+0.1
Bouley Bay	49 14N	2 05W	+0002	+0002	+0004	+0004	−0.3	−0.3	−0.1	−0.1
Les Ecrehou	49 17N	1 56W	+0005	+0009	+0011	+0009	−0.2	+0.1	−0.2	0.0
Les Minquiers	48 57N	2 08W	−0014	−0018	−0001	−0008	+0.5	+0.6	+0.1	+0.1

FRANCE *Time zone −0100*

Location	Lat	Long	High Water		Low Water		MHWS	MHWN	MLWN	MLWS
			0100	0800	0300	0800				
ST MALO	48 38N	2 02W	and	and	and	and	12.2	9.3	4.2	1.5
Standard port			1300	2000	1500	2000				
Les Ardentes	48 58N	1 52W	+0010	+0010	+0020	+0010	0.0	−0.1	0.0	−0.1
Iles Chausey	48 52N	1 49W	+0005	+0005	+0015	+0015	+0.8	+0.7	+0.6	+0.4
Diélette	49 33N	1 52W	+0045	+0035	+0020	+0035	−2.5	−1.9	−0.7	−0.3
Carteret	49 22N	1 47W	+0030	+0020	+0015	+0030	−1.6	−1.2	−0.5	−0.2
Portbail	49 18N	1 45W	+0030	+0025	+0025	+0030	−0.8	−0.6	−0.2	−0.1
St Germain sur Ay	49 14N	1 36W	+0025	+0025	+0035	+0035	−0.7	−0.5	0.0	+0.1
Le Sénéquet	49 05N	1 40W	+0015	+0015	+0025	+0025	−0.3	−0.3	+0.1	+0.1
Regnéville sur Mer	49 01N	1 33W	+0010	+0010	+0030	+0020	+0.5	+0.4	+0.2	0.0
Granville	48 50N	1 36W	+0005	+0005	+0020	+0010	+0.7	+0.5	+0.3	+0.1
Cancale	48 40N	1 51W	0000	0000	+0010	+0010	+0.8	+0.6	+0.3	+0.1
Ile des Hebihens	48 37N	2 11W	0000	0000	−0005	−0005	−0.2	−0.2	−0.1	−0.1
St Cast	48 38N	2 15W	0000	0000	−0005	−0005	−0.2	−0.2	−0.1	−0.1
Erquy	48 38N	2 28W	−0010	−0005	−0025	−0015	−0.6	−0.5	0.0	0.0
Dahouët	48 35N	2 34W	−0010	−0010	−0025	−0020	−0.9	−0.7	−0.2	−0.2
Le Légué (Buoy)	48 34N	2 41W	−0010	−0005	−0020	−0015	−0.8	−0.5	−0.2	−0.1
Binic	48 36N	2 49W	−0010	−0010	−0030	−0015	−0.8	−0.7	−0.2	−0.2
St Quay-Portrieux	48 38N	2 49W	−0010	−0005	−0025	−0020	−0.9	−0.7	−0.2	−0.1
Paimpol	48 47N	3 02W	−0010	−0005	−0035	−0025	−1.4	−1.0	−0.4	−0.2
Ile de Bréhat	48 51N	3 00W	−0015	−0015	−0045	−0035	−1.9	−1.4	−0.6	−0.3
Les Héaux de Bréhat	48 55N	3 05W	−0020	−0020	−0055	−0045	−2.4	−1.7	−0.7	−0.3
Lézardrieux	48 47N	3 06W	−0020	−0015	−0055	−0045	−1.7	−1.3	−0.5	−0.2
Port-Béni	48 51N	3 10W	−0025	−0025	−0105	−0050	−2.4	−1.7	−0.6	−0.2
Tréguier	48 47N	3 13W	−0020	−0020	−0100	−0045	−2.3	−1.6	−0.6	−0.2
Perros-Guirec	48 49N	3 28W	−0040	−0045	−0120	−0105	−2.9	−2.0	−0.8	−0.3
Ploumanac'h	48 50N	3 29W	−0035	−0040	−0120	−0100	−2.9	−2.0	−0.7	−0.2
			0000	0600	0000	0600				
BREST	48 23N	4 30W	and	and	and	and	7.0	5.5	2.7	1.1
Standard port			1200	1800	1200	1800				
Trébeurden	48 46N	3 35W	+0100	+0110	+0120	+0100	+2.2	+1.8	+0.8	+0.3
Locquirec	48 42N	3 38W	+0100	+0110	+0120	+0100	+2.1	+1.7	+0.7	+0.2
Anse de Primel	48 43N	3 50W	+0100	+0110	+0120	+0100	+2.0	+1.6	+0.7	+0.2
Chateau du Taureau (Morlaix)	48 41N	3 53W	+0055	+0105	+0115	+0055	+1.9	+1.6	+0.7	+0.2
Roscoff	48 43N	3 58W	+0055	+0105	+0115	+0055	+1.8	+1.5	+0.7	+0.2
Ile de Batz	48 44N	4 00W	+0045	+0100	+0105	+0055	+1.9	+1.5	+0.8	+0.3
Brignogan	48 40N	4 19W	+0040	+0045	+0100	+0040	+1.4	+1.1	+0.5	+0.1
L'Aber Wrac'h	48 36N	4 34W	+0030	+0030	+0040	+0035	+0.7	+0.6	+0.1	−0.1
Aber Benoit	48 35N	4 37W	+0022	+0025	+0035	+0020	+0.9	+0.8	+0.3	+0.1
Portsall	48 34N	4 43W	+0015	+0020	+0025	+0015	+0.5	+0.4	0.0	−0.1
L'Aber-Ildut	48 28N	4 45W	+0010	+0010	+0023	+0010	+0.3	+0.2	−0.1	−0.1
Ouessant, Baie de Lampaul	48 27N	5 06W	+0010	+0010	0000	+0005	−0.1	−0.1	−0.1	−0.1
Molene	48 24N	4 58W	+0015	+0010	+0020	+0020	+0.3	+0.3	+0.1	+0.1
Le Conquet	48 22N	4 47W	0000	0000	+0005	+0005	−0.2	−0.2	−0.1	0.0
Le Trez Hir	48 21N	4 42W	−0005	−0005	−0015	−0010	−0.4	−0.4	−0.2	−0.1
Camaret	48 17N	4 35W	−0010	−0010	−0015	−0010	−0.4	−0.4	−0.3	−0.1
Morgat	48 13N	4 30W	−0005	−0010	−0020	−0005	−0.5	−0.4	−0.2	0.0

Location	Lat	Long	High Water		Low Water		MHWS	MHWN	MLWN	MLWS
Douarnenez	48 06N	4 19W	−0010	−0010	−0020	−0010	−0.4	−0.4	−0.2	−0.1
Ile de Sein	48 02N	4 51W	−0005	−0005	−0015	−0010	−0.9	−0.8	−0.4	−0.2
Anse de Feunteun Aod	48 02N	4 42W	−0030	−0040	−0035	−0025	−1.4	−1.2	−0.6	−0.2
Audierne	48 01N	4 33W	−0035	−0030	−0035	−0030	−1.8	−1.4	−0.7	−0.3
Le Guilvinec	47 48N	4 17W	−0010	−0025	−0025	−0015	−1.9	−1.5	−0.7	−0.2
Lesconil	47 48N	4 13W	−0010	−0030	−0030	−0020	−2.0	−1.5	−0.7	−0.2
Pont l'Abbe River, Loctudy	47 50N	4 10W	−0010	−0030	−0030	−0020	−2.1	−1.7	−0.8	−0.4
Odet River										
Bénodet	47 53N	4 07W	0000	−0020	−0025	−0015	−1.8	−1.4	−0.6	−0.2
Corniguel	47 58N	4 06W	+0015	+0010	−0015	−0010	−2.1	−1.7	−1.1	−0.8
Concarneau	47 52N	3 55W	−0010	−0030	−0030	−0020	−2.0	−1.6	−0.8	−0.3
Iles de Glenan, Ile de Penfret	47 44N	3 57W	−0005	−0030	−0030	−0020	−2.0	−1.6	−0.8	−0.3
Port Louis	47 42N	3 21W	+0005	−0020	−0020	−0010	−1.9	−1.5	−0.7	−0.2
Lorient	47 45N	3 21W	+0005	−0020	−0020	−0010	−1.9	−1.5	−0.7	−0.3
Hennebont	47 48N	3 17W	+0015	−0015	+0005	+0003	−2.0	−1.6	−0.9	−0.3
Ile de Groix, Port Tudy	47 39N	3 27W	0000	−0025	−0025	−0015	−1.9	−1.5	−0.7	−0.2
Port d'Etel	47 39N	3 12W	+0020	−0010	+0030	+0010	−2.1	−1.4	−0.5	+0.4
Port Haliguen	47 29N	3 06W	+0010	−0020	−0015	−0010	−1.7	−1.3	−0.7	−0.3
Port Maria	47 29N	3 08W	+0010	−0025	−0025	−0015	−1.7	−1.4	−0.7	−0.2
Belle Ile, Le Palais	47 21N	3 09W	+0005	−0025	−0025	−0010	−1.9	−1.4	−0.8	−0.3
Crac'h River, La Trinité	47 35N	3 01W	+0025	−0020	−0015	−0010	−1.7	−1.2	−0.6	−0.3
Golfe du Morbihan										
Port Navalo	47 33N	2 55W	+0030	−0005	−0010	−0005	−2.1	−1.6	−0.9	−0.4
Auray	47 40N	2 59W	+0035	0000	+0015	−0005	−2.3	−1.9	−1.2	−0.5
Arradon	47 37N	2 50W	+0135	+0145	+0140	+0115	−3.9	−3.1	−1.9	−0.8
Vannes	47 39N	2 46W	+0200	+0150	+0140	+0120	−3.8	−3.0	−2.1	−0.9
St Armel (Le Passage)	47 36N	2 43W	+0200	+0200	+0210	+0135	−3.8	−3.0	−2.0	−0.9
Le Logeo	47 33N	2 51W	+0140	+0140	+0145	+0115	−4.1	−3.2	−2.1	−0.9
Port du Crouesty	47 32N	2 54W	+0010	−0025	−0025	−0030	−1.7	−1.3	−0.7	−0.4
Ile de Houat	47 24N	2 57W	+0005	−0025	−0025	−0010	−1.8	−1.4	−0.7	−0.4
Ile de Hoëdic	47 20N	2 52W	+0010	−0035	−0025	−0020	−1.9	−1.5	−0.8	−0.4
Pénerf	47 31N	2 37W	+0015	−0025	−0015	−0015	−1.6	−1.2	−0.7	−0.4
Tréhiguier	47 30N	2 27W	+0035	−0020	−0005	−0010	−1.5	−1.1	−0.6	−0.4
Le Croisic	47 18N	2 31W	+0015	−0040	−0020	−0015	−1.6	−1.2	−0.7	−0.4
Le Pouliguen	47 17N	2 25W	+0020	−0025	−0020	−0025	−1.6	−1.2	−0.7	−0.4
Le Grand-Charpentier	47 13N	2 19W	+0015	−0045	−0025	−0020	−1.6	−1.2	−0.7	−0.4
Pornichet	47 16N	2 21W	+0020	−0045	−0022	−0022	−1.5	−1.1	−0.6	−0.3
La Loire										
St Nazaire	47 16N	2 12W	+0030	−0040	−0010	−0010	−1.2	−0.9	−0.5	−0.3
Donges	47 18N	2 05W	+0035	−0035	+0005	+0005	−1.1	−0.8	−0.6	−0.5
Cordemais	47 17N	1 54W	+0055	−0005	+0105	+0030	−0.8	−0.6	−0.8	−0.5
Le Pellerin	47 12N	1 46W	+0110	+0010	+0145	+0100	−0.8	−0.6	−1.0	−0.5
Nantes (Chantenay)	47 12N	1 35W	+0135	+0055	+0215	+0125	−0.7	−0.4	−0.9	−0.2
			0500	1100	0500	1100				
BREST	48 23N	4 30W	and	and	and	and	7.0	5.5	2.7	1.1
Standard port			1700	2300	1700	2300				
Pointe de Saint–Gildas	47 08N	2 15W	−0045	+0025	−0020	−0020	−1.4	−1.1	−0.6	−0.3
Pornic	47 06N	2 07W	−0050	+0030	−0010	−0010	−1.2	−0.9	−0.5	−0.3
Ile de Noirmoutier, L'Herbaudière	47 02N	2 18W	−0045	+0025	−0020	−0020	−1.5	−1.1	−0.6	−0.3
Fromentine	46 54N	2 10W	−0045	+0020	−0015	+0005	−1.8	−1.4	−0.9	−0.2
Ile de Yeu, Port Joinville	46 44N	2 21W	−0040	+0015	−0030	−0035	−2.0	−1.5	−0.8	−0.4
St Gilles-Croix-de-Vie	46 41N	1 56W	−0030	+0015	−0030	−0030	−1.9	−1.4	−0.7	−0.4
Les Sables d'Olonne	46 30N	1 48W	−0030	+0015	−0035	−0035	−1.8	−1.4	−0.7	−0.4
			0000	0600	0000	0500				
POINTE DE GRAVE	45 34N	1 04W	and	and	and	and	5.4	4.4	2.1	1.0
Standard port			1200	1800	1200	1700				
Ile de Ré, St Martin	46 12N	1 22W	+0005	−0030	−0025	−0030	+0.5	+0.3	+0.2	−0.1
La Pallice	46 10N	1 13W	+0015	−0030	−0020	−0025	+0.6	+0.5	+0.3	−0.1
La Rochelle	46 09N	1 09W	+0015	−0030	−0020	−0025	+0.6	+0.5	+0.3	−0.1
Ile d'Aix	46 01N	1 10W	+0015	−0040	−0025	−0030	+0.7	+0.5	+0.3	−0.1
La Charente, Rochefort	45 57N	0 58W	+0035	−0010	+0125	+0030	+1.1	+0.9	+0.1	−0.2
Le Chapus	45 51N	1 11W	+0015	−0040	−0015	−0025	+0.6	+0.6	+0.4	+0.2
La Cayenne	45 47N	1 08W	+0030	−0015	−0005	−0010	+0.2	+0.2	+0.3	0.0
Pointe de Gatseau	45 48N	1 14W	+0055	0000	−0020	−0015	−0.1	−0.1	+0.2	+0.1

TIDES

TIDES

Location	Lat	Long	High Water		Low Water		MHWS	MHWN	MLWN	MLWS
Cordouan	45 35N	1 10W	−0010	−0010	−0025	−0015	−0.5	−0.4	−0.1	−0.2
La Gironde										
Royan	45 37N	1 01W	0000	−0005	0000	0000	−0.2	−0.1	0.0	0.0
Richard	45 27N	0 56W	+0020	+0020	+0035	+0030	−0.1	−0.1	−0.4	−0.5
Lamena	45 20N	0 48W	+0035	+0045	+0125	+0100	+0.2	+0.1	−0.5	−0.3
Pauillac	45 12N	0 45W	+0100	+0100	+0205	+0135	+0.1	0.0	−1.0	−0.5
La Reuille	45 03N	0 36W	+0135	+0145	+0230	+0305	−0.2	−0.3	−1.3	−0.7
La Garonne										
Le Marquis	45 00N	0 33W	+0145	+0150	+0320	+0245	−0.3	−0.4	−1.5	−0.9
Bordeaux	44 52N	0 33W	+0200	+0225	+0405	+0330	−0.1	−0.2	−1.7	−1.0
La Dordogne										
Libourne	44 55N	0 15W	+0250	+0305	+0540	+0525	−0.7	−0.9	−2.0	−0.4
Bassin d'Arcachon										
Cap Ferret	44 37N	1 15W	−0015	+0005	+0020	−0005	−1.4	−1.2	−0.8	−0.6
Arcachon (Eyrac)	44 40N	1 10W	+0010	+0020	+0030	+0005	−1.1	−1.0	−0.8	−0.6
L'Adour, Boucau	43 31N	1 31W	−0030	−0035	−0040	−0025	−1.2	−1.1	−0.4	−0.3
St Jean de Luz, Socoa	43 23N	1 40W	−0040	−0045	−0045	−0030	−1.1	−1.1	−0.6	−0.4

SPAIN *Time zone −0100*

Location	Lat	Long	High Water		Low Water		MHWS	MHWN	MLWN	MLWS
Pasajes	43 20N	1 56W	−0050	−0030	−0045	−0015	−1.2	−1.3	−0.5	−0.5
San Sebastian	43 19N	1 59W	−0110	−0030	−0040	−0020	−1.2	−1.2	−0.5	−0.4
Guetaria	43 18N	2 12W	−0110	−0030	−0040	−0020	−1.0	−1.0	−0.5	−0.4
Lequeitio	43 22N	2 30W	−0115	−0035	−0045	−0025	−1.2	−1.2	−0.5	−0.4
Bermeo	43 25N	2 43W	−0055	−0015	−0025	−0005	−0.8	−0.7	−0.5	−0.4
Abra de Bilbao	43 21N	3 02W	−0125	−0045	−0055	−0035	−1.2	−1.2	−0.5	−0.4
Portugalete (Bilbao)	43 20N	3 02W	−0100	−0020	−0030	−0010	−0.7	−1.2	−0.2	−0.6
Castro Urdiales	43 23N	3 13W	−0040	−0120	−0110	−0020	−1.4	−1.5	−0.6	−0.6
Ria de Santona	43 26N	3 28W	−0005	−0045	−0035	+0015	−0.7	−1.2	−0.3	−0.7
Santander	43 28N	3 47W	−0020	−0100	−0050	0000	−0.7	−1.2	−0.3	−0.7
Ria de Suances	43 27N	4 03W	0000	−0030	−0020	+0020	−1.5	−1.5	−0.6	−0.6
San Vicente de la Barquera	43 23N	4 24W	−0020	−0100	−0050	0000	−1.5	−1.5	−0.6	−0.6
Ria de Tina Mayor	43 24N	4 31W	−0020	−0100	−0050	0000	−1.4	−1.5	−0.6	−0.6
Ribadesella	43 28N	5 04W	+0005	−0020	−0020	+0020	−1.4	−1.3	−0.6	−0.4
Gijon	43 34N	5 42W	−0005	−0030	−0030	+0010	−1.0	−1.4	−0.4	−0.7
Luanco	43 37N	5 47W	−0010	−0035	−0035	+0005	−1.4	−1.3	−0.6	−0.4
Aviles	43 35N	5 56W	−0100	−0040	−0050	−0015	−1.2	−1.6	−0.5	−0.7
San Esteban de Pravia	43 34N	6 05W	−0005	−0030	−0030	+0010	−1.4	−1.3	−0.6	−0.4
Luarca	43 33N	6 32W	+0010	−0015	−0015	+0025	−1.2	−1.1	−0.5	−0.3
Ribadeo	43 33N	7 02W	+0010	−0015	−0015	+0025	−1.3	−1.5	−0.7	−0.8
Burela	43 39N	7 21W	+0010	−0015	−0015	+0025	−1.5	−1.5	−0.7	−0.6
Ria de Vivero	43 43N	7 36W	+0010	−0015	−0015	+0025	−1.4	−1.3	−0.6	−0.4

Location	Lat	Long	High Water		Low Water		MHWS	MHWN	MLWN	MLWS
LA CORUÑA	43 22N	8 24W	0000 and 1200	0600 and 1800	0000 and 1200	0500 and 1700	4.2	2.8	1.6	0.3
Standard port										
Santa Marta de Ortigueira	43 41N	7 51W	+0050	+0050	+0050	+0050	−0.1	+0.4	−0.1	+0.3
Ferrol (La Grana)	43 28N	8 16W	−0002	−0002	+0001	+0001	0.0	0.0	0.0	0.0
Ria de Corme	43 16N	8 58W	−0005	−0005	+0004	+0004	−0.3	−0.2	−0.1	0.0
Ria de Camarinas	43 08N	9 11W	−0005	−0005	−0005	−0005	−0.2	−0.2	−0.1	0.0

Location	Lat	Long	High Water		Low Water		MHWS	MHWN	MLWN	MLWS
LISBOA	38 42N	9 07W	0500 and 1700	1000 and 2200	0300 and 1500	0800 and 2000	3.8	3.0	1.5	0.6
Standard port										
Corcubion	42 57N	9 12W	+0055	+0110	+0120	+0135	−0.5	−0.4	−0.3	−0.1
Muros	42 46N	9 03W	+0050	+0105	+0115	+0130	−0.3	−0.3	−0.2	−0.1
Ria de Arosa, Villagarcia	42 37N	8 47W	+0040	+0100	+0110	+0120	+0.2	−0.3	0.0	−0.4
Ria de Pontevedra, Marin	42 24N	8 42W	+0050	+0110	+0120	+0130	−0.4	−0.3	−0.1	0.0
Vigo	42 15N	8 43W	+0040	+0100	+0105	+0125	+0.1	−0.4	0.0	−0.3
Bayona	42 07N	8 51W	+0035	+0050	+0100	+0115	−0.3	−0.3	−0.2	−0.1
La Guardia	41 54N	8 53W	+0040	+0055	+0105	+0120	−0.5	−0.4	−0.3	−0.2

PORTUGAL *Time zone UT*

Location	Lat	Long	High Water		Low Water		MHWS	MHWN	MLWN	MLWS
LISBOA	38 42N	9 07W	0400 and 1600	0900 and 2100	0400 and 1600	0900 and 2100	3.8	3.0	1.5	0.6
Standard port										
Viana do Castelo	41 41N	8 50W	−0020	0000	+0010	+0015	−0.3	−0.3	−0.2	−0.1
Esposende	41 32N	8 47W	−0020	0000	+0010	+0015	−0.6	−0.5	−0.2	−0.1

Location	Lat	Long	High Water		Low Water		MHWS	MHWN	MLWN	MLWS
Povoa de Varzim	41 22N	8 46W	−0020	0000	+0010	+0015	−0.3	−0.3	−0.1	−0.1
Porto de Leixoes	41 11N	8 42W	−0025	−0010	0000	+0010	−0.3	−0.3	−0.2	−0.1
Rio Douro										
Entrance	41 09N	8 40W	−0010	+0005	+0015	+0025	−0.6	−0.4	−0.1	+0.1
Oporto (Porto)	41 08N	8 37W	+0002	+0002	+0040	+0040	−0.5	−0.4	−0.2	0.0
Porto de Aveiro	40 39N	8 45W	+0005	+0010	+0010	+0015	−0.5	−0.4	−0.1	0.0
Figueira da Foz	40 09N	8 51W	−0015	0000	+0010	+0020	−0.4	−0.4	−0.1	−0.1
Nazaré (Pederneira)	39 35N	9 04W	−0030	−0015	−0005	+0005	−0.5	−0.4	−0.1	0.0
Peniche	39 21N	9 22W	−0035	−0015	−0005	0000	−0.3	−0.4	−0.1	0.0
Ericeira	38 58N	9 25W	−0040	−0025	−0010	−0010	−0.4	−0.3	−0.1	0.0
River Tagus (Rio Tejo)										
Cascais	38 42N	9 25W	−0040	−0025	−0015	−0010	−0.3	−0.2	0.0	+0.1
Paco de Arcos	38 41N	9 18W	−0020	−0030	−0005	−0005	−0.4	−0.4	−0.2	−0.1
Pedroucos	38 42N	9 13W	−0010	−0015	0000	0000	−0.3	−0.2	−0.1	0.0
Sesimbra	38 26N	9 07W	−0045	−0030	−0020	−0010	−0.4	−0.4	−0.1	0.0
Setubal	38 30N	8 54W	−0020	−0015	−0005	+0005	−0.4	−0.3	−0.1	−0.1
Porto de Sines	37 57N	8 53W	−0050	−0030	−0020	−0010	−0.4	−0.4	−0.1	0.0
Milfontes	37 43N	8 47W	−0040	−0030	*No data*	*No data*	−0.1	−0.1	0.0	+0.1
Arrifana	37 17N	8 52W	−0030	−0020	*No data*	*No data*	−0.1	0.0	−0.1	+0.1
Enseada de Belixe	37 01N	8 58W	−0050	−0030	−0020	−0015	+0.3	+0.2	+0.2	+0.2
Lagos	37 06N	8 40W	−0100	−0040	−0030	−0025	−0.4	−0.4	−0.1	0.0
Portimao	37 07N	8 32W	−0100	−0040	−0030	−0025	−0.5	−0.4	−0.1	+0.1
Ponta do Altar	37 06N	8 31W	−0100	−0040	−0030	−0025	−0.3	−0.3	−0.1	0.0
Enseada de Albufeira	37 05N	8 15W	−0035	+0015	−0005	0000	−0.2	−0.2	0.0	+0.1
Porto de Faro-Olhao	36 59N	7 52W	−0050	−0030	−0015	+0005	−0.4	−0.4	−0.1	0.0
Rio Guadiana										
Vila Real de Santo António	37 12N	7 25W	−0050	−0015	−0010	0000	−0.4	−0.4	−0.1	+0.1

			0500	1000	0500	1100				
LISBOA	38 42N	9 07W	and	and	and	and	**3.8**	**3.0**	**1.5**	**0.6**
Standard port			1700	2200	1700	2300				

SPAIN *Time zone −0100*

Ayamonte	37 13N	7 25W	+0005	+0015	+0025	+0045	−0.7	−0.6	−0.1	−0.2
Ria de Huelva										
Bar	37 08N	6 52W	0000	+0015	+0035	+0030	−0.1	−0.6	−0.1	−0.4
Rio Guadalquivir										
Bar (Chipiona)	36 45N	6 26W	−0005	+0005	+0020	+0030	−0.7	−0.5	−0.2	−0.1
Bonanza	36 48N	6 20W	+0025	+0040	+0100	+0120	−0.8	−0.7	−0.5	−0.2
Corta de los Jerónimos	37 08N	6 06W	+0210	+0230	+0255	+0345	−1.2	−0.9	−0.5	−0.1
Sevilla	37 23N	6 00W	+0400	+0430	+0510	+0545	−1.8	−1.3	−0.7	−0.7
Bahia de Cadiz										
Rota	36 37N	6 21W	−0010	+0010	+0025	+0015	−0.7	−0.6	−0.3	−0.1
Puerto de Santa Maria	36 36N	6 13W	+0006	+0006	+0027	+0027	−0.6	−0.4	−0.4	−0.1
La Carraca	36 30N	6 11W	+0020	+0050	+0100	+0040	−0.5	−0.4	−0.1	0.0
Cabo Trafalgar	36 11N	6 02W	−0008	−0006	−0003	−0001	−1.0	−0.7	−0.4	−0.2
Barbate	36 11N	5 56W	−0012	−0010	−0010	−0012	−0.8	−0.9	−0.4	−0.4
Punta Camarinal	36 05N	5 48W	−0014	−0012	−0015	−0015	−1.3	−1.0	−0.5	−0.3

			0000	0700	0100	0600				
GIBRALTAR (UK)	36 08N	5 21W	and	and	and	and	**1.0**	**0.7**	**0.3**	**0.1**
Standard port. Time zone −0100			1200	1900	1300	1800				
Tarifa	36 00N	5 36W	−0038	−0038	−0042	−0042	+0.3	+0.3	+0.2	+0.1
Punta Carnero	36 04N	5 26W	−0010	−0010	0000	0000	0.0	+0.1	+0.1	+0.1
Algeciras	36 07N	5 27W	−0010	−0010	−0010	−0010	+0.1	+0.2	+0.1	+0.1
Ceuta (to Spain)	35 53N	5 16W	−0045	−0045	−0050	−0050	0.0	+0.1	+0.1	+0.1
Morocco, Tangier (*Time UT*)	35 47N	5 48W	−0030	−0030	−0020	−0020	+1.3	+1.0	+0.5	+0.3

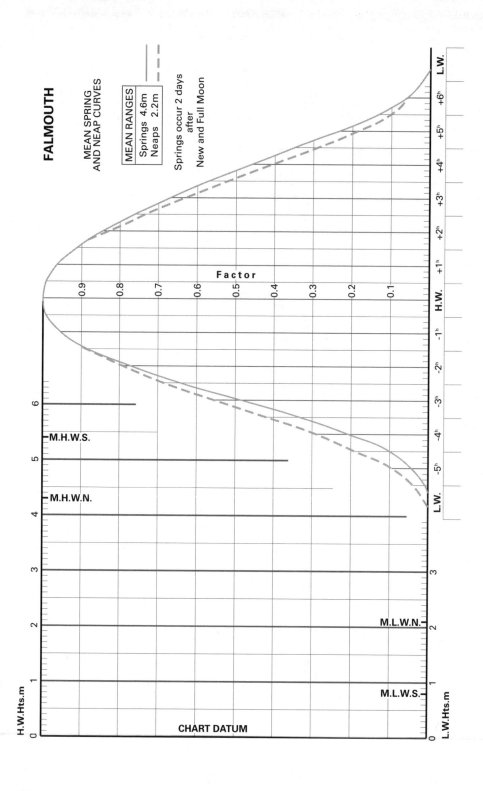

FALMOUTH

MEAN SPRING
AND NEAP CURVES

MEAN RANGES	
Springs	4.6m
Neaps	2.2m

Springs occur 2 days
after
New and Full Moon

Factor

FALMOUTH
LAT 50°09'N   LONG 5°03'W
TIMES AND HEIGHTS OF HIGH AND LOW WATERS

Dates in amber are **SPRINGS**
Dates in yellow are **NEAPS**

2011

JANUARY

Day	Time m	Time m	Time m	Time m	Day	Time m	Time m	Time m	Time m
1	0215 4.7	0859 1.7	SA 1444 4.7	2130 1.6	16	0141 4.4	0819 2.0	SU 1416 4.4	2047 1.8
2	0315 4.9	1001 1.5	SU 1543 4.8	2226 1.4	17	0248 4.6	0923 1.7	M 1520 4.6	2148 1.5
3	0407 5.1	1054 1.3	M 1633 4.9	2315 1.2	18	0343 4.9	1021 1.4	TU 1613 4.9	2243 1.3
4	0453 5.2	1141 1.1	TU 1717 5.0	● 2359 1.1	19	0432 5.2	1114 1.1	W 1701 5.1	○ 2334 1.0
5	0533 5.3	1225 1.0	W 1758 5.0		20	0517 5.4	1203 0.8	TH 1749 5.2	
6	0040 1.1	0614 5.3	TH 1304 1.0	1836 5.0	21	0021 0.8	0604 5.6	F 1250 0.6	1835 5.3
7	0117 1.1	0649 5.3	F 1339 1.1	1910 5.0	22	0107 0.6	0651 5.6	SA 1334 0.5	1921 5.3
8	0149 1.2	0723 5.2	SA 1411 1.2	1942 4.9	23	0149 0.6	0736 5.6	SU 1416 0.5	2004 5.3
9	0218 1.4	0755 5.1	SU 1439 1.4	2016 4.8	24	0229 0.7	0821 5.5	M 1456 0.7	2047 5.3
10	0244 1.5	0829 5.0	M 1506 1.5	2051 4.7	25	0309 0.9	0904 5.3	TU 1535 1.0	2129 5.0
11	0310 1.7	0904 4.8	TU 1534 1.7	2129 4.5	26	0349 1.2	0949 5.0	W 1617 1.4	● 2216 4.7
12	0340 1.9	0943 4.6	W 1609 1.9	◑ 2213 4.4	27	0436 1.5	1041 4.7	TH 1708 1.7	2316 4.5
13	0424 2.1	1032 4.4	TH 1703 2.1	2309 4.2	28	0537 1.9	1153 4.4	F 1819 1.9	
14	0536 2.3	1135 4.2	F 1823 2.2		29	0036 4.3	0706 2.1	SA 1316 4.3	1959 2.1
15	0020 4.2	0704 2.2	SA 1254 4.2	1940 2.1	30	0154 4.4	0846 2.0	SU 1430 4.3	2119 1.8
					31	0259 4.6	0953 1.6	M 1531 4.5	2216 1.5

FEBRUARY

Day	Time m	Time m	Time m	Time m	Day	Time m	Time m	Time m	Time m
1	0353 4.9	1044 1.4	TU 1620 4.8	2304 1.3	16	0319 4.9	1002 1.3	W 1554 4.8	2226 1.2
2	0437 5.1	1129 1.1	W 1702 4.9	2346 1.1	17	0411 5.2	1057 0.9	TH 1643 5.1	2318 0.8
3	0516 5.3	1210 0.9	TH 1739 5.0		18	0500 5.5	1147 0.5	F 1730 5.3	○
4	0024 0.9	0553 5.3	F 1247 0.8	1814 5.1	19	0006 0.5	0547 5.7	SA 1234 0.3	1817 5.4
5	0059 0.9	0628 5.3	SA 1319 0.9	1846 5.1	20	0051 0.3	0634 5.7	SU 1317 0.2	1902 5.5
6	0128 1.0	0701 5.3	SU 1346 1.0	1917 5.0	21	0133 0.2	0719 5.7	M 1357 0.2	1944 5.5
7	0153 1.1	0731 5.2	M 1409 1.2	1948 4.9	22	0212 0.4	0802 5.6	TU 1435 0.5	2023 5.3
8	0214 1.3	0802 5.0	TU 1430 1.3	2018 4.8	23	0249 0.7	0842 5.3	W 1512 0.9	2101 5.1
9	0233 1.5	0831 4.8	W 1451 1.5	2048 4.6	24	0327 1.1	0924 4.9	TH 1550 1.4	◑ 2141 4.7
10	0258 1.6	0902 4.6	TH 1519 1.6	2123 4.5	25	0410 1.5	1010 4.5	F 1636 1.7	2234 4.4
11	0333 1.8	0943 4.4	F 1600 1.9	◑ 2213 4.3	26	0506 1.9	1125 4.1	SA 1741 2.2	
12	0426 2.1	1041 4.2	SA 1707 2.2	2324 4.2	27	0008 4.2	0632 2.2	SU 1300 4.0	1935 2.3
13	0607 2.2	1202 4.1	SU 1857 2.2		28	0134 4.2	0835 2.0	M 1415 4.2	2105 2.0
14	0048 4.2	0744 2.1	M 1340 4.2	2018 2.1					
15	0216 4.5	0858 1.7	TU 1457 4.5	2127 1.5					

MARCH

Day	Time m	Time m	Time m	Time m	Day	Time m	Time m	Time m	Time m
1	0240 4.5	0939 1.6	TU 1514 4.4	2159 1.5	16	0144 4.5	0835 1.6	W 1434 4.5	2104 1.5
2	0332 4.8	1026 1.3	W 1600 4.7	2244 1.3	17	0254 4.9	0940 1.2	TH 1531 4.8	2205 1.1
3	0415 5.0	1108 1.0	TH 1640 4.9	2324 1.0	18	0348 5.2	1035 0.7	F 1621 5.2	2257 0.7
4	0453 5.2	1146 0.8	F 1713 5.0	●	19	0438 5.5	1125 0.4	SA 1707 5.4	○ 2345 0.3
5	0001 0.8	0527 5.3	SA 1222 0.8	1746 5.1	20	0524 5.7	1211 0.2	SU 1753 5.5	
6	0034 0.8	0601 5.3	SU 1252 0.8	1819 5.1	21	0030 0.2	0612 5.7	M 1255 0.2	1837 5.6
7	0102 0.9	0634 5.2	M 1317 0.9	1849 5.1	22	0112 0.2	0658 5.7	TU 1335 0.2	1919 5.5
8	0125 1.0	0706 5.1	TU 1338 1.0	1919 5.0	23	0151 0.3	0740 5.5	W 1413 0.5	1958 5.4
9	0144 1.1	0734 5.0	W 1358 1.2	1947 4.9	24	0229 0.6	0821 5.2	TH 1450 0.9	2034 5.1
10	0204 1.3	0801 4.8	TH 1419 1.4	2013 4.8	25	0307 1.1	0901 4.8	F 1528 1.4	2109 4.7
11	0229 1.5	0830 4.6	F 1447 1.5	2046 4.6	26	0350 1.5	0945 4.4	SA 1613 1.8	◑ 2155 4.4
12	0304 1.6	0911 4.4	SA 1526 1.8	◑ 2135 4.4	27	0445 1.9	1043 4.0	SU 1715 2.2	2338 4.1
13	0353 1.9	1013 4.2	SU 1626 2.1	2245 4.2	28	0603 2.2	1240 3.9	M 1854 2.3	
14	0522 2.1	1132 4.0	M 1820 2.2		29	0107 4.2	0804 2.0	TU 1350 4.1	2033 2.0
15	0010 4.2	0715 2.0	TU 1309 4.2	1952 1.9	30	0212 4.4	0909 1.7	W 1446 4.4	2129 1.6
					31	0302 4.7	0956 1.4	TH 1530 4.6	2214 1.4

APRIL

Day	Time m	Time m	Time m	Time m	Day	Time m	Time m	Time m	Time m
1	0345 4.9	1037 1.1	F 1608 4.9	2254 1.1	16	0321 5.2	1009 0.7	SA 1555 5.2	2232 0.7
2	0423 5.1	1115 0.9	SA 1643 5.0	2330 0.9	17	0413 5.4	1100 0.4	SU 1641 5.4	2321 0.4
3	0459 5.2	1149 0.9	SU 1716 5.1		18	0501 5.5	1147 0.3	M 1727 5.5	○
4	0003 0.9	0532 5.2	M 1219 0.9	1750 5.1	19	0007 0.3	0549 5.6	TU 1232 0.3	1813 5.6
5	0032 0.9	0607 5.1	TU 1245 1.0	1823 5.1	20	0051 0.3	0636 5.5	W 1313 0.4	1855 5.5
6	0057 1.0	0640 5.1	W 1309 1.1	1852 5.1	21	0132 0.4	0721 5.5	TH 1353 0.7	1934 5.3
7	0119 1.1	0711 4.9	TH 1332 1.2	1921 5.0	22	0212 0.7	0803 5.2	F 1432 1.0	2011 5.1
8	0143 1.2	0739 4.8	F 1358 1.3	1950 4.9	23	0252 1.1	0844 4.7	SA 1511 1.4	2048 4.8
9	0211 1.4	0812 4.6	SA 1429 1.5	2025 4.7	24	0336 1.5	0929 4.4	SU 1556 1.7	2131 4.5
10	0248 1.5	0856 4.4	SU 1510 1.7	2115 4.5	25	0427 1.8	1036 4.1	M 1652 2.1	◑ 2245 4.3
11	0340 1.7	0956 4.2	M 1612 2.0	◑ 2222 4.4	26	0533 2.0	1204 4.0	TU 1805 2.2	
12	0505 1.9	1111 4.1	TU 1752 2.1	2342 4.4	27	0025 4.2	0658 2.0	W 1311 4.1	1933 2.1
13	0648 1.8	1242 4.2	W 1924 1.8		28	0131 4.3	0817 1.8	TH 1406 4.3	2041 1.8
14	0110 4.6	0807 1.5	TH 1404 4.5	2037 1.5	29	0223 4.5	0911 1.5	F 1451 4.6	2131 1.5
15	0224 4.9	0912 1.1	F 1503 4.9	2138 1.1	30	0308 4.7	0955 1.4	SA 1531 4.8	2214 1.4

Chart Datum: 2·91 metres below Ordnance Datum (Newlyn)
HAT is 5·8 metres above Chart Datum

TIDES

FALMOUTH
LAT 50°09'N   LONG 5°03'W
TIMES AND HEIGHTS OF HIGH AND LOW WATERS

2011

TIME ZONE (UT)
For Summer Time add ONE hour in **non-shaded areas**

Dates in amber are **SPRINGS**
Dates in yellow are NEAPS

MAY

Time	m		Time	m
1 0349	4.9	**16** 0348	5.2
1035	1.2	1034	0.7
SU 1609	4.9	M 1616	5.3
2253	1.2	2258	0.7
2 0428	5.0	**17** 0440	5.3
1111	1.1	1124	0.6
M 1646	5.0	TU 1704	5.4
2328	1.1	○ 2347	0.5
3 0506	5.0	**18** 0528	5.3
1144	1.1	1210	0.6
TU 1721	5.1	W 1750	5.4
●			
4 0001	1.1	**19** 0033	0.5
0543	5.0	0618	5.3
W 1215	1.1	TH 1255	0.7
1757	5.1	1835	5.4
5 0032	1.1	**20** 0117	0.6
0619	5.0	0705	5.1
TH 1245	1.1	F 1337	0.8
1830	5.1	1917	5.3
6 0101	1.1	**21** 0159	0.8
0653	4.9	0749	4.9
F 1315	1.2	SA 1417	1.1
1902	5.1	1955	5.1
7 0132	1.2	**22** 0239	1.1
0726	4.8	0830	4.7
SA 1347	1.3	SU 1457	1.4
1935	5.0	2031	4.9
8 0206	1.3	**23** 0321	1.4
0804	4.7	0911	4.5
SU 1424	1.5	M 1539	1.6
2016	4.9	2110	4.7
9 0248	1.5	**24** 0406	1.6
0851	4.5	0958	4.3
M 1509	1.6	TU 1625	1.8
2105	4.7	◑ 2159	4.5
10 0341	1.5	**25** 0457	1.8
0947	4.4	1101	4.2
TU 1610	1.8	W 1702	2.0
◑ 2206	4.6	2307	4.3
11 0453	1.7	**26** 0556	1.9
1056	4.3	1209	4.1
W 1728	1.8	TH 1824	2.1
2318	4.6		
12 0617	1.6	**27** 0025	4.3
1215	4.4	0700	1.9
TH 1851	1.7	F 1310	4.3
		1930	2.0
13 0037	4.6	**28** 0130	4.4
0734	1.5	0803	1.8
F 1330	4.6	SA 1403	4.4
2005	1.5	2032	1.8
14 0151	4.8	**29** 0223	4.5
0841	1.2	0859	1.6
SA 1432	4.8	SU 1450	4.6
2109	1.2	2125	1.6
15 0253	5.0	**30** 0311	4.7
0940	0.9	0946	1.5
SU 1526	5.1	M 1534	4.8
2206	0.9	2211	1.5
		31 0357	4.8
		1030	1.4
		TU 1616	4.9
		2253	1.3

JUNE

Time	m		Time	m
1 0440	4.9	**16** 0512	5.1
1110	1.2	1155	0.8
W 1656	5.0	TH 1732	5.3
● 2333	1.2		
2 0520	4.9	**17** 0019	0.7
1149	1.2	0602	5.1
TH 1734	5.1	F 1241	0.8
		1818	5.3
3 0011	1.1	**18** 0104	0.7
0601	4.9	0648	5.0
F 1228	1.1	SA 1323	0.9
1813	5.1	1900	5.3
4 0050	1.1	**19** 0146	0.8
0641	4.9	0731	4.9
SA 1306	1.2	SU 1403	1.0
1850	5.2	1937	5.2
5 0128	1.1	**20** 0225	1.0
0721	4.9	0808	4.8
SU 1344	1.2	M 1440	1.2
1928	5.1	2011	5.0
6 0208	1.1	**21** 0301	1.2
0802	4.8	0843	4.6
M 1425	1.3	TU 1515	1.5
2011	5.1	2046	4.8
7 0251	1.2	**22** 0337	1.5
0848	4.7	0920	4.5
TU 1510	1.4	W 1552	1.6
2059	5.0	2123	4.7
8 0340	1.3	**23** 0416	1.6
0939	4.6	1001	4.4
W 1602	1.5	TH 1633	1.8
2152	4.9	◑ 2208	4.5
9 0436	1.5	**24** 0501	1.8
1038	4.5	1053	4.3
TH 1703	1.6	F 1725	2.0
◑ 2255	4.7	2303	4.3
10 0543	1.5	**25** 0556	1.9
1146	4.5	1155	4.2
F 1814	1.6	SA 1826	2.1
11 0007	4.7	**26** 0012	4.3
0657	1.6	0658	1.9
SA 1257	4.6	SU 1302	4.3
1930	1.6	1931	2.0
12 0121	4.7	**27** 0128	4.3
0809	1.5	0801	1.8
SU 1402	4.7	M 1405	4.4
2040	1.5	2034	1.8
13 0228	4.8	**28** 0232	4.4
0914	1.3	0859	1.7
M 1501	4.9	TU 1459	4.6
2143	1.2	2130	1.6
14 0327	4.6	**29** 0326	4.6
1013	1.1	0952	1.5
TU 1556	5.1	W 1548	4.8
2240	1.0	2221	1.5
15 0422	5.0	**30** 0415	4.8
1106	0.9	1042	1.3
W 1645	5.2	TH 1633	5.0
○ 2331	0.8	2309	1.2

JULY

Time	m		Time	m
1 0500	4.9	**16** 0008	0.8
1129	1.2	0545	5.0
F 1714	5.1	SA 1227	0.9
● 2355	1.0	1759	5.3
2 0545	5.0	**17** 0051	0.7
1214	1.0	0628	5.0
SA 1757	5.2	SU 1307	0.8
		1838	5.3
3 0040	0.9	**18** 0129	0.8
0630	5.0	0706	5.0
SU 1258	1.0	M 1344	0.9
1840	5.3	1913	5.2
4 0123	0.8	**19** 0204	0.9
0714	5.0	0738	4.9
M 1340	0.9	TU 1416	1.1
1922	5.3	1945	5.1
5 0205	0.8	**20** 0234	1.1
0757	5.0	0809	4.8
TU 1421	1.0	W 1445	1.3
2005	5.3	2016	5.0
6 0246	0.9	**21** 0302	1.3
0840	5.0	0841	4.6
W 1502	1.1	TH 1512	1.5
2050	5.2	2049	4.8
7 0328	1.0	**22** 0329	1.5
0926	4.9	0918	4.5
TH 1546	1.2	F 1540	1.7
2138	5.0	2125	4.6
8 0415	1.3	**23** 0400	1.7
1016	4.7	0958	4.4
F 1637	1.5	SA 1616	1.9
◑ 2231	4.8	◑ 2208	4.4
9 0510	1.5	**24** 0445	1.9
1116	4.6	1050	4.2
SA 1738	1.6	SU 1717	2.1
2339	4.6	2304	4.2
10 0619	1.6	**25** 0557	2.1
1226	4.5	1156	4.2
SU 1856	1.7	M 1839	2.2
11 0056	4.5	**26** 0019	4.1
0740	1.7	0713	2.1
M 1339	4.6	TU 1316	4.3
2018	1.7	1952	2.0
12 0210	4.5	**27** 0152	4.2
0856	1.5	0822	1.9
TU 1444	4.7	W 1427	4.5
2129	1.5	2057	1.7
13 0314	4.7	**28** 0300	4.5
1000	1.4	0923	1.6
W 1541	4.9	TH 1522	4.8
2229	1.3	2156	1.5
14 0410	4.8	**29** 0353	4.7
1054	1.2	1019	1.4
TH 1631	5.1	F 1610	5.0
2321	1.0	2250	1.2
15 0500	4.9	**30** 0441	4.9
1143	1.0	1111	1.1
F 1716	5.3	SA 1655	5.2
○		● 2340	0.9
		31 0526	5.1
		1200	0.8
		SU 1741	5.4

AUGUST

Time	m		Time	m
1 0026	0.6	**16** 0106	0.7
0613	5.2	0634	5.1
M 1245	0.7	TU 1319	0.9
1826	5.5	1844	5.3
2 0111	0.5	**17** 0136	0.9
0658	5.3	0705	5.0
TU 1328	0.6	W 1347	1.0
1910	5.5	1915	5.2
3 0152	0.5	**18** 0201	1.1
0741	5.3	0735	5.0
W 1408	0.6	TH 1410	1.2
1953	5.5	1945	5.0
4 0231	0.6	**19** 0222	1.3
0823	5.2	0806	4.8
TH 1447	0.8	F 1430	1.4
2035	5.3	2015	4.9
5 0310	0.8	**20** 0241	1.5
0905	5.0	0837	4.7
F 1527	1.1	SA 1450	1.6
2119	5.1	2047	4.6
6 0351	1.2	**21** 0304	1.6
0950	4.8	0910	4.5
SA 1612	1.4	SU 1518	1.8
◑ 2207	4.8	◑ 2124	4.4
7 0439	1.5	**22** 0339	1.9
1046	4.6	0958	4.3
SU 1708	1.7	M 1604	2.1
2312	4.4	2218	4.2
8 0545	1.8	**23** 0438	2.2
1202	4.4	1102	4.2
M 1828	2.0	TU 1743	2.3
		2331	4.1
9 0039	4.2	**24** 0632	2.2
0719	2.0	1223	4.2
TU 1323	4.4	W 1920	2.2
2008	1.9		
10 0201	4.3	**25** 0111	4.1
0848	1.8	0753	2.0
W 1432	4.6	TH 1354	4.4
2123	1.6	2032	1.8
11 0307	4.5	**26** 0237	4.4
0951	1.5	0900	1.6
TH 1528	4.9	F 1457	4.8
2220	1.3	2134	1.5
12 0400	4.7	**27** 0332	4.7
1043	1.2	0959	1.3
F 1616	5.1	SA 1548	5.1
2308	1.0	2229	1.0
13 0444	4.9	**28** 0420	5.0
1127	1.0	1052	0.9
SA 1658	5.3	SU 1635	5.4
○ 2351	0.8	2320	0.7
14 0523	5.0	**29** 0505	5.2
1209	0.8	1141	0.6
SU 1735	5.3	M 1719	5.6
		●	
15 0030	0.7	**30** 0007	0.4
0601	5.1	0550	5.4
M 1246	0.8	TU 1226	0.4
1812	5.3	1805	5.7
		31 0051	0.3
		0636	5.5
		W 1309	0.4
		1850	5.7

Chart Datum: 2·91 metres below Ordnance Datum (Newlyn)
HAT is 5·8 metres above Chart Datum

TIME ZONE (UT)
For Summer Time add ONE hour in **non-shaded areas**

FALMOUTH
LAT 50°09'N   LONG 5°03'W
TIMES AND HEIGHTS OF HIGH AND LOW WATERS

Dates in amber are **SPRINGS**
Dates in yellow are **NEAPS**

2011

SEPTEMBER

Time	m	Time	m
1 0132	0.3	**16** 0126	1.1
0719	5.5	0704	5.1
TH 1349	0.4	F 1336	1.2
1934	5.6	1916	5.1
2 0211	0.5	**17** 0145	1.3
0800	5.4	0733	5.0
F 1428	0.7	SA 1354	1.4
2016	5.4	1945	4.9
3 0249	0.8	**18** 0203	1.5
0841	5.2	0803	4.8
SA 1507	1.0	SU 1415	1.5
2058	5.0	2015	4.7
4 0328	1.3	**19** 0228	1.6
0925	4.9	0835	4.6
SU 1546	1.5	M 1445	1.7
☽ 2144	4.6	2052	4.5
5 0413	1.7	**20** 0302	1.9
1018	4.5	0921	4.4
M 1645	1.8	TU 1528	2.0
2251	4.3	☽ 2146	4.2
6 0518	2.1	**21** 0354	2.2
1143	4.3	1023	4.3
TU 1808	2.1	W 1647	2.3
		2258	4.1
7 0030	4.1	**22** 0548	2.3
0706	2.2	1142	4.3
W 1308	4.3	TH 1849	2.2
2002	2.0		
8 0153	4.2	**23** 0031	4.1
0838	2.0	0725	2.1
TH 1417	4.6	F 1315	4.5
2111	1.7	2006	1.8
9 0255	4.5	**24** 0210	4.4
0936	1.5	0836	1.7
F 1512	4.8	SA 1429	4.8
2202	1.4	2110	1.4
10 0343	4.8	**25** 0307	4.8
1023	1.3	0936	1.3
SA 1556	1.5	SU 1522	5.2
2246	1.0	2205	1.0
11 0423	5.0	**26** 0356	5.1
1105	1.0	1029	0.9
SU 1635	5.3	M 1610	5.5
2326	0.8	2256	0.6
12 0458	5.1	**27** 0441	5.4
1143	0.8	1118	0.6
M 1710	5.3	TU 1657	5.6
○		● 2343	0.4
13 0003	0.8	**28** 0525	5.5
0529	5.2	1204	0.4
TU 1218	0.8	W 1743	5.7
1743	5.3		
14 0036	0.8	**29** 0027	0.3
0601	5.2	0610	5.6
W 1249	0.9	TH 1247	0.3
1815	5.3	1829	5.7
15 0103	0.9	**30** 0110	0.4
0633	5.2	0654	5.6
TH 1315	1.0	F 1329	0.4
1845	5.2	1914	5.6

OCTOBER

Time	m	Time	m
1 0149	0.6	**16** 0115	1.3
0736	5.5	0707	5.1
SA 1409	0.7	SU 1329	1.4
1957	5.3	1921	4.9
2 0228	1.0	**17** 0138	1.5
0818	5.2	0736	5.0
SU 1449	1.1	M 1354	1.5
2039	5.0	1952	4.7
3 0308	1.4	**18** 0206	1.6
0901	4.9	0810	4.8
M 1533	1.5	TU 1427	1.7
2126	4.6	2032	4.5
4 0354	1.8	**19** 0243	1.8
0953	4.6	0856	4.6
TU 1628	1.9	W 1512	1.9
☽ 2236	4.2	2126	4.3
5 0456	2.2	**20** 0336	2.1
1120	4.3	0956	4.5
W 1748	2.2	TH 1624	2.1
		☽ 2234	4.2
6 0015	4.1	**21** 0507	2.3
0637	2.3	1109	4.4
TH 1246	4.3	F 1814	2.1
1936	2.1	2358	4.3
7 0131	4.2	**22** 0651	2.1
0810	2.1	1233	4.6
F 1352	4.5	SA 1935	1.8
2044	1.8		
8 0229	4.5	**23** 0132	4.5
0907	1.7	0806	1.7
SA 1444	4.8	SU 1353	4.9
2133	1.5	2041	1.5
9 0314	4.8	**24** 0236	4.9
0954	1.4	0908	1.4
SU 1526	5.0	M 1453	5.2
2216	1.2	2138	1.1
10 0354	5.0	**25** 0327	5.2
1035	1.2	1003	1.0
M 1606	5.2	TU 1545	5.4
2255	1.0	2230	0.7
11 0428	5.1	**26** 0415	5.4
1112	1.0	1054	0.7
TU 1641	5.3	W 1634	5.6
2330	1.0	● 2318	0.5
12 0500	5.2	**27** 0501	5.6
1147	1.0	1141	0.5
W 1714	5.3	TH 1720	5.7
○			
13 0002	1.0	**28** 0004	0.5
0531	5.3	0547	5.7
TH 1218	1.0	F 1227	0.5
1747	5.3	1808	5.6
14 0030	1.1	**29** 0048	0.5
0604	5.3	0632	5.7
F 1244	1.1	SA 1310	0.6
1820	5.2	1855	5.5
15 0053	1.2	**30** 0130	0.8
0636	5.3	0716	5.5
SA 1307	1.3	SU 1353	0.8
1851	5.1	1940	5.2
		31 0211	1.1
		0759	5.3
		M 1435	1.2
		2026	4.9

NOVEMBER

Time	m	Time	m
1 0252	1.5	**16** 0159	1.5
0842	5.0	0756	5.0
TU 1520	1.5	W 1423	1.6
2113	4.6	2022	4.7
2 0338	1.8	**17** 0239	1.7
0932	4.7	0841	4.8
W 1611	1.8	TH 1509	1.7
◐ 2215	4.3	2112	4.5
3 0433	2.1	**18** 0330	1.9
1043	4.5	0937	4.7
TH 1715	2.1	F 1610	1.9
2340	4.2	◑ 2214	4.4
4 0546	2.3	**19** 0439	2.1
1206	4.4	1042	4.6
F 1839	2.1	SA 1732	1.9
		2328	4.4
5 0051	4.2	**20** 0607	2.0
0716	2.2	1157	4.7
SA 1312	4.5	SU 1856	1.8
1956	2.0		
6 0148	4.4	**21** 0047	4.6
0823	2.0	0729	1.8
SU 1406	4.7	M 1314	4.8
2052	1.7	2007	1.5
7 0237	4.7	**22** 0159	4.8
0915	1.7	0837	1.5
M 1452	4.9	TU 1421	5.0
2138	1.5	2109	1.3
8 0317	4.9	**23** 0258	5.1
0959	1.6	0937	1.2
TU 1533	5.0	W 1519	5.3
2218	1.4	2205	1.0
9 0356	5.1	**24** 0351	5.3
1038	1.3	1031	0.9
W 1611	5.1	TH 1613	5.4
2255	1.3	2257	0.8
10 0431	5.2	**25** 0440	5.5
1114	1.3	1122	0.7
TH 1648	5.2	F 1703	5.5
○ 2328	1.2	● 2345	0.7
11 0506	5.3	**26** 0527	5.6
1147	1.2	1210	0.7
F 1723	5.2	SA 1753	5.5
2358	1.2		
12 0539	5.3	**27** 0031	0.7
1218	1.3	0615	5.6
SA 1759	5.1	SU 1257	0.7
		1841	5.4
13 0028	1.3	**28** 0116	0.9
0615	5.2	0701	5.5
SU 1247	1.3	M 1341	0.8
1834	5.0	1927	5.2
14 0056	1.4	**29** 0158	1.1
0647	5.0	0745	5.4
M 1316	1.4	TU 1423	1.1
1907	4.9	2012	5.0
15 0126	1.5	**30** 0239	1.4
0720	5.1	0827	5.2
TU 1347	1.5	W 1506	1.4
1941	4.8	2055	4.7

DECEMBER

Time	m	Time	m
1 0320	1.6	**16** 0237	1.5
0908	4.9	0833	5.1
TH 1549	1.6	F 1506	1.5
2140	4.5	2102	4.7
2 0405	1.9	**17** 0322	1.5
0954	4.7	0922	5.0
F 1638	1.9	SA 1555	1.5
◐ 2233	4.3	2154	4.6
3 0457	2.1	**18** 0416	1.7
1055	4.5	1019	4.8
SA 1734	2.1	SU 1655	1.7
2342	4.3	◑ 2257	4.7
4 0559	2.2	**19** 0523	1.8
1207	4.4	1125	4.7
SU 1839	2.1	M 1809	1.8
5 0049	4.3	**20** 0009	4.6
0711	2.2	0645	1.9
M 1312	4.6	TU 1239	4.7
1947	2.0	1930	1.7
6 0146	4.5	**21** 0124	4.7
0819	2.0	0806	1.7
TU 1408	4.6	W 1353	4.8
2046	1.8	2042	1.5
7 0237	4.7	**22** 0232	4.9
0914	1.8	0915	1.5
W 1457	4.7	TH 1459	4.9
2135	1.6	2145	1.2
8 0321	4.9	**23** 0331	5.1
1000	1.6	1015	1.2
TH 1542	4.9	F 1557	5.1
2217	1.5	2241	1.1
9 0403	5.1	**24** 0424	5.3
1042	1.5	1109	1.0
F 1624	5.0	SA 1650	5.2
2257	1.4	● 2332	0.9
10 0442	5.2	**25** 0512	5.5
1120	1.4	1159	0.8
SA 1704	5.0	SU 1741	5.3
○ 2334	1.3		
11 0520	5.2	**26** 0019	0.8
1157	1.3	0600	5.6
SU 1744	5.1	M 1246	0.7
		1828	5.3
12 0009	1.3	**27** 0104	0.8
0558	5.3	0645	5.5
M 1234	1.3	TU 1329	0.8
1823	5.0	1913	5.2
13 0045	1.3	**28** 0145	0.9
0635	5.3	0727	5.4
TU 1310	1.3	W 1409	0.9
1900	5.0	1952	5.1
14 0121	1.3	**29** 0223	1.1
0712	5.2	0805	5.3
W 1346	1.3	TH 1447	1.1
1936	4.9	2027	4.9
15 0158	1.4	**30** 0258	1.4
0750	5.2	0839	5.1
TH 1424	1.4	F 1522	1.4
2017	4.8	2100	4.7
		31 0333	1.5
		0913	4.9
		SA 1558	1.6
		2137	4.5

Chart Datum: 2·91 metres below Ordnance Datum (Newlyn)
HAT is 5·8 metres above Chart Datum

TIDES

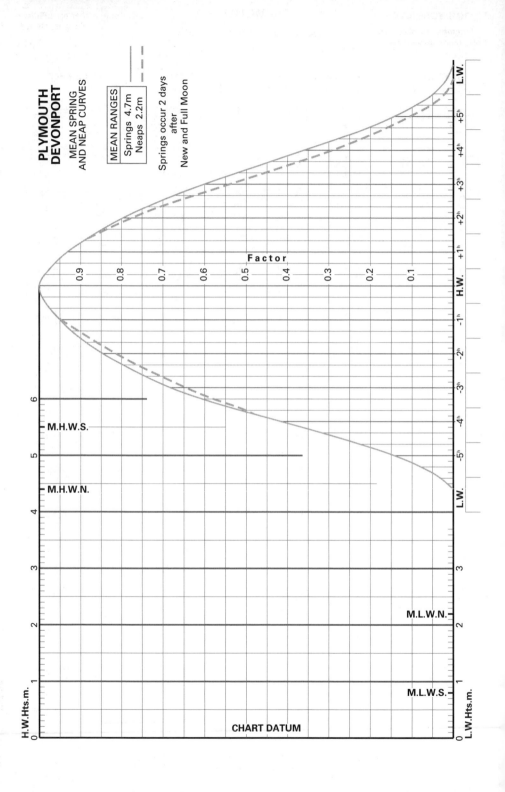

PLYMOUTH DEVONPORT

MEAN SPRING AND NEAP CURVES

MEAN RANGES
Springs 4.7m
Neaps 2.2m

Springs occur 2 days after New and Full Moon

Factor

0.9 0.8 0.7 0.6 0.5 0.4 0.3 0.2 0.1

H.W.Hts.m.

M.H.W.S.

M.H.W.N.

CHART DATUM

L.W.Hts.m.

M.L.W.N.

M.L.W.S.

H.W. +1ʰ +2ʰ +3ʰ +4ʰ +5ʰ L.W.

-1ʰ -2ʰ -3ʰ -4ʰ -5ʰ L.W.

TIME ZONE (UT)
For Summer Time add ONE hour in **non-shaded areas**

PLYMOUTH (DEVONPORT)
LAT 50°22'N   LONG 4°11'W
TIMES AND HEIGHTS OF HIGH AND LOW WATERS

Dates in amber are **SPRINGS**
Dates in yellow are **NEAPS**

2011

JANUARY

Day		Day	
1 SA 0244 4.8 / 0909 1.8 / 1514 4.8 / 2140 1.7		**16** SU 0209 4.5 / 0829 2.1 / 1447 4.5 / 2057 1.9	
2 SU 0346 5.0 / 1011 1.6 / 1614 4.9 / 2236 1.5		**17** M 0320 4.8 / 0933 1.8 / 1553 4.7 / 2157 1.6	
3 M 0439 5.2 / 1104 1.3 / 1706 5.0 / 2325 1.3		**18** TU 0416 5.0 / 1030 1.4 / 1647 5.0 / 2252 1.3	
4 TU 0526 5.3 / 1151 1.1 / 1751 5.1 / ●		**19** W 0505 5.3 / 1123 1.1 / 1736 5.2 / ○ 2343 1.0	
5 W 0009 1.1 / 0608 5.4 / 1235 1.0 / 1832 5.1		**20** TH 0553 5.5 / 1213 0.8 / 1823 5.3	
6 TH 0050 1.1 / 0646 5.4 / 1314 1.0 / 1908 5.1		**21** F 0031 0.8 / 1300 0.6 / 1909 5.4	
7 F 0127 1.1 / 0721 5.4 / 1349 1.1 / 1942 5.1		**22** SA 0116 0.6 / 0724 5.7 / 1344 0.5 / 1953 5.4	
8 SA 0159 1.2 / 0754 5.3 / 1421 1.2 / 2013 5.0		**23** SU 0159 0.6 / 0808 5.7 / 1425 0.5 / 2035 5.4	
9 SU 0228 1.4 / 0826 5.2 / 1449 1.4 / 2046 4.9		**24** M 0239 0.7 / 0851 5.6 / 1505 0.7 / 2116 5.3	
10 M 0255 1.6 / 0859 5.1 / 1516 1.6 / 2120 4.8		**25** TU 0318 0.9 / 0933 5.4 / 1544 1.0 / 2157 5.1	
11 TU 0320 1.8 / 0933 4.9 / 1544 1.8 / 2156 4.6		**26** W 0359 1.2 / 1017 5.1 / 1626 1.4 / 2242 4.8	
12 W 0350 2.0 / 1011 4.9 / 1619 2.0 / ◑ 2240 4.5		**27** TH 0446 1.6 / 1108 4.8 / 1717 1.8 / 2342 4.6	
13 TH 0433 2.2 / 1059 4.6 / 1713 2.2 / 2335 4.4		**28** F 0546 2.0 / 1218 4.5 / 1826 2.0	
14 F 0547 2.4 / 1200 4.4 / 1834 2.3		**29** SA 0102 4.4 / 0714 2.2 / 1343 4.4 / 2007 2.2	
15 SA 0046 4.3 / 0715 2.3 / 1321 4.4 / 1950 2.2		**30** SU 0222 4.4 / 0856 2.1 / 1500 4.4 / 2129 1.9	
		31 M 0330 4.7 / 1003 1.7 / 1602 4.7 / 2227 1.6	

FEBRUARY

Day		Day	
1 TU 0424 5.0 / 1055 1.4 / 1653 4.9 / 2314 1.3		**16** W 0351 5.0 / 1012 1.3 / 1627 4.9 / 2235 1.2	
2 W 0510 5.2 / 1140 1.1 / 1736 5.0 / 2356 1.1		**17** TH 0445 5.3 / 1107 0.9 / 1717 5.2 / 2328 0.8	
3 TH 0551 5.4 / 1220 0.9 / 1814 5.1 / ●		**18** F 0534 5.6 / 1157 0.5 / 1805 5.4 / ○	
4 F 0034 0.9 / 0627 5.4 / 1257 0.8 / 1847 5.2		**19** SA 0016 0.5 / 0621 5.8 / 1244 0.3 / 1850 5.5	
5 SA 0109 0.9 / 0700 5.4 / 1329 0.9 / 1919 5.2		**20** SU 0101 0.3 / 0707 5.8 / 1327 0.2 / 1934 5.6	
6 SU 0138 1.0 / 0732 5.4 / 1356 1.0 / 1949 5.1		**21** M 0142 0.3 / 0751 5.8 / 1407 0.2 / 2015 5.4	
7 M 0203 1.1 / 0803 5.3 / 1419 1.2 / 2019 5.0		**22** TU 0221 0.4 / 0832 5.7 / 1445 0.5 / 2053 5.4	
8 TU 0224 1.2 / 0832 5.1 / 1440 1.3 / 2048 4.9		**23** W 0259 0.7 / 0912 5.4 / 1521 0.9 / 2130 5.2	
9 W 0244 1.5 / 0901 4.9 / 1501 1.5 / 2117 4.8		**24** TH 0337 1.1 / 0951 5.0 / 1600 1.4 / ◑ 2208 4.8	
10 TH 0308 1.7 / 0931 4.7 / 1529 1.7 / 2151 4.6		**25** F 0420 1.6 / 1036 4.6 / 1646 1.8 / 2259 4.5	
11 F 0343 1.9 / 1012 4.5 / 1610 2.0 / ◑ 2240 4.4		**26** SA 0516 2.0 / 1149 4.2 / 1749 2.3	
12 SA 0436 2.2 / 1111 4.3 / 1717 2.3 / 2349 4.3		**27** SU 0033 4.3 / 0639 2.3 / 1327 4.1 / 1942 2.4	
13 SU 0619 2.4 / 1258 4.2 / 1908 2.3		**28** M 0202 4.3 / 0846 2.1 / 1445 4.3 / 2115 2.1	
14 M 0115 4.3 / 0755 2.2 / 1408 4.3 / 2028 2.0			
15 TU 0245 4.6 / 0909 1.8 / 1529 4.6 / 2136 1.6			

MARCH

Day		Day	
1 TU 0311 4.6 / 0950 1.7 / 1546 4.5 / 2210 1.6		**16** W 0211 4.6 / 0845 1.7 / 1504 4.6 / 2114 1.6	
2 W 0404 4.9 / 1037 1.3 / 1633 4.8 / 2255 1.3		**17** TH 0324 5.0 / 0950 1.2 / 1603 4.9 / 2214 1.1	
3 TH 0448 5.1 / 1119 1.0 / 1713 5.0 / 2335 1.0		**18** F 0420 5.3 / 1045 0.7 / 1654 5.2 / 2307 0.7	
4 F 0527 5.3 / 1157 0.8 / 1748 5.1		**19** SA 0511 5.6 / 1135 0.4 / 1741 5.5 / ○ 2355 0.3	
5 SA 0011 0.9 / 0602 5.4 / 1232 0.8 / 1820 5.2		**20** SU 0559 5.8 / 1221 0.1 / 1827 5.6	
6 SU 0044 0.8 / 0635 5.4 / 1302 0.8 / 1852 5.2		**21** M 0040 0.2 / 0645 5.8 / 1305 0.1 / 1910 5.7	
7 M 0111 0.9 / 0707 5.3 / 1327 0.9 / 1922 5.2		**22** TU 0122 0.1 / 0730 5.8 / 1345 0.2 / 1951 5.6	
8 TU 0134 1.0 / 0737 5.2 / 1348 1.1 / 1952 5.1		**23** W 0201 0.3 / 0812 5.6 / 1423 0.5 / 2028 5.5	
9 W 0154 1.1 / 0806 5.1 / 1408 1.2 / 2018 5.0		**24** TH 0239 0.6 / 0851 5.3 / 1500 0.9 / 2103 5.2	
10 TH 0214 1.3 / 0833 4.9 / 1429 1.4 / 2044 4.9		**25** F 0318 1.1 / 0929 4.9 / 1538 1.4 / 2137 4.9	
11 F 0240 1.5 / 0901 4.7 / 1457 1.6 / 2114 4.7		**26** SA 0401 1.5 / 1011 4.5 / 1623 1.9 / ◑ 2222 4.5	
12 SA 0314 1.7 / 0940 4.5 / 1536 1.9 / ◑ 2203 4.5		**27** SU 0455 2.0 / 1126 4.1 / 1724 2.3	
13 SU 0403 2.0 / 1041 4.3 / 1636 2.2 / 2312 4.3		**28** M 0002 4.2 / 0612 2.3 / 1306 4.0 / 1900 2.4	
14 M 0533 2.2 / 1158 4.2 / 1831 2.3		**29** TU 0135 4.3 / 0816 2.2 / 1420 4.2 / 2044 2.1	
15 TU 0035 4.3 / 0726 2.1 / 1336 4.3 / 2002 2.0		**30** W 0242 4.5 / 0920 1.8 / 1517 4.5 / 2140 1.7	
		31 TH 0334 4.8 / 1007 1.4 / 1603 4.7 / 2224 1.4	

APRIL

Day		Day	
1 F 0418 5.0 / 1048 1.1 / 1642 5.0 / 2304 1.1		**16** SA 0352 5.3 / 1018 0.7 / 1626 5.3 / 2242 0.7	
2 SA 0457 5.2 / 1125 0.9 / 1717 5.1 / 2340 1.0		**17** SU 0445 5.5 / 1109 0.4 / 1715 5.5 / 2331 0.4	
3 SU 0533 5.3 / 1159 0.9 / 1751 5.2		**18** M 0535 5.6 / 1157 0.3 / 1801 5.6 / ○	
4 M 0012 0.9 / 0607 5.3 / 1229 0.9 / 1824 5.2		**19** TU 0017 0.3 / 0622 5.7 / 1241 0.3 / 1845 5.7	
5 TU 0041 0.9 / 0641 5.2 / 1255 1.0 / 1856 5.2		**20** W 0101 0.3 / 0708 5.6 / 1323 0.4 / 1927 5.6	
6 W 0106 1.0 / 0713 5.2 / 1319 1.1 / 1925 5.2		**21** TH 0142 0.4 / 0752 5.4 / 1403 0.7 / 2006 5.4	
7 TH 0129 1.1 / 0743 5.1 / 1342 1.2 / 1953 5.1		**22** F 0222 0.7 / 0833 5.1 / 1442 1.0 / 2042 5.2	
8 F 0154 1.2 / 0811 4.9 / 1408 1.3 / 2021 5.0		**23** SA 0302 1.1 / 0912 4.8 / 1521 1.4 / 2116 4.9	
9 SA 0222 1.4 / 0843 4.7 / 1439 1.5 / 2055 4.8		**24** SU 0346 1.5 / 0955 4.4 / 1606 1.8 / 2157 4.6	
10 SU 0259 1.6 / 0925 4.5 / 1520 1.8 / 2144 4.6		**25** M 0437 1.9 / 1100 4.2 / 1702 2.2 / ◑ 2309 4.4	
11 M 0350 1.9 / 1024 4.3 / 1622 2.1 / ◑ 2249 4.5		**26** TU 0542 2.1 / 1229 4.1 / 1813 2.3	
12 TU 0515 2.0 / 1138 4.2 / 1802 2.2		**27** W 0052 4.3 / 0707 2.1 / 1339 4.2 / 1941 2.2	
13 W 0007 4.5 / 0658 1.9 / 1308 4.3 / 1933 1.8		**28** TH 0159 4.4 / 0828 1.9 / 1435 4.4 / 2051 1.9	
14 TH 0137 4.7 / 0817 1.6 / 1432 4.6 / 2046 1.5		**29** F 0253 4.6 / 0922 1.6 / 1522 4.7 / 2141 1.6	
15 F 0253 5.0 / 0922 1.1 / 1534 5.0 / 2148 1.1		**30** SA 0339 4.8 / 1006 1.4 / 1604 4.9 / 2224 1.4	

Chart Datum: 3·22 metres below Ordnance Datum (Newlyn)
HAT is 5·9 metres above Chart Datum

TIDES

TIDES

PLYMOUTH (DEVONPORT)
LAT 50°22'N   LONG 4°11'W
TIMES AND HEIGHTS OF HIGH AND LOW WATERS

Dates in amber are **SPRINGS**
Dates in yellow are **NEAPS**

2011

MAY

Day	T1	T2	T3	T4	Day	T1	T2	T3	T4
1 SU	0421 5.0	1045 1.2	1642 5.0	2302 1.2	**16** M	0420 5.3	1044 0.7	1649 5.4	2308 0.7
2 M	0501 5.1	1120 1.1	1720 5.2	2337 1.1	**17** TU	0512 5.4	1133 0.6	1737 5.5	2356 0.6
3 TU	0540 5.1	1153 1.1	1756 5.2		**18** W	0602 5.4	1220 0.6	1824 5.5	
4 W	0010 1.1	0616 5.1	1225 1.1	1831 5.2	**19** TH	0042 0.5	0650 5.4	1305 0.7	1907 5.5
5 TH	0041 1.1	0652 5.1	1255 1.1	1903 5.2	**20** F	0126 0.6	0736 5.2	1347 0.8	1948 5.4
6 F	0111 1.1	0725 5.0	1325 1.2	1934 5.2	**21** SA	0208 0.8	0818 5.0	1427 1.1	2025 5.2
7 SA	0142 1.2	0758 4.9	1357 1.3	2007 5.1	**22** SU	0249 1.1	0858 4.8	1507 1.4	2100 5.0
8 SU	0217 1.3	0835 4.8	1434 1.5	2046 5.0	**23** M	0331 1.4	0938 4.6	1549 1.7	2138 4.8
9 M	0258 1.5	0920 4.6	1520 1.7	2134 4.8	**24** TU	0416 1.7	1024 4.4	1635 2.0	2225 4.6
10 TU	0352 1.6	1015 4.5	1619 1.9	2233 4.7	**25** W	0507 1.9	1124 4.3	1730 2.1	2330 4.4
11 W	0503 1.8	1122 4.4	1737 1.9	2344 4.7	**26** TH	0605 2.0	1234 4.2	1832 2.2	
12 TH	0626 1.7	1240 4.5	1900 1.8		**27** F	0051 4.4	0709 2.0	1337 4.4	1938 2.1
13 F	0104 4.7	0743 1.6	1357 4.7	2014 1.6	**28** SA	0158 4.5	0812 1.9	1432 4.5	2040 1.9
14 SA	0219 4.9	0851 1.2	1501 4.9	2118 1.2	**29** SU	0253 4.6	0908 1.7	1521 4.7	2133 1.7
15 SU	0323 5.1	0950 1.0	1557 5.2	2215 0.9	**30** M	0343 4.8	0956 1.5	1606 4.9	2219 1.5
					31 TU	0429 4.9	1039 1.4	1649 5.1	2302 1.3

JUNE

Day	T1	T2	T3	T4	Day	T1	T2	T3	T4
1 W	0513 5.0	1119 1.2	1730 5.2	2342 1.2	**16** TH	0546 5.2	1205 0.9	1806 5.4	
2 TH	0555 5.0	1158 1.2	1809 5.2		**17** F	0029 0.8	0635 5.2	1251 0.8	1850 5.4
3 F	0020 1.1	0635 5.0	1237 1.1	1846 5.3	**18** SA	0114 0.8	0720 5.1	1333 0.9	1931 5.4
4 SA	0059 1.1	0714 5.0	1315 1.2	1923 5.3	**19** SU	0156 0.9	0801 5.0	1413 1.1	2008 5.3
5 SU	0138 1.1	0752 5.0	1354 1.2	2001 5.2	**20** M	0235 1.0	0838 4.9	1450 1.3	2041 5.1
6 M	0218 1.1	0833 4.9	1435 1.3	2042 5.2	**21** TU	0311 1.2	0911 4.7	1525 1.5	2114 5.0
7 TU	0301 1.2	0917 4.8	1520 1.4	2128 5.1	**22** W	0347 1.5	0947 4.6	1602 1.7	2151 4.8
8 W	0350 1.3	1007 4.7	1612 1.5	2220 5.0	**23** TH	0426 1.7	1028 4.5	1643 2.0	2234 4.6
9 TH	0446 1.5	1104 4.6	1712 1.7	2322 4.8	**24** F	0511 1.9	1118 4.4	1734 2.1	2327 4.4
10 F	0552 1.6	1211 4.6	1823 1.7		**25** SA	0606 2.0	1219 4.3	1836 2.2	
11 SA	0033 4.8	0706 1.6	1322 4.4	1938 1.7	**26** SU	0036 4.4	0708 2.1	1329 4.4	1940 2.1
12 SU	0148 4.8	0818 1.5	1430 4.8	2049 1.5	**27** M	0156 4.4	0810 2.0	1434 4.5	2042 2.0
13 M	0257 4.9	0924 1.3	1531 5.0	2153 1.3	**28** TU	0303 4.5	0908 1.8	1531 4.7	2139 1.7
14 TU	0358 5.0	1022 1.1	1627 5.2	2249 1.0	**29** W	0359 4.7	1002 1.6	1620 5.0	2230 1.5
15 W	0454 5.1	1115 0.9	1718 5.3	2341 0.9	**30** TH	0448 4.9	1051 1.4	1706 5.1	2319 1.2

JULY

Day	T1	T2	T3	T4	Day	T1	T2	T3	T4
1 F	0535 5.0	1138 1.2	1750 5.3		**16** SA	0018 0.8	0619 5.1	1237 0.9	1832 5.4
2 SA	0005 1.0	0619 5.1	1224 1.0	1831 5.4	**17** SU	0101 0.8	0700 5.1	1318 0.9	1911 5.4
3 SU	0050 0.9	0703 5.1	1308 1.0	1913 5.4	**18** M	0139 0.8	0737 5.1	1354 0.9	1945 5.3
4 M	0133 0.8	0746 5.1	1350 0.9	1955 5.4	**19** TU	0214 0.9	0809 5.0	1426 1.1	2015 5.2
5 TU	0215 0.8	0828 5.1	1431 1.0	2037 5.4	**20** W	0244 1.1	0839 4.9	1455 1.3	2046 5.1
6 W	0256 0.9	0910 5.1	1512 1.1	2120 5.3	**21** TH	0312 1.3	0911 4.8	1522 1.6	2118 4.9
7 TH	0338 1.0	0954 5.0	1556 1.2	2206 5.1	**22** F	0339 1.6	0945 4.7	1550 1.8	2153 4.7
8 F	0424 1.3	1043 4.8	1646 1.5	2258 4.9	**23** SA	0410 1.8	1025 4.5	1626 2.0	2234 4.5
9 SA	0519 1.5	1142 4.7	1747 1.7		**24** SU	0456 2.1	1115 4.4	1728 2.3	2329 4.3
10 SU	0004 4.7	0627 1.7	1252 4.6	1903 1.8	**25** M	0608 2.2	1221 4.3	1850 2.3	
11 M	0122 4.6	0748 1.8	1406 4.7	2027 1.8	**26** TU	0045 4.2	0724 2.2	1343 4.4	2002 2.1
12 TU	0238 4.6	0905 1.7	1513 4.8	2139 1.6	**27** W	0222 4.3	0832 2.0	1457 4.6	2107 1.8
13 W	0345 4.8	1009 1.4	1612 5.0	2239 1.3	**28** TH	0332 4.6	0933 1.7	1554 4.9	2206 1.5
14 TH	0443 4.9	1104 1.2	1703 5.2	2331 1.0	**29** F	0427 4.8	1029 1.4	1644 5.1	2259 1.2
15 F	0533 5.0	1153 1.0	1750 5.4		**30** SA	0515 5.0	1121 1.1	1730 5.4	2349 0.9
					31 SU	0602 5.2	1209 0.9	1815 5.5	

AUGUST

Day	T1	T2	T3	T4	Day	T1	T2	T3	T4
1 M	0036 0.7	0647 5.3	1255 0.7	1859 5.6	**16** TU	0116 0.8	0707 5.0	1329 0.8	1917 5.4
2 TU	0120 0.5	0731 5.4	1338 0.6	1942 5.6	**17** W	0146 0.9	0737 5.0	1357 1.0	1947 5.3
3 W	0202 0.5	0813 5.4	1418 0.6	2024 5.6	**18** TH	0211 1.1	0806 5.1	1421 1.2	2016 5.2
4 TH	0241 0.6	0853 5.3	1457 0.8	2105 5.4	**19** F	0233 1.3	0836 5.0	1440 1.5	2045 5.0
5 F	0320 0.9	0934 5.1	1537 1.1	2147 5.2	**20** SA	0252 1.5	0907 4.8	1500 1.7	2116 4.8
6 SA	0401 1.2	1018 4.9	1622 1.4	2234 4.9	**21** SU	0314 1.7	0941 4.6	1528 1.9	2153 4.5
7 SU	0449 1.6	1112 4.7	1717 1.8	2337 4.5	**22** M	0349 2.0	1026 4.4	1614 2.2	2245 4.3
8 M	0553 1.9	1227 4.5	1836 2.1		**23** TU	0448 2.3	1128 4.3	1755 2.4	2356 4.2
9 TU	0105 4.3	0726 2.1	1350 4.5	2017 2.0	**24** W	0643 2.4	1249 4.2	1930 2.3	
10 W	0230 4.4	0857 1.9	1501 4.7	2134 1.7	**25** TH	0139 4.2	0803 2.1	1423 4.5	2042 1.9
11 TH	0338 4.6	1002 1.6	1600 5.0	2230 1.3	**26** F	0308 4.5	0910 1.7	1529 4.9	2144 1.5
12 F	0433 4.8	1053 1.2	1649 5.2	2318 1.0	**27** SA	0405 4.9	1009 1.3	1621 5.2	2239 1.0
13 SA	0518 5.0	1138 1.0	1732 5.4		**28** SU	0454 5.1	1102 1.0	1708 5.5	2330 0.7
14 SU	0001 0.8	0558 5.1	1219 0.8	1810 5.4	**29** M	0540 5.3	1151 0.7	1754 5.7	
15 M	0041 0.7	0634 5.2	1256 0.8	1845 5.4	**30** TU	0016 0.4	0625 5.4	1236 0.5	1839 5.8
					31 W	0101 0.3	0709 5.6	1319 0.4	1923 5.8

Chart Datum: 3·22 metres below Ordnance Datum (Newlyn)
HAT is 5·9 metres above Chart Datum

TIME ZONE (UT)
For Summer Time add ONE hour in **non-shaded areas**

PLYMOUTH (DEVONPORT)
LAT 50°22'N   LONG 4°11'W
TIMES AND HEIGHTS OF HIGH AND LOW WATERS

Dates in amber are **SPRINGS**
Dates in yellow are **NEAPS**
2011

SEPTEMBER

Time	m	Time	m
1 0142 0.3 / 0751 5.6 / TH 1359 0.4 / 2006 5.7		**16** 0136 1.1 / 0736 5.2 / F 1346 1.2 / 1948 5.2	
2 0221 0.5 / 0831 5.5 / F 1438 0.7 / 2046 5.5		**17** 0155 1.3 / 0805 5.1 / SA 1404 1.4 / 2016 5.0	
3 0258 0.8 / 0911 5.3 / SA 1517 1.0 / 2127 5.2		**18** 0214 1.5 / 0834 4.9 / SU 1425 1.6 / 2045 4.8	
4 0338 1.3 / 0952 5.0 / SU 1600 1.5 / ◗ 2211 4.8		**19** 0238 1.7 / 0905 4.7 / M 1455 1.8 / 2121 4.6	
5 0423 1.7 / 1044 4.7 / M 1655 1.9 / 2316 4.4		**20** 0312 2.0 / 0949 4.5 / TU 1538 2.1 / ◑ 2215 4.3	
6 0527 2.2 / 1207 4.4 / TU 1816 2.2		21 0404 2.3 / 1051 4.4 / W 1657 2.4 / 2325 4.2	
7 0056 4.2 / 0713 2.4 / W 1336 4.4 / 2012 2.2		**22** 0600 2.5 / 1208 4.4 / TH 1900 2.3	
8 0221 4.3 / 0848 2.1 / TH 1447 4.7 / 2122 1.8		**23** 0059 4.2 / 0735 2.2 / F 1343 4.6 / 2016 1.9	
9 0326 4.6 / 0946 1.7 / F 1543 5.0 / 2213 1.4		**24** 0240 4.6 / 0846 1.8 / SA 1459 4.9 / 2120 1.4	
10 0415 4.9 / 1033 1.3 / SA 1628 5.2 / 2257 1.0		**25** 0339 4.9 / 0946 1.3 / SU 1554 5.3 / 2215 1.0	
11 0456 5.1 / 1115 1.0 / SU 1708 5.4 / 2337 0.8		**26** 0428 5.2 / 1039 0.9 / M 1643 5.6 / 2306 0.6	
12 0532 5.2 / 1154 0.9 / M 1744 5.4 / ○		**27** 0515 5.5 / 1128 0.6 / TU 1731 5.8 / ● 2353 0.4	
13 0013 0.8 / 0604 5.3 / TU 1229 0.8 / 1817 5.4		**28** 0600 5.6 / 1213 0.4 / W 1817 5.8	
14 0046 0.8 / 0635 5.3 / W 1259 0.9 / 1848 5.4		**29** 0037 0.3 / 0644 5.7 / TH 1257 0.3 / 1902 5.8	
15 0113 0.9 / 0706 5.3 / TH 1325 1.1 / 1918 5.3		**30** 0119 0.4 / 0727 5.7 / F 1338 0.4 / 1945 5.7	

OCTOBER

Time	m	Time	m
1 0159 0.6 / 0808 5.6 / SA 1418 0.7 / 2027 5.4		**16** 0126 1.3 / 0739 5.2 / SU 1340 1.4 / 1953 5.0	
2 0238 1.0 / 0848 5.3 / SU 1459 1.1 / 2108 5.1		**17** 0149 1.5 / 0808 5.1 / M 1405 1.6 / 2024 4.8	
3 0318 1.4 / 0929 5.0 / M 1543 1.6 / 2154 4.7		**18** 0217 1.7 / 0841 4.9 / TU 1437 1.8 / 2102 4.6	
4 0404 1.9 / 1020 4.7 / TU 1638 2.0 / ◗ 2301 4.3		**19** 0254 1.9 / 0926 4.7 / W 1522 2.0 / 2155 4.4	
5 0506 2.3 / 1145 4.5 / W 1756 2.3		**20** 0346 2.2 / 1025 4.6 / TH 1634 2.3 / ◑ 2302 4.3	
6 0041 4.2 / 0644 2.4 / TH 1313 4.4 / 1947 2.2		21 0518 2.4 / 1136 4.5 / F 1824 2.2	
7 0159 4.3 / 0821 2.2 / F 1421 4.6 / 2055 1.9		**22** 0025 4.4 / 0701 2.2 / SA 1301 4.7 / 1945 1.9	
8 0300 4.6 / 0918 1.8 / SA 1515 4.9 / 2144 1.5		**23** 0159 4.6 / 0816 1.8 / SU 1421 5.0 / 2051 1.5	
9 0347 4.9 / 1004 1.5 / SU 1600 5.1 / 2227 1.2		**24** 0306 5.0 / 0918 1.4 / M 1523 5.3 / 2148 1.1	
10 0426 5.1 / 1045 1.2 / M 1639 5.3 / 2306 1.0		**25** 0359 5.4 / 1013 1.0 / TU 1617 5.5 / 2240 0.7	
11 0501 5.3 / 1123 1.0 / TU 1715 5.4 / 2341 1.0		**26** 0448 5.5 / 1103 0.7 / W 1707 5.7 / ● 2328 0.5	
12 0534 5.3 / 1157 1.0 / W 1749 5.4 / ○		**27** 0535 5.7 / 1151 0.5 / TH 1755 5.8	
13 0012 1.0 / 0606 5.4 / TH 1227 1.1 / 1821 5.4		**28** 0014 0.5 / 0620 5.8 / F 1237 0.5 / 1842 5.7	
14 0039 1.1 / 0638 5.4 / F 1254 1.2 / 1853 5.3		**29** 0058 0.5 / 0705 5.8 / SA 1320 0.6 / 1927 5.6	
15 0103 1.2 / 0709 5.3 / SA 1317 1.3 / 1924 5.2		**30** 0140 0.7 / 0748 5.6 / SU 1403 0.8 / 2011 5.3	
		31 0221 1.1 / 0830 5.4 / M 1445 1.1 / 2055 5.0	

NOVEMBER

Time	m	Time	m
1 0303 1.5 / 0912 5.1 / TU 1530 1.5 / 2141 4.7		**16** 0210 1.6 / 0828 5.1 / W 1434 1.7 / 2052 4.8	
2 0348 1.9 / 1000 4.8 / W 1621 1.9 / ◗ 2241 4.4		**17** 0249 1.8 / 0912 4.9 / TH 1520 1.8 / 2142 4.6	
3 0443 2.2 / 1109 4.6 / TH 1725 2.2		**18** 0340 2.0 / 1006 4.8 / F 1621 2.0 / ◑ 2242 4.5	
4 0004 4.3 / 0554 2.4 / F 1232 4.5 / 1848 2.3		**19** 0449 2.2 / 1110 4.7 / SA 1742 2.0 / 2354 4.5	
5 0118 4.3 / 0725 2.3 / SA 1340 4.6 / 2007 2.1		20 0617 2.1 / 1223 4.8 / SU 1906 1.9	
6 0218 4.5 / 0838 2.1 / SU 1436 4.8 / 2103 1.8		**21** 0114 4.7 / 0738 1.9 / M 1341 4.9 / 2017 1.6	
7 0307 4.8 / 0925 1.8 / M 1523 5.0 / 2148 1.5		**22** 0228 4.9 / 0847 1.6 / TU 1450 5.1 / 2119 1.3	
8 0350 5.0 / 1009 1.5 / TU 1605 5.1 / 2228 1.4		**23** 0328 5.2 / 0947 1.2 / W 1550 5.4 / 2215 1.0	
9 0428 5.2 / 1048 1.4 / W 1644 5.2 / 2305 1.3		**24** 0422 5.4 / 1041 0.9 / TH 1645 5.5 / 2306 0.8	
10 0504 5.3 / 1124 1.3 / TH 1722 5.3 / ○ 2338 1.2		**25** 0513 5.6 / 1132 0.7 / F 1736 5.6 / ● 2355 0.7	
11 0540 5.4 / 1156 1.2 / F 1758 5.3		**26** 0601 5.7 / 1220 0.7 / SA 1826 5.5	
12 0008 1.2 / 0614 5.4 / SA 1227 1.3 / 1833 5.2		27 0041 0.7 / 0647 5.7 / SU 1306 0.7 / 1913 5.5	
13 0038 1.3 / 0646 5.3 / SU 1257 1.3 / 1907 5.1		**28** 0126 0.9 / 0732 5.6 / M 1350 0.8 / 1959 5.3	
14 0107 1.4 / 0720 5.3 / M 1326 1.4 / 1939 5.0		**29** 0208 1.1 / 0815 5.5 / TU 1433 1.1 / 2042 5.1	
15 0136 1.5 / 0752 5.2 / TU 1358 1.5 / 2013 4.9		**30** 0249 1.4 / 0856 5.3 / W 1516 1.4 / 2123 4.8	

DECEMBER

Time	m	Time	m
1 0331 1.7 / 0937 5.0 / TH 1559 1.7 / 2207 4.6		**16** 0248 1.5 / 0903 5.2 / F 1517 1.5 / 2132 4.8	
2 0415 2.0 / 1021 4.8 / F 1647 2.0 / ◗ 2259 4.4		**17** 0333 1.6 / 0951 5.1 / SA 1605 1.6 / 2223 4.7	
3 0507 2.2 / 1119 4.6 / SA 1743 2.2		**18** 0426 1.8 / 1046 4.9 / SU 1704 1.8 / ◑ 2323 4.7	
4 0006 4.4 / 0608 2.3 / SU 1232 4.5 / 1848 2.2		**19** 0532 2.0 / 1151 4.8 / M 1818 1.9	
5 0116 4.4 / 0720 2.3 / M 1340 4.6 / 1956 2.1		20 0035 4.7 / 0654 2.0 / TU 1306 4.8 / 1939 1.8	
6 0215 4.6 / 0828 2.2 / TU 1437 4.7 / 2055 2.0		**21** 0151 4.8 / 0815 1.8 / W 1421 4.9 / 2052 1.6	
7 0307 4.8 / 0923 1.9 / W 1528 4.8 / 2144 1.7		**22** 0301 5.0 / 0924 1.5 / TH 1529 5.1 / 2155 1.4	
8 0353 5.0 / 1010 1.7 / TH 1614 5.0 / 2227 1.6		**23** 0402 5.2 / 1025 1.2 / F 1629 5.2 / 2251 1.1	
9 0436 5.2 / 1051 1.5 / F 1657 5.1 / 2306 1.4		**24** 0456 5.4 / 1119 1.0 / SA 1723 5.3 / ● 2342 0.9	
10 0516 5.3 / 1130 1.4 / SA 1738 5.2 / ○ 2343 1.3		**25** 0546 5.6 / 1209 0.8 / SU 1814 5.4	
11 0555 5.4 / 1207 1.3 / SU 1818 5.2		26 0029 0.8 / 0633 5.7 / M 1256 0.7 / 1900 5.4	
12 0019 1.3 / 0632 5.4 / M 1243 1.3 / 1856 5.2		**27** 0114 0.8 / 0718 5.6 / TU 1339 0.8 / 1944 5.3	
13 0055 1.3 / 0709 5.4 / TU 1320 1.3 / 1932 5.1		**28** 0155 0.9 / 0759 5.5 / W 1419 0.9 / 2023 5.1	
14 0131 1.3 / 0744 5.3 / W 1356 1.3 / 2009 5.0		**29** 0233 1.1 / 0835 5.4 / TH 1456 1.1 / 2057 5.0	
15 0208 1.3 / 0822 5.3 / TH 1435 1.4 / 2048 4.9		**30** 0308 1.4 / 0908 5.2 / F 1532 1.4 / 2128 4.8	
		31 0343 1.7 / 0941 5.0 / SA 1608 1.7 / 2204 4.6	

Chart Datum: 3·22 metres below Ordnance Datum (Newlyn)
HAT is 5·9 metres above Chart Datum

TIDES

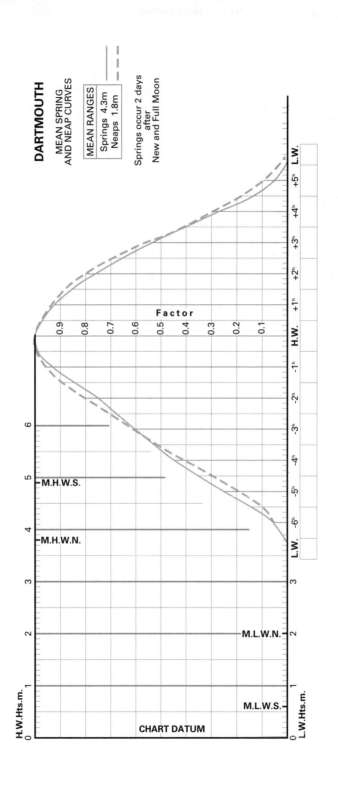

DARTMOUTH

MEAN SPRING
AND NEAP CURVES

MEAN RANGES
Springs 4.3m
Neaps 1.8m

Springs occur 2 days
after
New and Full Moon

DARTMOUTH

LAT 50°21'N   LONG 3°34'W

TIMES AND HEIGHTS OF HIGH AND LOW WATERS

Dates in amber are **SPRINGS**
Dates in yellow are **NEAPS**

2011

JANUARY

Day	Time m	Time m	Time m	Time m		Day	Time m	Time m	Time m	Time m
1 SA	0302 4.2	0906 1.6	1533 4.2	2138 1.5		**16** SU	0226 3.9	0825 1.9	1506 3.9	2054 1.7
2 SU	0407 4.4	1009 1.4	1635 4.3	2235 1.3		**17** M	0340 4.2	0931 1.6	1614 4.1	2155 1.4
3 M	0501 4.6	1103 1.1	1729 4.6	2324 1.1		**18** TU	0438 4.4	1029 1.2	1710 4.4	2251 1.1
4 TU	0550 4.7	1150 0.9	1816 4.5			**19** W	0528 4.7	1122 0.9	1800 4.6	2342 0.8
5 W	0008 0.9	0633 4.8	1235 0.8	1856 4.5		**20** TH	0618 4.9	1212 0.6	1848 4.7	
6 TH	0050 0.9	0710 4.8	1314 0.8	1932 4.5		**21** F	0031 0.6	0702 5.1	1300 0.4	1933 4.8
7 F	0127 0.9	0744 4.8	1348 0.9	2005 4.5		**22** SA	0116 0.4	0747 5.1	1343 0.3	2015 4.8
8 SA	0158 1.0	0816 4.7	1420 1.0	2035 4.4		**23** SU	0158 0.4	0830 5.1	1424 0.3	2056 4.8
9 SU	0227 1.2	0848 4.6	1447 1.2	2107 4.3		**24** M	0237 0.5	0912 5.0	1503 0.5	2136 4.7
10 M	0253 1.4	0920 4.5	1514 1.4	2140 4.2		**25** TU	0316 0.7	0953 4.8	1541 0.8	2216 4.5
11 TU	0318 1.6	0953 4.3	1541 1.6	2215 4.0		**26** W	0356 1.0	1036 4.5	1623 1.0	2300 4.2
12 W	0347 1.8	1030 4.1	1616 1.8	2258 3.9		**27** TH	0442 1.4	1126 4.2	1713 1.6	2359 4.0
13 TH	0429 2.0	1117 3.9	1709 2.0	2352 3.8		**28** F	0541 1.8	1234 3.9	1821 1.9	
14 F	0542 2.2	1216 3.8	1830 2.1			**29** SA	0117 3.8	0710 2.0	1359 3.8	2003 2.0
15 SA	0101 3.7	0711 2.1	1337 3.8	1946 2.0		**30** SU	0240 3.9	0853 1.9	1519 3.8	2126 1.7
						31 M	0350 4.1	1001 1.5	1623 4.1	2225 1.4

FEBRUARY

Day	Time m	Time m	Time m	Time m		Day	Time m	Time m	Time m	Time m
1 TU	0446 4.4	1054 1.2	1716 4.3	2313 1.1		**16** W	0412 4.4	1010 1.1	1649 4.3	2234 1.0
2 W	0533 4.6	1139 0.9	1800 4.4	2355 0.9		**17** TH	0508 4.7	1106 0.7	1741 4.6	2327 0.6
3 TH	0616 4.8	1219 0.7	1839 4.5			**18** F	0558 5.0	1156 0.3	1830 4.8	
4 F	0034 0.7	0652 4.8	1257 0.6	1911 4.6		**19** SA	0015 0.3	0646 5.2	1244 0.1	1914 4.9
5 SA	0109 0.7	0724 4.8	1329 0.7	1942 4.6		**20** SU	0101 0.1	0731 5.2	1327 0.0	1957 5.0
6 SU	0137 0.8	0755 4.8	1355 0.8	2011 4.5		**21** M	0141 0.1	0813 5.2	1406 0.0	2037 5.0
7 M	0202 0.9	0825 4.7	1418 1.0	2041 4.4		**22** TU	0220 0.2	0853 5.1	1443 0.3	2114 4.8
8 TU	0223 1.1	0853 4.5	1438 1.1	2109 4.3		**23** W	0257 0.5	0933 4.8	1519 0.7	2150 4.6
9 W	0242 1.3	0922 4.3	1459 1.3	2137 4.2		**24** TH	0334 0.9	1010 4.4	1557 1.2	2227 4.2
10 TH	0306 1.5	0951 4.1	1527 1.6	2210 4.0		**25** F	0417 1.4	1054 4.0	1642 1.6	2317 3.9
11 F	0340 1.7	1031 3.9	1607 1.8	2258 3.8		**26** SA	0512 1.8	1205 3.6	1744 2.1	
12 SA	0432 2.0	1129 3.7	1713 2.1			**27** SU	0048 3.7	0635 2.1	1343 3.5	1938 2.2
13 SU	0005 3.7	0614 2.2	1245 3.6	1904 2.1		**28** M	0219 3.7	0843 1.9	1504 3.7	2112 1.9
14 M	0131 3.7	0751 2.0	1425 3.7	2024 1.8						
15 TU	0304 4.0	0906 1.6	1549 4.0	2134 1.4						

MARCH

Day	Time m	Time m	Time m	Time m		Day	Time m	Time m	Time m	Time m
1 TU	0330 4.0	0948 1.5	1607 3.9	2208 1.4		**16** W	0228 4.0	0842 1.5	1523 4.0	2111 1.4
2 W	0425 4.3	1036 1.1	1655 4.2	2254 1.1		**17** TH	0344 4.4	0948 1.0	1624 4.3	2212 0.9
3 TH	0511 4.5	1118 0.8	1736 4.4	2334 0.8		**18** F	0442 4.7	1044 0.5	1717 4.6	2306 0.5
4 F	0551 4.7	1156 0.6	1813 4.5			**19** SA	0534 5.0	1134 0.2	1805 4.9	2354 0.1
5 SA	0010 0.7	0627 4.8	1232 0.6	1845 4.6		**20** SU	0624 5.2	1220 -0.1	1852 5.0	
6 SU	0044 0.6	0659 4.8	1302 0.6	1916 4.6		**21** M	0040 0.0	0709 5.2	1305 -0.1	1934 5.1
7 M	0111 0.7	0731 4.7	1327 0.7	1945 4.6		**22** TU	0122 -0.1	0753 5.2	1344 0.0	2013 5.0
8 TU	0133 0.8	0800 4.6	1347 0.9	2014 4.5		**23** W	0200 0.1	0834 5.0	1422 0.3	2050 4.9
9 W	0153 0.9	0828 4.5	1407 1.0	2040 4.4		**24** TH	0237 0.4	0912 4.7	1458 0.7	2124 4.6
10 TH	0213 1.1	0854 4.3	1428 1.2	2105 4.3		**25** F	0316 0.9	0949 4.3	1535 1.2	2157 4.3
11 F	0238 1.3	0922 4.1	1455 1.4	2135 4.1		**26** SA	0358 1.3	1030 3.9	1620 1.7	2241 3.9
12 SA	0312 1.5	1000 3.9	1533 1.7	2222 3.9		**27** SU	0451 1.8	1143 3.5	1720 2.1	
13 SU	0400 1.8	1059 3.7	1632 2.0	2330 3.7		**28** M	0018 3.6	0607 2.1	1321 3.4	1856 2.2
14 M	0528 2.0	1214 3.6	1827 2.1			**29** TU	0151 3.7	0812 2.0	1438 3.6	2041 1.9
15 TU	0050 3.7	0722 1.9	1352 3.7	1958 1.8		**30** W	0300 3.9	0917 1.6	1537 3.9	2138 1.5
						31 TH	0354 4.2	1005 1.2	1624 4.1	2222 1.2

APRIL

Day	Time m	Time m	Time m	Time m		Day	Time m	Time m	Time m	Time m
1 F	0440 4.4	1047 0.9	1704 4.4	2303 0.9		**16** SA	0413 4.7	1016 0.5	1648 4.7	2241 0.5
2 SA	0520 4.6	1124 0.7	1741 4.5	2339 0.8		**17** SU	0508 4.9	1108 0.2	1739 4.9	2330 0.2
3 SU	0557 4.7	1158 0.7	1816 4.6			**18** M	0559 5.0	1156 0.0	1826 5.0	
4 M	0011 0.7	0632 4.7	1228 0.7	1849 4.6		**19** TU	0016 0.1	0647 5.1	1241 0.1	1909 5.1
5 TU	0041 0.7	0705 4.6	1255 0.8	1920 4.6		**20** W	0101 0.1	0732 5.0	1323 0.2	1950 5.0
6 W	0106 0.8	0737 4.6	1319 0.9	1948 4.6		**21** TH	0141 0.2	0814 4.8	1402 0.5	2028 4.8
7 TH	0129 0.9	0806 4.5	1341 1.0	2015 4.5		**22** F	0221 0.5	0854 4.5	1440 0.9	2103 4.6
8 F	0153 1.0	0833 4.3	1407 1.1	2043 4.4		**23** SA	0300 0.9	0933 4.2	1519 1.2	2136 4.3
9 SA	0221 1.2	0904 4.1	1437 1.3	2116 4.2		**24** SU	0343 1.3	1014 3.9	1603 1.6	2216 4.0
10 SU	0257 1.4	0945 3.9	1518 1.6	2204 4.0		**25** M	0433 1.7	1118 3.6	1658 2.0	2327 3.8
11 M	0347 1.7	1043 3.7	1619 1.9	2307 3.9		**26** TU	0537 1.9	1245 3.5	1808 2.1	
12 TU	0511 1.8	1155 3.6	1757 2.0			**27** W	0107 3.7	0703 2.0	1355 3.6	1937 2.0
13 W	0023 3.9	0654 1.7	1323 3.7	1929 1.8		**28** TH	0216 3.8	0824 1.7	1453 3.8	2048 1.7
14 TH	0153 4.1	0813 1.4	1450 4.0	2043 1.3		**29** F	0312 4.0	0919 1.4	1542 4.1	2139 1.4
15 F	0312 4.4	0919 0.9	1554 4.4	2146 0.9		**30** SA	0359 4.2	1004 1.2	1625 4.3	2222 1.2

Chart Datum: 2·62 metres below Ordnance Datum (Newlyn)
HAT is 5·3 metres above Chart Datum

TIDES

<table>
<tr><td>

TIME ZONE (UT)
For Summer Time add ONE hour in **non-shaded areas**

</td><td>

DARTMOUTH
LAT 50°21′N   LONG 3°34′W
TIMES AND HEIGHTS OF HIGH AND LOW WATERS

</td><td>

Dates in amber are **SPRINGS**
Dates in yellow are **NEAPS**
2011

</td></tr>
</table>

MAY

Day	Time m	Day	Time m
1 SU	0443 4.4 / 1044 1.0 / 1704 4.4 / 2301 1.0	**16** M	0442 4.7 / 1043 0.5 / 1712 4.8 / 2307 0.5
2 M	0524 4.5 / 1119 0.9 / 1744 4.6 / 2336 0.9	**17** TU	0535 4.8 / 1132 0.4 / 1801 4.9 / ○ 2355 0.4
3 TU ●	0604 4.5 / 1152 0.9 / 1821 4.6	**18** W	0627 4.8 / 1219 0.4 / 1849 4.9
4 W	0009 0.9 / 0641 4.5 / 1224 0.9 / 1855 4.6	**19** TH	0042 0.3 / 0714 4.8 / 1305 0.5 / 1931 4.9
5 TH	0041 0.9 / 0716 4.5 / 1255 0.9 / 1927 4.6	**20** F	0126 0.4 / 0759 4.6 / 1346 0.6 / 2010 4.8
6 F	0111 0.9 / 0748 4.4 / 1325 1.0 / 1957 4.6	**21** SA	0207 0.6 / 0840 4.4 / 1426 0.9 / 2047 4.6
7 SA	0141 1.0 / 0820 4.3 / 1356 1.1 / 2029 4.5	**22** SU	0247 0.9 / 0919 4.2 / 1505 1.2 / 2121 4.4
8 SU	0216 1.1 / 0856 4.2 / 1432 1.3 / 2107 4.4	**23** M	0328 1.2 / 0958 4.0 / 1546 1.5 / 2158 4.2
9 M	0256 1.3 / 0940 4.0 / 1518 1.5 / 2154 4.2	**24** TU	0413 1.5 / 1043 3.8 / 1631 1.8 / ◑ 2244 4.0
10 TU	0349 1.4 / 1034 3.9 / 1616 1.7 / ◑ 2251 4.1	**25** W	0503 1.7 / 1141 3.7 / 1725 1.9 / 2347 3.8
11 W	0459 1.6 / 1139 3.8 / 1732 1.7	**26** TH	0600 1.8 / 1249 3.6 / 1828 2.0
12 TH	0001 4.1 / 0621 1.9 / 1255 3.9 / 1856 1.6	**27** F	0106 3.8 / 0705 1.8 / 1353 3.8 / 1934 1.9
13 F	0119 4.1 / 0739 1.9 / 1414 4.1 / 2010 1.4	**28** SA	0215 3.9 / 0808 1.7 / 1450 3.9 / 2037 1.7
14 SA	0237 4.3 / 0848 1.6 / 1520 4.3 / 2115 1.0	**29** SU	0312 4.0 / 0905 1.6 / 1541 4.1 / 2131 1.5
15 SU	0343 4.5 / 0948 0.8 / 1618 4.6 / 2213 0.7	**30** M	0403 4.2 / 0954 1.3 / 1627 4.3 / 2217 1.3
		31 TU	0451 4.3 / 1038 1.2 / 1712 4.5 / 2301 1.1

JUNE

Day	Time m	Day	Time m
1 W ●	0536 4.4 / 1118 1.0 / 1754 4.6 / 2341 1.0	**16** TH	0611 4.6 / 1204 0.7 / 1831 4.8
2 TH	0620 4.4 / 1157 1.0 / 1834 4.6	**17** F	0028 0.6 / 0659 4.6 / 1251 0.6 / 1914 4.8
3 F	0019 0.9 / 0659 4.4 / 1237 0.9 / 1910 4.7	**18** SA	0114 0.6 / 0743 4.5 / 1332 0.7 / 1954 4.8
4 SA	0059 0.9 / 0738 4.4 / 1315 1.0 / 1946 4.7	**19** SU	0155 0.7 / 0823 4.4 / 1412 0.9 / 2030 4.7
5 SU	0137 0.9 / 0814 4.4 / 1353 1.0 / 2023 4.6	**20** M	0233 0.8 / 0859 4.3 / 1448 1.1 / 2102 4.5
6 M	0217 0.9 / 0854 4.3 / 1433 1.1 / 2103 4.6	**21** TU	0309 1.0 / 0932 4.1 / 1523 1.3 / 2135 4.4
7 TU	0259 1.0 / 0937 4.2 / 1518 1.2 / 2148 4.5	**22** W	0344 1.3 / 1006 4.0 / 1559 1.5 / 2210 4.2
8 W	0347 1.1 / 1026 4.1 / 1609 1.3 / 2239 4.4	**23** TH	0423 1.5 / 1047 3.9 / 1639 1.8 / ◑ 2252 4.0
9 TH ●	0442 1.3 / 1122 4.0 / 1708 1.5 / 2339 4.2	**24** F	0507 1.7 / 1135 3.8 / 1729 1.9 / 2344 3.8
10 F	0547 1.4 / 1227 4.0 / 1818 1.5	**25** SA	0601 1.8 / 1235 3.7 / 1832 2.0
11 SA	0048 4.2 / 0702 1.4 / 1338 4.1 / 1934 1.5	**26** SU	0051 3.8 / 0704 1.9 / 1345 3.8 / 1936 1.9
12 SU	0205 4.2 / 0814 1.5 / 1448 4.2 / 2046 1.3	**27** M	0213 3.8 / 0806 1.8 / 1452 3.9 / 2039 1.8
13 M	0316 4.3 / 0921 1.1 / 1551 4.4 / 2151 1.1	**28** TU	0322 3.9 / 0905 1.6 / 1551 4.1 / 2137 1.5
14 TU	0419 4.4 / 1020 0.9 / 1649 4.6 / 2248 0.8	**29** W	0420 4.1 / 1000 1.4 / 1642 4.4 / 2229 1.3
15 W	0517 4.5 / 1114 0.7 / 1742 4.7 / ○ 2340 0.7	**30** TH	0511 4.3 / 1050 1.2 / 1729 4.5 / 2318 1.0

JULY

Day	Time m	Day	Time m
1 F ●	0559 4.4 / 1137 1.0 / 1815 4.7	**16** SA	0017 0.6 / 0644 4.5 / 1237 0.7 / 1856 4.8
2 SA	0004 0.8 / 0644 4.5 / 1223 0.8 / 1855 4.8	**17** SU	0101 0.6 / 0724 4.5 / 1318 0.7 / 1935 4.8
3 SU	0050 0.7 / 0727 4.5 / 1308 0.8 / 1937 4.8	**18** M	0138 0.6 / 0800 4.5 / 1353 0.7 / 2007 4.7
4 M	0132 0.6 / 0808 4.5 / 1349 0.7 / 2017 4.8	**19** TU	0213 0.7 / 0831 4.4 / 1425 0.9 / 2037 4.6
5 TU	0214 0.6 / 0850 4.5 / 1429 0.8 / 2058 4.8	**20** W	0242 0.9 / 0900 4.3 / 1453 1.1 / 2107 4.5
6 W	0254 0.7 / 0931 4.5 / 1510 0.9 / 2140 4.7	**21** TH	0310 1.1 / 0932 4.2 / 1520 1.4 / 2138 4.3
7 TH	0335 0.8 / 1013 4.4 / 1553 1.0 / 2225 4.5	**22** F	0336 1.4 / 1004 4.1 / 1547 1.6 / 2212 4.1
8 F	0421 1.1 / 1101 4.2 / 1642 1.3 / ◑ 2316 4.3	**23** SA	0407 1.6 / 1044 3.9 / 1623 1.8 / ◑ 2252 3.9
9 SA	0515 1.3 / 1159 4.1 / 1742 1.5	**24** SU	0452 1.9 / 1132 3.8 / 1724 2.1 / 2346 3.7
10 SU	0020 4.1 / 0622 1.5 / 1307 4.0 / 1859 1.6	**25** M	0603 2.0 / 1237 3.7 / 1846 2.1
11 M	0138 4.0 / 0744 1.6 / 1423 4.1 / 2023 1.6	**26** TU	0100 3.6 / 0720 2.0 / 1359 3.8 / 1958 1.9
12 TU	0256 4.0 / 0902 1.5 / 1532 4.2 / 2137 1.4	**27** W	0240 3.7 / 0831 1.9 / 1516 4.0 / 2104 1.6
13 W	0406 4.2 / 1007 1.2 / 1633 4.4 / 2238 1.1	**28** TH	0352 4.0 / 0931 1.5 / 1615 4.3 / 2204 1.3
14 TH	0505 4.3 / 1103 1.0 / 1726 4.6 / 2330 0.8	**29** F	0449 4.2 / 1027 1.2 / 1706 4.5 / 2258 1.0
15 F	0557 4.4 / 1152 0.8 / 1815 4.8 / ○	**30** SA ●	0539 4.4 / 1120 0.9 / 1754 4.8 / 2348 0.7
		31 SU	0627 4.6 / 1208 0.7 / 1840 4.9

AUGUST

Day	Time m	Day	Time m
1 M	0036 0.5 / 0711 4.7 / 1255 0.5 / 1923 5.0	**16** TU	0116 0.6 / 0731 4.6 / 1329 0.7 / 1940 4.8
2 TU	0120 0.3 / 0754 4.8 / 1337 0.4 / 2005 5.0	**17** W	0145 0.7 / 0800 4.6 / 1356 0.8 / 2009 4.7
3 W	0201 0.3 / 0835 4.8 / 1417 0.4 / 2046 5.0	**18** TH	0210 0.9 / 0828 4.5 / 1420 1.0 / 2038 4.6
4 TH	0239 0.4 / 0914 4.7 / 1455 0.6 / 2126 4.8	**19** F	0231 1.1 / 0857 4.4 / 1438 1.3 / 2106 4.4
5 F	0318 0.7 / 0954 4.5 / 1534 0.9 / 2206 4.6	**20** SA	0250 1.3 / 0928 4.2 / 1458 1.5 / 2136 4.2
6 SA	0358 1.0 / 1037 4.3 / 1619 1.2 / ◑ 2252 4.3	**21** SU	0312 1.5 / 1001 4.0 / 1526 1.7 / ◑ 2212 3.9
7 SU	0445 1.4 / 1130 4.1 / 1713 1.6 / 2354 3.9	**22** M	0346 1.8 / 1045 3.8 / 1611 2.0 / 2303 3.7
8 M	0548 1.7 / 1243 3.9 / 1832 1.9	**23** TU	0444 2.1 / 1145 3.7 / 1750 2.2
9 TU	0120 3.7 / 0722 1.9 / 1407 3.9 / 2013 1.8	**24** W	0012 3.6 / 0639 2.2 / 1304 3.7 / 1926 2.1
10 W	0248 3.8 / 0854 1.7 / 1520 4.1 / 2132 1.5	**25** TH	0155 3.6 / 0759 2.0 / 1441 3.9 / 2039 1.7
11 TH	0358 4.0 / 1000 1.4 / 1621 4.4 / 2229 1.1	**26** F	0327 3.9 / 0907 1.5 / 1549 4.3 / 2142 1.3
12 F	0455 4.2 / 1052 1.0 / 1712 4.6 / 2317 0.8	**27** SA	0426 4.3 / 1007 1.1 / 1643 4.6 / 2238 0.8
13 SA	0542 4.4 / 1137 0.8 / 1756 4.8 / ○	**28** SU	0517 4.5 / 1101 0.8 / 1731 4.9 / 2329 0.5
14 SU	0000 0.6 / 0623 4.5 / 1218 0.6 / 1835 4.8	**29** M ●	0604 4.7 / 1150 0.5 / 1819 5.1
15 M	0041 0.5 / 0658 4.6 / 1256 0.6 / 1909 4.8	**30** TU	0015 0.2 / 0650 4.9 / 1236 0.3 / 1903 5.2
		31 W	0101 0.1 / 0733 5.0 / 1319 0.2 / 1946 5.2

Chart Datum: 2·62 metres below Ordnance Datum (Newlyn)
HAT is 5·3 metres above Chart Datum

DARTMOUTH

LAT 50°21'N   LONG 3°34'W

TIMES AND HEIGHTS OF HIGH AND LOW WATERS

Dates in amber are **SPRINGS**
Dates in yellow are **NEAPS**

2011

SEPTEMBER

Time	m	Time	m
1 0141 0.1 0813 5.0 TH 1358 0.2 2028 5.1		**16** 0135 0.9 0759 4.6 F 1345 1.0 2010 4.6	
2 0220 0.3 0852 4.9 F 1436 0.5 2107 4.9		**17** 0154 1.1 0827 4.5 SA 1403 1.2 2038 4.4	
3 0256 0.6 0932 4.7 SA 1515 0.8 2147 4.6		**18** 0213 1.3 0855 4.3 SU 1424 1.4 2106 4.2	
4 0335 1.1 1011 4.4 SU 1557 1.6 ◖ 2230 4.2		**19** 0236 1.5 0926 4.1 M 1453 1.6 2141 4.0	
5 0420 1.5 1102 4.1 M 1651 1.9 2333 3.8		**20** 0310 1.8 1008 3.9 TU 1535 1.9 ◗ 2234 3.7	
6 0523 2.0 1223 3.8 TU 1811 2.0		**21** 0401 2.1 1109 3.8 W 1653 2.2 2342 3.6	
7 0111 3.6 0709 2.1 W 1352 3.8 2008 2.0		**22** 0555 2.3 1224 3.8 TH 1856 2.1	
8 0239 3.7 0845 1.9 TH 1506 4.1 2119 1.6		**23** 0114 3.6 0731 2.0 F 1359 4.0 2012 1.7	
9 0346 4.0 0944 1.5 F 1603 4.4 2211 1.2		**24** 0258 4.0 0843 1.6 SA 1518 4.3 2117 1.2	
10 0437 4.3 1032 1.1 SA 1650 4.6 2256 0.8		**25** 0359 4.3 0944 1.1 SU 1615 4.7 2213 0.8	
11 0519 4.5 1114 0.8 SU 1731 4.8 2336 0.6		**26** 0450 4.6 1038 0.7 M 1705 5.0 2305 0.4	
12 0556 4.6 1153 0.7 M 1808 4.8 ○		**27** 0539 4.9 1127 0.4 TU 1755 5.2 ● 2352 0.2	
13 0012 0.6 0629 4.7 TU 1228 0.6 1842 4.8		**28** 0625 5.0 1212 0.2 W 1842 5.2	
14 0046 0.6 0659 4.7 W 1259 0.7 1912 4.8		**29** 0037 0.1 0708 5.1 TH 1257 0.1 1926 5.2	
15 0113 0.7 0730 4.7 TH 1325 0.9 1941 4.7		**30** 0119 0.2 0750 5.1 F 1337 0.2 2007 5.1	

OCTOBER

Time	m	Time	m
1 0158 0.4 0830 5.0 SA 1417 0.5 2049 4.8		**16** 0126 1.1 0802 4.6 SU 1339 1.2 2015 4.4	
2 0236 0.8 0909 4.7 SU 1457 0.9 2129 4.5		**17** 0148 1.3 0830 4.5 M 1404 1.4 2046 4.2	
3 0316 1.2 0949 4.4 M 1540 1.4 2213 4.1		**18** 0216 1.5 0902 4.3 TU 1435 1.6 2123 4.0	
4 0401 1.7 1039 4.1 TU 1634 1.8 ◗ 2319 3.7		**19** 0252 1.7 0946 4.1 W 1520 1.8 2214 3.8	
5 0502 2.1 1201 3.9 W 1751 2.1		**20** 0343 2.0 1044 4.0 TH 1630 2.1 ◗ 2320 3.7	
6 0056 3.6 0640 2.2 TH 1328 3.8 1943 2.0		**21** 0514 2.2 1153 3.9 F 1819 2.0	
7 0216 3.7 0817 2.0 F 1439 4.0 2052 1.7		**22** 0041 3.8 0657 2.0 SA 1316 4.1 1941 1.7	
8 0319 4.0 0915 1.6 SA 1535 4.3 2142 1.3		**23** 0216 4.0 0812 1.6 SU 1439 4.4 2048 1.3	
9 0408 4.3 1002 1.3 SU 1621 4.5 2225 1.0		**24** 0325 4.4 0915 1.2 M 1543 4.7 2146 0.9	
10 0448 4.5 1044 1.0 M 1701 4.7 2305 0.8		**25** 0420 4.7 1011 0.8 TU 1639 4.9 2239 0.5	
11 0524 4.7 1122 0.8 TU 1739 4.8 2340 0.8		**26** 0511 4.9 1102 0.5 W 1730 5.1 ● 2327 0.3	
12 0558 4.7 1156 0.8 W 1814 4.8 ○		**27** 0559 5.1 1150 0.3 TH 1820 5.2	
13 0011 0.8 0631 4.8 TH 1226 0.9 1846 4.8		**28** 0013 0.3 0645 5.2 F 1237 0.3 1906 5.1	
14 0039 0.9 0702 4.8 F 1254 1.0 1917 4.7		**29** 0058 0.3 0729 5.2 SA 1320 0.4 1950 5.0	
15 0103 1.0 0733 4.7 SA 1317 1.1 1947 4.6		**30** 0139 0.5 0810 5.0 SU 1402 0.6 2033 4.7	
		31 0220 0.9 0851 4.8 M 1443 0.9 2116 4.4	

NOVEMBER

Time	m	Time	m
1 0301 1.3 0933 4.5 TU 1527 1.3 2201 4.1		**16** 0209 1.4 0850 4.5 W 1432 1.5 2113 4.2	
2 0345 1.7 1019 4.2 W 1618 1.7 ◗ 2259 3.8		**17** 0247 1.6 0933 4.3 TH 1518 1.6 2202 4.0	
3 0439 2.0 1127 4.0 TH 1721 2.0		**18** 0337 1.8 1025 4.2 F 1618 1.8 ◗ 2300 3.9	
4 0020 3.7 0549 2.2 F 1247 3.9 1844 2.1		**19** 0445 2.0 1128 4.1 SA 1737 1.8	
5 0134 3.7 0721 2.1 SA 1356 4.0 2003 1.9		**20** 0010 3.9 0612 1.9 SU 1239 4.2 1902 1.7	
6 0236 3.9 0831 1.9 SU 1454 4.2 2100 1.6		**21** 0129 4.1 0734 1.7 M 1357 4.3 2013 1.4	
7 0326 4.2 0922 1.6 M 1543 4.4 2146 1.4		**22** 0246 4.3 0844 1.4 TU 1509 4.5 2116 1.1	
8 0411 4.4 1007 1.3 TU 1626 4.5 2226 1.2		**23** 0348 4.6 0945 1.0 W 1611 4.8 2213 0.8	
9 0450 4.6 1047 1.2 W 1706 4.6 2304 1.1		**24** 0444 4.8 1040 0.7 TH 1708 4.9 2305 0.6	
10 0527 4.6 1123 1.1 TH 1746 4.7 ○ 2337 1.0		**25** 0536 5.0 1131 0.5 F 1800 5.0 ● 2354 0.5	
11 0604 4.8 1155 1.0 F 1823 4.7		**26** 0626 5.1 1219 0.5 SA 1851 4.9	
12 0007 1.0 0639 4.8 SA 1226 1.1 1857 4.6		**27** 0041 0.5 0711 5.1 SU 1306 0.5 1937 4.9	
13 0038 1.1 0712 4.8 SU 1257 1.1 1931 4.5		**28** 0126 0.7 0755 5.0 M 1349 0.6 2021 4.7	
14 0107 1.2 0743 4.7 M 1326 1.2 2002 4.4		**29** 0207 0.9 0837 4.9 TU 1431 0.9 2103 4.5	
15 0135 1.3 0814 4.6 TU 1357 1.3 2035 4.3		**30** 0247 1.2 0917 4.7 W 1514 1.2 2143 4.2	

DECEMBER

Time	m	Time	m
1 0328 1.5 0957 4.5 TH 1556 1.5 2226 4.0		**16** 0246 1.3 0924 4.6 F 1515 1.3 2152 4.2	
2 0412 1.8 1040 4.2 F 1643 1.8 ◗ 2317 3.8		**17** 0330 1.4 1010 4.5 SA 1602 1.4 2242 4.1	
3 0503 2.0 1136 4.0 SA 1738 2.0		**18** 0423 1.6 1104 4.3 SU 1700 1.6 ◗ 2340 4.1	
4 0022 3.8 0603 2.1 SU 1247 3.9 1844 2.0		**19** 0527 1.8 1207 4.2 M 1813 1.7	
5 0132 3.8 0716 2.1 M 1356 4.0 1952 1.9		**20** 0050 4.1 0650 1.8 TU 1321 4.2 1935 1.6	
6 0233 4.0 0824 2.0 TU 1455 4.1 2202 1.8		**21** 0208 4.2 0811 1.6 W 1439 4.3 2049 1.4	
7 0326 4.2 0920 1.7 W 1548 4.2 2142 1.5		**22** 0320 4.4 0921 1.3 TH 1549 4.5 2153 1.2	
8 0414 4.4 1008 1.5 TH 1635 4.4 2225 1.4		**23** 0423 4.6 1023 1.0 F 1651 4.6 2250 0.9	
9 0458 4.6 1050 1.3 F 1720 4.5 2305 1.3		**24** 0519 4.8 1118 0.8 SA 1747 4.7 ● 2341 0.7	
10 0540 4.7 1129 1.2 SA 1802 4.6 ○ 2342 1.1		**25** 0611 5.0 1208 0.6 SU 1839 4.8	
11 0620 4.8 1206 1.1 SU 1843 4.6		**26** 0028 0.6 0657 5.1 M 1256 0.5 1924 4.8	
12 0018 1.1 0656 4.8 M 1243 1.1 1920 4.6		**27** 0114 0.6 0741 5.0 TU 1338 0.6 2007 4.7	
13 0055 1.1 0733 4.8 TU 1320 1.1 1955 4.5		**28** 0154 0.7 0821 4.9 W 1418 0.7 2045 4.5	
14 0130 1.1 0807 4.7 W 1355 1.1 2031 4.4		**29** 0231 0.9 0856 4.8 TH 1454 0.9 2118 4.4	
15 0207 1.2 0844 4.7 TH 1433 1.2 2109 4.3		**30** 0306 1.2 0929 4.6 F 1529 1.2 2148 4.2	
		31 0340 1.5 1001 4.5 SA 1605 1.5 2223 4.0	

Chart Datum: 2·62 metres below Ordnance Datum (Newlyn)
HAT is 5·3 metres above Chart Datum

TIDES

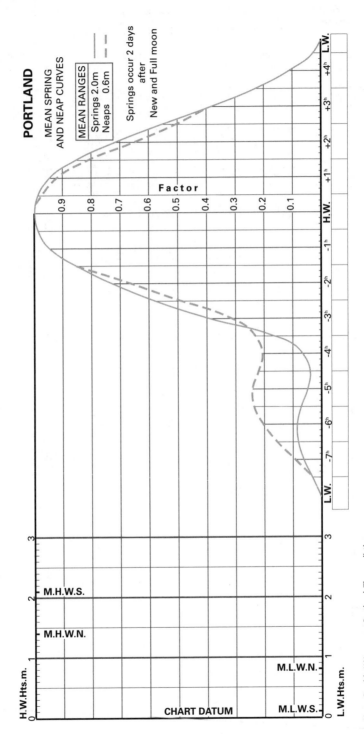

PORTLAND

MEAN SPRING
AND NEAP CURVES

MEAN RANGES
Springs 2.0m
Neaps 0.6m

Springs occur 2 days
after
New and Full moon

Note - Double LWs occur at Portland. The predictions are for the first LW. The second LW occurs from 3 to 4 Hrs later and may, at Springs, on occasions be lower than the first.

PORTLAND
LAT 50°34'N   LONG 2°26'W

Dates in amber are **SPRINGS**
Dates in yellow are **NEAPS**

2011

TIMES AND HEIGHTS OF HIGH AND LOW WATERS

JANUARY

Day	Time m	Time m	Time m	Time m
1 SA	0340 1.7	0904 0.7	1605 1.6	2126 0.6
16 SU	0259 1.5	0819 0.7	1534 1.4	2043 0.6
2 SU	0444 1.8	1006 0.6	1711 1.7	2221 0.5
17 M	0410 1.7	0927 0.6	1644 1.6	2145 0.5
3 M	0539 1.9	1056 0.5	1808 1.8	2309 0.4
18 TU	0509 1.9	1020 0.5	1744 1.7	2238 0.3
4 TU	0628 2.0	1140 0.4	1857 1.9	● 2351 0.4
19 W	0604 2.0	1109 0.3	1839 1.9	○ 2328 0.2
5 W	0711 2.1	1221 0.3	1939 1.9	
20 TH	0655 2.2	1155 0.2	1929 2.0	
6 TH	0031 0.3	0749 2.1	1300 0.3	2014 1.9
21	0014 0.1	0742 2.3	1241 0.1	2013 2.1
7 F	0108 0.3	0821 2.1	1337 0.3	2043 1.8
22 SA	0059 0.1	0825 2.3	1325 0.1	2054 2.1
8 SA	0144 0.3	0848 2.0	1412 0.3	2108 1.7
23 SU	0142 0.1	0905 2.3	1408 0.1	2131 2.0
9 SU	0215 0.4	0914 1.9	1443 0.3	2134 1.6
24 M	0224 0.1	0942 2.1	1451 0.1	2206 1.9
10 M	0239 0.4	0941 1.7	1506 0.4	2203 1.5
25 TU	0306 0.2	1018 1.9	1535 0.2	2243 1.8
11 TU	0259 0.5	1008 1.6	1525 0.5	2234 1.5
26 W	0349 0.4	1056 1.8	1622 0.4	○ 2325 1.6
12 W	0324 0.6	1036 1.5	1556 0.6	◑ 2313 1.4
27 TH	0438 0.5	1140 1.6	1717 0.5	
13 TH	0405 0.7	1116 1.4	1646 0.6	
28 F	0018 1.5	0714 0.8	1238 1.5	1827 0.7
14 F	0010 1.3	0508 0.8	1223 1.3	1759 0.6
29 SA	0137 1.5	0714 0.8	1409 1.4	1956 0.7
15 SA	0133 1.4	0643 0.8	1404 1.3	1927 0.6
30 SU	0315 1.5	0858 0.7	1554 1.4	2115 0.7
31 M	0430 1.6	1001 0.6	1705 1.5	2211 0.6

FEBRUARY

Day	Time m	Time m	Time m	Time m
1 TU	0527 1.8	1046 0.5	1800 1.7	2255 0.5
16 W	0448 1.8	1007 0.4	1730 1.7	2225 0.3
2 W	0615 1.9	1126 0.4	1845 1.8	2335 0.3
17 TH	0547 2.0	1056 0.2	1825 1.9	2313 0.1
3 TH	0657 2.0	1203 0.2	1924 1.9	
18 F	0640 2.2	1141 0.0	1913 2.1	○ 2359 0.0
4	0013 0.2	0733 2.1	1240 0.1	1957 1.9
19 SA	0728 2.3	1225 -0.1	1957 2.2	
5 SA	0050 0.2	0804 2.1	1316 0.1	2024 1.9
20 SU	0043 -0.1	0810 2.4	1309 -0.1	2036 2.2
6	0125 0.1	0831 2.0	1349 0.1	2049 1.8
21 M	0125 -0.1	0849 2.3	1350 -0.1	2112 2.1
7 M	0155 0.2	0857 1.9	1416 0.2	2113 1.7
22 TU	0205 -0.1	0925 2.2	1431 0.1	2146 2.0
8 TU	0217 0.2	0923 1.8	1433 0.2	2137 1.6
23 W	0244 0.1	1000 2.0	1510 0.2	2220 1.8
9 W	0239 0.3	0947 1.6	1449 0.3	2159 1.5
24 TH	0324 0.3	1035 1.8	1551 0.4	◑ 2257 1.6
10 TH	0254 0.4	1007 1.5	1513 0.4	2226 1.4
25 F	0409 0.5	1115 1.5	1639 0.6	2343 1.5
11 F	0324 0.5	1035 1.4	1550 0.5	◑ 2308 1.4
26 SA	0511 0.7	1208 1.3	1749 0.7	
12 SA	0411 0.6	1124 1.3	1651 0.6	
27	0056 1.4	0654 0.8	1350 1.2	1932 0.8
13	0015 1.3	0535 0.7	1254 1.2	1834 0.7
28 M	0254 1.4	0855 0.7	1549 1.3	2100 0.7
14 M	0158 1.4	0742 0.7	1459 1.4	2020 0.6
15 TU	0336 1.5	0911 0.6	1626 1.5	2130 0.5

MARCH

Day	Time m	Time m	Time m	Time m
1 TU	0412 1.6	0949 0.6	1653 1.5	2151 0.6
16 W	0300 1.5	0851 0.5	1605 1.5	2111 0.5
2 W	0506 1.7	1027 0.4	1740 1.6	2232 0.4
17 TH	0421 1.7	0947 0.3	1708 1.7	2205 0.3
3 TH	0552 1.9	1102 0.3	1822 1.8	2310 0.3
18 F	0523 2.0	1036 0.1	1802 1.9	2253 0.1
4 F	0633 2.0	1137 0.2	1859 1.9	● 2348 0.2
19 SA	0617 2.2	1121 -0.1	1849 2.1	○ 2339 -0.1
5 SA	0709 2.1	1214 0.1	1931 1.9	
20 SU	0705 2.3	1205 -0.2	1933 2.2	
6	0025 0.1	0745 2.1	1250 0.1	1959 1.9
21	0022 -0.1	0748 2.4	1248 -0.2	2013 2.3
7 M	0101 0.1	0809 2.0	1322 0.1	2025 1.9
22 TU	0104 -0.1	0829 2.3	1329 -0.1	2050 2.2
8 TU	0130 0.1	0836 1.9	1347 0.1	2049 1.8
23 W	0144 -0.1	0906 2.2	1408 0.0	2126 2.1
9 W	0152 0.1	0902 1.8	1404 0.2	2111 1.7
24 TH	0223 0.1	0942 2.0	1445 0.2	2200 1.9
10 TH	0209 0.2	0924 1.6	1420 0.2	2131 1.6
25 F	0303 0.3	1017 1.7	1524 0.4	2235 1.7
11 F	0229 0.3	0945 1.5	1443 0.3	2155 1.5
26 SA	0348 0.5	1056 1.5	1608 0.6	◑ 2317 1.5
12 SA	0257 0.4	1012 1.4	1515 0.4	◑ 2232 1.4
27 SU	0450 0.7	1150 1.3	1714 0.8	
13 SU	0339 0.5	1057 1.3	1606 0.6	2332 1.4
28	0023 1.4	0629 0.8	1345 1.2	1853 0.8
14	0458 0.7	1222 1.2	1802 0.7	
29 TU	0223 1.4	0832 0.7	1528 1.3	2027 0.8
15 TU	0107 1.4	0720 0.3	1431 1.3	2000 0.6
30 W	0339 1.5	0920 0.6	1624 1.5	2119 0.6
31 TH	0432 1.6	0954 0.4	1708 1.6	2159 0.5

APRIL

Day	Time m	Time m	Time m	Time m
1 F	0517 1.8	1029 0.3	1748 1.7	2239 0.3
16 SA	0452 1.9	1010 0.1	1732 1.9	2229 0.2
2 SA	0558 1.9	1105 0.2	1825 1.9	2318 0.2
17 SU	0548 2.1	1057 0.0	1821 2.1	2316 0.0
3 SU	0635 2.0	1142 0.1	1858 2.0	● 2356 0.1
18 M	0639 2.2	1142 -0.1	1907 2.3	○
4 M	0710 2.0	1218 0.1	1929 2.0	
19 TU	0001 0.0	0725 2.3	1226 -0.1	1950 2.3
5 TU	0032 0.1	0742 2.0	1251 0.1	1958 2.0
20 W	0044 0.0	0809 2.2	1307 0.0	2030 2.2
6 W	0102 0.1	0813 1.9	1316 0.1	2025 1.9
21 TH	0125 0.0	0849 2.1	1347 0.1	2107 2.1
7 TH	0126 0.2	0841 1.8	1338 0.2	2048 1.8
22 F	0206 0.2	0927 1.9	1425 0.3	2143 1.9
8 F	0148 0.3	0905 1.7	1359 0.3	2109 1.7
23 SA	0248 0.3	1003 1.7	1503 0.5	2216 1.7
9 SA	0212 0.3	0929 1.5	1424 0.4	2135 1.6
24 SU	0333 0.5	1043 1.5	1546 0.7	2254 1.6
10 SU	0243 0.4	1001 1.4	1459 0.5	2212 1.6
25 M	0431 0.6	1134 1.3	1643 0.8	◑ 2347 1.4
11 M	0329 0.5	1051 1.3	1554 0.6	◑ 2310 1.4
26	0548 0.7	1302 1.2	1804 0.9	
12	0452 0.6	1213 1.3	1747 0.7	
27 W	0112 1.4	0721 0.7	1440 1.3	1929 0.8
13 W	0038 1.4	0652 0.6	1406 1.3	1933 0.7
28 TH	0243 1.4	0826 0.6	1538 1.4	2032 0.7
14 TH	0224 1.5	0819 0.5	1534 1.5	2044 0.5
29 F	0341 1.5	0909 0.5	1623 1.6	2120 0.6
15 F	0347 1.7	0919 0.3	1637 1.8	2140 0.3
30 SA	0429 1.7	0948 0.4	1704 1.7	2204 0.4

Chart Datum: 0·93 metres below Ordnance Datum (Newlyn)
HAT is 2·5 metres above Chart Datum

TIDES

TIME ZONE (UT)
For Summer Time add ONE hour in **non-shaded areas**

PORTLAND
LAT 50°34'N   LONG 2°26'W

TIMES AND HEIGHTS OF HIGH AND LOW WATERS

Dates in amber are **SPRINGS**
Dates in yellow are **NEAPS**

2011

MAY

Day	Time m	Time m	Time m	Time m
1 SU	0514 1.8	1028 0.3	1743 1.8	2245 0.3
16 M	0520 2.0	1033 0.2	1754 2.1	2256 0.2
2 M	0556 1.8	1107 0.2	1821 1.9	2325 0.3
17 TU ○	0616 2.1	1121 0.1	1844 2.2	2343 0.2
3 TU ●	0637 1.9	1144 0.2	1857 2.0	
18 W	0707 2.1	1207 0.1	1930 2.2	
4 W	0001 0.2	0715 1.9	1219 0.2	1932 2.0
19 TH	0028 0.1	0753 2.1	1251 0.2	2013 2.2
5 TH	0034 0.2	0751 1.9	1249 0.2	2003 2.0
20 F	0112 0.2	0837 2.0	1332 0.2	2052 2.1
6 F	0104 0.3	0824 1.8	1319 0.3	2032 1.9
21 SA	0154 0.2	0916 1.9	1410 0.4	2128 2.0
7 SA	0133 0.3	0854 1.7	1350 0.4	2058 1.8
22 SU	0236 0.3	0953 1.7	1449 0.5	2200 1.8
8 SU	0206 0.3	0924 1.6	1424 0.4	2128 1.7
23 M	0319 0.4	1028 1.5	1528 0.6	2232 1.6
9 M	0245 0.4	1002 1.5	1506 0.5	2208 1.6
24 TU ◑	0406 0.5	1108 1.4	1614 0.7	2310 1.5
10 TU ◑	0337 0.5	1053 1.4	1605 0.6	2303 1.6
25 W	0502 0.6	1159 1.3	1714 0.8	
11 W	0450 0.5	1205 1.4	1730 0.7	
26 TH	0003 1.4	0609 0.6	1306 1.3	1828 0.8
12 TH	0018 1.5	0618 0.5	1335 1.4	1857 0.7
27 F	0110 1.4	0716 0.6	1419 1.4	1938 0.8
13 F	0148 1.6	0739 0.5	1455 1.6	2010 0.6
28 SA	0224 1.4	0814 0.5	1521 1.5	2037 0.7
14 SA	0310 1.7	0845 0.5	1602 1.8	2111 0.4
29 SU	0329 1.5	0903 0.5	1612 1.6	2127 0.6
15 SU	0419 1.8	0941 0.4	1701 1.9	2205 0.3
30 M	0426 1.6	0948 0.4	1700 1.8	2212 0.5
31 TU	0518 1.7	1030 0.3	1745 1.9	2254 0.4

JUNE

Day	Time m	Time m	Time m	Time m
1 W ●	0607 1.8	1111 0.3	1829 2.0	2333 0.4
16 TH	0655 2.0	1155 0.3	1916 2.2	
2 TH	0653 1.8	1151 0.3	1910 2.0	
17 F	0019 0.3	0743 2.0	1239 0.3	2000 2.2
3 F	0011 0.3	0736 1.9	1230 0.3	1949 2.0
18 SA	0102 0.2	0827 2.0	1319 0.3	2040 2.1
4 SA	0048 0.3	0816 1.9	1308 0.3	2025 2.0
19 SU	0143 0.2	0905 1.9	1357 0.3	2114 2.0
5 SU	0126 0.3	0853 1.8	1348 0.3	2058 1.9
20 M	0222 0.3	0938 1.8	1434 0.4	2142 1.9
6 M	0206 0.3	0929 1.7	1429 0.4	2133 1.8
21 TU	0300 0.3	1005 1.6	1509 0.5	2208 1.7
7 TU	0250 0.3	1007 1.7	1513 0.5	2212 1.8
22 W	0337 0.4	1034 1.5	1543 0.6	2238 1.6
8 W	0339 0.4	1053 1.6	1605 0.5	2300 1.7
23 TH ◑	0414 0.5	1111 1.4	1619 0.7	2315 1.5
9 TH ◐	0437 0.4	1149 1.6	1707 0.6	2359 1.6
24 F	0456 0.6	1159 1.4	1709 0.8	
10 F	0545 0.5	1258 1.5	1819 0.6	
25 SA	0005 1.4	0552 0.6	1300 1.4	1825 0.8
11 SA	0111 1.6	0658 0.5	1414 1.6	1933 0.6
26 SU	0112 1.3	0702 0.6	1411 1.4	1942 0.8
12 SU	0231 1.6	0810 0.5	1528 1.7	2043 0.5
27 M	0229 1.4	0808 0.6	1521 1.5	2046 0.7
13 M	0348 1.7	0916 0.4	1634 1.8	2146 0.5
28 TU	0343 1.5	0906 0.5	1621 1.7	2139 0.6
14 TU	0458 1.8	1015 0.3	1733 2.0	2242 0.4
29 W	0446 1.6	0957 0.5	1715 1.8	2227 0.5
15 W ○	0600 1.9	1107 0.3	1827 2.1	2333 0.3
30 TH	0543 1.7	1045 0.4	1806 1.9	2311 0.4

JULY

Day	Time m	Time m	Time m	Time m
1 F ●	0636 1.8	1131 0.3	1854 2.0	2354 0.3
16 SA	0007 0.3	0733 1.9	1224 0.3	1947 2.2
2 SA	0725 1.9	1215 0.3	1940 2.1	
17 SU	0048 0.2	0813 2.0	1303 0.2	2024 2.2
3 SU	0036 0.2	0809 1.9	1259 0.2	2021 2.1
18 M	0126 0.2	0847 1.9	1339 0.2	2054 2.1
4 M	0119 0.2	0850 1.9	1341 0.2	2100 2.1
19 TU	0202 0.2	0913 1.8	1414 0.3	2119 1.9
5 TU	0201 0.2	0927 1.9	1423 0.2	2136 2.0
20 W	0236 0.2	0936 1.7	1445 0.3	2143 1.8
6 W	0244 0.2	1003 1.8	1506 0.3	2212 1.9
21 TH	0305 0.3	1000 1.6	1510 0.4	2208 1.6
7 TH	0329 0.2	1042 1.8	1551 0.4	2252 1.8
22 F	0327 0.4	1029 1.5	1530 0.5	2235 1.5
8 F ◑	0418 0.3	1127 1.7	1643 0.5	2339 1.7
23 SA ◑	0348 0.5	1104 1.4	1559 0.6	2305 1.4
9 SA	0515 0.4	1222 1.6	1745 0.6	
24 SU	0424 0.6	1151 1.3	1649 0.7	2353 1.3
10 SU	0037 1.6	0623 0.6	1335 1.6	1900 0.7
25 M	0523 0.6	1301 1.3	1815 0.8	
11 M	0155 1.5	0742 0.6	1459 1.6	2024 0.7
26 TU	0121 1.3	0654 0.7	1428 1.4	2001 0.8
12 TU	0326 1.5	0901 0.6	1615 1.7	2139 0.6
27 W	0303 1.3	0828 0.6	1546 1.6	2113 0.7
13 W	0446 1.6	1006 0.5	1720 1.9	2236 0.5
28 TH	0420 1.5	0933 0.5	1650 1.7	2206 0.5
14 TH	0551 1.8	1058 0.4	1815 2.0	2324 0.4
29 F	0524 1.6	1026 0.4	1746 1.9	2253 0.4
15 F ○	0646 1.9	1143 0.3	1904 2.1	
30 SA ●	0620 1.8	1114 0.3	1839 2.1	2338 0.2
31 SU	0711 2.0	1159 0.2	1927 2.2	

AUGUST

Day	Time m	Time m	Time m	Time m
1 M	0022 0.1	0756 2.1	1244 0.1	2010 2.3
16 TU	0101 0.1	0819 2.0	1315 0.1	2028 2.1
2 TU	0105 0.0	0836 2.1	1326 0.0	2049 2.3
17 W	0136 0.1	0843 1.9	1349 0.2	2052 2.0
3 W	0148 0.0	0913 2.1	1408 0.1	2125 2.2
18 TH	0207 0.2	0904 1.8	1417 0.2	2115 1.8
4 TH	0229 0.1	0947 2.0	1449 0.1	2200 2.0
19 F	0230 0.2	0927 1.7	1436 0.4	2139 1.7
5 F	0312 0.2	1023 1.9	1531 0.3	2236 1.9
20 SA	0244 0.3	0950 1.6	1513 0.4	2200 1.5
6 SA	0356 0.3	1102 1.7	1618 0.5	2317 1.7
21 SU ◑	0301 0.4	1015 1.5	1513 0.6	2221 1.4
7 SU	0448 0.5	1152 1.6	1717 0.6	
22 M	0330 0.5	1051 1.4	1553 0.7	2259 1.3
8 M	0010 1.5	0555 0.6	1304 1.5	1839 0.7
23 TU	0420 0.6	1150 1.3	1709 0.8	
9 TU	0131 1.4	0726 0.7	1443 1.5	2023 0.8
24 W	0014 1.2	0557 0.7	1328 1.4	1925 0.8
10 W	0323 1.4	0857 0.7	1607 1.6	2137 0.7
25 TH	0228 1.3	0802 0.7	1512 1.5	2052 0.7
11 TH	0444 1.6	0958 0.6	1709 1.8	2228 0.5
26 F	0401 1.4	0913 0.6	1625 1.7	2146 0.5
12 F	0543 1.7	1044 0.5	1801 2.0	2309 0.4
27 SA	0505 1.7	1006 0.4	1724 1.9	2233 0.3
13 SA ○	0631 1.8	1124 0.3	1846 2.1	2347 0.3
28 SU	0600 1.9	1053 0.2	1817 2.1	2318 0.1
14 SU	0713 1.9	1202 0.2	1926 2.2	
29 M ●	0649 2.1	1138 0.1	1905 2.2	
15 M	0024 0.2	0749 2.0	1239 0.2	2000 2.2
30 TU	0001 0.0	0733 2.2	1222 0.0	1949 2.4
31 W	0045 -0.1	0813 2.2	1305 0.0	2029 2.4

Chart Datum: 0·93 metres below Ordnance Datum (Newlyn)
HAT is 2·5 metres above Chart Datum

PORTLAND
LAT 50°34'N LONG 2°26'W
TIMES AND HEIGHTS OF HIGH AND LOW WATERS

Dates in amber are **SPRINGS**
Dates in yellow are **NEAPS**

2011

SEPTEMBER				OCTOBER				NOVEMBER				DECEMBER			
Time	m	Time	m	Time	m	Time	m	Time	m	Time	m	Time	m	Time	m

SEPTEMBER

1 TH 0127 -0.1 / 0851 2.2 / 1346 0.0 / 2106 2.3 **16** F 0134 0.2 / 0832 1.9 / 1346 0.3 / 2046 1.9

2 F 0208 0.0 / 0926 2.1 / 1427 0.1 / 2141 2.1 **17** SA 0154 0.3 / 0855 1.8 / 1402 0.4 / 2110 1.7

3 SA 0249 0.2 / 1001 1.9 / 1508 0.3 / 2217 1.9 **18** SU 0207 0.4 / 0916 1.7 / 1417 0.4 / 2130 1.5

4 SU 0331 0.4 / 1039 1.8 / 1555 0.5 / ◐ 2257 1.6 **19** M 0224 0.4 / 0938 1.6 / 1439 0.5 / 2153 1.4

5 M 0420 0.6 / 1127 1.6 / 1658 0.7 / 2351 1.4 **20** TU 0249 0.5 / 1011 1.5 / 1515 0.6 / ◑ 2231 1.3

6 TU 0529 0.8 / 1241 1.5 / 1832 0.8 **21** W 0330 0.7 / 1105 1.4 / 1627 0.6 / 2344 1.2

7 W 0133 1.3 / 0715 0.8 / 1436 1.5 / 2028 0.8 **22** TH 0513 0.8 / 1233 1.4 / 1858 0.9

8 TH 0329 1.4 / 0849 0.8 / 1554 1.6 / 2128 0.7 **23** F 0201 1.3 / 0737 0.8 / 1433 1.5 / 2027 0.6

9 F 0435 1.6 / 0941 0.7 / 1649 1.6 / 2208 0.5 **24** SA 0339 1.5 / 0850 0.6 / 1554 1.7 / 2121 0.5

10 SA 0523 1.7 / 1020 0.5 / 1736 1.9 / 2243 0.4 **25** SU 0441 1.7 / 0942 0.4 / 1655 2.0 / 2208 0.3

11 SU 0605 1.8 / 1057 0.4 / 1818 2.0 / 2318 0.2 **26** M 0533 2.0 / 1029 0.2 / 1748 2.2 / 2253 0.1

12 M 0643 2.0 / 1855 2.1 / ○ 2354 0.2 **27** TU 0620 2.2 / 1114 0.1 / 1837 2.3 / ● 2337 0.0

13 TU 0717 2.0 / 1210 0.2 / 1928 2.1 **28** W 0705 2.3 / 1158 0.0 / 1923 2.4

14 W 0030 0.1 / 0744 2.0 / 1247 0.2 / 1955 2.1 **29** TH 0020 -0.1 / 0746 2.3 / 1241 0.0 / 2005 2.4

15 TH 0105 0.1 / 0808 2.0 / 1320 0.2 / 2021 2.0 **30** F 0102 0.0 / 0826 2.3 / 1323 0.1 / 2044 2.3

OCTOBER

1 SA 0143 0.1 / 0903 2.2 / 1404 0.2 / 2122 2.1 **16** SU 0120 0.3 / 0827 1.9 / 1334 0.4 / 2046 1.7

2 SU 0223 0.3 / 0940 2.0 / 1447 0.4 / 2200 1.8 **17** M 0139 0.4 / 0849 1.8 / 1354 0.5 / 2109 1.6

3 M 0304 0.5 / 1018 1.8 / 1536 0.6 / 2242 1.6 **18** TU 0159 0.5 / 0913 1.7 / 1420 0.5 / 2137 1.5

4 TU 0351 0.7 / 1104 1.6 / 1641 0.7 / ◑ 2340 1.4 **19** W 0227 0.6 / 0946 1.6 / 1500 0.6 / 2219 1.4

5 W 0458 0.9 / 1219 1.5 / 1820 0.8 **20** TH 0309 0.7 / 1037 1.5 / 1614 0.7 / ◑ 2331 1.3

6 TH 0140 1.3 / 0641 1.0 / 1413 1.5 / 2010 0.8 **21** F 0447 0.9 / 1157 1.5 / 1822 0.8

7 F 0315 1.4 / 0823 0.9 / 1525 1.6 / 2101 0.7 **22** SA 0131 1.4 / 0700 0.8 / 1347 1.6 / 1949 0.6

8 SA 0409 1.6 / 0912 0.8 / 1616 1.8 / 2136 0.5 **23** SU 0307 1.5 / 0817 0.7 / 1516 1.7 / 2048 0.5

9 SU 0451 1.7 / 0948 0.6 / 1700 1.9 / 2208 0.4 **24** M 0409 1.8 / 0913 0.6 / 1621 1.9 / 2138 0.3

10 M 0529 1.9 / 1024 0.5 / 1740 2.0 / 2243 0.3 **25** TU 0501 2.0 / 1003 0.4 / 1717 2.1 / 2225 0.1

11 TU 0605 2.0 / 1101 0.4 / 1817 2.0 / 2320 0.2 **26** W 0550 2.2 / 1049 0.2 / 1808 2.2 / ● 2311 0.1

12 W 0637 2.0 / 1139 0.3 / 1850 2.0 / ○ 2356 0.2 **27** TH 0637 2.3 / 1135 0.1 / 1857 2.3 / 2355 0.1

13 TH 0707 2.1 / 1216 0.3 / 1922 2.0 **28** F 0721 2.4 / 1219 0.1 / 1943 2.3

14 F 0030 0.2 / 0735 2.1 / 1249 0.3 / 1952 2.0 **29** SA 0039 0.1 / 0803 2.4 / 1303 0.2 / 2025 2.2

15 SA 0059 0.3 / 0802 2.0 / 1315 0.3 / 2020 1.9 **30** SU 0121 0.2 / 0843 2.2 / 1347 0.3 / 2106 2.0

31 M 0201 0.4 / 0922 2.1 / 1431 0.4 / 2146 1.8

NOVEMBER

1 TU 0242 0.6 / 1000 1.9 / 1521 0.6 / 2229 1.6 **16** W 0154 0.5 / 0904 1.8 / 1420 0.5 / 2134 1.6

2 W 0326 0.7 / 1041 1.7 / 1620 0.7 / ◐ 2324 1.4 **17** TH 0229 0.6 / 0939 1.7 / 1504 0.6 / 2218 1.5

3 TH 0423 0.9 / 1137 1.6 / 1736 0.8 **18** F 0315 0.7 / 1026 1.6 / 1610 0.7 / ◑ 2320 1.4

4 F 0100 1.4 / 0542 1.0 / 1313 1.5 / 1905 0.9 **19** SA 0433 0.8 / 1132 1.6 / 1740 0.7

5 SA 0231 1.4 / 0713 1.0 / 1435 1.5 / 2007 0.7 **20** SU 0049 1.4 / 0612 0.8 / 1301 1.6 / 1902 0.6

6 SU 0327 1.5 / 0821 0.9 / 1530 1.6 / 2048 0.6 **21** M 0221 1.6 / 0735 0.7 / 1431 1.7 / 2009 0.5

7 M 0410 1.7 / 0907 0.7 / 1614 1.7 / 2126 0.5 **22** TU 0331 1.8 / 0840 0.6 / 1544 1.8 / 2107 0.4

8 TU 0447 1.8 / 0948 0.6 / 1655 1.8 / 2205 0.4 **23** W 0430 2.0 / 0936 0.5 / 1647 2.0 / 2159 0.3

9 W 0522 1.9 / 1028 0.5 / 1734 1.9 / 2243 0.3 **24** TH 0523 2.1 / 1028 0.4 / 1744 2.1 / 2249 0.2

10 TH 0557 2.0 / 1108 0.4 / 1813 1.9 / ○ 2321 0.3 **25** F 0613 2.3 / 1117 0.3 / ● 1837 2.2 / 2336 0.2

11 F 0632 2.1 / 1145 0.4 / 1851 1.9 / 2356 0.3 **26** SA 0701 2.3 / 1204 0.3 / 1927 2.2

12 SA 0707 2.1 / 1220 0.4 / 1928 1.9 **27** SU 0021 0.2 / 0746 2.3 / 1250 0.3 / 2012 2.1

13 SU 0028 0.3 / 0739 2.1 / 1249 0.4 / 2002 1.9 **28** M 0105 0.3 / 0829 2.3 / 1335 0.3 / 2056 2.0

14 M 0057 0.3 / 0809 2.0 / 1317 0.4 / 2032 1.8 **29** TU 0146 0.4 / 0908 2.1 / 1419 0.4 / 2136 1.8

15 TU 0125 0.5 / 0835 1.9 / 1346 0.5 / 2101 1.7 **30** W 0226 0.5 / 0944 2.0 / 1503 0.5 / 2213 1.7

DECEMBER

1 TH 0306 0.7 / 1017 1.8 / 1551 0.6 / 2251 1.5 **16** F 0237 0.5 / 0941 1.8 / 1506 0.4 / 2216 1.6

2 F 0350 0.8 / 1053 1.6 / 1646 0.7 / ◐ 2337 1.4 **17** SA 0321 0.6 / 1023 1.7 / 1558 0.5 / 2304 1.6

3 SA 0446 0.9 / 1140 1.5 / 1749 0.8 **18** SU 0416 0.6 / 1115 1.7 / 1703 0.5 / ◑

4 SU 0040 1.4 / 0558 0.9 / 1243 1.5 / 1853 0.7 **19** M 0007 1.5 / 0527 0.7 / 1222 1.6 / 1816 0.6

5 M 0200 1.4 / 0714 0.9 / 1359 1.5 / 1950 0.7 **20** TU 0126 1.6 / 0648 0.7 / 1342 1.6 / 1929 0.6

6 TU 0305 1.5 / 0818 0.8 / 1508 1.5 / 2040 0.6 **21** W 0248 1.7 / 0806 0.7 / 1508 1.7 / 2038 0.5

7 W 0354 1.7 / 0911 0.7 / 1604 1.6 / 2126 0.5 **22** TH 0400 1.8 / 0915 0.6 / 1623 1.8 / 2140 0.4

8 TH 0438 1.8 / 0957 0.6 / 1655 1.7 / 2209 0.4 **23** F 0501 2.0 / 1015 0.5 / 1728 1.9 / 2235 0.4

9 F 0522 1.9 / 1039 0.5 / 1743 1.8 / 2250 0.4 **24** SA 0557 2.1 / 1108 0.4 / ● 1825 2.0 / 2325 0.3

10 SA 0604 2.0 / 1119 0.5 / 1829 1.9 / ○ 2329 0.4 **25** SU 0648 2.2 / 1156 0.3 / 1918 2.0

11 SU 0646 2.1 / 1156 0.5 / 1912 1.9 **26** M 0011 0.3 / 0735 2.3 / 1241 0.3 / 2004 2.0

12 M 0007 0.4 / 0725 2.1 / 1232 0.4 / 1952 1.9 **27** TU 0054 0.3 / 0818 2.3 / 1324 0.2 / 2045 2.0

13 TU 0045 0.4 / 0801 2.1 / 1307 0.4 / 2029 1.8 **28** W 0133 0.3 / 0855 2.2 / 1404 0.3 / 2120 1.9

14 W 0121 0.4 / 0834 2.0 / 1344 0.4 / 2103 1.8 **29** TH 0211 0.4 / 0927 2.0 / 1442 0.3 / 2149 1.7

15 TH 0158 0.5 / 0906 1.9 / 1422 0.4 / 2136 1.7 **30** F 0246 0.5 / 0953 1.9 / 1520 0.4 / 2216 1.6

31 SA 0320 0.6 / 1021 1.7 / 1558 0.5 / 2247 1.5

Chart Datum: 0·93 metres below Ordnance Datum (Newlyn)
HAT is 2·5 metres above Chart Datum

TIDES

221

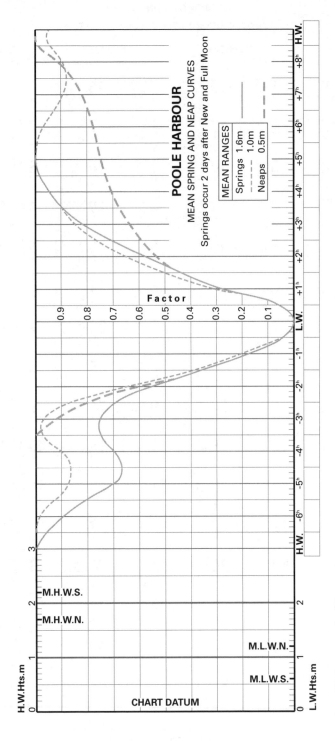

POOLE HARBOUR

MEAN SPRING AND NEAP CURVES

Springs occur 2 days after New and Full Moon

MEAN RANGES	
Springs	1.6m
	1.0m
Neaps	0.5m

Note - HW times are not shown because they cannot be predicted with reasonable accuracy. Approximate times can be gained using LW times and the Tidal Curves at the start of this section.

TIME ZONE (UT)	POOLE HARBOUR	Dates in amber are SPRINGS
For Summer Time add ONE hour in non-shaded areas	LAT 50°42′N LONG 1°59′W	Dates in yellow are NEAPS
	TIMES AND HEIGHTS OF HIGH AND LOW WATERS	2011

JANUARY

Day	Time m	Time m	Day	Time m	Time m
1 SA	0121 1.0 / 2.0	1402 1.0 / 1.9	16 SU	0056 1.3 / 1.9	1338 1.2 / 1.8
2 SU	0223 2.1	1459 0.9 / 2.0	17 M	0200 1.1 / 1.9	1432 0.9 / 1.9
3 M	0317 0.9 / 2.1	1547 0.8 / 2.1	18 TU	0252 1.0 / 2.0	1520 0.8 / 2.1
4 TU ●	0404 0.8 / 2.1	1631 0.7 / 2.1	19 W ○	0339 0.8 / 2.1	1606 0.7 / 2.1
5 W	0446 0.8 / 2.1	1711 0.7 / 2.3	20 TH	0423 0.7 / 2.2	1650 0.5 / 2.3
6 TH	2.1 / 0525 0.8	1747 0.7	21 F	0508 0.6 / 2.1	1734 0.4
7 F	2.1 / 0602 0.8	1822 0.7	22 SA	0552 0.6 / 2.3	1818 0.4
8 SA	2.1 / 0637 0.8 / 2.0	1854 0.7	23 SU	0637 0.6 / 2.3	1902 0.4
9 SU	2.0 / 0710 0.9 / 2.0	1925 0.8	24 M	0722 0.6 / 2.3	1946 0.5
10 M	2.0 / 0743 1.0 / 1.9	1957 0.9	25 TU	0808 0.7 / 2.2	2031 0.7
11 TU	2.0 / 0818 1.0 / 1.8	2033 1.0	26 W ◐	0859 0.8 / 2.0	2122 0.8
12 W ◑	1.9 / 0859 1.2 / 1.8	2117 1.2	27 TH	0957 1.0 / 1.9	2224 1.0
13 TH	1.8 / 0952 1.3 / 1.7	2216 1.3	28 F	1111 1.1 / 1.8	2342 1.2
14 F	1.8 / 1106 1.3 / 1.6	2335 1.3	29 SA	1235 1.2 / 1.8	
15 SA	1.8 / 1230 1.3 / 1.7		30 SU	0105 1.2 / 1.9	1350 1.0 / 1.9
			31 M	0216 1.1 / 1.9	1449 0.9 / 2.0

FEBRUARY

Day	Time m	Time m	Day	Time m	Time m
1 TU	0310 0.9 / 2.0	1536 0.8 / 2.0	16 W	0236 0.9 / 2.0	1503 0.7 / 2.1
2 W	0354 0.8 / 2.1	1616 0.7 / 2.1	17 TH	0324 0.7 / 2.1	1549 0.6 / 2.2
3 TH ●	0432 0.8 / 2.1	1653 0.6	18 F ○	0409 0.6 / 2.2	1634 0.4 / 2.3
4 F	2.1 / 0508 0.7	1727 0.6	19 SA	0453 0.4 / 2.3	1717 0.3
5 SA	2.1 / 0541 0.6	1759 0.6	20 SU	0536 0.4 / 2.4	1800 0.3
6 SU	2.1 / 0613 0.6 / 2.0	1828 0.7	21 M	0619 0.4 / 2.4	1842 0.3
7 M	2.1 / 0641 0.8 / 2.0	1855 0.7	22 TU	0702 0.4 / 2.3	1924 0.4
8 TU	2.1 / 0707 0.8 / 2.0	1921 0.8	23 W	0745 0.6 / 2.3	2007 0.7
9 W	2.1 / 0736 0.9 / 1.9	1951 0.9	24 TH ◑	0831 0.7 / 2.0	2055 0.9
10 TH	1.9 / 0810 1.0 / 1.8	2029 1.1	25 F	0926 0.9 / 1.9	2157 1.1
11 F ◐	1.8 / 0855 1.1 / 1.7	2120 1.2	26 SA	1041 1.2 / 1.8	2321 1.3
12 SA	1.8 / 0958 1.3 / 1.6	2235 1.3	27 SU	1213 1.2 / 1.6	1.7
13 SU	1.7 / 1134 1.3	1.6	28 M	0053 1.3 / 1.7	1335 1.1 / 1.8
14 M	0020 1.3 / 1.7	1310 1.2 / 1.8			
15 TU	0140 1.2 / 1.9	1412 0.9 / 1.9			

MARCH

Day	Time m	Time m	Day	Time m	Time m
1 TU	0207 1.1 / 1.8	1433 1.0 / 2.0	16 W	0116 1.1 / 1.8	1346 0.9 / 1.9
2 W	0257 0.9 / 1.9	1516 0.8 / 2.0	17 TH	0214 0.9 / 2.0	1439 0.7 / 2.1
3 TH	0337 0.8 / 2.0	1553 0.7 / 2.1	18 F	0303 0.7 / 2.1	1526 0.5 / 2.2
4 F	0412 0.7 / 2.1	1628 0.6 / 2.1	19 SA ○	0348 0.5 / 2.2	1611 0.4 / 2.3
5 SA	2.1 / 0445 0.7	1701 0.6	20 SU	0433 0.4 / 2.3	1655 0.3 / 2.4
6 SU	2.1 / 0516 0.6	1732 0.6	21 M	0516 0.3 / 2.3	1738 0.3
7 M	2.1 / 0546 0.6	1801 0.6	22 TU	0559 0.4 / 2.4	1820 0.3
8 TU	2.1 / 0612 0.7 / 2.0	1826 0.7	23 W	0641 0.4 / 2.3	1902 0.5
9 W	2.0 / 0636 0.7	1851 0.8	24 TH	0723 0.6 / 2.1	1945 0.7
10 TH	2.0 / 0704 0.8 / 2.0	1920 0.9	25 F	0808 0.7 / 2.1	2033 0.9
11 F	1.9 / 0737 1.0 / 1.9	1957 1.0	26 SA ◐	0900 0.9 / 1.9	2134 1.1
12 SA ◐	1.9 / 0820 1.0 / 1.8	2047 1.2	27 SU	1012 1.1 / 1.7	2258 1.3
13 SU	1.7 / 0919 1.2 / 1.6	2200 1.3	28 M	1143 1.2 / 1.6	1.7
14 M	1.6 / 1052 1.2	2350 1.3	29 TU	0030 1.3 / 1.6	1304 1.1 / 1.8
15 TU	1.6 / 1238 1.1	1.8	30 W	0142 1.2 / 1.8	1402 1.0 / 1.9
			31 TH	0231 1.0 / 1.9	1445 0.9 / 2.0

APRIL

Day	Time m	Time m	Day	Time m	Time m
1 F	0309 0.8 / 1.9	1522 0.8 / 2.1	16 SA	0236 0.7 / 2.1	1457 0.6 / 2.3
2 SA	0343 0.7 / 2.0	1557 0.7 / 2.1	17 SU	0324 0.5 / 2.2	1545 0.4 / 2.3
3 SU ●	0416 0.7 / 2.0	1631 0.6 / 2.1	18 M ○	0410 0.4 / 2.3	1631 0.4 / 2.4
4 M	0448 0.6 / 2.0	1703 0.6	19 TU	0455 0.3 / 2.3	1716 0.4
5 TU	2.1 / 0517 0.6	1732 0.7	20 W	0539 0.4 / 2.4	1759 0.4
6 W	2.1 / 0544 0.7	1759 0.7	21 TH	0622 0.4 / 2.3	1842 0.6
7 TH	2.1 / 0610 0.7	1826 0.8	22 F	0704 0.6 / 2.2	1926 0.7
8 F	2.0 / 0640 0.7	1859 0.9	23 SA	0749 0.7 / 2.0	2014 0.9
9 SA	2.0 / 0716 0.8	1939 1.0	24 SU	0839 0.9 / 1.9	2112 1.1
10 SU	1.9 / 0800 0.9	2030 1.1	25 M ◐	0941 1.0 / 1.8	2224 1.2
11 M ◐	1.8 / 0900 1.0	2143 1.2	26 TU	1059 1.2 / 1.6	2346 1.3
12 TU	1.7 / 1025 1.1	2317 1.2	27 W	1215 1.2 / 1.6	
13 W	1.7 / 1200 1.1	1.8	28 TH	0056 1.2 / 1315 1.0	1.9
14 TH	0041 1.0 / 1312 0.9	2.0	29 F	0149 1.0 / 1402 0.9	2.0
15 F	0144 0.9 / 1408 0.7	2.1	30 SA	0230 0.9 / 1443 0.9	2.0

Chart Datum: 1·40 metres below Ordnance Datum (Newlyn)
HAT is 2·6 metres above Chart Datum

TIDES

TIME ZONE (UT)
For Summer Time add ONE hour in **non-shaded areas**

POOLE HARBOUR

LAT 50°42′N LONG 1°59′W

TIMES AND HEIGHTS OF HIGH AND LOW WATERS

Dates in amber are **SPRINGS**
Dates in yellow are **NEAPS**

2011

MAY

Date	Day	Time	m	Time	m	Time	m	Time	m
1	SU	0308	0.8		1.9	1521	0.8		2.0
2	M	0344	0.8		2.0	1558	0.7		2.1
3	TU ●	0418	0.7		2.0	1633	0.7		2.1
4	W	0450	0.7		2.1	1705	0.7		
5	TH		2.1	0520	0.7		2.1	1736	0.8
6	F		2.1	0551	0.7		2.1	1809	0.8
7	SA		2.0	0625	0.7		2.0	1846	0.8
8	SU		2.0	0705	0.8		2.0	1930	0.9
9	M		1.9	0753	0.9		1.9	2023	1.0
10	TU ◐		1.9	0852	0.9		1.9	2129	1.1
11	W		1.8	1003	1.0		1.9	2245	1.1
12	TH		1.8	1121	0.9		1.9		
13	F	0001	1.0		1.9	1232	0.9		2.0
14	SA	0108	0.9		2.0	1334	0.8		2.1
15	SU	0206	0.7		2.1	1429	0.7		2.2
16	M	0259	0.6		2.1	1520	0.6		2.3
17	TU ○	0349	0.5		2.2	1609	0.6		2.3
18	W	0437	0.5		2.3	1656	0.6		
19	TH		2.3	0522	0.5		2.3	1741	0.6
20	F		2.3	0606	0.5		2.2	1826	0.7
21	SA		2.1	0649	0.6		2.1	1910	0.8
22	SU		2.0	0732	0.7		2.0	1955	0.9
23	M		1.9	0816	0.9		1.9	2044	1.0
24	TU ◑		1.8	0907	1.0		1.9	2141	1.2
25	W		1.7	1005	1.1		1.8	2247	1.2
26	TH		1.6	1111	1.2		1.8	2355	1.2
27	F		1.6	1216	1.2		1.8		
28	SA	0055	1.2		1.7	1312	1.1		1.9
29	SU	0145	1.0		1.8	1401	1.0		1.9
30	M	0229	0.9		1.9	1445	0.9		2.0
31	TU	0310	0.9		1.9	1526	0.9		2.0

JUNE

Date	Day	Time	m	Time	m	Time	m	Time	m
1	W ●	0349	0.8		2.0	1605	0.8		2.1
2	TH	0425	0.7		2.1	1642	0.8		2.1
3	F	0502	0.7		2.1	1719	0.8		
4	SA		2.1	0538	0.7		2.1	1757	0.8
5	SU		2.1	0618	0.7		2.1	1839	0.8
6	M		2.1	0701	0.7		2.1	1924	0.8
7	TU		2.0	0748	0.7		2.0	2015	0.9
8	W		2.0	0842	0.8		2.0	2112	0.9
9	TH ◐		1.9	0941	0.8		2.0	2216	1.0
10	F		1.9	1046	0.9		2.0	2326	1.0
11	SA		1.9	1155	0.9		2.0		
12	SU	0036	0.9		1.9	1303	0.9		2.1
13	M	0142	0.8		2.0	1405	0.8		2.1
14	TU	0241	0.7		2.1	1502	0.8		2.2
15	W ○	0335	0.7		2.1	1554	0.7		2.2
16	TH	0424	0.6		2.2	1642	0.7		2.2
17	F	0510	0.6		2.2	1728	0.7		
18	SA		2.2	0553	0.6		2.2	1810	0.7
19	SU		2.1	0633	0.6		2.1	1851	0.8
20	M		2.0	0711	0.7		2.1	1931	0.8
21	TU		2.0	0749	0.8		2.0	2012	0.9
22	W		1.9	0829	0.9		1.9	2056	1.0
23	TH ◑		1.8	0913	1.0		1.9	2146	1.2
24	F		1.7	1005	1.2		1.8	2245	1.2
25	SA		1.6	1108	1.2		1.8	2353	1.2
26	SU		1.6	1216	1.2		1.8		
27	M	0057	1.2		1.7	1317	1.2		1.9
28	TU	0152	1.0		1.8	1411	1.1		1.9
29	W	0240	0.9		1.9	1458	1.0		2.0
30	TH	0324	0.8		2.0	1542	0.9		2.1

JULY

Date	Day	Time	m	Time	m	Time	m	Time	m
1	F ●	0406	0.7		2.1	1623	0.8		2.1
2	SA	0447	0.7		2.1	1705	0.7		
3	SU		2.1	0527	0.6		2.1	1746	0.7
4	M		2.1	0609	0.6		2.2	1829	0.7
5	TU		2.1	0653	0.6		2.2	1914	0.7
6	W		2.1	0737	0.6		2.2	2001	0.7
7	TH		2.1	0825	0.7		2.1	2052	0.8
8	F ◐		2.0	0917	0.8		2.0	2150	0.9
9	SA		1.9	1017	0.9		2.0	2256	1.0
10	SU		1.9	1126	1.0		2.0		
11	M	0011	1.0		1.8	1241	1.0		2.0
12	TU	0126	1.0		1.9	1351	1.0		2.0
13	W	0231	0.9		2.0	1452	0.9		2.1
14	TH	0325	0.8		2.1	1544	0.8		2.1
15	F ○	0413	0.7		2.1	1630	0.7		2.1
16	SA	0456	0.6		2.2	1713	0.7		
17	SU		2.1	0535	0.6		2.2	1751	0.7
18	M		2.1	0612	0.6		2.1	1828	0.7
19	TU		2.0	0646	0.7		2.1	1903	0.8
20	W		2.0	0718	0.7		2.1	1936	0.9
21	TH		1.9	0750	0.8		2.0	2011	0.9
22	F		1.9	0823	0.9		1.9	2048	1.0
23	SA ◑		1.8	0904	1.1		1.9	2135	1.2
24	SU		1.7	0957	1.2		1.8	2241	1.3
25	M		1.6	1112	1.3		1.8		
26	TU	0007	1.3		1.6	1238	1.3		1.8
27	W	0120	1.2		1.8	1344	1.2		1.9
28	TH	0216	1.0		1.9	1436	1.0		2.0
29	F	0304	0.8		2.0	1522	0.9		2.1
30	SA ●	0348	0.7		2.1	1606	0.8		2.1
31	SU	0430	0.6		2.2	1649	0.7		2.2

AUGUST

Date	Day	Time	m	Time	m	Time	m	Time	m
1	M	0513	0.5		2.3	1731	0.6		
2	TU		2.2	0554	0.4		2.3	1814	0.6
3	W		2.3	0637	0.4		2.3	1858	0.6
4	TH		2.2	0720	0.5		2.3	1942	0.6
5	F		2.1	0804	0.6		2.2	2030	0.7
6	SA ◐		2.0	0853	0.8		2.1	2125	0.9
7	SU		1.9	0951	0.9		1.9	2232	1.0
8	M		1.8	1105	1.1		1.9	2355	1.1
9	TU		1.8	1229	1.2		1.9		
10	W	0117	1.0		1.9	1346	1.1		1.9
11	TH	0223	0.9		2.0	1446	1.0		2.0
12	F	0315	0.8		2.1	1534	0.9		2.1
13	SA ○	0358	0.7		2.1	1615	0.8		2.1
14	SU	0437	0.6		2.2	1653	0.7		2.1
15	M	0513	0.6		2.2	1728	0.7		
16	TU		2.1	0546	0.6		2.1	1801	0.7
17	W		2.1	0617	0.6		2.1	1831	0.7
18	TH		2.0	0645	0.7		2.1	1900	0.8
19	F		2.0	0712	0.8		2.0	1928	0.9
20	SA		1.9	0741	0.9		2.0	2001	1.0
21	SU ◑		1.9	0816	1.0		1.9	2042	1.2
22	M		1.8	0904	1.2		1.8	2140	1.3
23	TU		1.6	1015	1.4		1.7	2313	1.3
24	W		1.6	1202	1.4		1.7		
25	TH	0051	1.2		1.8	1321	1.3		1.8
26	F	0153	1.0		1.9	1415	1.0		2.0
27	SA	0242	0.8		2.0	1502	0.8		2.1
28	SU	0326	0.7		2.2	1545	0.7		2.2
29	M ●	0409	0.5		2.3	1628	0.6		2.3
30	TU	0451	0.4		2.3	1711	0.4		
31	W		2.3	0533	0.4		2.4	1753	0.4

Chart Datum: 1·40 metres below Ordnance Datum (Newlyn)
HAT is 2·6 metres above Chart Datum

POOLE HARBOUR

LAT 50°42′N   LONG 1°59′W

TIMES AND HEIGHTS OF HIGH AND LOW WATERS

Dates in amber are **SPRINGS**
Dates in yellow are **NEAPS**

2011

SEPTEMBER

Day	Time	m	m	Day	Time	m	m
1 TH	0616	2.3	0.4	16 F	0613	2.1	0.7
	1836	2.4	0.5		1825	2.1	0.8
2 F	0658	2.3	0.5	17 SA	0638	2.1	0.8
	1920	2.3	0.6		1852	2.1	0.9
3 SA	0742	2.2	0.6	18 SU	0707	2.0	0.9
	2007	2.2	0.7		1924	2.0	1.0
4 SU ◑	0831	2.1	0.8	19 M	0741	1.9	1.1
	2101	2.0	0.9		2004	1.9	1.1
5 M	0931	1.9	1.0	20 TU ◑	0828	1.8	1.2
	2211	1.9	1.1		2100	1.8	1.2
6 TU	1050	1.8	1.8	21 W	0937	1.7	1.4
	2340	1.2			2227	1.7	1.3
7 W	1220	1.8	1.3	22 TH	1125	1.7	1.4
		1.8				1.7	
8 TH	0105	1.2	1.9	23 F	0015	1.2	1.8
	1337	1.2	1.9		1251	1.3	1.8
9 F	0210	1.0	2.0	24 SA	0123	1.0	1.9
	1433	1.0	2.0		1348	1.0	2.0
10 SA	0256	0.8	2.1	25 SU	0214	0.8	2.1
	1515	0.9	2.1		1436	0.8	2.1
11 SU	0335	0.7	2.2	26 M	0259	0.6	2.3
	1552	0.8	2.1		1520	0.7	2.3
12 M ○	0411	0.7	2.2	27 TU ●	0343	0.5	2.3
	1627	0.7	2.1		1603	0.6	2.3
13 TU	0444	0.6	2.2	28 W	0426	0.4	2.4
	1700	0.7	2.1		1647	0.4	2.4
14 W	0517	0.6	2.2	29 TH	0510	0.4	2.4
	1731	0.7			1731	0.4	2.4
15 TH	0546	2.1	0.7	30 F	0553	2.4	0.4
	1759	2.1	0.7		1814	2.4	0.4

OCTOBER

Day	Time	m	m	Day	Time	m	m
1 SA	0636	2.3	0.6	16 SU	0611	2.1	0.9
	1859	2.3	0.6		1825	2.1	0.8
2 SU	0722	2.3	0.7	17 M	0641	2.0	0.9
	1946	2.2	0.8		1858	2.0	0.9
3 M	0812	2.1	0.9	18 TU	0718	2.0	1.0
	2040	2.0	0.9		1940	1.9	1.0
4 TU ◑	0913	1.9	1.1	19 W	0806	1.9	1.2
	2148	1.9	1.2		2034	1.8	1.2
5 W	1032	1.8	1.3	20 TH	0912	1.8	1.3
	2315	1.8	1.2		2152	1.8	1.3
6 TH	1200	1.8	1.3	21 F ○	1044	1.8	1.3
		1.8			2326	1.8	1.2
7 F	0039	1.2	1.8	22 SA	1210	1.8	1.2
	1315	1.2	1.9			1.8	
8 SA	0142	1.0	2.0	23 SU	0041	1.0	2.0
	1407	1.0	2.0		1313	1.0	2.0
9 SU	0227	0.8	2.1	24 M	0139	0.9	2.1
	1448	0.9	2.0		1405	0.8	2.1
10 M	0305	0.8	2.1	25 TU	0228	0.7	2.3
	1524	0.8	2.1		1453	0.7	2.3
11 TU	0340	0.7	2.2	26 W ●	0315	0.6	2.4
	1557	0.7	2.1		1539	0.6	2.3
12 W ○	0414	0.7	2.2	27 TH	0401	0.5	2.4
	1630	0.7	2.1		1625	0.4	2.4
13 TH	0446	0.7	2.2	28 F	0447	0.4	2.4
	1702	0.7	2.1		1711	0.4	2.4
14 F	0517	2.1	0.7	29 SA	0532	2.4	0.5
	1730	2.1	0.7		1756	2.4	0.5
15 SA	0544	2.1	0.8	30 SU	0618	2.3	0.6
	1756	2.1	0.8		1841	2.3	0.6
				31 M	0704	2.3	0.8
					1928	2.1	0.8

NOVEMBER

Day	Time	m	m	Day	Time	m	m
1 TU	0755	2.1	0.9	16 W	0705	2.0	1.0
	2020	2.0	0.9		1927	2.0	0.9
2 W ●	0853	2.1	1.1	17 TH	0753	2.0	1.1
	2121	1.9	1.1		2019	1.9	1.0
3 TH	1002	1.9	1.3	18 F ◑	0853	1.9	1.2
	2234	1.8	1.2		2125	1.8	1.1
4 F	1121	1.3	1.7	19 SA	1007	1.9	1.2
	2351	1.7	1.2		2240	1.9	1.1
5 SA	1233	1.9	1.3	20 SU	1124	1.9	1.2
		1.8			2354	1.9	1.1
6 SU	0056	1.2	2.0	21 M	1234	2.0	1.0
	1329	1.2	1.9			1.9	
7 M	0146	1.0	2.0	22 TU	0100	0.9	2.0
	1413	1.0	2.0		1334	0.9	2.0
8 TU	0228	0.9	2.1	23 W	0157	0.8	2.3
	1451	0.8	2.1		1428	0.7	2.2
9 W	0306	0.9	2.1	24 TH	0250	0.7	2.3
	1527	0.8	2.1		1520	0.6	2.3
10 TH ○	0342	0.8	2.1	25 F ●	0341	0.6	2.4
	1602	0.8	2.1		1609	0.6	2.4
11 F	0417	0.8	2.1	26 SA	0429	0.6	2.4
	1635	0.8	2.1		1657	0.5	
12 SA	0451	0.8	2.1	27 SU	0516	2.3	0.6
	1706	0.8	2.1		1743		0.6
13 SU	0521	2.1	0.8	28 M	0603	2.3	0.6
	1736	2.1	0.8		1828	2.3	0.6
14 M	0551	2.1	0.9	29 TU	0649	2.3	0.7
	1807	2.1	0.8		1913	2.1	0.7
15 TU	0625	2.1	0.9	30 W	0736	2.1	0.8
	1844	2.0	0.9		1959	2.0	0.8

DECEMBER

Day	Time	m	m	Day	Time	m	m
1 TH	0826	2.0	1.0	16 F	0742	2.1	0.9
	2048	2.0	1.0		2006	2.0	0.8
2 F ●	0922	2.0	1.2	17 SA	0834	2.0	1.0
	2143	1.8	1.1		2101	1.9	0.9
3 SA	1026	1.9	1.3	18 SU	0935	2.0	1.0
	2247	1.7	1.2		2204	1.9	1.0
4 SU	1134	1.9	1.3	19 M	1044	2.0	1.1
	2354	1.7	1.2		2313	1.9	1.0
5 M	1237	1.9	1.2	20 TU	1158	2.0	1.0
		1.8				2.0	
6 TU	0054	1.2	1.9	21 W	0025	1.0	2.0
	1330	1.2	1.8		1308	1.0	2.0
7 W	0146	1.1	2.0	22 TH	0133	0.9	2.1
	1416	1.1	1.9		1412	0.8	2.1
8 TH	0232	1.0	2.1	23 F	0234	0.8	2.2
	1457	0.9	2.0		1508	0.7	2.1
9 F	0313	1.0	2.1	24 SA ●	0329	0.7	2.3
	1536	0.9	2.0		1600	0.6	2.3
10 SA ○	0352	0.9	2.1	25 SU	0419	0.7	2.3
	1613	0.8	2.1		1648	0.6	2.3
11 SU	0429	0.8	2.1	26 M	0506	0.7	2.3
	1649	0.8	2.1		1733	0.6	
12 M	0504	0.8	2.1	27 TU	0550	2.3	0.7
	1723	0.7	2.1		1815	2.3	0.6
13 TU	0538	2.1	0.8	28 W	0633	2.3	0.7
	1758	2.1	0.7		1855	2.1	0.7
14 W	0615	2.1	0.8	29 TH	0714	2.2	0.8
	1836	2.1	0.8		1933	2.1	0.8
15 TH	0656	2.1	0.9	30 F	0754	2.1	0.9
	1919	2.1	0.8		2012	2.0	0.9
				31 SA	0837	2.0	1.0
					2053	1.9	1.0

Chart Datum: 1·40 metres below Ordnance Datum (Newlyn)
HAT is 2·6 metres above Chart Datum

TIDES

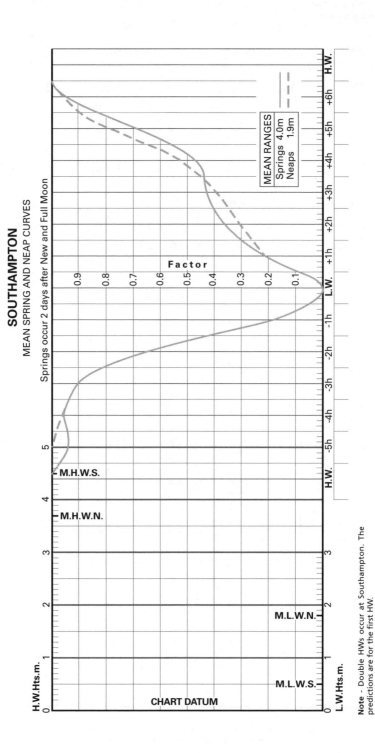

SOUTHAMPTON

MEAN SPRING AND NEAP CURVES

Springs occur 2 days after New and Full Moon

MEAN RANGES	
Springs	4.0m
Neaps	1.9m

Factor

0.9 0.8 0.7 0.6 0.5 0.4 0.3 0.2 0.1

H.W. +6h +5h +4h +3h +2h +1h L.W. -1h -2h -3h -4h -5h H.W.

M.H.W.S.

M.H.W.N.

M.L.W.N.

M.L.W.S.

CHART DATUM

H.W.Hts.m.

L.W.Hts.m.

Note - Double HWs occur at Southampton. The predictions are for the first HW.

TIME ZONE (UT)	SOUTHAMPTON	Dates in amber are SPRINGS
For Summer Time add ONE hour in non-shaded areas	LAT 50°54′N LONG 1°24′W	Dates in yellow are NEAPS
	TIMES AND HEIGHTS OF HIGH AND LOW WATERS	2011

JANUARY

Day	Time m	Time m	Day	Time m	Time m
1 SA	0122 1.5 / 0801 4.2	1403 1.4 / 2033 4.1	**16** SU	0059 2.0 / 0735 3.9	1340 1.8 / 2011 3.9
2 SU	0224 1.4 / 0859 4.3	1501 1.2 / 2129 4.2	**17** M	0202 1.7 / 0834 4.1	1436 1.4 / 2105 4.1
3 M	0319 1.3 / 0950 4.4	1550 1.0 / 2217 4.3	**18** TU	0254 1.4 / 0923 4.3	1525 1.1 / 2151 4.3
4 TU	0407 1.1 / 1034 4.5	1635 0.9 / ●2300 4.4	**19** W	0343 1.1 / 1008 4.5	1612 0.8 / ○2234 4.5
5 W	0452 1.0 / 1114 4.5	1716 0.8 / 2339 4.4	**20** TH	0429 0.8 / 1051 4.6	1657 0.5 / 2317 4.6
6 TH	0532 0.9 / 1151 4.5	1753 0.7	**21** F	0515 0.6 / 1134 4.7	1741 0.4
7 F	0015 4.4 / 0610 0.9	1227 4.4 / 1827 0.8	**22** SA	0000 4.7 / 0558 0.5	1217 4.8 / 1823 0.3
8 SA	0051 4.4 / 0644 1.0	1302 4.4 / 1858 0.9	**23** SU	0043 4.7 / 0642 0.5	1300 4.7 / 1905 0.4
9 SU	0126 4.3 / 0716 1.2	1337 4.2 / 1928 1.1	**24** M	0128 4.3 / 0725 0.6	1345 4.6 / 1947 0.5
10 M	0201 4.3 / 0748 1.3	1411 4.1 / 1958 1.3	**25** TU	0214 4.6 / 0809 0.8	1431 4.5 / 2032 0.8
11 TU	0239 4.1 / 0822 1.6	1451 4.0 / 2034 1.5	**26** W	0303 4.4 / 0858 1.1	1522 4.2 / 2121 1.2
12 W	0320 4.0 / 0902 1.8	1536 3.8 / ◐2118 1.8	**27** TH	0358 4.2 / 0954 1.4	1623 4.0 / 2222 1.5
13 TH	0409 3.9 / 0957 2.0	1632 3.7 / 2219 2.0	**28** F	0506 4.0 / 1107 1.7	1740 3.8 / 2341 1.8
14 F	0512 3.8 / 1111 2.1	1745 3.6 / 2341 2.1	**29** SA	0627 3.9 / 1232 1.8	1910 3.8
15 SA	0625 3.8 / 1232 2.0	1905 3.7	**30** SU	0106 1.8 / 0748 4.0	1352 1.6 / 2027 3.9
			31 M	0217 1.6 / 0853 4.1	1452 1.4 / 2125 4.1

FEBRUARY

Day	Time m	Time m	Day	Time m	Time m
1 TU	0312 1.4 / 0944 4.3	1540 1.1 / 2211 4.3	**16** W	0235 1.4 / 0902 4.2	1506 1.0 / 2131 4.3
2 W	0358 1.1 / 1025 4.4	1622 0.9 / 2249 4.4	**17** TH	0326 1.0 / 0949 4.5	1555 0.6 / 2215 4.5
3 TH	0438 0.9 / 1101 4.4	1659 0.7 / ●2322 4.4	**18** F	0414 0.6 / 1033 4.7	1640 0.3 / ○2258 4.7
4 F	0515 0.8 / 1133 4.4	1734 0.6 / 2353 4.4	**19** SA	0459 0.3 / 1116 4.8	1724 0.1 / 2340 4.8
5 SA	0549 0.7 / 1204 4.4	1806 0.6	**20** SU	0543 0.2 / 1158 4.9	1806 0.0
6 SU	0023 4.4 / 0620 0.6	1235 4.4 / 1833 0.7	**21** M	0022 4.9 / 0624 0.2	1241 4.8 / 1846 0.1
7 M	0055 4.4 / 0647 0.9	1307 4.3 / 1858 0.9	**22** TU	0105 4.8 / 0705 0.3	1324 4.7 / 1926 0.4
8 TU	0126 4.3 / 0713 1.1	1339 4.2 / 1924 1.1	**23** W	0149 4.6 / 0747 0.6	1408 4.5 / 2007 0.7
9 W	0158 4.2 / 0741 1.3	1412 4.1 / 1953 1.3	**24** TH	0235 4.4 / 0831 1.0	1457 4.2 / ◐2054 1.2
10 TH	0233 4.0 / 0814 1.5	1449 3.9 / 2029 1.6	**25** F	0327 4.1 / 0924 1.4	1556 3.9 / 2153 1.6
11 F	0313 3.9 / 0857 1.8	1537 3.7 / ◐2119 1.9	**26** SA	0433 3.8 / 1036 1.7	1718 3.6 / 2318 1.9
12 SA	0409 3.7 / 1000 2.0	1646 3.6 / 2237 2.1	**27** SU	0603 3.7 / 1212 1.9	1859 3.6
13 SU	0526 3.6 / 1107 2.0	1816 3.6	**28** M	0056 1.9 / 0736 3.7	1338 1.7 / 2019 3.8
14 M	0018 2.1 / 0653 3.7	1306 1.8 / 1939 3.8			
15 TU	0136 1.8 / 0806 3.9	1412 1.4 / 2041 4.0			

MARCH

Day	Time m	Time m	Day	Time m	Time m
1 TU	0209 1.7 / 0842 4.0	1438 1.4 / 2113 4.1	**16** W	0109 1.7 / 0736 3.9	1345 1.4 / 2014 4.1
2 W	0300 1.4 / 0930 4.1	1522 1.1 / 2154 4.3	**17** TH	0212 1.3 / 0836 4.2	1442 0.9 / 2106 4.4
3 TH	0340 1.1 / 1008 4.3	1559 0.9 / 2228 4.4	**18** F	0305 0.8 / 0926 4.5	1531 0.5 / 2152 4.6
4 F	0417 0.9 / 1040 4.4	1635 0.7 / 2258 4.4	**19** SA	0353 0.5 / 1011 4.7	1618 0.2 / ○2235 4.8
5 SA	0451 0.7 / 1109 4.4	1708 0.6 / 2326 4.4	**20** SU	0439 0.2 / 1054 4.8	1702 0.0 / 2317 4.9
6 SU	0523 0.6 / 1137 4.4	1739 0.6 / 2353 4.4	**21** M	0522 0.0 / 1137 4.9	1744 0.0
7 M	0552 0.6 / 1206 4.4	1806 0.7	**22** TU	0000 4.9 / 0604 0.0	1220 4.8 / 1825 0.1
8 TU	0022 4.4 / 0618 0.7	1237 4.3 / 1829 0.8	**23** W	0043 4.8 / 0645 0.2	1304 4.7 / 1905 0.4
9 W	0052 4.3 / 0642 0.9	1308 4.3 / 1853 1.0	**24** TH	0126 4.6 / 0725 0.5	1349 4.4 / 1946 0.8
10 TH	0123 4.2 / 0708 1.1	1340 4.1 / 1921 1.2	**25** F	0212 4.3 / 0809 0.9	1439 4.2 / 2032 1.3
11 F	0155 4.1 / 0739 1.3	1416 4.0 / 1956 1.5	**26** SA	0303 4.0 / 0900 1.4	1539 3.9 / 2131 1.7
12 SA	0233 3.9 / 0820 1.5	1501 3.8 / ◐2044 1.8	**27** SU	0408 3.7 / 1009 1.7	1700 3.6 / 2257 2.0
13 SU	0324 3.7 / 0918 1.8	1608 3.6 / 2156 2.0	**28** M	0536 3.6 / 1142 1.9	1837 3.6
14 M	0442 3.6 / 1049 1.9	1739 3.6 / 2342 2.0	**29** TU	0034 2.0 / 0709 3.6	1307 1.8 / 1953 3.8
15 TU	0616 3.6 / 1231 1.8	1907 3.8	**30** W	0145 1.8 / 0816 3.8	1406 1.5 / 2046 4.1
			31 TH	0233 1.5 / 0903 4.0	1450 1.2 / 2126 4.2

APRIL

Day	Time m	Time m	Day	Time m	Time m
1 F	0312 1.2 / 0940 4.2	1527 1.0 / 2159 4.3	**16** SA	0238 0.8 / 0859 4.4	1503 0.6 / 2126 4.7
2 SA	0347 0.9 / 1012 4.2	1603 0.8 / 2228 4.4	**17** SU	0328 0.5 / 0947 4.6	1551 0.3 / 2211 4.8
3 SU	0421 0.8 / 1041 4.3	1636 0.7 / ●2255 4.4	**18** M	0415 0.2 / 1032 4.7	1638 0.2 / ○2255 4.9
4 M	0453 0.7 / 1109 4.3	1708 0.7 / 2323 4.4	**19** TU	0500 0.1 / 1117 4.8	1722 0.2 / 2339 4.8
5 TU	0523 0.7 / 1138 4.3	1737 0.7 / 2352 4.4	**20** W	0544 0.2 / 1202 4.7	1805 0.3
6 W	0550 0.7 / 1209 4.3	1803 0.9	**21** TH	0022 4.7 / 0626 0.3	1248 4.6 / 1846 0.6
7 TH	0023 4.3 / 0616 0.8	1242 4.3 / 1829 1.0	**22** F	0107 4.5 / 0707 0.6	1335 4.4 / 1929 1.0
8 F	0055 4.2 / 0644 1.0	1316 4.2 / 1859 1.2	**23** SA	0154 4.3 / 0751 0.9	1426 4.1 / 2016 1.3
9 SA	0130 4.1 / 0718 1.2	1355 4.0 / 1937 1.4	**24** SU	0244 4.0 / 0839 1.3	1523 3.9 / 2112 1.7
10 SU	0210 4.0 / 0802 1.4	1443 3.9 / 2027 1.7	**25** M	0343 3.7 / 0940 1.6	1633 3.8 / ◐2226 2.0
11 M	0303 3.8 / 0900 1.6	1550 3.8 / 2139 1.9	**26** TU	0457 3.6 / 1057 1.8	1754 3.7 / 2349 2.0
12 TU	0417 3.7 / 1023 1.7	1713 3.7 / 2313 1.9	**27** W	0620 3.6 / 1214 1.8	1908 3.8
13 W	0545 3.7 / 1156 1.6	1836 3.9	**28** TH	0058 1.9 / 0731 3.7	1317 1.6 / 2003 4.0
14 TH	0037 1.6 / 0703 3.9	1311 1.3 / 1943 4.1	**29** F	0151 1.6 / 0823 3.9	1406 1.4 / 2046 4.1
15 F	0143 1.2 / 0807 4.2	1411 0.9 / 2038 4.4	**30** SA	0233 1.4 / 0904 4.0	1447 1.2 / 2122 4.2

Chart Datum: 2·74 metres below Ordnance Datum (Newlyn)
HAT is 5·0 metres above Chart Datum

TIDES

TIDES

TIME ZONE (UT)
For Summer Time add ONE hour in **non-shaded areas**

SOUTHAMPTON
LAT 50°54'N   LONG 1°24'W
TIMES AND HEIGHTS OF HIGH AND LOW WATERS

Dates in amber are **SPRINGS**
Dates in yellow are **NEAPS**

2011

MAY

Time	m		Time	m
1 0311	1.1	**16**	0303	0.7
0939	4.1		0925	4.5
SU 1526	1.1	M	1525	0.6
2154	4.3		2149	4.7
2 0347	0.9	**17**	0353	0.5
1011	4.2		1014	4.6
M 1602	0.9	TU	1615	0.5
2224	4.3	○	2236	4.7
3 0421	0.8	**18**	0441	0.4
1041	4.3		1101	4.6
TU 1637	0.9	W	1702	0.5
● 2254	4.4		2322	4.7
4 0454	0.8	**19**	0527	0.4
1113	4.3		1148	4.6
W 1709	0.9	TH	1748	0.6
2326	4.4			
5 0526	0.8	**20**	0007	4.6
1147	4.3		0610	0.5
TH 1741	1.0	F	1236	4.5
			1832	0.8
6 0000	4.4	**21**	0052	4.4
0556	0.8		0652	0.7
F 1223	4.3	SA	1323	4.4
1812	1.1		1916	1.0
7 0037	4.3	**22**	0138	4.3
0630	0.9		0734	0.9
SA 1302	4.2	SU	1410	4.2
1848	1.2		2000	1.3
8 0115	4.2	**23**	0224	4.1
0709	1.1		0818	1.2
SU 1345	4.1	M	1500	4.1
1930	1.4		2049	1.6
9 0200	4.1	**24**	0314	3.9
0755	1.2		0906	1.5
M 1436	4.0	TU	1555	3.9
2023	1.5	◐	2145	1.8
10 0254	4.0	**25**	0410	3.7
0852	1.4		1004	1.7
TU 1538	3.9	W	1656	3.8
◐ 2128	1.7		2250	1.9
11 0400	3.9	**26**	0515	3.6
1004	1.5		1110	1.8
W 1651	3.9	TH	1802	3.8
2246	1.7		2357	1.9
12 0516	3.9	**27**	0626	3.6
1122	1.4		1216	1.8
TH 1805	4.0	F	1905	3.9
13 0002	1.5	**28**	0057	1.8
0631	4.0		0730	3.7
F 1234	1.3	SA	1314	1.7
1911	4.2		1957	4.0
14 0110	1.2	**29**	0147	1.6
0736	4.1		0821	3.9
SA 1337	1.0	SU	1404	1.5
2009	4.4		2041	4.1
15 0209	0.9	**30**	0232	1.4
0833	4.3		0904	4.0
SU 1433	0.8	M	1448	1.4
2101	4.6		2119	4.2
		31	0313	1.2
			0942	4.1
		TU	1529	1.2
			2155	4.3

JUNE

Time	m		Time	m
1 0352	1.0	**16**	0427	0.7
1018	4.2		1052	4.4
W 1609	1.1	TH	1649	0.8
● 2230	4.3		2310	4.5
2 0429	0.9	**17**	0514	0.6
1053	4.3		1139	4.5
TH 1647	1.0	F	1736	0.8
2306	4.4		2354	4.5
3 0507	0.8	**18**	0558	0.6
1131	4.3		1223	4.4
F 1725	1.0	SA	1820	0.9
2344	4.4			
4 0544	0.8	**19**	0037	4.4
1210	4.3		0638	0.7
SA 1803	1.0	SU	1307	4.4
			1901	1.0
5 0024	4.4	**20**	0118	4.3
0623	0.8		0716	0.8
SU 1252	4.3	M	1348	4.3
1843	1.1		1940	1.2
6 0106	4.3	**21**	0159	4.1
0704	0.9		0752	1.0
M 1337	4.3	TU	1429	4.2
1928	1.2		2019	1.4
7 0152	4.2	**22**	0240	4.0
0750	1.0		0830	1.3
TU 1427	4.2	W	1512	4.1
2017	1.3		2100	1.6
8 0244	4.1	**23**	0324	3.8
0843	1.1		0912	1.5
W 1523	4.2	TH	1558	3.9
2114	1.4	◐	2149	1.8
9 0342	4.1	**24**	0414	3.7
0942	1.3		1003	1.8
TH 1625	4.1	F	1652	3.8
2219	1.5		2248	1.9
10 0448	4.0	**25**	0515	3.6
1048	1.3		1107	1.9
F 1732	4.1	SA	1754	3.8
2328	1.4		2355	1.9
11 0559	4.0	**26**	0626	3.6
1158	1.3		1216	1.9
SA 1839	4.2	SU	1859	3.8
12 0038	1.3	**27**	0058	1.8
0708	4.1		0734	3.7
SU 1306	1.2	M	1320	1.8
1942	4.3		1956	4.0
13 0143	1.2	**28**	0154	1.6
0811	4.2		0830	3.9
M 1408	1.1	TU	1413	1.7
2040	4.4		2046	4.1
14 0242	1.0	**29**	0242	1.4
0909	4.3		0916	4.0
TU 1506	1.0	W	1501	1.5
2133	4.5		2129	4.2
15 0337	0.8	**30**	0327	1.2
1002	4.4		0957	4.2
W 1559	0.9	TH	1546	1.3
○ 2223	4.5		2210	4.3

JULY

Time	m		Time	m
1 0410	0.9	**16**	0502	0.7
1037	4.3		1128	4.4
F 1629	1.1	SA	1724	0.9
● 2250	4.4		2340	4.4
2 0452	0.8	**17**	0542	0.6
1116	4.4		1207	4.4
SA 1712	0.9	SU	1804	0.8
2330	4.5			
3 0533	0.7	**18**	0017	4.4
1157	4.4		0619	0.6
SU 1754	0.9	M	1244	4.4
			1840	0.9
4 0011	4.5	**19**	0053	4.3
0615	0.6		0652	0.7
M 1240	4.5	TU	1318	4.4
1836	0.8		1914	1.0
5 0055	4.5	**20**	0128	4.2
0657	0.6		0723	0.9
TU 1324	4.5	W	1353	4.3
1920	0.9		1945	1.2
6 0139	4.4	**21**	0204	4.1
0740	0.7		0752	1.2
W 1411	4.4	TH	1429	4.2
2005	1.0		2016	1.4
7 0227	4.3	**22**	0241	4.0
0827	0.9		0824	1.4
TH 1501	4.4	F	1507	4.0
2055	1.1		2052	1.6
8 0319	4.1	**23**	0323	3.8
0918	1.1		0903	1.7
F 1557	4.3	SA	1551	3.9
2151	1.3	◐	2139	1.9
9 0419	4.1	**24**	0415	3.7
1018	1.3		0957	2.0
SA 1700	4.2	SU	1647	3.8
2258	1.5		2244	2.0
10 0529	3.9	**25**	0523	3.6
1127	1.5		1113	2.1
SU 1811	4.1	M	1758	3.7
11 0012	1.5	**26**	0006	2.0
0646	3.9		0644	3.6
M 1243	1.5	TU	1237	2.1
1922	4.1		1912	3.8
12 0126	1.4	**27**	0118	1.8
0800	4.0		0756	3.8
TU 1354	1.5	W	1344	1.9
2028	4.2		2015	4.0
13 0232	1.2	**28**	0216	1.6
0900	4.2		0851	4.0
W 1457	1.3	TH	1439	1.6
2126	4.3		2105	4.2
14 0328	1.0	**29**	0306	1.2
0959	4.3		0937	4.2
TH 1551	1.1	F	1527	1.3
2216	4.4		2150	4.3
15 0417	0.8	**30**	0352	0.9
1046	4.4		1018	4.4
F 1640	1.0	SA	1613	1.0
○ 2300	4.4	●	2231	4.5
		31	0436	0.6
			1059	4.5
		SU	1657	0.8
			2313	4.6

AUGUST

Time	m		Time	m
1 0520	0.4	**16**	0554	0.6
1139	4.6		1214	4.5
M 1740	0.6	TU	1813	0.8
2354	4.7			
2 0602	0.3	**17**	0023	4.4
1221	4.7		0624	0.7
TU 1823	0.5	W	1245	4.4
			1842	0.9
3 0036	4.7	**18**	0055	4.3
0643	0.4		0651	0.9
W 1304	4.7	TH	1316	4.3
1904	0.6		1909	1.1
4 0120	4.6	**19**	0127	4.2
0724	0.5		0716	1.1
TH 1349	4.6	F	1348	4.2
1947	0.7		1935	1.3
5 0206	4.5	**20**	0201	4.1
0807	0.7		0743	1.4
F 1436	4.5	SA	1422	4.1
2033	1.0		2005	1.5
6 0255	4.3	**21**	0238	3.9
0854	1.1		0817	1.7
SA 1529	4.3	SU	1501	3.9
◐ 2126	1.3	◐	2044	1.8
7 0353	4.1	**22**	0324	3.8
0951	1.4		0902	2.0
SU 1632	4.1	M	1552	3.8
2232	1.6		2142	2.0
8 0506	3.9	**23**	0429	3.6
1104	1.7		1013	2.2
M 1749	4.0	TU	1704	3.7
2355	1.7		2311	2.1
9 0635	3.8	**24**	0557	3.6
1231	1.8		1154	2.2
TU 1913	4.0	W	1830	3.7
10 0119	1.7	**25**	0044	2.0
0758	3.9		0721	3.7
W 1350	1.7	TH	1317	2.0
2024	4.1		1944	3.9
11 0228	1.4	**26**	0151	1.6
0903	4.1		0824	4.0
TH 1453	1.5	F	1416	1.6
2121	4.3		2040	4.2
12 0320	1.1	**27**	0244	1.2
0953	4.3		0912	4.3
F 1542	1.2	SA	1506	1.2
2206	4.4		2127	4.4
13 0405	0.9	**28**	0332	0.8
1035	4.4		0955	4.5
SA 1625	1.0	SU	1553	0.9
○ 2245	4.4		2209	4.6
14 0444	0.7	**29**	0417	0.5
1111	4.5		1036	4.7
SU 1704	0.8	M	1638	0.6
2319	4.5	●	2251	4.8
15 0521	0.6	**30**	0500	0.3
1144	4.5		1117	4.8
M 1741	0.8	TU	1721	0.4
2351	4.4		2333	4.9
		31	0542	0.2
			1159	4.9
		W	1803	0.3

Chart Datum: 2·74 metres below Ordnance Datum (Newlyn)
HAT is 5·0 metres above Chart Datum

TIME ZONE (UT)
For Summer Time add ONE hour in **non-shaded areas**

SOUTHAMPTON
LAT 50°54′N   LONG 1°24′W
TIMES AND HEIGHTS OF HIGH AND LOW WATERS

Dates in amber are **SPRINGS**
Dates in yellow are **NEAPS**

2011

SEPTEMBER

Time m	Time m
1 TH 0015 4.9 / 0623 0.2 / 1242 4.8 / 1844 0.4	**16** F 0021 4.4 / 0619 0.9 / 1240 4.4 / 1834 1.1
2 F 0059 4.8 / 0704 0.4 / 1325 4.7 / 1927 0.6	**17** SA 0054 4.3 / 0643 1.1 / 1311 4.3 / 1859 1.2
3 SA 0144 4.6 / 0746 0.7 / 1412 4.5 / 2011 1.0	**18** SU 0127 4.2 / 0710 1.4 / 1344 4.2 / 1928 1.5
4 SU 0234 4.3 / 0832 1.1 / 1505 4.3 / ◐ 2103 1.4	**19** M 0202 4.0 / 0742 1.6 / 1421 4.0 / 2006 1.7
5 M 0333 4.0 / 0929 1.6 / 1609 4.0 / 2211 1.7	**20** TU 0246 3.9 / 0827 1.9 / 1510 3.8 / ◐ 2100 2.0
6 TU 0451 3.8 / 1049 1.9 / 1734 3.8 / 2342 1.9	**21** W 0350 3.7 / 0934 2.2 / 1622 3.7 / 2225 2.1
7 W 0629 3.8 / 1225 2.0 / 1905 3.9	**22** TH 0517 3.7 / 1116 2.2 / 1751 3.7
8 TH 0111 1.8 / 0753 3.9 / 1345 1.8 / 2016 4.1	**23** F 0007 2.0 / 0645 3.8 / 1246 2.0 / 1911 3.9
9 F 0216 1.5 / 0852 4.2 / 1441 1.5 / 2108 4.2	**24** SA 0120 1.6 / 0752 4.1 / 1349 1.6 / 2011 4.2
10 SA 0303 1.2 / 0937 4.4 / 1524 1.3 / 2148 4.4	**25** SU 0216 1.2 / 0843 4.4 / 1441 1.2 / 2100 4.5
11 SU 0342 1.0 / 1014 4.5 / 1602 1.0 / 2223 4.4	**26** M 0305 0.8 / 0928 4.6 / 1528 0.8 / 2145 4.7
12 M 0418 0.8 / 1046 4.5 / 1638 0.9 / ○ 2254 4.5	**27** TU 0351 0.5 / 1011 4.8 / 1614 0.5 / ● 2227 4.9
13 TU 0452 0.7 / 1711 0.8 / 2322 4.5	**28** W 0436 0.3 / 1053 4.9 / 1658 0.3 / 2310 5.0
14 W 0524 0.7 / 1742 0.8 / 2351 4.4	**29** TH 0519 0.2 / 1135 5.0 / 1741 0.3 / 2354 4.9
15 TH 0554 0.8 / 1210 4.4 / 1810 0.9	**30** F 0602 0.3 / 1219 4.9 / 1824 0.4

OCTOBER

Time m	Time m
1 SA 0038 4.8 / 0643 0.5 / 1304 4.7 / 1906 0.7	**16** SU 0026 4.4 / 0616 1.2 / 1242 4.3 / 1832 1.2
2 SU 0126 4.6 / 0726 0.9 / 1351 4.5 / 1951 1.0	**17** M 0101 4.3 / 0645 1.4 / 1317 4.2 / 1904 1.4
3 M 0217 4.3 / 0814 1.3 / 1445 4.2 / 2043 1.4	**18** TU 0139 4.2 / 0721 1.6 / 1356 4.1 / 1944 1.6
4 TU 0318 4.0 / 0913 1.7 / 1550 4.0 / 2150 1.8	**19** W 0225 4.0 / 0807 1.9 / 1445 3.9 / 2037 1.8
5 W 0437 3.8 / 1033 2.0 / 1714 3.8 / 2318 1.9	**20** TH 0327 3.9 / 0912 2.1 / 1553 3.8 / ◐ 2153 2.0
6 TH 0611 3.8 / 1206 2.1 / 1843 3.8	**21** F 0446 3.8 / 1041 2.1 / 1716 3.8 / 2325 1.9
7 F 0044 1.9 / 0729 4.0 / 1322 1.9 / 1952 4.0	**22** SA 0608 3.9 / 1208 1.9 / 1835 4.0
8 SA 0146 1.6 / 0825 4.2 / 1414 1.6 / 2042 4.2	**23** SU 0042 1.6 / 0716 4.2 / 1315 1.6 / 1939 4.2
9 SU 0232 1.4 / 0908 4.4 / 1455 1.4 / 2122 4.3	**24** M 0142 1.2 / 0812 4.5 / 1411 1.2 / 2032 4.5
10 M 0310 1.1 / 0944 4.5 / 1531 1.1 / 2155 4.4	**25** TU 0235 0.9 / 0900 4.7 / 1501 0.8 / 2120 4.7
11 TU 0345 1.0 / 1015 4.5 / 1606 1.0 / 2225 4.4	**26** W 0323 0.6 / 0945 4.9 / 1549 0.6 / ○ 2205 4.9
12 W 0419 0.9 / 1043 4.5 / 1639 0.9 / ○ 2253 4.5	**27** TH 0410 0.4 / 1030 5.0 / 1635 0.4 / 2250 4.9
13 TH 0452 0.8 / 1110 4.5 / 1710 0.9 / 2322 4.5	**28** F 0456 0.4 / 1114 5.0 / 1720 0.4 / 2336 4.9
14 F 0522 0.9 / 1139 4.5 / 1739 0.9 / 2353 4.4	**29** SA 0541 0.5 / 1159 4.9 / 1805 0.5
15 SA 0550 1.0 / 1209 4.4 / 1806 1.1	**30** SU 0023 4.8 / 0625 0.7 / 1246 4.7 / 1849 0.7
	31 M 0112 4.6 / 0710 1.0 / 1334 4.5 / 1934 1.0

NOVEMBER

Time m	Time m
1 TU 0204 4.4 / 0758 1.3 / 1426 4.2 / 2024 1.3	**16** W 0126 4.3 / 0709 1.5 / 1340 4.2 / 1932 1.4
2 W 0302 4.1 / 0854 1.7 / 1526 4.0 / ◐ 2123 1.7	**17** TH 0212 4.2 / 0756 1.7 / 1429 4.1 / 2023 1.6
3 TH 0411 4.0 / 1004 2.0 / 1637 3.8 / 2236 1.9	**18** F 0309 4.1 / 0855 1.8 / 1529 4.0 / ◐ 2127 1.7
4 F 0529 3.9 / 1124 2.1 / 1757 3.8 / 2352 1.9	**19** SA 0416 4.0 / 1008 1.9 / 1640 3.9 / 2243 1.7
5 SA 0645 4.0 / 1236 2.0 / 1909 3.9	**20** SU 0530 4.1 / 1126 1.8 / 1756 4.0 / 2359 1.6
6 SU 0057 1.8 / 0744 4.1 / 1333 1.8 / 2004 4.0	**21** M 0639 4.2 / 1237 1.6 / 1904 4.2
7 M 0148 1.6 / 0830 4.3 / 1417 1.6 / 2047 4.2	**22** TU 0105 1.3 / 0739 4.5 / 1340 1.3 / 2004 4.4
8 TU 0231 1.4 / 0908 4.4 / 1456 1.3 / 2124 4.3	**23** W 0203 1.1 / 0833 4.7 / 1435 1.0 / 2057 4.6
9 W 0309 1.2 / 0942 4.5 / 1533 1.2 / 2157 4.4	**24** TH 0257 0.8 / 0923 4.8 / 1527 0.7 / 2147 4.7
10 TH 0346 1.1 / 1012 4.5 / 1608 1.0 / ○ 2228 4.4	**25** F 0347 0.7 / 1011 4.9 / 1617 0.6 / 2235 4.8
11 F 0421 1.0 / 1042 4.5 / 1642 1.0 / 2259 4.5	**26** SA 0436 0.6 / 1058 4.9 / 1704 0.5 / 2323 4.8
12 SA 0455 1.0 / 1114 4.5 / 1714 1.0 / 2332 4.5	**27** SU 0524 0.7 / 1145 4.8 / 1750 0.6
13 SU 0527 1.1 / 1147 4.5 / 1745 1.0	**28** M 0011 4.7 / 0610 0.8 / 1232 4.7 / 1834 0.7
14 M 0007 4.4 / 0558 1.2 / 1222 4.4 / 1816 1.1	**29** TU 0100 4.6 / 0656 1.0 / 1318 4.5 / 1918 0.9
15 TU 0045 4.4 / 0631 1.3 / 1259 4.3 / 1851 1.3	**30** W 0148 4.4 / 0741 1.3 / 1405 4.3 / 2002 1.2

DECEMBER

Time m	Time m
1 TH 0238 4.3 / 0830 1.5 / 1454 4.1 / 2049 1.4	**16** F 0158 4.3 / 0746 1.3 / 1413 4.3 / 2009 1.2
2 F 0332 4.1 / 0923 1.8 / 1549 3.9 / 2143 1.7	**17** SA 0248 4.3 / 0837 1.5 / 1505 4.2 / 2102 1.4
3 SA 0432 4.0 / 1026 2.0 / 1651 3.8 / 2247 1.9	**18** SU 0345 4.2 / 0936 1.8 / 1606 4.1 / 2205 1.5
4 SU 0538 3.9 / 1135 2.0 / 1802 3.7 / 2355 1.9	**19** M 0451 4.2 / 1046 1.7 / 1715 4.0 / 2316 1.5
5 M 0645 4.0 / 1239 2.0 / 1911 3.8	**20** TU 0601 4.2 / 1200 1.6 / 1829 4.1
6 TU 0056 1.9 / 0742 4.1 / 1334 1.8 / 2006 4.0	**21** W 0029 1.5 / 0709 4.3 / 1311 1.4 / 1938 4.2
7 W 0149 1.7 / 0829 4.2 / 1421 1.6 / 2052 4.1	**22** TH 0136 1.3 / 0811 4.4 / 1415 1.2 / 2040 4.3
8 TH 0234 1.5 / 0910 4.3 / 1502 1.4 / 2131 4.2	**23** F 0237 1.1 / 0907 4.6 / 1512 1.0 / 2136 4.5
9 F 0316 1.4 / 0946 4.4 / 1541 1.2 / 2207 4.3	**24** SA 0333 1.0 / 0959 4.7 / 1605 0.7 / 2227 4.6
10 SA 0355 1.2 / 1021 4.5 / 1619 1.0 / 2242 4.4	**25** SU 0424 0.8 / 1048 4.7 / 1653 0.6 / 2315 4.6
11 SU 0433 1.1 / 1055 4.5 / 1655 1.0 / 2317 4.4	**26** M 0513 0.8 / 1133 4.7 / 1739 0.5
12 M 0509 1.1 / 1130 4.5 / 1731 0.9 / 2353 4.4	**27** TU 0000 4.6 / 0557 0.8 / 1217 4.6 / 1820 0.6
13 TU 0545 1.1 / 1207 4.5 / 1806 0.9	**28** W 0044 4.6 / 0640 0.9 / 1259 4.6 / 1900 0.7
14 W 0032 4.4 / 0622 1.2 / 1246 4.4 / 1843 1.0	**29** TH 0126 4.5 / 0720 1.0 / 1340 4.4 / 1937 0.9
15 TH 0113 4.4 / 0701 1.2 / 1328 4.4 / 1923 1.1	**30** F 0208 4.3 / 0759 1.2 / 1420 4.2 / 2013 1.2
	31 SA 0250 4.2 / 0839 1.5 / 1503 4.0 / 2053 1.5

Chart Datum: 2·74 metres below Ordnance Datum (Newlyn)
HAT is 5·0 metres above Chart Datum

TIDES

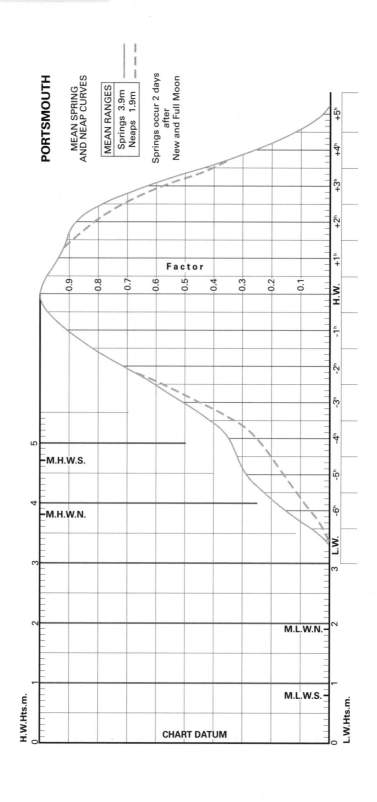

PORTSMOUTH

LAT 50°48′N   LONG 1°07′W

2011

TIMES AND HEIGHTS OF HIGH AND LOW WATERS

JANUARY

#	Time	m	#	Time	m
1 SA	0136	1.6	16 SU	0111	2.0
	0831	4.4		0802	4.1
	1417	1.5		1353	1.8
	2106	4.2		2039	4.0
2 SU	0238	1.5	17 M	0215	1.7
	0930	4.5		0901	4.2
	1514	1.3		1447	1.4
	2205	4.4		2135	4.2
3 M	0332	1.3	18 TU	0307	1.5
	1021	4.6		0951	4.4
	1602	1.1		1535	1.1
	2255	4.5		2224	4.5
4 TU	0419	1.2	19 W	0354	1.2
	1106	4.6		1037	4.6
	1646	1.0		1621	0.9
	● 2339	4.6		○ 2310	4.6
5 W	0501	1.1	20 TH	0438	0.9
	1147	4.6		1122	4.7
	1726	0.9		1705	0.6
				2355	4.8
6 TH	0019	4.6	21 F	0523	0.8
	0540	1.1		1207	4.8
	1225	4.6		1749	0.5
	1802	0.9			
7 F	0055	4.6	22 SA	0039	4.9
	0617	1.1		0607	0.7
	1300	4.5		1243	4.8
	1837	0.9		1833	0.5
8 SA	0129	4.5	23 SU	0124	4.9
	0652	1.2		0652	0.7
	1334	4.4		1338	4.8
	1909	1.0		1917	0.5
9 SU	0202	4.5	24 M	0209	4.9
	0725	1.2		0737	0.7
	1409	4.3		1423	4.7
	1940	1.0		2001	0.6
10 M	0237	4.4	25 TU	0253	4.7
	0758	1.4		0823	0.8
	1444	4.2		1510	4.5
	2012	1.4		2046	0.9
11 TU	0313	4.3	26 W	0340	4.6
	0833	1.6		0914	1.2
	1522	4.0		1600	4.3
	2048	1.6		◐ 2137	1.2
12 W	0353	4.1	27 TH	0432	4.3
	0914	1.8		1012	1.5
	1604	3.9		1658	4.1
	◐ 2132	1.8		2239	1.6
13 TH	0441	4.0	28 F	0535	4.1
	1007	2.0		1126	1.7
	1659	3.8		1814	3.9
	2231	2.0		2357	1.8
14 F	0541	3.9	29 SA	0655	4.0
	1121	2.1		1250	1.8
	1811	3.7		1945	3.9
	2350	2.1			
15 SA	0653	3.9	30 SU	0120	1.8
	1245	2.0		0816	4.1
	1930	3.8		1405	1.6
				2101	4.0
			31 M	0231	1.7
				0921	4.2
				1504	1.4
				2159	4.3

FEBRUARY

#	Time	m	#	Time	m
1 TU	0325	1.4	16 W	0251	1.4
	1012	4.4		0929	4.3
	1551	1.2		1518	1.0
	2246	4.4		2205	4.5
2 W	0409	1.2	17 TH	0339	1.0
	1055	4.5		1019	4.5
	1631	1.0		1604	0.7
	2326	4.5		2252	4.7
3 TH	0447	1.1	18 F	0424	0.7
	1133	4.5		1105	4.7
	1708	0.8		1649	0.4
	●			○ 2337	4.9
4 F	0001	4.6	19 SA	0508	0.5
	0523	1.0		1151	4.8
	1207	4.5		1732	0.3
	1742	0.8			
5 SA	0033	4.6	20 SU	0021	5.0
	0556	0.9		0551	0.4
	1239	4.5		1238	4.9
	1814	0.8		1815	0.3
6 SU	0103	4.6	21 M	0105	5.0
	0628	1.0		0634	0.4
	1311	4.4		1322	4.9
	1843	0.9		1857	0.3
7 M	0133	4.5	22 TU	0147	4.9
	0656	1.1		0717	0.5
	1343	4.4		1407	4.8
	1910	1.0		1939	0.5
8 TU	0203	4.5	23 W	0229	4.8
	0722	1.2		0800	0.7
	1415	4.3		1451	4.6
	1936	1.2		2022	0.9
9 W	0234	4.5	24 TH	0312	4.5
	0751	1.3		0846	1.0
	1447	4.2		1539	4.3
	2006	1.4		◑ 2110	1.3
10 TH	0307	4.2	25 F	0400	4.2
	0825	1.5		0941	1.4
	1523	4.0		1636	4.0
	2044	1.6		2212	1.7
11 F	0346	4.0	26 SA	0501	3.9
	0910	1.7		1056	1.8
	1610	3.8		1755	3.8
	◐ 2135	1.9		2336	2.0
12 SA	0441	3.9	27 SU	0629	3.7
	1013	2.0		1228	1.9
	1720	3.7		1934	3.8
	2250	2.1			
13 SU	0558	3.8	28 M	0108	2.0
	1149	2.0		0803	3.8
	1849	3.7		1350	1.7
				2050	4.0
14 M	0035	2.1			
	0722	3.8			
	1325	1.8			
	2011	3.9			
15 TU	0155	1.8			
	0833	4.1			
	1427	1.4			
	2114	4.2			

MARCH

#	Time	m	#	Time	m
1 TU	0222	1.7	16 W	0131	1.7
	0909	4.0		0803	4.0
	1448	1.5		1401	1.4
	2144	4.3		2047	4.2
2 W	0312	1.4	17 TH	0229	1.3
	0958	4.2		0904	4.3
	1531	1.2		1454	1.0
	2227	4.4		2140	4.5
3 TH	0352	1.2	18 F	0318	0.9
	1038	4.4		0955	4.5
	1608	1.0		1541	0.6
	2304	4.5		2227	4.7
4 F	0427	1.0	19 SA	0403	0.6
	1113	4.4		1044	4.7
	1643	0.8		1626	0.4
	● 2336	4.6		2313	4.9
5 SA	0500	0.9	20 SU	0448	0.4
	1144	4.4		1131	4.9
	1716	0.8		1710	0.2
				2358	5.0
6 SU	0005	4.6	21 M	0531	0.3
	0531	0.8		1218	4.9
	1215	4.5		1753	0.2
	1747	0.8			
7 M	0033	4.6	22 TU	0042	5.0
	0601	0.8		0614	0.3
	1246	4.5		1304	4.9
	1816	0.8		1835	0.4
8 TU	0102	4.5	23 W	0125	4.9
	0627	0.9		0656	0.4
	1317	4.4		1349	4.8
	1841	0.9		1917	0.6
9 W	0132	4.5	24 TH	0206	4.8
	0651	1.0		0738	0.7
	1348	4.4		1434	4.6
	1906	1.1		2000	0.9
10 TH	0201	4.4	25 F	0248	4.5
	0719	1.1		0823	1.0
	1420	4.3		1522	4.3
	1935	1.3		2048	1.3
11 F	0231	4.2	26 SA	0335	4.2
	0752	1.3		0915	1.4
	1455	4.1		1619	4.0
	2012	1.5		2149	1.7
12 SA	0307	4.1	27 SU	0433	3.8
	0835	1.5		1027	1.7
	1541	3.9		1737	3.8
	◑ 2102	1.8		2313	2.0
13 SU	0359	3.8	28 M	0601	3.6
	0934	1.8		1158	1.9
	1649	3.7		1911	3.8
	2215	2.0			
14 M	0516	3.7	29 TU	0045	2.0
	1107	1.9		0738	3.7
	1817	3.7		1319	1.7
				2023	4.0
15 TU	0005	2.0	30 W	0157	1.7
	0645	3.7		0843	3.9
	1253	1.7		1417	1.5
	1941	3.9		2115	4.2
			31 TH	0246	1.5
				0931	4.1
				1500	1.3
				2157	4.4

APRIL

#	Time	m	#	Time	m
1 F	0324	1.2	16 SA	0251	0.9
	1010	4.2		0928	4.5
	1537	1.1		1512	0.7
	2232	4.5		2200	4.8
2 SA	0358	1.0	17 SU	0339	0.6
	1044	4.3		1020	4.7
	1612	0.9		1600	0.5
	2304	4.5		2248	4.9
3 SU	0431	0.9	18 M	0425	0.4
	1116	4.4		1109	4.8
	1646	0.8		1646	0.4
	● 2333	4.5		○ 2334	5.0
4 M	0503	0.8	19 TU	0510	0.3
	1147	4.4		1158	4.9
	1718	0.8		1731	0.4
5 TU	0002	4.5	20 W	0019	5.0
	0532	0.8		0554	0.4
	1219	4.5		1246	4.9
	1747	0.9		1814	0.5
6 W	0033	4.5	21 TH	0104	4.9
	0559	0.9		0637	0.5
	1252	4.5		1333	4.8
	1814	1.0		1857	0.7
7 TH	0103	4.5	22 F	0146	4.7
	0625	0.9		0719	0.7
	1325	4.4		1419	4.6
	1841	1.1		1941	1.0
8 F	0134	4.4	23 SA	0229	4.4
	0655	1.0		0804	1.0
	1359	4.3		1508	4.4
	1914	1.3		2029	1.4
9 SA	0206	4.3	24 SU	0315	4.1
	0731	1.2		0854	1.3
	1437	4.2		1602	4.1
	1954	1.5		2127	1.7
10 SU	0244	4.1	25 M	0409	3.9
	0815	1.4		0956	1.6
	1525	4.0		1710	3.9
	2045	1.7		◑ 2239	1.9
11 M	0336	3.9	26 TU	0522	3.7
	0915	1.6		1114	1.8
	1630	3.9		1829	3.9
	◐ 2158	1.9			
12 TU	0449	3.8	27 W	0001	2.0
	1040	1.7		0650	3.7
	1750	3.9		1230	1.8
	2332	1.9		1938	4.0
13 W	0612	3.8	28 TH	0111	1.8
	1215	1.6		0759	3.8
	1910	4.0		1330	1.6
				2032	4.1
14 TH	0056	1.6	29 F	0204	1.6
	0729	4.0		0850	3.9
	1327	1.3		1417	1.4
	2015	4.3		2115	4.3
15 F	0159	1.3	30 SA	0245	1.4
	0833	4.3		0932	4.1
	1423	1.0		1458	1.3
	2110	4.6		2153	4.4

TIDES

Chart Datum: 2·73 metres below Ordnance Datum (Newlyn)
HAT is 5·1 metres above Chart Datum

TIME ZONE (UT)
For Summer Time add ONE hour in **non-shaded areas**

PORTSMOUTH
LAT 50°48′N   LONG 1°07′W
TIMES AND HEIGHTS OF HIGH AND LOW WATERS

Dates in amber are **SPRINGS**
Dates in yellow are **NEAPS**

2011

MAY

Day	Time m	Time m	Time m	Time m	Day	Time m	Time m	Time m	Time m
1 SU	0323 1.2	1009 4.2	1536 1.1	2227 4.4	16 M	0314 0.8	0958 4.6	1535 0.7	2225 4.8
2 M	0359 1.1	1044 4.3	1613 1.0	2300 4.5	17 TU	0404 0.6	1051 4.7	1624 0.7	○2314 4.9
3 TU	0433 1.0	1118 4.4	1648 1.0	●2333 4.5	18 W	0452 0.6	1142 4.8	1711 0.7	
4 W	0505 0.9	1153 4.5	1720 1.0		19 TH	0001 4.9	0537 0.6	1231 4.8	1756 0.7
5 TH	0006 4.5	0535 0.9	1229 4.5	1751 1.1	20 F	0046 4.8	0621 0.6	1319 4.7	1841 0.9
6 F	0040 4.5	0606 0.9	1305 4.5	1824 1.1	21 SA	0130 4.6	0704 0.8	1405 4.6	1925 1.1
7 SA	0114 4.4	0640 1.0	1343 4.4	1901 1.4	22 SU	0212 4.4	0747 1.0	1451 4.4	2010 1.3
8 SU	0150 4.3	0720 1.1	1426 4.3	1945 1.4	23 M	0256 4.2	0831 1.3	1538 4.2	2059 1.6
9 M	0232 4.2	0808 1.3	1515 4.2	2038 1.5	24 TU	0342 4.0	0922 1.5	1630 4.1	☽2156 1.8
10 TU	0324 4.1	0907 1.4	1615 4.1	☽2144 1.7	25 W	0436 3.8	1020 1.7	1728 4.0	2302 1.9
11 W	0429 4.0	1018 1.5	1725 4.1	2300 1.7	26 TH	0539 3.7	1126 1.8	1830 3.9	
12 TH	0542 4.0	1136 1.4	1837 4.2		27 F	0010 1.9	0647 3.8	1231 1.8	1929 4.0
13 F	0016 1.5	0655 4.1	1247 1.3	1942 4.4	28 SA	0110 1.8	0751 3.9	1327 1.7	2021 4.1
14 SA	0123 1.3	0802 4.3	1349 1.1	2040 4.6	29 SU	0200 1.6	0844 3.9	1416 1.5	2107 4.2
15 SU	0221 1.0	0902 4.5	1444 0.9	2134 4.7	30 M	0244 1.4	0929 4.1	1500 1.4	2149 4.3
					31 TU	0325 1.3	1011 4.2	1541 1.3	2228 4.4

JUNE

Day	Time m	Time m	Time m	Time m	Day	Time m	Time m	Time m	Time m
1 W	0404 1.1	1052 4.4	1620 1.2	●2306 4.5	16 TH	0439 0.8	1131 4.7	1657 0.9	2346 4.7
2 TH	0440 1.0	1131 4.5	1657 1.1	2343 4.5	17 F	0525 0.7	1219 4.7	1743 0.9	
3 F	0517 1.0	1210 4.5	1734 1.1		18 SA	0030 4.7	0608 0.7	1305 4.7	1825 1.0
4 SA	0020 4.5	0553 0.9	1250 4.5	1812 1.1	19 SU	0113 4.6	0648 0.8	1347 4.6	1906 1.1
5 SU	0059 4.5	0633 0.9	1332 4.5	1854 1.1	20 M	0152 4.4	0726 1.0	1427 4.5	1946 1.2
6 M	0140 4.5	0716 1.0	1416 4.5	1939 1.2	21 TU	0231 4.3	0804 1.1	1506 4.4	2027 1.4
7 TU	0224 4.4	0803 1.0	1504 4.4	2030 1.3	22 W	0310 4.1	0844 1.3	1546 4.2	2111 1.6
8 W	0314 4.3	0857 1.1	1558 4.4	2127 1.4	23 TH	0353 4.0	0928 1.6	1630 4.1	☽2201 1.8
9 TH	0410 4.2	0956 1.2	1658 4.3	☽2231 1.5	24 F	0441 3.8	1020 1.8	1720 4.0	2300 1.9
10 F	0514 4.1	1101 1.3	1803 4.3	2341 1.5	25 SA	0537 3.7	1123 1.9	1818 4.0	
11 SA	0624 4.1	1210 1.3	1910 4.4		26 SU	0008 1.9	0644 3.7	1231 1.9	1921 4.0
12 SU	0051 1.4	0735 4.2	1318 1.3	2013 4.5	27 M	0112 1.8	0752 3.8	1332 1.8	2021 4.1
13 M	0157 1.2	0842 4.3	1420 1.2	2113 4.6	28 TU	0207 1.6	0853 4.0	1426 1.7	2113 4.2
14 TU	0256 1.0	0943 4.5	1517 1.1	2207 4.7	29 W	0255 1.4	0943 4.2	1513 1.5	2159 4.4
15 W	0350 0.9	1039 4.6	1609 1.0	○2258 4.7	30 TH	0339 1.2	1029 4.4	1557 1.3	2242 4.5

JULY

Day	Time m	Time m	Time m	Time m	Day	Time m	Time m	Time m	Time m
1 F	0421 1.0	1112 4.5	1638 1.1	●2323 4.5	16 SA	0511 0.8	1207 4.7	1728 1.0	
2 SA	0502 0.9	1154 4.6	1720 1.0		17 SU	0014 4.6	0550 0.8	1247 4.7	1806 1.0
3 SU	0004 4.6	0542 0.8	1237 4.6	1801 0.9	18 M	0052 4.5	0627 0.8	1324 4.6	1843 1.0
4 M	0046 4.6	0624 0.7	1320 4.7	1844 0.9	19 TU	0127 4.4	0701 0.9	1357 4.5	1918 1.1
5 TU	0129 4.6	0708 0.7	1404 4.7	1929 0.9	20 W	0202 4.4	0733 1.0	1430 4.5	1951 1.3
6 W	0213 4.6	0752 0.8	1449 4.7	2016 1.0	21 TH	0236 4.2	0805 1.2	1504 4.4	2026 1.4
7 TH	0300 4.5	0840 0.9	1537 4.6	2107 1.1	22 F	0313 4.1	0838 1.4	1541 4.2	2103 1.6
8 F	0351 4.4	0932 1.1	1630 4.4	☽2205 1.3	23 SA	0353 4.0	0919 1.7	1623 4.1	☽2150 1.8
9 SA	0449 4.2	1032 1.3	1730 4.3	2311 1.5	24 SU	0443 3.8	1012 1.9	1717 3.9	2256 2.0
10 SU	0557 4.1	1141 1.5	1840 4.3		25 M	0549 3.7	1127 2.1	1825 3.9	
11 M	0026 1.5	0715 4.0	1256 1.6	1952 4.3	26 TU	0022 2.0	0707 3.7	1253 2.0	1938 4.0
12 TU	0141 1.5	0831 4.1	1406 1.5	2059 4.4	27 W	0135 1.8	0821 3.9	1359 1.9	2042 4.1
13 W	0246 1.3	0937 4.3	1507 1.3	2157 4.5	28 TH	0231 1.5	0920 4.2	1451 1.6	2134 4.3
14 TH	0340 1.1	1033 4.5	1559 1.2	2247 4.5	29 F	0319 1.2	1009 4.4	1537 1.3	2220 4.5
15 F	0428 0.9	1122 4.6	1645 1.1	○2333 4.6	30 SA	0403 0.9	1053 4.6	1621 1.1	●2303 4.6
					31 SU	0445 0.7	1136 4.7	1704 0.9	2346 4.7

AUGUST

Day	Time m	Time m	Time m	Time m	Day	Time m	Time m	Time m	Time m
1 M	0528 0.6	1219 4.8	1746 0.7		16 TU	0026 4.5	0601 0.8	1254 4.6	1816 0.9
2 TU	0029 4.7	0609 0.5	1303 4.9	1829 0.7	17 W	0059 4.5	0632 0.8	1323 4.6	1846 1.0
3 W	0114 4.8	0652 0.5	1345 4.9	1913 0.7	18 TH	0130 4.4	0700 1.0	1353 4.5	1915 1.2
4 TH	0158 4.7	0735 0.6	1428 4.8	1957 0.8	19 F	0203 4.4	0727 1.2	1425 4.4	1943 1.3
5 F	0243 4.6	0819 0.8	1513 4.7	2045 1.1	20 SA	0237 4.2	0756 1.4	1458 4.3	2016 1.5
6 SA	0331 4.4	0908 1.1	1602 4.5	☽2140 1.3	21 SU	0313 4.1	0831 1.6	1535 4.1	☽2057 1.8
7 SU	0426 4.2	1006 1.4	1700 4.2	2247 1.6	22 M	0358 3.9	0919 1.9	1624 3.9	2155 2.0
8 M	0537 4.0	1120 1.7	1815 4.1		23 TU	0502 3.7	1030 2.2	1733 3.8	2328 2.1
9 TU	0010 1.7	0706 3.9	1244 1.8	1940 4.1	24 W	0628 3.7	1217 2.2	1858 3.8	
10 W	0132 1.6	0830 4.1	1401 1.7	2053 4.2	25 TH	0106 1.9	0752 3.9	1336 2.0	2012 4.0
11 TH	0238 1.4	0934 4.3	1501 1.5	2149 4.4	26 F	0208 1.6	0856 4.2	1430 1.6	2109 4.3
12 F	0330 1.2	1025 4.5	1549 1.3	2236 4.5	27 SA	0257 1.2	0946 4.4	1517 1.2	2156 4.5
13 SA	0413 0.9	1109 4.6	1630 1.1	○2317 4.6	28 SU	0341 1.0	1030 4.6	1600 0.9	2241 4.7
14 SU	0452 0.8	1147 4.7	1708 1.0	2353 4.6	29 M	0424 0.6	1113 4.8	1643 0.7	●2325 4.8
15 M	0528 0.7	1222 4.7	1743 0.9		30 TU	0506 0.4	1157 4.9	1726 0.5	
					31 W	0009 4.9	0548 0.5	1240 5.0	1808 0.5

Chart Datum: 2·73 metres below Ordnance Datum (Newlyn)
HAT is 5·1 metres above Chart Datum

PORTSMOUTH

LAT 50°48'N LONG 1°07'W

2011

TIMES AND HEIGHTS OF HIGH AND LOW WATERS

SEPTEMBER

Time	m		Time	m
1 0054	4.9	**16** 0100	4.5
0631	0.4	0628	1.0
TH 1323	5.0	F 1319	4.6
1851	0.6	1840	1.1
2 0139	4.9	**17** 0132	4.5
0713	0.6	0653	1.2
F 1405	4.9	SA 1349	4.5
1935	0.7	1907	1.3
3 0224	4.7	**18** 0205	4.3
0757	0.8	0722	1.4
SA 1449	4.7	SU 1421	4.3
2022	1.0	1939	1.5
4 0312	4.5	**19** 0240	4.2
0846	1.2	0756	1.7
SU 1536	4.4	M 1455	4.1
◑ 2116	1.4	2019	1.7
5 0408	4.2	**20** 0323	4.0
0946	1.6	0843	1.9
M 1635	4.1	TU 1542	3.9
2226	1.7	◐ 2115	1.9
6 0524	3.9	**21** 0426	3.8
1105	1.9	0952	2.2
TU 1757	3.9	W 1651	3.8
2355	1.9	2242	2.1
7 0702	3.9	**22** 0552	3.8
1235	2.0	1140	2.2
W 1933	4.0	TH 1818	3.8
8 0120	1.8	**23** 0030	1.9
0823	4.1	0718	3.9
TH 1352	1.8	F 1306	2.0
2043	4.2	1938	4.0
9 0225	1.5	**24** 0138	1.6
0921	4.4	0824	4.2
F 1448	1.5	SA 1403	1.6
2135	4.4	2039	4.3
10 0311	1.2	**25** 0229	1.2
1007	4.6	0916	4.5
SA 1530	1.3	SU 1451	1.2
2218	4.5	2129	4.6
11 0350	1.0	**26** 0314	0.8
1046	4.7	1002	4.8
SU 1607	1.1	M 1535	0.9
2255	4.6	2216	4.8
12 0426	0.9	**27** 0358	0.6
1121	4.7	1046	4.9
M 1642	1.0	TU 1618	0.6
○ 2328	4.6	● 2302	4.9
13 0459	0.8	**28** 0441	0.4
1220	4.7	1131	5.0
TU 1715	0.9	W 1702	0.5
2358	4.6	2348	5.0
14 0532	0.8	**29** 0525	0.4
0601	0.9	1215	5.1
W 1746	0.9	TH 1746	0.6
15 0028	4.6	**30** 0034	5.0
0601	0.9	0608	0.5
TH 1249	4.6	F 1259	5.0
1814	1.0	1829	0.5

OCTOBER

Time	m		Time	m
1 0120	4.9	**16** 0106	4.5
0651	0.7	0626	1.3
SA 1343	4.9	SU 1319	4.5
1914	0.8	1840	1.2
2 0207	4.8	**17** 0140	4.4
0737	1.0	0656	1.4
SU 1427	4.7	M 1351	4.4
2001	1.1	1913	1.4
3 0256	4.5	**18** 0216	4.3
0827	1.3	0733	1.6
M 1515	4.4	TU 1427	4.2
2055	1.4	1955	1.6
4 0354	4.2	**19** 0301	4.1
0928	1.7	0821	1.9
TU 1614	4.1	W 1514	4.0
◑ 2203	1.8	2049	1.8
5 0510	4.0	**20** 0401	4.0
1047	2.0	0927	2.1
W 1738	3.9	TH 1619	3.9
2330	1.9	◐ 2207	2.0
6 0644	4.0	**21** 0518	3.9
1215	2.0	1059	2.1
TH 1914	3.9	F 1739	3.9
		2341	1.9
7 0054	1.8	**22** 0639	4.0
0759	4.2	1225	1.9
F 1330	1.9	SA 1859	4.0
2021	4.1		
8 0157	1.6	**23** 0056	1.6
0854	4.4	0747	4.3
SA 1422	1.6	SU 1328	1.6
2111	4.3	2004	4.3
9 0242	1.4	**24** 0154	1.3
0938	4.5	0842	4.6
SU 1503	1.4	M 1420	1.2
2152	4.4	2100	4.6
10 0320	1.2	**25** 0243	0.9
1016	4.6	0932	4.8
M 1539	1.2	TU 1508	0.9
2228	4.5	2150	4.8
11 0355	1.0	**26** 0330	0.7
1048	4.7	1019	5.0
TU 1612	1.0	W 1554	0.7
2259	4.6	● 2239	4.9
12 0429	1.0	**27** 0416	0.6
1118	4.7	1106	5.1
W 1645	1.0	TH 1640	0.5
○ 2329	4.6	2328	5.0
13 0501	1.0	**28** 0502	0.5
1147	4.7	1152	5.1
TH 1717	1.0	F 1726	0.5
14 0000	4.6	**29** 0016	5.0
0532	1.0	0547	0.6
F 1218	4.6	SA 1238	5.0
1745	1.0	1811	0.6
15 0033	4.6	**30** 0105	4.8
0559	1.1	0633	0.8
SA 1248	4.6	SU 1324	4.9
1811	1.1	1856	0.8
		31 0153	4.8
		0719	1.1
		M 1409	4.6
		1943	1.1

NOVEMBER

Time	m		Time	m
1 0243	4.6	**16** 0200	4.4
0810	1.4	0720	1.5
TU 1458	4.4	W 1409	4.3
2035	1.4	1942	1.4
2 0339	4.3	**17** 0245	4.3
0908	1.7	0808	1.7
W 1554	4.1	TH 1455	4.2
2136	1.7	2034	1.6
3 0446	4.1	**18** 0340	4.2
1017	2.0	0908	1.8
TH 1705	3.9	F 1554	4.1
2249	1.9	◑ 2140	1.7
4 0605	4.1	**19** 0446	4.1
1136	2.0	1022	1.9
F 1830	3.8	SA 1704	4.0
		2255	1.7
5 0006	1.9	**20** 0559	4.2
0716	4.1	1139	1.8
SA 1248	1.9	SU 1818	4.1
1940	4.0		
6 0111	1.8	**21** 0009	1.6
0814	4.3	0708	4.4
SU 1344	1.8	M 1249	1.6
2035	4.1	1929	4.3
7 0201	1.6	**22** 0115	1.3
0900	4.4	0809	4.6
M 1428	1.6	TU 1349	1.3
2118	4.3	2031	4.5
8 0243	1.4	**23** 0212	1.1
0938	4.5	0904	4.8
TU 1506	1.4	W 1443	1.0
2156	4.4	2128	4.7
9 0321	1.3	**24** 0305	0.9
1013	4.6	0956	4.9
W 1542	1.2	TH 1535	0.8
2229	4.5	2222	4.8
10 0357	1.2	**25** 0356	0.8
1045	4.6	1046	5.0
TH 1617	1.1	F 1624	0.7
○ 2302	4.5	● 2313	4.9
11 0432	1.2	**26** 0444	0.8
1117	4.6	1134	5.0
F 1650	1.1	SA 1712	0.6
2336	4.6		
12 0506	1.2	**27** 0004	4.9
1150	4.6	0531	0.8
SA 1721	1.1	SU 1222	4.9
		1758	0.7
13 0010	4.6	**28** 0053	4.9
0536	1.2	0618	0.9
SU 1223	4.6	M 1308	4.8
1751	1.1	1843	0.8
14 0045	4.6	**29** 0141	4.8
0606	1.3	0704	1.1
M 1256	4.5	TU 1353	4.6
1822	1.2	1928	1.0
15 0121	4.5	**30** 0229	4.6
0640	1.4	0751	1.3
TU 1331	4.4	W 1439	4.4
1859	1.3	2014	1.2

DECEMBER

Time	m		Time	m
1 0317	4.4	**16** 0232	4.5
0841	1.6	0757	1.4
TH 1526	4.2	F 1441	4.4
2103	1.5	2021	1.2
2 0409	4.3	**17** 0321	4.4
0937	1.8	0849	1.5
F 1619	4.0	SA 1533	4.3
◐ 2158	1.7	2116	1.3
3 0507	4.1	**18** 0417	4.3
1041	2.0	0950	1.6
SA 1720	3.8	SU 1632	4.2
2302	1.9	◑ 2219	1.5
4 0610	4.1	**19** 0521	4.3
1149	2.0	1059	1.7
SU 1830	3.8	M 1741	4.1
		2328	1.5
5 0009	1.9	**20** 0630	4.3
0712	4.1	1213	1.6
M 1252	1.9	TU 1856	4.2
1937	3.9		
6 0109	1.9	**21** 0040	1.5
0807	4.2	0738	4.4
TU 1345	1.8	W 1323	1.5
2033	4.0	2008	4.3
7 0201	1.7	**22** 0148	1.4
0855	4.3	0842	4.6
W 1431	1.6	TH 1427	1.2
2120	4.2	2113	4.5
8 0247	1.6	**23** 0249	1.2
0936	4.4	0939	4.7
TH 1512	1.4	F 1523	1.0
2200	4.3	2212	4.6
9 0328	1.4	**24** 0344	1.0
1014	4.5	1032	4.8
F 1551	1.3	SA 1615	0.8
2238	4.4	● 2305	4.7
10 0407	1.3	**25** 0434	0.9
1051	4.6	1122	4.9
SA 1628	1.2	SU 1703	0.7
○ 2315	4.5	2355	4.8
11 0444	1.3	**26** 0521	0.9
1127	4.6	1209	4.8
SU 1704	1.1	M 1748	0.7
2352	4.6		
12 0519	1.2	**27** 0042	4.8
1203	4.6	0605	0.9
M 1738	1.0	TU 1254	4.8
		1830	0.7
13 0029	4.6	**28** 0127	4.8
0553	1.2	0648	1.0
TU 1239	4.6	W 1336	4.6
1813	1.0	1910	0.9
14 0108	4.6	**29** 0208	4.7
0630	1.2	0729	1.2
W 1317	4.5	TH 1416	4.5
1851	1.1	1948	1.0
15 0148	4.6	**30** 0247	4.5
0713	1.3	0809	1.4
TH 1357	4.4	F 1455	4.3
1934	1.1	2027	1.3
		31 0327	4.4
		0852	1.6
		SA 1535	4.1
		2108	1.5

Chart Datum: 2·73 metres below Ordnance Datum (Newlyn)
HAT is 5·1 metres above Chart Datum

TIDES

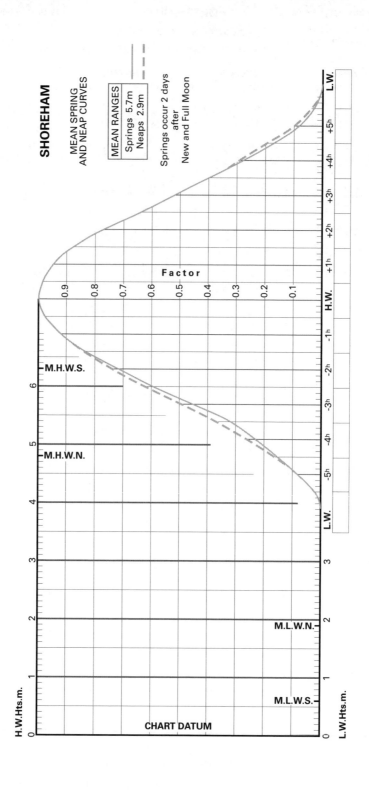

SHOREHAM
LAT 50°50′N   LONG 0°15′W
TIMES AND HEIGHTS OF HIGH AND LOW WATERS

Dates in amber are **SPRINGS**
Dates in yellow are **NEAPS**

2011

JANUARY

Day	Time	m	Time	m	Time	m	Time	m
1 SA	0214	1.5	0830	5.5	1447	1.3	2105	5.4
16 SU	0146	2.0	0758	5.1	1425	1.8	2032	5.1
2 SU	0314	1.4	0929	5.7	1542	1.1	2202	5.7
17 M	0253	1.8	0855	5.4	1523	1.4	2127	5.5
3 M	0406	1.2	1020	5.9	1631	1.0	2251	5.9
18 TU	0345	1.4	0945	5.8	1611	1.1	2216	5.9
4 TU	0452	1.1	1106	6.1	1716	0.9	2335	6.1
19 W	0431	1.1	1031	6.1	1655	1.0	2302	6.2
5 W	0535	1.0	1148	6.1	1757	0.8		
20 TH	0514	0.9	1116	6.3	1738	0.6	2347	6.4
6 TH	0015	6.1	0614	1.0	1227	6.1	1835	0.8
21 F	0557	0.7	1201	6.5	1822	0.4		
7 F	0053	6.1	0650	1.0	1301	6.0	1911	0.9
22 SA	0032	6.5	0641	0.6	1246	6.5	1906	0.4
8 SA	0126	6.0	0725	1.1	1333	5.8	1945	1.0
23 SU	0115	6.6	0726	0.5	1330	6.5	1951	0.4
9 SU	0157	5.9	0759	1.2	1403	5.7	2019	1.1
24 M	0159	6.5	0812	0.6	1414	6.3	2036	0.5
10 M	0225	5.7	0835	1.4	1433	5.5	2055	1.3
25 TU	0243	6.3	0859	0.8	1500	6.1	2123	0.8
11 TU	0253	5.5	0914	1.6	1507	5.3	2134	1.6
26 W	0329	6.0	0950	1.1	1551	5.7	2215	1.2
12 W	0329	5.3	0958	1.8	1550	5.0	2219	1.8
27 TH	0423	5.6	1050	1.4	1651	5.3	2319	1.6
13 TH	0416	5.1	1052	2.0	1649	4.8	2316	2.1
28 F	0527	5.3	1204	1.7	1806	4.9		
14 F	0528	4.9	1158	2.1	1818	4.7		
29 SA	0039	1.8	0648	5.0	1325	1.8	1939	4.9
15 SA	0029	2.2	0652	4.9	1313	2.0	1930	4.8
30 SU	0158	1.8	0815	5.1	1434	1.6	2058	5.1
31 M	0303	1.6	0922	5.4	1532	1.3	2156	5.5

FEBRUARY

Day	Time	m	Time	m	Time	m	Time	m
1 TU	0355	1.4	1013	5.7	1620	1.1	2242	5.8
16 W	0325	1.4	0926	5.7	1550	1.0	2158	5.9
2 W	0440	1.1	1057	5.9	1701	0.9	2323	6.0
17 TH	0412	1.0	1015	6.1	1635	0.6	2246	6.3
3 TH	0519	1.0	1136	6.0	1739	0.8		
18 F	0456	0.6	1102	6.4	1719	0.4	2331	6.6
4 F	0000	6.1	0555	0.9	1211	6.1	1814	0.7
19 SA	0539	0.4	1147	6.6	1803	0.2		
5 SA	0033	6.1	0629	0.9	1242	6.0	1847	0.8
20 SU	0015	6.7	0623	0.3	1232	6.7	1846	0.1
6 SU	0102	6.1	0700	0.9	1308	5.9	1919	0.8
21 M	0058	6.8	0707	0.3	1315	6.6	1930	0.2
7 M	0125	6.0	0731	1.0	1331	5.8	1949	0.8
22 TU	0140	6.7	0751	0.4	1357	6.5	2014	0.4
8 TU	0146	5.9	0802	1.1	1357	5.7	2019	1.1
23 W	0221	6.4	0836	0.6	1440	6.2	2058	0.7
9 W	0212	5.8	0832	1.3	1427	5.5	2048	1.3
24 TH	0304	6.1	0923	1.0	1527	5.7	2147	1.2
10 TH	0244	5.5	0906	1.5	1503	5.3	2123	1.6
25 F	0354	5.6	1017	1.4	1625	5.2	2247	1.7
11 F	0325	5.2	0949	1.8	1550	5.0	2213	1.9
26 SA	0456	5.0	1132	1.8	1739	4.8		
12 SA	0418	4.9	1053	2.0	1659	4.6	2328	2.2
27 SU	0016	2.0	0618	4.7	1306	1.9	1922	4.7
13 SU	0549	4.7	1221	2.1	1853	4.6		
28 M	0143	2.0	0802	4.8	1419	1.7	2046	5.0
14 M	0105	2.1	0726	4.8	1351	1.9	2006	5.0
15 TU	0227	1.8	0832	5.2	1459	1.4	2106	5.4

MARCH

Day	Time	m	Time	m	Time	m	Time	m
1 TU	0249	1.7	0910	5.1	1515	1.4	2141	5.4
16 W	0200	1.8	0808	5.2	1432	1.4	2044	5.5
2 W	0339	1.4	0958	5.5	1601	1.1	2224	5.8
17 TH	0300	1.3	0905	5.7	1525	0.9	2137	6.0
3 TH	0421	1.1	1039	5.8	1639	0.9	2302	6.0
18 F	0348	0.8	0955	6.1	1611	0.5	2225	6.4
4 F	0458	0.9	1116	5.9	1715	0.8	2336	6.1
19 SA	0433	0.5	1043	6.4	1655	0.3	2310	6.7
5 SA	0532	0.8	1149	6.0	1749	0.7		
20 SU	0517	0.2	1128	6.6	1740	0.1	2354	6.8
6 SU	0007	6.1	0603	0.8	1217	6.0	1820	0.7
21 M	0602	0.1	1213	6.7	1824	0.1		
7 M	0032	6.1	0634	0.8	1240	6.0	1851	0.8
22 TU	0037	6.8	0645	0.2	1257	6.7	1908	0.2
8 TU	0052	6.0	0704	0.8	1303	5.9	1920	0.9
23 W	0119	6.7	0730	0.3	1340	6.5	1951	0.4
9 W	0114	6.0	0731	0.9	1329	5.8	1946	1.0
24 TH	0159	6.4	0814	0.6	1423	6.1	2036	0.8
10 TH	0140	5.9	0758	1.1	1358	5.7	2013	1.2
25 F	0242	6.0	0859	1.0	1510	5.7	2123	1.3
11 F	0212	5.7	0830	1.3	1433	5.5	2049	1.5
26 SA	0330	5.4	0951	1.4	1606	5.2	2222	1.7
12 SA	0251	5.4	0913	1.6	1517	5.1	2139	1.8
27 SU	0431	4.9	1101	1.8	1715	4.8	2350	2.1
13 SU	0341	5.0	1013	1.9	1621	4.7	2251	2.1
28 M	0549	4.6	1239	2.0	1852	4.7		
14 M	0458	4.6	1137	2.0	1819	4.6		
29 TU	0120	2.0	0734	4.6	1352	1.8	2018	4.9
15 TU	0031	2.1	0656	4.7	1318	1.8	1940	5.0
30 W	0224	1.8	0844	5.0	1448	1.5	2112	5.3
31 TH	0313	1.4	0932	5.3	1532	1.2	2155	5.7

APRIL

Day	Time	m	Time	m	Time	m	Time	m
1 F	0354	1.2	1012	5.6	1610	1.0	2232	5.9
16 SA	0321	0.8	0931	6.0	1544	0.6	2159	6.4
2 SA	0430	1.0	1048	5.8	1646	0.9	2305	6.0
17 SU	0408	0.4	1020	6.3	1630	0.3	2246	6.6
3 SU	0504	0.9	1119	5.9	1720	0.8	2334	6.0
18 M	0454	0.3	1108	6.5	1716	0.2	2331	6.7
4 M	0536	0.8	1146	5.9	1753	0.8	2358	6.0
19 TU	0540	0.2	1154	6.6	1802	0.3		
5 TU	0608	0.8	1211	5.9	1825	0.8		
20 W	0015	6.7	0625	0.2	1240	6.5	1847	0.4
6 W	0021	6.0	0638	0.8	1238	5.9	1853	0.9
21 TH	0059	6.5	0710	0.4	1324	6.4	1932	0.6
7 TH	0047	5.9	0705	0.9	1307	5.9	1920	1.0
22 F	0141	6.2	0754	0.6	1409	6.1	2016	0.9
8 F	0116	5.9	0734	1.0	1338	5.8	1951	1.2
23 SA	0224	5.9	0840	1.0	1455	5.7	2104	1.3
9 SA	0150	5.7	0809	1.2	1415	5.5	2030	1.4
24 SU	0312	5.4	0930	1.4	1548	5.3	2159	1.7
10 SU	0229	5.4	0854	1.4	1501	5.2	2122	1.7
25 M	0409	5.0	1030	1.7	1649	5.0	2312	2.0
11 M	0321	5.1	0953	1.7	1605	4.9	2232	1.9
26 TU	0515	4.7	1154	1.9	1801	4.8		
12 TU	0435	4.8	1110	1.8	1747	4.8	2350	2.1
27 W	0041	2.0	0638	4.6	1311	1.8	1927	4.9
13 W	0002	1.9	0624	4.8	1243	1.7	1910	5.1
28 TH	0146	1.8	0759	4.8	1408	1.7	2028	5.2
14 TH	0128	1.6	0739	5.2	1359	1.3	2015	5.6
29 F	0237	1.6	0853	5.1	1455	1.4	2115	5.4
15 F	0231	1.2	0839	5.6	1455	0.9	2110	6.0
30 SA	0320	1.5	0935	5.3	1536	1.2	2153	5.6

TIDES

Chart Datum: 3·27 metres below Ordnance Datum (Newlyn)
HAT is 6·9 metres above Chart Datum

SHOREHAM
LAT 50°50'N LONG 0°15'W
TIMES AND HEIGHTS OF HIGH AND LOW WATERS

TIME ZONE (UT)
For Summer Time add ONE hour in **non-shaded areas**

Dates in amber are **SPRINGS**
Dates in yellow are **NEAPS**

2011

MAY

#	Time m	#	Time m
1 SU	0358 1.1 / 1011 5.6 / 1614 1.1 / 2226 5.8	16 M	0345 0.6 / 0959 6.1 / 1608 0.6 / 2223 6.4
2 M	0433 1.0 / 1043 5.7 / 1650 1.0 / 2256 5.9	17 TU	0433 0.4 / 1049 6.3 / 1656 0.5 / O 2311 6.5
3 TU	0508 0.9 / 1114 5.8 / 1725 1.0 / ● 2325 5.9	18 W	0521 0.4 / 1138 6.4 / 1744 0.5 / 2357 6.4
4 W	0542 0.9 / 1145 5.9 / 1759 1.0 / 2355 5.9	19 TH	0608 0.4 / 1225 6.3 / 1830 0.6
5 TH	0615 0.9 / 1217 5.9 / 1832 1.0	20 F	0042 6.3 / 0653 0.5 / 1311 6.2 / 1915 0.8
6 F	0026 5.9 / 0646 0.9 / 1251 5.9 / 1903 1.0	21 SA	0126 6.1 / 0738 0.7 / 1355 6.1 / 1959 1.0
7 SA	0100 5.9 / 0719 1.0 / 1326 5.8 / 1939 1.1	22 SU	0209 5.8 / 0822 1.0 / 1440 5.8 / 2044 1.3
8 SU	0137 5.7 / 0758 1.1 / 1407 5.7 / 2021 1.3	23 M	0254 5.5 / 0907 1.2 / 1526 5.5 / 2132 1.5
9 M	0220 5.5 / 0844 1.2 / 1456 5.5 / 2114 1.5	24 TU	0343 5.1 / 0957 1.5 / 1617 5.2 / ◐ 2227 1.8
10 TU	0313 5.3 / 0941 1.4 / 1557 5.2 / ◑ 2218 1.6	25 W	0438 4.9 / 1053 1.7 / 1712 5.0 / 2333 1.9
11 W	0421 5.1 / 1050 1.5 / 1715 5.2 / 2336 1.6	26 TH	0538 4.7 / 1200 1.9 / 1812 5.0
12 TH	0547 5.0 / 1210 1.5 / 1834 5.3	27 F	0047 1.9 / 0641 4.7 / 1311 1.8 / 1914 5.0
13 F	0053 1.5 / 0704 5.2 / 1324 1.3 / 1942 5.6	28 SA	0149 1.8 / 0745 4.9 / 1408 1.7 / 2012 5.2
14 SA	0159 1.1 / 0809 5.6 / 1424 1.0 / 2040 5.9	29 SU	0239 1.6 / 0839 5.1 / 1457 1.5 / 2100 5.4
15 SU	0254 0.9 / 0906 5.9 / 1518 0.7 / 2133 6.2	30 M	0322 1.4 / 0924 5.3 / 1540 1.4 / 2141 5.6
		31 TU	0402 1.2 / 1005 5.5 / 1620 1.2 / 2219 5.7

JUNE

#	Time m	#	Time m
1 W	0441 1.1 / 1044 5.7 / 1659 1.1 / ● 2256 5.8	16 TH	0507 0.6 / 1127 6.1 / 1730 0.8 / 2344 6.2
2 TH	0518 1.0 / 1123 5.9 / 1737 1.1 / 2333 5.9	17 F	0554 0.6 / 1214 6.2 / 1816 0.8
3 F	0556 0.9 / 1200 5.9 / 1814 1.0	18 SA	0029 6.1 / 0638 0.7 / 1259 6.2 / 1859 0.9
4 SA	0010 6.0 / 0632 0.9 / 1239 6.0 / 1851 1.0	19 SU	0112 6.0 / 0721 0.8 / 1340 6.1 / 1941 1.0
5 SU	0049 5.9 / 0710 0.9 / 1319 6.0 / 1931 1.0	20 M	0152 5.8 / 0801 0.9 / 1420 5.9 / 2021 1.2
6 M	0130 5.9 / 0751 0.9 / 1401 5.9 / 2015 1.1	21 TU	0231 5.6 / 0840 1.1 / 1459 5.7 / 2101 1.3
7 TU	0215 5.8 / 0837 1.0 / 1449 5.8 / 2105 1.2	22 W	0311 5.4 / 0921 1.3 / 1539 5.5 / 2144 1.5
8 W	0305 5.6 / 0930 1.1 / 1543 5.6 / 2203 1.3	23 TH	0355 5.1 / 1005 1.5 / 1624 5.2 / ◐ 2232 1.7
9 TH	0404 5.4 / 1030 1.2 / 1645 5.5 / ◐ 2310 1.4	24 F	0446 4.9 / 1055 1.8 / 1715 5.0 / 2328 1.9
10 F	0512 5.3 / 1140 1.3 / 1755 5.5	25 SA	0544 4.7 / 1153 1.9 / 1814 4.9
11 SA	0021 1.4 / 0626 5.3 / 1252 1.3 / 1905 5.6	26 SU	0032 1.9 / 0645 4.7 / 1300 2.0 / 1914 5.0
12 SU	0129 1.2 / 0738 5.4 / 1358 1.2 / 2012 5.7	27 M	0143 1.8 / 0746 4.9 / 1409 1.8 / 2012 5.1
13 M	0231 1.0 / 0844 5.6 / 1457 1.0 / 2112 5.9	28 TU	0243 1.6 / 0843 5.1 / 1506 1.6 / 2104 5.4
14 TU	0326 0.9 / 0943 5.8 / 1551 0.9 / 2206 6.1	29 W	0332 1.4 / 0933 5.4 / 1554 1.4 / 2150 5.6
15 W	0418 0.7 / 1037 6.0 / 1642 0.8 / O 2257 6.2	30 TH	0416 1.2 / 1019 5.7 / 1636 1.2 / 2233 5.8

JULY

#	Time m	#	Time m
1 F	0457 1.0 / 1103 5.9 / 1717 1.1 / ● 2315 6.0	16 SA	0540 0.7 / 1202 6.2 / 1801 0.6
2 SA	0538 0.8 / 1145 6.1 / 1758 0.9 / 2356 6.1	17 SU	0016 6.1 / 0621 0.7 / 1243 6.2 / 1840 0.9
3 SU	0618 0.7 / 1226 6.2 / 1839 0.8	18 M	0055 6.0 / 0659 0.8 / 1320 6.1 / 1917 0.9
4 M	0038 6.1 / 0659 0.7 / 1309 6.2 / 1920 0.8	19 TU	0130 5.9 / 0734 0.9 / 1353 6.0 / 1952 1.0
5 TU	0121 6.1 / 0742 0.7 / 1351 6.2 / 2005 0.9	20 W	0202 5.7 / 0809 1.0 / 1424 5.9 / 2026 1.2
6 W	0205 6.1 / 0827 0.7 / 1436 6.1 / 2052 0.9	21 TH	0232 5.5 / 0844 1.2 / 1453 5.6 / 2103 1.4
7 TH	0251 5.9 / 0915 0.8 / 1524 6.0 / 2144 1.0	22 F	0303 5.3 / 0921 1.4 / 1524 5.4 / 2144 1.6
8 F	0343 5.7 / 1009 1.0 / 1618 5.8 / ◐ 2244 1.2	23 SA	0341 5.1 / 1004 1.7 / 1604 5.1 / ◐ 2233 1.8
9 SA	0443 5.4 / 1111 1.3 / 1720 5.5 / 2352 1.4	24 SU	0434 4.8 / 1056 1.9 / 1706 4.9 / 2333 2.0
10 SU	0554 5.2 / 1223 1.5 / 1833 5.4	25 M	0554 4.6 / 1203 2.1 / 1826 4.8
11 M	0105 1.5 / 0714 5.1 / 1338 1.5 / 1950 5.4	26 TU	0045 2.0 / 0706 4.7 / 1321 2.1 / 1934 4.9
12 TU	0214 1.3 / 0832 5.3 / 1444 1.4 / 2100 5.6	27 W	0204 1.9 / 0811 5.0 / 1435 1.8 / 2034 5.2
13 W	0315 1.1 / 0936 5.6 / 1541 1.2 / 2158 5.8	28 TH	0306 1.5 / 0908 5.3 / 1530 1.5 / 2126 5.6
14 TH	0408 0.9 / 1031 5.8 / 1632 1.0 / 2248 6.0	29 F	0354 1.2 / 0958 5.7 / 1615 1.2 / 2213 5.9
15 F	0456 0.8 / 1119 6.1 / 1718 0.9 / O 2334 6.1	30 SA	0436 1.0 / 1044 6.0 / 1657 0.9 / ● 2257 6.1
		31 SU	0518 0.7 / 1128 6.3 / 1739 0.7 / 2341 6.3

AUGUST

#	Time m	#	Time m
1 M	0600 0.5 / 1211 6.4 / 1821 0.6	16 TU	0032 6.1 / 0632 0.8 / 1253 6.2 / 1849 0.9
2 TU	0024 6.4 / 0642 0.4 / 1253 6.5 / 1904 0.5	17 W	0102 6.0 / 0704 0.8 / 1321 6.1 / 1921 1.0
3 W	0107 6.4 / 0725 0.4 / 1335 6.5 / 1948 0.6	18 TH	0127 5.9 / 0736 0.9 / 1343 5.9 / 1952 1.1
4 TH	0149 6.3 / 0809 0.5 / 1418 6.4 / 2034 0.7	19 F	0151 5.7 / 0807 1.1 / 1405 5.8 / 2024 1.2
5 F	0234 6.1 / 0855 0.7 / 1503 6.2 / 2122 0.9	20 SA	0218 5.5 / 0838 1.3 / 1434 5.6 / 2058 1.5
6 SA	0322 5.8 / 0945 1.0 / 1553 5.8 / ◐ 2218 1.2	21 SU	0251 5.3 / 0913 1.6 / 1511 5.3 / ◐ 2139 1.8
7 SU	0419 5.4 / 1045 1.4 / 1653 5.4 / 2326 1.6	22 M	0334 5.0 / 1000 1.9 / 1601 4.9 / 2237 2.0
8 M	0530 5.1 / 1201 1.7 / 1809 5.1	23 TU	0442 4.6 / 1101 2.2 / 1729 4.7 / 2358 2.2
9 TU	0048 1.7 / 0700 4.9 / 1325 1.8 / 1939 5.1	24 W	0632 4.6 / 1241 2.2 / 1904 4.8
10 W	0204 1.6 / 0828 5.1 / 1435 1.6 / 2055 5.3	25 TH	0127 2.0 / 0744 4.9 / 1407 2.0 / 2009 5.1
11 TH	0306 1.3 / 0932 5.5 / 1532 1.3 / 2152 5.7	26 F	0240 1.6 / 0845 5.4 / 1506 1.5 / 2105 5.6
12 F	0357 1.1 / 1022 5.8 / 1620 1.1 / 2239 5.9	27 SA	0330 1.2 / 0936 5.8 / 1552 1.1 / 2153 6.0
13 SA	0441 0.9 / 1105 6.1 / 1702 0.9 / O 2320 6.1	28 SU	0413 0.8 / 1023 6.2 / 1635 0.8 / 2238 6.3
14 SU	0521 0.7 / 1144 6.2 / 1740 0.8 / 2358 6.1	29 M	0455 0.6 / 1107 6.5 / 1717 0.6 / ● 2322 6.5
15 M	0558 0.7 / 1220 6.2 / 1816 0.8	30 TU	0537 0.4 / 1150 6.7 / 1759 0.4
		31 W	0005 6.6 / 0620 0.4 / 1233 6.7 / 1842 0.4

Chart Datum: 3·27 metres below Ordnance Datum (Newlyn)
HAT is 6·9 metres above Chart Datum

SHOREHAM

LAT 50°50'N   LONG 0°15'W

Dates in amber are **SPRINGS**
Dates in yellow are **NEAPS**

2011

TIMES AND HEIGHTS OF HIGH AND LOW WATERS

SEPTEMBER

Day	Time	m	Time	m	Time	m	Time	m
1 TH	0049	6.6	0703	0.3	1315	6.7	1927	0.4
2 F	0131	6.5	0748	0.5	1357	6.5	2012	0.6
3 SA	0215	6.2	0833	0.7	1441	6.2	2100	0.9
4 SU	0303	5.9	0923	1.1	1530	5.7	2154	1.3
5 M	0400	5.4	1022	1.6	1631	5.3	2303	1.7
6 TU	0514	5.0	1144	2.0	1751	4.9		
7 W	0033	1.9	0650	4.8	1314	2.0	1930	4.9
8 TH	0152	1.8	0819	5.1	1424	1.8	2045	5.2
9 F	0252	1.5	0918	5.5	1518	1.4	2137	5.6
10 SA	0340	1.2	1003	5.9	1601	1.1	2220	5.9
11 SU	0420	0.9	1043	6.1	1639	0.9	2259	6.1
12 M	0457	0.8	1119	6.2	1715	0.9	2334	6.1
13 TU	0531	0.8	1152	6.2	1748	0.8		
14 W	0005	6.1	0603	0.8	1221	6.2	1820	0.9
15 TH	0031	6.0	0634	0.9	1244	6.1	1850	0.9
16 F	0053	6.0	0705	1.0	1305	6.0	1920	1.0
17 SA	0117	5.9	0733	1.1	1329	5.9	1949	1.2
18 SU	0145	5.7	0802	1.3	1359	5.7	2019	1.4
19 M	0217	5.5	0836	1.6	1435	5.4	2059	1.7
20 TU	0258	5.1	0923	1.9	1522	5.0	2155	2.0
21 W	0358	4.8	1032	2.2	1635	4.7	2315	2.2
22 TH	0557	4.6	1205	2.3	1833	4.7		
23 F	0051	2.1	0716	4.9	1335	2.0	1943	5.1
24 SA	0209	1.6	0819	5.4	1438	1.5	2040	5.6
25 SU	0302	1.2	0911	5.9	1526	1.0	2130	6.1
26 M	0347	0.8	0958	6.4	1609	0.7	2216	6.4
27 TU	0429	0.5	1042	6.6	1652	0.4	2300	6.6
28 W	0512	0.3	1126	6.8	1735	0.3	2345	6.7
29 TH	0556	0.3	1209	6.8	1820	0.3		
30 F	0029	6.7	0640	0.4	1252	6.7	1905	0.4

OCTOBER

Day	Time	m	Time	m	Time	m	Time	m
1 SA	0113	6.6	0726	0.6	1335	6.5	1951	0.7
2 SU	0158	6.3	0812	0.8	1420	6.1	2039	1.0
3 M	0247	5.9	0903	1.3	1511	5.7	2132	1.4
4 TU	0345	5.4	1002	1.7	1612	5.2	2240	1.8
5 W	0456	5.0	1125	2.1	1730	4.8		
6 TH	0011	2.0	0627	4.9	1254	2.1	1907	4.8
7 F	0128	1.9	0752	5.1	1401	1.8	2020	5.1
8 SA	0227	1.6	0849	5.5	1453	1.5	2111	5.5
9 SU	0313	1.3	0934	5.8	1535	1.2	2153	5.8
10 M	0353	1.1	1013	6.0	1612	1.0	2231	6.0
11 TU	0429	1.0	1048	6.1	1647	0.9	2305	6.1
12 W	0503	0.9	1119	6.2	1721	0.9	2334	6.1
13 TH	0536	0.9	1145	6.1	1753	0.9	2359	6.1
14 F	0608	1.0	1209	6.1	1824	1.0		
15 SA	0025	6.0	0638	1.1	1234	6.0	1853	1.1
16 SU	0052	5.9	0706	1.2	1302	5.9	1922	1.2
17 M	0121	5.8	0736	1.4	1333	5.7	1954	1.4
18 TU	0155	5.6	0813	1.6	1410	5.5	2035	1.6
19 W	0237	5.3	0901	1.8	1458	5.1	2129	1.9
20 TH	0335	5.0	1006	2.1	1605	4.8	2241	2.0
21 F	0513	4.9	1131	2.1	1755	4.8		
22 SA	0010	2.0	0642	5.1	1257	1.9	1911	5.1
23 SU	0129	1.7	0747	5.5	1403	1.5	2011	5.6
24 M	0228	1.2	0841	6.0	1455	1.0	2103	6.0
25 TU	0317	0.9	0930	6.4	1542	0.7	2151	6.4
26 W	0403	0.6	1016	6.6	1627	0.5	2238	6.6
27 TH	0449	0.5	1102	6.8	1713	0.4	2325	6.7
28 F	0535	0.4	1147	6.8	1759	0.4		
29 SA	0012	6.7	0620	0.5	1232	6.7	1846	0.5
30 SU	0058	6.5	0707	0.8	1317	6.4	1933	0.7
31 M	0145	6.3	0755	1.0	1403	6.1	2021	1.0

NOVEMBER

Day	Time	m	Time	m	Time	m	Time	m
1 TU	0235	5.9	0845	1.3	1454	5.7	2113	1.4
2 W	0329	5.6	0941	1.7	1552	5.2	2213	1.7
3 TH	0431	5.2	1053	2.0	1658	4.9	2331	2.0
4 F	0543	5.0	1217	2.1	1819	4.8		
5 SA	0047	2.0	0704	5.1	1324	1.9	1937	5.0
6 SU	0148	1.8	0807	5.3	1418	1.7	2034	5.3
7 M	0238	1.6	0856	5.6	1503	1.4	2119	5.5
8 TU	0321	1.4	0937	5.8	1543	1.2	2158	5.7
9 W	0359	1.2	1012	5.9	1619	1.1	2231	5.9
10 TH	0435	1.1	1043	6.0	1654	1.0	2302	6.0
11 F	0510	1.1	1112	6.1	1729	1.0	2332	6.0
12 SA	0544	1.1	1141	6.1	1802	1.0		
13 SU	0003	6.0	0616	1.1	1212	6.0	1834	1.1
14 M	0034	6.0	0648	1.2	1243	5.9	1905	1.2
15 TU	0107	5.9	0720	1.3	1318	5.8	1939	1.3
16 W	0143	5.8	0759	1.5	1357	5.6	2021	1.4
17 TH	0226	5.6	0846	1.6	1444	5.4	2111	1.6
18 F	0320	5.3	0945	1.8	1544	5.1	2214	1.8
19 SA	0431	5.2	1057	1.9	1704	5.1	2330	1.8
20 SU	0557	5.3	1216	1.8	1829	5.2		
21 M	0047	1.6	0709	5.5	1326	1.5	1937	5.5
22 TU	0153	1.3	0809	5.9	1425	1.1	2035	5.8
23 W	0250	1.0	0903	6.2	1518	0.8	2129	6.2
24 TH	0341	0.8	0953	6.5	1607	0.6	2220	6.4
25 F	0430	0.7	1042	6.6	1656	0.5	2310	6.5
26 SA	0518	0.6	1130	6.6	1744	0.5	2359	6.5
27 SU	0606	0.7	1217	6.5	1831	0.6		
28 M	0047	6.5	0652	0.8	1303	6.3	1918	0.7
29 TU	0134	6.3	0739	1.0	1349	6.1	2004	0.9
30 W	0220	6.1	0826	1.2	1436	5.8	2051	1.2

DECEMBER

Day	Time	m	Time	m	Time	m	Time	m
1 TH	0307	5.8	0915	1.5	1525	5.4	2140	1.5
2 F	0358	5.5	1009	1.8	1619	5.1	2235	1.8
3 SA	0453	5.2	1113	2.0	1718	4.9	2340	1.9
4 SU	0553	5.1	1227	2.0	1823	4.8		
5 M	0051	2.0	0657	5.1	1332	1.9	1931	4.9
6 TU	0153	1.9	0759	5.2	1425	1.7	2030	5.1
7 W	0245	1.7	0850	5.4	1511	1.5	2117	5.4
8 TH	0329	1.5	0931	5.6	1553	1.3	2156	5.6
9 F	0410	1.4	1009	5.8	1631	1.2	2233	5.8
10 SA	0448	1.3	1044	5.9	1708	1.1	2309	5.9
11 SU	0524	1.2	1119	6.0	1744	1.0	2345	6.0
12 M	0559	1.1	1154	6.0	1820	1.0		
13 TU	0020	6.1	0633	1.1	1230	6.0	1854	1.0
14 W	0056	6.0	0709	1.2	1307	6.0	1929	1.0
15 TH	0134	6.0	0747	1.2	1347	5.9	2009	1.1
16 F	0216	5.9	0832	1.3	1432	5.7	2055	1.2
17 SA	0304	5.7	0923	1.4	1524	5.5	2149	1.4
18 SU	0401	5.6	1025	1.6	1626	5.3	2253	1.5
19 M	0508	5.5	1137	1.6	1740	5.3		
20 TU	0008	1.6	0624	5.5	1251	1.5	1859	5.3
21 W	0122	1.5	0737	5.6	1359	1.3	2010	5.5
22 TH	0227	1.3	0841	5.8	1459	1.1	2113	5.8
23 F	0325	1.1	0938	6.1	1554	0.8	2210	6.1
24 SA	0418	0.9	1030	6.3	1644	0.7	2302	6.3
25 SU	0507	0.8	1120	6.4	1733	0.6	2351	6.4
26 M	0554	0.7	1206	6.4	1819	0.6		
27 TU	0037	6.4	0638	0.8	1251	6.3	1903	0.7
28 W	0120	6.3	0722	0.9	1333	6.1	1945	0.8
29 TH	0201	6.2	0803	1.1	1414	5.9	2025	1.0
30 F	0240	6.0	0843	1.3	1454	5.6	2104	1.2
31 SA	0320	5.7	0924	1.5	1536	5.3	2145	1.5

Chart Datum: 3·27 metres below Ordnance Datum (Newlyn)
HAT is 6·9 metres above Chart Datum

TIDES

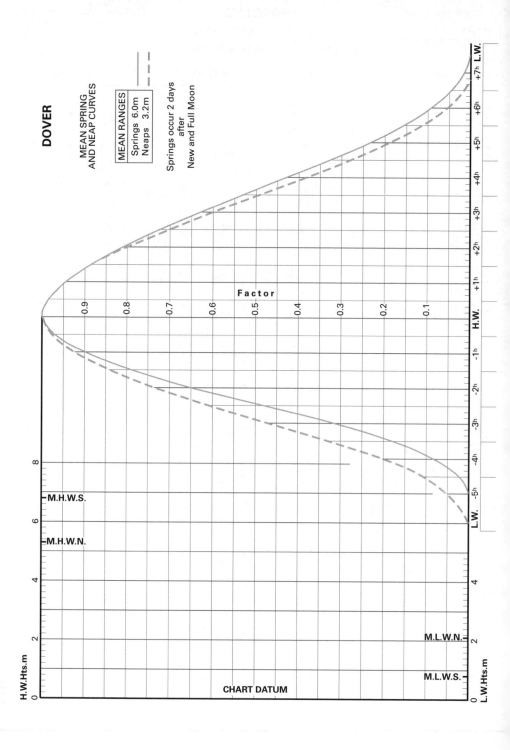

DOVER

MEAN SPRING
AND NEAP CURVES

MEAN RANGES
Springs 6.0m
Neaps 3.2m

Springs occur 2 days
after
New and Full Moon

Factor

0.9 0.8 0.7 0.6 0.5 0.4 0.3 0.2 0.1

+7ʰ L.W. +6ʰ +5ʰ +4ʰ +3ʰ +2ʰ +1ʰ H.W. -1ʰ -2ʰ -3ʰ -4ʰ -5ʰ L.W.

H.W.Hts.m

M.H.W.S.

M.H.W.N.

CHART DATUM

M.L.W.N.

M.L.W.S.

L.W.Hts.m

TIME ZONE (UT)	**DOVER**	Dates in amber are **SPRINGS**
For Summer Time add ONE hour in **non-shaded areas**	**LAT 51°07'N LONG 1°19'E**	Dates in yellow are **NEAPS**
	TIMES AND HEIGHTS OF HIGH AND LOW WATERS	**2011**

JANUARY

Day	Time m	Time m	Time m	Time m
1 SA	0249 1.9	0823 5.9	1528 1.7	2059 5.9
2 SU	0403 1.7	0925 6.1	1641 1.5	2152 6.1
3 M	0509 1.4	1018 6.2	1739 1.3	2238 6.3
4 TU	0602 1.2	1103 6.4	1826 1.2	●2319 6.5
5 W	0647 1.1	1142 6.4	1906 1.2	2357 6.6
6 TH	0727 1.1	1218 6.4	1941 1.3	
7 F	0034 6.6	0802 1.1	1254 6.3	2011 1.3
8 SA	0111 6.6	0832 1.2	1329 6.2	2036 1.4
9 SU	0144 6.4	0859 1.3	1402 6.0	2102 1.5
10 M	0214 6.3	0926 1.5	1433 5.9	2133 1.6
11 TU	0244 6.1	0959 1.6	1505 5.6	2209 1.8
12 W	0319 5.8	1038 1.8	1547 5.4	◑2252 2.1
13 TH	0408 5.6	1128 2.1	1655 5.2	2349 2.3
14 F	0522 5.3	1238 2.2	1825 5.1	
15 SA	0113 2.4	0644 5.3	1400 2.2	1932 5.3
16 SU	0233 2.2	0751 5.5	1508 1.9	2029 5.6
17 M	0338 1.9	0846 5.8	1607 1.6	2118 5.8
18 TU	0434 1.5	0936 6.1	1701 1.3	2204 6.3
19 W	0525 1.2	1022 6.4	1752 1.1	○2247 6.6
20 TH	0616 1.0	1106 6.6	1842 1.0	2330 6.8
21 F	0705 0.8	1149 6.8	1929 0.8	
22 SA	0012 7.0	0752 0.6	1232 6.8	2011 0.8
23 SU	0055 7.1	0836 0.6	1315 6.8	2051 0.8
24 M	0140 7.0	0917 0.6	1400 6.7	2129 0.9
25 TU	0226 6.9	0958 0.8	1448 6.4	2210 1.1
26 W	0316 6.6	1041 1.1	1542 6.1	◑2256 1.5
27 TH	0412 6.2	1132 1.5	1647 5.7	2353 1.8
28 F	0519 5.7	1234 1.9	1806 5.4	
29 SA	0105 2.1	0643 5.5	1347 2.1	1933 5.3
30 SU	0224 2.1	0814 5.5	1507 2.0	2049 5.5
31 M	0351 1.9	0927 5.8	1635 1.7	2146 5.9

FEBRUARY

Day	Time m	Time m	Time m	Time m
1 TU	0504 1.5	1019 6.0	1734 1.5	2230 6.2
2 W	0556 1.2	1058 6.2	1818 1.3	2307 6.4
3 TH	0639 1.1	1132 6.3	1855 1.2	●2342 6.6
4 F	0714 1.0	1203 6.4	1925 1.1	
5 SA	0016 6.6	0743 1.0	1234 6.4	1949 1.2
6 SU	0048 6.6	0807 1.1	1303 6.3	2010 1.2
7 M	0115 6.5	0830 1.1	1327 6.2	2035 1.2
8 TU	0136 6.4	0855 1.2	1348 6.1	2103 1.3
9 W	0159 6.3	0925 1.4	1413 6.0	2136 1.5
10 TH	0230 6.1	0958 1.6	1448 5.8	2212 1.8
11 F	0311 5.8	1038 1.9	1534 5.5	◑2258 2.1
12 SA	0405 5.4	1133 2.2	1646 5.1	
13 SU	0007 2.4	0553 5.2	1308 2.3	1857 5.1
14 M	0152 2.3	0726 5.3	1437 2.1	2004 5.4
15 TU	0308 2.0	0829 5.7	1543 1.7	2059 5.9
16 W	0410 1.5	0922 6.1	1642 1.4	2147 6.3
17 TH	0507 1.1	1009 6.5	1737 1.0	2231 6.7
18 F	0602 0.8	1053 6.7	1829 0.8	○2314 7.0
19 SA	0653 0.5	1134 6.9	1916 0.6	2356 7.2
20 SU	0740 0.3	1215 7.0	1957 0.5	
21 M	0037 7.2	0821 0.3	1257 7.0	2034 0.5
22 TU	0120 7.2	0859 0.4	1339 6.8	2110 0.6
23 W	0204 7.0	0937 0.7	1425 6.5	2149 0.9
24 TH	0251 6.6	1016 1.1	1516 6.1	○2232 1.4
25 F	0345 6.1	1104 1.6	1617 5.7	2326 1.9
26 SA	0450 5.6	1206 2.1	1733 5.3	◑2258 2.1
27 SU	0040 2.2	0616 5.2	1325 2.3	1906 5.2
28 M	0206 2.2	0811 5.3	1452 2.2	2035 5.4

MARCH

Day	Time m	Time m	Time m	Time m
1 TU	0344 1.9	0921 5.6	1622 1.8	2131 5.8
2 W	0453 1.5	1007 5.9	1717 1.5	2213 6.1
3 TH	0541 1.2	1042 6.2	1758 1.2	2248 6.4
4 F	0620 1.0	1112 6.3	1832 1.1	●2322 6.5
5 SA	0651 1.0	1140 6.4	1859 1.1	2353 6.6
6 SU	0716 1.0	1208 6.4	1920 1.1	
7 M	0021 6.5	0737 1.0	1234 6.4	1942 1.1
8 TU	0044 6.5	0800 1.0	1254 6.3	2008 1.1
9 W	0101 6.4	0826 1.1	1313 6.3	2037 1.2
10 TH	0124 6.4	0855 1.3	1339 6.2	2108 1.4
11 F	0156 6.3	0926 1.5	1415 6.1	2143 1.6
12 SA	0236 6.0	1004 1.8	1500 5.7	◑2226 2.0
13 SU	0327 5.6	1054 2.1	1603 5.3	2328 2.3
14 M	0457 5.2	1213 2.4	1824 5.1	
15 TU	0113 2.3	0703 5.3	1406 2.2	1938 5.4
16 W	0238 1.9	0809 5.7	1516 1.8	2036 5.9
17 TH	0343 1.4	0903 6.1	1617 1.3	2126 6.4
18 F	0444 1.0	0951 6.5	1714 1.0	2211 6.8
19 SA	0541 0.7	1034 6.8	1807 0.7	○2254 7.1
20 SU	0634 0.4	1115 7.0	1854 0.5	2336 7.2
21 M	0721 0.2	1156 7.0	1936 0.4	
22 TU	0017 7.3	0801 0.2	1237 7.0	2014 0.4
23 W	0100 7.1	0839 0.4	1320 6.8	2051 0.6
24 TH	0143 6.9	0916 0.7	1405 6.6	2130 1.0
25 F	0230 6.5	0955 1.2	1456 6.2	2213 1.4
26 SA	0324 6.0	1041 1.7	1555 5.7	○2306 2.0
27 SU	0428 5.5	1143 2.2	1703 5.3	◑2226 2.0
28 M	0021 2.2	0547 5.1	1303 2.4	1827 5.2
29 TU	0146 2.2	0744 5.2	1426 2.2	2002 5.4
30 W	0313 1.9	0856 5.5	1546 1.8	2101 5.7
31 TH	0420 1.6	0939 5.8	1639 1.6	2144 6.1

APRIL

Day	Time m	Time m	Time m	Time m
1 F	0508 1.3	1014 6.1	1722 1.3	2221 6.3
2 SA	0546 1.1	1043 6.2	1757 1.2	2254 6.4
3 SU	0616 1.1	1111 6.3	1824 1.1	●2324 6.5
4 M	0641 1.1	1139 6.4	1848 1.1	2351 6.4
5 TU	0705 1.0	1204 6.4	1915 1.1	
6 W	0012 6.4	0732 1.1	1225 6.3	1944 1.1
7 TH	0033 6.4	0801 1.1	1247 6.4	2015 1.2
8 F	0059 6.4	0831 1.2	1317 6.3	2047 1.3
9 SA	0132 6.3	0904 1.5	1355 6.2	2123 1.5
10 SU	0214 6.0	0943 1.7	1443 5.8	2208 1.8
11 M	0308 5.7	1033 2.0	1551 5.4	◑2309 2.1
12 TU	0440 5.3	1145 2.2	1747 5.3	
13 W	0042 2.1	0636 5.4	1332 2.1	1906 5.6
14 TH	0207 1.8	0744 5.7	1444 1.7	2007 6.0
15 F	0313 1.4	0839 6.1	1546 1.3	2100 6.4
16 SA	0415 1.0	0928 6.5	1645 1.0	2147 6.8
17 SU	0515 0.7	1012 6.7	1740 0.8	2232 7.0
18 M	0610 0.5	1055 6.9	1829 0.6	○2315 7.1
19 TU	0658 0.4	1137 6.9	1914 0.5	2358 7.1
20 W	0741 0.4	1219 6.9	1956 0.6	
21 TH	0041 7.0	0821 0.6	1303 6.8	2035 0.7
22 F	0127 6.7	0859 0.9	1349 6.6	2116 1.0
23 SA	0214 6.4	0939 1.3	1439 6.2	2200 1.4
24 SU	0307 6.0	1024 1.7	1534 5.9	2252 1.8
25 M	0406 5.5	1121 2.1	1634 5.6	○2359 2.1
26 TU	0514 5.2	1223 2.3	1744 5.4	
27 W	0112 2.1	0646 5.2	1345 2.2	1906 5.4
28 TH	0223 2.0	0807 5.6	1450 2.0	2015 5.6
29 F	0324 1.7	0856 5.6	1546 1.7	2104 5.9
30 SA	0415 1.5	0934 5.9	1633 1.5	2144 6.1

Chart Datum: 3·67 metres below Ordnance Datum (Newlyn)
HAT is 7·4 metres above Chart Datum

TIDES

TIME ZONE (UT)
For Summer Time add ONE hour in **non-shaded areas**

DOVER
LAT 51°07'N LONG 1°19'E
TIMES AND HEIGHTS OF HIGH AND LOW WATERS

Dates in amber are **SPRINGS**
Dates in yellow are **NEAPS**

2011

MAY

Time	m		Time	m
1 SU 0456 1007 1712 2219	1.3 6.1 1.4 6.2	**16** M 0446 0951 1712 2212	0.9 6.5 0.9 6.7
2 M 0531 1037 1745 2250	1.2 6.2 1.2 6.3	**17** TU 0546 1037 1807 ○2259	0.7 6.7 0.8 6.8
3 TU 0604 1107 1817 ●2318	1.2 6.3 1.2 6.3	**18** W 0638 1122 1856 2345	0.7 6.7 0.7 6.8
4 W 0636 1135 1851 2344	1.1 6.3 1.1 6.3	**19** TH 0724 1206 1941	0.7 6.7 0.7
5 TH 0710 1202 1925	1.1 6.4 1.1	**20** F 0029 0806 1250 2024	6.7 0.8 6.7 0.9
6 F 0012 0742 1231 1959	6.3 1.2 6.4 1.2	**21** SA 0114 0846 1335 2106	6.5 1.0 6.6 1.1
7 SA 0044 0816 1306 2035	6.3 1.3 6.3 1.3	**22** SU 0200 0926 1422 2148	6.3 1.3 6.4 1.3
8 SU 0121 0851 1348 2114	6.2 1.4 6.2 1.4	**23** M 0249 1006 1510 2233	6.0 1.6 6.1 1.6
9 M 0207 0932 1440 2201	6.0 1.6 1.6 1.6	**24** TU 0341 1051 1602 ◑2325	5.7 1.9 5.8 1.9
10 TU 0305 1022 1547 ◑2300	5.8 1.8 1.8 1.8	**25** W 0438 1147 1700	5.4 2.1 5.6
11 W 0425 1129 1709	5.6 1.9 5.7	**26** TH 0024 0543 1250 1805	2.0 5.3 2.2 5.5
12 TH 0018 0600 1256 1827	1.8 5.6 1.9 5.8	**27** F 0125 0655 1352 1913	2.0 5.3 2.1 5.5
13 F 0135 0711 1408 1934	1.6 5.8 1.7 6.0	**28** SA 0222 0757 1449 2011	1.9 5.4 2.0 5.7
14 SA 0240 0811 1511 2031	1.3 6.0 1.4 6.3	**29** SU 0315 0845 1541 2058	1.7 5.7 1.8 5.8
15 SU 0342 0903 1612 2123	1.1 6.3 1.2 6.6	**30** M 0404 0925 1628 2137	1.6 5.9 1.5 6.0
			31 TU 0449 1002 1710 2213	1.4 6.0 1.4 6.1

JUNE

Time	m		Time	m
1 W 0531 1036 1750 2248	1.3 6.2 1.2 6.2	**16** TH 0623 1112 1843 2338	1.0 6.5 0.9 6.5
2 TH 0612 1111 1830 2323	1.2 6.3 1.1 6.3	**17** F 0712 1156 1931	1.0 6.6 0.9
3 F 0651 1145 1910 2359	1.2 6.4 1.1 6.3	**18** SA 0021 0754 1238 2014	6.5 1.0 6.6 0.9
4 SA 0730 1222 1950	1.2 6.4 1.1	**19** SU 0103 0834 1320 2054	6.4 1.1 6.5 1.0
5 SU 0036 0808 1302 2030	6.3 1.2 6.5 1.1	**20** M 0144 0909 1401 2130	6.3 1.3 6.5 1.2
6 M 0118 0847 1346 2112	6.3 1.3 6.4 1.4	**21** TU 0226 0941 1443 2205	6.1 1.5 6.3 1.4
7 TU 0205 0929 1436 2159	6.2 1.4 6.3 1.4	**22** W 0310 1011 1527 2240	5.8 1.7 6.0 1.6
8 W 0259 1016 1532 2252	6.1 1.5 6.2 1.4	**23** TH 0358 1046 1613 ◑2322	5.6 1.9 5.8 1.8
9 TH 0402 1113 1636 ◑2354	5.9 1.6 6.0 1.5	**24** F 0452 1134 1707	5.4 2.1 5.6
10 F 0516 1221 1746	5.8 1.7 6.0	**25** SA 0017 0553 1240 1809	2.0 5.3 2.2 5.4
11 SA 0101 0633 1331 1858	1.5 5.8 1.7 6.0	**26** SU 0121 0656 1350 1912	2.1 5.3 2.2 5.4
12 SU 0207 0741 1437 2004	1.4 5.9 1.6 6.1	**27** M 0224 0755 1454 2009	2.0 5.4 2.0 5.6
13 M 0312 0841 1544 2105	1.3 6.0 1.4 6.3	**28** TU 0322 0845 1550 2059	1.8 5.6 1.8 5.8
14 TU 0420 0936 1650 2201	1.2 6.2 1.2 6.4	**29** W 0415 0930 1640 2143	1.6 5.9 1.5 6.0
15 W 0527 1026 1750 ○2252	1.1 6.4 1.0 6.5	**30** TH 0504 1011 1727 2226	1.4 6.1 1.3 6.2

JULY

Time	m		Time	m
1 F 0551 1050 1812 ●2306	1.2 6.3 1.1 6.3	**16** SA 0701 1144 1921	1.1 6.6 0.9
2 SA 0636 1130 1857 2347	1.2 6.5 1.0 6.4	**17** SU 0010 0741 1223 2000	6.4 1.1 6.7 0.9
3 SU 0720 1210 1942	1.1 6.6 0.9	**18** M 0047 0815 1301 2034	6.4 1.1 6.7 1.0
4 M 0027 0802 1251 2025	6.5 1.0 6.7 0.9	**19** TU 0122 0843 1337 2102	6.3 1.2 6.6 1.1
5 TU 0109 0843 1335 2108	6.5 1.0 6.7 0.9	**20** W 0158 0912 1412 2127	6.2 1.4 6.4 1.3
6 W 0154 0923 1421 2150	6.4 1.1 6.7 0.9	**21** TH 0232 0929 1444 2153	6.0 1.5 6.2 1.5
7 TH 0242 1005 1511 2236	6.3 1.2 6.5 1.1	**22** F 0307 0959 1518 2226	5.8 1.7 5.9 1.7
8 F 0337 1052 1607 ◑2328	6.1 1.4 6.3 1.3	**23** SA 0347 1038 1601 ◑2309	5.6 1.9 5.7 2.0
9 SA 0440 1149 1711	5.9 1.6 6.0	**24** SU 0448 1128 1706	5.3 2.2 5.4
10 SU 0029 0556 1258 1826	1.6 5.7 1.8 5.8	**25** M 0012 0604 1246 1823	2.2 5.2 2.4 5.3
11 M 0138 0716 1410 1946	1.7 5.6 1.8 5.8	**26** TU 0137 0714 1411 1932	2.2 5.2 2.3 5.4
12 TU 0248 0827 1523 2058	1.7 5.8 1.7 6.0	**27** W 0248 0813 1518 2031	2.0 5.5 2.0 5.7
13 W 0405 0928 1639 2200	1.5 6.0 1.4 6.1	**28** TH 0348 0904 1614 2121	1.7 5.8 1.6 6.0
14 TH 0518 1020 1743 2251	1.3 6.2 1.2 6.3	**29** F 0441 0949 1705 2207	1.5 6.2 1.3 6.3
15 F 0614 1104 1835 ○2333	1.2 6.5 1.0 6.4	**30** SA 0532 1031 1755 ●2249	1.2 6.5 1.0 6.5
			31 SU 0620 1112 1843 2330	1.1 6.7 0.9 6.7

AUGUST

Time	m		Time	m
1 M 0707 1152 1930	0.9 6.9 0.7	**16** TU 0024 0747 1237 2004	6.5 1.1 6.7 1.0
2 TU 0011 0750 1234 2014	6.7 0.8 7.0 0.6	**17** W 0055 0808 1309 2026	6.4 1.2 6.6 1.1
3 W 0052 0829 1316 2054	6.8 0.8 7.0 0.6	**18** TH 0124 0828 1335 2047	6.3 1.3 6.5 1.2
4 TH 0135 0907 1401 2133	6.7 0.8 6.9 0.7	**19** F 0148 0852 1356 2112	6.1 1.4 6.3 1.4
5 F 0221 0946 1448 2214	6.5 1.0 6.7 1.0	**20** SA 0209 0922 1422 2143	6.0 1.5 6.1 1.6
6 SA 0312 1029 1542 ◑2301	6.3 1.3 6.4 1.4	**21** SU 0238 0958 1458 ◑2221	5.8 1.8 5.8 1.9
7 SU 0413 1122 1645	5.9 1.7 5.9	**22** M 0320 1041 1550 2311	5.5 2.1 5.4 2.2
8 M 0001 0528 1231 1803	1.8 5.5 2.0 5.6	**23** TU 0445 1142 1743	5.1 2.4 5.2
9 TU 0115 0657 1350 1938	2.0 5.4 2.1 5.6	**24** W 0039 0639 1329 1905	2.4 5.1 2.4 5.3
10 W 0235 0818 1516 2101	2.0 5.6 1.9 5.8	**25** TH 0217 0745 1448 2008	2.3 5.4 2.1 5.6
11 TH 0406 0923 1639 2200	1.8 5.9 1.5 6.0	**26** F 0323 0839 1548 2100	1.9 5.8 1.7 6.0
12 F 0514 1011 1738 2244	1.5 6.2 1.2 6.3	**27** SA 0419 0926 1642 2147	1.5 6.3 1.3 6.4
13 SA 0604 1051 1825 ○2320	1.2 6.5 1.0 6.4	**28** SU 0511 1009 1734 2229	1.2 6.6 1.0 6.7
14 SU 0645 1127 1905 2352	1.0 6.7 0.9 6.5	**29** M 0600 1050 1825 ●2310	1.0 6.9 0.7 6.9
15 M 0720 1203 1938	1.1 6.7 0.9	**30** TU 0647 1131 1912 2350	0.8 7.1 0.5 7.0
			31 W 0730 1212 1955	0.7 7.2 0.5

Chart Datum: 3·67 metres below Ordnance Datum (Newlyn)
HAT is 7·4 metres above Chart Datum

DOVER
LAT 51°07'N   LONG 1°19'E
TIMES AND HEIGHTS OF HIGH AND LOW WATERS

Dates in amber are **SPRINGS**
Dates in yellow are **NEAPS**

2011

SEPTEMBER

Day	Time	m	Day	Time	m
1 TH	0030 / 0808 / 1254 / 2033	7.0 / 0.7 / 7.2 / 0.5	**16** F	0049 / 0754 / 1257 / 2011	6.4 / 1.2 / 6.5 / 1.2
2 F	0113 / 0846 / 1338 / 2111	6.9 / 0.8 / 7.1 / 0.7	**17** SA	0107 / 0821 / 1315 / 2039	6.3 / 1.3 / 6.4 / 1.4
3 SA	0158 / 0924 / 1426 / 2151	6.7 / 1.0 / 6.8 / 1.1	**18** SU	0127 / 0852 / 1341 / 2110	6.2 / 1.5 / 6.2 / 1.6
4 SU	0250 / 1007 / 1520 / 2237 ◑	6.3 / 1.3 / 6.3 / 1.5	**19**	0158 / 0927 / 1418 / 2146	6.0 / 1.8 / 6.0 / 1.9
5 M	0351 / 1059 / 1625 / 2337	5.9 / 1.8 / 5.8 / 2.0	**20** TU	0240 / 1008 / 1506 / 2232 ◐	5.7 / 2.1 / 5.6 / 2.3
6 TU	0505 / 1211 / 1746	5.5 / 2.2 / 5.4	**21** W	0340 / 1103 / 1648 / 2339	5.3 / 2.4 / 5.2 / 2.5
7 W	0057 / 0635 / 1339 / 1935	2.3 / 5.3 / 2.3 / 5.4	**22** TH	0604 / 1242 / 1840	5.2 / 2.5 / 5.3
8 TH	0229 / 0806 / 1517 / 2056	2.2 / 5.5 / 2.0 / 5.7	**23** F	0141 / 0714 / 1416 / 1944	2.4 / 5.5 / 2.1 / 5.7
9 F	0359 / 0908 / 1630 / 2147	1.9 / 5.9 / 1.5 / 6.0	**24** SA	0254 / 0811 / 1520 / 2037	2.0 / 5.9 / 1.7 / 6.1
10 SA	0457 / 0953 / 1721 / 2226	1.5 / 6.3 / 1.4 / 6.3	**25** SU	0352 / 0859 / 1615 / 2123	1.6 / 6.4 / 1.2 / 6.5
11 SU	0541 / 1030 / 1803 / 2258	1.3 / 6.6 / 1.0 / 6.4	**26** M	0444 / 0943 / 1709 / 2206	1.2 / 6.8 / 0.9 / 6.8
12 M	0618 / 1104 / 1838 / 2327 ○	1.1 / 6.7 / 0.9 / 6.5	**27** TU	0534 / 1025 / 1800 / 2246 ●	0.9 / 7.1 / 0.6 / 7.0
13 TU	0649 / 1138 / 1906 / 2356	1.1 / 6.7 / 1.0 / 6.5	**28** W	0622 / 1107 / 1848 / 2327	0.8 / 7.3 / 0.5 / 7.1
14 W	0712 / 1209 / 1927	1.2 / 6.7 / 1.1	**29** TH	0705 / 1149 / 1932	0.7 / 7.3 / 0.5
15 TH	0024 / 0731 / 1237 / 1947	6.5 / 1.2 / 6.6 / 1.2	**30** F	0008 / 0746 / 1232 / 2011	7.1 / 0.7 / 7.2 / 0.6

OCTOBER

Day	Time	m	Day	Time	m
1 SA	0052 / 0826 / 1317 / 2050	7.0 / 0.8 / 7.0 / 0.8	**16** SU	0036 / 0757 / 1245 / 2013	6.4 / 1.3 / 6.4 / 1.4
2 SU	0138 / 0906 / 1405 / 2131	6.7 / 1.0 / 6.7 / 1.2	**17** M	0101 / 0829 / 1315 / 2045	6.3 / 1.5 / 6.3 / 1.6
3 M	0231 / 0950 / 1501 / 2217	6.4 / 1.4 / 6.2 / 1.7	**18** TU	0134 / 0905 / 1352 / 2122	6.2 / 1.7 / 6.0 / 1.9
4 TU	0331 / 1044 / 1607 / 2318 ◑	6.0 / 1.9 / 5.7 / 2.2	**19** W	0218 / 0946 / 1442 / 2207	5.9 / 2.0 / 5.7 / 2.2
5 W	0440 / 1156 / 1724	5.6 / 2.2 / 5.4	**20** TH	0318 / 1040 / 1559 / 2308 ◐	5.6 / 2.2 / 5.4 / 2.4
6	0039 / 0601 / 1324 / 1915	2.4 / 5.4 / 2.3 / 5.4	**21** F	0516 / 1201 / 1808	5.4 / 2.3 / 5.4
7 F	0208 / 0734 / 1454 / 2032	2.3 / 5.6 / 2.0 / 5.6	**22** SA	0053 / 0637 / 1338 / 1914	2.4 / 5.6 / 2.1 / 5.7
8 SA	0326 / 0838 / 1600 / 2120	2.0 / 5.9 / 1.6 / 6.0	**23** SU	0217 / 0738 / 1445 / 2009	2.1 / 6.0 / 1.6 / 6.1
9 SU	0422 / 0923 / 1639 / 2157	1.6 / 6.2 / 1.3 / 6.2	**24** M	0318 / 0829 / 1543 / 2057	1.6 / 6.4 / 1.2 / 6.5
10 M	0506 / 1001 / 1729 / 2228	1.4 / 6.5 / 1.2 / 6.4	**25** TU	0413 / 0916 / 1639 / 2141	1.3 / 6.8 / 0.9 / 6.8
11 TU	0542 / 1036 / 1801 / 2256	1.3 / 6.6 / 1.1 / 6.5	**26** W	0506 / 1000 / 1734 / 2224 ●	1.0 / 7.0 / 0.7 / 7.0
12 W	0612 / 1108 / 1827 / 2325 ○	1.2 / 6.6 / 1.2 / 6.5	**27** TH	0556 / 1044 / 1824 / 2306	0.8 / 7.2 / 0.6 / 7.1
13 TH	0635 / 1138 / 1850 / 2353	1.2 / 6.6 / 1.2 / 6.5	**28** F	0643 / 1128 / 1910 / 2349	0.7 / 7.2 / 0.6 / 7.1
14 F	0659 / 1203 / 1915	1.2 / 6.5 / 1.2	**29** SA	0728 / 1213 / 1953	0.7 / 7.1 / 0.7
15 SA	0016 / 0727 / 1224 / 1943	6.5 / 1.3 / 6.4 / 1.3	**30** SU	0035 / 0811 / 1259 / 2034	7.0 / 0.9 / 6.9 / 1.0
			31 M	0123 / 0854 / 1349 / 2116	6.8 / 1.1 / 6.6 / 1.3

NOVEMBER

Day	Time	m	Day	Time	m
1 TU	0214 / 0940 / 1444 / 2203	6.5 / 1.4 / 6.2 / 1.7	**16** W	0124 / 0852 / 1341 / 2107	6.3 / 1.6 / 6.1 / 1.7
2 W	0311 / 1032 / 1455 / 2259 ◐	6.1 / 1.8 / 5.8 / 2.1	**17** TH	0209 / 0934 / 1431 / 2151	6.1 / 1.7 / 5.9 / 1.9
3 TH	0412 / 1137 / 1654	5.8 / 2.1 / 5.5	**18** F	0307 / 1026 / 1537 / 2247 ◑	5.9 / 1.9 / 5.7 / 2.1
4	0009 / 0520 / 1251 / 1820	2.4 / 5.6 / 2.2 / 5.4	**19** SA	0423 / 1133 / 1715	5.7 / 2.0 / 5.6
5 SA	0125 / 0640 / 1404 / 1944	2.4 / 5.6 / 2.0 / 5.5	**20**	0004 / 0548 / 1255 / 1836	2.2 / 5.8 / 1.9 / 5.7
6 SU	0234 / 0752 / 1509 / 2037	2.2 / 5.8 / 1.8 / 5.8	**21** M	0130 / 0659 / 1405 / 1937	2.0 / 6.0 / 1.6 / 6.0
7 M	0332 / 0844 / 1601 / 2118	1.9 / 6.0 / 1.6 / 6.0	**22** TU	0238 / 0757 / 1508 / 2030	1.7 / 6.3 / 1.3 / 6.3
8 TU	0420 / 0926 / 1643 / 2153	1.7 / 6.2 / 1.4 / 6.2	**23** W	0339 / 0850 / 1609 / 2119	1.4 / 6.6 / 1.1 / 6.5
9 W	0500 / 1003 / 1717 / 2224	1.5 / 6.4 / 1.3 / 6.3	**24** TH	0438 / 0940 / 1709 / 2207	1.2 / 6.8 / 0.9 / 6.7
10 TH	0533 / 1036 / 1748 / 2255 ○	1.4 / 6.4 / 1.3 / 6.4	**25** F	0535 / 1028 / 1805 / 2253 ●	1.0 / 6.9 / 0.8 / 6.9
11 F	0603 / 1104 / 1818 / 2324	1.3 / 6.4 / 1.3 / 6.5	**26** SA	0627 / 1115 / 1855 / 2338	0.8 / 7.0 / 0.8 / 6.9
12 SA	0634 / 1134 / 1850 / 2351	1.3 / 6.4 / 1.3 / 6.5	**27** SU	0716 / 1201 / 1941	0.8 / 6.9 / 0.9
13 SU	0707 / 1200 / 1923	1.3 / 6.4 / 1.4	**28** M	0024 / 0802 / 1248 / 2024	6.9 / 0.9 / 6.7 / 1.1
14 M	0017 / 0740 / 1228 / 1956	6.5 / 1.3 / 6.3 / 1.4	**29** TU	0110 / 0847 / 1336 / 2106	6.8 / 0.8 / 6.5 / 1.3
15 TU	0047 / 0815 / 1301 / 2029	6.4 / 1.4 / 6.3 / 1.6	**30** W	0158 / 0931 / 1426 / 2148	6.6 / 1.3 / 6.2 / 1.6

DECEMBER

Day	Time	m	Day	Time	m
1 TH	0247 / 1016 / 1519 / 2232	6.3 / 1.6 / 5.9 / 1.9	**16** F	0201 / 0928 / 1420 / 2141	6.4 / 1.4 / 6.2 / 1.6
2 F	0340 / 1106 / 1616 / 2323 ◐	6.0 / 1.8 / 5.6 / 2.2	**17** SA	0251 / 1014 / 1515 / 2230	6.3 / 1.5 / 6.0 / 1.7
3 SA	0437 / 1202 / 1720	5.8 / 2.0 / 5.4	**18** SU	0350 / 1109 / 1621 / 2330 ◑	6.1 / 1.6 / 5.8 / 1.9
4	0025 / 0541 / 1303 / 1832	2.3 / 5.6 / 2.1 / 5.4	**19** M	0459 / 1215 / 1743	6.0 / 1.7 / 5.7
5 M	0130 / 0651 / 1404 / 1938	2.3 / 5.6 / 2.1 / 5.5	**20**	0044 / 0615 / 1326 / 1902	1.9 / 5.9 / 1.7 / 5.8
6 TU	0232 / 0753 / 1500 / 2031	2.2 / 5.7 / 1.9 / 5.7	**21** W	0158 / 0728 / 1435 / 2008	1.9 / 6.0 / 1.6 / 6.0
7 W	0328 / 0844 / 1550 / 2114	2.0 / 5.9 / 1.7 / 5.9	**22** TH	0308 / 0832 / 1543 / 2106	1.7 / 6.2 / 1.4 / 6.2
8 TH	0416 / 0927 / 1635 / 2152	1.7 / 6.0 / 1.5 / 6.1	**23** F	0416 / 0929 / 1652 / 2159	1.4 / 6.4 / 1.2 / 6.4
9 F	0457 / 1003 / 1715 / 2227	1.5 / 6.2 / 1.4 / 6.3	**24** SA	0521 / 1023 / 1749 / 2248 ●	1.1 / 6.6 / 1.0 / 6.6
10 SA	0535 / 1037 / 1753 / 2300 ○	1.4 / 6.3 / 1.3 / 6.4	**25** SU	0618 / 1112 / 1847 / 2332	1.0 / 6.7 / 0.9 / 6.8
11 SU	0613 / 1111 / 1831 / 2332	1.3 / 6.3 / 1.3 / 6.5	**26**	0709 / 1156 / 1934	1.0 / 6.7 / 0.9
12 M	0651 / 1144 / 1909	1.2 / 6.4 / 1.3	**27** TU	0015 / 0755 / 1239 / 2015	6.8 / 0.8 / 6.6 / 1.0
13 TU	0005 / 0729 / 1218 / 1945	6.5 / 1.2 / 6.4 / 1.3	**28** W	0057 / 0837 / 1321 / 2052	6.8 / 0.9 / 6.5 / 1.2
14 W	0040 / 0807 / 1254 / 2022	6.5 / 1.2 / 6.4 / 1.4	**29** TH	0139 / 0916 / 1403 / 2126	6.7 / 1.0 / 6.3 / 1.4
15 TH	0118 / 0846 / 1334 / 2100	6.5 / 1.3 / 6.3 / 1.5	**30** F	0221 / 0951 / 1447 / 2156	6.5 / 1.3 / 6.0 / 1.6
			31 SA	0305 / 1025 / 1534 / 2228	6.3 / 1.6 / 5.8 / 1.8

Chart Datum: 3·67 metres below Ordnance Datum (Newlyn)
HAT is 7·4 metres above Chart Datum

TIDES

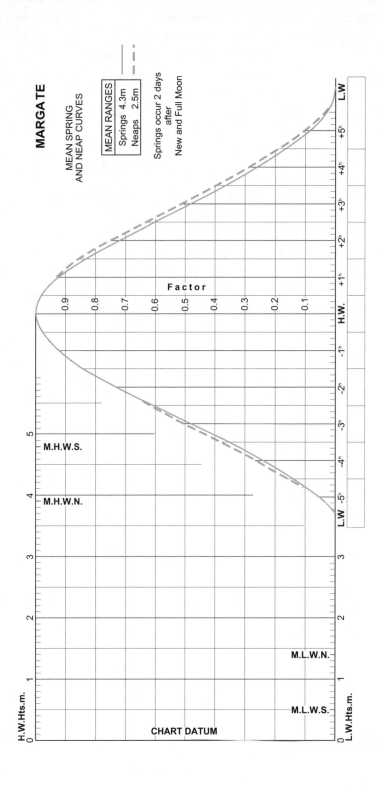

MARGATE

MEAN SPRING
AND NEAP CURVES

MEAN RANGES	
Springs	4.3m
Neaps	2.5m

Springs occur 2 days
after
New and Full Moon

TIME ZONE (UT)	MARGATE	Dates in amber are SPRINGS
For Summer Time add ONE hour in non-shaded areas	LAT 51°23′N LONG 1°23′E	Dates in yellow are NEAPS
	TIMES AND HEIGHTS OF HIGH AND LOW WATERS	2011

JANUARY

Day	Time m	Time m	Time m	Time m
1 SA	0259 1.2	0908 4.3	1532 1.0	2150 4.3
16 SU	0245 1.4	0841 3.9	1509 1.3	2126 4.1
2 SU	0406 1.0	1015 4.4	1628 1.0	2246 4.4
17 M	0349 1.2	0946 4.1	1607 1.2	2221 4.3
3 M	0508 0.9	1112 4.5	1718 1.0	2332 4.5
18 TU	0444 0.9	1042 4.3	1656 1.0	2309 4.4
4 TU ●	0600 0.7	1200 4.6	1801 1.0	
19 W ○	0534 0.7	1132 4.5	1741 0.9	2352 4.6
5 W	0011 4.6	0644 0.6	1242 4.6	1839 1.0
20 TH	0621 0.6	1218 4.7	1824 0.8	
6 TH	0047 4.6	0723 0.6	1321 4.6	1915 1.0
21 F	0034 4.7	0705 0.4	1306 4.8	1906 0.7
7 F	0123 4.6	0757 0.6	1357 4.5	1949 1.0
22 SA	0117 4.9	0749 0.3	1352 4.9	1948 0.7
8 SA	0158 4.6	0829 0.6	1431 4.5	2022 1.0
23 SU	0201 4.9	0832 0.2	1438 4.8	2031 0.7
9 SU	0234 4.6	0859 0.7	1505 4.4	2055 1.1
24 M	0244 4.9	0914 0.3	1522 4.7	2114 0.8
10 M	0309 4.5	0931 0.8	1539 4.2	2131 1.2
25 TU	0327 4.6	0956 0.4	1605 4.5	2159 0.9
11 TU	0344 4.4	1006 0.9	1615 4.1	2211 1.3
26 W ◑	0412 4.7	1041 0.6	1651 4.3	2250 1.1
12 W ◑	0423 4.2	1046 1.1	1656 4.0	2258 1.5
27 TH	0506 4.5	1134 0.8	1750 4.1	2353 1.2
13 TH	0509 4.1	1135 1.2	1746 3.8	2356 1.6
28 F	0614 4.3	1243 1.1	1904 4.0	
14 F	0605 3.9	1238 1.4	1855 3.8	
29 SA	0116 1.3	0734 4.1	1401 1.2	2021 4.0
15 SA	0118 1.6	0721 3.8	1358 1.4	2020 3.9
30 SU	0243 1.3	0857 4.1	1515 1.3	2136 4.1
31 M	0406 1.1	1013 4.2	1621 1.2	2238 4.3

FEBRUARY

Day	Time m	Time m	Time m	Time m
1 TU	0510 0.9	1110 4.4	1712 1.1	2325 4.4
16 W	0420 0.9	1025 4.3	1636 1.0	2249 4.4
2 W	0556 0.7	1155 4.5	1751 1.0	
17 TH	0514 0.6	1117 4.6	1724 0.9	2335 4.6
3 TH ●	0003 4.5	0633 0.6	1232 4.5	1824 1.0
18 F	0603 0.4	1204 4.8	1808 1.0	
4 F	0035 4.6	0704 0.6	1304 4.5	1856 0.9
19 SA	0018 4.8	0647 0.3	1250 4.9	1850 0.7
5 SA	0105 4.7	0732 0.6	1334 4.5	1928 0.9
20 SU	0101 5.0	0729 0.2	1335 4.9	1932 0.6
6 SU	0137 4.7	0800 0.6	1404 4.5	1959 0.9
21 M	0144 5.1	0810 0.2	1419 4.9	2014 0.6
7 M	0210 4.7	0828 0.6	1435 4.4	2030 0.9
22 TU	0227 5.1	0848 0.3	1459 4.7	2055 0.7
8 TU	0242 4.6	0856 0.7	1506 4.3	2101 1.0
23 W	0308 5.0	0926 0.4	1538 4.6	2137 0.8
9 W	0313 4.6	0926 0.8	1537 4.2	2135 1.1
24 TH ◑	0352 4.8	1007 0.7	1620 4.3	2224 1.0
10 TH	0347 4.6	0958 1.0	1612 4.1	2214 1.3
25 F	0443 4.5	1057 1.0	1713 4.1	2326 1.2
11 F ◑	0426 4.2	1038 1.2	1655 3.9	2305 1.4
26 SA	0550 4.2	1208 1.3	1831 3.9	
12 SA	0518 4.0	1136 1.4	1753 3.8	
27 SU	0054 1.3	0716 4.0	1336 1.5	1957 3.9
13 SU	0019 1.5	0627 3.8	1301 1.5	1918 3.7
28 M	0231 1.3	0848 4.0	1500 1.4	2116 4.0
14 M	0159 1.4	0734 3.8	1432 1.4	2049 3.9
15 TU	0318 1.2	0920 4.1	1541 1.2	2156 4.2

MARCH

Day	Time m	Time m	Time m	Time m
1 TU	0359 1.0	1003 4.2	1610 1.3	2220 4.2
16 W	0248 1.1	0856 4.1	1514 1.2	2126 4.2
2 W	0458 0.8	1057 4.4	1659 1.2	2308 4.4
17 TH	0354 0.8	1003 4.4	1612 1.0	2223 4.4
3 TH	0540 0.7	1139 4.4	1734 1.0	2344 4.5
18 F	0450 0.5	1056 4.6	1701 0.8	2311 4.7
4 F ●	0611 0.6	1212 4.5	1804 0.9	
19 SA ○	0538 0.3	1143 4.8	1746 0.7	2355 4.9
5 SA	0013 4.6	0636 0.6	1240 4.5	1834 0.9
20 SU	0622 0.2	1228 4.9	1830 0.6	
6 SU	0041 4.7	0701 0.6	1305 4.5	1905 0.8
21 M	0038 5.0	0704 0.2	1312 4.9	1913 0.5
7 M	0112 4.7	0728 0.5	1334 4.5	1936 0.8
22 TU	0123 5.1	0743 0.2	1354 4.8	1956 0.5
8 TU	0144 4.7	0755 0.6	1405 4.5	2006 0.8
23 W	0208 5.1	0821 0.3	1434 4.7	2038 0.6
9 W	0216 4.6	0822 0.6	1435 4.4	2036 0.9
24 TH	0251 4.9	0858 0.5	1512 4.5	2120 0.7
10 TH	0246 4.6	0850 0.8	1504 4.3	2108 1.0
25 F	0336 4.7	0938 0.8	1553 4.3	2207 0.9
11 F	0316 4.4	0921 0.9	1534 4.2	2143 1.1
26 SA ◑	0426 4.4	1028 1.1	1645 4.1	2309 1.1
12 SA ◑	0353 4.2	0958 1.1	1616 4.0	2231 1.2
27 SU	0531 4.1	1137 1.4	1759 3.9	
13 SU	0445 4.0	1054 1.3	1716 3.9	2342 1.3
28 M	0033 1.2	0657 3.9	1309 1.6	1926 3.8
14 M	0556 3.9	1219 1.5	1835 3.8	
29 TU	0207 1.2	0825 3.9	1434 1.5	2042 3.9
15 TU	0123 1.3	0727 3.8	1358 1.4	2013 3.9
30 W	0330 1.0	0935 4.1	1541 1.3	2146 4.1
31 TH	0427 0.8	1028 4.3	1629 1.2	2235 4.3

APRIL

Day	Time m	Time m	Time m	Time m
1 F	0506 0.7	1109 4.4	1705 1.0	2312 4.4
16 SA	0420 0.4	1029 4.6	1634 0.8	2241 4.7
2 SA	0534 0.7	1141 4.4	1737 0.9	2343 4.5
17 SU	0509 0.3	1117 4.7	1721 0.7	2328 4.9
3 SU	0601 0.6	1207 4.5	1810 0.8	
18 M ○	0554 0.3	1201 4.8	1808 0.6	
4 M	0012 4.6	0628 0.6	1234 4.5	1841 0.7
19 TU	0014 5.0	0636 0.3	1245 4.8	1855 0.5
5 TU	0044 4.6	0657 0.6	1304 4.5	1913 0.7
20 W	0102 5.0	0717 0.3	1328 4.8	1941 0.5
6 W	0118 4.6	0724 0.6	1337 4.5	1944 0.7
21 TH	0150 5.0	0757 0.5	1409 4.7	2025 0.5
7 TH	0152 4.6	0753 0.7	1409 4.4	2016 0.8
22 F	0236 4.8	0836 0.7	1450 4.5	2109 0.6
8 F	0224 4.5	0823 0.8	1439 4.3	2049 0.8
23 SA	0322 4.6	0916 0.9	1532 4.4	2156 0.8
9 SA	0256 4.4	0856 0.9	1510 4.2	2127 0.9
24 SU	0411 4.3	1004 1.2	1621 4.1	2253 1.0
10 SU	0336 4.2	0938 1.1	1555 4.1	2216 1.0
25 M ◑	0510 4.1	1104 1.4	1725 4.0	
11 M ◑	0429 4.1	1034 1.2	1654 4.0	2325 1.1
26 TU	0005 1.1	0627 3.9	1227 1.6	1846 3.9
12 TU	0538 4.0	1154 1.4	1807 3.9	
27 W	0126 1.1	0744 3.9	1351 1.5	1957 3.9
13 W	0056 1.1	0703 4.0	1326 1.3	1937 4.0
28 TH	0237 1.1	0849 4.0	1457 1.4	2057 4.1
14 TH	0218 0.9	0828 4.1	1443 1.1	2051 4.2
29 F	0332 0.9	0942 4.1	1548 1.2	2148 4.2
15 F	0325 0.6	0934 4.3	1543 0.9	2150 4.5
30 SA	0415 0.8	1026 4.3	1630 1.0	2231 4.3

Chart Datum: 2·50 metres below Ordnance Datum (Newlyn)
HAT is 5·2 metres above Chart Datum

TIME ZONE (UT)
For Summer Time add ONE hour in non-shaded areas

MARGATE
LAT 51°23'N   LONG 1°23'E
TIMES AND HEIGHTS OF HIGH AND LOW WATERS

Dates in amber are **SPRINGS**
Dates in yellow are NEAPS

2011

MAY

Day	Time	m	Time	m	Time	m	Time	m
1 SU	0451	0.8	1102	4.3	1708	0.9	2308	4.4
2 M	0525	0.7	1133	4.4	1744	0.8	2343	4.5
3 TU ●	0558	0.7	1204	4.5	1819	0.7		
4 W	0017	4.5	0628	0.7	1237	4.6	1853	0.7
5 TH	0054	4.6	0658	0.7	1313	4.6	1927	0.6
6 F	0131	4.6	0730	0.7	1348	4.5	2002	0.6
7 SA	0210	4.5	0804	0.8	1424	4.4	2039	0.7
8 SU	0249	4.4	0843	0.9	1502	4.3	2122	0.7
9 M	0332	4.3	0929	1.0	1547	4.2	2213	0.8
10 TU ☽	0423	4.2	1025	1.1	1641	4.1	2317	0.9
11 W	0525	4.1	1135	1.2	1745	4.1		
12 TH	0032	0.8	0639	4.1	1253	1.2	1902	4.1
13 F	0147	0.7	0757	4.2	1409	1.1	2015	4.3
14 SA	0253	0.6	0903	4.4	1512	1.0	2117	4.5
15 SU	0350	0.5	1000	4.6	1608	0.8	2213	4.6
16 M	0440	0.4	1051	4.6	1659	0.6	2305	4.8
17 TU ○	0527	0.4	1137	4.6	1750	0.6	2356	4.9
18 W	0613	0.5	1222	4.7	1841	0.5		
19 TH	0046	4.9	0656	0.5	1306	4.7	1930	0.5
20 F	0135	4.8	0738	0.6	1350	4.6	2017	0.5
21 SA	0222	4.7	0819	0.8	1432	4.5	2101	0.6
22 SU	0307	4.5	0858	1.0	1513	4.4	2144	0.7
23 M	0353	4.3	0941	1.1	1558	4.3	2231	0.8
24 TU ☾	0443	4.1	1029	1.3	1649	4.1	2326	1.0
25 W	0545	3.9	1129	1.5	1755	4.0		
26 TH	0032	1.1	0653	3.9	1249	1.5	1905	4.0
27 F	0139	1.1	0755	3.9	1405	1.4	2006	4.2
28 SA	0237	1.0	0849	4.0	1503	1.3	2100	4.1
29 SU	0326	1.0	0938	4.1	1552	1.1	2150	4.2
30 M	0411	0.9	1022	4.2	1637	1.0	2234	4.3
31 TU	0452	0.8	1101	4.3	1719	0.8	2315	4.4

JUNE

Day	Time	m	Time	m	Time	m	Time	m
1 W ●	0530	0.8	1138	4.4	1759	0.7	2354	4.5
2 TH	0605	0.8	1214	4.5	1837	0.7		
3 F	0033	4.5	0638	0.8	1253	4.5	1914	0.6
4 SA	0115	4.6	0714	0.7	1332	4.5	1953	0.6
5 SU	0158	4.6	0753	0.8	1412	4.5	2034	0.5
6 M	0242	4.5	0836	0.8	1454	4.5	2119	0.6
7 TU	0327	4.5	0923	0.9	1538	4.4	2209	0.6
8 W	0415	4.4	1015	1.0	1627	4.4	2304	0.6
9 TH ☽	0510	4.3	1114	1.1	1723	4.3		
10 F	0006	0.7	0613	4.2	1220	1.1	1830	4.3
11 SA	0114	0.7	0725	4.2	1325	1.1	1942	4.3
12 SU	0221	0.7	0832	4.2	1444	1.0	2049	4.4
13 M	0321	0.7	0934	4.3	1546	0.9	2152	4.5
14 TU	0417	0.7	1031	4.4	1645	0.9	2252	4.6
15 W ○	0508	0.7	1121	4.5	1741	0.6	2346	4.7
16 TH	0556	0.7	1207	4.6	1834	0.6		
17 F	0036	4.7	0641	0.7	1251	4.6	1922	0.5
18 SA	0123	4.7	0723	0.8	1333	4.6	2006	0.5
19 SU	0207	4.6	0802	0.9	1414	4.6	2046	0.6
20 M	0249	4.5	0839	1.0	1453	4.5	2123	0.7
21 TU	0329	4.4	0916	1.1	1532	4.4	2200	0.8
22 W	0409	4.2	0956	1.2	1612	4.3	2240	0.8
23 TH ◐	0452	4.1	1041	1.3	1658	4.1	2328	1.0
24 F	0544	3.9	1134	1.4	1753	4.0		
25 SA	0027	1.1	0651	3.8	1245	1.5	1903	3.9
26 SU	0137	1.2	0755	3.9	1410	1.4	2009	4.0
27 M	0239	1.2	0853	4.0	1513	1.3	2108	4.1
28 TU	0334	1.1	0945	4.1	1606	1.1	2202	4.2
29 W	0422	1.0	1033	4.3	1654	0.9	2250	4.3
30 TH	0506	1.0	1116	4.4	1739	0.8	2334	4.4

JULY

Day	Time	m	Time	m	Time	m	Time	m
1 F ●	0546	0.9	1156	4.5	1821	0.7		
2 SA	0017	4.6	0624	0.8	1236	4.6	1902	0.5
3 SU	0101	4.7	0703	0.8	1317	4.7	1944	0.4
4 M	0146	4.7	0744	0.7	1359	4.7	2026	0.4
5 TU	0232	4.7	0827	0.7	1442	4.7	2110	0.4
6 W	0317	4.6	0911	0.8	1524	4.7	2155	0.4
7 TH	0401	4.5	0958	0.9	1609	4.6	2243	0.5
8 F ☽	0449	4.4	1049	1.0	1700	4.5	2336	0.7
9 SA	0545	4.2	1148	1.1	1801	4.4		
10 SU	0040	0.8	0653	4.1	1303	1.2	1914	4.3
11 M	0151	0.9	0805	4.1	1421	1.2	2029	4.3
12 TU	0259	1.0	0915	4.2	1533	1.0	2143	4.4
13 W	0402	1.0	1019	4.3	1641	0.9	2248	4.5
14 TH	0458	0.9	1114	4.4	1740	0.7	2342	4.6
15 F ○	0546	0.9	1159	4.5	1829	0.6		
16 SA	0028	4.6	0627	0.9	1239	4.6	1911	0.5
17 SU	0111	4.6	0705	0.9	1316	4.7	1949	0.5
18 M	0149	4.6	0741	0.9	1353	4.7	2022	0.6
19 TU	0225	4.5	0815	0.9	1428	4.7	2053	0.6
20 W	0258	4.4	0849	1.0	1503	4.6	2124	0.7
21 TH	0331	4.3	0923	1.1	1537	4.5	2157	0.8
22 F	0405	4.2	1001	1.2	1615	4.4	2234	1.0
23 SA ◐	0444	4.0	1044	1.3	1658	4.2	2320	1.2
24 SU	0531	3.9	1139	1.5	1751	4.0		
25 M	0021	1.4	0636	3.8	1257	1.5	1902	3.9
26 TU	0143	1.4	0801	3.8	1427	1.4	2022	3.9
27 W	0256	1.3	0909	4.0	1533	1.2	2130	4.1
28 TH	0354	1.2	1006	4.2	1629	1.0	2227	4.3
29 F	0444	1.1	1054	4.4	1718	0.8	2316	4.5
30 SA ●	0528	0.9	1137	4.6	1803	0.6		
31 SU	0001	4.7	0608	0.8	1219	4.7	1846	0.5

AUGUST

Day	Time	m	Time	m	Time	m	Time	m
1 M	0045	4.8	0648	0.7	1300	4.8	1928	0.4
2 TU	0130	4.9	0730	0.7	1342	4.9	2010	0.3
3 W	0215	4.8	0812	0.7	1424	4.9	2051	0.3
4 TH	0258	4.8	0854	0.8	1506	4.9	2131	0.4
5 F	0340	4.6	0937	0.9	1549	4.8	2214	0.6
6 SA ◐	0422	4.4	1024	1.0	1637	4.6	2303	0.8
7 SU	0514	4.2	1121	1.1	1738	4.4		
8 M	0008	1.0	0623	4.1	1239	1.3	1855	4.2
9 TU	0128	1.2	0744	4.0	1407	1.2	2020	4.2
10 W	0245	1.3	0903	4.1	1531	1.1	2142	4.3
11 TH	0355	1.2	1012	4.3	1643	0.9	2247	4.5
12 F	0452	1.1	1106	4.5	1736	0.7	2336	4.6
13 SA ○	0535	1.0	1149	4.6	1818	0.6		
14 SU	0017	4.6	0610	1.0	1224	4.7	1852	0.6
15 M	0053	4.6	0644	0.9	1255	4.7	1921	0.6
16 TU	0123	4.6	0717	0.9	1326	4.8	1950	0.6
17 W	0153	4.6	0750	0.9	1359	4.7	2018	0.6
18 TH	0223	4.5	0822	0.9	1432	4.7	2047	0.7
19 F	0254	4.4	0853	1.0	1505	4.6	2116	0.9
20 SA	0326	4.3	0926	1.1	1539	4.4	2147	1.0
21 SU ◐	0400	4.2	1003	1.2	1618	4.2	2226	1.2
22 M	0442	4.0	1051	1.4	1707	4.0	2320	1.5
23 TU	0537	3.8	1200	1.5	1811	3.9		
24 W	0041	1.6	0656	3.8	1338	1.5	1937	3.9
25 TH	0215	1.5	0829	3.9	1459	1.3	2100	4.1
26 F	0326	1.3	0936	4.2	1601	1.0	2204	4.4
27 SA	0420	1.1	1030	4.4	1654	0.7	2256	4.6
28 SU	0506	0.9	1114	4.6	1740	0.5	2341	4.8
29 M ●	0548	0.8	1155	4.8	1824	0.4		
30 TU	0024	4.9	0629	0.7	1237	5.0	1905	0.3
31 W	0108	4.9	0710	0.6	1319	5.1	1945	0.3

Chart Datum: 2·50 metres below Ordnance Datum (Newlyn)
HAT is 5·2 metres above Chart Datum

TIME ZONE (UT)
For Summer Time add ONE hour in **non-shaded areas**

MARGATE
LAT 51°23′N   LONG 1°23′E
TIMES AND HEIGHTS OF HIGH AND LOW WATERS

Dates in amber are **SPRINGS**
Dates in yellow are **NEAPS**

2011

SEPTEMBER

Day	T1 (m)	T2 (m)	T3 (m)	T4 (m)
1	0152 4.9	0752 0.7	TH 1402 5.1	2024 0.3
16	0149 4.6	0756 0.8	F 1403 4.7	2011 0.8
2	0233 4.8	0834 0.7	F 1445 5.0	2103 0.5
17	0220 4.5	0826 0.9	SA 1436 4.6	2038 0.9
3	0313 4.6	0916 0.8	SA 1529 4.9	2143 0.7
18	0251 4.4	0857 0.9	SU 1508 4.4	2108 1.1
4	0355 4.4	1002 0.9	SU 1619 4.6	☽ 2232 1.0
19	0322 4.2	0932 1.1	M 1544 4.3	2144 1.3
5	0446 4.2	1101 1.1	M 1721 4.4	2340 1.3
20	0401 4.1	1016 1.3	TU 1632 4.1	☽ 2235 1.5
6	0556 4.0	1223 1.3	TU 1842 4.1	
21	0456 3.9	1121 1.4	W 1736 3.9	2353 1.6
7	0107 1.5	0724 3.9	W 1356 1.3	2015 4.1
22	0608 3.8	1255 1.4	TH 1859 3.9	
8	0233 1.5	0847 4.1	TH 1526 1.1	2135 4.3
23	0131 1.6	0743 3.9	F 1422 1.2	2027 4.1
9	0345 1.3	0955 4.3	F 1632 0.8	2234 4.5
24	0252 1.4	0900 4.2	SA 1529 0.9	2136 4.4
10	0439 1.2	1048 4.5	SA 1719 0.7	2320 4.6
25	0350 1.1	0957 4.5	SU 1624 0.6	2229 4.7
11	0517 1.1	1128 4.6	SU 1755 0.7	2357 4.6
26	0439 0.9	1045 4.7	M 1712 0.5	2315 4.8
12	0549 1.0	1159 4.7	M 1822 0.6	○
27	0523 0.8	1127 4.9	TU 1756 0.4	● 2358 4.9
13	0025 4.6	0620 0.9	TU 1227 4.7	1847 0.6
28	0606 0.7	1209 5.0	W 1837 0.3	
14	0051 4.6	0652 0.8	W 1257 4.8	1915 0.6
29	0040 5.0	0649 0.6	TH 1254 5.1	1917 0.3
15	0118 4.6	0725 0.8	TH 1330 4.8	1943 0.7
30	0123 4.9	0733 0.6	F 1340 5.1	1957 0.4

OCTOBER

Day	T1 (m)	T2 (m)	T3 (m)	T4 (m)
1	0205 4.8	0816 0.6	SA 1427 5.0	2036 0.6
16	0151 4.6	0803 0.8	SU 1411 4.6	2008 0.9
2	0246 4.7	0900 0.7	SU 1514 4.8	2117 0.9
17	0222 4.4	0836 0.9	M 1445 4.4	2040 1.1
3	0330 4.5	0948 0.9	M 1605 4.6	2206 1.2
18	0252 4.3	0912 1.0	TU 1522 4.3	2118 1.2
4	0421 4.2	1048 1.1	TU 1706 4.3	☽ 2313 1.5
19	0332 4.2	0957 1.1	W 1610 4.1	2209 1.4
5	0530 4.0	1207 1.2	W 1828 4.1	
20	0426 4.0	1057 1.2	TH 1711 4.0	☽ 2320 1.5
6	0042 1.6	0658 3.9	TH 1337 1.2	1956 4.1
21	0533 3.9	1219 1.2	F 1826 4.0	
7	0209 1.6	0817 4.1	F 1500 1.0	2110 4.3
22	0048 1.5	0656 4.0	SA 1343 1.1	1952 4.2
8	0319 1.4	0923 4.3	SA 1603 0.9	2207 4.5
23	0212 1.4	0818 4.2	SU 1453 0.8	2101 4.4
9	0411 1.2	1015 4.4	SU 1647 0.8	2252 4.5
24	0316 1.1	0919 4.4	M 1550 0.6	2158 4.6
10	0450 1.1	1056 4.5	M 1719 0.7	2246 4.6
25	0409 0.9	1011 4.7	TU 1640 0.5	2246 4.8
11	0523 1.0	1127 4.6	TU 1746 0.7	2352 4.6
26	0457 0.8	1058 4.9	W 1726 0.4	2330 4.9
12	0556 0.9	1157 4.7	W 1814 0.7	○
27	0543 0.7	1144 5.0	TH 1809 0.4	
13	0016 4.6	0629 0.8	TH 1228 4.7	1843 0.7
28	0013 4.9	0630 0.6	F 1233 5.1	1851 0.5
14	0046 4.7	0701 0.8	F 1302 4.9	1911 0.7
29	0057 4.9	0717 0.5	SA 1323 5.1	1933 0.6
15	0118 4.6	0733 0.8	SA 1337 4.7	1939 0.8
30	0141 4.8	0804 0.6	SU 1412 5.0	2015 0.8
31	0225 4.7	0851 0.6	M 1501 4.8	2057 1.0

NOVEMBER

Day	T1 (m)	T2 (m)	T3 (m)	T4 (m)
1	0310 4.5	0939 0.8	TU 1551 4.5	2145 1.3
16	0238 4.4	0901 0.8	W 1510 4.4	2104 1.1
2	0400 4.3	1035 0.9	W 1649 4.3	◐ 2244 1.5
17	0318 4.3	0947 0.9	TH 1556 4.3	2154 1.3
3	0501 4.1	1143 1.1	TH 1803 4.1	
18	0407 4.2	1042 1.0	F 1650 4.2	◑ 2256 1.4
4	0002 1.6	0621 4.0	F 1300 1.1	1920 4.1
19	0505 4.1	1150 1.0	SA 1756 4.1	
5	0127 1.6	0734 4.0	SA 1413 1.1	2027 4.2
20	0008 1.4	0614 4.1	SU 1303 0.9	1913 4.2
6	0236 1.5	0836 4.1	SU 1512 1.0	2124 4.3
21	0127 1.3	0733 4.2	M 1414 0.8	2025 4.4
7	0331 1.3	0930 4.3	M 1558 0.9	2210 4.4
22	0239 1.2	0842 4.4	TU 1515 0.7	2125 4.5
8	0416 1.1	1015 4.4	TU 1635 0.9	2247 4.5
23	0339 1.0	0941 4.6	W 1609 0.6	2219 4.6
9	0455 1.0	1053 4.5	W 1710 0.8	2318 4.6
24	0433 0.8	1035 4.8	TH 1659 0.6	2308 4.7
10	0532 0.9	1128 4.6	TH 1744 0.8	○ 2347 4.6
25	0525 0.7	1128 4.9	F 1746 0.6	● 2354 4.8
11	0607 0.8	1202 4.6	F 1815 0.8	
26	0617 0.6	1220 4.9	SA 1833 0.6	
12	0019 4.6	0641 0.7	SA 1238 4.6	1844 0.8
27	0039 4.8	0707 0.5	SU 1311 4.9	1917 0.7
13	0053 4.6	0714 0.7	SU 1314 4.6	1913 0.9
28	0125 4.8	0756 0.5	M 1400 4.9	2000 0.9
14	0128 4.6	0746 0.7	M 1352 4.6	1946 0.9
29	0209 4.7	0843 0.6	TU 1448 4.7	2041 1.0
15	0203 4.5	0822 0.8	TU 1430 4.5	2023 1.0
30	0253 4.6	0928 0.7	W 1535 4.5	2124 1.2

DECEMBER

Day	T1 (m)	T2 (m)	T3 (m)	T4 (m)
1	0338 4.4	1015 0.8	TH 1625 4.3	2211 1.4
16	0306 4.5	0937 0.7	F 1543 4.4	2141 1.1
2	0428 4.3	1107 1.0	F 1724 4.1	◐ 2306 1.5
17	0350 4.4	1025 0.7	SA 1630 4.3	2233 1.2
3	0530 4.1	1208 1.1	SA 1830 4.0	
18	0441 4.4	1120 0.8	SU 1725 4.2	◑ 2333 1.3
4	0021 1.6	0641 4.0	SU 1314 1.2	1933 4.0
19	0540 4.3	1223 0.8	M 1833 4.2	
5	0142 1.6	0745 4.0	M 1415 1.2	2030 4.1
20	0044 1.3	0652 4.3	TU 1334 0.8	1948 4.2
6	0245 1.5	0842 4.1	TU 1508 1.1	2122 4.2
21	0203 1.2	0809 4.3	W 1443 0.8	2057 4.3
7	0338 1.3	0934 4.2	W 1555 1.0	2208 4.3
22	0313 1.1	0918 4.5	TH 1544 0.8	2159 4.4
8	0425 1.1	1021 4.3	TH 1638 1.0	2248 4.4
23	0416 0.9	1021 4.6	F 1640 0.8	2254 4.6
9	0508 0.9	1103 4.4	F 1717 1.0	2324 4.5
24	0516 0.7	1121 4.7	SA 1732 0.8	● 2343 4.7
10	0547 0.8	1141 4.4	SA 1752 0.9	○ 2358 4.6
25	0612 0.6	1213 4.8	SU 1820 0.8	
11	0624 0.7	1218 4.5	SU 1824 0.9	
26	0029 4.7	0702 0.5	M 1303 4.8	1904 0.8
12	0033 4.6	0658 0.7	M 1257 4.6	1856 0.9
27	0113 4.8	0748 0.5	TU 1349 4.8	1945 0.9
13	0111 4.6	0734 0.6	TU 1337 4.6	1932 0.9
28	0155 4.7	0830 0.5	W 1433 4.7	2023 1.0
14	0148 4.6	0812 0.6	W 1418 4.6	2011 0.9
29	0235 4.7	0908 0.6	TH 1514 4.5	2100 1.1
15	0227 4.6	0853 0.6	TH 1500 4.5	2054 1.0
30	0314 4.6	0944 0.7	F 1553 4.3	2138 1.2
31	0353 4.4	1021 0.6	SA 1633 4.2	2220 1.3

Chart Datum: 2·50 metres below Ordnance Datum (Newlyn)
HAT is 5·2 metres above Chart Datum

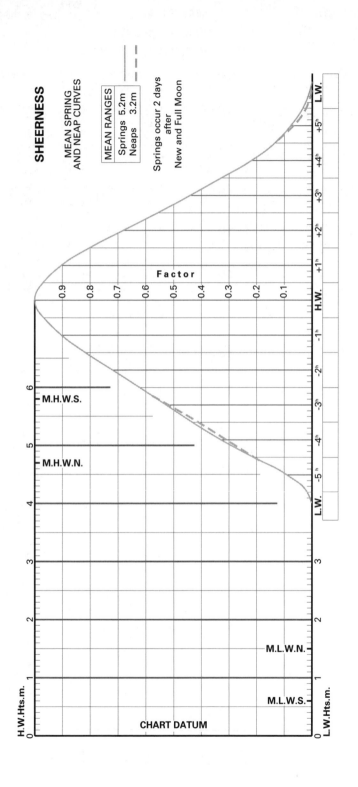

SHEERNESS

MEAN SPRING
AND NEAP CURVES

MEAN RANGES
Springs 5.2m
Neaps 3.2m

Springs occur 2 days
after
New and Full Moon

TIME ZONE (UT)	SHEERNESS	Dates in amber are **SPRINGS**
For Summer Time add ONE hour in **non-shaded areas**	**LAT 51°27'N LONG 0°45'E** TIMES AND HEIGHTS OF HIGH AND LOW WATERS	Dates in yellow are NEAPS **2011**

JANUARY

Time	m		Time	m
1 0311 0935 SA 1558 2213	1.4 5.2 1.2 5.2	**16**	0252 0909 SU 1532 2149	1.6 4.7 1.5 4.9
2 0425 1042 SU 1700 2312	1.2 5.3 1.1 5.3	**17**	0402 1017 M 1632 2249	1.4 5.0 1.3 5.2
3 0532 1139 M 1752	1.0 5.5 1.1	**18**	0501 1115 TU 1724 2341	1.1 5.3 1.1 5.4
4 0002 0626 TU 1229 ● 1835	5.4 0.9 5.6 1.0	**19**	0556 1205 W 1813 ○	0.9 5.6 0.9
5 0047 0713 W 1314 1913	5.5 0.8 5.7 1.0	**20**	0027 0648 TH 1252 1900	5.6 0.6 5.8 0.8
6 0126 0753 TH 1354 1948	5.6 0.7 5.7 1.0	**21**	0110 0738 F 1336 1945	5.8 0.4 6.0 0.7
7 0203 0829 F 1431 2020	5.6 0.7 5.6 1.0	**22**	0152 0825 SA 1420 2029	5.9 0.3 6.1 0.7
8 0236 0900 SA 1506 2051	5.5 0.8 5.5 1.1	**23**	0233 0909 SU 1503 2110	6.0 0.2 6.0 0.7
9 0308 0927 SU 1539 2121	5.4 0.9 5.4 1.1	**24**	0314 0951 M 1547 2148	5.9 0.3 5.9 0.8
10 0340 0953 M 1613 2153	5.4 0.9 5.2 1.2	**25**	0357 1030 TU 1632 2226	5.8 0.4 5.7 0.9
11 0415 1023 TU 1649 2229	5.2 1.1 5.0 1.4	**26**	0443 1108 W 1722 ◑ 2310	5.7 0.7 5.4 1.1
12 0453 1059 W 1731 ◑ 2311	5.1 1.2 4.9 1.5	**27**	0536 1153 TH 1818	5.4 1.0 5.1
13 0538 1144 TH 1822	4.9 1.4 4.7	**28**	0004 0640 F 1256 1926	1.3 5.1 1.2 4.9
14 0006 0637 F 1247 1926	1.7 4.7 1.6 4.6	**29**	0121 0759 SA 1417 2042	1.5 4.9 1.4 4.8
15 0122 0753 SA 1415 2040	1.8 4.6 1.6 4.7	**30**	0253 0922 SU 1536 2157	1.4 4.9 1.4 4.9
		31	0421 1035 M 1647 2301	1.3 5.1 1.3 5.1

FEBRUARY

Time	m		Time	m
1 0531 1133 TU 1741 2352	1.0 5.4 1.2 5.3	**16**	0439 1054 W 1703 2319	1.0 5.3 1.1 5.4
2 0621 1220 W 1823	0.8 5.5 1.1	**17**	0540 1147 TH 1757	0.7 5.7 0.9
3 0034 0701 TH 1301 ● 1857	5.5 0.7 5.6 1.0	**18**	0007 0634 F 1235 ○ 1845	5.7 0.5 5.9 0.7
4 0111 0736 F 1336 1929	5.5 0.7 5.6 0.9	**19**	0051 0723 SA 1318 1930	5.9 0.3 6.1 0.6
5 0143 0807 SA 1409 2000	5.6 0.7 5.6 0.9	**20**	0132 0808 SU 1401 2013	6.1 0.1 6.2 0.5
6 0213 0835 SU 1439 2030	5.6 0.7 5.6 0.9	**21**	0213 0851 M 1443 2053	6.2 0.1 6.1 0.5
7 0242 0901 M 1508 2058	5.6 0.7 5.5 0.9	**22**	0254 0929 TU 1524 2130	6.1 0.2 6.0 0.6
8 0312 0927 TU 1538 2126	5.6 0.8 5.4 1.0	**23**	0336 1005 W 1607 2206	6.0 0.4 5.7 0.8
9 0342 0952 W 1610 2155	5.4 0.9 5.2 1.2	**24**	0421 1039 TH 1652 ◐ 2245	5.8 0.7 5.4 1.0
10 0416 1019 TH 1645 2227	5.3 1.1 5.0 1.3	**25**	0512 1120 F 1746 2337	5.4 1.1 5.1 1.2
11 0455 1053 F 1729 ◐ 2312	5.1 1.3 4.8 1.5	**26**	0617 1220 SA 1854	5.0 1.4 4.8
12 0546 1144 SA 1828	4.8 1.5 4.6	**27**	0056 0739 SU 1348 2016	1.5 4.8 1.6 4.6
13 0019 0657 SU 1308 1948	1.6 4.6 1.7 4.6	**28**	0242 0908 M 1515 2139	1.5 4.8 1.6 4.8
14 0204 0827 M 1453 2113	1.6 4.6 1.6 4.7	**29**		
15 0332 0949 TU 1604 2223	1.4 4.9 1.3 5.1	**30**		

MARCH

Time	m		Time	m
1 0413 1023 TU 1629 2244	1.2 5.1 1.4 5.1	**16**	0303 0920 W 1535 2153	1.3 5.0 1.4 5.1
2 0518 1118 W 1723 2333	1.0 5.4 1.2 5.3	**17**	0415 1029 TH 1637 2252	0.9 5.4 1.1 5.4
3 0603 1202 TH 1802	0.8 5.6 1.1	**18**	0519 1124 F 1733 2341	0.6 5.8 0.9 5.7
4 0013 0639 F 1240 ● 1835	5.5 0.7 5.6 1.0	**19**	0614 1211 SA 1824 ○	0.4 6.0 0.7
5 0048 0709 SA 1312 1906	5.6 0.7 5.6 0.9	**20**	0025 0702 SU 1256 1909	6.0 0.2 6.1 0.6
6 0118 0738 SU 1341 1936	5.6 0.6 5.6 0.8	**21**	0108 0746 M 1338 1953	6.1 0.1 6.2 0.5
7 0146 0806 M 1408 2007	5.7 0.6 5.6 0.8	**22**	0150 0827 TU 1419 2034	6.2 0.1 6.1 0.5
8 0215 0833 TU 1436 2036	5.7 0.7 5.6 0.8	**23**	0233 0904 W 1500 2112	6.2 0.3 6.0 0.5
9 0244 0859 W 1505 2104	5.6 0.6 5.5 0.9	**24**	0316 0939 TH 1542 2149	6.0 0.5 5.7 0.7
10 0315 0924 TH 1536 2129	5.5 0.9 5.4 1.1	**25**	0402 1014 F 1626 2229	5.7 0.7 5.4 0.9
11 0348 0946 F 1610 2157	5.4 1.1 5.2 1.2	**26**	0454 1054 SA 1717 ◐ 2319	5.4 1.0 5.0 1.2
12 0426 1015 SA 1651 ◐ 2238	5.2 1.3 5.0 1.3	**27**	0559 1151 SU 1824	5.0 1.5 4.7
13 0516 1104 M 1746 2343	4.9 1.5 4.7 1.5	**28**	0038 0718 M 1317 1946	1.4 4.8 1.8 4.6
14 0623 1225 M 1904	4.7 1.7 4.6	**29**	0223 0844 TU 1445 2109	1.4 4.8 1.7 4.7
15 0124 0752 TU 1417 2037	1.5 4.7 1.6 4.7	**30**	0346 0956 W 1556 2214	1.2 5.0 1.5 5.0
		31	0447 1051 TH 1651 2304	1.0 5.3 1.3 5.3

APRIL

Time	m		Time	m
1 0531 1134 F 1731 2344	0.9 5.5 1.1 5.4	**16**	0450 1056 SA 1703 2312	0.6 5.7 0.9 5.7
2 0606 1210 SA 1806	0.8 5.6 1.0	**17**	0547 1145 SU 1757 2359	0.4 5.9 0.7 6.0
3 0018 0635 SU 1241 ● 1838	5.5 0.8 5.6 0.9	**18**	0636 1230 M 1846 ○	0.3 6.0 0.6
4 0049 0705 M 1310 1911	5.5 0.7 5.6 0.8	**19**	0044 0720 TU 1314 1932	6.1 0.3 6.1 0.5
5 0118 0734 TU 1338 1943	5.6 0.7 5.7 0.8	**20**	0130 0801 W 1356 2016	6.2 0.3 6.0 0.4
6 0148 0804 W 1407 2015	5.7 0.7 5.6 0.8	**21**	0215 0840 TH 1438 2058	6.1 0.5 5.9 0.5
7 0219 0833 TH 1437 2045	5.6 0.8 5.6 0.9	**22**	0301 0916 F 1521 2137	5.9 0.7 5.6 0.7
8 0252 0900 F 1509 2113	5.5 1.0 5.5 1.0	**23**	0348 0952 SA 1604 2218	5.7 1.0 5.4 0.9
9 0327 0926 SA 1545 2144	5.4 1.1 5.3 1.1	**24**	0440 1032 SU 1654 2305	5.4 1.3 5.1 1.1
10 0408 0959 SU 1627 2227	5.3 1.3 5.1 1.2	**25**	0540 1124 M 1754 ◐	5.0 1.5 4.8
11 0459 1050 M 1722 2330	5.1 1.5 4.9 1.3	**26**	0015 0648 TU 1237 1907	1.3 4.8 1.8 4.6
12 0605 1206 TU 1835	4.9 1.6 4.7	**27**	0146 0804 W 1401 2024	1.4 4.8 1.7 4.7
13 0101 0727 W 1343 2003	1.3 4.9 1.6 4.8	**28**	0259 0914 TH 1509 2131	1.2 5.0 1.6 4.9
14 0234 0851 TH 1502 2119	1.1 5.1 1.4 5.1	**29**	0357 1011 F 1605 2224	1.1 5.2 1.4 5.1
15 0345 0959 F 1605 2220	0.8 5.5 1.1 5.5	**30**	0444 1056 SA 1652 2307	1.0 5.3 1.2 5.3

Chart Datum: 2·90 metres below Ordnance Datum (Newlyn)
HAT is 6·3 metres above Chart Datum

TIDES

TIME ZONE (UT)	SHEERNESS	Dates in amber are SPRINGS
For Summer Time add ONE hour in non-shaded areas	LAT 51°27'N LONG 0°45'E	Dates in yellow are NEAPS
	TIMES AND HEIGHTS OF HIGH AND LOW WATERS	2011

MAY

Day	Time m	Time m	Time m	Time m
1 SU	0523 0.9	1134 5.4	1732 1.0	2344 5.4
2 M	0558 0.9	1207 5.5	1809 0.9	
3 TU ●	0018 5.5	0630 0.8	1239 5.6	1844 0.8
4 W	0051 5.6	0703 0.8	1310 5.6	1920 0.8
5 TH	0125 5.6	0737 0.8	1342 5.6	1956 0.8
6 F	0159 5.6	0810 0.9	1416 5.6	2032 0.8
7 SA	0236 5.6	0844 1.0	1451 5.5	2108 0.9
8 SU	0315 5.5	0918 1.1	1529 5.4	2145 0.9
9 M	0359 5.4	0957 1.2	1614 5.2	2231 1.1
10 TU ◗	0451 5.2	1047 1.4	1707 5.0	2329 1.1
11 W	0553 5.1	1153 1.5	1814 4.9	
12 TH	0043 1.1	0705 5.1	1311 1.5	1930 5.0
13 F	0203 1.0	0820 5.2	1425 1.3	2043 5.2
14 SA	0313 0.8	0928 5.4	1531 1.1	2147 5.4
15 SU	0417 0.7	1027 5.6	1632 1.0	2244 5.7
16 M	0517 0.6	1119 5.8	1731 0.8	2336 5.8
17 TU ○	0609 0.5	1207 5.8	1826 0.6	
18 W	0026 6.0	0655 0.5	1253 5.9	1916 0.5
19 TH	0114 6.0	0738 0.6	1338 5.9	2003 0.5
20 F	0202 6.0	0819 0.7	1421 5.8	2048 0.5
21 SA	0249 5.8	0857 0.9	1504 5.6	2129 0.7
22 SU	0336 5.6	0933 1.1	1546 5.4	2209 0.9
23 M	0424 5.4	1011 1.3	1631 5.2	2250 1.0
24 TU ◗	0514 5.1	1054 1.5	1722 5.0	2340 1.2
25 W	0610 4.9	1149 1.7	1820 4.8	
26 TH	0047 1.3	0711 4.8	1259 1.7	1926 4.7
27 F	0158 1.3	0815 4.8	1412 1.7	2032 4.8
28 SA	0258 1.3	0916 4.9	1514 1.5	2132 4.9
29 SU	0351 1.2	1008 5.1	1607 1.3	2223 5.1
30 M	0437 1.1	1053 5.3	1655 1.1	2308 5.2
31 TU	0520 1.0	1133 5.4	1739 1.0	2349 5.4

JUNE

Day	Time m	Time m	Time m	Time m
1 W ●	0559 1.0	1211 5.5	1820 0.9	
2 TH	0028 5.5	0637 0.9	1248 5.6	1901 0.8
3 F	0107 5.6	0715 0.9	1325 5.6	1942 0.7
4 SA	0146 5.6	0753 0.9	1402 5.6	2024 0.7
5 SU	0226 5.7	0833 0.9	1440 5.6	2107 0.6
6 M	0308 5.7	0913 1.0	1521 5.5	2150 0.7
7 TU	0353 5.6	0955 1.1	1605 5.4	2235 0.8
8 W	0443 5.5	1041 1.2	1655 5.3	2325 0.8
9 TH	0538 5.3	1135 1.3	1753 5.2	
10 F	0023 0.9	0641 5.2	1238 1.3	1859 5.2
11 SA	0131 0.9	0750 5.2	1349 1.3	2011 5.2
12 SU	0240 0.9	0857 5.2	1459 1.2	2119 5.3
13 M	0347 0.9	1000 5.4	1607 1.1	2223 5.5
14 TU	0450 0.8	1058 5.5	1714 0.9	2321 5.6
15 W ○	0547 0.8	1151 5.6	1814 0.8	
16 TH ●	0015 5.7	0636 0.8	1240 5.7	1907 0.6
17 F	0106 5.8	0720 0.8	1325 5.7	1955 0.6
18 SA	0153 5.8	0801 0.9	1408 5.7	2039 0.6
19 SU	0237 5.8	0839 1.0	1448 5.6	2119 0.7
20 M	0320 5.6	0914 1.1	1527 5.5	2154 0.8
21 TU	0401 5.5	0947 1.2	1605 5.3	2226 0.9
22 W	0442 5.3	1022 1.3	1645 5.2	2300 1.1
23 TH ◗	0525 5.1	1103 1.5	1730 5.0	2341 1.2
24 F	0613 4.9	1154 1.6	1823 4.8	
25 SA	0036 1.4	0708 4.7	1258 1.7	1925 4.7
26 SU	0147 1.4	0810 4.7	1414 1.7	2033 4.7
27 M	0256 1.4	0912 4.9	1522 1.5	2137 4.9
28 TU	0354 1.3	1010 5.1	1619 1.3	2234 5.1
29 W	0445 1.2	1102 5.3	1711 1.1	2324 5.3
30 TH ○	0532 1.0	1148 5.5	1759 0.9	

JULY

Day	Time m	Time m	Time m	Time m
1 F ●	0009 5.5	0615 1.0	1231 5.6	1845 0.8
2 SA	0052 5.6	0658 0.9	1311 5.7	1932 0.7
3 SU	0134 5.7	0741 0.9	1350 5.7	2018 0.5
4 M	0216 5.8	0824 0.8	1430 5.7	2103 0.4
5 TU	0258 5.9	0906 0.8	1510 5.7	2147 0.5
6 W	0342 5.8	0947 0.9	1553 5.7	2229 0.5
7 TH	0428 5.7	1028 1.0	1638 5.6	2311 0.7
8 F ◗	0518 5.5	1112 1.2	1730 5.5	2358 0.8
9 SA	0615 5.3	1206 1.3	1831 5.3	
10 SU	0057 1.0	0720 5.2	1315 1.4	1943 5.2
11 M	0210 1.1	0830 5.1	1435 1.3	2058 5.2
12 TU	0323 1.1	0940 5.2	1553 1.2	2211 5.3
13 W	0432 1.1	1045 5.3	1708 1.0	2315 5.5
14 TH	0533 1.1	1141 5.5	1811 0.8	
15 F ○	0010 5.6	0623 1.0	1230 5.6	1901 0.7
16 SA	0058 5.7	0706 1.0	1313 5.7	1945 0.6
17 SU	0141 5.8	0744 1.0	1352 5.7	2024 0.6
18 M	0221 5.8	0819 1.0	1429 5.7	2059 0.6
19 TU	0258 5.7	0851 1.0	1503 5.6	2129 0.7
20 W	0332 5.5	0921 1.1	1535 5.5	2155 0.8
21 TH	0406 5.4	0951 1.2	1608 5.4	2222 1.0
22 F	0441 5.2	1024 1.3	1645 5.2	2254 1.1
23 SA	0519 5.0	1103 1.5	1727 5.0	2334 1.3
24 SU	0606 4.8	1153 1.7	1821 4.7	
25 M	0030 1.5	0705 4.7	1303 1.8	1932 4.6
26 TU	0154 1.6	0818 4.7	1434 1.7	2050 4.7
27 W	0313 1.5	0930 4.9	1546 1.4	2201 4.9
28 TH	0415 1.3	1033 5.2	1646 1.2	2300 5.2
29 F	0508 1.2	1125 5.4	1740 0.9	2350 5.5
30 SA ●	0556 1.0	1211 5.6	1831 0.7	
31 SU	0035 5.8	0642 0.9	1254 5.8	1919 0.5

AUGUST

Day	Time m	Time m	Time m	Time m
1 M	0119 5.9	0727 0.8	1334 5.9	2005 0.4
2 TU	0200 6.0	0811 0.8	1413 6.0	2050 0.3
3 W	0242 6.1	0853 0.7	1453 6.0	2132 0.3
4 TH	0324 6.0	0932 0.8	1534 5.9	2211 0.4
5 F	0407 5.8	1009 0.9	1617 5.8	2248 0.6
6 SA ◗	0454 5.6	1049 1.1	1707 5.6	2329 0.9
7 SU	0547 5.3	1139 1.3	1807 5.3	
8 M	0025 1.2	0651 5.1	1249 1.4	1922 5.1
9 TU	0143 1.4	0806 4.9	1421 1.4	2046 5.0
10 W	0306 1.4	0925 5.0	1551 1.3	2206 5.2
11 TH	0421 1.3	1035 5.2	1708 1.0	2310 5.5
12 F	0523 1.2	1131 5.5	1804 0.8	
13 SA ○	0001 5.7	0609 1.1	1217 5.6	1848 0.7
14 SU	0045 5.8	0648 1.0	1256 5.7	1926 0.7
15 M	0123 5.8	0722 1.0	1331 5.7	1959 0.6
16 TU	0157 5.8	0754 1.0	1403 5.8	2029 0.7
17 W	0229 5.7	0825 1.0	1434 5.7	2057 0.7
18 TH	0259 5.6	0854 1.0	1503 5.7	2122 0.9
19 F	0329 5.5	0921 1.1	1534 5.5	2147 1.0
20 SA	0359 5.3	0949 1.3	1607 5.3	2213 1.2
21 SU ◗	0433 5.2	1021 1.4	1644 5.1	2247 1.4
22 M	0514 4.9	1103 1.6	1732 4.9	2334 1.6
23 TU	0608 4.7	1205 1.7	1837 4.6	
24 W	0049 1.8	0723 4.6	1342 1.8	2004 4.6
25 TH	0232 1.7	0850 4.8	1513 1.5	2128 4.9
26 F	0344 1.5	1002 5.1	1620 1.2	2234 5.3
27 SA	0443 1.2	1059 5.5	1719 0.9	2327 5.7
28 SU	0534 1.0	1147 5.7	1812 0.6	
29 M ●	0013 5.9	0622 0.9	1230 5.9	1900 0.4
30 TU	0057 6.1	0707 0.8	1311 6.1	1945 0.3
31 W	0139 6.2	0751 0.6	1351 6.2	2028 0.2

Chart Datum: 2·90 metres below Ordnance Datum (Newlyn)
HAT is 6·3 metres above Chart Datum

SHEERNESS

LAT 51°27'N   LONG 0°45'E

TIMES AND HEIGHTS OF HIGH AND LOW WATERS

2011

SEPTEMBER

Day	Time	m	Time	m	Time	m	Time	m
1 TH	0220	6.2	0833	0.7	1431	6.2	2109	0.3
16 F	0225	5.7	0826	1.0	1433	5.7	2048	0.9
2 F	0301	6.1	0912	0.7	1513	6.1	2146	0.5
17 SA	0253	5.6	0854	1.1	1503	5.6	2113	1.0
3 SA	0343	5.8	0950	0.9	1557	5.9	2222	0.8
18 SU	0323	5.5	0921	1.1	1536	5.4	2138	1.2
4 SU ◔	0428	5.6	1029	1.0	1647	5.6	2302	1.1
19 M	0356	5.3	0949	1.3	1613	5.2	2207	1.4
5 M	0519	5.2	1118	1.3	1749	5.3	2357	1.4
20 TU ◔	0434	5.1	1027	1.5	1659	5.0	2251	1.6
6 TU	0624	5.0	1231	1.5	1908	5.0		
21	0525	4.8	1125	1.6	1800	4.8		
7 W	0119	1.6	0744	4.8	1414	1.4	2035	5.0
22 TH	0002	1.8	0635	4.7	1256	1.7	1923	4.7
8 TH	0248	1.6	0908	4.9	1545	1.3	2154	5.2
23 F	0147	1.8	0807	4.7	1438	1.5	2052	5.0
9 F	0405	1.5	1018	5.2	1656	1.0	2255	5.5
24 SA	0309	1.6	0926	5.1	1549	1.1	2203	5.4
10 SA	0504	1.3	1112	5.5	1746	0.8	2343	5.7
25 SU	0411	1.3	1026	5.5	1650	0.8	2258	5.7
11 SU	0548	1.2	1155	5.6	1825	0.8		
26 M	0506	1.0	1116	5.8	1746	0.6	2346	6.0
12 M ○	0023	5.8	0622	1.1	1232	5.7	1857	0.7
27 TU ●	0556	0.9	1201	6.0	1835	0.4		
13 TU	0058	5.8	0654	1.0	1304	5.8	1926	0.7
28 W	0031	6.1	0643	0.8	1244	6.2	1920	0.3
14 W	0128	5.8	0725	0.9	1334	5.8	1954	0.7
29 TH	0113	6.2	0728	0.7	1326	6.3	2003	0.3
15 TH	0157	5.7	0756	0.9	1403	5.8	2022	0.8
30 F	0155	6.2	0812	0.6	1409	6.3	2043	0.4

OCTOBER

Day	Time	m	Time	m	Time	m	Time	m
1 SA	0237	6.1	0853	0.7	1453	6.2	2121	0.6
16 SU	0223	5.7	0830	1.0	1438	5.6	2045	1.1
2 SU	0319	5.8	0933	0.8	1540	5.9	2157	0.9
17 M	0254	5.5	0900	1.1	1513	5.5	2112	1.2
3 M	0404	5.5	1014	1.0	1632	5.6	2238	1.3
18 TU	0328	5.4	0930	1.2	1551	5.3	2143	1.4
4 TU ◔	0455	5.2	1104	1.2	1734	5.2	2331	1.6
19 W	0407	5.2	1009	1.3	1638	5.1	2227	1.6
5 W	0600	4.9	1218	1.5	1850	5.0		
20 TH	0456	5.0	1104	1.5	1737	5.0	2333	1.8
6	0050	1.8	0718	4.8	1358	1.5	2013	5.0
21	0602	4.8	1224	1.5	1852	4.9		
7 F	0219	1.8	0839	4.9	1521	1.3	2129	5.2
22 SA	0103	1.8	0725	4.8	1359	1.4	2015	5.1
8 SA	0332	1.6	0949	5.2	1626	1.0	2228	5.5
23 SU	0228	1.6	0845	5.1	1513	1.1	2127	5.4
9 SU	0431	1.4	1043	5.4	1714	0.9	2315	5.6
24 M	0334	1.3	0949	5.4	1616	0.8	2226	5.7
10 M	0515	1.2	1126	5.6	1751	0.9	2354	5.7
25 TU	0431	1.1	1043	5.7	1714	0.6	2317	5.9
11 TU	0551	1.1	1202	5.6	1821	0.9		
26 W ●	0526	0.9	1132	6.0	1806	0.5		
12 W ○	0027	5.7	0623	1.0	1235	5.7	1849	0.8
27 TH	0004	6.1	0617	0.8	1219	6.1	1853	0.5
13 TH	0057	5.7	0656	0.9	1305	5.7	1918	0.8
28 F	0049	6.1	0706	0.6	1305	6.2	1937	0.5
14 F	0125	5.7	0728	0.9	1335	5.8	1947	0.9
29 SA	0132	6.1	0753	0.6	1351	6.2	2018	0.6
15 SA	0153	5.7	0800	0.9	1406	5.7	2016	0.9
30 SU	0216	6.0	0838	0.6	1438	6.1	2058	0.8
31 M	0259	5.8	0921	0.8	1527	5.8	2136	1.1

NOVEMBER

Day	Time	m	Time	m	Time	m	Time	m
1 TU	0345	5.5	1004	1.0	1619	5.6	2216	1.3
16 W	0309	5.4	0924	1.1	1538	5.4	2132	1.3
2 W ◔	0435	5.2	1052	1.2	1717	5.3	2305	1.6
17 TH	0350	5.3	1005	1.1	1625	5.3	2216	1.4
3 TH	0533	5.0	1157	1.4	1824	5.0		
18 F	0438	5.1	1055	1.2	1720	5.2	2312	1.6
4	0011	1.8	0642	4.8	1322	1.4	1935	5.0
19 SA	0536	5.0	1159	1.3	1825	5.1		
5 SA	0133	1.8	0757	4.8	1436	1.3	2047	5.0
20	0023	1.6	0647	5.0	1317	1.2	1939	5.1
6 SU	0245	1.7	0906	5.0	1538	1.2	2149	5.2
21 M	0142	1.5	0803	5.1	1433	1.1	2050	5.3
7 M	0344	1.5	1003	5.2	1627	1.1	2238	5.4
22 TU	0253	1.4	0912	5.4	1540	0.9	2153	5.5
8 TU	0433	1.3	1050	5.4	1707	1.0	2318	5.5
23 W	0357	1.2	1012	5.6	1641	0.8	2249	5.7
9 W	0515	1.2	1129	5.5	1742	1.0	2353	5.6
24 TH	0457	1.0	1108	5.8	1737	0.7	2340	5.9
10 TH ○	0552	1.0	1204	5.6	1814	0.9		
25 F ●	0556	0.8	1159	6.0	1828	0.6		
11 F	0025	5.6	0628	0.9	1238	5.6	1845	0.9
26 SA	0028	5.9	0650	0.7	1250	6.1	1915	0.6
12 SA	0056	5.7	0703	0.9	1311	5.7	1917	0.9
27 SU	0115	5.9	0741	0.6	1339	6.1	1958	0.7
13 SU	0127	5.7	0737	0.9	1345	5.7	1950	1.0
28 M	0200	5.7	0828	0.6	1427	6.0	2039	0.9
14 M	0200	5.6	0813	0.9	1420	5.6	2023	1.0
29 TU	0244	5.7	0912	0.7	1515	5.8	2117	1.1
15 TU	0233	5.6	0848	1.0	1457	5.5	2056	1.2
30 W	0328	5.6	0955	0.9	1604	5.6	2155	1.3

DECEMBER

Day	Time	m	Time	m	Time	m	Time	m
1 TH	0414	5.3	1036	1.0	1654	5.3	2236	1.5
16 F	0338	5.5	1003	0.9	1612	5.5	2205	1.2
2 F ◔	0503	5.1	1123	1.2	1747	5.1	2325	1.6
17 SA	0422	5.4	1046	0.9	1702	5.3	2251	1.3
3 SA	0558	5.0	1221	1.4	1847	4.9		
18 SU ◔	0513	5.3	1135	1.0	1759	5.2	2347	1.4
4	0028	1.8	0701	4.8	1331	1.4	1950	4.8
19 M	0613	5.2	1236	1.1	1905	5.1		
5 M	0142	1.8	0808	4.8	1436	1.4	2053	4.9
20	0055	1.4	0724	5.2	1351	1.1	2015	5.2
6 TU	0250	1.7	0912	4.9	1531	1.3	2150	5.0
21 W	0213	1.4	0838	5.2	1506	1.0	2123	5.3
7 W	0347	1.5	1007	5.1	1620	1.2	2238	5.2
22 TH	0328	1.2	0948	5.4	1614	1.0	2226	5.4
8 TH	0438	1.3	1055	5.2	1703	1.1	2320	5.4
23 F	0438	1.0	1051	5.6	1716	0.9	2323	5.6
9 F	0522	1.1	1137	5.4	1742	1.1	2358	5.5
24 SA ●	0545	0.8	1149	5.7	1811	0.8		
10 SA ○	0604	1.0	1215	5.5	1819	1.0		
25 SU	0015	5.7	0642	0.7	1242	5.9	1859	0.8
11 SU	0034	5.6	0642	0.9	1253	5.6	1854	1.0
26 M	0103	5.8	0733	0.6	1331	5.9	1942	0.8
12 M	0109	5.6	0721	0.8	1330	5.6	1930	0.9
27 TU	0147	5.8	0820	0.5	1417	5.9	2022	0.9
13 TU	0144	5.6	0801	0.8	1407	5.7	2008	0.9
28 W	0229	5.7	0902	0.6	1500	5.8	2058	1.0
14 W	0220	5.6	0842	0.8	1446	5.7	2046	1.0
29 TH	0310	5.6	0939	0.7	1542	5.6	2132	1.1
15 TH	0258	5.5	0923	0.8	1528	5.6	2125	1.1
30 F	0349	5.5	1011	0.9	1623	5.4	2205	1.3
31 SA	0428	5.3	1042	1.0	1705	5.2	2241	1.4

Chart Datum: 2·90 metres below Ordnance Datum (Newlyn)
HAT is 6·3 metres above Chart Datum

TIDES

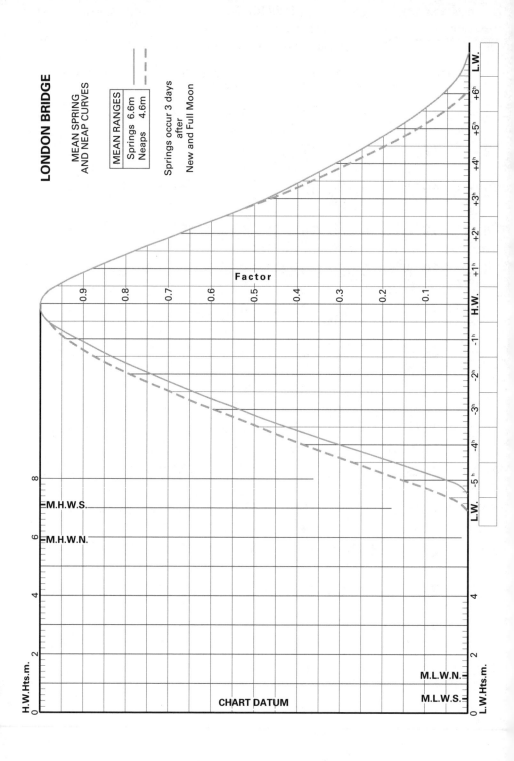

LONDON BRIDGE

MEAN SPRING
AND NEAP CURVES

MEAN RANGES	
Springs	6.6m
Neaps	4.6m

Springs occur 3 days
after
New and Full Moon

LONDON BRIDGE

LAT 51°30′N   LONG 0°05′W

TIMES AND HEIGHTS OF HIGH AND LOW WATERS

2011

	JANUARY		FEBRUARY		MARCH		APRIL	
	Time m	Time m	Time m	Time m	Time m	Time m	Time m	Time m

JANUARY

	Time m		Time m
1 SA	0452 1.4 / 1056 6.3 / 1725 1.2 / 2335 6.2	**16** SU	0417 1.7 / 1030 5.9 / 1642 1.5 / 2305 6.0
2 SU	0611 1.2 / 1202 6.5 / 1838 1.2	**17** M	0535 1.4 / 1135 6.2 / 1751 1.3
3 M	0036 6.4 / 0716 0.9 / 1259 6.6 / 1934 1.1	**18** TU	0009 6.3 / 0640 1.0 / 1232 6.6 / 1854 1.1
4 TU	0128 6.5 / 0810 0.7 / 1349 6.6 / ● 2021 1.1	**19** W	0104 6.6 / 0743 0.7 / 1324 6.9 / ○ 1957 1.1
5 W	0212 6.6 / 0857 0.6 / 1433 6.6 / 2103 1.1	**20** TH	0153 6.8 / 0841 0.5 / 1413 7.1 / 2053 0.9
6 TH	0252 6.7 / 0939 0.6 / 1513 6.9 / 2139 1.1	**21** F	0239 6.9 / 0932 0.3 / 1459 7.3 / 2142 0.8
7 F	0327 6.7 / 1014 0.7 / 1550 6.8 / 2208 1.2	**22** SA	0322 7.1 / 1018 0.1 / 1543 7.4 / 2226 0.7
8 SA	0400 6.7 / 1041 0.8 / 1623 6.7 / 2234 1.2	**23** SU	0403 7.2 / 1100 0.0 / 1626 7.4 / 2306 0.7
9 SU	0431 6.6 / 1102 0.8 / 1654 6.6 / 2304 1.2	**24** M	0443 7.1 / 1137 0.1 / 1710 7.2 / 2343 0.8
10 M	0501 6.5 / 1128 0.8 / 1725 6.4 / 2336 1.3	**25** TU	0524 7.0 / 1211 0.3 / 1755 6.9
11 TU	0533 6.4 / 1156 0.9 / 1759 6.2	**26** W	0020 0.9 / 0607 6.8 / 1246 0.5 / ◑ 1843 6.6
12 W	0009 1.4 / 0608 6.2 / 1227 1.1 / ◑ 1837 6.0	**27** TH	0101 1.1 / 0658 6.6 / 1327 0.9 / 1939 6.3
13 TH	0044 1.6 / 0652 5.9 / 1302 1.3 / 1925 5.8	**28** F	0151 1.4 / 0801 6.3 / 1424 1.2 / 2043 6.0
14 F	0128 1.7 / 0747 5.6 / 1349 1.5 / 2034 5.6	**29** SA	0259 1.6 / 0916 6.1 / 1535 1.5 / 2157 5.8
15 SA	0229 1.8 / 0911 5.7 / 1500 1.6 / 2155 5.7	**30** SU	0421 1.6 / 1036 6.0 / 1654 1.5 / 2319 5.9
		31 M	0553 1.3 / 1152 6.2 / 1818 1.4

FEBRUARY

	Time m		Time m
1 TU	0026 6.2 / 0703 0.9 / 1252 6.5 / 1917 1.2	**16** W	0613 1.0 / 1209 6.6 / 1833 1.2
2 W	0118 6.5 / 0756 0.7 / 1340 6.7 / 2005 1.1	**17** TH	0043 6.6 / 0726 0.6 / 1305 7.0 / 1945 1.0
3 TH	0201 6.6 / 0841 0.6 / 1421 6.8 / ● 2046 1.1	**18** F	0134 6.9 / 0826 0.3 / 1355 7.2 / ○ 2042 0.8
4 F	0237 6.7 / 0920 0.6 / 1458 6.8 / 2122 1.1	**19** SA	0219 7.1 / 0917 0.1 / 1441 7.4 / 2130 0.7
5 SA	0310 6.8 / 0952 0.7 / 1529 6.8 / 2153 1.1	**20** SU	0302 7.3 / 1002 -0.1 / 1524 7.5 / 2214 0.6
6 SU	0339 6.8 / 1018 0.7 / 1557 6.8 / 2219 1.0	**21** M	0342 7.4 / 1042 -0.1 / 1606 7.4 / 2252 0.5
7 M	0407 6.8 / 1039 0.7 / 1624 6.6 / 2246 1.1	**22** TU	0422 7.4 / 1117 0.0 / 1648 7.2 / 2327 0.6
8 TU	0435 6.7 / 1102 0.7 / 1652 6.6 / 2314 1.1	**23** W	0502 7.2 / 1147 0.3 / 1729 6.8
9 W	0505 6.6 / 1127 0.8 / 1723 6.4 / 2341 1.2	**24** TH	0000 0.8 / 0544 7.0 / 1216 0.6 / ◐ 1813 6.5
10 TH	0537 6.4 / 1150 0.8 / 1758 6.1	**25** F	0034 1.0 / 0632 6.6 / 1251 1.0 / 1902 6.1
11 F	0008 1.4 / 0615 6.2 / 1219 1.1 / ◐ 1839 5.9	**26** SA	0117 1.3 / 0731 6.2 / 1343 1.4 / 2005 5.8
12 SA	0044 1.5 / 0703 5.9 / 1300 1.3 / 1933 5.6	**27** SU	0222 1.6 / 0848 5.9 / 1501 1.7 / 2126 5.6
13 SU	0136 1.6 / 0807 5.7 / 1400 1.6 / 2057 5.5	**28** M	0350 1.6 / 1015 5.8 / 1627 1.7 / 2259 5.7
14 M	0301 1.8 / 0943 5.7 / 1552 1.7 / 2228 5.7		
15 TU	0459 1.4 / 1104 6.1 / 1720 1.4 / 2343 6.1		

MARCH

	Time m		Time m
1 TU	0534 1.3 / 1136 6.1 / 1756 1.4	**16** W	0425 1.4 / 1033 6.1 / 1652 1.5 / 2312 6.1
2 W	0007 6.1 / 0646 0.9 / 1236 6.5 / 1855 1.2	**17** TH	0544 0.9 / 1143 6.6 / 1807 1.2
3 TH	0058 6.5 / 0735 0.7 / 1321 6.7 / 1941 1.0	**18** F	0015 6.6 / 0702 0.6 / 1241 7.0 / 1922 0.9
4 F	0139 6.6 / 0816 0.6 / 1400 6.8 / ● 2022 1.0	**19** SA	0107 7.0 / 0804 0.3 / 1331 7.2 / ○ 2020 0.8
5 SA	0214 6.7 / 0850 0.7 / 1433 6.8 / 2058 1.0	**20** SU	0153 7.2 / 0854 0.1 / 1417 7.4 / 2110 0.6
6 SU	0244 6.8 / 0921 0.7 / 1502 6.8 / 2129 0.9	**21** M	0236 7.4 / 0939 0.0 / 1501 7.4 / 2154 0.5
7 M	0312 6.9 / 0946 0.7 / 1527 6.8 / 2157 0.9	**22** TU	0318 7.5 / 1018 0.1 / 1542 7.3 / 2233 0.5
8 TU	0339 6.9 / 1010 0.6 / 1553 6.8 / 2225 0.9	**23** W	0359 7.5 / 1051 0.3 / 1623 7.1 / 2307 0.5
9 W	0408 6.9 / 1034 0.7 / 1622 6.7 / 2252 0.9	**24** TH	0440 7.3 / 1118 0.5 / 1704 6.7 / 2338 0.7
10 TH	0438 6.7 / 1057 0.8 / 1653 6.5 / 2317 1.1	**25** F	0523 7.0 / 1145 0.8 / 1746 6.4
11 F	0511 6.5 / 1120 0.9 / 1727 6.2 / 2341 1.2	**26** SA	0009 0.9 / 0611 6.6 / 1220 1.2 / ◐ 1832 6.0
12 SA	0548 6.3 / 1148 1.0 / 1806 6.0 / ◐	**27** SU	0049 1.2 / 0708 6.1 / 1310 1.6 / 1931 5.7
13 SU	0013 1.2 / 0634 6.1 / 1227 1.2 / 1858 5.7	**28** M	0149 1.5 / 0822 5.8 / 1428 1.8 / 2051 5.5
14 M	0102 1.4 / 0734 5.9 / 1324 1.5 / 2012 5.5	**29** TU	0318 1.6 / 0946 5.8 / 1555 1.8 / 2222 5.7
15 TU	0217 1.6 / 0905 5.8 / 1511 1.8 / 2151 5.7	**30** W	0450 1.4 / 1106 6.0 / 1717 1.5 / 2334 6.0
		31 TH	0608 1.0 / 1207 6.4 / 1819 1.2

APRIL

	Time m		Time m
1 F	0025 6.4 / 0657 0.8 / 1252 6.6 / 1907 1.1	**16** SA	0628 0.5 / 1213 7.0 / 1852 0.9
2 SA	0107 6.6 / 0737 0.6 / 1330 6.7 / 1949 1.0	**17** SU	0037 7.0 / 0733 0.3 / 1305 7.1 / 1954 0.8
3 SU	0142 6.7 / 0812 0.7 / 1402 6.7 / 2027 0.9	**18** M	0125 7.2 / 0825 0.2 / 1352 7.2 / ○ 2046 0.6
4 M	0213 6.8 / 0843 0.7 / 1430 6.7 / 2101 0.9	**19** TU	0210 7.4 / 0911 0.3 / 1436 7.2 / 2131 0.5
5 TU	0242 6.9 / 0912 0.7 / 1456 6.8 / 2133 0.8	**20** W	0254 7.5 / 0950 0.4 / 1519 7.1 / 2212 0.4
6 W	0311 7.0 / 0938 0.7 / 1524 6.8 / 2203 0.8	**21** TH	0338 7.5 / 1024 0.5 / 1601 7.0 / 2248 0.5
7 TH	0342 6.9 / 1004 0.7 / 1556 6.7 / 2231 0.8	**22** F	0421 7.3 / 1052 0.8 / 1642 6.7 / 2318 0.7
8 F	0415 6.8 / 1029 0.8 / 1629 6.5 / 2257 0.9	**23** SA	0506 6.9 / 1120 1.0 / 1724 6.3 / 2348 0.9
9 SA	0450 6.7 / 1056 0.9 / 1704 6.3 / 2322 1.0	**24** SU	0553 6.5 / 1156 1.3 / 1809 6.0
10 SU	0529 6.5 / 1128 1.0 / 1744 6.1 / 2356 1.0	**25** M	0026 1.1 / 0647 6.1 / 1243 1.6 / ◐ 1903 5.8
11 M	0617 6.3 / 1209 1.2 / 1837 5.9 / ◐	**26** TU	0120 1.3 / 0753 5.9 / 1350 1.8 / 2014 5.6
12 TU	0044 1.2 / 0717 6.1 / 1307 1.5 / 1947 5.7	**27** W	0239 1.4 / 0905 5.8 / 1513 1.8 / 2132 5.7
13 W	0157 1.4 / 0841 6.0 / 1449 1.7 / 2118 5.8	**28** TH	0357 1.3 / 1017 5.9 / 1628 1.6 / 2243 5.9
14 TH	0355 1.2 / 1004 6.3 / 1623 1.4 / 2238 6.2	**29** F	0502 1.1 / 1122 6.2 / 1730 1.3 / 2341 6.2
15 F	0511 0.9 / 1113 6.7 / 1737 1.1 / 2342 6.6	**30** SA	0558 1.0 / 1212 6.4 / 1824 1.1

Chart Datum: 3·20 metres below Ordnance Datum (Newlyn)
HAT is 7·6 metres above Chart Datum

TIDES

251

LONDON BRIDGE

TIME ZONE (UT)	LAT 51°30'N LONG 0°05'W	Dates in amber are **SPRINGS**
For Summer Time add ONE hour in **non-shaded areas**	TIMES AND HEIGHTS OF HIGH AND LOW WATERS	Dates in yellow are **NEAPS** **2011**

MAY

Day				
1 SU	0027 6.5	0645 0.9	1253 6.5	1911 1.0
2 M	0107 6.7	0728 0.8	1327 6.6	1953 0.9
3 TU	0141 6.8	0806 0.8	1359 6.7	● 2033 0.8
4 W	0214 6.9	0839 0.8	1430 6.7	2109 0.7
5 TH	0246 6.9	0910 0.8	1502 6.7	2144 0.7
6 F	0321 6.9	0939 0.8	1537 6.6	2216 0.7
7 SA	0357 6.9	1010 0.8	1613 6.5	2245 0.7
8 SU	0436 6.8	1043 0.9	1651 6.3	2316 0.8
9 M	0518 6.6	1121 1.0	1734 6.2	2353 0.8
10 TU	0608 6.5	1205 1.2	1827 6.1	◐
11 W	0041 1.0	0707 6.3	1305 1.4	1931 6.0
12 TH	0154 1.1	0822 6.3	1432 1.5	2051 6.1
13 F	0326 0.9	0937 6.4	1555 1.3	2206 6.3
14 SA	0438 0.7	1044 6.6	1707 1.1	2311 6.6
15 SU	0549 0.6	1145 6.8	1822 1.0	
16 M	0009 6.9	0659 0.5	1240 6.9	1927 0.8
17 TU	0101 7.1	0756 0.5	1330 6.9	○ 2022 0.6
18 W	0149 7.3	0843 0.5	1416 7.0	2111 0.5
19 TH	0236 7.3	0926 0.6	1501 7.0	2154 0.4
20 F	0321 7.3	1002 0.8	1544 6.9	2233 0.5
21 SA	0407 7.1	1033 0.9	1626 6.7	2306 0.6
22 SU	0452 6.9	1103 1.1	1707 6.4	2335 0.8
23 M	0537 6.5	1138 1.2	1749 6.2	
24 TU	0009 1.0	0625 6.2	1220 1.4	◑ 1835 6.0
25 W	0053 1.1	0719 6.0	1311 1.6	1933 5.8
26 TH	0151 1.2	0820 5.9	1416 1.7	2042 5.8
27 F	0302 1.3	0922 5.9	1531 1.6	2148 5.9
28 SA	0406 1.2	1023 6.0	1639 1.5	2249 6.1
29 SU	0503 1.1	1120 6.1	1737 1.2	2343 6.3
30 M	0556 1.0	1210 6.3	1831 1.0	
31 TU	0029 6.6	0646 0.9	1253 6.5	1920 0.9

JUNE

Day				
1 W	0111 6.7	0732 0.9	1333 6.6	● 2006 0.7
2 TH	0150 6.8	0813 0.8	1411 6.7	2050 0.6
3 F	0228 6.9	0850 0.9	1449 6.7	2131 0.6
4 SA	0307 7.0	0926 0.9	1527 6.7	2210 0.5
5 SU	0347 7.0	1004 0.8	1606 6.6	2248 0.5
6 M	0428 7.0	1043 0.9	1646 6.6	2324 0.5
7 TU	0513 6.9	1125 0.9	1729 6.5	
8 W	0002 0.6	0601 6.7	1212 1.1	1817 6.4
9 TH	0049 0.7	0657 6.5	1306 1.2	◑ 1915 6.3
10 F	0148 0.8	0802 6.4	1413 1.3	2025 6.3
11 SA	0257 0.8	0910 6.4	1526 1.3	2137 6.4
12 SU	0405 0.8	1016 6.4	1640 1.2	2243 6.5
13 M	0514 0.8	1120 6.5	1755 1.0	2346 6.7
14 TU	0627 0.8	1221 6.6	1905 0.8	
15 W	0043 6.9	0730 0.8	1315 6.7	○ 2003 0.6
16 TH	0136 7.0	0822 0.8	1404 6.8	2055 0.4
17 F	0224 7.1	0907 0.8	1449 6.8	2141 0.4
18 SA	0311 7.2	0947 0.9	1532 6.8	2223 0.4
19 SU	0355 7.1	1022 1.0	1612 6.7	2258 0.6
20 M	0437 6.9	1051 1.1	1650 6.6	2325 0.7
21 TU	0517 6.6	1122 1.2	1727 6.4	2351 0.8
22 W	0557 6.4	1157 1.2	1805 6.3	
23 TH	0024 0.9	0638 6.2	1236 1.4	◑ 1848 6.1
24 F	0103 1.0	0726 6.0	1322 1.5	1944 5.9
25 SA	0151 1.2	0824 5.8	1418 1.7	2052 5.8
26 SU	0255 1.4	0926 5.8	1537 1.7	2157 5.9
27 M	0409 1.4	1027 5.9	1651 1.4	2258 6.1
28 TU	0512 1.2	1128 6.1	1752 1.1	2354 6.4
29 W	0608 1.1	1222 6.4	1849 0.9	
30 TH	0044 6.6	0702 1.0	1311 6.6	1943 0.7

JULY

Day				
1 F	0130 6.8	0753 1.0	1356 6.7	● 2034 0.6
2 SA	0213 7.0	0841 1.0	1438 6.8	2122 0.4
3 SU	0256 7.1	0927 0.9	1519 6.9	2208 0.3
4 M	0338 7.2	1011 0.8	1559 6.9	2250 0.2
5 TU	0420 7.2	1052 0.7	1638 6.9	2329 0.2
6 W	0503 7.1	1132 0.8	1719 6.8	
7 TH	0006 0.3	0549 6.9	1213 0.9	1803 6.7
8 F	0044 0.5	0639 6.6	1257 1.1	◑ 1854 6.6
9 SA	0129 0.7	0737 6.4	1350 1.3	1956 6.4
10 SU	0226 0.9	0842 6.3	1457 1.4	2108 6.4
11 M	0333 1.0	0949 6.2	1612 1.3	2220 6.4
12 TU	0444 1.1	1100 6.2	1732 1.1	2330 6.5
13 W	0603 1.1	1210 6.3	1849 0.9	
14 TH	0035 6.7	0711 1.0	1307 6.5	1950 0.6
15 F	0130 6.9	0806 0.9	1356 6.7	○ 2042 0.4
16 SA	0218 7.0	0852 0.9	1439 6.8	2128 0.4
17 SU	0301 7.1	0934 0.9	1519 6.9	2209 0.4
18 M	0341 7.0	1009 1.0	1554 6.9	2242 0.5
19 TU	0417 6.9	1038 1.0	1627 6.8	2306 0.6
20 W	0450 6.7	1104 1.0	1659 6.7	2327 0.7
21 TH	0522 6.5	1132 1.1	1731 6.5	2352 0.8
22 F	0554 6.3	1204 1.2	1805 6.3	
23 SA	0020 1.0	0629 6.0	1238 1.4	◑ 1845 6.0
24 SU	0053 1.2	0714 5.8	1319 1.6	1937 5.8
25 M	0136 1.4	0818 5.6	1416 1.8	2057 5.7
26 TU	0242 1.6	0937 5.6	1559 1.7	2214 5.8
27 W	0425 1.6	1049 5.9	1715 1.3	2320 6.2
28 TH	0534 1.3	1154 6.2	1819 0.9	
29 F	0018 6.5	0636 1.1	1249 6.5	1921 0.7
30 SA	0109 6.8	0737 1.0	1337 6.8	● 2019 0.5
31 SU	0156 7.1	0833 0.9	1422 6.9	2110 0.3

AUGUST

Day				
1 M	0240 7.3	0922 0.8	1503 7.1	2157 0.1
2 TU	0323 7.4	1007 0.7	1543 7.2	2240 0.0
3 W	0405 7.3	1048 0.6	1622 7.2	2318 0.0
4 TH	0446 7.2	1125 0.7	1701 7.1	2352 0.2
5 F	0529 6.9	1201 0.8	1743 6.9	
6 SA	0024 0.5	0614 6.6	1239 1.0	◑ 1829 6.7
7 SU	0101 0.8	0707 6.3	1325 1.2	1928 6.4
8 M	0152 1.1	0810 6.0	1427 1.4	2041 6.2
9 TU	0303 1.4	0923 5.9	1547 1.4	2201 6.1
10 W	0421 1.4	1045 6.0	1716 1.2	2320 6.3
11 TH	0548 1.3	1159 6.2	1839 0.9	
12 F	0027 6.6	0656 1.1	1257 6.6	1937 0.5
13 SA	0121 6.9	0749 0.9	1343 6.8	○ 2026 0.4
14 SU	0205 7.0	0834 0.9	1423 6.9	2108 0.4
15 M	0244 7.0	0914 0.9	1458 6.9	2144 0.5
16 TU	0319 7.0	0948 1.0	1529 7.0	2213 0.6
17 W	0349 6.9	1016 1.0	1559 6.9	2236 0.6
18 TH	0417 6.8	1040 1.0	1627 6.9	2255 0.7
19 F	0444 6.6	1107 1.0	1657 6.7	2318 0.8
20 SA	0513 6.4	1134 1.2	1728 6.4	2341 1.0
21 SU	0545 6.1	1200 1.3	1804 6.2	◑
22 M	0007 1.2	0623 5.9	1231 1.5	1847 5.9
23 TU	0042 1.4	0713 5.6	1317 1.7	1947 5.7
24 W	0136 1.7	0831 5.4	1435 1.8	2122 5.6
25 TH	0323 1.9	1008 5.6	1638 1.5	2244 6.0
26 F	0459 1.5	1122 6.1	1748 1.0	2349 6.5
27 SA	0608 1.2	1222 6.5	1857 0.5	
28 SU	0044 6.9	0716 1.0	1312 6.9	1959 0.4
29 M	0133 7.2	0816 0.9	1357 7.1	● 2051 0.2
30 TU	0218 7.4	0906 0.8	1439 7.3	2138 0.1
31 W	0301 7.4	0952 0.8	1519 7.4	2220 0.2

Chart Datum: 3·20 metres below Ordnance Datum (Newlyn)
HAT is 7·6 metres above Chart Datum

TIME ZONE (UT)	LONDON BRIDGE	Dates in amber are SPRINGS
For Summer Time add ONE hour in **non-shaded areas**	LAT 51°30′N LONG 0°05′W	Dates in yellow are NEAPS
	TIMES AND HEIGHTS OF HIGH AND LOW WATERS	**2011**

SEPTEMBER

Day	Time m	Day	Time m
1 TH	0343 7.4 / 1033 0.6 / 1559 7.4 / 2257 0.1	**16** F	0342 6.8 / 1014 0.9 / 1556 7.0 / 2220 0.8
2 F	0424 7.2 / 1110 0.6 / 1638 7.3 / 2329 0.4	**17** SA	0409 6.7 / 1041 1.0 / 1626 6.8 / 2244 0.9
3 SA	0504 6.9 / 1143 0.8 / 1720 7.0 / 2358 0.7	**18** SU	0439 6.5 / 1106 1.1 / 1657 6.6 / 2306 1.0
4 SU ☽	0547 6.5 / 1217 1.0 / 1807 6.7	**19** M	0510 6.3 / 1129 1.2 / 1732 6.3 / 2331 1.2
5 M	0031 1.0 / 0636 6.2 / 1259 1.2 / 1903 6.4	**20** TU ○	0546 6.0 / 1156 1.3 / 1815 6.1
6 TU	0120 1.4 / 0738 5.9 / 1359 1.5 / 2018 6.1	**21** W	0005 1.3 / 0632 5.7 / 1238 1.4 / 1909 5.8
7 W	0234 1.7 / 0858 5.7 / 1524 1.5 / 2143 6.0	**22** TH	0056 1.6 / 0737 5.5 / 1342 1.6 / 2031 5.7
8 TH	0359 1.7 / 1026 5.8 / 1700 1.3 / 2306 6.3	**23** F	0217 1.9 / 0918 5.6 / 1557 1.5 / 2205 6.0
9 F	0528 1.4 / 1141 6.2 / 1822 0.8	**24** SA	0423 1.7 / 1043 6.0 / 1713 1.0 / 2315 6.5
10 SA	0011 6.7 / 0634 1.1 / 1237 6.6 / 1916 0.6	**25** SU	0534 1.3 / 1147 6.5 / 1823 0.7
11 SU	0102 6.9 / 0725 1.0 / 1321 6.8 / 2000 0.5	**26** M	0013 7.0 / 0645 1.0 / 1240 6.9 / 1930 0.4
12 M ○	0143 7.0 / 0808 0.9 / 1358 6.9 / 2038 0.5	**27** TU ●	0104 7.2 / 0750 0.9 / 1327 7.2 / 2025 0.2
13 TU	0219 6.9 / 0846 0.9 / 1430 6.9 / 2110 0.6	**28** W	0151 7.4 / 0843 0.8 / 1411 7.4 / 2112 0.2
14 W	0250 6.9 / 0919 0.9 / 1459 7.0 / 2137 0.7	**29** TH	0235 7.4 / 0930 0.6 / 1453 7.5 / 2155 0.2
15 TH	0316 6.9 / 0948 0.9 / 1527 7.0 / 2159 0.7	**30** F	0318 7.3 / 1012 0.6 / 1535 7.5 / 2231 0.4

OCTOBER

Day	Time m	Day	Time m
1 SA	0359 7.2 / 1050 0.6 / 1617 7.4 / 2302 0.6	**16** SU	0340 6.8 / 1016 0.9 / 1559 6.9 / 2212 0.9
2 SU	0441 6.8 / 1124 0.7 / 1700 7.1 / 2330 0.9	**17** M	0411 6.6 / 1042 1.0 / 1633 6.7 / 2239 1.0
3 M	0523 6.5 / 1156 0.9 / 1748 6.7	**18** TU	0444 6.4 / 1106 1.1 / 1710 6.5 / 2308 1.1
4 TU ☽	0003 1.2 / 0610 6.1 / 1235 1.2 / 1844 6.3	**19** W	0520 6.1 / 1136 1.1 / 1753 6.3 / 2345 1.3
5 W ○	0051 1.6 / 0709 5.8 / 1333 1.4 / 1957 6.0	**20** TH ○	0607 5.9 / 1217 1.2 / 1847 6.1
6 TH	0204 1.8 / 0828 5.7 / 1458 1.5 / 2117 6.0	**21** F	0034 1.5 / 0708 5.7 / 1317 1.4 / 1959 6.0
7 F	0331 1.8 / 0954 5.8 / 1626 1.3 / 2237 6.2	**22** SA	0149 1.8 / 0833 5.7 / 1512 1.4 / 2128 6.2
8 SA	0453 1.5 / 1108 6.1 / 1746 1.0 / 2343 6.5	**23** SU	0345 1.7 / 1002 6.1 / 1635 1.0 / 2239 6.6
9 SU	0600 1.2 / 1205 6.5 / 1841 0.8	**24** M	0500 1.3 / 1109 6.5 / 1743 0.7 / 2340 6.9
10 M	0033 6.8 / 0651 1.1 / 1250 6.7 / 1922 0.7	**25** TU	0611 1.1 / 1206 6.9 / 1854 0.6
11 TU	0114 6.8 / 0734 1.0 / 1326 6.8 / 1957 0.7	**26** W ●	0034 7.1 / 0720 0.9 / 1257 7.2 / 1954 0.4
12 W ○	0148 6.8 / 0813 0.9 / 1359 6.9 / 2029 0.8	**27** TH	0124 7.2 / 0817 0.7 / 1344 7.4 / 2044 0.4
13 TH	0217 6.8 / 0847 0.9 / 1428 7.0 / 2057 0.8	**28** F	0210 7.3 / 0907 0.6 / 1429 7.5 / 2128 0.5
14 F	0243 6.9 / 0919 0.8 / 1457 7.0 / 2122 0.8	**29** SA	0255 7.2 / 0952 0.5 / 1514 7.5 / 2206 0.8
15 SA	0310 6.8 / 0949 0.8 / 1527 7.0 / 2147 0.8	**30** SU	0338 7.1 / 1032 0.5 / 1559 7.4 / 2239 0.8
		31 M	0421 6.8 / 1107 0.7 / 1645 7.1 / 2308 1.1

NOVEMBER

Day	Time m	Day	Time m
1 TU	0505 6.5 / 1139 0.8 / 1733 6.7 / 2342 1.3	**16** W	0428 6.5 / 1056 0.9 / 1655 6.7 / 2257 1.1
2 W ●	0551 6.2 / 1216 1.1 / 1827 6.3	**17** TH	0507 6.3 / 1129 0.9 / 1740 6.6 / 2337 1.3
3 TH	0027 1.6 / 0643 5.9 / 1307 1.3 / 1931 6.1	**18** F ○	0553 6.2 / 1210 1.0 / 1833 6.4
4 F	0129 1.8 / 0752 5.8 / 1422 1.4 / 2041 6.0	**19** SA	0026 1.4 / 0649 6.0 / 1305 1.1 / 1936 6.3
5 SA	0249 1.9 / 0909 5.8 / 1538 1.3 / 2152 6.0	**20** SU	0134 1.6 / 0759 6.0 / 1430 1.2 / 2054 6.3
6 SU	0406 1.7 / 1020 6.0 / 1643 1.2 / 2300 6.2	**21** M	0306 1.6 / 0923 6.2 / 1557 1.0 / 2205 6.5
7 M	0511 1.4 / 1121 6.2 / 1741 1.0 / 2354 6.4	**22** TU	0426 1.4 / 1034 6.5 / 1706 0.8 / 2309 6.7
8 TU	0607 1.2 / 1210 6.5 / 1829 0.9	**23** W	0540 1.2 / 1135 6.8 / 1816 0.7
9 W	0037 6.6 / 0654 1.0 / 1251 6.7 / 1911 0.9	**24** TH	0008 6.9 / 0652 1.0 / 1231 7.1 / 1923 0.6
10 TH ○	0114 6.7 / 0738 0.9 / 1327 6.8 / 1950 0.8	**25** F ●	0101 7.0 / 0754 0.7 / 1322 7.2 / 2017 0.5
11 F	0146 6.7 / 0817 0.8 / 1400 6.9 / 2024 0.9	**26** SA	0150 7.1 / 0847 0.5 / 1411 7.4 / 2105 0.7
12 SA	0216 6.8 / 0853 0.8 / 1431 6.9 / 2053 0.9	**27** SU	0238 7.1 / 0935 0.4 / 1459 7.4 / 2147 0.8
13 SU	0246 6.8 / 0927 0.8 / 1504 7.0 / 2120 0.9	**28** M	0323 7.0 / 1019 0.5 / 1546 7.3 / 2223 1.0
14 M	0319 6.7 / 0959 0.8 / 1539 6.9 / 2150 1.0	**29** TU	0407 6.8 / 1057 0.6 / 1633 7.1 / 2255 1.1
15 TU	0353 6.6 / 1028 0.9 / 1616 6.8 / 2222 1.0	**30** W	0450 6.6 / 1130 0.7 / 1719 6.8 / 2327 1.3

DECEMBER

Day	Time m	Day	Time m
1 TH	0533 6.4 / 1202 0.9 / 1807 6.4	**16** F	0500 6.6 / 1133 0.7 / 1729 6.8 / 2339 1.1
2 F ●	0005 1.6 / 0617 6.1 / 1241 1.1 / 1858 6.2	**17** SA	0542 6.5 / 1211 0.8 / 1818 6.6
3 SA	0052 1.6 / 0711 5.9 / 1333 1.2 / 1956 6.0	**18** SU	0024 1.3 / 0631 6.4 / 1257 0.9 / 1914 6.4
4 SU	0151 1.8 / 0817 5.8 / 1439 1.3 / 2058 5.9	**19** M	0119 1.5 / 0730 6.3 / 1358 1.0 / 2022 6.3
5 M	0305 1.8 / 0924 5.8 / 1545 1.3 / 2159 5.9	**20** TU	0230 1.6 / 0846 6.2 / 1517 1.1 / 2133 6.3
6 TU	0417 1.7 / 1027 6.0 / 1644 1.3 / 2300 6.1	**21** W	0353 1.5 / 1002 6.4 / 1631 1.0 / 2241 6.4
7 W	0518 1.4 / 1124 6.2 / 1738 1.2 / 2353 6.3	**22** TH	0512 1.3 / 1110 6.6 / 1745 1.0 / 2346 6.5
8 TH	0613 1.2 / 1214 6.4 / 1829 1.1	**23** F	0630 1.0 / 1213 6.8 / 1859 0.9
9 F	0039 6.5 / 0703 1.0 / 1257 6.6 / 1916 1.0	**24** SA ●	0045 6.7 / 0736 0.7 / 1310 7.0 / 1958 0.8
10 SA ○	0119 6.6 / 0750 0.8 / 1336 6.8 / 1958 1.0	**25** SU	0139 6.8 / 0832 0.5 / 1401 7.1 / 2049 0.8
11 SU	0156 6.7 / 0832 0.8 / 1413 6.8 / 2034 1.1	**26** M	0227 6.9 / 0923 0.4 / 1450 7.2 / 2134 0.9
12 M	0232 6.7 / 0913 0.7 / 1449 6.9 / 2107 1.0	**27** TU	0313 7.0 / 1008 0.4 / 1536 7.2 / 2213 1.0
13 TU	0308 6.7 / 0951 0.6 / 1526 7.0 / 2141 1.0	**28** W	0355 6.9 / 1048 0.5 / 1620 7.1 / 2246 1.1
14 W	0344 6.7 / 1027 0.6 / 1605 7.0 / 2218 1.0	**29** TH	0434 6.8 / 1120 0.6 / 1701 6.8 / 2314 1.2
15 TH	0421 6.7 / 1101 0.6 / 1646 6.9 / 2258 1.0	**30** F	0511 6.8 / 1144 0.8 / 1740 6.6 / 2343 1.3
		31 SA	0548 6.7 / 1210 0.9 / 1819 6.3

Chart Datum: 3·20 metres below Ordnance Datum (Newlyn)
HAT is 7·6 metres above Chart Datum

TIDES

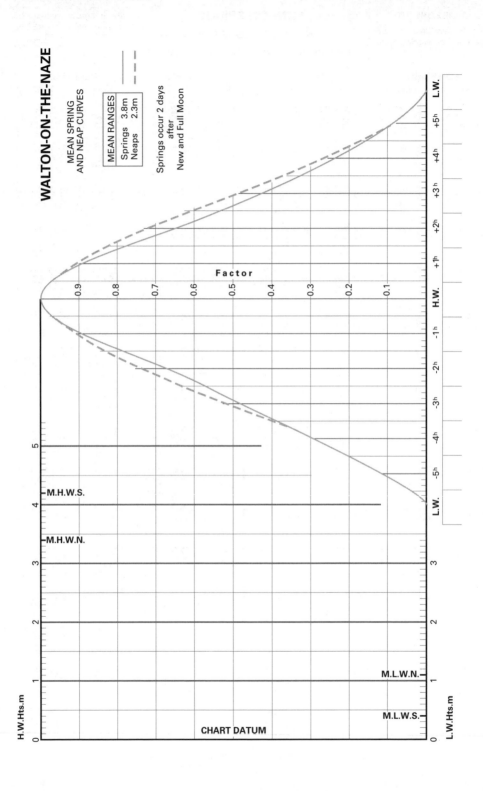

WALTON-ON-THE-NAZE

MEAN SPRING
AND NEAP CURVES

MEAN RANGES	
Springs	3.8m
Neaps	2.3m

Springs occur 2 days
after
New and Full Moon

Factor

0.9 0.8 0.7 0.6 0.5 0.4 0.3 0.2 0.1

H.W. -1ʰ -2ʰ -3ʰ -4ʰ -5ʰ L.W.

L.W. +5ʰ +4ʰ +3ʰ +2ʰ +1ʰ H.W.

M.H.W.S.
M.H.W.N.

M.L.W.N.
M.L.W.S.

CHART DATUM

H.W.Hts.m

L.W.Hts.m

WALTON-ON-THE-NAZE

LAT 51°51′N   LONG 1°17′E

TIMES AND HEIGHTS OF HIGH AND LOW WATERS

Dates in amber are **SPRINGS**
Dates in yellow are **NEAPS**

2011

JANUARY

Day	Time	m	Time	m		Day	Time	m	Time	m
1 SA	0227	1.0	0850	3.8		16 SU	0219	1.2	0817	3.5
	1503	0.8	2128	3.8			1443	1.1	2057	3.6
2 SU	0337	0.9	0950	3.9		17 M	0320	1.0	0922	3.6
	1604	0.9	2223	3.9			1539	1.0	2157	3.7
3 M	0439	0.7	1042	4.0		18 TU	0414	0.7	1017	3.9
	1655	0.9	2311	4.0			1628	0.9	2248	3.9
4 TU	0531	0.5	1129	4.1		19 W	0503	0.5	1106	4.1
	1739	0.8	2354	4.1			1712	0.8	2335	4.1
5 W	0616	0.4	1212	4.1		20 TH	0549	0.3	1152	4.3
	1819	0.8					1755	0.7		
6 TH	0034	4.1	0656	0.4		21 F	0020	4.3	0634	0.2
	1252	4.1	1854	0.8			1238	4.4	1837	0.6
7 F	0111	4.1	0732	0.4		22 SA	0105	4.4	0719	0.1
	1331	4.1	1928	0.9			1324	4.5	1919	0.6
8 SA	0145	4.1	0804	0.4		23 SU	0148	4.4	0803	0.0
	1408	4.0	1958	0.9			1409	4.4	2003	0.6
9 SU	0218	4.0	0833	0.5		24 M	0230	4.3	0846	0.1
	1444	3.9	2027	0.9			1454	4.3	2047	0.7
10 M	0252	4.0	0902	0.6		25 TU	0313	4.3	0930	0.2
	1530	3.8	2100	1.0			1541	4.1	2134	0.8
11 TU	0328	3.9	0934	0.7		26 W	0358	4.2	1017	0.4
	1557	3.6	2140	1.1			1631	3.9	2228	0.9
12 W	0408	3.7	1012	0.8		27 TH	0450	4.0	1112	0.6
	1640	3.5	(2226	1.2			1729	3.7	2331	1.0
13 TH	0455	3.6	1101	1.0		28 F	0554	3.8	1217	0.8
	1734	3.4	2328	1.3			1838	3.5		
14 F	0556	3.4	1211	1.1		29 SA	0046	1.1	0715	3.6
	1840	3.3					1330	1.0	1959	3.5
15 SA	0100	1.3	0706	3.4		30 SU	0212	1.0	0835	3.6
	1337	1.1	1949	3.4			1449	1.1	2115	3.6
						31 M	0337	0.9	0943	3.8
							1558	1.0	2215	3.8

FEBRUARY

Day	Time	m	Time	m		Day	Time	m	Time	m
1 TU	0439	0.7	1037	3.9		16 W	0350	0.7	0958	3.8
	1648	1.0	2302	3.9			1608	0.9	2229	3.9
2 W	0526	0.5	1121	4.0		17 TH	0443	0.4	1049	4.1
	1728	0.9	2343	4.0			1655	0.7	2316	4.1
3 TH	0604	0.4	1200	4.0		18 F	0531	0.2	1136	4.3
	1802	0.8					1739	0.6		
4 F	0019	4.1	0637	0.4		19 SA	0001	4.3	0616	0.1
	1236	4.1	1834	0.8			1221	4.4	1821	0.6
5 SA	0052	4.1	0707	0.4		20 SU	0045	4.5	0700	0.0
	1310	4.1	1905	0.8			1305	4.5	1903	0.5
6 SU	0122	4.2	0737	0.4		21 M	0127	4.6	0742	0.0
	1343	4.0	1933	0.8			1349	4.5	1946	0.5
7 M	0153	4.1	0801	0.4		22 TU	0208	4.6	0821	0.1
	1414	3.9	2001	0.8			1433	4.3	2028	0.6
8 TU	0223	4.1	0826	0.5		23 W	0250	4.5	0901	0.2
	1444	3.8	2031	0.8			1517	4.1	2112	0.7
9 W	0254	4.0	0853	0.6		24 TH	0333	4.3	0944	0.5
	1515	3.7	2105	0.9			1604	3.9	(2202	0.8
10 TH	0328	3.8	0925	0.7		25 F	0423	4.0	1037	0.8
	1551	3.6	2144	1.0			1658	3.6	2303	0.9
11 F	0407	3.7	1004	0.9		26 SA	0528	3.7	1143	1.0
	1636	3.5	(2235	1.1			1807	3.4		
12 SA	0458	3.5	1100	1.1		27 SU	0021	1.0	0654	3.5
	1738	3.3	2351	1.3			1304	1.2	1935	3.3
13 SU	0607	3.3	1234	1.2		28 M	0203	1.0	0822	3.5
	1858	3.3					1436	1.2	2059	3.5
14 M	0136	1.2	0734	3.3						
	1408	1.2	2022	3.4						
15 TU	0249	0.9	0856	3.5						
	1514	1.0	2133	3.6						

MARCH

Day	Time	m	Time	m		Day	Time	m	Time	m
1 TU	0331	0.8	0932	3.7		16 W	0220	0.8	0829	3.6
	1546	1.1	2158	3.7			1445	1.0	2105	3.6
2 W	0427	0.6	1024	3.9		17 TH	0323	0.6	0935	3.9
	1632	1.0	2244	3.9			1542	0.8	2203	3.9
3 TH	0509	0.5	1105	3.9		18 F	0418	0.3	1027	4.1
	1708	0.9	2322	4.0			1631	0.7	2251	4.2
4 F	0542	0.4	1140	4.0		19 SA	0507	0.1	1114	4.3
	1739	0.8	2355	4.1			1716	0.6	2336	4.4
5 SA	0609	0.4	1213	4.0		20 SU	0552	0.0	1158	4.4
	1810	0.7					1801	0.5		
6 SU	0025	4.1	0635	0.4		21 M	0019	4.6	0635	0.0
	1244	4.0	1840	0.7			1243	4.5	1844	0.4
7 M	0055	4.2	0702	0.4		22 TU	0102	4.6	0716	0.0
	1315	4.0	1909	0.7			1326	4.4	1927	0.4
8 TU	0124	4.2	0727	0.4		23 W	0144	4.6	0755	0.2
	1344	4.0	1937	0.7			1409	4.3	2010	0.5
9 W	0155	4.1	0752	0.5		24 TH	0227	4.5	0833	0.4
	1412	3.9	2006	0.7			1452	4.1	2054	0.5
10 TH	0225	4.0	0817	0.6		25 F	0311	4.2	0916	0.7
	1443	3.8	2038	0.7			1538	3.8	2142	0.7
11 F	0258	3.9	0847	0.7		26 SA	0402	3.9	1007	0.9
	1518	3.7	2114	0.8			1631	3.6	(2240	0.8
12 SA	0336	3.8	0925	0.9		27 SU	0507	3.6	1111	1.2
	1600	3.6	(2200	0.9			1738	3.4	2357	1.0
13 SU	0424	3.6	1018	1.1		28 M	0631	3.4	1234	1.3
	1657	3.4	2309	1.1			1902	3.3		
14 M	0529	3.4	1147	1.3		29 TU	0139	1.0	0756	3.5
	1815	3.3					1406	1.3	2026	3.4
15 TU	0058	1.1	0656	3.4		30 W	0306	0.9	0907	3.6
	1335	1.2	1946	3.3			1517	1.2	2128	3.6
						31 TH	0401	0.6	0958	3.8
							1604	1.0	2214	3.8

APRIL

Day	Time	m	Time	m		Day	Time	m	Time	m
1 F	0439	0.6	1038	3.9		16 SA	0349	0.3	1001	4.1
	1640	0.9	2252	3.9			1603	0.7	2223	4.2
2 SA	0509	0.5	1113	3.9		17 SU	0439	0.1	1049	4.3
	1712	0.8	2324	4.0			1652	0.6	2309	4.4
3 SU	0535	0.5	1144	4.0		18 M	0525	0.1	1135	4.3
	1743	0.7	● 2354	4.1			1740	0.5	○ 2354	4.5
4 M	0602	0.4	1215	4.0		19 TU	0609	0.1	1219	4.4
	1814	0.6					1827	0.4		
5 TU	0024	4.2	0629	0.4		20 W	0038	4.6	0651	0.2
	1245	4.0	1844	0.6			1304	4.3	1912	0.4
6 W	0056	4.2	0655	0.5		21 TH	0122	4.5	0732	0.4
	1315	4.0	1915	0.6			1348	4.2	1957	0.4
7 TH	0128	4.1	0721	0.5		22 F	0207	4.4	0812	0.6
	1346	3.9	1945	0.6			1431	4.0	2041	0.5
8 F	0200	4.1	0748	0.6		23 SA	0253	4.2	0854	0.8
	1418	3.9	2018	0.6			1517	3.8	2128	0.6
9 SA	0235	4.0	0822	0.7		24 SU	0344	3.9	0941	1.0
	1455	3.7	2055	0.7			1607	3.6	2221	0.7
10 SU	0316	3.9	0903	0.9		25 M	0446	3.6	1040	1.2
	1538	3.6	2142	0.8			1709	3.5	(2329	0.9
11 M	0405	3.7	0959	1.1		26 TU	0559	3.5	1153	1.3
	1634	3.5	(2251	0.9			1820	3.4		
12 TU	0509	3.6	1125	1.2		27 W	0054	0.9	0714	3.6
	1748	3.4	2357	1.0			1317	1.3	1935	3.4
13 W	0029	0.9	0630	3.5		28 TH	0215	0.9	0824	3.6
	1302	1.2	1913	3.4			1429	1.2	2042	3.5
14 TH	0149	0.7	0758	3.7		29 F	0315	0.8	0919	3.7
	1413	1.0	2031	3.7			1523	1.1	2132	3.7
15 F	0253	0.5	0906	3.9		30 SA	0356	0.7	1002	3.8
	1512	0.8	2132	3.9			1605	0.9	2213	3.8

Chart Datum: 2·16 metres below Ordnance Datum (Newlyn)
HAT is 4·7 metres above Chart Datum

TIDES

TIME ZONE (UT)	WALTON-ON-THE-NAZE	Dates in amber are SPRINGS
For Summer Time add ONE hour in **non-shaded areas**	LAT 51°51′N LONG 1°17′E	Dates in yellow are NEAPS

TIMES AND HEIGHTS OF HIGH AND LOW WATERS

2011

MAY

Time	m	Time	m
1 0429	0.6	**16** 0411	0.3
1039	3.9	1026	4.1
SU 1642	0.8	M 1631	0.6
2248	3.9	2245	4.3
2 0500	0.6	**17** 0500	0.3
1113	3.9	1114	4.2
M 1717	0.7	TU 1723	0.5
2322	4.0	O 2332	4.4
3 0531	0.6	**18** 0547	0.4
1145	4.0	1200	4.2
TU 1750	0.6	W 1813	0.4
● 2356	4.1		
4 0600	0.6	**19** 0018	4.5
1218	4.0	0632	0.5
W 1823	0.5	TH 1246	4.2
		1902	0.3
5 0031	4.1	**20** 0105	4.4
0628	0.6	0715	0.6
TH 1252	4.0	F 1330	4.2
1856	0.5	1948	0.4
6 0106	4.1	**21** 0151	4.3
0657	0.6	0756	0.7
F 1327	4.0	SA 1414	4.1
1931	0.5	2032	0.4
7 0142	4.1	**22** 0238	4.1
0730	0.7	0836	0.9
SA 1404	3.9	SU 1459	3.9
2008	0.5	2115	0.5
8 0221	4.0	**23** 0327	3.9
0808	0.8	0918	1.0
SU 1443	3.8	M 1545	3.8
2049	0.6	2200	0.6
9 0305	3.9	**24** 0421	3.7
0855	0.9	1006	1.2
M 1528	3.7	TU 1637	3.6
2139	0.6	◑ 2253	0.7
10 0355	3.8	**25** 0521	3.6
0954	1.0	1105	1.3
TU 1623	3.6	W 1735	3.5
◑ 2246	0.7	2358	0.8
11 0456	3.7	**26** 0623	3.5
1109	1.1	1220	1.3
W 1729	3.6	TH 1836	3.5
12 0006	0.7	**27** 0106	0.9
0609	3.7	0725	3.5
TH 1229	1.1	F 1333	1.3
1843	3.6	1938	3.5
13 0118	0.5	**28** 0208	0.9
0727	3.8	0825	3.6
F 1340	1.0	SA 1435	1.1
1957	3.8	2038	3.6
14 0221	0.4	**29** 0301	0.8
0836	3.9	0917	3.7
SA 1441	0.9	SU 1526	1.0
2101	4.0	2128	3.7
15 0318	0.3	**30** 0346	0.8
0935	4.0	1001	3.8
SU 1538	0.7	M 1611	0.8
2156	4.2	2212	3.9
		31 0427	0.7
		1041	3.9
		TU 1651	0.7
		2252	4.0

JUNE

Time	m	Time	m
1 0503	0.7	**16** 0532	0.6
1119	3.9	1147	4.1
W 1729	0.6	TH 1806	0.4
● 2331	4.0		
2 0536	0.7	**17** 0006	4.3
1157	4.0	0618	0.7
TH 1806	0.5	F 1233	4.2
		1854	0.3
3 0010	4.1	**18** 0052	4.3
0608	0.7	0701	0.7
F 1236	4.1	SA 1317	4.2
1843	0.5	1939	0.3
4 0050	4.2	**19** 0137	4.2
0643	0.7	0741	0.8
SA 1316	4.1	SU 1359	4.1
1923	0.4	2020	0.4
5 0131	4.2	**20** 0221	4.1
0721	0.7	0817	0.9
SU 1356	4.0	M 1439	4.1
2005	0.4	2057	0.5
6 0213	4.2	**21** 0305	4.0
0804	0.8	0853	1.0
M 1438	4.0	TU 1519	4.0
2049	0.4	2133	0.6
7 0258	4.1	**22** 0350	3.8
0852	0.9	0930	1.1
TU 1523	3.9	W 1602	3.8
2139	0.5	2212	0.7
8 0347	4.0	**23** 0438	3.7
0946	1.0	1016	1.2
W 1613	3.9	TH 1650	3.7
2236	0.5	◑ 2259	0.8
9 0443	3.9	**24** 0530	3.5
1048	1.0	1111	1.3
TH 1710	3.8	F 1743	3.6
◑ 2340	0.5		
10 0547	3.8	**25** 0000	0.9
1157	1.1	0624	3.5
F 1815	3.8	SA 1228	1.3
		1841	3.5
11 0046	0.5	**26** 0108	1.0
0656	3.8	0723	3.5
SA 1307	1.0	SU 1342	1.2
1925	3.8	1943	3.5
12 0150	0.5	**27** 0210	1.0
0806	3.8	0824	3.5
SU 1413	0.9	M 1444	1.1
2033	3.9	2044	3.6
13 0250	0.5	**28** 0307	1.0
0911	3.9	0921	3.7
M 1516	0.8	TU 1538	0.9
2134	4.1	2138	3.7
14 0348	0.6	**29** 0357	0.9
1009	4.0	1011	3.8
TU 1617	0.6	W 1626	0.8
2228	4.2	2226	3.9
15 0443	0.6	**30** 0440	0.9
1100	4.1	1056	3.9
W 1713	0.5	TH 1710	0.6
O 2318	4.3	2311	4.0

JULY

Time	m	Time	m
1 0519	0.8	**16** 0606	0.8
1139	4.0	1222	4.2
F 1751	0.5	SA 1845	0.3
● 2354	4.1		
2 0555	0.8	**17** 0040	4.2
1222	4.1	0644	0.8
SA 1832	0.4	SU 1302	4.2
		1924	0.4
3 0036	4.3	**18** 0121	4.2
0633	0.7	0721	0.8
SU 1304	4.2	M 1339	4.2
1914	0.3	1958	0.4
4 0120	4.3	**19** 0200	4.1
0714	0.7	0754	0.9
M 1347	4.2	TU 1414	4.2
1957	0.3	2029	0.5
5 0203	4.3	**20** 0237	4.0
0757	0.7	0825	0.9
TU 1428	4.2	W 1448	4.1
2041	0.3	2058	0.5
6 0248	4.2	**21** 0314	3.9
0842	0.8	0856	0.9
W 1511	4.2	TH 1524	4.0
2126	0.3	2128	0.6
7 0334	4.1	**22** 0352	3.7
0930	0.9	0932	1.0
TH 1556	4.1	F 1603	3.8
2216	0.4	2203	0.8
8 0425	4.0	**23** 0433	3.6
1025	1.0	1016	1.1
F 1646	4.0	SA 1649	3.7
◑ 2312	0.5	◑ 2249	1.0
9 0523	3.8	**24** 0524	3.5
1127	1.0	1114	1.3
SA 1746	3.9	SU 1745	3.5
2357	1.1		
10 0015	0.6	**25** 0625	3.4
0628	3.7	1241	1.3
SU 1238	1.0	M 1852	3.4
1857	3.8		
11 0121	0.7	**26** 0121	1.2
0741	3.7	0732	3.4
M 1351	1.0	TU 1401	1.2
2013	3.8	2002	3.5
12 0229	0.8	**27** 0231	1.2
0855	3.7	0842	3.5
TU 1504	0.9	W 1505	1.0
2121	3.9	2108	3.6
13 0335	0.9	**28** 0330	1.1
0959	3.9	0944	3.7
W 1613	0.7	TH 1601	0.8
2220	4.1	2204	3.8
14 0434	0.9	**29** 0419	1.0
1052	4.0	1034	3.9
TH 1712	0.5	F 1649	0.6
2311	4.2	2252	4.0
15 0523	0.8	**30** 0501	0.9
1139	4.1	1120	4.1
F 1801	0.4	SA 1733	0.5
O 2357	4.2	● 2336	4.2
		31 0540	0.8
		1203	4.2
		SU 1816	0.3

AUGUST

Time	m	Time	m
1 0020	4.4	**16** 0058	4.2
0619	0.7	0656	0.8
M 1246	4.4	TU 1313	4.3
1858	0.2	1927	0.4
2 0104	4.5	**17** 0132	4.1
0700	0.6	0728	0.8
TU 1328	4.5	W 1344	4.2
1941	0.2	1955	0.5
3 0147	4.5	**18** 0205	4.1
0742	0.7	0757	0.8
W 1409	4.5	TH 1415	4.2
2022	0.2	2020	0.6
4 0230	4.4	**19** 0236	3.9
0825	0.7	0825	0.9
TH 1451	4.4	F 1446	4.1
2104	0.3	2045	0.7
5 0315	4.2	**20** 0307	3.8
0910	0.8	0858	0.9
F 1533	4.3	SA 1520	3.9
2149	0.4	2114	0.8
6 0402	4.0	**21** 0340	3.7
1001	0.9	0936	1.0
SA 1621	4.1	SU 1558	3.8
◑ 2241	0.6	◑ 2151	1.0
7 0456	3.8	**22** 0423	3.5
1100	1.0	1023	1.2
SU 1720	3.9	M 1646	3.6
2344	0.8	2243	1.2
8 0602	3.6	**23** 0522	3.4
1212	1.0	1135	1.3
M 1837	3.8	TU 1752	3.4
9 0057	1.0	**24** 0018	1.4
0721	3.5	0639	3.3
TU 1335	1.0	W 1317	1.3
2000	3.7	1919	3.4
10 0215	1.1	**25** 0155	1.3
0844	3.6	0802	3.4
W 1503	0.9	TH 1431	1.0
2114	3.9	2038	3.6
11 0331	1.1	**26** 0300	1.2
0950	3.8	0913	3.7
TH 1615	0.7	F 1531	0.8
2214	4.0	2139	3.9
12 0428	1.0	**27** 0353	1.0
1043	4.0	1008	3.9
F 1707	0.5	SA 1623	0.6
2303	4.1	2229	4.1
13 0512	0.9	**28** 0437	0.8
1126	4.1	1055	4.1
SA 1750	0.4	SU 1709	0.4
O 2344	4.2	2314	4.3
14 0549	0.9	**29** 0518	0.7
1205	4.2	1139	4.3
SU 1826	0.4	M 1753	0.2
		● 2358	4.5
15 0022	4.2	**30** 0600	0.7
0623	0.8	1221	4.5
M 1240	4.2	TU 1836	0.1
1857	0.4		
		31 0641	0.6
		1303	4.6
		W 1916	0.1

Chart Datum: 2·16 metres below Ordnance Datum (Newlyn)
HAT is 4·7 metres above Chart Datum

| TIME ZONE (UT) | WALTON-ON-THE-NAZE | Dates in amber are SPRINGS |
For Summer Time add ONE hour in **non-shaded areas** | **LAT 51°51'N   LONG 1°17'E** | Dates in yellow are NEAPS

2011

TIMES AND HEIGHTS OF HIGH AND LOW WATERS

SEPTEMBER

Time	m		Time	m
1 TH	0125 4.5 / 0723 0.6 / 1345 4.6 / 1957 0.2	**16** F	0131 4.1 / 0730 0.7 / 1342 4.2 / 1942 0.6
2 F	0208 4.4 / 0806 0.6 / 1426 4.6 / 2036 0.4	**17** SA	0200 4.0 / 0758 0.8 / 1413 4.1 / 2006 0.8
3 SA	0251 4.2 / 0850 0.7 / 1509 4.4 / 2119 0.6	**18** SU	0229 3.9 / 0829 0.8 / 1445 4.0 / 2034 0.9
4 SU ◑	0337 4.0 / 0939 0.8 / 1558 4.2 / 2211 0.8	**19** M	0302 3.8 / 0903 0.9 / 1521 3.8 / 2109 1.0
5 M	0430 3.7 / 1038 0.9 / 1659 3.9 / 2317 1.1	**20** TU ◑	0341 3.6 / 0946 1.0 / 1606 3.7 / 2157 1.2
6 TU	0537 3.5 / 1153 1.0 / 1821 3.7	**21** W	0433 3.5 / 1048 1.2 / 1706 3.5 / 2314 1.4
7 W	0036 1.3 / 0702 3.4 / 1326 1.0 / 1949 3.7	**22** TH	0548 3.3 / 1232 1.2 / 1830 3.4
8 TH	0203 1.3 / 0828 3.6 / 1457 0.9 / 2104 3.9	**23** F	0112 1.4 / 0719 3.4 / 1355 1.0 / 2003 3.6
9 F	0319 1.2 / 0934 3.8 / 1603 0.7 / 2201 4.0	**24** SA	0225 1.2 / 0837 3.6 / 1458 0.7 / 2109 3.9
10 SA	0412 1.1 / 1024 4.0 / 1650 0.5 / 2246 4.1	**25** SU	0320 1.0 / 0936 3.9 / 1552 0.5 / 2202 4.2
11 SU	0452 1.0 / 1105 4.1 / 1727 0.5 / 2324 4.2	**26** M	0408 0.8 / 1025 4.2 / 1640 0.3 / 2248 4.4
12 M ○	0526 0.9 / 1140 4.2 / 1757 0.5 / 2358 4.2	**27** TU ●	0452 0.7 / 1110 4.4 / 1725 0.2 / 2332 4.5
13 TU	0558 0.8 / 1211 4.2 / 1825 0.5	**28** W	0536 0.6 / 1153 4.6 / 1808 0.1
14 W	0030 4.2 / 0629 0.7 / 1242 4.3 / 1852 0.5	**29** TH	0016 4.5 / 0620 0.6 / 1236 4.7 / 1849 0.2
15 TH	0101 4.2 / 0701 0.7 / 1311 4.3 / 1918 0.6	**30** F	0100 4.5 / 0704 0.5 / 1319 4.7 / 1930 0.3

OCTOBER

Time	m		Time	m
1 SA	0144 4.4 / 0748 0.5 / 1403 4.6 / 2010 0.5	**16** SU	0130 4.1 / 0735 0.7 / 1345 4.1 / 1934 0.8
2 SU	0228 4.2 / 0834 0.6 / 1448 4.4 / 2054 0.8	**17** M	0201 4.0 / 0806 0.7 / 1419 4.0 / 2004 0.9
3 M	0314 4.0 / 0923 0.7 / 1538 4.1 / 2146 1.0	**18** TU	0235 3.9 / 0841 0.8 / 1457 3.9 / 2042 1.0
4 TU	0406 3.7 / 1021 0.8 / 1641 3.8 / 2250 1.3	**19** W	0314 3.7 / 0924 0.9 / 1542 3.8 / 2132 1.2
5 W	0513 3.5 / 1135 0.9 / 1803 3.6	**20** TH ◑	0405 3.6 / 1023 1.0 / 1640 3.6 / 2243 1.4
6 TH ◑	0009 1.4 / 0635 3.5 / 1307 1.0 / 1927 3.7	**21** F	0512 3.5 / 1153 1.0 / 1754 3.6
7 F	0135 1.4 / 0758 3.5 / 1433 0.8 / 2040 3.8	**22** SA	0024 1.4 / 0635 3.5 / 1317 0.8 / 1921 3.7
8 SA	0251 1.3 / 0905 3.8 / 1536 0.7 / 2136 4.0	**23** SU	0144 1.2 / 0756 3.7 / 1422 0.6 / 2033 3.9
9 SU	0345 1.1 / 0955 3.9 / 1621 0.6 / 2219 4.1	**24** M	0244 1.0 / 0900 3.9 / 1518 0.4 / 2130 4.2
10 M	0425 1.0 / 1035 4.0 / 1655 0.6 / 2256 4.1	**25** TU	0337 0.8 / 0953 4.2 / 1608 0.3 / 2220 4.3
11 TU	0458 0.9 / 1109 4.1 / 1723 0.6 / 2329 4.1	**26** W ●	0426 0.7 / 1041 4.4 / 1656 0.3 / 2307 4.4
12 W ○	0531 0.8 / 1139 4.2 / 1750 0.6	**27** TH	0514 0.6 / 1127 4.6 / 1741 0.4 / 2352 4.5
13 TH	0000 4.2 / 0603 0.7 / 1210 4.2 / 1817 0.6	**28** F	0602 0.5 / 1212 4.7 / 1825 0.5
14 F	0030 4.2 / 0635 0.7 / 1241 4.2 / 1844 0.6	**29** SA	0038 4.5 / 0649 0.4 / 1258 4.7 / 1908 0.5
15 SA	0100 4.1 / 0705 0.7 / 1313 4.2 / 1908 0.7	**30** SU	0123 4.4 / 0736 0.4 / 1343 4.5 / 1951 0.7
		31 M	0208 4.2 / 0823 0.5 / 1431 4.3 / 2035 0.9

NOVEMBER

Time	m		Time	m
1 TU	0254 4.0 / 0912 0.6 / 1522 4.1 / 2124 1.1	**16** W	0220 3.9 / 0830 0.6 / 1442 4.0 / 2029 1.0
2 W ◐	0345 3.8 / 1006 0.7 / 1623 3.8 / 2221 1.3	**17** TH	0300 3.8 / 0914 0.7 / 1528 3.9 / 2119 1.1
3 TH	0446 3.6 / 1112 0.8 / 1735 3.6 / 2331 1.4	**18** F ◐	0349 3.7 / 1010 0.8 / 1622 3.8 / 2223 1.2
4 F	0557 3.5 / 1229 0.9 / 1849 3.6	**19** SA	0448 3.7 / 1122 0.8 / 1727 3.7 / 2342 1.3
5 SA	0051 1.4 / 0712 3.5 / 1346 0.9 / 2000 3.7	**20** SU	0558 3.6 / 1238 0.7 / 1843 3.8
6 SU	0205 1.3 / 0821 3.6 / 1452 0.8 / 2059 3.8	**21** M	0101 1.2 / 0714 3.7 / 1344 0.6 / 1956 3.9
7 M	0305 1.2 / 0915 3.8 / 1540 0.8 / 2145 3.9	**22** TU	0208 1.0 / 0824 3.9 / 1443 0.5 / 2100 4.0
8 TU	0351 1.0 / 0958 3.9 / 1615 0.7 / 2224 4.0	**23** W	0307 0.9 / 0924 4.1 / 1538 0.4 / 2155 4.2
9 W	0429 0.9 / 1034 4.0 / 1647 0.7 / 2258 4.1	**24** TH	0403 0.7 / 1017 4.3 / 1630 0.4 / 2246 4.3
10 TH ○	0505 0.8 / 1107 4.1 / 1718 0.7 / 2330 4.1	**25** F	0457 0.5 / 1106 4.5 / 1720 0.4 / 2334 4.4
11 F	0539 0.7 / 1141 4.1 / 1748 0.7	**26** SA	0549 0.4 / 1154 4.5 / 1808 0.5
12 SA	0002 4.1 / 0612 0.6 / 1215 4.2 / 1816 0.7	**27** SU	0021 4.4 / 0639 0.4 / 1241 4.5 / 1853 0.6
13 SU	0035 4.1 / 0645 0.6 / 1249 4.2 / 1843 0.8	**28** M	0107 4.3 / 0728 0.3 / 1329 4.4 / 1937 0.8
14 M	0108 4.1 / 0718 0.6 / 1325 4.1 / 1912 0.8	**29** TU	0153 4.2 / 0816 0.4 / 1417 4.3 / 2020 0.9
15 TU	0143 4.0 / 0753 0.6 / 1401 4.1 / 1947 0.9	**30** W	0238 4.1 / 0901 0.5 / 1506 4.1 / 2102 1.1

DECEMBER

Time	m		Time	m
1 TH	0325 3.9 / 0947 0.6 / 1559 3.9 / 2148 1.2	**16** F	0252 4.0 / 0907 0.5 / 1516 4.0 / 2109 1.0
2 F ◐	0415 3.8 / 1037 0.7 / 1657 3.7 / 2243 1.3	**17** SA	0336 3.9 / 0956 0.5 / 1605 3.9 / 2204 1.1
3 SA	0512 3.6 / 1136 0.8 / 2352 1.4	**18** SU ◐	0426 3.9 / 1053 0.6 / 1702 3.8 / 2308 1.1
4 SU	0613 3.5 / 1241 0.9 / 1902 3.5	**19** M	0526 3.8 / 1159 0.6 / 1809 3.8
5 M	0107 1.4 / 0718 3.5 / 1344 0.9 / 2006 3.6	**20** TU	0021 1.1 / 0635 3.8 / 1308 0.6 / 1921 3.8
6 TU	0214 1.3 / 0821 3.6 / 1441 0.9 / 2101 3.7	**21** W	0135 1.0 / 0751 3.8 / 1412 0.6 / 2032 3.8
7 W	0311 1.1 / 0914 3.7 / 1530 0.9 / 2147 3.8	**22** TH	0243 0.9 / 0900 4.0 / 1514 0.6 / 2137 4.0
8 TH	0358 0.9 / 0958 3.8 / 1613 0.9 / 2227 3.9	**23** F	0346 0.7 / 1000 4.1 / 1612 0.6 / 2233 4.1
9 F	0440 0.8 / 1038 3.9 / 1651 0.8 / 2304 4.0	**24** SA ●	0447 0.5 / 1053 4.3 / 1707 0.6 / 2323 4.2
10 SA	0518 0.7 / 1117 4.0 / 1725 0.8 / 2341 4.1	**25** SU	0542 0.4 / 1143 4.4 / 1756 0.6
11 SU	0554 0.6 / 1154 4.1 / 1756 0.8	**26** M	0010 4.3 / 0633 0.3 / 1231 4.4 / 1841 0.7
12 M	0017 4.1 / 0629 0.5 / 1233 4.1 / 1826 0.8	**27** TU	0056 4.3 / 0720 0.3 / 1317 4.3 / 1923 0.8
13 TU	0055 4.1 / 0705 0.5 / 1311 4.1 / 1900 0.8	**28** W	0139 4.3 / 0804 0.3 / 1402 4.2 / 2002 0.9
14 W	0133 4.1 / 0743 0.4 / 1350 4.1 / 1939 0.8	**29** TH	0220 4.2 / 0843 0.4 / 1446 4.1 / 2038 0.9
15 TH	0212 4.1 / 0824 0.4 / 1431 4.1 / 2022 0.9	**30** F	0300 4.1 / 0919 0.5 / 1530 3.9 / 2114 1.0
		31 SA	0340 3.9 / 0955 0.6 / 1615 3.7 / 2154 1.1

Chart Datum: 2·16 metres below Ordnance Datum (Newlyn)
HAT is 4·7 metres above Chart Datum

TIDES

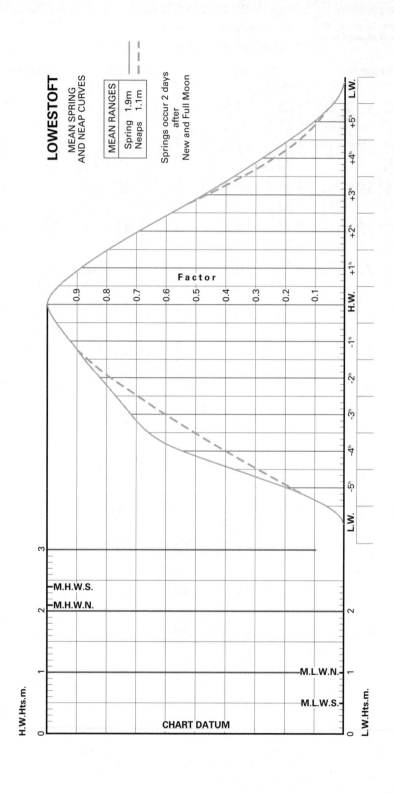

LOWESTOFT

MEAN SPRING
AND NEAP CURVES

MEAN RANGES

Spring 1.9m
Neaps 1.1m

Springs occur 2 days
after
New and Full Moon

LOWESTOFT
LAT 52°28′N   LONG 1°45′E

TIMES AND HEIGHTS OF HIGH AND LOW WATERS

Dates in amber are **SPRINGS**
Dates in yellow are **NEAPS**

2011

JANUARY

Day	Time m	Time m	Time m	Time m		Day	Time m	Time m	Time m	Time m
1 SA	0014 1.1	0621 2.4	1251 0.9	1910 2.3		16 SU	0000 1.2	0612 2.2	1230 1.1	1855 2.2
2 SU	0122 1.0	0729 2.4	1347 0.9	1959 2.4		17 M	0058 1.1	0712 2.2	1319 1.0	1941 2.3
3 M	0223 0.8	0832 2.4	1439 0.9	2044 2.5		18 TU	0150 0.9	0807 2.3	1406 0.9	2024 2.4
4 TU	0315 0.7	0925 2.4	1524 0.9	● 2126 2.5		19 W	0242 0.7	0857 2.4	1454 0.9	○ 2105 2.5
5 W	0400 0.6	1010 2.4	1603 0.9	2206 2.6		20 TH	0332 0.6	0943 2.5	1541 0.8	2147 2.6
6 TH	0442 0.5	1052 2.4	1639 0.9	2244 2.6		21 F	0421 0.4	1026 2.5	1626 0.8	2229 2.7
7 F	0521 0.6	1131 2.3	1710 1.0	2320 2.6		22 SA	0508 0.3	1109 2.5	1709 0.7	2311 2.8
8 SA	0557 0.6	1207 2.3	1740 1.0	2354 2.6		23 SU	0553 0.3	1152 2.5	1750 0.8	2354 2.8
9 SU	0631 0.7	1241 2.2	1810 1.0			24 M	0636 0.3	1235 2.4	1830 0.9	
10 M	0030 2.5	0703 0.8	1316 2.2	1844 1.1		25 TU	0039 2.7	0720 0.4	1322 2.3	1913 0.9
11 TU	0109 2.5	0738 0.8	1355 2.1	1925 1.2		26 W	0127 2.6	0807 0.6	1415 2.2	◑ 2001 1.0
12 W	0152 2.4	0818 1.0	1443 2.1	◐ 2012 1.3		27 TH	0222 2.5	0903 0.8	1529 2.1	2102 1.1
13 TH	0242 2.3	0908 1.1	1600 2.1	2110 1.3		28 F	0338 2.4	1015 1.0	1648 2.1	2235 1.1
14 F	0345 2.2	1021 1.1	1711 2.1	2237 1.3		29 SA	0507 2.3	1132 1.1	1751 2.2	
15 SA	0507 2.2	1135 1.1	1805 2.2			30 SU	0005 1.0	0626 2.3	1241 1.1	1852 2.2
						31 M	0119 0.9	0744 2.3	1342 1.1	1948 2.3

FEBRUARY

Day	Time m	Time m	Time m	Time m		Day	Time m	Time m	Time m	Time m
1 TU	0219 0.8	0838 2.3	1433 1.0	2033 2.4		16 W	0129 0.8	0756 2.3	1349 1.0	1958 2.4
2 W	0306 0.6	0920 2.4	1514 1.0	2111 2.5		17 TH	0223 0.6	0843 2.4	1438 0.9	2042 2.5
3 TH	0347 0.6	0957 2.4	1549 0.9	● 2147 2.5		18 F	0315 0.4	0926 2.5	1526 0.8	○ 2125 2.7
4 F	0423 0.5	1032 2.4	1620 0.9	2222 2.6		19 SA	0403 0.3	1007 2.5	1610 0.7	2208 2.8
5 SA	0457 0.5	1104 2.3	1648 0.9	2255 2.6		20 SU	0448 0.2	1047 2.5	1652 0.6	2251 2.8
6 SU	0529 0.6	1133 2.3	1715 0.9	2328 2.6		21 M	0531 0.2	1128 2.5	1732 0.6	2334 2.8
7 M	0558 0.6	1202 2.3	1744 0.9			22 TU	0612 0.3	1210 2.4	1813 0.7	
8 TU	0002 2.5	0625 0.7	1234 2.2	1816 0.9		23 W	0020 2.7	0653 0.4	1254 2.3	1855 0.8
9 W	0039 2.5	0655 0.8	1309 2.2	1854 1.0		24 TH	0109 2.6	0738 0.7	1342 2.2	◑ 1944 0.9
10 TH	0118 2.4	0730 0.9	1350 2.1	1938 1.1		25 F	0209 2.4	0829 0.9	1443 2.1	2046 1.0
11 F	0203 2.3	0812 1.0	1441 2.1	2031 1.2		26 SA	0339 2.3	0944 1.1	1607 2.1	2227 1.0
12 SA	0259 2.2	0908 1.1	1554 2.1	2144 1.2		27 SU	0509 2.2	1118 1.2	1719 2.1	2355 0.9
13 SU	0427 2.1	1041 1.2	1718 2.1	2327 1.2		28 M	0634 2.2	1231 1.2	1829 2.2	
14 M	0552 2.1	1201 1.2	1818 2.2							
15 TU	0033 1.0	0658 2.2	1258 1.1	1911 2.3						

MARCH

Day	Time m	Time m	Time m	Time m		Day	Time m	Time m	Time m	Time m
1 TU	0105 0.8	0742 2.3	1333 1.2	1930 2.3		16 W	0007 0.9	0643 2.2	1234 1.1	1836 2.2
2 W	0202 0.7	0828 2.3	1419 1.1	2015 2.3		17 TH	0105 0.7	0737 2.3	1327 1.0	1927 2.4
3 TH	0246 0.6	0904 2.3	1456 1.0	2050 2.4		18 F	0200 0.5	0822 2.4	1417 0.9	2014 2.5
4 F	0323 0.6	0936 2.3	1527 0.9	● 2123 2.5		19 SA	0251 0.3	0903 2.5	1504 0.7	○ 2059 2.7
5 SA	0356 0.5	1006 2.3	1556 0.8	2156 2.5		20 SU	0339 0.2	0943 2.5	1549 0.6	2145 2.8
6 SU	0427 0.5	1033 2.3	1623 0.8	2228 2.6		21 M	0424 0.2	1023 2.5	1632 0.5	2230 2.8
7 M	0456 0.6	1100 2.3	1651 0.9	2302 2.5		22 TU	0506 0.2	1104 2.5	1714 0.5	2316 2.8
8 TU	0523 0.6	1128 2.3	1720 0.9	2336 2.5		23 W	0547 0.3	1146 2.4	1757 0.5	
9 W	0550 0.7	1200 2.3	1753 0.9			24 TH	0005 2.7	0627 0.6	1229 2.4	1841 0.6
10 TH	0011 2.4	0619 0.8	1235 2.3	1829 1.0		25 F	0059 2.5	0710 0.8	1316 2.3	◑ 1932 0.7
11 F	0049 2.3	0653 0.9	1314 2.2	1911 1.0		26 SA	0206 2.3	0759 1.0	1411 2.2	◑ 2037 0.8
12 SA	0133 2.2	0734 1.0	1401 2.2	2003 1.0		27 SU	0339 2.2	0908 1.3	1524 2.1	2214 0.9
13 SU	0229 2.1	0827 1.2	1501 2.1	2112 1.1		28 M	0500 2.2	1055 1.3	1641 2.1	2333 0.8
14 M	0355 2.1	0944 1.3	1621 2.1	2257 1.0		29 TU	0619 2.2	1207 1.3	1751 2.2	
15 TU	0537 2.1	1131 1.2	1738 2.1			30 W	0036 0.8	0721 2.3	1307 1.2	1857 2.2
						31 TH	0131 0.7	0805 2.3	1353 1.1	1945 2.3

APRIL

Day	Time m	Time m	Time m	Time m		Day	Time m	Time m	Time m	Time m
1 F	0214 0.7	0840 2.3	1429 1.0	2021 2.3		16 SA	0131 0.4	0756 2.4	1350 0.9	1945 2.5
2 SA	0250 0.6	0910 2.3	1500 0.9	2054 2.4		17 SU	0224 0.3	0837 2.5	1440 0.7	2035 2.6
3 SU	0323 0.6	0936 2.3	1528 0.8	● 2128 2.5		18 M	0313 0.3	0918 2.5	1528 0.6	○ 2124 2.7
4 M	0353 0.6	1001 2.4	1557 0.7	2202 2.5		19 TU	0358 0.3	0959 2.5	1614 0.5	2213 2.7
5 TU	0421 0.6	1028 2.4	1628 0.7	2237 2.4		20 W	0441 0.4	1041 2.5	1659 0.4	2303 2.7
6 W	0450 0.7	1059 2.4	1700 0.7	2312 2.4		21 TH	0523 0.5	1124 2.5	1744 0.5	2355 2.5
7 TH	0519 0.7	1131 2.4	1735 0.7	2348 2.3		22 F	0604 0.7	1208 2.4	1831 0.5	
8 F	0550 0.8	1207 2.3	1812 0.8			23 SA	0052 2.4	0646 0.9	1254 2.4	1922 0.6
9 SA	0028 2.3	0625 0.9	1247 2.3	1854 0.8		24 SU	0201 2.3	0732 1.1	1345 2.3	2025 0.7
10 SU	0114 2.2	0708 1.0	1333 2.2	1946 0.9		25 M	0323 2.2	0828 1.3	1444 2.2	◑ 2147 0.8
11 M	0211 2.1	0801 1.2	1429 2.2	2055 0.9		26 TU	0436 2.2	1008 1.4	1553 2.2	2258 0.8
12 TU	0337 2.1	0910 1.3	1536 2.1	2229 0.9		27 W	0545 2.2	1127 1.3	1702 2.3	2357 0.8
13 W	0518 2.1	1052 1.3	1654 2.2	2339 0.7		28 TH	0647 2.2	1226 1.3	1805 2.4	
14 TH	0620 2.2	1202 1.2	1800 2.3			29 F	0049 0.7	0734 2.2	1314 1.2	1859 2.4
15 F	0037 0.6	0711 2.3	1258 1.0	1854 2.4		30 SA	0134 0.7	0810 2.3	1353 1.0	1943 2.3

Chart Datum: 1·50 metres below Ordnance Datum (Newlyn)
HAT is 3·0 metres above Chart Datum

TIDES

TIME ZONE (UT)	LOWESTOFT	Dates in amber are SPRINGS
For Summer Time add ONE hour in **non-shaded areas**	LAT 52°28'N LONG 1°45'E	Dates in yellow are NEAPS
	TIMES AND HEIGHTS OF HIGH AND LOW WATERS	**2011**

MAY

Time	m	Time	m
1 SU 0211 / 0839 / 1427 / 2022	0.7 / 2.3 / 0.9 / 2.3	**16** M 0156 / 0812 / 1418 / 2014	0.5 / 2.4 / 0.7 / 2.6
2 M 0245 / 0904 / 1459 / 2059	0.7 / 2.3 / 0.8 / 2.3	**17** TU 0247 / 0855 / 1511 / ○2108	0.4 / 2.5 / 0.6 / 0.6
3 TU 0316 / 0930 / 1532 / ●2137	0.7 / 2.4 / 0.7 / 2.4	**18** W 0335 / 0938 / 1600 / 2202	0.5 / 2.5 / 0.5 / 2.6
4 W 0347 / 1000 / 1607 / 2215	0.7 / 2.4 / 0.7 / 2.4	**19** TH 0420 / 1022 / 1648 / 2256	0.6 / 2.5 / 0.4 / 2.5
5 TH 0420 / 1033 / 1643 / 2253	0.7 / 2.4 / 0.7 / 2.3	**20** F 0502 / 1106 / 1734 / 2349	0.7 / 2.5 / 0.4 / 2.4
6 F 0454 / 1108 / 1722 / 2332	0.8 / 2.4 / 0.7 / 2.3	**21** SA 0544 / 1150 / 1821	0.8 / 2.5 / 0.5
7 SA 0529 / 1145 / 1802	0.8 / 2.4 / 0.7	**22** SU 0043 / 0623 / 1234 / 1909	2.3 / 1.0 / 2.4 / 0.5
8 SU 0014 / 0607 / 1227 / 1847	2.3 / 0.9 / 2.3 / 0.7	**23** M 0142 / 0704 / 1319 / 2003	2.2 / 1.1 / 2.4 / 0.6
9 M 0103 / 0651 / 1313 / 1939	2.2 / 1.0 / 2.3 / 0.7	**24** TU 0250 / 0749 / 1407 / ○2106	2.2 / 1.2 / 2.3 / 0.7
10 TU 0159 / 0743 / 1406 / ◑2044	2.2 / 1.1 / 2.3 / 0.7	**25** W 0359 / 0842 / 1501 / 2213	2.1 / 1.3 / 2.2 / 0.8
11 W 0315 / 0845 / 1504 / 2200	2.1 / 1.2 / 2.3 / 0.7	**26** TH 0501 / 1015 / 1605 / 2313	2.1 / 1.4 / 2.2 / 0.8
12 TH 0450 / 1005 / 1612 / 2308	2.2 / 1.2 / 2.3 / 0.6	**27** F 0559 / 1132 / 1711	2.1 / 1.3 / 2.2
13 F 0551 / 1123 / 1724	2.2 / 1.2 / 2.3	**28** SA 0004 / 0650 / 1227 / 1809	0.8 / 2.2 / 1.2 / 2.2
14 SA 0007 / 0642 / 1226 / 1824	0.5 / 2.3 / 1.0 / 2.4	**29** SU 0050 / 0731 / 1311 / 1902	0.8 / 2.2 / 1.1 / 2.2
15 SU 0103 / 0728 / 1323 / 1920	0.5 / 2.4 / 0.9 / 2.5	**30** M 0130 / 0803 / 1351 / 1950	0.8 / 2.3 / 1.0 / 2.2
		31 TU 0206 / 0832 / 1429 / 2034	0.8 / 2.3 / 0.9 / 2.3

JUNE

Time	m	Time	m
1 W 0241 / 0902 / 1508 / ●2116	0.8 / 2.4 / 0.8 / 2.3	**16** TH 0318 / 0922 / 1552 / 2159	0.7 / 2.5 / 0.5 / 2.5
2 TH 0318 / 0936 / 1548 / 2158	0.8 / 2.4 / 0.7 / 2.3	**17** F 0403 / 1006 / 1639 / 2249	0.7 / 2.6 / 0.4 / 2.4
3 F 0356 / 1012 / 1630 / 2239	0.8 / 2.5 / 0.6 / 2.3	**18** SA 0446 / 1049 / 1724 / 2337	0.8 / 2.6 / 0.4 / 2.4
4 SA 0435 / 1049 / 1713 / 2321	0.8 / 2.5 / 0.6 / 2.3	**19** SU 0524 / 1131 / 1807	0.9 / 2.6 / 0.4
5 SU 0515 / 1129 / 1757	0.8 / 2.5 / 0.6	**20** M 0024 / 0601 / 1211 / 1849	2.3 / 1.0 / 2.5 / 0.5
6 M 0005 / 0556 / 1211 / 1843	2.3 / 0.9 / 2.5 / 0.6	**21** TU 0111 / 0635 / 1251 / 1931	2.2 / 1.1 / 2.5 / 0.6
7 TU 0052 / 0639 / 1256 / 1932	2.3 / 1.0 / 2.4 / 0.6	**22** W 0200 / 0711 / 1332 / 2016	2.1 / 1.1 / 2.4 / 0.7
8 W 0144 / 0727 / 1344 / 2027	2.2 / 1.1 / 2.4 / 0.6	**23** TH 0258 / 0752 / 1417 / ◑2108	2.1 / 1.2 / 2.3 / 0.8
9 TH 0245 / 0820 / 1437 / 2129	2.2 / 1.1 / 2.4 / 0.6	**24** F 0402 / 0841 / 1510 / 2212	2.1 / 1.3 / 2.3 / 0.9
10 F 0412 / 0923 / 1539 / 2236	2.2 / 1.2 / 2.4 / 0.6	**25** SA 0459 / 0950 / 1618 / 2314	2.1 / 1.4 / 2.2 / 1.0
11 SA 0518 / 1042 / 1653 / 2339	2.2 / 1.2 / 2.4 / 0.6	**26** SU 0550 / 1128 / 1727	2.1 / 1.3 / 2.1
12 SU 0612 / 1156 / 1801	2.3 / 1.1 / 2.4	**27** M 0005 / 0637 / 1228 / 1827	1.0 / 2.2 / 1.2 / 2.1
13 M 0037 / 0702 / 1302 / 1902	0.6 / 2.3 / 0.9 / 2.4	**28** TU 0050 / 0702 / 1317 / 1923	1.0 / 2.3 / 1.1 / 2.2
14 TU 0134 / 0750 / 1404 / 2004	0.7 / 2.4 / 0.8 / 2.5	**29** W 0132 / 0759 / 1402 / 2015	1.0 / 2.3 / 0.9 / 2.2
15 W 0228 / 0836 / 1501 / ○2104	0.7 / 2.5 / 0.6 / 2.5	**30** TH 0213 / 0836 / 1447 / 2101	0.9 / 2.4 / 0.8 / 2.3

JULY

Time	m	Time	m
1 F 0255 / 0914 / 1532 / ●2145	0.9 / 2.5 / 0.7 / 2.3	**16** SA 0351 / 0950 / 1627 / 2236	0.9 / 2.6 / 0.4 / 2.4
2 SA 0338 / 0952 / 1618 / 2227	0.8 / 2.5 / 0.6 / 2.4	**17** SU 0429 / 1030 / 1708 / 2317	0.9 / 2.6 / 0.4 / 2.4
3 SU 0421 / 1032 / 1704 / 2309	0.8 / 2.6 / 0.5 / 2.4	**18** M 0504 / 1109 / 1745 / 2355	0.9 / 2.6 / 0.5 / 2.3
4 M 0504 / 1112 / 1748 / 2351	0.8 / 2.6 / 0.4 / 2.4	**19** TU 0536 / 1145 / 1821	0.9 / 2.6 / 0.5
5 TU 0545 / 1154 / 1832	0.8 / 2.6 / 0.4	**20** W 0031 / 0605 / 1221 / 1854	2.3 / 1.0 / 2.6 / 0.6
6 W 0034 / 0626 / 1237 / 1916	2.4 / 0.9 / 2.6 / 0.5	**21** TH 0107 / 0637 / 1258 / 1928	2.2 / 1.0 / 2.5 / 0.8
7 TH 0121 / 0709 / 1322 / 2004	2.3 / 1.0 / 2.6 / 0.5	**22** F 0143 / 0714 / 1339 / 2004	2.2 / 1.1 / 2.4 / 0.9
8 F 0213 / 0756 / 1413 / 2058	2.2 / 1.0 / 2.5 / 0.6	**23** SA 0228 / 0758 / 1426 / ◑2048	2.1 / 1.2 / 2.3 / 1.0
9 SA 0322 / 0852 / 1513 / 2204	2.2 / 1.1 / 2.5 / 0.7	**24** SU 0331 / 0852 / 1526 / 2152	2.1 / 1.3 / 2.2 / 1.1
10 SU 0443 / 1008 / 1634 / 2314	2.2 / 1.1 / 2.4 / 0.8	**25** M 0447 / 1012 / 1649 / 2315	2.1 / 1.3 / 2.1 / 1.2
11 M 0544 / 1137 / 1750	2.2 / 1.1 / 2.4	**26** TU 0545 / 1147 / 1759	2.2 / 1.2 / 2.1
12 TU 0019 / 0639 / 1251 / 1900	0.9 / 2.3 / 0.9 / 2.4	**27** W 0014 / 0637 / 1246 / 1902	1.1 / 2.3 / 1.1 / 2.2
13 W 0120 / 0732 / 1358 / 2009	0.9 / 2.4 / 0.8 / 2.4	**28** TH 0104 / 0726 / 1337 / 1959	1.1 / 2.3 / 1.0 / 2.2
14 TH 0217 / 0822 / 1455 / 2106	0.9 / 2.5 / 0.6 / 2.4	**29** F 0150 / 0809 / 1426 / 2047	1.0 / 2.4 / 0.8 / 2.3
15 F 0307 / 0908 / 1544 / ○2153	0.9 / 2.6 / 0.5 / 2.4	**30** SA 0236 / 0850 / 1515 / ●2129	0.9 / 2.5 / 0.6 / 2.4
		31 SU 0321 / 0930 / 1602 / 2209	0.8 / 2.6 / 0.5 / 2.5

AUGUST

Time	m	Time	m
1 M 0406 / 1011 / 1647 / 2249	0.8 / 2.7 / 0.4 / 2.5	**16** TU 0439 / 1042 / 1717 / 2322	0.9 / 2.7 / 0.5 / 2.4
2 TU 0449 / 1052 / 1730 / 2330	0.8 / 2.8 / 0.3 / 2.5	**17** W 0508 / 1116 / 1747 / 2352	0.9 / 2.7 / 0.6 / 2.3
3 W 0529 / 1133 / 1812	0.8 / 2.8 / 0.3	**18** TH 0537 / 1151 / 1816	0.9 / 2.6 / 0.7
4 TH 0011 / 0609 / 1216 / 1854	2.4 / 0.8 / 2.8 / 0.4	**19** F 0023 / 0607 / 1227 / 1844	2.3 / 1.0 / 2.5 / 0.8
5 F 0055 / 0650 / 1302 / 1938	2.4 / 0.9 / 2.7 / 0.5	**20** SA 0057 / 0643 / 1305 / 1916	2.3 / 1.0 / 2.4 / 0.9
6 SA 0143 / 0736 / 1353 / ◑2028	2.3 / 1.0 / 2.6 / 0.7	**21** SU 0137 / 0725 / 1350 / ◑1955	2.2 / 1.1 / 2.3 / 1.1
7 SU 0242 / 0832 / 1459 / 2132	2.2 / 1.0 / 2.5 / 0.9	**22** M 0225 / 0816 / 1444 / 2045	2.2 / 1.2 / 2.2 / 1.2
8 M 0404 / 0951 / 1631 / 2255	2.2 / 1.1 / 2.4 / 1.1	**23** TU 0330 / 0923 / 1610 / 2202	2.2 / 1.3 / 2.1 / 1.3
9 TU 0515 / 1130 / 1753 / 2339	2.2 / 1.0 / 2.3 / 1.3	**24** W 0454 / 1109 / 1738 / 2339	2.2 / 1.2 / 2.2 / 1.3
10 W 0008 / 0617 / 1246 / 1912	1.1 / 2.3 / 0.9 / 2.3	**25** TH 0557 / 1217 / 1844	2.3 / 1.1 / 2.2
11 TH 0114 / 0718 / 1353 / 2015	1.1 / 2.4 / 0.8 / 2.4	**26** F 0037 / 0651 / 1311 / 1940	1.2 / 2.3 / 0.9 / 2.3
12 F 0211 / 0809 / 1445 / 2101	1.1 / 2.5 / 0.6 / 2.4	**27** SA 0127 / 0738 / 1402 / 2026	1.1 / 2.5 / 0.7 / 2.4
13 SA 0256 / 0852 / 1529 / ○2140	1.0 / 2.6 / 0.5 / 2.4	**28** SU 0215 / 0822 / 1452 / 2106	1.0 / 2.6 / 0.5 / 2.5
14 SU 0335 / 0930 / 1608 / 2216	0.9 / 2.6 / 0.5 / 2.4	**29** M 0301 / 0903 / 1539 / ●2145	0.9 / 2.7 / 0.4 / 2.6
15 M 0408 / 1007 / 1644 / 2250	0.9 / 2.7 / 0.5 / 2.4	**30** TU 0346 / 0945 / 1624 / 2225	0.8 / 2.7 / 0.3 / 2.6
		31 W 0429 / 1028 / 1707 / 2305	0.7 / 2.7 / 0.3 / 2.6

Chart Datum: 1·50 metres below Ordnance Datum (Newlyn)
HAT is 3·0 metres above Chart Datum

TIME ZONE (UT)	LOWESTOFT	Dates in amber are SPRINGS
For Summer Time add ONE hour in **non-shaded areas**	LAT 52°28'N LONG 1°45'E	Dates in yellow are NEAPS
		2011

TIMES AND HEIGHTS OF HIGH AND LOW WATERS

SEPTEMBER

Time	m		Time	m
1 0510	0.7	**16** 0510	0.9
1111	2.9	1122	2.6
TH 1748	0.3	F 1738	0.8
2346	2.5	2347	2.4
2 0551	0.7	**17** 0542	0.9
1156	2.8	1158	2.5
F 1829	0.5	SA 1806	0.9
3 0029	2.5	**18** 0021	2.4
0634	0.8	0617	1.0
SA 1244	2.7	SU 1236	2.4
1912	0.7	1837	1.0
4 0116	2.4	**19** 0100	2.4
0722	0.9	0658	1.0
SU 1340	2.6	M 1319	2.3
◑ 2000	0.9	1916	1.1
5 0211	2.3	**20** 0145	2.3
0820	1.0	0747	1.1
M 1458	2.4	TU 1412	2.2
2103	1.1	◐ 2005	1.2
6 0326	2.3	**21** 0241	2.3
0948	1.0	0852	1.2
TU 1636	2.3	W 1531	2.1
2238	1.3	2110	1.4
7 0445	2.3	**22** 0354	2.2
1122	1.0	1031	1.2
W 1757	2.3	TH 1717	2.2
2356	1.3	2256	1.4
8 0553	2.3	**23** 0513	2.3
1233	0.9	1146	1.0
TH 1913	2.4	F 1821	2.3
9 0102	1.2	**24** 0007	1.3
0658	2.4	0612	2.4
F 1336	0.7	SA 1242	0.8
2005	2.4	1914	2.4
10 0156	1.2	**25** 0100	1.1
0749	2.5	0703	2.5
SA 1424	0.7	SU 1333	0.7
2045	2.4	1959	2.5
11 0237	1.1	**26** 0148	1.0
0829	2.5	0749	2.6
SU 1505	0.6	M 1423	0.5
2118	2.4	2039	2.5
12 0311	1.0	**27** 0236	0.9
0905	2.6	0834	2.8
M 1540	0.6	TU 1511	0.4
○ 2150	2.4	● 2119	2.6
13 0343	0.9	**28** 0322	0.8
0940	2.7	0946	2.9
TU 1613	0.6	W 1557	0.3
2219	2.5	2159	2.6
14 0412	0.9	**29** 0407	0.7
1014	2.7	1005	2.9
W 1643	0.6	TH 1641	0.3
2248	2.4	2240	2.6
15 0441	0.9	**30** 0451	0.6
1048	2.6	1051	2.9
TH 1711	0.7	F 1723	0.4
2316	2.4	2322	2.6

OCTOBER

Time	m		Time	m
1 0535	0.6	**16** 0520	0.9
1140	2.8	1133	2.4
SA 1805	0.6	SU 1733	0.9
		2351	2.5
2 0005	2.5	**17** 0557	0.9
0621	0.7	1212	2.4
SU 1233	2.7	M 1807	1.0
1847	0.8		
3 0053	2.5	**18** 0029	2.4
0711	0.8	0638	1.0
M 1335	2.5	TU 1256	2.3
1935	1.1	1847	1.1
4 0147	2.4	**19** 0115	2.4
0812	0.9	0727	1.0
TU 1502	2.4	W 1348	2.2
◑ 2035	1.3	1936	1.3
5 0253	2.3	**20** 0207	2.3
0939	0.9	0829	1.1
W 1629	2.3	TH 1459	2.2
2212	1.4	◐ 2037	1.4
6 0410	2.3	**21** 0309	2.3
1102	0.9	0955	1.0
TH 1745	2.4	F 1650	2.2
2332	1.4	2202	1.4
7 0520	2.3	**22** 0422	2.3
1207	0.8	1111	0.9
F 1853	2.4	SA 1752	2.3
		2327	1.3
8 0035	1.3	**23** 0532	2.4
0625	2.4	1209	0.7
SA 1305	0.8	SU 1844	2.4
1942	2.4		
9 0128	1.2	**24** 0025	1.2
0719	2.4	0627	2.5
SU 1353	0.7	M 1302	0.6
2020	2.4	1929	2.5
10 0208	1.1	**25** 0118	1.0
0800	2.5	0718	2.6
M 1432	0.7	TU 1353	0.5
2052	2.4	2011	2.6
11 0243	1.0	**26** 0209	0.9
0836	2.5	0807	2.8
TU 1506	0.7	W 1443	0.4
2121	2.5	● 2052	2.6
12 0314	0.9	**27** 0259	0.8
0911	2.6	0856	2.8
W 1538	0.7	TH 1530	0.4
○ 2147	2.5	2134	2.7
13 0344	0.9	**28** 0348	0.6
0946	2.6	0946	2.9
TH 1607	0.7	F 1616	0.4
2214	2.5	2216	2.7
14 0415	0.8	**29** 0435	0.6
1021	2.6	1037	2.8
F 1634	0.8	SA 1659	0.6
2244	2.5	2300	2.6
15 0447	0.8	**30** 0523	0.6
1057	2.5	1129	2.7
SA 1703	0.8	SU 1742	0.7
2316	2.5	2345	2.6
		31 0611	0.6
		1225	2.6
		M 1826	0.9

NOVEMBER

Time	m		Time	m
1 0032	2.5	**16** 0007	2.5
0702	0.7	0626	0.9
TU 1329	2.4	W 1240	2.3
1911	1.1	1827	1.1
2 0124	2.5	**17** 0051	2.4
0801	0.8	0715	0.9
W 1448	2.3	TH 1330	2.2
◑ 2004	1.3	1915	1.2
3 0221	2.4	**18** 0140	2.4
0915	0.8	0812	0.9
TH 1607	2.3	F 1431	2.2
2121	1.4	◐ 2010	1.3
4 0327	2.4	**19** 0235	2.4
1029	0.8	0921	0.9
F 1716	2.3	SA 1604	2.2
2250	1.4	2117	1.3
5 0438	2.3	**20** 0337	2.4
1131	0.8	1033	0.8
SA 1819	2.3	SU 1718	2.3
2355	1.4	2238	1.3
6 0541	2.3	**21** 0449	2.4
1226	0.8	1135	0.7
SU 1911	2.4	M 1811	2.4
		2349	1.2
7 0049	1.3	**22** 0554	2.5
0637	2.4	1231	0.6
M 1314	0.8	TU 1859	2.4
1951	2.4		
8 0133	1.2	**23** 0048	1.1
0724	2.4	0650	2.6
TU 1354	0.8	W 1325	0.6
2023	2.4	1944	2.5
9 0210	1.1	**24** 0145	0.9
0805	2.4	0745	2.7
W 1429	0.8	TH 1417	0.6
2051	2.5	2028	2.6
10 0244	1.0	**25** 0241	0.7
0843	2.5	0839	2.7
TH 1501	0.8	F 1507	0.6
○ 2116	2.5	● 2112	2.6
11 0318	0.9	**26** 0334	0.6
0921	2.3	0934	2.7
F 1531	0.8	SA 1555	0.6
2145	2.5	2157	2.7
12 0352	0.8	**27** 0424	0.5
0958	2.5	1029	2.7
SA 1602	0.8	SU 1640	0.7
2216	2.6	2242	2.7
13 0427	0.8	**28** 0513	0.5
1036	2.4	1122	2.6
SU 1635	0.9	M 1723	0.8
2251	2.6	2327	2.6
14 0505	0.8	**29** 0601	0.5
1115	2.4	1216	2.5
M 1709	0.9	TU 1805	1.0
2327	2.6		
15 0544	0.8	**30** 0013	2.6
1155	2.3	0649	0.6
TU 1746	1.0	W 1312	2.4
		1847	1.1

DECEMBER

Time	m		Time	m
1 0059	2.5	**16** 0031	2.5
0741	0.7	0703	0.7
TH 1416	2.3	F 1311	2.3
1930	1.2	1857	1.1
2 0148	2.5	**17** 0117	2.5
0839	0.8	0752	0.7
F 1529	2.2	SA 1402	2.2
◑ 2020	1.4	1946	1.2
3 0240	2.5	**18** 0206	2.5
0944	0.9	0848	0.7
SA 1634	2.2	SU 1506	2.2
2129	1.4	◐ 2042	1.2
4 0343	2.3	**19** 0301	2.5
1048	0.9	0954	0.8
SU 1734	2.2	M 1635	2.2
2300	1.4	2150	1.2
5 0452	2.3	**20** 0412	2.5
1143	0.9	1102	0.8
M 1828	2.2	TU 1737	2.3
		2314	1.2
6 0003	1.3	**21** 0527	2.5
0552	2.3	1205	0.8
TU 1233	1.0	W 1830	2.3
1914	2.3		
7 0054	1.2	**22** 0025	1.0
0646	2.3	0631	2.5
W 1315	1.0	TH 1303	0.8
1950	2.4	1920	2.4
8 0137	1.1	**23** 0130	0.9
0736	2.3	0732	2.5
TH 1353	1.0	F 1358	0.7
2020	2.4	2008	2.5
9 0216	1.0	**24** 0230	0.7
0821	2.3	0834	2.6
F 1427	0.9	SA 1452	0.8
2048	2.5	● 2055	2.6
10 0254	0.9	**25** 0326	0.6
0903	2.4	0931	2.6
SA 1501	0.9	SU 1541	0.8
○ 2120	2.5	2141	2.6
11 0333	0.8	**26** 0417	0.5
0942	2.4	1023	2.6
SU 1537	0.9	M 1625	0.8
2154	2.6	2226	2.7
12 0413	0.7	**27** 0503	0.4
1022	2.4	1112	2.5
M 1614	0.9	TU 1707	0.9
2231	2.6	2310	2.7
13 0454	0.7	**28** 0547	0.4
1102	2.4	1158	2.4
TU 1653	0.9	W 1745	0.9
2309	2.6	2352	2.6
14 0536	0.7	**29** 0630	0.5
1142	2.4	1244	2.3
W 1732	1.0	TH 1821	1.0
2349	2.6		
15 0619	0.7	**30** 0033	2.6
1225	2.3	0712	0.6
TH 1813	1.0	F 1331	2.2
		1856	1.1
		31 0114	2.5
		0755	0.7
		SA 1424	2.1
		1935	1.2

Chart Datum: 1·50 metres below Ordnance Datum (Newlyn)
HAT is 3·0 metres above Chart Datum

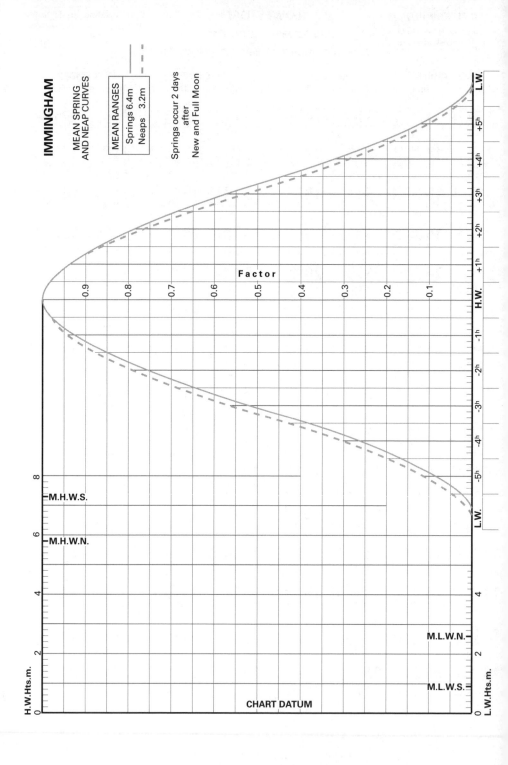

IMMINGHAM

MEAN SPRING
AND NEAP CURVES

MEAN RANGES	
Springs 6.4m	Neaps 3.2m

Springs occur 2 days
after
New and Full Moon

Factor

IMMINGHAM
LAT 53°38'N   LONG 0°11'W
TIMES AND HEIGHTS OF HIGH AND LOW WATERS

Dates in amber are **SPRINGS**
Dates in yellow are **NEAPS**

2011

JANUARY

Day	Time m	Time m	Time m	Time m	Day	Time m	Time m	Time m	Time m
1 SA	0251 6.3	0917 2.0	1528 6.3	2150 2.1	16 SU	0226 5.8	0839 2.4	1510 5.9	2114 2.4
2 SU	0358 6.4	1015 1.9	1623 6.6	2249 1.7	17 M	0332 6.1	0943 2.2	1604 6.3	2219 2.0
3 M	0458 6.6	1106 1.7	1711 6.8	2341 1.4	18 TU	0429 6.4	1039 1.9	1652 6.7	2316 1.6
4 TU	0549 6.8	1153 1.6	1754 7.0 ●		19 W	0520 6.8	1131 1.6	1736 7.0 ○	
5 W	0028 1.3	0633 6.8	1236 1.6	1833 7.1	20 TH	0008 1.1	0607 7.0	1218 1.3	1817 7.3
6 TH	0111 1.2	0712 6.8	1315 1.5	1910 7.2	21 F	0055 0.8	0652 7.2	1303 1.1	1858 7.5
7 F	0148 1.2	0747 6.7	1349 1.6	1944 7.1	22 SA	0140 0.6	0734 7.3	1345 1.1	1938 7.7
8 SA	0222 1.3	0820 6.6	1420 1.7	2017 7.0	23 SU	0222 0.5	0816 7.3	1425 1.1	2019 7.7
9 SU	0251 1.5	0850 6.4	1450 1.9	2048 6.8	24 M	0304 0.6	0857 7.1	1506 1.2	2102 7.5
10 M	0321 1.7	0920 6.3	1521 2.1	2123 6.6	25 TU	0346 0.9	0941 6.8	1547 1.5	2149 7.2
11 TU	0353 1.9	0956 6.1	1557 2.3	2202 6.3	26 W	0430 1.3	1031 6.5	1633 1.9	2244 6.7
12 W	0433 2.2	1039 5.8	1642 2.5	◖ 2249 6.0	27 TH	0521 1.8	1129 6.1	1730 2.3	2352 6.2
13 TH	0522 2.4	1134 5.7	1739 2.8	2350 5.8	28 F	0625 2.3	1239 5.8	1847 2.6	
14 F	0623 2.6	1247 5.6	1849 2.9		29 SA	0115 5.9	0744 2.5	1355 5.8	2025 2.6
15 SA	0107 5.7	0731 2.6	1405 5.7	2002 2.7	30 SU	0242 5.9	0900 2.4	1506 6.0	2143 2.2
					31 M	0359 6.1	1002 2.2	1607 6.3	2241 1.8

FEBRUARY

Day	Time m	Time m	Time m	Time m	Day	Time m	Time m	Time m	Time m
1 TU	0459 6.4	1053 2.0	1656 6.7	2330 1.5	16 W	0415 6.4	1019 1.9	1629 6.6	2259 1.4
2 W	0544 6.6	1138 1.7	1738 6.9		17 TH	0506 6.8	1113 1.5	1715 7.1	2351 0.9
3 TH	0014 1.2	0621 6.7	1220 1.5	● 1815 7.1	18 F	0553 7.1	1201 1.2	1758 7.5 ○	
4 F	0054 1.1	0654 6.8	1257 1.4	1850 7.2	19 SA	0038 0.5	0635 7.4	1247 0.9	1840 7.8
5 SA	0129 1.1	0724 6.8	1330 1.4	1923 7.2	20 SU	0123 0.3	0716 7.5	1329 0.7	1921 7.9
6 SU	0159 1.2	0751 6.7	1359 1.5	1953 7.1	21 M	0204 0.3	0754 7.5	1409 0.7	2002 7.9
7 M	0226 1.3	0816 6.6	1426 1.6	2021 6.9	22 TU	0243 0.4	0833 7.3	1448 0.9	2044 7.5
8 TU	0251 1.5	0842 6.5	1452 1.7	2050 6.8	23 W	0321 0.8	0913 7.0	1527 1.2	2129 7.2
9 W	0316 1.7	0912 6.3	1521 1.9	2122 6.5	24 TH	0401 1.4	0956 6.5	1609 1.7	◑ 2221 6.6
10 TH	0345 2.0	0947 6.1	1556 2.2	2200 6.2	25 F	0446 2.0	1050 6.1	1700 2.2	2330 6.0
11 F	0424 2.3	1031 5.8	1645 2.5	◖ 2251 5.9	26 SA	0547 2.5	1202 5.7	1817 2.6	
12 SA	0522 2.6	1131 5.5	1757 2.8		27 SU	0103 5.6	0717 2.9	1326 5.6	2015 2.6
13 SU	0005 5.6	0640 2.8	1308 5.4	1920 2.8	28 M	0236 5.6	0844 2.7	1444 5.8	2131 2.2
14 M	0153 5.6	0802 2.7	1436 5.7	2042 2.5					
15 TU	0314 5.9	0916 2.4	1539 6.2	2159 2.0					

MARCH

Day	Time m	Time m	Time m	Time m	Day	Time m	Time m	Time m	Time m
1 TU	0356 6.0	0946 2.4	1547 6.2	2225 1.8	16 W	0255 5.9	0850 2.4	1508 6.2	2134 1.8
2 W	0448 6.3	1034 2.0	1636 6.6	2310 1.5	17 TH	0356 6.4	0955 1.9	1601 6.7	2235 1.2
3 TH	0527 6.5	1118 1.7	1716 6.8	2350 1.2	18 F	0446 6.8	1050 1.5	1649 7.2	2327 0.7
4 F	0559 6.7	1157 1.5	1753 7.0 ●		19 SA	0531 7.2	1139 1.1	1734 7.5 ○	
5 SA	0027 1.1	0628 6.8	1234 1.4	1826 7.1	20 SU	0014 0.4	0612 7.4	1226 0.8	1818 7.8
6 SU	0101 1.1	0655 6.8	1307 1.3	1857 7.1	21 M	0059 0.2	0652 7.5	1309 0.6	1901 7.9
7 M	0131 1.2	0719 6.6	1335 1.3	1926 7.0	22 TU	0140 0.3	0730 7.5	1351 0.6	1944 7.8
8 TU	0157 1.3	0744 6.8	1401 1.4	1954 6.9	23 W	0219 0.5	0808 7.3	1430 0.8	2027 7.5
9 W	0221 1.4	0809 6.7	1427 1.5	2022 6.8	24 TH	0257 0.9	0846 7.0	1509 1.1	2113 7.0
10 TH	0243 1.6	0837 6.5	1453 1.7	2052 6.6	25 F	0335 1.5	0928 6.6	1551 1.6	2205 6.4
11 F	0309 1.8	0909 6.3	1526 2.0	2128 6.3	26 SA	0417 2.1	1019 6.1	1642 2.1	◑ 2317 5.8
12 SA	0344 2.1	0949 6.0	1611 2.3	◖ 2217 5.9	27 SU	0515 2.7	1131 5.7	1758 2.5	
13 SU	0438 2.5	1045 5.6	1723 2.6	2329 5.6	28 M	0051 5.5	0644 3.0	1258 5.6	1952 2.5
14 M	0600 2.8	1211 5.5	1850 2.6		29 TU	0216 5.6	0817 2.9	1415 5.8	2104 2.2
15 TU	0129 5.5	0730 2.8	1400 5.7	2016 2.3	30 W	0329 5.9	0918 2.5	1517 6.1	2155 1.8
					31 TH	0419 6.2	1007 2.1	1607 6.4	2238 1.5

APRIL

Day	Time m	Time m	Time m	Time m	Day	Time m	Time m	Time m	Time m
1 F	0456 6.5	1049 1.8	1648 6.7	2317 1.4	16 SA	0419 6.8	1022 1.4	1621 7.2	2258 0.7
2 SA	0528 6.6	1129 1.5	1724 6.8	2354 1.2	17 SU	0505 7.1	1114 1.1	1710 7.5	2347 0.5
3 SU	0557 6.7	1206 1.4	1757 6.9		18 M	0548 7.3	1203 0.8	1758 7.6 ○	
4 M	0028 1.2	0622 6.8	1240 1.3	1829 6.9	19 TU	0033 0.4	0628 7.4	1250 0.6	1844 7.7
5 TU	0100 1.2	0648 6.8	1310 1.3	1900 6.9	20 W	0116 0.5	0707 7.4	1333 0.6	1930 7.6
6 W	0128 1.3	0715 6.8	1338 1.4	1931 6.9	21 TH	0157 0.7	0746 7.3	1415 0.8	2015 7.3
7 TH	0153 1.4	0742 6.8	1406 1.4	2001 6.7	22 F	0235 1.1	0825 7.0	1457 1.1	2102 6.8
8 F	0218 1.6	0811 6.6	1435 1.6	2033 6.5	23 SA	0314 1.5	0907 6.7	1540 1.5	2155 6.3
9 SA	0247 1.8	0844 6.4	1511 1.8	2112 6.3	24 SU	0356 2.2	0956 6.2	1630 2.0	2304 5.8
10 SU	0324 2.1	0925 6.1	1559 2.1	2203 5.9	25 M	0449 2.6	1101 5.9	1738 2.3	◑
11 M	0418 2.4	1021 5.8	1708 2.3	◖ 2317 5.6	26 TU	0024 5.5	0601 2.9	1222 5.7	1905 2.4
12 TU	0534 2.7	1140 5.7	1830 2.3		27 W	0138 5.5	0728 2.9	1335 5.8	2018 2.2
13 W	0107 5.6	0701 2.7	1320 5.9	1951 2.0	28 TH	0243 5.7	0837 2.6	1437 6.0	2112 2.0
14 TH	0228 6.0	0820 2.3	1432 6.3	2104 1.6	29 F	0335 6.0	0929 2.3	1528 6.2	2156 1.8
15 F	0328 6.4	0926 1.9	1530 6.7	2204 1.1	30 SA	0417 6.2	1014 2.0	1611 6.4	2237 1.6

TIDES

Chart Datum: 3·90 metres below Ordnance Datum (Newlyn)
HAT is 8·0 metres above Chart Datum

TIDES

TIME ZONE (UT)
For Summer Time add ONE hour in **non-shaded areas**

IMMINGHAM
LAT 53°38'N LONG 0°11'W
TIMES AND HEIGHTS OF HIGH AND LOW WATERS

Dates in amber are **SPRINGS**
Dates in yellow are **NEAPS**

2011

Each daily entry lists up to four readings as *Time m* (24-hour time, height in metres). Weekday abbreviations precede the third reading. Moon-phase symbols (●, ○, ◑, ◐) are shown where marked.

MAY

#	Reading 1	Reading 2	Reading 3	Reading 4
1	0451 6.5	1055 1.7	SU 1650 6.6	2316 1.5
2	0522 6.6	1134 1.5	M 1726 6.7	2353 1.4
3	0551 6.7	1211 1.4	TU 1802 6.7 ●	
4	0028 1.4	0621 6.8	W 1246 1.4	1837 6.8
5	0101 1.4	0652 6.8	TH 1319 1.3	1912 6.8
6	0131 1.5	0723 6.8	F 1351 1.4	1948 6.7
7	0201 1.6	0755 6.7	SA 1426 1.5	2025 6.5
8	0235 1.7	0830 6.6	SU 1507 1.6	2108 6.3
9	0316 2.0	0914 6.4	M 1557 1.8	2202 6.1
10	0409 2.3	1010 6.2	TU 1700 1.9	◑ 2312 5.9
11	0516 2.4	1121 6.1	W 1811 1.9	
12	0039 5.9	0633 2.4	TH 1243 6.1	1923 1.7
13	0154 6.1	0748 2.2	F 1356 6.4	2031 1.5
14	0243 6.4	0855 1.9	SA 1459 6.7	2133 1.2
15	0349 6.7	0955 1.5	SU 1555 7.0	2229 1.0
16	0438 7.0	1051 1.2	M 1650 7.2	2321 0.8
17	0524 7.1	1143 1.0	TU 1742 7.3 ○	
18	0009 0.8	0607 7.3	W 1233 0.8	1832 7.3
19	0055 0.9	0649 7.3	TH 1320 0.8	1921 7.2
20	0137 1.0	0729 7.2	F 1404 0.9	2007 7.0
21	0217 1.3	0809 7.0	SA 1447 1.1	2053 6.7
22	0256 1.7	0850 6.8	SU 1530 1.4	2143 6.3
23	0336 2.1	0936 6.4	M 1615 1.8	2239 5.9
24	0422 2.4	1030 6.1	TU 1707 2.0	◑ 2342 5.7
25	0517 2.7	1135 5.9	W 1806 2.2	
26	0045 5.6	0622 2.8	TH 1242 5.8	1909 2.3
27	0146 5.6	0732 2.7	F 1344 5.9	2010 2.2
28	0241 5.8	0836 2.5	SA 1440 6.0	2103 2.1
29	0328 6.0	0930 2.2	SU 1529 6.2	2152 1.9
30	0409 6.3	1017 2.0	M 1614 6.3	2236 1.8
31	0446 6.5	1101 1.8	TU 1656 6.5	2319 1.6

JUNE

#	Reading 1	Reading 2	Reading 3	Reading 4
1	0522 6.6	1143 1.6	W 1738 6.6	● 2359 1.5
2	0558 6.8	1224 1.4	TH 1819 6.7	
3	0037 1.5	0634 6.9	F 1304 1.3	1900 6.8
4	0114 1.5	0710 6.9	SA 1344 1.2	1940 6.8
5	0151 1.5	0746 6.9	SU 1424 1.2	2022 6.7
6	0229 1.6	0824 6.8	M 1507 1.3	2107 6.5
7	0311 1.8	0908 6.7	TU 1555 1.4	2158 6.4
8	0400 1.9	1000 6.6	W 1650 1.5	2258 6.2
9	0458 2.1	1102 6.5	TH 1750 1.6	
10	0007 6.1	0604 2.2	F 1213 6.4	1854 1.6
11	0117 6.1	0715 2.2	SA 1324 6.4	2001 1.6
12	0221 6.3	0826 2.0	SU 1433 6.5	2105 1.5
13	0321 6.5	0933 1.8	M 1537 6.7	2205 1.4
14	0415 6.7	1033 1.5	TU 1638 6.8	2300 1.3
15	0505 6.9	1130 1.2	W 1735 6.9	○ 2351 1.2
16	0551 7.1	1222 1.0	TH 1828 7.0	
17	0038 1.2	0634 7.2	F 1310 0.9	1915 7.0
18	0122 1.3	0715 7.2	SA 1355 0.9	1959 6.9
19	0202 1.4	0755 7.1	SU 1436 1.1	2040 6.7
20	0239 1.6	0833 6.9	M 1515 1.3	2120 6.4
21	0315 1.9	0912 6.7	TU 1552 1.6	2201 6.1
22	0352 2.1	0955 6.4	W 1630 1.8	2245 5.9
23	0434 2.4	1044 6.1	TH 1714 2.1	◐ 2336 5.7
24	0523 2.6	1140 5.9	F 1804 2.3	
25	0033 5.6	0621 2.7	SA 1243 5.8	1900 2.4
26	0135 5.6	0726 2.7	SU 1346 5.8	2002 2.4
27	0234 5.8	0834 2.5	M 1447 5.9	2103 2.2
28	0327 6.0	0936 2.3	TU 1542 6.1	2158 2.1
29	0414 6.3	1031 2.0	W 1632 6.3	2249 1.9
30	0457 6.6	1121 1.7	TH 1720 6.5	2336 1.7

JULY

#	Reading 1	Reading 2	Reading 3	Reading 4
1	0539 6.8	1208 1.4	F 1806 6.7 ●	
2	0020 1.5	0618 7.0	SA 1254 1.1	1849 6.9
3	0102 1.4	0657 7.1	SU 1337 1.0	1932 7.0
4	0142 1.3	0736 7.2	M 1419 0.9	2014 7.0
5	0222 1.3	0816 7.2	TU 1501 0.9	2057 6.9
6	0303 1.4	0858 7.2	W 1545 1.0	2143 6.7
7	0347 1.6	0946 7.0	TH 1632 1.2	2234 6.5
8	0437 1.8	1041 6.7	F 1725 1.5	◐ 2333 6.3
9	0535 2.1	1145 6.5	SA 1826 1.7	
10	0040 6.1	0645 2.2	SU 1300 6.3	1934 1.9
11	0150 6.1	0804 2.2	M 1416 6.4	2044 2.0
12	0257 6.2	0919 2.0	TU 1530 6.3	2149 1.9
13	0358 6.5	1025 1.7	W 1637 6.5	2246 1.7
14	0451 6.7	1122 1.3	TH 1735 6.7	2337 1.5
15	0537 7.0	1212 1.1	F 1823 6.8 ○	
16	0024 1.4	0619 7.1	SA 1259 0.9	1905 6.9
17	0106 1.4	0659 7.2	SU 1340 0.9	1942 6.8
18	0144 1.4	0736 7.2	M 1418 1.0	2017 6.7
19	0218 1.5	0811 7.1	TU 1451 1.2	2048 6.6
20	0250 1.7	0845 6.9	W 1521 1.5	2118 6.4
21	0320 1.9	0919 6.6	TH 1551 1.7	2150 6.2
22	0353 2.1	0956 6.4	F 1625 2.0	2228 5.9
23	0433 2.4	1041 6.0	SA 1709 2.3	◐ 2318 5.7
24	0525 2.6	1139 5.8	SU 1803 2.5	
25	0027 5.6	0629 2.8	M 1254 5.6	1908 2.6
26	0144 5.6	0741 2.7	TU 1410 5.7	2018 2.5
27	0251 5.8	0857 2.5	W 1517 5.9	2126 2.3
28	0347 6.2	1005 2.1	TH 1614 6.2	2225 2.0
29	0435 6.5	1102 1.6	F 1705 6.6	2317 1.7
30	0519 6.9	1153 1.2	SA 1752 6.9 ●	
31	0004 1.5	0600 7.2	SU 1240 0.9	1835 7.1

AUGUST

#	Reading 1	Reading 2	Reading 3	Reading 4
1	0048 1.2	0640 7.4	M 1324 0.7	1917 7.2
2	0129 1.1	0720 7.6	TU 1406 0.5	1957 7.3
3	0209 1.1	0800 7.6	W 1446 0.6	2038 7.2
4	0248 1.1	0842 7.5	TH 1527 0.8	2119 7.0
5	0329 1.3	0927 7.2	F 1609 1.2	2205 6.7
6	0414 1.7	1019 6.8	SA 1657 1.6	◑ 2259 6.3
7	0508 2.1	1123 6.4	SU 1756 2.1	
8	0007 6.0	0619 2.4	M 1244 6.0	1911 2.4
9	0123 5.9	0751 2.5	TU 1411 5.9	2031 2.4
10	0238 6.0	0915 2.2	W 1533 6.1	2139 2.2
11	0344 6.3	1018 1.8	TH 1639 6.4	2234 1.9
12	0436 6.7	1111 1.4	F 1730 6.7	2322 1.7
13	0521 7.0	1157 1.1	SA 1810 6.8 ○	
14	0005 1.5	0600 7.1	SU 1240 1.0	1845 6.9
15	0046 1.4	0637 7.2	M 1317 1.0	1916 6.9
16	0122 1.4	0712 7.2	TU 1351 1.1	1946 6.8
17	0153 1.4	0744 7.2	W 1420 1.2	2012 6.7
18	0221 1.5	0814 7.0	TH 1446 1.4	2037 6.6
19	0248 1.7	0844 6.8	F 1511 1.7	2104 6.4
20	0316 1.9	0915 6.5	SA 1539 2.0	2137 6.2
21	0350 2.2	0952 6.2	SU 1615 2.3	◑ 2218 5.9
22	0436 2.5	1042 5.8	M 1707 2.6	2317 5.6
23	0542 2.8	1200 5.5	TU 1819 2.8	
24	0054 5.5	0701 2.8	W 1341 5.6	1940 2.8
25	0218 5.7	0824 2.6	TH 1457 5.9	2058 2.5
26	0320 6.1	0942 2.1	F 1556 6.3	2202 2.1
27	0410 6.6	1041 1.5	SA 1647 6.7	2255 1.7
28	0454 7.0	1132 1.1	SU 1732 7.0	2342 1.4
29	0537 7.4	1218 0.7	M 1815 7.3 ●	
30	0027 1.1	0618 7.7	TU 1303 0.4	1855 7.4
31	0110 0.9	0659 7.8	W 1344 0.4	1934 7.5

Chart Datum: 3·90 metres below Ordnance Datum (Newlyn)
HAT is 8·0 metres above Chart Datum

TIME ZONE (UT)
For Summer Time add ONE hour in **non-shaded areas**

IMMINGHAM
LAT 53°38'N   LONG 0°11'W
TIMES AND HEIGHTS OF HIGH AND LOW WATERS

Dates in amber are **SPRINGS**
Dates in yellow are **NEAPS**

2011

SEPTEMBER

Day	Time m	Time m	Time m	Time m		Day	Time m	Time m	Time m	Time m
1 TH	0150 0.8	0741 7.9	1424 0.5	2013 7.4		**16** F	0153 1.5	0745 7.0	1412 1.5	2001 6.8
2 F	0230 0.9	0823 7.7	1502 0.8	2052 7.1		**17** SA	0218 1.6	0813 6.8	1435 1.7	2027 6.8
3 SA	0310 1.2	0908 7.3	1542 1.3	2135 6.8		**18** SU	0245 1.8	0843 6.6	1500 1.9	2057 6.4
4 SU	0352 1.6	1000 6.8	1627 1.9	2227 6.3 ◐		**19** M	0317 2.1	0917 6.3	1532 2.2	2135 6.1
5 M	0445 2.1	1106 6.2	1726 2.4	2336 5.9		**20** TU	0400 2.4	1004 5.9	1621 2.6	2227 5.7 ◑
6 TU	0600 2.5	1235 5.8	1851 2.8			**21** W	0506 2.7	1117 5.6	1735 2.9	2354 5.5
7 W	0059 5.8	0746 2.6	1407 5.8	2018 2.7		**22** TH	0629 2.8	1313 5.5	1904 2.9	
8 TH	0218 6.0	0906 2.2	1529 6.1	2123 2.4		**23** F	0140 5.7	0754 2.5	1433 5.9	2026 2.6
9 F	0324 6.3	1003 1.8	1628 6.4	2215 2.1		**24** SA	0247 6.2	0912 2.0	1532 6.4	2133 2.2
10 SA	0415 6.7	1050 1.4	1627 6.7	2300 1.7		**25** SU	0339 6.7	1012 1.4	1622 6.8	2227 1.7
11 SU	0457 7.0	1132 1.2	1745 6.8	2341 1.5		**26** M	0425 7.1	1103 1.0	1707 7.2	2316 1.3
12 M	0535 7.1	1211 1.1	1816 6.9 ○			**27** TU	0510 7.5	1150 0.6	1749 7.4 ●	
13 TU	0019 1.4	0610 7.2	1247 1.1	1845 6.9		**28** W	0002 1.0	0553 7.8	1236 0.4	1829 7.6
14 W	0055 1.3	0644 7.2	1319 1.2	1911 6.9		**29** TH	0047 0.8	0637 7.9	1318 0.4	1909 7.6
15 TH	0126 1.4	0715 7.1	1347 1.3	1936 6.9		**30** F	0130 0.7	0721 7.9	1358 0.6	1947 7.5

OCTOBER

Day	Time m	Time m	Time m	Time m		Day	Time m	Time m	Time m	Time m
1 SA	0211 0.9	0805 7.7	1438 0.9	2027 7.2		**16** SU	0153 1.6	0749 6.8	1405 1.7	1959 6.8
2 SU	0252 1.2	0852 7.2	1517 1.5	2109 6.9		**17** M	0222 1.7	0820 6.6	1432 1.9	2029 6.6
3 M	0335 1.6	0945 6.7	1600 2.1	2159 6.4		**18** TU	0255 2.0	0857 6.3	1506 2.2	2106 6.3
4 TU	0428 2.1	1055 6.1	1657 2.6	2308 6.0 ◐		**19** W	0339 2.2	0944 6.0	1553 2.5	2157 6.0
5 W	0545 2.5	1224 5.7	1822 3.0			**20** TH	0441 2.5	1054 5.7	1701 2.8	2310 5.8 ◑
6 TH	0033 5.8	0726 2.5	1347 5.8	1951 2.9		**21** F	0601 2.5	1238 5.7	1826 2.9	
7 F	0150 6.0	0841 2.2	1502 6.0	2056 2.6		**22** SA	0050 5.9	0721 2.3	1359 6.0	1948 2.6
8 SA	0254 6.3	0934 1.8	1557 6.3	2147 2.2		**23** SU	0205 6.2	0835 1.9	1500 6.4	2057 2.2
9 SU	0346 6.6	1019 1.6	1638 6.6	2231 1.9		**24** M	0303 6.7	0936 1.4	1552 6.8	2155 1.8
10 M	0429 6.9	1059 1.4	1712 6.8	2312 1.6		**25** TU	0354 7.1	1030 1.0	1648 7.1	2247 1.4
11 TU	0507 7.0	1137 1.3	1743 6.9	2350 1.5		**26** W	0443 7.5	1120 0.8	1722 7.4 ●	2337 1.0
12 W	0542 7.1	1212 1.3	1811 7.0 ○			**27** TH	0531 7.7	1207 0.6	1804 7.5	
13 TH	0025 1.4	0615 7.1	1245 1.3	1838 7.0		**28** F	0025 0.8	0618 7.8	1252 0.6	1845 7.6
14 F	0057 1.4	0647 7.1	1314 1.4	1905 7.0		**29** SA	0111 0.8	0705 7.7	1335 0.8	1925 7.5
15 SA	0126 1.5	0719 7.0	1340 1.5	1931 6.9		**30** SU	0155 0.8	0752 7.5	1415 1.1	2006 7.3
						31 M	0238 1.1	0840 7.1	1455 1.6	2048 7.0

NOVEMBER

Day	Time m	Time m	Time m	Time m		Day	Time m	Time m	Time m	Time m
1 TU	0323 1.5	0934 6.6	1538 2.1	2137 6.6		**16** W	0244 1.8	0847 6.4	1451 2.1	2050 6.5
2 W	0414 1.9	1040 6.1	1629 2.6	2238 6.2 ◐		**17** TH	0328 1.9	0935 6.2	1537 2.3	2139 6.3
3 TH	0521 2.3	1158 5.8	1739 3.0	2356 6.0		**18** F	0425 2.1	1036 6.0	1636 2.6	2241 6.2 ◑
4 F	0644 2.4	1309 5.8	1903 3.0			**19** SA	0533 2.2	1157 5.9	1749 2.7	2359 6.2
5 SA	0110 6.0	0757 2.3	1415 5.9	2014 2.8		**20** SU	0646 2.1	1316 6.0	1906 2.6	
6 SU	0214 6.2	0853 2.1	1512 6.1	2110 2.4		**21** M	0118 6.3	0756 1.8	1422 6.3	2019 2.3
7 M	0309 6.4	0939 1.9	1557 6.4	2157 2.1		**22** TU	0226 6.6	0900 1.5	1518 6.6	2123 1.9
8 TU	0355 6.6	1020 1.7	1635 6.6	2239 1.8		**23** W	0325 7.0	0958 1.3	1610 6.9	2221 1.5
9 W	0435 6.8	1059 1.6	1708 6.8	2319 1.7		**24** TH	0421 7.2	1052 1.1	1658 7.2	2316 1.2
10 TH	0512 6.8	1136 1.5	1739 6.9	2356 1.5 ○		**25** F	0514 7.4	1142 1.0	1743 7.4 ●	
11 F	0548 6.9	1211 1.5	1809 7.0			**26** SA	0007 1.0	0606 7.5	1231 1.0	1826 7.5
12 SA	0031 1.5	0623 6.9	1244 1.5	1840 7.0		**27** SU	0057 0.8	0656 7.4	1315 1.0	1909 7.5
13 SU	0104 1.5	0658 6.9	1314 1.6	1910 7.0		**28** M	0143 0.9	0744 7.3	1357 1.3	1950 7.4
14 M	0135 1.5	0733 6.8	1343 1.7	1940 6.9		**29** TU	0227 1.0	0831 7.0	1438 1.6	2032 7.1
15 TU	0208 1.6	0808 6.6	1415 1.9	2012 6.7		**30** W	0311 1.3	0920 6.6	1518 2.0	2116 6.8

DECEMBER

Day	Time m	Time m	Time m	Time m		Day	Time m	Time m	Time m	Time m
1 TH	0357 1.7	1014 6.3	1601 2.4	2207 6.5		**16** F	0320 1.5	0923 6.5	1524 2.0	2124 6.7
2 F	0446 2.0	1115 5.9	1651 2.7	2308 6.2 ◐		**17** SA	0408 1.8	1015 6.3	1614 2.2	2218 6.6
3 SA	0544 2.3	1218 5.8	1753 2.9			**18** SU	0505 1.8	1117 6.1	1715 2.3	2322 6.4 ◑
4 SU	0016 6.0	0647 2.4	1319 5.7	1905 2.9		**19** M	0609 1.9	1229 6.1	1826 2.4	
5 M	0122 6.0	0751 2.4	1417 5.9	2016 2.7		**20** TU	0036 6.4	0718 1.9	1340 6.2	1942 2.3
6 TU	0222 6.1	0847 2.3	1509 6.1	2115 2.5		**21** W	0153 6.4	0828 1.8	1446 6.4	2056 2.1
7 W	0316 6.2	0936 2.1	1555 6.3	2204 2.2		**22** TH	0304 6.6	0932 1.7	1545 6.6	2202 1.8
8 TH	0402 6.4	1020 1.9	1634 6.6	2248 1.9		**23** F	0408 6.8	1031 1.5	1639 6.9	2302 1.4
9 F	0445 6.5	1102 1.8	1711 6.7	2330 1.7		**24** SA	0507 7.0	1124 1.3	1728 7.2	2356 1.1 ●
10 SA	0525 6.7	1142 1.7	1746 6.9 ○			**25** SU	0602 7.2	1214 1.2	1813 7.3	
11 SU	0009 1.6	0604 6.8	1220 1.6	1820 7.0		**26** M	0047 0.9	0651 7.2	1300 1.2	1856 7.4
12 M	0048 1.5	0643 6.8	1255 1.6	1855 7.0		**27** TU	0133 0.8	0736 7.2	1342 1.3	1936 7.4
13 TU	0124 1.4	0721 6.8	1329 1.6	1928 7.0		**28** W	0216 0.9	0818 7.0	1420 1.5	2015 7.3
14 W	0201 1.4	0800 6.8	1404 1.7	2002 7.0		**29** TH	0255 1.0	0858 6.7	1456 1.7	2054 7.0
15 TH	0239 1.4	0839 6.6	1441 1.8	2040 6.9		**30** F	0332 1.5	0939 6.4	1531 2.0	2133 6.7
						31 SA	0408 1.8	1020 6.1	1609 2.3	2218 6.4

Chart Datum: 3·90 metres below Ordnance Datum (Newlyn)
HAT is 8·0 metres above Chart Datum

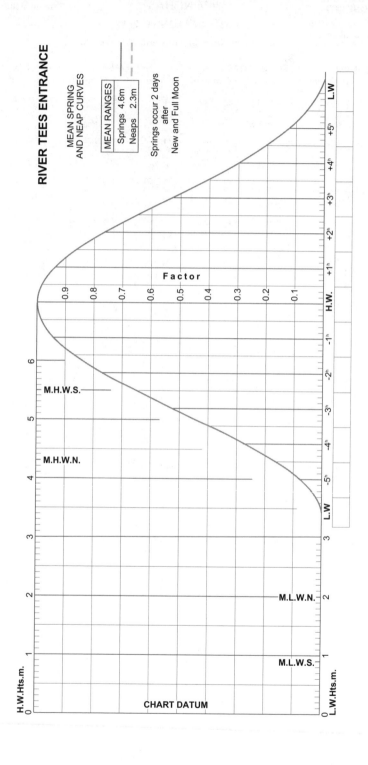

RIVER TEES ENTRANCE

MEAN SPRING
AND NEAP CURVES

MEAN RANGES
Springs 4.6m
Neaps 2.3m

Springs occur 2 days
after
New and Full Moon

RIVER TEES
LAT 54°38'N LONG 0°90'W

TIMES AND HEIGHTS OF HIGH AND LOW WATERS

Dates in amber are **SPRINGS**
Dates in yellow are **NEAPS**

2011

JANUARY

Day	Time m	Time m	Time m	Time m
1 SA	0036 4.7	0707 1.6	1313 4.8	1938 1.6
2 SU	0143 4.8	0805 1.5	1409 4.9	2035 1.3
3 M	0239 5.0	0854 1.4	1456 5.1	2124 1.1
4 TU	0326 5.1	0938 1.3	1537 5.2	●2207 1.0
5 W	0409 5.1	1017 1.3	1615 5.3	2246 0.9
6 TH	0448 5.1	1054 1.3	1650 5.4	2322 0.9
7 F	0526 5.1	1128 1.4	1725 5.3	2357 1.0
8 SA	0602 5.0	1200 1.5	1800 5.2	
9 SU	0030 1.1	0637 4.9	1233 1.6	1836 5.1
10 M	0103 1.3	0714 4.7	1307 1.6	1915 4.9
11 TU	0137 1.5	0755 4.5	1345 1.9	1959 4.7
12 W	0216 1.7	0841 4.4	1432 2.1	●2049 4.5
13 TH	0306 2.0	0936 4.2	1534 2.3	2149 4.3
14 F	0411 2.1	1038 4.2	1653 2.3	2257 4.2
15 SA	0527 2.1	1144 4.2	1809 2.2	
16 SU	0008 4.3	0638 2.0	1247 4.4	1913 1.9
17 M	0114 4.5	0737 1.8	1342 4.7	2008 1.5
18 TU	0209 4.8	0828 1.5	1429 5.0	2057 1.2
19 W	0257 5.0	0913 1.3	1513 5.3	○2143 0.8
20 TH	0342 5.3	0957 1.1	1555 5.5	2228 0.5
21 F	0427 5.4	1040 1.0	1637 5.7	2311 0.4
22 SA	0511 5.5	1122 0.9	1719 5.8	2354 0.3
23 SU	0556 5.5	1204 0.9	1803 5.7	
24 M	0037 0.4	0641 5.3	1246 1.0	1848 5.6
25 TU	0122 0.6	0728 5.1	1330 1.3	1937 5.3
26 W	0210 1.0	0820 4.8	1421 1.6	●2034 5.0
27 TH	0305 1.4	0918 4.6	1524 1.8	2141 4.7
28 F	0412 1.8	1025 4.4	1645 2.0	2300 4.4
29 SA	0534 2.0	1142 4.3	1820 1.9	
30 SU	0029 4.4	0656 1.9	1301 4.5	1937 1.7
31 M	0142 4.6	0757 1.8	1400 4.7	2033 1.4

FEBRUARY

Day	Time m	Time m	Time m	Time m
1 TU	0235 4.8	0845 1.6	1447 5.0	2118 1.1
2 W	0318 4.9	0925 1.4	1526 5.2	2155 1.0
3 TH	0355 5.0	1001 1.3	1600 5.3	●2229 0.9
4 F	0430 5.1	1034 1.2	1632 5.3	2300 0.9
5 SA	0502 5.1	1104 1.2	1702 5.4	2329 1.0
6 SU	0532 5.1	1133 1.2	1733 5.3	2357 1.0
7 M	0602 5.0	1202 1.3	1805 5.2	
8 TU	0026 1.1	0634 4.9	1234 1.4	1840 5.0
9 W	0057 1.3	0710 4.7	1307 1.6	1918 4.8
10 TH	0132 1.6	0752 4.5	1347 1.9	2003 4.6
11 F	0214 1.8	0842 4.3	1437 2.1	●2059 4.3
12 SA	0311 2.1	0944 4.1	1550 2.2	2210 4.2
13 SU	0432 2.2	1055 4.1	1724 2.2	2329 4.2
14 M	0603 2.1	1208 4.3	1845 1.9	
15 TU	0046 4.4	0714 1.9	1313 4.6	1947 1.4
16 W	0148 4.7	0809 1.5	1406 5.0	2039 1.0
17 TH	0238 5.1	0856 1.2	1452 5.3	2126 0.6
18 F	0324 5.3	0941 0.9	1535 5.6	○2210 0.3
19 SA	0407 5.5	1023 0.7	1617 5.9	2253 0.1
20 SU	0450 5.6	1104 0.6	1659 6.0	2334 0.1
21 M	0533 5.6	1144 0.6	1743 5.9	
22 TU	0015 0.2	0616 5.5	1225 0.8	1827 5.7
23 W	0057 0.6	0700 5.2	1307 1.0	1916 5.4
24 TH	0142 1.0	0748 4.9	1354 1.4	●2011 4.9
25 F	0233 1.5	0844 4.5	1456 1.7	2120 4.5
26 SA	0342 2.0	0953 4.2	1624 2.0	2245 4.2
27 SU	0514 2.2	1118 4.2	1813 1.9	
28 M	0022 4.2	0642 2.1	1244 4.3	1928 1.6

MARCH

Day	Time m	Time m	Time m	Time m
1 TU	0133 4.4	0743 1.9	1344 4.6	2020 1.4
2 W	0221 4.7	0828 1.7	1429 4.9	2100 1.1
3 TH	0300 4.9	0905 1.4	1506 5.1	2133 1.0
4 F	0333 5.0	0938 1.3	1538 5.2	●2203 0.9
5 SA	0404 5.1	1008 1.1	1608 5.3	2231 0.9
6 SU	0433 5.1	1037 1.1	1636 5.3	2258 0.9
7 M	0500 5.1	1105 1.0	1705 5.3	2325 0.9
8 TU	0528 5.1	1134 1.1	1735 5.2	2352 1.1
9 W	0559 5.0	1204 1.2	1808 5.0	
10 TH	0023 1.2	0632 4.8	1238 1.4	1845 4.8
11 F	0058 1.5	0711 4.6	1316 1.6	1929 4.6
12 SA	0138 1.8	0759 4.4	1403 1.9	●2025 4.3
13 SU	0231 2.1	0900 4.2	1511 2.1	2137 4.1
14 M	0351 2.3	1015 4.1	1647 2.0	2259 4.1
15 TU	0530 2.2	1132 4.2	1815 1.7	
16 W	0018 4.4	0646 1.9	1241 4.6	1921 1.3
17 TH	0123 4.7	0744 1.5	1338 5.0	2014 0.8
18 F	0214 5.1	0832 1.1	1426 5.4	2102 0.4
19 SA	0259 5.4	0917 0.8	1510 5.7	○2147 0.2
20 SU	0343 5.6	1000 0.6	1554 5.9	2229 0.0
21 M	0425 5.7	1042 0.4	1638 6.0	2311 0.1
22 TU	0508 5.6	1123 0.5	1723 5.9	2352 0.3
23 W	0550 5.5	1204 0.8	1809 5.6	
24 TH	0033 0.7	0633 5.2	1248 0.9	1859 5.2
25 F	0117 1.2	0720 4.9	1336 1.2	1955 4.8
26 SA	0207 1.7	0814 4.5	1439 1.6	●2103 4.3
27 SU	0315 2.1	0923 4.3	1605 1.9	2226 4.1
28 M	0446 2.3	1047 4.2	1748 1.8	2358 4.1
29 TU	0612 2.2	1211 4.3	1900 1.6	
30 W	0106 4.3	0713 2.0	1313 4.5	1950 1.4
31 TH	0153 4.6	0758 1.7	1359 4.8	2029 1.2

APRIL

Day	Time m	Time m	Time m	Time m
1 F	0231 4.8	0835 1.5	1436 5.0	2101 1.1
2 SA	0304 4.9	0908 1.3	1509 5.1	2131 1.0
3 SU	0334 5.0	0939 1.1	1540 5.2	●2159 0.9
4 M	0402 5.1	1009 1.0	1609 5.2	2226 0.9
5 TU	0428 5.1	1039 1.0	1638 5.2	2254 1.0
6 W	0457 5.1	1109 1.0	1709 5.1	2323 1.1
7 TH	0528 5.0	1141 1.1	1744 5.0	2356 1.1
8 F	0603 4.9	1216 1.3	1823 4.8	
9 SA	0032 1.5	0642 4.7	1256 1.5	1909 4.6
10 SU	0114 1.7	0729 4.5	1346 1.7	2007 4.4
11 M	0207 2.0	0830 4.3	1453 1.8	●2116 4.2
12 TU	0324 2.2	0942 4.2	1620 1.8	2234 4.2
13 W	0458 2.1	1058 4.4	1741 1.5	2349 4.4
14 TH	0612 1.9	1207 4.7	1848 1.1	
15 F	0053 4.8	0711 1.5	1306 5.0	1944 0.8
16 SA	0146 5.1	0803 1.1	1358 5.4	2034 0.4
17 SU	0233 5.3	0851 0.8	1446 5.6	2120 0.3
18 M	0317 5.5	0936 0.6	1532 5.8	●2205 0.2
19 TU	0401 5.6	1021 0.5	1619 5.8	2248 0.3
20 W	0444 5.5	1105 0.5	1706 5.7	2331 0.5
21 TH	0527 5.4	1149 0.6	1755 5.4	
22 F	0013 0.9	0611 5.2	1235 0.8	1846 5.1
23 SA	0057 1.3	0657 4.9	1325 1.1	1941 4.7
24 SU	0146 1.7	0749 4.6	1424 1.5	2044 4.3
25 M	0248 2.1	0852 4.4	1537 1.7	●2156 4.1
26 TU	0405 2.3	1007 4.3	1659 1.8	2313 4.1
27 W	0523 2.3	1122 4.3	1811 1.7	
28 TH	0020 4.2	0627 2.1	1227 4.4	1904 1.5
29 F	0112 4.3	0717 1.8	1318 4.6	1947 1.4
30 SA	0153 4.6	0758 1.6	1400 4.8	2023 1.3

TIDES

TIME ZONE (UT)
For Summer Time add ONE hour in **non-shaded areas**

RIVER TEES
LAT 54°38′N   LONG 0°90′W
TIMES AND HEIGHTS OF HIGH AND LOW WATERS

Dates in amber are **SPRINGS**
Dates in yellow are **NEAPS**

2011

MAY

Day	Time m	Time m	Time m	Time m	Day	Time m	Time m	Time m	Time m
1 SU	0229 4.8	0835 1.4	1437 4.9	2056 1.2	16 M	0208 5.2	0827 0.9	1426 5.4	2057 0.6
2 M	0301 4.9	0909 1.2	1511 5.0	2127 1.1	17 TU	0255 5.3	0917 0.7	1516 5.5	2144 0.5
3 TU	0331 5.0	0942 1.1	1543 5.0	2157 1.0	18 W	0340 5.4	1005 0.6	1606 5.5	2230 0.7
4 W	0400 5.1	1015 1.0	1615 5.0	2228 1.1	19 TH	0425 5.4	1052 0.6	1655 5.4	2314 0.8
5 TH	0431 5.1	1049 1.0	1650 5.0	2301 1.1	20 F	0508 5.3	1138 0.7	1745 5.2	2357 1.1
6 F	0506 5.0	1125 1.0	1728 5.0	2337 1.3	21 SA	0552 5.2	1224 0.8	1834 5.0	
7 SA	0543 4.9	1203 1.1	1811 4.8		22 SU	0040 1.4	0637 5.0	1312 1.0	1924 4.7
8 SU	0016 1.4	0624 4.8	1248 1.3	1859 4.7	23 M	0126 1.7	0725 4.8	1403 1.3	2018 4.5
9 M	0101 1.7	0711 4.7	1339 1.4	1955 4.5	24 TU	0217 1.9	0818 4.6	1459 1.6	2116 4.3
10 TU	0154 1.9	0809 4.6	1443 1.5	2100 4.4	25 W	0317 2.1	0920 4.4	1602 1.7	2218 4.2
11 W	0305 2.0	0916 4.5	1556 1.5	2209 4.4	26 TH	0424 2.2	1026 4.3	1706 1.8	2320 4.2
12 TH	0424 2.0	1027 4.6	1707 1.3	2318 4.5	27 F	0530 2.2	1130 4.3	1806 1.8	
13 F	0535 1.8	1134 4.8	1813 1.1		28 SA	0017 4.3	0627 2.0	1229 4.4	1857 1.7
14 SA	0021 4.8	0638 1.5	1237 5.0	1912 0.9	29 SU	0108 4.5	0717 1.8	1319 4.6	1942 1.5
15 SU	0117 5.0	0734 1.2	1333 5.3	2006 0.7	30 M	0150 4.6	0801 1.6	1403 4.7	2021 1.4
					31 TU	0227 4.8	0840 1.3	1443 4.8	2057 1.3

JUNE

Day	Time m	Time m	Time m	Time m	Day	Time m	Time m	Time m	Time m
1 W	0302 4.9	0918 1.2	1521 4.9	2132 1.2	16 TH	0327 5.3	0955 0.8	1559 5.3	2216 1.0
2 TH	0337 5.0	0955 1.1	1558 5.0	2208 1.2	17 F	0411 5.3	1042 0.7	1647 5.3	2300 1.1
3 F	0412 5.1	1034 1.0	1637 5.0	2246 1.2	18 SA	0453 5.3	1127 0.7	1732 5.2	2341 1.2
4 SA	0449 5.1	1114 0.9	1718 5.0	2326 1.2	19 SU	0535 5.2	1209 0.8	1816 5.0	
5 SU	0529 5.1	1156 0.9	1803 5.0		20 M	0020 1.3	0615 5.2	1251 1.0	1859 4.8
6 M	0007 1.3	0611 5.1	1242 1.0	1850 4.9	21 TU	0100 1.5	0657 5.0	1333 1.2	1943 4.6
7 TU	0053 1.5	0657 5.0	1332 1.1	1943 4.8	22 W	0140 1.7	0742 4.8	1416 1.5	2029 4.5
8 W	0144 1.6	0750 4.8	1428 1.1	2041 4.7	23 TH	0225 1.9	0832 4.6	1504 1.7	2120 4.3
9 TH	0244 1.8	0851 4.6	1530 1.2	2143 4.6	24 F	0320 2.1	0929 4.4	1559 1.9	2216 4.2
10 F	0352 1.8	0958 4.8	1635 1.3	2247 4.6	25 SA	0425 2.2	1031 4.3	1700 2.0	2316 4.2
11 SA	0501 1.8	1106 4.8	1741 1.2	2351 4.7	26 SU	0532 2.1	1135 4.3	1803 1.9	
12 SU	0608 1.6	1212 4.9	1845 1.1		27 M	0015 4.3	0633 2.0	1237 4.4	1859 1.8
13 M	0052 4.8	0711 1.4	1316 5.0	1945 1.1	28 TU	0109 4.5	0727 1.8	1331 4.5	1948 1.6
14 TU	0149 5.0	0811 1.1	1415 5.2	2040 1.0	29 W	0156 4.7	0811 1.1	1418 4.7	2032 1.5
15 W	0240 5.2	0905 0.9	1509 5.3	2130 0.9	30 TH	0237 4.9	0857 1.3	1501 4.9	2114 1.3

JULY

Day	Time m	Time m	Time m	Time m	Day	Time m	Time m	Time m	Time m
1 F	0317 5.0	0939 1.0	1543 5.1	2154 1.2	16 SA	0359 5.3	1032 0.8	1634 5.2	2243 1.2
2 SA	0356 5.2	1022 0.8	1624 5.2	2235 1.1	17 SU	0438 5.4	1111 0.8	1713 5.2	2320 1.2
3 SU	0435 5.3	1104 0.7	1707 5.2	2316 1.1	18 M	0514 5.4	1147 0.8	1751 5.1	2354 1.3
4 M	0515 5.4	1147 0.6	1751 5.2	2358 1.1	19 TU	0550 5.3	1222 1.0	1827 5.0	
5 TU	0557 5.4	1231 0.6	1837 5.2		20 W	0027 1.4	0626 5.2	1256 1.2	1903 4.8
6 W	0041 1.2	0641 5.3	1318 0.7	1925 5.0	21 TH	0100 1.5	0705 5.0	1330 1.4	1942 4.6
7 TH	0127 1.3	0731 5.2	1408 0.9	2017 4.9	22 F	0136 1.7	0747 4.8	1407 1.6	2025 4.5
8 F	0219 1.5	0827 5.0	1503 1.2	2114 4.7	23 SA	0219 2.0	0836 4.5	1453 1.9	2116 4.3
9 SA	0320 1.7	0932 4.9	1606 1.4	2217 4.6	24 SU	0316 2.2	0935 4.3	1553 2.1	2216 4.2
10 SU	0431 1.8	1043 4.7	1714 1.5	2325 4.5	25 M	0432 2.2	1043 4.2	1707 2.1	2322 4.2
11 M	0546 1.7	1157 4.7	1827 1.5		26 TU	0550 2.2	1155 4.3	1820 2.1	
12 TU	0034 4.6	0701 1.6	1311 4.8	1934 1.5	27 W	0028 4.3	0656 1.9	1301 4.4	1921 1.8
13 W	0138 4.8	0806 1.3	1413 5.0	2031 1.3	28 TH	0126 4.6	0750 1.6	1355 4.7	2011 1.6
14 TH	0232 5.0	0901 1.1	1505 5.1	2120 1.2	29 F	0214 4.9	0838 1.2	1442 5.0	2056 1.4
15 F	0318 5.2	0949 0.9	1552 5.2	2204 1.2	30 SA	0256 5.1	0923 0.9	1525 5.2	2139 1.1
					31 SU	0337 5.4	1006 0.6	1607 5.4	2221 1.0

AUGUST

Day	Time m	Time m	Time m	Time m	Day	Time m	Time m	Time m	Time m
1 M	0416 5.6	1049 0.4	1649 5.5	2301 0.9	16 TU	0449 5.4	1117 0.9	1720 5.2	2324 1.2
2 TU	0457 5.7	1131 0.4	1732 5.5	2342 0.9	17 W	0520 5.4	1147 1.0	1751 5.1	2353 1.2
3 W	0538 5.7	1213 0.4	1816 5.4		18 TH	0553 5.3	1216 1.2	1823 5.0	
4 TH	0023 0.9	0622 5.6	1257 0.6	1901 5.3	19 F	0024 1.4	0628 5.2	1246 1.4	1858 4.6
5 F	0106 1.1	0709 5.4	1343 0.9	1950 5.0	20 SA	0057 1.6	0707 4.9	1320 1.6	1938 4.6
6 SA	0153 1.4	0804 5.1	1435 1.2	2045 4.7	21 SU	0135 1.8	0749 4.6	1401 1.9	2026 4.4
7 SU	0252 1.6	0909 4.8	1539 1.6	2149 4.5	22 M	0223 2.1	0847 4.3	1456 2.2	2126 4.2
8 M	0408 1.9	1027 4.6	1655 1.9	2303 4.4	23 TU	0334 2.3	0956 4.2	1616 2.3	2235 4.1
9 TU	0537 1.9	1153 4.5	1819 1.9		24 W	0508 2.2	1115 4.2	1745 2.2	2349 4.3
10 W	0024 4.5	0702 1.7	1313 4.7	1929 1.7	25 TH	0627 2.0	1231 4.4	1855 2.0	
11 TH	0132 4.7	0805 1.3	1411 4.9	2023 1.6	26 F	0054 4.5	0727 1.6	1331 4.7	1949 1.7
12 F	0224 5.0	0855 1.1	1458 5.1	2107 1.4	27 SA	0147 4.9	0817 1.1	1419 5.0	2035 1.3
13 SA	0306 5.2	0937 0.9	1538 5.2	2146 1.2	28 SU	0231 5.3	0902 0.8	1502 5.3	2118 1.0
14 SU	0343 5.4	1013 0.8	1614 5.2	2221 1.2	29 M	0313 5.6	0945 0.4	1544 5.6	2159 0.8
15 M	0417 5.4	1046 0.8	1648 5.2	2253 1.1	30 TU	0353 5.8	1027 0.3	1626 5.7	2240 0.7
					31 W	0434 5.9	1109 0.3	1708 5.7	2321 0.6

RIVER TEES

LAT 54°38′N   LONG 0°90′W

Dates in amber are **SPRINGS**
Dates in yellow are **NEAPS**

2011

TIMES AND HEIGHTS OF HIGH AND LOW WATERS

SEPTEMBER

Day	Time m	Time m	Time m	Time m
1 TH	0516 5.9	1150 0.3	1751 5.6	
16 F	0522 5.2	1139 1.2	1746 5.1	2353 1.3
2 F	0001 0.7	0601 5.8	1233 0.6	1835 5.4
17 SA	0555 5.1	1209 1.4	1820 4.9	
3 SA	0044 0.9	0649 5.5	1318 1.0	1923 5.1
18 SU	0025 1.5	0632 4.9	1243 1.6	1859 4.7
4 SU	0131 1.3	0745 5.1	◗ 2017 4.7	
19 M	0103 1.7	0716 4.6	1324 1.9	1946 4.5
5 M	0231 1.6	0853 4.7	1515 1.9	2124 4.5
20 TU	0149 2.0	0811 4.4	1415 2.2	◗ 2044 4.3
6 TU	0353 1.9	1016 4.4	1640 2.1	2244 4.3
21 W	0253 2.2	0919 4.2	1532 2.4	2154 4.2
7 W	0535 1.9	1151 4.4	1810 2.1	
22 TH	0429 2.2	1040 4.2	1709 2.3	2309 4.3
8 TH	0011 4.5	0657 1.6	1306 4.6	1916 1.9
23 F	0554 1.9	1158 4.4	1824 2.1	
9 F	0118 4.7	0754 1.3	1358 4.9	2006 1.7
24 SA	0018 4.6	0657 1.5	1301 4.8	1919 1.7
10 SA	0206 5.0	0838 1.1	1440 5.0	2046 1.5
25 SU	0114 5.0	0749 1.0	1351 5.1	2007 1.3
11 SU	0246 5.2	0915 1.0	1516 5.2	2121 1.3
26 M	0202 5.4	0835 0.6	1435 5.4	2052 1.0
12 M	0320 5.3	0946 0.9	1548 5.2	○ 2153 1.2
27 TU	0245 5.7	0919 0.4	1518 5.7	● 2135 0.7
13 TU	0352 5.4	1016 0.9	1618 5.3	2224 1.1
28 W	0328 5.9	1002 0.2	1600 5.8	2217 0.6
14 W	0421 5.4	1044 0.9	1647 5.2	2253 1.1
29 TH	0411 6.0	1044 0.2	1642 5.8	2259 0.5
15 TH	0451 5.3	1111 1.0	1715 5.2	2322 1.2
30 F	0456 6.0	1127 0.4	1726 5.7	2342 0.6

OCTOBER

Day	Time m	Time m	Time m	Time m
1 SA	0544 5.8	1210 0.7	1811 5.4	
16 SU	0529 5.1	1140 1.4	1750 5.0	
2 SU	0026 0.9	0634 5.4	1255 1.1	1858 5.1
17 M	0003 1.4	0608 4.9	1216 1.6	1829 4.8
3 M	0116 1.2	0731 5.0	1347 1.6	1952 4.8
18 TU	0041 1.6	0652 4.7	1256 1.9	1914 4.6
4 TU	0218 1.6	0840 4.6	1453 2.1	◗ 2059 4.5
19 W	0128 1.8	0747 4.5	1346 2.1	2010 4.4
5 W	0340 1.8	1002 4.3	1618 2.3	2219 4.4
20 TH	0229 2.0	0853 4.3	1457 2.3	◗ 2116 4.4
6 TH	0517 1.8	1132 4.4	1744 2.3	2343 4.5
21 F	0353 2.0	1008 4.3	1629 2.3	2229 4.4
7 F	0633 1.6	1242 4.5	1849 2.1	
22 SA	0514 1.7	1122 4.5	1744 2.1	2338 4.7
8 SA	0049 4.7	0727 1.4	1333 4.8	1938 1.8
23 SU	0620 1.4	1226 4.8	1845 1.8	
9 SU	0138 4.9	0809 1.2	1413 5.0	2018 1.6
24 M	0038 5.0	0716 1.0	1320 5.1	1936 1.4
10 M	0218 5.1	0844 1.1	1448 5.1	2052 1.4
25 TU	0131 5.4	0805 0.7	1407 5.4	2024 1.0
11 TU	0253 5.2	0919 1.1	1519 5.2	2125 1.2
26 W	0219 5.7	0852 0.5	1452 5.6	● 2111 0.8
12 W	0324 5.3	0944 1.0	1548 5.2	○ 2156 1.1
27 TH	0306 5.8	0938 0.4	1536 5.7	2156 0.6
13 TH	0355 5.3	1011 1.1	1615 5.3	2226 1.1
28 F	0353 5.9	1022 0.4	1620 5.7	2242 0.6
14 F	0425 5.3	1039 1.1	1644 5.2	2257 1.1
29 SA	0441 5.8	1107 0.6	1704 5.6	2327 0.6
15 SA	0456 5.2	1108 1.2	1715 5.2	2328 1.2
30 SU	0531 5.6	1151 0.9	1750 5.5	
31 M	0015 0.8	0623 5.3	1238 1.3	1837 5.2

NOVEMBER

Day	Time m	Time m	Time m	Time m
1 TU	0106 1.1	0720 4.9	1328 1.7	1930 4.9
16 W	0028 1.4	0637 4.8	1239 1.8	1851 4.8
2 W	0204 1.4	0823 4.6	1428 2.1	◑ 2031 4.7
17 TH	0115 1.5	0729 4.6	1327 2.0	1942 4.7
3 TH	0314 1.7	0935 4.4	1542 2.3	2142 4.5
18 F	0211 1.6	0830 4.5	1429 2.2	◗ 2043 4.6
4 F	0434 1.8	1051 4.3	1659 2.3	2256 4.5
19 SA	0320 1.7	0937 4.5	1546 2.2	2151 4.6
5 SA	0549 1.7	1200 4.4	1806 2.2	
20 SU	0433 1.6	1045 4.6	1701 2.1	2259 4.8
6 SU	0004 4.6	0646 1.6	1255 4.6	1900 2.0
21 M	0540 1.4	1149 4.8	1807 1.8	
7 M	0059 4.7	0730 1.5	1338 4.8	1944 1.7
22 TU	0003 5.0	0641 1.1	1248 5.0	1906 1.5
8 TU	0144 4.9	0808 1.4	1415 5.0	2022 1.4
23 W	0103 5.2	0737 0.9	1341 5.3	2000 1.2
9 W	0222 5.0	0841 1.3	1449 5.1	2057 1.4
24 TH	0158 5.5	0829 0.8	1429 5.5	2052 0.9
10 TH	0258 5.1	0913 1.2	1519 5.2	○ 2131 1.2
25 F	0250 5.6	0918 0.7	1516 5.6	● 2142 0.7
11 F	0331 5.1	0943 1.2	1549 5.2	2204 1.2
26 SA	0341 5.6	1005 0.7	1602 5.6	2230 0.6
12 SA	0404 5.1	1013 1.2	1619 5.2	2237 1.2
27 SU	0432 5.6	1052 0.9	1648 5.6	2318 0.6
13 SU	0437 5.1	1044 1.3	1652 5.1	2311 1.2
28 M	0522 5.5	1137 1.1	1733 5.5	
14 M	0513 5.0	1119 1.4	1728 5.1	2348 1.3
29 TU	0006 0.8	0612 5.2	1222 1.3	1818 5.3
15 TU	0553 4.9	1157 1.6	1807 5.0	
30 W	0054 1.0	0703 5.0	1308 1.6	1906 5.1

DECEMBER

Day	Time m	Time m	Time m	Time m
1 TH	0143 1.2	0757 4.7	1357 1.9	1958 4.9
16 F	0103 1.2	0712 4.9	1311 1.7	1919 5.0
2 F	0237 1.5	0854 4.5	1454 2.2	◑ 2056 4.7
17 SA	0153 1.3	0806 4.7	1403 1.9	2013 4.9
3 SA	0338 1.7	0956 4.3	1600 2.3	2200 4.5
18 SU	0250 1.4	0905 4.6	1507 2.0	2116 4.8
4 SU	0444 1.9	1100 4.3	1708 2.3	2306 4.4
19 M	0354 1.5	1009 4.6	1619 2.0	2224 4.8
5 M	0548 1.9	1201 4.4	1812 2.2	
20 TU	0502 1.5	1114 4.7	1731 1.9	2334 4.8
6 TU	0008 4.5	0643 1.8	1254 4.5	1905 2.0
21 W	0610 1.4	1219 4.8	1840 1.6	
7 W	0104 4.6	0729 1.7	1339 4.7	1951 1.7
22 TH	0042 5.0	0715 1.3	1320 5.0	1944 1.4
8 TH	0151 4.7	0810 1.6	1418 4.9	2031 1.5
23 F	0146 5.1	0813 1.1	1414 5.2	2042 1.1
9 F	0233 4.8	0846 1.5	1453 5.0	2109 1.3
24 SA	0243 5.3	0906 1.0	1504 5.4	● 2135 0.8
10 SA	0311 4.9	0920 1.4	1527 5.2	○ 2146 1.2
25 SU	0336 5.4	0954 1.0	1551 5.5	2224 0.7
11 SU	0348 5.0	0954 1.3	1600 5.2	2222 1.1
26 M	0425 5.4	1040 1.0	1635 5.6	2309 0.6
12 M	0424 5.1	1029 1.3	1635 5.2	2259 1.1
27 TU	0512 5.4	1123 1.1	1717 5.6	2352 0.7
13 TU	0501 5.1	1106 1.4	1712 5.2	2338 1.1
28 W	0556 5.2	1203 1.3	1759 5.5	
14 W	0541 5.0	1145 1.4	1750 5.2	
29 TH	0033 0.8	0639 5.1	1242 1.5	1839 5.3
15 TH	0019 1.1	0625 5.0	1227 1.6	1832 5.1
30 F	0114 1.1	0723 4.8	1321 1.7	1923 5.1
31 SA	0155 1.4	0808 4.6	1403 1.9	2010 4.8

TIDES

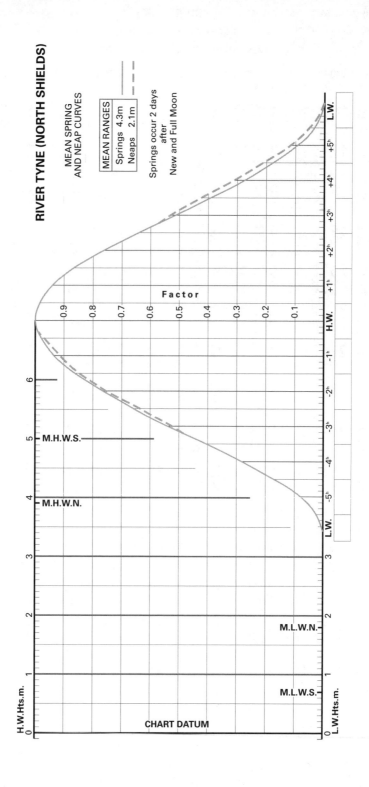

RIVER TYNE (NORTH SHIELDS)

MEAN SPRING
AND NEAP CURVES

MEAN RANGES
Springs 4.3m
Neaps 2.1m

Springs occur 2 days
after
New and Full Moon

NORTH SHIELDS
LAT 55°01'N   LONG 1°26'W

Dates in amber are SPRINGS
Dates in yellow are NEAPS

2011

TIMES AND HEIGHTS OF HIGH AND LOW WATERS

JANUARY

Day	Time m	Time m	Time m	Time m	Day	Time m	Time m	Time m	Time m
1 SA	0026 4.5	0654 1.5	1259 4.5	1927 1.5	16 SU	0629 1.9	1242 4.2	1905 1.8	
2 SU	0130 4.6	0752 1.4	1353 4.7	2024 1.3	17 M	0106 4.2	0728 1.7	1336 4.4	1958 1.5
3 M	0225 4.7	0841 1.4	1439 4.9	2112 1.1	18 TU	0200 4.5	0817 1.5	1420 4.7	2046 1.2
4 TU	0313 4.8	0924 1.3	1520 5.0	2155 0.9	19 W	0246 4.8	0902 1.2	1501 5.0	2131 0.8
5 W	0355 4.9	1003 1.3	1558 5.1	2234 0.9	20 TH	0329 5.0	0945 1.0	1541 5.2	2215 0.5
6 TH	0434 4.8	1038 1.3	1634 5.1	2310 0.9	21 F	0412 5.2	1026 0.9	1621 5.4	2258 0.4
7 F	0511 4.8	1111 1.3	1709 5.0	2344 1.0	22 SA	0455 5.2	1107 0.8	1702 5.4	2342 0.3
8 SA	0546 4.7	1143 1.4	1744 5.0		23 SU	0539 5.2	1148 0.9	1745 5.4	
9 SU	0016 1.1	0622 4.6	1215 1.5	1820 4.8	24 M	0025 0.4	0623 5.0	1230 1.0	1831 5.3
10 M	0050 1.2	0659 4.4	1250 1.6	1859 4.7	25 TU	0111 0.6	0711 4.8	1314 1.2	1922 5.1
11 TU	0126 1.4	0739 4.2	1329 1.8	1942 4.5	26 W	0159 1.0	0804 4.6	1405 1.5	2020 4.8
12 W	0208 1.6	0826 4.1	1416 2.0	2032 4.2	27 TH	0255 1.3	0904 4.2	1511 1.7	2130 4.4
13 TH	0259 1.9	0921 4.0	1519 2.2	2132 4.1	28 F	0403 1.7	1014 4.2	1635 1.9	2252 4.2
14 F	0404 2.0	1026 3.9	1639 2.2	2243 4.0	29 SA	0524 1.8	1132 4.1	1808 1.8	
15 SA	0519 2.0	1137 4.0	1758 2.1	2359 4.1	30 SU	0018 4.2	0643 1.8	1246 4.3	1924 1.6
					31 M	0129 4.4	0745 1.7	1345 4.5	2020 1.3

FEBRUARY

Day	Time m	Time m	Time m	Time m	Day	Time m	Time m	Time m	Time m
1 TU	0223 4.5	0833 1.5	1431 4.7	2106 1.1	16 W	0140 4.5	0759 1.5	1357 4.7	2027 1.0
2 W	0306 4.7	0913 1.4	1510 4.9	2144 0.9	17 TH	0228 4.8	0845 1.2	1440 5.0	2113 0.6
3 TH	0342 4.8	0947 1.2	1544 5.0	2217 0.8	18 F	0311 5.1	0927 0.9	1520 5.3	2157 0.3
4 F	0416 4.8	1019 1.1	1616 5.1	2248 0.8	19 SA	0353 5.3	1008 0.7	1601 5.5	2240 0.1
5 SA	0447 4.8	1049 1.1	1647 5.1	2317 0.8	20 SU	0434 5.3	1048 0.6	1642 5.6	2322 0.1
6 SU	0517 4.8	1118 1.1	1718 5.0	2346 0.9	21 M	0516 5.3	1129 0.6	1726 5.6	
7 M	0548 4.7	1147 1.2	1750 4.9		22 TU	0003 0.3	0558 5.1	1210 0.8	1811 5.4
8 TU	0015 1.1	0619 4.5	1218 1.4	1824 4.8	23 W	0046 0.6	0643 4.9	1253 1.0	1902 5.0
9 W	0047 1.3	0653 4.4	1251 1.5	1901 4.6	24 TH	0131 1.0	0733 4.6	1343 1.3	2000 4.7
10 TH	0121 1.5	0732 4.2	1330 1.8	1944 4.3	25 F	0224 1.5	0831 4.3	1447 1.6	2112 4.3
11 F	0202 1.8	0819 4.0	1422 2.0	2038 4.1	26 SA	0333 1.9	0943 4.1	1617 1.8	2239 4.0
12 SA	0300 2.0	0922 3.9	1537 2.1	2152 3.9	27 SU	0504 2.1	1109 4.0	1759 1.8	
13 SU	0423 2.1	1042 3.9	1711 2.1	2320 3.9	28 M	0009 4.0	0631 2.0	1230 4.2	1915 1.5
14 M	0553 2.1	1204 4.0	1834 1.8						
15 TU	0040 4.1	0705 1.8	1308 4.3	1936 1.4					

MARCH

Day	Time m	Time m	Time m	Time m	Day	Time m	Time m	Time m	Time m
1 TU	0120 4.2	0732 1.8	1330 4.4	2007 1.3	16 W	0013 4.1	0637 1.8	1236 4.3	1909 1.2
2 W	0210 4.4	0817 1.6	1415 4.6	2048 1.1	17 TH	0115 4.5	0734 1.4	1329 4.7	2002 0.8
3 TH	0248 4.6	0853 1.4	1451 4.8	2122 0.9	18 F	0204 4.8	0821 1.1	1414 5.0	2049 0.4
4 F	0321 4.7	0925 1.2	1523 4.9	2152 0.8	19 SA	0247 5.1	0904 0.8	1456 5.3	2133 0.2
5 SA	0351 4.8	0955 1.1	1553 5.0	2220 0.8	20 SU	0328 5.3	0946 0.5	1538 5.5	2216 0.0
6 SU	0419 4.8	1024 1.0	1622 5.0	2248 0.8	21 M	0409 5.3	1027 0.4	1622 5.6	2258 0.1
7 M	0447 4.8	1052 1.0	1652 5.0	2315 0.9	22 TU	0451 5.3	1109 0.5	1707 5.5	2340 0.3
8 TU	0516 4.7	1121 1.0	1722 4.9	2343 1.0	23 W	0533 5.1	1151 0.6	1755 5.3	
9 W	0545 4.6	1150 1.2	1755 4.8		24 TH	0022 0.7	0617 4.9	1237 0.9	1847 4.9
10 TH	0012 1.2	0616 4.5	1223 1.3	1830 4.6	25 F	0106 1.2	0706 4.6	1327 1.2	1946 4.5
11 F	0044 1.4	0652 4.3	1300 1.5	1912 4.3	26 SA	0158 1.6	0803 4.3	1431 1.5	2057 4.1
12 SA	0122 1.7	0736 4.1	1349 1.8	2006 4.1	27 SU	0306 2.0	0914 4.1	1559 1.7	2220 3.9
13 SU	0215 2.0	0835 4.0	1500 1.9	2120 3.9	28 M	0438 2.2	1038 4.0	1736 1.7	2346 4.0
14 M	0340 2.1	0957 3.9	1635 1.9	2251 3.9	29 TU	0605 2.1	1200 4.1	1849 1.5	
15 TU	0520 2.1	1125 4.0	1803 1.7		30 W	0054 4.1	0705 1.8	1302 4.3	1939 1.3
					31 TH	0142 4.3	0750 1.6	1347 4.5	2018 1.1

APRIL

Day	Time m	Time m	Time m	Time m	Day	Time m	Time m	Time m	Time m
1 F	0220 4.5	0825 1.4	1423 4.6	2050 1.0	16 SA	0136 4.8	0752 1.1	1346 5.0	2021 0.4
2 SA	0252 4.6	0858 1.2	1456 4.8	2120 0.9	17 SU	0221 5.0	0839 0.8	1432 5.3	2108 0.3
3 SU	0321 4.7	0929 1.0	1526 4.9	2149 0.8	18 M	0303 5.2	0923 0.6	1517 5.4	2152 0.2
4 M	0350 4.8	0959 1.0	1556 4.9	2217 0.8	19 TU	0345 5.3	1008 0.4	1604 5.4	2235 0.3
5 TU	0418 4.8	1028 0.9	1627 4.9	2246 0.9	20 W	0427 5.2	1052 0.4	1652 5.3	2318 0.6
6 W	0447 4.8	1058 0.9	1659 4.8	2314 1.0	21 TH	0511 5.1	1137 0.6	1742 5.1	
7 TH	0517 4.7	1130 1.1	1733 4.7	2344 1.2	22 F	0000 0.9	0555 4.9	1225 0.8	1835 4.8
8 F	0549 4.6	1204 1.2	1811 4.5		23 SA	0045 1.3	0644 4.6	1316 1.1	1933 4.4
9 SA	0017 1.4	0625 4.4	1244 1.3	1855 4.3	24 SU	0135 1.7	0739 4.4	1415 1.4	2037 4.1
10 SU	0058 1.6	0711 4.3	1335 1.5	1950 4.1	25 M	0236 2.0	0843 4.2	1529 1.6	2148 3.9
11 M	0153 1.9	0809 4.1	1443 1.7	2102 4.0	26 TU	0355 2.1	0957 4.0	1650 1.6	2303 3.9
12 TU	0313 2.0	0925 4.0	1608 1.6	2225 4.0	27 W	0516 2.1	1112 4.0	1802 1.6	
13 W	0446 2.0	1047 4.1	1730 1.4	2343 4.2	28 TH	0009 4.0	0621 1.9	1217 4.2	1855 1.4
14 TH	0603 1.7	1159 4.4	1837 1.1		29 F	0101 4.2	0710 1.7	1307 4.3	1937 1.3
15 F	0044 4.5	0702 1.4	1257 4.7	1932 0.7	30 SA	0142 4.4	0750 1.5	1348 4.5	2012 1.2

Chart Datum: 2·60 metres below Ordnance Datum (Newlyn)
HAT is 5·7 metres above Chart Datum

TIDES

TIME ZONE (UT)	NORTH SHIELDS	Dates in amber are SPRINGS
For Summer Time add ONE hour in **non-shaded** areas	LAT 55°01′N LONG 1°26′W	Dates in yellow are NEAPS

2011
TIMES AND HEIGHTS OF HIGH AND LOW WATERS

MAY

Day	Time m	Time m	Time m	Time m
1 SU	0217 4.5	0826 1.3	1424 4.6	2045 1.1
2 M	0250 4.6	0900 1.1	1458 4.7	2117 1.0
3 TU ●	0321 4.7	0933 1.0	1532 4.7	2148 1.0
4 W	0351 4.8	1006 1.0	1605 4.7	2220 1.0
5 TH	0422 4.8	1040 0.9	1640 4.7	2252 1.1
6 F	0454 4.7	1115 1.0	1718 4.7	2326 1.2
7 SA	0529 4.7	1154 1.0	1759 4.5	
8 SU	0004 1.4	0609 4.6	1238 1.1	1845 4.4
9 M	0048 1.5	0656 4.4	1329 1.3	1941 4.3
10 TU ◑	0142 1.7	0752 4.3	1431 1.3	2046 4.2
11 W	0251 1.8	0859 4.2	1543 1.3	2159 4.2
12 TH	0410 1.8	1013 4.3	1656 1.2	2309 4.3
13 F	0524 1.7	1123 4.5	1802 1.0	
14 SA	0012 4.5	0628 1.4	1225 4.7	1901 0.8
15 SU	0107 4.7	0724 1.1	1321 4.9	1954 0.6
16 M	0155 4.9	0816 0.9	1412 5.1	2044 0.5
17 TU ○	0241 5.1	0905 0.7	1502 5.2	2131 0.6
18 W	0325 5.1	0953 0.5	1552 5.2	2216 0.6
19 TH	0408 5.1	1040 0.5	1641 5.1	2259 0.8
20 F	0452 5.1	1127 0.6	1731 4.9	2342 1.1
21 SA	0537 4.9	1213 0.8	1822 4.7	
22 SU	0025 1.3	0623 4.7	1301 1.0	1913 4.4
23 M	0110 1.6	0713 4.5	1351 1.2	2008 4.2
24 TU ◑	0200 1.8	0808 4.3	1447 1.4	2106 4.0
25 W	0300 2.0	0908 4.2	1549 1.6	2207 3.9
26 TH	0410 2.1	1013 4.1	1654 1.6	2310 3.9
27 F	0519 2.0	1118 4.1	1754 1.6	
28 SA	0008 4.0	0618 1.9	1217 4.1	1846 1.5
29 SU	0058 4.2	0709 1.7	1308 4.3	1930 1.4
30 M	0140 4.4	0753 1.5	1352 4.4	2010 1.3
31 TU	0218 4.5	0833 1.3	1432 4.5	2047 1.2

JUNE

Day	Time m	Time m	Time m	Time m
1 W ●	0253 4.6	0910 1.1	1510 4.9	2123 1.1
2 TH	0327 4.7	0947 1.0	1548 4.7	2159 1.1
3 F	0402 4.8	1025 0.9	1626 4.7	2236 1.1
4 SA	0437 4.8	1105 0.8	1706 4.7	2314 1.1
5 SU	0515 4.8	1147 0.9	1749 4.7	2355 1.2
6 M	0557 4.8	1231 0.9	1836 4.6	
7 TU	0039 1.4	0642 4.7	1320 0.9	1928 4.5
8 W	0129 1.5	0735 4.6	1415 1.0	2026 4.4
9 TH ◑	0227 1.6	0835 4.5	1517 1.1	2130 4.3
10 F	0335 1.7	0942 4.5	1623 1.1	2236 4.3
11 SA	0447 1.6	1051 4.5	1730 1.1	2341 4.4
12 SU	0557 1.5	1200 4.6	1834 1.1	
13 M	0041 4.6	0702 1.3	1304 4.7	1933 1.0
14 TU	0135 4.7	0801 1.0	1401 4.9	2027 0.9
15 W ○	0225 4.9	0855 0.8	1455 4.9	2116 0.9
16 TH	0311 5.0	0945 0.7	1545 5.0	2201 0.9
17 F	0354 5.1	1031 0.6	1632 4.9	2244 1.0
18 SA	0437 5.0	1116 0.6	1718 4.8	2324 1.1
19 SU	0519 5.0	1157 0.7	1802 4.7	
20 M	0002 1.3	0601 4.9	1238 0.9	1845 4.5
21 TU	0041 1.4	0643 4.7	1318 1.1	1930 4.3
22 W	0121 1.6	0729 4.5	1400 1.3	2017 4.1
23 TH ◑	0206 1.8	0818 4.3	1448 1.5	2109 4.0
24 F	0301 2.0	0913 4.2	1544 1.7	2206 3.9
25 SA	0408 2.0	1015 4.0	1646 1.8	2307 3.9
26 SU	0518 2.0	1120 4.0	1750 1.8	
27 M	0008 4.0	0623 1.9	1225 4.1	1848 1.7
28 TU	0102 4.2	0719 1.7	1321 4.2	1938 1.5
29 W	0148 4.4	0807 1.4	1408 4.4	2022 1.4
30 TH	0229 4.6	0850 1.2	1450 4.6	2103 1.2

JULY

Day	Time m	Time m	Time m	Time m
1 F	0307 4.8	0931 1.0	1545 4.7	2143 1.1
2 SA	0344 4.9	1012 0.8	1611 4.9	2222 1.0
3 SU	0421 5.0	1053 0.6	1653 4.9	2302 1.0
4 M	0500 5.1	1136 0.5	1735 4.9	2343 1.0
5 TU	0542 5.1	1219 0.5	1820 4.8	
6 W	0025 1.1	0626 5.0	1305 0.6	1908 4.7
7 TH	0111 1.2	0715 4.9	1354 0.8	2000 4.6
8 F ◑	0202 1.4	0810 4.8	1449 1.0	2059 4.4
9 SA	0303 1.6	0915 4.6	1553 1.2	2205 4.3
10 SU	0416 1.6	1027 4.5	1703 1.4	2314 4.3
11 M	0535 1.6	1144 4.4	1815 1.4	
12 TU	0022 4.4	0651 1.4	1257 4.5	1921 1.4
13 W	0123 4.6	0756 1.2	1359 4.6	2017 1.3
14 TH	0215 4.8	0850 0.9	1452 4.8	2105 1.2
15 F ○	0301 4.9	0938 0.7	1538 4.9	2148 1.1
16 SA	0342 5.0	1020 0.6	1619 4.9	2226 1.1
17 SU	0421 5.1	1059 0.6	1658 4.9	2302 1.1
18 M	0458 5.1	1134 0.7	1735 4.8	2335 1.2
19 TU	0534 5.0	1208 0.8	1812 4.6	
20 W	0008 1.3	0611 4.9	1241 1.0	1848 4.5
21 TH	0042 1.4	0649 4.7	1316 1.2	1927 4.3
22 F	0120 1.6	0731 4.5	1355 1.5	2011 4.1
23 SA ◑	0204 1.8	0819 4.3	1442 1.7	2103 4.0
24 SU	0302 2.0	0917 4.1	1541 1.9	2205 3.9
25 M	0417 2.1	1025 3.9	1654 2.0	2314 3.9
26 TU	0537 2.0	1141 3.9	1808 1.9	
27 W	0023 4.1	0651 1.7	1251 4.1	1910 1.7
28 TH	0119 4.3	0742 1.5	1345 4.4	2000 1.5
29 F	0205 4.6	0829 1.2	1431 4.6	2044 1.3
30 SA ○	0245 4.8	0912 0.8	1512 4.9	2125 1.1
31 SU ●	0323 5.1	0954 0.6	1553 5.0	2206 0.9

AUGUST

Day	Time m	Time m	Time m	Time m
1 M	0401 5.3	1036 0.4	1633 5.1	2246 0.8
2 TU	0441 5.4	1118 0.3	1715 5.2	2326 0.8
3 W	0522 5.4	1201 0.3	1758 5.1	
4 TH	0006 0.9	0605 5.3	1244 0.5	1843 4.9
5 F	0050 1.0	0654 5.1	1330 0.8	1933 4.7
6 SA ◑	0138 1.3	0748 4.9	1422 1.1	2030 4.5
7 SU	0238 1.5	0854 4.6	1526 1.5	2137 4.3
8 M	0355 1.7	1013 4.3	1643 1.7	2253 4.2
9 TU	0526 1.7	1140 4.3	1805 1.7	
10 W	0010 4.3	0649 1.5	1257 4.4	1915 1.6
11 TH	0115 4.5	0753 1.2	1357 4.6	2009 1.5
12 F	0207 4.7	0843 1.0	1444 4.7	2053 1.3
13 SA ○	0249 4.9	0925 0.8	1524 4.8	2131 1.2
14 SU	0326 5.1	1001 0.7	1559 4.9	2205 1.1
15 M	0400 5.1	1034 0.7	1632 4.9	2236 1.0
16 TU	0433 5.1	1105 0.7	1704 4.8	2307 1.1
17 W	0505 5.1	1134 0.8	1735 4.7	2337 1.1
18 TH	0538 5.0	1203 1.0	1808 4.6	
19 F	0007 1.3	0612 4.8	1234 1.1	1842 4.5
20 SA	0041 1.5	0650 4.6	1308 1.4	1920 4.3
21 SU ◑	0121 1.7	0734 4.3	1349 1.6	2007 4.1
22 M	0212 1.9	0828 4.1	1443 2.0	2106 4.0
23 TU	0323 2.1	0938 3.9	1601 2.2	2222 3.9
24 W	0452 2.1	1102 3.9	1730 2.1	2342 4.0
25 TH	0614 1.9	1221 4.1	1843 1.9	
26 F	0047 4.3	0716 1.5	1320 4.4	1937 1.6
27 SA	0137 4.6	0805 1.1	1407 4.7	2022 1.3
28 SU	0219 5.0	0850 0.7	1449 5.0	2103 1.0
29 M ●	0258 5.3	0932 0.4	1529 5.2	2144 0.8
30 TU	0337 5.5	1014 0.2	1609 5.3	2224 0.6
31 W	0417 5.6	1056 0.1	1650 5.3	2304 0.6

Chart Datum: 2·60 metres below Ordnance Datum (Newlyn)
HAT is 5·7 metres above Chart Datum

NORTH SHIELDS

LAT 55°01'N LONG 1°26'W

2011

TIMES AND HEIGHTS OF HIGH AND LOW WATERS

Dates in amber are **SPRINGS**
Dates in yellow are **NEAPS**

SEPTEMBER

Day	Time	m	Time	m	Time	m	Time	m
1 TH	0500	5.6	1138	0.2	1732	5.2	2346	0.7
16 F	0508	5.0	1128	1.0	1731	4.8	2338	1.2
2 F	0545	5.5	1220	0.5	1817	5.0		
17 SA	0542	4.8	1157	1.2	1804	4.6		
3 SA	0029	0.9	0635	5.2	1305	0.9	1905	4.8
18 SU	0011	1.4	0618	4.6	1229	1.5	1839	4.5
4 SU	0119	1.2	0732	4.8	1357	1.3	2002	4.5
19 M	0049	1.6	0700	4.4	1307	1.7	1923	4.3
5 M	0221	1.5	0842	4.4	1503	1.7	2112	4.3
20 TU	0138	1.8	0753	4.1	1358	2.0	2019	4.1
6 TU	0344	1.7	1005	4.2	1628	2.0	2234	4.2
21 W	0245	2.0	0903	3.9	1515	2.2	2136	4.0
7 W	0522	1.7	1135	4.2	1757	2.0	2357	4.3
22 TH	0413	2.0	1028	3.9	1652	2.2	2300	4.1
8 TH	0644	1.5	1250	4.3	1905	1.8		
23 F	0539	1.8	1149	4.1	1811	2.0		
9 F	0102	4.5	0742	1.2	1345	4.5	1954	1.6
24 SA	0011	4.3	0644	1.4	1251	4.5	1908	1.6
10 SA	0151	4.7	0826	1.0	1427	4.7	2034	1.4
25 SU	0105	4.7	0736	1.0	1340	4.8	1955	1.3
11 SU	0230	4.9	0903	0.9	1502	4.8	2108	1.2
26 M	0150	5.1	0822	0.6	1422	5.1	2038	0.9
12 M	0304	5.0	0935	0.8	1533	4.9	2139	1.1
27 TU	0231	5.4	0906	0.3	1503	5.3	2120	0.7
13 TU	0335	5.1	1004	0.8	1603	4.9	2209	1.0
28 W	0312	5.6	0949	0.2	1543	5.4	2201	0.6
14 W	0406	5.1	1032	0.8	1632	4.9	2239	1.0
29 TH	0355	5.7	1031	0.2	1625	5.4	2244	0.5
15 TH	0436	5.1	1100	0.9	1701	4.8	2308	1.1
30 F	0440	5.6	1114	0.4	1707	5.3	2327	0.6

OCTOBER

Day	Time	m	Time	m	Time	m	Time	m
1 SA	0528	5.4	1157	0.7	1752	5.1		
16 SU	0518	4.8	1128	1.3	1734	4.7	2350	1.3
2 SU	0014	0.9	0620	5.1	1243	1.1	1841	4.8
17 M	0556	4.6	1201	1.5	1810	4.6		
3 M	0106	1.1	0720	4.7	1335	1.6	1938	4.6
18 TU	0029	1.5	0638	4.4	1239	1.8	1852	4.4
4 TU	0209	1.5	0831	4.4	1441	2.0	2048	4.3
19 W	0118	1.7	0730	4.2	1329	2.0	1947	4.2
5 W	0332	1.7	0952	4.1	1608	2.2	2210	4.2
20 TH	0220	1.8	0837	4.1	1441	2.2	2057	4.1
6 TH	0505	1.7	1116	4.1	1734	2.1	2331	4.3
21 F	0339	1.8	0956	4.1	1611	2.2	2217	4.2
7 F	0622	1.5	1227	4.3	1840	1.9		
22 SA	0500	1.6	1113	4.2	1731	2.0	2329	4.4
8 SA	0036	4.5	0717	1.3	1320	4.5	1928	1.7
23 SU	0608	1.3	1217	4.5	1833	1.7		
9 SU	0125	4.7	0758	1.2	1400	4.6	2007	1.5
24 M	0028	4.7	0703	1.0	1309	4.8	1924	1.3
10 M	0204	4.8	0833	1.1	1434	4.8	2040	1.3
25 TU	0119	5.1	0753	0.7	1355	5.1	2011	1.0
11 TU	0238	4.9	0903	1.0	1505	4.9	2112	1.2
26 W	0205	5.4	0840	0.5	1437	5.4	2057	0.8
12 W	0309	5.0	0932	0.9	1534	4.9	2143	1.1
27 TH	0251	5.5	0925	0.4	1519	5.4	2142	0.6
13 TH	0340	5.0	1001	0.9	1602	5.0	2213	1.1
28 F	0337	5.6	1009	0.4	1602	5.4	2228	0.6
14 F	0411	5.0	1029	1.0	1631	4.9	2244	1.1
29 SA	0425	5.5	1053	0.6	1646	5.3	2314	0.6
15 SA	0444	4.9	1058	1.1	1701	4.8	2316	1.2
30 SU	0516	5.3	1137	0.9	1731	5.2		
31 M	0003	0.8	0609	5.0	1224	1.3	1820	4.9

NOVEMBER

Day	Time	m	Time	m	Time	m	Time	m
1 TU	0055	1.1	0708	4.7	1314	1.7	1915	4.7
16 W	0018	1.3	0623	4.5	1224	1.7	1832	4.6
2 W	0155	1.4	0813	4.4	1414	2.0	2020	4.4
17 TH	0105	1.4	0713	4.4	1312	1.9	1923	4.5
3 TH	0307	1.6	0923	4.2	1530	2.2	2133	4.3
18 F	0201	1.5	0813	4.3	1413	2.0	2024	4.4
4 F	0426	1.7	1037	4.1	1650	2.1	2248	4.3
19 SA	0307	1.6	0922	4.2	1528	2.1	2135	4.4
5 SA	0539	1.7	1146	4.2	1759	2.1	2355	4.4
20 SU	0420	1.5	1034	4.3	1646	2.0	2247	4.5
6 SU	0637	1.5	1242	4.3	1852	1.9		
21 M	0529	1.3	1140	4.5	1755	1.7	2353	4.6
7 M	0048	4.5	0721	1.4	1326	4.5	1934	1.7
22 TU	0630	1.1	1237	4.7	1854	1.4		
8 TU	0132	4.6	0757	1.3	1402	4.7	2011	1.5
23 W	0051	5.0	0725	0.9	1329	5.0	1948	1.1
9 W	0210	4.7	0830	1.2	1436	4.8	2046	1.3
24 TH	0145	5.2	0817	0.8	1416	5.2	2039	0.9
10 TH	0244	4.8	0902	1.2	1507	4.9	2119	1.2
25 F	0236	5.3	0905	0.7	1500	5.3	2129	0.7
11 F	0318	4.9	0933	1.1	1537	4.9	2152	1.1
26 SA	0326	5.4	0952	0.7	1545	5.3	2217	0.6
12 SA	0352	4.9	1003	1.2	1608	4.9	2226	1.1
27 SU	0416	5.3	1037	0.9	1629	5.3	2305	0.7
13 SU	0426	4.9	1035	1.2	1639	4.9	2300	1.1
28 M	0507	5.2	1121	1.1	1715	5.2	2353	0.8
14 M	0502	4.8	1108	1.4	1713	4.8	2337	1.2
29 TU	0558	5.0	1205	1.3	1802	5.0		
15 TU	0541	4.7	1143	1.5	1750	4.7		
30 W	0041	1.0	0650	4.7	1251	1.6	1851	4.8

DECEMBER

Day	Time	m	Time	m	Time	m	Time	m
1 TH	0132	1.2	0745	4.4	1339	1.9	1945	4.6
16 F	0052	1.1	0655	4.6	1255	1.6	1902	4.8
2 F	0227	1.5	0843	4.2	1436	2.1	2046	4.4
17 SA	0141	1.2	0748	4.5	1346	1.7	1955	4.7
3 SA	0328	1.7	0944	4.1	1544	2.2	2151	4.3
18 SU	0237	1.3	0848	4.4	1448	1.8	2058	4.6
4 SU	0433	1.8	1048	4.1	1656	2.2	2257	4.2
19 M	0342	1.4	0955	4.3	1601	1.9	2209	4.6
5 M	0537	1.8	1150	4.1	1801	2.1		
20 TU	0452	1.4	1103	4.4	1718	1.8	2322	4.6
6 TU	0001	4.3	0632	1.7	1244	4.3	1856	1.9
21 W	0600	1.3	1209	4.6	1829	1.6		
7 W	0055	4.4	0718	1.6	1329	4.5	1941	1.7
22 TH	0032	4.7	0704	1.2	1308	4.8	1933	1.3
8 TH	0142	4.5	0759	1.5	1408	4.6	2022	1.5
23 F	0134	4.9	0801	1.0	1401	5.0	2030	1.0
9 F	0222	4.6	0836	1.4	1443	4.8	2059	1.3
24 SA	0230	5.1	0853	1.0	1448	5.1	2122	0.8
10 SA	0300	4.7	0911	1.3	1517	4.9	2135	1.2
25 SU	0322	5.1	0941	1.0	1533	5.2	2211	0.6
11 SU	0336	4.8	0945	1.3	1549	4.9	2211	1.1
26 M	0410	5.2	1025	1.0	1617	5.3	2257	0.6
12 M	0412	4.8	1019	1.3	1622	5.0	2248	1.0
27 TU	0456	5.1	1106	1.1	1659	5.2	2340	0.7
13 TU	0449	4.8	1055	1.3	1657	5.0	2327	1.0
28 W	0541	4.9	1145	1.2	1742	5.1		
14 W	0528	4.8	1132	1.4	1735	4.9		
29 TH	0021	0.8	0624	4.7	1224	1.4	1824	5.0
15 TH	0008	1.0	0609	4.7	1212	1.5	1815	4.9
30 F	0101	1.1	0708	4.5	1302	1.6	1908	4.8
31 SA	0142	1.3	0755	4.3	1344	1.8	1956	4.5

Chart Datum: 2·60 metres below Ordnance Datum (Newlyn)
HAT is 5·7 metres above Chart Datum

TIDES

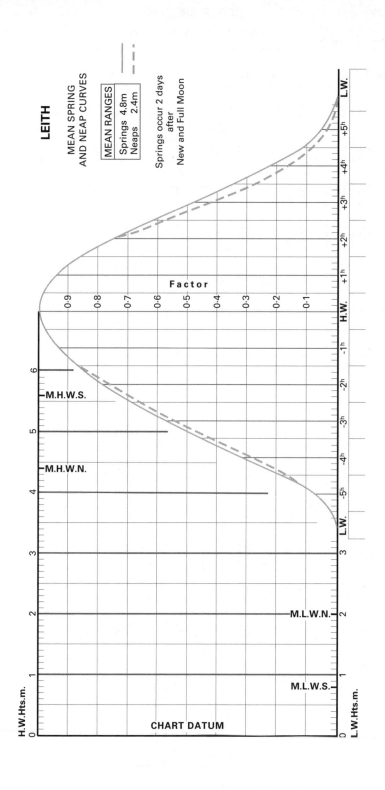

SCOTLAND – LEITH
LAT 55°59′N   LONG 3°11′W
TIMES AND HEIGHTS OF HIGH AND LOW WATERS

Dates in amber are **SPRINGS**
Dates in yellow are **NEAPS**

2011

JANUARY

Day			
1 SA	0546 1.7	1159 5.0	SA 1813 1.6
2 SU	0035 5.1	0644 1.6	SU 1257 5.1 / 1914 1.4
3 M	0131 5.2	0733 1.4	M 1347 5.3 / 2006 1.1
4 TU	0220 5.3	0815 1.3	TU 1432 5.4 / ●2051 1.0
5 W	0303 5.4	0852 1.3	W 1513 5.5 / 2130 0.9
6 TH	0343 5.4	0925 1.3	TH 1551 5.4 / 2203 0.9
7 F	0421 5.3	0953 1.3	F 1628 5.4 / 2229 1.0
8 SA	0457 5.2	1019 1.4	SA 1703 5.3 / 2251 1.1
9 SU	0533 5.0	1048 1.5	SU 1739 5.1 / 2317 1.3
10 M	0611 4.9	1120 1.7	M 1817 5.0 / 2349 1.5
11 TU	0651 4.7	1157 1.9	TU 1858 4.8
12 W	0028 1.7	0736 4.5	W 1244 2.1 / ◐1946 4.6
13 TH	0118 2.0	0828 4.4	TH 1353 2.3 / 2045 4.4
14 F	0226 2.2	0929 4.3	F 1524 2.4 / 2153 4.4
15 SA	0400 2.3	1035 4.4	SA 1649 2.2 / 2303 4.4
16 SU	0519 2.1	1141 4.6	SU 1751 2.0
17 M	0010 4.7	0615 1.9	M 1242 4.9 / 1843 1.6
18 TU	0108 5.0	0703 1.6	TU 1332 5.1 / 1932 1.2
19 W	0155 5.3	0748 1.3	W 1415 5.4 / ○2020 0.9
20 TH	0238 5.5	0834 1.1	TH 1454 5.6 / 2108 0.5
21 F	0320 5.7	0919 0.8	F 1534 5.8 / 2154 0.3
22 SA	0402 5.8	1003 0.8	SA 1615 5.9 / 2239 0.3
23 SU	0445 5.8	1045 0.8	SU 1659 5.9 / 2322 0.4
24 M	0530 5.6	1124 1.0	M 1745 5.7
25 TU	0003 0.7	0617 5.4	TU 1201 1.3 / 1834 5.5
26 W	0044 1.1	0709 5.1	W 1242 1.5 / ◐1933 5.2
27 TH	0130 1.5	0809 4.8	TH 1344 1.9 / 2044 4.9
28 F	0239 1.9	0919 4.6	F 1519 2.1 / 2201 4.6
29 SA	0415 2.1	1031 4.6	SA 1658 2.0 / 2319 4.7
30 SU	0537 2.0	1146 4.7	SU 1821 1.7
31 M	0032 4.8	0639 1.8	M 1252 4.9 / 1919 1.4

FEBRUARY

Day			
1 TU	0129 5.0	0725 1.6	TU 1342 5.1 / 2004 1.2
2 W	0214 5.2	0802 1.4	W 1423 5.3 / 2041 1.0
3 TH	0251 5.3	0834 1.2	TH 1500 5.4 / ●2114 0.9
4 F	0325 5.3	0903 1.1	F 1533 5.4 / 2141 0.8
5 SA	0357 5.3	0932 1.1	SA 1605 5.4 / 2205 0.9
6 SU	0429 5.2	0959 1.1	SU 1636 5.4 / 2226 1.0
7 M	0501 5.1	1025 1.2	M 1708 5.3 / 2248 1.1
8 TU	0535 5.0	1049 1.4	TU 1742 5.1 / 2310 1.3
9 W	0611 4.8	1113 1.6	W 1819 4.9 / 2337 1.6
10 TH	0650 4.6	1144 1.8	TH 1901 4.7
11 F	0011 1.9	0736 4.4	F 1231 2.1 / ◐1953 4.4
12 SA	0107 2.2	0835 4.3	SA 1401 2.3 / 2101 4.3
13 SU	0249 2.4	0948 4.3	SU 1603 2.3 / 2222 4.3
14 M	0449 2.3	1104 4.4	M 1728 2.0 / 2340 4.5
15 TU	0557 2.0	1214 4.7	TU 1828 1.6
16 W	0044 4.9	0647 1.6	W 1309 5.1 / 1919 1.1
17 TH	0135 5.3	0733 1.2	TH 1353 5.5 / 2007 0.7
18 F	0218 5.6	0818 0.9	F 1433 5.8 / ○2053 0.3
19 SA	0259 5.8	0902 0.6	SA 1513 6.0 / 2138 0.1
20 SU	0340 5.9	0945 0.5	SU 1555 6.1 / 2220 0.0
21 M	0423 5.9	1026 0.5	M 1639 6.1 / 2301 0.2
22 TU	0507 5.7	1104 0.7	TU 1725 5.8 / 2339 0.6
23 W	0553 5.4	1138 1.0	W 1815 5.5
24 TH	0015 1.1	0642 5.1	TH 1215 1.4 / ◑1913 5.1
25 F	0054 1.6	0740 4.7	F 1313 1.8 / 2024 4.7
26 SA	0202 2.1	0851 4.5	SA 1504 2.1 / 2142 4.5
27 SU	0356 2.3	1008 4.4	SU 1703 2.0 / 2306 4.5
28 M	0527 2.2	1131 4.5	M 1819 1.7

MARCH

Day			
1 TU	0023 4.7	0627 2.0	TU 1239 4.8 / 1910 1.4
2 W	0118 4.9	0708 1.7	W 1327 5.0 / 1949 1.2
3 TH	0158 5.1	0740 1.4	TH 1406 5.2 / 2020 1.0
4 F	0232 5.2	0809 1.2	F 1439 5.3 / ●2047 0.9
5 SA	0302 5.2	0839 1.0	SA 1510 5.4 / 2112 0.8
6 SU	0330 5.3	0909 0.9	SU 1539 5.4 / 2136 0.8
7 M	0400 5.2	0938 1.0	M 1609 5.4 / 2159 0.9
8 TU	0430 5.2	1002 1.1	TU 1641 5.3 / 2219 1.0
9 W	0502 5.1	1021 1.2	W 1714 5.1 / 2234 1.2
10 TH	0536 4.9	1040 1.4	TH 1749 4.9 / 2255 1.5
11 F	0613 4.7	1108 1.6	F 1831 4.7 / 2326 1.7
12 SA	0656 4.5	1151 1.9	SA 1921 4.4
13 SU	0013 2.1	0750 4.3	SU 1310 2.1 / 2025 4.3
14 M	0201 2.4	0904 4.2	M 1521 2.2 / 2147 4.3
15 TU	0419 2.3	1029 4.4	TU 1703 1.9 / 2309 4.5
16 W	0531 2.0	1142 4.7	W 1806 1.4
17 TH	0016 4.9	0623 1.5	TH 1240 5.1 / 1857 0.9
18 F	0109 5.3	0709 1.1	F 1326 5.5 / 1945 0.5
19 SA	0153 5.6	0754 0.8	SA 1408 5.8 / ○2031 0.2
20 SU	0234 5.8	0839 0.5	SU 1450 6.1 / 2116 0.0
21 M	0316 5.9	0924 0.3	M 1534 6.1 / 2158 0.1
22 TU	0359 5.9	1007 0.4	TU 1620 6.0 / 2239 0.3
23 W	0443 5.7	1047 0.6	W 1708 5.8 / 2317 0.8
24 TH	0530 5.4	1124 0.9	TH 1800 5.4 / 2351 1.3
25 F	0619 5.1	1202 1.3	F 1859 5.0
26 SA	0029 1.8	0717 4.7	SA 1300 1.7 / ◑2006 4.6
27 SU	0135 2.2	0827 4.5	SU 1458 2.0 / 2119 4.4
28 M	0330 2.4	0942 4.4	M 1645 1.9 / 2240 4.4
29 TU	0454 2.3	1101 4.4	TU 1754 1.7 / 2357 4.5
30 W	0552 2.0	1210 4.7	W 1843 1.5
31 TH	0051 4.8	0633 1.7	TH 1259 4.9 / 1918 1.3

APRIL

Day			
1 F	0131 5.0	0706 1.5	F 1338 5.1 / 1947 1.1
2 SA	0204 5.1	0738 1.2	SA 1412 5.2 / 2013 1.0
3 SU	0233 5.2	0811 1.0	SU 1442 5.3 / ●2039 0.9
4 M	0301 5.2	0844 0.9	M 1513 5.3 / 2106 0.9
5 TU	0331 5.2	0915 0.9	TU 1544 5.3 / 2131 1.0
6 W	0402 5.2	0942 1.0	W 1617 5.2 / 2152 1.1
7 TH	0434 5.1	1004 1.1	TH 1651 5.1 / 2208 1.3
8 F	0508 5.0	1024 1.3	F 1728 5.0 / 2229 1.5
9 SA	0545 4.8	1054 1.5	SA 1811 4.8 / 2302 1.7
10 SU	0629 4.6	1142 1.7	SU 1902 4.6 / 2355 2.0
11 M	0722 4.5	1305 1.9	M 2004 4.5
12 TU	0149 2.3	0831 4.4	TU 1454 1.9 / 2120 4.5
13 W	0344 2.2	0955 4.5	W 1630 1.6 / 2238 4.6
14 TH	0456 1.9	1107 4.8	TH 1734 1.2 / 2344 5.0
15 F	0550 1.5	1206 5.1	F 1828 0.8
16 SA	0038 5.3	0638 1.1	SA 1257 5.5 / 1917 0.5
17 SU	0125 5.6	0727 0.8	SU 1343 5.8 / 2005 0.3
18 M	0209 5.8	0816 0.5	M 1428 6.0 / ○2052 0.2
19 TU	0252 5.8	0904 0.4	TU 1515 6.0 / 2136 0.3
20 W	0337 5.8	0950 0.4	W 1604 5.9 / 2218 0.6
21 TH	0423 5.6	1035 0.6	TH 1654 5.6 / 2257 1.0
22 F	0510 5.4	1116 0.9	F 1747 5.3 / 2332 1.4
23 SA	0601 5.1	1158 1.2	SA 1843 5.0
24 SU	0009 1.8	0657 4.8	SU 1251 1.6 / 1944 4.6
25 M	0106 2.2	0801 4.6	M 1427 1.8 / ◑2048 4.4
26 TU	0240 2.3	0908 4.4	TU 1600 1.9 / 2157 4.3
27 W	0401 2.3	1017 4.4	W 1705 1.7 / 2309 4.4
28 TH	0459 2.1	1124 4.5	TH 1755 1.5
29 F	0008 4.6	0544 1.8	F 1218 4.7 / 1831 1.5
30 SA	0052 4.8	0625 1.6	SA 1302 4.9 / 1903 1.3

Chart Datum: 2·90 metres below Ordnance Datum (Newlyn)
HAT is 6·3 metres above Chart Datum

TIDES

TIDES

TIME ZONE (UT)
For Summer Time add ONE hour in **non-shaded areas**

SCOTLAND – LEITH
LAT 55°59'N   LONG 3°11'W
TIMES AND HEIGHTS OF HIGH AND LOW WATERS

Dates in amber are **SPRINGS**
Dates in yellow are **NEAPS**

2011

MAY

Day	Time	m	Time	m	Time	m	Time	m
1 SU	0128	4.9	0704	1.3	1339	5.0	1933	1.3
2 M	0200	5.1	0741	1.2	1413	5.1	2003	1.1
3 TU ●	0232	5.2	0817	1.0	1447	5.2	2034	1.0
4 W	0304	5.2	0852	1.0	1521	5.2	2105	1.1
5 TH	0337	5.2	0926	1.0	1556	5.2	2134	1.2
6 F	0411	5.2	0958	1.0	1633	5.2	2201	1.3
7 SA	0447	5.1	1032	1.1	1713	5.1	2230	1.5
8 SU	0526	5.0	1111	1.3	1757	5.0	2308	1.7
9 M	0610	4.8	1203	1.4	1848	4.8		
10 TU ◐	0012	1.9	0702	4.7	1310	1.5	1946	4.7
11 W	0140	2.1	0807	4.6	1430	1.4	2055	4.7
12 TH	0306	2.0	0923	1.4	1551	1.4	2207	4.8
13 F	0417	1.8	1034	4.9	1658	1.2	2311	5.0
14 SA	0516	1.5	1135	5.1	1755	0.9		
15 SU	0008	5.2	0609	1.2	1231	5.4	1848	0.7
16 M	0059	5.4	0702	0.9	1322	5.6	1940	0.6
17 TU ○	0146	5.6	0756	0.7	1412	5.7	2029	0.6
18 W	0232	5.6	0849	0.5	1501	5.8	2115	0.7
19 TH	0319	5.6	0938	0.5	1551	5.7	2158	0.8
20 F	0406	5.5	1024	0.6	1641	5.5	2238	1.1
21 SA	0454	5.4	1108	0.9	1732	5.3	2313	1.4
22 SU	0543	5.1	1148	1.1	1822	5.0	2345	1.7
23 M	0634	4.9	1228	1.4	1915	4.7		
24 TU ○	0029	2.0	0728	4.7	1320	1.7	2009	4.5
25 W	0131	2.2	0826	4.6	1438	1.8	2105	4.4
26 TH	0251	2.2	0925	4.5	1551	1.9	2204	4.4
27 F	0400	2.2	1024	4.4	1647	1.8	2304	4.4
28 SA	0457	2.0	1123	4.5	1734	1.7	2358	4.6
29 SU	0546	1.8	1216	4.7	1815	1.6		
30 M	0045	4.8	0630	1.5	1302	4.8	1853	1.4
31 TU	0126	5.0	0712	1.3	1344	5.0	1930	1.3

JUNE

Day	Time	m	Time	m	Time	m	Time	m
1 W ●	0204	5.1	0752	1.2	1423	5.1	2007	1.2
2 TH	0240	5.2	0832	1.0	1501	5.2	2044	1.2
3 F	0317	5.3	0912	0.9	1538	5.3	2123	1.2
4 SA	0353	5.3	0953	0.8	1618	5.3	2203	1.2
5 SU	0431	5.3	1036	0.9	1659	5.3	2244	1.3
6 M	0511	5.2	1121	1.0	1744	5.2	2328	1.5
7 TU	0556	5.1	1209	1.1	1833	5.1		
8 W	0018	1.6	0646	5.0	1302	1.2	1927	4.9
9 TH ◐	0118	1.8	0744	4.9	1403	1.3	2029	4.8
10 F	0227	1.8	0852	4.9	1513	1.3	2136	4.8
11 SA	0339	1.8	1004	4.8	1622	1.3	2241	4.9
12 SU	0445	1.6	1110	5.0	1726	1.2	2342	5.1
13 M	0547	1.4	1211	5.2	1825	1.1		
14 TU	0038	5.2	0647	1.1	1309	5.4	1920	1.0
15 W ○	0130	5.4	0746	0.9	1402	5.5	2011	1.0
16 TH	0219	5.5	0840	0.7	1452	5.5	2058	0.9
17 F	0306	5.5	0929	0.6	1540	5.5	2140	1.0
18 SA	0352	5.5	1013	0.7	1626	5.4	2217	1.1
19 SU	0437	5.4	1053	0.8	1711	5.3	2249	1.3
20 M	0521	5.3	1126	1.0	1755	5.1	2317	1.5
21 TU	0604	5.1	1152	1.2	1839	4.8	2351	1.7
22 W	0649	4.9	1225	1.5	1924	4.6		
23 TH ◐	0036	1.9	0737	4.7	1310	1.7	2012	4.5
24 F	0135	2.1	0829	4.5	1409	1.9	2104	4.4
25 SA	0249	2.2	0925	4.4	1524	2.0	2200	4.4
26 SU	0405	2.2	1024	4.4	1636	2.0	2259	4.5
27 M	0507	2.0	1125	4.5	1733	1.9	2358	4.6
28 TU	0600	1.8	1224	4.6	1821	1.7		
29 W	0052	4.8	0647	1.5	1316	4.8	1904	1.5
30 TH	0138	5.0	0731	1.3	1401	5.1	1946	1.3

JULY

Day	Time	m	Time	m	Time	m	Time	m
1 F ●	0220	5.2	0815	1.0	1442	5.2	2028	1.2
2 SA	0258	5.4	0859	0.8	1522	5.4	2111	1.1
3 SU	0336	5.5	0945	0.6	1602	5.5	2155	1.0
4 M	0415	5.5	1030	0.6	1643	5.5	2239	1.0
5 TU	0456	5.5	1114	0.6	1727	5.4	2321	1.1
6 W	0540	5.5	1158	0.7	1814	5.3		
7 TH	0003	1.3	0627	5.4	1243	0.9	1904	5.1
8 F ◐	0050	1.5	0721	5.2	1333	1.2	2002	4.9
9 SA	0148	1.7	0826	5.0	1435	1.4	2107	4.8
10 SU	0303	1.8	0940	4.9	1552	1.6	2215	4.8
11 M	0424	1.7	1052	4.9	1707	1.6	2322	4.9
12 TU	0538	1.6	1201	5.0	1812	1.5		
13 W	0025	5.0	0646	1.3	1304	5.1	1909	1.4
14 TH	0122	5.2	0745	1.0	1357	5.3	1958	1.2
15 F	0210	5.4	0835	0.8	1444	5.4	2040	1.1
16 SA	0254	5.5	0918	0.7	1526	5.4	2119	1.1
17 SU	0336	5.5	0956	0.7	1607	5.4	2152	1.1
18 M	0416	5.5	1029	0.7	1645	5.3	2220	1.2
19 TU	0454	5.4	1054	0.9	1723	5.1	2246	1.3
20 W	0531	5.2	1115	1.1	1800	5.0	2315	1.5
21 TH	0608	5.0	1142	1.3	1839	4.8	2350	1.7
22 F	0649	4.8	1217	1.6	1922	4.6		
23 SA	0034	1.9	0735	4.6	1303	1.8	2011	4.5
24 SU	0136	2.2	0830	4.4	1405	2.1	2108	4.4
25 M	0300	2.3	0933	4.3	1533	2.2	2210	4.4
26 TU	0429	2.2	1040	4.3	1658	2.1	2316	4.5
27 W	0535	1.9	1148	4.5	1757	1.9		
28 TH	0020	4.7	0627	1.6	1250	4.8	1844	1.7
29 F	0114	5.0	0714	1.3	1339	5.1	1928	1.4
30 SA ●	0158	5.3	0800	0.9	1422	5.4	2012	1.1
31 SU	0238	5.5	0846	0.6	1502	5.6	2056	0.9

AUGUST

Day	Time	m	Time	m	Time	m	Time	m
1 M	0316	5.7	0931	0.4	1542	5.7	2140	0.7
2 TU	0355	5.8	1015	0.2	1623	5.7	2223	0.7
3 W	0436	5.9	1058	0.3	1706	5.7	2304	0.8
4 TH	0520	5.8	1139	0.5	1751	5.5	2342	1.1
5 F	0607	5.6	1220	0.8	1840	5.2		
6 SA ◐	0021	1.3	0700	5.3	1304	1.3	1935	5.0
7 SU	0116	1.6	0805	5.0	1403	1.7	2041	4.7
8 M	0240	1.9	0923	4.8	1532	1.9	2154	4.7
9 TU	0420	1.9	1042	4.7	1659	1.9	2309	4.7
10 W	0546	1.6	1158	4.8	1808	1.8		
11 TH	0019	4.9	0652	1.3	1302	5.0	1901	1.6
12 F	0115	5.2	0742	1.1	1351	5.2	1943	1.4
13 SA ○	0200	5.4	0824	0.9	1432	5.3	2019	1.2
14 SU	0239	5.5	0859	0.7	1508	5.4	2052	1.0
15 M	0316	5.5	0931	0.7	1542	5.4	2123	1.0
16 TU	0350	5.5	0958	0.7	1615	5.3	2151	1.0
17 W	0423	5.4	1020	0.9	1648	5.2	2217	1.1
18 TH	0457	5.3	1039	1.0	1722	5.1	2241	1.3
19 F	0532	5.1	1101	1.2	1758	4.9	2306	1.5
20 SA	0609	4.9	1127	1.5	1838	4.7	2338	1.8
21 SU ◐	0652	4.7	1201	1.8	1924	4.5		
22 M	0026	2.1	0742	4.5	1256	2.2	2019	4.4
23 TU	0154	2.3	0846	4.3	1432	2.4	2127	4.3
24 W	0346	2.3	1000	4.3	1627	2.3	2239	4.4
25 TH	0512	2.0	1114	4.5	1735	2.0	2349	4.7
26 F	0609	1.7	1221	4.8	1825	1.7		
27 SA	0046	5.0	0657	1.2	1314	5.2	1909	1.3
28 SU	0132	5.4	0742	0.8	1357	5.5	1951	1.0
29 M ●	0212	5.7	0827	0.4	1438	5.8	2035	0.7
30 TU	0251	6.0	0911	0.2	1518	5.9	2119	0.5
31 W	0332	6.1	0955	0.1	1559	5.9	2202	1.0

Chart Datum: 2·90 metres below Ordnance Datum (Newlyn)
HAT is 6·3 metres above Chart Datum

TIME ZONE (UT)
For Summer Time add ONE hour in **non-shaded areas**

SCOTLAND – LEITH
LAT 55°59′N   LONG 3°11′W
TIMES AND HEIGHTS OF HIGH AND LOW WATERS

Dates in amber are **SPRINGS**
Dates in yellow are **NEAPS**
2011

SEPTEMBER

Day	Time	m		Day	Time	m
1	0414	6.1		**16**	0426	5.3
	1037	0.2			1004	1.1
	TH 1642	5.8			F 1648	5.2
	2243	0.7			2211	1.3
2	0500	5.9		**17**	0500	5.2
	1117	0.5			1022	1.3
	F 1727	5.6			SA 1722	5.0
	2322	0.9			2232	1.4
3	0548	5.7		**18**	0537	5.0
	1156	1.0			1043	1.5
	SA 1815	5.3			SU 1800	4.8
					2300	1.7
4	0001	1.3		**19**	0619	4.8
	0643	5.3			1113	1.8
	SU 1238	1.5			M 1843	4.6
	◐ 1911	5.0			2342	2.0
5	0058	1.7		**20**	0708	4.6
	0751	4.9			1157	2.2
	M 1339	2.0			TU 1936	4.5
	2020	4.7			◯	
6	0233	1.9		**21**	0103	2.2
	0910	4.6			0809	4.4
	TU 1520	2.2			W 1342	2.5
	2138	4.6			2044	4.4
7	0427	1.9		**22**	0259	2.3
	1032	4.6			0924	4.4
	W 1652	2.2			TH 1551	2.4
	2256	4.7			2203	4.5
8	0548	1.6		**23**	0443	2.0
	1151	4.8			1041	4.5
	TH 1757	2.1			F 1707	2.1
					2315	4.7
9	0007	4.9		**24**	0543	1.9
	0644	1.3			1150	4.9
	F 1251	5.0			SA 1758	1.7
	1844	1.7				
10	0101	5.2		**25**	0014	5.1
	0727	1.1			0631	1.1
	SA 1336	5.2			SU 1244	5.3
	1920	1.5			1842	1.3
11	0142	5.3		**26**	0102	5.5
	0802	1.0			0717	0.7
	SU 1412	5.3			M 1329	5.6
	1951	1.2			1925	1.0
12	0218	5.5		**27**	0144	5.8
	0831	0.8			0802	0.4
	M 1444	5.4			TU 1410	5.9
	◯ 2022	1.1			● 2010	0.7
13	0251	5.5		**28**	0225	6.1
	0858	0.8			0847	0.2
	TU 1514	5.4			W 1452	6.0
	2054	1.0			2055	0.5
14	0323	5.5		**29**	0308	6.2
	0922	0.8			0931	0.1
	W 1544	5.3			TH 1534	6.0
	2123	1.0			2141	0.5
15	0354	5.4		**30**	0354	6.2
	0945	0.9			1014	0.3
	TH 1615	5.3			F 1618	5.9
	2149	1.1			2225	0.6

OCTOBER

Day	Time	m		Day	Time	m
1	0442	6.0		**16**	0436	5.2
	1055	0.7			0954	1.4
	SA 1704	5.6			SU 1652	5.1
	2308	0.9			2215	1.4
2	0533	5.6		**17**	0513	5.0
	1134	1.2			1016	1.6
	SU 1754	5.3			M 1729	5.0
	2352	1.3			2244	1.6
3	0631	5.2		**18**	0555	4.9
	1217	1.7			1046	1.8
	M 1852	5.0			TU 1811	4.8
					2328	1.8
4	0051	1.7		**19**	0644	4.7
	0739	4.9			1131	2.1
	TU 1319	2.1			W 1902	4.6
	◐ 2002	4.7				
5	0230	1.9		**20**	0043	2.0
	0854	4.6			0741	4.6
	W 1459	2.4			TH 1308	2.4
	2117	4.6			◯ 2006	4.5
6	0414	1.9		**21**	0221	2.1
	1011	4.6			0852	4.5
	TH 1626	2.3			F 1507	2.4
	2232	4.7			2124	4.6
7	0527	1.7		**22**	0400	1.8
	1128	5.0			1007	4.7
	F 1727	2.1			SA 1628	2.1
	2341	4.9			2237	4.8
8	0620	1.5		**23**	0507	1.5
	1226	4.9			1115	5.0
	SA 1812	1.8			SU 1724	1.8
					2338	5.2
9	0034	5.1		**24**	0559	1.1
	0659	1.3			1211	5.3
	SU 1310	5.1			M 1812	1.4
	1847	1.6				
10	0116	5.2		**25**	0030	5.5
	0730	1.2			0647	0.8
	M 1345	5.2			TU 1300	5.6
	1919	1.3			1858	1.0
11	0152	5.3		**26**	0117	5.8
	0756	1.1			0734	0.5
	TU 1416	5.3			W 1344	5.8
	1952	1.2			● 1945	0.7
12	0224	5.4		**27**	0203	6.0
	0821	1.0			0822	0.4
	W 1445	5.4			TH 1427	6.0
	◯ 2026	1.1			2035	0.5
13	0256	5.4		**28**	0249	6.1
	0846	1.0			0908	0.4
	TH 1515	5.4			F 1512	6.0
	2058	1.0			2125	0.5
14	0327	5.4		**29**	0337	6.1
	0912	1.0			0953	0.6
	F 1546	5.3			SA 1557	5.8
	2126	1.1			2213	0.6
15	0401	5.3		**30**	0428	5.9
	0934	1.2			1036	0.9
	SA 1618	5.2			SU 1645	5.6
	2151	1.2			2259	0.9
				31	0521	5.6
					1117	1.4
					M 1736	5.4
					2347	1.2

NOVEMBER

Day	Time	m		Day	Time	m
1	0618	5.2		**16**	0537	5.0
	1158	1.8			1043	1.8
	TU 1833	5.1			W 1748	5.0
					2335	1.6
2	0042	1.6		**17**	0624	4.9
	0720	4.9			1129	2.0
	W 1252	2.2			TH 1837	4.9
	◑ 1939	4.8				
3	0204	1.8		**18**	0034	1.7
	0827	4.7			0718	4.8
	TH 1414	2.4			F 1246	2.2
	2047	4.7			◐ 1934	4.8
4	0334	1.9		**19**	0148	1.8
	0935	4.6			0821	4.7
	F 1537	2.4			SA 1420	2.2
	2155	4.7			2045	4.8
5	0444	1.8		**20**	0311	1.7
	1044	4.6			0932	4.8
	SA 1639	2.2			SU 1542	2.1
	2300	4.7			2159	4.9
6	0538	1.7		**21**	0424	1.5
	1145	4.7			1039	5.0
	SU 1728	2.0			M 1646	1.8
	2356	4.9			2304	5.1
7	0618	1.6		**22**	0524	1.2
	1233	4.9			1139	5.2
	M 1810	1.8			TU 1741	1.5
8	0043	5.0		**23**	0002	5.4
	0649	1.5			0618	1.0
	TU 1313	5.1			W 1233	5.5
	1848	1.5			1834	1.2
9	0123	5.1		**24**	0055	5.7
	0716	1.3			0710	0.8
	W 1346	5.2			TH 1321	5.7
	1925	1.3			1928	0.8
10	0158	5.2		**25**	0146	5.8
	0745	1.2			0801	0.7
	TH 1418	5.3			F 1408	5.8
	◯ 2001	1.2			● 2022	0.5
11	0232	5.3		**26**	0236	5.9
	0815	1.2			0849	0.7
	F 1449	5.4			SA 1454	5.8
	2035	1.1			2115	0.6
12	0305	5.3		**27**	0326	5.9
	0845	1.2			0936	0.9
	SA 1521	5.4			SU 1541	5.8
	2108	1.1			2204	0.6
13	0340	5.3		**28**	0416	5.7
	0914	1.3			1019	1.1
	SU 1555	5.3			M 1630	5.6
	2141	1.2			2251	0.8
14	0416	5.2		**29**	0507	5.5
	0943	1.4			1059	1.4
	M 1629	5.2			TU 1719	5.4
	2214	1.3			2336	1.1
15	0455	5.1		**30**	0559	5.2
	1011	1.6			1134	1.7
	TU 1707	5.1			W 1812	5.2
	2250	1.4				

DECEMBER

Day	Time	m		Day	Time	m
1	0019	1.4		**16**	0605	5.1
	0653	5.0			1130	1.7
	TH 1212	2.0			F 1816	5.4
	1907	5.0				
2	0108	1.7		**17**	0022	1.3
	0749	4.7			0655	5.0
	F 1305	2.2			SA 1221	1.9
	◑ 2007	4.8			1907	5.0
3	0214	1.9		**18**	0116	1.5
	0847	4.6			0751	4.9
	SA 1420	2.4			SU 1329	2.0
	2107	4.6			◐ 2008	4.9
4	0330	2.0		**19**	0223	1.6
	0946	4.5			0856	4.8
	SU 1536	2.4			M 1451	2.0
	2207	4.6			2121	4.9
5	0432	2.0		**20**	0340	1.6
	1046	4.5			1005	4.9
	M 1639	2.2			TU 1609	1.9
	2306	4.6			2234	5.0
6	0522	1.9		**21**	0452	1.5
	1144	4.7			1110	5.0
	TU 1732	2.0			W 1717	1.7
					2341	5.2
7	0002	4.7		**22**	0556	1.4
	0603	1.8			1216	5.2
	W 1234	4.9			TH 1820	1.4
	1818	1.8				
8	0050	4.9		**23**	0041	5.4
	0640	1.6			0653	1.2
	TH 1315	5.0			F 1305	5.4
	1900	1.6			1920	1.1
9	0132	5.0		**24**	0137	5.6
	0716	1.5			0747	1.1
	F 1352	5.2			SA 1355	5.6
	1939	1.4			● 2017	0.8
10	0210	5.1		**25**	0228	5.7
	0750	1.4			0836	1.0
	SA 1428	5.3			SU 1443	5.7
	◯ 2017	1.2			2109	0.6
11	0247	5.2		**26**	0316	5.7
	0826	1.3			0921	1.0
	SU 1503	5.4			M 1529	5.7
	2054	1.1			2155	0.6
12	0323	5.3		**27**	0403	5.6
	0902	1.3			1002	1.1
	M 1537	5.4			TU 1615	5.7
	2133	1.0			2238	0.7
13	0400	5.3		**28**	0449	5.5
	0939	1.3			1037	1.2
	TU 1613	5.4			W 1700	5.5
	2213	1.0			2315	0.9
14	0439	5.3		**29**	0534	5.3
	1015	1.4			1105	1.4
	W 1650	5.3			TH 1745	5.3
	2253	1.1			2344	1.2
15	0520	5.2		**30**	0619	5.0
	1052	1.5			1132	1.7
	TH 1730	5.2			F 1830	5.1
	2336	1.2				
				31	0008	1.5
					0704	4.8
					SA 1210	1.9
					1917	4.9

Chart Datum: 2·90 metres below Ordnance Datum (Newlyn)
HAT is 6·3 metres above Chart Datum

TIDES

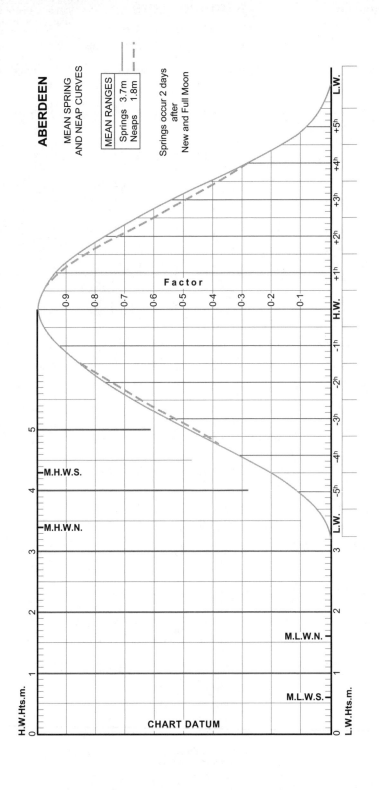

ABERDEEN

MEAN SPRING
AND NEAP CURVES

MEAN RANGES
Springs 3.7m
Neaps 1.8m

Springs occur 2 days
after
New and Full Moon

TIME ZONE (UT)	SCOTLAND – ABERDEEN	Dates in amber are SPRINGS
For Summer Time add ONE hour in non-shaded areas	LAT 57°09′N LONG 2°05′W	Dates in yellow are NEAPS
	TIMES AND HEIGHTS OF HIGH AND LOW WATERS	2011

JANUARY

	Time m	Time m		Time m	Time m
1 SA	0434 1.4 / 1053 3.9	1707 1.4 / 2324 4.0	**16** SU	0407 1.8 / 1036 3.6	1645 1.7 / 2300 3.6
2 SU	0531 1.3 / 1146 4.0	1801 1.2	**17** M	0506 1.6 / 1128 3.8	1737 1.4 / 2353 3.8
3 M	0019 4.0 / 0618 1.3	1232 4.2 / 1847 1.0	**18** TU	0554 1.4 / 1213 4.0	1822 1.1
4 TU	0107 4.1 / 0700 1.2	1313 4.3 / ●1930 0.9	**19** W	0040 4.1 / 0637 1.2	○1254 4.2 / 1905 0.8
5 W	0149 4.1 / 0738 1.2	1351 4.3 / 2009 0.8	**20** TH	0124 4.2 / 0719 1.0	1334 4.4 / 1949 0.5
6 TH	0229 4.1 / 0814 1.2	1428 4.3 / 2045 0.8	**21** F	0206 4.4 / 0801 0.9	1414 4.6 / 2032 0.4
7 F	0306 4.1 / 0848 1.2	1503 4.3 / 2119 0.9	**22** SA	0249 4.4 / 0842 0.8	1456 4.6 / 2116 0.3
8 SA	0342 4.0 / 0921 1.2	1538 4.2 / 2153 1.0	**23** SU	0333 4.4 / 0923 0.9	1539 4.6 / 2200 0.4
9 SU	0418 3.8 / 0954 1.4	1613 4.1 / 2227 1.1	**24** M	0418 4.2 / 1005 1.0	1625 4.5 / 2246 0.6
10 M	0455 3.7 / 1029 1.5	1652 3.9 / 2304 1.3	**25** TU	0506 4.1 / 1051 1.1	1717 4.3 / 2336 0.9
11 TU	0537 3.6 / 1109 1.7	1736 3.8 / 2346 1.5	**26** W	0559 3.9 / 1145 1.4	1816 4.0
12 W	0624 3.5 / 1157 1.8	1828 3.6 ●	**27** TH	0033 1.2 / 0659 3.7	1252 1.6 / 1925 3.8
13 TH	0038 1.7 / 0719 3.4	1302 2.0 / 1929 3.5	**28** F	0140 1.5 / 0808 3.5	1414 1.7 / 2047 3.6
14 F	0142 1.8 / 0822 3.4	1419 2.0 / 2038 3.4	**29** SA	0302 1.7 / 0927 3.6	1550 1.6 / 2214 3.6
15 SA	0255 1.8 / 0932 3.4	1538 1.9 / 2154 3.5	**30** SU	0424 1.7 / 1040 3.7	1703 1.4 / 2323 3.7
			31 M	0523 1.6 / 1137 3.9	1756 1.2

FEBRUARY

	Time m	Time m		Time m	Time m
1 TU	0016 3.9 / 0608 1.4	1223 4.0 / 1839 1.0	**16** W	0535 1.4 / 1150 4.0	1803 0.9
2 W	0059 4.0 / 0647 1.3	1302 4.2 / 1917 0.9	**17** TH	0021 4.1 / 0619 1.1	1233 4.2 / 1847 0.6
3 TH	0136 4.0 / 0722 1.1	1337 4.3 / ○1951 0.8	**18** F	0105 4.3 / 0701 0.8	1314 4.5 / 1930 0.3
4 F	0209 4.1 / 0754 1.1	1409 4.3 / 2023 0.8	**19** SA	0147 4.4 / 0742 0.7	1354 4.7 / 2011 0.2
5 SA	0241 4.1 / 0825 1.0	1440 4.3 / 2053 0.8	**20** SU	0228 4.5 / 0822 0.6	1436 4.8 / 2055 0.1
6 SU	0312 4.0 / 0854 1.1	1511 4.2 / 2121 0.9	**21** M	0309 4.4 / 0902 0.6	1519 4.7 / 2137 0.3
7 M	0342 3.9 / 0922 1.1	1543 4.1 / 2151 1.0	**22** TU	0352 4.3 / 0944 0.7	1605 4.5 / 2221 0.6
8 TU	0414 3.8 / 0955 1.2	1617 4.0 / 2222 1.2	**23** W	0438 4.1 / 1029 0.9	1657 4.3 / 2308 0.9
9 W	0449 3.7 / 1029 1.4	1655 3.8 / 2257 1.4	**24** TH	0528 3.9 / 1122 1.2	1757 3.9 ◐
10 TH	0529 3.6 / 1109 1.6	1740 3.7 / 2340 1.6	**25** F	0003 1.3 / 0628 3.6	1229 1.5 / 1909 3.6
11 F	0619 3.4 / 1202 1.8	1838 3.5 ◐	**26** SA	0112 1.7 / 0739 3.4	1356 1.6 / 2034 3.4
12 SA	0038 1.8 / 0723 3.3	1318 1.9 / 1951 3.3	**27** SU	0243 1.7 / 0902 3.4	1543 1.6 / 2207 3.5
13 SU	0159 1.9 / 0837 3.3	1451 1.9 / 2113 3.3	**28** M	0412 1.8 / 1023 3.5	1653 1.4 / 2315 3.6
14 M	0330 1.9 / 0956 3.4	1616 1.6 / 2234 3.5			
15 TU	0443 1.7 / 1101 3.7	1715 1.3 / 2334 3.8			

MARCH

	Time m	Time m		Time m	Time m
1 TU	0509 1.6 / 1122 3.7	1742 1.2	**16** W	0417 1.6 / 1028 3.6	1648 1.1 / 2309 3.8
2 W	0003 3.7 / 0552 1.4	1207 3.9 / 1822 1.0	**17** TH	0512 1.3 / 1122 3.9	1738 0.8 / 2358 4.1
3 TH	0042 3.9 / 0628 1.2	1243 4.0 / 1856 0.9	**18** F	0557 1.0 / 1207 4.2	1823 0.4
4 F	0114 4.0 / 0700 1.1	1315 4.2 / ●1927 0.8	**19** SA	0041 4.3 / 0638 0.7	1250 4.5 / ○1906 0.2
5 SA	0144 4.0 / 0731 1.0	1346 4.2 / 1955 0.7	**20** SU	0122 4.4 / 0720 0.5	1332 4.7 / 1949 0.1
6 SU	0213 4.0 / 0800 0.9	1415 4.2 / 2023 0.7	**21** M	0203 4.5 / 0800 0.4	1416 4.7 / 2031 0.1
7 M	0240 4.0 / 0828 0.9	1445 4.2 / 2050 0.8	**22** TU	0244 4.4 / 0842 0.4	1501 4.7 / 2113 0.4
8 TU	0309 4.0 / 0857 1.0	1515 4.1 / 2118 0.9	**23** W	0326 4.3 / 0925 0.6	1549 4.4 / 2156 0.7
9 W	0338 3.9 / 0926 1.1	1549 4.0 / 2147 1.1	**24** TH	0411 4.1 / 1012 0.8	1642 4.1 / 2243 1.1
10 TH	0411 3.8 / 0959 1.2	1625 3.8 / 2219 1.3	**25** F	0501 3.9 / 1106 1.1	1744 3.8 / 2337 1.5
11 F	0447 3.6 / 1037 1.4	1709 3.6 / 2258 1.5 ◐	**26** SA	0601 3.6 / 1212 1.3	1855 3.5
12 SA	0532 3.5 / 1127 1.6	1805 3.4 / 2353 1.7	**27** SU	0046 1.8 / 0711 3.4	1338 1.5 / 2016 3.3
13 SU	0636 3.3 / 1240 1.7	1921 3.3	**28** M	0216 1.9 / 0831 3.4	1521 1.5 / 2146 3.4
14 M	0118 1.9 / 0755 3.3	1414 1.7 / 2043 3.3	**29** TU	0346 1.8 / 0954 3.4	1629 1.3 / 2251 3.5
15 TU	0258 1.9 / 0916 3.4	1544 1.5 / 2207 3.5	**30** W	0443 1.7 / 1054 3.6	1716 1.2 / 2337 3.6
			31 TH	0526 1.4 / 1139 3.8	1754 1.0

APRIL

	Time m	Time m		Time m	Time m
1 F	0014 3.8 / 0601 1.2	1216 3.9 / 1826 0.9	**16** SA	0530 1.0 / 1140 4.2	1757 0.4
2 SA	0045 3.9 / 0634 1.1	1248 4.0 / 1856 0.8	**17** SU	0015 4.2 / 0614 0.7	1227 4.4 / 1841 0.3
3 SU	0115 4.0 / 0705 0.9	1319 4.1 / 1925 0.8	**18** M	0057 4.4 / 0658 0.5	1312 4.6 / ○1925 0.2
4 M	0143 4.0 / 0735 0.9	1349 4.1 / 1953 0.8	**19** TU	0138 4.4 / 0741 0.4	1358 4.6 / 2008 0.3
5 TU	0211 4.0 / 0804 0.9	1420 4.1 / 2020 0.8	**20** W	0220 4.4 / 0826 0.4	1446 4.5 / 2051 0.6
6 W	0239 4.0 / 0834 0.9	1452 4.0 / 2049 0.9	**21** TH	0303 4.3 / 0912 0.5	1536 4.3 / 2135 0.9
7 TH	0309 3.9 / 0905 1.0	1527 3.9 / 2119 1.1	**22** F	0349 4.1 / 1000 0.7	1631 4.0 / 2222 1.2
8 F	0342 3.8 / 0939 1.1	1605 3.8 / 2153 1.3	**23** SA	0439 3.9 / 1053 1.0	1732 3.7 / 2314 1.5
9 SA	0419 3.7 / 1019 1.2	1651 3.6 / 2234 1.5	**24** SU	0536 3.7 / 1155 1.2	1836 3.5
10 SU	0504 3.6 / 1111 1.4	1749 3.5 / 2331 1.7	**25** M	0017 1.8 / 0640 3.5	1308 1.4 / ◐1944 3.3
11 M	0605 3.4 / 1221 1.5	1902 3.4 ◐	**26** TU	0133 1.9 / 0750 3.4	1432 1.4 / 2101 3.3
12 TU	0053 1.8 / 0722 3.4	1347 1.5 / 2018 3.4	**27** W	0257 1.9 / 0906 3.4	1545 1.4 / 2209 3.4
13 W	0226 1.8 / 0839 3.4	1509 1.3 / 2135 3.5	**28** TH	0403 1.7 / 1011 3.5	1636 1.3 / 2258 3.5
14 TH	0343 1.6 / 0951 3.6	1616 1.0 / 2239 3.8	**29** F	0450 1.5 / 1101 3.6	1716 1.1 / 2337 3.6
15 F	0441 1.3 / 1050 3.9	1710 0.7 / 2330 4.0	**30** SA	0530 1.3 / 1142 3.7	1751 1.0

Chart Datum: 2·25 metres below Ordnance Datum (Newlyn)
HAT is 4·9 metres above Chart Datum

TIDES

TIDES

TIME ZONE (UT)
For Summer Time add ONE hour in **non-shaded areas**

SCOTLAND – ABERDEEN
LAT 57°09'N   LONG 2°05'W
TIMES AND HEIGHTS OF HIGH AND LOW WATERS

Dates in amber are **SPRINGS**
Dates in yellow are **NEAPS**

2011

MAY

Day	Time m	Time m	Time m	Time m
1 SU	0011 3.8	0605 1.2	1218 3.8	1823 1.0
16 M	0554 0.8	1207 4.3	1820 0.5	
2 M	0043 3.9	0638 1.0	1252 3.9	1854 0.9
17 TU	0034 4.2	0641 0.6	1257 4.4 ○	1906 0.5
3 TU	0114 4.0	0710 0.9	1326 4.0 ●	1924 0.9
18 W	0118 4.3	0728 0.5	1346 4.4	1950 0.6
4 W	0144 4.0	0742 0.9	1359 4.0	1955 0.9
19 TH	0201 4.3	0815 0.5	1435 4.3	2034 0.8
5 TH	0214 4.0	0816 0.9	1434 4.0	2027 1.0
20 F	0245 4.2	0901 0.5	1526 4.1	2118 1.0
6 F	0247 4.0	0851 0.9	1512 3.9	2102 1.1
21 SA	0331 4.1	0949 0.7	1619 3.9	2202 1.2
7 SA	0322 3.9	0929 1.0	1553 3.8	2140 1.2
22 SU	0419 4.0	1038 0.9	1712 3.7	2249 1.4
8 SU	0402 3.8	1013 1.0	1641 3.7	2224 1.4
23 M	0510 3.8	1130 1.1	1806 3.5	2341 1.6
9 M	0448 3.7	1105 1.1	1738 3.6	2321 1.5
24 TU	0605 3.6	1226 1.3	1902 3.4 ☽	
10 TU	0547 3.6	1209 1.2	1844 3.5 ●	
25 W	0042 1.8	0703 3.5	1328 1.4	2003 3.3
11 W	0032 1.6	0656 3.5	1322 1.2	1952 3.5
26 TH	0149 1.8	0806 3.4	1435 1.4	2107 3.3
12 TH	0152 1.6	0806 3.6	1434 1.1	2102 3.6
27 F	0300 1.8	0913 3.4	1539 1.4	2206 3.4
13 F	0304 1.5	0915 3.7	1541 0.9	2206 3.8
28 SA	0403 1.6	1013 3.5	1630 1.4	2254 3.5
14 SA	0408 1.3	1019 3.9	1640 0.7	2301 3.9
29 SU	0452 1.5	1103 3.6	1712 1.3	2335 3.7
15 SU	0503 1.0	1116 4.1	1732 0.6	2349 4.1
30 M	0534 1.3	1147 3.7	1750 1.2	
31 TU	0012 3.8	0611 1.2	1227 3.8	1825 1.1

JUNE

Day	Time m	Time m	Time m	Time m
1 W	0047 3.9	0648 1.0	1304 3.9	1900 1.0 ●
16 TH	0104 4.2	0720 0.6	1339 4.2	1937 0.9
2 TH	0120 4.0	0724 0.9	1342 3.9	1935 1.0
17 F	0148 4.2	0806 0.5	1427 4.1	2019 0.9
3 F	0155 4.0	0802 0.8	1420 4.0	2012 1.0
18 SA	0231 4.2	0850 0.6	1514 4.1	2100 1.0
4 SA	0230 4.1	0841 0.8	1501 4.0	2051 1.1
19 SU	0313 4.2	0933 0.6	1559 3.9	2139 1.1
5 SU	0308 4.0	0922 0.8	1544 3.9	2132 1.1
20 M	0356 4.1	1014 0.8	1643 3.8	2219 1.3
6 M	0349 4.0	1007 0.8	1631 3.8	2216 1.2
21 TU	0440 3.9	1056 1.0	1728 3.6	2301 1.4
7 TU	0436 3.9	1057 0.8	1724 3.7	2308 1.3
22 W	0525 3.8	1140 1.2	1815 3.5	2349 1.6
8 W	0529 3.9	1153 0.9	1823 3.7	
23 TH	0614 3.6	1229 1.3	1905 3.4 ☽	
9 TH	0008 1.4	0630 3.8	1256 1.0	1924 3.6 ☽
24 F	0045 1.7	0708 3.5	1325 1.5	2000 3.3
10 F	0117 1.5	0736 3.8	1401 1.0	2029 3.6
25 SA	0150 1.8	0808 3.4	1426 1.6	2103 3.3
11 SA	0227 1.5	0845 3.8	1508 1.0	2135 3.7
26 SU	0301 1.8	0915 3.4	1532 1.6	2204 3.4
12 SU	0337 1.3	0954 3.8	1614 1.0	2236 3.8
27 M	0409 1.7	1021 3.4	1631 1.5	2257 3.6
13 M	0443 1.2	1059 4.0	1713 0.9	2330 4.0
28 TU	0503 1.5	1116 3.5	1719 1.4	2342 3.7
14 TU	0540 0.9	1156 4.1	1805 0.9	
29 W	0547 1.3	1203 3.7	1801 1.3	
15 W	0018 4.1	0632 0.8	1249 4.2	1852 0.8 ○
30 TH	0022 3.9	0627 1.1	1245 3.8	1840 1.2

JULY

Day	Time m	Time m	Time m	Time m
1 F	0100 4.0	0707 0.9	1326 4.0	1919 1.0 ●
16 SA	0136 4.2	0755 0.6	1414 4.1	2002 1.0
2 SA	0137 4.1	0748 0.7	1407 4.1	1959 1.0
17 SU	0215 4.3	0833 0.6	1454 4.1	2038 1.0
3 SU	0215 4.2	0829 0.6	1448 4.1	2039 0.9
18 M	0252 4.3	0909 0.6	1531 4.0	2112 1.0
4 M	0254 4.3	0911 0.5	1531 4.1	2120 0.9
19 TU	0329 4.2	0944 0.8	1608 3.9	2146 1.1
5 TU	0335 4.3	0955 0.5	1616 4.0	2202 1.0
20 W	0405 4.1	1018 0.9	1645 3.7	2221 1.3
6 W	0420 4.2	1041 0.6	1704 3.9	2248 1.1
21 TH	0443 3.9	1053 1.1	1725 3.6	2259 1.4
7 TH	0510 4.1	1131 0.7	1757 3.8	2342 1.3
22 F	0526 3.7	1133 1.3	1809 3.5	2346 1.6
8 F	0606 4.0	1228 0.8	1855 3.7 ☽	
23 SA	0615 3.6	1221 1.5	1901 3.4 ☽	
9 SA	0045 1.4	0710 3.9	1331 1.1	1958 3.6
24 SU	0045 1.8	0713 3.4	1321 1.7	2000 3.3
10 SU	0157 1.5	0822 3.7	1441 1.2	2108 3.6
25 M	0159 1.9	0820 3.3	1432 1.8	2109 3.3
11 M	0316 1.4	0939 3.7	1556 1.3	2217 3.7
26 TU	0320 1.8	0936 3.3	1549 1.7	2217 3.5
12 TU	0434 1.2	1053 3.8	1702 1.2	2317 3.9
27 W	0432 1.6	1046 3.5	1656 1.6	2312 3.7
13 W	0535 1.1	1154 3.9	1756 1.2	
28 TH	0524 1.4	1140 3.7	1739 1.4	2358 3.9
14 TH	0009 4.0	0627 0.9	1247 4.0	1842 1.1
29 F	0607 1.1	1226 3.9	1821 1.2	
15 F	0054 4.2	0713 0.7	1333 4.1	1923 1.0 ○
30 SA	0038 4.1	0648 0.8	1308 4.1	1901 1.0 ●
31 SU	0117 4.3	0730 0.5	1348 4.2	1941 0.8

AUGUST

Day	Time m	Time m	Time m	Time m
1 M	0156 4.4	0811 0.4	1429 4.3	2021 0.7
16 TU	0227 4.3	0840 0.7	1459 4.4	2043 1.0
2 TU	0235 4.5	0853 0.3	1510 4.3	2101 0.7
17 W	0259 4.3	0910 0.8	1530 4.0	2114 1.1
3 W	0316 4.5	0935 0.3	1553 4.3	2142 0.8
18 TH	0332 4.2	0939 0.9	1602 3.9	2145 1.2
4 TH	0400 4.5	1019 0.5	1638 4.1	2226 1.0
19 F	0406 4.0	1010 1.1	1637 3.7	2219 1.3
5 F	0449 4.3	1107 0.7	1729 3.9	2317 1.2
20 SA	0444 3.8	1045 1.3	1717 3.6	2259 1.5
6 SA	0545 4.1	1201 1.0	1826 3.7 ●	
21 SU	0530 3.6	1126 1.5	1806 3.5	2351 1.7 ☽
7 SU	0019 1.4	0651 3.8	1305 1.3	1932 3.6
22 M	0627 3.4	1221 1.8	1907 3.4	
8 M	0136 1.5	0808 3.6	1421 1.5	2046 3.6
23 TU	0104 1.9	0736 3.3	1339 1.9	2018 3.3
9 TU	0309 1.5	0935 3.6	1548 1.6	2204 3.7
24 W	0234 1.9	0855 3.3	1509 1.9	2134 3.4
10 W	0432 1.3	1053 3.9	1656 1.5	2309 3.8
25 TH	0359 1.7	1016 3.4	1624 1.7	2241 3.6
11 TH	0531 1.1	1152 3.8	1747 1.3	
26 F	0458 1.4	1116 3.7	1716 1.5	2331 3.9
12 F	0000 4.0	0619 0.9	1239 4.0	1829 1.2
27 SA	0544 1.0	1202 4.0	1759 1.2	
13 SA	0042 4.2	0700 0.7	1319 4.0	1906 1.1 ○
28 SU	0013 4.2	0625 0.7	1245 4.2	1839 0.9
14 SU	0119 4.3	0736 0.7	1354 4.1	1940 1.0
29 M	0053 4.4	0707 0.4	1325 4.4	1919 0.7 ●
15 M	0154 4.3	0809 0.6	1427 4.1	2013 0.9
30 TU	0132 4.6	0748 0.2	1404 4.5	1959 0.6
31 W	0213 4.7	0830 0.1	1445 4.5	2039 0.6

Chart Datum: 2·25 metres below Ordnance Datum (Newlyn)
HAT is 4·9 metres above Chart Datum

SCOTLAND – ABERDEEN
LAT 57°09′N   LONG 2°05′W
TIMES AND HEIGHTS OF HIGH AND LOW WATERS

Dates in amber are **SPRINGS**
Dates in yellow are **NEAPS**

2011

SEPTEMBER

Day	Time m	Time m	Time m	Time m
1 TH	0255 4.7	0911 0.3	1527 4.4	2120 0.7
16 F	0302 4.2	0904 1.0	1525 4.0	2115 1.1
2 F	0340 4.6	0955 0.5	1612 4.2	2205 0.9
17 SA	0335 4.0	0933 1.1	1558 3.9	2148 1.3
3 SA	0430 4.4	1042 0.8	1701 4.0	2257 1.1
18 SU	0413 3.9	1006 1.3	1634 3.7	2226 1.4
4 SU ◐	0529 4.1	1136 1.2	1800 3.8	
19 M	0456 3.7	1044 1.6	1719 3.6	2315 1.6
5 M	0002 1.4	0639 3.8	1243 1.6	1908 3.6
20 TU ◑	0552 3.5	1136 1.8	1820 3.5	
6 TU	0125 1.5	0800 3.6	1406 1.8	2027 3.5
21 W	0024 1.8	0704 3.4	1255 2.0	1935 3.4
7 W	0306 1.5	0933 3.5	1539 1.8	2150 3.6
22 TH	0154 1.8	0822 3.4	1431 2.0	2052 3.5
8 TH	0425 1.3	1047 3.7	1643 1.6	2255 3.8
23 F	0321 1.6	0942 3.5	1552 1.8	2203 3.7
9 F	0519 1.1	1140 3.8	1730 1.4	2343 4.0
24 SA	0426 1.3	1046 3.8	1648 1.5	2258 4.0
10 SA	0602 1.0	1222 3.9	1809 1.3	
25 SU	0515 0.9	1135 4.1	1733 1.2	2344 4.3
11 SU	0022 4.1	0638 0.8	1257 4.0	1843 1.1
26 M	0559 0.6	1217 4.3	1814 0.9	
12 M ○	0057 4.2	0710 0.8	1328 4.1	1915 1.0
27 TU ●	0026 4.5	0641 0.3	1258 4.5	1855 0.7
13 TU	0129 4.3	0740 0.7	1357 4.1	1946 0.9
28 W	0108 4.7	0723 0.2	1338 4.6	1936 0.5
14 W	0159 4.3	0808 0.8	1426 4.1	2015 1.0
29 TH	0150 4.8	0805 0.2	1419 4.6	2018 0.5
15 TH	0230 4.3	0836 0.8	1455 4.1	2044 1.0
30 F	0235 4.8	0847 0.4	1501 4.5	2102 0.6

OCTOBER

Day	Time m	Time m	Time m	Time m
1 SA	0323 4.6	0931 0.7	1546 4.3	2149 0.8
16 SU	0312 4.0	0904 1.2	1527 4.0	2126 1.2
2 SU	0416 4.3	1019 1.0	1637 4.1	2244 1.1
17 M	0350 3.9	0938 1.4	1603 3.9	2206 1.4
3 M	0518 4.0	1114 1.4	1736 3.9	2350 1.4
18 TU	0434 3.7	1017 1.6	1647 3.7	2254 1.5
4 TU ◐	0629 3.7	1221 1.8	1846 3.7	
19 W	0529 3.6	1108 1.8	1743 3.6	2358 1.6
5 W	0111 1.5	0747 3.5	1344 1.9	2003 3.6
20 TH ◑	0638 3.5	1221 2.0	1857 3.5	
6 TH	0247 1.5	0915 3.5	1515 1.9	2124 3.6
21 F	0119 1.6	0751 3.5	1351 2.0	2011 3.6
7 F	0403 1.4	1026 3.6	1619 1.7	2229 3.8
22 SA	0240 1.5	0905 3.6	1511 1.8	2121 3.7
8 SA	0455 1.2	1116 3.8	1705 1.6	2318 3.9
23 SU	0347 1.2	1011 3.8	1612 1.5	2222 4.0
9 SU	0535 1.1	1155 3.9	1744 1.4	2356 4.1
24 M	0442 0.9	1104 4.1	1703 1.2	2313 4.3
10 M	0609 1.0	1228 4.0	1818 1.2	
25 TU	0530 0.7	1149 4.3	1749 1.0	
11 TU	0030 4.2	0640 0.9	1258 4.1	1849 1.1
26 W ●	0000 4.5	0615 0.5	1232 4.5	1832 0.7
12 W ○	0102 4.2	0709 0.9	1327 4.2	1920 1.0
27 TH	0046 4.7	0659 0.4	1314 4.6	1916 0.6
13 TH	0134 4.2	0737 0.9	1356 4.2	1950 1.0
28 F	0132 4.8	0743 0.5	1356 4.6	2002 0.6
14 F	0205 4.2	0806 1.0	1425 4.1	2020 1.0
29 SA	0220 4.7	0827 0.6	1439 4.5	2048 0.6
15 SA	0238 4.1	0834 1.1	1455 4.1	2052 1.1
30 SU	0310 4.5	0912 0.9	1525 4.4	2138 0.8
31 M	0406 4.3	1000 1.2	1616 4.2	2232 1.0

NOVEMBER

Day	Time m	Time m	Time m	Time m
1 TU	0506 4.0	1052 1.5	1713 4.0	2334 1.2
16 W	0419 3.8	1001 1.5	1625 3.9	2241 1.3
2 W ◐	0611 3.7	1154 1.8	1818 3.8	
17 TH	0511 3.7	1050 1.7	1717 3.8	2338 1.4
3 TH	0044 1.4	0719 3.6	1306 2.0	1927 3.7
18 F	0612 3.6	1153 1.8	1822 3.7	
4 F	0204 1.5	0834 3.5	1426 2.0	2040 3.6
19 SA	0046 1.4	0719 3.6	1310 1.9	1931 3.7
5 SA	0321 1.5	0945 3.6	1538 1.9	2149 3.7
20 SU	0158 1.4	0826 3.7	1426 1.8	2040 3.8
6 SU	0417 1.4	1039 3.7	1631 1.7	2242 3.8
21 M	0306 1.2	0933 3.8	1533 1.6	2146 4.0
7 M	0500 1.3	1121 3.8	1713 1.5	2325 3.9
22 TU	0408 1.0	1032 4.0	1633 1.3	2246 4.2
8 TU	0536 1.2	1156 3.9	1750 1.4	
23 W	0503 0.9	1123 4.2	1726 1.1	2340 4.4
9 W	0002 4.0	0608 1.2	1229 4.1	1824 1.2
24 TH	0553 0.7	1209 4.4	1816 0.9	
10 TH ○	0038 4.1	0640 1.1	1300 4.1	1857 1.1
25 F ●	0030 4.5	0640 0.7	1254 4.5	1904 0.7
11 F	0111 4.1	0710 1.1	1330 4.2	1929 1.1
26 SA	0120 4.6	0726 0.7	1338 4.5	1951 0.6
12 SA	0145 4.1	0741 1.1	1400 4.2	2002 1.1
27 SU	0210 4.5	0812 0.9	1423 4.5	2039 0.6
13 SU	0219 4.1	0812 1.2	1432 4.2	2037 1.1
28 M	0301 4.4	0856 1.0	1508 4.4	2128 0.7
14 M	0256 4.0	0845 1.3	1505 4.1	2113 1.1
29 TU	0354 4.2	0941 1.2	1557 4.3	2217 0.9
15 TU	0335 3.9	0921 1.4	1543 4.0	2154 1.2
30 W	0448 4.0	1028 1.5	1648 4.1	2309 1.1

DECEMBER

Day	Time m	Time m	Time m	Time m
1 TH	0543 3.8	1119 1.7	1744 3.9	
16 F	0452 3.9	1033 1.5	1656 4.1	2317 1.1
2 F ◐	0005 1.3	0639 3.6	1217 1.9	1842 3.7
17 SA	0545 3.8	1126 1.6	1752 4.0	
3 SA	0105 1.5	0739 3.5	1322 2.0	1944 3.6
18 SU ◐	0015 1.2	0645 3.7	1230 1.7	1855 3.9
4 SU	0211 1.6	0845 3.5	1433 2.0	2051 3.6
19 M	0120 1.3	0749 3.7	1343 1.7	2004 3.9
5 M	0319 1.6	0948 3.5	1543 1.9	2156 3.6
20 TU	0228 1.3	0856 3.8	1456 1.6	2116 3.9
6 TU	0416 1.6	1039 3.7	1638 1.7	2250 3.7
21 W	0337 1.2	1003 3.9	1608 1.5	2226 4.0
7 W	0501 1.5	1122 3.8	1722 1.6	2335 3.8
22 TH	0443 1.2	1102 4.1	1712 1.2	2328 4.2
8 TH	0539 1.4	1200 3.9	1801 1.4	
23 F	0539 1.1	1154 4.2	1807 1.0	
9 F	0015 3.9	0614 1.3	1236 4.1	1837 1.2
24 SA ●	0024 4.3	0629 1.0	1241 4.4	1857 0.8
10 SA ○	0053 4.0	0648 1.3	1309 4.2	1912 1.1
25 SU	0115 4.4	0715 1.0	1326 4.5	1945 0.6
11 SU	0129 4.1	0722 1.2	1342 4.2	1948 1.0
26 M	0204 4.4	0759 1.0	1410 4.5	2030 0.5
12 M	0205 4.1	0756 1.2	1415 4.2	2025 1.0
27 TU	0251 4.3	0840 1.0	1453 4.5	2113 0.7
13 TU	0243 4.1	0832 1.2	1450 4.2	2103 1.0
28 W	0336 4.2	0920 1.2	1536 4.4	2156 0.8
14 W	0322 4.1	0909 1.3	1527 4.2	2143 1.0
29 TH	0421 4.0	1000 1.3	1620 4.2	2237 1.0
15 TH	0405 4.0	0949 1.4	1609 4.1	2227 1.0
30 F	0506 3.8	1040 1.5	1704 4.0	2320 1.2
31 SA	0552 3.7	1125 1.5	1753 3.8	

Chart Datum: 2·25 metres below Ordnance Datum (Newlyn)
HAT is 4·9 metres above Chart Datum

TIDES

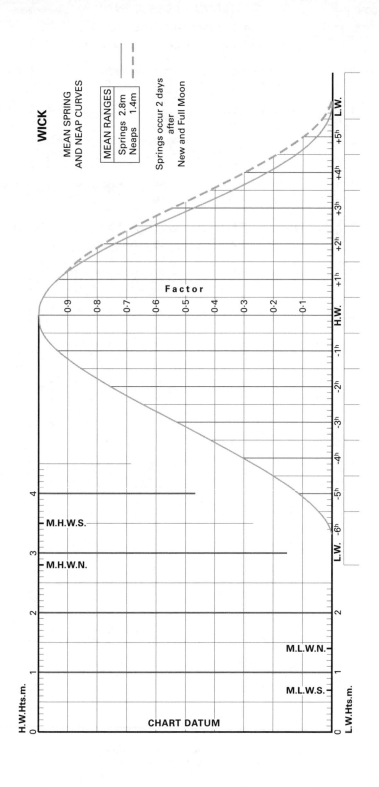

WICK

MEAN SPRING
AND NEAP CURVES

MEAN RANGES	
Springs	2.8m
Neaps	1.4m

Springs occur 2 days
after
New and Full Moon

TIME ZONE (UT)	SCOTLAND – WICK	Dates in amber are SPRINGS
For Summer Time add ONE hour in non-shaded areas	LAT 58°26′N LONG 3°05′W	Dates in yellow are NEAPS
	TIMES AND HEIGHTS OF HIGH AND LOW WATERS	2011

JANUARY

Time	m	Time	m	Time	m	Time	m
1 0226	1.2	**16** 0158	1.5
0840	3.1	0818	2.9
SA 1458	1.2	SU 1439	1.4
2114	3.2	2041	2.9
2 0319	1.2	**17** 0254	1.4
0936	3.3	0913	3.1
SU 1550	1.1	M 1529	1.2
2210	3.3	2139	3.1
3 0403	1.2	**18** 0340	1.2
1023	3.4	1001	3.3
M 1635	0.9	TU 1613	1.0
2258	3.3	2229	3.3
4 0443	1.1	**19** 0423	1.1
1106	3.5	1046	3.5
TU 1716	0.8	W 1655	0.7
● 2341	3.4	○ 2316	3.5
5 0521	1.1	**20** 0504	0.9
1146	3.6	1129	3.7
W 1755	0.7	TH 1737	0.5
6 0021	3.3	**21** 0000	3.6
0556	1.1	0544	0.8
TH 1224	3.6	F 1213	3.8
1831	0.8	1819	0.4
7 0059	3.3	**22** 0045	3.6
0630	1.1	0624	0.8
F 1300	3.6	SA 1255	3.8
1905	0.8	1902	0.4
8 0134	3.2	**23** 0128	3.5
0703	1.1	0705	0.6
SA 1334	3.5	SU 1338	3.8
1938	0.9	1945	0.4
9 0208	3.1	**24** 0212	3.4
0735	1.2	0747	0.9
SU 1408	3.4	M 1423	3.7
2012	1.0	2032	0.6
10 0244	3.0	**25** 0258	3.3
0809	1.3	0831	1.0
M 1444	3.3	TU 1511	3.5
2048	1.1	2122	0.8
11 0323	2.9	**26** 0347	3.1
0847	1.4	0922	1.2
TU 1525	3.1	W 1606	3.3
2130	1.3	◑ 2223	1.1
12 0408	2.8	**27** 0444	3.0
0934	1.6	1032	1.4
W 1612	3.0	TH 1713	3.1
◑ 2225	1.4	2335	1.3
13 0502	2.7	**28** 0551	2.9
1044	1.7	1206	1.5
TH 1711	2.8	F 1832	2.9
2335	1.5	
14 0607	2.7	**29** 0100	1.4
1210	1.7	0706	2.9
F 1821	2.8	SA 1348	1.4
		1959	2.9
15 0048	1.5	**30** 0217	1.4
0714	2.8	0823	3.0
SA 1333	1.6	SU 1458	1.2
1933	2.8	2112	3.0
		31 0312	1.4
		0924	3.2
		M 1548	1.1
		2205	3.1

FEBRUARY

Time	m	Time	m
1 0355	1.3	**16** 0323	1.2
1012	3.3	0938	3.2
TU 1629	0.9	W 1554	0.8
2248	3.2	2212	3.3
2 0431	1.1	**17** 0406	1.0
1053	3.4	1025	3.5
W 1704	0.8	TH 1636	0.5
2327	3.3	2258	3.5
3 0505	1.0	**18** 0446	0.8
1131	3.5	1110	3.7
TH 1737	0.7	F 1718	0.3
●		○ 2342	3.6
4 0002	3.3	**19** 0526	0.6
0536	1.0	1153	3.9
F 1206	3.6	SA 1759	0.2
1808	0.7	
5 0035	3.3	**20** 0024	3.6
0607	0.9	0605	0.5
SA 1238	3.5	SU 1236	3.9
1838	0.7	1840	0.2
6 0106	3.2	**21** 0106	3.6
0544	0.9	0645	0.6
SU 1308	3.5	M 1319	3.9
1907	0.8	1922	0.3
7 0135	3.2	**22** 0148	3.5
0707	1.0	0726	0.7
M 1339	3.4	TU 1404	3.7
1936	0.9	2005	0.6
8 0206	3.1	**23** 0230	3.3
0738	1.1	0809	0.8
TU 1411	3.3	W 1451	3.5
2006	1.0	2051	0.9
9 0238	3.0	**24** 0317	3.1
0810	1.2	0858	1.0
W 1446	3.1	TH 1546	3.2
2039	1.2	◑ 2147	1.2
10 0316	2.9	**25** 0411	2.9
0847	1.4	1008	1.3
TH 1527	3.0	F 1654	2.9
2118	1.3	2302	1.5
11 0401	2.8	**26** 0519	2.8
0936	1.5	1154	1.4
F 1619	2.8	SA 1819	2.8
◑ 2216	1.5	
12 0501	2.7	**27** 0040	1.6
1106	1.6	0639	2.8
SA 1730	2.7	SU 1343	1.3
2350	1.6	1953	2.8
13 0618	2.7	**28** 0206	1.5
1249	1.6	0804	2.9
SU 1855	2.7	M 1449	1.2
		2102	2.9
14 0121	1.6		
0735	2.8		
M 1412	1.4		
2015	2.8		
15 0232	1.4		
0843	3.0		
TU 1509	1.1		
2120	3.0		

MARCH

Time	m	Time	m
1 0300	1.4	**16** 0206	1.4
0907	3.0	0809	2.9
TU 1535	1.0	W 1442	0.9
2150	3.0	2056	3.0
2 0339	1.2	**17** 0259	1.1
0954	3.2	0909	3.2
W 1611	0.9	TH 1529	0.6
2230	3.1	2149	3.2
3 0412	1.1	**18** 0343	0.9
1033	3.3	1000	3.4
TH 1642	0.8	F 1612	0.4
2305	3.2	2235	3.4
4 0443	1.0	**19** 0424	0.7
1109	3.4	1046	3.7
F 1711	0.7	SA 1654	0.2
● 2337	3.2	○ 2318	3.6
5 0513	0.9	**20** 0504	0.5
1141	3.4	1131	3.8
SA 1740	0.6	SU 1735	0.1
6 0007	3.2	**21** 0000	3.6
0543	0.8	0544	0.4
SU 1212	3.4	M 1216	3.9
1807	0.6	1816	0.2
7 0036	3.2	**22** 0042	3.6
0612	0.8	0625	0.4
M 1241	3.4	TU 1300	3.8
1835	0.7	1857	0.3
8 0104	3.2	**23** 0123	3.5
0641	0.8	0708	0.5
TU 1311	3.3	W 1346	3.6
1903	0.8	1939	0.6
9 0132	3.1	**24** 0205	3.3
0711	0.9	0752	0.7
W 1343	3.2	TH 1435	3.3
1931	0.9	2024	1.0
10 0203	3.1	**25** 0250	3.1
0742	1.0	0844	0.9
TH 1417	3.1	F 1530	3.0
2001	1.1	2117	1.3
11 0238	3.0	**26** 0343	2.9
0817	1.2	0958	1.2
F 1458	2.9	SA 1639	2.8
2037	1.3	◑ 2231	1.5
12 0320	2.8	**27** 0450	2.8
0902	1.3	1138	1.3
SA 1548	2.8	SU 1802	2.6
◑ 2126	1.5	
13 0416	2.7	**28** 0008	1.6
1019	1.4	0609	2.7
SU 1657	2.7	M 1320	1.2
2303	1.6	1930	2.6
14 0532	2.7	**29** 0139	1.5
1214	1.4	0730	2.8
M 1826	2.6	TU 1423	1.1
		2037	2.8
15 0048	1.5	**30** 0233	1.4
0657	2.7	0837	2.9
TU 1341	1.2	W 1507	1.0
1949	2.6	2124	2.9
		31 0313	1.2
		0925	3.0
		TH 1541	0.8
		2202	3.0

APRIL

Time	m	Time	m
1 0346	1.1	**16** 0316	0.8
1005	3.2	0932	3.4
F 1611	0.8	SA 1546	0.3
2236	3.1	2209	3.4
2 0417	0.9	**17** 0400	0.6
1041	3.2	1022	3.6
SA 1640	0.7	SU 1629	0.2
2308	3.2	2253	3.5
3 0448	0.8	**18** 0442	0.5
1113	3.3	1110	3.7
SU 1709	0.7	M 1711	0.2
● 2337	3.2	2336	3.5
4 0518	0.7	**19** 0526	0.4
1144	3.3	1157	3.7
M 1737	0.7	TU 1753	0.3
5 0005	3.2	**20** 0018	3.5
0547	0.7	0609	0.4
TU 1215	3.3	W 1244	3.6
1804	0.7	1835	0.5
6 0034	3.2	**21** 0100	3.5
0618	0.7	0654	0.5
W 1247	3.2	TH 1331	3.4
1833	0.8	1918	0.8
7 0104	3.2	**22** 0143	3.3
0649	0.8	0742	0.6
TH 1320	3.2	F 1421	3.2
1903	0.9	2002	1.0
8 0136	3.1	**23** 0228	3.2
0723	0.9	0837	0.8
F 1357	3.0	SA 1516	2.9
1935	1.1	2052	1.3
9 0212	3.0	**24** 0319	3.0
0801	1.0	0945	1.0
SA 1440	2.9	SU 1620	2.7
2013	1.2	2157	1.5
10 0255	2.9	**25** 0421	2.8
0849	1.1	1104	1.1
SU 1532	2.8	M 1731	2.6
2105	1.4	◑ 2317	1.6
11 0349	2.8	**26** 0532	2.7
1006	1.2	1230	1.1
M 1640	2.6	TU 1845	2.6
◑ 2235	1.5	
12 0501	2.7	**27** 0044	1.5
1147	1.2	0643	2.7
TU 1803	2.6	W 1338	1.1
		1953	2.7
13 0015	1.5	**28** 0150	1.4
0622	2.8	0750	2.8
W 1307	1.0	TH 1426	1.0
1920	2.8	2045	2.8
14 0132	1.3	**29** 0236	1.3
0734	2.9	0845	2.9
TH 1410	0.8	F 1503	0.9
2026	3.0	2126	2.9
15 0229	1.1	**30** 0314	1.1
0837	3.1	0929	3.0
F 1501	0.5	SA 1536	0.8
2121	3.2	2202	3.0

Chart Datum: 1·71 metres below Ordnance Datum (Newlyn)
HAT is 4·0 metres above Chart Datum

TIDES

TIDES

TIME ZONE (UT)
For Summer Time add ONE hour in **non-shaded areas**

SCOTLAND – WICK
LAT 58°26′N   LONG 3°05′W
TIMES AND HEIGHTS OF HIGH AND LOW WATERS

Dates in amber are **SPRINGS**
Dates in yellow are **NEAPS**

2011

MAY

Date	Time	m	Time	m	Time	m	Time	m
1 SU	0349	1.0	1008	3.1	1607	0.8	2236	3.1
2 M	0422	0.9	1043	3.1	1638	0.8	2307	3.2
3 TU ●	0454	0.8	1118	3.2	1708	0.8	2338	3.2
4 W	0527	0.7	1152	3.2	1738	0.8		
5 TH	0009	3.2	0600	0.7	1228	3.2	1810	0.8
6 F	0042	3.2	0635	0.7	1305	3.1	1844	0.9
7 SA	0117	3.2	0713	0.8	1345	3.0	1921	1.0
8 SU	0156	3.1	0755	0.9	1430	2.9	2004	1.2
9 M	0240	3.0	0848	0.9	1522	2.8	2057	1.3
10 TU ◖	0333	2.9	0959	1.0	1626	2.7	2214	1.4
11 W	0438	2.9	1119	1.0	1738	2.7	2340	1.4
12 TH	0552	2.9	1231	0.9	1848	2.8		
13 F	0053	1.3	0701	3.0	1336	0.7	1952	2.9
14 SA	0156	1.1	0806	3.1	1431	0.6	2050	3.1
15 SU	0250	0.9	0906	3.2	1520	0.5	2142	3.3
16 M	0339	0.7	1001	3.4	1606	0.5	2229	3.4
17 TU ○	0426	0.5	1053	3.5	1650	0.5	2314	3.5
18 W	0512	0.5	1143	3.5	1734	0.6	2358	3.5
19 TH	0559	0.4	1231	3.4	1817	0.7		
20 F	0041	3.4	0646	0.5	1319	3.3	1900	0.9
21 SA	0125	3.4	0734	0.6	1407	3.1	1943	1.1
22 SU	0209	3.2	0824	0.7	1457	2.9	2027	1.2
23 M	0256	3.1	0918	0.9	1551	2.7	2118	1.4
24 TU ◖	0348	2.9	1017	1.0	1649	2.6	2219	1.5
25 W	0448	2.8	1120	1.1	1749	2.6	2330	1.5
26 TH	0550	2.7	1228	1.1	1851	2.6		
27 F	0044	1.5	0652	2.7	1329	1.1	1950	2.7
28 SA	0148	1.4	0753	2.8	1417	1.1	2041	2.8
29 SU	0238	1.2	0847	2.9	1458	1.0	2124	2.9
30 M	0320	1.0	0933	2.9	1535	1.0	2202	3.0
31 TU	0358	1.0	1015	3.0	1609	0.9	2238	3.1

JUNE

Date	Time	m	Time	m	Time	m	Time	m
1 W ●	0434	0.9	1054	3.1	1643	0.9	2313	3.2
2 TH	0510	0.8	1133	3.1	1718	0.9	2349	3.3
3 F	0548	0.7	1212	3.2	1754	0.9		
4 SA	0026	3.3	0626	0.7	1254	3.1	1832	0.9
5 SU	0104	3.3	0707	0.6	1336	3.1	1913	1.0
6 M	0145	3.2	0752	0.7	1421	3.0	1957	1.0
7 TU	0229	3.2	0843	0.7	1511	2.9	2047	1.1
8 W	0319	3.1	0942	0.8	1608	2.9	2149	1.2
9 TH	0417	3.0	1049	0.8	1710	2.8	2302	1.3
10 F	0523	3.0	1157	0.8	1815	2.8		
11 SA	0016	1.2	0631	3.0	1304	0.8	1919	2.9
12 SU	0127	1.1	0740	3.1	1406	0.8	2022	3.0
13 M	0231	1.0	0848	3.1	1501	0.8	2120	3.2
14 TU	0327	0.8	0949	3.2	1551	0.8	2211	3.3
15 W ○	0418	0.7	1044	3.3	1636	0.8	2259	3.4
16 TH	0506	0.6	1133	3.3	1720	0.8	2343	3.5
17 F	0552	0.5	1220	3.3	1802	0.8		
18 SA	0026	3.5	0636	0.5	1306	3.2	1842	0.9
19 SU	0108	3.4	0719	0.6	1349	3.1	1920	1.0
20 M	0149	3.3	0800	0.7	1431	3.0	1958	1.1
21 TU	0230	3.2	0841	0.8	1514	2.8	2038	1.2
22 W	0312	3.1	0925	1.0	1600	2.7	2124	1.3
23 TH ◖	0359	2.9	1016	1.1	1652	2.6	2223	1.4
24 F	0453	2.8	1113	1.2	1748	2.6	2333	1.5
25 SA	0554	2.7	1217	1.3	1847	2.6		
26 SU	0048	1.5	0657	2.7	1322	1.3	1947	2.7
27 M	0158	1.4	0800	2.7	1419	1.2	2042	2.8
28 TU	0253	1.2	0858	2.8	1505	1.1	2129	3.0
29 W	0337	1.1	0948	2.9	1546	1.1	2211	3.1
30 TH	0417	0.9	1033	3.0	1624	1.0	2251	3.2

JULY

Date	Time	m	Time	m	Time	m	Time	m
1 F ●	0456	0.8	1116	3.2	1702	0.9	2331	3.4
2 SA	0535	0.6	1159	3.2	1741	0.8		
3 SU	0011	3.4	0615	0.5	1241	3.3	1821	0.8
4 M	0052	3.5	0657	0.4	1324	3.3	1902	0.8
5 TU	0133	3.5	0741	0.4	1408	3.2	1944	0.9
6 W	0216	3.4	0827	0.5	1454	3.1	2029	1.0
7 TH	0303	3.3	0918	0.6	1544	3.0	2121	1.1
8 F ◖	0356	3.2	1018	0.8	1641	2.9	2227	1.2
9 SA	0458	3.1	1125	0.9	1744	2.9	2345	1.3
10 SU	0609	3.0	1236	1.0	1851	2.9		
11 M	0109	1.2	0724	3.0	1349	1.1	2000	3.0
12 TU	0226	1.1	0841	3.0	1452	1.1	2105	3.1
13 W	0326	0.9	0946	3.1	1543	1.0	2200	3.2
14 TH	0416	0.7	1038	3.2	1626	1.0	2247	3.4
15 F ○	0500	0.6	1125	3.3	1707	0.9	2330	3.5
16 SA	0541	0.5	1207	3.3	1744	0.9		
17 SU	0010	3.5	0619	0.5	1247	3.2	1820	0.9
18 M	0049	3.5	0655	0.6	1324	3.2	1854	0.9
19 TU	0125	3.4	0729	0.6	1359	3.1	1927	0.9
20 W	0200	3.3	0802	0.8	1434	3.0	2001	1.1
21 TH	0235	3.2	0836	0.9	1511	2.9	2038	1.2
22 F	0314	3.0	0915	1.1	1553	2.8	2122	1.4
23 SA ◖	0359	2.9	1005	1.2	1644	2.7	2227	1.5
24 SU	0455	2.7	1110	1.4	1745	2.6	2350	1.6
25 M	0603	2.6	1223	1.4	1852	2.7		
26 TU	0115	1.5	0716	2.6	1338	1.4	1957	2.8
27 W	0226	1.3	0826	2.7	1439	1.3	2056	2.9
28 TH	0317	1.1	0925	2.9	1526	1.2	2145	3.1
29 F	0359	0.9	1013	3.1	1607	1.0	2229	3.3
30 SA ●	0439	0.7	1058	3.2	1646	0.9	2311	3.5
31 SU	0518	0.5	1141	3.4	1725	0.8	2352	3.6

AUGUST

Date	Time	m	Time	m	Time	m	Time	m
1 M	0558	0.3	1224	3.5	1804	0.7		
2 TU	0034	3.7	0639	0.3	1306	3.5	1844	0.7
3 W	0116	3.7	0721	0.3	1348	3.4	1925	0.7
4 TH	0158	3.6	0804	0.4	1432	3.3	2008	0.8
5 F	0244	3.5	0852	0.6	1518	3.1	2056	1.0
6 SA ◖	0336	3.3	0947	0.9	1612	3.0	2159	1.2
7 SU	0438	3.1	1056	1.1	1715	2.9	2327	1.3
8 M	0554	2.9	1218	1.3	1828	2.9		
9 TU	0108	1.3	0720	2.9	1343	1.3	1945	2.9
10 W	0229	1.1	0842	2.9	1447	1.3	2055	3.1
11 TH	0325	0.9	0942	3.1	1535	1.2	2149	3.3
12 F	0410	0.8	1029	3.2	1614	1.1	2233	3.4
13 SA ○	0447	0.7	1110	3.2	1649	1.0	2313	3.5
14 SU	0521	0.6	1147	3.3	1722	0.9	2350	3.5
15 M	0554	0.6	1221	3.3	1755	0.8		
16 TU	0024	3.5	0624	0.5	1254	3.2	1826	0.8
17 W	0057	3.5	0654	0.7	1325	3.2	1856	0.9
18 TH	0128	3.4	0723	0.8	1355	3.1	1927	1.0
19 F	0200	3.2	0753	0.9	1427	3.0	2000	1.1
20 SA	0236	3.1	0826	1.1	1504	2.9	2038	1.3
21 SU ◖	0316	2.9	0904	1.3	1548	2.8	2127	1.4
22 M	0407	2.8	0958	1.5	1645	2.7	2256	1.6
23 TU	0514	2.6	1130	1.6	1758	2.7		
24 W	0035	1.5	0637	2.6	1300	1.6	1914	2.8
25 TH	0157	1.4	0756	2.7	1413	1.4	2021	2.9
26 F	0252	1.1	0900	2.9	1504	1.2	2116	3.2
27 SA	0336	0.8	0951	3.1	1545	1.0	2203	3.4
28 SU	0416	0.6	1036	3.4	1625	0.8	2247	3.6
29 M ●	0455	0.4	1119	3.5	1704	0.7	2330	3.8
30 TU	0535	0.2	1201	3.6	1743	0.6		
31 W	0012	3.9	0615	0.2	1243	3.6	1823	0.5

Chart Datum: 1·71 metres below Ordnance Datum (Newlyn)
HAT is 4·0 metres above Chart Datum

TIME ZONE (UT)	SCOTLAND – WICK	Dates in amber are **SPRINGS**
For Summer Time add ONE hour in **non-shaded areas**	LAT 58°26'N LONG 3°05'W	Dates in yellow are **NEAPS**
	TIMES AND HEIGHTS OF HIGH AND LOW WATERS	**2011**

SEPTEMBER

Day	Time m	Time m	Time m	Time m
1 TH	0055 3.9	0657 0.3	1324 3.5	1904 0.6
2 F	0139 3.7	0739 0.5	1406 3.4	1947 0.8
3 SA	0226 3.5	0825 0.8	1452 3.2	2036 0.8
4 SU	0319 3.3	0919 1.1	1545 3.1	◑ 2143 1.2
5 M	0425 3.0	1032 1.4	1650 2.9	2322 1.3
6 TU	0546 2.8	1203 1.5	1807 2.9	
7 W	0108 1.3	0718 2.8	1334 1.5	1929 2.9
8 TH	0222 1.1	0835 2.9	1435 1.4	2039 3.1
9 F	0313 0.9	0928 3.2	1519 1.2	2131 3.3
10 SA	0352 0.8	1010 3.2	1554 1.1	2213 3.4
11 SU	0424 0.7	1047 3.2	1626 1.0	2250 3.5
12 M	0454 0.7	1117 3.2	1657 0.9	○ 2324 3.5
13 TU	0523 0.6	1222 3.3	1728 0.8	2356 3.5
14 W	0552 0.7	1251 3.3	1758 0.8	
15 TH	0027 3.5	0620 0.7	1251 3.3	1828 0.9
16 F	0058 3.4	0648 0.8	1319 3.2	1858 1.0
17 SA	0130 3.3	0717 1.0	1351 3.1	1931 1.1
18 SU	0205 3.1	0747 1.1	1426 3.0	2006 1.2
19 M	0245 3.0	0822 1.3	1507 2.9	2051 1.4
20 TU	0334 2.8	0908 1.5	1600 2.8	◑ 2208 1.5
21 W	0439 2.7	1037 1.7	1711 2.7	2358 1.5
22 TH	0604 2.7	1223 1.6	1833 2.8	
23 F	0121 1.3	0724 2.8	1341 1.5	1944 3.0
24 SA	0221 1.1	0831 3.0	1435 1.3	2043 3.2
25 SU	0307 0.8	0923 3.2	1519 1.0	2133 3.5
26 M	0349 0.5	1010 3.4	1600 0.8	2220 3.7
27 TU	0429 0.3	1053 3.6	1640 0.6	● 2305 3.9
28 W	0510 0.2	1135 3.7	1721 0.5	2350 3.9
29 TH	0551 0.2	1217 3.7	1802 0.5	
30 F	0035 3.9	0632 0.4	1259 3.6	1845 0.6

OCTOBER

Day	Time m	Time m	Time m	Time m
1 SA	0122 3.7	0715 0.6	1342 3.5	1931 0.7
2 SU	0211 3.5	0801 0.9	1428 3.3	2024 0.9
3 M	0306 3.2	0854 1.3	1521 3.1	2136 1.2
4 TU	0414 3.0	1007 1.5	1626 3.0	◑ 2312 1.3
5 W	0534 2.8	1138 1.7	1743 2.9	
6 TH	0050 1.3	0659 2.8	1310 1.6	1901 3.0
7 F	0200 1.1	0811 2.9	1411 1.5	2011 3.1
8 SA	0248 1.0	0902 3.0	1454 1.3	2103 3.2
9 SU	0324 0.9	0943 3.1	1531 1.2	2145 3.3
10 M	0355 0.9	1019 3.2	1600 1.1	2222 3.4
11 TU	0424 0.9	1051 3.3	1632 1.0	2257 3.4
12 W	0452 0.8	1122 3.4	1703 0.9	○ 2329 3.4
13 TH	0521 0.8	1151 3.4	1734 0.9	
14 F	0000 3.4	0549 0.8	1220 3.4	1804 0.9
15 SA	0032 3.4	0618 0.9	1250 3.3	1836 1.0
16 SU	0106 3.3	0648 1.1	1322 3.3	1909 1.1
17 M	0142 3.2	0719 1.2	1357 3.2	1947 1.2
18 TU	0223 3.0	0755 1.4	1438 3.1	2033 1.3
19 W	0312 2.9	0842 1.5	1529 2.9	2142 1.4
20 TH	0415 2.8	0956 1.7	1634 2.9	◑ 2321 1.4
21 F	0534 2.8	1142 1.7	1753 2.9	
22 SA	0039 1.2	0650 2.9	1301 1.5	1905 3.0
23 SU	0143 1.0	0756 3.1	1401 1.3	2007 3.2
24 M	0235 0.8	0852 3.3	1450 1.1	2102 3.5
25 TU	0320 0.6	0941 3.5	1534 0.9	2154 3.7
26 W	0403 0.4	1026 3.6	1618 0.7	● 2243 3.8
27 TH	0446 0.4	1110 3.7	1701 0.6	2331 3.9
28 F	0528 0.5	1154 3.7	1746 0.6	
29 SA	0018 3.8	0611 0.6	1237 3.7	1832 0.6
30 SU	0108 3.7	0655 0.8	1321 3.6	1921 0.7
31 M	0158 3.4	0741 1.1	1408 3.4	2016 0.9

NOVEMBER

Day	Time m	Time m	Time m	Time m
1 TU	0253 3.2	0832 1.4	1459 3.3	2123 1.1
2 W	0357 3.0	0934 1.6	1600 3.1	◐ 2241 1.2
3 TH	0506 2.8	1051 1.7	1709 3.0	
4 F	0006 1.3	0618 2.8	1217 1.7	1819 3.0
5 SA	0119 1.2	0728 2.8	1329 1.6	1927 3.0
6 SU	0210 1.2	0824 3.0	1419 1.5	2025 3.1
7 M	0249 1.1	0908 3.1	1459 1.3	2112 3.2
8 TU	0322 1.1	0946 3.2	1534 1.2	2152 3.3
9 W	0353 1.0	1021 3.3	1608 1.1	2229 3.3
10 TH	0424 1.0	1053 3.4	1641 1.0	○ 2303 3.4
11 F	0454 1.0	1124 3.4	1714 1.0	2337 3.4
12 SA	0524 1.0	1155 3.4	1747 0.9	
13 SU	0012 3.3	0555 1.0	1227 3.4	1821 1.0
14 M	0048 3.3	0627 1.1	1301 3.4	1857 1.0
15 TU	0127 3.2	0702 1.2	1338 3.3	1937 1.1
16 W	0209 3.1	0741 1.3	1419 3.2	2023 1.1
17 TH	0257 3.0	0827 1.5	1507 3.1	2124 1.2
18 F	0354 2.9	0929 1.6	1605 3.1	◑ 2242 1.2
19 SA	0502 2.9	1056 1.6	1715 3.1	2356 1.2
20 SU	0613 2.9	1215 1.5	1827 3.1	
21 M	0103 1.0	0718 3.1	1323 1.4	1932 3.3
22 TU	0202 0.9	0818 3.2	1421 1.2	2034 3.4
23 W	0254 0.8	0913 3.4	1513 1.0	2132 3.6
24 TH	0341 0.7	1003 3.6	1602 0.8	2226 3.7
25 F	0427 0.7	1050 3.7	1649 0.7	● 2317 3.7
26 SA	0511 0.7	1135 3.7	1737 0.6	
27 SU	0007 3.7	0555 0.8	1220 3.7	1824 0.6
28 M	0056 3.6	0639 1.0	1305 3.7	1913 0.7
29 TU	0146 3.4	0723 1.2	1350 3.6	2004 0.8
30 W	0236 3.2	0807 1.3	1437 3.4	2057 1.0

DECEMBER

Day	Time m	Time m	Time m	Time m
1 TH	0329 3.0	0855 1.5	1529 3.2	2155 1.2
2 F	0426 2.9	0953 1.6	1626 3.1	◐ 2258 1.3
3 SA	0526 2.8	1102 1.7	1728 3.0	
4 SU	0007 1.4	0627 2.8	1219 1.7	1831 2.9
5 M	0113 1.4	0730 2.9	1331 1.6	1934 3.0
6 TU	0205 1.3	0825 3.0	1425 1.5	2032 3.0
7 W	0247 1.3	0911 3.1	1509 1.3	2121 3.1
8 TH	0325 1.2	0951 3.2	1549 1.2	2203 3.2
9 F	0359 1.2	1027 3.3	1625 1.1	2242 3.3
10 SA	0432 1.1	1101 3.4	1700 1.0	2319 3.3
11 SU	0505 1.1	1135 3.5	1735 0.9	2357 3.3
12 M	0539 1.1	1210 3.5	1811 0.9	
13 TU	0035 3.3	0614 1.1	1247 3.5	1848 0.9
14 W	0115 3.3	0651 1.2	1324 3.5	1928 0.9
15 TH	0156 3.2	0730 1.2	1404 3.4	2012 0.9
16 F	0241 3.1	0814 1.3	1449 3.3	2103 1.0
17 SA	0332 3.1	0904 1.4	1541 3.3	2205 1.1
18 SU	0430 3.0	1010 1.5	1642 3.2	2315 1.1
19 M	0535 3.0	1130 1.5	1751 3.2	
20 TU	0024 1.1	0641 3.0	1247 1.5	1902 3.2
21 W	0133 1.1	0747 3.1	1359 1.3	2013 3.3
22 TH	0234 1.0	0850 3.3	1501 1.1	2120 3.4
23 F	0327 1.0	0945 3.5	1555 0.9	2218 3.5
24 SA	0415 0.9	1036 3.6	1644 0.7	● 2310 3.6
25 SU	0500 0.9	1122 3.7	1731 0.6	2358 3.6
26 M	0542 0.9	1206 3.7	1816 0.6	
27 TU	0044 3.5	0623 1.0	1250 3.7	1859 0.6
28 W	0129 3.4	0702 1.1	1332 3.6	1941 0.7
29 TH	0211 3.3	0740 1.2	1413 3.5	2022 0.9
30 F	0254 3.1	0818 1.3	1455 3.4	2104 1.1
31 SA	0339 3.0	0859 1.4	1540 3.2	2150 1.3

Chart Datum: 1·71 metres below Ordnance Datum (Newlyn)
HAT is 4·0 metres above Chart Datum

TIDES

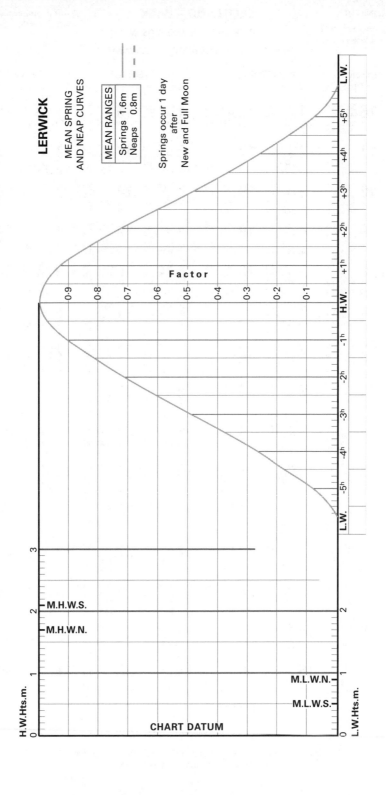

LERWICK

MEAN SPRING
AND NEAP CURVES

MEAN RANGES
Springs 1.6m
Neaps 0.8m

Springs occur 1 day
after
New and Full Moon

TIME ZONE (UT)
For Summer Time add ONE hour in **non-shaded areas**

SCOTLAND – LERWICK
LAT 60°09'N   LONG 1°08'W
TIMES AND HEIGHTS OF HIGH AND LOW WATERS

Dates in amber are **SPRINGS**
Dates in yellow are **NEAPS**

2011

JANUARY

Day				
1 SA	0207 0.9	0818 2.0	1441 0.8	2055 2.0
2 SU	0300 0.9	0912 2.1	1534 0.7	2152 2.1
3 M	0347 0.8	1001 2.2	1619 0.6	2241 2.1
4 TU	0429 0.8	1045 2.2	1701 0.6	● 2324 2.1
5 W	0508 0.8	1125 2.3	1740 0.5	
6 TH	0003 2.1	0545 0.8	1203 2.3	1817 0.5
7 F	0040 2.1	0621 0.8	1239 2.2	1853 0.6
8 SA	0115 2.0	0654 0.8	1313 2.2	1928 0.6
9 SU	0149 1.9	0727 0.9	1346 2.1	2003 0.7
10 M	0223 1.9	0801 0.9	1421 2.0	2039 0.8
11 TU	0300 1.8	0840 1.0	1501 1.9	2120 0.9
12 W	0343 1.7	0928 1.1	1547 1.8	◐ 2211 1.0
13 TH	0434 1.7	1038 1.1	1643 1.8	2323 1.1
14 F	0537 1.7	1209 1.1	1754 1.7	
15 SA	0037 1.1	0655 1.8	1321 1.1	1919 1.7
16 SU	0140 1.0	0759 1.8	1419 1.0	2025 1.8
17 M	0234 1.0	0849 2.0	1509 0.8	2118 1.9
18 TU	0322 0.9	0935 2.1	1554 0.7	2206 2.1
19 W	0407 0.8	1020 2.2	1637 0.5	○ 2254 2.2
20 TH	0449 0.7	1104 2.3	1719 0.4	2340 2.2
21 F	0530 0.6	1148 2.4	1802 0.3	
22 SA	0025 2.2	0611 0.6	1232 2.4	1844 0.2
23 SU	0110 2.2	0653 0.6	1316 2.4	1928 0.3
24 M	0154 2.1	0736 0.6	1402 2.3	2014 0.4
25 TU	0239 2.0	0822 0.7	1451 2.2	2103 0.6
26 W	0327 1.9	0913 0.8	1546 2.0	2200 0.8
27 TH	0422 1.8	1020 0.9	1652 1.9	2316 0.9
28 F	0529 1.8	1204 1.0	1817 1.8	
29 SA	0045 1.0	0651 1.8	1334 0.9	1944 1.8
30 SU	0157 1.0	0805 1.9	1440 0.8	2054 1.9
31 M	0253 0.9	0904 2.0	1531 0.7	2147 1.9

FEBRUARY

Day				
1 TU	0338 0.9	0952 2.1	1612 0.6	2230 2.0
2 W	0417 0.8	1034 2.2	1649 0.5	2307 2.0
3 TH	0452 0.7	1110 2.2	1722 0.5	● 2342 2.0
4 F	0526 0.7	1144 2.2	1754 0.5	
5 SA	0014 2.0	0556 0.7	1216 2.2	1825 0.5
6 SU	0045 2.0	0627 0.7	1246 2.2	1854 0.5
7 M	0114 2.0	0656 0.7	1315 2.1	1924 0.6
8 TU	0143 1.9	0728 0.8	1346 2.0	1955 0.7
9 W	0215 1.9	0802 0.8	1421 1.9	2030 0.8
10 TH	0253 1.8	0843 0.9	1504 1.8	2111 0.9
11 F	0339 1.7	0937 1.0	1558 1.7	◐ 2206 1.0
12 SA	0437 1.7	1102 1.1	1705 1.6	2339 1.1
13 SU	0549 1.7	1243 1.0	1835 1.6	
14 M	0109 1.1	0718 1.7	1352 0.9	2001 1.7
15 TU	0214 1.0	0823 1.9	1448 0.7	2059 1.9
16 W	0305 0.8	0914 2.0	1535 0.5	2149 2.0
17 TH	0350 0.7	1001 2.2	1618 0.3	2235 2.1
18 F	0431 0.5	1045 2.3	1700 0.2	○ 2320 2.2
19 SA	0512 0.4	1129 2.4	1741 0.1	
20 SU	0003 2.2	0552 0.4	1214 2.5	1823 0.1
21 M	0046 2.2	0633 0.4	1258 2.4	1905 0.2
22 TU	0127 2.1	0715 0.4	1343 2.3	1948 0.4
23 W	0209 2.0	0800 0.6	1431 2.1	2035 0.6
24 TH	0254 1.9	0851 0.7	1526 1.9	◑ 2128 0.8
25 F	0346 1.8	0959 0.8	1631 1.8	2244 1.0
26 SA	0452 1.7	1153 0.9	1804 1.6	
27 SU	0027 1.1	0625 1.7	1324 0.8	1939 1.7
28 M	0143 1.0	0748 1.8	1429 0.7	2044 1.7

MARCH

Day				
1 TU	0239 0.9	0847 1.9	1516 0.6	2130 1.8
2 W	0322 0.8	0933 2.0	1554 0.6	2208 1.9
3 TH	0358 0.7	1013 2.1	1626 0.5	2242 1.9
4 F	0431 0.6	1047 2.1	1657 0.4	2314 2.0
5 SA	0501 0.6	1119 2.1	1725 0.4	2344 2.0
6 SU	0530 0.5	1149 2.1	1753 0.4	
7 M	0012 2.0	0559 0.5	1217 2.1	1821 0.5
8 TU	0039 2.0	0629 0.6	1245 2.1	1849 0.5
9 W	0106 1.9	0700 0.6	1316 2.0	1919 0.6
10 TH	0136 1.9	0735 0.7	1351 1.9	1952 0.8
11 F	0211 1.8	0815 0.8	1433 1.8	2031 0.9
12 SA	0255 1.7	0906 0.9	1527 1.7	◐ 2122 1.0
13 SU	0352 1.7	1018 0.9	1636 1.6	2243 1.1
14 M	0504 1.6	1205 0.9	1803 1.6	
15 TU	0040 1.0	0635 1.6	1322 0.8	1936 1.7
16 W	0150 0.9	0753 1.8	1421 0.6	2036 1.8
17 TH	0242 0.7	0848 1.9	1509 0.4	2125 1.9
18 F	0327 0.6	0936 2.1	1554 0.2	2211 2.1
19 SA	0408 0.4	1022 2.3	1636 0.1	○ 2255 2.1
20 SU	0449 0.3	1107 2.4	1718 0.0	2337 2.2
21 M	0531 0.2	1152 2.4	1759 0.1	
22 TU	0018 2.2	0612 0.2	1238 2.3	1841 0.2
23 W	0059 2.1	0656 0.3	1325 2.2	1924 0.4
24 TH	0141 2.0	0743 0.4	1415 2.0	2010 0.6
25 F	0226 1.9	0837 0.6	1510 1.9	2102 0.9
26 SA	0317 1.8	0948 0.7	1615 1.6	◑ 2217 1.0
27 SU	0420 1.7	1133 0.8	1744 1.5	2358 1.1
28 M	0551 1.6	1258 0.8	1915 1.5	
29 TU	0115 1.0	0717 1.7	1402 0.7	2015 1.6
30 W	0212 0.9	0817 1.7	1448 0.6	2059 1.7
31 TH	0256 0.8	0903 1.8	1525 0.5	2136 1.8

APRIL

Day				
1 F	0332 0.7	0942 1.9	1557 0.5	2210 1.9
2 SA	0404 0.6	1017 1.9	1625 0.4	2242 1.9
3 SU	0434 0.5	1050 2.0	1653 0.4	● 2311 2.0
4 M	0503 0.5	1120 2.0	1721 0.4	2340 2.0
5 TU	0534 0.5	1150 2.0	1749 0.5	
6 W	0007 2.0	0605 0.5	1220 2.0	1819 0.5
7 TH	0035 1.9	0638 0.5	1253 1.9	1850 0.6
8 F	0106 1.9	0715 0.6	1330 1.8	1925 0.7
9 SA	0142 1.8	0758 0.6	1415 1.7	2006 0.8
10 SU	0225 1.7	0850 0.7	1511 1.6	2100 0.9
11 M	0322 1.7	0957 0.8	1620 1.5	◐ 2217 1.0
12 TU	0434 1.6	1129 0.7	1740 1.5	
13 W	0005 0.9	0558 1.6	1248 0.6	1905 1.6
14 TH	0118 0.8	0719 1.7	1349 0.5	2007 1.8
15 F	0213 0.7	0818 1.9	1440 0.3	2057 1.9
16 SA	0300 0.5	0909 2.0	1527 0.2	2143 2.0
17 SU	0344 0.4	0958 2.2	1611 0.1	2227 2.1
18 M	0428 0.3	1046 2.2	1654 0.1	○ 2310 2.1
19 TU	0511 0.2	1134 2.2	1736 0.2	2352 2.1
20 W	0556 0.2	1222 2.2	1819 0.3	
21 TH	0034 2.1	0641 0.3	1312 2.1	1903 0.5
22 F	0118 2.0	0730 0.4	1403 1.9	1949 0.7
23 SA	0204 1.9	0825 0.5	1456 1.7	2041 0.9
24 SU	0254 1.8	0932 0.6	1554 1.6	2147 1.0
25 M	0352 1.7	1054 0.7	1707 1.5	◑ 2310 1.0
26 TU	0505 1.6	1212 0.7	1827 1.5	
27 W	0029 1.0	0630 1.6	1318 0.7	1928 1.5
28 TH	0132 0.9	0733 1.6	1408 0.6	2016 1.6
29 F	0221 0.8	0823 1.7	1447 0.5	2056 1.7
30 SA	0300 0.7	0906 1.8	1520 0.5	2133 1.8

Chart Datum: 1·22 metres below Ordnance Datum (Local)
HAT is 2·5 metres above Chart Datum

TIDES

TIME ZONE (UT)	SCOTLAND – LERWICK	Dates in amber are SPRINGS
For Summer Time add ONE hour in non-shaded areas	LAT 60°09'N LONG 1°08'W	Dates in yellow are NEAPS
	TIMES AND HEIGHTS OF HIGH AND LOW WATERS	2011

MAY

Time m	Time m
1 0334 0.6 / 0944 1.8 / SU 1550 0.5 / 2207 1.9	**16** 0323 0.4 / 0938 2.1 / M 1548 0.3 / 2202 2.0
2 0406 0.5 / 1019 1.9 / M 1620 0.5 / 2239 1.9	**17** 0410 0.3 / 1030 2.1 / TU 1633 0.3 / ○ 2247 2.1
3 0438 0.5 / 1053 1.9 / TU 1650 0.5 / ● 2309 2.0	**18** 0457 0.2 / 1121 2.1 / W 1717 0.4 / 2332 2.1
4 0511 0.5 / 1126 1.9 / W 1722 0.5 / 2340 2.0	**19** 0543 0.2 / 1212 2.1 / TH 1801 0.5
5 0546 0.4 / 1201 1.9 / TH 1755 0.6	**20** 0016 2.1 / 0630 0.3 / F 1301 2.0 / 1845 0.6
6 0011 2.0 / 0622 0.5 / F 1238 1.9 / 1830 0.6	**21** 0101 2.0 / 0719 0.3 / SA 1349 1.8 / 1931 0.7
7 0046 1.9 / 0702 0.5 / SA 1320 1.8 / 1909 0.7	**22** 0146 2.0 / 0810 0.4 / SU 1436 1.7 / 2019 0.8
8 0125 1.9 / 0748 0.5 / SU 1407 1.7 / 1955 0.8	**23** 0233 1.8 / 0904 0.5 / M 1525 1.6 / 2111 0.9
9 0210 1.8 / 0840 0.6 / M 1503 1.6 / 2050 0.8	**24** 0322 1.7 / 1004 0.6 / TU 1620 1.5 / ◑ 2213 0.9
10 0307 1.7 / 0942 0.6 / TU 1606 1.6 / ◑ 2157 0.9	**25** 0417 1.6 / 1108 0.7 / W 1724 1.5 / 2323 0.9
11 0414 1.7 / 1055 0.6 / W 1716 1.6 / 2321 0.9	**26** 0525 1.6 / 1212 0.7 / TH 1830 1.5
12 0528 1.7 / 1211 0.5 / TH 1831 1.6	**27** 0033 0.9 / 0631 1.6 / F 1311 0.7 / 1926 1.6
13 0039 0.8 / 0644 1.7 / F 1315 0.4 / 1934 1.7	**28** 0134 0.8 / 0738 1.6 / SA 1358 0.7 / 2013 1.7
14 0141 0.7 / 0748 1.8 / SA 1411 0.4 / 2027 1.8	**29** 0221 0.8 / 0826 1.7 / SU 1438 0.7 / 2055 1.8
15 0234 0.5 / 0845 2.0 / SU 1501 0.3 / 2116 1.9	**30** 0302 0.7 / 0910 1.7 / M 1514 0.6 / 2132 1.8
	31 0339 0.6 / 0950 1.8 / TU 1549 0.6 / 2208 1.9

JUNE

Time m	Time m
1 0416 0.5 / 1029 1.8 / W 1625 0.6 / ● 2243 2.0	**16** 0448 0.3 / 1115 2.0 / TH 1703 0.5 / 2319 2.1
2 0453 0.5 / 1108 1.8 / TH 1701 0.6 / 2319 2.0	**17** 0534 0.3 / 1202 2.0 / F 1747 0.6
3 0531 0.4 / 1148 1.9 / F 1739 0.6 / 2355 2.0	**18** 0003 2.1 / 0618 0.3 / SA 1247 1.9 / 1828 0.6
4 0611 0.4 / 1229 1.9 / SA 1818 0.6	**19** 0046 2.1 / 0702 0.3 / SU 1329 1.9 / 1910 0.7
5 0034 2.0 / 0653 0.4 / SU 1314 1.8 / 1900 0.6	**20** 0127 2.0 / 0745 0.4 / M 1410 1.8 / 1950 0.7
6 0116 2.0 / 0738 0.4 / M 1401 1.8 / 1946 0.7	**21** 0208 1.9 / 0829 0.5 / TU 1450 1.7 / 2032 0.8
7 0203 1.9 / 0828 0.4 / TU 1453 1.7 / 2037 0.7	**22** 0249 1.8 / 0913 0.6 / W 1533 1.6 / 2118 0.9
8 0256 1.9 / 0922 0.5 / W 1548 1.7 / 2134 0.8	**23** 0332 1.7 / 1002 0.7 / TH 1620 1.6 / ◑ 2215 0.9
9 0355 1.8 / 1024 0.5 / TH 1649 1.7 / ◑ 2241 0.8	**24** 0422 1.6 / 1059 0.8 / F 1717 1.5 / 2326 0.9
10 0501 1.8 / 1134 0.5 / F 1755 1.7	**25** 0522 1.6 / 1201 0.8 / SA 1826 1.6
11 0000 0.8 / 0613 1.8 / SA 1244 0.5 / 1901 1.7	**26** 0037 0.9 / 0640 1.6 / SU 1301 0.8 / 1927 1.6
12 0113 0.7 / 0724 1.8 / SU 1346 0.5 / 2000 1.8	**27** 0139 0.9 / 0746 1.6 / M 1354 0.8 / 2017 1.7
13 0215 0.6 / 0827 1.9 / M 1441 0.6 / 2054 1.9	**28** 0230 0.8 / 0838 1.7 / TU 1441 0.8 / 2101 1.8
14 0310 0.5 / 0926 1.9 / TU 1532 0.5 / 2144 2.0	**29** 0315 0.7 / 0924 1.8 / W 1524 0.7 / 2142 1.9
15 0400 0.4 / 1022 1.9 / W 1619 0.5 / ○ 2232 2.1	**30** 0356 0.6 / 1008 1.8 / TH 1606 0.7 / 2222 2.0

JULY

Time m	Time m
1 0437 0.5 / 1052 1.9 / F 1646 0.6 / ● 2302 2.1	**16** 0522 0.3 / 1148 2.0 / SA 1730 0.6 / 2349 2.2
2 0517 0.4 / 1135 2.0 / SA 1726 0.6 / 2343 2.1	**17** 0601 0.3 / 1226 2.0 / SU 1808 0.6
3 0558 0.3 / 1219 2.0 / SU 1807 0.6	**18** 0026 2.1 / 0638 0.4 / M 1302 1.9 / 1843 0.6
4 0024 2.1 / 0640 0.3 / M 1303 2.0 / 1848 0.6	**19** 0103 2.1 / 0714 0.4 / TU 1337 1.9 / 1918 0.7
5 0107 2.1 / 0723 0.3 / TU 1348 1.9 / 1932 0.6	**20** 0137 2.0 / 0750 0.5 / W 1411 1.8 / 1952 0.7
6 0152 2.1 / 0809 0.3 / W 1435 1.9 / 2018 0.7	**21** 0212 1.9 / 0825 0.6 / TH 1447 1.7 / 2030 0.8
7 0241 2.0 / 0859 0.4 / TH 1524 1.8 / 2109 0.7	**22** 0250 1.8 / 0903 0.7 / F 1527 1.7 / 2115 0.9
8 0335 1.9 / 0954 0.5 / F 1619 1.7 / ◑ 2209 0.8	**23** 0333 1.7 / 0950 0.8 / SA 1613 1.6 / ◑ 2218 1.0
9 0437 1.8 / 1100 0.6 / SA 1721 1.7 / 2329 0.8	**24** 0425 1.6 / 1054 0.9 / SU 1710 1.6 / 2345 1.0
10 0550 1.8 / 1217 0.7 / SU 1831 1.7	**25** 0530 1.6 / 1211 1.0 / M 1825 1.6
11 0056 0.8 / 0709 1.8 / M 1329 0.7 / 1940 1.8	**26** 0100 1.0 / 0659 1.6 / TU 1318 1.0 / 1938 1.7
12 0208 0.7 / 0821 1.8 / TU 1430 0.7 / 2040 1.9	**27** 0201 0.9 / 0809 1.7 / W 1415 0.9 / 2032 1.8
13 0306 0.6 / 0924 1.9 / W 1523 0.7 / 2135 2.0	**28** 0252 0.7 / 0902 1.8 / TH 1504 0.8 / 2118 1.9
14 0356 0.5 / 1019 1.9 / TH 1609 0.6 / 2224 2.1	**29** 0337 0.6 / 0949 1.9 / F 1548 0.7 / 2201 2.0
15 0441 0.4 / 1106 2.0 / F 1651 0.6 / ○ 2308 2.1	**30** 0419 0.5 / 1034 2.0 / SA 1630 0.6 / ● 2244 2.2
	31 0459 0.3 / 1118 2.1 / SU 1710 0.5 / 2326 2.2

AUGUST

Time m	Time m
1 0540 0.2 / 1201 2.1 / M 1750 0.5	**16** 0001 2.2 / 0609 0.4 / TU 1231 2.0 / 1814 0.6
2 0008 2.3 / 0621 0.2 / TU 1244 2.1 / 1830 0.5	**17** 0033 2.1 / 0640 0.5 / W 1301 2.0 / 1845 0.6
3 0051 2.3 / 0703 0.2 / W 1327 2.1 / 1912 0.5	**18** 0104 2.1 / 0710 0.6 / TH 1331 1.9 / 1917 0.7
4 0135 2.2 / 0746 0.3 / TH 1410 2.0 / 1956 0.6	**19** 0135 2.0 / 0741 0.7 / F 1403 1.9 / 1951 0.8
5 0223 2.1 / 0833 0.4 / F 1457 1.9 / 2046 0.7	**20** 0210 1.9 / 0817 0.8 / SA 1439 1.8 / 2032 0.9
6 0316 2.0 / 0926 0.6 / SA 1549 1.8 / ◑ 2145 0.8	**21** 0252 1.8 / 0854 0.9 / SU 1523 1.7 / ◑ 2125 1.1
7 0417 1.9 / 1031 0.8 / SU 1650 1.7 / 2313 0.9	**22** 0344 1.7 / 0947 1.0 / M 1617 1.7 / 2249 1.1
8 0535 1.8 / 1201 0.9 / M 1807 1.7	**23** 0447 1.6 / 1116 1.1 / TU 1723 1.7
9 0054 0.9 / 0705 1.7 / TU 1321 0.9 / 1927 1.8	**24** 0025 1.0 / 0610 1.6 / W 1248 1.1 / 1853 1.7
10 0207 0.8 / 0822 1.8 / W 1424 0.9 / 2033 1.9	**25** 0133 0.9 / 0742 1.7 / TH 1352 1.0 / 2002 1.8
11 0304 0.6 / 0921 1.9 / TH 1514 0.8 / 2126 2.0	**26** 0227 0.7 / 0839 1.8 / F 1443 0.9 / 2052 2.0
12 0349 0.5 / 1008 1.9 / F 1556 0.7 / 2212 2.1	**27** 0313 0.6 / 0927 1.9 / SA 1527 0.7 / 2137 2.1
13 0428 0.4 / 1048 2.0 / SA 1634 0.7 / ○ 2252 2.2	**28** 0356 0.4 / 1011 2.1 / SU 1608 0.6 / 2221 2.2
14 0503 0.4 / 1125 2.0 / SU 1709 0.6 / 2328 2.2	**29** 0436 0.2 / 1054 2.2 / M 1648 0.5 / ● 2304 2.4
15 0537 0.4 / 1159 2.0 / M 1742 0.6	**30** 0517 0.2 / 1137 2.2 / TU 1728 0.4 / 2347 2.4
	31 0558 0.1 / 1218 2.2 / W 1809 0.4

Chart Datum: 1·22 metres below Ordnance Datum (Local)
HAT is 2·5 metres above Chart Datum

SCOTLAND – LERWICK
LAT 60°09'N LONG 1°08'W
2011

TIMES AND HEIGHTS OF HIGH AND LOW WATERS

SEPTEMBER

Time	m		Time	m
1 0030	2.4	**16** 0032	2.1
0639	0.2	0634	0.6
TH 1301	2.2	F 1253	2.0
1851	0.4	1847	0.7
2 0116	2.3	**17** 0103	2.0
0722	0.4	0704	0.7
F 1343	2.1	SA 1323	2.0
1936	0.5	1922	0.8
3 0205	2.2	**18** 0138	1.9
0808	0.6	0736	0.8
SA 1429	2.0	SU 1357	1.9
2027	0.7	2002	0.9
4 0300	2.0	**19** 0219	1.8
0900	0.8	0814	1.0
SU 1520	1.9	M 1440	1.8
◖ 2130	0.8	2052	1.0
5 0404	1.8	**20** 0312	1.7
1008	1.0	0903	1.1
M 1623	1.8	TU 1534	1.7
2312	0.9	◗ 2203	1.0
6 0526	1.7	**21** 0417	1.6
1150	1.1	1020	1.1
TU 1747	1.8	W 1642	1.7
		2349	1.6
7 0049	0.8	**22** 0536	1.6
0704	1.7	1217	1.1
W 1311	1.0	TH 1806	1.7
1914	1.8		
8 0159	0.7	**23** 0101	0.9
0814	1.8	0710	1.7
TH 1411	1.0	F 1325	1.0
2018	1.9	1928	1.8
9 0251	0.6	**24** 0158	0.7
0905	1.9	0811	1.8
F 1458	0.9	SA 1417	0.9
2109	2.0	2023	2.0
10 0331	0.6	**25** 0245	0.5
0946	1.9	0900	2.0
SA 1537	0.8	SU 1502	0.7
2151	2.1	2110	2.2
11 0406	0.5	**26** 0329	0.4
1023	2.0	0944	2.1
SU 1611	0.7	M 1544	0.6
2228	2.2	2155	2.3
12 0438	0.5	**27** 0411	0.2
1056	2.0	1027	2.2
M 1644	0.6	TU 1625	0.5
○ 2302	2.2	● 2240	2.4
13 0508	0.5	**28** 0452	0.2
1127	2.1	1110	2.3
TU 1715	0.6	W 1706	0.4
2333	2.2	2325	2.5
14 0537	0.5	**29** 0534	0.2
1157	2.1	1151	2.3
W 1745	0.6	TH 1749	0.4
15 0002	2.2	**30** 0011	2.4
0605	0.5	0616	0.3
TH 1225	2.0	F 1234	2.3
1815	0.6	1833	0.5

OCTOBER

Time	m		Time	m
1 0059	2.3	**16** 0039	2.0
0700	0.5	0634	0.8
SA 1317	2.2	SU 1252	2.1
1920	0.5	1900	0.8
2 0151	2.2	**17** 0115	2.0
0746	0.7	0708	0.9
SU 1404	2.1	M 1327	2.0
2013	0.7	1942	0.8
3 0248	2.0	**18** 0158	1.9
0839	0.9	0747	1.0
M 1457	2.0	TU 1409	1.9
2120	0.8	2032	0.9
4 0352	1.8	**19** 0251	1.8
1126	1.1	0837	1.1
TU 1600	1.9	W 1503	1.8
◖ 2302	0.9	2136	0.9
5 0512	1.7	**20** 0355	1.7
1126	1.1	0948	1.1
W 1722	1.9	TH 1610	1.8
		◗ 2304	0.9
6 0030	0.8	**21** 0509	1.7
0644	1.7	1133	1.1
TH 1246	1.1	F 1727	1.8
1848	1.8		
7 0136	0.8	**22** 0023	0.8
0749	1.8	0632	1.7
F 1347	1.0	SA 1250	1.0
1951	1.9	1848	1.9
8 0226	0.7	**23** 0123	0.7
0836	1.8	0738	1.8
SA 1433	0.9	SU 1346	0.9
2041	2.0	1950	2.0
9 0305	0.7	**24** 0214	0.6
0916	1.9	0829	2.0
SU 1512	0.8	M 1434	0.8
2122	2.1	2042	2.2
10 0339	0.6	**25** 0301	0.4
0951	2.0	0916	2.2
M 1546	0.7	TU 1519	0.6
2159	2.1	2130	2.3
11 0409	0.6	**26** 0345	0.3
1024	2.1	1000	2.3
TU 1618	0.7	W 1603	0.5
2233	2.1	● 2218	2.4
12 0438	0.6	**27** 0429	0.3
1055	2.1	1044	2.3
W 1648	0.6	TH 1647	0.4
○ 2304	2.2	2306	2.4
13 0505	0.6	**28** 0512	0.4
1124	2.1	1127	2.4
TH 1719	0.6	F 1732	0.4
2335	2.1	2356	2.4
14 0534	0.6	**29** 0556	0.5
1153	2.1	1211	2.3
F 1751	0.7	SA 1819	0.4
15 0006	2.1	**30** 0047	2.3
0603	0.7	0641	0.6
SA 1221	2.1	SU 1257	2.3
1824	0.7	1908	0.5
		31 0141	2.1
		0728	0.8
		M 1345	2.2
		2002	0.6

NOVEMBER

Time	m		Time	m
1 0235	2.0	**16** 0145	1.9
0820	1.0	0732	1.0
TU 1437	2.1	W 1350	2.0
2107	0.8	2017	0.8
2 0334	1.8	**17** 0237	1.9
0922	1.1	0822	1.0
W 1535	1.9	TH 1442	2.0
◖ 2228	0.8	2114	0.8
3 0441	1.7	**18** 0336	1.8
1042	1.2	0923	1.1
TH 1644	1.9	F 1544	1.9
2349	0.9	◗ 2221	0.8
4 0559	1.7	**19** 0441	1.8
1203	1.1	1038	1.1
F 1805	1.8	SA 1653	1.9
		2338	0.8
5 0057	0.9	**20** 0553	1.8
0705	1.7	1204	1.1
SA 1310	1.1	SU 1808	1.9
1912	1.9		
6 0150	0.8	**21** 0045	0.7
0756	1.8	0701	1.9
SU 1402	1.0	M 1311	1.0
2005	1.9	1917	2.0
7 0232	0.8	**22** 0143	0.6
0839	1.9	0758	2.0
M 1444	0.9	TU 1407	0.8
2049	2.0	2016	2.1
8 0307	0.8	**23** 0235	0.6
0917	2.0	0849	2.1
TU 1520	0.8	W 1458	0.7
2128	2.0	2110	2.3
9 0338	0.7	**24** 0323	0.5
0952	2.1	0936	2.2
W 1553	0.8	TH 1546	0.6
2205	2.1	2203	2.3
10 0407	0.7	**25** 0410	0.5
1025	2.1	1023	2.3
TH 1626	0.7	F 1634	0.5
○ 2239	2.1	● 2255	2.4
11 0437	0.7	**26** 0455	0.6
1056	2.2	1109	2.4
F 1658	0.7	SA 1721	0.4
2313	2.1	2348	2.3
12 0508	0.7	**27** 0540	0.6
1127	2.2	1155	2.4
SA 1732	0.7	SU 1809	0.4
2347	2.1		
13 0540	0.8	**28** 0039	2.2
1158	2.2	0625	0.7
SU 1808	0.7	M 1242	2.3
		1857	0.5
14 0022	2.1	**29** 0129	2.1
0613	0.8	0711	0.8
M 1231	2.1	TU 1329	2.2
1846	0.7	1948	0.6
15 0102	2.0	**30** 0217	2.0
0650	0.9	0758	0.9
TU 1308	2.1	W 1417	2.1
1928	0.8	2042	0.7

DECEMBER

Time	m		Time	m
1 0306	1.9	**16** 0222	1.9
0849	1.0	0806	0.9
TH 1506	2.0	F 1425	2.1
2140	0.8	2051	0.7
2 0359	1.8	**17** 0314	1.9
0947	1.1	0858	1.0
F 1600	1.9	SA 1520	2.0
◖ 2246	0.9	2147	0.7
3 0459	1.7	**18** 0411	1.8
1057	1.1	0958	1.0
SA 1704	1.8	SU 1622	2.0
2355	0.9	◗ 2253	0.8
4 0607	1.7	**19** 0515	1.8
1213	1.1	1114	1.0
SU 1818	1.8	M 1733	2.0
5 0059	1.0	**20** 0007	0.8
0707	1.8	0624	1.9
M 1320	1.1	TU 1238	1.0
1921	1.8	1848	2.0
6 0150	0.9	**21** 0116	0.8
0759	1.9	0730	2.0
TU 1412	1.0	W 1347	0.9
2013	1.9	1957	2.1
7 0232	0.9	**22** 0215	0.7
0843	2.0	0828	2.1
W 1455	0.9	TH 1445	0.8
2059	1.9	2059	2.1
8 0307	0.9	**23** 0308	0.7
0922	2.0	0921	2.2
TH 1532	0.9	F 1538	0.6
2140	2.0	2157	2.2
9 0341	0.9	**24** 0357	0.7
0958	2.1	1011	2.3
F 1607	0.8	SA 1627	0.5
2218	2.0	● 2251	2.2
10 0415	0.8	**25** 0443	0.7
1033	2.2	1059	2.4
SA 1642	0.7	SU 1714	0.4
○ 2256	2.1	2341	2.2
11 0449	0.8	**26** 0527	0.7
1108	2.2	1145	2.4
SU 1718	0.7	M 1759	0.4
2334	2.1		
12 0524	0.8	**27** 0027	2.2
1142	2.2	0610	0.7
M 1756	0.6	TU 1229	2.4
		1843	0.4
13 0012	2.1	**28** 0111	2.1
0600	0.8	0651	0.8
TU 1218	2.2	W 1311	2.3
1834	0.6	1926	0.5
14 0053	2.1	**29** 0152	2.0
0639	0.8	0732	0.8
W 1257	2.2	TH 1352	2.2
1916	0.6	2009	0.6
15 0135	2.0	**30** 0232	1.9
0721	0.9	0813	0.9
TH 1338	2.1	F 1433	2.1
2001	0.6	2053	0.8
		31 0314	1.8
		0856	1.0
		SA 1516	2.0
		2140	0.9

Chart Datum: 1·22 metres below Ordnance Datum (Local)
HAT is 2·5 metres above Chart Datum

TIDES

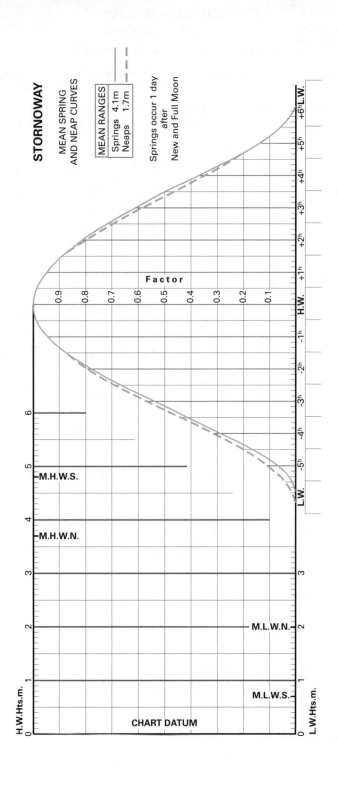

STORNOWAY

MEAN SPRING
AND NEAP CURVES

MEAN RANGES
Springs 4.1m
Neaps 1.7m

Springs occur 1 day
after
New and Full Moon

Factor

0.9
0.8
0.7
0.6
0.5
0.4
0.3
0.2
0.1

H.W.Hts.m.

M.H.W.S.

M.H.W.N.

CHART DATUM

L.W.Hts.m.

M.L.W.N.

M.L.W.S.

H.W.

L.W.

TIME ZONE (UT)	SCOTLAND – STORNOWAY	Dates in amber are SPRINGS
For Summer Time add ONE hour in **non-shaded areas**	LAT 58°12′N LONG 6°23′W	Dates in yellow are NEAPS
	TIMES AND HEIGHTS OF HIGH AND LOW WATERS	**2011**

JANUARY

Day	Time m	Day	Time m
1 SA	0422 4.1 / 1038 1.6 / 1651 4.1 / 2307 1.4	**16** SU	0406 3.8 / 1023 1.9 / 1628 3.8 / 2239 1.7
2 SU	0513 4.3 / 1136 1.4 / 1741 4.0 / 2355 1.2	**17** M	0454 4.1 / 1118 1.6 / 1720 4.1 / 2330 1.5
3 M	0557 4.5 / 1225 1.2 / 1825 4.2	**18** TU	0537 4.4 / 1206 1.3 / 1805 4.3
4 TU	0038 1.1 / 0637 4.7 / 1309 1.0 / 1903 4.3	**19** W	0015 1.2 / 0617 4.7 / 1251 0.9 / 1846 4.6
5 W	0119 1.0 / 0714 4.8 / 1348 0.9 / 1939 4.3	**20** TH	0058 0.9 / 0657 4.9 / 1333 0.6 / 1926 4.7
6 TH	0156 1.0 / 0750 4.8 / 1425 0.9 / 2013 4.3	**21** F	0139 0.7 / 0736 5.1 / 1414 0.4 / 2005 4.8
7 F	0232 1.0 / 0825 4.8 / 1500 0.9 / 2046 4.2	**22** SA	0219 0.5 / 0815 5.2 / 1455 0.3 / 2045 4.7
8 SA	0307 1.1 / 0859 4.6 / 1534 1.0 / 2119 4.1	**23** SU	0259 0.5 / 0856 5.1 / 1537 0.3 / 2127 4.6
9 SU	0342 1.2 / 0936 4.4 / 1609 1.2 / 2156 3.9	**24** M	0340 0.7 / 0941 4.8 / 1620 0.6 / 2215 4.3
10 M	0419 1.5 / 1016 4.2 / 1646 1.4 / 2238 3.7	**25** TU	0424 0.9 / 1034 4.5 / 1707 0.9 / 2313 4.0
11 TU	0459 1.7 / 1103 4.0 / 1728 1.6 / 2331 3.6	**26** W	0514 1.3 / 1141 4.2 / 1801 1.3
12 W	0545 1.9 / 1158 3.8 / 1815 1.8	**27** TH	0027 3.8 / 0613 1.6 / 1303 3.9 / 1905 1.6
13 TH	0035 3.5 / 0641 2.1 / 1301 3.6 / 1911 1.9	**28** F	0147 3.7 / 0732 1.8 / 1427 3.7 / 2030 1.8
14 F	0148 3.5 / 0749 2.2 / 1410 3.6 / 2019 2.0	**29** SA	0305 3.7 / 0916 1.9 / 1546 3.7 / 2158 1.7
15 SA	0304 3.6 / 0911 2.2 / 1525 3.7 / 2135 1.9	**30** SU	0412 3.9 / 1038 1.7 / 1650 3.8 / 2300 1.4
		31 M	0505 4.1 / 1135 1.4 / 1739 3.9 / 2348 1.3

FEBRUARY

Day	Time m	Day	Time m
1 TU	0548 4.3 / 1220 1.2 / 1817 4.0	**16** W	0517 4.3 / 1148 1.1 / 1747 4.4 / 2357 1.1
2 W	0028 1.1 / 0624 4.5 / 1259 0.9 / 1849 4.2	**17** TH	0600 4.7 / 1232 0.7 / 1828 4.7
3 TH	0105 0.9 / 0657 4.7 / 1332 0.8 / 1919 4.3	**18** F	0040 0.7 / 0639 5.1 / 1314 0.3 / 1906 4.9
4 F	0139 0.8 / 0728 4.8 / 1404 0.7 / 1947 4.3	**19** SA	0121 0.4 / 0717 5.3 / 1354 0.1 / 1943 5.0
5 SA	0212 0.7 / 0758 4.7 / 1434 0.7 / 2015 4.3	**20** SU	0200 0.3 / 0755 5.4 / 1433 0.0 / 2021 5.0
6 SU	0243 0.8 / 0828 4.6 / 1504 0.8 / 2043 4.2	**21** M	0240 0.3 / 0835 5.2 / 1513 0.2 / 2101 4.8
7 M	0314 0.9 / 0859 4.5 / 1535 0.9 / 2113 4.1	**22** TU	0320 0.4 / 0918 5.0 / 1554 0.5 / 2145 4.5
8 TU	0346 1.1 / 0932 4.2 / 1608 1.1 / 2146 3.9	**23** W	0403 0.7 / 1007 4.5 / 1638 0.9 / 2239 4.1
9 W	0420 1.4 / 1010 4.0 / 1644 1.4 / 2226 3.7	**24** TH	0449 1.2 / 1114 4.1 / 1727 1.4 / 2356 3.8
10 TH	0459 1.7 / 1058 3.7 / 1726 1.7 / 2323 3.5	**25** F	0546 1.6 / 1246 3.7 / 1830 1.8
11 F	0546 1.9 / 1205 3.5 / 1817 1.9	**26** SA	0124 3.6 / 0708 1.9 / 1417 3.5 / 2004 2.0
12 SA	0042 3.4 / 0648 2.1 / 1324 3.4 / 1923 2.1	**27** SU	0246 3.6 / 0910 1.9 / 1541 3.5 / 2145 1.9
13 SU	0206 3.4 / 0817 2.2 / 1451 3.5 / 2051 2.1	**28** M	0357 3.8 / 1034 1.7 / 1647 3.6 / 2247 1.7
14 M	0328 3.6 / 0955 1.9 / 1606 3.7 / 2214 1.8		
15 TU	0429 3.9 / 1059 1.6 / 1701 4.0 / 2310 1.5		

MARCH

Day	Time m	Day	Time m
1 TU	0451 4.0 / 1125 1.4 / 1730 3.8 / 2332 1.4	**16** W	0400 4.0 / 1033 1.4 / 1638 4.1 / 2245 1.5
2 W	0531 4.2 / 1204 1.2 / 1802 4.0	**17** TH	0452 4.4 / 1123 1.0 / 1723 4.4 / 2333 1.1
3 TH	0010 1.1 / 0605 4.4 / 1238 0.9 / 1829 4.1	**18** F	0536 4.8 / 1207 0.5 / 1804 4.8
4 F	0045 0.9 / 0635 4.6 / 1308 0.8 / 1855 4.3	**19** SA	0017 0.7 / 0616 5.1 / 1249 0.2 / 1842 5.0
5 SA	0117 0.8 / 0704 4.7 / 1337 0.7 / 1920 4.4	**20** SU	0059 0.4 / 0656 5.3 / 1329 0.0 / 1920 5.1
6 SU	0148 0.7 / 0731 4.7 / 1405 0.7 / 1945 4.4	**21** M	0139 0.3 / 0735 5.4 / 1409 0.0 / 1958 5.1
7 M	0217 0.7 / 0758 4.6 / 1432 0.7 / 2011 4.4	**22** TU	0220 0.3 / 0815 5.2 / 1448 0.2 / 2038 4.9
8 TU	0246 0.8 / 0827 4.5 / 1501 0.8 / 2039 4.2	**23** W	0301 0.4 / 0859 4.9 / 1529 0.6 / 2122 4.6
9 W	0316 1.0 / 0857 4.3 / 1533 1.0 / 2108 4.1	**24** TH	0344 0.8 / 0950 4.5 / 1612 1.0 / 2216 4.3
10 TH	0348 1.2 / 0930 4.0 / 1607 1.3 / 2139 3.8	**25** F	0432 1.2 / 1059 4.0 / 1700 1.5 / 2333 3.9
11 F	0424 1.5 / 1013 3.7 / 1645 1.6 / 2223 3.6	**26** SA	0529 1.6 / 1232 3.6 / 1802 1.9
12 SA	0507 1.8 / 1124 3.5 / 1732 1.8 / 2352 3.5	**27** SU	0059 3.7 / 0652 1.9 / 1359 3.4 / 1936 2.2
13 SU	0607 2.0 / 1256 3.4 / 1839 2.1	**28** M	0218 3.7 / 0846 2.0 / 1523 3.5 / 2115 2.1
14 M	0127 3.4 / 0741 2.1 / 1426 3.5 / 2014 2.1	**29** TU	0329 3.8 / 1009 1.7 / 1628 3.6 / 2219 1.9
15 TU	0252 3.6 / 0926 1.8 / 1542 3.7 / 2145 1.9	**30** W	0424 4.0 / 1058 1.5 / 1709 3.8 / 2304 1.6
		31 TH	0505 4.2 / 1135 1.3 / 1740 4.0 / 2343 1.3

APRIL

Day	Time m	Day	Time m
1 F	0540 4.3 / 1208 1.1 / 1804 4.1	**16** SA	0510 4.8 / 1139 0.6 / 1739 4.8 / 2351 0.8
2 SA	0018 1.1 / 0610 4.5 / 1238 0.9 / 1829 4.3	**17** SU	0554 5.0 / 1222 0.4 / 1819 5.0
3 SU	0051 0.9 / 0637 4.5 / 1307 0.8 / 1853 4.4	**18** M	0035 0.6 / 0635 5.2 / 1305 0.3 / 1858 5.1
4 M	0122 0.8 / 0704 4.6 / 1334 0.7 / 1917 4.5	**19** TU	0119 0.4 / 0717 5.2 / 1346 0.3 / 1938 5.1
5 TU	0151 0.8 / 0732 4.5 / 1402 0.8 / 1944 4.5	**20** W	0202 0.5 / 0800 5.0 / 1426 0.5 / 2020 4.9
6 W	0221 0.9 / 0802 4.4 / 1432 0.9 / 2013 4.4	**21** TH	0246 0.6 / 0846 4.7 / 1508 0.8 / 2106 4.7
7 TH	0252 1.0 / 0834 4.2 / 1503 1.0 / 2043 4.2	**22** F	0331 0.9 / 0939 4.3 / 1551 1.2 / 2200 4.4
8 F	0325 1.2 / 0910 4.0 / 1538 1.3 / 2117 4.0	**23** SA	0421 1.2 / 1046 3.9 / 1639 1.6 / 2309 4.1
9 SA	0402 1.4 / 0957 3.8 / 1616 1.5 / 2204 3.8	**24** SU	0518 1.6 / 1205 3.6 / 1738 2.0
10 SU	0447 1.6 / 1111 3.6 / 1703 1.8 / 2329 3.6	**25** M	0024 3.9 / 0630 1.8 / 1324 3.5 / 1857 2.2
11 M	0550 1.8 / 1238 3.5 / 1810 2.0	**26** TU	0137 3.8 / 0757 1.9 / 1442 3.4 / 2025 2.2
12 TU	0059 3.6 / 0721 1.8 / 1300 3.5 / 1943 2.0	**27** W	0245 3.8 / 0916 1.8 / 1549 3.5 / 2135 2.0
13 W	0219 3.8 / 0852 1.6 / 1512 3.8 / 2109 1.8	**28** TH	0344 3.9 / 1013 1.7 / 1634 3.7 / 2226 1.8
14 TH	0327 4.1 / 1000 1.3 / 1609 4.1 / 2213 1.5	**29** F	0430 4.0 / 1055 1.5 / 1707 3.9 / 2309 1.5
15 F	0423 4.4 / 1053 0.9 / 1657 4.5 / 2304 1.1	**30** SA	0508 4.2 / 1132 1.3 / 1736 4.1 / 2347 1.3

Chart Datum: 2·71 metres below Ordnance Datum (Local)
HAT is 5·5 metres above Chart Datum

TIME ZONE (UT)	SCOTLAND – STORNOWAY	Dates in amber are SPRINGS
For Summer Time add ONE hour in non-shaded areas	LAT 58°12'N LONG 6°23'W	Dates in yellow are NEAPS
	TIMES AND HEIGHTS OF HIGH AND LOW WATERS	2011

MAY

Day	Time m	Time m	Time m	Day	Time m	Time m	Time m
1 SU	0542 4.3	1205 1.1	1802 4.3	16 M	0533 4.7	1159 0.7	1758 4.8
2 M	0022 1.2 / 0611 4.4	1235 1.0	1827 4.4	17 TU	0016 0.8 / 0618 4.8	1244 0.6	○ 1840 4.9
3 TU	0055 1.0 / 0641 4.4	1305 0.9	● 1854 4.5	18 W	0104 0.7 / 0704 4.8	1327 0.6	1923 4.9
4 W	0127 1.0 / 0712 4.4	1336 0.9	1924 4.5	19 TH	0151 0.7 / 0750 4.7	1410 0.8	2006 4.9
5 TH	0200 1.0 / 0745 4.3	1408 0.9	1956 4.4	20 F	0236 0.8 / 0837 4.5	1452 1.0	2052 4.7
6 F	0234 1.0 / 0822 4.2	1442 1.1	2031 4.3	21 SA	0322 0.9 / 0927 4.2	1535 1.2	2142 4.5
7 SA	0311 1.1 / 0904 4.0	1518 1.2	2111 4.1	22 SU	0410 1.2 / 1021 4.0	1621 1.5	2237 4.3
8 SU	0353 1.3 / 0956 3.8	1559 1.4	2203 4.0	23 M	0500 1.4 / 1122 3.7	1712 1.8	2339 4.1
9 M	0442 1.4 / 1103 3.7	1648 1.7	2315 3.9	24 TU	0556 1.6	1230 3.5	1813 2.0
10 TU	0545 1.5 / 1217 3.6	1753 1.8	◐	25 W	0043 3.9 / 0658 1.8	1343 3.4	1925 2.1
11 W	0033 3.8 / 0659 1.5	1329 3.6	1912 1.9	26 TH	0150 3.8 / 0808 1.9	1453 3.5	2038 2.1
12 TH	0145 3.9 / 0815 1.4	1437 3.8	2031 1.8	27 F	0253 3.8 / 0914 1.8	1549 3.6	2140 2.0
13 F	0252 4.1 / 0923 1.2	1538 4.1	2137 1.5	28 SA	0348 3.8 / 1007 1.7	1631 3.8	2231 1.8
14 SA	0352 4.3 / 1021 1.0	1629 4.3	2235 1.2	29 SU	0433 3.9 / 1051 1.6	1706 4.0	2314 1.6
15 SU	0445 4.6 / 1111 0.8	1715 4.6	2326 1.0	30 M	0512 4.0 / 1130 1.4	1736 4.1	2354 1.4
				31 TU	0548 4.1	1205 1.3	1805 4.3

JUNE

Day	Time m	Time m	Time m	Day	Time m	Time m	Time m
1 W	0031 1.3 / 0622 4.2	1240 1.1	● 1835 4.4	16 TH	0057 0.9 / 0657 4.5	1315 0.9	1910 4.8
2 TH	0108 1.1 / 0658 4.3	1315 1.0	1909 4.5	17 F	0143 0.8 / 0741 4.4	1358 0.9	1952 4.8
3 F	0145 1.0 / 0736 4.3	1351 1.0	1944 4.5	18 SA	0227 0.8 / 0824 4.3	1438 1.0	2034 4.8
4 SA	0223 0.9 / 0816 4.2	1428 1.0	2022 4.5	19 SU	0309 0.8 / 0906 4.2	1518 1.1	2116 4.6
5 SU	0304 0.9 / 0859 4.2	1507 1.1	2105 4.4	20 M	0350 1.0 / 0948 4.0	1559 1.3	2200 4.4
6 M	0347 1.0 / 0948 4.0	1549 1.2	2154 4.2	21 TU	0432 1.2 / 1033 3.8	1641 1.6	2248 4.2
7 TU	0436 1.1 / 1044 3.9	1637 1.4	2255 4.1	22 W	0515 1.4 / 1123 3.6	1728 1.8	2342 4.0
8 W	0530 1.2 / 1148 3.8	1734 1.6	◐	23 TH	0601 1.6	1224 3.5	1821 2.0
9 TH	0003 4.0 / 0631 1.2	1255 3.7	1840 1.7	24 F	0041 3.8 / 0653 1.8	1337 3.4	1925 2.1
10 F	0112 4.0 / 0737 1.3	1402 3.8	1952 1.7	25 SA	0147 3.7 / 0754 1.9	1451 3.5	2040 2.1
11 SA	0221 4.0 / 0845 1.3	1506 3.9	2105 1.6	26 SU	0254 3.6 / 0904 1.9	1549 3.6	2147 2.0
12 SU	0326 4.1 / 0951 1.2	1604 4.1	2211 1.4	27 M	0354 3.7 / 1006 1.8	1633 3.8	2241 1.8
13 M	0426 4.2 / 1050 1.1	1656 4.4	2311 1.2	28 TU	0444 3.8 / 1056 1.6	1710 4.0	2327 1.6
14 TU	0520 4.4 / 1142 1.0	1743 4.6		29 W	0527 3.9 / 1139 1.5	1744 4.2	
15 W	0005 1.0 / 0610 4.4	1231 0.9	○ 1827 4.7	30 TH	0010 1.4 / 0608 4.1	1220 1.3	1819 4.4

JULY

Day	Time m	Time m	Time m	Day	Time m	Time m	Time m
1 F	0051 1.1 / 0647 4.2	1259 1.1	● 1855 4.6	16 SA	0133 0.8 / 0727 4.3	1344 0.9	1934 4.8
2 SA	0131 0.9 / 0726 4.4	1338 0.9	1932 4.7	17 SU	0212 0.7 / 0803 4.3	1421 0.9	2010 4.8
3 SU	0211 0.7 / 0805 4.4	1416 0.8	2010 4.7	18 M	0248 0.7 / 0837 4.2	1457 0.9	2045 4.7
4 M	0252 0.6 / 0846 4.4	1455 0.8	2050 4.7	19 TU	0323 0.8 / 0911 4.1	1532 1.1	2121 4.5
5 TU	0334 0.6 / 0929 4.3	1536 0.9	2135 4.6	20 W	0357 1.0 / 0947 4.0	1608 1.3	2200 4.2
6 W	0418 0.7 / 1018 4.1	1620 1.1	2228 4.4	21 TH	0433 1.2 / 1027 3.8	1646 1.6	2245 4.0
7 TH	0506 0.9 / 1115 4.0	1710 1.3	2332 4.2	22 F	0511 1.5 / 1115 3.6	1729 1.8	2339 3.7
8 F	0600 1.1 / 1220 3.8	1809 1.5	◐	23 SA	0555 1.7	1214 3.5	1821 2.1 / ◐
9 SA	0043 4.0 / 0701 1.3	1330 3.8	1918 1.6	24 SU	0041 3.6 / 0646 1.9	1325 3.4	1925 2.2
10 SU	0158 3.9 / 0812 1.4	1441 3.8	2041 1.7	25 M	0153 3.5 / 0750 2.0	1447 3.5	2052 2.2
11 M	0312 3.9 / 0930 1.4	1548 4.0	2202 1.6	26 TU	0312 3.5 / 0912 2.0	1554 3.7	2210 2.0
12 TU	0419 3.9 / 1038 1.4	1645 4.2	2308 1.3	27 W	0417 3.6 / 1024 1.9	1642 3.9	2305 1.7
13 W	0517 4.0 / 1134 1.2	1734 4.4		28 TH	0507 3.9 / 1116 1.6	1723 4.2	2350 1.4
14 TH	0003 1.1 / 0605 4.2	1222 1.1	1817 4.6	29 F	0551 4.1	1200 1.3	1801 4.5
15 F	0051 0.9 / 0648 4.2	1305 0.9	○ 1857 4.7	30 SA	0032 1.0 / 0630 4.4	1242 1.0	● 1838 4.8
				31 SU	0113 0.7 / 0709 4.6	1321 0.8	1914 5.0

AUGUST

Day	Time m	Time m	Time m	Day	Time m	Time m	Time m
1 M	0153 0.4 / 0747 4.7	1359 0.6	1952 5.1	16 TU	0219 0.7 / 0805 4.3	1431 0.8	2013 4.7
2 TU	0232 0.3 / 0825 4.7	1438 0.5	2030 5.0	17 W	0249 0.8 / 0834 4.3	1502 1.0	2044 4.5
3 W	0312 0.3 / 0905 4.6	1517 0.6	2113 4.9	18 TH	0320 0.9 / 0905 4.1	1534 1.2	2117 4.3
4 TH	0354 0.5 / 0950 4.4	1559 0.8	2201 4.6	19 F	0352 1.2 / 0939 4.0	1608 1.5	2155 4.0
5 F	0438 0.7 / 1044 4.2	1646 1.1	2304 4.3	20 SA	0428 1.4 / 1020 3.8	1646 1.8	2244 3.8
6 SA	0529 1.1 / 1151 3.9	1741 1.5	◐	21 SU	0509 1.7 / 1116 3.6	1732 2.1	2352 3.5 / ◐
7 SU	0023 3.9 / 0628 1.4	1308 3.8	1852 1.7	22 M	0557 2.0	1228 3.5	1832 2.2
8 M	0148 3.7 / 0745 1.7	1426 3.8	2033 1.8	23 TU	0110 3.4 / 0658 2.1	1348 3.5	1958 2.3
9 TU	0310 3.7 / 0921 1.7	1538 3.9	2207 1.7	24 W	0237 3.5 / 0823 2.2	1510 3.6	2140 2.1
10 W	0421 3.8 / 1034 1.6	1638 4.1	2310 1.4	25 TH	0350 4.0 / 0953 2.0	1611 3.9	2241 1.7
11 TH	0516 3.9 / 1126 1.4	1725 4.4	2358 1.1	26 F	0444 4.0 / 1051 1.7	1658 4.3	2327 1.3
12 F	0559 4.1 / 1210 1.2	1804 4.6		27 SA	0528 4.3 / 1136 1.3	1738 4.7	
13 SA	0039 0.9 / 0634 4.2	1249 1.0	○ 1839 4.7	28 SU	0009 0.9 / 0607 4.6	1219 1.0	1816 5.0
14 SU	0115 0.8 / 0706 4.3	1325 0.8	1912 4.8	29 M	0049 0.5 / 0646 4.9	1258 0.7	● 1853 5.3
15 M	0148 0.7 / 0736 4.4	1359 0.8	1943 4.8	30 TU	0128 0.3 / 0723 5.0	1338 0.5	1930 5.4
				31 W	0207 0.1 / 0801 5.0	1417 0.4	2009 5.3

Chart Datum: 2·71 metres below Ordnance Datum (Local)
HAT is 5·5 metres above Chart Datum

SCOTLAND – STORNOWAY
LAT 58°12′N   LONG 6°23′W
2011

TIMES AND HEIGHTS OF HIGH AND LOW WATERS

SEPTEMBER

Day	Time	m	Time	m		Day	Time	m	Time	m
1 TH	0247	0.2	1457	0.5		16 F	0244	1.0	1503	1.2
	0840	4.9	2051	5.1			0828	4.3	2042	4.4
2 F	0328	0.5	1539	0.8		17 SA	0316	1.2	1536	1.4
	0924	4.7	2140	4.7			0859	4.2	2116	4.1
3 SA	0411	0.8	1625	1.1		18 SU	0350	1.4	1612	1.7
	1018	4.4	2244	4.3			0935	4.0	2200	3.8
4 SU ◐	0500	1.3	1720	1.6		19 M	0429	1.7	1657	2.0
	1130	4.1					1025	3.8	2314	3.6
5 M	0015	3.9	1252	3.9		20 TU ◑	0516	2.0	1753	2.2
	0559	1.7	1837	1.9			1148	3.6		
6 TU	0143	3.7	1412	3.8		21 W	0043	3.5	1311	3.6
	0727	2.0	2035	2.0			0618	2.2	1920	2.3
7 W	0307	3.7	1526	4.0		22 TH	0207	3.5	1429	3.7
	0913	2.0	2206	1.7			0745	2.3	2104	2.1
8 TH	0419	3.8	1626	4.2		23 F	0320	3.8	1536	4.0
	1022	1.8	2301	1.5			0918	2.1	2210	1.7
9 F	0510	3.9	1711	4.4		24 SA	0415	4.1	1628	4.4
	1110	1.5	2342	1.4			1020	1.8	2258	1.3
10 SA	0545	4.1	1746	4.6		25 SU	0501	4.5	1712	4.8
	1150	1.3					1108	1.4	2340	0.8
11 SU	0017	1.0	1227	1.1		26 M	0542	4.8	1752	5.2
	0614	4.3	1817	4.7			1151	1.0		
12 M ○	0049	0.9	1301	0.9		27 TU ●	0021	0.5	1233	0.7
	0642	4.4	1847	4.8			0620	5.1	1831	5.4
13 TU	0119	0.8	1333	0.9		28 W	0102	0.3	1314	0.5
	0708	4.5	1915	4.8			0658	5.2	1910	5.5
14 W	0147	0.8	1403	0.9		29 TH	0142	0.2	1356	0.5
	0734	4.5	1942	4.7			0737	5.3	1950	5.4
15 TH	0215	0.9	1433	1.0		30 F	0222	0.4	1437	0.6
	0800	4.5	2011	4.6			0818	5.1	2034	5.1

OCTOBER

Day	Time	m	Time	m		Day	Time	m	Time	m
1 SA	0304	0.6	1521	0.9		16 SU	0246	1.2	1512	1.4
	0904	4.9	2125	4.7			0832	4.3	2054	4.2
2 SU	0347	1.1	1609	1.3		17 M	0321	1.5	1548	1.6
	0959	4.6	2235	4.3			0908	4.1	2140	3.9
3 M	0436	1.5	1707	1.7		18 TU	0359	1.7	1632	1.9
	1113	4.2					0956	3.9	2253	3.7
4 TU ◗	0005	3.9	1233	4.0		19 W	0445	2.0	1731	2.0
	0536	2.0	1827	2.0			1116	3.8		
5 W	0129	3.7	1349	4.0		20 TH ◑	0018	3.6	1238	3.8
	0705	2.2	2016	2.0			0547	2.2	1853	2.1
6 TH	0252	3.7	1502	4.1		21 F	0135	3.7	1351	3.9
	0847	2.2	2143	1.8			0712	2.3	2021	1.9
7 F	0403	3.8	1602	4.2		22 SA	0245	3.9	1458	4.1
	0956	2.0	2235	1.6			0837	2.1	2131	1.6
8 SA	0450	4.0	1647	4.4		23 SU	0343	4.2	1555	4.5
	1044	1.7	2314	1.4			0943	1.8	2224	1.2
9 SU	0522	4.1	1722	4.5		24 M	0431	4.5	1644	4.8
	1123	1.5	2347	1.2			1036	1.4	2310	0.9
10 M	0550	4.3	1753	4.6		25 TU	0515	4.9	1728	5.1
	1200	1.3					1123	1.1	2354	0.7
11 TU	0018	1.1	1234	1.1		26 W ●	0556	5.1	1810	5.3
	0616	4.4	1822	4.7			1209	0.9		
12 W ○	0048	1.0	1306	1.1		27 TH	0036	0.5	1254	0.7
	0641	4.6	1849	4.7			0636	5.3	1852	5.3
13 TH	0116	1.0	1336	1.0		28 F	0119	0.5	1338	0.7
	0705	4.6	1916	4.7			0717	5.3	1936	5.2
14 F	0144	1.0	1407	1.1		29 SA	0201	0.6	1423	0.7
	0732	4.6	1946	4.6			0801	5.2	2023	5.0
15 SA	0214	1.1	1438	1.2		30 SU	0244	0.9	1510	1.0
	0801	4.5	2018	4.4			0848	5.0	2117	4.6
						31 M	0329	1.2	1559	1.3
							0944	4.7	2222	4.3

NOVEMBER

Day	Time	m	Time	m		Day	Time	m	Time	m
1 TU	0417	1.6	1656	1.6		16 W	0340	1.6	1621	1.6
	1050	4.5	2339	3.9			0942	4.1	2234	3.8
2 W ◐	0515	2.0	1805	1.9		17 TH	0426	1.8	1717	1.7
	1202	4.2					1047	4.0	2347	3.8
3 TH	0056	3.7	1312	4.1		18 F ◑	0524	2.0	1825	1.8
	0630	2.3	1929	2.0			1202	4.0		
4 F	0213	3.7	1420	4.1		19 SA	0058	3.8	1312	4.0
	0758	2.3	2051	2.0			0637	2.1	1938	1.7
5 SA	0324	3.8	1522	4.1		20 SU	0205	3.9	1419	4.2
	0912	2.2	2151	1.8			0753	2.0	2048	1.5
6 SU	0415	3.9	1613	4.2		21 M	0307	4.1	1521	4.4
	1007	1.9	2236	1.7			0904	1.8	2148	1.3
7 M	0452	4.1	1653	4.3		22 TU	0401	4.4	1616	4.6
	1051	1.7	2313	1.5			1004	1.5	2241	1.1
8 TU	0523	4.1	1728	4.4		23 W	0449	4.7	1707	4.8
	1130	1.5	2346	1.4			1059	1.3	2330	0.9
9 W	0551	4.4	1759	4.5		24 TH	0535	4.9	1755	5.0
	1207	1.4					1150	1.0		
10 TH ○	0018	1.2	1241	1.3		25 F ●	0017	0.8	1240	0.9
	0617	4.5	1828	4.5			0618	5.1	1841	5.0
11 F	0048	1.2	1314	1.2		26 SA	0102	0.8	1328	0.8
	0644	4.6	1858	4.5			0703	5.2	1928	4.9
12 SA	0119	1.1	1347	1.2		27 SU	0146	0.8	1415	0.8
	0712	4.6	1930	4.5			0748	5.2	2015	4.8
13 SU	0151	1.1	1421	1.2		28 M	0230	1.0	1501	0.9
	0743	4.6	2006	4.4			0834	5.0	2105	4.6
14 M	0225	1.2	1457	1.3		29 TU	0314	1.2	1548	1.1
	0817	4.5	2045	4.2			0924	4.9	2158	4.3
15 TU	0301	1.4	1536	1.5		30 W	0400	1.5	1638	1.4
	0856	4.3	2133	4.0			1018	4.6	2257	4.0

DECEMBER

Day	Time	m	Time	m		Day	Time	m	Time	m
1 TH	0449	1.8	1731	1.7		16 F	0410	1.4	1658	1.3
	1117	4.4					1018	4.3	2309	3.9
2 F	0004	3.8	1221	4.2		17 SA	0501	1.6	1754	1.4
	0547	2.0	1831	1.9			1121	4.1		
3 SA	0116	3.6	1327	4.0		18 SU ◑	0016	3.8	1232	4.1
	0655	2.2	1939	2.0			0601	1.7	1857	1.5
4 SU	0227	3.6	1432	3.9		19 M	0124	3.9	1341	4.1
	0811	2.2	2049	2.0			0710	1.8	2005	1.5
5 M	0329	3.7	1531	4.0		20 TU	0231	4.0	1450	4.1
	0919	2.1	2148	1.9			0825	1.8	2115	1.4
6 TU	0417	3.9	1621	4.0		21 W	0333	4.2	1555	4.3
	1015	2.0	2235	1.8			0937	1.6	2218	1.3
7 W	0456	4.1	1702	4.1		22 TH	0430	4.4	1654	4.4
	1101	1.8	2315	1.6			1043	1.4	2315	1.1
8 TH	0529	4.2	1739	4.2		23 F	0520	4.6	1747	4.5
	1142	1.6	2352	1.4			1141	1.2		
9 F	0559	4.4	1814	4.3		24 SA ●	0005	1.0	1234	1.0
	1221	1.4					0607	4.8	1835	4.6
10 SA ○	0026	1.3	1257	1.3		25 SU	0052	0.9	1322	0.8
	0628	4.5	1847	4.4			0652	5.0	1920	4.7
11 SU	0101	1.2	1333	1.2		26 M	0136	0.8	1407	0.7
	0659	4.6	1922	4.4			0735	5.1	2003	4.6
12 M	0136	1.1	1409	1.1		27 TU	0218	0.9	1449	0.7
	0732	4.6	1958	4.4			0817	5.0	2044	4.5
13 TU	0212	1.1	1447	1.1		28 W	0258	1.0	1530	0.9
	0807	4.6	2037	4.3			0858	4.9	2125	4.3
14 W	0248	1.1	1527	1.1		29 TH	0339	1.2	1611	1.1
	0844	4.5	2119	4.2			0941	4.7	2207	4.1
15 TH	0327	1.3	1610	1.2		30 F	0420	1.4	1653	1.4
	0926	4.4	2209	4.0			1026	4.4	2255	3.8
						31 SA	0505	1.7	1738	1.6
							1117	4.2	2354	3.6

Chart Datum: 2·71 metres below Ordnance Datum (Local)
HAT is 5·5 metres above Chart Datum

TIDES

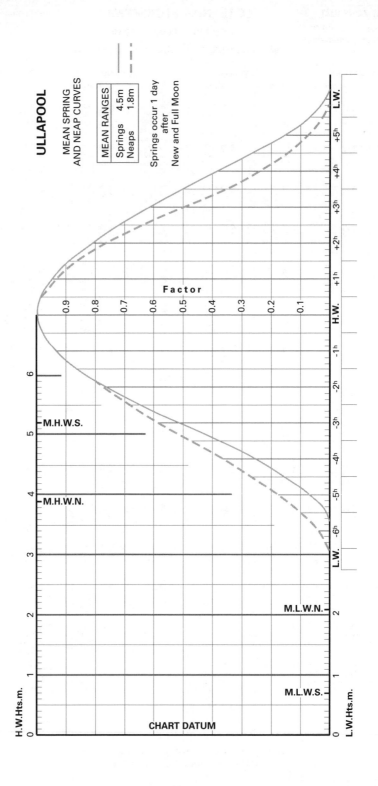

ULLAPOOL

MEAN SPRING
AND NEAP CURVES

MEAN RANGES	
Springs	4.5m
Neaps	1.8m

Springs occur 1 day
after
New and Full Moon

Factor

0.9
0.8
0.7
0.6
0.5
0.4
0.3
0.2
0.1

H.W.

+1ʰ +2ʰ +3ʰ +4ʰ +5ʰ L.W.

-1ʰ -2ʰ -3ʰ -4ʰ -5ʰ -6ʰ L.W.

M.H.W.S.

M.H.W.N.

M.L.W.N.

M.L.W.S.

H.W.Hts.m.

L.W.Hts.m.

CHART DATUM

SCOTLAND – ULLAPOOL

LAT 57°54'N LONG 5°10'W

TIMES AND HEIGHTS OF HIGH AND LOW WATERS

Dates in amber are SPRINGS
Dates in yellow are NEAPS

2011

JANUARY

Day	Time m	Time m	Time m	Time m
1 SA	0433 4.6	1046 1.8	1703 4.6	2317 1.7
16 SU	0417 4.2	1034 2.2	1637 4.3	2250 2.0
2 SU	0524 4.5	1143 1.6	1754 4.7	
17 M	0505 4.5	1126 1.9	1726 4.5	2339 1.7
3 M	0006 1.5	0607 5.1	1233 1.4	1836 4.9
18 TU	0546 4.8	1212 1.5	1810 4.8	
4 TU	0050 1.3	0647 5.2	1316 1.2	1915 4.9
19 W	0023 1.4	0624 5.1	1256 1.1	1850 5.1
5 W	0130 1.3	0723 5.3	1355 1.1	1950 4.9
20 TH	0106 1.1	0702 5.4	1338 0.8	1931 5.3
6 TH	0207 1.2	0758 5.3	1431 1.1	2024 4.9
21 F	0147 0.9	0741 5.6	1420 0.6	2012 5.4
7 F	0242 1.3	0831 5.2	1506 1.1	2055 4.8
22 SA	0228 0.7	0821 5.6	1501 0.5	2054 5.3
8 SA	0316 1.4	0904 5.1	1540 1.3	2127 4.6
23 SU	0309 0.7	0904 5.6	1543 0.6	2139 5.1
9 SU	0350 1.5	0937 4.9	1615 1.4	2201 4.4
24 M	0351 0.9	0949 5.4	1626 0.8	2227 4.9
10 M	0426 1.7	1014 4.7	1651 1.6	2239 4.2
25 TU	0436 1.2	1041 5.0	1713 1.2	2324 4.6
11 TU	0503 2.0	1057 4.4	1730 1.9	2328 4.1
26 W	0526 1.5	1144 4.7	1806 1.6	
12 W	0547 2.2	1153 4.2	1816 2.1	
27 TH	0033 4.3	0624 1.9	1303 4.3	1911 2.0
13 TH	0037 3.9	0643 2.4	1307 4.0	1914 2.3
28 F	0152 4.2	0743 2.2	1432 4.2	2039 2.2
14 F	0159 3.6	0759 2.5	1424 4.0	2031 2.3
29 SA	0314 4.2	0921 2.2	1558 4.2	2207 2.1
15 SA	0315 4.0	0926 2.5	1536 4.1	2149 2.2
30 SU	0424 4.4	1044 2.0	1703 4.3	2310 1.9
31 M	0517 4.6	1141 1.7	1751 4.5	2358 1.6

FEBRUARY

Day	Time m	Time m	Time m	Time m
1 TU	0559 4.9	1226 1.4	1829 4.7	
16 W	0525 4.7	1154 1.3	1752 4.8	
2 W	0039 1.4	0634 5.1	1305 1.2	1901 4.8
17 TH	0006 1.3	0604 5.1	1238 0.9	1832 5.2
3 TH	0116 1.2	0707 5.2	1339 1.0	1930 4.9
18 F	0048 0.9	0642 5.5	1319 0.5	1910 5.4
4 F	0149 1.1	0737 5.3	1411 1.0	1958 4.9
19 SA	0129 0.6	0721 5.7	1400 0.2	1949 5.5
5 SA	0221 1.1	0806 5.2	1441 1.0	2025 4.9
20 SU	0209 0.4	0800 5.8	1440 0.2	2030 5.5
6 SU	0252 1.1	0834 5.1	1511 1.0	2052 4.8
21 M	0249 0.4	0842 5.7	1520 0.3	2112 5.3
7 M	0322 1.2	0904 5.0	1541 1.2	2120 4.6
22 TU	0331 0.6	0927 5.4	1601 0.7	2157 5.0
8 TU	0352 1.4	0936 4.8	1612 1.4	2152 4.4
23 W	0414 0.9	1017 5.0	1645 1.1	2251 4.6
9 W	0425 1.6	1012 4.5	1646 1.6	2229 4.2
24 TH	0501 1.4	1121 4.5	1734 1.4	
10 TH	0502 1.9	1056 4.3	1724 1.9	2318 4.0
25 F	0001 4.3	0558 1.8	1247 4.1	1837 2.1
11 F	0547 2.2	1159 4.0	1813 2.2	
26 SA	0126 4.1	0718 2.2	1423 3.9	2014 2.3
12 SA	0040 3.8	0651 2.4	1332 3.8	1923 2.4
27 SU	0255 4.1	0911 2.2	1551 4.0	2154 2.2
13 SU	0220 3.8	0832 2.5	1500 3.9	2105 2.4
28 M	0408 4.2	1036 2.0	1653 4.1	2257 2.0
14 M	0341 4.0	1006 2.2	1613 4.1	2225 2.1
15 TU	0440 4.3	1106 1.8	1708 4.4	2320 1.7

MARCH

Day	Time m	Time m	Time m	Time m
1 TU	0501 4.5	1128 1.7	1737 4.4	2342 1.7
16 W	0408 4.3	1040 1.6	1643 4.4	2256 1.6
2 W	0541 4.7	1208 1.4	1810 4.6	
17 TH	0457 4.7	1129 1.1	1728 4.8	2342 1.2
3 TH	0020 1.4	0614 4.9	1243 1.2	1839 4.7
18 F	0539 5.1	1213 0.7	1808 5.2	
4 F	0055 1.2	0644 5.0	1315 1.0	1905 4.9
19 SA	0025 0.7	0618 5.5	1255 0.3	1846 5.4
5 SA	0126 1.0	0711 5.1	1344 0.9	1930 4.9
20 SU	0107 0.4	0658 5.7	1336 0.1	1925 5.6
6 SU	0156 1.0	0739 5.1	1412 0.8	1955 4.9
21 M	0148 0.2	0739 5.7	1416 0.1	2005 5.5
7 M	0225 1.0	0806 5.1	1440 0.9	2020 4.8
22 TU	0229 0.3	0821 5.6	1456 0.3	2047 5.3
8 TU	0254 1.1	0834 5.0	1508 1.0	2047 4.7
23 W	0311 0.5	0908 5.2	1537 0.7	2132 5.0
9 W	0323 1.2	0905 4.8	1538 1.2	2117 4.6
24 TH	0355 0.8	1001 4.8	1620 1.1	2226 4.6
10 TH	0354 1.4	0940 4.5	1610 1.4	2151 4.4
25 F	0443 1.3	1109 4.3	1709 1.7	2336 4.3
11 F	0429 1.7	1023 4.3	1646 1.7	2235 4.1
26 SA	0540 1.7	1234 3.9	1811 2.1	
12 SA	0512 2.0	1123 4.0	1731 2.0	2344 3.9
27 SU	0100 4.0	0659 2.1	1404 3.8	1946 2.3
13 SU	0611 2.2	1258 3.8	1838 2.3	
28 M	0226 4.0	0847 2.1	1528 3.8	2126 2.2
14 M	0134 3.8	0749 2.3	1430 3.8	2026 2.4
29 TU	0339 4.1	1008 1.9	1629 4.0	2229 2.0
15 TU	0302 3.9	0935 2.1	1546 4.0	2158 2.1
30 W	0433 4.3	1059 1.7	1711 4.2	2315 1.7
31 TH	0513 4.5	1138 1.4	1744 4.4	2353 1.4

APRIL

Day	Time m	Time m	Time m	Time m
1 F	0547 4.7	1212 1.2	1812 4.6	
16 SA	0511 5.0	1145 0.6	1742 5.1	2359 0.7
2 SA	0027 1.2	0616 4.8	1244 1.0	1838 4.7
17 SU	0554 5.4	1229 0.4	1823 5.3	
3 SU	0059 1.1	0644 4.9	1314 0.9	1902 4.8
18 M	0043 0.5	0637 5.5	1311 0.2	1902 5.4
4 M	0129 1.0	0712 5.0	1342 0.9	1927 4.9
19 TU	0127 0.3	0720 5.5	1353 0.3	1944 5.4
5 TU	0159 1.0	0740 4.9	1410 0.9	1952 4.8
20 W	0211 0.4	0806 5.3	1434 0.5	2027 5.2
6 W	0228 1.0	0810 4.8	1439 1.0	2020 4.8
21 TH	0255 0.5	0856 5.0	1517 0.8	2114 5.0
7 TH	0258 1.1	0843 4.7	1510 1.1	2051 4.6
22 F	0340 0.8	0952 4.6	1601 1.2	2208 4.6
8 F	0331 1.3	0921 4.4	1543 1.4	2128 4.4
23 SA	0429 1.2	1058 4.2	1650 1.6	2313 4.3
9 SA	0408 1.5	1008 4.2	1621 1.6	2215 4.2
24 SU	0525 1.6	1211 3.9	1749 2.0	
10 SU	0453 1.8	1114 4.0	1708 1.9	2324 4.0
25 M	0026 4.1	0634 1.9	1328 3.7	1907 2.3
11 M	0554 2.0	1240 3.8	1815 2.2	
26 TU	0142 4.0	0758 2.0	1445 3.7	2035 2.2
12 TU	0101 3.9	0723 2.1	1402 3.9	1953 2.2
27 W	0254 4.0	0916 1.9	1548 3.9	2145 2.1
13 W	0224 4.0	0859 1.8	1514 4.1	2122 1.9
28 TH	0352 4.1	1014 1.7	1635 4.0	2236 1.8
14 TH	0331 4.3	1006 1.4	1613 4.4	2224 1.5
29 F	0437 4.2	1058 1.5	1711 4.2	2318 1.6
15 F	0425 4.6	1059 1.0	1700 4.8	2314 1.1
30 SA	0514 4.4	1136 1.3	1742 4.4	2356 1.4

Chart Datum: 2·75 metres below Ordnance Datum (Newlyn)
HAT is 5·9 metres above Chart Datum

TIDES

TIDES

SCOTLAND – ULLAPOOL
LAT 57°54'N   LONG 5°10'W

Dates in amber are **SPRINGS**
Dates in yellow are **NEAPS**

2011

TIMES AND HEIGHTS OF HIGH AND LOW WATERS

MAY

Day	Time	m	Day	Time	m
1 SU	0547 / 1209 / 1810	4.6 / 1.2 / 4.6	16 M	0536 / 1206 / 1803	5.0 / 0.7 / 5.1
2 M	0030 / 0618 / 1242 / 1836	1.2 / 4.7 / 1.1 / 4.7	17 TU	0024 / 0622 / 1251 / ○ 1845	0.7 / 5.1 / 0.6 / 5.3
3 TU	0103 / 0648 / 1313 / ● 1902	1.1 / 4.7 / 1.0 / 4.8	18 W	0112 / 0710 / 1335 / 1929	0.6 / 5.1 / 0.6 / 5.3
4 W	0135 / 0720 / 1344 / 1931	1.0 / 4.7 / 1.0 / 4.8	19 TH	0158 / 0758 / 1418 / 2013	0.6 / 5.0 / 0.7 / 5.2
5 TH	0207 / 0753 / 1415 / 2002	1.0 / 4.7 / 1.0 / 4.8	20 F	0243 / 0848 / 1501 / 2100	0.7 / 4.8 / 1.0 / 5.0
6 F	0241 / 0831 / 1449 / 2037	1.1 / 4.6 / 1.1 / 4.7	21 SA	0329 / 0940 / 1545 / 2149	0.9 / 4.5 / 1.2 / 4.7
7 SA	0317 / 0914 / 1525 / 2119	1.2 / 4.4 / 1.3 / 4.5	22 SU	0416 / 1034 / 1631 / 2243	1.1 / 4.2 / 1.5 / 4.4
8 SU	0357 / 1006 / 1607 / 2210	1.3 / 4.2 / 1.5 / 4.3	23 M	0505 / 1132 / 1722 / 2343	1.4 / 4.0 / 1.8 / 4.2
9 M	0445 / 1109 / 1657 / 2315	1.5 / 4.1 / 1.7 / 4.2	24 TU	0559 / 1235 / 1822 / ◑	1.7 / 3.8 / 2.0
10 TU	0545 / 1221 / 1801 / ☾	1.7 / 4.0 / 1.9	25 W	0047 / 0700 / 1342 / 1931	4.0 / 1.8 / 3.7 / 2.2
11 W	0033 / 0659 / 1332 / 1922	4.1 / 1.7 / 4.1 / 2.0	26 TH	0153 / 0807 / 1450 / 2044	3.9 / 1.9 / 3.8 / 2.1
12 TH	0148 / 0819 / 1440 / 2042	4.2 / 1.6 / 4.1 / 1.8	27 F	0257 / 0913 / 1547 / 2147	3.9 / 1.9 / 3.9 / 2.0
13 F	0254 / 0928 / 1540 / 2149	4.3 / 1.4 / 4.4 / 1.5	28 SA	0351 / 1008 / 1631 / 2238	4.0 / 1.8 / 4.1 / 1.8
14 SA	0354 / 1027 / 1633 / 2245	4.6 / 1.1 / 4.7 / 1.2	29 SU	0437 / 1054 / 1709 / 2322	4.2 / 1.6 / 4.3 / 1.6
15 SU	0447 / 1118 / 1719 / 2336	4.8 / 0.8 / 4.9 / 0.9	30 M	0517 / 1134 / 1741	4.3 / 1.5 / 4.4
			31 TU	0001 / 0553 / 1212 / 1812	1.5 / 4.4 / 1.3 / 4.6

JUNE

Day	Time	m	Day	Time	m
1 W	0038 / 0629 / 1247 / ● 1843	1.3 / 4.5 / 1.2 / 4.7	16 TH	0103 / 0705 / 1323 / 1918	0.8 / 4.9 / 0.9 / 5.2
2 TH	0115 / 0705 / 1322 / 1915	1.2 / 4.6 / 1.1 / 4.8	17 F	0149 / 0751 / 1406 / 2001	0.8 / 4.8 / 0.9 / 5.1
3 F	0151 / 0743 / 1358 / 1951	1.1 / 4.6 / 1.1 / 4.8	18 SA	0233 / 0834 / 1447 / 2042	0.8 / 4.7 / 1.0 / 5.0
4 SA	0229 / 0823 / 1436 / 2029	1.0 / 4.6 / 1.1 / 4.8	19 SU	0315 / 0916 / 1528 / 2124	0.9 / 4.5 / 1.2 / 4.8
5 SU	0308 / 0908 / 1515 / 2113	1.0 / 4.6 / 1.2 / 4.7	20 M	0356 / 0959 / 1609 / 2206	1.0 / 4.4 / 1.4 / 4.6
6 M	0351 / 0957 / 1559 / 2202	1.1 / 4.5 / 1.3 / 4.6	21 TU	0437 / 1042 / 1651 / 2252	1.2 / 4.1 / 1.6 / 4.4
7 TU	0438 / 1053 / 1648 / 2259	1.2 / 4.3 / 1.5 / 4.5	22 W	0519 / 1131 / 1736 / 2345	1.5 / 4.0 / 1.8 / 4.1
8 W	0531 / 1155 / 1744 / ☽	1.3 / 4.2 / 1.6	23 TH	0605 / 1230 / 1829 / ◑	1.7 / 3.8 / 2.1
9 TH	0005 / 0632 / 1301 / ◑ 1850	4.4 / 1.4 / 4.2 / 1.7	24 F	0046 / 0657 / 1336 / 1932	4.0 / 1.9 / 3.8 / 2.2
10 F	0115 / 0741 / 1407 / 2003	4.3 / 1.5 / 4.2 / 1.8	25 SA	0153 / 0800 / 1444 / 2045	3.9 / 2.0 / 3.8 / 2.2
11 SA	0223 / 0851 / 1511 / 2115	4.3 / 1.4 / 4.3 / 1.7	26 SU	0258 / 0908 / 1545 / 2153	3.9 / 2.0 / 3.9 / 2.1
12 SU	0330 / 0958 / 1610 / 2221	4.4 / 1.3 / 4.5 / 1.5	27 M	0358 / 1010 / 1634 / 2248	4.0 / 1.9 / 4.1 / 1.9
13 M	0432 / 1057 / 1703 / 2320	4.6 / 1.2 / 4.7 / 1.2	28 TU	0449 / 1101 / 1715 / 2335	4.1 / 1.7 / 4.3 / 1.7
14 TU	0528 / 1149 / 1751	4.8 / 1.1 / 4.9	29 W	0533 / 1145 / 1752	4.3 / 1.6 / 4.5
15 W	0013 / 0618 / 1238 / ○ 1835	1.0 / 4.8 / 1.0 / 5.1	30 TH	0017 / 0613 / 1226 / 1826	1.4 / 4.5 / 1.4 / 4.7

JULY

Day	Time	m	Day	Time	m
1 F	0058 / 0651 / 1306 / ● 1902	1.2 / 4.6 / 1.2 / 4.9	16 SA	0139 / 0736 / 1352 / 1943	0.8 / 4.8 / 1.0 / 5.2
2 SA	0137 / 0730 / 1345 / 1938	1.0 / 4.8 / 1.0 / 5.0	17 SU	0218 / 0812 / 1430 / 2018	0.8 / 4.8 / 1.0 / 5.1
3 SU	0217 / 0811 / 1424 / 2018	0.8 / 4.8 / 0.9 / 5.1	18 M	0254 / 0845 / 1505 / 2052	0.8 / 4.7 / 1.1 / 5.0
4 M	0257 / 0853 / 1505 / 2059	0.7 / 4.8 / 0.9 / 5.1	19 TU	0329 / 0918 / 1541 / 2127	0.9 / 4.5 / 1.2 / 4.8
5 TU	0339 / 0939 / 1547 / 2145	0.7 / 4.8 / 1.0 / 5.0	20 W	0403 / 0952 / 1616 / 2203	1.1 / 4.4 / 1.4 / 4.6
6 W	0423 / 1028 / 1632 / 2236	0.8 / 4.6 / 1.2 / 4.8	21 TH	0438 / 1029 / 1653 / 2245	1.3 / 4.2 / 1.7 / 4.3
7 TH	0510 / 1125 / 1722 / 2336	1.0 / 4.5 / 1.4 / 4.6	22 F	0516 / 1114 / 1735 / 2338	1.6 / 4.0 / 1.9 / 4.1
8 F	0604 / 1228 / 1821 / ◑	1.3 / 4.3 / 1.6	23 SA	0558 / 1218 / 1826 / ☽	1.8 / 3.8 / 2.2
9 SA	0046 / 0705 / 1337 / 1930	4.4 / 1.5 / 4.2 / 1.8	24 SU	0049 / 0650 / 1337 / 1936	3.9 / 2.1 / 3.8 / 2.3
10 SU	0201 / 0819 / 1448 / 2050	4.3 / 1.7 / 4.2 / 1.8	25 M	0206 / 0801 / 1453 / 2104	3.8 / 2.2 / 3.8 / 2.3
11 M	0319 / 0937 / 1556 / 2209	4.2 / 1.7 / 4.4 / 1.7	26 TU	0320 / 0925 / 1559 / 2218	3.8 / 2.2 / 4.0 / 2.1
12 TU	0431 / 1045 / 1655 / 2315	4.3 / 1.6 / 4.6 / 1.5	27 W	0423 / 1031 / 1649 / 2312	4.0 / 2.0 / 4.2 / 1.8
13 W	0529 / 1141 / 1744	4.5 / 1.4 / 4.8	28 TH	0513 / 1123 / 1731 / 2358	4.2 / 1.7 / 4.5 / 1.5
14 TH	0010 / 0617 / 1230 / 1827	1.2 / 4.6 / 1.2 / 5.0	29 F	0555 / 1207 / 1808	4.5 / 1.4 / 4.8
15 F	0057 / 0659 / 1313 / ○ 1906	1.0 / 4.7 / 1.1 / 5.1	30 SA	0039 / 0634 / 1248 / ● 1843	1.1 / 4.8 / 1.1 / 5.1
			31 SU	0120 / 0712 / 1328 / 1920	0.8 / 5.0 / 0.9 / 5.3

AUGUST

Day	Time	m	Day	Time	m
1 M	0200 / 0750 / 1408 / 1958	0.5 / 5.1 / 0.7 / 5.4	16 TU	0227 / 0812 / 1439 / 2020	0.8 / 4.8 / 1.0 / 5.1
2 TU	0239 / 0830 / 1448 / 2039	0.4 / 5.2 / 0.6 / 5.4	17 W	0257 / 0839 / 1510 / 2050	0.9 / 4.7 / 1.1 / 4.9
3 W	0319 / 0913 / 1528 / 2122	0.4 / 5.1 / 0.7 / 5.3	18 TH	0328 / 0908 / 1542 / 2122	1.0 / 4.6 / 1.3 / 4.7
4 TH	0401 / 0959 / 1611 / 2211	0.6 / 4.9 / 0.9 / 5.0	19 F	0359 / 0939 / 1615 / 2158	1.2 / 4.4 / 1.5 / 4.4
5 F	0445 / 1053 / 1659 / 2310	0.9 / 4.6 / 1.2 / 4.7	20 SA	0433 / 1016 / 1652 / 2243	1.5 / 4.2 / 1.8 / 4.2
6 SA	0534 / 1158 / 1754 / ◑	1.3 / 4.4 / 1.6	21 SU	0510 / 1105 / 1736 / ◐ 2349	1.8 / 4.0 / 2.1 / 3.9
7 SU	0026 / 0634 / 1314 / 1904	4.3 / 1.7 / 4.2 / 1.9	22 M	0556 / 1227 / 1837	2.1 / 3.8 / 2.4
8 M	0152 / 0754 / 1434 / 2038	4.1 / 2.0 / 4.2 / 2.0	23 TU	0121 / 0700 / 1404 / 2013	3.7 / 2.3 / 3.8 / 2.4
9 TU	0321 / 0927 / 1549 / 2209	4.1 / 2.0 / 4.3 / 1.9	24 W	0245 / 0840 / 1522 / 2148	3.8 / 2.4 / 3.9 / 2.2
10 W	0433 / 1040 / 1649 / 2314	4.2 / 1.8 / 4.5 / 1.6	25 TH	0356 / 1004 / 1641 / 2249	4.0 / 2.1 / 4.2 / 1.8
11 TH	0527 / 1134 / 1735	4.4 / 1.6 / 4.8	26 F	0450 / 1100 / 1705 / 2335	4.3 / 1.8 / 4.6 / 1.4
12 F	0004 / 0608 / 1219 / 1814	1.3 / 4.6 / 1.3 / 5.0	27 SA	0533 / 1145 / 1743	4.6 / 1.4 / 5.0
13 SA	0045 / 0643 / 1258 / ○ 1848	1.1 / 4.7 / 1.1 / 5.1	28 SU	0016 / 0610 / 1226 / 1819	1.0 / 5.0 / 1.0 / 5.3
14 SU	0122 / 0715 / 1333 / 1920	0.9 / 4.8 / 1.0 / 5.2	29 M	0057 / 0648 / 1306 / ● 1856	0.6 / 5.2 / 0.7 / 5.6
15 M	0155 / 0744 / 1407 / 1950	0.8 / 4.9 / 0.9 / 5.2	30 TU	0136 / 0725 / 1346 / 1935	0.3 / 5.4 / 0.5 / 5.7
			31 W	0215 / 0804 / 1426 / 2015	0.2 / 5.5 / 0.4 / 5.6

Chart Datum: 2·75 metres below Ordnance Datum (Newlyn)
HAT is 5·9 metres above Chart Datum

TIME ZONE (UT)	SCOTLAND – ULLAPOOL	Dates in amber are SPRINGS
For Summer Time add ONE hour in non-shaded areas	LAT 57°54′N LONG 5°10′W	Dates in yellow are NEAPS
	TIMES AND HEIGHTS OF HIGH AND LOW WATERS	2011

SEPTEMBER

Day	Time m	Time m	Time m	Time m		Day	Time m	Time m	Time m	Time m
1 TH	0255 0.3	0846 5.3	1507 0.5	2059 5.4		16 F	0254 1.1	0832 4.8	1510 1.3	2049 4.8
2 F	0336 0.5	0931 5.1	1550 0.8	2149 5.0		17 SA	0324 1.3	0902 4.6	1542 1.5	2125 4.5
3 SA	0419 0.9	1024 4.7	1637 1.2	2252 4.6		18 SU	0356 1.5	0936 4.4	1618 1.8	2208 4.2
4 SU	0508 1.4	1133 4.4	1733 1.6			19 M	0432 1.8	1020 4.2	1700 2.0	2310 4.0
5 M	0017 4.2	0608 1.9	1256 4.2	1848 2.0		20 TU	0515 2.1	1129 3.9	1757 2.3	
6 TU	0150 4.0	0736 2.2	1339 4.1	2033 2.1		21 W	0045 3.8	0616 2.4	1319 3.8	1929 2.4
7 W	0319 4.0	0918 2.2	1538 4.3	2206 1.9		22 TH	0213 3.8	0757 2.4	1442 4.0	2114 2.2
8 TH	0427 4.2	1029 1.9	1636 4.5	2303 1.6		23 F	0325 4.0	0932 2.2	1546 4.3	2218 1.8
9 F	0515 4.4	1118 1.7	1719 4.7	2346 1.3		24 SA	0421 4.3	1031 1.8	1634 4.6	2306 1.3
10 SA	0551 4.6	1159 1.4	1754 4.9			25 SU	0505 4.7	1118 1.4	1715 5.0	2348 0.9
11 SU	0023 1.1	0621 4.8	1236 1.2	1825 5.1		26 M	0545 5.1	1200 1.0	1754 5.4	
12 M	0057 1.0	0649 4.9	1309 1.0	1854 5.2		27 TU	0029 0.5	0622 5.4	1242 0.6	1832 5.7
13 TU	0127 0.9	0715 4.9	1340 1.0	1922 5.2		28 W	0110 0.3	0700 5.6	1323 0.4	1912 5.8
14 W	0156 0.9	0740 4.9	1410 1.0	1950 5.1		29 TH	0150 0.2	0739 5.6	1404 0.4	1955 5.7
15 TH	0225 0.9	0805 4.9	1440 1.1	2018 5.0		30 F	0231 0.3	0821 5.5	1447 0.5	2041 5.4

OCTOBER

Day	Time m	Time m	Time m	Time m		Day	Time m	Time m	Time m	Time m
1 SA	0313 0.7	0907 5.2	1532 0.8	2134 5.0		16 SU	0255 1.3	0835 4.8	1518 1.5	2104 4.6
2 SU	0357 1.1	1001 4.8	1621 1.2	2242 4.5		17 M	0327 1.5	0911 4.6	1554 1.7	2149 4.3
3 M	0446 1.6	1112 4.5	1719 1.7			18 TU	0404 1.8	0955 4.3	1637 1.9	2251 4.1
4 TU	0008 4.2	0547 2.0	1236 4.3	1834 2.0		19 W	0449 2.1	1059 4.1	1733 2.2	
5 W	0137 4.0	0715 2.3	1400 4.2	2015 2.1		20 TH	0015 3.9	0549 2.3	1235 4.0	1854 2.3
6 TH	0301 4.0	0853 2.3	1515 4.3	2141 2.0		21 F	0137 3.9	0718 2.4	1359 4.1	2029 2.1
7 F	0406 4.1	1003 2.1	1611 4.4	2236 1.7		22 SA	0248 4.1	0851 2.2	1505 4.3	2139 1.7
8 SA	0452 4.3	1052 1.8	1654 4.6	2318 1.5		23 SU	0347 4.4	0956 1.8	1559 4.7	2232 1.3
9 SU	0527 4.5	1133 1.5	1729 4.8	2354 1.3		24 M	0436 4.8	1047 1.4	1646 5.1	2319 0.9
10 M	0556 4.7	1209 1.3	1800 5.0			25 TU	0518 5.1	1133 1.1	1729 5.4	
11 TU	0026 1.1	0622 4.9	1242 1.2	1828 5.0		26 W	0002 0.6	0558 5.4	1218 0.7	1811 5.6
12 W	0057 1.0	0647 5.0	1314 1.1	1856 5.1		27 TH	0046 0.5	0638 5.6	1302 0.6	1855 5.7
13 TH	0126 1.0	0712 5.0	1344 1.1	1925 5.0		28 F	0128 0.4	0720 5.6	1346 0.5	1941 5.5
14 F	0155 1.1	0738 5.0	1414 1.2	1955 4.9		29 SA	0211 0.6	0803 5.5	1432 0.6	2030 5.3
15 SA	0224 1.2	0805 4.9	1445 1.3	2027 4.8		30 SU	0254 0.9	0850 5.3	1518 0.9	2125 4.9
						31 M	0340 1.2	0944 5.0	1609 1.3	2230 4.5

NOVEMBER

Day	Time m	Time m	Time m	Time m		Day	Time m	Time m	Time m	Time m
1 TU	0429 1.7	1049 4.7	1705 1.6	2345 4.2		16 W	0347 1.7	0944 4.6	1624 1.7	2236 4.3
2 W	0527 2.0	1203 4.4	1812 1.9			17 TH	0433 1.9	1041 4.4	1717 1.9	2345 4.2
3 TH	0103 4.0	0640 2.3	1321 4.3	1931 2.1		18 F	0529 2.1	1154 4.3	1824 2.0	
4 F	0222 4.0	0805 2.4	1434 4.2	2051 2.1		19 SA	0058 4.1	0642 2.2	1313 4.3	1941 1.9
5 SA	0329 4.1	0920 2.2	1535 4.3	2153 1.9		20 SU	0208 4.2	0803 2.2	1423 4.4	2055 1.7
6 SU	0419 4.2	1016 2.0	1622 4.5	2240 1.7		21 M	0311 4.5	0915 1.9	1525 4.7	2157 1.5
7 M	0457 4.4	1101 1.8	1700 4.6	2320 1.6		22 TU	0406 4.7	1015 1.6	1620 4.9	2251 1.2
8 TU	0529 4.6	1140 1.6	1734 4.8	2355 1.4		23 W	0455 5.1	1109 1.3	1710 5.2	2340 1.0
9 W	0558 4.6	1215 1.5	1806 4.9			24 TH	0540 5.3	1159 1.0	1759 5.4	
10 TH	0027 1.3	0624 4.9	1249 1.4	1836 4.9		25 F	0026 0.8	0623 5.5	1247 0.8	1846 5.4
11 F	0059 1.2	0651 5.0	1321 1.3	1907 4.9		26 SA	0112 0.8	0707 5.6	1335 0.7	1934 5.4
12 SA	0130 1.2	0719 5.0	1354 1.3	1940 4.9		27 SU	0156 0.8	0751 5.5	1421 0.8	2023 5.2
13 SU	0201 1.3	0748 5.0	1427 1.3	2014 4.8		28 M	0241 1.0	0838 5.4	1508 0.9	2114 4.9
14 M	0234 1.4	0821 4.9	1502 1.4	2054 4.6		29 TU	0325 1.3	0926 5.1	1556 1.2	2207 4.6
15 TU	0309 1.5	0858 4.8	1540 1.6	2140 4.5		30 W	0412 1.6	1019 4.9	1645 1.5	2305 4.3

DECEMBER

Day	Time m	Time m	Time m	Time m		Day	Time m	Time m	Time m	Time m
1 TH	0501 1.9	1118 4.6	1738 1.8			16 F	0419 1.6	1021 4.8	1659 1.5	2312 4.5
2 F	0008 4.1	0557 2.1	1224 4.3	1836 2.0		17 SA	0509 1.8	1119 4.6	1754 1.7	
3 SA	0119 4.0	0703 2.3	1333 4.2	1942 2.1		18 SU	0018 4.4	0608 2.0	1230 4.5	1858 1.8
4 SU	0232 4.0	0817 2.4	1441 4.2	2051 2.2		19 M	0127 4.3	0718 2.1	1344 4.5	2011 1.8
5 M	0334 4.1	0927 2.3	1540 4.2	2152 2.1		20 TU	0236 4.4	0835 2.0	1455 4.6	2123 1.7
6 TU	0422 4.3	1024 2.1	1628 4.4	2242 1.9		21 W	0340 4.6	0948 1.8	1602 4.7	2228 1.5
7 W	0501 4.5	1110 1.9	1709 4.5	2323 1.7		22 TH	0438 4.9	1052 1.6	1703 4.9	2325 1.3
8 TH	0535 4.6	1150 1.8	1746 4.7			23 F	0529 5.1	1149 1.3	1756 5.1	
9 F	0001 1.6	0606 4.8	1228 1.6	1821 4.8		24 SA	0015 1.2	0615 5.4	1241 1.0	1844 5.2
10 SA	0036 1.5	0636 4.9	1304 1.4	1855 4.8		25 SU	0102 1.0	0659 5.5	1328 0.9	1929 5.2
11 SU	0111 1.4	0706 5.0	1339 1.3	1929 4.9		26 M	0146 1.0	0741 5.5	1413 0.8	2012 5.1
12 M	0145 1.3	0737 5.1	1415 1.3	2005 4.9		27 TU	0228 1.0	0823 5.5	1456 0.9	2054 5.0
13 TU	0220 1.3	0815 5.0	1451 1.3	2044 4.8		28 W	0309 1.1	0904 5.3	1537 1.0	2135 4.8
14 W	0256 1.4	0849 5.0	1530 1.3	2127 4.7		29 TH	0350 1.3	0945 5.1	1618 1.3	2217 4.5
15 TH	0336 1.5	0932 4.9	1612 1.4	2215 4.5		30 F	0431 1.6	1029 4.8	1659 1.5	2302 4.3
						31 SA	0514 1.9	1118 4.5	1743 1.8	2358 4.1

Chart Datum: 2·75 metres below Ordnance Datum (Newlyn)
HAT is 5·9 metres above Chart Datum

TIDES

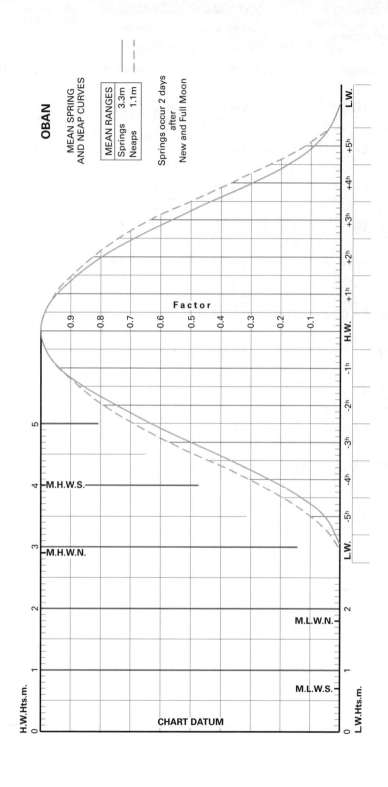

OBAN

MEAN SPRING
AND NEAP CURVES

MEAN RANGES	
Springs	3.3m
Neaps	1.1m

Springs occur 2 days
after
New and Full Moon

SCOTLAND – OBAN

LAT 56°25′N   LONG 5°29′W

Dates in amber are **SPRINGS**
Dates in yellow are **NEAPS**

2011

TIMES AND HEIGHTS OF HIGH AND LOW WATERS

JANUARY

Time	m		Time	m
1 SA 0320	3.4	**16** SU 0249	3.1
0916	1.4	0853	1.9
1550	3.4	1540	3.3
2200	1.4	2118	1.6
2 SU 0410	3.6	**17** M 0346	3.3
1019	1.3	1006	1.6
1636	3.5	1626	3.5
2248	1.3	2210	1.3
3 M 0451	3.8	**18** TU 0433	3.6
1111	1.2	1058	1.4
1714	3.6	1707	3.7
2330	1.1	2256	1.0
4 TU 0530	3.9	**19** W 0514	3.8
1156	1.2	1142	1.1
1749	3.7	1745	3.9
●		2339	0.7
5 W 0009	1.0	**20** TH 0554	4.0
0608	4.0	1224	0.9
1237	1.2	1820	4.0
1823	3.8		
6 TH 0048	1.0	**21** F 0021	0.5
0644	4.1	0631	4.2
1316	1.2	1304	0.7
1856	3.8	1855	4.0
7 F 0125	1.0	**22** SA 0104	0.4
0720	4.1	0710	4.2
1352	1.3	1345	0.7
1928	3.8	1932	3.9
8 SA 0201	1.1	**23** SU 0148	0.4
0754	4.0	0749	4.1
1427	1.4	1426	0.8
2000	3.7	2010	3.8
9 SU 0236	1.2	**24** M 0232	0.5
0829	3.8	0829	4.0
1501	1.5	1509	0.9
2032	3.6	2052	3.6
10 M 0310	1.4	**25** TU 0319	0.7
0903	3.7	0913	3.7
1538	1.7	1556	1.2
2105	3.4	2138	3.4
11 TU 0345	1.6	**26** W 0410	0.9
0940	3.5	1001	3.4
1619	1.8	1650	1.4
2141	3.3	2233	3.2
12 W 0425	1.8	**27** TH 0509	1.2
1021	3.3	1104	3.1
1708	1.9	1756	1.6
◑ 2225	3.1	2355	3.0
13 TH 0514	2.0	**28** F 0618	1.5
1117	3.1	1253	2.9
1807	2.0	1915	1.8
2323	3.0		
14 F 0617	2.1	**29** SA 0145	3.0
1303	2.9	0738	1.6
1912	2.0	1502	2.9
		2045	1.7
15 SA 0111	2.9	**30** SU 0312	3.1
0731	2.1	0911	1.6
1442	3.1	1620	3.1
2018	1.9	2153	1.5
		31 M 0407	3.4
		1020	1.5
		1653	3.3
		2241	1.3

FEBRUARY

Time	m		Time	m
1 TU 0445	3.6	**16** W 0418	3.5
1108	1.3	1047	1.2
1714	3.5	1654	3.6
2321	1.1	2238	0.9
2 W 0520	3.8	**17** TH 0459	3.9
1147	1.2	1129	0.9
1741	3.6	1729	3.8
2358	1.0	2322	0.5
3 TH 0554	4.0	**18** F 0538	4.1
1223	1.1	1209	0.6
1810	3.8	1803	4.0
●		○	
4 F 0033	0.9	**19** SA 0005	0.3
0628	4.1	0615	4.3
1256	1.1	1247	0.4
1839	3.9	1837	4.1
5 SA 0107	0.9	**20** SU 0048	0.1
0700	4.1	0652	4.3
1328	1.1	1325	0.4
1908	3.9	1912	4.1
6 SU 0139	0.9	**21** M 0131	0.1
0731	4.0	0730	4.2
1359	1.1	1403	0.5
1936	3.8	1949	3.9
7 M 0208	1.1	**22** TU 0214	0.2
0801	3.9	0808	4.0
1428	1.3	1444	0.7
2003	3.7	2028	3.7
8 TU 0234	1.3	**23** W 0300	0.5
0829	3.7	0857	3.7
1456	1.4	1528	1.0
2031	3.6	2110	3.5
9 W 0259	1.5	**24** TH 0349	0.9
0857	3.5	0931	3.3
1527	1.6	1619	1.3
2102	3.4	◑ 2201	3.2
10 TH 0326	1.7	**25** F 0446	1.2
0929	3.3	1025	2.9
1607	1.8	1722	1.6
2138	3.2	2316	2.9
11 F 0403	1.9	**26** SA 0554	1.5
1011	3.1	1226	2.7
1706	1.9	1841	1.7
◑ 2225	3.0		
12 SA 0511	2.0	**27** 0123	2.8
1117	2.9	0721	1.7
1821	2.0	SU 1529	2.7
2337	2.9	2025	1.7
13 0651	2.1	**28** 0307	3.0
1424	2.9	0913	1.7
SU 1938	1.9	M 1625	2.9
		2139	1.5
14 0222	2.9		
0832	1.9		
M 1530	3.1		
2048	1.6		
15 0312	3.2		
0957	1.6		
TU 1615	3.4		
2148	1.3		

MARCH

Time	m		Time	m
1 0358	3.2	**16** 0306	3.2
1015	1.5	0934	1.4
TU 1652	3.1	W 1553	3.3
2226	1.3	2121	1.2
2 0427	3.5	**17** 0354	3.6
1055	1.3	1024	1.1
W 1656	3.3	TH 1631	3.6
2304	1.1	2214	0.8
3 0459	3.7	**18** 0436	3.9
1128	1.1	1106	0.7
TH 1719	3.6	F 1706	3.8
2339	0.9	2301	0.4
4 0532	3.9	**19** 0515	4.1
1159	1.0	1145	0.5
F 1747	3.8	SA 1739	4.0
●		○ 2345	0.1
5 0011	0.8	**20** 0553	4.3
0604	4.0	1223	0.3
SA 1229	0.9	SU 1814	4.1
1815	3.9		
6 0043	0.8	**21** 0029	0.0
0635	4.0	0631	4.3
SU 1259	0.9	M 1301	0.3
1842	3.9	1850	4.1
7 0112	0.9	**22** 0113	0.1
0704	4.0	0708	4.1
M 1328	1.0	TU 1340	0.4
1908	3.9	1927	4.0
8 0138	1.0	**23** 0157	0.2
0732	3.9	0746	3.9
TU 1355	1.1	W 1421	0.6
1934	3.8	2007	3.8
9 0200	1.2	**24** 0242	0.5
0757	3.7	0825	3.6
W 1419	1.2	TH 1505	0.9
2000	3.7	2049	3.5
10 0219	1.4	**25** 0331	0.9
0823	3.5	0906	3.2
TH 1445	1.4	F 1555	1.2
2030	3.5	◑ 2138	3.2
11 0244	1.5	**26** 0427	1.3
0853	3.3	0957	2.8
F 1522	1.6	SA 1655	1.5
2105	3.3	◑ 2249	2.9
12 0320	1.7	**27** 0534	1.6
0933	3.1	1152	2.5
SA 1616	1.8	SU 1810	1.7
◑ 2150	3.1		
13 0420	1.9	**28** 0057	2.8
1036	2.8	0703	1.8
SU 1737	1.9	M 1503	2.6
2301	2.9	1950	1.7
14 0627	2.0	**29** 0234	2.9
1359	1.7	0853	1.7
M 1901	1.8	TU 1557	2.8
		2108	1.5
15 0146	2.9	**30** 0325	3.1
0817	1.8	0949	1.5
TU 1507	3.0	W 1615	3.0
2017	1.5	2158	1.3
		31 0358	3.4
		1026	1.3
		TH 1622	3.2
		2238	1.1

APRIL

Time	m		Time	m
1 0430	3.6	**16** 0407	3.9
1058	1.1	1038	0.7
F 1647	3.5	SA 1638	3.8
2312	1.0	2237	0.5
2 0503	3.7	**17** 0449	4.1
1127	1.0	1119	0.5
SA 1717	3.7	SU 1714	4.0
2344	0.9	2324	0.3
3 0536	3.9	**18** 0530	4.2
1156	0.9	1158	0.4
SU 1746	3.8	M 1751	4.1
●		○	
4 0013	0.9	**19** 0010	0.2
0607	3.9	0609	4.1
M 1226	0.9	TU 1238	0.4
1814	3.9	1830	4.1
5 0042	0.9	**20** 0055	0.2
0637	3.9	0648	4.0
TU 1256	0.9	W 1319	0.5
1841	3.8	1909	4.0
6 0109	1.0	**21** 0141	0.4
0705	3.8	0727	3.8
W 1324	1.0	TH 1400	0.7
1908	3.8	1950	3.8
7 0133	1.2	**22** 0227	0.7
0731	3.6	0807	3.4
TH 1349	1.1	F 1445	0.9
1936	3.7	2034	3.6
8 0155	1.5	**23** 0316	1.0
0800	3.5	0849	3.1
F 1420	1.3	SA 1534	1.2
2008	3.5	2123	3.3
9 0224	1.5	**24** 0409	1.4
0834	3.3	0939	2.8
SA 1459	1.4	SU 1630	1.4
2045	3.3	2225	3.0
10 0307	1.6	**25** 0512	1.6
0919	3.0	1055	2.6
SU 1552	1.6	M 1735	1.6
2135	3.2	◑	
11 0416	1.8	**26** 0004	2.9
1026	2.8	0629	1.8
M 1705	1.7	TU 1338	2.6
◑ 2249	3.0	1856	1.6
12 0612	1.8	**27** 0142	2.9
1308	2.7	0800	1.7
TU 1826	1.6	W 1443	2.7
		2020	1.6
13 0052	3.0	**28** 0240	3.1
0750	1.7	0903	1.6
W 1432	2.9	TH 1513	2.9
1942	1.4	2119	1.4
14 0228	3.3	**29** 0320	3.2
0901	1.3	0945	1.4
TH 1522	3.2	F 1540	3.1
2050	1.1	2202	1.3
15 0322	3.6	**30** 0356	3.3
0953	1.0	1019	1.3
F 1602	3.5	SA 1612	3.3
2147	0.8	2239	1.2

TIDES

Chart Datum: 2·10 metres below Ordnance Datum (Newlyn)
HAT is 4·5 metres above Chart Datum

TIDES

TIME ZONE (UT)
For Summer Time add ONE hour in **non-shaded areas**

SCOTLAND – OBAN
LAT 56°25'N   LONG 5°29'W

Dates in amber are SPRINGS
Dates in yellow are NEAPS

2011

TIMES AND HEIGHTS OF HIGH AND LOW WATERS

MAY

Day	Time m	Time m	Time m	Time m		Day	Time m	Time m	Time m	Time m
1 SU	0431 3.6	1050 1.1	1644 3.5	2311 1.1		16 M	0427 3.9	1054 0.7	1653 3.9	2305 0.5
2 M	0506 3.7	1121 1.0	1716 3.7	2341 1.1		17 TU	0510 3.9	1137 0.6	1734 4.0	2354 0.5
3 TU ●	0541 3.8	1154 0.9	1748 3.7			18 W	0553 3.9	1219 0.6	1815 4.0	
4 W	0013 1.1	0613 3.8	1226 0.9	1817 3.8		19 TH	0041 0.5	0634 3.8	1301 0.6	1856 4.0
5 TH	0045 1.1	0644 3.7	1258 1.0	1848 3.7		20 F	0128 0.7	0714 3.6	1344 0.8	1938 3.8
6 F	0116 1.2	0715 3.6	1330 1.0	1921 3.7		21 SA	0214 0.9	0755 3.4	1428 0.9	2021 3.7
7 SA	0148 1.3	0749 3.4	1406 1.1	1957 3.6		22 SU	0300 1.1	0836 3.2	1513 1.1	2106 3.4
8 SU	0225 1.4	0829 3.3	1448 1.2	2040 3.4		23 M	0349 1.4	0920 3.0	1602 1.3	2156 3.2
9 M	0314 1.5	0918 3.1	1540 1.3	2132 3.3		24 TU ◑	0442 1.6	1013 2.8	1655 1.5	2257 3.1
10 TU ◑	0423 1.6	1021 2.9	1642 1.4	2240 3.2		25 W	0540 1.7	1126 2.7	1754 1.6	
11 W	0550 1.6	1149 2.8	1754 1.4			26 TH	0016 3.0	0645 1.8	1306 2.7	1900 1.7
12 TH	0007 3.2	0713 1.5	1341 3.0	1907 1.3		27 F	0136 3.0	0751 1.7	1408 2.8	2010 1.7
13 F	0141 3.3	0824 1.3	1443 3.2	2016 1.1		28 SA	0232 3.1	0847 1.6	1453 3.0	2110 1.6
14 SA	0247 3.5	0921 0.9	1531 3.4	2118 0.9		29 SU	0318 3.2	0932 1.5	1533 3.2	2156 1.5
15 SU	0340 3.5	1010 0.9	1612 3.7	2214 0.7		30 M	0359 3.4	1011 1.3	1612 3.4	2234 1.4
						31 TU	0440 3.5	1048 1.2	1650 3.5	2312 1.3

JUNE

Day	Time m	Time m	Time m	Time m		Day	Time m	Time m	Time m	Time m
1 W ●	0519 3.6	1125 1.0	1727 3.6	2350 1.2		16 TH	0545 3.7	1206 0.8	1806 4.0	
2 TH	0557 3.7	1201 0.9	1802 3.7			17 F	0031 0.8	0626 3.7	1249 0.8	1846 4.0
3 F	0028 1.1	0632 3.7	1238 0.9	1837 3.7		18 SA	0117 0.9	0705 3.6	1330 0.8	1926 3.9
4 SA	0108 1.1	0707 3.6	1315 0.9	1913 3.7		19 SU	0200 1.0	0742 3.5	1411 0.9	2005 3.8
5 SU	0147 1.1	0743 3.5	1355 0.9	1952 3.7		20 M	0241 1.2	0819 3.4	1451 1.1	2044 3.6
6 M	0230 1.2	0824 3.4	1439 1.0	2036 3.6		21 TU	0323 1.3	0855 3.2	1531 1.3	2125 3.5
7 TU	0318 1.3	0911 3.2	1527 1.0	2125 3.5		22 W	0405 1.5	0934 3.1	1614 1.4	2208 3.3
8 W	0414 1.4	1005 3.1	1622 1.1	2223 3.4		23 TH ◑	0451 1.7	1018 3.0	1700 1.6	2259 3.1
9 TH	0521 1.4	1112 3.0	1725 1.2	2333 3.3		24 F	0542 1.8	1114 2.9	1751 1.8	
10 F	0634 1.5	1237 3.0	1834 1.2			25 SA	0005 3.0	0640 1.8	1234 2.8	1849 1.8
11 SA	0057 3.3	0745 1.4	1402 3.1	1945 1.2		26 SU	0127 3.0	0741 1.8	1356 2.9	1953 1.8
12 SU	0217 3.3	0850 1.3	1505 3.3	2053 1.1		27 M	0239 3.1	0841 1.7	1458 3.0	2101 1.8
13 M	0320 3.5	0946 1.1	1556 3.5	2156 1.0		28 TU	0334 3.2	0934 1.5	1547 3.2	2202 1.6
14 TU	0414 3.6	1036 1.0	1641 3.7	2252 0.9		29 W	0422 3.4	1020 1.3	1632 3.4	2252 1.4
15 W ○	0502 3.7	1122 0.9	1724 3.9	2343 0.8		30 TH	0505 3.5	1102 1.1	1713 3.6	2336 1.2

JULY

Day	Time m	Time m	Time m	Time m		Day	Time m	Time m	Time m	Time m
1 F ●	0546 3.6	1141 0.9	1752 3.7			16 SA	0021 1.0	0618 3.7	1236 0.8	1834 4.0
2 SA	0018 1.0	0623 3.7	1221 0.8	1829 3.9		17 SU	0102 0.9	0651 3.7	1314 0.8	1909 4.0
3 SU	0059 0.9	0659 3.7	1301 0.6	1906 3.9		18 M	0140 1.0	0723 3.7	1351 0.9	1944 3.9
4 M	0140 0.9	0734 3.7	1342 0.6	1944 3.9		19 TU	0216 1.1	0754 3.6	1425 1.0	2017 3.8
5 TU	0222 0.9	0812 3.6	1425 0.6	2025 3.8		20 W	0250 1.2	0824 3.5	1458 1.2	2051 3.6
6 W	0306 1.0	0854 3.4	1511 0.7	2110 3.7		21 TH	0326 1.4	0856 3.4	1533 1.4	2125 3.4
7 TH	0354 1.1	0942 3.3	1602 0.9	2200 3.5		22 F	0405 1.6	0931 3.2	1612 1.6	2203 3.2
8 F ◑	0450 1.3	1039 3.1	1700 1.1	2301 3.3		23 SA ◑	0451 1.8	1013 3.1	1658 1.8	2251 3.1
9 SA	0557 1.4	1154 3.0	1807 1.3			24 SU	0547 1.8	1107 2.9	1756 2.0	
10 SU	0022 3.1	0710 1.5	1332 3.0	1919 1.4		25 M	0011 2.9	0650 1.9	1249 2.8	1904 2.0
11 M	0200 3.1	0825 1.5	1452 3.2	2035 1.4		26 TU	0209 2.9	0758 1.8	1432 2.9	2024 1.9
12 TU	0319 3.2	0933 1.3	1552 3.4	2147 1.3		27 W	0321 3.1	0903 1.6	1533 3.1	2147 1.7
13 W	0421 3.3	1028 1.2	1639 3.6	2247 1.1		28 TH	0410 3.3	0957 1.4	1619 3.4	2243 1.4
14 TH	0506 3.5	1114 1.0	1719 3.8	2337 1.0		29 F	0453 3.5	1043 1.1	1701 3.7	2326 1.1
15 F ○	0544 3.6	1156 0.9	1757 4.0			30 SA ●	0533 3.7	1124 0.8	1740 3.9	
						31 SU	0006 0.9	0609 3.8	1204 0.5	1816 4.0

AUGUST

Day	Time m	Time m	Time m	Time m		Day	Time m	Time m	Time m	Time m
1 M	0046 0.7	0642 3.9	1244 0.4	1852 4.1		16 TU	0112 0.9	0657 3.8	1326 0.8	1916 4.0
2 TU	0124 0.6	0715 3.9	1326 0.3	1929 4.1		17 W	0145 1.0	0725 3.8	1356 1.0	1947 3.9
3 W	0203 0.6	0751 3.8	1408 0.4	2007 4.0		18 TH	0216 1.1	0752 3.7	1425 1.2	2016 3.8
4 TH	0245 0.8	0831 3.6	1453 0.5	2048 3.8		19 F	0248 1.3	0820 3.6	1454 1.4	2045 3.5
5 F	0330 0.9	0915 3.4	1543 0.8	2134 3.5		20 SA	0322 1.5	0852 3.4	1525 1.6	2116 3.3
6 SA ◑	0422 1.2	1008 3.2	1639 1.1	2229 3.2		21 SU ◑	0403 1.7	0928 3.2	1604 1.9	2154 3.1
7 SU	0526 1.4	1122 3.0	1745 1.3	2355 2.9		22 M	0458 1.9	1015 3.0	1707 2.1	2252 2.9
8 M	0642 1.6	1319 3.0	1902 1.5			23 TU	0608 1.9	1130 2.8	1833 2.1	
9 TU	0204 2.9	0809 1.6	1450 3.1	2029 1.6		24 W	0156 2.8	0722 1.9	1418 2.9	2008 2.0
10 W	0346 3.0	0927 1.4	1553 3.3	2151 1.4		25 TH	0309 3.0	0835 1.7	1520 3.2	2138 1.7
11 TH	0437 3.2	1021 1.2	1633 3.6	2245 1.3		26 F	0356 3.3	0934 1.3	1603 3.5	2227 1.3
12 F	0505 3.4	1104 1.0	1707 3.8	2327 1.1		27 SA	0436 3.5	1021 1.0	1642 3.8	2308 0.7
13 SA ○	0530 3.6	1142 0.8	1740 4.0			28 SU	0512 3.7	1103 0.6	1719 4.1	2346 0.7
14 SU	0004 1.0	0559 3.7	1219 0.8	1813 4.1		29 M ●	0546 3.9	1144 0.4	1755 4.2	
15 M	0039 0.9	0629 3.8	1254 0.7	1846 4.1		30 TU	0024 0.5	0618 4.0	1225 0.2	1831 4.3
						31 W	0101 0.4	0651 4.0	1307 0.2	1907 4.2

Chart Datum: 2·10 metres below Ordnance Datum (Newlyn)
HAT is 4·5 metres above Chart Datum

SCOTLAND – OBAN
LAT 56°25′N   LONG 5°29′W
TIMES AND HEIGHTS OF HIGH AND LOW WATERS

Dates in amber are **SPRINGS**
Dates in yellow are **NEAPS**

2011

SEPTEMBER

Day	Time m	Time m	Time m	Time m
1 TH	0140 0.5	0727 4.0	1350 0.2	1944 4.1
16 F	0142 1.1	0721 3.8	1353 1.2	1944 3.8
2 F	0220 0.6	0807 3.8	1435 0.5	2024 3.8
17 SA	0212 1.2	0749 3.7	1417 1.5	2011 3.6
3 SA	0305 0.9	0850 3.5	1525 0.8	2108 3.4
18 SU	0242 1.4	0819 3.5	1442 1.7	2040 3.4
4 SU ☽	0357 1.2	0942 3.3	1621 1.2	2200 3.1
19 M	0317 1.6	0854 3.3	1514 1.9	2116 3.1
5 M	0459 1.4	1058 3.0	1728 1.5	2335 2.7
20 TU ☽	0410 1.8	1019 3.0	1619 2.1	2212 2.9
6 TU	0617 1.6	1312 2.9	1849 1.7	
21 W	0525 1.9	1050 2.9	1812 2.2	
7 W	0234 2.7	0754 1.6	1446 3.1	2035 1.7
22 TH	0138 2.8	0645 1.9	1352 3.2	1955 2.0
8 TH	0354 2.9	0912 1.4	1543 3.3	2148 1.5
23 F	0246 3.0	0800 1.7	1454 3.3	2112 1.7
9 F	0433 3.1	1004 1.2	1615 3.6	2232 1.3
24 SA	0333 3.3	0902 1.2	1537 3.6	2201 1.3
10 SA	0443 3.3	1045 1.0	1644 3.8	2307 1.2
25 SU	0411 3.5	0953 1.0	1615 3.9	2242 0.8
11 SU	0503 3.5	1121 0.9	1715 4.0	2339 1.0
26 M	0446 3.8	1038 0.6	1653 4.2	2320 0.7
12 M ○	0531 3.7	1155 0.8	1746 4.1	
27 TU ●	0518 4.0	1121 0.3	1730 4.3	2358 0.5
13 TU	0009 0.9	0559 3.9	1228 0.8	1817 4.1
28 W	0552 4.1	1204 0.2	1807 4.4	
14 W	0041 0.9	0627 3.9	1258 0.9	1847 4.1
29 TH	0036 0.4	0627 4.2	1248 0.2	1844 4.3
15 TH	0112 1.0	0654 3.9	1326 1.0	1916 4.0
30 F	0115 0.4	0705 4.1	1332 0.3	1922 4.1

OCTOBER

Day	Time m	Time m	Time m	Time m
1 SA	0157 0.6	0746 3.9	1419 0.6	2002 3.7
16 SU	0142 1.2	0724 3.8	1351 1.5	1946 3.6
2 SU	0242 0.9	0830 3.7	1509 0.9	2045 3.4
17 M	0212 1.4	0756 3.6	1417 1.7	2018 3.4
3 M	0334 1.2	0922 3.4	1605 1.3	2136 3.0
18 TU	0248 1.6	0832 3.4	1455 1.9	2057 3.2
4 TU ☽	0434 1.4	1037 3.1	1712 1.6	2308 2.7
19 W	0336 1.7	0919 3.3	1601 2.1	2156 2.9
5 W	0549 1.6	1254 3.0	1835 1.8	
20 TH ☽	0443 1.8	1028 3.1	1749 2.1	2350 2.8
6 TH	0221 2.7	0723 1.7	1423 3.2	2021 1.8
21 F	0602 1.8	1235 3.1	1924 2.0	
7 F	0331 2.9	0843 1.5	1515 3.3	2124 1.6
22 SA	0210 3.0	0717 1.7	1413 3.4	2035 1.7
8 SA	0404 3.1	0936 1.3	1545 3.5	2204 1.4
23 SU	0301 3.2	0824 1.4	1503 3.7	2127 1.3
9 SU	0407 3.3	1018 1.2	1614 3.7	2237 1.3
24 M	0341 3.5	0921 1.0	1545 3.9	2211 1.0
10 M	0430 3.5	1055 1.0	1645 3.9	2307 1.1
25 TU	0416 3.8	1012 0.7	1625 4.2	2252 0.8
11 TU	0500 3.7	1128 1.0	1717 4.0	2337 1.0
26 W ●	0451 4.0	1059 0.5	1704 4.3	2332 0.6
12 W ○	0529 3.9	1159 1.0	1748 4.1	
27 TH	0528 4.2	1145 0.4	1744 4.3	
13 TH	0008 1.0	0558 4.0	1229 1.1	1819 4.1
28 F	0012 0.5	0607 4.2	1231 0.4	1823 4.2
14 F	0040 1.0	0627 4.0	1258 1.2	1849 4.0
29 SA	0054 0.5	0647 4.2	1317 0.5	1904 4.0
15 SA	0112 1.1	0655 3.9	1326 1.4	1918 3.8
30 SU	0137 0.7	0730 4.0	1404 0.8	1945 3.7
31 M	0223 0.9	0815 3.8	1454 1.1	2028 3.4

NOVEMBER

Day	Time m	Time m	Time m	Time m
1 TU	0313 1.2	0906 3.5	1549 1.4	2117 3.1
16 W	0230 1.4	0821 3.6	1453 1.8	2050 3.3
2 W ●	0409 1.4	1010 3.3	1650 1.7	2224 2.8
17 TH	0315 1.5	0908 3.5	1551 1.9	2144 3.1
3 TH	0514 1.6	1202 3.1	1804 1.9	
18 F ☽	0411 1.6	1008 3.4	1713 1.9	2256 3.0
4 F	0106 2.7	0633 1.7	1335 3.2	1930 1.9
19 SA	0519 1.6	1128 3.3	1837 1.9	
5 SA	0229 2.8	0756 1.7	1431 3.3	2040 1.8
20 SU	0048 3.0	0632 1.6	1309 3.4	1950 1.7
6 SU	0302 3.0	0859 1.5	1510 3.4	2125 1.6
21 M	0216 3.2	0743 1.4	1422 3.6	2050 1.5
7 M	0326 3.2	0947 1.4	1543 3.6	2200 1.5
22 TU	0306 3.5	0849 1.2	1515 3.8	2141 1.2
8 TU	0356 3.4	1026 1.3	1615 3.8	2232 1.3
23 W	0349 3.7	0947 1.0	1602 4.0	2227 1.0
9 W	0428 3.6	1100 1.3	1649 3.9	2305 1.2
24 TH	0430 3.9	1040 0.8	1646 4.1	2311 0.8
10 TH	0501 3.8	1131 1.2	1723 4.0	2338 1.1
25 F ●	0511 4.1	1130 0.7	1728 4.1	2354 0.7
11 F	0534 3.9	1203 1.3	1757 4.0	
26 SA	0553 4.2	1218 0.7	1810 4.1	
12 SA	0012 1.1	0605 3.9	1236 1.3	1829 3.9
27 SU	0038 0.7	0635 4.2	1306 0.8	1851 3.9
13 SU	0046 1.1	0637 3.9	1308 1.4	1901 3.8
28 M	0122 0.8	0719 4.1	1353 0.9	1933 3.7
14 M	0119 1.2	0709 3.8	1340 1.5	1933 3.7
29 TU	0207 0.9	0803 3.9	1440 1.2	2014 3.5
15 TU	0152 1.3	0742 3.7	1412 1.7	2008 3.5
30 W	0253 1.1	0849 3.7	1528 1.4	2056 3.3

DECEMBER

Day	Time m	Time m	Time m	Time m
1 TH	0342 1.3	0939 3.5	1620 1.7	2144 3.1
16 F	0258 1.2	0855 3.7	1534 1.6	2125 3.3
2 F ●	0434 1.5	1038 3.3	1716 1.8	2245 2.9
17 SA	0347 1.3	0946 3.6	1633 1.7	2221 3.2
3 SA	0533 1.7	1202 3.2	1819 2.0	
18 SU ☽	0445 1.4	1048 3.4	1745 1.7	2332 3.1
4 SU	0024 2.9	0641 1.8	1331 3.2	1926 1.9
19 M	0553 1.5	1208 3.4	1901 1.7	
5 M	0147 2.9	0758 1.8	1427 3.3	2027 1.8
20 TU	0106 3.1	0707 1.5	1341 3.4	2012 1.6
6 TU	0238 3.1	0905 1.8	1510 3.4	2116 1.7
21 W	0232 3.3	0820 1.4	1454 3.5	2114 1.4
7 W	0320 3.3	0955 1.7	1548 3.5	2157 1.5
22 TH	0331 3.6	0928 1.2	1551 3.7	2209 1.2
8 TH	0400 3.5	1035 1.6	1626 3.7	2235 1.4
23 F	0420 3.8	1028 1.0	1639 3.8	2258 1.0
9 F	0438 3.7	1110 1.5	1705 3.8	2312 1.2
24 SA ●	0504 4.0	1121 0.9	1723 3.9	2343 0.9
10 SA ○	0515 3.8	1144 1.4	1742 3.9	2349 1.1
25 SU	0546 4.1	1210 0.9	1804 3.9	
11 SU	0551 3.9	1220 1.4	1818 3.9	
26 M	0027 0.8	0627 4.2	1256 0.9	1843 3.9
12 M	0025 1.1	0625 3.9	1257 1.4	1851 3.8
27 TU	0110 0.8	0708 4.2	1340 1.0	1921 3.8
13 TU	0101 1.1	0659 3.9	1333 1.4	1924 3.7
28 W	0152 0.9	0747 4.1	1422 1.1	1957 3.7
14 W	0137 1.1	0734 3.8	1409 1.4	1959 3.6
29 TH	0232 1.0	0826 3.9	1502 1.3	2032 3.5
15 TH	0215 1.1	0812 3.8	1447 1.5	2039 3.5
30 F	0313 1.2	0906 3.7	1543 1.5	2108 3.3
31 SA	0355 1.4	0947 3.5	1627 1.7	2148 3.2

Chart Datum: 2·10 metres below Ordnance Datum (Newlyn)
HAT is 4·5 metres above Chart Datum

TIDES

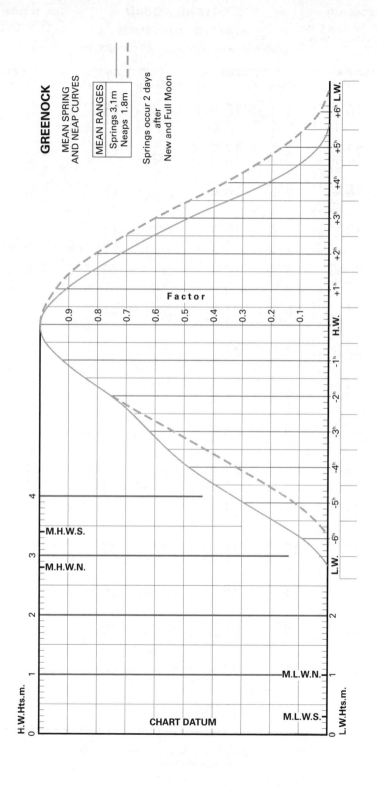

GREENOCK

MEAN SPRING
AND NEAP CURVES

MEAN RANGES
Springs 3.1m
Neaps 1.8m

Springs occur 2 days
after
New and Full Moon

| TIME ZONE (UT) | SCOTLAND – GREENOCK | Dates in amber are SPRINGS |
For Summer Time add ONE hour in **non-shaded areas**
LAT 55°57′N LONG 4°46′W
Dates in yellow are NEAPS
2011
TIMES AND HEIGHTS OF HIGH AND LOW WATERS

JANUARY

Day	Time m	Time m	Time m	Time m		Day	Time m	Time m	Time m	Time m
1 SA	0247 0.8	0953 3.2	1528 0.7	2205 3.2		**16** SU	0238 1.0	0910 3.0	1500 1.1	2149 2.9
2 SU	0346 0.8	1050 3.3	1622 0.6	2308 3.3		**17** M	0335 0.9	1016 3.1	1556 0.9	2252 3.1
3 M	0437 0.7	1138 3.5	1709 0.4			**18** TU	0422 0.7	1106 3.3	1642 0.6	2344 3.2
4 TU	0001 3.3	0523 0.7	1222 3.6	●1751 0.4		**19** W	0506 0.6	1149 3.5	1724 0.4	○
5 W	0048 3.3	0604 0.7	1302 3.7	1830 0.3		**20**	0031 3.3	0547 0.5	1232 3.7	1805 0.2
6 TH	0128 3.3	0642 0.7	1339 3.7	1907 0.4		**21** F	0117 3.4	0629 0.4	1314 3.8	1847 0.1
7 F	0205 3.2	0718 0.7	1415 3.7	1943 0.4		**22** SA	0201 3.4	0713 0.3	1357 3.9	1931 0.1
8 SA	0240 3.2	0753 0.7	1449 3.6	2020 0.5		**23** SU	0244 3.4	0758 0.3	1441 3.9	2016 0.1
9 SU	0315 3.2	0830 0.7	1525 3.6	2100 0.6		**24** M	0326 3.4	0845 0.3	1524 3.9	2104 0.2
10 M	0352 3.2	0908 0.8	1601 3.5	2142 0.7		**25** TU	0407 3.4	0934 0.4	1608 3.8	2155 0.3
11 TU	0431 3.2	0949 0.9	1640 3.3	2228 0.8		**26** W	0449 3.3	1028 0.5	1654 3.6	●2251 0.5
12 W	0511 3.1	1033 1.0	1723 3.2	●2321 0.9		**27** TH	0535 3.2	1129 0.7	1743 3.4	2357 0.8
13 TH	0555 3.0	1125 1.2	1814 3.0			**28** F	0629 3.0	1245 0.9	1842 3.1	
14 F	0022 1.0	0647 3.0	1230 1.3	1916 2.9		**29** SA	0117 1.0	0757 2.9	1407 1.0	2019 2.9
15 SA	0131 1.1	0753 3.0	1346 1.3	2031 2.9		**30** SU	0234 1.0	0935 3.0	1516 0.7	2207 2.9
						31 M	0337 0.9	1038 3.2	1611 0.5	2308 3.0

FEBRUARY

Day	Time m	Time m	Time m	Time m		Day	Time m	Time m	Time m	Time m
1 TU	0429 0.8	1127 3.4	1658 0.4	2357 3.1		**16** W	0401 0.7	1042 3.2	1621 0.5	2330 3.1
2 W	0513 0.7	1210 3.5	1739 0.3			**17** TH	0446 0.5	1129 3.4	1704 0.2	
3 TH	0039 3.2	0552 0.6	1250 3.6	●1814 0.3		**18** F	0017 3.3	0528 0.3	1214 3.6	○1745 0.0
4 F	0115 3.2	0626 0.6	1325 3.6	1847 0.3		**19** SA	0101 3.3	0609 0.1	1259 3.7	1826 -0.1
5 SA	0146 3.2	0656 0.6	1357 3.6	1918 0.4		**20** SU	0144 3.4	0652 0.1	1343 3.8	1909 -0.1
6 SU	0216 3.2	0726 0.6	1428 3.6	1950 0.4		**21** M	0225 3.4	0736 0.0	1426 3.9	1953 -0.1
7 M	0248 3.3	0758 0.5	1459 3.5	2024 0.5		**22** TU	0304 3.5	0822 0.1	1509 3.9	2039 0.1
8 TU	0321 3.3	0832 0.6	1532 3.5	2059 0.5		**23** W	0342 3.4	0909 0.2	1551 3.7	2128 0.3
9 W	0354 3.3	0909 0.6	1608 3.3	2139 0.7		**24** TH	0420 3.3	1001 0.3	1633 3.5	◐2221 0.6
10 TH	0429 3.2	0950 0.8	1647 3.2	2224 0.8		**25** F	0502 3.2	1103 0.6	1719 3.2	2328 0.9
11 F	0507 3.1	1038 0.9	1733 3.0	◐2319 1.0		**26** SA	0550 3.0	1225 0.8	1812 2.9	
12 SA	0552 2.9	1137 1.1	1831 2.8			**27** SU	0058 1.1	0705 2.8	1351 0.8	2005 2.6
13 SU	0027 1.1	0651 2.8	1250 1.2	1947 2.7		**28** M	0219 1.1	0915 2.8	1459 0.7	2204 2.7
14 M	0151 1.1	0814 2.8	1418 1.1	2124 2.8						
15 TU	0306 1.0	0942 3.0	1530 0.8	2238 3.0						

MARCH

Day	Time m	Time m	Time m	Time m		Day	Time m	Time m	Time m	Time m
1 TU	0322 1.0	1019 3.1	1553 0.5	2257 2.9		**16** W	0234 0.9	0904 2.9	1459 0.6	2218 2.9
2 W	0413 0.8	1107 3.3	1638 0.3	2340 3.0		**17** TH	0335 0.7	1013 3.2	1553 0.3	2309 3.1
3 TH	0456 0.6	1150 3.4	1718 0.2			**18** F	0422 0.4	1105 3.4	1639 0.0	2354 3.3
4 F	0017 3.1	0532 0.5	1229 3.5	●1751 0.2		**19** SA	0506 0.1	1152 3.6	1721 -0.1	○
5 SA	0050 3.2	0603 0.5	1304 3.5	1821 0.3		**20** SU	0038 3.4	0548 0.0	1239 3.7	1803 -0.2
6 SU	0119 3.2	0630 0.5	1334 3.4	1850 0.3		**21** M	0120 3.4	0630 -0.1	1324 3.8	1846 -0.2
7 M	0148 3.3	0657 0.5	1403 3.4	1918 0.4		**22** TU	0200 3.5	0714 -0.1	1409 3.8	1930 -0.1
8 TU	0218 3.3	0726 0.4	1433 3.4	1949 0.4		**23** W	0239 3.5	0759 -0.1	1452 3.7	2016 0.1
9 W	0248 3.4	0759 0.4	1505 3.4	2023 0.4		**24** TH	0316 3.5	0846 0.0	1534 3.6	2104 0.3
10 TH	0319 3.4	0836 0.4	1540 3.3	2102 0.5		**25** F	0355 3.4	0939 0.2	1616 3.3	2157 0.6
11 F	0352 3.3	0918 0.6	1618 3.1	2148 0.7		**26** SA	0436 3.2	1042 0.5	1702 3.0	◐2303 0.9
12 SA	0427 3.2	1006 0.7	1701 2.9	◐2242 0.9		**27** SU	0524 3.0	1206 0.6	1756 2.7	
13 SU	0509 3.0	1105 0.9	1756 2.7	2348 1.1		**28** M	0031 1.1	0633 2.8	1326 0.7	1954 2.5
14 M	0604 2.8	1216 1.0	1914 2.6			**29** TU	0151 1.1	0840 2.8	1431 0.6	2139 2.6
15 TU	0110 1.1	0724 2.8	1342 0.9	2102 2.7		**30** W	0255 1.0	0949 3.0	1524 0.4	2229 2.8
						31 TH	0347 0.8	1038 3.2	1609 0.3	2309 3.0

APRIL

Day	Time m	Time m	Time m	Time m		Day	Time m	Time m	Time m	Time m
1 F	0430 0.6	1121 3.3	1648 0.2	2345 3.1		**16** SA	0356 0.3	1037 3.4	1611 0.0	2327 3.3
2 SA	0506 0.5	1159 3.3	1722 0.2			**17** SU	0443 0.1	1127 3.5	1656 -0.1	
3 SU	0017 3.2	0536 0.5	1235 3.3	●1752 0.2		**18** M	0011 3.4	0526 -0.1	1217 3.6	○1740 -0.1
4 M	0048 3.2	0602 0.5	1306 3.3	1820 0.3		**19** TU	0054 3.4	0610 -0.1	1304 3.6	1824 -0.1
5 TU	0117 3.3	0628 0.4	1336 3.3	1848 0.4		**20** W	0135 3.5	0654 -0.1	1351 3.6	1909 0.1
6 W	0147 3.4	0657 0.4	1407 3.3	1920 0.4		**21** TH	0214 3.5	0739 -0.1	1435 3.5	1956 0.2
7 TH	0217 3.4	0731 0.4	1440 3.3	1956 0.4		**22** F	0253 3.5	0827 0.0	1518 3.4	2045 0.5
8 F	0248 3.5	0810 0.4	1517 3.2	2038 0.5		**23** SA	0333 3.4	0920 0.2	1602 3.2	2138 0.7
9 SA	0321 3.4	0855 0.4	1556 3.1	2126 0.7		**24** SU	0416 3.2	1021 0.4	1650 2.9	2238 0.9
10 SU	0358 3.4	0946 0.6	1640 2.9	2222 0.8		**25** M	0505 3.0	1135 0.5	1746 2.7	◐2351 1.1
11 M	0439 3.1	1046 0.7	1735 2.8	2326 1.0		**26** TU	0609 2.8	1249 0.6	1904 2.6	
12 TU	0533 3.0	1155 0.7	1851 2.7			**27** W	0107 1.1	0744 2.8	1352 0.5	2041 2.6
13 W	0041 1.0	0648 2.9	1313 0.6	2031 2.7		**28** TH	0215 1.0	0904 2.9	1446 0.5	2140 2.8
14 TH	0159 0.9	0826 2.9	1425 0.4	2148 2.9		**29** F	0310 0.9	0959 3.0	1532 0.4	2225 2.9
15 F	0304 0.6	0941 3.2	1522 0.2	2240 3.1		**30** SA	0356 0.7	1044 3.2	1612 0.3	2304 3.1

TIDES

Chart Datum: 1·62 metres below Ordnance Datum (Newlyn)
HAT is 3·9 metres above Chart Datum

TIDES

TIME ZONE (UT)	SCOTLAND – GREENOCK	Dates in amber are SPRINGS
For Summer Time add ONE hour in non-shaded areas	LAT 55°57'N LONG 4°46'W	Dates in yellow are NEAPS
		2011

TIMES AND HEIGHTS OF HIGH AND LOW WATERS

MAY

Day	Time m	Time m	Time m	Time m
1 SU	0434 0.6	1124 3.2	1649 0.3	2340 3.2
2 M	0507 0.5	1201 3.2	1722 0.4	
3 TU ●	0014 3.3	0535 0.5	1235 3.2	1752 0.4
4 W	0047 3.3	0604 0.4	1308 3.2	1824 0.4
5 TH	0117 3.4	0635 0.4	1342 3.2	1858 0.5
6 F	0149 3.5	0712 0.3	1419 3.2	1938 0.5
7 SA	0223 3.5	0753 0.3	1459 3.2	2023 0.5
8 SU	0259 3.5	0839 0.4	1541 3.1	2113 0.6
9 M	0338 3.4	0931 0.4	1628 3.0	2208 0.7
10 TU ◑	0422 3.3	1031 0.5	1723 2.9	2308 0.8
11 W	0515 3.1	1136 0.5	1831 2.8	
12 TH	0015 0.8	0624 3.0	1246 0.5	1953 2.8
13 F	0125 0.8	0751 3.1	1352 0.3	2108 2.9
14 SA	0232 0.6	0907 3.2	1452 0.2	2207 3.1
15 SU	0330 0.4	1009 3.3	1545 0.1	2258 3.2
16 M	0421 0.2	1104 3.4	1634 0.1	2346 3.3
17 TU ○	0508 0.0	1155 3.5	1720 0.1	
18 W	0030 3.4	0553 -0.1	1246 3.5	1806 0.2
19 TH	0114 3.5	0638 -0.1	1334 3.4	1853 0.3
20 F	0155 3.5	0723 0.0	1421 3.3	1939 0.4
21 SA	0235 3.5	0810 0.1	1505 3.2	2027 0.5
22 SU	0315 3.5	0859 0.2	1550 3.1	2116 0.7
23 M	0357 3.3	0953 0.3	1636 2.9	2208 0.8
24 TU ◑	0444 3.2	1054 0.5	1726 2.8	2304 0.9
25 W	0537 3.0	1159 0.6	1822 2.7	
26 TH	0007 1.0	0642 2.9	1302 0.6	1922 2.7
27 F	0115 1.1	0757 2.8	1359 0.6	2027 2.8
28 SA	0219 1.0	0904 2.9	1449 0.5	2126 2.9
29 SU	0313 0.9	0958 3.0	1534 0.5	2217 3.0
30 M	0358 0.8	1045 3.0	1615 0.5	2302 3.2
31 TU	0437 0.6	1126 3.1	1653 0.5	2342 3.3

JUNE

Day	Time m	Time m	Time m	Time m
1 W ●	0512 0.6	1205 3.1	1729 0.5	
2 TH	0017 3.4	0545 0.5	1243 3.1	1804 0.5
3 F	0051 3.5	0619 0.4	1322 3.1	1843 0.5
4 SA	0127 3.5	0657 0.3	1403 3.1	1925 0.5
5 SU	0204 3.6	0740 0.3	1445 3.2	2011 0.5
6 M	0243 3.6	0827 0.3	1530 3.1	2100 0.5
7 TU	0324 3.6	0918 0.3	1617 3.1	2153 0.5
8 W	0409 3.5	1013 0.3	1709 3.0	2248 0.6
9 TH	0500 3.4	1114 0.4	1806 3.0	2348 0.7
10 F	0600 3.2	1217 0.4	1913 2.9	
11 SA	0054 0.7	0714 3.1	1323 0.4	2026 2.9
12 SU	0202 0.6	0834 3.1	1425 0.4	2135 3.0
13 M	0307 0.5	0945 3.2	1523 0.3	2234 3.2
14 TU	0404 0.3	1046 3.3	1617 0.3	2326 3.3
15 W ○	0455 0.2	1142 3.3	1707 0.3	
16 TH	0013 3.4	0542 0.1	1235 3.3	1754 0.4
17 F	0058 3.5	0626 0.0	1324 3.2	1839 0.4
18 SA	0140 3.5	0709 0.0	1409 3.2	1923 0.5
19 SU	0219 3.5	0751 0.1	1452 3.1	2007 0.5
20 M	0258 3.5	0835 0.2	1532 3.0	2050 0.6
21 TU	0337 3.4	0920 0.3	1613 3.0	2134 0.7
22 W	0417 3.3	1010 0.4	1655 2.9	2220 0.8
23 TH ◑	0501 3.1	1104 0.5	1739 2.9	2310 0.9
24 F	0549 3.0	1202 0.6	1827 2.9	2348 0.7
25 SA	0006 1.0	0644 2.9	1303 0.6	1920 2.8
26 SU	0111 1.1	0749 2.8	1402 0.7	2021 2.9
27 M	0220 1.0	0900 2.8	1455 0.7	2125 3.0
28 TU	0320 0.9	1003 2.9	1544 0.6	2223 3.1
29 W	0409 0.8	1055 3.0	1628 0.6	2311 3.2
30 TH ○	0451 0.6	1141 3.0	1708 0.5	2351 3.3

JULY

Day	Time m	Time m	Time m	Time m
1 F ●	0529 0.5	1224 3.1	1747 0.5	
2 SA	0029 3.5	0605 0.3	1307 3.1	1827 0.4
3 SU	0108 3.6	0644 0.2	1350 3.1	1910 0.4
4 M	0148 3.7	0726 0.1	1434 3.2	1955 0.4
5 TU	0229 3.7	0810 0.1	1517 3.2	2042 0.3
6 W	0311 3.7	0859 0.1	1602 3.2	2132 0.4
7 TH	0355 3.7	0951 0.2	1648 3.2	2224 0.4
8 F ◑	0442 3.5	1047 0.3	1737 3.1	2321 0.5
9 SA	0533 3.3	1149 0.4	1833 3.0	
10 SU	0025 0.7	0637 3.1	1256 0.5	1944 2.9
11 M	0138 0.7	0800 3.0	1406 0.6	2108 2.9
12 TU	0251 0.6	0930 3.0	1511 0.6	2218 3.1
13 W	0354 0.5	1041 3.1	1608 0.4	2314 3.3
14 TH	0447 0.3	1139 3.1	1659 0.5	
15 F ○	0002 3.4	0532 0.1	1230 3.1	1744 0.5
16 SA	0047 3.5	0614 0.1	1315 3.1	1826 0.5
17 SU	0126 3.5	0653 0.1	1355 3.1	1904 0.5
18 M	0203 3.5	0729 0.1	1431 3.1	1941 0.5
19 TU	0238 3.5	0806 0.2	1505 3.1	2018 0.5
20 W	0312 3.5	0844 0.3	1540 3.1	2056 0.6
21 TH	0347 3.4	0926 0.4	1618 3.1	2136 0.6
22 F	0424 3.3	1012 0.6	1657 3.1	2220 0.8
23 SA ◑	0504 3.1	1104 0.7	1739 3.0	2308 0.9
24 SU	0552 2.9	1203 0.9	1826 2.9	
25 M	0007 1.1	0651 2.8	1310 0.9	1922 2.9
26 TU	0120 1.2	0803 2.7	1417 0.9	2031 2.9
27 W	0241 1.1	0925 2.8	1516 0.8	2144 3.0
28 TH	0343 0.8	1031 3.0	1605 0.7	2241 3.2
29 F	0430 0.6	1124 3.0	1648 0.5	2327 3.3
30 SA ●	0510 0.4	1209 3.1	1728 0.4	
31 SU	0008 3.5	0547 0.2	1253 3.2	1807 0.3

AUGUST

Day	Time m	Time m	Time m	Time m
1 M	0050 3.6	0626 0.1	1335 3.2	1849 0.3
2 TU	0132 3.7	0706 0.0	1417 3.2	1933 0.2
3 W	0214 3.8	0749 0.0	1459 3.3	2019 0.2
4 TH	0257 3.8	0835 0.0	1540 3.3	2107 0.2
5 F	0340 3.8	0924 0.2	1621 3.3	2159 0.3
6 SA ◑	0423 3.6	1019 0.4	1705 3.2	2255 0.5
7 SU	0511 3.4	1121 0.6	1755 3.0	
8 M	0003 0.7	0605 3.1	1237 0.8	1902 2.9
9 TU	0124 0.8	0726 2.8	1356 0.9	2050 2.9
10 W	0242 0.7	0936 2.8	1505 0.8	2208 3.1
11 TH	0345 0.5	1044 3.0	1601 0.7	2303 3.3
12 F	0436 0.3	1135 3.1	1649 0.6	2349 3.4
13 SA ○	0519 0.2	1219 3.1	1731 0.5	
14 SU	0031 3.5	0557 0.1	1258 3.1	1808 0.5
15 M	0109 3.5	0632 0.2	1332 3.1	1841 0.5
16 TU	0143 3.5	0703 0.2	1401 3.1	1912 0.5
17 W	0214 3.5	0734 0.3	1432 3.2	1944 0.5
18 TH	0245 3.5	0808 0.4	1504 3.2	2018 0.5
19 F	0316 3.4	0844 0.5	1539 3.3	2055 0.6
20 SA	0350 3.3	0922 0.6	1615 3.2	2136 0.7
21 SU ◑	0428 3.2	1007 0.8	1654 3.1	2221 0.9
22 M	0512 3.0	1102 1.0	1739 3.0	2317 1.1
23 TU	0609 2.7	1213 1.1	1835 2.9	
24 W	0027 1.2	0722 2.6	1337 1.1	1944 2.9
25 TH	0159 1.1	0856 2.7	1448 1.0	2105 3.0
26 F	0315 0.9	1016 2.9	1541 0.9	2212 3.2
27 SA	0405 0.5	1107 3.1	1624 0.6	2302 3.4
28 SU ○	0446 0.3	1150 3.2	1705 0.3	2346 3.6
29 M ●	0524 0.1	1232 3.3	1745 0.2	
30 TU	0030 3.7	0603 0.1	1314 3.3	1826 0.1
31 W	0114 3.8	0643 -0.1	1355 3.4	1910 0.1

Chart Datum: 1·62 metres below Ordnance Datum (Newlyn)
HAT is 3·9 metres above Chart Datum

SCOTLAND – GREENOCK
LAT 55°57'N   LONG 4°46'W
TIMES AND HEIGHTS OF HIGH AND LOW WATERS

2011

SEPTEMBER

Time	m	Time	m
1 0158	3.9	**16** 0216	3.5
0726	-0.1	0734	0.5
TH 1435	3.4	F 1429	3.4
1955	0.1	1943	0.5
2 0241	3.9	**17** 0248	3.4
0811	0.1	0807	0.5
F 1514	3.4	SA 1502	3.4
2043	0.2	2020	0.6
3 0323	3.8	**18** 0322	3.4
0859	0.3	0844	0.6
SA 1554	3.4	SU 1537	3.4
2134	0.4	2101	0.7
4 0405	3.6	**19** 0359	3.2
0952	0.5	0927	0.8
SU 1637	3.3	M 1614	3.3
◑ 2234	0.5	2147	0.8
5 0450	3.3	**20** 0442	3.0
1057	0.8	1020	1.0
M 1726	3.1	TU 1658	3.1
2349	0.7	◐ 2243	1.0
6 0543	2.9	**21** 0536	2.8
1224	1.0	1127	1.2
TU 1832	2.9	W 1753	3.0
		2351	1.1
7 0115	0.8	**22** 0650	2.7
0710	2.7	1252	1.2
W 1347	1.1	TH 1903	2.9
2034	2.9		
8 0229	0.7	**23** 0118	1.1
0937	2.6	0830	2.7
TH 1453	1.0	F 1414	1.1
2151	3.1	2026	3.0
9 0328	0.5	**24** 0238	0.8
1033	2.9	0952	2.9
F 1547	0.8	SA 1511	0.8
2243	3.3	2139	3.2
10 0417	0.3	**25** 0333	0.5
1118	3.1	1043	3.2
SA 1632	0.6	SU 1558	0.5
2328	3.4	2233	3.5
11 0459	0.2	**26** 0417	0.2
1157	3.2	1126	3.3
SU 1712	0.5	M 1640	0.3
		2321	3.6
12 0008	3.6	**27** 0458	0.0
0534	0.2	1207	3.4
M 1231	3.2	TU 1722	0.2
○ 1745	0.5	●	
13 0045	3.5	**28** 0008	3.8
0606	0.2	0538	-0.1
TU 1300	3.2	W 1248	3.5
1814	0.5	1804	0.1
14 0117	3.5	**29** 0054	3.8
0635	0.3	0620	-0.1
W 1328	3.3	TH 1329	3.5
1841	0.5	1847	0.1
15 0146	3.5	**30** 0140	3.9
0703	0.4	0704	0.0
TH 1357	3.3	F 1410	3.6
1910	0.5	1933	0.1

OCTOBER

Time	m	Time	m
1 0224	3.8	**16** 0223	3.4
0749	0.2	0740	0.6
SA 1450	3.6	SU 1431	3.6
2021	0.2	1953	0.6
2 0307	3.7	**17** 0258	3.4
0837	0.4	0818	0.7
SU 1531	3.5	M 1506	3.6
2114	0.4	2035	0.7
3 0350	3.5	**18** 0337	3.3
0931	0.7	0903	0.8
M 1614	3.4	TU 1544	3.5
2216	0.6	2123	0.8
4 0437	3.2	**19** 0420	3.1
1037	1.0	0956	1.1
TU 1704	3.2	W 1626	3.3
◑ 2336	0.7	2219	0.9
5 0532	2.9	**20** 0512	2.9
1204	1.2	1059	1.2
W 1812	3.0	TH 1718	3.2
		◐ 2325	1.0
6 0057	0.8	**21** 0622	2.8
0718	2.7	1214	1.3
TH 1325	1.2	F 1826	3.1
2002	3.0		
7 0204	0.7	**22** 0042	1.0
0914	2.8	0755	2.8
F 1429	1.1	SA 1332	1.1
2120	3.1	1947	3.1
8 0301	0.6	**23** 0157	0.8
1007	3.0	0918	3.0
SA 1523	0.9	SU 1437	0.9
2214	3.3	2103	3.3
9 0349	0.4	**24** 0257	0.5
1048	3.1	1012	3.2
SU 1608	0.7	M 1529	0.6
2258	3.5	2203	3.5
10 0431	0.3	**25** 0347	0.3
1124	3.3	1058	3.4
M 1647	0.6	TU 1616	0.4
2339	3.5	2256	3.7
11 0507	0.3	**26** 0432	0.1
1156	3.3	1141	3.5
TU 1720	0.6	W 1700	0.2
		● 2346	3.8
12 0015	3.5	**27** 0516	0.1
0538	0.4	1223	3.6
W 1226	3.4	TH 1744	0.1
○ 1748	0.6		
13 0048	3.5	**28** 0035	3.8
0607	0.5	0600	0.1
TH 1256	3.5	F 1306	3.7
1814	0.6	1829	0.1
14 0118	3.5	**29** 0123	3.8
0636	0.5	0645	0.2
F 1326	3.5	SA 1348	3.7
1843	0.6	1915	0.1
15 0149	3.5	**30** 0209	3.7
0706	0.6	0732	0.4
SA 1358	3.6	SU 1430	3.7
1916	0.6	2004	0.2
		31 0254	3.6
		0820	0.6
		M 1512	3.6
		2056	0.4

NOVEMBER

Time	m	Time	m
1 0340	3.4	**16** 0321	3.3
0913	0.8	0847	0.9
TU 1557	3.5	W 1522	3.6
2157	0.6	2106	0.7
2 0428	3.2	**17** 0404	3.2
1014	1.1	0938	1.0
W 1647	3.3	TH 1605	3.5
◐ 2309	0.7	2200	0.8
3 0525	2.9	**18** 0454	3.1
1128	1.2	1036	1.1
TH 1749	3.2	F 1654	3.4
		◑ 2301	0.8
4 0024	0.8	**19** 0555	3.0
0642	2.8	1141	1.2
F 1246	1.3	SA 1754	3.3
1912	3.1		
5 0130	0.8	**20** 0008	0.8
0818	2.8	0711	2.9
SA 1353	1.2	SU 1252	1.1
2034	3.1	1908	3.3
6 0226	0.7	**21** 0118	0.7
0921	3.0	0833	3.0
SU 1450	1.1	M 1401	1.0
2134	3.3	2026	3.3
7 0315	0.6	**22** 0222	0.6
1006	3.1	0937	3.2
M 1538	0.9	TU 1501	0.7
2223	3.4	2134	3.5
8 0358	0.5	**23** 0319	0.4
1046	3.3	1030	3.4
TU 1618	0.8	W 1554	0.5
2306	3.4	2233	3.6
9 0436	0.5	**24** 0410	0.3
1121	3.4	1118	3.5
W 1654	0.7	TH 1643	0.3
2344	3.4	2327	3.7
10 0511	0.5	**25** 0458	0.3
1155	3.5	1204	3.6
TH 1724	0.7	F 1729	0.2
○			
11 0019	3.4	**26** 0019	3.7
0543	0.6	0544	0.3
F 1228	3.6	SA 1249	3.7
1753	0.7	1815	0.1
12 0053	3.4	**27** 0110	3.7
0614	0.6	0631	0.4
SA 1300	3.7	SU 1332	3.8
1823	0.7	1901	0.2
13 0127	3.4	**28** 0158	3.6
0645	0.7	0717	0.5
SU 1333	3.7	M 1415	3.8
1856	0.7	1949	0.2
14 0203	3.4	**29** 0245	3.5
0721	0.7	0805	0.6
M 1407	3.7	TU 1457	3.7
1934	0.7	2038	0.4
15 0240	3.4	**30** 0330	3.3
0802	0.8	0854	0.8
TU 1443	3.7	W 1541	3.6
2018	0.7	2131	0.6

DECEMBER

Time	m	Time	m
1 0416	3.2	**16** 0350	3.3
0945	1.0	0920	0.8
TH 1628	3.5	F 1549	3.7
2230	0.6	2139	0.6
2 0505	3.1	**17** 0435	3.2
1042	1.1	1012	0.9
F 1720	3.3	SA 1635	3.6
◐ 2335	0.8	2235	0.6
3 0559	3.0	**18** 0526	3.1
1146	1.2	1110	0.9
SA 1819	3.2	SU 1727	3.5
		◑ 2336	0.7
4 0042	0.8	**19** 0626	3.0
0659	2.9	1215	1.0
SU 1259	1.3	M 1830	3.4
1927	3.1		
5 0143	0.8	**20** 0042	0.7
0805	2.9	0742	3.0
M 1406	1.2	TU 1326	1.0
2037	3.1	1946	3.3
6 0236	0.8	**21** 0151	0.7
0909	3.1	0901	3.1
TU 1501	1.1	W 1435	0.8
2139	3.2	2106	3.3
7 0324	0.7	**22** 0256	0.7
1002	3.2	1007	3.3
W 1548	1.0	TH 1537	0.6
2230	3.2	2216	3.4
8 0407	0.7	**23** 0354	0.6
1048	3.4	1101	3.5
TH 1628	0.9	F 1630	0.4
2315	3.3	2316	3.5
9 0446	0.7	**24** 0446	0.5
1128	3.5	1150	3.6
F 1704	0.8	SA 1719	0.3
2355	3.3	●	
10 0523	0.7	**25** 0011	3.5
1205	3.6	0534	0.5
SA 1737	0.7	SU 1237	3.7
○		1805	0.2
11 0033	3.3	**26** 0103	3.5
0557	0.7	0620	0.5
SU 1239	3.7	M 1321	3.8
1808	0.7	1849	0.2
12 0110	3.3	**27** 0150	3.4
0631	0.7	0704	0.5
M 1312	3.7	TU 1403	3.8
1842	0.6	1932	0.2
13 0148	3.4	**28** 0234	3.4
0707	0.7	0747	0.6
TU 1348	3.8	W 1444	3.8
1920	0.6	2016	0.3
14 0227	3.3	**29** 0314	3.3
0748	0.7	0830	0.7
W 1426	3.8	TH 1524	3.7
2003	0.6	2100	0.4
15 0308	3.3	**30** 0354	3.3
0832	0.7	0912	0.8
TH 1506	3.8	F 1605	3.6
2049	0.6	2147	0.6
		31 0434	3.2
		0957	0.9
		SA 1647	3.4
		2239	0.7

Chart Datum: 1·62 metres below Ordnance Datum (Newlyn)
HAT is 3·9 metres above Chart Datum

TIDES

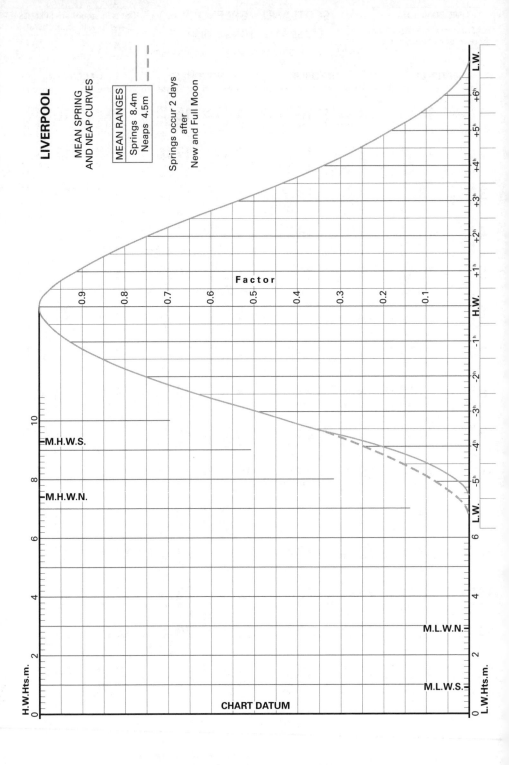

LIVERPOOL

MEAN SPRING
AND NEAP CURVES

MEAN RANGES	
Springs	8.4m
Neaps	4.5m

Springs occur 2 days
after
New and Full Moon

LIVERPOOL (GLADSTONE DOCK)

LAT 53°27'N   LONG 3°01'W

Dates in amber are **SPRINGS**
Dates in yellow are **NEAPS**

2011

TIMES AND HEIGHTS OF HIGH AND LOW WATERS

JANUARY

Day	Time	m	Time	m	Time	m	Time	m
1 SA	0242	2.4	0824	8.2	1511	2.5	2055	8.3
16 SU	0214	3.2	0803	7.6	1451	3.0	2030	7.8
2 SU	0345	2.2	0923	8.6	1614	2.1	2152	8.6
17 M	0315	2.7	0900	8.1	1549	2.5	2125	8.2
3 M	0439	2.0	1013	8.9	1708	1.9	2241	8.8
18 TU	0408	2.3	0949	8.6	1642	1.9	2213	8.7
4 TU	0526	1.9	1057	9.1	1756	1.6	● 2324	8.9
19 W	0458	1.8	1033	9.1	1733	1.4	○ 2258	9.1
5 W	0608	1.8	1137	9.3	1837	1.6		
20 TH	0546	1.4	1116	9.5	1820	1.0	2342	9.5
6 TH	0002	8.9	0645	1.8	1214	9.3	1914	1.6
21 F	0631	1.1	1159	9.8	1906	0.7		
7 F	0038	8.8	0718	1.9	1249	9.2	1947	1.7
22 SA	0025	9.6	0714	1.0	1243	9.8	1949	0.6
8 SA	0111	8.7	0749	2.0	1323	9.0	2016	1.9
23 SU	0109	9.6	0756	1.0	1326	9.9	2030	0.7
9 SU	0143	8.5	0819	2.3	1357	8.8	2044	2.1
24 M	0153	9.4	0837	1.2	1410	9.6	2111	1.1
10 M	0217	8.3	0850	2.5	1433	8.5	2115	2.4
25 TU	0238	9.1	0918	1.5	1457	9.2	2153	1.6
11 TU	0254	8.0	0925	2.9	1513	8.1	2151	2.8
26 W	0326	8.6	1003	2.0	1548	8.7	◐ 2242	2.1
12 W	0335	7.6	1008	3.2	1559	7.8	◐ 2237	3.1
27 TH	0421	8.1	1058	2.5	1651	8.1	2344	2.7
13 TH	0426	7.3	1103	3.5	1657	7.4	2338	3.4
28 F	0530	7.7	1210	2.9	1809	7.7		
14 F	0534	7.1	1218	3.7	1810	7.3		
29 SA	0104	3.0	0651	7.6	1340	3.0	1935	7.6
15 SA	0058	3.4	0652	7.2	1342	3.5	1925	7.4
30 SU	0226	2.9	0810	7.8	1504	2.7	2051	7.9
31 M	0335	2.6	0914	8.2	1611	2.3	2148	8.2

FEBRUARY

Day	Time	m	Time	m	Time	m	Time	m
1 TU	0431	2.2	1004	8.7	1703	1.9	2234	8.5
16 W	0347	2.3	0927	8.5	1624	1.7	2155	8.7
2 W	0517	1.9	1046	9.0	1745	1.6	2312	8.8
17 TH	0441	1.7	1014	9.2	1716	1.1	2240	9.3
3 TH	0555	1.7	1122	9.2	1821	1.5	○ 2345	8.9
18 F	0530	1.1	1057	9.7	1804	0.6	○ 2324	9.7
4 F	0628	1.6	1155	9.3	1853	1.4		
19 SA	0616	0.7	1140	10.0	1848	0.2		
5 SA	0016	8.9	0657	1.6	1227	9.3	1920	1.5
20 SU	0006	9.9	0658	0.5	1223	10.2	1929	0.2
6 SU	0045	8.9	0724	1.7	1257	9.2	1946	1.6
21 M	0048	9.9	0739	0.5	1306	10.1	2009	0.4
7 M	0114	8.8	0752	1.8	1328	9.0	2012	1.8
22 TU	0130	9.6	0818	0.8	1348	9.8	2048	0.9
8 TU	0144	8.6	0821	2.1	1358	8.7	2040	2.1
23 W	0212	9.3	0857	1.2	1433	9.3	2127	1.5
9 W	0213	8.3	0853	2.4	1430	8.4	2112	2.4
24 TH	0258	8.7	0940	1.8	1522	8.6	◐ 2212	2.2
10 TH	0246	8.0	0928	2.8	1506	8.0	2149	2.9
25 F	0351	8.1	1034	2.5	1624	7.9	2312	2.9
11 F	0327	7.6	1013	3.2	1554	7.5	2239	3.3
26 SA	0501	7.6	1149	3.0	1748	7.3		
12 SA	0425	7.2	1118	3.6	1706	7.1	2355	3.6
27 SU	0039	3.3	0627	7.4	1328	3.1	1923	7.3
13 SU	0552	7.0	1253	3.6	1838	7.1		
28 M	0211	3.2	0753	7.6	1454	2.8	2041	7.6
14 M	0131	3.4	0722	7.3	1419	3.1	2001	7.5
15 TU	0246	2.9	0832	7.8	1526	2.4	2104	8.1

MARCH

Day	Time	m	Time	m	Time	m	Time	m
1 TU	0323	2.7	0859	8.1	1558	2.3	2135	8.1
16 W	0215	2.9	0801	7.9	1459	2.3	2038	8.1
2 W	0417	2.3	0947	8.5	1646	1.9	2216	8.4
17 TH	0321	2.2	0859	8.6	1600	1.5	2131	8.8
3 TH	0459	1.9	1026	8.8	1724	1.6	2250	8.7
18 F	0417	1.6	0948	9.2	1653	0.9	2217	9.4
4 F	0533	1.7	1059	9.1	1755	1.5	● 2321	8.9
19 SA	0508	1.0	1033	9.7	1740	0.4	○ 2300	9.7
5 SA	0603	1.5	1130	9.2	1823	1.4	2349	9.0
20 SU	0554	0.6	1117	10.1	1824	0.1	2342	9.9
6 SU	0631	1.5	1200	9.2	1849	1.4		
21 M	0637	0.3	1200	10.2	1906	0.1		
7 M	0017	9.0	0658	1.5	1230	9.2	1915	1.4
22 TU	0024	9.9	0718	0.4	1244	10.0	1945	0.4
8 TU	0045	8.9	0726	1.6	1259	9.0	1942	1.6
23 W	0106	9.7	0759	0.6	1327	9.7	2024	0.9
9 W	0112	8.7	0755	1.8	1328	8.8	2010	1.9
24 TH	0149	9.3	0839	1.1	1412	9.1	2103	1.6
10 TH	0140	8.5	0826	2.1	1358	8.5	2041	2.2
25 F	0234	8.8	0923	1.8	1502	8.4	2147	2.4
11 F	0211	8.2	0900	2.5	1433	8.1	2115	2.7
26 SA	0327	8.2	1017	2.4	1604	7.7	◐ 2246	3.1
12 SA	0249	7.8	0941	2.9	1520	7.4	◐ 2201	3.1
27 SU	0435	7.6	1133	3.0	1725	7.2		
13 SU	0344	7.4	1040	3.3	1627	7.2	2311	3.5
28 M	0013	3.4	0558	7.4	1306	3.1	1857	7.1
14 M	0509	7.1	1213	3.4	1801	7.1		
29 TU	0144	3.3	0722	7.5	1426	2.8	2015	7.5
15 TU	0050	3.4	0645	7.0	1347	3.0	1930	7.5
30 W	0254	2.9	0828	7.9	1527	2.3	2108	7.9
31 TH	0347	2.5	0917	8.3	1613	2.0	2148	8.3

APRIL

Day	Time	m	Time	m	Time	m	Time	m
1 F	0428	2.1	0955	8.6	1650	1.8	2221	8.6
16 SA	0347	1.6	0919	9.2	1624	0.9	2150	9.3
2 SA	0502	1.8	1029	8.9	1721	1.6	2251	8.8
17 SU	0440	1.1	1007	9.6	1713	0.6	2235	9.6
3 SU	0532	1.6	1101	9.0	1749	1.5	○ 2319	8.9
18 M	0529	0.7	1053	9.9	1758	0.4	○ 2318	9.8
4 M	0602	1.5	1132	9.1	1817	1.4	2348	9.0
19 TU	0615	0.5	1139	9.9	1841	0.4		
5 TU	0631	1.4	1202	9.0	1846	1.4		
20 W	0002	9.8	0658	0.5	1225	9.7	1922	0.7
6 W	0016	8.9	0702	1.5	1233	8.9	1915	1.6
21 TH	0045	9.6	0741	0.8	1310	9.4	2002	1.2
7 TH	0045	8.8	0733	1.7	1303	8.7	1946	1.8
22 F	0129	9.2	0825	1.2	1356	8.8	2043	1.8
8 F	0115	8.6	0806	1.9	1336	8.5	2018	2.2
23 SA	0214	8.8	0911	1.8	1445	8.2	2127	2.5
9 SA	0149	8.4	0842	2.3	1415	8.2	2054	2.5
24 SU	0306	8.3	1003	2.3	1544	7.6	2222	3.0
10 SU	0230	8.1	0924	2.6	1504	7.8	2140	2.9
25 M	0409	7.8	1110	2.8	1654	7.2	◐ 2337	3.4
11 M	0326	7.7	1022	2.9	1610	7.4	2247	3.2
26 TU	0521	7.5	1227	3.0	1813	7.1		
12 TU	0445	7.4	1145	3.0	1735	7.4		
27 W	0058	3.4	0634	7.5	1339	2.8	1927	7.3
13 W	0015	3.2	0612	7.6	1314	2.6	1858	7.7
28 TH	0207	3.1	0741	7.7	1438	2.6	2025	7.7
14 TH	0139	2.8	0726	8.0	1427	2.1	2006	8.2
29 F	0302	2.8	0834	8.0	1526	2.3	2108	8.0
15 F	0248	2.2	0827	8.6	1529	1.5	2101	8.8
30 SA	0346	2.4	0917	8.3	1606	2.1	2145	8.3

Chart Datum: 4·93 metres below Ordnance Datum (Newlyn)
HAT is 10·4m above Chart Datum

TIDES

TIME ZONE (UT)
For Summer Time add ONE hour in **non-shaded areas**

LIVERPOOL (GLADSTONE DOCK)
LAT 53°27'N   LONG 3°01'W
TIMES AND HEIGHTS OF HIGH AND LOW WATERS

Dates in amber are **SPRINGS**
Dates in yellow are **NEAPS**

2011

MAY

Day	Time m	Time m	Time m	Time m	Day	Time m	Time m	Time m	Time m
1 SU	0424 2.1	0955 8.6	1641 1.9	2217 8.6	16 M	0412 1.4	0944 9.3	1645 1.0	2211 9.4
2 M	0458 1.9	1030 8.7	1713 1.7	2249 8.8	17 TU ○	0506 1.0	1034 9.5	1734 0.9	2258 9.5
3 TU ●	0532 1.7	1104 8.8	1746 1.6	2320 8.9	18 W	0555 0.8	1123 9.5	1819 0.9	2343 9.6
4 W	0606 1.6	1137 8.9	1819 1.6	2351 8.9	19 TH	0643 0.8	1210 9.3	1903 1.1	
5 TH	0641 1.6	1210 8.8	1853 1.6		20 F	0028 9.4	0728 1.0	1256 9.1	1944 1.5
6 F	0024 8.9	0716 1.6	1246 8.7	1927 1.8	21 SA	0112 9.2	0813 1.3	1342 8.7	2026 1.9
7 SA	0059 8.8	0753 1.8	1323 8.5	2003 2.0	22 SU	0157 8.9	0857 1.7	1428 8.2	2108 2.4
8 SU	0137 8.6	0832 2.0	1406 8.3	2043 2.3	23 M	0244 8.5	0944 2.2	1517 7.8	2154 2.8
9 M	0222 8.3	0918 2.3	1457 8.0	2131 2.6	24 TU ◐	0337 8.1	1035 2.6	1613 7.5	2249 3.2
10 TU ◐	0318 8.1	1014 2.4	1559 7.8	2232 2.8	25 W	0436 7.8	1134 2.8	1716 7.2	2355 3.4
11 W	0427 7.9	1124 2.5	1711 7.7	2345 2.8	26 TH	0540 7.6	1237 2.9	1823 7.2	
12 TH	0542 8.0	1239 2.3	1825 7.9		27 F	0103 3.3	0643 7.6	1338 2.9	1926 7.4
13 F	0100 2.6	0651 8.2	1350 2.0	1932 8.3	28 SA	0205 3.1	0742 7.7	1431 2.7	2020 7.7
14 SA	0210 2.2	0755 8.6	1455 1.6	2031 8.7	29 SU	0257 2.8	0834 8.0	1518 2.5	2104 8.0
15 SU	0314 1.6	0852 9.0	1553 1.2	2123 9.1	30 M	0342 2.5	0919 8.2	1600 2.2	2143 8.3
					31 TU	0424 2.2	1000 8.4	1640 2.0	2220 8.6

JUNE

Day	Time m	Time m	Time m	Time m	Day	Time m	Time m	Time m	Time m
1 W ●	0505 1.9	1038 8.6	1718 1.8	2255 8.8	16 TH	0543 1.2	1113 9.1	1803 1.4	2330 9.3
2 TH	0545 1.7	1115 8.7	1756 1.7	2331 8.9	17 F	0632 1.1	1159 9.0	1847 1.4	
3 F	0625 1.6	1153 8.8	1835 1.7		18 SA	0014 9.3	0717 1.2	1243 8.9	1928 1.6
4 SA	0008 9.0	0705 1.5	1232 8.8	1914 1.7	19 SU	0056 9.2	0759 1.3	1324 8.7	2007 1.9
5 SU	0048 9.0	0746 1.5	1314 8.8	1954 1.8	20 M	0137 9.0	0838 1.6	1403 8.4	2044 2.2
6 M	0130 8.9	0828 1.6	1359 8.6	2036 2.0	21 TU	0217 8.7	0915 2.0	1443 8.1	2120 2.5
7 TU	0216 8.7	0914 1.8	1448 8.4	2123 2.2	22 W	0300 8.4	0951 2.3	1527 7.8	2200 2.9
8 W	0308 8.6	1004 1.9	1543 8.2	2216 2.4	23 TH ◐	0348 8.0	1032 2.7	1617 7.5	2247 3.2
9 TH	0406 8.4	1101 2.1	1645 8.1	2317 2.5	24 F ◐	0442 7.7	1122 3.0	1716 7.3	2347 3.4
10 F	0511 8.3	1205 2.1	1752 8.1		25 SA	0543 7.5	1224 3.1	1821 7.2	
11 SA	0024 2.5	0619 8.3	1315 2.1	1859 8.2	26 SU	0058 3.4	0647 7.4	1331 3.1	1925 7.4
12 SU	0136 2.3	0726 8.4	1423 1.9	2004 8.4	27 M	0205 3.2	0749 7.6	1431 2.9	2023 7.7
13 M	0246 2.1	0830 8.6	1526 1.7	2102 8.7	28 TU	0303 2.8	0845 7.8	1523 2.6	2111 8.1
14 TU	0351 1.8	0929 8.8	1623 1.5	2155 9.0	29 W	0354 2.4	0933 8.2	1610 2.3	2154 8.4
15 W ○	0449 1.5	1022 9.0	1715 1.4	2244 9.2	30 TH	0441 2.1	1016 8.5	1655 2.0	2234 8.8

JULY

Day	Time m	Time m	Time m	Time m	Day	Time m	Time m	Time m	Time m
1 F ●	0527 1.7	1057 8.7	1739 1.7	2314 9.0	16 SA	0622 1.3	1147 8.9	1833 1.5	2359 9.3
2 SA	0612 1.5	1137 8.7	1822 1.5	2354 9.2	17 SU	0702 1.2	1225 8.9	1910 1.6	
3 SU	0656 1.2	1219 9.1	1905 1.4		18 M	0036 9.3	0738 1.3	1300 8.8	1944 1.7
4 M	0035 9.3	0739 1.1	1302 9.1	1946 1.4	19 TU	0111 9.1	0810 1.5	1333 8.6	2015 2.0
5 TU	0119 9.3	0821 1.1	1346 9.1	2028 1.5	20 W	0146 8.9	0839 1.8	1407 8.4	2044 2.2
6 W	0203 9.2	0903 1.3	1432 8.9	2110 1.7	21 TH	0222 8.6	0907 2.1	1443 8.1	2117 2.6
7 TH	0250 9.0	0947 1.5	1522 8.6	2157 2.0	22 F	0301 8.3	0939 2.5	1523 7.8	2155 3.0
8 F	0342 8.8	1036 1.8	1617 8.3	2250 2.3	23 SA ◐	0345 7.8	1019 2.9	1611 7.4	2244 3.3
9 SA	0442 8.4	1134 2.2	1721 8.1	2354 2.5	24 SU	0439 7.5	1113 3.2	1713 7.2	2351 3.5
10 SU	0551 8.2	1244 2.4	1832 8.0		25 M	0548 7.2	1226 3.4	1829 7.1	
11 M	0110 2.6	0706 8.1	1359 2.4	1944 8.1	26 TU	0114 3.5	0704 7.2	1345 3.3	1942 7.4
12 TU	0229 2.4	0819 8.2	1509 2.2	2049 8.4	27 W	0227 3.1	0812 7.5	1450 2.9	2042 7.9
13 W	0341 2.1	0923 8.4	1610 2.0	2146 8.8	28 TH	0327 2.6	0909 8.0	1545 2.4	2131 8.4
14 TH	0443 1.7	1018 8.7	1704 1.8	2235 9.1	29 F	0421 2.1	0956 8.5	1635 2.0	2214 8.9
15 F ○	0536 1.4	1105 8.8	1751 1.6	2319 9.2	30 SA ●	0511 1.6	1039 8.9	1723 1.6	2255 9.3
					31 SU	0558 1.2	1120 9.2	1808 1.3	2336 9.6

AUGUST

Day	Time m	Time m	Time m	Time m	Day	Time m	Time m	Time m	Time m
1 M	0643 0.8	1202 9.5	1852 1.0		16 TU	0011 9.3	0709 1.4	1232 8.9	1915 1.6
2 TU	0018 9.8	0725 0.7	1244 9.5	1933 1.0	17 W	0043 9.2	0736 1.5	1301 8.8	1943 1.8
3 W	0101 9.8	0806 0.7	1327 9.5	2013 1.1	18 TH	0114 9.1	0801 1.7	1331 8.6	2011 2.0
4 TH	0143 9.7	0845 0.9	1411 9.2	2053 1.4	19 F	0146 8.8	0828 2.0	1402 8.4	2041 2.4
5 F	0228 9.4	0926 1.3	1457 8.8	2136 1.8	20 SA	0218 8.4	0858 2.4	1435 8.0	2116 2.8
6 SA ◐	0317 8.9	1010 1.9	1549 8.4	2227 2.2	21 SU ◐	0255 8.0	0934 2.8	1515 7.7	2159 3.2
7 SU	0416 8.4	1106 2.4	1653 8.0	2332 2.7	22 M	0341 7.5	1021 3.3	1609 7.3	2259 3.5
8 M	0529 7.9	1220 2.8	1811 7.7		23 TU	0448 7.1	1129 3.6	1732 7.1	
9 TU	0057 2.8	0654 7.7	1345 2.9	1932 7.9	24 W	0027 3.6	0617 7.0	1301 3.5	1901 7.3
10 W	0225 2.7	0816 7.8	1501 2.6	2043 8.2	25 TH	0154 3.2	0740 7.4	1419 3.1	2012 7.8
11 TH	0339 2.2	0921 8.2	1604 2.2	2138 8.7	26 F	0301 2.6	0844 8.0	1520 2.5	2105 8.4
12 F	0438 1.8	1011 8.6	1655 1.9	2224 9.0	27 SA	0359 2.0	0933 8.6	1614 1.9	2150 9.0
13 SA ○	0525 1.5	1052 8.8	1737 1.7	2303 9.2	28 SU	0450 1.4	1017 9.1	1703 1.4	2232 9.5
14 SU	0605 1.3	1128 8.9	1814 1.6	2338 9.3	29 M ●	0538 0.9	1058 9.5	1750 1.0	2314 9.9
15 M	0639 1.3	1201 9.0	1846 1.6		30 TU	0622 0.5	1140 9.8	1833 0.8	2356 10.1
					31 W	0705 0.4	1221 9.9	1915 0.7	

Chart Datum: 4·93 metres below Ordnance Datum (Newlyn)
HAT is 10·4m above Chart Datum

LIVERPOOL (GLADSTONE DOCK)
LAT 53°27'N   LONG 3°01'W
TIMES AND HEIGHTS OF HIGH AND LOW WATERS

Dates in amber are **SPRINGS**
Dates in yellow are **NEAPS**

2011

SEPTEMBER

Time	m		Time	m
1 0038	10.1	**16** 0043	9.1	
0744	0.5		0727	1.7
TH 1304	9.7	F 1258	8.8	
1955	0.8		1941	2.0
2 0121	9.9	**17** 0113	8.8	
0823	0.8		0755	2.0
F 1347	9.4	SA 1327	8.6	
2035	1.2		2012	2.3
3 0206	9.4	**18** 0144	8.5	
0903	1.4		0825	2.4
SA 1432	9.0	SU 1358	8.3	
2118	1.7		2046	2.7
4 0255	8.8	**19** 0219	8.1	
0947	2.1		0900	2.8
SU 1524	8.4	M 1435	7.9	
☾ 2209	2.3		2127	3.1
5 0355	8.1	**20** 0303	7.7	
1043	2.7		0944	3.2
M 1631	7.9	TU 1526	7.5	
2319	2.8		☾ 2223	3.4
6 0515	7.6	**21** 0406	7.2	
1203	3.2		1048	3.6
TU 1754	7.6	W 1645	7.2	
			2348	3.6
7 0052	3.0	**22** 0536	7.1	
0647	7.4		1219	3.6
W 1335	3.4	TH 1820	7.3	
1920	7.8			
8 0220	2.7	**23** 0120	3.2	
0810	7.7		0705	7.4
TH 1451	2.8	F 1345	3.2	
2030	8.2		1936	7.9
9 0329	2.2	**24** 0232	2.5	
0910	8.2		0813	8.0
F 1551	2.3	SA 1451	2.5	
2123	8.7		2034	8.5
10 0422	1.8	**25** 0331	1.8	
0955	8.5		0905	8.7
SA 1637	2.0	SU 1548	1.9	
2204	9.0		2122	9.2
11 0504	1.6	**26** 0424	1.2	
1031	8.8		0951	9.3
SU 1715	1.8	M 1638	1.4	
2240	9.2		2206	9.7
12 0539	1.5	**27** 0512	0.7	
1103	9.0		1033	9.7
M 1748	1.6	TU 1726	0.9	
○ 2312	9.3		● 2249	10.1
13 0608	1.4	**28** 0557	0.4	
1133	9.0		1115	10.0
TU 1817	1.6	W 1811	0.7	
2343	9.3		2332	10.2
14 0635	1.5	**29** 0640	0.4	
1201	9.1		1158	10.0
W 1845	1.6	TH 1854	0.6	
15 0013	9.3	**30** 0016	10.2	
0700	1.5		0721	0.6
TH 1230	9.0	F 1241	9.9	
1912	1.7		1936	0.8

OCTOBER

Time	m		Time	m
1 0101	9.8	**16** 0048	8.8	
0801	1.0		0728	2.0
SA 1324	9.5	SU 1300	8.8	
2018	1.2		1950	2.2
2 0148	9.3	**17** 0121	8.6	
0842	1.6		0801	2.3
SU 1411	9.0	M 1333	8.5	
2104	1.8		2026	2.5
3 0238	8.7	**18** 0157	8.2	
0927	2.3		0836	2.7
M 1504	8.5	TU 1411	8.2	
2158	2.4		2107	2.9
4 0340	8.0	**19** 0243	7.9	
1025	3.0		0921	3.1
TU 1612	7.9	W 1502	7.8	
☾ 2311	2.9		2202	3.2
5 0458	7.4	**20** 0343	7.5	
1146	3.4		1021	3.4
W 1732	7.7	TH 1614	7.5	
			☾ 2317	3.3
6 0038	3.0	**21** 0503	7.4	
0627	7.3		1142	3.5
TH 1314	3.3	F 1741	7.6	
1854	7.8			
7 0158	2.7	**22** 0043	3.0	
0748	7.6		0626	7.6
F 1427	3.0	SA 1306	3.2	
2003	8.1		1856	8.0
8 0302	2.4	**23** 0157	2.5	
0846	8.1		0737	8.1
SA 1523	2.5	SU 1416	2.6	
2055	8.5		1958	8.6
9 0352	2.0	**24** 0258	1.8	
0929	8.4		0833	8.8
SU 1608	2.2	M 1516	2.0	
2137	8.8		2051	9.2
10 0431	1.8	**25** 0354	1.3	
1004	8.7		0922	9.3
M 1645	2.0	TU 1610	1.5	
2212	9.0		2139	9.7
11 0504	1.7	**26** 0444	0.9	
1035	8.9		1008	9.7
TU 1717	1.8	W 1701	1.1	
2244	9.2		● 2226	10.0
12 0533	1.7	**27** 0531	0.7	
1104	9.0		1052	9.9
W 1746	1.7	TH 1749	0.8	
○ 2315	9.2		2312	10.1
13 0601	1.6	**28** 0616	0.6	
1132	9.1		1136	10.0
TH 1816	1.7	F 1835	0.7	
2346	9.2		2359	10.0
14 0629	1.7	**29** 0700	0.8	
1201	9.1		1221	9.9
F 1846	1.8	SA 1921	0.9	
15 0017	9.1	**30** 0046	9.6	
0657	1.8		0742	1.2
SA 1231	8.9	SU 1307	9.6	
1917	1.9		2006	1.3
		31 0134	9.1	
			0825	1.8
		M 1354	9.1	
			2054	1.8

NOVEMBER

Time	m		Time	m
1 0225	8.6	**16** 0145	8.4	
0911	2.4		0822	2.5
TU 1446	8.6	W 1359	8.5	
2148	2.3		2057	2.5
2 0323	8.0	**17** 0231	8.2	
1006	3.0		0907	2.8
W 1548	8.2	TH 1448	8.2	
☽ 2253	2.7		2148	2.7
3 0431	7.5	**18** 0326	7.9	
1116	3.4		1002	3.1
TH 1658	7.8	F 1550	8.0	
			☽ 2251	2.8
4 0006	2.9	**19** 0433	7.8	
0547	7.3		1109	3.2
F 1234	3.4	SA 1703	8.0	
1811	7.8			
5 0117	2.9	**20** 0004	2.7	
0704	7.5		0547	7.8
SA 1344	3.2	SU 1224	3.0	
1919	7.9		1816	8.2
6 0218	2.7	**21** 0117	2.4	
0806	7.8		0658	8.2
SU 1442	2.9	M 1337	2.7	
2016	8.2		1922	8.5
7 0309	2.4	**22** 0223	2.0	
0853	8.2		0800	8.6
M 1529	2.6	TU 1443	2.2	
2102	8.5		2022	9.0
8 0351	2.2	**23** 0323	1.6	
0931	8.5		0856	9.1
TU 1609	2.3	W 1543	1.7	
2141	8.7		2117	9.3
9 0426	2.1	**24** 0418	1.3	
1004	8.7		0946	9.4
W 1644	2.1	TH 1639	1.4	
2216	8.9		2208	9.6
10 0458	1.9	**25** 0509	1.1	
1036	8.9		1034	9.7
TH 1718	2.0	F 1731	1.1	
○ 2250	9.0		● 2258	9.7
11 0530	1.9	**26** 0557	1.0	
1107	9.0		1121	9.8
F 1751	1.9	SA 1821	0.9	
2323	9.0		2347	9.6
12 0601	1.8	**27** 0643	1.1	
1138	9.1		1207	9.8
SA 1825	1.8	SU 1909	1.0	
2356	9.0			
13 0634	1.9	**28** 0035	9.4	
1210	9.0		0727	1.4
SU 1900	1.9	M 1253	9.6	
			1956	1.2
14 0030	8.8	**29** 0123	9.1	
0708	2.0		0810	1.8
M 1243	8.9	TU 1339	9.3	
1936	2.1		2043	1.6
15 0106	8.7	**30** 0209	8.8	
0744	2.2		0855	2.3
TU 1318	8.7	W 1426	8.9	
2014	2.3		2130	2.1

DECEMBER

Time	m		Time	m
1 0258	8.2	**16** 0219	8.6	
0941	2.7		0856	2.3
TH 1517	8.5	F 1435	8.7	
2221	2.5		2133	2.2
2 0352	7.8	**17** 0308	8.4	
1034	3.2		0943	2.5
F 1614	8.1	SA 1527	8.5	
☽ 2317	2.9		2225	2.3
3 0452	7.5	**18** 0404	8.2	
1137	3.4		1039	2.7
SA 1717	7.8	SU 1628	8.4	
			☽ 2325	2.3
4 0019	3.1	**19** 0510	8.0	
0559	7.3		1144	2.8
SU 1245	3.5	M 1737	8.3	
1822	7.7			
5 0121	3.1	**20** 0036	2.5	
0707	7.5		0620	8.1
M 1349	3.4	TU 1258	2.7	
1925	7.8		1849	8.3
6 0217	2.9	**21** 0149	2.3	
0807	7.7		0730	8.3
TU 1444	3.1	W 1413	2.5	
2021	8.0		1959	8.5
7 0306	2.7	**22** 0257	2.0	
0854	8.1		0834	8.7
W 1531	2.8	TH 1522	2.1	
2109	8.3		2102	8.8
8 0348	2.5	**23** 0357	1.7	
0935	8.4		0931	9.0
TH 1613	2.5	F 1624	1.7	
2150	8.5		2159	9.1
9 0427	2.3	**24** 0452	1.5	
1012	8.7		1023	9.4
F 1653	2.2	SA 1721	1.3	
2228	8.7		● 2252	9.3
10 0504	2.1	**25** 0543	1.3	
1046	8.9		1111	9.6
SA 1731	2.0	SU 1813	1.1	
○ 2304	8.8		2340	9.4
11 0541	1.9	**26** 0630	1.3	
1120	9.0		1157	9.7
SU 1809	1.8	M 1900	1.0	
2340	8.9			
12 0618	1.9	**27** 0025	9.3	
1155	9.1		0713	1.4
M 1848	1.8	TU 1240	9.6	
			1944	1.1
13 0016	8.9	**28** 0108	9.1	
0655	1.9		0754	1.6
TU 1231	9.1	W 1321	9.4	
1927	1.8		2025	1.4
14 0054	8.9	**29** 0147	8.8	
0734	1.9		0833	2.0
W 1309	9.1	TH 1401	9.1	
2007	1.8		2103	1.7
15 0135	8.8	**30** 0226	8.4	
0813	2.1		0909	2.4
TH 1350	8.9	F 1442	8.7	
2049	2.0		2140	2.2
		31 0308	8.1	
			0947	2.8
		SA 1527	8.3	
			2218	2.7

Chart Datum: 4·93 metres below Ordnance Datum (Newlyn)
HAT is 10·4m above Chart Datum

TIDES

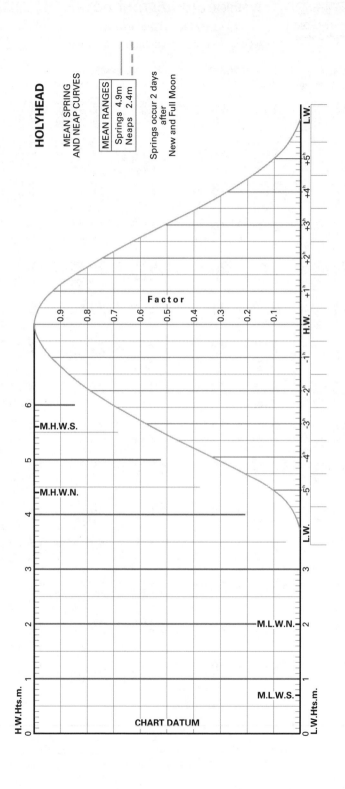

HOLYHEAD

MEAN SPRING
AND NEAP CURVES

MEAN RANGES
Springs 4.9m
Neaps 2.4m

Springs occur 2 days
after
New and Full Moon

Factor

WALES – HOLYHEAD

LAT 53°19′N   LONG 4°37′W

2011

TIMES AND HEIGHTS OF HIGH AND LOW WATERS

JANUARY

#	Time	m	Time	m	#	Time	m	Time	m
1 SA	0125 / 0745	1.6 / 5.0	1354 / 2014	1.6 / 5.1	16 SU	0059 / 0729	2.1 / 4.6	1337 / 1952	2.0 / 4.7
2 SU	0224 / 0839	1.5 / 5.3	1451 / 2109	1.4 / 5.2	17 M	0157 / 0821	1.8 / 4.9	1431 / 2044	1.6 / 5.0
3 M	0314 / 0926	1.3 / 5.5	1541 / 2155	1.2 / 5.3	18 TU	0246 / 0906	1.5 / 5.2	1517 / 2129	1.3 / 5.2
4 TU	0358 / 1009	1.2 / 5.6	1624 / ●2237	1.0 / 5.3	19 W	0330 / 0947	1.2 / 5.5	1601 / ○2211	1.0 / 5.5
5 W	0437 / 1048	1.1 / 5.7	1704 / 2316	1.0 / 5.3	20 TH	0412 / 1027	0.9 / 5.8	1643 / 2253	0.6 / 5.6
6 TH	0514 / 1125	1.1 / 5.7	1741 / 2352	1.0 / 5.3	21 F	0454 / 1109	0.7 / 6.0	1725 / 2336	0.4 / 5.7
7 F	0550 / 1201	1.2 / 5.6	1816	1.1	22 SA	0536 / 1151	0.6 / 6.1	1808	1.0
8 SA	0026 / 0624	5.2 / 1.4	1236 / 1850	5.5 / 1.2	23 SU	0019 / 0618	5.7 / 0.6	1236 / 1853	6.0 / 0.5
9 SU	0100 / 0659	5.0 / 1.6	1311 / 1926	5.4 / 1.3	24 M	0104 / 0703	5.6 / 0.8	1321 / 1939	5.9 / 0.7
10 M	0135 / 0736	4.9 / 1.6	1347 / 2004	5.2 / 1.5	25 TU	0150 / 0751	5.4 / 1.0	1410 / 2030	5.6 / 1.0
11 TU	0213 / 0817	4.7 / 1.9	1428 / 2046	5.0 / 1.8	26 W	0241 / 0845	5.1 / 1.3	1505 / ◐2128	5.3 / 1.4
12 W	0257 / 0904	4.6 / 2.1	1515 / ◐2136	4.7 / 2.0	27 TH	0341 / 0949	4.8 / 1.7	1612 / 2238	4.9 / 1.7
13 TH	0353 / 1002	4.4 / 2.3	1616 / 2238	4.5 / 2.2	28 F	0456 / 1109	4.7 / 1.9	1737 / 2356	4.7 / 1.9
14 F	0506 / 1115	4.3 / 2.4	1731 / 2349	4.5 / 2.2	29 SA	0620 / 1233	4.6 / 1.9	1905	4.7
15 SA	0623 / 1231	4.4 / 2.3	1847	4.5	30 SU	0113 / 0735	1.9 / 4.8	1350 / 2015	1.7 / 4.8
					31 M	0218 / 0833	1.7 / 5.1	1449 / 2108	1.5 / 5.0

FEBRUARY

#	Time	m	Time	m	#	Time	m	Time	m
1 TU	0308 / 0919	1.5 / 5.3	1535 / 2150	1.2 / 5.1	16 W	0226 / 0844	1.5 / 5.2	1457 / 2111	1.1 / 5.2
2 W	0348 / 0958	1.3 / 5.5	1613 / 2225	1.0 / 5.2	17 TH	0311 / 0927	1.1 / 5.6	1541 / 2153	0.7 / 5.5
3 TH	0423 / 1033	1.1 / 5.6	1647 / ●2257	0.9 / 5.3	18 F	0353 / 1008	0.7 / 5.9	1623 / ○2234	0.3 / 5.8
4 F	0456 / 1105	1.0 / 5.6	1718 / 2328	0.9 / 5.3	19 SA	0434 / 1049	0.4 / 6.1	1704 / 2315	0.1 / 5.9
5 SA	0527 / 1137	1.0 / 5.6	1749 / 2357	0.9 / 5.3	20 SU	0515 / 1131	0.3 / 6.2	1746 / 2357	0.1 / 5.9
6 SU	0557 / 1208	1.0 / 5.6	1819	1.0	21 M	0557 / 1215	0.3 / 6.2	1829	0.2
7 M	0027 / 0628	5.2 / 1.2	1240 / 1850	5.5 / 1.1	22 TU	0039 / 0641	5.7 / 0.5	1300 / 1914	6.0 / 0.6
8 TU	0059 / 0701	5.1 / 1.3	1313 / 1923	5.3 / 1.3	23 W	0124 / 0728	5.5 / 0.8	1348 / 2002	5.6 / 1.0
9 W	0132 / 0736	4.9 / 1.6	1348 / 1959	5.1 / 1.6	24 TH	0213 / 0821	5.2 / 1.2	1441 / ◑2058	5.2 / 1.5
10 TH	0209 / 0816	4.7 / 1.8	1428 / 2041	4.8 / 1.8	25 F	0310 / 0926	4.8 / 1.6	1550 / 2209	4.7 / 1.9
11 F	0253 / 0907	4.5 / 2.1	1519 / ◑2137	4.5 / 2.1	26 SA	0425 / 1049	4.6 / 1.9	1723 / 2335	4.4 / 2.1
12 SA	0355 / 1017	4.3 / 2.3	1641 / 2252	4.3 / 2.3	27 SU	0558 / 1220	4.5 / 1.9	1900	4.4
13 SU	0526 / 1146	4.3 / 2.3	1809	4.3	28 M	0059 / 0720	2.1 / 4.7	1340 / 2009	1.7 / 4.6
14 M	0019 / 0651	2.2 / 4.5	1307 / 1927	2.0 / 4.5					
15 TU	0131 / 0755	1.9 / 4.8	1408 / 2025	1.6 / 4.9					

MARCH

#	Time	m	Time	m	#	Time	m	Time	m
1 TU	0205 / 0820	1.8 / 4.9	1437 / 2057	1.5 / 4.8	16 W	0101 / 0723	1.9 / 4.8	1340 / 2001	1.4 / 4.9
2 W	0253 / 0903	1.5 / 5.2	1518 / 2134	1.2 / 5.0	17 TH	0159 / 0816	1.4 / 5.2	1431 / 2048	0.9 / 5.2
3 TH	0330 / 0939	1.3 / 5.4	1553 / 2205	1.0 / 5.2	18 F	0246 / 0901	1.0 / 5.6	1515 / 2129	0.5 / 5.6
4 F	0403 / 1010	1.1 / 5.5	1623 / ●2233	0.9 / 5.3	19 SA	0329 / 0943	0.6 / 5.9	1558 / ○2210	0.2 / 5.8
5 SA	0432 / 1041	0.9 / 5.6	1651 / 2300	0.8 / 5.3	20 SU	0411 / 1026	0.3 / 6.1	1639 / 2251	0.0 / 5.9
6 SU	0501 / 1110	0.9 / 5.6	1719 / 2328	0.8 / 5.3	21 M	0453 / 1109	0.1 / 6.2	1722 / 2333	0.1 / 5.9
7 M	0530 / 1140	0.9 / 5.5	1747 / 2357	0.9 / 5.3	22 TU	0536 / 1154	0.2 / 6.1	1805	0.3
8 TU	0600 / 1211	1.0 / 5.4	1817	1.0	23 W	0016 / 0621	5.8 / 0.4	1241 / 1850	5.8 / 0.6
9 W	0027 / 0631	5.2 / 1.1	1243 / 1848	5.3 / 1.2	24 TH	0102 / 0710	5.6 / 0.7	1330 / 1939	5.4 / 1.1
10 TH	0059 / 0705	5.1 / 1.4	1317 / 1922	5.1 / 1.4	25 F	0150 / 0804	5.2 / 1.1	1425 / 2034	5.0 / 1.6
11 F	0133 / 0743	4.9 / 1.6	1355 / 2002	4.8 / 1.7	26 SA	0246 / 0908	4.9 / 1.5	1533 / ◑2143	4.5 / 2.0
12 SA	0215 / 0831	4.7 / 1.9	1444 / ◑2055	4.5 / 2.0	27 SU	0358 / 1029	4.6 / 1.8	1705 / 2309	4.3 / 2.2
13 SU	0311 / 0939	4.4 / 2.1	1556 / 2210	4.3 / 2.2	28 M	0527 / 1157	4.5 / 1.9	1839	4.3
14 M	0437 / 1109	4.3 / 2.1	1736 / 2343	4.3 / 2.2	29 TU	0032 / 0650	2.1 / 4.6	1313 / 1946	1.7 / 4.5
15 TU	0613 / 1235	4.4 / 1.8	1901	4.5	30 W	0138 / 0751	1.8 / 4.8	1408 / 2032	1.5 / 4.7
					31 TH	0226 / 0835	1.6 / 5.0	1449 / 2107	1.3 / 4.9

APRIL

#	Time	m	Time	m	#	Time	m	Time	m
1 F	0304 / 0910	1.4 / 5.2	1523 / 2137	1.1 / 5.1	16 SA	0218 / 0832	1.0 / 5.6	1447 / 2103	0.5 / 5.5
2 SA	0336 / 0942	1.2 / 5.3	1553 / 2204	1.0 / 5.2	17 SU	0303 / 0918	0.6 / 5.8	1532 / 2145	0.3 / 5.8
3 SU	0405 / 1013	1.0 / 5.4	1621 / 2232	0.9 / 5.3	18 M	0348 / 1004	0.4 / 6.0	1616 / ○2228	0.2 / 5.9
4 M	0434 / 1043	0.9 / 5.4	1649 / 2300	0.9 / 5.3	19 TU	0433 / 1050	0.2 / 6.0	1700 / 2312	0.3 / 5.9
5 TU	0504 / 1114	0.9 / 5.4	1718 / 2329	0.9 / 5.3	20 W	0519 / 1137	0.3 / 5.9	1745 / 2357	0.5 / 5.8
6 W	0535 / 1146	1.0 / 5.3	1748	1.0	21 TH	0607 / 1225	0.4 / 5.6	1831	0.8
7 TH	0000 / 0607	5.3 / 1.1	1219 / 1820	5.2 / 1.2	22 F	0043 / 0656	5.6 / 0.7	1316 / 1919	5.2 / 1.2
8 F	0034 / 0643	5.2 / 1.2	1255 / 1856	5.0 / 1.4	23 SA	0132 / 0750	5.3 / 1.1	1410 / 2013	4.9 / 1.6
9 SA	0110 / 0723	5.0 / 1.4	1336 / 1938	4.8 / 1.6	24 SU	0225 / 0851	5.0 / 1.4	1514 / 2116	4.5 / 1.9
10 SU	0153 / 0813	4.8 / 1.6	1427 / 2032	4.6 / 1.9	25 M	0329 / 1001	4.7 / 1.7	1632 / ◑2231	4.3 / 2.2
11 M	0250 / 0919	4.6 / 1.8	1537 / ◑2144	4.4 / 2.1	26 TU	0444 / 1117	4.5 / 1.8	1754 / 2347	4.3 / 2.2
12 TU	0407 / 1041	4.5 / 1.8	1708 / 2311	4.4 / 2.1	27 W	0601 / 1227	4.5 / 1.8	1903	4.4
13 W	0535 / 1201	4.6 / 1.6	1829	4.3	28 TH	0054 / 0705	2.0 / 4.6	1324 / 1952	1.6 / 4.6
14 TH	0027 / 0646	1.8 / 4.8	1307 / 1930	1.2 / 4.9	29 F	0146 / 0754	1.8 / 4.8	1409 / 2030	1.4 / 4.8
15 F	0128 / 0743	1.5 / 5.2	1400 / 2019	0.8 / 5.2	30 SA	0228 / 0834	1.6 / 5.0	1446 / 2103	1.3 / 5.0

TIDES

Chart Datum: 3·05 metres below Ordnance Datum (Newlyn)
HAT is 6·3m above Chart Datum

WALES – HOLYHEAD

LAT 53°19'N   LONG 4°37'W

TIMES AND HEIGHTS OF HIGH AND LOW WATERS

TIME ZONE (UT)
For Summer Time add ONE hour in **non-shaded areas**

Dates in amber are **SPRINGS**
Dates in yellow are **NEAPS**

2011

MAY

Day	Time	m		Day	Time	m
1 SU	0304 / 0910 / 1519 / 2134	1.4 / 5.1 / 1.2 / 5.1		**16** M	0241 / 0857 / 1510 / 2124	0.8 / 5.6 / 0.6 / 5.6
2 M	0336 / 0943 / 1549 / 2203	1.2 / 5.2 / 1.1 / 5.2		**17** TU ○	0330 / 0946 / 1556 / 2209	0.6 / 5.7 / 0.5 / 5.7
3 TU ●	0408 / 1016 / 1620 / 2233	1.4 / 5.3 / 1.0 / 5.3		**18** W	0418 / 1035 / 1643 / 2255	0.5 / 5.8 / 0.6 / 5.8
4 W	0440 / 1049 / 1651 / 2305	1.0 / 5.3 / 1.0 / 5.3		**19** TH	0506 / 1124 / 1729 / 2341	0.5 / 5.6 / 0.7 / 5.7
5 TH	0514 / 1124 / 1725 / 2340	1.0 / 5.2 / 1.1 / 5.3		**20** F	0555 / 1213 / 1815	0.6 / 5.4 / 0.9
6 F	0551 / 1201 / 1801	1.1 / 5.1 / 1.2		**21** SA	0027 / 0643 / 1302 / 1901	5.6 / 0.8 / 5.1 / 1.2
7 SA	0016 / 0629 / 1241 / 1840	5.3 / 1.1 / 5.0 / 1.3		**22** SU	0114 / 0733 / 1351 / 1950	5.4 / 1.0 / 4.8 / 1.5
8 SU	0057 / 0713 / 1326 / 1925	5.1 / 1.3 / 4.9 / 1.5		**23** M	0202 / 0825 / 1444 / 2042	5.1 / 1.3 / 4.6 / 1.8
9 M	0143 / 0804 / 1419 / 2019	5.0 / 1.4 / 4.7 / 1.7		**24** TU ◑	0255 / 0922 / 1544 / 2143	4.9 / 1.6 / 4.4 / 2.0
10 TU ◑	0238 / 0905 / 1523 / 2125	4.8 / 1.5 / 4.6 / 1.8		**25** W	0354 / 1024 / 1651 / 2250	4.7 / 1.7 / 4.3 / 2.2
11 W	0344 / 1016 / 1639 / 2240	4.8 / 1.5 / 4.5 / 1.8		**26** TH	0458 / 1128 / 1759 / 2356	4.5 / 1.8 / 4.3 / 2.1
12 TH	0500 / 1128 / 1753 / 2352	4.8 / 1.4 / 4.7 / 1.7		**27** F	0603 / 1228 / 1858	4.5 / 1.8 / 4.4
13 F	0610 / 1233 / 1856	5.0 / 1.1 / 4.9		**28** SA	0055 / 0702 / 1320 / 1946	2.0 / 4.6 / 1.7 / 4.6
14 SA	0054 / 0711 / 1330 / 1950	1.4 / 5.2 / 0.9 / 5.2		**29** SU	0146 / 0752 / 1405 / 2026	1.8 / 4.7 / 1.6 / 4.8
15 SU	0150 / 0806 / 1421 / 2038	1.1 / 5.4 / 0.7 / 5.4		**30** M	0228 / 0836 / 1444 / 2102	1.6 / 4.9 / 1.4 / 5.0
				31 TU	0307 / 0915 / 1519 / 2136	1.4 / 5.0 / 1.3 / 5.1

JUNE

Day	Time	m		Day	Time	m
1 W ●	0344 / 0952 / 1554 / 2210	1.2 / 5.1 / 1.2 / 5.3		**16** TH	0410 / 1026 / 1630 / 2242	0.7 / 5.4 / 0.8 / 5.7
2 TH	0420 / 1029 / 1630 / 2246	1.1 / 5.2 / 1.1 / 5.4		**17** F	0458 / 1113 / 1715 / 2327	0.7 / 5.4 / 0.9 / 5.7
3 F	0458 / 1108 / 1708 / 2323	1.0 / 5.2 / 1.1 / 5.4		**18** SA	0543 / 1158 / 1758	0.7 / 5.3 / 1.0
4 SA	0538 / 1148 / 1747	1.0 / 5.2 / 1.0		**19** SU	0010 / 0626 / 1242 / 1839	5.6 / 0.8 / 5.1 / 1.2
5 SU	0003 / 0619 / 1231 / 1829	5.4 / 1.0 / 5.1 / 1.2		**20** M	0052 / 0709 / 1324 / 1921	5.4 / 1.0 / 4.9 / 1.4
6 M	0046 / 0704 / 1317 / 1915	5.3 / 1.0 / 5.0 / 1.3		**21** TU	0134 / 0752 / 1406 / 2005	5.2 / 1.2 / 4.7 / 1.6
7 TU	0132 / 0753 / 1407 / 2006	5.3 / 1.1 / 4.9 / 1.4		**22** W	0216 / 0837 / 1451 / 2052	5.0 / 1.4 / 4.6 / 1.8
8 W	0224 / 0848 / 1503 / 2104	5.2 / 1.2 / 4.8 / 1.5		**23** TH ◑	0303 / 0926 / 1543 / 2146	4.8 / 1.7 / 4.4 / 2.1
9 TH ◑	0322 / 0949 / 1608 / 2209	5.1 / 1.2 / 4.7 / 1.6		**24** F	0356 / 1021 / 1643 / 2248	4.6 / 1.8 / 4.3 / 2.2
10 F	0427 / 1055 / 1717 / 2318	5.0 / 1.3 / 4.7 / 1.6		**25** SA	0458 / 1122 / 1749 / 2355	4.5 / 1.9 / 4.3 / 2.2
11 SA	0537 / 1201 / 1824	5.0 / 1.2 / 4.9		**26** SU	0604 / 1224 / 1853	4.5 / 1.9 / 4.4
12 SU	0025 / 0644 / 1304 / 1924	1.5 / 5.1 / 1.1 / 5.0		**27** M	0058 / 0708 / 1321 / 1947	2.1 / 4.5 / 1.8 / 4.6
13 M	0128 / 0747 / 1402 / 2019	1.3 / 5.2 / 1.0 / 5.2		**28** TU	0153 / 0803 / 1410 / 2032	1.8 / 4.7 / 1.7 / 4.8
14 TU	0226 / 0844 / 1455 / 2109	1.1 / 5.3 / 0.9 / 5.4		**29** W	0240 / 0850 / 1453 / 2112	1.6 / 4.8 / 1.5 / 5.1
15 W ○	0320 / 0937 / 1544 / 2156	0.9 / 5.4 / 0.9 / 5.6		**30** TH	0323 / 0932 / 1533 / 2150	1.3 / 5.0 / 1.3 / 5.3

JULY

Day	Time	m		Day	Time	m
1 F ●	0403 / 1012 / 1613 / 2228	1.1 / 5.1 / 1.1 / 5.4		**16** SA	0447 / 1100 / 1659 / 2310	0.8 / 5.3 / 1.0 / 5.6
2 SA	0443 / 1052 / 1652 / 2308	0.9 / 5.3 / 1.0 / 5.6		**17** SU	0526 / 1139 / 1737 / 2348	0.8 / 5.2 / 1.0 / 5.6
3 SU	0524 / 1133 / 1733 / 2349	0.8 / 5.3 / 0.9 / 5.6		**18** M	0603 / 1215 / 1813	0.8 / 5.2 / 1.1
4 M	0605 / 1216 / 1815	0.7 / 5.4 / 0.9		**19** TU	0025 / 0639 / 1251 / 1849	5.5 / 0.9 / 5.1 / 1.2
5 TU	0031 / 0649 / 1301 / 1859	5.6 / 0.7 / 5.3 / 1.0		**20** W	0101 / 0715 / 1326 / 1926	5.4 / 1.1 / 4.9 / 1.4
6 W	0116 / 0735 / 1348 / 1946	5.6 / 0.8 / 5.2 / 1.1		**21** TH	0137 / 0752 / 1402 / 2005	5.2 / 1.3 / 4.8 / 1.7
7 TH	0204 / 0825 / 1438 / 2039	5.5 / 0.9 / 5.0 / 1.3		**22** F	0216 / 0832 / 1444 / 2050	5.0 / 1.6 / 4.6 / 1.9
8 F	0257 / 0921 / 1536 / 2139	5.3 / 1.1 / 4.9 / 1.5		**23** SA ◑	0300 / 0918 / 1535 / 2145	4.7 / 1.8 / 4.4 / 2.1
9 SA	0359 / 1025 / 1644 / 2249	5.1 / 1.3 / 4.8 / 1.6		**24** SU	0356 / 1015 / 1641 / 2253	4.5 / 2.1 / 4.3 / 2.3
10 SU	0511 / 1135 / 1757	4.9 / 1.5 / 4.8		**25** M	0508 / 1125 / 1757	4.3 / 2.2 / 4.3
11 M	0004 / 0628 / 1246 / 1907	1.6 / 4.9 / 1.5 / 4.9		**26** TU	0011 / 0625 / 1238 / 1907	2.2 / 4.4 / 2.1 / 4.5
12 TU	0117 / 0740 / 1351 / 2008	1.5 / 4.9 / 1.4 / 5.1		**27** W	0120 / 0734 / 1339 / 2004	2.0 / 4.5 / 1.9 / 4.8
13 W	0221 / 0842 / 1448 / 2101	1.3 / 5.0 / 1.3 / 5.3		**28** TH	0216 / 0826 / 1430 / 2050	1.7 / 4.8 / 1.6 / 5.0
14 TH	0317 / 0934 / 1536 / 2148	1.1 / 5.2 / 1.1 / 5.5		**29** F	0302 / 0914 / 1513 / 2130	1.3 / 5.0 / 1.3 / 5.3
15 F ○	0404 / 1019 / 1620 / 2230	0.9 / 5.3 / 1.0 / 5.6		**30** SA ●	0344 / 0954 / 1554 / 2209	1.0 / 5.2 / 1.0 / 5.6
				31 SU	0424 / 1034 / 1633 / 2248	0.7 / 5.4 / 0.8 / 5.8

AUGUST

Day	Time	m		Day	Time	m
1 M	0504 / 1114 / 1713 / 2329	0.5 / 5.6 / 0.6 / 5.9		**16** TU	0534 / 1144 / 1744 / 2355	0.8 / 5.3 / 1.0 / 5.6
2 TU	0545 / 1155 / 1755	0.4 / 5.6 / 0.6		**17** W	0606 / 1215 / 1816	0.9 / 5.2 / 1.1
3 W	0011 / 0627 / 1239 / 1838	5.9 / 0.4 / 5.6 / 0.7		**18** TH	0027 / 0637 / 1247 / 1849	5.4 / 1.1 / 5.1 / 1.3
4 TH	0055 / 0711 / 1324 / 1924	5.8 / 0.6 / 5.4 / 0.9		**19** F	0100 / 0710 / 1320 / 1925	5.3 / 1.3 / 5.0 / 1.5
5 F	0142 / 0759 / 1412 / 2015	5.6 / 0.8 / 5.2 / 1.1		**20** SA	0136 / 0746 / 1357 / 2005	5.0 / 1.5 / 4.8 / 1.8
6 SA	0233 / 0853 / 1507 / 2115	5.4 / 1.2 / 5.0 / 1.4		**21** SU ◑	0215 / 0827 / 1441 / 2055	4.8 / 1.8 / 4.6 / 2.1
7 SU	0335 / 0958 / 1616 / 2229	5.0 / 1.5 / 4.7 / 1.7		**22** M	0305 / 0920 / 1540 / 2201	4.5 / 2.1 / 4.4 / 2.3
8 M	0455 / 1116 / 1738 / 2354	4.7 / 1.8 / 4.7 / 1.8		**23** TU	0415 / 1030 / 1704 / 2326	4.3 / 2.3 / 4.3 / 2.3
9 TU	0625 / 1235 / 1858	4.6 / 1.8 / 4.8		**24** W	0548 / 1155 / 1829	4.3 / 2.3 / 4.5
10 W	0114 / 0743 / 1346 / 2003	1.7 / 4.7 / 1.7 / 5.0		**25** TH	0047 / 0708 / 1309 / 1934	2.1 / 4.4 / 2.0 / 4.7
11 TH	0221 / 0842 / 1442 / 2054	1.4 / 4.9 / 1.5 / 5.3		**26** F	0149 / 0806 / 1405 / 2023	1.7 / 4.8 / 1.7 / 5.1
12 F	0312 / 0929 / 1527 / 2137	1.1 / 5.1 / 1.2 / 5.5		**27** SA	0238 / 0852 / 1450 / 2105	1.3 / 5.1 / 1.3 / 5.4
13 SA	0353 / 1007 / 1605 / 2214	1.0 / 5.2 / 1.1 / 5.6		**28** SU	0320 / 0932 / 1530 / 2144	0.8 / 5.4 / 0.9 / 5.8
14 SU	0430 / 1041 / 1639 / 2249	0.8 / 5.3 / 1.0 / 5.6		**29** M ●	0359 / 1011 / 1610 / 2224	0.5 / 5.6 / 0.6 / 6.0
15 M	0503 / 1113 / 1712 / 2322	0.8 / 5.4 / 0.9 / 5.6		**30** TU	0439 / 1050 / 1650 / 2305	0.3 / 5.8 / 0.4 / 6.2
				31 W	0520 / 1131 / 1732 / 2348	0.2 / 5.9 / 0.4 / 6.1

Chart Datum: 3·05 metres below Ordnance Datum (Newlyn)
HAT is 6·3m above Chart Datum

TIME ZONE (UT)
For Summer Time add ONE hour in **non-shaded areas**

WALES – HOLYHEAD
LAT 53°19'N   LONG 4°37'W

Dates in amber are **SPRINGS**
Dates in yellow are **NEAPS**

2011

TIMES AND HEIGHTS OF HIGH AND LOW WATERS

SEPTEMBER

Day	Time	m	Time	m	Day	Time	m	Time	m
1 TH	0602 / 1214 / 1815	0.3 / 5.8 / 0.5			16 F	0602 / 1213 / 1818	1.1 / 5.3 / 1.3		
2 F	0033 / 0646 / 1259 / 1902	6.0 / 0.5 / 5.6 / 0.7			17 SA	0028 / 0633 / 1246 / 1852	5.3 / 1.3 / 5.1 / 1.5		
3 SA	0121 / 0734 / 1347 / 1954	5.7 / 0.9 / 5.3 / 1.1			18 SU	0103 / 0708 / 1321 / 1931	5.1 / 1.6 / 5.0 / 1.7		
4 SU	0214 / 0829 / 1443 / 2057	5.3 / 1.3 / 5.0 / 1.5			19 M	0141 / 0747 / 1402 / 2018	4.8 / 1.8 / 4.8 / 2.0		
5 M	0319 / 0937 / 1554 / 2216	4.9 / 1.8 / 4.8 / 1.8			20 TU	0229 / 0837 / 1457 / 2123	4.6 / 2.1 / 4.5 / 2.2		
6 TU	0447 / 1100 / 1723 / 2346	4.6 / 2.0 / 4.7 / 1.9			21 W	0336 / 0947 / 1616 / 2248	4.3 / 2.3 / 4.4 / 2.3		
7 W	0624 / 1224 / 1847	4.5 / 2.0 / 4.8			22 TH	0512 / 1116 / 1749	4.3 / 2.3 / 4.5		
8 TH	0108 / 0740 / 1335 / 1952	1.7 / 4.7 / 1.8 / 5.0			23 F	0012 / 0637 / 1236 / 1859	2.0 / 4.5 / 2.1 / 4.8		
9 F	0210 / 0833 / 1428 / 2040	1.4 / 4.9 / 1.6 / 5.3			24 SA	0117 / 0737 / 1334 / 1952	1.6 / 4.8 / 1.7 / 5.2		
10 SA	0256 / 0913 / 1509 / 2118	1.2 / 5.1 / 1.3 / 5.4			25 SU	0207 / 0824 / 1421 / 2036	1.2 / 5.2 / 1.2 / 5.6		
11 SU	0333 / 0946 / 1544 / 2151	1.0 / 5.2 / 1.1 / 5.6			26 M	0251 / 0905 / 1503 / 2117	0.7 / 5.5 / 0.8 / 5.9		
12 M	0405 / 1016 / 1615 / ○2223	0.9 / 5.3 / 1.0 / 5.6			27 TU	0332 / 0945 / 1544 / ●2159	0.4 / 5.8 / 0.5 / 6.1		
13 TU	0435 / 1045 / 1645 / 2254	0.9 / 5.4 / 1.0 / 5.6			28 W	0413 / 1025 / 1626 / 2242	0.2 / 6.0 / 0.4 / 6.3		
14 W	0503 / 1113 / 1715 / 2324	0.9 / 5.4 / 1.0 / 5.6			29 TH	0455 / 1107 / 1710 / 2327	0.2 / 6.0 / 0.3 / 6.2		
15 TH	0532 / 1143 / 1746 / 2356	1.0 / 5.3 / 1.1 / 5.5			30 F	0539 / 1151 / 1756	0.3 / 5.9 / 0.5		

OCTOBER

Day	Time	m	Day	Time	m
1 SA	0014 / 0624 / 1237 / 1844	6.0 / 0.6 / 5.7 / 0.7	16 SU	0003 / 0604 / 1219 / 1828	5.3 / 1.4 / 5.3 / 1.5
2 SU	0104 / 0713 / 1327 / 1939	5.6 / 1.1 / 5.5 / 1.1	17 M	0039 / 0640 / 1255 / 1908	5.1 / 1.6 / 5.1 / 1.7
3 M	0200 / 0809 / 1424 / 2044	5.2 / 1.5 / 5.1 / 1.5	18 TU	0119 / 0720 / 1337 / 1955	4.9 / 1.8 / 4.9 / 1.9
4 TU	0308 / 0917 / 1534 / 2203	4.8 / 1.9 / 4.9 / 1.8	19 W	0207 / 0810 / 1430 / 2057	4.7 / 2.1 / 4.8 / 2.0
5 W	0436 / 1039 / 1700 / 2328	4.5 / 2.2 / 4.7 / 1.9	20 TH	0311 / 0917 / 1540 / 2214	4.5 / 2.3 / 4.6 / 2.1
6 TH	0608 / 1201 / 1823	4.5 / 2.2 / 4.8	21 F	0437 / 1039 / 1706 / 2333	4.4 / 2.3 / 4.7 / 1.9
7 F	0045 / 0719 / 1310 / 1926	1.8 / 4.7 / 2.0 / 5.0	22 SA	0600 / 1157 / 1819	4.6 / 2.1 / 4.9
8 SA	0145 / 0810 / 1403 / 2014	1.6 / 4.9 / 1.7 / 5.2	23 SU	0039 / 0703 / 1259 / 1916	1.5 / 4.9 / 1.7 / 5.3
9 SU	0230 / 0848 / 1444 / 2052	1.4 / 5.1 / 1.5 / 5.3	24 M	0134 / 0753 / 1350 / 2006	1.1 / 5.3 / 1.3 / 5.6
10 M	0305 / 0920 / 1518 / 2125	1.2 / 5.2 / 1.3 / 5.5	25 TU	0221 / 0837 / 1437 / 2051	0.8 / 5.6 / 0.9 / 5.9
11 TU	0336 / 0948 / 1549 / 2156	1.1 / 5.3 / 1.2 / 5.5	26 W	0306 / 0920 / 1521 / ●2137	0.5 / 5.8 / 0.6 / 6.1
12 W	0405 / 1016 / 1619 / ○2226	1.1 / 5.4 / 1.1 / 5.6	27 TH	0349 / 1002 / 1606 / 2223	0.4 / 6.0 / 0.4 / 6.2
13 TH	0433 / 1045 / 1649 / 2257	1.1 / 5.4 / 1.1 / 5.5	28 F	0434 / 1046 / 1653 / 2310	0.4 / 6.1 / 0.4 / 6.1
14 F	0502 / 1114 / 1720 / 2329	1.1 / 5.4 / 1.2 / 5.4	29 SA	0519 / 1132 / 1741	0.5 / 6.0 / 0.5
15 SA	0532 / 1145 / 1753	1.2 / 5.4 / 1.3	30 SU	0000 / 0606 / 1220 / 1832	5.9 / 0.8 / 5.8 / 0.8
			31 M	0052 / 0656 / 1310 / 1927	5.5 / 1.2 / 5.6 / 1.1

NOVEMBER

Day	Time	m	Day	Time	m
1 TU	0147 / 0750 / 1405 / 2028	5.1 / 1.6 / 5.3 / 1.5	16 W	0105 / 0703 / 1321 / 1940	5.0 / 1.7 / 5.2 / 1.6
2 W	0251 / 0853 / 1509 / ◐2138	4.8 / 1.9 / 5.0 / 1.7	17 TH	0153 / 0752 / 1411 / 2036	4.8 / 1.9 / 5.0 / 1.7
3 TH	0407 / 1006 / 1623 / 2253	4.5 / 2.2 / 4.8 / 1.9	18 F	0251 / 0852 / 1512 / ◐2142	4.7 / 2.0 / 4.9 / 1.7
4 F	0529 / 1122 / 1739	4.5 / 2.3 / 4.8	19 SA	0402 / 1002 / 1624 / 2253	4.6 / 2.1 / 4.9 / 1.7
5 SA	0004 / 0639 / 1230 / 1845	1.9 / 4.6 / 2.2 / 4.9	20 SU	0518 / 1116 / 1737	4.7 / 2.0 / 5.0
6 SU	0105 / 0733 / 1327 / 1937	1.8 / 4.8 / 2.0 / 5.0	21 M	0001 / 0625 / 1223 / 1841	1.5 / 4.9 / 1.7 / 5.3
7 M	0153 / 0815 / 1412 / 2019	1.6 / 4.9 / 1.8 / 5.1	22 TU	0101 / 0722 / 1321 / 1938	1.2 / 5.2 / 1.4 / 5.5
8 TU	0232 / 0849 / 1449 / 2055	1.5 / 5.1 / 1.6 / 5.3	23 W	0154 / 0812 / 1414 / 2030	1.0 / 5.5 / 1.1 / 5.7
9 W	0306 / 0921 / 1523 / 2129	1.4 / 5.1 / 1.4 / 5.4	24 TH	0244 / 0859 / 1504 / 2120	0.8 / 5.7 / 0.8 / 5.9
10 TH	0336 / 0950 / 1555 / ○2202	1.3 / 5.4 / 1.3 / 5.4	25 F	0331 / 0945 / 1553 / ●2210	0.7 / 5.9 / 0.6 / 5.9
11 F	0406 / 1020 / 1627 / 2235	1.2 / 5.5 / 1.2 / 5.4	26 SA	0418 / 1031 / 1642 / 2259	0.7 / 6.0 / 0.6 / 5.7
12 SA	0437 / 1051 / 1700 / 2309	1.2 / 5.5 / 1.2 / 5.4	27 SU	0505 / 1118 / 1732 / 2349	0.8 / 6.0 / 0.6 / 5.7
13 SU	0510 / 1124 / 1735 / 2344	1.3 / 5.5 / 1.3 / 5.3	28 M	0552 / 1205 / 1822	0.9 / 5.9 / 0.8
14 M	0544 / 1159 / 1813	1.4 / 5.4 / 1.4	29 TU	0039 / 0639 / 1254 / 1912	5.5 / 1.2 / 5.7 / 1.0
15 TU	0022 / 0621 / 1238 / 1853	5.2 / 1.5 / 5.3 / 1.5	30 W	0130 / 0729 / 1343 / 2005	5.3 / 1.5 / 5.4 / 1.3

DECEMBER

Day	Time	m	Day	Time	m
1 TH	0223 / 0821 / 1436 / 2101	4.9 / 1.8 / 5.2 / 1.6	16 F	0137 / 0735 / 1353 / 2014	5.1 / 1.5 / 5.3 / 1.4
2 F	0322 / 0920 / 1534 / ◐2203	4.6 / 2.1 / 4.9 / 1.8	17 SA	0228 / 0827 / 1445 / 2111	5.0 / 1.7 / 5.2 / 1.4
3 SA	0428 / 1026 / 1638 / 2308	4.5 / 2.2 / 4.8 / 2.0	18 SU	0326 / 0928 / 1546 / 2215	4.9 / 1.8 / 5.1 / 1.5
4 SU	0538 / 1135 / 1745	4.5 / 2.3 / 4.7	19 M	0435 / 1036 / 1657 / 2324	4.8 / 1.8 / 5.1 / 1.5
5 M	0010 / 0641 / 1238 / 1847	2.0 / 4.6 / 2.2 / 4.7	20 TU	0547 / 1148 / 1809	4.9 / 1.8 / 5.1
6 TU	0106 / 0734 / 1333 / 1941	1.9 / 4.7 / 2.0 / 4.9	21 W	0031 / 0653 / 1257 / 1917	1.4 / 5.0 / 1.6 / 5.2
7 W	0154 / 0816 / 1419 / 2026	1.8 / 4.9 / 1.8 / 5.0	22 TH	0133 / 0752 / 1358 / 2018	1.3 / 5.3 / 1.3 / 5.4
8 TH	0234 / 0851 / 1458 / 2105	1.6 / 5.1 / 1.6 / 5.1	23 F	0229 / 0845 / 1455 / 2113	1.1 / 5.5 / 1.0 / 5.6
9 F	0310 / 0927 / 1535 / 2142	1.5 / 5.3 / 1.5 / 5.2	24 SA	0321 / 0934 / 1547 / ●2204	1.0 / 5.7 / 0.8 / 5.6
10 SA	0344 / 1000 / 1610 / ○2217	1.4 / 5.4 / 1.3 / 5.3	25 SU	0409 / 1021 / 1636 / 2251	0.9 / 5.9 / 0.7 / 5.7
11 SU	0418 / 1033 / 1646 / 2253	1.3 / 5.5 / 1.2 / 5.3	26 M	0454 / 1106 / 1722 / 2337	0.9 / 6.0 / 0.7 / 5.6
12 M	0453 / 1108 / 1722 / 2330	1.3 / 5.6 / 1.2 / 5.3	27 TU	0538 / 1150 / 1807	0.9 / 5.9 / 0.7
13 TU	0530 / 1145 / 1801	1.2 / 5.6 / 1.1	28 W	0021 / 0620 / 1234 / 1850	5.4 / 1.1 / 5.8 / 0.9
14 W	0009 / 0608 / 1225 / 1841	5.3 / 1.3 / 5.5 / 1.2	29 TH	0104 / 0702 / 1316 / 1933	5.2 / 1.3 / 5.6 / 1.2
15 TH	0052 / 0649 / 1307 / 1925	5.2 / 1.4 / 5.4 / 1.3	30 F	0147 / 0745 / 1358 / 2017	5.0 / 1.5 / 5.3 / 1.4
			31 SA	0230 / 0831 / 1443 / 2105	4.8 / 1.8 / 5.1 / 1.7

Chart Datum: 3·05 metres below Ordnance Datum (Newlyn)
HAT is 6·3m above Chart Datum

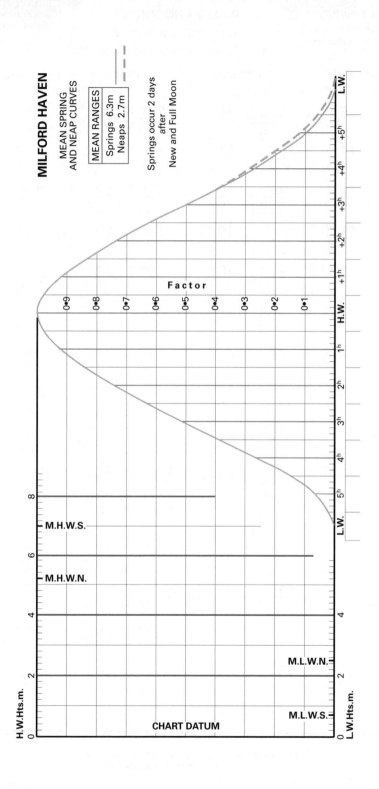

MILFORD HAVEN

MEAN SPRING
AND NEAP CURVES

MEAN RANGES
Springs 6.3m
Neaps 2.7m

Springs occur 2 days
after
New and Full Moon

Factor

0•9 0•8 0•7 0•6 0•5 0•4 0•3 0•2 0•1

H.W.Hts.m.

M.H.W.S.

M.H.W.N.

M.L.W.N.

M.L.W.S.

CHART DATUM

L.W.Hts.m.

H.W.

L.W.

TIME ZONE (UT)
For Summer Time add ONE hour in **non-shaded areas**

WALES – MILFORD HAVEN
LAT 51°42'N   LONG 5°03'W
TIMES AND HEIGHTS OF HIGH AND LOW WATERS

Dates in amber are **SPRINGS**
Dates in yellow are **NEAPS**

2011

JANUARY

Day	Time	m	Time	m		Day	Time	m	Time	m
1 SA	0320 / 0947	5.9 / 1.9	1552 / 2219	6.0 / 1.8		16 SU	0255 / 0924	5.4 / 2.4	1528 / 2150	5.5 / 2.2
2 SU	0423 / 1047	6.2 / 1.6	1651 / 2312	6.2 / 1.5		17 M	0357 / 1023	5.8 / 2.0	1625 / 2244	5.9 / 1.7
3 M	0516 / 1138	6.5 / 1.4	1742 / 2358	6.4 / 1.3		18 TU	0449 / 1114	6.3 / 1.5	1715 / 2332	6.4 / 1.3
4 TU ●	0603 / 1222	6.7 / 1.2	1825	6.6		19 W ○	0536 / 1200	6.7 / 1.1	1801	6.8
5 W	0039 / 0643	1.2 / 6.9	1303 / 1904	1.1 / 6.6		20 TH	0017 / 0620	0.9 / 7.1	1245 / 1845	0.7 / 7.0
6 TH	0117 / 0721	1.2 / 6.9	1340 / 1940	1.1 / 6.6		21 F	0101 / 0704	0.7 / 7.4	1329 / 1929	0.5 / 7.2
7 F	0152 / 0757	1.2 / 6.8	1414 / 2014	1.2 / 6.5		22 SA	0144 / 0748	0.5 / 7.5	1412 / 2012	0.4 / 7.2
8 SA	0225 / 0830	1.3 / 6.7	1447 / 2046	1.3 / 6.3		23 SU	0227 / 0831	0.5 / 7.4	1454 / 2055	0.5 / 7.1
9 SU	0256 / 0903	1.5 / 6.5	1518 / 2118	1.5 / 6.1		24 M	0309 / 0915	0.7 / 7.2	1537 / 2139	0.8 / 6.8
10 M	0327 / 0937	1.7 / 6.3	1551 / 2151	1.8 / 5.9		25 TU	0352 / 1000	1.0 / 6.9	1620 / 2224	1.2 / 6.4
11 TU	0400 / 1013	2.0 / 6.0	1627 / 2229	2.1 / 5.6		26 W ◑	0438 / 1048	1.4 / 6.4	1708 / 2316	1.6 / 6.0
12 W ◑	0439 / 1054	2.3 / 5.7	1710 / 2315	2.4 / 5.3		27 TH	0532 / 1146	1.8 / 5.9	1809	2.1
13 TH	0529 / 1146	2.6 / 5.4	1808	2.6		28 F	0020 / 0643	5.6 / 2.2	1257 / 1930	5.5 / 2.4
14 F	0015 / 0641	5.1 / 2.8	1256 / 1926	5.2 / 2.7		29 SA	0141 / 0814	5.4 / 2.4	1423 / 2058	5.4 / 2.3
15 SA	0136 / 0809	5.1 / 2.7	1417 / 2045	5.2 / 2.5		30 SU	0306 / 0937	5.6 / 2.2	1544 / 2210	5.6 / 2.1
						31 M	0416 / 1041	5.9 / 1.8	1645 / 2304	5.9 / 1.7

FEBRUARY

Day	Time	m	Time	m		Day	Time	m	Time	m
1 TU	0508 / 1130	6.3 / 1.5	1732 / 2348	6.2 / 1.4		16 W	0427 / 1054	6.2 / 1.4	1656 / 2312	6.4 / 1.2
2 W	0551 / 1211	6.6 / 1.2	1812	6.5		17 TH	0517 / 1142	6.8 / 0.9	1743 / 2359	6.9 / 0.7
3 TH ●	0026 / 0628	1.2 / 6.8	1247 / 1847	1.1 / 6.6		18 F	0603 / 1227	7.2 / 0.4	1828	7.3
4 F	0100 / 0703	1.1 / 6.9	1319 / 1919	1.0 / 6.7		19 SA	0043 / 0646	0.4 / 7.6	1311 / 1910	0.2 / 7.5
5 SA	0131 / 0734	1.0 / 6.9	1350 / 1949	1.0 / 6.6		20 SU	0127 / 0729	0.2 / 7.7	1353 / 1952	0.1 / 7.5
6 SU	0200 / 0804	1.1 / 6.8	1419 / 2017	1.1 / 6.6		21 M	0208 / 0812	0.1 / 7.7	1434 / 2033	0.2 / 7.3
7 M	0229 / 0834	1.2 / 6.7	1447 / 2046	1.2 / 6.4		22 TU	0249 / 0853	0.4 / 7.4	1513 / 2114	0.6 / 7.0
8 TU	0256 / 0903	1.4 / 6.5	1515 / 2114	1.5 / 6.2		23 W	0330 / 0936	0.7 / 6.9	1554 / 2157	1.1 / 6.5
9 W	0325 / 0934	1.6 / 6.2	1546 / 2146	1.8 / 5.9		24 TH	0413 / 1021	1.3 / 6.3	1637 / 2246	1.7 / 6.0
10 TH	0357 / 1008	2.0 / 5.8	1620 / 2223	2.1 / 5.6		25 F	0503 / 1114	1.8 / 5.7	1733 / 2348	2.2 / 5.5
11 F ◑	0436 / 1051	2.3 / 5.5	1704 / 2313	2.4 / 5.2		26 SA	0614 / 1227	2.3 / 5.2	1859	2.6
12 SA	0532 / 1152	2.7 / 5.1	1813	2.7		27 SU	0115 / 0755	5.2 / 2.5	1405 / 2042	5.1 / 2.5
13 SU	0029 / 0708	5.0 / 2.8	1322 / 1957	5.0 / 2.7		28 M	0250 / 0925	5.4 / 2.3	1533 / 2156	5.3 / 2.2
14 M	0209 / 0848	5.1 / 2.5	1455 / 2120	5.3 / 2.3						
15 TU	0329 / 0959	5.6 / 2.0	1603 / 2221	5.8 / 1.8						

MARCH

Day	Time	m	Time	m		Day	Time	m	Time	m
1 TU	0401 / 1027	5.8 / 1.9	1631 / 2249	5.8 / 1.8		16 W	0258 / 0930	5.6 / 1.9	1536 / 2155	5.8 / 1.7
2 W	0450 / 1113	6.2 / 1.5	1714 / 2329	6.2 / 1.4		17 TH	0400 / 1028	6.2 / 1.3	1631 / 2248	6.4 / 1.1
3 TH	0530 / 1150	6.5 / 1.2	1750	6.4		18 F	0452 / 1118	6.8 / 0.7	1719 / 2336	6.9 / 0.6
4 F ●	0004 / 0605	1.2 / 6.7	1223 / 1822	1.0 / 6.6		19 SA ○	0539 / 1204	7.3 / 0.3	1804	7.3
5 SA	0036 / 0637	1.0 / 6.8	1253 / 1852	0.9 / 6.7		20 SU	0021 / 0623	0.2 / 7.6	1248 / 1847	0.1 / 7.6
6 SU	0105 / 0707	0.9 / 6.9	1322 / 1920	0.9 / 6.7		21 M	0105 / 0707	0.0 / 7.7	1330 / 1929	0.0 / 7.6
7 M	0133 / 0736	0.9 / 6.8	1349 / 1948	0.9 / 6.7		22 TU	0147 / 0749	0.1 / 7.6	1411 / 2010	0.2 / 7.4
8 TU	0201 / 0804	1.0 / 6.7	1417 / 2015	1.1 / 6.6		23 W	0228 / 0831	0.3 / 7.3	1450 / 2051	0.6 / 7.0
9 W	0228 / 0832	1.2 / 6.5	1444 / 2042	1.3 / 6.4		24 TH	0309 / 0914	0.7 / 6.8	1530 / 2134	1.1 / 6.5
10 TH	0257 / 0901	1.4 / 6.3	1513 / 2112	1.6 / 6.1		25 F	0353 / 0958	1.3 / 6.2	1613 / 2222	1.7 / 6.0
11 F	0328 / 0934	1.8 / 5.9	1545 / 2147	1.9 / 5.8		26 SA ◑	0443 / 1051	1.9 / 5.6	1707 / 2323	2.3 / 5.5
12 SA ◑	0404 / 1014	2.1 / 5.6	1626 / 2234	2.3 / 5.4		27 SU	0552 / 1201	2.4 / 5.1	1830	2.6
13 SU	0456 / 1113	2.5 / 5.2	1729 / 2346	2.6 / 5.1		28 M	0047 / 0728	5.2 / 2.5	1338 / 2012	4.9 / 2.6
14 M	0623 / 1242	2.7 / 5.0	1915	2.7		29 TU	0220 / 0856	5.3 / 2.3	1503 / 2127	5.2 / 2.3
15 TU	0128 / 0814	5.1 / 2.5	1424 / 2049	5.2 / 2.3		30 W	0329 / 0956	5.7 / 1.9	1601 / 2219	5.6 / 1.9
						31 TH	0420 / 1041	6.0 / 1.6	1644 / 2259	6.0 / 1.5

APRIL

Day	Time	m	Time	m		Day	Time	m	Time	m
1 F	0500 / 1118	6.3 / 1.3	1720 / 2334	6.3 / 1.3		16 SA	0423 / 1049	6.8 / 0.8	1651 / 2309	6.9 / 0.7
2 SA	0535 / 1151	6.6 / 1.1	1752	6.5		17 SU	0512 / 1137	7.2 / 0.4	1738 / 2357	7.2 / 0.4
3 SU ●	0006 / 0607	1.1 / 6.7	1222 / 1822	1.0 / 6.6		18 M ○	0559 / 1223	7.4 / 0.3	1823	7.4
4 M	0037 / 0637	1.0 / 6.7	1252 / 1850	1.0 / 6.7		19 TU	0042 / 0644	0.2 / 7.5	1307 / 1906	0.3 / 7.4
5 TU	0106 / 0706	1.0 / 6.7	1320 / 1919	1.0 / 6.7		20 W	0126 / 0728	0.3 / 7.3	1349 / 1949	0.5 / 7.3
6 W	0135 / 0736	1.0 / 6.7	1349 / 1947	1.1 / 6.6		21 TH	0210 / 0812	0.5 / 7.0	1430 / 2032	0.8 / 7.0
7 TH	0204 / 0805	1.2 / 6.5	1419 / 2017	1.3 / 6.5		22 F	0253 / 0855	0.9 / 6.6	1511 / 2116	1.3 / 6.5
8 F	0235 / 0837	1.4 / 6.3	1450 / 2049	1.5 / 6.2		23 SA	0337 / 0941	1.4 / 6.1	1555 / 2204	1.8 / 6.1
9 SA	0309 / 0912	1.7 / 6.0	1524 / 2127	1.8 / 5.9		24 SU	0427 / 1031	1.8 / 5.6	1646 / 2300	2.2 / 5.6
10 SU	0349 / 0956	2.0 / 5.6	1608 / 2217	2.1 / 5.6		25 M	0529 / 1134	2.2 / 5.2	1756	2.5
11 M	0443 / 1056	2.2 / 5.3	1711 / 2327	2.4 / 5.4		26 TU ◑	0011 / 0646	5.3 / 2.4	1254 / 1922	5.0 / 2.6
12 TU ◑	0603 / 1219	2.4 / 5.2	1844	2.5		27 W	0132 / 0805	5.3 / 2.4	1414 / 2038	5.1 / 2.4
13 W	0058 / 0741	5.4 / 2.2	1351 / 2014	5.4 / 2.2		28 TH	0241 / 0909	5.5 / 2.1	1515 / 2134	5.4 / 2.1
14 TH	0223 / 0857	5.6 / 1.8	1504 / 2122	5.8 / 1.7		29 F	0336 / 0958	5.8 / 1.8	1603 / 2219	5.8 / 1.8
15 F	0328 / 0957	6.3 / 1.2	1601 / 2219	6.4 / 1.1		30 SA	0420 / 1039	6.1 / 1.6	1642 / 2258	6.1 / 1.5

Chart Datum: 3·71 metres below Ordnance Datum (Newlyn)
HAT is 7·9m above Chart Datum

WALES – MILFORD HAVEN
LAT 51°42'N   LONG 5°03'W
TIMES AND HEIGHTS OF HIGH AND LOW WATERS

TIME ZONE (UT)
For Summer Time add ONE hour in **non-shaded areas**

Dates in amber are **SPRINGS**
Dates in yellow are **NEAPS**

2011

MAY

Day	Time	m	Day	Time	m
1 SU	0459	6.3	16 M	0447	6.9
	1115	1.4		1112	0.8
	1717	6.3		1713	7.0
	2333	1.4		2334	0.7
2 M	0534	6.4	17 TU	0537	7.0
	1149	1.2		1200	0.6
	1750	6.5		1801	7.1 ○
3 TU	0007	1.2	18 W	0023	0.6
	0607	6.5		0625	7.1
	1222	1.1		1246	0.6
	● 1821	6.6		1847	7.2
4 W	0040	1.2	19 TH	0110	0.6
	0639	6.6		0712	7.0
	1254	1.1		1330	0.8
	1853	6.6		1933	7.1
5 TH	0112	1.2	20 F	0155	0.7
	0712	6.5		0757	6.8
	1326	1.2		1413	1.0
	1925	6.6		2017	6.9
6 F	0146	1.2	21 SA	0239	1.0
	0746	6.5		0840	6.4
	1400	1.3		1455	1.3
	1959	6.5		2101	6.6
7 SA	0221	1.3	22 SU	0322	1.3
	0822	6.3		0924	6.1
	1436	1.4		1537	1.7
	2036	6.4		2145	6.2
8 SU	0300	1.5	23 M	0408	1.7
	0902	6.1		1009	5.7
	1515	1.7		1623	2.0
	2119	6.1		2233	5.9
9 M	0344	1.7	24 TU	0457	2.0
	0950	5.8		1059	5.4
	1603	1.9		1716	2.3
	2212	5.9		☽ 2328	5.6
10 TU	0438	1.9	25 W	0555	2.3
	1049	5.6		1159	5.2
	1702	2.1		1820	2.5
	☽ 2317	5.7			
11 W	0548	2.0	26 TH	0033	5.4
	1200	5.5		0659	2.3
	1819	2.2		1309	5.1
				1930	2.5
12 TH	0032	5.7	27 F	0141	5.4
	0707	1.9		0805	2.3
	1317	5.6		1416	5.3
	1938	2.0		2035	2.3
13 F	0148	5.9	28 SA	0242	5.5
	0820	1.7		0904	2.1
	1428	5.9		1512	5.5
	2047	1.7		2131	2.1
14 SA	0254	6.2	29 SU	0334	5.7
	0924	1.3		0953	1.9
	1529	6.3		1600	5.8
	2148	1.3		2218	1.9
15 SU	0353	6.6	30 M	0420	6.0
	1020	1.0		1037	1.7
	1623	6.7		1641	6.1
	2243	0.9		2300	1.7
			31 TU	0501	6.2
				1116	1.5
				1719	6.3
				2339	1.5

JUNE

Day	Time	m	Day	Time	m
1 W	0539	6.3	16 TH	0009	0.9
	1154	1.3		0613	6.7
	1756	6.5		1231	1.0
				● 1835	6.9
2 TH	0016	1.3	17 F	0057	0.9
	0616	6.4		0700	6.7
	1231	1.2		1316	1.0
	1832	6.6		1920	6.9
3 F	0054	1.2	18 SA	0141	0.9
	0654	6.5		0743	6.6
	1309	1.2		1358	1.1
	1910	6.7		2002	6.8
4 SA	0132	1.2	19 SU	0223	1.0
	0733	6.5		0823	6.5
	1347	1.2		1437	1.3
	1949	6.7		2042	6.6
5 SU	0212	1.2	20 M	0302	1.2
	0814	6.4		0902	6.2
	1427	1.2		1515	1.5
	2030	6.6		2122	6.4
6 M	0254	1.2	21 TU	0341	1.5
	0857	6.3		0941	6.0
	1510	1.4		1553	1.8
	2116	6.5		2201	6.1
7 TU	0339	1.4	22 W	0420	1.8
	0944	6.1		1020	5.7
	1557	1.5		1632	2.0
	2206	6.3		2243	5.8
8 W	0430	1.5	23 TH	0502	2.0
	1037	6.0		1104	5.4
	1650	1.7		1719	2.3
	2302	6.1		☽ 2332	5.6
9 TH	0528	1.7	24 F	0553	2.3
	1137	5.8		1157	5.2
	1752	1.8		1817	2.5
10 F	0005	6.0	25 SA	0030	5.4
	0634	1.8		0653	2.4
	1244	5.8		1304	5.1
	1902	1.9		1925	2.5
11 SA	0114	6.0	26 SU	0139	5.3
	0744	1.7		0800	2.4
	1354	5.8		1414	5.2
	2014	1.8		2035	2.4
12 SU	0223	6.1	27 M	0244	5.4
	0853	1.6		0904	2.2
	1459	6.1		1515	5.5
	2122	1.6		2137	2.2
13 M	0328	6.2	28 TU	0341	5.6
	0956	1.4		0959	2.0
	1600	6.3		1607	5.8
	2223	1.3		2229	1.9
14 TU	0428	6.4	29 W	0431	5.9
	1052	1.2		1047	1.7
	1656	6.6		1652	6.1
	2318	1.1		2314	1.6
15 W	0523	6.6	30 TH	0516	6.2
	1144	1.0		1130	1.5
	1747	6.8 ○		1735	6.4
				2357	1.4

JULY

Day	Time	m	Day	Time	m
1 F	0558	6.4	16 SA	0045	1.0
	1212	1.2		0647	6.6
	1816	6.7 ●		1301	1.0
				1905	6.9
2 SA	0038	1.1	17 SU	0125	0.9
	0639	6.6		0725	6.6
	1254	1.0		1339	1.0
	1857	6.8		1943	6.9
3 SU	0120	0.9	18 M	0202	1.0
	0721	6.7		0801	6.6
	1335	0.9		1414	1.1
	1939	6.9		2018	6.8
4 M	0202	0.9	19 TU	0236	1.1
	0804	6.8		0835	6.4
	1417	0.9		1447	1.3
	2021	7.0		2052	6.6
5 TU	0245	0.9	20 W	0308	1.3
	0847	6.7		0907	6.2
	1500	1.0		1518	1.5
	2105	6.9		2125	6.3
6 W	0328	1.0	21 TH	0340	1.6
	0931	6.5		0940	6.0
	1544	1.1		1550	1.8
	2152	6.7		2200	6.0
7 TH	0413	1.2	22 F	0413	1.8
	1019	6.3		1016	5.7
	1631	1.4		1626	2.1
	2241	6.4		2239	5.7
8 F	0503	1.5	23 SA	0452	2.2
	1111	6.0		1057	5.4
	1725	1.6		1711	2.4
	● 2337	6.1		☽ 2326	5.4
9 SA	0602	1.7	24 SU	0543	2.4
	1212	5.8		1151	5.2
	1831	1.9		1814	2.6
10 SU	0043	5.9	25 M	0028	5.1
	0711	1.9		0654	2.6
	1323	5.7		1306	5.1
	1947	2.0		1938	2.7
11 M	0157	5.8	26 TU	0149	5.1
	0829	2.0		0815	2.6
	1437	5.8		1430	5.2
	2104	1.9		2058	2.5
12 TU	0311	5.8	27 W	0305	5.3
	0941	1.8		0925	2.3
	1547	6.0		1536	5.6
	2213	1.6		2201	2.1
13 W	0419	6.0	28 TH	0405	5.7
	1042	1.6		1021	1.9
	1647	6.4		1629	6.0
	2311	1.4		2252	1.7
14 TH	0516	6.3	29 F	0455	6.1
	1134	1.3		1109	1.5
	1739	6.6		1715	6.5
				2338	1.3
15 F	0001	1.1	30 SA	0540	6.5
	0604	6.5		1154	1.1
	1220	1.1		1758	6.8 ●
	○ 1824	6.8			
			31 SU	0021	0.9
				0622	6.8
				1237	0.8
				1841	7.1

AUGUST

Day	Time	m	Day	Time	m
1 M	0105	0.6	16 TU	0134	0.9
	0705	7.0		0734	6.7
	1320	0.6		1346	1.0
	1923	7.3		1949	6.9
2 TU	0147	0.5	17 W	0204	1.0
	0747	7.1		0803	6.6
	1402	0.5		1415	1.2
	2005	7.4		2020	6.7
3 W	0228	0.5	18 TH	0233	1.2
	0829	7.1		0832	6.4
	1443	0.6		1444	1.4
	2048	7.2		2049	6.5
4 TH	0310	0.7	19 F	0302	1.4
	0911	6.9		0902	6.2
	1525	0.8		1512	1.6
	2131	7.0		2120	6.2
5 F	0352	1.0	20 SA	0331	1.7
	0955	6.6		0933	5.9
	1609	1.2		1544	2.0
	2218	6.6		2154	5.9
6 SA	0437	1.4	21 SU	0405	2.1
	1044	6.2		1008	5.6
	1700	1.6		1622	2.4
	☽ 2311	6.1		☽ 2234	5.5
7 SU	0532	1.9	22 M	0447	2.4
	1143	5.8		1055	5.3
	1804	2.0		1714	2.7
				2331	5.1
8 M	0017	5.6	23 TU	0550	2.7
	0645	2.2		1205	5.0
	1259	5.5		1843	2.8
	1929	2.3			
9 TU	0140	5.4	24 W	0055	4.9
	0815	2.3		0729	2.7
	1425	5.5		1343	5.1
	2058	2.2		2024	2.7
10 W	0306	5.5	25 TH	0231	5.1
	0934	2.1		0854	2.4
	1542	5.9		1506	5.5
	2209	1.8		2135	2.2
11 TH	0416	5.8	26 F	0340	5.6
	1035	1.7		0956	1.9
	1641	6.3		1604	6.0
	2305	1.5		2229	1.6
12 F	0508	6.2	27 SA	0432	6.2
	1124	1.4		1047	1.4
	1728	6.6		1652	6.6
	2349	1.2		2316	1.1
13 SA	0551	6.5	28 SU	0518	6.7
	1205	1.2		1132	0.9
	1809	6.8 ○		1737	7.1
14 SU	0028	1.0	29 M	0000	0.7
	0628	6.6		0601	7.1
	1242	1.0		● 1217	0.7
	1845	6.9		1819	7.4
15 M	0103	0.9	30 TU	0044	0.4
	0702	6.7		0643	7.4
	1315	1.0		1259	0.3
	1918	6.9		1902	7.6
			31 W	0126	0.2
				0725	7.5
				1341	0.3
				1944	7.6

Chart Datum: 3·71 metres below Ordnance Datum (Newlyn)
HAT is 7·9m above Chart Datum

TIME ZONE (UT)	WALES – MILFORD HAVEN	Dates in amber are SPRINGS
For Summer Time add ONE hour in non-shaded areas	LAT 51°42′N LONG 5°03′W	Dates in yellow are NEAPS
	TIMES AND HEIGHTS OF HIGH AND LOW WATERS	2011

SEPTEMBER

Time	m		Time	m
1 0207	0.3	**16** 0201	1.2
0807	7.4	0759	6.6
TH 1423	0.4	F 1412	1.3
2026	7.4	2016	6.6
2 0248	0.6	**17** 0228	1.4
0848	7.1	0827	6.4
F 1505	0.7	SA 1441	1.4
2109	7.0	2046	6.3
3 0329	1.0	**18** 0257	1.7
0932	6.7	0857	6.1
SA 1548	1.2	SU 1512	1.9
2155	6.5	2118	6.0
4 0413	1.5	**19** 0329	2.0
1020	6.2	0932	5.8
SU 1638	1.7	M 1549	2.3
☽ 2248	5.9	2156	5.6
5 0507	2.1	**20** 0409	2.4
1120	5.7	1016	5.5
M 1746	2.2	TU 1638	2.6
2356	5.4	☽ 2251	5.2
6 0626	2.5	**21** 0507	2.7
1241	5.4	1123	5.2
TU 1921	2.5	W 1759	2.8
7 0128	5.2	**22** 0014	5.0
0806	2.5	0646	2.8
W 1416	5.5	TH 1300	5.1
2053	2.3	1949	2.7
8 0300	5.4	**23** 0156	5.2
0926	2.2	0822	2.5
TH 1531	5.9	F 1432	5.5
2200	1.9	2105	2.2
9 0404	5.8	**24** 0310	5.7
1023	1.8	0928	2.0
F 1626	6.3	SA 1534	6.1
2249	1.5	2202	1.6
10 0451	6.2	**25** 0405	6.3
1107	1.4	1020	1.4
SA 1709	6.6	SU 1625	6.7
2329	1.2	2250	1.0
11 0530	6.5	**26** 0452	6.8
1144	1.2	1108	0.9
SU 1746	6.8	M 1711	7.2
		2336	0.6
12 0003	1.1	**27** 0536	7.3
0603	6.8	1152	0.5
M 1217	1.1	TU 1755	7.6
○ 1819	6.9	●	
13 0035	1.0	**28** 0019	0.3
0635	6.8	0619	7.5
TU 1247	1.0	W 1237	0.3
1850	6.9	1839	7.7
14 0104	1.0	**29** 0103	0.3
0704	6.8	0702	7.6
W 1316	1.0	TH 1320	0.2
1919	6.9	1922	7.7
15 0133	1.0	**30** 0145	0.3
0732	6.7	0744	7.5
TH 1345	1.1	F 1403	0.4
1948	6.8	2006	7.4

OCTOBER

Time	m		Time	m
1 0226	0.7	**16** 0202	1.4
0827	7.2	0801	6.5
SA 1446	0.8	SU 1418	1.6
2050	7.0	2020	6.3
2 0308	1.1	**17** 0233	1.7
0912	6.8	0833	6.3
SU 1531	1.3	M 1452	1.9
2136	6.4	2054	6.1
3 0353	1.7	**18** 0307	2.0
1002	6.2	0909	6.0
M 1623	1.9	TU 1530	2.2
2230	5.8	2135	5.7
4 0448	2.2	**19** 0348	2.3
1102	5.7	0955	5.7
TU 1732	2.3	W 1621	2.5
☽ 2338	5.3	2230	5.4
5 0608	2.6	**20** 0445	2.6
1222	5.4	1100	5.4
W 1905	2.5	TH 1733	2.6
		☽ 2347	5.2
6 0109	5.1	**21** 0611	2.7
0746	2.6	1226	5.4
TH 1352	5.5	F 1912	2.5
2032	2.4		
7 0236	5.3	**22** 0117	5.3
0903	2.3	0744	2.5
F 1505	5.8	SA 1352	5.7
2135	2.0	2029	2.1
8 0338	5.7	**23** 0234	5.8
0957	1.9	0854	2.0
SA 1558	6.2	SU 1500	6.2
2222	1.7	2129	1.6
9 0423	6.1	**24** 0333	6.3
1040	1.6	0950	1.5
SU 1640	6.5	M 1554	6.7
2300	1.4	2222	1.1
10 0501	6.4	**25** 0423	6.8
1116	1.4	1041	1.0
M 1717	6.7	TU 1644	7.2
2333	1.2	2310	0.7
11 0535	6.6	**26** 0510	7.2
1148	1.2	1129	0.6
TU 1750	6.8	W 1731	7.5
		● 2356	0.5
12 0004	1.1	**27** 0556	7.5
0605	6.7	1215	0.4
W 1219	1.1	TH 1818	7.6
○ 1820	6.9		
13 0035	1.1	**28** 0041	0.4
0634	6.8	0640	7.6
TH 1249	1.2	F 1301	0.4
1850	6.8	1903	7.5
14 0104	1.2	**29** 0125	0.5
0703	6.8	0725	7.5
F 1318	1.2	SA 1347	0.6
1920	6.7	1949	7.3
15 0132	1.3	**30** 0208	0.8
0732	6.7	0811	7.2
SA 1347	1.4	SU 1432	0.9
1949	6.6	2035	6.9
		31 0252	1.3
		0857	6.8
		M 1519	1.4
		2122	6.4

NOVEMBER

Time	m		Time	m
1 0338	1.7	**16** 0255	1.8
0946	6.4	0859	6.3
TU 1610	1.8	W 1522	1.9
2214	5.9	2126	5.9
2 0431	2.2	**17** 0339	2.1
1043	5.9	0946	6.0
W 1712	2.3	TH 1611	2.1
☽ 2314	5.4	2219	5.7
3 0539	2.5	**18** 0432	2.3
1151	5.6	1044	5.8
TH 1828	2.5	F 1713	2.3
		☽ 2324	5.5
4 0030	5.2	**19** 0541	2.4
0702	2.7	1155	5.7
F 1309	5.5	SA 1831	2.3
1946	2.5		
5 0150	5.3	**20** 0039	5.6
0819	2.5	0702	2.3
SA 1420	5.7	SU 1312	5.9
2051	2.2	1948	2.1
6 0255	5.6	**21** 0154	5.8
0917	2.2	0815	2.0
SU 1518	5.9	M 1422	6.2
2142	2.0	2054	1.7
7 0346	5.9	**22** 0259	6.2
1004	1.9	0919	1.6
M 1604	6.2	TU 1524	6.5
2224	1.7	2153	1.4
8 0427	6.2	**23** 0355	6.6
1044	1.7	1016	1.2
TU 1644	6.4	W 1619	6.9
2301	1.5	2246	1.0
9 0504	6.4	**24** 0447	7.0
1119	1.5	1109	0.9
W 1720	6.6	TH 1712	7.1
2335	1.4	2336	0.8
10 0537	6.6	**25** 0537	7.3
1153	1.4	1159	0.7
TH 1754	6.7	F 1802	7.3
○		●	
11 0007	1.3	**26** 0024	0.7
0609	6.7	0625	7.4
F 1226	1.3	SA 1248	0.6
1826	6.7	1850	7.2
12 0039	1.3	**27** 0110	0.8
0640	6.7	0712	7.4
SA 1257	1.3	SU 1335	0.7
1858	6.7	1937	7.1
13 0111	1.3	**28** 0155	0.9
0711	6.7	0758	7.2
SU 1330	1.4	M 1421	0.9
1931	6.6	2022	6.8
14 0144	1.4	**29** 0238	1.2
0744	6.6	0844	6.9
M 1404	1.5	TU 1506	1.3
2005	6.4	2107	6.4
15 0218	1.6	**30** 0322	1.6
0819	6.5	0929	6.6
TU 1441	1.7	W 1552	1.6
2042	6.2	2153	6.0

DECEMBER

Time	m		Time	m
1 0408	2.0	**16** 0330	1.6
1017	6.2	0937	6.4
TH 1642	2.0	F 1600	1.7
2242	5.7	2205	6.1
2 0500	2.3	**17** 0417	1.8
1110	5.8	1028	6.3
F 1737	2.3	SA 1651	1.8
2338	5.4	2300	5.9
3 0601	2.5	**18** 0513	2.0
1211	5.6	1126	6.1
SA 1841	2.5	SU 1753	2.0
		☽	
4 0046	5.3	**19** 0003	5.8
0711	2.6	0620	2.1
SU 1320	5.5	M 1234	6.0
1948	2.5	1905	2.0
5 0157	5.3	**20** 0115	5.8
0821	2.5	0736	2.1
M 1425	5.6	TU 1347	6.0
2051	2.3	2019	1.9
6 0258	5.5	**21** 0227	5.9
0920	2.3	0850	1.9
TU 1521	5.8	W 1457	6.2
2143	2.1	2128	1.7
7 0349	5.8	**22** 0332	6.3
1009	2.1	0957	1.6
W 1610	6.0	TH 1601	6.4
2228	1.9	2229	1.4
8 0433	6.1	**23** 0432	6.6
1052	1.8	1056	1.2
TH 1652	6.2	F 1700	6.7
2307	1.7	2323	1.1
9 0512	6.4	**24** 0526	6.9
1130	1.6	1149	1.0
F 1731	6.4	SA 1753	6.9
2344	1.5	●	
10 0548	6.5	**25** 0013	0.9
1207	1.5	0616	7.2
SA 1807	6.5	SU 1239	0.8
○		1841	7.0
11 0020	1.4	**26** 0059	0.9
0622	6.7	0702	7.3
SU 1242	1.4	M 1325	0.8
1842	6.6	1926	7.0
12 0055	1.3	**27** 0142	0.9
0657	6.8	0746	7.2
M 1318	1.3	TU 1408	0.9
1919	6.6	2008	6.8
13 0131	1.3	**28** 0223	1.1
0734	6.8	0827	7.0
TU 1355	1.3	W 1448	1.1
1956	6.6	2048	6.6
14 0209	1.3	**29** 0302	1.3
0811	6.7	0907	6.8
W 1434	1.3	TH 1527	1.4
2035	6.5	2126	6.3
15 0248	1.5	**30** 0339	1.6
0852	6.6	0946	6.4
TH 1515	1.5	F 1605	1.7
2118	6.3	2205	6.0
		31 0417	1.9
		1027	6.1
		SA 1645	2.0
		2246	5.6

Chart Datum: 3·71 metres below Ordnance Datum (Newlyn)
HAT is 7·9m above Chart Datum

TIDES

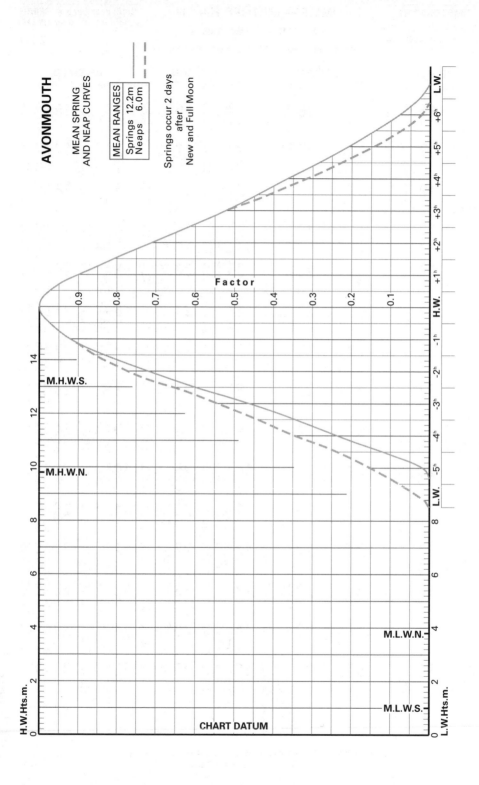

AVONMOUTH

MEAN SPRING
AND NEAP CURVES

MEAN RANGES
Springs 12.2m
Neaps 6.0m

Springs occur 2 days
after
New and Full Moon

Factor

0.9
0.8
0.7
0.6
0.5
0.4
0.3
0.2
0.1

M.H.W.S.

M.H.W.N.

M.L.W.N.

M.L.W.S.

CHART DATUM

H.W.Hts.m.

L.W.Hts.m.

TIME ZONE (UT)
For Summer Time add ONE hour in **non-shaded areas**

AVONMOUTH
LAT 51°30'N   LONG 2°44'W
TIMES AND HEIGHTS OF HIGH AND LOW WATERS

Dates in amber are **SPRINGS**
Dates in yellow are **NEAPS**

2011

JANUARY

Time m	Time m
1 SA 0412 10.9 / 1048 3.0 / 1643 11.2 / 2322 2.8	**16** SU 0335 10.1 / 1008 3.6 / 1616 10.5 / 2246 3.1
2 SU 0513 11.5 / 1150 2.5 / 1741 11.8	**17** M 0446 10.9 / 1120 2.9 / 1719 11.3 / 2351 2.4
3 M 0020 2.2 / 0606 12.1 / 1245 2.0 / 1832 12.2	**18** TU 0542 11.9 / 1222 2.2 / 1813 12.1
4 TU 0112 1.8 / 0654 12.6 / 1337 1.6 / ● 1919 12.5	**19** W 0048 1.9 / 0632 12.7 / 1320 1.7 / ○ 1901 12.8
5 W 0201 1.6 / 0738 12.9 / 1424 1.5 / 2003 12.6	**20** TH 0144 1.5 / 0719 13.3 / 1415 1.4 / 1949 13.2
6 TH 0245 1.6 / 0820 12.9 / 1507 1.6 / 2042 12.5	**21** F 0235 1.2 / 0805 13.7 / 1505 1.1 / 2034 13.5
7 F 0324 1.7 / 0857 12.7 / 1543 1.8 / 2117 12.3	**22** SA 0322 1.0 / 0850 13.9 / 1548 1.0 / 2117 13.6
8 SA 0353 2.0 / 0930 12.4 / 1609 2.1 / 2146 12.0	**23** SU 0402 0.9 / 0932 13.9 / 1626 1.0 / 2157 13.5
9 SU 0413 2.3 / 1000 12.0 / 1631 2.3 / 2214 11.7	**24** M 0437 1.0 / 1013 13.6 / 1658 1.2 / 2236 13.1
10 M 0432 2.4 / 1028 11.6 / 1655 2.4 / 2242 11.4	**25** TU 0508 1.3 / 1054 13.1 / 1727 1.6 / 2316 12.5
11 TU 0459 2.5 / 1059 11.2 / 1725 2.6 / 2315 10.9	**26** W 0541 1.8 / 1138 12.3 / 1800 2.2 / ◐
12 W 0533 2.8 / 1136 10.7 / 1804 2.9 / ◑ 2356 10.4	**27** TH 0000 11.6 / 0619 2.5 / 1229 11.3 / 1842 3.0
13 TH 0616 3.3 / 1224 10.2 / 1854 3.4	**28** F 0057 10.7 / 0710 3.3 / 1340 10.4 / 1940 3.7
14 F 0051 10.0 / 0715 3.8 / 1332 9.8 / 2004 3.8	**29** SA 0224 10.0 / 0836 3.9 / 1510 10.1 / 2139 4.1
15 SA 0207 9.8 / 0841 4.0 / 1457 9.9 / 2129 3.7	**30** SU 0349 10.2 / 1025 3.7 / 1625 10.4 / 2302 3.4
	31 M 0457 10.9 / 1133 2.9 / 1728 11.1

FEBRUARY

Time m	Time m
1 TU 0002 2.6 / 0553 11.7 / 1228 2.2 / 1820 11.9	**16** W 0522 11.7 / 1206 2.3 / 1756 12.1
2 W 0055 1.9 / 0641 12.4 / 1319 1.6 / 1905 12.4	**17** TH 0032 1.9 / 0615 12.7 / 1306 1.5 / 1845 13.0
3 TH 0143 1.4 / 0724 12.9 / 1406 1.3 / ● 1946 12.7	**18** F 0129 1.2 / 0703 13.6 / 1401 1.0 / ○ 1932 13.7
4 F 0228 1.3 / 0802 13.0 / 1449 1.3 / 2023 12.7	**19** SA 0222 0.7 / 0744 14.1 / 1450 0.6 / 2016 14.1
5 SA 0307 1.4 / 0837 12.9 / 1526 1.4 / 2054 12.6	**20** SU 0308 0.4 / 0832 14.4 / 1533 0.4 / 2058 14.2
6 SU 0339 1.6 / 0907 12.7 / 1553 1.7 / 2121 12.3	**21** M 0348 0.3 / 0914 14.4 / 1609 0.5 / 2137 14.0
7 M 0358 2.0 / 0934 12.4 / 1610 2.0 / 2146 12.1	**22** TU 0421 0.5 / 0954 14.0 / 1638 0.9 / 2214 13.5
8 TU 0410 2.1 / 0959 12.0 / 1626 2.0 / 2211 11.8	**23** W 0449 1.0 / 1032 13.3 / 1702 1.5 / 2251 12.7
9 W 0430 2.1 / 1025 11.7 / 1650 2.1 / 2239 11.5	**24** TH 0516 1.6 / 1111 12.3 / 1729 2.2 / ◑ 2330 11.6
10 TH 0458 2.3 / 1056 11.2 / 1721 2.5 / 2314 11.0	**25** F 0548 2.5 / 1156 11.0 / 1806 3.1
11 F 0534 2.8 / 1138 10.6 / 1802 3.1	**26** SA 0020 10.5 / 0633 3.4 / 1304 9.9 / 1858 4.0
12 SA 0001 10.3 / 0620 3.4 / 1235 9.9 / 1859 3.8	**27** SU 0154 9.6 / 0749 4.2 / 1449 9.5 / 2103 4.5
13 SU 0107 9.8 / 0733 4.1 / 1357 9.5 / 2035 4.1	**28** M 0328 9.7 / 1005 4.0 / 1607 9.9 / 2243 3.7
14 M 0242 9.7 / 0925 4.0 / 1542 10.0 / 2213 3.6	
15 TU 0417 10.5 / 1055 3.2 / 1658 11.0 / 2329 2.7	

MARCH

Time m	Time m
1 TU 0438 10.5 / 1113 3.1 / 1709 10.8 / 2341 2.7	**16** W 0347 10.4 / 1032 3.2 / 1635 10.9 / 2307 2.7
2 W 0534 11.5 / 1206 2.1 / 1800 11.7	**17** TH 0458 11.6 / 1146 2.2 / 1734 12.1
3 TH 0031 1.8 / 0620 12.3 / 1255 1.5 / 1843 12.4	**18** F 0011 1.8 / 0553 12.8 / 1245 1.3 / 1824 13.2
4 F 0118 1.3 / 0701 12.8 / 1340 1.1 / ● 1921 12.7	**19** SA 0108 1.0 / 0641 13.7 / 1338 0.7 / ○ 1909 13.9
5 SA 0202 1.1 / 0737 13.0 / 1423 1.1 / 1955 12.8	**20** SU 0159 0.5 / 0727 14.3 / 1427 0.3 / 1953 14.3
6 SU 0242 1.2 / 0810 12.9 / 1500 1.4 / 2025 12.7	**21** M 0245 0.2 / 0811 14.5 / 1510 0.2 / 2034 14.3
7 M 0315 1.5 / 0840 12.7 / 1529 1.6 / 2052 12.4	**22** TU 0326 0.1 / 0852 14.4 / 1546 0.5 / 2114 14.1
8 TU 0337 1.8 / 0906 12.4 / 1546 1.9 / 2117 12.2	**23** W 0400 0.4 / 0932 13.9 / 1614 0.9 / 2151 13.5
9 W 0347 2.0 / 0930 12.1 / 1558 1.9 / 2140 12.1	**24** TH 0428 1.0 / 1011 13.1 / 1638 1.6 / 2228 12.6
10 TH 0403 1.9 / 0956 11.9 / 1619 2.0 / 2208 11.8	**25** F 0454 1.7 / 1049 12.0 / 1703 2.3 / 2306 11.5
11 F 0430 2.0 / 1027 11.5 / 1649 2.2 / 2243 11.3	**26** SA 0525 2.5 / 1132 10.8 / 1738 3.2 / ◐ 2354 10.3
12 SA 0503 2.4 / 1108 10.8 / 1726 2.8 / ◑ 2329 10.7	**27** SU 0610 3.5 / 1236 9.6 / 1830 4.1
13 SU 0546 3.1 / 1202 10.1 / 1817 3.5	**28** M 0129 9.5 / 0722 4.2 / 1425 9.3 / 2009 4.6
14 M 0031 10.0 / 0649 3.8 / 1319 9.5 / 1942 4.1	**29** TU 0302 9.6 / 0931 4.1 / 1539 9.8 / 2213 3.9
15 TU 0200 9.7 / 0844 4.0 / 1509 9.8 / 2143 3.7	**30** W 0407 10.4 / 1042 3.2 / 1638 10.6 / 2310 2.9
	31 TH 0502 11.3 / 1134 2.2 / 1728 11.5 / 2359 2.0

APRIL

Time m	Time m
1 F 0549 12.0 / 1221 1.6 / 1811 12.2	**16** SA 0526 12.7 / 1215 1.4 / 1757 13.0
2 SA 0045 1.4 / 0629 12.5 / 1307 1.2 / 1848 12.5	**17** SU 0038 1.0 / 0616 13.5 / 1309 0.8 / 1843 13.7
3 SU 0130 1.2 / 0705 12.7 / 1349 1.2 / ● 1922 12.6	**18** M 0130 0.5 / 0703 14.0 / 1358 0.5 / ○ 1927 14.1
4 M 0210 1.3 / 0739 12.6 / 1428 1.3 / 1953 12.6	**19** TU 0218 0.3 / 0748 14.2 / 1442 0.4 / 2010 14.1
5 TU 0245 1.5 / 0810 12.5 / 1459 1.6 / 2023 12.4	**20** W 0301 0.3 / 0831 14.0 / 1521 0.7 / 2051 13.8
6 W 0311 1.8 / 0839 12.3 / 1520 1.8 / 2049 12.3	**21** TH 0338 0.6 / 0913 13.5 / 1553 1.2 / 2131 13.2
7 TH 0325 2.0 / 0906 12.1 / 1534 1.9 / 2116 12.1	**22** F 0410 1.2 / 0953 12.7 / 1619 1.8 / 2210 12.4
8 F 0343 1.9 / 0934 11.9 / 1557 1.9 / 2146 11.9	**23** SA 0439 1.9 / 1033 11.7 / 1646 2.5 / 2249 11.4
9 SA 0411 2.0 / 1008 11.6 / 1628 2.1 / 2224 11.5	**24** SU 0511 2.6 / 1115 10.7 / 1721 3.2 / 2337 10.4
10 SU 0445 2.3 / 1051 11.0 / 1707 2.6 / 2311 10.9	**25** M 0555 3.3 / 1212 9.8 / 1811 3.9 / ◐
11 M 0529 2.8 / 1145 10.4 / 1758 3.3 / ◐	**26** TU 0056 9.7 / 0656 3.8 / 1343 9.4 / 1925 4.3
12 TU 0012 10.3 / 0631 3.5 / 1258 9.9 / 1915 3.8	**27** W 0223 9.7 / 0817 3.9 / 1457 9.7 / 2107 4.0
13 W 0135 10.1 / 0811 3.7 / 1436 10.0 / 2111 3.6	**28** TH 0326 10.2 / 0945 3.4 / 1556 10.3 / 2223 3.3
14 TH 0313 10.6 / 0959 3.1 / 1604 10.9 / 2236 2.7	**29** F 0421 10.9 / 1048 2.7 / 1647 11.0 / 2317 2.5
15 F 0428 11.6 / 1115 2.2 / 1706 12.1 / 2341 1.8	**30** SA 0508 11.5 / 1139 2.1 / 1731 11.7

Chart Datum: 6·50 metres below Ordnance Datum (Newlyn)
HAT is 14·7m above Chart Datum

TIDES

TIME ZONE (UT)
For Summer Time add ONE hour in **non-shaded areas**

AVONMOUTH
LAT 51°30'N LONG 2°44'W
TIMES AND HEIGHTS OF HIGH AND LOW WATERS

Dates in amber are **SPRINGS**
Dates in yellow are NEAPS

2011

MAY

Time m	Time m
1 SU 0005 1.9 / 0550 11.9 / 1227 1.7 / 1810 12.1	**16** M 0007 1.3 / 0550 12.9 / 1239 1.2 / 1818 13.2
2 M 0051 1.6 / 0629 12.2 / 1311 1.5 / 1847 12.4	**17** TU 0102 0.9 / 0640 13.3 / 1330 0.9 / 1904 13.5 ○
3 TU 0133 1.6 / 0706 12.3 / 1351 1.5 / ● 1922 12.4	**18** W 0152 0.7 / 0727 13.5 / 1417 0.9 / 1949 13.6
4 W 0211 1.6 / 0741 12.3 / 1427 1.6 / 1955 12.4	**19** TH 0239 0.7 / 0813 13.3 / 1500 1.1 / 2033 13.4
5 TH 0244 1.8 / 0815 12.2 / 1456 1.8 / 2027 12.3	**20** F 0321 1.0 / 0857 13.0 / 1538 1.5 / 2115 12.9
6 F 0309 1.9 / 0848 12.1 / 1520 1.9 / 2059 12.2	**21** SA 0358 1.4 / 0939 12.4 / 1608 2.0 / 2156 12.3
7 SA 0333 2.0 / 0922 11.9 / 1547 1.9 / 2135 12.0	**22** SU 0429 1.9 / 1019 11.7 / 1636 2.4 / 2236 11.6
8 SU 0403 2.0 / 1000 11.7 / 1620 2.1 / 2215 11.7	**23** M 0501 2.4 / 1059 11.0 / 1708 2.9 / 2318 10.9
9 M 0441 2.2 / 1045 11.3 / 1702 2.4 / 2303 11.3	**24** TU 0538 2.8 / 1142 10.4 / 1750 3.3 ◔
10 TU 0528 2.6 / 1137 10.9 / 1753 2.9 ◑	**25** W 0011 10.3 / 0626 3.2 / 1239 9.9 / 1844 3.7
11 W 0001 10.9 / 0627 2.9 / 1242 10.5 / 1903 3.3	**26** TH 0121 9.9 / 0723 3.4 / 1350 9.7 / 1950 3.8
12 TH 0115 10.7 / 0746 3.1 / 1403 10.5 / 2035 3.2	**27** F 0229 10.0 / 0827 3.4 / 1456 10.0 / 2101 3.6
13 F 0239 10.9 / 0919 2.8 / 1525 11.0 / 2159 2.6	**28** SA 0328 10.3 / 0935 3.1 / 1554 10.5 / 2213 3.1
14 SA 0353 11.6 / 1038 2.3 / 1632 11.8 / 2308 1.9	**29** SU 0420 10.8 / 1042 2.7 / 1645 11.0 / 2315 2.6
15 SU 0456 12.3 / 1142 1.7 / 1728 12.6	**30** M 0509 11.3 / 1139 2.2 / 1731 11.6
	31 TU 0007 2.1 / 0553 11.7 / 1230 1.9 / 1813 12.0

JUNE

Time m	Time m
1 W 0055 1.8 / 0635 12.0 / 1316 1.7 / ● 1854 12.3	**16** TH 0132 1.2 / 0711 12.8 / 1358 1.3 / 1933 13.1
2 TH 0139 1.8 / 0717 12.2 / 1359 1.7 / 1933 12.4	**17** F 0222 1.1 / 0759 12.8 / 1445 1.3 / 2018 13.0
3 F 0221 1.8 / 0757 12.2 / 1438 1.7 / 2012 12.5	**18** SA 0308 1.2 / 0844 12.7 / 1527 1.5 / 2101 12.8
4 SA 0259 1.8 / 0837 12.2 / 1513 1.8 / 2050 12.4	**19** SU 0348 1.5 / 0926 12.4 / 1601 1.9 / 2141 12.4
5 SU 0334 1.9 / 0917 12.2 / 1547 1.9 / 2130 12.4	**20** M 0421 1.8 / 1003 12.0 / 1628 2.2 / 2217 11.9
6 M 0409 1.9 / 0958 12.1 / 1623 1.9 / 2212 12.2	**21** TU 0448 2.1 / 1036 11.5 / 1653 2.5 / 2252 11.4
7 TU 0447 2.0 / 1041 11.9 / 1704 2.1 / 2259 11.9	**22** W 0517 2.4 / 1109 11.0 / 1724 2.7 / 2328 10.9
8 W 0530 2.1 / 1129 11.6 / 1751 2.3 / 2351 11.6	**23** TH 0553 2.6 / 1147 10.6 / 1804 3.1 ◑
9 TH 0621 2.4 / 1224 11.2 / 1848 2.6 ◑	**24** F 0013 10.4 / 0637 2.9 / 1235 10.2 / 1854 3.4
10 F 0053 11.3 / 0721 2.6 / 1331 11.0 / 1958 2.8	**25** SA 0111 10.0 / 0731 3.2 / 1337 9.9 / 1958 3.6
11 SA 0206 11.1 / 0835 2.8 / 1447 11.0 / 2121 2.8	**26** SU 0219 9.9 / 0835 3.3 / 1449 10.0 / 2110 3.6
12 SU 0320 11.3 / 1000 2.7 / 1559 11.3 / 2236 2.4	**27** M 0326 10.2 / 0945 3.2 / 1556 10.5 / 2222 3.1
13 M 0428 11.7 / 1111 2.3 / 1702 11.9 / 2340 1.9	**28** TU 0427 10.7 / 1053 2.7 / 1654 11.1 / 2326 2.6
14 TU 0528 12.2 / 1212 1.8 / 1756 12.5	**29** W 0521 11.3 / 1153 2.2 / 1744 11.7
15 W 0038 1.5 / 0621 12.6 / 1307 1.5 / ○ 1846 12.9	**30** TH 0022 2.1 / 0610 11.8 / 1247 1.9 / 1830 12.3

JULY

Time m	Time m
1 F 0114 1.8 / 0657 12.2 / 1337 1.7 / ● 1915 12.6	**16** SA 0207 1.2 / 0746 12.7 / 1431 1.3 / 2005 13.0
2 SA 0205 1.7 / 0742 12.4 / 1426 1.6 / 1959 12.8	**17** SU 0254 1.2 / 0829 12.7 / 1514 1.4 / 2045 13.0
3 SU 0253 1.6 / 0826 12.6 / 1510 1.6 / 2042 12.9	**18** M 0335 1.3 / 0907 12.5 / 1550 1.6 / 2121 12.7
4 M 0337 1.6 / 0909 12.7 / 1550 1.5 / 2124 13.0	**19** TU 0407 1.6 / 0940 12.2 / 1615 2.0 / 2153 12.3
5 TU 0415 1.6 / 0951 12.7 / 1626 1.5 / 2205 12.9	**20** W 0430 1.9 / 1008 11.9 / 1633 2.2 / 2221 11.8
6 W 0450 1.6 / 1032 12.6 / 1702 1.6 / 2248 12.6	**21** TH 0451 2.1 / 1035 11.5 / 1654 2.4 / 2250 11.4
7 TH 0525 1.7 / 1115 12.2 / 1740 1.9 / 2334 12.2	**22** F 0517 2.3 / 1105 11.1 / 1724 2.6 / 2323 10.8
8 F 0604 2.0 / 1202 11.7 / ◑ 1825 2.3	**23** SA 0551 2.7 / 1142 10.6 / 1802 3.1
9 SA 0027 11.6 / 0651 2.5 / 1259 11.1 / 1921 2.8	**24** SU 0006 10.2 / 0635 3.1 / 1231 10.1 / 1855 3.6
10 SU 0134 11.0 / 0752 3.0 / 1413 10.7 / 2041 3.2	**25** M 0108 9.8 / 0738 3.6 / 1341 9.7 / 2014 4.0
11 M 0252 10.8 / 0925 3.3 / 1532 10.7 / 2211 3.1	**26** TU 0231 9.7 / 0858 3.7 / 1508 9.9 / 2140 3.7
12 TU 0407 10.9 / 1048 3.0 / 1641 11.2 / 2321 2.6	**27** W 0350 10.1 / 1016 3.2 / 1622 10.6 / 2255 3.0
13 W 0512 11.4 / 1153 2.4 / 1741 11.9	**28** TH 0455 10.9 / 1124 2.6 / 1720 11.5 / 2359 2.3
14 TH 0021 2.0 / 0608 12.0 / 1250 1.9 / 1833 12.5	**29** F 0550 11.7 / 1224 2.0 / 1811 12.3
15 F 0116 1.5 / 0659 12.4 / 1343 1.5 / ○ 1920 12.9	**30** SA 0057 1.8 / 0639 12.4 / 1321 1.6 / ● 1858 12.9
	31 SU 0153 1.5 / 0726 12.9 / 1414 1.4 / 1944 13.4

AUGUST

Time m	Time m
1 M 0244 1.3 / 0811 13.2 / 1502 1.2 / 2028 13.6	**16** TU 0313 1.1 / 0841 12.7 / 1530 1.4 / 2055 12.9
2 TU 0330 1.1 / 0855 13.3 / 1544 1.0 / 2110 13.7	**17** W 0346 1.5 / 0911 12.4 / 1555 1.8 / 2124 12.5
3 W 0409 1.1 / 0935 13.4 / 1620 1.1 / 2151 13.5	**18** TH 0407 1.9 / 0936 12.1 / 1609 2.2 / 2149 12.1
4 TH 0441 1.2 / 1015 13.1 / 1651 1.3 / 2231 13.2	**19** F 0421 2.1 / 1001 11.8 / 1623 2.3 / 2213 11.6
5 F 0510 1.5 / 1054 12.7 / 1722 1.7 / 2313 12.5	**20** SA 0440 2.2 / 1027 11.4 / 1646 2.4 / 2241 11.1
6 SA 0540 2.0 / 1137 11.9 / 1758 2.3 ◑	**21** SU 0507 2.5 / 1058 10.9 / 1718 2.9 / 2318 10.5 ◑
7 SU 0000 11.6 / 0618 2.7 / 1229 11.0 / 1845 3.1	**22** M 0544 3.0 / 1141 10.3 / 1800 3.5
8 M 0104 10.6 / 0711 3.5 / 1345 10.3 / 2002 3.8	**23** TU 0010 9.8 / 0636 3.7 / 1243 9.7 / 1907 4.2
9 TU 0233 10.1 / 0858 4.0 / 1515 10.2 / 2155 3.7	**24** W 0132 9.4 / 0807 4.1 / 1419 9.6 / 2101 4.2
10 W 0354 10.3 / 1034 3.5 / 1628 10.8 / 2308 2.9	**25** TH 0318 9.7 / 0945 3.7 / 1554 10.3 / 2231 3.4
11 TH 0501 11.0 / 1138 2.7 / 1729 11.6	**26** F 0433 10.7 / 1102 2.9 / 1658 11.4 / 2342 2.5
12 F 0006 2.1 / 0556 11.8 / 1234 1.9 / 1820 12.4	**27** SA 0531 11.8 / 1206 2.1 / 1751 12.5
13 SA 0059 1.4 / 0645 12.4 / 1324 1.4 / ○ 1905 13.0	**28** SU 0041 1.7 / 0620 12.7 / 1304 1.5 / 1839 13.3
14 SU 0148 1.1 / 0728 12.8 / 1411 1.1 / 1946 13.2	**29** M 0136 1.2 / 0706 13.3 / 1357 1.1 / ● 1924 13.9
15 M 0233 1.0 / 0807 12.9 / 1454 1.1 / 2023 13.1	**30** TU 0227 0.9 / 0751 13.7 / 1446 0.9 / 2008 14.1
	31 W 0312 0.7 / 0833 13.9 / 1527 0.7 / 2050 14.2

Chart Datum: 6·50 metres below Ordnance Datum (Newlyn)
HAT is 14·7m above Chart Datum

TIME ZONE (UT)	AVONMOUTH	Dates in amber are **SPRINGS**
For Summer Time add ONE hour in **non-shaded areas**	LAT 51°30'N LONG 2°44'W	Dates in yellow are NEAPS
	TIMES AND HEIGHTS OF HIGH AND LOW WATERS	**2011**

SEPTEMBER

Time m	Time m
1 0351 0.8 / 0914 13.8 / TH 1603 0.8 / 2131 13.9	**16** 0339 1.9 / 0904 12.2 / F 1542 2.2 / 2118 12.1
2 0422 1.1 / 0953 13.5 / F 1633 1.1 / 2210 13.4	**17** 0350 2.2 / 0928 11.9 / SA 1553 2.3 / 2141 11.7
3 0448 1.6 / 1031 12.8 / SA 1701 1.7 / 2250 12.5	**18** 0407 2.3 / 0953 11.6 / SU 1616 2.4 / 2209 11.3
4 0514 2.2 / 1112 11.9 / SU 1733 2.5 / ◑ 2335 11.3	**19** 0433 2.5 / 1025 11.2 / M 1646 2.7 / 2246 10.7
5 0548 3.0 / 1202 10.8 / M 1816 3.4	**20** 0507 2.9 / 1107 10.5 / TU 1724 3.3 / ◑ 2335 10.0
6 0039 10.2 / 0638 3.9 / TU 1328 9.9 / 1933 4.2	**21** 0553 3.6 / 1205 9.9 / W 1821 4.1
7 0222 9.6 / 0846 4.5 / W 1502 9.9 / 2144 4.0	**22** 0049 9.4 / 0709 4.3 / TH 1333 9.6 / 2016 4.4
8 0341 10.0 / 1020 3.7 / TH 1612 10.7 / 2252 3.1	**23** 0243 9.6 / 0912 4.0 / F 1523 10.2 / 2206 3.6
9 0444 10.7 / 1119 2.7 / F 1710 11.6 / 2345 2.1	**24** 0408 10.6 / 1037 3.1 / SA 1632 11.4 / 2320 2.5
10 0537 11.8 / 1210 1.8 / SA 1759 12.5	**25** 0507 11.8 / 1143 2.1 / SU 1727 12.6
11 0034 1.3 / 0621 12.5 / SU 1258 1.2 / 1841 13.1	**26** 0018 1.7 / 0556 12.8 / M 1240 1.4 / 1815 13.5
12 0121 0.9 / 0702 12.9 / M 1343 1.0 / ○ 1920 13.2	**27** 0112 1.0 / 0642 13.6 / TU 1332 0.9 / ● 1901 14.1
13 0205 0.9 / 0738 12.9 / TU 1426 1.1 / 1954 13.1	**28** 0201 0.7 / 0726 14.0 / W 1420 0.6 / 1945 14.4
14 0244 1.1 / 0810 12.8 / W 1502 1.4 / 2026 12.8	**29** 0246 0.5 / 0809 14.2 / TH 1503 0.5 / 2028 14.4
15 0317 1.5 / 0839 12.5 / TH 1529 1.9 / 2053 12.5	**30** 0326 0.7 / 0850 14.0 / F 1541 0.7 / 2110 14.0

OCTOBER

Time m	Time m
1 0359 1.1 / 0930 13.5 / SA 1614 1.2 / 2150 13.3	**16** 0325 2.2 / 0901 12.0 / SU 1531 2.4 / 2118 11.8
2 0426 1.7 / 1010 12.8 / SU 1643 1.9 / 2231 12.3	**17** 0343 2.3 / 0929 11.8 / M 1555 2.4 / 2148 11.5
3 0452 2.4 / 1052 11.8 / M 1714 2.7 / 2316 11.1	**18** 0411 2.4 / 1004 11.4 / TU 1627 2.7 / 2227 11.0
4 0526 3.3 / 1143 10.6 / TU 1757 3.6 / ◑	**19** 0447 2.8 / 1047 10.9 / W 1707 3.1 / 2317 10.3
5 0021 10.0 / 0615 4.1 / W 1313 9.8 / 1910 4.3	**20** 0533 3.4 / 1144 10.3 / TH 1801 3.7 / ◑
6 0203 9.5 / 0809 4.6 / TH 1441 9.9 / 2117 4.1	**21** 0023 9.8 / 0639 4.0 / F 1301 10.0 / 1930 4.1
7 0316 9.9 / 0953 3.9 / F 1545 10.6 / 2223 3.2	**22** 0157 9.8 / 0829 4.0 / SA 1441 10.4 / 2126 3.6
8 0416 10.8 / 1050 2.9 / SA 1641 11.5 / 2315 2.3	**23** 0332 10.6 / 1002 3.2 / SU 1559 11.4 / 2246 2.7
9 0507 11.6 / 1139 2.0 / SU 1729 12.3	**24** 0436 11.7 / 1111 2.3 / M 1658 12.4 / 2347 1.8
10 0003 1.6 / 0550 12.3 / M 1226 1.4 / 1810 12.8	**25** 0529 12.7 / 1209 1.5 / TU 1749 13.3
11 0048 1.2 / 0629 12.7 / TU 1311 1.2 / 1848 13.0	**26** 0041 1.2 / 0616 13.5 / W 1303 1.0 / ● 1837 13.9
12 0131 1.1 / 0705 12.8 / W 1352 1.3 / ○ 1923 12.9	**27** 0132 0.8 / 0701 14.0 / TH 1352 0.7 / 1923 14.2
13 0211 1.2 / 0738 12.7 / TH 1430 1.5 / 1955 12.7	**28** 0219 0.7 / 0745 14.1 / F 1438 0.6 / 2007 14.2
14 0245 1.6 / 0808 12.5 / F 1459 1.9 / 2025 12.4	**29** 0301 0.8 / 0829 14.0 / SA 1520 0.8 / 2051 13.8
15 0310 1.9 / 0836 12.3 / SA 1518 2.2 / 2052 12.1	**30** 0338 1.2 / 0911 13.5 / SU 1557 1.3 / 2134 13.1
	31 0410 1.8 / 0953 12.7 / M 1630 1.9 / 2217 12.2

NOVEMBER

Time m	Time m
1 0439 2.5 / 1037 11.8 / TU 1703 2.6 / 2302 11.2	**16** 0402 2.4 / 0954 11.7 / W 1621 2.6 / 2220 11.3
2 0512 3.2 / 1127 10.9 / W 1744 3.4 / ◐ 2359 10.2	**17** 0439 2.6 / 1038 11.4 / TH 1703 2.8 / 2307 10.9
3 0558 3.9 / 1241 10.2 / TH 1842 3.9	**18** 0525 3.0 / 1131 11.0 / F 1754 3.2 / ◐
4 0123 9.7 / 0707 4.4 / F 1404 10.1 / 2004 4.1	**19** 0005 10.5 / 0623 3.4 / SA 1237 10.7 / 1902 3.5
5 0237 9.9 / 0854 4.2 / SA 1508 10.5 / 2132 3.6	**20** 0118 10.3 / 0743 3.6 / SU 1357 10.7 / 2032 3.5
6 0336 10.4 / 1007 3.5 / SU 1602 11.1 / 2232 2.9	**21** 0245 10.6 / 0917 3.3 / M 1518 11.3 / 2204 3.0
7 0428 11.1 / 1100 2.7 / M 1651 11.7 / 2323 2.2	**22** 0400 11.4 / 1035 2.6 / TU 1626 12.0 / 2313 2.2
8 0514 11.8 / 1148 2.1 / TU 1735 12.2	**23** 0500 12.3 / 1139 1.9 / W 1723 12.8
9 0010 1.7 / 0554 12.3 / W 1234 1.7 / 1815 12.5	**24** 0012 1.6 / 0552 13.0 / TH 1235 1.3 / 1815 13.4
10 0054 1.5 / 0632 12.5 / TH 1316 1.6 / ○ 1852 12.6	**25** 0105 1.2 / 0640 13.6 / F 1328 1.0 / ● 1904 13.7
11 0135 1.5 / 0707 12.6 / F 1355 1.7 / 1928 12.5	**26** 0155 1.0 / 0726 13.8 / SA 1417 0.9 / 1951 13.7
12 0212 1.6 / 0740 12.7 / SA 1430 1.9 / 2002 12.3	**27** 0241 1.0 / 0812 13.7 / SU 1503 1.0 / 2037 13.5
13 0244 1.9 / 0814 12.4 / SU 1458 2.2 / 2034 12.1	**28** 0323 1.3 / 0857 13.4 / M 1545 1.3 / 2122 13.0
14 0308 2.1 / 0845 12.2 / M 1521 2.3 / 2106 11.9	**29** 0400 1.8 / 0940 12.9 / TU 1621 1.8 / 2204 12.3
15 0332 2.2 / 0917 12.0 / TU 1547 2.4 / 2140 11.7	**30** 0430 2.3 / 1023 12.2 / W 1654 2.3 / 2246 11.6

DECEMBER

Time m	Time m
1 0500 2.8 / 1106 11.5 / TH 1728 2.8 / 2328 10.9	**16** 0438 2.2 / 1032 12.1 / F 1701 2.4 / 2258 11.7
2 0537 3.3 / 1156 10.8 / F 1810 3.3 / ◐	**17** 0519 2.4 / 1118 11.8 / SA 1745 2.6 / 2347 11.3
3 0019 10.2 / 0623 3.7 / SA 1302 10.3 / 1902 3.6	**18** 0608 2.7 / 1213 11.4 / SU 1837 2.9 / ◐
4 0130 9.9 / 0723 4.0 / SU 1412 10.2 / 2003 3.7	**19** 0045 10.9 / 0706 3.1 / M 1319 11.1 / 1941 3.2
5 0240 10.0 / 0834 3.9 / M 1513 10.4 / 2114 3.5	**20** 0159 10.7 / 0825 3.3 / TU 1438 11.0 / 2114 3.3
6 0339 10.4 / 0952 3.6 / TU 1607 10.8 / 2226 3.1	**21** 0322 10.9 / 0958 3.1 / W 1555 11.4 / 2241 2.9
7 0432 11.0 / 1059 3.0 / W 1657 11.3 / 2325 2.5	**22** 0433 11.5 / 1112 2.5 / TH 1701 12.0 / 2347 2.2
8 0518 11.6 / 1152 2.4 / TH 1742 11.8	**23** 0532 12.3 / 1213 1.9 / F 1758 12.6
9 0015 2.0 / 0601 12.1 / F 1239 2.0 / 1824 12.1	**24** 0044 1.7 / 0624 13.0 / SA 1310 1.4 / ● 1850 13.1
10 0101 1.7 / 0641 12.4 / SA 1324 1.9 / ○ 1904 12.3	**25** 0138 1.3 / 0713 13.4 / SU 1402 1.1 / 1939 13.3
11 0144 1.7 / 0720 12.5 / SU 1406 1.9 / 1943 12.3	**26** 0227 1.1 / 0800 13.6 / M 1451 1.0 / 2025 13.3
12 0224 1.8 / 0757 12.6 / M 1445 2.0 / 2022 12.3	**27** 0312 1.2 / 0844 13.5 / TU 1535 1.2 / 2109 13.1
13 0259 1.9 / 0834 12.5 / TU 1519 2.2 / 2059 12.2	**28** 0351 1.5 / 0926 13.2 / W 1612 1.5 / 2148 12.7
14 0330 2.1 / 0911 12.4 / W 1550 2.2 / 2136 12.1	**29** 0422 1.9 / 1004 12.7 / TH 1640 1.9 / 2223 12.1
15 0402 2.3 / 0950 12.3 / TH 1623 2.3 / 2215 12.0	**30** 0445 2.3 / 1039 12.1 / F 1706 2.3 / 2255 11.5
	31 0511 2.6 / 1114 11.4 / SA 1736 2.6 / 2328 11.0

Chart Datum: 6·50 metres below Ordnance Datum (Newlyn)
HAT is 14·7m above Chart Datum

TIDES

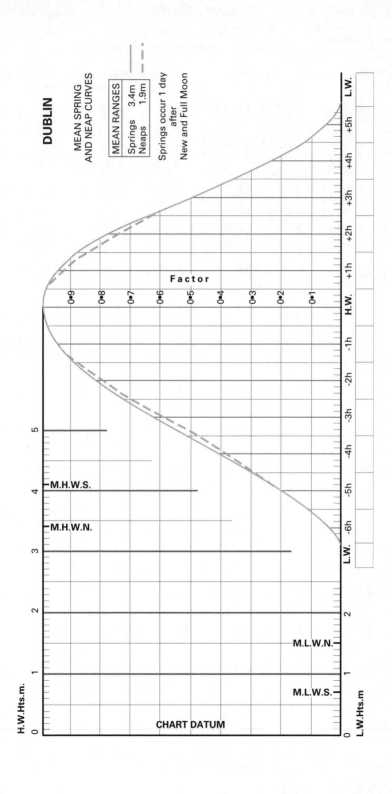

DUBLIN

MEAN SPRING AND NEAP CURVES

MEAN RANGES	
Springs	3.4m
Neaps	1.9m

Springs occur 1 day after
New and Full Moon

IRELAND – DUBLIN (NORTH WALL)

LAT 53°21'N   LONG 6°13'W

TIMES AND HEIGHTS OF HIGH AND LOW WATERS

Dates in amber are **SPRINGS**
Dates in yellow are **NEAPS**

2011

JANUARY

Day	Time m	Time m	Time m	Time m
1 SA	0222 1.2	0903 3.8	1453 1.2	2134 3.8
2 SU	0322 1.1	0959 3.9	1550 1.1	2231 3.8
3 M	0411 1.0	1048 4.0	1639 0.9	2320 3.8
4 TU	0453 1.0	1129 4.1	1721 0.8 ●	
5 W	0000 3.8	0530 0.9	1205 4.1	1800 0.7
6 TH	0035 3.8	0606 0.9	1238 4.1	1837 0.7
7 F	0108 3.7	0641 0.9	1314 4.1	1913 0.8
8 SA	0143 3.7	0717 1.0	1351 4.0	1951 0.8
9 SU	0221 3.6	0757 1.1	1430 3.9	2029 1.0
10 M	0302 3.5	0839 1.2	1512 3.8	2109 1.1
11 TU	0346 3.4	0925 1.4	1556 3.6	2153 1.3
12 W	0435 3.3	1018 1.5	1646 3.5	◑ 2243 1.4
13 TH	0536 3.3	1120 1.6	1746 3.3	2344 1.5
14 F	0647 3.3	1226 1.7	1859 3.3	
15 SA	0052 1.6	0752 3.3	1331 1.6	2009 3.3
16 SU	0156 1.5	0848 3.5	1430 1.4	2108 3.5
17 M	0251 1.4	0935 3.7	1520 1.2	2157 3.6
18 TU	0337 1.2	1017 3.9	1603 0.9	2241 3.8
19 W	0417 0.9	1057 4.1	1644 0.6	○ 2322 4.0
20 TH	0456 0.7	1137 4.2	1726 0.4	
21 F	0003 4.1	0535 0.6	1218 4.4	1808 0.3
22 SA	0046 4.1	0617 0.6	1302 4.4	1853 0.2
23 SU	0131 4.1	0701 0.6	1349 4.4	1941 0.3
24 M	0218 4.0	0750 0.7	1439 4.3	2032 0.5
25 TU	0309 3.9	0843 0.9	1532 4.1	2126 0.7
26 W	0404 3.8	0943 1.1	1630 3.9	◑ 2225 1.0
27 TH	0508 3.6	1050 1.3	1740 3.7	2331 1.2
28 F	0622 3.5	1206 1.4	1859 3.6	
29 SA	0047 1.4	0736 3.5	1331 1.4	2017 3.5
30 SU	0208 1.6	0846 3.6	1447 1.3	2128 3.6
31 M	0312 1.2	0948 3.8	1545 1.1	2227 3.6

FEBRUARY

Day	Time m	Time m	Time m	Time m
1 TU	0401 1.1	1039 3.9	1630 0.9	2314 3.7
2 W	0441 1.0	1120 4.0	1709 0.8	2350 3.7
3 TH	0516 0.9	1151 4.0	1743 0.7 ●	
4 F	0017 3.7	0548 0.8	1219 4.0	1815 0.7
5 SA	0042 3.7	0619 0.8	1249 4.0	1846 0.7
6 SU	0111 3.7	0650 0.8	1321 4.0	1915 0.8
7 M	0143 3.7	0721 0.9	1357 3.9	1945 0.8
8 TU	0218 3.6	0755 1.0	1435 3.8	2018 0.9
9 W	0257 3.6	0834 1.1	1516 3.7	2056 1.1
10 TH	0340 3.4	0917 1.3	1602 3.5	2139 1.3
11 F	0431 3.3	1010 1.5	1656 3.3	◑ 2233 1.5
12 SA	0535 3.2	1116 1.6	1805 3.2	2352 1.6
13 SU	0658 3.2	1247 1.6	1932 3.2	
14 M	0117 1.6	0811 3.3	1359 1.4	2041 3.3
15 TU	0226 1.4	0907 3.6	1457 1.0	2136 3.6
16 W	0317 1.1	0954 3.8	1544 0.7	2222 3.8
17 TH	0359 0.8	1036 4.1	1626 0.4	2303 4.0
18 F	0438 0.5	1117 4.3	1707 0.1	○ 2342 4.1
19 SA	0517 0.4	1158 4.4	1748 0.0	
20 SU	0022 4.2	0557 0.3	1241 4.4	1831 0.0
21 M	0105 4.1	0640 0.3	1327 4.4	1916 0.1
22 TU	0150 4.1	0727 0.4	1416 4.2	2005 0.4
23 W	0238 3.9	0820 0.6	1509 4.0	2058 0.7
24 TH	0331 3.8	0919 0.9	1609 3.8	◑ 2155 1.1
25 F	0434 3.6	1026 1.1	1722 3.5	2300 1.3
26 SA	0552 3.4	1143 1.3	1843 3.4	
27 SU	0018 1.5	0711 3.4	1316 1.4	2004 3.3
28 M	0150 1.5	0826 3.5	1434 1.2	2118 3.4

MARCH

Day	Time m	Time m	Time m	Time m
1 TU	0256 1.4	0931 3.7	1530 1.0	2215 3.5
2 W	0344 1.2	1022 3.8	1612 0.9	2258 3.6
3 TH	0422 1.0	1102 3.9	1647 0.7	2330 3.6
4 F	0455 0.8	1132 3.9	1719 0.7	● 2353 3.7
5 SA	0526 0.7	1157 3.9	1749 0.7	
6 SU	0014 3.7	0555 0.7	1224 3.9	1815 0.7
7 M	0039 3.7	0622 0.7	1254 3.9	1839 0.7
8 TU	0108 3.7	0650 0.7	1328 3.8	1907 0.8
9 W	0143 3.7	0722 0.8	1405 3.8	1940 0.9
10 TH	0222 3.6	0800 0.9	1447 3.6	2018 1.0
11 F	0304 3.5	0843 1.1	1533 3.4	2103 1.2
12 SA	0353 3.4	0935 1.2	1625 3.3	◑ 2156 1.4
13 SU	0452 3.2	1045 1.4	1732 3.1	2311 1.6
14 M	0609 3.1	1212 1.4	1857 3.1	
15 TU	0043 1.6	0732 3.3	1329 1.2	2013 3.3
16 W	0157 1.3	0836 3.5	1431 0.9	2110 3.6
17 TH	0253 1.0	0928 3.8	1521 0.5	2158 3.8
18 F	0337 0.7	1013 4.1	1604 0.2	2239 4.0
19 SA	0418 0.4	1056 4.3	1646 0.0	○ 2319 4.1
20 SU	0458 0.2	1138 4.4	1727 -0.1	2359 4.2
21 M	0539 0.1	1222 4.4	1809 0.0	
22 TU	0040 4.2	0622 0.2	1308 4.3	1853 0.2
23 W	0125 4.1	0709 0.3	1358 4.1	1941 0.5
24 TH	0212 3.9	0803 0.5	1453 3.9	2033 0.8
25 F	0305 3.8	0902 0.8	1554 3.6	2130 1.1
26 SA	0407 3.6	1007 1.0	1706 3.4	2232 1.4
27 SU	0524 3.4	1120 1.2	1824 3.3	◑ 2346 1.6
28 M	0643 3.4	1248 1.2	1944 3.3	
29 TU	0115 1.6	0757 3.5	1406 1.2	2055 3.3
30 W	0226 1.6	0902 3.6	1501 1.0	2149 3.5
31 TH	0316 1.2	0953 3.7	1543 0.9	2229 3.6

APRIL

Day	Time m	Time m	Time m	Time m
1 F	0355 1.0	1033 3.8	1619 0.8	2259 3.6
2 SA	0429 0.8	1105 3.8	1650 0.7	2324 3.7
3 SU	0501 0.7	1132 3.8	1718 0.7	● 2346 3.7
4 M	0529 0.7	1159 3.8	1743 0.7	
5 TU	0010 3.7	0555 0.7	1229 3.8	1807 0.8
6 W	0039 3.8	0623 0.7	1303 3.8	1836 0.8
7 TH	0115 3.8	0657 0.8	1342 3.7	1911 0.9
8 F	0155 3.7	0736 0.8	1425 3.6	1952 1.0
9 SA	0239 3.6	0823 0.9	1512 3.5	2040 1.2
10 SU	0329 3.5	0919 1.1	1606 3.3	2137 1.3
11 M	0426 3.3	1027 1.2	1711 3.2	◑ 2248 1.5
12 TU	0536 3.3	1145 1.1	1827 3.2	
13 W	0010 1.4	0653 3.4	1259 1.0	1939 3.4
14 TH	0123 1.3	0801 3.6	1401 0.7	2039 3.6
15 F	0222 1.0	0858 3.8	1454 0.4	2130 3.8
16 SA	0311 0.7	0948 4.0	1541 0.2	2215 4.0
17 SU	0356 0.4	1035 4.2	1625 0.1	2257 4.1
18 M	0439 0.3	1121 4.3	1707 0.1	○ 2338 4.1
19 TU	0523 0.2	1207 4.3	1750 0.2	
20 W	0020 4.1	0608 0.2	1255 4.2	1834 0.4
21 TH	0106 4.1	0657 0.3	1346 4.0	1921 0.6
22 F	0153 4.0	0750 0.5	1440 3.8	2012 0.9
23 SA	0246 3.8	0848 0.7	1540 3.6	2107 1.1
24 SU	0345 0.9	0949 0.9	1645 3.4	2206 1.3
25 M	0455 3.5	1055 1.1	1755 3.3	◑ 2312 1.5
26 TU	0608 3.4	1208 1.2	1906 3.2	
27 W	0026 1.5	0717 3.4	1322 1.1	2012 3.3
28 TH	0140 1.4	0820 3.5	1420 1.1	2106 3.4
29 F	0237 1.3	0912 3.6	1506 1.0	2147 3.5
30 SA	0321 1.1	0955 3.7	1544 0.9	2221 3.6

Chart Datum: 0·20 metres above Ordnance Datum (Dublin)
HAT is 4·5m above Chart Datum

TIDES

TIME ZONE (UT)	IRELAND – DUBLIN (NORTH WALL)	Dates in amber are SPRINGS
For Summer Time add ONE hour in **non-shaded areas**	LAT 53°21′N LONG 6°13′W	Dates in yellow are NEAPS

TIMES AND HEIGHTS OF HIGH AND LOW WATERS   **2011**

MAY

Day	Time m	Time m	Day	Time m	Time m
1 SU	0358 1.0 / 1032 3.7	1617 0.9 / 2251 3.7	**16** M	0337 0.6 / 1018 4.1	1606 0.4 / 2238 4.0
2 M	0431 0.9 / 1104 3.7	1646 0.8 / 2318 3.7	**17** TU	0425 0.5 / 1109 4.1	1651 0.4 / ○ 2323 4.1
3 TU	0502 0.8 / 1134 3.7	1712 0.8 / ● 2344 3.8	**18** W	0512 0.4 / 1157 4.1	1735 0.4
4 W	0530 0.8 / 1206 3.7	1739 0.8	**19** TH	0006 4.1 / 0558 0.4	1227 4.0 / 1818 0.6
5 TH	0015 3.8 / 0601 0.8	1242 3.7 / 1811 0.9	**20** F	0051 4.1 / 0647 0.5	1334 3.9 / 1904 0.7
6 F	0053 3.8 / 0638 0.8	1323 3.7 / 1850 0.9	**21** SA	0137 4.0 / 0738 0.6	1425 3.7 / 1952 0.9
7 SA	0135 3.8 / 0721 0.8	1408 3.6 / 1934 1.0	**22** SU	0227 3.9 / 0831 0.7	1518 3.6 / 2043 1.1
8 SU	0221 3.7 / 0811 0.8	1458 3.6 / 2024 1.1	**23** M	0320 3.8 / 0926 0.9	1615 3.4 / 2137 1.3
9 M	0312 3.7 / 0908 0.9	1552 3.5 / 2122 1.2	**24** TU	0420 3.6 / 1023 1.0	1716 3.3 / ☽ 2236 1.4
10 TU	0408 3.6 / 1012 0.9	1652 3.4 / ☽ 2227 1.3	**25** W	0525 3.5 / 1123 1.1	1818 3.2 / 2338 1.5
11 W	0512 3.6 / 1120 0.9	1759 3.4 / 2338 1.3	**26** TH	0630 3.5 / 1225 1.2	1918 3.3
12 TH	0620 3.6 / 1227 0.8	1906 3.5	**27** F	0042 1.5 / 0731 3.4	1327 1.2 / 2012 3.4
13 F	0047 1.2 / 0727 3.7	1330 0.7 / 2007 3.6	**28** SA	0145 1.4 / 0825 3.5	1420 1.2 / 2059 3.5
14 SA	0150 1.0 / 0828 3.8	1427 0.6 / 2102 3.8	**29** SU	0238 1.3 / 0914 3.5	1504 1.1 / 2141 3.6
15 SU	0245 0.8 / 0925 4.0	1519 0.4 / 2152 3.9	**30** M	0322 1.2 / 0957 3.6	1541 1.1 / 2218 3.7
			31 TU	0400 1.1 / 1035 3.6	1614 1.0 / 2250 3.7

JUNE

Day	Time m	Time m	Day	Time m	Time m
1 W	0434 1.0 / 1111 3.7	1644 1.0 / ● 2321 3.8	**16** TH	0506 0.6 / 1149 4.0	1723 0.7 / 2354 4.1
2 TH	0507 0.9 / 1146 3.7	1716 0.9 / 2355 3.9	**17** F	0552 0.6 / 1234 3.9	1805 0.7
3 F	0542 0.8 / 1224 3.8	1752 0.9	**18** SA	0035 4.1 / 0636 0.6	1318 3.8 / 1845 0.8
4 SA	0034 3.9 / 0622 0.7	1306 3.8 / 1832 0.9	**19** SU	0118 4.0 / 0721 0.6	1401 3.7 / 1928 0.9
5 SU	0117 3.9 / 0707 0.7	1352 3.8 / 1918 0.9	**20** M	0202 4.0 / 0808 0.7	1446 3.6 / 2014 1.0
6 M	0204 3.9 / 0757 0.7	1441 3.7 / 2008 1.0	**21** TU	0248 3.9 / 0856 0.8	1534 3.5 / 2103 1.2
7 TU	0255 3.9 / 0853 0.7	1533 3.7 / 2103 1.1	**22** W	0337 3.7 / 0945 1.0	1625 3.4 / 2155 1.3
8 W	0349 3.9 / 0952 0.7	1629 3.6 / 2203 1.1	**23** TH	0431 3.6 / 1037 1.1	1721 3.3 / ☽ 2251 1.4
9 TH	0447 3.8 / 1053 0.8	1730 3.6 / ☽ 2306 1.2	**24** F	0532 3.5 / 1131 1.3	1821 3.3 / 2350 1.5
10 F	0551 3.8 / 1157 0.8	1834 3.6	**25** SA	0637 3.4 / 1227 1.4	1920 3.3
11 SA	0013 1.2 / 0658 3.8	1301 0.8 / 1938 3.6	**26** SU	0051 1.5 / 0738 3.4	1325 1.4 / 2014 3.4
12 SU	0121 1.1 / 0805 3.8	1403 0.8 / 2039 3.7	**27** M	0151 1.5 / 0834 3.4	1419 1.4 / 2103 3.5
13 M	0224 1.0 / 0909 3.9	1500 0.8 / 2135 3.8	**28** TU	0244 1.4 / 0924 3.5	1505 1.3 / 2146 3.6
14 TU	0323 0.9 / 1008 3.9	1553 0.7 / 2226 4.0	**29** W	0329 1.2 / 1009 3.6	1545 1.2 / 2224 3.8
15 W	0417 0.7 / 1101 4.0	1640 0.7 / ○ 2312 4.0	**30** TH	0409 1.0 / 1049 3.7	1621 1.0 / 2300 3.9

JULY

Day	Time m	Time m	Day	Time m	Time m
1 F	0446 0.9 / 1127 3.8	1657 0.9 / ● 2336 4.0	**16** SA	0542 0.7 / 1222 3.8	1749 0.8
2 SA	0524 0.7 / 1206 3.9	1734 0.8	**17** SU	0018 4.1 / 0620 0.6	1256 3.8 / 1824 0.8
3 SU	0015 4.1 / 0604 0.6	1247 3.9 / 1814 0.8	**18** M	0054 4.1 / 0659 0.7	1331 3.7 / 1901 0.9
4 M	0058 4.1 / 0649 0.5	1332 3.9 / 1858 0.8	**19** TU	0131 4.0 / 0737 0.7	1408 3.6 / 1941 0.9
5 TU	0144 4.2 / 0738 0.5	1419 3.9 / 1946 0.8	**20** W	0211 3.9 / 0818 0.9	1447 3.6 / 2023 1.0
6 W	0233 4.1 / 0830 0.6	1509 3.8 / 2038 0.9	**21** TH	0253 3.8 / 0900 1.0	1530 3.5 / 2109 1.2
7 TH	0325 4.1 / 0926 0.6	1602 3.8 / 2135 1.0	**22** F	0338 3.7 / 0945 1.2	1617 3.4 / 2200 1.4
8 F	0421 4.0 / 1025 0.8	1700 3.7 / ☽ 2237 1.1	**23** SA	0429 3.5 / 1035 1.3	1712 3.3 / ☽ 2258 1.5
9 SA	0524 3.8 / 1128 0.9	1805 3.6 / 2345 1.2	**24** SU	0530 3.3 / 1132 1.5	1821 3.2
10 SU	0636 3.7 / 1234 1.0	1915 3.6	**25** M	0002 1.6 / 0647 3.2	1235 1.6 / 1929 3.3
11 M	0059 1.3 / 0751 3.7	1343 1.1 / 2023 3.7	**26** TU	0107 1.6 / 0757 3.3	1338 1.5 / 2028 3.4
12 TU	0212 1.2 / 0901 3.7	1447 1.1 / 2124 3.8	**27** W	0210 1.5 / 0856 3.4	1434 1.4 / 2118 3.6
13 W	0318 1.1 / 1004 3.8	1543 1.0 / 2219 3.9	**28** TH	0303 1.2 / 0945 3.6	1521 1.2 / 2200 3.8
14 TH	0413 0.9 / 1058 3.8	1630 1.0 / 2304 4.0	**29** F	0346 1.0 / 1028 3.7	1600 1.0 / 2238 4.0
15 F	0500 0.8 / 1143 3.8	1711 0.8 / ○ 2343 4.1	**30** SA	0426 0.9 / 1107 3.9	1637 0.8 / ● 2315 4.1
			31 SU	0504 0.5 / 1145 4.0	1715 0.6 / 2354 4.3

AUGUST

Day	Time m	Time m	Day	Time m	Time m
1 M	0545 0.3 / 1224 4.0	1754 0.5	**16** TU	0027 4.1 / 0631 0.7	1258 3.7 / 1834 0.8
2 TU	0034 4.3 / 0627 0.3	1307 4.1 / 1836 0.5	**17** W	0101 4.0 / 0702 0.8	1331 3.7 / 1907 0.8
3 W	0119 4.3 / 0713 0.3	1352 4.0 / 1922 0.6	**18** TH	0137 3.9 / 0735 0.8	1406 3.7 / 1943 0.9
4 TH	0207 4.3 / 0803 0.4	1440 4.0 / 2012 0.7	**19** F	0216 3.8 / 0809 1.0	1444 3.6 / 2022 1.1
5 F	0259 4.2 / 0858 0.6	1532 3.8 / 2109 0.9	**20** SA	0258 3.7 / 0848 1.1	1527 3.5 / 2106 1.3
6 SA	0355 4.0 / 0957 0.9	1630 3.7 / ☽ 2212 1.1	**21** SU	0344 3.5 / 0933 1.3	1615 3.4 / ☽ 2200 1.5
7 SU	0502 3.8 / 1100 1.1	1739 3.6 / 2324 1.3	**22** M	0439 3.3 / 1031 1.5	1717 3.2 / 2312 1.6
8 M	0623 3.6 / 1211 1.3	1857 3.6	**23** TU	0553 3.2 / 1147 1.7	1839 3.2
9 TU	0045 1.4 / 0744 3.5	1328 1.3 / 2010 3.6	**24** W	0029 1.6 / 0722 3.2	1302 1.6 / 1952 3.3
10 W	0208 1.3 / 0858 3.6	1437 1.3 / 2115 3.8	**25** TH	0139 1.4 / 0829 3.3	1407 1.5 / 2049 3.6
11 TH	0315 1.1 / 1001 3.7	1533 1.1 / 2211 3.9	**26** F	0238 1.2 / 0922 3.5	1457 1.2 / 2134 3.8
12 F	0406 0.9 / 1052 3.8	1617 1.0 / 2255 4.0	**27** SA	0324 0.8 / 1005 3.8	1538 0.9 / 2214 4.1
13 SA	0448 0.8 / 1133 3.8	1655 0.9 / ○ 2330 4.1	**28** SU	0404 0.5 / 1044 4.0	1616 0.7 / 2252 4.3
14 SU	0525 0.7 / 1205 3.8	1729 0.8 / 2358 4.1	**29** M	0443 0.3 / 1122 4.1	1654 0.5 / ● 2331 4.4
15 M	0559 0.7 / 1230 3.7	1802 0.8	**30** TU	0522 0.1 / 1200 4.2	1732 0.4
			31 W	0011 4.5 / 0603 0.1	1241 4.2 / 1813 0.4

Chart Datum: 0·20 metres above Ordnance Datum (Dublin)
HAT is 4·5m above Chart Datum

IRELAND – DUBLIN (NORTH WALL)

LAT 53°21'N   LONG 6°13'W

TIMES AND HEIGHTS OF HIGH AND LOW WATERS

Dates in amber are **SPRINGS**
Dates in yellow are **NEAPS**

2011

SEPTEMBER

Day	Time m	Time m	Time m	Time m
1 TH	0055 4.4	0648 0.2	1325 4.1	1859 0.4
2 F	0143 4.3	0736 0.4	1413 4.0	1949 0.6
3 SA	0235 4.1	0830 0.7	1505 3.9	2047 0.9
4 SU	0335 3.9	0930 1.0	1604 3.7	☽2153 1.1
5 M	0447 3.6	1035 1.3	1716 3.6	2308 1.3
6 TU	0613 3.5	1149 1.5	1838 3.5	
7 W	0035 1.4	0736 3.4	1311 1.5	1954 3.6
8 TH	0201 1.3	0851 3.6	1422 1.4	2101 3.8
9 F	0303 1.1	0950 3.7	1515 1.2	2156 3.9
10 SA	0349 0.9	1037 3.7	1558 1.0	2239 4.0
11 SU	0428 0.8	1114 3.8	1634 0.9	2311 4.0
12 M	0502 0.7	1143 3.8	1707 0.8	○2337 4.0
13 TU	0533 0.7	1204 3.8	1738 0.8	
14 W	0003 4.0	0601 0.7	1229 3.8	1808 0.8
15 TH	0034 4.0	0627 0.8	1259 3.8	1838 0.8
16 F	0108 3.9	0655 0.9	1332 3.8	1910 0.9
17 SA	0145 3.8	0727 1.0	1410 3.7	1947 1.0
18 SU	0227 3.7	0805 1.1	1452 3.6	2030 1.2
19 M	0313 3.5	0850 1.3	1540 3.5	2121 1.4
20 TU	0407 3.3	0945 1.5	1636 3.3	☽2230 1.5
21 W	0515 3.2	1103 1.5	1749 3.3	2353 1.5
22 TH	0644 3.2	1227 1.7	1911 3.3	
23 F	0108 1.4	0758 3.3	1336 1.5	2014 3.6
24 SA	0209 1.0	0854 3.6	1430 1.2	2104 3.8
25 SU	0258 0.7	0939 3.8	1513 0.9	2148 4.1
26 M	0340 0.4	1019 4.0	1553 0.6	2228 4.3
27 TU	0420 0.2	1057 4.2	1632 0.4	●2309 4.4
28 W	0500 0.1	1136 4.3	1712 0.3	2351 4.5
29 TH	0542 0.1	1217 4.3	1755 0.3	
30 F	0625 0.2	1302 4.2	1841 0.4	

OCTOBER

Day	Time m	Time m	Time m	Time m
1 SA	0125 4.3	0713 0.5	1350 4.1	1933 0.6
2 SU	0220 4.0	0806 0.8	1443 4.0	2032 0.8
3 M	0322 3.8	0906 1.1	1543 3.8	2138 1.1
4 TU	0437 3.6	1011 1.4	1656 3.7	☽2251 1.2
5 W	0558 3.4	1123 1.6	1814 3.6	
6 TH	0015 1.3	0717 3.4	1244 1.6	1928 3.6
7 F	0137 1.2	0830 3.5	1356 1.5	2035 3.8
8 SA	0237 1.1	0927 3.6	1449 1.3	2129 3.9
9 SU	0324 0.9	1012 3.7	1533 1.1	2212 3.9
10 M	0402 0.8	1047 3.8	1610 1.0	2246 4.0
11 TU	0435 0.8	1114 3.8	1644 0.9	2314 4.0
12 W	0505 0.8	1139 3.8	1716 0.8	○2342 3.9
13 TH	0532 0.8	1204 3.9	1745 0.8	
14 F	0011 3.9	0556 0.9	1232 3.9	1814 0.9
15 SA	0044 3.9	0623 0.9	1305 3.9	1845 0.9
16 SU	0122 3.8	0656 1.0	1344 3.8	1923 1.0
17 M	0204 3.7	0735 1.2	1427 3.7	2007 1.1
18 TU	0251 3.6	0821 1.3	1515 3.6	2059 1.3
19 W	0345 3.4	0917 1.5	1609 3.5	2203 1.4
20 TH	0449 3.3	1028 1.6	1713 3.4	☽2318 1.4
21 F	0605 3.3	1148 1.6	1825 3.5	
22 SA	0032 1.2	0718 3.4	1259 1.5	1932 3.6
23 SU	0135 1.0	0818 3.6	1356 1.2	2029 3.9
24 M	0228 0.7	0908 3.9	1445 0.9	2119 4.1
25 TU	0315 0.4	0952 4.1	1530 0.7	2206 4.3
26 W	0358 0.3	1034 4.2	1613 0.5	●2251 4.4
27 TH	0441 0.2	1116 4.3	1657 0.4	2336 4.4
28 F	0523 0.2	1159 4.3	1742 0.3	
29 SA	0024 4.3	0607 0.4	1244 4.3	1830 0.4
30 SU	0115 4.2	0654 0.6	1333 4.2	1922 0.6
31 M	0210 4.0	0746 0.9	1426 4.1	2019 0.8

NOVEMBER

Day	Time m	Time m	Time m	Time m
1 TU	0311 3.8	0843 1.2	1525 3.9	2121 1.0
2 W	0419 3.6	0945 1.4	1631 3.8	●2227 1.2
3 TH	0531 3.4	1051 1.6	1742 3.7	2339 1.3
4 F	0644 3.4	1204 1.6	1851 3.7	
5 SA	0056 1.3	0752 3.5	1316 1.6	1955 3.7
6 SU	0200 1.2	0849 3.6	1416 1.4	2051 3.8
7 M	0251 1.1	0935 3.7	1504 1.3	2137 3.8
8 TU	0332 1.0	1011 3.8	1544 1.1	2216 3.8
9 W	0407 1.0	1043 3.9	1620 1.0	2250 3.9
10 TH	0438 1.0	1113 3.9	1654 1.0	○2321 3.9
11 F	0505 1.0	1141 3.9	1725 1.0	2352 3.8
12 SA	0531 1.0	1210 3.9	1755 1.0	
13 SU	0025 3.8	0559 1.0	1244 3.9	1827 1.0
14 M	0103 3.8	0633 1.1	1323 3.9	1905 1.0
15 TU	0146 3.7	0713 1.2	1406 3.9	1950 1.0
16 W	0233 3.7	0800 1.3	1454 3.8	2041 1.1
17 TH	0326 3.6	0854 1.4	1545 3.7	2139 1.1
18 F	0424 3.5	0957 1.5	1643 3.7	☽2244 1.1
19 SA	0529 3.5	1107 1.5	1746 3.7	2352 1.1
20 SU	0637 3.5	1217 1.4	1851 3.7	
21 M	0058 1.0	0739 3.7	1321 1.3	1954 3.9
22 TU	0157 0.8	0836 3.9	1418 1.1	2052 4.0
23 W	0251 0.6	0928 4.0	1510 0.9	2147 4.2
24 TH	0340 0.5	1016 4.2	1600 0.7	2239 4.2
25 F	0426 0.5	1101 4.3	1647 0.5	○2328 4.3
26 SA	0510 0.5	1146 4.3	1734 0.5	
27 SU	0016 4.2	0554 0.6	1232 4.3	1822 0.5
28 M	0106 4.1	0639 0.7	1319 4.3	1911 0.6
29 TU	0158 3.9	0727 0.9	1409 4.2	2003 0.7
30 W	0252 3.8	0819 1.1	1502 4.0	2058 0.9

DECEMBER

Day	Time m	Time m	Time m	Time m
1 TH	0351 3.6	0915 1.3	1559 3.9	2155 1.1
2 F	0453 3.5	1014 1.5	1701 3.7	●2255 1.2
3 SA	0557 3.4	1117 1.6	1805 3.6	
4 SU	0000 1.3	0659 3.4	1225 1.6	1907 3.6
5 M	0108 1.4	0756 3.5	1331 1.6	2005 3.6
6 TU	0209 1.3	0848 3.6	1429 1.4	2058 3.6
7 W	0258 1.3	0932 3.7	1517 1.3	2144 3.7
8 TH	0337 1.2	1011 3.8	1557 1.2	2224 3.7
9 F	0411 1.2	1047 3.9	1632 1.1	2301 3.8
10 SA	0441 1.1	1119 4.0	1705 1.0	○2334 3.8
11 SU	0510 1.1	1150 4.0	1737 1.0	
12 M	0008 3.8	0540 1.0	1224 4.0	1810 0.9
13 TU	0046 3.8	0615 1.0	1303 4.0	1848 0.8
14 W	0128 3.8	0655 1.0	1346 4.0	1932 0.8
15 TH	0213 3.8	0740 1.0	1432 4.0	2020 0.8
16 F	0303 3.8	0830 1.2	1521 4.0	2113 0.9
17 SA	0356 3.7	0926 1.3	1614 3.9	2211 0.9
18 SU	0454 3.6	1028 1.3	1712 3.8	☽2314 1.0
19 M	0558 3.6	1136 1.4	1816 3.8	
20 TU	0021 1.0	0704 3.7	1247 1.3	1924 3.8
21 W	0129 1.0	0809 3.8	1355 1.2	2033 3.9
22 TH	0231 0.9	0909 3.9	1457 1.0	2136 4.0
23 F	0327 0.8	1003 4.1	1553 0.8	2233 4.0
24 SA	0417 0.7	1052 4.2	1644 0.7	●2324 4.1
25 SU	0502 0.7	1137 4.3	1730 0.6	
26 M	0010 4.1	0543 0.7	1221 4.3	1814 0.5
27 TU	0055 4.0	0625 0.8	1303 4.3	1858 0.5
28 W	0139 3.9	0707 0.9	1347 4.2	1943 0.6
29 TH	0224 3.8	0752 1.0	1432 4.1	2029 0.8
30 F	0311 3.6	0840 1.1	1520 3.9	2117 1.0
31 SA	0403 3.5	0933 1.3	1611 3.8	2208 1.2

Chart Datum: 0·20 metres above Ordnance Datum (Dublin)
HAT is 4·5m above Chart Datum

TIDES

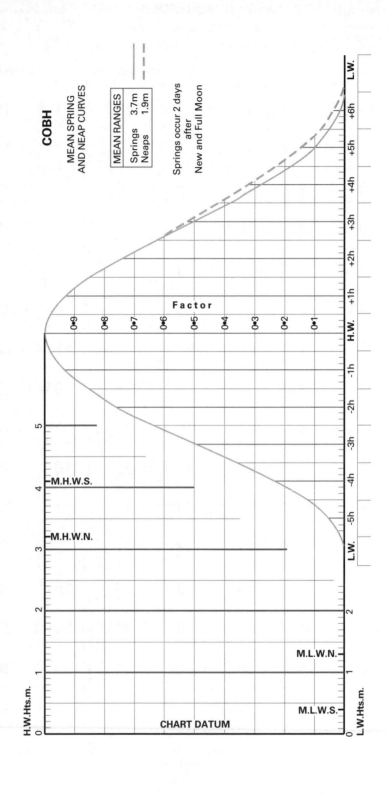

COBH

MEAN SPRING
AND NEAP CURVES

MEAN RANGES	
Springs	3.7m
Neaps	1.9m

Springs occur 2 days
after
New and Full Moon

Factor

CHART DATUM

TIME ZONE (UT)
For Summer Time add ONE hour in **non-shaded areas**

IRELAND – COBH
LAT 51°51'N   LONG 8°18'W
TIMES AND HEIGHTS OF HIGH AND LOW WATERS

Dates in amber are **SPRINGS**
Dates in yellow are **NEAPS**

2011

JANUARY

Time	m		Time	m
1 SA 0220 / 0904 / 1457 / 2134	3.6 / 1.0 / 3.6 / 1.0	**16** SU 0154 / 0838 / 1430 / 2105	3.4 / 1.3 / 3.5 / 1.2
2 SU 0327 / 1008 / 1557 / 2232	3.8 / 0.9 / 3.8 / 0.8	**17** M 0303 / 0940 / 1533 / 2202	3.6 / 1.1 / 3.6 / 1.0
3 M 0424 / 1101 / 1649 / 2320	3.9 / 0.8 / 3.9 / 0.7	**18** TU 0401 / 1034 / 1626 / 2252	3.8 / 0.9 / 3.8 / 0.7
4 TU 0513 / 1146 / 1733 ●	4.1 / 0.7 / 4.0	**19** W 0451 / 1122 / 1712 / 2337 ○	4.0 / 0.6 / 4.0 / 0.5
5 W 0002 / 0554 / 1225 / 1811	0.6 / 4.1 / 0.7 / 4.0	**20** TH 0536 / 1205 / 1755	4.2 / 0.5 / 4.1
6 TH 0040 / 0633 / 1300 / 1845	0.6 / 4.1 / 0.7 / 4.0	**21** F 0019 / 0619 / 1247 / 1837	0.4 / 4.3 / 0.4 / 4.2
7 F 0115 / 0708 / 1333 / 1918	0.6 / 4.1 / 0.8 / 3.9	**22** SA 0101 / 0701 / 1329 / 1919	0.3 / 4.3 / 0.3 / 4.2
8 SA 0149 / 0743 / 1405 / 1951	0.7 / 4.0 / 0.9 / 3.8	**23** SU 0144 / 0744 / 1411 / 2002	0.3 / 4.3 / 0.4 / 4.1
9 SU 0222 / 0818 / 1439 / 2026	0.8 / 3.9 / 1.0 / 3.8	**24** M 0228 / 0829 / 1455 / 2046	0.4 / 4.2 / 0.5 / 4.0
10 M 0257 / 0854 / 1515 / 2103	1.0 / 3.8 / 1.1 / 3.7	**25** TU 0314 / 0914 / 1541 / 2133	0.5 / 4.0 / 0.7 / 3.9
11 TU 0336 / 0933 / 1555 / 2145	1.1 / 3.7 / 1.2 / 3.6	**26** W 0403 / 1002 / 1630 / 2223	0.7 / 3.8 / 0.9 / 3.7
12 W 0420 / 1015 / 1643 / 2233 ◐	1.2 / 3.6 / 1.4 / 3.5	**27** TH 0457 / 1056 / 1728 / 2322	0.9 / 3.6 / 1.1 / 3.5
13 TH 0514 / 1105 / 1742 / 2331	1.4 / 3.5 / 1.5 / 3.4	**28** F 0601 / 1202 / 1840	1.1 / 3.4 / 1.2
14 F 0621 / 1207 / 1851	1.5 / 3.4 / 1.5	**29** SA 0036 / 0720 / 1322 / 2003	3.4 / 1.2 / 3.3 / 1.3
15 SA 0039 / 0731 / 1318 / 2000	3.3 / 1.4 / 3.4 / 1.4	**30** SU 0201 / 0849 / 1441 / 2122	3.4 / 1.2 / 3.4 / 1.1
		31 M 0315 / 1000 / 1546 / 2224	3.6 / 1.0 / 3.6 / 0.9

FEBRUARY

Time	m		Time	m
1 TU 0413 / 1054 / 1637 / 2311	3.8 / 0.8 / 3.8 / 0.7	**16** W 0337 / 1012 / 1605 / 2230	3.7 / 0.8 / 3.8 / 0.6
2 W 0459 / 1136 / 1719 / 2350	4.0 / 0.7 / 3.9 / 0.6	**17** TH 0430 / 1102 / 1653 / 2317	4.0 / 0.5 / 4.0 / 0.4
3 TH 0539 / 1211 / 1756 ●	4.1 / 0.6 / 4.0	**18** F 0516 / 1146 / 1737 ○	4.2 / 0.3 / 4.2
4 F 0023 / 0614 / 1241 / 1827	0.5 / 4.1 / 0.6 / 4.0	**19** SA 0000 / 0558 / 1228 / 1818	0.2 / 4.3 / 0.1 / 4.3
5 SA 0053 / 0647 / 1308 / 1856	0.6 / 4.1 / 0.7 / 3.9	**20** SU 0042 / 0640 / 1309 / 1859	0.1 / 4.4 / 0.1 / 4.3
6 SU 0121 / 0717 / 1335 / 1925	0.6 / 4.0 / 0.7 / 3.9	**21** M 0124 / 0722 / 1350 / 1941	0.1 / 4.4 / 0.2 / 4.2
7 M 0149 / 0747 / 1405 / 1956	0.7 / 4.0 / 0.8 / 3.9	**22** TU 0207 / 0805 / 1433 / 2023	0.2 / 4.2 / 0.3 / 4.1
8 TU 0220 / 0818 / 1437 / 2029	0.8 / 3.9 / 0.9 / 3.8	**23** W 0252 / 0848 / 1516 / 2107	0.3 / 4.0 / 0.5 / 3.9
9 W 0254 / 0852 / 1512 / 2105	1.0 / 3.8 / 1.1 / 3.7	**24** TH 0338 / 0934 / 1604 / 2154 ◐	0.6 / 3.7 / 0.8 / 3.7
10 TH 0333 / 0930 / 1553 / 2147	1.1 / 3.7 / 1.2 / 3.6	**25** F 0430 / 1025 / 1659 / 2251	0.9 / 3.5 / 1.0 / 3.4
11 F 0420 / 1015 / 1644 / 2240 ◐	1.3 / 3.5 / 1.4 / 3.4	**26** SA 0533 / 1131 / 1810	1.1 / 3.2 / 1.2
12 SA 0524 / 1114 / 1755 / 2348	1.4 / 3.3 / 1.5 / 3.3	**27** SU 0010 / 0653 / 1300 / 1940	3.2 / 1.3 / 3.1 / 1.3
13 SU 0644 / 1228 / 1918	1.5 / 3.2 / 1.5	**28** M 0144 / 0834 / 1426 / 2109	3.2 / 1.2 / 3.2 / 1.1
14 M 0110 / 0803 / 1352 / 2032	3.3 / 1.4 / 3.3 / 1.3		
15 TU 0232 / 0912 / 1507 / 2137	3.4 / 1.1 / 3.5 / 1.0		

MARCH

Time	m		Time	m
1 TU 0259 / 0946 / 1530 / 2209	3.4 / 1.0 / 3.4 / 0.8	**16** W 0200 / 0841 / 1437 / 2106	3.4 / 1.0 / 3.4 / 0.9
2 W 0354 / 1037 / 1619 / 2255	3.7 / 0.8 / 3.7 / 0.6	**17** TH 0308 / 0943 / 1538 / 2203	3.7 / 0.7 / 3.7 / 0.6
3 TH 0439 / 1117 / 1700 / 2332	3.9 / 0.6 / 3.8 / 0.5	**18** F 0403 / 1035 / 1628 / 2253	4.0 / 0.4 / 4.0 / 0.3
4 F 0517 / 1150 / 1735 ●	4.0 / 0.5 / 3.9	**19** SA 0450 / 1122 / 1713 / 2338	4.2 / 0.1 / 4.2 / 0.1
5 SA 0002 / 0550 / 1217 / 1805	0.5 / 4.1 / 0.5 / 4.0	**20** SU 0535 / 1205 / 1756	4.3 / 0.0 / 4.3
6 SU 0028 / 0621 / 1241 / 1832	0.5 / 4.1 / 0.6 / 4.0	**21** M 0021 / 0617 / 1248 / 1837	0.0 / 4.3 / 0.0 / 4.3
7 M 0052 / 0649 / 1305 / 1858	0.6 / 4.0 / 0.6 / 3.9	**22** TU 0104 / 0700 / 1330 / 1919	0.0 / 4.3 / 0.1 / 4.3
8 TU 0118 / 0716 / 1333 / 1926	0.6 / 3.9 / 0.7 / 3.9	**23** W 0148 / 0743 / 1413 / 2001	0.1 / 4.1 / 0.2 / 4.1
9 W 0148 / 0744 / 1404 / 1957	0.7 / 3.9 / 0.8 / 3.8	**24** TH 0233 / 0826 / 1457 / 2045 ◐	0.3 / 3.9 / 0.4 / 3.9
10 TH 0222 / 0816 / 1438 / 2032	0.9 / 3.8 / 0.9 / 3.8	**25** F 0320 / 0911 / 1545 / 2133	0.5 / 3.7 / 0.7 / 3.6
11 F 0259 / 0854 / 1517 / 2112	1.0 / 3.7 / 1.1 / 3.6	**26** SA 0411 / 1001 / 1640 / 2230	0.8 / 3.4 / 1.0 / 3.3
12 SA 0345 / 0939 / 1605 / 2203 ◐	1.2 / 3.5 / 1.3 / 3.4	**27** SU 0512 / 1106 / 1749 / 2348	1.1 / 3.1 / 1.2 / 3.1
13 SU 0445 / 1037 / 1714 / 2311	1.3 / 3.3 / 1.4 / 3.3	**28** M 0631 / 1235 / 1916	1.2 / 3.0 / 1.2
14 M 0605 / 1152 / 1839	1.4 / 3.1 / 1.4	**29** TU 0119 / 0804 / 1400 / 2039	3.1 / 1.2 / 3.1 / 1.1
15 TU 0034 / 0728 / 1319 / 1959	3.2 / 1.3 / 3.2 / 1.2	**30** W 0231 / 0915 / 1502 / 2139	3.3 / 1.0 / 3.3 / 0.8
		31 TH 0324 / 1006 / 1550 / 2225	3.6 / 0.8 / 3.6 / 0.7

APRIL

Time	m		Time	m
1 F 0409 / 1046 / 1631 / 2302	3.8 / 0.6 / 3.7 / 0.6	**16** SA 0332 / 1006 / 1559 / 2227	3.9 / 0.4 / 4.0 / 0.3
2 SA 0447 / 1119 / 1707 / 2333	3.9 / 0.6 / 3.8 / 0.5	**17** SU 0423 / 1056 / 1648 / 2316	4.1 / 0.2 / 4.2 / 0.1
3 SU 0522 / 1146 / 1738 / 2358 ●	3.9 / 0.5 / 3.9 / 0.5	**18** M 0511 / 1143 / 1734 ○	4.2 / 0.1 / 4.3
4 M 0553 / 1210 / 1805	3.9 / 0.6 / 3.9	**19** TU 0002 / 0556 / 1229 / 1817	0.0 / 4.2 / 0.0 / 4.3
5 TU 0023 / 0620 / 1237 / 1832	0.6 / 3.9 / 0.6 / 3.9	**20** W 0047 / 0640 / 1313 / 1901	0.0 / 4.2 / 0.1 / 4.2
6 W 0051 / 0647 / 1306 / 1901	0.6 / 3.9 / 0.9 / 3.9	**21** TH 0132 / 0724 / 1357 / 1944	0.2 / 4.0 / 0.2 / 4.1
7 TH 0123 / 0716 / 1339 / 1933	0.7 / 3.8 / 0.8 / 3.8	**22** F 0218 / 0807 / 1443 / 2029	0.3 / 3.8 / 0.4 / 3.9
8 F 0158 / 0751 / 1416 / 2009	0.8 / 3.8 / 0.9 / 3.8	**23** SA 0305 / 0853 / 1531 / 2117	0.6 / 3.6 / 0.7 / 3.6
9 SA 0238 / 0830 / 1457 / 2051	0.9 / 3.7 / 1.0 / 3.7	**24** SU 0356 / 0942 / 1625 / 2212	0.8 / 3.4 / 0.9 / 3.4
10 SU 0326 / 0918 / 1547 / 2143	1.1 / 3.5 / 1.1 / 3.5	**25** M 0454 / 1041 / 1728 / 2320 ◐	1.0 / 3.1 / 1.1 / 3.2
11 M 0425 / 1016 / 1652 / 2248 ◐	1.2 / 3.3 / 1.2 / 3.4	**26** TU 0602 / 1157 / 1841	1.2 / 3.0 / 1.1
12 TU 0539 / 1128 / 1810	1.2 / 3.2 / 1.2	**27** W 0040 / 0717 / 1317 / 1952	3.2 / 1.1 / 3.1 / 1.1
13 W 0006 / 0657 / 1248 / 1926	3.3 / 1.2 / 3.3 / 1.1	**28** TH 0149 / 0824 / 1419 / 2052	3.3 / 1.0 / 3.2 / 0.9
14 TH 0127 / 0809 / 1403 / 2034	3.5 / 0.9 / 3.5 / 0.8	**29** F 0243 / 0917 / 1510 / 2141	3.4 / 0.9 / 3.4 / 0.8
15 F 0235 / 0911 / 1505 / 2134	3.7 / 0.6 / 3.7 / 0.5	**30** SA 0330 / 1002 / 1553 / 2222	3.6 / 0.8 / 3.6 / 0.7

Chart Datum: 0·13 metres above Ordnance Datum (Dublin)
HAT is 4·5m above Chart Datum

TIDES

TIME ZONE (UT)
For Summer Time add ONE hour in **non-shaded areas**

Dates in amber are **SPRINGS**
Dates in yellow are **NEAPS**

MAY

Day	Time m	Day	Time m
1 SU	0411 3.7 / 1039 0.7 / 1631 3.7 / 2256 0.7	**16** M	0358 4.0 / 1033 0.3 / 1624 4.1 / 2256 0.3
2 M	0448 3.8 / 1111 0.6 / 1706 3.8 / 2327 0.6	**17** TU	0450 4.1 / 1124 0.2 / 1714 4.2 / ○2346 0.2
3 TU	0522 3.8 / 1141 0.6 / 1738 3.9 / ●2357 0.6	**18** W	0539 4.1 / 1212 0.2 / 1801 4.2
4 W	0553 3.8 / 1212 0.6 / 1809 3.9	**19** TH	0033 0.2 / 0624 4.0 / 1258 0.2 / 1846 4.1
5 TH	0029 0.7 / 0624 3.8 / 1246 0.7 / 1841 3.9	**20** F	0118 0.3 / 0708 3.9 / 1343 0.3 / 1930 4.0
6 F	0105 0.7 / 0657 3.8 / 1323 0.7 / 1917 3.9	**21** SA	0203 0.4 / 0751 3.8 / 1429 0.5 / 2014 3.8
7 SA	0144 0.8 / 0735 3.8 / 1403 0.8 / 1956 3.8	**22** SU	0249 0.6 / 0835 3.6 / 1515 0.6 / 2059 3.7
8 SU	0227 0.8 / 0818 3.7 / 1448 0.9 / 2041 3.7	**23** M	0336 0.8 / 0921 3.4 / 1604 0.8 / 2148 3.5
9 M	0316 0.9 / 0907 3.6 / 1539 1.0 / 2133 3.6	**24** TU	0427 1.0 / 1010 3.3 / 1658 1.0 / ◐2243 3.3
10 TU	0412 1.0 / 1004 3.5 / 1638 1.0 / ◐2234 3.5	**25** W	0523 1.1 / 1108 3.2 / 1757 1.1 / 2346 3.2
11 W	0517 1.0 / 1109 3.4 / 1746 1.0 / 2343 3.5	**26** TH	0624 1.2 / 1214 3.2 / 1858 1.1
12 TH	0628 1.0 / 1219 3.4 / 1857 0.9	**27** F	0052 3.3 / 0724 1.1 / 1320 3.2 / 1955 1.1
13 F	0055 3.6 / 0736 0.9 / 1329 3.6 / 2003 0.8	**28** SA	0151 3.3 / 0818 1.1 / 1416 3.3 / 2047 1.0
14 SA	0203 3.7 / 0840 0.7 / 1432 3.7 / 2105 0.6	**29** SU	0243 3.5 / 0908 1.0 / 1506 3.5 / 2134 0.9
15 SU	0303 3.9 / 0939 0.5 / 1530 3.9 / 2203 0.4	**30** M	0330 3.6 / 0954 0.9 / 1552 3.6 / 2217 0.8
		31 TU	0413 3.7 / 1036 0.8 / 1634 3.7 / 2257 0.7

JUNE

Day	Time m	Day	Time m
1 W	0453 3.8 / 1115 0.7 / 1713 3.8 / ●2335 0.7	**16** TH	0525 3.9 / 1158 0.4 / 1748 4.0
2 TH	0531 3.8 / 1153 0.7 / 1750 3.9	**17** F	0020 0.4 / 0610 3.9 / 1244 0.4 / 1832 4.1
3 F	0013 0.6 / 0607 3.8 / 1231 0.6 / 1827 3.9	**18** SA	0104 0.4 / 0653 3.9 / 1327 0.4 / 1914 4.0
4 SA	0052 0.6 / 0645 3.8 / 1311 0.6 / 1906 3.9	**19** SU	0146 0.5 / 0733 3.8 / 1409 0.5 / 1955 3.9
5 SU	0133 0.6 / 0726 3.8 / 1353 0.7 / 1948 3.9	**20** M	0227 0.6 / 0813 3.7 / 1451 0.6 / 2036 3.8
6 M	0217 0.7 / 0810 3.8 / 1439 0.7 / 2033 3.8	**21** TU	0308 0.8 / 0853 3.6 / 1533 0.8 / 2117 3.6
7 TU	0305 0.7 / 0859 3.7 / 1528 0.8 / 2123 3.8	**22** W	0350 0.9 / 0934 3.5 / 1617 0.9 / 2201 3.5
8 W	0357 0.8 / 0951 3.7 / 1621 0.8 / 2218 3.7	**23** TH	0436 1.1 / 1023 3.4 / 1705 1.1 / ◐2249 3.4
9 TH	0454 0.9 / 1048 3.6 / 1720 0.9 / ◐2319 3.6	**24** F	0526 1.2 / 1111 3.3 / 1758 1.2 / 2344 3.3
10 F	0557 0.9 / 1150 3.6 / 1826 0.9	**25** SA	0623 1.2 / 1210 3.3 / 1856 1.2
11 SA	0024 3.6 / 0703 0.9 / 1256 3.6 / 1933 0.8	**26** SU	0046 3.3 / 0721 1.2 / 1315 3.3 / 1953 1.2
12 SU	0131 3.6 / 0810 0.8 / 1402 3.7 / 2039 0.7	**27** M	0150 3.4 / 0819 1.2 / 1417 3.4 / 2049 1.1
13 M	0236 3.7 / 0914 0.7 / 1506 3.8 / 2143 0.6	**28** TU	0248 3.5 / 0914 1.0 / 1514 3.6 / 2143 1.0
14 TU	0337 3.8 / 1014 0.6 / 1606 3.9 / 2241 0.5	**29** W	0340 3.6 / 1006 0.9 / 1605 3.7 / 2232 0.8
15 W	0434 3.9 / 1109 0.4 / 1700 4.0 / ○2333 0.4	**30** TH	0428 3.7 / 1053 0.8 / 1651 3.8 / 2316 0.7

JULY

Day	Time m	Day	Time m
1 F	0512 3.8 / 1135 0.6 / 1733 3.9 / ●2358 0.6	**16** SA	0007 0.5 / 0556 3.9 / 1229 0.4 / 1816 4.1
2 SA	0553 3.9 / 1216 0.5 / 1814 4.0	**17** SU	0047 0.5 / 0635 3.9 / 1307 0.4 / 1854 4.0
3 SU	0038 0.5 / 0633 3.9 / 1257 0.5 / 1854 4.0	**18** M	0122 0.5 / 0711 3.9 / 1344 0.5 / 1930 4.0
4 M	0120 0.5 / 0714 3.9 / 1339 0.5 / 1936 4.0	**19** TU	0157 0.6 / 0745 3.8 / 1419 0.6 / 2006 3.9
5 TU	0203 0.5 / 0758 3.9 / 1424 0.5 / 2020 4.0	**20** W	0231 0.8 / 0820 3.7 / 1454 0.8 / 2041 3.8
6 W	0248 0.6 / 0844 3.9 / 1510 0.5 / 2107 3.9	**21** TH	0306 0.9 / 0856 3.6 / 1530 0.9 / 2118 3.6
7 TH	0336 0.6 / 0932 3.8 / 1559 0.6 / 2157 3.9	**22** F	0344 1.0 / 0935 3.5 / 1609 1.0 / 2158 3.5
8 F	0427 0.8 / 1023 3.7 / 1652 0.8 / ◐2251 3.7	**23** SA	0427 1.1 / 1019 3.4 / 1656 1.2 / ◐2244 3.4
9 SA	0524 0.9 / 1120 3.6 / 1753 0.9 / 2353 3.6	**24** SU	0520 1.3 / 1111 3.3 / 1755 1.3 / 2341 3.3
10 SU	0631 1.0 / 1225 3.5 / 1903 0.9	**25** M	0625 1.3 / 1216 3.2 / 1903 1.3
11 M	0103 3.5 / 0743 1.0 / 1337 3.5 / 2017 0.9	**26** TU	0050 3.3 / 0734 1.3 / 1330 3.3 / 2010 1.3
12 TU	0215 3.5 / 0855 0.9 / 1449 3.6 / 2130 0.8	**27** W	0205 3.5 / 0839 1.2 / 1440 3.4 / 2112 1.1
13 W	0323 3.6 / 1002 0.7 / 1554 3.8 / 2232 0.7	**28** TH	0310 3.5 / 0938 1.0 / 1539 3.6 / 2207 0.9
14 TH	0422 3.7 / 1058 0.6 / 1649 3.9 / 2323 0.6	**29** F	0405 3.7 / 1030 0.8 / 1629 3.8 / 2256 0.6
15 F	0512 3.9 / 1146 0.5 / 1735 4.0 / ○	**30** SA	0451 3.8 / 1115 0.5 / 1714 4.0 / ●2339 0.5
		31 SU	0534 4.0 / 1157 0.4 / 1755 4.1

AUGUST

Day	Time m	Day	Time m
1 M	0020 0.3 / 0615 4.1 / 1238 0.3 / 1836 4.2	**16** TU	0054 0.6 / 0645 3.9 / 1313 0.5 / 1902 4.0
2 TU	0101 0.3 / 0656 4.1 / 1319 0.3 / 1917 4.2	**17** W	0122 0.6 / 0715 3.9 / 1341 0.6 / 1933 3.9
3 W	0143 0.3 / 0738 4.1 / 1402 0.3 / 2000 4.1	**18** TH	0151 0.7 / 0745 3.8 / 1411 0.7 / 2004 3.8
4 TH	0226 0.4 / 0822 4.0 / 1447 0.4 / 2045 4.0	**19** F	0223 0.9 / 0818 3.7 / 1443 0.9 / 2036 3.6
5 F	0312 0.5 / 0908 3.9 / 1534 0.5 / 2131 3.9	**20** SA	0258 1.0 / 0854 3.6 / 1519 1.0 / 2113 3.6
6 SA	0400 0.7 / 0957 3.7 / 1625 0.7 / ◐2223 3.6	**21** SU	0337 1.1 / 0935 3.5 / 1603 1.2 / ◐2156 3.5
7 SU	0455 0.9 / 1052 3.6 / 1724 0.9 / 2324 3.4	**22** M	0426 1.3 / 1024 3.4 / 1700 1.4 / 2250 3.3
8 M	0602 1.1 / 1200 3.4 / 1837 1.1	**23** TU	0532 1.4 / 1127 3.2 / 1815 1.4
9 TU	0040 3.3 / 0722 1.1 / 1322 3.3 / 2003 1.1	**24** W	0000 3.2 / 0651 1.4 / 1246 3.2 / 1933 1.4
10 W	0203 3.3 / 0845 1.0 / 1441 3.5 / 2124 1.0	**25** TH	0124 3.2 / 0805 1.3 / 1408 3.3 / 2042 1.1
11 TH	0314 3.5 / 0955 0.8 / 1545 3.7 / 2225 0.8	**26** F	0240 3.4 / 0909 1.0 / 1513 3.6 / 2141 0.9
12 F	0411 3.7 / 1049 0.6 / 1636 3.9 / 2313 0.6	**27** SA	0338 3.7 / 1003 0.7 / 1604 3.9 / 2231 0.6
13 SA	0458 3.8 / 1133 0.5 / 1719 4.0 / ○2352 0.5	**28** SU	0427 3.9 / 1050 0.4 / 1649 4.1 / 2316 0.4
14 SU	0538 3.9 / 1210 0.4 / 1757 4.1	**29** M	0510 4.1 / 1133 0.3 / 1732 4.3 / ●2357 0.3
15 M	0025 0.5 / 0613 4.0 / 1243 0.4 / 1830 4.1	**30** TU	0552 4.2 / 1215 0.1 / 1813 4.3
		31 W	0038 0.2 / 0633 4.2 / 1257 0.1 / 1854 4.3

Chart Datum: 0·13 metres above Ordnance Datum (Dublin)
HAT is 4·5m above Chart Datum

IRELAND – COBH

LAT 51°51'N   LONG 8°18'W

TIMES AND HEIGHTS OF HIGH AND LOW WATERS

Dates in amber are **SPRINGS**
Dates in yellow are **NEAPS**

2011

SEPTEMBER

Days 1–15

Day	Time	m	Time	m	Time	m	Time	m
1 TH	0121	0.2	0715	4.2	1340	0.2	1937	4.2
2 F	0204	0.3	0759	4.1	1425	0.3	2021	4.0
3 SA	0249	0.5	0844	3.9	1512	0.5	2107	3.8
4 SU	0338	0.7	0933	3.7	1603	0.8	◑2158	3.6
5 M	0434	0.9	1030	3.5	1703	1.0	2300	3.3
6 TU	0542	1.1	1143	3.3	1819	1.2		
7 W	0024	3.1	0708	1.2	1314	3.2	1955	1.2
8 TH	0153	3.2	0837	1.0	1431	3.4	2115	1.0
9 F	0301	3.4	0943	0.8	1530	3.7	2210	0.8
10 SA	0354	3.7	1032	0.6	1617	3.9	2254	0.6
11 SU	0437	3.8	1113	0.5	1657	4.0	2329	0.5
12 M	0515	3.9	1732	4.1	○2359	0.5		
13 TU	0548	4.0	1215	0.5	1804	4.1		
14 W	0023	0.6	0617	4.0	1240	0.6	1832	4.0
15 TH	0048	0.7	0644	3.9	1305	0.7	1859	3.9

Days 16–30

Day	Time	m	Time	m	Time	m	Time	m
16 F	0114	0.8	0712	3.9	1333	0.8	1928	3.9
17 SA	0145	0.9	0744	3.8	1405	0.9	1959	3.8
18 SU	0220	1.0	0819	3.7	1442	1.1	2035	3.7
19 M	0300	1.1	0859	3.6	1525	1.2	2119	3.5
20 TU	0348	1.3	0948	3.4	1621	1.4	○2213	3.4
21 W	0453	1.4	1051	3.3	1736	1.5	2323	3.2
22 TH	0614	1.4	1209	3.2	1858	1.4		
23 F	0046	3.2	0731	1.3	1333	3.4	2010	1.2
24 SA	0206	3.4	0838	1.0	1441	3.6	2111	0.9
25 SU	0307	3.7	0934	0.7	1535	3.9	2203	0.6
26 M	0358	4.0	1024	0.4	1622	4.2	2250	0.3
27 TU	0444	4.2	1109	0.2	1706	4.3	●2334	0.2
28 W	0528	4.3	1153	0.1	1750	4.4		
29 TH	0017	0.1	0610	4.3	1237	0.1	1832	4.3
30 F	0101	0.2	0654	4.3	1322	0.2	1916	4.2

OCTOBER

Days 1–15

Day	Time	m	Time	m	Time	m	Time	m
1 SA	0145	0.3	0738	4.1	1407	0.3	2000	4.0
2 SU	0232	0.5	0825	4.0	1455	0.6	2047	3.8
3 M	0322	0.7	0915	3.7	1548	0.8	2138	3.5
4 TU	0419	0.9	1014	3.5	1648	1.1	◑2241	3.3
5 W	0527	1.1	1128	3.3	1804	1.3		
6 TH	0005	3.1	0652	1.2	1256	3.2	1936	1.2
7 F	0132	3.2	0815	1.1	1408	3.4	2049	1.1
8 SA	0237	3.4	0916	0.9	1503	3.6	2142	0.9
9 SU	0328	3.6	1004	0.7	1554	3.8	2224	0.7
10 M	0410	3.8	1044	0.6	1628	4.0	2259	0.7
11 TU	0447	3.9	1117	0.6	1704	4.0	2328	0.7
12 W	0520	4.0	1145	0.6	1735	4.0	○2352	0.7
13 TH	0549	4.0	1209	0.7	1804	4.0		
14 F	0017	0.7	0616	4.0	1236	0.8	1830	4.0
15 SA	0048	0.8	0645	3.9	1305	0.8	1858	3.9

Days 16–31

Day	Time	m	Time	m	Time	m	Time	m
16 SU	0118	0.9	0717	3.9	1339	1.0	1931	3.9
17 M	0154	1.0	0753	3.8	1418	1.1	2009	3.8
18 TU	0236	1.1	0835	3.7	1503	1.2	2053	3.6
19 W	0326	1.2	0925	3.5	1558	1.3	2148	3.5
20 TH	0428	1.4	1026	3.4	1707	1.4	◑2256	3.3
21 F	0542	1.4	1139	3.4	1825	1.4		
22 SA	0013	3.4	0657	1.2	1257	3.5	1937	1.2
23 SU	0129	3.5	0805	1.0	1406	3.7	2040	0.9
24 M	0233	3.8	0904	0.7	1503	3.8	2135	0.6
25 TU	0328	4.0	0958	0.5	1554	4.2	2226	0.4
26 W	0418	4.2	1048	0.3	1643	4.3	●2313	0.3
27 TH	0506	4.3	1135	0.2	1729	4.3	2359	0.2
28 F	0552	4.4	1222	0.2	1814	4.3		
29 SA	0044	0.2	0637	4.3	1308	0.3	1859	4.2
30 SU	0131	0.3	0723	4.2	1355	0.4	1944	4.0
31 M	0218	0.5	0811	4.0	1443	0.6	2031	3.8

NOVEMBER

Days 1–15

Day	Time	m	Time	m	Time	m	Time	m
1 TU	0309	0.7	0901	3.8	1534	0.9	2121	3.5
2 W	0404	0.9	0957	3.5	1632	1.1	◑2219	3.3
3 TH	0508	1.1	1103	3.4	1739	1.3	2330	3.2
4 F	0621	1.2	1218	3.3	1856	1.3		
5 SA	0050	3.2	0734	1.1	1328	3.4	2005	1.2
6 SU	0158	3.4	0835	1.0	1425	3.6	2059	1.1
7 M	0250	3.6	0925	0.9	1512	3.7	2144	0.9
8 TU	0335	3.7	1007	0.8	1554	3.9	2223	0.9
9 W	0415	3.9	1043	0.8	1632	3.9	2255	0.8
10 TH	0451	3.9	1115	0.8	1707	4.0	○2324	0.8
11 F	0524	4.0	1144	0.8	1738	4.0	2353	0.8
12 SA	0555	4.0	1214	0.8	1808	4.0		
13 SU	0025	0.8	0626	4.0	1248	0.9	1839	4.0
14 M	0100	0.9	0700	4.0	1324	0.9	1913	3.9
15 TU	0139	0.9	0738	3.9	1405	1.0	1953	3.8

Days 16–30

Day	Time	m	Time	m	Time	m	Time	m
16 W	0222	1.0	0821	3.8	1450	1.1	2039	3.7
17 TH	0312	1.1	0910	3.7	1543	1.2	2132	3.6
18 F	0408	1.2	1007	3.6	1643	1.3	◑2233	3.5
19 SA	0513	1.2	1111	3.6	1751	1.3	2341	3.5
20 SU	0623	1.2	1221	3.6	1903	1.2		
21 M	0052	3.6	0731	1.0	1329	3.8	2008	1.0
22 TU	0158	3.8	0835	0.9	1432	3.9	2108	0.9
23 W	0259	4.0	0935	0.7	1529	4.1	2204	0.6
24 TH	0355	4.2	1030	0.5	1623	4.2	2256	0.4
25 F	0448	4.3	1122	0.4	1713	4.2	●2345	0.3
26 SA	0538	4.3	1210	0.3	1801	4.2		
27 SU	0032	0.3	0625	4.3	1257	0.4	1845	4.2
28 M	0119	0.4	0711	4.2	1343	0.5	1930	4.0
29 TU	0205	0.5	0757	4.1	1429	0.7	2014	3.8
30 W	0253	0.7	0844	3.9	1517	0.9	2100	3.7

DECEMBER

Days 1–15

Day	Time	m	Time	m	Time	m	Time	m
1 TH	0342	0.9	0933	3.7	1607	1.1	2148	3.5
2 F	0436	1.1	1026	3.5	1701	1.2	◑2243	3.3
3 SA	0535	1.2	1126	3.4	1802	1.3	2347	3.3
4 SU	0638	1.3	1230	3.4	1905	1.3		
5 M	0056	3.3	0738	1.2	1333	3.5	2003	1.3
6 TU	0159	3.4	0834	1.2	1427	3.6	2056	1.2
7 W	0252	3.6	0923	1.1	1516	3.7	2143	1.1
8 TH	0339	3.7	1008	1.0	1601	3.8	2224	1.0
9 F	0423	3.9	1048	0.9	1642	3.9	2302	0.9
10 SA	0502	4.0	1125	0.9	1719	4.0	○2337	0.8
11 SU	0539	4.0	1201	0.8	1753	4.0		
12 M	0012	0.8	0614	4.1	1237	0.8	1827	4.0
13 TU	0049	0.8	0650	4.1	1315	0.8	1903	4.0
14 W	0128	0.8	0728	4.0	1355	0.8	1943	3.9
15 TH	0211	0.9	0810	4.0	1438	1.0	2027	3.9

Days 16–31

Day	Time	m	Time	m	Time	m	Time	m
16 F	0257	0.9	0856	3.9	1526	1.0	2116	3.8
17 SA	0348	1.0	0947	3.8	1618	1.1	2209	3.7
18 SU	0444	1.1	1044	3.8	1717	1.2	◑2309	3.7
19 M	0547	1.1	1146	3.7	1824	1.2		
20 TU	0016	3.6	0656	1.2	1254	3.7	1935	1.1
21 W	0125	3.7	0807	1.0	1403	3.7	2043	1.0
22 TH	0234	3.8	0915	0.9	1508	3.9	2147	0.8
23 F	0339	4.0	1018	0.7	1609	4.0	2244	0.6
24 SA	0437	4.1	1113	0.6	1702	4.1	2335	0.5
25 SU	0528	4.3	1201	0.5	1750	4.1		
26 M	0021	0.4	0614	4.3	1247	0.5	1833	4.1
27 TU	0105	0.4	0658	4.3	1329	0.5	1914	4.1
28 W	0147	0.5	0739	4.2	1410	0.6	1954	3.9
29 TH	0230	0.6	0820	4.0	1451	0.8	2033	3.8
30 F	0312	0.8	0902	3.9	1532	1.0	2112	3.7
31 SA	0355	1.0	0944	3.7	1615	1.1	2155	3.5

Chart Datum: 0·13 metres above Ordnance Datum (Dublin)
HAT is 4·5m above Chart Datum

TIDES

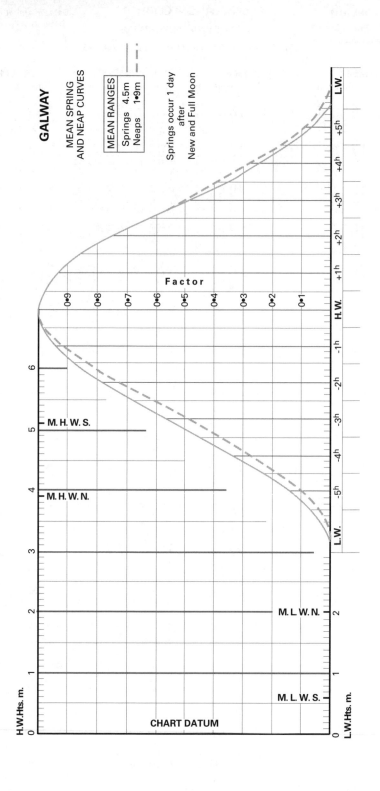

IRELAND – GALWAY
LAT 53°16'N LONG 9°03'W

Dates in amber are **SPRINGS**
Dates in yellow are NEAPS

2011

TIMES AND HEIGHTS OF HIGH AND LOW WATERS

JANUARY

Time m	Time m
1 SA 0221 4.5 / 0824 1.5 / 1452 4.4 / 2055 1.5	**16** SU 0201 3.9 / 0823 1.8 / 1430 3.9 / 2036 1.7
2 SU 0315 4.7 / 0916 1.3 / 1545 4.6 / 2141 1.3	**17** M 0301 4.2 / 0913 1.5 / 1528 4.2 / 2124 1.4
3 M 0403 4.9 / 1003 1.1 / 1632 4.7 / 2223 1.2	**18** TU 0348 4.5 / 0957 1.1 / 1615 4.5 / 2207 1.1
4 TU 0448 5.0 / 1046 1.0 / 1716 4.7 / ● 2304 1.1	**19** W 0432 4.8 / 1039 0.7 / 1659 4.8 / 2249 0.8
5 W 0531 5.0 / 1128 0.8 / 1758 4.7 / 2343 1.1	**20** TH 0516 5.0 / 1119 0.4 / 1742 5.0 / 2330 0.5
6 TH 0613 5.0 / 1206 0.8 / 1838 4.7	**21** F 0559 5.2 / 1158 0.2 / 1825 5.1
7 F 0021 1.1 / 0652 5.0 / 1243 0.8 / 1916 4.6	**22** SA 0011 0.4 / 0641 5.3 / 1238 0.1 / 1907 5.1
8 SA 0058 1.1 / 0731 4.9 / 1319 0.9 / 1955 4.5	**23** SU 0053 0.4 / 0724 5.3 / 1319 0.2 / 1950 5.0
9 SU 0135 1.3 / 0808 4.7 / 1355 1.1 / 2034 4.4	**24** M 0136 0.6 / 0807 5.1 / 1401 0.5 / 2036 4.8
10 M 0213 1.5 / 0846 4.5 / 1432 1.3 / 2114 4.2	**25** TU 0222 0.9 / 0854 4.8 / 1446 0.9 / 2128 4.5
11 TU 0254 1.7 / 0925 4.3 / 1511 1.5 / 2158 4.0	**26** W 0313 1.2 / 0949 4.5 / 1539 1.3 / 2229 4.2
12 W 0342 2.0 / 1008 4.1 / 1556 1.8 / ◑ 2246 3.9	**27** TH 0415 1.6 / 1055 4.2 / 1646 1.7 / 2338 4.1
13 TH 0442 2.2 / 1056 3.9 / 1651 2.0 / 2339 3.8	**28** F 0532 1.8 / 1210 4.0 / 1821 1.9
14 F 0603 2.2 / 1153 3.8 / 1810 2.1	**29** SA 0055 4.0 / 0659 1.8 / 1334 3.9 / 1949 1.8
15 SA 0043 3.8 / 0721 2.1 / 1306 3.7 / 1935 2.0	**30** SU 0210 4.2 / 0815 1.7 / 1446 4.1 / 2047 1.6
	31 M 0308 4.4 / 0911 1.0 / 1539 4.3 / 2131 1.4

FEBRUARY

Time m	Time m
1 TU 0355 4.6 / 0955 1.1 / 1623 4.5 / 2211 1.2	**16** W 0331 4.4 / 0940 0.9 / 1558 4.5 / 2151 0.9
2 W 0438 4.8 / 1034 0.9 / 1704 4.6 / 2249 1.0	**17** TH 0416 4.8 / 1021 0.5 / 1641 4.9 / 2232 0.5
3 TH 0519 4.9 / 1111 0.7 / 1742 4.7 / ● 2325 0.8	**18** F 0459 5.1 / 1100 0.1 / 1723 5.1 / ○ 2313 0.2
4 F 0557 5.0 / 1145 0.6 / 1819 4.7	**19** SA 0542 5.3 / 1139 -0.1 / 1805 5.3 / 2353 0.1
5 SA 0000 0.8 / 0633 5.0 / 1219 0.6 / 1854 4.7	**20** SU 0624 5.4 / 1218 -0.1 / 1846 5.3
6 SU 0034 0.8 / 0709 4.9 / 1251 0.7 / 1928 4.6	**21** M 0034 0.1 / 0705 5.4 / 1258 0.0 / 1926 5.2
7 M 0107 0.9 / 0743 4.8 / 1323 0.8 / 2001 4.5	**22** TU 0116 0.2 / 0747 5.1 / 1338 0.3 / 2008 4.9
8 TU 0140 1.1 / 0815 4.6 / 1355 1.0 / 2033 4.3	**23** W 0200 0.6 / 0831 4.8 / 1421 0.8 / 2055 4.5
9 W 0214 1.4 / 0848 4.3 / 1429 1.3 / 2108 4.1	**24** TH 0248 1.0 / 0922 4.4 / 1510 1.3 / ◑ 2153 4.2
10 TH 0252 1.7 / 0926 4.1 / 1507 1.6 / 2152 3.9	**25** F 0347 1.6 / 1028 4.0 / 1616 1.8 / 2308 3.9
11 F 0336 1.9 / 1016 3.8 / 1554 1.9 / ◑ 2247 3.7	**26** SA 0506 1.8 / 1150 3.7 / 1755 2.0
12 SA 0437 2.1 / 1115 3.7 / 1656 2.1 / 2350 3.6	**27** 0035 3.8 / 0636 1.8 / 1322 3.7 / 1932 1.9
13 SU 0646 2.1 / 1223 3.6 / 1904 2.1	**28** 0155 3.9 / 0807 1.7 / 1435 3.9 / 2036 1.7
14 M 0108 3.7 / 0801 1.9 / 1400 3.7 / 2018 1.8	
15 TU 0239 4.0 / 0855 1.6 / 1511 4.1 / 2108 1.4	

MARCH

Time m	Time m
1 TU 0253 4.2 / 0902 1.4 / 1525 4.2 / 2116 1.4	**16** W 0207 4.0 / 0828 1.3 / 1446 4.1 / 2044 1.3
2 W 0339 4.4 / 0938 1.1 / 1606 4.4 / 2152 1.1	**17** TH 0307 4.4 / 0914 0.9 / 1534 4.6 / 2128 0.8
3 TH 0420 4.6 / 1012 0.9 / 1644 4.6 / 2227 0.9	**18** F 0353 4.8 / 0956 0.4 / 1617 5.0 / 2210 0.4
4 F 0459 4.8 / 1046 0.7 / 1720 4.7 / 2302 0.7	**19** SA 0436 5.1 / 1036 0.1 / 1659 5.3 / 2251 0.1
5 SA 0535 4.9 / 1119 0.6 / 1754 4.8 / 2336 0.7	**20** SU 0520 5.4 / 1115 -0.1 / 1740 5.4 / 2332 -0.1
6 SU 0611 4.9 / 1151 0.6 / 1828 4.8	**21** M 0603 5.4 / 1155 -0.1 / 1822 5.4
7 M 0008 0.7 / 0644 4.8 / 1221 0.6 / 1859 4.7	**22** TU 0014 0.0 / 0645 5.4 / 1235 0.1 / 1902 5.3
8 TU 0039 0.8 / 0716 4.7 / 1251 0.8 / 1929 4.6	**23** W 0056 0.2 / 0727 5.1 / 1316 0.4 / 1944 5.0
9 W 0110 1.0 / 0747 4.6 / 1321 1.0 / 1958 4.4	**24** TH 0140 0.5 / 0812 4.8 / 1358 0.9 / 2029 4.6
10 TH 0142 1.2 / 0818 4.3 / 1354 1.2 / 2028 4.2	**25** F 0228 0.9 / 0902 4.3 / 1447 1.4 / 2124 4.2
11 F 0219 1.5 / 0856 4.1 / 1432 1.5 / 2109 4.0	**26** SA 0326 1.4 / 1006 3.9 / 1554 1.9 / ◑ 2239 3.9
12 SA 0302 1.7 / 0946 3.8 / 1519 1.8 / ◑ 2209 3.8	**27** SU 0444 1.7 / 1130 3.7 / 1729 2.1
13 SU 0358 2.0 / 1048 3.7 / 1620 2.1 / 2316 3.7	**28** 0010 3.8 / 0608 1.8 / 1300 3.7 / 1857 2.0
14 0556 2.1 / 1158 3.6 / 1831 2.1	**29** TU 0129 3.9 / 0731 1.7 / 1412 3.9 / 2007 1.8
15 0030 3.7 / 0733 1.8 / 1328 3.8 / 1953 1.8	**30** W 0228 4.1 / 0832 1.5 / 1501 4.1 / 2050 1.5
	31 TH 0314 4.3 / 0909 1.2 / 1541 4.4 / 2126 1.2

APRIL

Time m	Time m
1 F 0355 4.5 / 0943 1.0 / 1617 4.6 / 2201 0.9	**16** SA 0325 4.8 / 0929 0.5 / 1549 5.0 / 2145 0.5
2 SA 0433 4.7 / 1017 0.8 / 1652 4.7 / 2236 0.8	**17** SU 0411 5.1 / 1010 0.1 / 1632 5.3 / 2228 0.2
3 SU 0509 4.7 / 1050 0.7 / 1726 4.8 / ● 2310 0.7	**18** M 0456 5.3 / 1051 0.2 / 1715 5.4 / ○ 2311 0.1
4 M 0544 4.8 / 1121 0.7 / 1758 4.8 / 2342 0.7	**19** TU 0541 5.4 / 1132 0.2 / 1758 5.4 / 2354 0.1
5 TU 0617 4.7 / 1150 0.8 / 1829 4.7	**20** W 0626 5.3 / 1214 0.4 / 1841 5.3
6 W 0012 0.8 / 0650 4.7 / 1220 0.9 / 1859 4.6	**21** TH 0038 0.3 / 0710 5.0 / 1256 0.7 / 1924 5.0
7 TH 0044 1.0 / 0722 4.5 / 1252 1.1 / 1929 4.6	**22** F 0124 0.6 / 0755 4.7 / 1340 1.0 / 2010 4.7
8 F 0118 1.1 / 0747 4.4 / 1328 1.3 / 2001 4.3	**23** SA 0212 0.9 / 0845 4.3 / 1429 1.5 / 2103 4.3
9 SA 0156 1.4 / 0836 4.1 / 1408 1.5 / 2043 4.1	**24** SU 0308 1.3 / 0946 4.0 / 1532 1.9 / 2212 4.0
10 SU 0242 1.6 / 0927 3.9 / 1457 1.8 / 2143 3.9	**25** M 0417 1.6 / 1101 3.7 / 1656 2.1 / 2333 3.9
11 M 0339 1.8 / 1029 3.8 / 1559 2.0 / ◑ 2252 3.8	**26** 0531 1.7 / 1220 3.7 / 1813 2.0
12 0500 1.9 / 1137 3.8 / 1738 2.1	**27** W 0048 3.9 / 0639 1.7 / 1333 3.8 / 1919 1.9
13 W 0003 3.9 / 0656 1.8 / 1255 4.0 / 1919 1.8	**28** TH 0150 4.0 / 0741 1.6 / 1427 4.1 / 2012 1.6
14 TH 0126 4.1 / 0755 1.3 / 1410 4.3 / 2015 1.3	**29** F 0240 4.2 / 0829 1.4 / 1509 4.3 / 2054 1.4
15 F 0234 4.5 / 0845 0.9 / 1504 4.7 / 2102 0.9	**30** SA 0323 4.3 / 0909 1.2 / 1546 4.5 / 2132 1.2

Chart Datum: 0·20 metres above Ordnance Datum (Dublin)
HAT is 5·6m above Chart Datum

TIDES

TIME ZONE (UT)
For Summer Time add ONE hour in **non-shaded areas**

IRELAND – GALWAY
LAT 53°16'N   LONG 9°03'W
TIMES AND HEIGHTS OF HIGH AND LOW WATERS

Dates in amber are **SPRINGS**
Dates in yellow are **NEAPS**

2011

MAY

#	Time	m	#	Time	m
1 SU	0402	4.5	**16** M	0347	5.0
	0945	1.1		0947	0.6
	1621	4.6		1607	5.2
	2208	1.0		2207	0.5
2 M	0439	4.6	**17** TU	0435	5.1
	1019	1.0		1030	0.5
	1654	4.7		1652	5.3
	2243	0.9	○	2252	0.4
3 TU	0514	4.6	**18** W	0523	5.1
	1051	1.0		1113	0.6
	1726	4.7		1738	5.3
●	2317	0.9		2338	0.4
4 W	0550	4.6	**19** TH	0610	5.1
	1122	1.0		1156	0.7
	1759	4.7		1823	5.2
	2349	0.9			
5 TH	0626	4.6	**20** F	0023	0.5
	1155	1.0		0655	4.9
	1833	4.7		1240	0.9
				1908	5.0
6 F	0023	1.0	**21** SA	0109	0.6
	0702	4.6		0741	4.7
	1230	1.1		1324	1.1
	1908	4.6		1954	4.8
7 SA	0101	1.1	**22** SU	0156	0.9
	0740	4.4		0828	4.4
	1310	1.3		1410	1.4
	1946	4.5		2044	4.5
8 SU	0143	1.2	**23** M	0245	1.2
	0823	4.3		0921	4.1
	1353	1.5		1504	1.7
	2030	4.3		2141	4.2
9 M	0230	1.4	**24** TU	0342	1.4
	0913	4.2		1020	3.9
	1443	1.7		1610	1.9
	2127	4.2	◔	2245	4.0
10 TU	0326	1.5	**25** W	0444	1.6
	1012	4.1		1125	3.8
	1545	1.9		1723	2.0
◔	2232	4.1		2351	3.9
11 W	0435	1.6	**26** TH	0546	1.7
	1116	4.1		1231	3.8
	1704	1.9		1829	2.0
	2339	4.2			
12 TH	0607	1.5	**27** F	0054	3.9
	1223	4.2		0645	1.7
	1838	1.7		1335	3.9
				1927	1.8
13 F	0051	4.3	**28** SA	0154	3.9
	0718	1.3		0741	1.7
	1333	4.4		1427	4.1
	1942	1.4		2018	1.6
14 SA	0200	4.5	**29** SU	0244	4.1
	0814	1.1		0830	1.5
	1432	4.7		1510	4.2
	2034	1.0		2102	1.4
15 SU	0257	4.8	**30** M	0328	4.2
	0902	0.8		0911	1.2
	1522	5.0		1547	4.4
	2122	0.7		2141	1.2
			31 TU	0408	4.3
				0949	1.3
				1622	4.5
				2219	1.1

JUNE

#	Time	m	#	Time	m
1 W	0446	4.4	**16** TH	0509	4.9
	1026	1.2		1058	0.9
	1657	4.6		1723	5.1
●	2257	1.0		2325	0.6
2 TH	0525	4.5	**17** F	0556	4.8
	1101	1.1		1142	0.9
	1734	4.7		1809	5.1
	2333	0.9			
3 F	0605	4.6	**18** SA	0009	0.6
	1138	1.0		0641	4.8
	1812	4.8		1224	0.9
				1853	5.0
4 SA	0011	0.8	**19** SU	0052	0.6
	0644	4.6		0724	4.7
	1217	1.0		1305	1.1
	1851	4.7		1936	4.8
5 SU	0051	0.8	**20** M	0134	0.8
	0725	4.6		0807	4.5
	1258	1.1		1346	1.2
	1932	4.7		2021	4.6
6 M	0132	0.9	**21** TU	0216	1.0
	0808	4.5		0851	4.3
	1342	1.2		1430	1.5
	2017	4.6		2108	4.4
7 TU	0218	1.0	**22** W	0301	1.2
	0856	4.4		0938	4.1
	1431	1.4		1520	1.7
	2110	4.5		2158	4.1
8 W	0309	1.2	**23** TH	0351	1.5
	0951	4.3		1029	3.9
	1527	1.6		1620	1.9
	2211	4.3	◔	2251	3.9
9 TH	0409	1.3	**24** F	0446	1.7
	1050	4.3		1122	3.8
	1634	1.7		1730	2.0
◔	2316	4.3		2346	3.8
10 F	0518	1.4	**25** SA	0546	1.8
	1153	4.3		1220	3.8
	1753	1.6		1839	2.0
11 SA	0023	4.3	**26** SU	0049	3.7
	0636	1.4		0648	1.9
	1300	4.4		1328	3.8
	1909	1.5		1940	1.9
12 SU	0132	4.4	**27** M	0156	3.8
	0744	1.3		0749	1.8
	1405	4.6		1428	4.0
	2011	1.2		2033	1.6
13 M	0235	4.6	**28** TU	0253	3.9
	0840	1.1		0841	1.6
	1500	4.8		1514	4.2
	2103	1.0		2119	1.4
14 TU	0330	4.7	**29** W	0340	4.1
	0928	1.0		0926	1.4
	1549	5.0		1555	4.4
	2152	0.8		2200	1.1
15 W	0420	4.8	**30** TH	0423	4.3
	1014	0.9		1007	1.2
	1636	5.1		1633	4.6
○	2238	0.6		2240	0.9

JULY

#	Time	m	#	Time	m
1 F	0505	4.5	**16** SA	0543	4.7
	1047	1.0		1125	0.9
	1713	4.7		1754	5.0
●	2320	0.7		2351	0.5
2 SA	0547	4.7	**17** SU	0624	4.7
	1126	0.9		1204	0.8
	1755	4.9		1836	5.0
	2359	0.5			
3 SU	0628	4.8	**18** M	0029	0.6
	1206	0.8		0703	4.7
	1836	4.9		1242	0.9
				1915	4.9
4 M	0037	0.5	**19** TU	0107	0.7
	0709	4.8		0742	4.6
	1247	0.7		1318	1.0
	1917	4.9		1954	4.7
5 TU	0118	0.5	**20** W	0143	0.8
	0751	4.8		0820	4.4
	1329	0.8		1355	1.2
	2001	4.9		2034	4.5
6 W	0201	0.6	**21** TH	0221	1.1
	0835	4.7		0858	4.2
	1414	1.0		1435	1.5
	2049	4.7		2115	4.2
7 TH	0248	0.9	**22** F	0301	1.4
	0925	4.5		0938	4.1
	1505	1.2		1519	1.7
	2146	4.5		2159	4.0
8 F	0341	1.1	**23** SA	0346	1.6
	1021	4.3		1022	3.9
	1604	1.5		1616	2.0
◔	2250	4.3	◔	2249	3.8
9 SA	0443	1.4	**24** SU	0440	1.9
	1124	4.2		1110	3.7
	1717	1.6		1743	2.1
	2358	4.2		2345	3.6
10 SU	0559	1.6	**25** M	0553	2.0
	1232	4.2		1208	3.7
	1841	1.6		1906	2.0
11 M	0111	4.2	**26** TU	0056	3.6
	0720	1.6		0713	2.0
	1344	4.3		1332	3.7
	1955	1.4		2009	1.8
12 TU	0221	4.3	**27** W	0220	3.7
	0824	1.4		0816	1.8
	1447	4.5		1447	4.0
	2053	1.2		2059	1.4
13 W	0320	4.4	**28** TH	0318	4.0
	0916	1.3		0906	1.5
	1539	4.7		1534	4.3
	2142	0.9		2142	1.1
14 TH	0411	4.6	**29** F	0404	4.3
	1001	1.1		0950	1.2
	1626	4.9		1615	4.5
	2227	0.7		2222	0.7
15 F	0458	4.7	**30** SA	0446	4.5
	1044	1.0		1031	0.9
	1711	5.0		1655	4.8
○	2310	0.6	●	2301	0.4
			31 SU	0527	4.8
				1110	0.6
				1737	5.0
				2340	0.2

AUGUST

#	Time	m	#	Time	m
1 M	0608	5.0	**16** TU	0002	0.5
	1150	0.4		0638	4.8
	1818	5.1		1215	0.8
				1850	4.9
2 TU	0018	0.1	**17** W	0036	0.6
	0648	5.0		0714	4.7
	1230	0.4		1249	0.9
	1858	5.1		1926	4.7
3 W	0058	0.2	**18** TH	0109	0.8
	0728	5.0		0748	4.6
	1310	0.4		1322	1.1
	1940	5.0		2000	4.5
4 TH	0139	0.4	**19** F	0142	1.0
	0810	4.9		0821	4.5
	1353	0.7		1355	1.3
	2025	4.8		2036	4.3
5 F	0223	0.7	**20** SA	0217	1.3
	0855	4.6		0855	4.2
	1440	1.0		1431	1.6
	2118	4.5		2117	4.0
6 SA	0312	1.1	**21** SU	0255	1.6
	0949	4.3		0934	4.0
	1536	1.4		1514	1.9
◔	2224	4.2	◔	2206	3.8
7 SU	0413	1.5	**22** M	0340	1.9
	1053	4.1		1023	3.8
	1648	1.7		1613	2.2
	2338	4.0		2304	3.6
8 M	0534	1.8	**23** TU	0443	2.1
	1209	4.0		1121	3.7
	1822	1.7		1836	2.1
9 TU	0058	3.9	**24** W	0011	3.5
	0704	1.8		0645	2.2
	1332	4.1		1229	3.7
	1949	1.6		1945	1.9
10 W	0215	4.0	**25** TH	0147	3.6
	0812	1.6		0754	2.1
	1439	4.3		1416	3.9
	2049	1.3		2036	1.5
11 TH	0313	4.3	**26** F	0256	4.0
	0903	1.4		0845	1.5
	1530	4.6		1512	4.3
	2133	1.0		2119	1.0
12 F	0401	4.5	**27** SA	0341	4.3
	0946	1.2		0929	1.1
	1615	4.8		1554	4.6
	2212	0.8		2158	0.6
13 SA	0443	4.6	**28** SU	0422	4.7
	1026	1.0		1009	0.7
	1656	4.9		1634	5.0
○	2250	0.6		2237	0.3
14 SU	0524	4.7	**29** M	0502	5.0
	1104	0.8		1049	0.4
	1736	5.0		1714	5.2
	2327	0.5	●	2315	0.0
15 M	0602	4.8	**30** TU	0543	5.2
	1141	0.7		1128	0.2
	1814	5.0		1756	5.4
				2354	0.0
			31 W	0623	5.3
				1208	0.1
				1837	5.3

Chart Datum: 0·20 metres above Ordnance Datum (Dublin)
HAT is 5·6m above Chart Datum

TIME ZONE (UT)	IRELAND – GALWAY	Dates in amber are SPRINGS
For Summer Time add ONE hour in non-shaded areas	LAT 53°16′N LONG 9°03′W	Dates in yellow are NEAPS
	TIMES AND HEIGHTS OF HIGH AND LOW WATERS	2011

SEPTEMBER

Time	m	Time	m
1 TH 0033 0.1, 0703 5.2, 1249 0.2, 1918 5.2		**16** F 0035 0.9, 0716 4.6, 1250 1.1, 1930 4.6	
2 F 0115 0.3, 0743 5.0, 1331 0.5, 2002 4.9		**17** SA 0106 1.1, 0747 4.5, 1322 1.3, 2004 4.4	
3 SA 0158 0.7, 0827 4.7, 1417 0.9, 2053 4.5		**18** SU 0140 1.4, 0819 4.3, 1357 1.6, 2043 4.1	
4 SU 0247 1.2, 0918 4.4, ◐ 1511 1.4, 2200 4.1		**19** M 0217 1.7, 0857 4.1, 1438 1.8, 2134 3.8	
5 M 0349 1.7, 1025 4.1, 1625 1.7, 2322 3.8		**20** TU 0302 2.0, 0947 3.9, 1531 2.1, ◑ 2235 3.7	
6 TU 0519 2.0, 1151 3.9, 1807 1.8		**21** W 0401 2.2, 1048 3.8, 1757 2.2, 2341 3.6	
7 W 0048 3.8, 0649 1.9, 1319 4.0, 1947 1.6		**22** TH 0615 2.3, 1153 3.8, 1914 1.9	
8 TH 0205 4.0, 0756 1.9, 1425 4.3, 2042 1.4		**23** F 0102 3.8, 0820 2.0, 1318 4.0, 2006 1.5	
9 F 0259 4.3, 0845 1.5, 1514 4.5, 2117 1.1		**24** SA 0222 4.1, 0817 1.6, 1438 4.4, 2050 1.1	
10 SA 0342 4.5, 0925 1.2, 1556 4.8, 2151 0.9		**25** SU 0310 4.5, 0902 1.1, 1525 4.8, 2131 0.6	
11 SU 0422 4.7, 1003 1.0, 1635 4.9, 2225 0.7		**26** M 0352 4.9, 0944 0.7, 1607 5.1, 2210 0.3	
12 M 0459 4.8, 1040 0.8, 1713 5.0, ○ 2259 0.6		**27** TU 0433 5.2, 1024 0.4, ● 1649 5.4, 2249 0.1	
13 TU 0535 4.8, 1115 0.8, 1749 5.0, 2332 0.7		**28** W 0515 5.4, 1104 0.1, 1732 5.5, 2329 0.1	
14 W 0610 4.8, 1147 0.8, 1823 4.9		**29** TH 0556 5.5, 1146 0.1, 1815 5.5	
15 TH 0003 0.7, 0643 4.8, 1219 0.9, 1857 4.8		**30** F 0009 0.2, 0638 5.4, 1228 0.2, 1858 5.3	

OCTOBER

Time	m	Time	m
1 SA 0052 0.5, 0720 5.2, 1311 0.5, 1943 5.0		**16** SU 0035 1.3, 0717 4.6, 1257 1.3, 1939 4.4	
2 SU 0136 0.9, 0804 4.9, 1358 0.9, 2035 4.5		**17** M 0111 1.5, 0751 4.4, 1334 1.5, 2019 4.2	
3 M 0226 1.4, 0855 4.5, 1452 1.4, 2140 4.1		**18** TU 0151 1.8, 0829 4.3, 1416 1.7, 2110 4.0	
4 TU 0330 1.8, 1002 4.2, 1604 1.8, ◐ 2304 3.9		**19** W 0238 2.0, 0919 4.1, 1508 2.0, 2210 3.9	
5 W 0501 2.1, 1129 4.0, 1741 1.9		**20** TH 0337 2.2, 1020 4.0, 1619 2.1, ◑ 2315 3.9	
6 TH 0029 3.9, 0624 2.1, 1254 4.0, 1920 1.7		**21** F 0508 2.3, 1125 4.0, 1830 1.9	
7 F 0143 4.1, 0730 1.9, 1400 4.3, 2017 1.5		**22** SA 0024 4.0, 0648 2.0, 1236 4.2, 1929 1.6	
8 SA 0235 4.3, 0820 1.6, 1450 4.5, 2051 1.3		**23** SU 0137 4.3, 0745 1.6, 1354 4.5, 2018 1.2	
9 SU 0317 4.5, 0901 1.4, 1532 4.7, 2124 1.1		**24** M 0234 4.7, 0833 1.2, 1452 4.9, 2102 0.8	
10 M 0355 4.7, 0938 1.1, 1610 4.9, 2157 0.9		**25** TU 0321 5.1, 0917 0.8, 1540 5.2, 2143 0.5	
11 TU 0431 4.8, 1014 1.0, 1646 4.9, 2230 0.9		**26** W 0404 5.4, 1000 0.5, 1625 5.4, 2224 0.4	
12 W 0506 4.9, 1049 0.9, 1721 4.9, ○ 2301 0.9		**27** TH 0448 5.5, 1043 0.3, 1710 5.5, 2306 0.3	
13 TH 0540 4.9, 1121 0.9, 1755 4.8, 2332 1.0		**28** F 0532 5.6, 1126 0.3, 1756 5.5, 2348 0.5	
14 F 0613 4.8, 1152 1.0, 1829 4.8		**29** SA 0617 5.5, 1210 0.4, 1842 5.3	
15 SA 0002 1.1, 0645 4.7, 1223 1.1, 1903 4.6		**30** SU 0032 0.7, 0701 5.3, 1256 0.6, 1929 5.0	
		31 M 0119 1.1, 0747 5.0, 1343 0.9, 2020 4.6	

NOVEMBER

Time	m	Time	m
1 TU 0209 1.5, 0838 4.7, 1435 1.3, 2121 4.3		**16** W 0134 1.7, 0810 4.5, 1402 1.5, 2049 4.3	
2 W 0309 1.4, 0940 4.3, 1539 1.7, ◐ 2236 4.0		**17** TH 0222 1.9, 0857 4.4, 1452 1.7, 2146 4.2	
3 TH 0429 2.1, 1056 4.1, 1659 1.9, 2353 4.0		**18** F 0318 2.0, 0955 4.3, 1552 1.8, ◑ 2248 4.2	
4 F 0547 2.1, 1212 4.1, 1820 1.9		**19** SA 0429 2.1, 1057 4.3, 1710 1.8, 2352 4.3	
5 SA 0104 4.1, 0651 2.0, 1321 4.2, 1927 1.7		**20** SU 0555 2.0, 1203 4.4, 1842 1.6	
6 SU 0202 4.3, 0746 1.8, 1417 4.3, 2015 1.6		**21** M 0057 4.5, 0707 1.7, 1315 4.6, 1944 1.4	
7 M 0247 4.5, 0832 1.5, 1502 4.5, 2053 1.4		**22** TU 0200 4.8, 0804 1.4, 1421 4.8, 2034 1.1	
8 TU 0326 4.6, 0912 1.4, 1542 4.6, 2128 1.3		**23** W 0253 5.0, 0853 1.0, 1516 5.1, 2120 0.8	
9 W 0402 4.7, 0949 1.2, 1618 4.7, 2201 1.2		**24** TH 0340 5.3, 0940 0.8, 1605 5.3, 2204 0.7	
10 TH 0436 4.8, 1025 1.2, ○ 1654 4.8, 2233 1.2		**25** F 0427 5.4, 1025 0.6, ● 1654 5.3, 2248 0.7	
11 F 0510 4.8, 1059 1.1, 1729 4.8, 2305 1.2		**26** SA 0514 5.5, 1111 0.5, 1742 5.2, 2333 0.7	
12 SA 0544 4.8, 1131 1.1, 1805 4.8, 2338 1.3		**27** SU 0601 5.5, 1157 0.5, 1829 5.2	
13 SU 0619 4.8, 1205 1.2, 1842 4.7		**28** M 0018 0.9, 0647 5.3, 1243 0.6, 1916 5.0	
14 M 0013 1.4, 0655 4.7, 1240 1.2, 1920 4.6		**29** TU 0104 1.1, 0733 5.1, 1328 0.9, 2004 4.7	
15 TU 0052 1.5, 0731 4.6, 1319 1.3, 2001 4.4		**30** W 0151 1.4, 0821 4.8, 1415 1.2, 2057 4.4	

DECEMBER

Time	m	Time	m
1 TH 0243 1.7, 0914 4.5, 1507 1.5, 2158 4.2		**16** F 0208 1.5, 0838 4.7, 1435 1.2, 2120 4.4	
2 F 0345 2.0, 1014 4.3, 1608 1.7, ◑ 2304 4.0		**17** SA 0258 1.7, 0929 4.5, 1528 1.4, 2218 4.3	
3 SA 0456 2.1, 1118 4.1, 1716 1.9		**18** SU 0358 1.8, 1029 4.4, 1628 1.6, 2320 4.3	
4 SU 0008 4.0, 0603 2.1, 1223 4.0, 1824 1.9		**19** M 0507 1.9, 1134 4.4, 1742 1.6	
5 M 0112 4.1, 0704 2.0, 1328 4.0, 1926 1.9		**20** TU 0024 4.4, 0624 1.8, 1245 4.4, 1907 1.6	
6 TU 0208 4.2, 0758 1.9, 1425 4.1, 2017 1.7		**21** W 0131 4.6, 0736 1.6, 1358 4.6, 2012 1.4	
7 W 0254 4.4, 0845 1.7, 1511 4.3, 2058 1.6		**22** TH 0232 4.8, 0835 1.3, 1500 4.7, 2104 1.2	
8 TH 0333 4.5, 0926 1.5, 1552 4.4, 2136 1.5		**23** F 0325 5.0, 0927 1.0, 1553 4.9, 2151 1.0	
9 F 0409 4.6, 1005 1.2, 1630 4.5, 2212 1.3		**24** SA 0414 5.2, 1015 0.9, ● 1643 5.0, 2236 0.9	
10 SA 0445 4.7, 1042 1.2, 1708 4.6, 2248 1.3		**25** SU 0502 5.3, 1101 0.6, 1731 5.1, 2321 0.8	
11 SU 0522 4.8, 1119 1.1, 1746 4.7, 2324 1.2		**26** M 0549 5.3, 1146 0.5, 1818 5.0	
12 M 0600 4.9, 1154 1.0, 1825 4.7		**27** TU 0005 0.8, 0634 5.3, 1229 0.6, 1902 4.9	
13 TU 0001 1.2, 0637 4.9, 1231 1.0, 1904 4.7		**28** W 0048 1.0, 0718 5.1, 1310 0.7, 1945 4.8	
14 W 0041 1.2, 0716 4.8, 1309 1.0, 1945 4.7		**29** TH 0130 1.1, 0802 4.9, 1351 0.9, 2030 4.5	
15 TH 0123 1.3, 0755 4.8, 1350 1.1, 2029 4.5		**30** F 0213 1.4, 0846 4.7, 1433 1.2, 2118 4.3	
		31 SA 0300 1.7, 0932 4.4, 1519 1.5, 2210 4.1	

Chart Datum: 0·20 metres above Ordnance Datum (Dublin)
HAT is 5·6m above Chart Datum

TIDES

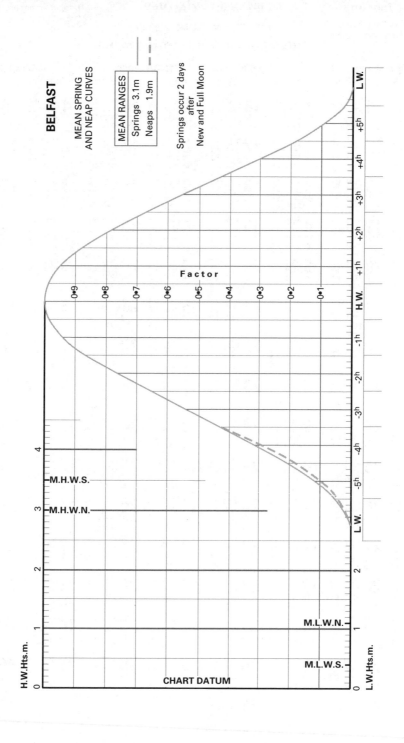

BELFAST

MEAN SPRING
AND NEAP CURVES

MEAN RANGES	
Springs	3.1m
Neaps	1.9m

Springs occur 2 days
after
New and Full Moon

Factor

0·9 0·8 0·7 0·6 0·5 0·4 0·3 0·2 0·1

H.W.Hts.m.

4

M.H.W.S.

3 M.H.W.N.

2

1

0   CHART DATUM

L.W.Hts.m.

M.L.W.N.

M.L.W.S.

L.W.   +5h +4h +3h +2h +1h H.W. -1h -2h -3h -4h -5h L.W.   2   1   0

TIME ZONE (UT)	NORTHERN IRELAND – BELFAST	Dates in amber are SPRINGS
For Summer Time add ONE hour in non-shaded areas	LAT 54°36′N LONG 5°55′W	Dates in yellow are NEAPS
	TIMES AND HEIGHTS OF HIGH AND LOW WATERS	**2011**

JANUARY

Time	m	Time	m
1 SA 0158 / 0830 / 1439 / 2055	0.9 / 3.2 / 0.9 / 3.3	**16** SU 0157 / 0800 / 1422 / 2028	1.1 / 3.1 / 1.1 / 3.0
2 SU 0257 / 0926 / 1537 / 2151	0.9 / 3.4 / 0.9 / 3.4	**17** M 0251 / 0858 / 1515 / 2125	1.0 / 3.2 / 0.9 / 3.1
3 M 0348 / 1016 / 1629 / 2240	0.9 / 3.5 / 0.7 / 3.4	**18** TU 0338 / 0946 / 1601 / 2212	0.8 / 3.4 / 0.7 / 3.3
4 TU 0435 / 1101 / 1714 / ●2324	0.8 / 3.6 / 0.6 / 3.4	**19** W 0421 / 1029 / 1644 / ○2253	0.7 / 3.6 / 0.5 / 3.3
5 W 0516 / 1142 / 1754	0.8 / 3.7 / 0.6	**20** TH 0502 / 1109 / 1724 / 2333	0.6 / 3.7 / 0.4 / 3.4
6 TH 0005 / 0553 / 1221 / 1830	3.3 / 0.8 / 3.7 / 0.6	**21** F 0542 / 1150 / 1805	0.6 / 3.8 / 0.3
7 F 0043 / 0628 / 1257 / 1904	3.2 / 0.9 / 3.6 / 0.6	**22** SA 0016 / 0623 / 1235 / 1847	3.4 / 0.6 / 3.8 / 0.2
8 SA 0121 / 0703 / 1335 / 1938	3.2 / 0.9 / 3.6 / 0.7	**23** SU 0102 / 0707 / 1322 / 1932	3.3 / 0.5 / 3.8 / 0.2
9 SU 0200 / 0739 / 1413 / 2013	3.2 / 0.9 / 3.5 / 0.7	**24** M 0151 / 0753 / 1411 / 2019	3.3 / 0.6 / 3.8 / 0.3
10 M 0242 / 0819 / 1452 / 2052	3.1 / 0.9 / 3.4 / 0.8	**25** TU 0242 / 0842 / 1502 / 2110	3.3 / 0.6 / 3.7 / 0.5
11 TU 0326 / 0901 / 1533 / 2135	3.1 / 1.0 / 3.3 / 0.9	**26** W 0335 / 0937 / 1557 / ◐2207	3.2 / 0.7 / 3.6 / 0.7
12 W 0413 / 0948 / 1619 / ◐2226	3.1 / 1.0 / 3.2 / 1.0	**27** TH 0432 / 1041 / 1658 / 2315	3.1 / 0.9 / 3.4 / 0.9
13 TH 0504 / 1043 / 1714 / 2329	3.0 / 1.2 / 3.1 / 1.1	**28** F 0540 / 1159 / 1813	3.0 / 1.0 / 3.2
14 F 0559 / 1151 / 1816	3.0 / 1.3 / 3.0	**29** SA 0031 / 0701 / 1317 / 1937	1.0 / 3.0 / 1.0 / 3.1
15 SA 0051 / 0659 / 1316 / 1922	1.2 / 3.0 / 1.3 / 2.9	**30** SU 0144 / 0816 / 1430 / 2047	1.0 / 3.1 / 0.9 / 3.1
		31 M 0248 / 0915 / 1533 / 2142	1.0 / 3.3 / 0.7 / 3.2

FEBRUARY

Time	m	Time	m
1 TU 0341 / 1005 / 1623 / 2229	0.9 / 3.4 / 0.6 / 3.2	**16** W 0319 / 0918 / 1542 / 2149	0.8 / 3.3 / 0.5 / 3.2
2 W 0425 / 1049 / 1704 / 2311	0.8 / 3.5 / 0.5 / 3.2	**17** TH 0403 / 1004 / 1625 / 2232	0.6 / 3.5 / 0.3 / 3.3
3 TH 0502 / 1128 / 1737 / ●2348	0.8 / 3.6 / 0.5 / 3.2	**18** F 0443 / 1047 / 1705 / ○2314	0.5 / 3.7 / 0.1 / 3.3
4 F 0534 / 1204 / 1807	0.7 / 3.5 / 0.5	**19** SA 0522 / 1130 / 1744 / 2357	0.4 / 3.8 / 0.1 / 3.4
5 SA 0022 / 0604 / 1237 / 1835	3.1 / 0.7 / 3.5 / 0.6	**20** SU 0603 / 1216 / 1826	0.3 / 3.8 / 0.1
6 SU 0055 / 0635 / 1309 / 1905	3.1 / 0.7 / 3.5 / 0.6	**21** M 0043 / 0645 / 1305 / 1909	3.4 / 0.3 / 3.8 / 0.1
7 M 0128 / 0708 / 1340 / 1937	3.1 / 0.7 / 3.4 / 0.6	**22** TU 0131 / 0730 / 1355 / 1954	3.4 / 0.3 / 3.8 / 0.3
8 TU 0203 / 0744 / 1413 / 2012	3.2 / 0.7 / 3.4 / 0.7	**23** W 0220 / 0818 / 1445 / 2043	3.3 / 0.4 / 3.7 / 0.5
9 W 0242 / 0823 / 1449 / 2051	3.2 / 0.8 / 3.3 / 0.8	**24** TH 0310 / 0911 / 1539 / ◑2138	3.2 / 0.6 / 3.4 / 0.7
10 TH 0323 / 0906 / 1528 / 2135	3.1 / 0.9 / 3.2 / 0.9	**25** F 0403 / 1017 / 1638 / 2246	3.1 / 0.8 / 3.2 / 1.0
11 F 0412 / 0956 / 1620 / ◐2230	3.0 / 1.0 / 3.0 / 1.1	**26** SA 0507 / 1140 / 1754	3.0 / 0.9 / 3.0
12 SA 0510 / 1057 / 1730 / 2348	2.9 / 1.2 / 2.8 / 1.2	**27** SU 0009 / 0635 / 1302 / 1925	1.1 / 2.9 / 0.9 / 2.9
13 SU 0615 / 1235 / 1844	2.9 / 1.2 / 2.8	**28** M 0126 / 0758 / 1418 / 2034	1.1 / 3.0 / 0.8 / 2.9
14 M 0130 / 0721 / 1359 / 1955	1.2 / 2.9 / 1.0 / 2.9		
15 TU 0230 / 0825 / 1455 / 2100	1.0 / 3.1 / 0.8 / 3.0		

MARCH

Time	m	Time	m
1 TU 0236 / 0858 / 1522 / 2127	1.0 / 3.1 / 0.6 / 3.0	**16** W 0204 / 0752 / 1429 / 2032	1.0 / 3.0 / 0.6 / 3.0
2 W 0331 / 0946 / 1609 / 2211	0.9 / 3.3 / 0.5 / 3.1	**17** TH 0255 / 0849 / 1517 / 2123	0.8 / 3.3 / 0.4 / 3.1
3 TH 0412 / 1028 / 1645 / 2250	0.8 / 3.4 / 0.4 / 3.1	**18** F 0340 / 0938 / 1600 / 2208	0.6 / 3.5 / 0.2 / 3.3
4 F 0442 / 1107 / 1712 / ●2325	0.7 / 3.4 / 0.5 / 3.1	**19** SA 0421 / 1024 / 1640 / ○2252	0.4 / 3.7 / 0.0 / 3.4
5 SA 0510 / 1141 / 1737 / 2357	0.7 / 3.4 / 0.5 / 3.1	**20** SU 0500 / 1110 / 1720 / 2336	0.3 / 3.8 / 0.0 / 3.4
6 SU 0538 / 1212 / 1805	0.6 / 3.4 / 0.5	**21** M 0541 / 1157 / 1801	0.2 / 3.8 / 0.1
7 M 0025 / 0608 / 1238 / 1834	3.1 / 0.6 / 3.3 / 0.6	**22** TU 0023 / 0623 / 1247 / 1845	3.4 / 0.2 / 3.8 / 0.2
8 TU 0053 / 0640 / 1304 / 1904	3.2 / 0.6 / 3.3 / 0.6	**23** W 0111 / 0709 / 1338 / 1931	3.4 / 0.2 / 3.7 / 0.3
9 W 0124 / 0713 / 1334 / 1937	3.2 / 0.6 / 3.3 / 0.6	**24** TH 0159 / 0758 / 1429 / ◑2020	3.4 / 0.3 / 3.5 / 0.5
10 TH 0159 / 0750 / 1410 / 2015	3.2 / 0.6 / 3.2 / 0.7	**25** F 0248 / 0853 / 1522 / 2114	3.3 / 0.5 / 3.3 / 0.8
11 F 0238 / 0832 / 1451 / 2058	3.2 / 0.7 / 3.1 / 0.9	**26** SA 0339 / 1000 / 1621 / ◐2221	3.2 / 0.7 / 3.1 / 1.0
12 SA 0323 / 0920 / 1543 / ◐2151	3.1 / 0.9 / 2.9 / 1.1	**27** SU 0439 / 1122 / 1735 / ◐2151	3.0 / 0.8 / 2.8 / 1.1
13 SU 0422 / 1020 / 1656 / 2300	2.9 / 1.0 / 2.8 / 1.2	**28** M 0601 / 1238 / 1906	2.9 / 0.8 / 2.8
14 M 0534 / 1146 / 1814	2.8 / 1.1 / 2.7	**29** TU 0058 / 0729 / 1352 / 2011	1.2 / 2.9 / 0.7 / 2.8
15 TU 0059 / 0645 / 1332 / 1927	1.2 / 2.9 / 0.9 / 2.8	**30** W 0208 / 0830 / 1453 / 2102	1.1 / 3.1 / 0.6 / 2.9
		31 TH 0305 / 0919 / 1539 / 2145	0.9 / 3.2 / 0.5 / 3.0

APRIL

Time	m	Time	m
1 F 0346 / 1001 / 1613 / 2222	0.8 / 3.3 / 0.5 / 3.1	**16** SA 0312 / 0913 / 1531 / 2144	0.6 / 3.5 / 0.2 / 3.3
2 SA 0416 / 1039 / 1639 / 2256	0.7 / 3.3 / 0.5 / 3.1	**17** SU 0356 / 1002 / 1614 / 2230	0.4 / 3.6 / 0.1 / 3.4
3 SU 0443 / 1113 / 1705 / ●2326	0.7 / 3.3 / 0.5 / 3.2	**18** M 0439 / 1050 / 1656 / ○2316	0.3 / 3.7 / 0.1 / 3.5
4 M 0513 / 1141 / 1735 / 2354	0.6 / 3.3 / 0.6 / 3.2	**19** TU 0523 / 1139 / 1740	0.2 / 3.7 / 0.2
5 TU 0544 / 1204 / 1806	0.6 / 3.3 / 0.6	**20** W 0004 / 0607 / 1230 / 1824	3.5 / 0.2 / 3.7 / 0.3
6 W 0021 / 0615 / 1231 / 1836	3.3 / 0.6 / 3.3 / 0.6	**21** TH 0052 / 0654 / 1321 / 1911	3.5 / 0.3 / 3.5 / 0.5
7 TH 0053 / 0648 / 1304 / 1909	3.3 / 0.6 / 3.2 / 0.7	**22** F 0139 / 0744 / 1412 / 2001	3.5 / 0.3 / 3.4 / 0.7
8 F 0128 / 0725 / 1343 / 1948	3.3 / 0.6 / 3.2 / 0.8	**23** SA 0227 / 0840 / 1505 / 2055	3.4 / 0.5 / 3.2 / 0.9
9 SA 0208 / 0807 / 1428 / 2033	3.3 / 0.6 / 3.1 / 0.9	**24** SU 0317 / 0945 / 1601 / 2158	3.3 / 0.6 / 3.0 / 1.0
10 SU 0253 / 0857 / 1524 / 2127	3.2 / 0.7 / 2.9 / 1.0	**25** M 0411 / 1057 / 1708 / ◑2309	3.1 / 0.7 / 2.8 / 1.2
11 M 0349 / 0957 / 1634 / ◐2233	3.0 / 0.9 / 2.8 / 1.2	**26** TU 0517 / 1205 / 1829	3.0 / 0.8 / 2.7
12 TU 0458 / 1115 / 1749 / 2343	3.0 / 0.9 / 2.8 / 1.2	**27** W 0018 / 0642 / 1310 / 1934	1.2 / 2.9 / 0.7 / 2.8
13 W 0010 / 0611 / 1254 / 1900	1.2 / 3.0 / 0.8 / 2.8	**28** TH 0123 / 0751 / 1407 / 2025	1.1 / 3.0 / 0.7 / 2.9
14 TH 0129 / 0720 / 1356 / 2004	1.0 / 3.1 / 0.5 / 3.0	**29** F 0220 / 0843 / 1454 / 2108	1.0 / 3.1 / 0.6 / 3.0
15 F 0224 / 0820 / 1446 / 2057	0.8 / 3.3 / 0.3 / 3.2	**30** SA 0306 / 0927 / 1531 / 2147	0.9 / 3.1 / 0.6 / 3.1

Chart Datum: 2·01 metres below Ordnance Datum (Belfast)
HAT is 3·9m above Chart Datum

TIDES

TIME ZONE (UT)
For Summer Time add ONE hour in **non-shaded areas**

NORTHERN IRELAND – BELFAST
LAT 54°36′N   LONG 5°55′W
TIMES AND HEIGHTS OF HIGH AND LOW WATERS

Dates in amber are **SPRINGS**
Dates in yellow are **NEAPS**

2011

MAY

Day	Time	m	Time	m	Time	m	Time	m
1 SU	0343	0.8	1005	3.2	1603	0.6	2221	3.2
2 M	0415	0.7	1040	3.2	1635	0.6	2254	3.3
3 TU ●	0448	0.7	1110	3.2	1708	0.6	2325	3.3
4 W	0522	0.6	1136	3.2	1741	0.7	2355	3.4
5 TH	0556	0.6	1205	3.2	1815	0.7		
6 F	0028	3.4	0630	0.6	1242	3.2	1851	0.7
7 SA	0106	3.4	0709	0.6	1325	3.2	1932	0.8
8 SU	0148	3.4	0752	0.6	1413	3.1	2018	0.9
9 M	0235	3.3	0842	0.6	1509	3.1	2112	1.0
10 TU ◑	0328	3.2	0941	0.6	1613	2.9	2215	1.0
11 W	0430	3.2	1052	0.7	1723	2.9	2328	1.1
12 TH	0539	3.2	1210	0.6	1833	2.9		
13 F	0043	1.0	0649	3.2	1318	0.5	1935	3.1
14 SA	0147	0.8	0753	3.4	1414	0.4	2031	3.2
15 SU	0243	0.7	0851	3.5	1504	0.3	2122	3.3
16 M	0334	0.5	0943	3.6	1551	0.3	2211	3.4
17 TU ○	0423	0.4	1034	3.6	1637	0.3	2259	3.5
18 W	0511	0.3	1124	3.6	1723	0.4	2346	3.6
19 TH	0558	0.3	1213	3.5	1809	0.5		
20 F	0033	3.6	0645	0.3	1303	3.4	1856	0.7
21 SA	0120	3.6	0734	0.4	1353	3.3	1944	0.8
22 SU	0207	3.5	0826	0.5	1443	3.1	2034	0.9
23 M	0253	3.4	0922	0.6	1535	3.0	2128	1.0
24 TU ◑	0343	3.3	1023	0.7	1634	2.9	2226	1.1
25 W	0436	3.1	1124	0.8	1728	2.8	2329	1.2
26 TH	0535	3.0	1222	0.8	1829	2.8		
27 F	0030	1.2	0642	3.0	1317	0.8	1927	2.9
28 SA	0129	1.1	0748	3.0	1406	0.8	2018	3.0
29 SU	0221	1.0	0842	3.1	1450	0.8	2103	3.1
30 M	0307	0.9	0927	3.1	1530	0.7	2144	3.2
31 TU	0348	0.8	1007	3.2	1607	0.7	2223	3.2

JUNE

Day	Time	m	Time	m	Time	m	Time	m
1 W ●	0426	0.7	1043	3.2	1644	0.7	2259	3.4
2 TH	0503	0.7	1115	3.2	1721	0.7	2333	3.5
3 F	0541	0.6	1147	3.2	1759	0.7		
4 SA	0008	3.5	0618	0.6	1225	3.2	1838	0.7
5 SU	0048	3.5	0658	0.5	1308	3.2	1921	0.8
6 M	0131	3.5	0742	0.5	1357	3.1	2007	0.8
7 TU	0217	3.5	0830	0.5	1451	3.1	2059	0.9
8 W	0309	3.5	0925	0.5	1550	3.0	2155	0.9
9 TH	0405	3.4	1027	0.6	1654	3.0	2258	0.9
10 F	0508	3.3	1135	0.6	1801	3.0		
11 SA	0006	0.9	0617	3.2	1244	0.6	1906	3.1
12 SU	0116	0.9	0728	3.3	1346	0.5	2007	3.2
13 M	0220	0.9	0832	3.4	1443	0.5	2104	3.3
14 TU	0319	0.6	0930	3.4	1535	0.5	2157	3.4
15 W ○	0413	0.5	1022	3.5	1624	0.5	2246	3.5
16 TH	0503	0.4	1112	3.4	1711	0.6	2332	3.6
17 F	0550	0.4	1159	3.4	1756	0.7		
18 SA	0017	3.6	0635	0.4	1245	3.3	1840	0.7
19 SU	0101	3.6	0719	0.4	1331	3.2	1923	0.8
20 M	0144	3.5	0802	0.5	1417	3.1	2005	0.9
21 TU	0228	3.5	0845	0.6	1503	3.0	2047	0.9
22 W	0312	3.4	0931	0.7	1550	3.0	2133	1.0
23 TH ◑	0358	3.2	1023	0.8	1639	2.9	2223	1.1
24 F	0448	3.1	1122	0.9	1730	2.9	2322	1.1
25 SA	0542	3.0	1224	1.0	1823	2.9		
26 SU	0030	1.2	0641	2.9	1321	1.0	1919	3.0
27 M	0136	1.1	0745	2.9	1413	0.9	2016	3.1
28 TU	0233	1.0	0846	3.0	1500	0.8	2108	3.2
29 W	0322	0.9	0937	3.1	1543	0.8	2154	3.3
30 TH ○	0406	0.7	1019	3.2	1624	0.7	2234	3.4

JULY

Day	Time	m	Time	m	Time	m	Time	m
1 F ●	0446	0.6	1055	3.2	1703	0.7	2310	3.5
2 SA	0525	0.5	1129	3.2	1743	0.7	2347	3.6
3 SU	0604	0.4	1207	3.2	1823	0.7		
4 M	0027	3.6	0644	0.3	1250	3.2	1905	0.7
5 TU	0112	3.6	0727	0.3	1338	3.2	1950	0.8
6 W	0158	3.6	0813	0.3	1429	3.2	2038	0.8
7 TH	0248	3.6	0903	0.4	1525	3.1	2131	0.7
8 F ◑	0342	3.5	0959	0.5	1624	3.1	2230	0.8
9 SA	0442	3.4	1103	0.6	1728	3.0	2338	0.9
10 SU	0550	3.3	1216	0.7	1839	3.0		
11 M	0054	0.9	0708	3.2	1326	0.8	1949	3.1
12 TU	0206	0.8	0821	3.2	1429	0.8	2053	3.2
13 W	0310	0.7	0923	3.3	1524	0.7	2148	3.4
14 TH	0407	0.5	1015	3.3	1614	0.7	2236	3.5
15 F ○	0455	0.4	1102	3.3	1659	0.7	2320	3.5
16 SA	0539	0.4	1145	3.2	1740	0.7		
17 SU	0001	3.6	0619	0.4	1226	3.2	1818	0.7
18 M	0041	3.5	0655	0.5	1306	3.1	1853	0.8
19 TU	0119	3.5	0728	0.5	1345	3.1	1928	0.8
20 W	0158	3.5	0800	0.6	1427	3.1	2006	0.8
21 TH	0238	3.4	0836	0.7	1510	3.1	2047	0.9
22 F	0319	3.3	0917	0.8	1556	3.1	2131	1.0
23 SA ◑	0403	3.1	1004	0.9	1644	3.0	2222	1.1
24 SU	0453	3.0	1104	1.0	1737	3.0	2325	1.2
25 M	0553	2.9	1231	1.1	1834	3.0		
26 TU	0052	1.2	0657	2.9	1339	1.1	1934	3.0
27 W	0203	1.1	0806	2.9	1434	1.0	2033	3.1
28 TH	0258	0.9	0908	3.0	1521	0.8	2124	3.3
29 F	0345	0.7	0955	3.1	1604	0.7	2206	3.4
30 SA ●	0427	0.5	1033	3.2	1643	0.6	2245	3.5
31 SU	0506	0.3	1109	3.3	1722	0.6	2324	3.6

AUGUST

Day	Time	m	Time	m	Time	m	Time	m
1 M	0544	0.2	1147	3.3	1801	0.5		
2 TU	0006	3.7	0623	0.2	1230	3.3	1842	0.5
3 W	0051	3.7	0705	0.2	1317	3.3	1926	0.5
4 TH	0139	3.7	0749	0.3	1407	3.3	2013	0.6
5 F	0229	3.7	0837	0.4	1459	3.2	2105	0.6
6 SA ◑	0322	3.5	0930	0.6	1556	3.1	2203	0.8
7 SU	0421	3.4	1033	0.8	1700	3.1	2317	0.9
8 M	0530	3.1	1152	0.9	1815	3.0		
9 TU	0041	0.9	0656	3.0	1312	1.0	1937	3.1
10 W	0158	0.8	0815	3.0	1419	0.9	2043	3.2
11 TH	0306	0.7	0916	3.1	1517	0.8	2137	3.4
12 F	0402	0.5	1005	3.2	1604	0.8	2223	3.5
13 SA ○	0446	0.4	1049	3.2	1645	0.7	2305	3.5
14 SU	0523	0.4	1128	3.2	1719	0.7	2342	3.5
15 M	0555	0.5	1203	3.1	1750	0.7		
16 TU	0017	3.5	0622	0.5	1237	3.1	1820	0.7
17 W	0051	3.4	0650	0.6	1311	3.1	1853	0.7
18 TH	0124	3.4	0720	0.6	1342	3.2	1928	0.7
19 F	0159	3.4	0753	0.7	1428	3.2	2007	0.8
20 SA	0235	3.3	0831	0.8	1511	3.2	2050	0.9
21 SU ◑	0314	3.2	0914	0.9	1558	3.1	2138	1.0
22 M	0404	3.0	1006	1.1	1653	3.0	2235	1.2
23 TU	0509	2.8	1117	1.2	1753	2.9		
24 W	0001	1.2	0619	2.7	1308	1.2	1855	3.0
25 TH	0135	1.1	0731	2.8	1408	1.1	1958	3.1
26 F	0233	0.8	0838	3.0	1458	0.9	2052	3.3
27 SA	0321	0.6	0927	3.1	1541	0.7	2137	3.5
28 SU	0403	0.4	1008	3.3	1620	0.6	2219	3.6
29 M ●	0441	0.2	1046	3.4	1658	0.5	2300	3.7
30 TU	0519	0.1	1126	3.4	1736	0.4	2344	3.8
31 W	0558	0.1	1209	3.4	1817	0.4		

Chart Datum: 2·01 metres below Ordnance Datum (Belfast)
HAT is 3·9m above Chart Datum

TIME ZONE (UT)
For Summer Time add ONE hour in **non-shaded areas**

NORTHERN IRELAND – BELFAST
LAT 54°36'N   LONG 5°55'W
TIMES AND HEIGHTS OF HIGH AND LOW WATERS

Dates in amber are **SPRINGS**
Dates in yellow are **NEAPS**

2011

SEPTEMBER

Time m	Time m
1 TH 0031 3.8 / 0639 0.2 / 1256 3.4 / 1901 3.4	**16** F 0047 3.4 / 0645 0.7 / 1309 3.3 / 1856 0.7
2 F 0121 3.8 / 0723 0.3 / 1346 3.4 / 1949 0.5	**17** SA 0118 3.3 / 0718 0.7 / 1346 3.3 / 1933 0.8
3 SA 0212 3.7 / 0811 0.5 / 1438 3.3 / 2041 0.6	**18** SU 0154 3.3 / 0754 0.8 / 1426 3.3 / 2015 0.9
4 SU 0307 3.5 / 0904 0.7 / 1533 3.2 / 2142 0.8	**19** M 0233 3.2 / 0836 0.9 / 1512 3.2 / 2102 1.0
5 M 0406 3.3 / 1006 0.9 / 1636 3.1 / 2302 0.9	**20** TU 0322 3.0 / 0927 1.1 / 1608 3.1 / 2159 1.1
6 TU 0517 3.0 / 1131 1.1 / 1755 3.0	**21** W 0432 2.8 / 0927 1.1 / 1713 3.0 / 2313 1.2
7 W 0030 0.9 / 0647 2.9 / 1256 1.2 / 1922 3.1	**22** TH 0547 2.8 / 1227 1.1 / 1820 3.0
8 TH 0149 0.8 / 0804 2.9 / 1408 1.1 / 2027 3.1	**23** F 0101 1.1 / 0659 2.8 / 1338 1.2 / 1923 3.1
9 F 0257 0.7 / 0901 3.0 / 1507 1.0 / 2119 3.4	**24** SA 0203 0.8 / 0805 3.0 / 1430 1.0 / 2020 3.3
10 SA 0349 0.5 / 0948 3.1 / 1551 0.8 / 2203 3.5	**25** SU 0252 0.6 / 0858 3.2 / 1514 0.8 / 2109 3.5
11 SU 0429 0.5 / 1028 3.2 / 1626 0.8 / 2243 3.5	**26** M 0334 0.4 / 0942 3.4 / 1554 0.6 / 2154 3.7
12 M 0500 0.5 / 1105 3.2 / 1654 0.8 / 2319 3.5	**27** TU 0412 0.2 / 1023 3.5 / 1632 0.5 / 2239 3.8
13 TU 0524 0.6 / 1137 3.2 / 1722 0.8 / 2351 3.4	**28** W 0451 0.2 / 1106 3.5 / 1711 0.4 / 2325 3.9
14 W 0549 0.6 / 1207 3.2 / 1751 0.7	**29** TH 0532 0.2 / 1151 3.6 / 1754 0.4
15 TH 0019 3.4 / 0616 0.7 / 1236 3.3 / 1822 0.7	**30** F 0015 3.8 / 0615 0.3 / 1239 3.6 / 1840 0.4

OCTOBER

Time m	Time m
1 SA 0106 3.8 / 0700 0.4 / 1328 3.6 / 1929 0.5	**16** SU 0047 3.4 / 0650 0.8 / 1314 3.5 / 1907 0.8
2 SU 0159 3.6 / 0749 0.6 / 1420 3.5 / 2023 0.6	**17** M 0124 3.3 / 0727 0.9 / 1353 3.5 / 1949 0.8
3 M 0254 3.4 / 0843 0.9 / 1514 3.4 / 2127 0.8	**18** TU 0207 3.2 / 0810 1.0 / 1437 3.4 / 2036 0.9
4 TU 0353 3.2 / 0946 1.1 / 1615 3.2 / 2248 0.9	**19** W 0257 3.1 / 0901 1.2 / 1529 3.2 / 2132 1.0
5 W 0503 3.0 / 1109 1.3 / 1730 3.1	**20** TH 0402 2.9 / 1003 1.3 / 1634 3.1 / 2241 1.1
6 TH 0010 0.9 / 0630 2.9 / 1231 1.3 / 1856 3.1	**21** F 0517 2.9 / 1123 1.4 / 1743 3.1
7 F 0125 0.9 / 0742 2.9 / 1342 1.2 / 2001 3.2	**22** SA 0008 1.0 / 0628 2.9 / 1255 1.2 / 1849 3.2
8 SA 0231 0.8 / 0837 3.0 / 1442 1.1 / 2053 3.3	**23** SU 0122 0.8 / 0733 3.1 / 1354 1.0 / 1949 3.4
9 SU 0321 0.6 / 0922 3.2 / 1527 1.0 / 2138 3.4	**24** M 0215 0.6 / 0828 3.3 / 1442 0.8 / 2043 3.6
10 M 0359 0.6 / 1002 3.2 / 1600 0.9 / 2218 3.5	**25** TU 0301 0.4 / 0916 3.4 / 1526 0.7 / 2132 3.8
11 TU 0427 0.7 / 1037 3.3 / 1627 0.8 / 2253 3.4	**26** W 0343 0.3 / 1002 3.6 / 1609 0.5 / 2221 3.8
12 W 0451 0.7 / 1109 3.3 / 1656 0.8 / 2324 3.4	**27** TH 0426 0.3 / 1047 3.7 / 1652 0.5 / 2310 3.9
13 TH 0518 0.7 / 1138 3.4 / 1738 0.8 / 2350 3.4	**28** F 0510 0.4 / 1134 3.7 / 1738 0.4
14 F 0548 0.8 / 1206 3.5 / 1758 0.8	**29** SA 0001 3.8 / 0555 0.5 / 1223 3.7 / 1825 0.4
15 SA 0015 3.4 / 0617 0.8 / 1238 3.5 / 1831 0.8	**30** SU 0053 3.7 / 0642 0.6 / 1313 3.7 / 1916 0.5
	31 M 0146 3.6 / 0732 0.8 / 1403 3.6 / 2011 0.6

NOVEMBER

Time m	Time m
1 TU 0240 3.4 / 0826 1.0 / 1455 3.5 / 2114 0.7	**16** W 0148 3.3 / 0753 1.0 / 1413 3.5 / 2018 0.8
2 W 0337 3.2 / 0927 1.2 / 1551 3.4 / 2226 0.9	**17** TH 0238 3.2 / 0843 1.1 / 1503 3.4 / 2112 0.9
3 TH 0441 3.0 / 1039 1.3 / 1655 3.3 / 2337 0.9	**18** F 0337 3.1 / 0941 1.2 / 1600 3.4 / 2214 0.9
4 F 0557 2.9 / 1152 1.3 / 1813 3.2	**19** SA 0444 3.0 / 1047 1.3 / 1705 3.3 / 2323 0.9
5 SA 0044 0.9 / 0706 3.0 / 1259 1.3 / 1923 3.2	**20** SU 0554 3.0 / 1201 1.2 / 1813 3.4
6 SU 0145 0.9 / 0802 3.1 / 1359 1.2 / 2019 3.3	**21** M 0034 0.8 / 0700 3.1 / 1311 1.1 / 1918 3.5
7 M 0237 0.9 / 0849 3.2 / 1449 1.1 / 2107 3.3	**22** TU 0137 0.7 / 0759 3.3 / 1411 0.9 / 2019 3.6
8 TU 0317 0.8 / 0930 3.3 / 1528 1.0 / 2149 3.4	**23** W 0231 0.6 / 0853 3.4 / 1504 0.8 / 2114 3.7
9 W 0350 0.8 / 1007 3.4 / 1601 0.9 / 2226 3.4	**24** TH 0320 0.5 / 0943 3.6 / 1553 0.6 / 2206 3.8
10 TH 0420 0.8 / 1041 3.5 / 1633 0.9 / 2259 3.4	**25** F 0408 0.5 / 1032 3.7 / 1642 0.5 / 2257 3.8
11 F 0452 0.9 / 1113 3.5 / 1706 0.9 / 2328 3.4	**26** SA 0455 0.6 / 1121 3.8 / 1730 0.5 / 2348 3.7
12 SA 0525 0.9 / 1144 3.6 / 1740 0.8 / 2354 3.4	**27** SU 0542 0.7 / 1209 3.8 / 1818 0.5
13 SU 0558 0.9 / 1215 3.6 / 1815 0.8	**28** M 0039 3.6 / 0629 0.8 / 1257 3.8 / 1907 0.5
14 M 0026 3.4 / 0632 0.9 / 1251 3.6 / 1851 0.8	**29** TU 0130 3.5 / 0718 0.9 / 1346 3.7 / 1959 0.6
15 TU 0104 3.3 / 0710 1.0 / 1330 3.6 / 1932 0.8	**30** W 0222 3.3 / 0808 1.0 / 1434 3.7 / 2054 0.7

DECEMBER

Time m	Time m
1 TH 0314 3.2 / 0901 1.1 / 1525 3.5 / 2154 0.8	**16** F 0217 3.2 / 0826 1.0 / 1440 3.6 / 2052 0.7
2 F 0408 3.1 / 1000 1.2 / 1618 3.4 / 2256 0.9	**17** SA 0310 3.2 / 0918 1.0 / 1532 3.5 / 2147 0.7
3 SA 0505 3.0 / 1103 1.3 / 1716 3.3 / 2356 1.0	**18** SU 0409 3.1 / 1016 1.1 / 1631 3.5 / 2249 0.8
4 SU 0606 3.0 / 1208 1.3 / 1821 3.2	**19** M 0514 3.1 / 1123 1.1 / 1737 3.4 / 2357 0.8
5 M 0053 1.0 / 0707 3.0 / 1309 1.3 / 1929 3.1	**20** TU 0624 3.1 / 1236 1.2 / 1848 3.4
6 TU 0147 1.0 / 0803 3.1 / 1405 1.2 / 2028 3.2	**21** W 0106 0.8 / 0732 3.2 / 1347 1.2 / 1958 3.4
7 W 0234 1.0 / 0852 3.3 / 1453 1.1 / 2117 3.2	**22** TH 0210 0.8 / 0835 3.3 / 1449 0.8 / 2101 3.5
8 TH 0316 1.0 / 0936 3.4 / 1535 1.0 / 2200 3.3	**23** F 0306 0.7 / 0932 3.5 / 1545 0.7 / 2157 3.6
9 F 0354 0.9 / 1016 3.5 / 1613 0.9 / 2238 3.3	**24** SA 0358 0.7 / 1023 3.6 / 1636 0.5 / 2249 3.6
10 SA 0430 0.9 / 1053 3.6 / 1650 0.8 / 2311 3.3	**25** SU 0446 0.7 / 1111 3.7 / 1725 0.5 / 2338 3.5
11 SU 0507 0.9 / 1126 3.6 / 1726 0.8 / 2339 3.3	**26** M 0533 0.7 / 1157 3.7 / 1812 0.4
12 M 0544 0.9 / 1157 3.7 / 1803 0.7	**27** TU 0025 3.5 / 0617 0.8 / 1243 3.8 / 1856 0.5
13 TU 0009 3.3 / 0620 0.9 / 1231 3.7 / 1840 0.7	**28** W 0113 3.4 / 0701 0.8 / 1327 3.8 / 1941 0.5
14 W 0047 3.3 / 0659 0.9 / 1310 3.7 / 1920 0.7	**29** TH 0159 3.3 / 0743 0.9 / 1411 3.7 / 2025 0.6
15 TH 0130 3.3 / 0740 0.9 / 1353 3.7 / 2004 0.7	**30** F 0244 3.2 / 0826 0.9 / 1456 3.6 / 2110 0.7
	31 SA 0330 3.2 / 0911 1.0 / 1542 3.5 / 2159 0.9

Chart Datum: 2·01 metres below Ordnance Datum (Belfast)
HAT is 3·9m above Chart Datum

TIDES

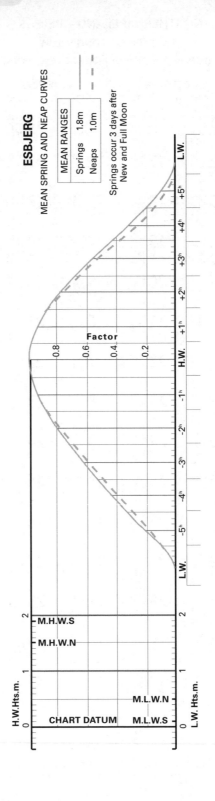

ESBJERG

MEAN SPRING AND NEAP CURVES

MEAN RANGES

Springs 1.8m
Neaps 1.0m

Springs occur 3 days after
New and Full Moon

DENMARK – ESBJERG

LAT 55°28'N   LONG 8°26'E

TIMES AND HEIGHTS OF HIGH AND LOW WATERS

2011

JANUARY

Day	Time m	Day	Time m
1 SA	0521 0.4 / 1203 1.9 / 1802 0.4	16 SU	0453 0.5 / 1130 1.7 / 1730 0.5
2 SU	0034 1.8 / 0630 0.4 / 1308 1.9 / 1900 0.4	17 M	0009 1.7 / 0609 0.5 / 1242 1.7 / 1837 0.5
3 M	0132 1.9 / 0730 0.3 / 1406 1.9 / 1953 0.4	18 TU	0112 1.8 / 0712 0.4 / 1343 1.8 / 1933 0.4
4 TU	0224 2.0 / 0824 0.2 / 1457 1.8 / ● 2040 0.4	19 W	0206 1.9 / 0806 0.3 / 1437 1.8 / ○ 2021 0.3
5 W	0311 2.0 / 0912 0.2 / 1542 1.8 / 2123 0.4	20 TH	0254 1.9 / 0854 0.2 / 1526 1.8 / 2106 0.3
6 TH	0353 2.0 / 0956 0.2 / 1621 1.8 / 2202 0.4	21 F	0339 2.0 / 0938 0.1 / 1611 1.8 / 2150 0.2
7 F	0430 2.0 / 1035 0.3 / 1655 1.7 / 2239 0.4	22 SA	0421 2.0 / 1021 0.1 / 1653 1.8 / 2233 0.1
8 SA	0503 2.0 / 1112 0.3 / 1726 1.7 / 2313 0.4	23 SU	0503 2.1 / 1105 0.0 / 1734 1.8 / 2315 0.1
9 SU	0533 2.0 / 1145 0.4 / 1755 1.7 / 2348 0.4	24 M	0545 2.1 / 1148 0.0 / 1815 1.8
10 M	0604 2.0 / 1219 0.4 / 1827 1.7	25 TU	0000 0.1 / 0630 2.1 / 1234 0.1 / 1900 1.7
11 TU	0024 0.4 / 0638 1.9 / 1255 0.4 / 1903 1.7	26 W	0047 0.1 / 0718 2.0 / 1322 0.2 / 1949 1.7
12 W	0103 0.4 / 0718 1.9 / 1335 0.4 / ◐ 1948 1.7	27 TH	0138 0.2 / 0814 1.9 / 1415 0.3 / 2045 1.7
13 TH	0148 0.4 / 0807 1.8 / 1421 0.5 / 2042 1.7	28 F	0236 0.3 / 0919 1.8 / 1516 0.4 / 2152 1.7
14 F	0239 0.5 / 0904 1.8 / 1515 0.5 / 2145 1.7	29 SA	0344 0.3 / 1033 1.8 / 1627 0.5 / 2305 1.7
15 SA	0340 0.5 / 1013 1.7 / 1619 0.5 / 2257 1.7	30 SU	0504 0.4 / 1147 1.7 / 1742 0.5
		31 M	0013 1.7 / 0619 0.3 / 1253 1.7 / 1845 0.4

FEBRUARY

Day	Time m	Day	Time m
1 TU	0115 1.8 / 0721 0.2 / 1351 1.7 / 1939 0.3	16 W	0037 1.7 / 0647 0.3 / 1318 1.7 / 1907 0.3
2 W	0209 1.9 / 0813 0.2 / 1442 1.7 / 2025 0.3	17 TH	0138 1.8 / 0744 0.2 / 1415 1.7 / 1959 0.2
3 TH	0257 1.9 / 0859 0.1 / 1525 1.7 / ● 2106 0.2	18 F	0230 1.9 / 0833 0.0 / 1505 1.8 / ○ 2045 0.1
4 F	0337 1.9 / 0939 0.2 / 1602 1.7 / 2144 0.2	19 SA	0318 2.0 / 0918 0.0 / 1549 1.8 / 2129 0.0
5 SA	0412 1.9 / 1014 0.2 / 1633 1.7 / 2217 0.2	20 SU	0402 2.0 / 1000 -0.1 / 1631 1.8 / 2212 0.0
6 SU	0443 1.9 / 1045 0.2 / 1700 1.7 / 2248 0.2	21 M	0445 2.0 / 1042 -0.1 / 1711 1.8 / 2255 -0.1
7 M	0509 1.9 / 1115 0.2 / 1725 1.7 / 2319 0.2	22 TU	0527 2.0 / 1125 0.0 / 1751 1.7 / 2339 -0.1
8 TU	0535 1.8 / 1144 0.2 / 1751 1.7 / 2353 0.2	23 W	0611 1.9 / 1209 0.0 / 1832 1.7
9 W	0604 1.8 / 1217 0.2 / 1823 1.7	24 TH	0024 0.0 / 0658 1.9 / 1255 0.1 / 1918 1.7
10 TH	0030 0.2 / 0641 1.8 / 1254 0.3 / 1903 1.7	25 F	0115 0.1 / 0752 1.8 / 1345 0.3 / ◐ 2013 1.6
11 F	0111 0.2 / 0725 1.8 / 1337 0.3 / ◐ 1951 1.7	26 SA	0212 0.2 / 0857 1.7 / 1445 0.4 / 2121 1.6
12 SA	0200 0.3 / 0819 1.7 / 1428 0.4 / 2048 1.6	27 SU	0323 0.3 / 1014 1.6 / 1600 0.5 / 2238 1.6
13 SU	0257 0.4 / 0924 1.6 / 1529 0.4 / 2159 1.6	28 M	0451 0.3 / 1129 1.6 / 1721 0.4 / 2350 1.7
14 M	0409 0.4 / 1048 1.6 / 1645 0.5 / 2323 1.6		
15 TU	0534 0.4 / 1211 1.6 / 1804 0.4		

MARCH

Day	Time m	Day	Time m
1 TU	0606 0.2 / 1234 1.6 / 1827 0.3	16 W	0504 0.3 / 1143 1.5 / 1732 0.4
2 W	0053 1.7 / 0706 0.1 / 1331 1.6 / 1920 0.2	17 TH	0003 1.6 / 0619 0.2 / 1252 1.6 / 1839 0.2
3 TH	0148 1.8 / 0755 0.1 / 1420 1.7 / 2005 0.2	18 F	0109 1.7 / 0718 0.0 / 1349 1.6 / 1933 0.1
4 F	0235 1.9 / 0838 0.1 / 1502 1.7 / ● 2045 0.1	19 SA	0204 1.8 / 0807 -0.1 / 1439 1.7 / ○ 2021 0.0
5 SA	0315 1.9 / 0915 0.1 / 1537 1.7 / 2121 0.1	20 SU	0254 1.9 / 0853 -0.2 / 1524 1.7 / 2106 -0.1
6 SU	0350 1.8 / 0948 0.1 / 1608 1.6 / 2153 0.1	21 M	0339 1.9 / 0936 -0.2 / 1606 1.7 / 2150 -0.2
7 M	0419 1.8 / 1016 0.1 / 1633 1.6 / 2222 0.1	22 TU	0424 1.9 / 1018 -0.2 / 1645 1.7 / 2233 -0.2
8 TU	0444 1.8 / 1043 0.1 / 1657 1.6 / 2252 0.1	23 W	0506 1.9 / 1100 -0.1 / 1724 1.7 / 2318 -0.2
9 W	0508 1.7 / 1112 0.1 / 1721 1.7 / 2324 0.1	24 TH	0551 1.8 / 1143 0.0 / 1806 1.7
10 TH	0536 1.7 / 1144 0.1 / 1751 1.7	25 F	0004 -0.1 / 0638 1.7 / 1228 0.1 / 1851 1.6
11 F	0001 0.1 / 0611 1.7 / 1221 0.1 / 1828 1.7	26 SA	0054 0.0 / 0731 1.6 / 1317 0.2 / ◐ 1944 1.6
12 SA	0042 0.1 / 0654 1.7 / 1304 0.2 / 1913 1.6	27 SU	0151 0.1 / 0836 1.5 / 1415 0.4 / 2051 1.6
13 SU	0130 0.2 / 0747 1.6 / 1354 0.3 / ◐ 2008 1.6	28 M	0304 0.2 / 0950 1.4 / 1530 0.4 / 2208 1.6
14 M	0227 0.2 / 0852 1.5 / 1454 0.3 / 2115 1.6	29 TU	0432 0.2 / 1103 1.4 / 1653 0.4 / 2321 1.6
15 TU	0339 0.3 / 1017 1.5 / 1610 0.4 / 2242 1.6	30 W	0544 0.2 / 1206 1.5 / 1759 0.3
		31 TH	0024 1.7 / 0641 0.1 / 1301 1.5 / 1853 0.2

APRIL

Day	Time m	Day	Time m
1 F	0118 1.7 / 0728 0.0 / 1350 1.6 / 1939 0.1	16 SA	0039 1.7 / 0648 0.0 / 1321 1.6 / 1905 0.0
2 SA	0206 1.8 / 0810 0.0 / 1432 1.6 / 2019 0.1	17 SU	0136 1.8 / 0739 -0.1 / 1411 1.6 / 1956 -0.1
3 SU	0247 1.8 / 0846 0.0 / 1509 1.6 / 2055 0.0	18 M	0229 1.8 / 0827 -0.2 / 1457 1.7 / ○ 2043 -0.2
4 M	0323 1.7 / 0918 0.0 / 1540 1.6 / 2127 0.0	19 TU	0318 1.8 / 0911 -0.2 / 1540 1.7 / 2129 -0.2
5 TU	0353 1.7 / 0945 0.1 / 1608 1.6 / 2157 0.0	20 W	0403 1.8 / 0954 -0.1 / 1621 1.7 / 2214 -0.2
6 W	0420 1.7 / 1013 0.1 / 1633 1.6 / 2227 0.0	21 TH	0448 1.7 / 1036 0.0 / 1701 1.7 / 2300 -0.2
7 TH	0446 1.6 / 1043 0.1 / 1657 1.6 / 2301 0.0	22 F	0532 1.6 / 1119 0.0 / 1742 1.7 / 2346 -0.1
8 F	0515 1.6 / 1118 0.1 / 1727 1.6 / 2339 0.0	23 SA	0618 1.5 / 1203 0.1 / 1827 1.6
9 SA	0551 1.6 / 1156 0.1 / 1803 1.7	24 SU	0036 0.0 / 0709 1.4 / 1251 0.2 / 1918 1.6
10 SU	0021 0.0 / 0634 1.6 / 1239 0.1 / 1848 1.6	25 M	0133 0.1 / 0809 1.4 / 1346 0.3 / ◐ 2019 1.6
11 M	0110 0.1 / 0727 1.5 / 1330 0.2 / ◐ 1941 1.6	26 TU	0240 0.2 / 0917 1.3 / 1454 0.4 / 2130 1.6
12 TU	0208 0.1 / 0832 1.4 / 1430 0.3 / 2047 1.6	27 W	0358 0.2 / 1024 1.4 / 1611 0.4 / 2241 1.6
13 W	0318 0.2 / 0954 1.4 / 1542 0.3 / 2209 1.6	28 TH	0509 0.2 / 1127 1.4 / 1721 0.3 / 2344 1.6
14 TH	0437 0.1 / 1115 1.4 / 1700 0.3 / 2330 1.6	29 F	0606 0.1 / 1223 1.5 / 1818 0.2
15 F	0549 0.1 / 1223 1.5 / 1808 0.2	30 SA	0040 1.7 / 0654 0.1 / 1312 1.6 / 1906 0.1

TIDES

Chart Datum: 0·69 metres below Dansk Normal Null
HAT is 2·2 metres above Chart Datum

DENMARK – ESBJERG

TIME ZONE -0100
(Danish Standard Time)
Subtract 1 hour for UT
For Danish Summer Time add
ONE hour in **non-shaded areas**

LAT 55°28′N   LONG 8°26′E

TIMES AND HEIGHTS OF HIGH AND LOW WATERS

Dates in amber are **SPRINGS**
Dates in yellow are NEAPS

2011

MAY

Day	Time	m	Time	m	Time	m	Time	m
1 SU	0130	1.7	0736	0.0	1357	1.6	1949	0.1
2 M	0214	1.7	0814	0.0	1437	1.6	2027	0.1
3 TU ●	0253	1.7	0846	0.0	1513	1.6	2101	0.0
4 W	0327	1.6	0917	0.1	1544	1.6	2133	0.0
5 TH	0400	1.6	0948	0.1	1613	1.6	2207	0.0
6 F	0430	1.6	1021	0.1	1641	1.6	2243	0.0
7 SA	0503	1.5	1057	0.1	1712	1.7	2324	0.0
8 SU	0540	1.5	1138	0.1	1749	1.7		
9 M	0008	0.0	0624	1.5	1223	0.1	1833	1.7
10 TU ◔	0057	0.0	0716	1.5	1313	0.1	1926	1.7
11 W	0154	0.0	0818	1.4	1412	0.2	2029	1.6
12 TH	0258	0.1	0930	1.4	1517	0.2	2143	1.6
13 F	0409	0.1	1045	1.4	1628	0.2	2300	1.7
14 SA	0517	0.0	1151	1.5	1736	0.1		
15 SU	0010	1.7	0618	0.0	1251	1.6	1837	0.0
16 M	0112	1.7	0713	-0.1	1345	1.6	1933	-0.1
17 TU ○	0207	1.8	0803	-0.1	1433	1.7	2024	-0.1
18 W	0259	1.7	0849	-0.1	1519	1.7	2112	-0.2
19 TH	0347	1.7	0933	0.0	1602	1.7	2159	-0.2
20 F	0433	1.6	1017	0.0	1643	1.7	2245	-0.1
21 SA	0516	1.5	1100	0.1	1724	1.7	2332	0.0
22 SU	0600	1.5	1142	0.1	1807	1.7		
23 M	0019	0.0	0645	1.4	1227	0.2	1853	1.7
24 TU ◑	0110	0.1	0736	1.4	1316	0.3	1945	1.6
25 W	0206	0.2	0832	1.3	1412	0.3	2045	1.6
26 TH	0308	0.2	0933	1.4	1515	0.3	2149	1.6
27 F	0414	0.2	1036	1.4	1624	0.3	2253	1.6
28 SA	0516	0.2	1134	1.5	1730	0.3	2353	1.6
29 SU	0609	0.2	1229	1.5	1826	0.2		
30 M	0048	1.6	0657	0.2	1318	1.6	1915	0.2
31 TU	0137	1.6	0738	0.1	1404	1.6	1957	0.1

JUNE

Day	Time	m	Time	m	Time	m	Time	m
1 W ●	0222	1.6	0815	0.1	1445	1.7	2036	0.1
2 TH	0303	1.6	0851	0.1	1522	1.7	2114	0.1
3 F	0342	1.6	0926	0.1	1557	1.7	2151	0.0
4 SA	0419	1.6	1003	0.1	1630	1.7	2230	0.0
5 SU	0456	1.5	1042	0.1	1704	1.7	2312	0.0
6 M	0536	1.5	1124	0.1	1742	1.8	2357	0.0
7 TU	0618	1.5	1209	0.1	1826	1.7		
8 W	0045	0.0	0707	1.5	1258	0.1	1915	1.8
9 TH ◑	0138	0.0	0802	1.5	1352	0.1	2014	1.7
10 F	0235	0.1	0904	1.5	1451	0.2	2121	1.7
11 SA	0339	0.1	1012	1.5	1557	0.2	2233	1.7
12 SU	0445	0.1	1120	1.5	1707	0.2	2345	1.7
13 M	0550	0.1	1224	1.6	1813	0.1		
14 TU	0051	1.7	0649	0.1	1321	1.6	1914	0.0
15 W ○	0151	1.7	0742	0.1	1415	1.7	2009	0.0
16 TH	0245	1.7	0832	0.1	1503	1.7	2100	0.0
17 F	0335	1.6	0918	0.1	1548	1.8	2148	0.0
18 SA	0420	1.6	1000	0.1	1630	1.8	2233	0.0
19 SU	0501	1.5	1042	0.1	1709	1.8	2317	0.0
20 M	0540	1.5	1122	0.2	1748	1.8	2359	0.1
21 TU	0618	1.5	1203	0.2	1826	1.7		
22 W	0041	0.2	0657	1.4	1245	0.2	1907	1.7
23 TH ◑	0124	0.2	0740	1.4	1330	0.3	1954	1.7
24 F ◑	0211	0.2	0831	1.4	1419	0.3	2048	1.6
25 SA	0303	0.3	0929	1.5	1516	0.4	2149	1.6
26 SU	0402	0.3	1033	1.5	1623	0.4	2255	1.6
27 M	0506	0.3	1136	1.5	1733	0.4	2345	1.7
28 TU	0000	1.6	0607	0.3	1236	1.6	1835	0.3
29 W	0059	1.6	0700	0.3	1329	1.6	1927	0.3
30 TH ○	0152	1.6	0745	0.2	1417	1.7	2013	0.2

JULY

Day	Time	m	Time	m	Time	m	Time	m
1 F ●	0241	1.6	0827	0.2	1500	1.7	2056	0.1
2 SA	0325	1.6	0908	0.2	1539	1.8	2136	0.1
3 SU	0406	1.6	0948	0.2	1618	1.8	2218	0.0
4 M	0447	1.6	1028	0.1	1655	1.9	2259	0.0
5 TU	0527	1.6	1110	0.1	1734	1.9	2342	0.0
6 W	0607	1.6	1154	0.1	1817	1.9		
7 TH	0028	0.0	0651	1.6	1241	0.1	1904	1.9
8 F ◑	0117	0.0	0740	1.6	1331	0.1	1957	1.8
9 SA	0209	0.1	0836	1.6	1427	0.2	2100	1.8
10 SU	0308	0.2	0940	1.5	1530	0.2	2211	1.7
11 M	0414	0.3	1051	1.6	1642	0.2	2326	1.7
12 TU	0524	0.3	1200	1.6	1756	0.2		
13 W	0036	1.7	0703	0.3	1303	1.7	1903	0.2
14 TH	0139	1.7	0727	0.2	1400	1.8	2000	0.1
15 F ○	0235	1.7	0818	0.2	1451	1.8	2051	0.1
16 SA	0324	1.7	0903	0.2	1536	1.9	2136	0.1
17 SU	0406	1.6	0945	0.2	1616	1.9	2218	0.1
18 M	0443	1.6	1024	0.2	1653	1.9	2257	0.1
19 TU	0516	1.6	1100	0.2	1726	1.9	2333	0.2
20 W	0547	1.6	1136	0.2	1757	1.8		
21 TH	0007	0.2	0618	1.6	1212	0.2	1830	1.8
22 F	0042	0.3	0651	1.6	1251	0.3	1907	1.8
23 SA	0120	0.3	0733	1.6	1333	0.3	1952	1.7
24 SU ◑	0203	0.4	0822	1.6	1421	0.4	2045	1.7
25 M	0253	0.4	0921	1.6	1518	0.4	2151	1.6
26 TU	0354	0.5	1033	1.6	1630	0.5	2307	1.6
27 W	0507	0.5	1146	1.6	1750	0.5		
28 TH	0020	1.6	0618	0.4	1251	1.7	1857	0.4
29 F	0123	1.7	0727	0.2	1346	1.8	1949	0.3
30 SA ●	0218	1.7	0803	0.2	1436	1.9	2036	0.1
31 SU	0306	1.8	0848	0.1	1520	1.9	2118	0.1

AUGUST

Day	Time	m	Time	m	Time	m	Time	m
1 M	0349	1.8	0929	0.1	1600	2.0	2200	0.0
2 TU	0430	1.8	1010	0.1	1640	2.0	2241	0.0
3 W	0509	1.8	1052	0.0	1721	2.0	2323	0.0
4 TH	0549	1.8	1136	0.0	1803	2.0		
5 F	0007	0.0	0630	1.7	1221	0.1	1848	2.0
6 SA	0053	0.1	0715	1.7	1309	0.1	1940	1.9
7 SU	0143	0.2	0807	1.7	1403	0.2	2041	1.8
8 M	0239	0.4	0910	1.7	1506	0.3	2154	1.7
9 TU	0346	0.5	1025	1.7	1624	0.4	2312	1.7
10 W	0503	0.5	1140	1.7	1745	0.3		
11 TH	0024	1.7	0615	0.4	1247	1.8	1854	0.3
12 F	0127	1.7	0713	0.4	1345	1.9	1949	0.2
13 SA	0221	1.8	0803	0.3	1436	2.0	2037	0.1
14 SU	0307	1.8	0847	0.2	1521	2.0	2120	0.1
15 M	0347	1.8	0927	0.2	1559	2.0	2158	0.2
16 TU	0421	1.8	1003	0.2	1632	2.0	2232	0.2
17 W	0450	1.7	1036	0.2	1701	1.9	2303	0.3
18 TH	0516	1.7	1109	0.2	1728	1.9	2333	0.3
19 F	0542	1.7	1141	0.3	1755	1.9		
20 SA	0003	0.3	0610	1.8	1215	0.3	1828	1.9
21 SU	0038	0.4	0646	1.8	1255	0.3	1909	1.8
22 M	0118	0.4	0731	1.8	1339	0.4	1959	1.8
23 TU	0205	0.5	0824	1.7	1433	0.5	2100	1.7
24 W	0302	0.5	0930	1.7	1540	0.5	2218	1.7
25 TH	0414	0.6	1052	1.6	1706	0.5	2343	1.7
26 F	0536	0.6	1210	1.6	1823	0.4		
27 SA	0053	1.7	0643	0.5	1313	1.9	1921	0.3
28 SU	0151	1.8	0736	0.4	1407	2.0	2010	0.2
29 M ●	0241	1.9	0824	0.3	1455	2.1	2054	0.1
30 TU	0326	1.9	0907	0.2	1539	2.1	2137	0.1
31 W	0407	1.9	0949	0.1	1621	2.1	2218	0.0

Chart Datum: 0·69 metres below Dansk Normal Null
HAT is 2·2 metres above Chart Datum

TIME ZONE -0100
(Danish Standard Time)
Subtract 1 hour for UT
For Danish Summer Time add
ONE hour in **non-shaded areas**

DENMARK – ESBJERG

LAT 55°28'N   LONG 8°26'E

TIMES AND HEIGHTS OF HIGH AND LOW WATERS

Dates in amber are **SPRINGS**
Dates in yellow are **NEAPS**

2011

SEPTEMBER

Day	Time m	Day	Time m
1 TH	0447 1.9 / 1032 0.1 / 1703 2.1 / 2300 0.1	**16** F	0448 1.9 / 1042 0.3 / 1700 1.9 / 2300 0.4
2 F	0526 1.9 / 1115 0.1 / 1745 2.1 / 2343 0.2	**17** SA	0511 1.9 / 1112 0.3 / 1726 1.9 / 2330 0.4
3 SA	0606 1.9 / 1200 0.1 / 1831 2.0	**18** SU	0537 1.9 / 1146 0.3 / 1757 1.9
4 SU	0028 0.3 / 0650 1.9 / 1248 0.2 / ◑ 1923 1.9	**19** M	0004 0.4 / 0611 1.9 / 1225 0.4 / 1836 1.9
5 M	0117 0.4 / 0741 1.8 / 1342 0.3 / 2024 1.8	**20** TU	0044 0.4 / 0654 1.9 / 1309 0.4 / ◑ 1925 1.8
6 TU	0212 0.5 / 0845 1.8 / 1448 0.4 / 2139 1.7	**21** W	0130 0.5 / 0745 1.9 / 1403 0.5 / 2024 1.8
7 W	0321 0.6 / 1002 1.8 / 1611 0.5 / 2258 1.7	**22** TH	0226 0.6 / 0846 1.9 / 1508 0.5 / 2141 1.7
8 TH	0444 0.6 / 1119 1.8 / 1734 0.4	**23** F	0336 0.6 / 1004 1.8 / 1629 0.5 / 2308 1.7
9 F	0008 1.8 / 0557 0.6 / 1226 1.9 / 1839 0.3	**24** SA	0457 0.6 / 1129 1.9 / 1748 0.5
10 SA	0108 1.8 / 0654 0.5 / 1324 2.0 / 1931 0.3	**25** SU	0021 1.8 / 0609 0.5 / 1238 2.0 / 1850 0.3
11 SU	0200 1.9 / 0743 0.4 / 1415 2.1 / 2017 0.2	**26** M	0121 1.9 / 0706 0.4 / 1336 2.1 / 1942 0.2
12 M	0244 1.9 / 0827 0.3 / 1459 2.1 / ○ 2057 0.2	**27** TU	0212 2.0 / 0757 0.3 / 1427 2.1 / ● 2028 0.2
13 TU	0322 1.9 / 0905 0.3 / 1536 2.1 / 2133 0.3	**28** W	0259 2.0 / 0842 0.2 / 1515 2.2 / 2112 0.1
14 W	0355 1.9 / 0940 0.3 / 1609 2.0 / 2203 0.3	**29** TH	0342 2.0 / 0927 0.1 / 1600 2.2 / 2154 0.1
15 TH	0423 1.9 / 1012 0.3 / 1636 2.0 / 2232 0.4	**30** F	0422 2.0 / 1011 0.1 / 1644 2.2 / 2236 0.2

OCTOBER

Day	Time m	Day	Time m
1 SA	0503 2.0 / 1055 0.1 / 1728 2.1 / 2320 0.3	**16** SU	0447 2.0 / 1048 0.4 / 1703 1.9 / 2302 0.4
2 SU	0543 2.0 / 1141 0.2 / 1815 2.0	**17** M	0513 2.0 / 1124 0.4 / 1735 1.9 / 2338 0.4
3 M	0004 0.4 / 0627 2.0 / 1230 0.3 / 1907 1.9	**18** TU	0546 2.0 / 1203 0.4 / 1815 1.9
4 TU	0053 0.5 / 0719 1.9 / 1326 0.4 / 2009 1.8	**19** W	0019 0.5 / 0627 2.0 / 1249 0.4 / 1903 1.9
5 W	0148 0.6 / 0822 1.9 / 1433 0.5 / 2121 1.7	**20** TH	0106 0.5 / 0716 2.0 / 1342 0.5 / ◑ 2001 1.8
6 TH	0256 0.7 / 0937 1.9 / 1555 0.5 / 2235 1.7	**21** F	0201 0.6 / 0815 2.0 / 1445 0.5 / 2112 1.8
7 F	0417 0.7 / 1052 1.9 / 1712 0.5 / 2341 1.8	**22** SA	0307 0.6 / 0928 2.0 / 1558 0.5 / 2234 1.8
8 SA	0530 0.6 / 1158 2.0 / 1814 0.4	**23** SU	0421 0.6 / 1050 2.0 / 1712 0.5 / 2347 1.8
9 SU	0039 1.9 / 0627 0.5 / 1256 2.1 / 1905 0.3	**24** M	0533 0.6 / 1203 2.0 / 1816 0.4
10 M	0130 1.9 / 0718 0.4 / 1346 2.1 / 1950 0.3	**25** TU	0048 1.9 / 0635 0.4 / 1306 2.1 / 1911 0.3
11 TU	0214 1.9 / 0801 0.4 / 1430 2.1 / 2030 0.3	**26** W	0142 1.9 / 0729 0.3 / 1401 2.2 / 2000 0.2
12 W	0254 2.0 / 0841 0.3 / 1509 2.1 / ○ 2104 0.4	**27** TH	0232 2.0 / 0818 0.2 / 1452 2.2 / 2047 0.2
13 TH	0328 2.0 / 0915 0.4 / 1542 2.0 / 2134 0.4	**28** F	0317 2.1 / 0906 0.2 / 1540 2.2 / 2131 0.2
14 F	0357 2.0 / 0947 0.4 / 1611 2.0 / 2202 0.4	**29** SA	0400 2.1 / 0952 0.2 / 1627 2.1 / 2215 0.3
15 SA	0423 2.0 / 1017 0.4 / 1637 1.9 / 2230 0.4	**30** SU	0442 2.1 / 1039 0.2 / 1712 2.0 / 2258 0.4
		31 M	0524 2.1 / 1126 0.2 / 1800 1.9 / 2343 0.5

NOVEMBER

Day	Time m	Day	Time m
1 TU	0609 2.0 / 1215 0.3 / 1851 1.8	**16** W	0531 2.0 / 1148 0.4 / 1803 1.9
2 W	0031 0.5 / 0700 2.0 / 1310 0.4 / ◐ 1948 1.8	**17** TH	0001 0.4 / 0611 2.1 / 1234 0.4 / 1849 1.8
3 TH	0124 0.6 / 0758 2.0 / 1413 0.5 / 2053 1.7	**18** F	0048 0.5 / 0659 2.1 / 1326 0.4 / ◐ 1944 1.8
4 F	0227 0.7 / 0906 2.0 / 1526 0.5 / 2200 1.7	**19** SA	0142 0.5 / 0754 2.1 / 1424 0.4 / 2048 1.8
5 SA	0339 0.7 / 1015 2.0 / 1638 0.5 / 2303 1.8	**20** SU	0242 0.5 / 0901 2.0 / 1529 0.4 / 2200 1.8
6 SU	0451 0.6 / 1121 2.0 / 1739 0.5	**21** M	0349 0.6 / 1016 2.0 / 1637 0.4 / 2312 1.8
7 M	0000 1.9 / 0553 0.6 / 1218 2.0 / 1832 0.4	**22** TU	0458 0.5 / 1130 2.0 / 1743 0.4
8 TU	0053 1.9 / 0646 0.5 / 1311 2.1 / 1918 0.4	**23** W	0016 1.9 / 0604 0.4 / 1237 2.1 / 1842 0.4
9 W	0140 2.0 / 0733 0.4 / 1358 2.1 / 1959 0.4	**24** TH	0114 1.9 / 0703 0.4 / 1338 2.1 / 1935 0.3
10 TH	0222 2.0 / 0815 0.4 / 1439 2.0 / ○ 2035 0.4	**25** F	0207 2.0 / 0757 0.3 / 1433 2.1 / 2024 0.3
11 F	0300 2.0 / 0851 0.4 / 1517 2.0 / 2106 0.4	**26** SA	0256 2.0 / 0849 0.2 / 1524 2.0 / 2111 0.3
12 SA	0333 2.0 / 0924 0.4 / 1549 1.9 / 2136 0.5	**27** SU	0342 2.1 / 0938 0.2 / 1612 2.0 / 2156 0.4
13 SU	0403 2.0 / 0957 0.4 / 1619 1.9 / 2207 0.5	**28** M	0426 2.1 / 1025 0.2 / 1659 1.9 / 2240 0.4
14 M	0430 2.0 / 1030 0.4 / 1650 1.9 / 2241 0.4	**29** TU	0509 2.1 / 1113 0.3 / 1745 1.9 / 2325 0.4
15 TU	0458 2.0 / 1107 0.4 / 1723 1.9 / 2319 0.4	**30** W	0553 2.1 / 1201 0.3 / 1830 1.8

DECEMBER

Day	Time m	Day	Time m
1 TH	0010 0.5 / 0639 2.0 / 1251 0.4 / 1920 1.7	**16** F	0602 2.1 / 1220 0.3 / 1838 1.8
2 F	0059 0.5 / 0730 2.0 / 1345 0.5 / ◐ 2013 1.7	**17** SA	0033 0.3 / 0647 2.1 / 1309 0.3 / 1927 1.8
3 SA	0152 0.6 / 0827 2.0 / 1443 0.5 / 2112 1.7	**18** SU	0122 0.4 / 0739 2.1 / 1402 0.3 / ◑ 2023 1.7
4 SU	0252 0.6 / 0929 2.0 / 1548 0.5 / 2213 1.7	**19** M	0218 0.4 / 0839 2.0 / 1500 0.4 / 2127 1.8
5 M	0400 0.6 / 1033 1.9 / 1651 0.5 / 2313 1.8	**20** TU	0319 0.4 / 0948 2.0 / 1604 0.4 / 2236 1.8
6 TU	0507 0.6 / 1133 1.9 / 1750 0.5	**21** W	0427 0.4 / 1103 1.9 / 1712 0.4 / 2346 1.8
7 W	0009 1.9 / 0608 0.6 / 1230 1.9 / 1841 0.5	**22** TH	0537 0.4 / 1215 1.9 / 1816 0.4
8 TH	0101 1.9 / 0701 0.5 / 1321 1.9 / 1925 0.5	**23** F	0050 1.9 / 0644 0.4 / 1321 1.9 / 1915 0.4
9 F	0148 2.0 / 0747 0.5 / 1409 1.9 / 2005 0.5	**24** SA	0148 1.9 / 0743 0.3 / 1420 1.9 / ● 2007 0.4
10 SA	0232 2.0 / 0827 0.4 / 1451 1.9 / ○ 2040 0.4	**25** SU	0240 2.0 / 0837 0.2 / 1513 1.9 / 2056 0.3
11 SU	0310 2.0 / 0904 0.4 / 1530 1.9 / 2115 0.4	**26** M	0328 2.0 / 0927 0.2 / 1601 1.9 / 2141 0.3
12 M	0345 2.0 / 0939 0.4 / 1606 1.9 / 2149 0.4	**27** TU	0413 2.1 / 1014 0.2 / 1645 1.8 / 2224 0.3
13 TU	0416 2.0 / 1015 0.4 / 1640 1.8 / 2225 0.4	**28** W	0455 2.1 / 1058 0.2 / 1726 1.8 / 2306 0.3
14 W	0448 2.0 / 1054 0.3 / 1716 1.8 / 2304 0.4	**29** TH	0535 2.0 / 1142 0.3 / 1805 1.7 / 2348 0.4
15 TH	0523 2.1 / 1136 0.3 / 1754 1.8 / 2347 0.3	**30** F	0615 2.0 / 1224 0.3 / 1845 1.7
		31 SA	0030 0.4 / 0657 2.0 / 1308 0.4 / 1927 1.7

Chart Datum: 0·69 metres below Dansk Normal Null
HAT is 2·2 metres above Chart Datum

TIDES

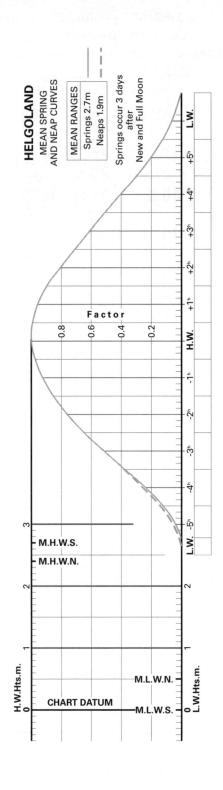

HELGOLAND

MEAN SPRING AND NEAP CURVES

MEAN RANGES

Springs 2.7m
Neaps 1.9m

Springs occur 3 days after New and Full Moon

TIME ZONE -0100
(German Standard Time)
Subtract 1 hour for UT
For German Summer Time add ONE hour in **non-shaded areas**

GERMANY – HELGOLAND
LAT 54°11'N   LONG 7°53'E
TIMES AND HEIGHTS OF HIGH AND LOW WATERS

Dates in amber are **SPRINGS**
Dates in yellow are **NEAPS**

2011

JANUARY

Time m	Time m
1 0305 0.9 / 0853 3.1 / SA 1540 0.9 / 2128 3.1	**16** 0228 1.0 / 0816 2.8 / SU 1500 0.9 / 2054 2.9
2 0416 0.9 / 1001 3.1 / SU 1645 0.9 / 2229 3.2	**17** 0342 0.9 / 0928 2.9 / M 1609 0.9 / 2159 3.0
3 0518 0.8 / 1100 3.1 / M 1740 0.8 / 2322 3.2	**18** 0447 0.8 / 1031 3.0 / TU 1710 0.8 / 2254 3.1
4 0613 0.7 / 1151 3.1 / TU 1828 0.8 ●	**19** 0545 0.7 / 1126 3.1 / W 1804 0.7 / ○ 2343 3.3
5 0008 3.3 / 0658 0.6 / W 1234 3.1 / 1910 0.7	**20** 0637 0.6 / 1216 3.1 / TH 1853 0.6
6 0048 3.3 / 0738 0.6 / TH 1314 3.1 / 1949 0.7	**21** 0030 3.3 / 0727 0.5 / F 1303 3.1 / 1940 0.5
7 0126 3.3 / 0817 0.6 / F 1352 3.1 / 2026 0.6	**22** 0116 3.4 / 0815 0.4 / SA 1348 3.1 / 2024 0.4
8 0203 3.3 / 0854 0.6 / SA 1427 3.0 / 2057 0.6	**23** 0159 3.4 / 0858 0.4 / SU 1429 3.1 / 2104 0.4
9 0236 3.3 / 0925 0.6 / SU 1458 3.0 / 2125 0.6	**24** 0239 3.4 / 0937 0.4 / M 1510 3.0 / 2145 0.4
10 0307 3.2 / 0954 0.7 / M 1528 2.9 / 2156 0.7	**25** 0322 3.4 / 1018 0.5 / TU 1553 3.0 / 2230 0.6
11 0339 3.2 / 1023 0.8 / TU 1600 2.9 / 2229 0.8	**26** 0408 3.3 / 1100 0.6 / W 1640 3.0 / ◑ 2316 0.7
12 0413 3.1 / 1053 0.8 / W 1635 2.8 / ◑ 2307 0.9	**27** 0458 3.2 / 1145 0.7 / TH 1731 2.9
13 0453 2.9 / 1133 0.9 / TH 1721 2.7	**28** 0009 0.8 / 0559 3.1 / F 1240 0.8 / 1832 2.9
14 0000 0.9 / 0548 2.8 / F 1231 0.9 / 1824 2.7	**29** 0116 0.9 / 0707 3.0 / SA 1354 1.0 / 1947 2.9
15 0110 1.0 / 0659 2.8 / SA 1344 1.0 / 1940 2.8	**30** 0239 0.9 / 0829 2.9 / SU 1517 1.0 / 2107 3.0
	31 0401 0.9 / 0948 3.0 / M 1631 0.9 / 2216 3.1

FEBRUARY

Time m	Time m
1 0510 0.8 / 1052 3.0 / TU 1729 0.8 / 2311 3.2	**16** 0424 0.7 / 1011 2.9 / W 1651 0.8 / 2234 3.1
2 0603 0.7 / 1141 3.0 / W 1817 0.7 / 2356 3.3	**17** 0528 0.6 / 1110 3.0 / TH 1749 0.7 / 2326 3.3
3 0646 0.6 / 1222 3.1 / TH 1858 0.6	**18** 0623 0.4 / 1200 3.1 / F 1839 0.5 ○
4 0034 3.3 / 0724 0.6 / F 1258 3.1 / 1934 0.6	**19** 0012 3.3 / 0711 0.3 / SA 1245 3.1 / 1925 0.4
5 0108 3.3 / 0758 0.5 / SA 1331 3.1 / 2007 0.5	**20** 0057 3.4 / 0756 0.2 / SU 1327 3.1 / 2009 0.3
6 0140 3.3 / 0829 0.5 / SU 1401 3.0 / 2035 0.5	**21** 0142 3.3 / 0839 0.2 / M 1409 3.1 / 2050 0.3
7 0210 3.3 / 0857 0.6 / M 1428 3.0 / 2101 0.5	**22** 0224 3.3 / 0919 0.3 / TU 1450 3.1 / 2131 0.3
8 0238 3.2 / 0923 0.6 / TU 1456 3.0 / 2130 0.5	**23** 0306 3.3 / 0957 0.4 / W 1530 3.0 / 2212 0.4
9 0308 3.1 / 0950 0.6 / W 1525 2.9 / 2159 0.6	**24** 0349 3.3 / 1036 0.5 / TH 1612 3.0 / 2254 0.5
10 0337 3.1 / 1014 0.7 / TH 1552 2.9 / 2227 0.7	**25** 0435 3.1 / 1116 0.7 / F 1658 2.9 / ◑ 2341 0.6
11 0408 2.9 / 1041 0.7 / F 1626 2.8 / ◑ 2305 0.8	**26** 0527 2.9 / 1207 0.8 / SA 1757 2.9
12 0451 2.8 / 1127 0.8 / SA 1720 2.7	**27** 0046 0.8 / 0638 2.8 / SU 1321 0.9 / 1915 2.8
13 0007 0.9 / 0559 2.7 / SU 1242 0.9 / 1839 2.7	**28** 0213 0.9 / 0807 2.7 / M 1452 1.0 / 2043 3.0
14 0134 0.9 / 0728 2.7 / M 1414 1.0 / 2009 2.8	
15 0305 0.9 / 0856 2.8 / TU 1539 0.9 / 2130 3.0	

MARCH

Time m	Time m
1 0345 0.8 / 0934 2.8 / TU 1616 0.9 / 2201 3.1	**16** 0233 0.8 / 0827 2.7 / W 1511 0.8 / 2059 3.0
2 0458 0.7 / 1041 2.9 / W 1716 0.8 / 2256 3.2	**17** 0359 0.6 / 0946 2.9 / TH 1627 0.7 / 2208 3.1
3 0549 0.6 / 1126 3.0 / TH 1800 0.6 / 2337 3.2	**18** 0506 0.4 / 1047 3.0 / F 1727 0.5 / 2302 3.2
4 0627 0.5 / 1201 3.0 / F 1838 0.5 ●	**19** 0600 0.3 / 1136 3.0 / SA 1818 0.4 / ○ 2349 3.3
5 0012 3.2 / 0701 0.5 / SA 1234 3.0 / 1912 0.4	**20** 0647 0.2 / 1220 3.1 / SU 1904 0.3
6 0044 3.2 / 0732 0.4 / SU 1304 3.0 / 1942 0.4	**21** 0035 3.3 / 0731 0.1 / M 1302 3.1 / 1948 0.2
7 0114 3.2 / 0800 0.4 / M 1332 3.0 / 2010 0.4	**22** 0120 3.3 / 0815 0.2 / TU 1344 3.1 / 2031 0.2
8 0142 3.2 / 0826 0.4 / TU 1358 3.0 / 2037 0.4	**23** 0205 3.3 / 0856 0.3 / W 1426 3.1 / 2113 0.2
9 0211 3.1 / 0853 0.5 / W 1426 3.0 / 2106 0.4	**24** 0249 3.2 / 0935 0.4 / TH 1506 3.1 / 2153 0.3
10 0241 3.0 / 0921 0.5 / TH 1455 3.0 / 2136 0.4	**25** 0331 3.1 / 1012 0.5 / F 1546 3.0 / 2234 0.4
11 0311 3.0 / 0946 0.5 / F 1522 2.9 / 2201 0.5	**26** 0414 3.0 / 1050 0.6 / SA 1630 3.0 / ◑ 2319 0.5
12 0339 2.9 / 1009 0.6 / SA 1551 2.8 / 2231 0.6	**27** 0505 2.8 / 1139 0.8 / SU 1727 2.9
13 0417 2.7 / 1048 0.7 / SU 1638 2.7 / ◑ 2326 0.7	**28** 0021 0.7 / 0613 2.6 / M 1250 0.9 / 1843 2.8
14 0520 2.6 / 1200 0.9 / M 1755 2.7	**29** 0145 0.8 / 0739 2.6 / TU 1421 0.9 / 2012 2.9
15 0054 0.8 / 0651 2.7 / TU 1336 0.9 / 1930 2.8	**30** 0318 0.7 / 0907 2.7 / W 1548 0.8 / 2132 3.0
	31 0433 0.6 / 1014 2.8 / TH 1651 0.7 / 2228 3.1

APRIL

Time m	Time m
1 0520 0.5 / 1057 2.9 / F 1732 0.5 / 2306 3.1	**16** 0434 0.3 / 1015 2.9 / SA 1657 0.5 / 2233 3.2
2 0554 0.4 / 1129 2.9 / SA 1807 0.4 / 2340 3.1	**17** 0528 0.2 / 1105 3.0 / SU 1751 0.4 / 2324 3.2
3 0628 0.4 / 1201 2.9 / SU 1842 0.4 ●	**18** 0619 0.2 / 1152 3.1 / M 1841 0.2 ○
4 0014 3.1 / 0700 0.3 / M 1233 3.0 / 1913 0.3	**19** 0012 3.2 / 0705 0.2 / TU 1236 3.1 / 1927 0.2
5 0045 3.0 / 0729 0.3 / TU 1303 3.0 / 1943 0.3	**20** 0058 3.2 / 0749 0.2 / W 1318 3.1 / 2011 0.2
6 0115 3.0 / 0757 0.4 / W 1330 3.0 / 2013 0.3	**21** 0144 3.2 / 0832 0.3 / TH 1402 3.1 / 2055 0.2
7 0145 3.0 / 0826 0.4 / TH 1400 3.0 / 2045 0.3	**22** 0229 3.1 / 0912 0.4 / F 1443 3.1 / 2137 0.2
8 0218 2.9 / 0857 0.4 / F 1431 3.0 / 2116 0.3	**23** 0313 2.9 / 0950 0.4 / SA 1524 3.0 / 2218 0.3
9 0252 2.9 / 0926 0.4 / SA 1502 3.0 / 2146 0.4	**24** 0357 2.8 / 1028 0.6 / SU 1609 3.0 / 2302 0.4
10 0325 2.8 / 0954 0.5 / SU 1534 2.9 / 2219 0.5	**25** 0446 2.7 / 1115 0.7 / M 1702 2.9 / ◑ 2358 0.6
11 0404 2.7 / 1032 0.6 / M 1620 2.8 / 2311 0.6	**26** 0546 2.6 / 1217 0.8 / TU 1810 2.9
12 0503 2.7 / 1138 0.8 / TU 1730 2.8	**27** 0110 0.7 / 0701 2.5 / W 1338 0.8 / 1929 2.8
13 0032 0.7 / 0626 2.7 / W 1309 0.8 / 1900 2.9	**28** 0233 0.7 / 0820 2.6 / TH 1500 0.8 / 2045 2.9
14 0206 0.7 / 0757 2.7 / TH 1442 0.8 / 2027 3.0	**29** 0346 0.5 / 0927 2.7 / F 1606 0.6 / 2143 3.0
15 0329 0.6 / 0915 2.9 / F 1557 0.6 / 2137 3.1	**30** 0435 0.4 / 1013 2.8 / SA 1651 0.5 / 2224 3.0

Chart Datum: 1·68 metres below Normal Null (German reference level)
HAT is 3·0 metres above Chart Datum

TIDES

TIDES

TIME ZONE -0100
(German Standard Time)
Subtract 1 hour for UT
For German Summer Time add
ONE hour in **non-shaded areas**

GERMANY – HELGOLAND
LAT 54°11'N   LONG 7°53'E
TIMES AND HEIGHTS OF HIGH AND LOW WATERS

Dates in amber are **SPRINGS**
Dates in yellow are **NEAPS**

2011

MAY

Date	Time m	Time m	Time m	Time m
1 SU	0511 0.4	1049 2.8	1728 0.4	2302 3.0
2 M	0547 0.4	1125 2.9	1807 0.4	2340 0.4
3 TU ●	0624 0.4	1201 3.0	1843 0.4	
4 W	0016 3.0	0658 0.4	1234 3.0	1918 0.3
5 TH	0050 3.0	0730 0.4	1305 3.1	1952 0.3
6 F	0125 3.0	0804 0.4	1338 3.1	2028 0.3
7 SA	0202 2.9	0838 0.4	1414 3.1	2103 0.3
8 SU	0239 2.9	0913 0.4	1450 3.1	2140 0.4
9 M	0319 2.9	0948 0.5	1529 3.0	2220 0.5
10 TU ◗	0403 2.8	1031 0.6	1616 3.0	2311 0.5
11 W	0458 2.7	1131 0.7	1718 3.0	
12 TH	0019 0.6	0608 2.7	1248 0.7	1835 3.0
13 F	0138 0.6	0726 2.8	1410 0.7	1953 3.1
14 SA	0254 0.5	0839 2.9	1522 0.6	2102 3.1
15 SU	0357 0.4	0939 3.0	1624 0.5	2203 3.2
16 M	0455 0.3	1034 3.0	1723 0.4	2259 3.2
17 TU ○	0551 0.3	1126 3.1	1819 0.3	2352 3.2
18 W	0641 0.3	1214 3.2	1908 0.2	
19 TH	0039 3.1	0726 0.3	1258 3.2	1953 0.2
20 F	0125 3.1	0809 0.4	1341 3.2	2038 0.2
21 SA	0211 3.0	0851 0.4	1425 3.2	2122 0.2
22 SU	0257 2.9	0931 0.4	1508 3.1	2204 0.3
23 M	0341 2.8	1009 0.5	1551 3.1	2246 0.4
24 TU ◗	0426 2.7	1051 0.6	1637 3.0	2332 0.6
25 W	0515 2.7	1142 0.7	1731 3.0	
26 TH	0027 0.6	0612 2.6	1245 0.8	1834 2.9
27 F	0132 0.6	0717 2.6	1356 0.7	1942 2.9
28 SA	0239 0.6	0822 2.7	1504 0.7	2045 2.9
29 SU	0335 0.5	0918 2.8	1600 0.5	2136 2.9
30 M	0421 0.5	1005 2.8	1647 0.5	2222 2.9
31 TU	0504 0.5	1048 2.9	1731 0.5	2306 3.0

JUNE

Date	Time m	Time m	Time m	Time m
1 W ●	0548 0.5	1129 3.0	1814 0.5	2349 3.0
2 TH	0630 0.5	1208 3.1	1855 0.4	
3 F	0029 3.0	0709 0.5	1245 3.2	1935 0.4
4 SA	0109 3.0	0748 0.5	1324 3.2	2016 0.4
5 SU	0150 3.0	0827 0.5	1402 3.2	2056 0.4
6 M	0231 3.0	0904 0.5	1442 3.2	2136 0.4
7 TU	0313 2.9	0945 0.5	1524 3.2	2221 0.4
8 W	0400 2.9	1031 0.6	1613 3.2	2311 0.5
9 TH	0452 2.8	1125 0.6	1709 3.1	
10 F	0006 0.5	0550 2.8	1228 0.7	1813 3.1
11 SA	0109 0.6	0656 2.9	1338 0.7	1922 3.1
12 SU	0217 0.6	0803 2.9	1449 0.7	2032 3.1
13 M	0324 0.6	0908 3.0	1556 0.6	2137 3.1
14 TU	0427 0.5	1008 3.1	1700 0.5	2239 3.1
15 W ○	0527 0.5	1106 3.1	1801 0.4	2335 3.1
16 TH	0621 0.5	1158 3.2	1853 0.4	
17 F	0025 3.1	0708 0.4	1243 3.2	1939 0.3
18 SA	0110 3.0	0751 0.5	1326 3.3	2024 0.4
19 SU	0155 3.0	0834 0.5	1410 3.3	2107 0.4
20 M	0239 2.9	0913 0.5	1451 3.2	2147 0.4
21 TU	0320 2.9	0948 0.5	1529 3.2	2223 0.5
22 W	0358 2.8	1024 0.6	1608 3.1	2259 0.6
23 TH ◗	0436 2.8	1104 0.7	1649 3.1	2338 0.7
24 F	0519 2.7	1150 0.8	1737 3.0	
25 SA	0025 0.7	0610 2.7	1248 0.8	1834 2.9
26 SU	0123 0.7	0711 2.7	1356 0.8	1940 2.8
27 M	0228 0.7	0817 2.8	1504 0.7	2044 2.8
28 TU	0329 0.6	0918 2.9	1604 0.7	2142 2.9
29 W	0424 0.6	1012 2.9	1658 0.6	2236 3.0
30 TH	0517 0.6	1101 3.1	1748 0.6	2326 3.0

JULY

Date	Time m	Time m	Time m	Time m
1 F ●	0606 0.6	1146 3.2	1835 0.5	
2 SA	0012 3.1	0652 0.6	1229 3.2	1921 0.5
3 SU	0056 3.1	0736 0.6	1311 3.3	2006 0.4
4 M	0140 3.1	0817 0.5	1351 3.3	2048 0.4
5 TU	0221 3.0	0856 0.4	1430 3.3	2128 0.4
6 W	0302 3.0	0937 0.4	1513 3.3	2212 0.4
7 TH	0348 2.9	1023 0.5	1602 3.3	2259 0.5
8 F ◗	0438 2.9	1114 0.6	1655 3.2	2346 0.6
9 SA	0530 2.9	1207 0.7	1751 3.2	
10 SU	0040 0.7	0627 2.9	1309 0.7	1855 3.1
11 M	0145 0.7	0733 3.0	1422 0.7	2008 3.1
12 TU	0258 0.8	0844 3.0	1537 0.7	2121 3.1
13 W	0409 0.7	0952 3.1	1647 0.6	2227 3.0
14 TH	0512 0.7	1052 3.2	1748 0.5	2325 3.0
15 F ○	0606 0.6	1145 3.2	1840 0.5	
16 SA	0014 3.0	0654 0.6	1231 3.3	1926 0.5
17 SU	0058 3.0	0737 0.5	1312 3.3	2008 0.5
18 M	0139 3.0	0817 0.5	1351 3.3	2047 0.5
19 TU	0217 3.0	0852 0.5	1428 3.3	2121 0.5
20 W	0250 3.0	0922 0.5	1501 3.2	2151 0.6
21 TH	0323 2.9	0953 0.6	1533 3.2	2220 0.7
22 F	0356 2.9	1027 0.7	1608 3.1	2250 0.7
23 SA ◗	0430 2.9	1102 0.8	1645 3.0	2324 0.8
24 SU	0509 2.8	1146 0.8	1731 2.9	
25 M	0012 0.8	0603 2.8	1249 0.9	1836 2.8
26 TU	0120 0.8	0714 2.8	1405 0.9	1952 2.8
27 W	0237 0.8	0830 2.8	1522 0.8	2106 2.8
28 TH	0349 0.8	0939 2.9	1628 0.7	2210 2.9
29 F	0452 0.7	1037 3.1	1726 0.7	2307 3.0
30 SA ●	0547 0.7	1126 3.2	1818 0.6	2356 3.1
31 SU	0636 0.6	1211 3.3	1906 0.5	

AUGUST

Date	Time m	Time m	Time m	Time m
1 M	0041 3.1	0721 0.5	1254 3.4	1952 0.4
2 TU	0124 3.1	0804 0.5	1335 3.4	2033 0.3
3 W	0204 3.1	0843 0.4	1415 3.3	2112 0.3
4 TH	0244 3.0	0923 0.4	1457 3.3	2153 0.4
5 F	0328 3.0	1008 0.5	1544 3.3	2237 0.5
6 SA ◗	0415 3.0	1055 0.6	1635 3.2	2321 0.7
7 SU	0504 3.0	1143 0.7	1728 3.1	
8 M	0011 0.8	0558 2.9	1243 0.8	1832 3.0
9 TU	0117 0.9	0707 2.9	1401 0.8	1951 2.9
10 W	0239 0.9	0827 3.0	1526 0.8	2113 2.9
11 TH	0359 0.9	0943 3.1	1641 0.7	2223 3.0
12 F	0503 0.8	1044 3.2	1739 0.6	2318 3.0
13 SA ○	0554 0.7	1133 3.3	1826 0.6	
14 SU	0002 3.1	0639 0.6	1215 3.3	1908 0.5
15 M	0041 3.1	0719 0.5	1253 3.3	1946 0.5
16 TU	0116 3.1	0755 0.5	1327 3.3	2019 0.5
17 W	0148 3.0	0826 0.5	1359 3.3	2048 0.5
18 TH	0217 3.0	0853 0.5	1429 3.2	2115 0.6
19 F	0246 3.0	0922 0.5	1459 3.1	2142 0.7
20 SA	0317 3.0	0953 0.6	1531 3.1	2209 0.7
21 SU ◗	0347 2.9	1023 0.7	1602 3.0	2235 0.8
22 M	0419 2.9	1057 0.8	1641 2.8	2314 0.9
23 TU	0506 2.8	1151 0.9	1741 2.7	
24 W	0021 0.9	0617 2.7	1311 0.9	1904 2.7
25 TH	0149 1.0	0745 2.8	1441 0.9	2032 2.8
26 F	0317 0.9	0907 2.9	1601 0.7	2148 2.9
27 SA	0428 0.8	1013 3.1	1705 0.6	2247 3.0
28 SU ○	0526 0.7	1104 3.2	1758 0.5	2336 3.1
29 M ●	0616 0.6	1149 3.3	1845 0.4	
30 TU	0019 3.1	0701 0.5	1232 3.3	1929 0.3
31 W	0100 3.1	0744 0.6	1314 3.3	2011 0.3

Chart Datum: 1·68 metres below Normal Null (German reference level)
HAT is 3·0 metres above Chart Datum

TIME ZONE -0100
(German Standard Time)
Subtract 1 hour for UT
For German Summer Time add
ONE hour in **non-shaded areas**

GERMANY – HELGOLAND
LAT 54°11'N   LONG 7°53'E
TIMES AND HEIGHTS OF HIGH AND LOW WATERS

Dates in amber are **SPRINGS**
Dates in yellow are NEAPS
2011

SEPTEMBER

Day	Time m	Time m	Day	Time m	Time m
1 TH	0141 3.1	1356 3.3	**16** F	0145 3.0	1358 3.1
	0825 0.3	2051 0.4		0825 0.5	2040 0.6
2 F	0222 3.1	1439 3.3	**17** SA	0213 3.0	1428 3.0
	0906 0.4	2131 0.4		0853 0.5	2108 0.6
3 SA	0304 3.1	1524 3.3	**18** SU	0242 3.0	1500 3.0
	0949 0.4	2212 0.6		0924 0.5	2135 0.7
4 SU ◐	0348 3.1	1612 3.1	**19** M	0312 3.0	1531 2.9
	1033 0.6	2254 0.7		0952 0.6	2201 0.8
5 M	0435 3.0	1705 3.0	**20** TU ◑	0343 2.9	1607 2.8
	1120 0.7	2343 0.9		1022 0.8	2235 0.9
6 TU	0531 2.9	1811 2.8	**21**	0426 2.8	1704 2.7
	1220 0.8			1110 0.9	2338 1.0
7 W	0051 1.0	1341 0.9	**22** TH	0534 2.8	1826 2.7
	0643 2.9	1936 2.7		1228 1.0	
8 TH	0220 1.0	1514 0.9	**23** F	0108 1.0	1404 0.9
	0811 3.0	2105 2.8		0704 2.8	2000 2.7
9 F	0347 1.0	1633 0.8	**24** SA	0243 1.0	1531 0.7
	0933 3.1	2217 2.9		0833 2.9	2120 2.9
10 SA	0454 0.9	1727 0.6	**25** SU	0400 0.8	1637 0.6
	1033 3.2	2306 3.0		0943 3.1	2220 3.0
11 SU	0539 0.7	1806 0.6	**26** M	0459 0.7	1730 0.4
	1115 3.2	2341 3.0		1037 3.2	2308 3.0
12 M	0617 0.6	1841 0.5	**27** TU ●	0549 0.5	1817 0.4
	1151 3.2 ○			1123 3.3	2351 3.1
13 TU	0015 3.0	1226 3.2	**28** W	0635 0.4	1901 0.3
	0654 0.5	1915 0.5		1207 3.3	
14 W	0048 3.0	1259 3.2	**29** TH	0033 3.1	1252 3.3
	0727 0.5	1946 0.5		0720 0.4	1945 0.4
15 TH	0118 3.0	1329 3.2	**30** F	0116 3.2	1337 3.3
	0757 0.6	2014 0.5		0804 0.4	2028 0.4

OCTOBER

Day	Time m	Time m	Day	Time m	Time m
1 SA	0159 3.2	1421 3.3	**16** SU	0145 3.1	1404 3.0
	0848 0.4	2109 0.5		0829 0.5	2040 0.6
2 SU	0241 3.1	1505 3.2	**17** M	0215 3.0	1436 2.9
	0930 0.4	2148 0.6		0900 0.5	2109 0.6
3 M	0323 3.1	1551 3.0	**18** TU	0247 3.0	1510 2.9
	1013 0.5	2228 0.7		0930 0.6	2138 0.7
4 TU ◐	0409 3.0	1644 2.8	**19** W	0320 3.0	1549 2.8
	1100 0.6	2317 0.9		1003 0.8	2214 0.9
5 W	0505 2.9	1750 2.7	**20** TH ◑	0403 2.9	1642 2.7
	1159 0.8			1049 0.9	2311 1.0
6	0024 1.0	1318 0.9	**21**	0505 2.9	1756 2.7
	0618 2.9	1914 2.6		1200 0.9	
7 F	0152 1.1	1450 0.9	**22** SA	0034 1.1	1329 0.9
	0745 2.9	2043 2.7		0628 2.9	1924 2.8
8 SA	0322 1.0	1610 0.8	**23** SU	0206 1.0	1454 0.8
	0909 3.0	2155 2.8		0755 3.0	2045 2.9
9 SU	0430 0.9	1702 0.6	**24** M	0325 0.9	1601 0.6
	1009 3.1	2240 2.9		0907 3.1	2146 3.0
10 M	0513 0.7	1734 0.6	**25** TU	0425 0.7	1656 0.5
	1047 3.2	2311 3.0		1005 3.2	2236 3.0
11 TU	0546 0.6	1806 0.6	**26** W	0518 0.6	1746 0.4
	1120 3.1	2343 3.0		1055 3.2	2323 3.1
12 W	0622 0.6	1840 0.5	**27** TH	0609 0.5	1835 0.4
	1156 3.1 ○			1144 3.2	
13 TH	0017 3.0	1230 3.1	**28** F	0007 3.1	1231 3.3
	0657 0.6	1912 0.5		0657 0.4	1920 0.4
14 F	0049 3.0	1301 3.0	**29** SA	0051 3.2	1318 3.2
	0729 0.5	1941 0.5		0743 0.4	2005 0.5
15 SA	0117 3.1	1332 3.0	**30** SU	0136 3.2	1404 3.2
	0759 0.6	2010 0.5		0830 0.4	2048 0.5
			31 M	0220 3.2	1449 3.0
				0915 0.4	2127 0.6

NOVEMBER

Day	Time m	Time m	Day	Time m	Time m
1 TU	0303 3.1	1535 3.0	**16** W	0231 3.1	1458 2.9
	0958 0.5	2207 0.7		0918 0.6	2126 0.7
2 W ●	0349 3.1	1625 2.8	**17** TH	0307 3.1	1539 2.8
	1043 0.6	2253 0.8		0955 0.7	2204 0.8
3 TH	0442 3.0	1725 2.6	**18** F	0350 3.1	1628 2.8
	1137 0.8	2354 1.0		1041 0.8	2256 0.9
4 F	0548 2.9	1838 2.6	**19** SA	0445 3.0	1732 2.6
	1246 0.9			1140 0.8	
5 SA	0110 1.0	1406 0.9	**20** SU	0006 1.0	1254 0.8
	0705 2.9	1957 2.6		0556 3.0	1847 2.8
6 SU	0233 1.0	1522 0.8	**21** M	0126 1.0	1411 0.8
	0823 2.9	2108 2.7		0714 3.1	2003 2.9
7 M	0344 0.9	1617 0.7	**22** TU	0243 0.9	1520 0.7
	0926 3.0	2158 2.8		0828 3.1	2108 3.0
8 TU	0433 0.7	1654 0.6	**23** W	0349 0.8	1621 0.6
	1010 3.0	2235 2.9		0932 3.2	2205 3.0
9 W	0511 0.7	1728 0.6	**24** TH	0449 0.6	1718 0.5
	1047 3.0	2310 3.0		1030 3.2	2257 3.1
10 TH ○	0549 0.6	1805 0.6	**25** F ●	0547 0.5	1812 0.5
	1125 3.0	2346 3.0		1124 3.2	2347 3.2
11 F	0627 0.6	1841 0.6	**26** SA	0639 0.4	1900 0.5
	1203 3.0			1214 3.2	
12 SA	0021 3.1	1237 3.0	**27** SU	0033 3.2	1301 3.1
	0703 0.5	1914 0.6		0726 0.4	1945 0.5
13 SU	0053 3.1	1311 3.0	**28** M	0118 3.2	1349 3.1
	0737 0.5	1947 0.6		0814 0.4	2030 0.6
14 M	0125 3.1	1346 3.0	**29** TU	0204 3.2	1436 3.0
	0811 0.6	2020 0.6		0901 0.4	2111 0.6
15 TU	0158 3.1	1422 2.9	**30** W	0249 3.2	1521 2.9
	0844 0.6	2053 0.7		0945 0.5	2150 0.6

DECEMBER

Day	Time m	Time m	Day	Time m	Time m
1 TH	0332 3.2	1605 2.8	**16** F	0257 3.2	1529 2.9
	1027 0.6	2231 0.7		0950 0.6	2158 0.7
2 F ◑	0418 3.1	1653 2.7	**17** SA	0339 3.2	1616 2.9
	1111 0.7	2319 0.9		1034 0.7	2245 0.8
3 SA	0511 3.0	1749 2.6	**18** SU ◑	0429 3.2	1709 2.9
	1203 0.8			1122 0.7	2342 0.9
4 SU	0018 1.0	1304 0.9	**19** M	0528 3.1	1811 2.9
	0612 2.9	1853 2.6		1220 0.8	
5 M	0128 1.0	1411 0.9	**20**	0049 1.0	1328 0.8
	0719 2.9	2000 2.7		0637 3.1	1921 2.9
6 TU	0240 0.9	1514 0.8	**21** W	0203 1.0	1441 0.9
	0826 2.9	2102 2.8		0751 3.1	2032 3.0
7 W	0343 0.9	1605 0.8	**22** TH	0317 0.9	1551 0.7
	0924 2.9	2153 2.9		0903 3.1	2138 3.0
8 TH	0433 0.8	1649 0.7	**23** F	0427 0.7	1657 0.7
	1011 2.9	2237 3.0		1010 3.1	2239 3.1
9 F	0518 0.7	1733 0.7	**24** SA ●	0531 0.6	1755 0.6
	1055 2.9	2318 3.1		1110 3.1	2334 3.2
10 SA	0600 0.7	1814 0.7	**25** SU ○	0626 0.5	1844 0.6
	1138 2.9	2357 3.1		1202 3.1	
11 SU	0640 0.7	1853 0.7	**26**	0021 3.2	1250 3.1
	1217 3.0			0715 0.4	1930 0.6
12 M	0034 3.2	1256 3.0	**27** TU	0105 3.3	1337 3.1
	0719 0.6	1931 0.7		0801 0.5	2015 0.6
13 TU	0111 3.2	1334 3.0	**28** W	0151 3.3	1422 3.0
	0759 0.6	2008 0.6		0848 0.5	2057 0.6
14 W	0147 3.2	1412 3.0	**29** TH	0235 3.3	1503 2.9
	0836 0.6	2042 0.6		0929 0.5	2133 0.6
15 TH	0221 3.2	1449 3.0	**30** F	0314 3.3	1539 2.9
	0911 0.6	2117 0.7		1005 0.6	2206 0.6
			31 SA	0351 3.2	1616 2.8
				1039 0.7	2243 0.8

Chart Datum: 1·68 metres below Normal Null (German reference level)
HAT is 3·0 metres above Chart Datum

TIDES

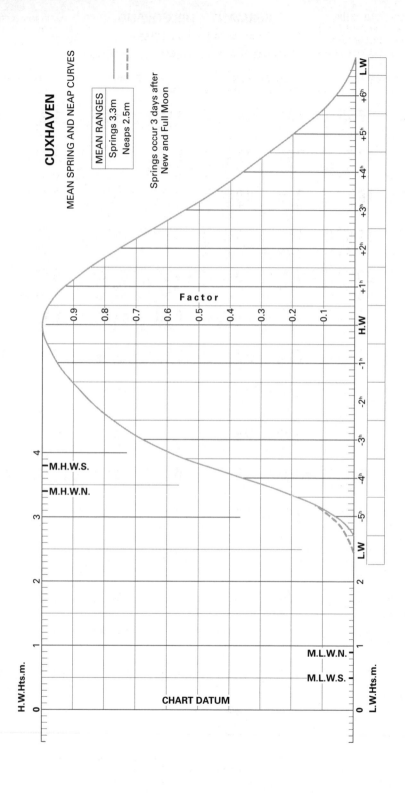

CUXHAVEN

MEAN SPRING AND NEAP CURVES

MEAN RANGES
Springs 3.3m
Neaps 2.5m

Springs occur 3 days after
New and Full Moon

Factor

0.9
0.8
0.7
0.6
0.5
0.4
0.3
0.2
0.1

L.W +6ʰ +5ʰ +4ʰ +3ʰ +2ʰ +1ʰ H.W -1ʰ -2ʰ -3ʰ -4ʰ -5ʰ L.W

H.W.Hts.m.

M.H.W.S.
M.H.W.N.

CHART DATUM

M.L.W.N.
M.L.W.S.

L.W.Hts.m.

TIME ZONE -0100
(German Standard Time)
Subtract 1 hour for UT
For German Summer Time add
ONE hour in **non-shaded areas**

GERMANY – CUXHAVEN
LAT 53°52′N   LONG 8°43′E
TIMES AND HEIGHTS OF HIGH AND LOW WATERS

Dates in amber are **SPRINGS**
Dates in yellow are **NEAPS**

2011

JANUARY
Time m | Time m

Day	Times (m)	Day	Times (m)
1 SA	0423 0.9 / 1003 3.6 / 1702 0.9 / 2240 3.6	16 SU	0340 0.9 / 0926 3.3 / 1613 0.9 / 2203 3.4
2 SU	0536 0.8 / 1112 3.6 / 1808 0.8 / 2340 3.7	17 M	0458 0.8 / 1037 3.4 / 1726 0.8 / 2308 3.5
3 M	0641 0.7 / 1213 3.6 / 1906 0.7	18 TU	0606 0.7 / 1141 3.5 / 1831 0.8
4 TU ●	0033 3.8 / 0737 0.7 / 1304 3.6 / 1954 0.7	19 W ○	0006 3.7 / 0706 0.7 / 1237 3.6 / 1927 0.7
5 W	0118 3.8 / 0822 0.6 / 1348 3.6 / 2035 0.6	20 TH	0056 3.8 / 0800 0.5 / 1328 3.6 / 2018 0.6
6 TH	0158 3.8 / 0902 0.6 / 1428 3.6 / 2113 0.6	21 F	0143 4.0 / 0852 0.4 / 1416 3.7 / 2106 0.5
7 F	0236 3.9 / 0940 0.6 / 1506 3.6 / 2150 0.6	22 SA	0228 4.0 / 0940 0.4 / 1501 3.7 / 2150 0.5
8 SA	0313 3.9 / 1016 0.6 / 1540 3.5 / 2220 0.6	23 SU	0310 4.0 / 1023 0.3 / 1543 3.7 / 2229 0.4
9 SU	0348 3.8 / 1047 0.6 / 1612 3.4 / 2247 0.7	24 M	0351 4.0 / 1101 0.3 / 1624 3.6 / 2307 0.4
10 M	0420 3.8 / 1115 0.6 / 1643 3.4 / 2315 0.7	25 TU	0434 4.0 / 1141 0.4 / 1707 3.5 / 2349 0.5
11 TU	0452 3.7 / 1143 0.7 / 1715 3.4 / 2345 0.8	26 W ☽	0520 3.9 / 1223 0.6 / 1753 3.5
12 W ☾	0525 3.6 / 1212 0.8 / 1749 3.3	27 TH	0033 0.6 / 0611 3.8 / 1306 0.7 / 1843 3.4
13 TH	0020 0.9 / 0604 3.4 / 1249 0.8 / 1834 3.2	28 F	0122 0.7 / 0704 3.6 / 1358 0.8 / 1943 3.4
14 F	0109 0.9 / 0658 3.3 / 1343 0.9 / 1936 3.2	29 SA	0228 0.9 / 0816 3.5 / 1510 0.9 / 2057 3.4
15 SA	0219 1.0 / 0809 3.3 / 1455 0.9 / 2050 3.3	30 SU	0351 0.9 / 0939 3.5 / 1633 1.0 / 2216 3.6
		31 M	0517 0.9 / 1058 3.5 / 1751 0.9 / 2326 3.7

FEBRUARY
Time m | Time m

Day	Times (m)	Day	Times (m)
1 TU	0630 0.8 / 1203 3.6 / 1853 0.8	16 W	0540 0.7 / 1119 3.5 / 1810 0.7 / 2342 3.7
2 W	0021 3.8 / 0726 0.7 / 1254 3.6 / 1942 0.7	17 TH	0649 0.5 / 1220 3.6 / 1912 0.6
3 TH ●	0105 3.8 / 0810 0.6 / 1334 3.6 / 2022 0.6	18 F ○	0037 3.9 / 0746 0.4 / 1311 3.7 / 2004 0.5
4 F	0143 3.8 / 0846 0.5 / 1410 3.6 / 2058 0.5	19 SA	0124 4.0 / 0835 0.3 / 1357 3.7 / 2050 0.3
5 SA	0217 3.9 / 0920 0.5 / 1443 3.6 / 2130 0.5	20 SU	0208 4.0 / 0921 0.2 / 1440 3.7 / 2133 0.3
6 SU	0249 3.9 / 0951 0.5 / 1513 3.6 / 2157 0.5	21 M	0251 4.0 / 1004 0.2 / 1522 3.7 / 2213 0.2
7 M	0320 3.9 / 1018 0.5 / 1541 3.5 / 2222 0.5	22 TU	0333 4.0 / 1044 0.3 / 1603 3.6 / 2251 0.3
8 TU	0350 3.8 / 1043 0.5 / 1609 3.5 / 2249 0.5	23 W	0417 4.0 / 1122 0.4 / 1644 3.6 / 2331 0.4
9 W	0421 3.7 / 1110 0.6 / 1639 3.5 / 2316 0.6	24 TH	0501 3.9 / 1159 0.5 / 1726 3.6
10 TH	0450 3.6 / 1133 0.6 / 1706 3.4 / 2342 0.7	25 F	0010 0.5 / 0546 3.7 / 1235 0.6 / 1810 3.5
11 F ☾	0519 3.5 / 1157 0.7 / 1739 3.3	26 SA	0053 0.6 / 0638 3.5 / 1320 0.8 / 1907 3.4
12 SA	0014 0.7 / 0601 3.4 / 1238 0.8 / 1831 3.2	27 SU	0154 0.7 / 0748 3.3 / 1430 0.9 / 2024 3.4
13 SU	0113 0.8 / 0708 3.2 / 1350 0.9 / 1949 3.2	28 M	0321 0.9 / 0917 3.3 / 1603 1.0 / 2152 3.5
14 M	0240 0.9 / 0835 3.2 / 1522 0.9 / 2116 3.3		
15 TU	0415 0.8 / 1003 3.4 / 1653 0.8 / 2236 3.5		

MARCH
Time m | Time m

Day	Times (m)	Day	Times (m)
1 TU	0458 0.8 / 1044 3.3 / 1732 0.9 / 2309 3.7	16 W	0342 0.7 / 0935 3.3 / 1624 0.8 / 2206 3.5
2 W	0617 0.7 / 1150 3.5 / 1837 0.8	17 TH	0514 0.5 / 1055 3.5 / 1746 0.7 / 2316 3.7
3 TH	0006 3.8 / 0711 0.6 / 1237 3.6 / 1923 0.6	18 F	0626 0.4 / 1158 3.6 / 1850 0.5
4 F ●	0046 3.8 / 0749 0.5 / 1313 3.6 / 2000 0.5	19 SA ○	0012 3.8 / 0722 0.3 / 1248 3.6 / 1942 0.3
5 SA	0120 3.8 / 0822 0.4 / 1345 3.6 / 2034 0.4	20 SU	0100 3.9 / 0810 0.1 / 1332 3.7 / 2028 0.2
6 SU	0152 3.8 / 0855 0.4 / 1415 3.6 / 2104 0.4	21 M	0145 4.0 / 0854 0.1 / 1415 3.7 / 2111 0.2
7 M	0222 3.8 / 0920 0.3 / 1443 3.6 / 2131 0.4	22 TU	0229 4.0 / 0937 0.2 / 1457 3.7 / 2152 0.2
8 TU	0251 3.8 / 0946 0.4 / 1509 3.6 / 2157 0.4	23 W	0314 4.0 / 1020 0.2 / 1539 3.7 / 2233 0.2
9 W	0322 3.7 / 1012 0.4 / 1538 3.6 / 2225 0.3	24 TH	0359 3.9 / 1058 0.3 / 1620 3.6 / 2311 0.2
10 TH	0353 3.6 / 1039 0.5 / 1608 3.6 / 2253 0.4	25 F	0443 3.7 / 1133 0.4 / 1700 3.6 / 2350 0.3
11 F	0423 3.6 / 1104 0.5 / 1635 3.5 / 2317 0.5	26 SA	0528 3.5 / 1206 0.6 / 1743 3.5
12 SA ☾	0451 3.4 / 1124 0.5 / 1703 3.4 / 2342 0.5	27 SU	0031 0.5 / 0617 3.3 / 1248 0.7 / 1838 3.4
13 SU	0527 3.3 / 1158 3.3 / 1750 3.3	28 M	0128 0.6 / 0724 3.1 / 1355 0.8 / 1953 3.3
14 M	0032 0.7 / 0630 3.1 / 1306 0.8 / 1905 3.3	29 TU	0252 0.7 / 0850 3.1 / 1527 0.9 / 2122 3.4
15 TU	0158 0.8 / 0759 3.2 / 1444 0.9 / 2038 3.4	30 W	0428 0.7 / 1017 3.2 / 1700 0.8 / 2242 3.6
		31 TH	0549 0.6 / 1124 3.3 / 1808 0.7 / 2338 3.7

APRIL
Time m | Time m

Day	Times (m)	Day	Times (m)
1 F	0641 0.5 / 1207 3.4 / 1852 0.5	16 SA	0554 0.3 / 1127 3.6 / 1819 0.4 / 2342 3.8
2 SA	0015 3.7 / 0715 0.4 / 1240 3.5 / 1927 0.4	17 SU	0650 0.2 / 1218 3.6 / 1914 0.3
3 SU ●	0048 3.7 / 0747 0.3 / 1312 3.5 / 2002 0.3	18 M ○	0034 3.8 / 0741 0.1 / 1305 3.7 / 2003 0.2
4 M	0121 3.7 / 0818 0.3 / 1344 3.6 / 2035 0.3	19 TU	0123 3.9 / 0826 0.1 / 1350 3.7 / 2048 0.2
5 TU	0154 3.7 / 0847 0.3 / 1413 3.6 / 2105 0.3	20 W	0209 3.9 / 0910 0.1 / 1433 3.8 / 2131 0.2
6 W	0225 3.7 / 0915 0.3 / 1441 3.6 / 2134 0.3	21 TH	0256 3.8 / 0954 0.3 / 1516 3.7 / 2214 0.2
7 TH	0256 3.6 / 0944 0.3 / 1511 3.6 / 2204 0.3	22 F	0342 3.7 / 1034 0.3 / 1558 3.7 / 2254 0.2
8 F	0330 3.5 / 1014 0.4 / 1544 3.6 / 2234 0.3	23 SA	0427 3.5 / 1109 0.4 / 1639 3.6 / 2334 0.3
9 SA	0404 3.5 / 1043 0.4 / 1616 3.6 / 2302 0.4	24 SU	0512 3.4 / 1144 0.5 / 1722 3.6
10 SU	0437 3.4 / 1110 0.5 / 1648 3.5 / 2332 0.5	25 M ☽	0016 0.4 / 0600 3.2 / 1225 0.7 / 1814 3.5
11 M ☾	0517 3.3 / 1145 0.6 / 1733 3.4	26 TU	0108 0.5 / 0659 3.1 / 1323 0.8 / 1921 3.4
12 TU	0020 0.6 / 0615 3.2 / 1247 0.7 / 1842 3.4	27 W	0219 0.6 / 0814 3.1 / 1443 0.8 / 2040 3.4
13 W	0138 0.6 / 0738 3.2 / 1418 0.8 / 2010 3.5	28 TH	0343 0.6 / 0933 3.1 / 1610 0.8 / 2155 3.5
14 TH	0315 0.6 / 0908 3.3 / 1555 0.7 / 2136 3.6	29 F	0500 0.5 / 1039 3.3 / 1720 0.6 / 2253 3.6
15 F	0444 0.5 / 1027 3.5 / 1716 0.6 / 2245 3.7	30 SA	0553 0.4 / 1125 3.3 / 1808 0.5 / 2334 3.6

TIDES

Chart Datum: 2·06 metres below Normal Null (German reference level)
HAT is 4·1 metres above Chart Datum

TIME ZONE -0100
(German Standard Time)
Subtract 1 hour for UT
For German Summer Time add
ONE hour in **non-shaded areas**

GERMANY – CUXHAVEN
LAT 53°52'N   LONG 8°43'E
TIMES AND HEIGHTS OF HIGH AND LOW WATERS

Dates in amber are **SPRINGS**
Dates in yellow are **NEAPS**

2011

MAY

Day	Time	m	Day	Time	m
1 SU	0630 / 1200 / 1847	0.3 / 3.4 / 0.4	16 M	0616 / 1148 / 1844	0.3 / 3.7 / 0.4
2 M	0011 / 0706 / 1236 / 1927	3.6 / 0.3 / 3.5 / 0.4	17 TU ○	0010 / 0713 / 1240 / 1940	3.8 / 0.3 / 3.7 / 0.3
3 TU ●	0050 / 0742 / 1312 / 2005	3.6 / 0.3 / 3.6 / 0.3	18 W	0104 / 0803 / 1329 / 2029	3.8 / 0.2 / 3.8 / 0.2
4 W	0127 / 0816 / 1345 / 2039	3.6 / 0.3 / 3.6 / 0.3	19 TH	0153 / 0847 / 1412 / 2113	3.8 / 0.3 / 3.8 / 0.2
5 TH	0202 / 0848 / 1418 / 2113	3.6 / 0.4 / 3.7 / 0.3	20 F	0240 / 0930 / 1455 / 2157	3.7 / 0.3 / 3.8 / 0.2
6 F	0237 / 0922 / 1452 / 2147	3.6 / 0.4 / 3.7 / 0.3	21 SA	0326 / 1012 / 1539 / 2240	3.6 / 0.4 / 3.8 / 0.2
7 SA	0314 / 0957 / 1528 / 2221	3.5 / 0.4 / 3.7 / 0.3	22 SU	0412 / 1050 / 1621 / 2321	3.5 / 0.4 / 3.7 / 0.3
8 SU	0353 / 1031 / 1605 / 2257	3.5 / 0.4 / 3.7 / 0.4	23 M	0456 / 1127 / 1705	3.3 / 0.5 / 3.7
9 M	0434 / 1107 / 1644 / 2336	3.5 / 0.5 / 3.7 / 0.4	24 TU ◑	0002 / 0540 / 1205 / 1751	0.4 / 3.2 / 0.6 / 3.6
10 TU ◐	0518 / 1148 / 1730	3.4 / 0.6 / 3.6	25 W	0046 / 0629 / 1252 / 1844	0.5 / 3.2 / 0.7 / 3.5
11 W	0025 / 0614 / 1244 / 1832	0.5 / 3.3 / 0.7 / 3.6	26 TH	0139 / 0727 / 1352 / 1947	0.6 / 3.1 / 0.8 / 3.4
12 TH	0131 / 0724 / 1401 / 1948	0.5 / 3.3 / 0.7 / 3.6	27 F	0243 / 0833 / 1505 / 2054	0.6 / 3.1 / 0.7 / 3.4
13 F	0252 / 0841 / 1525 / 2105	0.5 / 3.4 / 0.7 / 3.7	28 SA	0352 / 0938 / 1616 / 2156	0.6 / 3.2 / 0.6 / 3.5
14 SA	0410 / 0953 / 1641 / 2213	0.5 / 3.5 / 0.6 / 3.7	29 SU	0451 / 1032 / 1715 / 2248	0.5 / 3.3 / 0.5 / 3.5
15 SU	0517 / 1054 / 1744 / 2312	0.4 / 3.6 / 0.5 / 3.8	30 M	0539 / 1117 / 1804 / 2334	0.4 / 3.4 / 0.5 / 3.5
			31 TU	0623 / 1200 / 1851	0.4 / 3.5 / 0.5

JUNE

Day	Time	m	Day	Time	m
1 W ●	0019 / 0707 / 1241 / 1935	3.6 / 0.4 / 3.6 / 0.5	16 TH	0050 / 0744 / 1312 / 2014	3.7 / 0.4 / 3.8 / 0.4
2 TH	0103 / 0748 / 1321 / 2016	3.6 / 0.4 / 3.7 / 0.4	17 F	0141 / 0831 / 1357 / 2059	3.7 / 0.4 / 3.8 / 0.3
3 F	0143 / 0827 / 1400 / 2056	3.6 / 0.5 / 3.8 / 0.4	18 SA	0228 / 0913 / 1440 / 2143	3.7 / 0.4 / 3.9 / 0.4
4 SA	0223 / 0908 / 1439 / 2137	3.6 / 0.5 / 3.8 / 0.4	19 SU	0313 / 0955 / 1523 / 2226	3.6 / 0.5 / 3.9 / 0.4
5 SU	0304 / 0947 / 1518 / 2216	3.6 / 0.5 / 3.8 / 0.4	20 M	0355 / 1034 / 1604 / 2305	3.5 / 0.5 / 3.8 / 0.4
6 M	0346 / 1025 / 1557 / 2255	3.6 / 0.5 / 3.8 / 0.4	21 TU	0435 / 1108 / 1644 / 2342	3.4 / 0.5 / 3.8 / 0.5
7 TU	0430 / 1105 / 1640 / 2339	3.5 / 0.5 / 3.8 / 0.5	22 W	0513 / 1141 / 1723	3.4 / 0.6 / 3.7
8 W	0517 / 1150 / 1728	3.5 / 0.6 / 3.8	23 TH ◑	0018 / 0552 / 1218 / 1804	0.6 / 3.3 / 0.7 / 3.7
9 TH ◑	0029 / 0610 / 1242 / 1823	0.5 / 3.4 / 0.6 / 3.8	24 F	0055 / 0636 / 1301 / 1851	0.7 / 3.2 / 0.8 / 3.6
10 F	0124 / 0709 / 1344 / 1927	0.5 / 3.4 / 0.7 / 3.7	25 SA	0139 / 0728 / 1357 / 1948	0.7 / 3.2 / 0.8 / 3.4
11 SA	0228 / 0813 / 1455 / 2036	0.6 / 3.4 / 0.7 / 3.7	26 SU	0236 / 0829 / 1505 / 2053	0.7 / 3.2 / 0.8 / 3.4
12 SU	0336 / 0920 / 1606 / 2144	0.6 / 3.5 / 0.7 / 3.7	27 M	0341 / 0933 / 1616 / 2158	0.7 / 3.3 / 0.7 / 3.4
13 M	0443 / 1023 / 1714 / 2249	0.6 / 3.6 / 0.6 / 3.7	28 TU	0444 / 1032 / 1719 / 2257	0.6 / 3.4 / 0.6 / 3.4
14 TU	0548 / 1123 / 1820 / 2352	0.5 / 3.7 / 0.6 / 3.7	29 W	0542 / 1125 / 1816 / 2351	0.5 / 3.5 / 0.6 / 3.5
15 W ○	0649 / 1220 / 1921	0.4 / 3.7 / 0.4	30 TH	0636 / 1214 / 1908	3.6 / 0.6 / 0.6

JULY

Day	Time	m	Day	Time	m
1 F ●	0041 / 0726 / 1300 / 1957	3.6 / 0.6 / 3.8 / 0.5	16 SA	0132 / 0818 / 1345 / 2048	3.7 / 0.5 / 3.9 / 0.5
2 SA	0128 / 0813 / 1345 / 2044	3.7 / 0.6 / 3.9 / 0.5	17 SU	0216 / 0900 / 1427 / 2129	3.7 / 0.5 / 3.9 / 0.5
3 SU	0213 / 0858 / 1428 / 2130	3.7 / 0.6 / 3.9 / 0.4	18 M	0257 / 0940 / 1506 / 2208	3.7 / 0.5 / 3.9 / 0.5
4 M	0256 / 0941 / 1508 / 2211	3.7 / 0.5 / 4.0 / 0.4	19 TU	0334 / 1017 / 1542 / 2242	3.6 / 0.5 / 3.9 / 0.5
5 TU	0337 / 1019 / 1547 / 2249	3.6 / 0.4 / 3.9 / 0.4	20 W	0407 / 1043 / 1616 / 2312	3.5 / 0.5 / 3.8 / 0.5
6 W	0419 / 1059 / 1629 / 2333	3.6 / 0.5 / 3.9 / 0.4	21 TH	0439 / 1112 / 1650 / 2342	3.5 / 0.6 / 3.8 / 0.7
7 TH	0506 / 1144 / 1718	3.5 / 0.5 / 3.9	22 F	0512 / 1143 / 1724	3.4 / 0.7 / 3.7
8 F ◑	0021 / 0556 / 1233 / 1809	0.5 / 3.5 / 0.6 / 3.9	23 SA ◑	0011 / 0547 / 1216 / 1800	0.7 / 3.4 / 0.8 / 3.6
9 SA	0109 / 0648 / 1324 / 1905	0.6 / 3.5 / 0.7 / 3.8	24 SU	0041 / 0627 / 1247 / 1847	0.8 / 3.3 / 0.8 / 3.4
10 SU	0202 / 0745 / 1425 / 2010	0.6 / 3.5 / 0.7 / 3.7	25 M	0126 / 0722 / 1357 / 1951	0.8 / 3.3 / 0.9 / 3.4
11 M	0305 / 0851 / 1538 / 2123	0.7 / 3.5 / 0.8 / 3.7	26 TU	0231 / 0832 / 1515 / 2107	0.8 / 3.3 / 0.8 / 3.3
12 TU	0417 / 1000 / 1654 / 2236	0.8 / 3.6 / 0.7 / 3.6	27 W	0349 / 0945 / 1634 / 2221	0.8 / 3.3 / 0.8 / 3.3
13 W	0529 / 1107 / 1806 / 2343	0.7 / 3.7 / 0.7 / 3.6	28 TH	0504 / 1053 / 1745 / 2326	0.7 / 3.5 / 0.7 / 3.5
14 TH	0634 / 1207 / 1910	0.6 / 3.8 / 0.5	29 F	0611 / 1151 / 1846	0.7 / 3.7 / 0.6
15 F ○	0042 / 0730 / 1300 / 2003	3.6 / 0.6 / 3.8 / 0.5	30 SA ○	0023 / 0709 / 1241 / 1941	3.6 / 0.7 / 3.8 / 0.6
			31 SU	0113 / 0800 / 1328 / 2031	3.7 / 0.6 / 3.9 / 0.5

AUGUST

Day	Time	m	Day	Time	m
1 M	0159 / 0847 / 1411 / 2116	3.7 / 0.6 / 4.0 / 0.4	16 TU	0234 / 0919 / 1442 / 2142	3.7 / 0.5 / 3.9 / 0.5
2 TU	0241 / 0929 / 1452 / 2157	3.7 / 0.5 / 4.0 / 0.4	17 W	0306 / 0949 / 1514 / 2210	3.6 / 0.5 / 3.9 / 0.5
3 W	0321 / 1007 / 1531 / 2235	3.7 / 0.4 / 4.0 / 0.3	18 TH	0334 / 1014 / 1545 / 2236	3.6 / 0.5 / 3.8 / 0.6
4 TH	0401 / 1045 / 1613 / 2316	3.6 / 0.4 / 4.0 / 0.4	19 F	0403 / 1041 / 1617 / 2304	3.5 / 0.5 / 3.7 / 0.7
5 F	0445 / 1128 / 1700	3.6 / 0.5 / 3.9	20 SA	0433 / 1111 / 1648 / 2330	3.5 / 0.6 / 3.6 / 0.7
6 SA ◑	0001 / 0533 / 1214 / 1749	0.6 / 3.5 / 0.6 / 3.8	21 SU	0504 / 1139 / 1719 / 2354	3.5 / 0.7 / 3.5 / 0.8
7 SU	0046 / 0622 / 1301 / 1842	0.7 / 3.5 / 0.7 / 3.7	22 M	0536 / 1209 / 1757	3.4 / 0.8 / 3.3
8 M	0133 / 0717 / 1358 / 1947	0.8 / 3.5 / 0.8 / 3.5	23 TU	0029 / 0623 / 1259 / 1857	0.9 / 3.3 / 0.9 / 3.2
9 TU	0235 / 0825 / 1514 / 2107	0.9 / 3.5 / 0.8 / 3.5	24 W	0131 / 0735 / 1418 / 2019	0.9 / 3.2 / 0.9 / 3.2
10 W	0356 / 0944 / 1642 / 2230	0.9 / 3.5 / 0.8 / 3.5	25 TH	0259 / 0901 / 1552 / 2147	0.9 / 3.3 / 0.9 / 3.3
11 TH	0517 / 1059 / 1801 / 2341	0.9 / 3.7 / 0.7 / 3.5	26 F	0430 / 1021 / 1717 / 2303	0.9 / 3.4 / 0.7 / 3.4
12 F	0626 / 1200 / 1903	0.8 / 3.8 / 0.6	27 SA	0548 / 1127 / 1826	0.8 / 3.6 / 0.6
13 SA ○	0035 / 0719 / 1248 / 1951	3.6 / 0.7 / 3.9 / 0.6	28 SU	0004 / 0651 / 1220 / 1922	3.6 / 0.7 / 3.8 / 0.5
14 SU	0120 / 0804 / 1330 / 2031	3.6 / 0.6 / 3.9 / 0.6	29 M ●	0054 / 0743 / 1306 / 2010	3.7 / 0.6 / 3.9 / 0.4
15 M	0159 / 0844 / 1408 / 2108	3.7 / 0.5 / 3.9 / 0.5	30 TU	0138 / 0828 / 1348 / 2054	3.7 / 0.5 / 4.0 / 0.3
			31 W	0219 / 0910 / 1430 / 2136	3.7 / 0.4 / 4.0 / 0.3

Chart Datum: 2·06 metres below Normal Null (German reference level)
HAT is 4·1 metres above Chart Datum

GERMANY – CUXHAVEN

LAT 53°52'N   LONG 8°43'E

TIMES AND HEIGHTS OF HIGH AND LOW WATERS

Dates in amber are **SPRINGS**
Dates in yellow are **NEAPS**

2011

SEPTEMBER

Day	Time m	Time m	Time m	Time m
1 TH	0259 3.7	0950 0.3	1512 4.0	2216 0.4
16 F	0302 3.6	0947 0.5	1515 3.7	2202 0.5
2 F	0339 3.7	1028 0.4	1555 3.9	2255 0.4
17 SA	0329 3.6	1014 0.5	1546 3.6	2229 0.6
3 SA	0422 3.6	1110 0.5	1641 3.6	2337 0.6
18 SU	0359 3.6	1043 0.5	1617 3.5	2256 0.7
4 SU	0507 3.6	1153 0.6	1728 3.7 ☽	
19 M	0429 3.5	1110 0.6	1647 3.4	2320 0.8
5 M	0017 0.7	0554 3.5	1238 0.7	1820 3.5
20 TU	0459 3.4	1137 0.8	1723 3.3	☽ 2351 0.9
6 TU	0102 0.9	0648 3.4	1334 0.8	1926 3.3
21 W	0541 3.3	1221 0.9	1818 3.2	
7 W	0205 1.0	0800 3.4	1454 0.9	2052 3.4
22 TH	0049 1.0	0650 3.2	1337 0.9	1941 3.1
8 TH	0333 1.0	0927 3.5	1630 0.9	2222 3.4
23 F	0219 1.0	0820 3.3	1516 0.9	2115 3.2
9 F	0505 1.0	1049 3.6	1754 0.6	2335 3.4
24 SA	0358 1.0	0948 3.4	1648 0.7	2237 3.4
10 SA	0616 0.9	1149 3.8	1852 0.7	
25 SU	0522 0.8	1058 3.6	1800 0.5	2338 3.5
11 SU	0023 3.5	0704 0.7	1231 3.8	1931 0.6
26 M	0625 0.7	1152 3.7	1855 0.4	
12 M	0059 3.6	0741 0.6	1306 3.8	○ 2005 0.5
27 TU	0026 3.6	0717 0.5	1239 3.8	● 1943 0.4
13 TU	0132 3.6	0817 0.6	1340 3.8	2038 0.5
28 W	0110 3.7	0804 0.4	1323 3.9	2026 0.3
14 W	0205 3.6	0851 0.5	1413 3.8	2109 0.5
29 TH	0152 3.7	0847 0.4	1407 3.9	2110 0.3
15 TH	0235 3.6	0921 0.5	1445 3.8	2137 0.5
30 F	0234 3.7	0929 0.4	1452 3.9	2153 0.4

OCTOBER

Day	Time m	Time m	Time m	Time m
1 SA	0317 3.7	1011 0.4	1537 3.8	2234 0.5
16 SU	0301 3.6	0952 0.5	1521 3.5	2201 0.6
2 SU	0359 3.7	1052 0.4	1623 3.7	2312 0.6
17 M	0332 3.6	1020 0.5	1553 3.4	2230 0.6
3 M	0442 3.6	1133 0.5	1710 3.5	2349 0.7
18 TU	0404 3.5	1049 0.6	1626 3.4	2258 0.7
4 TU	0527 3.5	1218 0.6	1801 3.3	
19 W	0436 3.5	1120 0.7	1704 3.3	2332 0.9
5 W	0033 0.9	0622 3.4	1313 0.8	1905 3.1
20 TH	0517 3.4	1203 0.8	1757 3.2	☽
6 TH	0136 1.0	0734 3.4	1431 0.9	2028 3.1
21 F	0026 1.0	0619 3.4	1312 0.9	1912 3.2
7 F	0303 1.1	0901 3.4	1605 0.9	2158 3.2
22 SA	0148 1.1	0743 3.4	1443 0.9	2041 3.3
8 SA	0438 1.0	1024 3.6	1731 0.8	2311 3.3
23 SU	0323 1.0	0910 3.5	1613 0.7	2202 3.4
9 SU	0551 0.9	1125 3.7	1827 0.7	2357 3.4
24 M	0447 0.9	1022 3.6	1725 0.6	2304 3.5
10 M	0637 0.7	1202 3.7	1901 0.6	
25 TU	0552 0.7	1119 3.7	1821 0.6	2354 3.6
11 TU	0029 3.5	0710 0.6	1234 3.7	1930 0.5
26 W	0646 0.5	1210 3.8	1912 0.4 ●	
12 W	0059 3.5	0745 0.5	1308 3.6	○ 2003 0.5
27 TH	0041 3.6	0737 0.4	1258 3.8	2000 0.4
13 TH	0132 3.5	0821 0.5	1344 3.6	2035 0.5
28 F	0126 3.7	0824 0.4	1346 3.8	2045 0.4
14 F	0203 3.6	0854 0.5	1417 3.6	2105 0.5
29 SA	0210 3.7	0909 0.4	1433 3.8	2130 0.5
15 SA	0232 3.6	0924 0.5	1449 3.6	2133 0.5
30 SU	0255 3.8	0954 0.4	1521 3.7	2213 0.5
31 M	0338 3.7	1037 0.4	1608 3.5	2251 0.6

NOVEMBER

Day	Time m	Time m	Time m	Time m
1 TU	0421 3.6	1119 0.5	1654 3.4	2328 0.7
16 W	0348 3.6	1039 0.6	1615 3.4	2248 0.7
2 W	0506 3.6	1203 0.6	1743 3.2 ●	
17 TH	0424 3.6	1115 0.7	1655 3.3	2325 0.8
3 TH	0010 0.8	0557 3.5	1254 0.7	1840 3.1
18 F	0505 3.6	1159 0.8	1744 3.3	☽
4 F	0106 1.0	0702 3.4	1400 0.9	1951 3.0
19 SA	0015 0.9	0559 3.5	1257 0.8	1848 3.2
5 SA	0221 1.0	0819 3.4	1521 0.9	2111 3.1
20 SU	0123 1.0	0710 3.5	1412 0.8	2003 3.3
6 SU	0347 1.0	0937 3.5	1641 0.8	2223 3.2
21 M	0245 1.0	0828 3.6	1532 0.7	2119 3.4
7 M	0503 0.9	1039 3.5	1740 0.7	2314 3.3
22 TU	0405 0.9	0941 3.6	1644 0.7	2225 3.5
8 TU	0555 0.7	1123 3.6	1819 0.6	2350 3.4
23 W	0514 0.8	1045 3.7	1746 0.6	2321 3.6
9 W	0634 0.6	1159 3.5	1852 0.6	
24 TH	0615 0.6	1143 3.7	1844 0.5	
10 TH	0024 3.5	0713 0.6	1237 3.5	○ 1928 0.5
25 F	0014 3.6	0713 0.5	1238 3.7	● 1938 0.4
11 F	0100 3.5	0752 0.6	1317 3.5	2004 0.5
26 SA	0104 3.7	0805 0.4	1329 3.7	2025 0.5
12 SA	0135 3.6	0829 0.5	1353 3.5	2037 0.5
27 SU	0150 3.7	0852 0.4	1417 3.7	2110 0.5
13 SU	0208 3.6	0903 0.5	1428 3.5	2110 0.6
28 M	0235 3.8	0938 0.4	1506 3.6	2155 0.6
14 M	0241 3.6	0936 0.5	1503 3.5	2143 0.6
29 TU	0320 3.8	1024 0.4	1554 3.5	2236 0.6
15 TU	0315 3.6	1007 0.5	1538 3.4	2215 0.6
30 W	0404 3.8	1107 0.5	1639 3.4	2313 0.6

DECEMBER

Day	Time m	Time m	Time m	Time m
1 TH	0447 3.7	1148 0.6	1723 3.2	2350 0.7
16 F	0414 3.8	1111 0.6	1646 3.4	2321 0.7
2 F	0533 3.6	1231 0.7	1809 3.1	
17 SA	0455 3.8	1154 0.7	1731 3.4	
3 SA	0034 0.9	0624 3.5	1321 0.8	1903 3.1
18 SU	0006 0.8	0543 3.7	1243 0.8	☽ 1824 3.4
4 SU	0129 0.9	0723 3.4	1420 0.9	2006 3.0
19 M	0101 0.9	0640 3.7	1341 0.8	1926 3.4
5 M	0239 1.0	0831 3.4	1528 0.9	2114 3.1
20 TU	0207 1.0	0748 3.6	1450 0.8	2036 3.5
6 TU	0354 0.9	0937 3.4	1633 0.8	2215 3.2
21 W	0323 1.0	0902 3.6	1604 0.8	2146 3.5
7 W	0501 0.8	1035 3.4	1727 0.7	2305 3.4
22 TH	0438 0.9	1014 3.6	1715 0.7	2252 3.6
8 TH	0554 0.7	1123 3.4	1812 0.7	2349 3.5
23 F	0549 0.7	1122 3.6	1822 0.6	2353 3.6
9 F	0641 0.6	1208 3.4	1856 0.6	
24 SA	0655 0.5	1224 3.6	1921 0.5 ●	
10 SA	0031 3.5	0724 0.6	1252 3.5	○ 1937 0.6
25 SU	0047 3.7	0751 0.4	1317 3.6	2010 0.5
11 SU	0110 3.6	0805 0.6	1332 3.5	2016 0.6
26 M	0135 3.8	0839 0.4	1406 3.6	2055 0.5
12 M	0148 3.7	0845 0.5	1411 3.5	2055 0.6
27 TU	0219 3.8	0925 0.5	1452 3.6	2140 0.6
13 TU	0226 3.7	0925 0.5	1450 3.5	2133 0.6
28 W	0304 3.9	1011 0.5	1538 3.6	2222 0.6
14 W	0303 3.8	1001 0.5	1528 3.5	2207 0.6
29 TH	0347 3.9	1052 0.5	1619 3.5	2257 0.6
15 TH	0337 3.8	1035 0.5	1605 3.5	2242 0.6
30 F	0426 3.8	1128 0.5	1656 3.4	2328 0.6
31 SA	0504 3.7	1201 0.6	1732 3.3	

Chart Datum: 2·06 metres below Normal Null (German reference level)
HAT is 4·1 metres above Chart Datum

TIDES

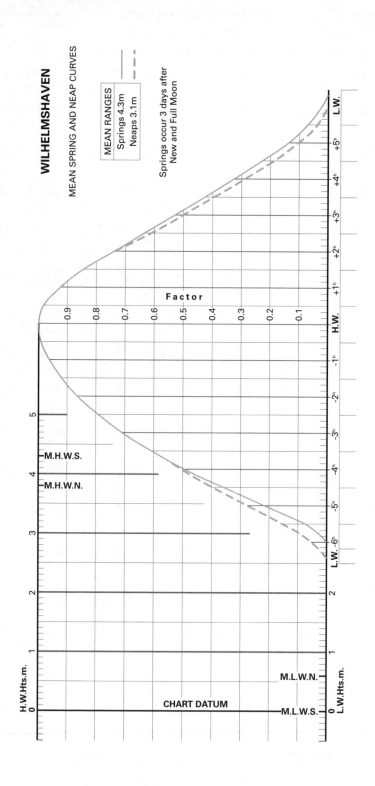

WILHELMSHAVEN

MEAN SPRING AND NEAP CURVES

MEAN RANGES
Springs 4.3m
Neaps 3.1m

Springs occur 3 days after
New and Full Moon

Factor

0.9 0.8 0.7 0.6 0.5 0.4 0.3 0.2 0.1

H.W.Hts.m.

L.W.Hts.m.

M.H.W.S.
M.H.W.N.

M.L.W.N.
M.L.W.S.

CHART DATUM

L.W. +5ʰ +4ʰ +3ʰ +2ʰ +1ʰ H.W. -1ʰ -2ʰ -3ʰ -4ʰ -5ʰ L.W. -6ʰ

GERMANY – WILHELMSHAVEN

LAT 53°31'N LONG 8°09'E

TIMES AND HEIGHTS OF HIGH AND LOW WATERS

TIME ZONE -0100 (German Standard Time) **Subtract 1 hour for UT.** For German Summer Time add ONE hour in **non-shaded areas**

Dates in amber are **SPRINGS** / Dates in yellow are **NEAPS**

2011

JANUARY

Day	Time m	Time m	Time m	Time m
1 SA	0321 1.1	0946 4.6	1604 1.0	2220 4.5
2 SU	0434 1.0	1056 4.6	1711 1.0	2323 4.6
3 M	0540 0.9	1157 4.6	1811 0.9	
4 TU	0018 4.7	0638 0.8	1248 4.6	● 1902 0.8
5 W	0105 4.8	0725 0.7	1335 4.6	1943 0.7
6 TH	0145 4.8	0806 0.7	1416 4.6	2021 0.7
7 F	0223 4.9	0846 0.6	1453 4.5	2057 0.7
8 SA	0300 4.9	0923 0.6	1526 4.5	2127 0.6
9 SU	0334 4.8	0954 0.6	1555 4.4	2153 0.6
10 M	0405 4.7	1022 0.7	1623 4.3	2221 0.8
11 TU	0436 4.7	1051 0.8	1653 4.3	2251 0.9
12 W	0507 4.5	1120 0.9	1727 4.2	◐ 2325 1.0
13 TH	0545 4.4	1155 1.0	1812 4.1	
14 F	0012 1.1	0639 4.2	1247 1.1	1915 4.1
15 SA	0121 1.2	0750 4.2	1358 1.2	2030 4.2
16 SU	0240 1.2	0907 4.2	1516 1.1	2145 4.3
17 M	0357 1.1	1020 4.3	1629 1.0	2252 4.5
18 TU	0506 0.9	1125 4.5	1735 1.0	2351 4.7
19 W	0608 0.8	1223 4.6	1833 0.9	○
20 TH	0043 4.8	0704 0.7	1316 4.6	1926 0.8
21 F	0132 4.9	0758 0.5	1405 4.6	2015 0.6
22 SA	0219 5.0	0848 0.4	1451 4.7	2059 0.6
23 SU	0303 5.0	0932 0.4	1534 4.6	2138 0.4
24 M	0343 5.0	1009 0.3	1614 4.5	2215 0.5
25 TU	0425 5.0	1048 0.5	1656 4.5	2256 0.6
26 W	0509 4.9	1129 0.6	1739 4.4	◑ 2338 0.7
27 TH	0556 4.8	1210 0.8	1825 4.4	
28 F	0025 0.9	0651 4.6	1301 0.9	1922 4.4
29 SA	0127 1.0	0801 4.4	1411 1.1	2036 4.4
30 SU	0247 1.1	0923 4.4	1535 1.2	2157 4.5
31 M	0413 1.1	1043 4.4	1653 1.1	2309 4.6

FEBRUARY

Day	Time m	Time m	Time m	Time m
1 TU	0528 0.9	1149 4.5	1757 1.0	
2 W	0006 4.7	0626 0.8	1241 4.5	1848 0.8
3 TH	0052 4.8	0713 0.7	1323 4.6	● 1929 0.7
4 F	0132 4.8	0752 0.6	1401 4.6	2005 0.6
5 SA	0208 4.9	0828 0.5	1434 4.6	2037 0.5
6 SU	0240 4.9	0900 0.5	1502 4.6	2105 0.5
7 M	0310 4.9	0927 0.5	1528 4.6	2129 0.5
8 TU	0339 4.8	0953 0.6	1554 4.5	2155 0.5
9 W	0408 4.7	1019 0.7	1622 4.4	2224 0.7
10 TH	0435 4.6	1043 0.7	1648 4.3	2249 0.8
11 F	0503 4.4	1106 0.8	1720 4.2	◐ 2319 0.9
12 SA	0544 4.2	1145 1.0	1813 4.1	
13 SU	0015 1.1	0651 4.1	1254 1.1	1931 4.1
14 M	0139 1.2	0820 4.1	1425 1.2	2101 4.2
15 TU	0312 1.1	0949 4.2	1555 1.1	2224 4.4
16 W	0437 0.9	1105 4.4	1712 1.0	2332 4.7
17 TH	0549 0.7	1209 4.6	1816 0.8	
18 F	0028 4.9	0649 0.5	1303 4.8	○ 1911 0.6
19 SA	0117 5.0	0741 0.3	1351 4.7	1959 0.4
20 SU	0203 5.0	0829 0.2	1435 4.7	2042 0.3
21 M	0247 5.0	0913 0.2	1517 4.7	2122 0.3
22 TU	0330 5.0	0953 0.2	1556 4.6	2200 0.3
23 W	0411 4.9	1030 0.2	1635 4.6	2238 0.4
24 TH	0453 4.9	1106 0.6	1714 4.5	2315 0.6
25 F	0536 4.7	1141 0.7	1755 4.4	◑ 2356 0.7
26 SA	0625 4.4	1224 0.9	1849 4.3	
27 SU	0053 0.9	0734 4.2	1333 1.1	2007 4.3
28 M	0217 1.1	0902 4.2	1504 1.2	2136 4.4

MARCH

Day	Time m	Time m	Time m	Time m
1 TU	0353 1.1	1030 4.2	1634 1.1	2255 4.6
2 W	0514 0.9	1139 4.4	1741 0.9	2353 4.7
3 TH	0611 0.7	1227 4.5	1828 0.7	
4 F	0035 4.8	0652 0.6	1304 4.6	● 1907 0.6
5 SA	0112 4.8	0728 0.5	1338 4.6	1941 0.5
6 SU	0146 4.8	0801 0.4	1409 4.6	2011 0.4
7 M	0216 4.8	0830 0.4	1436 4.6	2038 0.4
8 TU	0245 4.8	0856 0.4	1501 4.6	2104 0.4
9 W	0314 4.7	0923 0.5	1528 4.5	2132 0.4
10 TH	0344 4.6	0950 0.5	1556 4.5	2200 0.5
11 F	0412 4.5	1014 0.5	1622 4.4	2224 0.5
12 SA	0437 4.4	1034 0.6	1649 4.3	2248 0.7
13 SU	0513 4.2	1107 0.8	1735 4.2	◐ 2335 0.9
14 M	0615 4.0	1212 1.0	1851 4.1	
15 TU	0057 1.0	0745 4.0	1346 1.2	2027 4.3
16 W	0238 1.0	0922 4.2	1525 1.1	2157 4.5
17 TH	0411 0.7	1044 4.4	1648 0.9	2310 4.7
18 F	0525 0.5	1149 4.6	1753 0.6	
19 SA	0007 4.8	0625 0.3	1243 4.6	○ 1848 0.4
20 SU	0057 4.9	0717 0.2	1330 4.7	1936 0.3
21 M	0143 5.0	0803 0.1	1413 4.7	2020 0.3
22 TU	0228 5.0	0849 0.1	1455 4.7	2102 0.1
23 W	0313 4.9	0931 0.2	1535 4.7	2141 0.2
24 TH	0356 4.8	1008 0.3	1613 4.6	2218 0.2
25 F	0438 4.7	1041 0.5	1650 4.5	2254 0.4
26 SA	0519 4.5	1113 0.7	1731 4.4	◑ 2334 0.6
27 SU	0606 4.2	1154 0.9	1824 4.3	
28 M	0029 0.8	0710 4.0	1258 1.1	1939 4.2
29 TU	0150 1.0	0836 4.2	1429 1.2	2109 4.3
30 W	0326 1.0	1005 4.1	1603 1.1	2231 4.5
31 TH	0448 0.8	1115 4.3	1711 0.8	2328 4.6

APRIL

Day	Time m	Time m	Time m	Time m
1 F	0542 0.6	1200 4.4	1755 0.6	
2 SA	0006 4.7	0618 0.4	1234 4.5	1832 0.5
3 SU	0042 4.7	0653 0.4	1307 4.6	● 1908 0.4
4 M	0118 4.7	0727 0.3	1339 4.6	1942 0.3
5 TU	0150 4.7	0757 0.3	1408 4.6	2012 0.3
6 W	0220 4.7	0825 0.4	1436 4.6	2041 0.3
7 TH	0251 4.6	0854 0.4	1505 4.6	2111 0.3
8 F	0324 4.5	0924 0.4	1536 4.6	2141 0.3
9 SA	0356 4.4	0952 0.5	1605 4.5	2210 0.4
10 SU	0426 4.3	1019 0.5	1636 4.4	2239 0.5
11 M	0504 4.2	1054 0.7	1720 4.3	◐ 2324 0.7
12 TU	0602 4.1	1154 0.9	1830 4.3	
13 W	0039 0.8	0725 4.1	1322 1.0	2001 4.4
14 TH	0214 0.8	0857 4.2	1457 0.9	2129 4.5
15 F	0342 0.6	1018 4.4	1618 0.7	2241 4.7
16 SA	0454 0.4	1121 4.5	1722 0.5	2340 4.8
17 SU	0554 0.3	1215 4.6	1820 0.4	
18 M	0033 4.9	0649 0.2	1305 4.7	○ 1911 0.2
19 TU	0122 4.9	0737 0.1	1350 4.7	1957 0.1
20 W	0209 4.9	0822 0.1	1431 4.8	2040 0.1
21 TH	0255 4.8	0905 0.2	1512 4.7	2121 0.1
22 F	0339 4.7	0943 0.3	1552 4.6	2201 0.2
23 SA	0422 4.5	1017 0.5	1631 4.6	2238 0.3
24 SU	0504 4.3	1050 0.6	1712 4.5	2319 0.5
25 M	0549 4.1	1131 0.8	1802 4.4	◑
26 TU	0010 0.7	0645 4.0	1228 1.0	1909 4.3
27 W	0120 0.8	0759 3.9	1346 1.0	2029 4.3
28 TH	0243 0.8	0920 4.0	1513 1.0	2146 4.4
29 F	0400 0.7	1029 4.2	1622 0.7	2245 4.5
30 SA	0454 0.5	1117 4.3	1710 0.6	2327 4.6

Chart Datum: 2·7 metres below Normal Null (German reference level)
HAT is 5·1 metres above Chart Datum

TIDES

TIME ZONE -0100 (German Standard Time) **Subtract 1 hour for UT** For German Summer Time add ONE hour in **non-shaded areas**	**GERMANY – WILHELMSHAVEN** **LAT 53°31'N LONG 8°09'E** TIMES AND HEIGHTS OF HIGH AND LOW WATERS	Dates in amber are **SPRINGS** Dates in yellow are **NEAPS** **2011**

MAY

Time m	Time m
1 SU 0533 0.4 / 1154 4.4 / 1751 0.5	**16** M 0521 0.4 / 1144 4.6 / 1750 0.4
2 M 0005 4.6 / 0611 0.4 / 1230 4.5 / 1833 0.5	**17** TU 0008 4.8 / 0621 0.3 / 1239 4.7 / ○1847 0.3
3 TU 0045 4.6 / 0650 0.4 / 1307 4.6 / ●1912 0.4	**18** W 0103 4.8 / 0714 0.2 / 1327 4.8 / 1937 0.2
4 W 0123 4.6 / 0726 0.4 / 1341 4.6 / 1947 0.4	**19** TH 0152 4.7 / 0759 0.2 / 1410 4.8 / 2021 0.2
5 TH 0158 4.6 / 0759 0.4 / 1414 4.7 / 2021 0.4	**20** F 0238 4.7 / 0841 0.3 / 1452 4.8 / 2104 0.2
6 F 0233 4.6 / 0832 0.4 / 1447 4.7 / 2055 0.3	**21** SA 0323 4.5 / 0924 0.4 / 1534 4.7 / 2146 0.2
7 SA 0309 4.5 / 0907 0.4 / 1521 4.7 / 2129 0.3	**22** SU 0406 4.4 / 0957 0.6 / 1615 4.7 / 2226 0.3
8 SU 0346 4.4 / 0941 0.4 / 1556 4.6 / 2205 0.4	**23** M 0448 4.3 / 1033 0.5 / 1656 4.6 / 2307 0.5
9 M 0424 4.4 / 1016 0.6 / 1633 4.6 / 2245 0.5	**24** TU 0529 4.2 / 1111 0.7 / 1740 4.6 / ◑2352 0.6
10 TU 0506 4.3 / 1057 0.7 / 1719 4.5 / ◐2331 0.6	**25** W 0614 4.1 / 1158 0.9 / 1832 4.4
11 W 0601 4.2 / 1152 0.8 / 1822 4.5	**26** TH 0044 0.7 / 0710 4.0 / 1257 0.9 / 1936 4.4
12 TH 0034 0.6 / 0711 4.1 / 1306 0.9 / 1939 4.5	**27** F 0147 0.8 / 0817 4.0 / 1408 0.9 / 2045 4.4
13 F 0153 0.7 / 0830 4.3 / 1428 0.8 / 2058 4.6	**28** SA 0254 0.7 / 0924 4.1 / 1519 0.8 / 2148 4.5
14 SA 0311 0.6 / 0944 4.4 / 1544 0.7 / 2208 4.7	**29** SU 0354 0.6 / 1021 4.2 / 1618 0.7 / 2240 4.5
15 SU 0419 0.4 / 1047 4.5 / 1649 0.5 / 2309 4.8	**30** M 0443 0.5 / 1108 4.4 / 1708 0.5 / 2326 4.5
	31 TU 0529 0.5 / 1152 4.5 / 1757 0.6

JUNE

Time m	Time m
1 W 0012 4.5 / 0616 0.5 / 1234 4.6 / ●1843 0.5	**16** TH 0047 4.7 / 0655 0.4 / 1308 4.8 / 1921 0.4
2 TH 0056 4.5 / 0659 0.4 / 1315 4.7 / 1924 0.5	**17** F 0138 4.6 / 0742 0.4 / 1353 4.8 / 2006 0.4
3 F 0138 4.6 / 0739 0.5 / 1354 4.8 / 2005 0.5	**18** SA 0224 4.6 / 0824 0.4 / 1436 4.9 / 2051 0.4
4 SA 0219 4.6 / 0819 0.5 / 1433 4.8 / 2046 0.4	**19** SU 0308 4.5 / 0905 0.4 / 1518 4.9 / 2134 0.4
5 SU 0259 4.6 / 0859 0.5 / 1511 4.8 / 2126 0.4	**20** M 0349 4.4 / 0942 0.5 / 1558 4.8 / 2213 0.4
6 M 0340 4.5 / 0937 0.5 / 1549 4.8 / 2205 0.4	**21** TU 0426 4.3 / 1015 0.5 / 1635 4.8 / 2250 0.5
7 TU 0421 4.4 / 1016 0.6 / 1631 4.8 / 2249 0.5	**22** W 0501 4.3 / 1049 0.7 / 1712 4.7 / 2326 0.6
8 W 0507 4.4 / 1100 0.6 / 1719 4.8 / 2337 0.5	**23** TH 0537 4.2 / 1125 0.8 / 1752 4.6 ◑
9 TH 0558 4.3 / 1151 0.7 / 1813 4.7	**24** F 0004 0.7 / 0617 4.1 / 1208 0.9 / 1838 4.5
10 F 0030 0.5 / 0656 4.3 / 1251 0.7 / 1917 4.7	**25** SA 0048 0.8 / 0709 4.1 / 1303 0.9 / 1936 4.4
11 SA 0131 0.6 / 0801 4.4 / 1359 0.8 / 2026 4.7	**26** SU 0143 0.8 / 0811 4.1 / 1411 1.0 / 2042 4.3
12 SU 0240 0.7 / 0909 4.5 / 1511 0.7 / 2136 4.7	**27** M 0247 0.8 / 0918 4.2 / 1521 0.9 / 2147 4.3
13 M 0348 0.6 / 1014 4.5 / 1619 0.6 / 2243 4.7	**28** TU 0351 0.7 / 1019 4.3 / 1624 0.7 / 2246 4.4
14 TU 0453 0.6 / 1116 4.6 / 1725 0.5 / 2347 4.7	**29** W 0450 0.7 / 1115 4.5 / 1722 0.7 / 2341 4.5
15 W 0557 0.5 / 1215 4.7 / 1827 0.4 ○	**30** TH 0545 0.7 / 1205 4.6 / 1816 0.7

JULY

Time m	Time m
1 F 0032 4.6 / 0637 0.7 / 1253 4.7 / ●1905 0.6	**16** SA 0126 4.6 / 0730 0.6 / 1339 4.9 / 1956 0.5
2 SA 0121 4.6 / 0725 0.7 / 1338 4.9 / 1953 0.5	**17** SU 0210 4.6 / 0812 0.5 / 1420 4.9 / 2038 0.5
3 SU 0207 4.7 / 0811 0.6 / 1421 5.0 / 2040 0.5	**18** M 0251 4.6 / 0851 0.5 / 1500 5.0 / 2118 0.4
4 M 0250 4.7 / 0854 0.5 / 1502 5.0 / 2122 0.4	**19** TU 0326 4.5 / 0924 0.5 / 1535 4.9 / 2153 0.4
5 TU 0331 4.6 / 0932 0.5 / 1540 4.9 / 2200 0.4	**20** W 0357 4.5 / 0952 0.5 / 1608 4.8 / 2223 0.5
6 W 0412 4.5 / 1010 0.5 / 1622 4.9 / 2243 0.4	**21** TH 0426 4.4 / 1021 0.6 / 1640 4.8 / 2253 0.7
7 TH 0457 4.5 / 1054 0.6 / 1709 4.9 / 2330 0.5	**22** F 0456 4.4 / 1053 0.8 / 1711 4.7 / 2322 0.8
8 F 0545 4.5 / 1142 0.6 / 1759 4.8 ◐	**23** SA 0528 4.3 / 1125 0.9 / 1746 4.5 / ◑2353 0.9
9 SA 0017 0.5 / 0634 4.4 / 1232 0.7 / 1853 4.7	**24** SU 0607 4.2 / 1205 1.0 / 1831 4.3
10 SU 0107 0.7 / 0729 4.4 / 1330 0.8 / 1957 4.7	**25** M 0036 0.9 / 0702 4.2 / 1304 1.0 / 1936 4.2
11 M 0210 0.8 / 0835 4.5 / 1441 0.9 / 2111 4.6	**26** TU 0140 1.0 / 0813 4.2 / 1420 1.1 / 2053 4.2
12 TU 0322 0.9 / 0947 4.5 / 1558 0.8 / 2225 4.6	**27** W 0257 1.0 / 0929 4.3 / 1538 1.0 / 2208 4.3
13 W 0435 0.8 / 1057 4.6 / 1710 0.7 / 2334 4.6	**28** TH 0412 0.9 / 1039 4.4 / 1649 0.8 / 2314 4.4
14 TH 0541 0.7 / 1159 4.7 / 1814 0.6	**29** F 0519 0.8 / 1140 4.6 / 1752 0.8
15 F 0035 4.6 / 0641 0.6 / 1253 4.8 / ○1909 0.5	**30** SA 0012 4.6 / 0619 0.8 / 1233 4.8 / ●1849 0.7
	31 SU 0104 4.7 / 0712 0.7 / 1320 4.9 / 1940 0.5

AUGUST

Time m	Time m
1 M 0152 4.7 / 0800 0.6 / 1405 5.0 / 2028 0.4	**16** TU 0227 4.5 / 0829 0.5 / 1435 4.9 / 2053 0.5
2 TU 0236 4.7 / 0843 0.5 / 1446 5.0 / 2110 0.3	**17** W 0257 4.6 / 0859 0.5 / 1507 4.9 / 2123 0.5
3 W 0316 4.7 / 0921 0.4 / 1526 5.0 / 2148 0.3	**18** TH 0324 4.5 / 0925 0.5 / 1536 4.8 / 2149 0.6
4 TH 0356 4.6 / 0958 0.4 / 1607 4.9 / 2227 0.4	**19** F 0350 4.5 / 0951 0.6 / 1606 4.7 / 2216 0.7
5 F 0438 4.6 / 1039 0.5 / 1652 4.9 / 2311 0.6	**20** SA 0418 4.5 / 1021 0.7 / 1635 4.6 / 2243 0.8
6 SA 0522 4.6 / 1123 0.6 / 1739 4.8 / ◐2355 0.7	**21** SU 0447 4.4 / 1049 0.8 / 1703 4.5 / ◐2307 0.9
7 SU 0606 4.5 / 1208 0.7 / 1829 4.7	**22** M 0517 4.3 / 1118 0.9 / 1739 4.3 / 2340 1.0
8 M 0040 0.8 / 0657 4.4 / 1302 0.9 / 1932 4.5	**23** TU 0603 4.2 / 1205 1.1 / 1838 4.1
9 TU 0140 1.0 / 0806 4.4 / 1416 1.0 / 2051 4.4	**24** W 0040 1.1 / 0714 4.1 / 1322 1.2 / 2002 4.1
10 W 0300 1.0 / 0927 4.5 / 1542 1.0 / 2215 4.4	**25** TH 0206 1.2 / 0842 4.2 / 1454 1.1 / 2131 4.2
11 TH 0423 1.1 / 1045 4.6 / 1703 0.8 / 2328 4.5	**26** F 0337 1.1 / 1006 4.4 / 1619 0.9 / 2249 4.4
12 F 0533 0.9 / 1148 4.8 / 1807 0.7	**27** SA 0454 1.0 / 1115 4.6 / 1729 0.7 / 2351 4.5
13 SA 0025 4.5 / 0629 0.8 / 1238 4.9 / ○1857 0.7	**28** SU 0558 0.8 / 1210 4.8 / 1829 0.6
14 SU 0111 4.6 / 0715 0.7 / 1321 4.9 / 1940 0.6	**29** M 0044 4.6 / 0653 0.7 / 1258 4.9 / ●1919 0.5
15 M 0151 4.6 / 0755 0.6 / 1400 4.9 / 2019 0.5	**30** TU 0130 4.7 / 0740 0.5 / 1342 5.0 / 2005 0.4
	31 W 0213 4.7 / 0823 0.4 / 1425 5.0 / 2049 0.3

Chart Datum: 2·7 metres below Normal Null (German reference level)
HAT is 5·1 metres above Chart Datum

TIME ZONE -0100
(German Standard Time)
Subtract 1 hour for UT
For German Summer Time add
ONE hour in **non-shaded areas**

GERMANY – WILHELMSHAVEN
LAT 53°31′N   LONG 8°09′E
TIMES AND HEIGHTS OF HIGH AND LOW WATERS

Dates in amber are **SPRINGS**
Dates in yellow are **NEAPS**

2011

SEPTEMBER

Time m	Time m
1 TH 0254 4.7 / 0902 0.3 / 1506 5.0 / 2129 0.3	**16** F 0251 4.6 / 0857 0.5 / 1505 4.7 / 2114 0.6
2 F 0334 4.7 / 0940 0.4 / 1549 4.9 / 2207 0.4	**17** SA 0317 4.6 / 0923 0.6 / 1535 4.6 / 2141 0.7
3 SA 0414 4.6 / 1020 0.5 / 1632 4.8 / 2247 0.6	**18** SU 0345 4.5 / 0951 0.6 / 1604 4.5 / 2207 0.8
4 SU 0455 4.6 / 1100 0.6 / 1717 4.7 / ◑ 2326 0.8	**19** M 0413 4.5 / 1019 0.7 / 1631 4.4 / 2231 0.9
5 M 0537 4.5 / 1142 0.8 / 1806 4.5	**20** TU 0441 4.4 / 1045 0.9 / 1703 4.2 / ◑ 2301 1.0
6 TU 0009 1.0 / 0628 4.4 / 1235 0.9 / 1909 4.3	**21** W 0522 4.2 / 1126 1.0 / 1758 4.0 / 2357 1.2
7 W 0110 1.2 / 0740 4.3 / 1352 1.1 / 2033 4.2	**22** TH 0629 4.1 / 1239 1.2 / 1921 4.0
8 TH 0237 1.3 / 0908 4.4 / 1527 1.1 / 2203 4.2	**23** F 0124 1.3 / 0800 4.2 / 1416 1.2 / 2056 4.1
9 F 0409 1.2 / 1033 4.6 / 1654 0.9 / 2318 4.4	**24** SA 0302 1.2 / 0931 4.4 / 1548 0.9 / 2220 4.3
10 SA 0522 1.0 / 1135 4.7 / 1755 0.8	**25** SU 0425 1.0 / 1044 4.6 / 1701 0.7 / 2324 4.5
11 SU 0010 4.5 / 0612 0.8 / 1218 4.8 / 1837 0.6	**26** M 0529 0.8 / 1141 4.7 / 1800 0.5
12 M 0048 4.5 / 0651 0.7 / 1256 4.8 / ○ 1914 0.6	**27** TU 0016 4.6 / 0624 0.6 / 1229 4.8 / ● 1851 0.4
13 TU 0123 4.6 / 0727 0.6 / 1332 4.8 / 1949 0.5	**28** W 0103 4.7 / 0713 0.5 / 1315 4.9 / 1938 0.3
14 W 0156 4.6 / 0801 0.5 / 1406 4.8 / 2020 0.5	**29** TH 0146 4.7 / 0758 0.4 / 1400 4.9 / 2023 0.3
15 TH 0225 4.6 / 0831 0.5 / 1436 4.8 / 2048 0.5	**30** F 0228 4.8 / 0840 0.3 / 1446 4.9 / 2107 0.4

OCTOBER

Time m	Time m
1 SA 0310 4.7 / 0921 0.4 / 1530 4.8 / 2146 0.5	**16** SU 0249 4.6 / 0859 0.6 / 1508 4.5 / 2111 0.7
2 SU 0350 4.7 / 1000 0.4 / 1614 4.7 / 2221 0.6	**17** M 0318 4.6 / 0927 0.6 / 1539 4.4 / 2139 0.7
3 M 0429 4.6 / 1038 0.6 / 1657 4.6 / 2257 0.8	**18** TU 0347 4.5 / 0956 0.7 / 1610 4.3 / 2207 0.9
4 TU 0511 4.5 / 1119 0.7 / 1745 4.4 / ◑ 2339 1.0	**19** W 0418 4.4 / 1027 0.8 / 1644 4.2 / 2240 1.0
5 W 0602 4.4 / 1213 0.9 / 1847 4.0	**20** TH 0458 4.3 / 1108 1.0 / 1735 4.1 / ◑ 2332 1.2
6 TH 0039 1.2 / 0713 4.3 / 1328 1.1 / 2008 4.0	**21** F 0600 4.3 / 1214 1.1 / 1850 4.0
7 F 0205 1.4 / 0841 4.3 / 1502 1.1 / 2137 4.1	**22** SA 0052 1.3 / 0724 4.3 / 1342 1.1 / 2020 4.1
8 SA 0340 1.3 / 1006 4.5 / 1629 1.0 / 2252 4.2	**23** SU 0224 1.3 / 0851 4.4 / 1511 0.9 / 2142 4.3
9 SU 0455 1.0 / 1109 4.6 / 1728 0.8 / 2341 4.4	**24** M 0347 1.0 / 1006 4.6 / 1624 0.7 / 2248 4.4
10 M 0541 0.8 / 1149 4.7 / 1804 0.6	**25** TU 0453 0.8 / 1105 4.7 / 1724 0.5 / 2342 4.5
11 TU 0014 4.4 / 0615 0.7 / 1222 4.7 / 1836 0.6	**26** W 0550 0.6 / 1158 4.8 / 1819 0.5 ●
12 W 0046 4.5 / 0652 0.6 / 1258 4.6 / ○ 1911 0.6	**27** TH 0032 4.6 / 0644 0.5 / 1249 4.8 / 1910 0.4
13 TH 0120 4.5 / 0729 0.6 / 1334 4.6 / 1944 0.5	**28** F 0118 4.7 / 0732 0.4 / 1337 4.8 / 1957 0.4
14 F 0152 4.6 / 0802 0.5 / 1406 4.6 / 2014 0.6	**29** SA 0202 4.7 / 0817 0.4 / 1425 4.8 / 2042 0.4
15 SA 0221 4.6 / 0832 0.6 / 1437 4.6 / 2042 0.6	**30** SU 0245 4.7 / 0900 0.4 / 1512 4.7 / 2123 0.5
	31 M 0327 4.7 / 0942 0.4 / 1547 4.5 / 2159 0.6

NOVEMBER

Time m	Time m
1 TU 0408 4.6 / 1021 0.5 / 1640 4.3 / 2233 0.8	**16** W 0331 4.6 / 0946 0.7 / 1558 4.3 / 2155 0.8
2 W 0450 4.5 / 1103 0.7 / 1726 4.1 / ◐ 2314 1.0	**17** TH 0406 4.6 / 1022 0.8 / 1636 4.2 / 2232 1.0
3 TH 0539 4.4 / 1153 0.9 / 1821 4.0	**18** F 0447 4.5 / 1105 0.9 / 1723 4.2 / 2321 1.1
4 F 0008 1.2 / 0642 4.3 / 1258 1.0 / 1930 3.9	**19** SA 0541 4.5 / 1159 1.0 / 1826 4.1
5 SA 0122 1.3 / 0758 4.3 / 1418 1.1 / 2049 3.9	**20** SU 0026 1.2 / 0652 4.4 / 1311 1.0 / 1942 4.2
6 SU 0247 1.3 / 0918 4.4 / 1537 1.0 / 2201 4.1	**21** M 0145 1.2 / 0810 4.5 / 1430 1.0 / 2059 4.3
7 M 0403 1.1 / 1023 4.5 / 1638 0.8 / 2255 4.3	**22** TU 0304 1.1 / 0924 4.6 / 1543 0.8 / 2206 4.4
8 TU 0456 0.9 / 1108 4.5 / 1720 0.7 / 2333 4.4	**23** W 0414 0.9 / 1029 4.7 / 1647 0.7 / 2306 4.5
9 W 0536 0.7 / 1145 4.5 / 1756 0.7	**24** TH 0517 0.7 / 1129 4.7 / 1749 0.6
10 TH 0008 4.5 / 0617 0.7 / 1224 4.5 / ○ 1834 0.7	**25** F 0002 4.6 / 0616 0.6 / 1226 4.7 / 1845 0.5
11 F 0045 4.5 / 0658 0.7 / 1303 4.5 / 1911 0.6	**26** SA 0054 4.7 / 0709 0.5 / 1318 4.7 / 1934 0.5
12 SA 0121 4.6 / 0735 0.6 / 1340 4.5 / 1945 0.6	**27** SU 0140 4.7 / 0756 0.4 / 1407 4.6 / 2019 0.5
13 SU 0155 4.6 / 0809 0.6 / 1414 4.5 / 2018 0.7	**28** M 0224 4.8 / 0842 0.4 / 1455 4.6 / 2103 0.6
14 M 0227 4.6 / 0842 0.6 / 1449 4.4 / 2051 0.7	**29** TU 0308 4.8 / 0928 0.5 / 1541 4.4 / 2142 0.6
15 TU 0259 4.6 / 0914 0.6 / 1523 4.4 / 2123 0.7	**30** W 0351 4.7 / 1010 0.5 / 1624 4.3 / 2217 0.7

DECEMBER

Time m	Time m
1 TH 0432 4.6 / 1049 0.6 / 1705 4.2 / 2253 0.8	**16** F 0357 4.8 / 1019 0.7 / 1628 4.3 / 2227 0.8
2 F 0515 4.6 / 1132 0.8 / 1748 4.0 / ◐ 2336 1.0	**17** SA 0438 4.7 / 1101 0.8 / 1713 4.3 / 2312 0.9
3 SA 0605 4.4 / 1221 0.9 / 1840 3.9	**18** SU 0526 4.7 / 1147 0.8 / 1804 4.3 ◐
4 SU 0031 1.2 / 0704 4.3 / 1320 1.1 / 1942 3.9	**19** M 0005 1.0 / 0623 4.6 / 1242 0.9 / 1905 4.3
5 M 0139 1.2 / 0811 4.3 / 1426 1.1 / 2051 4.0	**20** TU 0108 1.1 / 0731 4.6 / 1349 1.0 / 2014 4.3
6 TU 0253 1.2 / 0919 4.3 / 1531 1.0 / 2154 4.2	**21** W 0222 1.1 / 0844 4.6 / 1503 1.0 / 2126 4.4
7 W 0400 1.1 / 1017 4.4 / 1627 0.9 / 2246 4.3	**22** TH 0337 1.0 / 0957 4.6 / 1615 0.9 / 2234 4.5
8 TH 0454 0.9 / 1106 4.4 / 1714 0.8 / 2331 4.4	**23** F 0448 0.8 / 1107 4.6 / 1723 0.8 / 2338 4.6
9 F 0543 0.8 / 1151 4.4 / 1800 0.8	**24** SA 0554 0.7 / 1210 4.6 / 1826 0.7 ●
10 SA 0013 4.5 / 0629 0.8 / 1236 4.4 / ○ 1843 0.7	**25** SU 0035 4.7 / 0652 0.6 / 1305 4.6 / 1917 0.6
11 SU 0054 4.6 / 0710 0.7 / 1317 4.4 / 1923 0.7	**26** M 0123 4.7 / 0742 0.5 / 1354 4.6 / 2003 0.6
12 M 0133 4.7 / 0751 0.7 / 1357 4.5 / 2002 0.7	**27** TU 0208 4.8 / 0828 0.5 / 1441 4.5 / 2048 0.6
13 TU 0211 4.7 / 0831 0.7 / 1435 4.5 / 2041 0.7	**28** W 0252 4.9 / 0915 0.5 / 1525 4.5 / 2128 0.6
14 W 0247 4.8 / 0909 0.6 / 1512 4.5 / 2116 0.7	**29** TH 0334 4.9 / 0957 0.5 / 1604 4.4 / 2201 0.6
15 TH 0321 4.8 / 0942 0.6 / 1549 4.4 / 2149 0.7	**30** F 0412 4.8 / 1032 0.6 / 1638 4.3 / 2231 0.7
	31 SA 0448 4.7 / 1105 0.7 / 1711 4.2 / 2304 0.9

Chart Datum: 2·7 metres below Normal Null (German reference level)
HAT is 5·1 metres above Chart Datum

TIDES

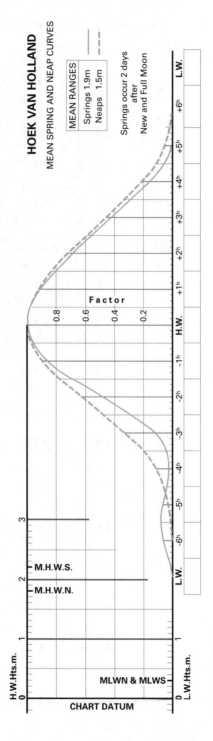

HOEK VAN HOLLAND
MEAN SPRING AND NEAP CURVES

MEAN RANGES	
Springs	1.9m
Neaps	1.5m

Springs occur 2 days
after
New and Full Moon

Factor

0.8   0.6   0.4   0.2

L.W.   -6ʰ   -5ʰ   -4ʰ   -3ʰ   -2ʰ   -1ʰ   H.W.   +1ʰ   +2ʰ   +3ʰ   +4ʰ   +5ʰ   +6ʰ   L.W.

3

M.H.W.S.

M.H.W.N.

H.W.Hts.m.

2

1

0

CHART DATUM

L.W.Hts.m.

MLWN & MLWS

Note - Double LWs often occur.
The predictions are for the lower
LW which is usually the first.

TIME ZONE -0100 (Dutch Standard Time) Subtract 1 hour for UT	NETHERLANDS – HOEK VAN HOLLAND	Dates in amber are SPRINGS Dates in yellow are NEAPS
For Dutch Summer Time add ONE hour in non-shaded areas	LAT 51°59'N LONG 4°07'E TIMES AND HEIGHTS OF HIGH AND LOW WATERS	2011

JANUARY

Day	Time m	Time m	Time m	Time m
1 SA	0740 0.5	1210 2.0	1739 0.4	
16 SU	0600 0.5	1206 1.9	1824 0.4	
2 SU	0045 2.0	0855 0.5	1306 2.1	1834 0.4
17 M	0029 1.9	0640 0.4	1256 2.0	1900 0.4
3 M	0139 2.1	0659 0.4	1355 2.1	1929 0.5
18 TU	0125 2.0	0655 0.4	1339 2.1	2137 0.4
4 TU	0236 2.1	0746 0.3	1446 2.2	●2004 0.5
19 W	0209 2.1	0725 0.3	1426 2.2	○1944 0.5
5 W	0319 2.1	0814 0.3	1525 2.3	2050 0.6
20 TH	0249 2.1	0759 0.3	1500 2.3	2256 0.5
6 TH	0355 2.1	0855 0.2	1605 2.3	2125 0.6
21 F	0328 2.1	0836 0.2	1545 2.4	2330 0.5
7 F	0435 2.1	0929 0.2	1646 2.3	2200 0.6
22 SA	0411 2.1	0911 0.1	1625 2.4	
8 SA	0509 2.1	1009 0.1	1725 2.2	2233 0.6
23 SU	0015 0.5	0456 2.1	0955 0.1	1711 2.4
9 SU	0545 2.1	1056 0.1	1806 2.2	2325 0.6
24 M	0054 0.5	0539 2.1	1045 0.1	1757 2.3
10 M	0614 2.1	1146 0.2	1845 2.1	
25 TU	0124 0.5	0625 2.1	1139 0.1	1847 2.3
11 TU	0030 0.5	0706 2.0	1215 0.2	1926 2.0
26 W	0200 0.5	0716 2.1	1300 0.1	1946 2.1
12 W	0115 0.5	0746 2.0	1314 0.2	◑2016 2.0
27 TH	0155 0.5	0816 2.0	1410 0.1	2045 2.0
13 TH	0205 0.5	0840 1.9	1405 0.3	2104 1.9
28 F	0256 0.4	0904 1.9	1515 0.2	2206 1.9
14 F	0304 0.5	0946 1.8	1520 0.4	2220 1.9
29 SA	0344 0.4	1033 1.9	1630 0.3	2330 1.8
15 SA	0450 0.5	1044 1.8	1727 0.4	2330 1.9
30 SU	0454 0.4	1155 1.9	1734 0.4	
31 M	0045 1.9	0825 0.4	1306 2.0	2120 0.4

FEBRUARY

Day	Time m	Time m	Time m	Time m
1 TU	0134 2.0	0941 0.3	1355 2.1	2220 0.5
16 W	0106 1.9	0905 0.3	1319 2.1	2130 0.4
2 W	0230 2.0	1020 0.2	1439 2.2	2235 0.5
17 TH	0144 2.0	0654 0.3	1401 2.2	2215 0.4
3 TH	0304 2.1	0806 0.2	1515 2.2	●2307 0.6
18 F	0227 2.0	0736 0.2	1440 2.4	○2246 0.5
4 F	0345 2.1	0835 0.2	1559 2.3	2335 0.6
19 SA	0307 2.1	0805 0.1	1522 2.4	2305 0.5
5 SA	0416 2.1	0905 0.2	1625 2.3	
20 SU	0347 2.2	0848 0.0	1605 2.4	
6 SU	0025 0.5	0445 2.2	0939 0.1	1659 2.2
21 M	0006 0.4	0431 2.2	0931 0.0	1649 2.4
7 M	0050 0.5	0520 2.2	1015 0.2	1736 2.2
22 TU	0034 0.4	0512 2.2	1026 0.1	1735 2.3
8 TU	0047 0.5	0550 2.1	1055 0.2	1805 2.1
23 W	0126 0.4	0557 2.2	1119 0.1	1825 2.2
9 W	0105 0.4	0620 2.1	1146 0.2	1831 2.1
24 TH	0130 0.4	0648 2.2	1257 0.1	1915 2.0
10 TH	0014 0.4	0655 2.1	1214 0.2	1905 2.0
25 F	0125 0.3	0745 2.1	1400 0.1	◑2019 1.9
11 F	0117 0.4	0729 2.0	1324 0.2	◑1955 1.9
26 SA	0214 0.3	0856 1.9	1454 0.3	2134 1.7
12 SA	0204 0.4	0845 1.9	1445 0.3	2125 1.8
27 SU	0324 0.3	1015 1.8	1604 0.4	2314 1.7
13 SU	0314 0.4	1016 1.8	1604 0.4	2245 1.7
28 M	0456 0.3	1150 1.9	1910 0.4	
14 M	0545 0.4	1130 1.8	1810 0.4	
15 TU	0006 1.8	0620 0.4	1235 1.9	2017 0.4

MARCH

Day	Time m	Time m	Time m	Time m
1 TU	0029 1.8	0544 0.3	1255 2.0	2115 0.4
16 W	0504 0.3	1206 2.0	1957 0.4	
2 W	0125 1.9	0925 0.2	1345 2.1	2215 0.4
17 TH	0036 1.8	0835 0.3	1256 2.1	2116 0.3
3 TH	0209 2.0	1004 0.2	1419 2.2	2240 0.4
18 F	0125 1.9	0626 0.2	1337 2.3	2145 0.4
4 F	0249 2.1	1044 0.2	1455 2.2	●2250 0.5
19 SA	0201 2.0	0706 0.1	1417 2.3	○2215 0.4
5 SA	0314 2.1	0815 0.2	1525 2.2	2325 0.5
20 SU	0242 2.1	0741 0.1	1459 2.4	2005 0.4
6 SU	0345 2.1	0846 0.2	1558 2.2	2340 0.4
21 M	0326 2.2	0825 0.0	1543 2.4	2048 0.4
7 M	0416 2.2	1157 0.2	1629 2.2	2140 0.4
22 TU	0407 2.3	0909 0.1	1626 2.3	
8 TU	0445 2.2	1234 0.2	1705 2.2	2205 0.4
23 W	0024 0.3	0449 2.3	0955 0.1	1710 2.2
9 W	0515 2.2	1254 0.2	1730 2.1	2240 0.3
24 TH	0115 0.3	0536 2.3	1055 0.2	1758 2.1
10 TH	0546 2.1	1054 0.2	1755 2.1	2315 0.3
25 F	0135 0.3	0618 2.2	1300 0.2	1855 1.9
11 F	0616 2.1	1134 0.2	1831 2.1	2354 0.3
26 SA	0054 0.2	0715 2.1	1334 0.2	◑1955 1.8
12 SA	0656 2.1	1234 0.2	1915 1.9	
27 SU	0144 0.2	0835 1.9	1439 0.3	2120 1.6
13 SU	0130 0.3	0746 2.0	1420 0.3	◑2024 1.7
28 M	0304 0.2	1005 1.8	1555 0.4	2254 1.6
14 M	0240 0.3	0914 1.8	1540 0.4	2210 1.6
29 TU	0430 0.2	1124 1.9	1840 0.4	
15 TU	0345 0.3	1056 1.8	1810 0.4	2324 1.7
30 W	0010 1.7	0524 0.2	1224 2.0	2035 0.3
31 TH	0105 1.9	0906 0.1	1320 2.1	2130 0.3

APRIL

Day	Time m	Time m	Time m	Time m
1 F	0146 1.9	0956 0.1	1355 2.1	2216 0.4
16 SA	0051 1.9	0556 0.1	1311 2.2	2130 0.3
2 SA	0225 2.0	1014 0.2	1426 2.1	2236 0.4
17 SU	0137 2.0	0635 0.1	1353 2.3	2205 0.4
3 SU	0249 2.0	0754 0.2	1455 2.1	●2247 0.4
18 M	0217 2.1	0719 0.1	1437 2.3	○1945 0.3
4 M	0316 2.1	1050 0.2	1530 2.2	2257 0.3
19 TU	0259 2.2	0805 0.1	1522 2.3	2025 0.3
5 TU	0345 2.2	1120 0.2	1559 2.2	2335 0.3
20 W	0345 2.3	0849 0.2	1607 2.2	2116 0.3
6 W	0415 2.2	1205 0.2	1629 2.1	2145 0.2
21 TH	0427 2.3	1235 0.2	1656 2.1	
7 TH	0446 2.2	1234 0.2	1659 2.1	2215 0.2
22 F	0115 0.2	0516 2.3	1340 0.2	1741 2.0
8 F	0515 2.2	1315 0.2	1731 2.1	2250 0.2
23 SA	0200 0.2	0606 2.2	1250 0.3	1835 1.9
9 SA	0548 2.2	1109 0.3	1808 2.0	2335 0.2
24 SU	0014 0.1	0659 2.1	1330 0.3	1934 1.7
10 SU	0625 2.1	1340 0.3	1855 1.9	
25 M	0114 0.1	0803 1.9	1425 0.4	◑2044 1.6
11 M	0035 0.2	0719 2.0	1414 0.3	◑1955 1.7
26 TU	0240 0.1	0929 1.9	1540 0.4	2214 1.6
12 TU	0154 0.2	0844 1.9	1514 0.4	2146 1.6
27 W	0355 0.1	1100 1.9	1757 0.4	2336 1.7
13 W	0305 0.2	1014 1.9	1757 0.4	2255 1.6
28 TH	0454 0.1	1155 1.9	1915 0.4	
14 TH	0415 0.2	1125 2.0	1945 0.3	
29 F	0030 1.8	0544 0.2	1246 2.0	2046 0.3
15 F	0005 1.7	0503 0.2	1226 2.1	2035 0.3
30 SA	0104 1.9	0850 0.2	1318 2.0	2124 0.3

Chart Datum: 0·92 metres below NAP Datum
HAT is 2·5 metres above Chart Datum

TIME ZONE -0100 (Dutch Standard Time) **Subtract 1 hour for UT** For Dutch Summer Time add ONE hour in **non-shaded areas**	**NETHERLANDS – HOEK VAN HOLLAND** LAT 51°59'N LONG 4°07'E TIMES AND HEIGHTS OF HIGH AND LOW WATERS	Dates in amber are **SPRINGS** Dates in yellow are **NEAPS** **2011**

MAY

Time m	Time m
1 0145 1.9 / 0715 0.2 / SU 1355 2.1 / 2155 0.3	**16** 0108 2.0 / 0615 0.1 / M 1335 2.2 / 1845 0.3
2 0215 2.0 / 0745 0.3 / M 1425 2.1 / 1959 0.3	**17** 0157 2.1 / 0706 0.2 / TU 1421 2.2 / ○ 1929 0.3
3 0245 2.1 / 1000 0.3 / TU 1455 2.1 / ● 2025 0.3	**18** 0241 2.2 / 0749 0.2 / W 1505 2.1 / 2015 0.3
4 0315 2.1 / 1050 0.3 / W 1535 2.1 / 2324 0.2	**19** 0327 2.3 / 0839 0.3 / TH 1552 2.1 / 2059 0.3
5 0349 2.2 / 1125 0.3 / TH 1605 2.1 / 2354 0.2	**20** 0412 2.3 / 1224 0.3 / F 1646 2.0
6 0426 2.2 / 1204 0.3 / F 1639 2.0	**21** 0056 0.1 / 0458 2.2 / SA 1314 0.3 / 1728 1.9
7 0034 0.2 / 0456 2.2 / SA 1244 0.3 / 1715 2.0	**22** 0140 0.1 / 0549 2.2 / SU 1415 0.4 / 1825 1.9
8 0125 0.2 / 0531 2.2 / SU 1325 0.3 / 1755 1.9	**23** 0220 0.2 / 0645 2.1 / M 1300 0.4 / 1915 1.8
9 0210 0.1 / 0615 2.1 / M 1407 0.3 / 1841 1.8	**24** 0044 0.0 / 0734 2.0 / TU 1354 0.4 / ◑ 2005 1.7
10 0015 0.1 / 0704 2.1 / TU 1504 0.3 / ◑ 1945 1.7	**25** 0145 0.0 / 0845 1.9 / W 1500 0.4 / 2055 1.6
11 0134 0.1 / 0825 2.0 / W 1610 0.4 / 2116 1.7	**26** 0330 0.1 / 0954 1.8 / TH 1555 0.4 / 2235 1.6
12 0246 0.1 / 0950 2.0 / TH 1745 0.4 / 2219 1.7	**27** 0425 0.1 / 1115 1.9 / F 1655 0.4 / 2346 1.7
13 0334 0.1 / 1056 2.1 / F 1915 0.4 / 2325 1.8	**28** 0525 0.2 / 1206 1.9 / SA 1745 0.4
14 0436 0.1 / 1155 2.1 / SA 2015 0.3	**29** 0026 1.8 / 0614 0.2 / SU 1256 1.9 / 1834 0.3
15 0022 1.9 / 0525 0.1 / SU 1248 2.2 / 2106 0.3	**30** 0110 1.9 / 0655 0.3 / M 1325 2.0 / 1910 0.3
	31 0139 1.9 / 0740 0.3 / TU 1359 2.0 / 1935 0.3

JUNE

Time m	Time m
1 0216 2.0 / 0755 0.3 / W 1435 2.1 / ● 2004 0.3	**16** 0227 2.2 / 0744 0.4 / TH 1459 2.1 / 2005 0.2
2 0249 2.1 / 1020 0.3 / TH 1509 2.1 / 2035 0.2	**17** 0315 2.2 / 0835 0.4 / F 1547 2.0 / 2044 0.1
3 0325 2.2 / 1104 0.3 / F 1545 2.1 / 2356 0.3	**18** 0405 2.3 / 1215 0.4 / SA 1631 2.0 / 2136 0.1
4 0401 2.2 / 1156 0.3 / SA 1626 2.0	**19** 0445 2.2 / 1316 0.5 / SU 1719 2.0 / 2219 0.1
5 0036 0.2 / 0438 2.2 / SU 1225 0.3 / 1705 1.9	**20** 0535 2.2 / 1405 0.5 / M 1754 1.9 / 2310 0.0
6 0116 0.1 / 0521 2.2 / M 1326 0.3 / 1745 1.9	**21** 0614 2.1 / 1446 0.5 / TU 1846 1.9
7 0150 0.1 / 0606 2.2 / TU 1405 0.3 / 1835 1.8	**22** 0005 0.0 / 0710 2.1 / W 1310 0.5 / 1925 1.9
8 0235 0.1 / 0654 2.1 / W 1447 0.4 / 1933 1.8	**23** 0054 0.1 / 0755 2.0 / TH 1410 0.4 / ◑ 2016 1.8
9 0105 0.1 / 0810 2.1 / TH 1540 0.4 / ◑ 2046 1.8	**24** 0210 0.1 / 0849 1.9 / F 1507 0.4 / 2110 1.7
10 0204 0.1 / 0920 2.1 / F 1700 0.4 / 2145 1.8	**25** 0405 0.2 / 0945 1.8 / SA 1625 0.4 / 2204 1.7
11 0310 0.1 / 1026 2.1 / SA 1610 0.4 / 2256 1.8	**26** 0505 0.2 / 1100 1.8 / SU 1714 0.4 / 2335 1.7
12 0410 0.1 / 1126 2.1 / SU 1930 0.4 / 2355 1.9	**27** 0545 0.3 / 1155 1.8 / M 1804 0.3
13 0504 0.2 / 1228 2.1 / M 2030 0.4	**28** 0026 1.8 / 0635 0.3 / TU 1256 1.9 / 1856 0.3
14 0050 2.0 / 0604 0.2 / TU 1317 2.1 / 1835 0.3	**29** 0104 1.9 / 0705 0.3 / W 1335 2.0 / 1914 0.3
15 0139 2.1 / 0705 0.3 / W 1408 2.1 / ○ 1926 0.3	**30** 0149 2.0 / 0740 0.3 / TH 1416 2.0 / 1944 0.3

JULY

Time m	Time m
1 0229 2.1 / 0754 0.4 / F 1455 2.0 / ● 2004 0.2	**16** 0305 2.2 / 0825 0.5 / SA 1535 2.1 / 2035 0.1
2 0308 2.2 / 1044 0.4 / SA 1528 2.0 / 2046 0.2	**17** 0345 2.3 / 1145 0.6 / SU 1619 2.1 / 2109 0.1
3 0345 2.3 / 1136 0.4 / SU 1611 2.0 / 2120 0.2	**18** 0429 2.3 / 1235 0.6 / M 1700 2.1 / 2155 0.1
4 0425 2.3 / 1215 0.4 / M 1655 2.0 / 2158 0.1	**19** 0509 2.2 / 1336 0.5 / TU 1736 2.1 / 2229 0.1
5 0507 2.3 / 1254 0.4 / TU 1735 1.9 / 2239 0.1	**20** 0549 2.2 / 1416 0.5 / W 1809 2.0 / 2320 0.1
6 0550 2.3 / 1345 0.4 / W 1825 1.9 / 2324 0.1	**21** 0629 2.1 / 1230 0.5 / TH 1845 2.0
7 0641 2.2 / 1414 0.4 / TH 1915 1.9	**22** 0004 0.1 / 0715 2.0 / F 1310 0.5 / 1930 1.9
8 0035 0.1 / 0734 2.2 / F 1450 0.4 / ◑ 2016 1.9	**23** 0104 0.2 / 0806 1.9 / SA 1400 0.4 / ◑ 2013 1.9
9 0144 0.1 / 0846 2.1 / SA 1444 0.4 / 2115 1.9	**24** 0154 0.2 / 0850 1.9 / SU 1445 0.4 / 2126 1.8
10 0255 0.1 / 0949 2.0 / SU 1534 0.4 / 2225 1.9	**25** 0255 0.3 / 0950 1.8 / M 1650 0.4 / 2230 1.7
11 0354 0.2 / 1059 2.0 / M 1639 0.4 / 2335 1.9	**26** 0520 0.4 / 1055 1.8 / TU 1735 0.4 / 2334 1.8
12 0510 0.3 / 1216 1.9 / TU 1745 0.4	**27** 0605 0.4 / 1226 1.8 / W 1836 0.4
13 0036 2.0 / 0605 0.4 / W 1316 2.0 / 1829 0.3	**28** 0039 1.9 / 0650 0.4 / TH 1309 1.9 / 1900 0.3
14 0131 2.1 / 0659 0.4 / TH 1410 2.0 / 1915 0.2	**29** 0124 2.0 / 0720 0.4 / F 1355 2.0 / 1920 0.3
15 0225 2.2 / 0745 0.5 / F 1455 2.0 / ○ 1956 0.2	**30** 0209 2.2 / 0734 0.5 / SA 1431 2.0 / ● 1946 0.3
	31 0246 2.3 / 0805 0.5 / SU 1515 2.1 / 2015 0.2

AUGUST

Time m	Time m
1 0325 2.4 / 1116 0.5 / M 1548 2.1 / 2056 0.1	**16** 0406 2.3 / 0910 0.6 / TU 1629 2.2 / 2114 0.2
2 0407 2.4 / 1149 0.5 / TU 1631 2.1 / 2135 0.1	**17** 0441 2.3 / 1245 0.6 / W 1706 2.2 / 2155 0.2
3 0447 2.4 / 1235 0.5 / W 1715 2.1 / 2215 0.1	**18** 0518 2.2 / 1019 0.5 / TH 1731 2.1 / 2235 0.2
4 0530 2.3 / 1320 0.4 / TH 1758 2.1 / 2306 0.1	**19** 0556 2.1 / 1059 0.5 / F 1806 2.1 / 2315 0.3
5 0617 2.3 / 1406 0.5 / F 1845 2.1	**20** 0619 2.1 / 1200 0.5 / SA 1835 2.1
6 0004 0.1 / 0715 2.2 / SA 1410 0.5 / ◐ 1935 2.0	**21** 0016 0.3 / 0656 2.0 / SU 1250 0.5 / ◑ 1915 2.0
7 0144 0.2 / 0816 2.0 / SU 1436 0.4 / 2045 2.0	**22** 0107 0.3 / 0735 1.9 / M 1345 0.4 / 2004 1.9
8 0245 0.2 / 0914 1.9 / M 1526 0.4 / 2153 1.9	**23** 0226 0.4 / 0844 1.8 / TU 1445 0.5 / 2146 1.8
9 0345 0.3 / 1045 1.8 / TU 1630 0.4 / 2319 1.9	**24** 0450 0.5 / 1016 0.5 / W 1725 0.4 / 2306 1.8
10 0455 0.4 / 1210 1.8 / W 1725 0.4	**25** 0554 0.5 / 1146 1.7 / TH 1815 0.4
11 0036 2.0 / 0837 0.5 / TH 1316 1.9 / 2105 0.3	**26** 0015 1.9 / 0650 0.5 / F 1245 1.8 / 1830 0.4
12 0124 2.1 / 0950 0.5 / F 1406 2.0 / 2154 0.3	**27** 0106 2.1 / 0855 0.5 / SA 1329 2.0 / 1839 0.3
13 0215 2.2 / 1141 0.5 / SA 1443 2.1 / ○ 1939 0.2	**28** 0146 2.2 / 0945 0.5 / SU 1409 2.1 / 1916 0.3
14 0256 2.3 / 1047 0.6 / SU 1526 2.1 / 2016 0.2	**29** 0225 2.4 / 0739 0.5 / M 1445 2.1 / ● 1945 0.2
15 0328 2.6 / 0835 0.6 / M 1600 2.1 / 2046 0.2	**30** 0302 2.5 / 0815 0.6 / TU 1526 2.2 / 2025 0.1
	31 0342 2.5 / 0845 0.6 / W 1607 2.2 / 2108 0.1

Chart Datum: 0·92 metres below NAP Datum
HAT is 2·5 metres above Chart Datum

SEPTEMBER

Time	m		Time	m
1 0426 1226 TH 1647 2149	2.5 0.5 2.2 0.1	**16**	0446 0943 F 1659 2205	2.2 0.5 2.2 0.4
2 0509 1254 F 1731 2245	2.4 0.5 2.2 0.2	**17**	0516 1026 SA 1729 2240	2.2 0.5 2.2 0.4
3 0555 1330 SA 1816 2344	2.3 0.5 2.2 0.3	**18**	0545 1100 SU 1800 2314	2.1 0.4 2.2 0.4
4 0645 1320 SU 1910 ◐	2.1 0.5 2.2 	**19**	0611 1139 M 1829 2354	2.1 0.4 2.2 0.4
5 0134 0746 M 1345 2016	0.3 2.0 0.4 2.0	**20**	0656 1244 TU 1915 ◑	2.0 0.4 2.0
6 0230 0900 TU 1444 2146	0.3 2.0 0.4 1.9	**21**	0150 0745 W 1416 2040	0.5 1.9 0.4 1.9
7 0334 1040 W 1610 2304	0.5 1.7 0.4 1.9	**22**	0304 0924 TH 1514 2231	0.5 1.7 0.4 1.9
8 0644 1155 TH 1714	0.5 1.8 0.4	**23**	0527 1106 F 1754 2340	0.5 1.7 0.4 2.0
9 0025 0840 F 1254 2055	2.1 0.5 1.9 0.3	**24**	0720 1205 SA 1724	0.5 1.8 0.4
10 0113 0937 SA 1343 2144	2.2 0.5 0.4 0.2	**25**	0036 0856 SU 1255 1805	2.2 0.5 2.0 0.3
11 0159 1030 SU 1425 2225	2.3 0.5 2.1 0.3	**26**	0118 0946 M 1339 1841	2.3 0.5 2.1 0.3
12 0235 1034 M 1459 ○ 1955	2.3 0.6 2.2 0.3	**27**	0156 0709 TU 1418 ● 1919	2.4 0.6 2.2 0.2
13 0306 0815 TU 1524 2026	2.3 0.6 2.3 0.3	**28**	0237 0746 W 1458 2002	2.5 0.5 2.3 0.2
14 0338 0846 W 1559 2056	2.3 0.6 2.2 0.3	**29**	0316 0825 TH 1541 2045	2.5 0.5 2.4 0.2
15 0415 0909 TH 1629 2125	2.3 0.5 2.3 0.3	**30**	0402 0906 F 1626 2129	2.4 0.5 2.4 0.2

OCTOBER

Time	m		Time	m
1 0447 0949 SA 1707 2225	2.3 0.5 2.4 0.3	**16**	0445 0953 SU 1659 2209	2.2 0.4 2.3 0.5
2 0536 1045 SU 1756 2335	2.2 0.6 2.3 0.4	**17**	0518 1036 M 1731 2243	2.2 0.4 2.3 0.5
3 0621 1200 M 1845	2.1 0.4 2.2	**18**	0550 1105 TU 1806 2325	2.1 0.4 2.2 0.5
4 0120 0719 TU 1315 ◑ 1955	0.4 1.9 0.3 2.1	**19**	0629 1154 W 1851	2.0 0.3 2.2
5 0215 0834 W 1415 2115	0.5 1.8 0.3 2.0	**20**	0130 0726 TH 1330 ◑ 1959	0.6 1.9 0.4 2.0
6 0315 1014 TH 1545 2306	0.6 1.7 0.4 2.0	**21**	0244 0905 F 1434 2150	0.6 1.8 0.4 2.0
7 0624 1135 F 1700	0.6 1.8 0.4	**22**	0520 1020 SA 1535 2300	0.6 1.8 0.4 2.1
8 0004 0800 SA 1235 2015	2.1 0.5 1.9 0.3	**23**	0700 1130 SU 1635 2355	0.6 1.8 0.4 2.2
9 0056 0916 SU 1319 2135	2.2 0.5 2.1 0.3	**24**	0826 1225 M 1729	0.5 2.0 0.4
10 0136 0935 M 1354 2205	2.2 0.5 2.1 0.3	**25**	0048 0910 TU 1309 1816	2.4 0.5 2.1 0.3
11 0209 1020 TU 1429 1935	2.3 0.6 2.2 0.4	**26**	0132 0646 W 1352 ● 1858	2.6 0.5 2.3 0.2
12 0245 0754 W 1459 ○ 2004	2.3 0.6 2.4 0.4	**27**	0215 0725 TH 1437 1946	2.5 0.6 2.4 0.2
13 0316 0825 TH 1529 2035	2.3 0.6 2.3 0.4	**28**	0258 0806 F 1517 2028	2.4 0.5 2.4 0.3
14 0345 0849 F 1559 2106	2.3 0.5 2.3 0.4	**29**	0342 0846 SA 1606 2115	2.4 0.4 2.4 0.4
15 0415 0925 SA 1632 2135	2.2 0.5 2.3 0.5	**30**	0429 0936 SU 1647 2204	2.3 0.4 2.4 0.5
		31	0516 1024 M 1735 2350	2.1 0.3 2.3 0.6

NOVEMBER

Time	m		Time	m
1 0605 1135 TU 1829	2.0 0.3 2.2	**16**	0116 0536 W 1053 1752	0.5 2.1 0.3 2.3
2 0045 0703 W 1245 ◑ 1940	0.5 1.9 0.2 2.1	**17**	0150 0615 TH 1155 1846	0.6 2.0 0.3 2.2
3 0144 0826 TH 1344 2044	0.6 1.8 0.3 2.0	**18**	0217 0709 F 1235 ◑ 1946	0.6 1.9 0.3 2.1
4 0455 0934 F 1520 2220	0.6 1.7 0.3 2.1	**19**	0300 0830 SA 1406 2110	0.6 1.8 0.3 2.1
5 0545 1105 SA 1640 2324	0.6 1.8 0.3 2.1	**20**	0320 0946 SU 1455 2214	0.6 1.8 0.3 2.1
6 0710 1200 SU 1926	0.6 1.9 0.3	**21**	0617 1050 M 1605 2321	0.6 1.9 0.3 2.2
7 0025 0820 M 1245 2020	2.1 0.5 2.0 0.3	**22**	0735 1149 TU 1654	2.0 0.2 0.3
8 0105 0916 TU 1330 1855	2.2 0.5 2.1 0.4	**23**	0018 0846 W 1245 1755	2.3 0.5 2.1 0.3
9 0146 0956 W 1405 1940	2.2 0.5 2.1 0.4	**24**	0108 0625 TH 1332 1845	2.3 0.5 2.2 0.3
10 0218 0744 TH 1436 ○ 2020	2.2 0.5 2.2 0.5	**25**	0157 0704 F 1417 ● 1930	2.3 0.5 2.3 0.4
11 0250 0805 F 1506 2024	2.2 0.5 2.3 0.5	**26**	0242 0749 SA 1505 2015	2.3 0.6 2.4 0.4
12 0325 0833 SA 1535 2255	2.2 0.4 2.3 0.5	**27**	0328 0838 SU 1549 2106	2.2 0.3 2.4 0.5
13 0356 0905 SU 1610 2350	2.2 0.4 2.3 0.5	**28**	0415 0926 M 1635 2200	2.2 0.3 2.4 0.6
14 0426 0939 M 1642	2.2 0.4 2.3	**29**	0506 1015 TU 1726	2.1 0.2 2.4
15 0036 0459 TU 1013 1715	0.5 2.1 0.4 2.3	**30**	0150 0555 W 1110 1815	0.6 2.0 0.2 2.3

DECEMBER

Time	m		Time	m
1 0010 0650 TH 1204 1916	0.6 2.0 0.2 2.2	**16**	0140 0609 F 1126 1829	0.5 2.0 0.2 2.3
2 0110 0739 F 1304 ◑ 2020	0.6 1.9 0.2 2.1	**17**	0220 0654 SA 1215 1926	0.5 1.9 0.2 2.2
3 0215 0846 SA 1415 2115	0.6 1.8 0.2 2.0	**18**	0247 0759 SU 1314 ◑ 2036	0.6 1.9 0.2 2.2
4 0315 0945 SU 1600 2234	0.6 1.8 0.3 1.9	**19**	0245 0910 M 1436 2145	0.6 1.9 0.2 2.1
5 0616 1116 M 1700 2346	0.6 1.8 0.3 2.0	**20**	0335 1015 TU 1535 2250	0.6 1.9 0.2 2.1
6 0720 1205 TU 1800	0.6 1.9 0.3	**21**	0424 1120 W 1635 2356	0.6 1.9 0.3 2.1
7 0035 0824 W 1256 1845	2.0 0.5 1.9 0.4	**22**	0519 1219 TH 1746	0.5 2.1 0.4
8 0115 0926 TH 1335 1930	2.1 0.5 2.0 0.4	**23**	0056 0604 F 1315 1833	2.1 0.5 2.2 0.4
9 0156 0735 F 1405 2010	2.1 0.4 2.1 0.5	**24**	0146 0659 SA 1406 ● 1925	2.1 0.4 2.3 0.5
10 0225 0754 SA 1439 ○ 2024	2.1 0.4 2.2 0.5	**25**	0238 0746 SU 1450 2015	2.2 0.3 2.4 0.5
11 0259 0805 SU 1515 2230	2.2 0.4 2.3 0.5	**26**	0320 0828 M 1539 2055	2.2 0.3 2.4 0.6
12 0336 0855 M 1549 2320	2.2 0.3 2.3 0.5	**27**	0415 0909 TU 1626	2.1 0.2 2.4
13 0415 0925 TU 1628	2.1 0.3 2.3	**28**	0034 0455 W 0955 1708	0.6 2.1 0.1 2.4
14 0010 0449 W 0954 1705	0.5 2.1 0.1 2.3	**29**	0124 0539 TH 1039 1758	0.6 2.1 0.1 2.3
15 0055 0530 TH 1039 1742	0.5 2.0 0.2 2.3	**30**	0220 0626 F 1136 1846	0.6 2.1 0.1 2.2
		31	0030 0706 SA 1224 1935	0.6 2.0 0.1 2.1

Chart Datum: 0·92 metres below NAP Datum
HAT is 2·5 metres above Chart Datum

TIDES

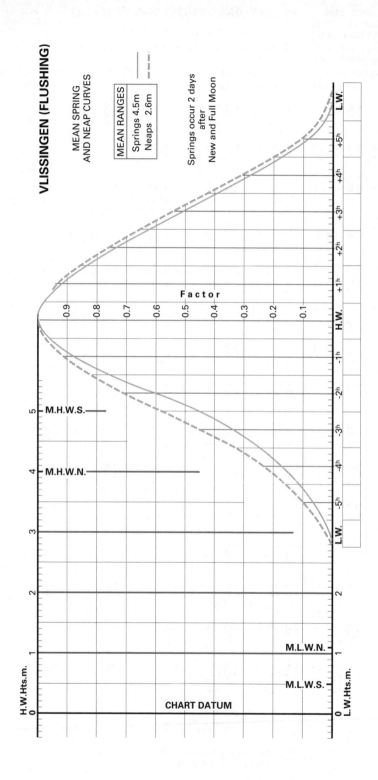

VLISSINGEN (FLUSHING)

MEAN SPRING
AND NEAP CURVES

MEAN RANGES	
Springs 4.5m	
Neaps 2.6m	

Springs occur 2 days
after
New and Full Moon

TIME ZONE -0100 (Dutch Standard Time) Subtract 1 hour for UT	NETHERLANDS – VLISSINGEN	Dates in amber are SPRINGS
For Dutch Summer Time add ONE hour in **non-shaded areas**	LAT 51°27'N LONG 3°36'E TIMES AND HEIGHTS OF HIGH AND LOW WATERS	Dates in yellow are NEAPS **2011**

JANUARY

Time m	Time m
1 0526 1.1 / 1118 4.4 / SA 1756 0.9 / 2359 4.5	**16** 0455 1.3 / 1111 4.1 / SU 1736 1.1 / 2342 4.3
2 0626 0.9 / 1226 4.6 / SU 1850 0.9	**17** 0600 1.1 / 1206 4.4 / M 1826 1.0
3 0056 4.6 / 0716 0.8 / M 1318 4.8 / 1936 0.9	**18** 0035 4.5 / 0656 0.9 / TU 1252 4.6 / 1910 0.9
4 0145 4.7 / 0801 0.6 / TU 1406 4.9 / ●2018 0.9	**19** 0118 4.7 / 0740 0.7 / W 1337 4.9 / ○1956 0.8
5 0228 4.8 / 0845 0.5 / W 1445 4.9 / 2055 0.9	**20** 0201 4.8 / 0825 0.5 / TH 1418 5.1 / 2040 0.7
6 0306 4.8 / 0925 0.5 / TH 1526 5.0 / 2132 0.9	**21** 0240 4.9 / 0912 0.4 / F 1459 5.2 / 2123 0.7
7 0345 4.9 / 1005 0.5 / F 1602 4.9 / 2208 1.0	**22** 0323 5.0 / 0958 0.3 / SA 1541 5.2 / 2211 0.7
8 0419 4.8 / 1046 0.6 / SA 1639 4.8 / 2242 1.0	**23** 0405 5.0 / 1046 0.2 / SU 1626 5.2 / 2256 0.7
9 0455 4.8 / 1118 0.6 / SU 1716 4.7 / 2318 1.0	**24** 0446 5.0 / 1130 0.2 / M 1716 5.1 / 2338 0.7
10 0530 4.7 / 1150 0.7 / M 1751 4.6 / 2350 1.0	**25** 0535 4.9 / 1215 0.3 / TU 1805 4.9
11 0605 4.5 / 1225 0.8 / TU 1832 4.4	**26** 0026 0.8 / 0625 4.7 / W 1259 0.5 / ☽1901 4.7
12 0025 1.1 / 0645 4.4 / W 1300 0.9 / ☽1915 4.2	**27** 0115 0.9 / 0728 4.5 / TH 1356 0.7 / 2006 4.4
13 0110 1.2 / 0746 4.2 / TH 1356 1.1 / 2015 4.1	**28** 0216 1.1 / 0832 4.3 / F 1455 0.9 / 2116 4.2
14 0209 1.3 / 0846 4.0 / F 1516 1.2 / 2121 4.0	**29** 0324 1.2 / 0955 4.2 / SA 1620 1.1 / 2240 4.1
15 0350 1.4 / 0955 4.0 / SA 1625 1.2 / 2238 4.1	**30** 0506 1.1 / 1116 4.2 / SU 1740 1.1 / 2349 4.3
	31 0615 0.9 / 1226 4.5 / M 1834 1.0

FEBRUARY

Time m	Time m
1 0049 4.5 / 0716 0.7 / TU 1316 4.7 / 1926 1.0	**16** 0015 4.3 / 0635 0.9 / W 1236 4.6 / 1849 0.9
2 0135 4.6 / 0756 0.6 / W 1358 4.8 / 2005 0.9	**17** 0057 4.6 / 0722 0.6 / TH 1317 4.9 / 1935 0.7
3 0216 4.7 / 0835 0.5 / TH 1435 4.9 / ●2040 0.9	**18** 0139 4.8 / 0810 0.4 / F 1358 5.1 / ○2019 0.6
4 0247 4.8 / 0909 0.5 / F 1505 4.9 / 2112 0.9	**19** 0219 5.0 / 0856 0.3 / SA 1438 5.3 / 2105 0.4
5 0321 4.9 / 0946 0.5 / SA 1538 4.9 / 2146 0.8	**20** 0300 5.1 / 0937 0.1 / SU 1522 5.3 / 2151 0.5
6 0352 4.9 / 1021 0.5 / SU 1611 4.9 / 2215 0.8	**21** 0343 5.2 / 1023 0.1 / M 1605 5.3 / 2233 0.5
7 0426 4.9 / 1050 0.5 / M 1646 4.8 / 2245 0.9	**22** 0426 5.1 / 1105 0.2 / TU 1650 5.1 / 2317 0.5
8 0456 4.8 / 1115 0.6 / TU 1716 4.7 / 2315 0.9	**23** 0510 5.0 / 1151 0.3 / W 1737 4.9
9 0525 4.7 / 1146 0.7 / W 1746 4.6 / 2346 0.9	**24** 0000 0.6 / 0602 4.9 / TH 1232 0.5 / 1831 4.6
10 0559 4.6 / 1216 0.8 / TH 1819 4.4	**25** 0050 0.8 / 0658 4.6 / F 1325 0.7 / ☽1935 4.3
11 0022 0.9 / 0640 4.4 / F 1301 0.9 / ☽1915 4.2	**26** 0150 0.9 / 0805 4.3 / SA 1430 1.0 / 2056 4.0
12 0115 1.1 / 0740 4.1 / SA 1353 1.1 / 2036 4.0	**27** 0310 1.1 / 0936 4.1 / SU 1554 1.2 / 2225 3.9
13 0224 1.3 / 0916 4.0 / SU 1535 1.2 / 2156 3.9	**28** 0456 1.1 / 1105 4.1 / M 1724 1.2 / 2339 4.1
14 0426 1.3 / 1035 4.0 / M 1656 1.2 / 2316 4.1	
15 0535 1.1 / 1146 4.3 / TU 1800 1.0	

MARCH

Time m	Time m
1 0606 0.9 / 1216 4.4 / TU 1830 1.0	**16** 0505 1.0 / 1116 4.3 / W 1736 1.0 / 2345 4.3
2 0035 4.4 / 0659 0.7 / W 1306 4.6 / 1915 1.0	**17** 0610 0.8 / 1209 4.6 / TH 1825 0.9
3 0119 4.6 / 0742 0.5 / TH 1339 4.8 / 1950 0.9	**18** 0030 4.6 / 0706 0.5 / F 1256 4.9 / 1915 0.7
4 0156 4.7 / 0816 0.5 / F 1410 4.8 / ●2018 0.9	**19** 0116 4.8 / 0748 0.3 / SA 1335 5.1 / ○2003 0.5
5 0222 4.8 / 0846 0.5 / SA 1440 4.9 / 2048 0.8	**20** 0155 5.0 / 0832 0.2 / SU 1415 5.3 / 2046 0.5
6 0256 4.9 / 0918 0.4 / SU 1511 4.9 / 2122 0.7	**21** 0235 5.2 / 0916 0.1 / M 1457 5.3 / 2128 0.4
7 0322 4.9 / 0949 0.4 / M 1541 4.9 / 2156 0.7	**22** 0318 5.3 / 0958 0.1 / TU 1543 5.2 / 2213 0.4
8 0353 4.9 / 1019 0.5 / TU 1611 4.8 / 2226 0.7	**23** 0403 5.2 / 1039 0.2 / W 1626 5.0 / 2255 0.4
9 0422 4.9 / 1051 0.6 / W 1639 4.7 / 2245 0.7	**24** 0448 5.1 / 1126 0.4 / TH 1715 4.8 / 2340 0.5
10 0456 4.8 / 1116 0.6 / TH 1707 4.7 / 2318 0.7	**25** 0535 4.9 / 1206 0.6 / F 1810 4.5
11 0526 4.7 / 1146 0.7 / F 1745 4.5 / 2356 0.8	**26** 0031 0.6 / 0635 4.6 / SA 1256 0.8 / ☽1904 4.2
12 0558 4.6 / 1222 0.8 / SA 1826 4.3	**27** 0124 0.8 / 0750 4.2 / SU 1406 1.1 / 2031 3.9
13 0046 0.9 / 0652 4.3 / SU 1320 1.0 / ☽1935 4.0	**28** 0256 1.0 / 0916 4.0 / M 1535 1.3 / 2206 3.8
14 0156 1.1 / 0830 4.0 / M 1450 1.2 / 2115 3.8	**29** 0436 1.0 / 1046 4.1 / TU 1715 1.2 / 2316 4.0
15 0334 1.2 / 1005 4.0 / TU 1625 1.2 / 2234 4.0	**30** 0546 0.8 / 1146 4.4 / W 1805 1.1
	31 0009 4.3 / 0635 0.6 / TH 1235 4.6 / 1849 0.9

APRIL

Time m	Time m
1 0051 4.5 / 0715 0.6 / F 1316 4.7 / 1919 0.9	**16** 0006 4.6 / 0639 0.5 / SA 1227 4.9 / 1852 0.7
2 0128 4.6 / 0750 0.5 / SA 1346 4.7 / 1956 0.8	**17** 0046 4.8 / 0722 0.3 / SU 1310 5.1 / 1938 0.5
3 0156 4.7 / 0821 0.5 / SU 1412 4.8 / ●2022 0.7	**18** 0130 5.0 / 0808 0.2 / M 1355 5.2 / ○2023 0.4
4 0226 4.8 / 0848 0.5 / M 1441 4.9 / 2056 0.6	**19** 0215 5.2 / 0852 0.2 / TU 1438 5.2 / 2108 0.4
5 0252 4.9 / 0920 0.5 / TU 1511 4.9 / 2125 0.6	**20** 0257 5.2 / 0936 0.3 / W 1526 5.1 / 2151 0.3
6 0326 4.9 / 0949 0.5 / W 1541 4.8 / 2206 0.6	**21** 0343 5.2 / 1017 0.4 / TH 1611 4.9 / 2238 0.4
7 0355 4.9 / 1026 0.6 / TH 1611 4.8 / 2230 0.7	**22** 0430 5.0 / 1058 0.5 / F 1658 4.7 / 2326 0.4
8 0425 4.8 / 1051 0.7 / F 1642 4.7 / 2300 0.7	**23** 0526 4.8 / 1146 0.7 / SA 1749 4.5
9 0457 4.7 / 1125 0.7 / SA 1717 4.5 / 2346 0.7	**24** 0016 0.6 / 0619 4.6 / SU 1229 0.9 / 1844 4.2
10 0540 4.6 / 1205 0.8 / SU 1806 4.3	**25** 0104 0.7 / 0725 4.3 / M 1335 1.1 / 1955 4.0
11 0030 0.8 / 0631 4.4 / M 1305 1.0 / ☽1916 1.0	**26** 0226 0.8 / 0839 4.1 / TU 1455 1.3 / 2126 3.8
12 0135 0.9 / 0806 4.1 / TU 1415 1.2 / 2046 3.9	**27** 0346 0.9 / 1006 4.1 / W 1615 1.2 / 2236 4.0
13 0305 1.0 / 0930 4.2 / W 1545 1.2 / 2201 4.0	**28** 0506 0.8 / 1110 4.3 / TH 1725 1.1 / 2335 4.2
14 0430 0.9 / 1045 4.4 / TH 1654 1.0 / 2309 4.3	**29** 0606 0.7 / 1155 4.9 / F 1816 1.0
15 0546 0.7 / 1139 4.7 / F 1806 0.9	**30** 0015 4.4 / 0646 0.7 / SA 1239 4.5 / 1850 0.9

Chart Datum: 2·56 metres below NAP Datum
HAT is 5·4 metres above Chart Datum

TIME ZONE -0100 (Dutch Standard Time) **Subtract 1 hour for UT** For Dutch Summer Time add ONE hour in **non-shaded areas**	**NETHERLANDS – VLISSINGEN** **LAT 51°27′N LONG 3°36′E** TIMES AND HEIGHTS OF HIGH AND LOW WATERS	Dates in amber are **SPRINGS** Dates in yellow are **NEAPS** **2011**

MAY

Time m	Time m
1 SU 0051 4.5 / 0716 0.6 / 1316 4.6 / 1919 0.8	**16** M 0023 4.8 / 0658 0.4 / 1249 5.0 / 1915 0.6
2 M 0126 4.6 / 0746 0.6 / 1341 4.7 / 1956 0.6	**17** TU 0109 5.0 / 0745 0.3 / 1335 5.0 / ○ 2006 0.4
3 TU 0156 4.7 / 0815 0.6 / 1412 4.8 / ● 2030 0.6	**18** W 0155 5.1 / 0830 0.4 / 1423 5.0 / 2052 0.4
4 W 0225 4.9 / 0850 0.6 / 1446 4.8 / 2105 0.6	**19** TH 0241 5.1 / 0916 0.4 / 1506 4.9 / 2138 0.3
5 TH 0257 4.9 / 0926 0.6 / 1517 4.8 / 2139 0.6	**20** F 0329 5.1 / 0955 0.5 / 1557 4.8 / 2221 0.3
6 F 0332 4.9 / 0955 0.6 / 1551 4.7 / 2216 0.6	**21** SA 0419 5.0 / 1041 0.7 / 1646 4.7 / 2305 0.4
7 SA 0407 4.8 / 1036 0.7 / 1627 4.6 / 2255 0.6	**22** SU 0509 4.8 / 1119 0.8 / 1735 4.5 / 2355 0.5
8 SU 0445 4.8 / 1116 0.8 / 1705 4.5 / 2335 0.6	**23** M 0606 4.6 / 1205 1.0 / 1826 4.3
9 M 0529 4.6 / 1156 0.9 / 1755 4.3	**24** TU 0050 0.6 / 0656 4.4 / 1254 1.1 / ◗ 1916 4.2
10 TU 0031 0.7 / 0626 4.5 / 1250 1.0 / ◗ 1859 4.1	**25** W 0145 0.7 / 0801 4.2 / 1405 1.2 / 2015 4.0
11 W 0135 0.8 / 0746 4.3 / 1400 1.1 / 2020 4.1	**26** TH 0244 0.8 / 0905 4.1 / 1516 1.2 / 2141 3.9
12 TH 0245 0.8 / 0855 4.4 / 1515 1.1 / 2132 4.1	**27** F 0356 0.9 / 1015 4.1 / 1615 1.2 / 2240 4.0
13 F 0401 0.7 / 1008 4.6 / 1636 1.0 / 2237 4.3	**28** SA 0454 0.9 / 1116 4.2 / 1715 1.1 / 2332 4.2
14 SA 0511 0.6 / 1110 4.7 / 1736 0.9 / 2333 4.6	**29** SU 0556 0.8 / 1200 4.4 / 1806 1.0
15 SU 0611 0.5 / 1201 4.8 / 1831 0.7	**30** M 0015 4.3 / 0635 0.8 / 1238 4.5 / 1851 0.9
	31 TU 0049 4.5 / 0710 0.7 / 1311 4.6 / 1926 0.8

JUNE

Time m	Time m
1 W 0126 4.6 / 0745 0.7 / 1348 4.7 / ● 2005 0.7	**16** TH 0147 4.9 / 0812 0.6 / 1415 4.9 / 2040 0.4
2 TH 0201 4.8 / 0819 0.7 / 1422 4.8 / 2046 0.6	**17** F 0233 5.0 / 0855 0.6 / 1459 4.9 / 2126 0.3
3 F 0240 4.9 / 0900 0.6 / 1457 4.8 / 2125 0.5	**18** SA 0321 5.0 / 0938 0.7 / 1546 4.8 / 2210 0.3
4 SA 0317 4.9 / 0941 0.7 / 1537 4.7 / 2206 0.5	**19** SU 0405 5.0 / 1018 0.8 / 1627 4.8 / 2249 0.4
5 SU 0356 4.9 / 1020 0.7 / 1617 4.6 / 2250 0.5	**20** M 0451 4.9 / 1108 0.9 / 1708 4.7 / 2335 0.5
6 M 0435 4.8 / 1102 0.8 / 1659 4.5 / 2340 0.5	**21** TU 0535 4.7 / 1135 1.0 / 1755 4.5
7 TU 0520 4.7 / 1145 0.9 / 1747 4.4	**22** W 0015 0.6 / 0622 4.5 / 1226 1.1 / 1835 4.4
8 W 0030 0.5 / 0616 4.6 / 1234 1.0 / ◗ 1845 4.3	**23** TH 0106 0.7 / 0708 4.3 / 1316 1.1 / ◗ 1925 4.2
9 TH 0125 0.6 / 0721 4.5 / 1335 1.0 / ◗ 1956 4.3	**24** F 0155 0.8 / 0806 4.2 / 1426 1.2 / 2020 4.1
10 F 0225 0.6 / 0832 4.5 / 1445 1.0 / 2056 4.3	**25** SA 0256 0.9 / 0859 4.1 / 1525 1.2 / 2125 4.0
11 SA 0326 0.6 / 0936 4.5 / 1550 1.0 / 2201 4.4	**26** SU 0356 1.0 / 1015 4.0 / 1626 1.2 / 2238 4.0
12 SU 0436 0.7 / 1039 4.6 / 1700 0.9 / 2305 4.5	**27** M 0506 1.0 / 1116 4.2 / 1726 1.1 / 2336 4.2
13 M 0546 0.6 / 1138 4.7 / 1806 0.8	**28** TU 0550 0.9 / 1206 4.3 / 1816 1.0
14 TU 0002 4.7 / 0638 0.6 / 1236 4.8 / 1906 0.6	**29** W 0026 4.3 / 0635 0.9 / 1245 4.5 / 1906 0.9
15 W 0055 4.8 / 0726 0.6 / 1325 4.8 / ○ 1952 0.5	**30** TH 0106 4.4 / 0720 0.8 / 1328 4.6 / 1946 0.7

JULY

Time m	Time m
1 F 0145 4.7 / 0800 0.8 / 1406 4.7 / ● 2028 0.6	**16** SA 0227 5.0 / 0838 0.8 / 1447 4.9 / 2112 0.4
2 SA 0220 4.9 / 0840 0.7 / 1446 4.8 / 2109 0.5	**17** SU 0309 5.0 / 0921 0.8 / 1527 4.9 / 2152 0.4
3 SU 0301 5.0 / 0926 0.7 / 1526 4.8 / 2156 0.4	**18** M 0347 5.0 / 0955 0.9 / 1605 4.9 / 2229 0.4
4 M 0340 5.0 / 1006 0.7 / 1606 4.8 / 2239 0.4	**19** TU 0427 4.9 / 1036 0.9 / 1642 4.8 / 2306 0.5
5 TU 0422 5.0 / 1056 0.8 / 1646 4.7 / 2330 0.4	**20** W 0506 4.8 / 1108 0.9 / 1717 4.7 / 2342 0.6
6 W 0507 4.9 / 1136 0.8 / 1732 4.7	**21** TH 0541 4.6 / 1145 1.0 / 1758 4.6
7 TH 0015 0.4 / 0559 4.8 / 1225 0.9 / 1825 4.6	**22** F 0020 0.7 / 0622 4.5 / 1220 1.1 / 1835 4.4
8 F 0105 0.4 / 0656 4.7 / 1316 0.9 / ◗ 1926 4.5	**23** SA 0056 0.8 / 0706 4.3 / 1254 1.2 / ◗ 1927 4.2
9 SA 0155 0.5 / 0759 4.4 / 1345 1.0 / 2028 4.4	**24** SU 0135 1.0 / 0755 4.1 / 1355 1.3 / 2026 4.0
10 SU 0252 0.7 / 0906 4.4 / 1520 1.0 / 2132 4.4	**25** M 0255 1.1 / 0859 4.0 / 1546 1.3 / 2135 3.9
11 M 0354 0.8 / 1016 4.4 / 1646 1.0 / 2245 4.4	**26** TU 0415 1.2 / 1016 4.0 / 1648 1.2 / 2256 4.0
12 TU 0526 0.8 / 1128 4.4 / 1750 0.9 / 2351 4.5	**27** W 0516 1.1 / 1136 4.1 / 1745 1.1 / 2355 4.3
13 W 0620 0.8 / 1226 4.6 / 1849 0.7	**28** TH 0616 1.0 / 1226 4.4 / 1846 0.9
14 TH 0056 4.7 / 0715 0.8 / 1318 4.7 / 1941 0.5	**29** F 0046 4.5 / 0656 0.9 / 1306 4.6 / 1926 0.8
15 F 0140 4.9 / 0758 0.8 / 1405 4.8 / ○ 2030 0.4	**30** SA 0126 4.8 / 0740 0.8 / 1347 4.8 / ● 2008 0.6
	31 SU 0206 5.0 / 0826 0.7 / 1423 4.9 / 2055 0.4

AUGUST

Time m	Time m
1 M 0242 5.1 / 0905 0.7 / 1505 5.0 / 2136 0.3	**16** TU 0325 5.0 / 0932 0.9 / 1537 5.0 / 2206 0.5
2 TU 0322 5.2 / 0948 0.7 / 1545 5.0 / 2226 0.3	**17** W 0357 4.9 / 1006 0.9 / 1611 5.0 / 2235 0.6
3 W 0403 5.2 / 1036 0.7 / 1625 5.0 / 2308 0.2	**18** TH 0431 4.9 / 1040 0.9 / 1646 4.9 / 2311 0.7
4 TH 0446 5.1 / 1118 0.7 / 1709 4.9 / 2352 0.3	**19** F 0502 4.7 / 1110 0.9 / 1715 4.7 / 2336 0.8
5 F 0535 4.9 / 1202 0.8 / 1756 4.8	**20** SA 0535 4.6 / 1136 1.0 / 1748 4.6
6 SA 0038 0.4 / 0627 4.7 / 1250 0.9 / ◗ 1856 4.6	**21** SU 0006 0.9 / 0605 4.4 / 1205 1.1 / ◗ 1825 4.4
7 SU 0128 0.6 / 0736 4.5 / 1348 1.0 / 1958 4.5	**22** M 0035 1.0 / 0649 4.2 / 1255 1.2 / 1926 4.1
8 M 0226 0.8 / 0840 4.3 / 1455 1.1 / 2116 4.3	**23** TU 0136 1.2 / 0806 4.0 / 1355 1.4 / 2046 3.9
9 TU 0335 1.0 / 1000 4.2 / 1627 1.1 / 2236 4.3	**24** W 0326 1.4 / 0926 3.9 / 1605 1.4 / 2205 4.0
10 W 0506 1.1 / 1120 4.2 / 1746 0.9 / 2356 4.5	**25** TH 0445 1.3 / 1055 4.0 / 1716 1.2 / 2325 4.2
11 TH 0615 1.0 / 1221 4.5 / 1846 0.7	**26** F 0545 1.1 / 1158 4.3 / 1816 1.0
12 F 0044 4.7 / 0705 0.9 / 1316 4.7 / 1936 0.6	**27** SA 0019 4.6 / 0636 1.0 / 1246 4.6 / 1906 0.7
13 SA 0136 4.9 / 0745 0.9 / 1356 4.8 / ○ 2021 0.5	**28** SU 0101 4.9 / 0718 0.8 / 1321 4.8 / 1948 0.5
14 SU 0216 5.0 / 0825 0.9 / 1429 4.9 / 2055 0.5	**29** M 0137 5.1 / 0800 0.7 / 1359 5.0 / ● 2029 0.4
15 M 0248 5.0 / 0856 0.9 / 1506 4.9 / 2132 0.5	**30** TU 0216 5.3 / 0842 0.7 / 1438 5.1 / 2113 0.3
	31 W 0258 5.3 / 0927 0.6 / 1518 5.2 / 2200 0.2

Chart Datum: 2·56 metres below NAP Datum
HAT is 5·4 metres above Chart Datum

TIME ZONE -0100
(Dutch Standard Time)
Subtract 1 hour for UT
For Dutch Summer Time add ONE hour in **non-shaded areas**

NETHERLANDS – VLISSINGEN

LAT 51°27'N   LONG 3°36'E

TIMES AND HEIGHTS OF HIGH AND LOW WATERS

Dates in amber are **SPRINGS**
Dates in yellow are **NEAPS**

2011

SEPTEMBER

Day	Time m	Time m	Time m	Time m
1 TH	0340 5.3 / 1010 0.6 / 1600 5.2 / 2242 0.3	**16** F	0357 4.9 / 1010 0.9 / 1612 4.9 / 2237 0.8	
2 F	0425 5.2 / 1056 0.7 / 1643 5.1 / 2326 0.4	**17** SA	0427 4.8 / 1036 0.9 / 1639 4.8 / 2255 0.9	
3 SA	0510 5.0 / 1138 0.7 / 1731 5.0	**18** SU	0457 4.7 / 1059 0.9 / 1709 4.7 / 2325 0.9	
4 SU	0010 0.6 / 0601 4.7 / 1226 0.8 / ☽1825 4.7	**19** M	0528 4.6 / 1136 1.0 / 1746 4.6	
5 M	0058 0.8 / 0706 4.4 / 1322 1.0 / 1936 4.4	**20** TU	0000 1.0 / 0606 4.4 / 1220 1.1 / ☽1828 4.3	
6 TU	0155 1.0 / 0816 4.1 / 1433 1.1 / 2058 4.2	**21** W	0056 1.2 / 0705 4.1 / 1314 1.3 / 1956 4.0	
7 W	0320 1.2 / 0946 4.0 / 1610 1.1 / 2230 4.2	**22** TH	0205 1.4 / 0834 3.9 / 1514 1.4 / 2129 4.0	
8 TH	0506 1.3 / 1110 4.2 / 1735 0.9 / 2346 4.5	**23** F	0405 1.4 / 1010 4.0 / 1640 1.2 / 2256 4.3	
9 F	0610 1.1 / 1209 4.4 / 1835 0.7	**24** SA	0515 1.2 / 1126 4.2 / 1746 1.0 / 2349 4.6	
10 SA	0040 4.7 / 0656 1.0 / 1256 4.7 / 1926 0.6	**25** SU	0608 1.0 / 1211 4.6 / 1836 0.7	
11 SU	0126 4.9 / 0729 1.0 / 1336 4.8 / 1959 0.5	**26** M	0030 4.9 / 0652 0.9 / 1252 4.8 / 1926 0.5	
12 M	0156 4.9 / 0801 1.0 / 1405 4.9 / ○2032 0.6	**27** TU	0113 5.2 / 0735 0.7 / 1333 5.1 / ●2005 0.4	
13 TU	0225 5.0 / 0831 0.9 / 1437 5.0 / 2105 0.6	**28** W	0153 5.3 / 0818 0.6 / 1413 5.3 / 2050 0.3	
14 W	0258 5.0 / 0906 0.9 / 1510 5.0 / 2136 0.6	**29** TH	0236 5.4 / 0903 0.6 / 1456 5.3 / 2133 0.3	
15 TH	0327 5.0 / 0940 1.0 / 1539 5.0 / 2208 0.6	**30** F	0317 5.3 / 0948 0.8 / 1535 5.3 / 2217 0.4	

OCTOBER

Day	Time m	Day	Time m
1 SA	0401 5.2 / 1032 0.6 / 1623 5.2 / 2258 0.5	**16** SU	0400 4.8 / 1011 0.9 / 1613 4.9 / 2236 0.9
2 SU	0446 4.9 / 1115 0.7 / 1711 5.0 / 2342 0.7	**17** M	0427 4.7 / 1046 0.9 / 1642 4.8 / 2255 1.0
3 M	0538 4.7 / 1205 0.8 / 1806 4.7	**18** TU	0502 4.6 / 1116 0.9 / 1719 4.7 / 2335 1.1
4 TU	0029 1.0 / 0639 4.4 / 1306 0.9 / ☽1915 4.4	**19** W	0539 4.4 / 1200 1.0 / 1805 4.5
5 W	0129 1.2 / 0756 4.1 / 1415 1.1 / 2040 4.2	**20** TH	0036 1.2 / 0638 4.2 / 1305 1.1 / ☽1920 4.2
6 TH	0254 1.4 / 0925 4.0 / 1545 1.1 / 2205 4.2	**21** F	0140 1.4 / 0805 4.0 / 1430 1.2 / 2056 4.2
7 F	0440 1.4 / 1041 4.1 / 1721 0.9 / 2319 4.5	**22** SA	0315 1.4 / 0925 4.0 / 1555 1.1 / 2210 4.4
8 SA	0545 1.2 / 1145 4.4 / 1818 0.7	**23** SU	0430 1.3 / 1039 4.3 / 1705 0.9 / 2316 4.7
9 SU	0015 4.7 / 0636 1.1 / 1235 4.6 / 1854 0.7	**24** M	0530 1.1 / 1135 4.6 / 1806 0.7
10 M	0056 4.8 / 0710 1.0 / 1309 4.7 / 1936 0.7	**25** TU	0001 5.0 / 0626 0.9 / 1223 4.9 / 1855 0.6
11 TU	0127 4.9 / 0738 1.0 / 1339 4.8 / 2001 0.7	**26** W	0046 5.2 / 0710 0.8 / 1305 5.1 / ●1943 0.5
12 W	0159 4.9 / 0811 0.9 / 1409 4.9 / ○2036 0.7	**27** TH	0129 5.3 / 0756 0.6 / 1348 5.3 / 2026 0.4
13 TH	0227 4.9 / 0842 0.8 / 1440 5.0 / 2105 0.7	**28** F	0214 5.3 / 0842 0.6 / 1434 5.3 / 2110 0.4
14 F	0257 4.9 / 0916 0.8 / 1509 5.0 / 2136 0.7	**29** SA	0258 5.2 / 0928 0.5 / 1518 5.3 / 2152 0.5
15 SA	0327 4.9 / 0948 0.8 / 1541 5.0 / 2206 0.8	**30** SU	0343 5.1 / 1016 0.5 / 1605 5.2 / 2236 0.7
		31 M	0432 4.9 / 1100 0.6 / 1655 5.0 / 2320 0.9

NOVEMBER

Day	Time m	Day	Time m
1 TU	0525 4.7 / 1148 0.7 / 1748 4.8	**16** W	0445 4.6 / 1110 0.8 / 1706 4.7 / 2325 1.1
2 W	0006 1.1 / 0622 4.4 / 1246 0.8 / ●1900 4.5	**17** TH	0530 4.5 / 1156 0.9 / 1756 4.6
3 TH	0106 1.3 / 0726 4.2 / 1356 1.0 / 2010 4.3	**18** F	0012 1.2 / 0626 4.3 / 1250 0.9 / ☽1854 4.4
4 F	0215 1.4 / 0846 4.0 / 1509 1.0 / 2130 4.2	**19** SA	0116 1.3 / 0741 4.2 / 1400 1.0 / 2020 4.4
5 SA	0344 1.5 / 1005 4.1 / 1647 1.0 / 2246 4.3	**20** SU	0225 1.3 / 0852 4.2 / 1516 1.0 / 2129 4.5
6 SU	0505 1.3 / 1108 4.2 / 1746 0.9 / 2335 4.5	**21** M	0346 1.3 / 1000 4.3 / 1619 0.9 / 2236 4.6
7 M	0554 1.2 / 1156 4.4 / 1826 0.8	**22** TU	0444 1.1 / 1100 4.5 / 1730 0.8 / 2331 4.8
8 TU	0021 4.6 / 0636 1.1 / 1238 4.6 / 1859 0.8	**23** W	0552 1.0 / 1153 4.8 / 1828 0.7
9 W	0100 4.7 / 0705 1.0 / 1309 4.7 / 1929 0.8	**24** TH	0026 5.0 / 0651 0.8 / 1245 5.0 / 1918 0.6
10 TH	0128 4.8 / 0746 0.9 / 1341 4.8 / ○2002 0.8	**25** F	0110 5.1 / 0741 0.7 / 1330 5.1 / ●2006 0.6
11 F	0201 4.8 / 0816 0.8 / 1413 4.9 / 2036 0.8	**26** SA	0156 5.1 / 0826 0.5 / 1418 5.2 / 2048 0.6
12 SA	0235 4.9 / 0850 0.8 / 1445 5.0 / 2108 0.8	**27** SU	0246 5.1 / 0916 0.5 / 1505 5.2 / 2133 0.7
13 SU	0306 4.9 / 0925 0.8 / 1517 4.9 / 2141 0.9	**28** M	0333 5.0 / 1000 0.5 / 1553 5.1 / 2216 0.8
14 M	0337 4.8 / 1001 0.8 / 1553 4.9 / 2210 0.9	**29** TU	0421 4.9 / 1048 0.5 / 1642 5.0 / 2258 0.9
15 TU	0409 4.7 / 1036 0.8 / 1625 4.8 / 2246 1.0	**30** W	0509 4.7 / 1136 0.6 / 1735 4.8 / 2342 1.1

DECEMBER

Day	Time m	Day	Time m
1 TH	0557 4.6 / 1214 0.7 / 1829 4.6	**16** F	0519 4.6 / 1156 0.7 / 1746 4.8
2 F	0024 1.2 / 0652 4.4 / 1316 0.8 / ●1930 4.4	**17** SA	0002 1.1 / 0607 4.5 / 1245 0.7 / 1839 4.6
3 SA	0124 1.4 / 0756 4.2 / 1415 1.0 / 2035 4.2	**18** SU	0056 1.1 / 0710 4.4 / 1340 0.8 / ☽1945 4.5
4 SU	0234 1.4 / 0900 4.0 / 1525 1.1 / 2156 4.1	**19** M	0156 1.2 / 0816 4.3 / 1446 0.8 / 2055 4.5
5 M	0343 1.4 / 1016 4.0 / 1646 1.1 / 2256 4.2	**20** TU	0254 1.2 / 0926 4.4 / 1545 0.9 / 2159 4.5
6 TU	0455 1.3 / 1112 4.2 / 1735 1.1 / 2346 4.3	**21** W	0416 1.2 / 1027 4.4 / 1706 0.9 / 2306 4.6
7 W	0550 1.2 / 1159 4.3 / 1820 1.0	**22** TH	0531 1.0 / 1131 4.6 / 1806 0.8
8 TH	0026 4.4 / 0640 1.1 / 1239 4.4 / 1900 1.0	**23** F	0006 4.7 / 0632 0.9 / 1227 4.8 / 1900 0.7
9 F	0106 4.6 / 0716 1.0 / 1316 4.6 / 1936 0.9	**24** SA	0059 4.8 / 0725 0.7 / 1320 4.9 / ●1948 0.7
10 SA	0137 4.7 / 0756 0.9 / 1356 4.7 / ○2005 0.9	**25** SU	0149 4.9 / 0815 0.5 / 1411 5.1 / 2036 0.7
11 SU	0211 4.8 / 0830 0.8 / 1425 4.8 / 2046 0.9	**26** M	0237 5.0 / 0906 0.4 / 1457 5.1 / 2116 0.8
12 M	0245 4.8 / 0911 0.7 / 1500 4.9 / 2120 0.9	**27** TU	0322 5.0 / 0948 0.4 / 1542 5.1 / 2155 0.9
13 TU	0322 4.8 / 0948 0.7 / 1537 4.9 / 2155 0.9	**28** W	0406 4.9 / 1029 0.4 / 1629 5.0 / 2235 0.9
14 W	0359 4.8 / 1025 0.7 / 1615 4.9 / 2235 0.9	**29** TH	0449 4.9 / 1112 0.5 / 1712 4.9 / 2315 1.0
15 TH	0437 4.7 / 1116 0.7 / 1657 4.9 / 2321 1.0	**30** F	0531 4.7 / 1156 0.7 / 1758 4.7 / 2356 1.1
		31 SA	0616 4.6 / 1236 0.7 / 1841 4.5

Chart Datum: 2·56 metres below NAP Datum
HAT is 5·4 metres above Chart Datum

TIDES

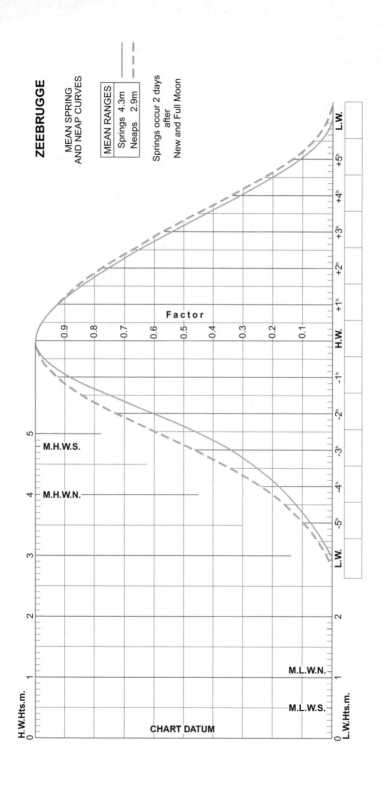

ZEEBRUGGE

MEAN SPRING
AND NEAP CURVES

MEAN RANGES	
Springs	4.3m
Neaps	2.9m

Springs occur 2 days
after
New and Full Moon

TIME ZONE −0100
(Belgian Standard Time)
Subtract 1 hour for UT
For Belgian Summer Time add
ONE hour in non-shaded areas

BELGIUM – ZEEBRUGGE
LAT 51°21′N   LONG 3°12′E
TIMES AND HEIGHTS OF HIGH AND LOW WATERS

Dates in amber are **SPRINGS**
Dates in yellow are **NEAPS**

2011

JANUARY

Day				
1 SA	0457 1.1	1105 4.3	1729 0.9	2343 4.3
2 SU	0603 0.9	1207 4.4	1826 0.9	
3 M	0037 4.4	0654 0.8	1257 4.4	1913 0.9
4 TU ●	0119 4.5	0737 0.7	1338 4.4	1953 0.9
5 W	0157 4.5	0816 0.6	1417 4.7	2030 0.9
6 TH	0234 4.6	0854 0.5	1454 4.7	2105 0.9
7 F	0310 4.6	0931 0.5	1532 4.7	2139 0.9
8 SA	0347 4.6	1008 0.5	1610 4.6	2214 0.9
9 SU	0424 4.6	1045 0.6	1647 4.5	2248 1.0
10 M	0459 4.5	1121 0.7	1725 4.4	2323 1.1
11 TU	0536 4.3	1158 0.8	1804 4.3	2359 1.2
12 W)	0617 4.2	1241 1.0	1850 4.1	
13 TH	0050 1.3	0708 4.0	1342 1.2	1948 4.0
14 F	0207 1.5	0815 3.8	1502 1.3	2101 3.8
15 SA	0339 1.5	0932 3.8	1608 1.3	2215 3.9
16 SU	0444 1.3	1043 3.9	1706 1.2	2319 4.0
17 M	0540 1.1	1142 4.1	1756 1.1	
18 TU	0010 4.2	0627 0.9	1229 4.4	1841 0.9
19 W ○	0052 4.4	0710 0.7	1311 4.6	1923 0.8
20 TH	0131 4.6	0751 0.5	1352 4.8	2006 0.7
21 F	0210 4.7	0834 0.4	1433 5.0	2049 0.6
22 SA	0251 4.8	0919 0.2	1516 5.1	2134 0.6
23 SU	0334 4.9	1004 0.2	1602 5.0	2220 0.6
24 M	0420 4.9	1051 0.2	1649 4.9	2307 0.7
25 TU	0507 4.8	1139 0.3	1740 4.7	2355 0.8
26 W (	0559 4.6	1230 0.5	1836 4.5	
27 TH	0048 1.0	0658 4.4	1329 0.7	1939 4.2
28 F	0154 1.2	0807 4.2	1441 1.0	2055 4.0
29 SA	0318 1.3	0931 4.0	1600 1.1	2221 3.9
30 SU	0443 1.4	1057 4.1	1717 1.1	2335 4.1
31 M	0554 1.1	1203 4.3	1819 1.0	

FEBRUARY

Day				
1 TU	0028 4.3	0645 0.8	1249 4.5	1904 1.0
2 W	0108 4.4	0726 0.6	1327 4.6	1940 1.0
3 TH ●	0142 4.5	0802 0.5	1401 4.6	2012 1.0
4 F	0215 4.6	0836 0.5	1435 4.7	2042 0.8
5 SA	0248 4.6	0909 0.4	1509 4.7	2114 0.8
6 SU	0321 4.7	0942 0.4	1543 4.7	2146 0.7
7 M	0354 4.7	1014 0.4	1615 4.7	2218 0.7
8 TU	0425 4.6	1045 0.6	1647 4.6	2250 0.8
9 W	0457 4.5	1116 0.7	1719 4.4	2323 0.9
10 TH	0533 4.4	1149 0.9	1757 4.3	2359 1.1
11 F)	0616 4.2	1231 1.1	1845 4.1	
12 SA	0051 1.3	0712 4.0	1336 1.3	1951 3.8
13 SU	0235 1.5	0803 3.8	1526 1.4	2126 3.7
14 M	0409 1.4	1005 3.8	1634 1.3	2245 3.8
15 TU	0511 1.2	1115 4.0	1730 1.1	2343 4.1
16 W	0604 0.9	1207 4.4	1820 0.9	
17 TH	0028 4.3	0649 0.6	1251 4.7	1904 0.8
18 F ○	0109 4.6	0733 0.4	1332 4.9	1948 0.6
19 SA	0149 4.8	0816 0.2	1414 5.1	2032 0.5
20 SU	0231 5.0	0900 0.1	1457 5.1	2116 0.4
21 M	0314 5.1	0945 0.0	1542 5.1	2201 0.4
22 TU	0359 5.0	1031 0.1	1628 4.9	2246 0.5
23 W	0445 4.9	1116 0.3	1715 4.7	2331 0.7
24 TH (	0535 4.7	1204 0.5	1807 4.4	
25 F	0021 0.9	0630 4.4	1259 0.8	1908 4.0
26 SA	0127 1.1	0740 4.1	1416 1.2	2028 3.8
27 SU	0257 1.2	0911 3.9	1539 1.3	2200 3.7
28 M	0421 1.2	1042 4.0	1658 1.2	2316 3.9

MARCH

Day				
1 TU	0533 1.0	1146 4.2	1802 1.1	
2 W	0008 4.2	0627 0.7	1232 4.4	1847 1.0
3 TH	0048 4.3	0707 0.6	1307 4.5	1920 0.9
4 F ●	0121 4.5	0741 0.5	1339 4.6	1949 0.8
5 SA	0152 4.6	0812 0.4	1411 4.7	2017 0.7
6 SU	0223 4.7	0841 0.4	1443 4.7	2047 0.6
7 M	0254 4.7	0912 0.4	1514 4.7	2118 0.6
8 TU	0324 4.7	0942 0.4	1543 4.7	2150 0.6
9 W	0354 4.7	1013 0.5	1613 4.6	2221 0.7
10 TH	0425 4.6	1043 0.6	1644 4.5	2253 0.8
11 F	0500 4.5	1115 0.8	1721 4.4	2329 0.9
12 SA	0541 4.4	1154 1.0	1805 4.1	
13 SU)	0014 1.1	0634 4.1	1249 1.2	1906 3.8
14 M	0130 1.4	0751 3.8	1443 1.4	2044 3.6
15 TU	0333 1.3	0932 3.8	1602 1.3	2211 3.7
16 W	0439 1.1	1045 4.1	1702 1.1	2313 4.0
17 TH	0535 0.8	1140 4.4	1755 0.9	2359 4.4
18 F	0624 0.5	1227 4.7	1842 0.7	
19 SA ○	0044 4.7	0710 0.3	1309 5.0	1927 0.5
20 SU	0127 4.9	0754 0.1	1352 5.1	2011 0.4
21 M	0209 5.1	0839 0.0	1436 5.1	2056 0.3
22 TU	0253 5.1	0924 0.0	1520 5.0	2140 0.3
23 W	0338 5.1	1008 0.2	1605 4.8	2225 0.4
24 TH	0424 4.9	1053 0.4	1652 4.6	2309 0.6
25 F	0513 4.6	1140 0.7	1742 4.3	2359 0.8
26 SA (	0607 4.3	1235 1.0	1841 3.9	
27 SU	0106 1.0	0729 4.0	1353 1.3	2000 3.7
28 M	0234 1.2	0846 3.8	1511 1.4	2127 3.6
29 TU	0348 1.1	1011 3.9	1624 1.3	2242 3.8
30 W	0458 0.9	1115 4.1	1730 1.2	2337 4.1
31 TH	0556 0.8	1202 4.3	1819 1.0	

APRIL

Day				
1 F	0019 4.3	0639 0.6	1240 4.5	1854 0.9
2 SA	0053 4.4	0713 0.5	1313 4.6	1923 0.8
3 SU ●	0125 4.5	0743 0.5	1345 4.6	1950 0.7
4 M	0156 4.6	0811 0.5	1415 4.7	2020 0.6
5 TU	0226 4.7	0841 0.5	1445 4.7	2052 0.6
6 W	0256 4.7	0912 0.5	1514 4.6	2124 0.6
7 TH	0326 4.6	0944 0.6	1544 4.5	2157 0.6
8 F	0358 4.6	1016 0.7	1617 4.5	2231 0.7
9 SA	0435 4.5	1050 0.8	1655 4.3	2308 0.8
10 SU	0518 4.4	1131 1.0	1742 4.1	2355 1.0
11 M)	0612 4.2	1228 1.2	1841 3.9	
12 TU	0112 1.1	0729 4.0	1407 1.3	2013 3.7
13 W	0258 1.1	0903 4.0	1529 1.2	2137 3.8
14 TH	0405 0.9	1014 4.2	1631 1.1	2240 4.1
15 F	0503 0.6	1112 4.5	1727 0.9	2333 4.4
16 SA	0557 0.4	1201 4.7	1818 0.7	
17 SU	0020 4.7	0646 0.3	1247 4.9	1906 0.5
18 M ○	0104 4.9	0732 0.2	1331 5.0	1951 0.4
19 TU	0149 5.0	0818 0.1	1415 5.0	2036 0.3
20 W	0234 5.0	0902 0.2	1500 4.9	2121 0.3
21 TH	0319 4.9	0947 0.4	1545 4.7	2205 0.4
22 F	0406 4.8	1031 0.6	1632 4.5	2251 0.6
23 SA	0455 4.6	1117 0.8	1721 4.2	2341 0.7
24 SU	0548 4.3	1210 1.1	1817 4.0	
25 M (	0047 0.9	0653 4.0	1322 1.3	1927 3.8
26 TU	0203 1.0	0810 3.9	1435 1.4	2044 3.7
27 W	0310 1.0	0926 3.9	1541 1.4	2156 3.8
28 TH	0413 0.9	1031 4.0	1644 1.2	2254 4.0
29 F	0513 0.8	1123 4.2	1739 1.1	2342 4.2
30 SA	0601 0.7	1206 4.4	1821 0.9	

Chart Datum: 0·19 metres below TAW Datum
HAT is 5·6 metres above Chart Datum

TIDES

TIME ZONE -0100 (Belgian Standard Time) Subtract 1 hour for UT For Belgian Summer Time add ONE hour in non-shaded areas	BELGIUM – ZEEBRUGGE LAT 51°21′N LONG 3°12′E TIMES AND HEIGHTS OF HIGH AND LOW WATERS	Dates in amber are SPRINGS Dates in yellow are NEAPS 2011

MAY

Day	Time	m	Time	m	Time	m	Time	m
1 SU	0021	4.3	0639	0.7	1243	4.5	1853	0.8
2 M	0057	4.4	0711	0.6	1317	4.5	1923	0.7
3 TU	0129	4.5	0740	0.6	1349	4.6	●1954	0.6
4 W	0200	4.5	0812	0.6	1419	4.5	2028	0.6
5 TH	0231	4.6	0845	0.6	1449	4.5	2102	0.6
6 F	0303	4.6	0919	0.7	1521	4.5	2138	0.6
7 SA	0339	4.6	0955	0.7	1557	4.4	2215	0.7
8 SU	0419	4.5	1034	0.8	1638	4.3	2257	0.7
9 M	0504	4.5	1119	1.0	1726	4.2	2349	0.8
10 TU ◑	0600	4.3	1217	1.1	1827	4.0		
11 W	0103	0.9	0713	4.2	1321	1.2	1947	3.9
12 TH	0224	0.8	0833	4.2	1454	1.1	2103	4.0
13 F	0330	0.7	0942	4.3	1558	1.0	2208	4.2
14 SA	0431	0.6	1043	4.6	1659	0.9	2305	4.4
15 SU	0529	0.5	1137	4.6	1755	0.7	2357	4.6
16 M	0623	0.4	1226	4.7	1847	0.6		
17 TU	0045	4.7	0712	0.4	1313	4.7	○1934	0.5
18 W	0132	4.8	0758	0.4	1358	4.7	2019	0.4
19 TH	0218	4.8	0842	0.5	1443	4.7	2104	0.4
20 F	0304	4.8	0926	0.6	1528	4.6	2149	0.4
21 SA	0350	4.7	1009	0.7	1613	4.4	2234	0.5
22 SU	0438	4.5	1054	0.9	1659	4.3	2324	0.6
23 M	0528	4.4	1143	1.1	1750	4.1		
24 TU	0021	0.7	0624	4.2	1242	1.2	◑1849	3.9
25 W	0126	0.9	0728	4.0	1350	1.3	1955	3.8
26 TH	0228	0.9	0834	3.9	1453	1.3	2101	3.8
27 F	0327	1.0	0938	3.9	1554	1.3	2203	3.9
28 SA	0424	0.9	1036	4.0	1651	1.2	2258	4.0
29 SU	0516	0.9	1127	4.2	1741	1.1	2345	4.1
30 M	0600	0.9	1211	4.3	1821	0.9		
31 TU	0026	4.3	0637	0.8	1249	4.4	1857	0.8

JUNE

Day	Time	m	Time	m	Time	m	Time	m
1 W	0102	4.4	0711	0.8	1323	4.4	●1931	0.7
2 TH	0136	4.4	0745	0.7	1355	4.4	2007	0.7
3 F	0210	4.5	0821	0.7	1428	4.5	2044	0.6
4 SA	0246	4.6	0859	0.7	1504	4.5	2123	0.6
5 SU	0325	4.6	0939	0.8	1543	4.5	2205	0.6
6 M	0407	4.6	1022	0.8	1626	4.4	2251	0.6
7 TU	0455	4.6	1110	0.9	1715	4.4	2344	0.6
8 W	0549	4.5	1206	1.0	1812	4.3		
9 TH	0046	0.6	0653	4.4	1311	1.0	1919	4.2
10 F	0152	0.6	0803	4.4	1419	1.0	2029	4.2
11 SA	0257	0.6	0910	4.3	1526	1.0	2136	4.2
12 SU	0402	0.6	1015	4.4	1633	1.0	2240	4.3
13 M	0505	0.6	1117	4.4	1736	0.8	2340	4.5
14 TU	0604	0.6	1212	4.5	1832	0.7		
15 W	0033	4.6	0656	0.6	1301	4.5	○1921	0.6
16 TH	0121	4.7	0742	0.7	1346	4.5	2006	0.5
17 F	0206	4.7	0825	0.7	1428	4.5	2049	0.5
18 SA	0250	4.7	0906	0.8	1510	4.5	2132	0.4
19 SU	0333	4.7	0947	0.8	1552	4.5	2216	0.4
20 M	0417	4.6	1029	0.9	1635	4.4	2300	0.5
21 TU	0502	4.5	1111	1.0	1720	4.3	2348	0.6
22 W	0549	4.4	1156	1.1	1807	4.2		
23 TH	0039	0.8	0640	4.2	1248	1.2	◑1900	4.0
24 F	0137	0.9	0737	4.0	1353	1.3	2000	3.9
25 SA	0236	1.0	0838	3.9	1501	1.3	2103	3.8
26 SU	0334	1.1	0941	3.9	1603	1.3	2206	3.9
27 M	0429	1.1	1041	4.0	1700	1.2	2305	4.0
28 TU	0520	1.0	1135	4.1	1749	1.1	2355	4.1
29 W	0604	1.0	1221	4.2	1832	0.9		
30 TH	0037	4.3	0644	0.9	1259	4.3	1910	0.8

JULY

Day	Time	m	Time	m	Time	m	Time	m
1 F	0115	4.4	0722	0.8	1334	4.4	●1948	0.7
2 SA	0152	4.6	0801	0.7	1410	4.5	2028	0.5
3 SU	0230	4.7	0842	0.7	1448	4.6	2110	0.4
4 M	0311	4.8	0925	0.7	1529	4.7	2154	0.4
5 TU	0354	4.8	1010	0.7	1613	4.7	2241	0.4
6 W	0441	4.8	1058	0.8	1700	4.6	2331	0.4
7 TH	0532	4.7	1148	0.8	1752	4.6		
8 F	0024	0.4	0628	4.6	1243	0.9	◑1851	4.5
9 SA	0122	0.6	0731	4.4	1345	1.0	1956	4.3
10 SU	0220	0.7	0839	4.3	1456	1.1	2108	4.2
11 M	0336	0.8	0951	4.2	1611	1.1	2222	4.2
12 TU	0446	0.9	1103	4.2	1723	1.0	2331	4.3
13 W	0551	0.9	1204	4.3	1823	0.8		
14 TH	0027	4.5	0644	0.9	1253	4.4	1911	0.7
15 F	0113	4.6	0729	0.9	1334	4.5	○1953	0.5
16 SA	0154	4.7	0808	0.9	1412	4.6	2033	0.5
17 SU	0233	4.7	0846	0.8	1450	4.6	2113	0.4
18 M	0313	4.7	0923	0.8	1529	4.7	2152	0.4
19 TU	0353	4.7	1001	0.8	1608	4.7	2231	0.4
20 W	0432	4.7	1037	0.8	1647	4.6	2310	0.5
21 TH	0512	4.5	1114	0.9	1725	4.5	2348	0.7
22 F	0551	4.4	1151	1.0	1804	4.3		
23 SA	0027	0.9	0633	4.2	1233	1.2	◑1850	4.1
24 SU	0118	1.1	0725	4.0	1334	1.4	1949	3.9
25 M	0235	1.3	0833	3.8	1512	1.4	2105	3.8
26 TU	0344	1.3	0950	3.8	1621	1.3	2221	3.8
27 W	0443	1.2	1057	3.9	1718	1.2	2323	4.0
28 TH	0534	1.1	1151	4.1	1806	1.0		
29 F	0011	4.3	0618	1.0	1233	4.3	1848	0.8
30 SA	0053	4.5	0700	0.8	1311	4.5	●1928	0.6
31 SU	0131	4.8	0741	0.7	1349	4.7	2010	0.4

AUGUST

Day	Time	m	Time	m	Time	m	Time	m
1 M	0211	4.9	0824	0.6	1429	4.9	2053	0.3
2 TU	0253	5.1	0909	0.6	1510	4.9	2138	0.2
3 W	0336	5.1	0954	0.6	1554	5.0	2224	0.2
4 TH	0422	5.0	1040	0.6	1640	4.9	2311	0.3
5 F	0510	4.9	1127	0.7	1729	4.8		
6 SA	0000	0.4	0602	4.7	1217	0.8	◑1823	4.6
7 SU	0054	0.6	0701	4.4	1316	1.0	1927	4.4
8 M	0159	0.9	0810	4.1	1431	1.2	2044	4.1
9 TU	0315	1.0	0932	4.0	1555	1.2	2210	4.1
10 W	0431	1.1	1053	4.0	1711	1.0	2325	4.3
11 TH	0540	1.1	1155	4.2	1812	0.8		
12 F	0019	4.5	0633	1.0	1240	4.4	1858	0.6
13 SA	0101	4.6	0714	0.9	1318	4.6	○1937	0.5
14 SU	0138	4.7	0749	0.9	1353	4.7	2014	0.4
15 M	0213	4.8	0823	0.8	1428	4.8	2049	0.4
16 TU	0249	4.8	0857	0.7	1504	4.8	2125	0.4
17 W	0326	4.8	0932	0.7	1539	4.8	2200	0.4
18 TH	0401	4.8	1005	0.7	1613	4.7	2232	0.5
19 F	0434	4.8	1038	0.8	1645	4.6	2304	0.7
20 SA	0507	4.5	1110	0.9	1719	4.5	2335	0.9
21 SU ◑	0541	4.6	1146	1.1	1758	4.3		
22 M	0013	1.1	0623	4.2	1230	1.3	1847	4.1
23 TU	0107	1.3	0721	3.9	1346	1.5	2001	3.9
24 W	0257	1.4	0854	1.4	1543	1.4	2137	3.8
25 TH	0408	1.3	1019	3.8	1645	1.2	2250	4.1
26 F	0505	1.2	1119	4.1	1737	1.0	2344	4.4
27 SA	0553	1.0	1206	4.4	1823	0.7		
28 SU	0028	4.7	0638	0.8	1246	4.7	1906	0.5
29 M	0109	5.0	0721	0.6	1326	4.9	●1949	0.3
30 TU	0150	5.2	0805	0.5	1407	5.1	2033	0.1
31 W	0232	5.3	0850	0.4	1449	5.2	2118	0.1

Chart Datum: 0·19 metres below TAW Datum
HAT is 5·6 metres above Chart Datum

TIME ZONE -0100
(Belgian Standard Time)
Subtract 1 hour for UT
For Belgian Summer Time add
ONE hour in **non-shaded areas**

Dates in amber are **SPRINGS**
Dates in yellow are **NEAPS**

2011

SEPTEMBER

Time	m	Time	m
1 0315	5.2	**16** 0330	4.8
0935	0.4	0936	0.6
TH 1533	5.2	F 1541	4.8
2204	0.1	2158	0.6
2 0400	5.1	**17** 0400	4.7
1020	0.5	1007	0.5
F 1619	5.1	SA 1612	4.7
2249	0.3	2228	0.7
3 0447	4.9	**18** 0430	4.8
1105	0.6	1039	0.8
SA 1706	4.9	SU 1644	4.6
2336	0.5	2259	0.9
4 0537	4.6	**19** 0503	4.5
1153	0.8	1113	1.0
SU 1759	4.6	M 1722	4.5
◐		2335	1.1
5 0028	0.8	**20** 0544	4.3
0633	4.3	1154	1.1
M 1251	1.0	TU 1810	4.3
1902	4.3	◑	
6 0135	1.1	**21** 0023	1.3
0746	4.0	0637	4.0
TU 1413	1.2	W 1256	1.4
2026	4.1	1918	4.0
7 0257	1.3	**22** 0158	1.5
0914	3.9	0804	3.8
W 1537	1.4	TH 1504	1.4
2157	4.1	2059	3.9
8 0414	1.3	**23** 0334	1.4
1036	4.0	0940	3.9
TH 1651	1.0	F 1611	1.2
2311	4.3	2217	4.2
9 0523	1.2	**24** 0434	1.2
1136	4.3	1045	4.1
F 1753	0.8	SA 1706	0.9
2359	4.5	2314	4.5
10 0616	1.0	**25** 0527	1.0
1221	4.5	1136	4.5
SA 1839	0.6	SU 1756	0.6
		2359	4.8
11 0043	4.7	**26** 0614	0.8
0655	0.9	1220	4.8
SU 1257	4.6	M 1842	0.4
1917	0.5		
12 0118	4.8	**27** 0045	5.1
0728	0.9	0700	0.6
M 1331	4.8	TU 1302	5.1
○ 1951	0.5	● 1927	0.2
13 0151	4.9	**28** 0127	5.3
0759	0.8	0745	0.4
TU 1404	4.8	W 1345	5.2
2023	0.4	2012	0.1
14 0225	4.9	**29** 0210	5.3
0831	0.7	0830	0.4
W 1438	4.9	TH 1428	5.3
2056	0.4	2057	0.1
15 0258	4.9	**30** 0254	5.2
0903	0.6	0915	0.4
TH 1510	4.9	F 1513	5.3
2127	0.5	2142	0.2

OCTOBER

Time	m	Time	m
1 0339	5.1	**16** 0331	4.7
1000	0.5	0942	0.7
SA 1559	5.1	SU 1544	4.7
2227	0.4	2159	0.8
2 0425	4.8	**17** 0401	4.6
1045	0.6	1015	0.8
SU 1647	4.9	M 1618	4.6
2313	0.7	2232	0.9
3 0514	4.5	**18** 0436	4.5
1133	0.8	1050	0.9
M 1739	4.6	TU 1658	4.6
		2310	1.1
4 0005	1.0	**19** 0518	4.3
0611	4.2	1133	1.0
TU 1233	1.0	W 1747	4.4
◑ 1844	4.3	2359	1.2
5 0114	1.3	**20** 0612	4.1
0723	4.0	1235	1.2
W 1355	1.1	TH 1854	4.2
2006	4.1	◑	
6 0234	1.4	**21** 0120	1.4
0848	3.9	0732	3.9
TH 1512	1.1	F 1424	1.2
2132	4.1	2026	4.1
7 0347	1.4	**22** 0258	1.4
1006	4.0	0903	4.0
F 1622	1.0	SA 1536	1.1
2244	4.3	2143	4.3
8 0455	1.2	**23** 0402	1.2
1108	4.2	1010	4.2
SA 1724	0.8	SU 1634	0.8
2337	4.5	2243	4.6
9 0551	1.1	**24** 0458	1.0
1155	4.5	1105	4.5
SU 1814	0.7	M 1728	0.6
		2335	4.8
10 0019	4.7	**25** 0550	0.8
0632	0.9	1154	4.8
M 1243	4.6	TU 1818	0.4
1853	0.6		
11 0055	4.8	**26** 0021	5.0
0706	0.8	0639	0.6
TU 1308	4.8	W 1240	5.0
1926	0.4	● 1906	0.3
12 0128	4.8	**27** 0106	5.1
0736	0.8	0726	0.5
W 1341	4.8	TH 1325	5.2
○ 1956	0.5	1952	0.2
13 0201	4.8	**28** 0151	5.2
0806	0.7	0812	0.4
TH 1413	4.8	F 1410	5.2
2027	0.4	2037	0.3
14 0232	4.8	**29** 0235	5.1
0837	0.6	0857	0.4
F 1444	4.8	SA 1455	5.2
2057	0.6	2122	0.4
15 0302	4.7	**30** 0321	4.9
0910	0.7	0942	0.5
SA 1514	4.8	SU 1542	5.0
2128	0.7	2207	0.6
		31 0407	4.7
		1028	0.6
		M 1631	4.8
		2253	0.8

NOVEMBER

Time	m	Time	m
1 0456	4.5	**16** 0418	4.5
1118	0.7	1037	0.8
TU 1723	4.6	W 1643	4.6
2344	1.1	2255	1.0
2 0550	4.4	**17** 0502	4.4
1217	0.9	1123	0.9
W 1825	4.3	TH 1733	4.5
◐		2346	1.2
3 0048	1.3	**18** 0556	4.3
0656	4.0	1224	1.0
TH 1330	1.0	F 1837	4.4
1938	4.2	◐	
4 0202	1.4	**19** 0056	1.3
0812	3.9	0706	4.1
F 1440	1.0	SA 1347	1.0
2055	4.1	1955	4.3
5 0311	1.4	**20** 0218	1.3
0925	4.0	0826	4.1
SA 1545	1.0	SU 1459	0.9
2204	4.2	2108	4.4
6 0417	1.3	**21** 0327	1.2
1030	4.2	0935	4.3
SU 1647	0.9	M 1601	0.7
2302	4.4	2212	4.5
7 0517	1.2	**22** 0429	1.0
1122	4.4	1036	4.5
M 1742	0.8	TU 1700	0.6
2349	4.5	2309	4.7
8 0605	1.0	**23** 0528	0.9
1206	4.5	1131	4.7
TU 1825	0.7	W 1756	0.5
		2359	4.8
9 0030	4.6	**24** 0622	0.7
0643	0.9	1221	4.9
W 1244	4.6	TH 1847	0.5
1900	0.7		
10 0106	4.7	**25** 0049	4.9
0714	0.8	0711	0.6
TH 1319	4.7	F 1309	5.0
○ 1930	0.7	● 1935	0.5
11 0139	4.7	**26** 0136	4.9
0744	0.8	0757	0.5
F 1351	4.7	SA 1356	5.0
2000	0.7	2020	0.5
12 0210	4.7	**27** 0221	4.8
0815	0.7	0843	0.5
SA 1421	4.7	SU 1442	5.0
2030	0.8	2104	0.6
13 0238	4.6	**28** 0305	4.8
0848	0.7	0928	0.5
SU 1452	4.7	M 1528	4.9
2103	0.8	2148	0.7
14 0308	4.6	**29** 0351	4.7
0922	0.7	1014	0.5
M 1524	4.7	TU 1615	4.8
2137	0.9	2233	0.9
15 0341	4.5	**30** 0437	4.6
0958	0.8	1102	0.6
TU 1601	4.7	W 1705	4.6
2213	0.9	2321	1.1

DECEMBER

Time	m	Time	m
1 0527	4.4	**16** 0450	4.5
1156	0.7	1116	0.7
TH 1800	4.4	F 1720	4.7
		2334	1.0
2 0016	1.2	**17** 0541	4.5
0623	4.2	1211	0.9
F 1257	0.8	SA 1817	4.6
◐ 1901	4.3		
3 0120	1.3	**18** 0033	1.1
0728	4.1	0641	4.4
SA 1401	1.0	SU 1315	0.8
2008	4.1	◐ 1923	4.4
4 0227	1.4	**19** 0141	1.3
0836	4.0	0750	4.3
SU 1504	1.0	M 1423	0.8
2115	4.1	2033	4.4
5 0333	1.4	**20** 0251	1.2
0942	4.0	0900	4.3
M 1605	1.0	TU 1530	0.8
2218	4.1	2141	4.4
6 0436	1.3	**21** 0401	1.1
1042	4.1	1008	4.3
TU 1703	1.0	W 1636	0.8
2314	4.3	2247	4.4
7 0533	1.2	**22** 0509	1.0
1135	4.2	1112	4.5
W 1753	1.0	TH 1738	0.7
2359	4.4	2347	4.5
8 0619	1.0	**23** 0609	0.8
1220	4.4	1210	4.6
TH 1833	0.9	F 1834	0.7
9 0043	4.5	**24** 0039	4.6
0655	0.9	0701	0.7
F 1258	4.4	SA 1300	4.7
1905	0.9	● 1922	0.7
10 0119	4.5	**25** 0125	4.6
0725	0.8	0747	0.6
SA 1332	4.5	SU 1346	4.8
○ 1936	0.9	2006	0.7
11 0150	4.5	**26** 0208	4.7
0757	0.8	0831	0.5
SU 1403	4.6	M 1430	4.9
2008	0.9	2048	0.8
12 0219	4.5	**27** 0250	4.7
0831	0.7	0914	0.4
M 1434	4.8	TU 1513	4.9
2043	0.8	2130	0.8
13 0251	4.6	**28** 0333	4.7
0907	0.6	0957	0.4
TU 1509	4.7	W 1557	4.8
2120	0.8	2212	0.8
14 0326	4.6	**29** 0416	4.7
0946	0.6	1042	0.4
W 1548	4.7	TH 1643	4.7
2200	0.9	2255	0.9
15 0405	4.6	**30** 0501	4.6
1028	0.6	1128	0.5
TH 1631	4.7	F 1730	4.6
2244	0.9	2339	1.0
		31 0548	4.6
		1218	0.7
		SA 1820	4.4

Chart Datum: 0·19 metres below TAW Datum
HAT is 5·6 metres above Chart Datum

TIDES

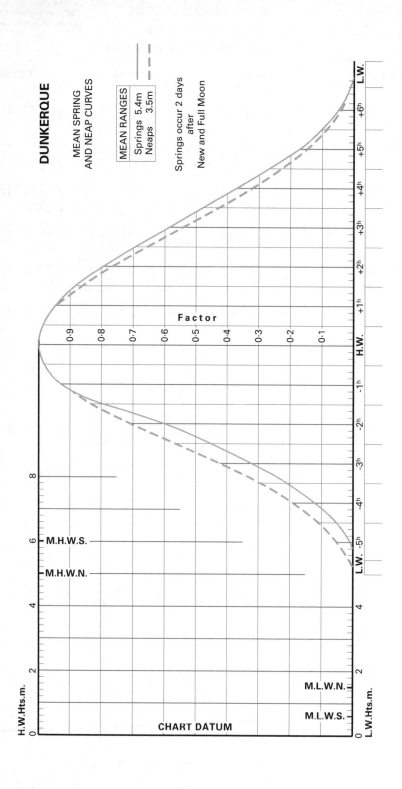

DUNKERQUE

MEAN SPRING
AND NEAP CURVES

MEAN RANGES	
Springs	5.4m
Neaps	3.5m

Springs occur 2 days
after
New and Full Moon

Factor

TIME ZONE -0100
(French Standard Time)
Subtract 1 hour for UT
For French Summer Time add
ONE hour in non-shaded areas

FRANCE – DUNKERQUE

LAT 51°03'N   LONG 2°22'E

TIMES AND HEIGHTS OF HIGH AND LOW WATERS

Dates in amber are **SPRINGS**
Dates in yellow are **NEAPS**

2011

JANUARY

Day	Time m	Time m	Day	Time m	Time m
1 SA	0433 1.4 / 1009 5.3	1711 1.2 / 2244 5.4	**16** SU	0401 1.7 / 0943 4.9	1638 1.5 / 2221 5.0
2 SU	0541 1.2 / 1109 5.5	1811 1.1 / 2339 5.5	**17** M	0507 1.5 / 1046 5.2	1738 1.3 / 2315 5.3
3 M	0635 1.0 / 1202 5.7	1859 1.0	**18** TU	0604 1.2 / 1137 5.5	1830 1.1
4 TU	0025 5.6 / 0721 0.8	1247 5.8 / ● 1942 0.9	**19** W	0001 5.6 / 0653 0.9	1220 5.8 / ○ 1916 0.8
5 W	0106 5.7 / 0803 0.7	1328 5.9 / 2020 0.9	**20** TH	0042 5.8 / 0738 0.6	1302 6.0 / 2000 0.7
6 TH	0144 5.8 / 0842 0.7	1407 5.9 / 2056 0.9	**21** F	0121 6.0 / 0823 0.4	1343 6.2 / 2044 0.6
7 F	0220 5.8 / 0918 0.7	1444 5.8 / 2131 1.0	**22** SA	0202 6.1 / 0907 0.3	1426 6.2 / 2127 0.6
8 SA	0253 5.8 / 0952 0.8	1518 5.7 / 2204 1.1	**23** SU	0243 6.1 / 0952 0.3	1509 6.2 / 2210 0.6
9 SU	0326 5.7 / 1025 0.9	1551 5.6 / 2236 1.2	**24** M	0325 6.1 / 1036 0.3	1554 6.0 / 2252 0.8
10 M	0400 5.6 / 1057 1.0	1627 5.6 / 2309 1.3	**25** TU	0410 6.0 / 1121 0.5	1643 5.8 / 2337 1.0
11 TU	0437 5.4 / 1131 1.2	1707 5.3 / 2345 1.4	**26** W	0500 5.8 / 1210 0.8	1737 5.6
12 W	0520 5.2 / 1211 1.3	◐ 1754 5.1	**27** TH	0029 1.2 / 0558 5.5	1308 1.1 / 1840 5.2
13 TH	0029 1.6 / 0612 5.0	1302 1.6 / 1852 4.9	**28** F	0133 1.5 / 0710 5.2	1417 1.3 / 1959 5.0
14 F	0127 1.8 / 0716 4.8	1413 1.7 / 1959 4.7	**29** SA	0250 1.6 / 0837 5.0	1537 1.5 / 2122 4.9
15 SA	0246 1.9 / 0828 4.7	1530 1.7 / 2113 4.8	**30** SU	0417 1.6 / 0958 5.1	1700 1.4 / 2235 5.0
			31 M	0532 1.3 / 1106 5.3	1801 1.2 / 2334 5.3

FEBRUARY

Day	Time m	Time m	Day	Time m	Time m
1 TU	0626 1.0 / 1159 5.5	1848 1.1	**16** W	0542 1.1 / 1118 5.5	1812 1.0 / 2342 5.5
2 W	0019 5.5 / 0710 0.8	1240 5.7 / 1927 0.9	**17** TH	0635 0.7 / 1203 5.8	1859 0.7
3 TH	0054 5.7 / 0748 0.7	1315 5.8 / ● 2003 0.9	**18** F	0023 5.8 / 0721 0.4	1244 6.1 / ○ 1942 0.6
4 F	0127 5.8 / 0824 0.6	1349 5.9 / 2035 0.8	**19** SA	0101 6.0 / 0805 0.2	1324 6.2 / 2024 0.5
5 SA	0158 5.8 / 0856 0.6	1421 5.9 / 2107 0.8	**20** SU	0140 6.2 / 0849 0.1	1405 6.3 / 2106 0.4
6 SU	0228 5.8 / 0927 0.6	1450 5.8 / 2137 0.8	**21** M	0220 6.3 / 0932 0.1	1447 6.2 / 2148 0.5
7 M	0257 5.8 / 0957 0.7	1518 5.7 / 2206 0.9	**22** TU	0302 6.2 / 1015 0.2	1531 6.1 / 2230 0.6
8 TU	0326 5.7 / 1025 0.8	1549 5.6 / 2235 1.0	**23** W	0346 6.1 / 1058 0.4	1617 5.9 / 2313 0.8
9 W	0357 5.6 / 1053 0.9	1621 5.4 / 2305 1.2	**24** TH	0435 5.9 / 1144 0.7	1709 5.5
10 TH	0429 5.4 / 1127 1.1	1657 5.2 / 2342 1.4	**25** F	0002 1.1 / 0532 5.5	1238 1.1 / 1811 5.1
11 F	0509 5.2 / 1209 1.4	◐ 1749 4.9	**26** SA	0103 1.4 / 0645 5.1	1349 1.5 / 1931 4.7
12 SA	0030 1.6 / 0612 4.9	1308 1.7 / 1904 4.7	**27** SU	0224 1.7 / 0817 4.8	1517 1.7 / 2102 4.6
13 SU	0140 1.8 / 0737 4.7	1433 1.8 / 2027 4.6	**28** M	0400 1.6 / 0946 4.9	1644 1.5 / 2221 4.8
14 M	0312 1.8 / 0904 4.7	1600 1.7 / 2150 4.8			
15 TU	0435 1.6 / 1021 5.0	1714 1.3 / 2254 5.2			

MARCH

Day	Time m	Time m	Day	Time m	Time m
1 TU	0516 1.3 / 1054 5.1	1744 1.3 / 2319 5.1	**16** W	0403 1.4 / 0954 5.1	1646 1.3 / 2228 5.1
2 W	0609 1.0 / 1144 5.4	1829 1.1	**17** TH	0516 1.0 / 1054 5.5	1747 1.0 / 2317 5.5
3 TH	0000 5.4 / 0651 0.8	1221 5.6 / 1906 0.9	**18** F	0612 0.6 / 1140 5.9	1835 0.7 / 2358 5.9
4 F	0033 5.6 / 0727 0.7	1254 5.7 / ● 1939 0.8	**19** SA	0659 0.3 / 1221 6.1	1919 0.5 ○
5 SA	0104 5.7 / 0758 0.6	1325 5.8 / 2009 0.8	**20** SU	0036 6.1 / 0743 0.2	1300 6.2 / 2001 0.4
6 SU	0133 5.8 / 0828 0.6	1354 5.9 / 2039 0.7	**21** M	0115 6.2 / 0826 0.1	1341 6.3 / 2043 0.4
7 M	0200 5.9 / 0858 0.6	1420 5.8 / 2109 0.7	**22** TU	0156 6.3 / 0909 0.1	1424 6.2 / 2126 0.4
8 TU	0226 5.9 / 0927 0.6	1446 5.8 / 2137 0.8	**23** W	0240 6.3 / 0952 0.2	1509 6.1 / 2208 0.5
9 W	0254 5.8 / 0954 0.7	1514 5.7 / 2205 0.9	**24** TH	0326 6.1 / 1035 0.5	1555 5.8 / 2252 0.7
10 TH	0322 5.7 / 1022 0.9	1541 5.5 / 2235 1.0	**25** F	0416 5.8 / 1121 0.9	1647 5.5 / 2340 1.0
11 F	0350 5.6 / 1054 1.0	1611 5.3 / ◐ 2310 1.2	**26** SA	0514 5.4 / 1213 1.3	1747 5.0
12 SA	0425 5.3 / 1134 1.3	1654 5.0 / 2357 1.4	**27** SU	0039 1.4 / 0624 5.0	1322 1.6 / 1904 4.7
13 SU	0520 5.0 / 1230 1.6	1817 4.7 ◐	**28** M	0159 1.6 / 0755 4.7	1450 1.8 / 2035 4.6
14 M	0102 1.7 / 0659 4.7	1351 1.7 / 1950 4.6	**29** TU	0332 1.6 / 0921 4.8	1614 1.6 / 2151 4.8
15 TU	0232 1.7 / 0830 4.7	1526 1.6 / 2119 4.7	**30** W	0447 1.5 / 1026 5.0	1715 1.4 / 2247 5.0
			31 TH	0541 1.0 / 1115 5.3	1801 1.1 / 2329 5.3

APRIL

Day	Time m	Time m	Day	Time m	Time m
1 F	0623 0.8 / 1152 5.5	1838 1.0	**16** SA	0544 0.6 / 1112 5.8	1808 0.7 / 2329 5.8
2 SA	0004 5.5 / 0657 0.7	1226 5.7 / 1908 0.9	**17** SU	0633 0.4 / 1155 6.1	1854 0.6
3 SU	0036 5.7 / 0727 0.7	1256 5.7 / ● 1938 0.8	**18** M	0010 6.1 / 0719 0.2	1236 6.2 / ○ 1938 0.5
4 M	0105 5.7 / 0757 0.6	1324 5.8 / 2009 0.7	**19** TU	0052 6.2 / 0803 0.2	1318 6.2 / 2022 0.4
5 TU	0131 5.8 / 0828 0.6	1349 5.8 / 2041 0.7	**20** W	0136 6.3 / 0847 0.3	1403 6.1 / 2105 0.4
6 W	0158 5.8 / 0859 0.7	1417 5.8 / 2112 0.7	**21** TH	0223 6.2 / 0931 0.4	1450 6.0 / 2150 0.5
7 TH	0227 5.8 / 0928 0.8	1446 5.7 / 2142 0.8	**22** F	0312 6.0 / 1015 0.7	1539 5.7 / 2235 0.7
8 F	0257 5.7 / 0958 0.9	1515 5.5 / 2214 0.9	**23** SA	0404 5.8 / 1101 1.0	1630 5.4 / 2323 1.0
9 SA	0328 5.6 / 1032 1.0	1549 5.3 / 2252 1.1	**24** SU	0459 5.4 / 1151 1.3	1725 5.1
10 SU	0408 5.3 / 1115 1.3	1635 5.1 / 2340 1.3	**25** M	0018 1.2 / 0602 5.0	1252 1.6 / ◐ 1832 4.8
11 M	0508 5.1 / 1211 1.5	◐ 1757 4.8	**26** TU	0128 1.5 / 0721 4.8	1409 1.7 / 1954 4.6
12 TU	0044 1.4 / 0638 4.9	1327 1.6 / 1920 4.7	**27** W	0249 1.5 / 0841 4.8	1526 1.7 / 2107 4.7
13 W	0206 1.5 / 0800 4.9	1455 1.5 / 2043 4.8	**28** TH	0401 1.3 / 0944 5.0	1630 1.5 / 2203 5.0
14 TH	0332 1.3 / 0922 5.2	1614 1.3 / 2155 5.2	**29** F	0458 1.1 / 1034 5.2	1720 1.2 / 2249 5.2
15 F	0445 0.9 / 1024 5.5	1717 0.9 / 2246 5.5	**30** SA	0543 1.0 / 1115 5.4	1800 1.1 / 2329 5.4

Chart Datum: 2·69 metres below IGN Datum
HAT is 6·4 metres above Chart Datum

TIDES

<table>
<tr><td>

TIME ZONE -0100
(French Standard Time)
Subtract 1 hour for UT
For French Summer Time add
ONE hour in **non-shaded areas**

</td><td>

FRANCE – DUNKERQUE
LAT 51°03′N LONG 2°22′E
TIMES AND HEIGHTS OF HIGH AND LOW WATERS

</td><td>

Dates in amber are **SPRINGS**
Dates in yellow are **NEAPS**
2011

</td></tr>
</table>

MAY

Time m	Time m
1 0620 0.9 / 1153 5.5 / SU 1834 1.0	**16** 0608 0.5 / 1132 5.9 / M 1832 0.7 / 2349 6.0
2 0005 5.5 / 0652 0.8 / M 1225 5.6 / 1907 0.9	**17** 0657 0.5 / 1216 6.1 / TU 1919 0.6 ○
3 0036 5.6 / 0725 0.8 / TU 1254 5.7 / ● 1941 0.8	**18** 0035 6.1 / 0744 0.5 / W 1302 6.0 / 2005 0.5
4 0104 5.7 / 0759 0.8 / W 1322 5.7 / 2016 0.7	**19** 0123 6.1 / 0829 0.5 / TH 1349 5.9 / 2051 0.5
5 0135 5.8 / 0834 0.8 / TH 1354 5.7 / 2051 0.7	**20** 0213 6.1 / 0914 0.6 / F 1438 5.7 / 2136 0.5
6 0209 5.8 / 0908 0.8 / F 1430 5.7 / 2126 0.8	**21** 0304 5.9 / 0958 0.8 / SA 1526 5.3 / 2220 0.7
7 0245 5.7 / 0944 0.9 / SA 1506 5.6 / 2203 0.8	**22** 0353 5.7 / 1042 1.0 / SU 1612 5.5 / 2305 0.9
8 0324 5.6 / 1022 1.0 / SU 1548 5.4 / 2245 0.9	**23** 0442 5.5 / 1127 1.3 / M 1700 5.2 / 2353 1.1
9 0412 5.4 / 1107 1.2 / M 1641 5.2 / 2334 1.1	**24** 0533 5.2 / 1217 1.5 / TU 1752 5.0 ◗
10 0513 5.2 / 1202 1.3 / TU 1745 5.0 ◖	**25** 0049 1.3 / 0633 4.9 / W 1317 1.6 / 1855 4.8
11 0034 1.2 / 0620 5.1 / W 1309 1.4 / 1852 4.9	**26** 0154 1.4 / 0744 4.8 / TH 1425 1.7 / 2007 4.8
12 0145 1.2 / 0730 5.1 / TH 1426 1.4 / 2005 5.0	**27** 0300 1.4 / 0850 4.9 / F 1530 1.6 / 2111 4.9
13 0303 1.1 / 0846 5.3 / F 1540 1.2 / 2117 5.3	**28** 0401 1.3 / 0945 5.0 / SA 1627 1.4 / 2205 5.0
14 0413 1.0 / 0952 5.5 / SA 1644 1.0 / 2214 5.5	**29** 0453 1.2 / 1034 5.2 / SU 1716 1.3 / 2251 5.2
15 0514 0.6 / 1045 5.7 / SU 1741 0.8 / 2303 5.8	**30** 0539 1.1 / 1117 5.3 / M 1759 1.1 / 2333 5.4
	31 0618 1.0 / 1155 5.4 / TU 1838 1.0

JUNE

Time m	Time m
1 0009 5.5 / 0657 0.9 / W 1229 5.5 / ● 1916 0.9	**16** 0030 5.9 / 0732 0.7 / TH 1255 5.8 / 1955 0.6
2 0043 5.6 / 0735 0.9 / TH 1302 5.6 / 1955 0.8	**17** 0119 6.0 / 0817 0.7 / F 1342 5.8 / 2040 0.5
3 0118 5.7 / 0814 0.8 / F 1339 5.7 / 2035 0.7	**18** 0206 6.0 / 0900 0.8 / SA 1427 5.8 / 2123 0.5
4 0157 5.8 / 0854 0.8 / SA 1419 5.7 / 2116 0.7	**19** 0253 5.9 / 0941 0.9 / SU 1509 5.7 / 2205 0.6
5 0239 5.8 / 0935 0.9 / SU 1502 5.7 / 2157 0.7	**20** 0336 5.7 / 1021 1.0 / M 1550 5.6 / 2244 0.8
6 0323 5.7 / 1017 0.9 / M 1546 5.5 / 2241 0.7	**21** 0417 5.6 / 1100 1.1 / TU 1629 5.4 / 2324 0.9
7 0411 5.6 / 1101 1.0 / TU 1633 5.4 / 2328 0.8	**22** 0458 5.4 / 1140 1.3 / W 1711 5.3
8 0502 5.5 / 1151 1.1 / W 1725 5.3	**23** 0007 1.1 / 0542 5.2 / TH 1225 1.4 / ◗ 1758 5.1
9 0021 0.9 / 0559 5.4 / TH 1248 1.2 / ◗ 1824 5.3	**24** 0056 1.3 / 0634 5.0 / F 1320 1.6 / 1855 4.9
10 0124 0.9 / 0701 5.3 / F 1356 1.3 / 1930 5.2	**25** 0156 1.4 / 0736 4.8 / SA 1426 1.7 / 2001 4.8
11 0234 0.9 / 0811 5.3 / SA 1507 1.2 / 2041 5.3	**26** 0300 1.5 / 0843 4.8 / SU 1531 1.6 / 2109 4.8
12 0342 0.9 / 0922 5.4 / SU 1615 1.1 / 2148 5.5	**27** 0402 1.4 / 0945 4.9 / M 1631 1.5 / 2210 5.0
13 0448 0.8 / 1023 5.5 / M 1718 1.0 / 2247 5.6	**28** 0458 1.3 / 1040 5.1 / TU 1725 1.3 / 2302 5.2
14 0549 0.8 / 1118 5.6 / TU 1816 0.8 / 2340 5.8	**29** 0549 1.2 / 1127 5.3 / W 1812 1.1 / 2346 5.4
15 0643 0.7 / 1208 5.7 / W 1908 0.7 ○	**30** 0634 1.1 / 1208 5.5 / TH 1856 0.9

JULY

Time m	Time m
1 0026 5.6 / 0716 0.9 / F 1246 5.6 / ● 1938 0.8	**16** 0113 5.9 / 0804 0.8 / SA 1331 5.8 / 2027 0.5
2 0104 5.7 / 0758 0.8 / SA 1325 5.8 / 2021 0.6	**17** 0154 5.9 / 0844 0.8 / SU 1409 5.8 / 2106 0.5
3 0144 5.9 / 0841 0.8 / SU 1405 5.8 / 2104 0.5	**18** 0234 5.9 / 0920 0.8 / M 1446 5.8 / 2143 0.6
4 0226 5.9 / 0923 0.7 / M 1446 5.8 / 2147 0.5	**19** 0311 5.8 / 0955 0.9 / TU 1520 5.7 / 2218 0.7
5 0309 5.9 / 1006 0.8 / TU 1528 5.8 / 2230 0.5	**20** 0345 5.7 / 1029 1.0 / W 1554 5.6 / 2251 0.8
6 0354 5.9 / 1048 0.8 / W 1612 5.7 / 2315 0.5	**21** 0419 5.5 / 1100 1.1 / TH 1630 5.5 / 2325 1.0
7 0442 5.8 / 1133 1.0 / TH 1700 5.6	**22** 0457 5.4 / 1138 1.3 / F 1711 5.3
8 0003 0.7 / 0534 5.6 / F 1225 1.1 / ◗ 1755 5.5	**23** 0003 1.2 / 0541 5.1 / SA 1220 1.5 / ◗ 1800 5.1
9 0100 0.8 / 0633 5.4 / SA 1327 1.2 / 1859 5.4	**24** 0050 1.4 / 0634 4.9 / SU 1315 1.7 / 1900 4.9
10 0206 1.0 / 0742 5.3 / SU 1438 1.3 / 2015 5.3	**25** 0155 1.6 / 0739 4.7 / M 1429 1.8 / 2011 4.7
11 0317 1.1 / 0859 5.2 / M 1552 1.3 / 2133 5.3	**26** 0310 1.7 / 0853 4.7 / TU 1544 1.7 / 2127 4.8
12 0430 1.1 / 1011 5.3 / TU 1706 1.2 / 2241 5.4	**27** 0419 1.6 / 1004 4.9 / W 1652 1.5 / 2233 5.0
13 0539 1.0 / 1113 5.4 / W 1809 0.9 / 2339 5.6	**28** 0522 1.4 / 1101 5.2 / TH 1750 1.2 / 2325 5.3
14 0635 0.9 / 1206 5.6 / TH 1900 0.7	**29** 0614 1.1 / 1148 5.4 / F 1838 0.9
15 0029 5.8 / 0722 0.8 / F 1251 5.7 / ○ 1945 0.6	**30** 0008 5.6 / 0659 0.9 / SA 1228 5.7 / ● 1922 0.7
	31 0047 5.9 / 0741 0.8 / SU 1305 5.9 / 2004 0.5

AUGUST

Time m	Time m
1 0125 6.0 / 0823 0.7 / M 1343 6.0 / 2047 0.3	**16** 0208 5.9 / 0854 0.8 / TU 1417 5.9 / 2116 0.6
2 0205 6.1 / 0905 0.6 / TU 1422 6.0 / 2130 0.3	**17** 0239 5.9 / 0926 0.9 / W 1447 5.9 / 2147 0.7
3 0247 6.1 / 0947 0.6 / W 1503 6.0 / 2212 0.3	**18** 0309 5.8 / 0957 0.9 / TH 1517 5.8 / 2217 0.8
4 0330 6.1 / 1028 0.7 / TH 1545 6.0 / 2256 0.4	**19** 0339 5.7 / 1027 1.0 / F 1549 5.6 / 2246 1.0
5 0416 5.9 / 1112 0.8 / F 1634 5.9 / 2342 0.6	**20** 0412 5.5 / 1057 1.2 / SA 1623 5.4 / 2318 1.2
6 0508 5.7 / 1200 1.1 / SA 1729 5.7 ◗	**21** 0449 5.2 / 1132 1.4 / SU 1704 5.2 / ◗ 2357 1.5
7 0035 0.9 / 0607 5.4 / SU 1300 1.3 / 1835 5.4	**22** 0540 5.0 / 1218 1.7 / M 1806 4.9
8 0141 1.2 / 0718 5.1 / M 1415 1.5 / 1957 5.1	**23** 0052 1.7 / 0650 4.7 / TU 1324 1.9 / 1925 4.7
9 0258 1.4 / 0844 5.0 / TU 1538 1.5 / 2125 5.1	**24** 0213 1.9 / 0808 4.7 / W 1454 1.9 / 2047 4.7
10 0422 1.4 / 1004 5.1 / W 1700 1.3 / 2238 5.3	**25** 0340 1.9 / 0929 4.8 / TH 1618 1.6 / 2203 5.0
11 0533 1.2 / 1108 5.3 / TH 1801 1.0 / 2335 5.6	**26** 0454 1.5 / 1035 5.1 / F 1725 1.2 / 2301 5.4
12 0625 1.0 / 1159 5.5 / F 1849 0.7	**27** 0551 1.2 / 1124 5.5 / SA 1816 0.8 / 2346 5.7
13 0021 5.7 / 0708 0.9 / SA 1237 5.7 / ○ 1930 0.6	**28** 0637 0.9 / 1204 5.8 / SU 1900 0.6
14 0058 5.9 / 0746 0.9 / SU 1311 5.8 / 2008 0.5	**29** 0024 6.0 / 0719 0.7 / M 1240 6.0 / ● 1943 0.4
15 0133 5.9 / 0821 0.8 / M 1344 5.9 / 2043 0.5	**30** 0101 6.2 / 0800 0.6 / TU 1316 6.2 / 2025 0.2
	31 0140 6.3 / 0842 0.5 / W 1355 6.2 / 2107 0.2

Chart Datum: 2·69 metres below IGN Datum
HAT is 6·4 metres above Chart Datum

TIME ZONE -0100
(French Standard Time)
Subtract 1 hour for UT
For French Summer Time add ONE hour in **non-shaded areas**

FRANCE – DUNKERQUE

LAT 51°03′N LONG 2°22′E

TIMES AND HEIGHTS OF HIGH AND LOW WATERS

Dates in amber are **SPRINGS**
Dates in yellow are **NEAPS**

2011

SEPTEMBER

	Time m		Time m
1 TH	0221 6.3 / 0923 0.6 / 1436 6.3 / 2150 0.3	**16** F	0233 5.9 / 0926 0.9 / 1442 5.9 / 2143 0.9
2 F	0304 6.2 / 1006 0.6 / 1520 6.2 / 2233 0.4	**17** SA	0301 5.8 / 0954 1.0 / 1511 5.7 / 2211 1.0
3 SA	0351 6.0 / 1049 0.8 / 1610 6.0 / 2318 0.7	**18** SU	0331 5.6 / 1023 1.2 / 1542 5.5 / 2241 1.2
4 SU	0443 5.7 / 1137 1.1 / 1707 5.7	**19** M	0401 5.3 / 1057 1.4 / 1614 5.3 / 2319 1.5
5 M	0011 1.1 / 0544 5.3 / 1237 1.4 / 1817 5.3	**20** TU	0440 5.0 / 1141 1.6 / 1705 5.0
6 TU	0120 1.4 / 0658 5.0 / 1356 1.6 / 1944 5.0	**21** W	0012 1.7 / 0729 4.7 / 1243 1.8 / 1846 4.7
7 W	0244 1.6 / 0829 4.8 / 1528 1.6 / 2116 5.0	**22** TH	0126 1.9 / 0729 4.6 / 1408 1.9 / 2009 4.7
8 TH	0412 1.6 / 0952 5.0 / 1648 1.3 / 2228 5.3	**23** F	0259 1.9 / 0851 4.8 / 1540 1.6 / 2130 5.0
9 F	0519 1.3 / 1055 5.3 / 1746 1.0 / 2322 5.5	**24** SA	0421 1.5 / 1003 5.1 / 1653 1.2 / 2232 5.5
10 SA	0608 1.1 / 1141 5.5 / 1831 0.8	**25** SU	0522 1.2 / 1054 5.5 / 1749 0.8 / 2318 5.8
11 SU	0003 5.7 / 0648 1.0 / 1215 5.7 / 1909 0.7	**26** M	0611 0.9 / 1135 5.9 / 1835 0.5 / 2357 6.1
12 M	0036 5.9 / 0722 0.9 / 1246 5.8 / ○ 1943 0.6	**27** TU	0654 0.7 / 1211 6.1 / ● 1918 0.3
13 TU	0107 5.9 / 0754 0.9 / 1317 5.9 / 2014 0.6	**28** W	0034 6.3 / 0736 0.6 / 1249 6.3 / 2000 0.2
14 W	0138 5.9 / 0824 0.9 / 1346 5.9 / 2045 0.7	**29** TH	0113 6.4 / 0817 0.5 / 1329 6.4 / 2043 0.2
15 TH	0206 5.9 / 0855 0.9 / 1413 5.9 / 2115 0.8	**30** F	0156 6.3 / 0900 0.5 / 1413 6.4 / 2126 0.4

OCTOBER

	Time m		Time m
1 SA	0240 6.2 / 0944 0.6 / 1500 6.3 / 2211 0.6	**16** SU	0231 5.8 / 0928 1.0 / 1444 5.8 / 2144 1.1
2 SU	0328 6.0 / 1029 0.8 / 1552 6.0 / 2257 0.9	**17** M	0302 5.7 / 0959 1.1 / 1516 5.6 / 2216 1.3
3 M	0421 5.7 / 1118 1.1 / 1651 5.7 / 2350 1.3	**18** TU	0334 5.4 / 1035 1.3 / 1551 5.4 / 2256 1.5
4 TU	0522 5.3 / 1218 1.4 / 1800 5.3	**19** W	0413 5.2 / 1120 1.5 / 1642 5.1 / 2347 1.7
5 W	0058 1.6 / 0635 4.9 / 1337 1.6 / 1926 5.0	**20** TH	0524 4.9 / 1218 1.6 / 1814 4.9
6 TH	0223 1.8 / 0806 4.8 / 1506 1.6 / 2055 5.0	**21** F	0055 1.8 / 0651 4.8 / 1334 1.7 / 1931 4.9
7 F	0347 1.7 / 0925 4.9 / 1623 1.3 / 2203 5.2	**22** SA	0218 1.8 / 0808 4.9 / 1501 1.5 / 2049 5.1
8 SA	0453 1.5 / 1025 5.2 / 1721 1.1 / 2255 5.5	**23** SU	0342 1.6 / 0922 5.2 / 1616 1.2 / 2155 5.5
9 SU	0542 1.2 / 1110 5.5 / 1805 0.9 / 2334 5.7	**24** M	0447 1.2 / 1018 5.6 / 1716 0.8 / 2246 5.9
10 M	0621 1.1 / 1146 5.7 / 1842 0.8	**25** TU	0541 1.0 / 1102 5.9 / 1807 0.5 / 2328 6.1
11 TU	0008 5.8 / 0654 1.0 / 1218 5.8 / 1914 0.8	**26** W	0627 0.8 / 1143 6.2 / ● 1853 0.4
12 W	0039 5.9 / 0724 0.9 / 1249 5.9 / ○ 1943 0.8	**27** TH	0009 6.3 / 0712 0.6 / 1225 6.3 / 1937 0.4
13 TH	0108 5.9 / 0755 0.9 / 1317 5.9 / 2014 0.8	**28** F	0051 6.3 / 0756 0.6 / 1309 6.4 / 2022 0.4
14 F	0134 5.9 / 0826 0.9 / 1344 5.9 / 2045 0.9	**29** SA	0135 6.3 / 0841 0.6 / 1356 6.4 / 2106 0.5
15 SA	0201 5.9 / 0858 0.9 / 1413 5.9 / 2115 1.0	**30** SU	0222 6.2 / 0926 0.6 / 1446 6.2 / 2152 0.7
		31 M	0312 5.9 / 1013 0.8 / 1539 6.0 / 2239 1.0

NOVEMBER

	Time m		Time m
1 TU	0404 5.7 / 1102 1.0 / 1636 5.7 / 2330 1.4	**16** W	0324 5.5 / 1024 1.1 / 1546 5.5 / 2243 1.4
2 W	0500 5.3 / 1158 1.3 / 1738 5.3 / ◐	**17** TH	0406 5.3 / 1108 1.3 / 1638 5.3 / 2332 1.5
3 TH	0030 1.7 / 0604 5.0 / 1307 1.5 / 1855 5.0	**18** F	0504 5.1 / 1202 1.4 / 1745 5.2
4 F	0144 1.9 / 0725 4.8 / 1426 1.6 / 2017 5.0	**19** SA	0030 1.6 / 0613 5.0 / 1306 1.4 / 1853 5.2
5 SA	0302 1.8 / 0842 4.9 / 1540 1.5 / 2122 5.1	**20** SU	0141 1.7 / 0722 5.1 / 1423 1.4 / 2004 5.3
6 SU	0409 1.6 / 0942 5.1 / 1641 1.3 / 2214 5.3	**21** M	0300 1.5 / 0834 5.2 / 1538 1.1 / 2115 5.5
7 M	0504 1.4 / 1031 5.3 / 1730 1.1 / 2258 5.5	**22** TU	0409 1.3 / 0940 5.5 / 1643 0.9 / 2214 5.7
8 TU	0547 1.3 / 1112 5.5 / 1809 1.0 / 2336 5.6	**23** W	0510 1.1 / 1034 5.8 / 1740 0.7 / 2304 6.0
9 W	0623 1.1 / 1149 5.7 / 1842 1.0	**24** TH	0604 0.9 / 1122 6.0 / 1832 0.6 / 2350 6.1
10 TH	0010 5.7 / 0655 1.1 / 1223 5.7 / ○ 1913 0.9	**25** F	0653 0.7 / 1210 6.2 / ● 1920 0.5
11 F	0040 5.8 / 0727 1.0 / 1252 5.8 / 1946 0.9	**26** SA	0036 6.2 / 0741 0.6 / 1257 6.3 / 2006 0.6
12 SA	0108 5.8 / 0801 0.9 / 1321 5.8 / 2020 1.0	**27** SU	0123 6.2 / 0828 0.6 / 1346 6.3 / 2052 0.7
13 SU	0138 5.9 / 0836 0.9 / 1353 5.9 / 2053 1.0	**28** M	0210 6.1 / 0914 0.6 / 1437 6.2 / 2138 0.8
14 M	0211 5.8 / 0910 1.0 / 1428 5.8 / 2127 1.1	**29** TU	0258 5.9 / 1000 0.7 / 1528 6.0 / 2222 1.1
15 TU	0247 5.7 / 0945 1.0 / 1505 5.7 / 2203 1.2	**30** W	0346 5.7 / 1047 0.9 / 1617 5.7 / 2308 1.3

DECEMBER

	Time m		Time m
1 TH	0434 5.5 / 1134 1.1 / 1709 5.4 / 2356 1.5	**16** F	0355 5.6 / 1058 0.9 / 1624 5.6 / 2317 1.2
2 F	0525 5.2 / 1228 1.4 / 1807 5.1 / ◐	**17** SA	0442 5.4 / 1145 1.0 / 1717 5.5
3 SA	0052 1.7 / 0625 5.0 / 1330 1.5 / 1918 4.9	**18** SU	0007 1.4 / 0538 5.3 / 1240 1.1 / ◑ 1818 5.4
4 SU	0158 1.8 / 0739 4.9 / 1438 1.6 / 2027 4.9	**19** M	0107 1.5 / 0643 5.3 / 1348 1.2 / 1925 5.3
5 M	0306 1.8 / 0848 4.9 / 1542 1.5 / 2126 5.0	**20** TU	0220 1.5 / 0753 5.3 / 1502 1.2 / 2038 5.4
6 TU	0408 1.7 / 0946 5.0 / 1641 1.4 / 2217 5.2	**21** W	0334 1.4 / 0907 5.4 / 1612 1.0 / 2149 5.5
7 W	0504 1.5 / 1036 5.2 / 1730 1.3 / 2303 5.3	**22** TH	0443 1.2 / 1016 5.6 / 1719 0.9 / 2250 5.7
8 TH	0549 1.3 / 1120 5.4 / 1811 1.2 / 2343 5.5	**23** F	0548 1.0 / 1114 5.8 / 1818 0.8 / 2343 5.8
9 F	0628 1.2 / 1159 5.5 / 1847 1.1	**24** SA	0644 0.8 / 1206 6.0 / ● 1910 0.7
10 SA	0018 5.6 / 0705 1.1 / 1233 5.7 / ○ 1923 1.0	**25** SU	0031 5.9 / 0733 0.6 / 1254 6.1 / 1957 0.7
11 SU	0049 5.7 / 0742 0.9 / 1305 5.8 / 2000 1.0	**26** M	0116 6.0 / 0820 0.5 / 1341 6.2 / 2041 0.7
12 M	0122 5.8 / 0820 0.9 / 1340 5.9 / 2038 1.0	**27** TU	0201 6.0 / 0904 0.5 / 1427 6.1 / 2123 0.8
13 TU	0158 5.8 / 0858 0.8 / 1418 5.9 / 2116 1.0	**28** W	0243 5.9 / 0946 0.6 / 1511 6.0 / 2203 1.0
14 W	0236 5.8 / 0936 0.8 / 1457 5.8 / 2154 1.0	**29** TH	0324 5.8 / 1027 0.7 / 1553 5.8 / 2242 1.1
15 TH	0314 5.7 / 1016 0.9 / 1538 5.7 / 2234 1.1	**30** F	0404 5.6 / 1106 0.9 / 1634 5.5 / 2320 1.3
		31 SA	0444 5.5 / 1146 1.1 / 1717 5.3

Chart Datum: 2·69 metres below IGN Datum
HAT is 6·4 metres above Chart Datum

TIDES

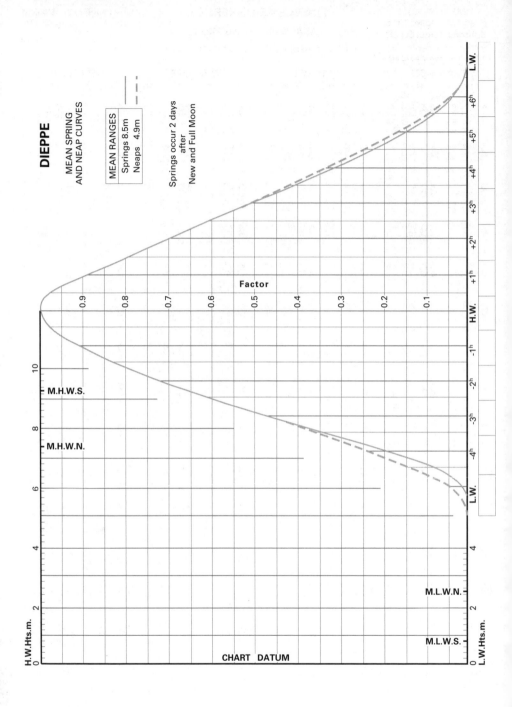

DIEPPE

MEAN SPRING
AND NEAP CURVES

MEAN RANGES
Springs 8.5m
Neaps 4.9m

Springs occur 2 days
after
New and Full Moon

TIME ZONE -0100
(French Standard Time)
Subtract 1 hour for UT
For French Summer Time add ONE hour in non-shaded areas

FRANCE – DIEPPE

LAT 49°56'N   LONG 1°05'E

TIMES AND HEIGHTS OF HIGH AND LOW WATERS

Dates in amber are **SPRINGS**
Dates in yellow are **NEAPS**

2011

JANUARY

Day	Time	m		Day	Time	m
1 SA	0318 / 0900 / 1554 / 2133	2.2 / 8.1 / 1.9 / 8.0		**16** SU	0234 / 0832 / 1520 / 2107	2.9 / 7.3 / 2.6 / 7.4
2 SU	0424 / 1001 / 1655 / 2230	1.9 / 8.4 / 1.6 / 8.3		**17** M	0349 / 0932 / 1624 / 2203	2.4 / 7.8 / 2.0 / 8.0
3 M	0520 / 1052 / 1748 / 2319	1.7 / 8.7 / 1.4 / 8.6		**18** TU	0448 / 1024 / 1719 / 2252	1.9 / 8.4 / 1.5 / 8.5
4 TU ●	0609 / 1137 / 1834	1.5 / 8.9 / 1.2		**19** W ○	0542 / 1112 / 1812 / 2339	1.5 / 8.8 / 1.1 / 8.9
5 W	0002 / 0652 / 1217 / 1915	8.8 / 1.4 / 9.0 / 1.1		**20** TH	0633 / 1157 / 1903	1.1 / 9.2 / 0.8
6 TH	0040 / 0731 / 1255 / 1953	8.9 / 1.3 / 9.0 / 1.1		**21** F	0024 / 0722 / 1242 / 1950	9.3 / 0.9 / 9.5 / 0.5
7 F	0116 / 0808 / 1330 / 2028	8.9 / 1.3 / 9.0 / 1.2		**22** SA	0108 / 0808 / 1326 / 2035	9.5 / 0.7 / 9.6 / 0.4
8 SA	0151 / 0841 / 1405 / 2058	8.8 / 1.5 / 8.8 / 1.3		**23** SU	0152 / 0852 / 1410 / 2116	9.6 / 0.7 / 9.6 / 0.5
9 SU	0225 / 0910 / 1438 / 2126	8.6 / 1.7 / 8.5 / 1.6		**24** M	0235 / 0934 / 1453 / 2155	9.4 / 0.8 / 9.4 / 0.8
10 M	0257 / 0939 / 1510 / 2154	8.4 / 1.9 / 8.2 / 1.9		**25** TU	0318 / 1014 / 1537 / 2234	9.1 / 1.1 / 9.0 / 1.2
11 TU	0329 / 1010 / 1543 / 2228	8.1 / 2.2 / 7.8 / 2.2		**26** W ◑	0402 / 1056 / 1625 / 2318	8.7 / 1.5 / 8.4 / 1.7
12 W ◑	0403 / 1050 / 1623 / 2309	7.7 / 2.5 / 7.4 / 2.5		**27** TH	0453 / 1147 / 1722	8.2 / 2.0 / 7.8
13 TH	0447 / 1139 / 1715	7.4 / 2.8 / 7.0		**28** F	0013 / 0559 / 1252 / 1838	2.3 / 7.6 / 2.4 / 7.3
14 F	0002 / 0548 / 1241 / 1830	2.9 / 7.1 / 3.0 / 6.8		**29** SA	0129 / 0722 / 1416 / 2008	2.6 / 7.4 / 2.5 / 7.2
15 SA	0110 / 0712 / 1359 / 1958	3.0 / 7.0 / 2.9 / 7.0		**30** SU	0256 / 0848 / 1539 / 2127	2.6 / 7.5 / 2.3 / 7.6
				31 M	0413 / 0954 / 1648 / 2225	2.3 / 8.0 / 1.8 / 8.1

FEBRUARY

Day	Time	m		Day	Time	m
1 TU	0514 / 1045 / 1742 / 2311	1.9 / 8.4 / 1.5 / 8.5		**16** W	0424 / 1003 / 1659 / 2233	1.9 / 8.3 / 1.5 / 8.5
2 W	0602 / 1127 / 1825 / 2350	1.5 / 8.7 / 1.2 / 8.7		**17** TH	0523 / 1054 / 1756 / 2322	1.3 / 8.9 / 0.9 / 9.1
3 TH ●	0641 / 1204 / 1902	1.3 / 8.9 / 1.0		**18** F ○	0618 / 1141 / 1849	0.9 / 9.4 / 0.5
4 F	0024 / 0716 / 1237 / 1935	8.9 / 1.2 / 9.1 / 1.0		**19** SA	0007 / 0709 / 1226 / 1936	9.5 / 0.5 / 9.7 / 0.2
5 SA	0055 / 0748 / 1309 / 2006	9.0 / 1.1 / 9.1 / 1.0		**20** SU	0051 / 0755 / 1309 / 2019	9.8 / 0.3 / 9.9 / 0.1
6 SU	0126 / 0818 / 1340 / 2033	9.0 / 1.2 / 9.0 / 1.1		**21** M	0133 / 0837 / 1352 / 2059	9.8 / 0.3 / 9.9 / 0.2
7 M	0156 / 0844 / 1409 / 2058	8.9 / 1.3 / 8.8 / 1.2		**22** TU	0214 / 0916 / 1433 / 2135	9.7 / 0.5 / 9.6 / 0.6
8 TU	0224 / 0909 / 1437 / 2123	8.7 / 1.5 / 8.6 / 1.5		**23** W	0254 / 0953 / 1515 / 2211	9.4 / 0.8 / 9.1 / 1.1
9 W	0251 / 0936 / 1506 / 2151	8.5 / 1.8 / 8.2 / 1.8		**24** TH	0336 / 1032 / 1559 / 2250	8.8 / 1.4 / 8.4 / 1.8
10 TH	0321 / 1009 / 1539 / 2225	8.1 / 2.1 / 7.8 / 2.3		**25** F ◑	0422 / 1118 / 1653 / 2343	8.1 / 2.0 / 7.6 / 2.4
11 F ◑	0357 / 1050 / 1622 / 2311	7.7 / 2.5 / 7.3 / 2.7		**26** SA	0525 / 1222 / 1811	7.4 / 2.5 / 7.0
12 SA	0447 / 1146 / 1725	7.2 / 2.9 / 6.8		**27** SU	0059 / 0657 / 1351 / 1954	2.9 / 7.0 / 2.8 / 6.9
13 SU	0014 / 0602 / 1302 / 1904	3.1 / 6.8 / 3.0 / 6.7		**28** M	0237 / 0835 / 1524 / 2116	2.9 / 7.2 / 2.5 / 7.4
14 M	0142 / 0748 / 1437 / 2036	3.1 / 6.9 / 2.8 / 7.2				
15 TU	0315 / 0905 / 1556 / 2140	2.6 / 7.6 / 2.1 / 7.8				

MARCH

Day	Time	m		Day	Time	m
1 TU	0401 / 0941 / 1635 / 2210	2.4 / 7.7 / 1.9 / 8.0		**16** W	0244 / 0835 / 1528 / 2114	2.6 / 7.5 / 2.1 / 7.9
2 W	0501 / 1029 / 1726 / 2252	1.9 / 8.3 / 1.5 / 8.4		**17** TH	0358 / 0937 / 1634 / 2209	1.9 / 8.3 / 1.4 / 8.6
3 TH	0545 / 1108 / 1806 / 2328	1.5 / 8.6 / 1.2 / 8.7		**18** F	0459 / 1030 / 1733 / 2259	1.2 / 9.0 / 0.8 / 9.2
4 F ●	0620 / 1142 / 1839 / 2359	1.2 / 8.9 / 1.0 / 8.9		**19** SA ○	0556 / 1119 / 1827 / 2344	0.7 / 9.5 / 0.4 / 9.6
5 SA	0652 / 1213 / 1910	1.1 / 9.0 / 0.9		**20** SU	0648 / 1204 / 1914	0.4 / 9.8 / 0.1
6 SU	0029 / 0723 / 1243 / 1939	9.0 / 1.0 / 9.1 / 0.9		**21** M	0028 / 0734 / 1248 / 1958	9.9 / 0.2 / 9.9 / 0.1
7 M	0058 / 0751 / 1312 / 2006	9.0 / 1.0 / 9.1 / 1.0		**22** TU	0110 / 0816 / 1330 / 2037	9.9 / 0.2 / 9.9 / 0.3
8 TU	0126 / 0817 / 1341 / 2030	9.0 / 1.1 / 8.9 / 1.1		**23** W	0150 / 0855 / 1412 / 2112	9.7 / 0.4 / 9.6 / 0.7
9 W	0153 / 0842 / 1408 / 2055	8.9 / 1.3 / 8.7 / 1.4		**24** TH	0231 / 0932 / 1454 / 2148	9.3 / 0.8 / 9.0 / 1.2
10 TH	0220 / 0908 / 1437 / 2122	8.7 / 1.5 / 8.4 / 1.7		**25** F	0312 / 1010 / 1538 / 2227	8.8 / 1.4 / 8.3 / 1.9
11 F	0250 / 0939 / 1510 / 2154	8.3 / 1.9 / 8.0 / 2.1		**26** SA ◑	0358 / 1055 / 1631 / 2319	8.0 / 2.0 / 7.6 / 2.5
12 SA	0325 / 1017 / 1551 / 2237	7.9 / 2.3 / 7.5 / 2.6		**27** SU	0459 / 1156 / 1746	7.3 / 2.6 / 6.9
13 SU ◑	0411 / 1110 / 1649 / 2339	7.4 / 2.7 / 7.0 / 3.0		**28** M	0033 / 0607 / 1320 / 1925	3.0 / 6.8 / 2.8 / 6.8
14 M	0521 / 1224 / 1824	6.9 / 2.9 / 6.7		**29** TU	0206 / 0805 / 1450 / 2047	2.9 / 7.0 / 2.6 / 7.3
15 TU	0106 / 0709 / 1402 / 2005	3.0 / 6.9 / 2.7 / 7.1		**30** W	0328 / 0913 / 1601 / 2140	2.5 / 7.5 / 2.1 / 7.8
				31 TH	0427 / 1000 / 1652 / 2222	2.0 / 8.0 / 1.6 / 8.3

APRIL

Day	Time	m		Day	Time	m
1 F	0511 / 1039 / 1732 / 2257	1.6 / 8.4 / 1.3 / 8.6		**16** SA	0430 / 1003 / 1704 / 2231	1.2 / 8.9 / 0.8 / 9.2
2 SA	0548 / 1112 / 1806 / 2328	1.3 / 8.7 / 1.2 / 8.8		**17** SU	0529 / 1053 / 1759 / 2318	0.8 / 9.4 / 0.5 / 9.5
3 SU ●	0621 / 1144 / 1838 / 2359	1.2 / 8.9 / 1.1 / 8.9		**18** M ○	0622 / 1141 / 1848	0.5 / 9.6 / 0.4
4 M	0653 / 1214 / 1909	1.1 / 8.9 / 1.0		**19** TU	0003 / 0710 / 1226 / 1932	9.7 / 0.4 / 9.7 / 0.4
5 TU	0028 / 0723 / 1245 / 1937	9.0 / 1.1 / 9.0 / 1.1		**20** W	0046 / 0753 / 1309 / 2013	9.7 / 0.4 / 9.6 / 0.5
6 W	0057 / 0751 / 1314 / 2004	9.0 / 1.1 / 8.9 / 1.2		**21** TH	0128 / 0834 / 1352 / 2051	9.6 / 0.5 / 9.4 / 0.9
7 TH	0126 / 0819 / 1344 / 2032	8.9 / 1.2 / 8.7 / 1.4		**22** F	0210 / 0912 / 1435 / 2128	9.2 / 0.9 / 8.9 / 1.4
8 F	0156 / 0848 / 1416 / 2101	8.7 / 1.4 / 8.5 / 1.6		**23** SA	0252 / 0952 / 1521 / 2209	8.7 / 1.4 / 8.3 / 1.9
9 SA	0228 / 0920 / 1452 / 2136	8.4 / 1.7 / 8.1 / 2.0		**24** SU	0339 / 1036 / 1612 / 2259	8.0 / 1.9 / 7.7 / 2.5
10 SU	0306 / 0959 / 1535 / 2221	8.0 / 2.1 / 7.6 / 2.4		**25** M ◑	0435 / 1131 / 1717	7.4 / 2.4 / 7.1
11 M ◑	0354 / 1051 / 1634 / 2321	7.5 / 2.4 / 7.2 / 2.7		**26** TU	0004 / 0547 / 1241 / 1835	2.8 / 7.0 / 2.7 / 6.9
12 TU	0502 / 1202 / 1801	7.1 / 2.6 / 7.0		**27** W	0120 / 0710 / 1356 / 1954	2.9 / 6.9 / 2.6 / 7.1
13 W	0042 / 0637 / 1333 / 1932	2.8 / 7.1 / 2.5 / 7.4		**28** TH	0232 / 0823 / 1504 / 2054	2.6 / 7.2 / 2.3 / 7.6
14 TH	0213 / 0801 / 1457 / 2042	2.4 / 7.0 / 1.9 / 8.0		**29** F	0333 / 0917 / 1600 / 2140	2.2 / 7.7 / 1.9 / 8.0
15 F	0327 / 0907 / 1604 / 2140	1.7 / 8.3 / 1.3 / 8.7		**30** SA	0424 / 1000 / 1646 / 2218	1.9 / 8.1 / 1.6 / 8.3

Chart Datum: 4·43 metres below IGN Datum
HAT is 10·1 metres above Chart Datum

TIDES

TIME ZONE -0100
(French Standard Time)
Subtract 1 hour for UT
For French Summer Time add
ONE hour in **non-shaded areas**

FRANCE – DIEPPE
LAT 49°56′N   LONG 1°05′E
TIMES AND HEIGHTS OF HIGH AND LOW WATERS

Dates in amber are **SPRINGS**
Dates in yellow are **NEAPS**

2011

MAY

Day	Time m	Time m	Time m	Time m
1 SU	0507 1.6	1037 8.4	1727 1.4	2254 8.6
16 M	0500 1.0	1029 9.0	1730 0.9	2253 9.3
2 M	0545 1.4	1112 8.6	1803 1.3	2327 8.7
17 TU	0555 0.8	1119 9.3	1821 0.7	○2341 9.4
3 TU	0621 1.3	1146 8.7	1837 1.3	●2359 8.8
18 W	0645 0.6	1206 9.3	1908 0.7	
4 W	0655 1.2	1219 8.8	1910 1.2	
19 TH	0026 9.4	0732 0.6	1256 9.3	1951 0.8
5 TH	0031 8.9	0727 1.1	1252 8.8	1942 1.3
20 F	0109 9.3	0815 0.7	1336 9.1	2032 1.1
6 F	0104 8.8	0800 1.2	1326 8.7	2015 1.4
21 SA	0152 9.0	0856 1.0	1420 8.8	2112 1.4
7 SA	0138 8.7	0834 1.3	1403 8.5	2050 1.6
22 SU	0236 8.7	0936 1.3	1504 8.4	2152 1.8
8 SU	0216 8.5	0911 1.5	1443 8.3	2129 1.8
23 M	0320 8.2	1017 1.7	1550 8.0	2236 2.2
9 M	0258 8.2	0953 1.8	1530 7.9	2215 2.1
24 TU	0409 7.7	1102 2.1	1641 7.5	◐2327 2.5
10 TU	0348 7.8	1045 2.1	1628 7.6	◐2313 2.3
25 W	0504 7.3	1155 2.4	1739 7.2	
11 W	0452 7.5	1149 2.2	1741 7.5	
26 TH	0026 2.7	0607 7.1	1256 2.6	1844 7.2
12 TH	0024 2.4	0610 7.5	1306 2.1	1858 7.7
27 F	0129 2.7	0715 7.1	1400 2.5	1950 7.3
13 F	0142 2.1	0726 7.8	1423 1.8	2007 8.1
28 SA	0232 2.5	0820 7.3	1501 2.3	2048 7.6
14 SA	0255 1.7	0834 8.3	1531 1.4	2109 8.6
29 SU	0331 2.2	0914 7.6	1557 2.0	2136 8.0
15 SU	0400 1.4	0934 8.7	1633 1.1	2203 9.0
30 M	0422 1.9	1000 8.0	1645 1.8	2218 8.2
31 TU	0509 1.7	1041 8.2	1729 1.6	2257 8.5

JUNE

Day	Time m	Time m	Time m	Time m
1 W	0550 1.5	1120 8.5	1809 1.5	●2334 8.6
16 TH	0626 0.9	1154 9.0	1849 1.1	
2 TH	0629 1.3	1158 8.6	1847 1.4	
17 F	0011 9.1	0715 0.9	1239 9.0	1934 1.1
3 F	0011 8.8	0708 1.2	1235 8.7	1924 1.3
18 SA	0055 9.1	0759 0.9	1323 9.0	2016 1.1
4 SA	0048 8.8	0747 1.1	1314 8.8	2003 1.3
19 SU	0137 9.0	0840 1.0	1404 8.9	2055 1.3
5 SU	0127 8.8	0827 1.1	1355 8.7	2044 1.4
20 M	0218 8.8	0917 1.2	1444 8.6	2132 1.6
6 M	0209 8.7	0909 1.2	1439 8.6	2126 1.5
21 TU	0258 8.5	0952 1.5	1523 8.3	2207 1.9
7 TU	0254 8.5	0952 1.4	1526 8.4	2212 1.7
22 W	0337 8.1	1027 1.8	1603 8.0	2244 2.2
8 W	0343 8.5	1040 1.6	1618 8.1	2304 1.9
23 TH	0419 7.7	1106 2.2	1646 7.6	◐2329 2.5
9 TH	0438 8.1	1135 1.8	1717 8.0	
24 F	0507 7.3	1153 2.5	1738 7.3	
10 F	0003 2.0	0542 7.9	1238 1.8	1824 8.0
25 SA	0022 2.7	0605 7.1	1251 2.7	1841 7.2
11 SA	0111 1.9	0652 7.9	1349 1.8	1933 8.1
26 SU	0126 2.7	0716 7.0	1357 2.7	1951 7.2
12 SU	0223 1.8	0804 8.1	1500 1.7	2040 8.4
27 M	0235 2.6	0825 7.2	1506 2.5	2053 7.5
13 M	0331 1.5	0910 8.3	1605 1.5	2140 8.6
28 TU	0339 2.3	0923 7.6	1606 2.2	2145 7.9
14 TU	0435 1.3	1010 8.6	1705 1.3	2235 8.9
29 W	0433 1.9	1013 7.9	1657 1.9	2231 8.2
15 W	0533 1.1	1104 8.8	1759 1.1	○2325 9.0
30 TH	0522 1.6	1058 8.3	1744 1.6	2313 8.5

JULY

Day	Time m	Time m	Time m	Time m
1 F	0609 1.4	1140 8.6	1828 1.4	●2355 8.8
16 SA	0001 9.0	0702 1.0	1228 9.0	1920 1.1
2 SA	0654 1.1	1222 8.8	1912 1.2	
17 SU	0042 9.1	0744 0.9	1306 9.0	1959 1.1
3 SU	0036 9.0	0739 1.0	1304 9.0	1956 1.1
18 M	0119 9.0	0821 1.0	1343 9.0	2034 1.2
4 M	0118 9.1	0823 0.8	1347 9.1	2039 1.0
19 TU	0155 8.9	0854 1.1	1417 8.8	2105 1.4
5 TU	0201 9.1	0905 0.8	1430 9.0	2122 1.1
20 W	0229 8.7	0923 1.3	1450 8.6	2133 1.6
6 W	0245 9.0	0947 1.0	1514 8.9	2205 1.2
21 TH	0303 8.4	0950 1.6	1523 8.3	2203 1.9
7 TH	0330 8.8	1029 1.2	1600 8.6	2249 1.5
22 F	0335 8.0	1020 1.9	1556 7.9	2238 2.3
8 F	0419 8.5	1115 1.5	1651 8.3	◐2340 1.7
23 SA	0411 7.6	1058 2.3	1635 7.5	◐2322 2.6
9 SA	0514 8.1	1210 1.8	1752 8.1	
24 SU	0457 7.1	1147 2.7	1728 7.1	
10 SU	0041 1.9	0622 7.8	1317 2.0	1903 7.9
25 M	0019 2.9	0604 6.8	1251 3.0	1845 6.9
11 M	0155 2.0	0740 7.7	1434 2.1	2018 8.0
26 TU	0133 2.9	0734 6.8	1412 3.0	2010 7.1
12 TU	0310 1.9	0856 7.9	1546 1.9	2127 8.2
27 W	0255 2.7	0856 7.9	1530 2.6	2114 7.6
13 W	0419 1.6	1002 8.2	1650 1.6	2226 8.5
28 TH	0402 2.2	0947 7.7	1630 2.1	2207 8.1
14 TH	0521 1.4	1058 8.6	1747 1.4	2317 8.8
29 F	0458 1.7	1037 8.3	1722 1.6	2254 8.6
15 F	0615 1.1	1146 8.8	1836 1.2	○
30 SA	0550 1.3	1122 8.7	1812 1.3	●2338 9.0
31 SU	0641 1.0	1206 9.1	1900 1.0	

AUGUST

Day	Time m	Time m	Time m	Time m
1 M	0021 9.3	0728 0.7	1249 9.3	1946 0.8
16 TU	0056 9.1	0755 1.0	1316 9.1	2007 1.1
2 TU	0104 9.5	0812 0.5	1331 9.5	2029 0.7
17 W	0128 9.0	0824 1.1	1346 9.0	2035 1.3
3 W	0146 9.5	0854 0.5	1412 9.5	2110 0.7
18 TH	0158 8.9	0850 1.3	1416 8.8	2100 1.5
4 TH	0229 9.4	0933 0.7	1454 9.3	2150 0.9
19 F	0227 8.6	0914 1.5	1444 8.5	2126 1.8
5 F	0311 9.1	1011 1.0	1537 8.9	2230 1.2
20 SA	0255 8.2	0940 1.9	1512 8.1	2156 2.1
6 SA	0356 8.7	1053 1.4	1624 8.5	◐2317 1.7
21 SU	0327 7.8	1013 2.3	1546 7.7	◐2235 2.5
7 SU	0449 8.1	1143 2.0	1722 7.9	
22 M	0407 7.3	1057 2.8	1632 7.2	2327 2.9
8 M	0015 2.1	0558 7.6	1252 2.4	1840 7.5
23 TU	0505 6.8	1157 3.2	1741 6.8	
9 TU	0134 2.4	0725 7.3	1417 2.5	2006 7.6
24 W	0038 3.1	0638 6.6	1322 3.2	1925 6.8
10 W	0259 2.2	0852 7.6	1537 2.2	2123 7.9
25 TH	0212 2.9	0817 6.8	1455 2.8	2044 7.4
11 TH	0414 1.8	0959 8.1	1645 1.8	2221 8.4
26 F	0332 2.3	0921 7.7	1603 2.1	2142 8.1
12 F	0517 1.5	1051 8.5	1741 1.5	2308 8.8
27 SA	0434 1.7	1013 8.4	1659 1.5	2231 8.7
13 SA	0607 1.2	1133 8.8	1825 1.3	○2348 9.0
28 SU	0529 1.2	1100 8.9	1752 1.1	2317 9.2
14 SU	0648 1.0	1211 9.0	1902 1.1	
29 M	0622 0.7	1144 9.4	1842 0.7	●
15 M	0023 9.1	0723 1.0	1244 9.1	1936 1.1
30 TU	0001 9.6	0710 0.5	1227 9.6	1929 0.5
31 W	0044 9.8	0754 0.3	1309 9.8	2012 0.4

Chart Datum: 4·43 metres below IGN Datum
HAT is 10·1 metres above Chart Datum

TIME ZONE -0100
(French Standard Time)
Subtract 1 hour for UT
For French Summer Time add
ONE hour in **non-shaded areas**

FRANCE – DIEPPE

LAT 49°56′N   LONG 1°05′E

TIMES AND HEIGHTS OF HIGH AND LOW WATERS

Dates in amber are **SPRINGS**
Dates in yellow are **NEAPS**

2011

SEPTEMBER		OCTOBER		NOVEMBER		DECEMBER	
Time m	Time m	Time m	Time m	Time m	Time m	Time m	Time m

1 0126 9.8 / 0835 0.4 / TH 1350 9.7 / 2052 0.5	**16** 0127 8.9 / 0818 1.3 / F 1342 8.9 / 2030 1.4	**1** 0147 9.7 / 0851 0.7 / SA 1408 9.5 / 2110 0.8	**16** 0128 8.7 / 0816 1.6 / SU 1341 8.7 / 2032 1.6	**1** 0301 8.6 / 0954 1.9 / TU 1522 8.4 / 2219 1.9	**16** 0221 8.3 / 0907 2.0 / W 1437 8.2 / 2129 2.0	**1** 0332 8.3 / 1022 2.2 / TH 1552 8.0 / 2245 2.1	**16** 0256 8.5 / 0944 1.8 / F 1513 8.4 / 2207 1.7
2 0208 9.6 / 0912 0.6 / F 1431 9.5 / 2130 0.8	**17** 0155 8.7 / 0842 1.5 / SA 1409 8.6 / 2055 1.7	**2** 0230 9.2 / 0929 1.2 / SU 1451 9.0 / 2150 1.3	**17** 0159 8.5 / 0845 1.9 / M 1412 8.4 / 2102 1.9	**2** 0353 8.0 / 1045 2.4 / W 1618 7.7 / ☾ 2314 2.4	**17** 0304 8.0 / 0950 2.3 / TH 1522 7.9 / 2215 2.3	**2** 0421 7.8 / 1111 2.5 / F 1644 7.6 / ☽ 2335 2.5	**17** 0342 8.2 / 1030 2.0 / SA 1602 8.1 / 2255 1.9
3 0250 9.2 / 0950 1.0 / SA 1513 9.0 / 2209 1.2	**18** 0223 8.4 / 0908 1.9 / SU 1437 8.3 / 2123 2.0	**3** 0316 8.6 / 1010 1.8 / M 1539 8.3 / 2236 1.9	**18** 0233 8.1 / 0917 2.2 / TU 1448 8.0 / 2138 2.3	**3** 0455 7.4 / 1148 2.8 / TH 1725 7.3	**18** 0355 7.7 / 1042 2.6 / F 1618 7.6 / ☾ 2312 2.5	**3** 0516 7.4 / 1207 2.8 / SA 1744 7.2	**18** 0435 8.0 / 1124 2.2 / SU 1659 7.9 / ☾ 2352 2.1
4 0335 8.7 / 1030 1.6 / SU 1559 8.4 / ☽ 2255 1.8	**19** 0254 8.0 / 0939 2.3 / M 1511 7.9 / 2159 2.4	**4** 0409 7.9 / 1102 2.4 / TU 1638 7.6 / ☽ 2335 2.5	**19** 0313 7.7 / 0959 2.6 / W 1533 7.5 / 2226 2.6	**4** 0022 2.7 / 0609 7.2 / F 1302 2.9 / 1843 7.1	**19** 0500 7.5 / 1147 2.7 / SA 1729 7.5	**4** 0033 2.7 / 0620 7.2 / SU 1310 2.9 / 1852 7.1	**19** 0538 7.9 / 1227 2.2 / M 1808 7.8
5 0427 7.9 / 1121 2.2 / M 1658 7.7 / 2354 2.3	**20** 0333 7.5 / 1020 2.7 / TU 1555 7.3 / ☽ 2248 2.8	**5** 0521 7.3 / 1214 2.9 / W 1759 7.2	**20** 0407 7.2 / 1056 3.0 / TH 1634 7.1 / ☽ 2331 2.9	**5** 0136 2.7 / 0728 7.3 / SA 1414 2.7 / 1959 7.3	**20** 0022 2.5 / 0617 7.6 / SU 1303 2.5 / 1847 7.6	**5** 0138 2.8 / 0729 7.3 / M 1417 2.7 / 2001 7.3	**20** 0100 2.2 / 0651 7.9 / TU 1341 2.2 / 1923 7.9
6 0539 7.3 / 1232 2.7 / TU 1821 7.3	**21** 0428 7.0 / 1119 3.2 / W 1659 6.9 / 2358 3.1	**6** 0057 2.8 / 0653 7.1 / TH 1343 2.9 / 1931 7.2	**21** 0524 7.0 / 1212 3.1 / F 1802 7.0	**6** 0245 2.5 / 0834 7.6 / SU 1518 2.3 / 2058 7.7	**21** 0142 2.2 / 0731 7.9 / M 1420 2.1 / 1958 8.1	**6** 0243 2.6 / 0832 7.5 / TU 1519 2.4 / 2100 7.6	**21** 0218 2.1 / 0803 8.2 / W 1457 1.9 / 2035 8.2
7 0117 2.6 / 0716 7.1 / W 1405 2.8 / 1957 7.3	**22** 0554 6.7 / 1242 3.3 / TH 1840 6.8	**7** 0225 2.6 / 0818 7.4 / F 1504 2.5 / 2046 7.6	**22** 0056 2.8 / 0658 7.2 / SA 1342 2.7 / 1929 7.5	**7** 0343 2.1 / 0924 8.0 / M 1610 2.0 / 2144 8.1	**22** 0256 1.8 / 0836 8.5 / TU 1528 1.6 / 2101 8.6	**7** 0343 2.3 / 0924 7.9 / W 1613 2.1 / 2147 7.9	**22** 0332 1.8 / 0909 8.5 / TH 1606 1.5 / 2139 8.5
8 0250 2.4 / 0845 7.5 / TH 1530 2.4 / 2112 7.8	**23** 0132 3.0 / 0740 7.0 / F 1420 2.9 / 2009 7.3	**8** 0337 2.1 / 0918 7.9 / SA 1605 2.0 / 2138 8.1	**23** 0224 2.3 / 0812 7.9 / SU 1459 2.1 / 2036 8.1	**8** 0431 1.8 / 1005 8.4 / TU 1653 1.7 / 2223 8.4	**23** 0400 1.4 / 0933 8.9 / W 1629 1.2 / 2158 9.0	**8** 0433 2.0 / 1007 8.2 / TH 1659 1.8 / 2229 8.2	**23** 0436 1.5 / 1008 8.9 / F 1707 1.2 / 2237 8.9
9 0406 1.9 / 0946 8.1 / F 1635 1.8 / 2206 8.3	**24** 0301 2.4 / 0849 7.7 / SA 1533 2.1 / 2111 8.1	**9** 0431 1.7 / 1003 8.4 / SU 1653 1.6 / 2220 8.5	**24** 0332 1.7 / 0910 8.4 / M 1601 1.5 / 2132 8.8	**9** 0511 1.6 / 1041 8.6 / W 1732 1.5 / 2258 8.6	**24** 0459 1.1 / 1026 9.3 / TH 1726 0.9 / 2251 9.3	**9** 0517 1.8 / 1046 8.5 / F 1740 1.6 / 2308 8.5	**24** 0534 1.2 / 1102 9.2 / SA 1803 0.9 / ● 2330 9.1
10 0503 1.5 / 1032 8.6 / SA 1724 1.5 / 2249 8.7	**25** 0405 1.7 / 0944 8.5 / SU 1632 1.4 / 2203 8.8	**10** 0514 1.4 / 1041 8.7 / M 1732 1.4 / 2256 8.8	**25** 0432 1.1 / 1002 9.1 / TU 1658 1.0 / 2224 9.3	**10** 0548 1.5 / 1114 8.8 / TH 1807 1.4 / ○ 2332 8.7	**25** 0553 0.9 / 1115 9.5 / F 1819 0.7 / ● 2340 9.5	**10** 0557 1.7 / 1123 8.7 / SA 1818 1.4 / ○ 2344 8.6	**25** 0627 1.1 / 1151 9.2 / SU 1855 0.8
11 0547 1.2 / 1111 8.9 / SU 1804 1.2 / 2325 9.0	**26** 0503 1.1 / 1033 9.1 / M 1726 1.0 / 2251 9.3	**11** 0550 1.3 / 1114 8.9 / TU 1806 1.3 / 2329 8.9	**26** 0527 0.8 / 1050 9.6 / W 1751 0.7 / ● 2312 9.6	**11** 0622 1.4 / 1146 8.9 / F 1841 1.4	**26** 0643 0.8 / 1202 9.6 / SA 1908 0.6	**11** 0633 1.5 / 1159 8.8 / SU 1855 1.3	**26** 0018 9.3 / 0716 1.0 / M 1237 9.4 / 1942 0.7
12 0623 1.1 / 1145 9.0 / M 1837 1.2 / ○ 2358 9.1	**27** 0556 0.7 / 1118 9.6 / TU 1818 0.7 / ● 2337 9.7	**12** 0621 1.2 / 1145 9.0 / W 1837 1.2 / ○ 2359 9.0	**27** 0618 0.6 / 1136 9.8 / TH 1841 0.5 / 2358 9.8	**12** 0004 8.8 / 0655 1.5 / SA 1218 8.9 / 1913 1.3	**27** 0028 9.5 / 0730 0.9 / SU 1249 9.6 / 1954 0.7	**12** 0020 8.8 / 0709 1.5 / M 1234 8.9 / 1931 1.3	**27** 0103 9.3 / 0801 1.0 / TU 1321 9.4 / 2025 0.8
13 0655 1.0 / 1216 9.1 / TU 1908 1.1	**28** 0645 0.4 / 1202 9.8 / W 1906 0.4	**13** 0652 1.2 / 1214 9.0 / TH 1908 1.2	**28** 0705 0.5 / 1221 9.9 / F 1927 0.4	**13** 0037 8.8 / 0726 1.5 / SU 1250 8.9 / 1944 1.4	**28** 0114 9.4 / 0814 1.0 / M 1334 9.4 / 2038 0.9	**13** 0056 8.8 / 0746 1.5 / TU 1310 8.9 / 2008 1.3	**28** 0145 9.2 / 0842 1.2 / W 1402 9.2 / 2104 1.1
14 0028 9.1 / 0724 1.0 / W 1245 9.1 / 1937 1.2	**29** 0021 9.9 / 0730 0.3 / TH 1245 9.9 / 1950 0.4	**14** 0029 9.0 / 0722 1.3 / F 1244 9.0 / 1937 1.3	**29** 0044 9.8 / 0749 0.7 / SA 1305 9.7 / 2011 0.6	**14** 0109 8.7 / 0757 1.6 / M 1322 8.8 / 2016 1.5	**29** 0200 9.1 / 0857 1.4 / TU 1419 9.0 / 2120 1.3	**14** 0134 8.8 / 0823 1.5 / W 1349 8.8 / 2046 1.4	**29** 0226 8.9 / 0919 1.5 / TH 1442 8.8 / 2139 1.4
15 0058 9.0 / 0752 1.1 / TH 1314 9.0 / 2005 1.3	**30** 0104 9.9 / 0812 0.4 / F 1327 9.8 / 2031 0.5	**15** 0059 9.0 / 0749 1.4 / SA 1312 8.9 / 2004 1.4	**30** 0129 9.5 / 0831 0.9 / SU 1349 9.4 / 2053 0.9	**15** 0144 8.6 / 0831 1.8 / TU 1357 8.5 / 2051 1.7	**30** 0245 8.7 / 0939 1.7 / W 1504 8.6 / 2201 1.7	**15** 0214 8.7 / 0903 1.6 / TH 1430 8.7 / 2125 1.5	**30** 0305 8.6 / 0954 1.8 / F 1521 8.4 / 2211 1.8
			31 0214 9.1 / 0911 1.4 / M 1434 9.0 / 2134 1.4				**31** 0343 8.2 / 1028 2.1 / SA 1601 7.9 / 2246 2.2

Chart Datum: 4·43 metres below IGN Datum
HAT is 10·1 metres above Chart Datum

TIDES

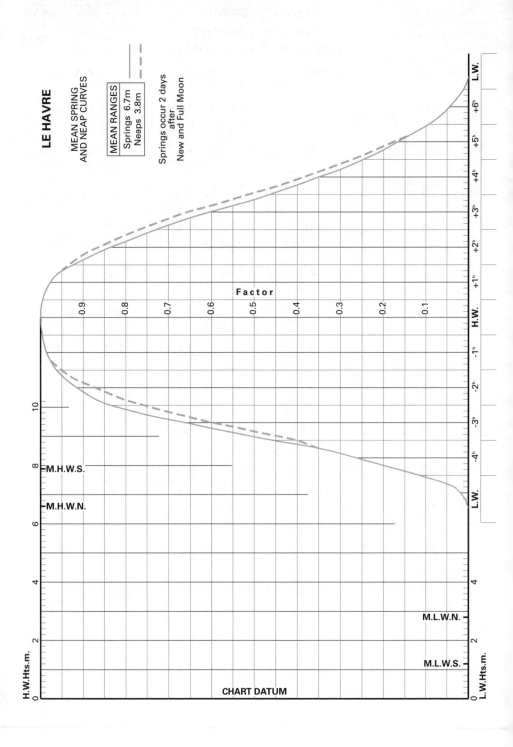

LE HAVRE

MEAN SPRING
AND NEAP CURVES

MEAN RANGES
Springs 6.7m
Neaps 3.8m

Springs occur 2 days
after
New and Full Moon

TIME ZONE -0100
(French Standard Time)
Subtract 1 hour for UT
For French Summer Time add
ONE hour in **non-shaded** areas

FRANCE – LE HAVRE

LAT 49°29'N   LONG 0°07'E

TIMES AND HEIGHTS OF HIGH AND LOW WATERS

Dates in amber are **SPRINGS**
Dates in yellow are **NEAPS**

2011

JANUARY

#	Time m	Time m	#	Time m	Time m
1 SA	0228 2.5 / 0806 7.2	1504 2.3 / 2041 7.1	**16** SU	0138 3.2 / 0737 6.6	1427 2.9 / 2013 6.6
2 SU	0333 2.3 / 0905 7.4	1606 2.0 / 2137 7.3	**17** M	0258 2.8 / 0835 6.8	1534 2.4 / 2108 7.0
3 M	0430 2.1 / 0955 7.6	1659 1.8 / 2225 7.5	**18** TU	0359 2.3 / 0925 7.3	1631 1.9 / 2156 7.4
4 TU	0520 1.9 / 1038 7.7	1746 1.6 / ● 2307 7.6	**19** W	0453 1.9 / 1010 7.6	1724 1.5 / ○ 2241 7.6
5 W	0603 1.8 / 1118 7.8	1826 1.5 / 2345 7.6	**20** TH	0545 1.2 / 1055 7.9	1815 1.1 / 2325 7.8
6 TH	0642 1.7 / 1154 7.8	1903 1.5	**21** F	0635 1.2 / 1139 8.1	1902 0.9
7 F	0020 7.6 / 0718 1.7	1229 7.7 / 1937 1.5	**22** SA	0009 8.0 / 0721 1.1	1223 8.1 / 1946 0.8
8 SA	0054 7.4 / 0751 1.8	1304 7.6 / 2008 1.7	**23** SU	0054 8.0 / 0804 1.0	1308 8.1 / 2027 0.9
9 SU	0128 7.4 / 0822 2.0	1337 7.4 / 2037 1.9	**24** M	0138 7.9 / 0844 1.2	1352 7.9 / 2105 1.1
10 M	0200 7.2 / 0851 2.3	1408 7.2 / 2105 2.2	**25** TU	0221 7.7 / 0923 1.5	1436 7.6 / 2143 1.6
11 TU	0231 7.0 / 0921 2.6	1441 7.0 / 2135 2.5	**26** W	0307 7.4 / 1004 1.9	1525 7.3 / ◐ 2225 2.1
12 W	0306 6.8 / 0956 2.8	1522 6.7 / ◑ 2213 2.8	**27** TH	0359 7.1 / 1052 2.4	1625 6.9 / 2319 2.6
13 TH	0352 6.6 / 1043 3.1	1616 6.4 / 2305 3.1	**28** F	0507 6.8 / 1156 2.8	1746 6.6
14 F	0455 6.5 / 1144 3.3	1734 6.3	**29** SA	0035 3.0 / 0632 6.7	1323 2.9 / 1920 6.6
15 SA	0013 3.3 / 0621 6.4	1302 3.2 / 1904 6.3	**30** SU	0205 2.9 / 0754 6.8	1448 2.6 / 2036 6.8
			31 M	0322 2.6 / 0857 7.0	1600 2.3 / 2131 7.1

FEBRUARY

#	Time m	Time m	#	Time m	Time m
1 TU	0428 2.3 / 0945 7.3	1657 1.9 / 2215 7.3	**16** W	0337 2.3 / 0904 7.2	1611 1.8 / 2137 7.4
2 W	0517 2.0 / 1026 7.5	1739 1.6 / 2252 7.5	**17** TH	0437 1.7 / 0952 7.6	1709 1.3 / 2223 7.7
3 TH	0555 1.7 / 1101 7.9	● 1814 1.5 / 2325 7.6	**18** F	0533 1.3 / 1038 8.0	1801 0.8 / ○ 2307 8.0
4 F	0627 1.6 / 1134 7.8	1846 1.4 / 2356 7.6	**19** SA	0622 0.9 / 1122 8.2	1848 0.5 / 2351 8.2
5 SA	0659 1.5 / 1206 7.8	1916 1.3	**20** SU	0707 0.7 / 1206 8.3	1930 0.4
6 SU	0027 7.6 / 0729 1.5	1237 7.7 / 1944 1.4	**21** M	0034 8.2 / 0748 0.6	1250 8.3 / 2009 0.6
7 M	0057 7.5 / 0756 1.7	1307 7.6 / 2009 1.6	**22** TU	0116 8.1 / 0827 0.8	1333 8.1 / 2046 1.0
8 TU	0126 7.4 / 0821 1.9	1335 7.4 / 2033 1.9	**23** W	0157 7.8 / 0903 1.2	1415 7.7 / 2121 1.5
9 W	0153 7.2 / 0846 2.2	1404 7.2 / 2058 2.2	**24** TH	0239 7.5 / 0940 1.8	1501 7.2 / 2158 2.1
10 TH	0223 7.0 / 0915 2.5	1439 6.9 / 2130 2.6	**25** F	0326 7.1 / 1023 2.3	1558 6.7 / 2248 2.8
11 F	0301 6.8 / 0952 2.8	1526 6.5 / ◑ 2214 3.0	**26** SA	0433 6.6 / 1124 2.9	1724 6.4
12 SA	0354 6.5 / 1046 3.1	1632 6.2 / 2317 3.3	**27** SU	0004 3.2 / 0608 6.4	1255 3.1 / 1909 6.3
13 SU	0513 6.3 / 1205 3.3	1816 6.4	**28** M	0145 3.2 / 0740 6.5	1432 2.8 / 2025 6.6
14 M	0048 3.4 / 0656 6.4	1346 3.0 / 1944 6.5			
15 TU	0227 2.9 / 0809 6.7	1507 2.5 / 2046 6.9			

MARCH

#	Time m	Time m	#	Time m	Time m
1 TU	0315 2.8 / 0843 6.8	1551 2.4 / 2116 6.9	**16** W	0158 2.9 / 0739 6.7	1439 2.4 / 2020 7.0
2 W	0418 2.3 / 0928 7.1	1642 1.9 / 2155 7.2	**17** TH	0312 2.2 / 0838 7.2	1546 1.7 / 2113 7.4
3 TH	0501 1.9 / 1005 7.4	1719 1.6 / 2229 7.4	**18** F	0414 1.6 / 0929 7.6	1646 1.2 / 2200 7.8
4 F	0534 1.6 / 1038 7.6	● 1751 1.4 / 2259 7.6	**19** SA	0511 1.1 / 1016 8.0	1739 0.7 / ○ 2244 8.1
5 SA	0605 1.5 / 1108 7.7	1821 1.3 / 2328 7.6	**20** SU	0601 0.7 / 1101 8.2	1826 0.5 / 2328 8.2
6 SU	0635 1.4 / 1139 7.7	1850 1.3 / 2357 7.6	**21** M	0646 0.5 / 1146 8.3	1908 0.4
7 M	0703 1.4 / 1210 7.7	1916 1.4	**22** TU	0011 8.2 / 0727 0.5	1230 8.2 / 1947 0.6
8 TU	0027 7.6 / 0728 1.5	1239 7.6 / 1940 1.5	**23** W	0053 8.1 / 0806 0.8	1313 8.0 / 2024 0.9
9 W	0054 7.5 / 0753 1.6	1308 7.5 / 2005 1.7	**24** TH	0134 7.8 / 0843 1.2	1356 7.6 / 2059 1.6
10 TH	0122 7.4 / 0819 1.9	1338 7.2 / 2031 2.1	**25** F	0215 7.4 / 0919 1.7	1442 7.1 / 2136 2.3
11 F	0152 7.2 / 0847 2.2	1413 6.9 / 2101 2.4	**26** SA	0301 7.0 / 1000 2.3	1538 6.6 / ◐ 2225 2.9
12 SA	0228 6.9 / 0922 2.6	1458 6.5 / 2141 2.9	**27** SU	0405 6.5 / 1059 2.8	1702 6.3 / 2340 3.3
13 SU	0318 6.5 / 1011 2.9	1601 6.3 / ◑ 2240 3.2	**28** M	0537 6.3 / 1224 3.1	1841 6.2
14 M	0433 6.2 / 1126 3.2	1741 6.2	**29** TU	0114 3.2 / 0709 6.3	1354 2.9 / 1957 6.5
15 TU	0013 3.3 / 0620 6.1	1313 3.0 / 1915 6.5	**30** W	0237 2.9 / 0814 6.6	1509 2.5 / 2048 6.8
			31 TH	0340 2.4 / 0900 6.9	1602 2.1 / 2126 7.1

APRIL

#	Time m	Time m	#	Time m	Time m
1 F	0425 2.0 / 0936 7.2	1642 1.8 / 2158 7.4	**16** SA	0344 1.6 / 0901 7.6	1615 1.2 / 2132 7.8
2 SA	0502 1.7 / 1008 7.4	1718 1.6 / 2227 7.5	**17** SU	0443 1.1 / 0951 7.9	1711 0.9 / 2219 8.0
3 SU	0535 1.5 / 1039 7.6	1750 1.5 / 2257 7.6	**18** M	0535 0.8 / 1039 8.1	1800 0.7 / ○ 2304 8.1
4 M	0606 1.4 / 1111 7.6	1819 1.4 / 2327 7.6	**19** TU	0622 0.6 / 1125 8.1	1844 0.7 / 2348 8.1
5 TU	0634 1.4 / 1143 7.6	1846 1.5 / 2357 7.6	**20** W	0705 0.7 / 1211 8.1	1925 0.9
6 W	0701 1.4 / 1214 7.6	1913 1.6	**21** TH	0031 8.0 / 0745 0.9	1256 7.8 / 2003 1.3
7 TH	0027 7.5 / 0729 1.5	1246 7.4 / 1941 1.7	**22** F	0113 7.8 / 0823 1.2	1341 7.5 / 2039 1.8
8 F	0058 7.4 / 0759 1.7	1321 7.2 / 2011 2.0	**23** SA	0156 7.4 / 0901 1.7	1427 7.1 / 2118 2.3
9 SA	0132 7.2 / 0830 2.0	1400 7.0 / 2043 2.4	**24** SU	0242 7.0 / 0942 2.2	1521 6.7 / 2207 2.8
10 SU	0212 6.9 / 0903 2.3	1446 6.7 / 2124 2.7	**25** M	0340 6.6 / 1037 2.7	1631 6.4 / ◐ 2313 3.1
11 M	0303 6.6 / 0951 2.7	1547 6.4 / 2223 3.0	**26** TU	0456 6.3 / 1147 2.9	1751 6.3
12 TU	0412 6.4 / 1106 2.9	1718 6.4 / 2353 3.1	**27** W	0029 3.1 / 0616 6.3	1259 2.9 / 1906 6.5
13 W	0548 6.4 / 1244 2.7	1844 6.6	**28** TH	0138 2.9 / 0726 6.5	1405 2.4 / 2003 6.7
14 TH	0128 2.7 / 0706 6.8	1406 2.2 / 1949 7.1	**29** F	0241 2.6 / 0819 6.8	1503 2.3 / 2045 7.0
15 F	0240 2.1 / 0808 7.2	1514 1.7 / 2043 7.5	**30** SA	0334 2.2 / 0859 7.0	1554 2.0 / 2121 7.2

Chart Datum: 4·38 metres below IGN Datum
HAT is 8·4 metres above Chart Datum

TIDES

FRANCE – LE HAVRE

LAT 49°29′N   LONG 0°07′E

TIMES AND HEIGHTS OF HIGH AND LOW WATERS

2011

TIME ZONE -0100
(French Standard Time)
Subtract 1 hour for UT
For French Summer Time add
ONE hour in **non-shaded** areas

Dates in amber are **SPRINGS**
Dates in yellow are **NEAPS**

MAY

Day	Time m	Time m	Time m	Time m
1 SU	0420 1.9	0935 7.2	1637 1.8	2153 7.4
16 M	0413 1.3	0929 7.7	1641 1.2	2155 7.9
2 M	0500 1.7	1010 7.4	1715 1.7	2226 7.5
17 TU	0509 1.1	1020 7.8	1733 1.1	2243 8.0 ○
3 TU	0534 1.6	1045 7.4	1747 1.7	2259 7.5 ●
18 W	0559 0.9	1109 7.9	1820 1.1	2328 8.0
4 W	0605 1.5	1119 7.5	1818 1.6	2332 7.6
19 TH	0644 0.9	1156 7.9	1903 1.2	
5 TH	0637 1.5	1154 7.5	1850 1.6	
20 F	0013 7.9	0726 1.0	1242 7.7	1944 1.5
6 F	0005 7.5	0709 1.5	1230 7.4	1923 1.8
21 SA	0056 7.7	0806 1.3	1326 7.5	2023 1.8
7 SA	0041 7.5	0744 1.6	1309 7.3	1958 1.9
22 SU	0139 7.4	0844 1.6	1411 7.2	2102 2.2
8 SU	0120 7.3	0820 1.8	1351 7.1	2035 2.2
23 M	0223 7.1	0924 2.0	1458 6.9	2146 2.6
9 M	0204 7.1	0859 2.1	1440 6.9	2119 2.5
24 TU	0312 6.8	1010 2.4	1551 6.6	2238 2.8 ◑
10 TU	0255 6.9	0948 2.3	1538 6.7	2218 2.7 ●
25 W	0409 6.5	1102 2.7	1643 6.5	2337 3.0
11 W	0357 6.7	1055 2.5	1654 6.7	2335 2.7
26 TH	0515 6.4	1202 2.8	1758 6.5	
12 TH	0517 6.7	1215 2.4	1810 6.9	
27 F	0039 3.0	0622 6.4	1304 2.8	1901 6.6
13 F	0054 2.5	0632 6.9	1331 2.1	1915 7.2
28 SA	0142 2.8	0724 6.6	1406 2.6	1955 6.8
14 SA	0206 2.1	0736 7.2	1439 1.8	2013 7.5
29 SU	0242 2.5	0816 6.8	1503 2.4	2040 7.0
15 SU	0312 1.6	0834 7.5	1543 1.4	2106 7.7
30 M	0335 2.3	0901 7.0	1554 2.2	2120 7.2
31 TU	0421 2.0	0942 7.1	1638 2.0	2158 7.4

JUNE

Day	Time m	Time m	Time m	Time m
1 W	0502 1.8	1021 7.3	1716 1.9	2234 7.5 ●
16 TH	0539 1.3	1058 7.7	1800 1.5	2314 7.8
2 TH	0539 1.6	1059 7.4	1754 1.8	2311 7.5
17 F	0627 1.2	1144 7.7	1846 1.5	2358 7.8
3 F	0617 1.5	1137 7.5	1833 1.7	2348 7.6
18 SA	0710 1.2	1227 7.6	1927 1.6	
4 SA	0656 1.4	1217 7.5	1912 1.7	
19 SU	0039 7.7	0749 1.3	1308 7.5	2006 1.7
5 SU	0028 7.6	0737 1.4	1259 7.4	1953 1.8
20 M	0119 7.5	0826 1.5	1348 7.3	2042 2.0
6 M	0111 7.5	0818 1.5	1343 7.3	2035 1.9
21 TU	0159 7.3	0901 1.8	1428 7.1	2119 2.3
7 TU	0156 7.4	0900 1.7	1431 7.2	2121 2.1
22 W	0239 7.0	0936 2.2	1508 6.9	2156 2.5
8 W	0245 7.2	0947 1.9	1524 7.1	2213 2.2
23 TH	0321 6.8	1013 2.5	1554 6.7	2239 2.8 ◑
9 TH	0340 7.1	1042 2.1	1627 7.0	2313 2.3
24 F	0411 6.5	1058 2.7	1648 6.5	2331 3.0
10 F	0447 7.0	1145 2.2	1735 7.0	
25 SA	0513 6.4	1153 2.9	1753 6.5	
11 SA	0021 2.3	0558 7.0	1255 2.2	1842 7.2
26 SU	0033 3.1	0623 6.3	1258 3.0	1859 6.5
12 SU	0133 2.2	0707 7.1	1407 2.0	1945 7.3
27 M	0143 2.9	0730 6.5	1409 2.8	1958 6.7
13 M	0243 1.9	0813 7.3	1514 1.8	2044 7.5
28 TU	0248 2.6	0828 6.7	1512 2.6	2048 7.0
14 TU	0347 1.7	0914 7.4	1615 1.7	2138 7.7
29 W	0344 2.3	0917 7.0	1604 2.3	2132 7.2
15 W	0445 1.4	1008 7.6	1710 1.5	2228 7.8 ○
30 TH	0432 2.0	1000 7.2	1651 2.0	2214 7.4

JULY

Day	Time m	Time m	Time m	Time m
1 F	0518 1.7	1042 7.4	1737 1.8	2254 7.6 ●
16 SA	0615 1.3	1130 7.6	1833 1.6	2341 7.8
2 SA	0604 1.4	1123 7.5	1822 1.6	2335 7.7
17 SU	0655 1.3	1209 7.6	1910 1.5	
3 SU	0649 1.2	1205 7.6	1907 1.5	
18 M	0018 7.8	0730 1.3	1245 7.6	1945 1.6
4 M	0017 7.8	0733 1.1	1248 7.7	1951 1.4
19 TU	0054 7.7	0802 1.4	1319 7.5	2016 1.8
5 TU	0100 7.8	0815 1.2	1332 7.7	2033 1.5
20 W	0129 7.5	0831 1.7	1353 7.3	2045 2.0
6 W	0145 7.7	0901 1.3	1417 7.6	2115 1.6
21 TH	0203 7.3	0858 2.0	1426 7.1	2114 2.3
7 TH	0231 7.5	0937 1.5	1505 7.4	2159 1.9
22 F	0236 7.0	0926 2.3	1458 6.9	2146 2.6
8 F	0320 7.3	1022 1.8	1557 7.2	2249 2.1 ◑
23 SA	0312 6.7	1000 2.6	1538 6.7	2227 2.9 ◑
9 SA	0418 7.1	1116 2.1	1701 7.1	2349 2.3
24 SU	0401 6.4	1046 3.0	1634 6.5	2323 3.0
10 SU	0529 6.9	1223 2.4	1812 7.0	
25 M	0512 6.2	1150 3.2	1754 6.3	
11 M	0104 2.4	0647 6.9	1341 2.4	1925 7.1
26 TU	0039 3.2	0643 6.2	1314 3.2	1917 6.5
12 TU	0221 2.3	0803 7.0	1453 2.3	2033 7.3
27 W	0204 2.9	0757 6.5	1436 2.9	2019 6.8
13 W	0329 2.0	0909 7.2	1557 2.1	2130 7.5
28 TH	0312 2.5	0853 6.8	1537 2.4	2110 7.1
14 TH	0431 1.7	1002 7.4	1657 1.8	2218 7.6
29 F	0408 2.0	0941 7.2	1631 2.0	2154 7.4
15 F	0528 1.5	1049 7.6	1750 1.7	2302 7.7 ○
30 SA	0501 1.7	1024 7.5	1723 1.7	2237 7.7 ●
31 SU	0552 1.3	1106 7.7	1812 1.4	2319 7.9

AUGUST

Day	Time m	Time m	Time m	Time m
1 M	0639 1.0	1149 7.9	1858 1.1	
16 TU	0704 1.3	1215 7.7	1918 1.5	
2 TU	0001 8.0	0723 0.8	1231 8.0	1940 1.0
17 W	0025 7.7	0733 1.4	1247 7.6	1946 1.6
3 W	0045 8.0	0803 0.8	1314 8.0	2021 1.1
18 TH	0058 7.6	0759 1.6	1317 7.5	2012 1.9
4 TH	0128 8.0	0842 1.0	1357 7.8	2100 1.3
19 F	0128 7.4	0823 1.9	1345 7.3	2036 2.1
5 F	0212 7.7	0920 1.3	1441 7.6	2139 1.7
20 SA	0156 7.2	0847 2.2	1413 7.1	2104 2.5
6 SA	0258 7.4	0959 1.8	1529 7.3	2224 2.1 ◑
21 SU	0229 6.8	0916 2.6	1449 6.6	2138 2.8 ◑
7 SU	0353 7.1	1048 2.3	1630 7.0	2322 2.5
22 M	0313 6.5	0957 3.0	1538 6.3	2228 3.2
8 M	0507 6.7	1156 2.7	1749 6.8	
23 TU	0415 6.2	1056 3.3	1650 6.1	2343 3.4
9 TU	0042 2.7	0637 6.6	1324 2.8	1915 6.8
24 W	0555 6.1	1224 3.4	1835 6.3	
10 W	0208 2.5	0802 6.8	1443 2.6	2028 7.1
25 TH	0125 3.2	0726 6.4	1405 3.1	1950 6.6
11 TH	0322 2.2	0905 7.1	1555 2.3	2122 7.3
26 F	0245 2.6	0828 6.8	1513 2.5	2045 7.1
12 F	0429 1.9	0953 7.4	1655 1.9	2206 7.5
27 SA	0345 2.0	0917 7.3	1610 1.9	2131 7.5
13 SA	0521 1.6	1034 7.5	1740 1.7	2245 7.7 ○
28 SU	0441 1.5	1002 7.6	1704 1.5	2215 7.9
14 SU	0601 1.4	1110 7.6	1816 1.5	2320 7.8
29 M	0533 1.1	1044 7.9	1754 1.1	2258 8.1 ●
15 M	0634 1.3	1143 7.7	1848 1.5	2353 7.8
30 TU	0620 0.8	1127 8.1	1840 0.9	2342 8.2
31 W	0704 0.8	1209 8.2	1922 0.8	

Chart Datum: 4·38 metres below IGN Datum
HAT is 8·4 metres above Chart Datum

TIME ZONE -0100
(French Standard Time)
Subtract 1 hour for UT
For French Summer Time add ONE hour in **non-shaded** areas

FRANCE – LE HAVRE
LAT 49°29'N   LONG 0°07'E
TIMES AND HEIGHTS OF HIGH AND LOW WATERS

Dates in amber are **SPRINGS**
Dates in yellow are **NEAPS**

2011

SEPTEMBER

Day	Time m	Time m	Time m	Time m
1 TH	0025 8.2	0744 0.7	1252 8.1	2002 0.9
2 F	0109 8.1	0823 0.9	1334 8.0	2041 1.2
3 SA	0152 7.8	0859 1.4	1417 7.6	2119 1.6
4 SU	0238 7.4	0937 2.0	1503 7.3	2202 2.2
5 M	0333 6.9	1025 2.6	1605 6.8	2259 2.7
6 TU	0452 6.5	1136 3.0	1732 6.6	
7 W	0027 2.9	0632 6.5	1314 3.1	1905 6.6
8 TH	0200 2.7	0756 6.7	1439 2.8	2016 6.9
9 F	0316 2.3	0853 7.1	1549 2.3	2107 7.4
10 SA	0416 1.9	0935 7.3	1640 1.9	2147 7.5
11 SU	0500 1.6	1012 7.5	1718 1.7	2222 7.7
12 M	0534 1.5	1044 7.6	1749 1.5	2253 7.8
13 TU	0605 1.4	1114 7.7	1820 1.5	2324 7.8
14 W	0634 1.4	1143 7.7	1849 1.5	2356 7.7
15 TH	0702 1.5	1213 7.6	1915 1.6	
16 F	0026 7.6	0727 1.7	1242 7.5	1940 1.8
17 SA	0056 7.4	0751 1.9	1309 7.4	2006 2.0
18 SU	0125 7.2	0817 2.2	1338 7.1	2034 2.3
19 M	0158 6.9	0846 2.6	1414 6.8	2104 2.7
20 TU	0242 6.6	0924 3.0	1502 6.5	2151 3.1
21 W	0342 6.3	1018 3.4	1611 6.3	2301 3.3
22 TH	0514 6.1	1144 3.5	1753 6.3	
23 F	0048 3.2	0653 6.4	1333 3.1	1916 6.6
24 SA	0214 2.6	0757 6.9	1445 2.5	2014 7.1
25 SU	0317 2.0	0848 7.4	1544 1.9	2104 7.6
26 M	0414 1.4	0934 7.8	1639 1.4	2150 7.9
27 TU	0507 1.0	1018 8.0	1730 1.0	2234 8.2
28 W	0556 0.7	1102 8.2	1817 0.8	2319 8.3
29 TH	0640 0.6	1145 8.3	1901 0.7	
30 F	0004 8.3	0722 0.7	1228 8.2	1942 0.9

OCTOBER

Day	Time m	Time m	Time m	Time m
1 SA	0049 8.1	0801 1.1	1311 8.0	2022 1.2
2 SU	0134 7.8	0839 1.6	1355 7.6	2101 1.7
3 M	0222 7.3	0919 2.2	1442 7.2	2144 2.2
4 TU	0318 6.9	1007 2.8	1544 6.8	2242 2.8
5 W	0437 6.5	1121 3.2	1710 6.5	
6 TH	0008 3.0	1116 3.3	1840 6.5	
7 F	0135 2.8	0732 6.7	1413 2.8	1951 6.8
8 SA	0245 2.5	0827 7.0	1516 2.4	2041 7.1
9 SU	0340 2.1	0908 7.3	1604 2.1	2120 7.4
10 M	0423 1.8	0943 7.5	1642 1.8	2154 7.6
11 TU	0459 1.7	1013 7.6	1717 1.7	2225 7.7
12 W	0532 1.6	1042 7.7	1749 1.6	2256 7.7
13 TH	0603 1.6	1113 7.7	1819 1.6	2328 7.7
14 F	0631 1.6	1142 7.6	1847 1.7	2359 7.6
15 SA	0658 1.8	1211 7.6	1914 1.8	
16 SU	0030 7.4	0725 2.0	1240 7.5	1943 2.0
17 M	0102 7.2	0754 2.2	1313 7.2	2013 2.2
18 TU	0140 7.0	0826 2.6	1353 7.0	2045 2.5
19 W	0225 6.7	0904 2.9	1441 6.7	2128 2.9
20 TH	0322 6.5	0957 3.2	1544 6.5	2234 3.1
21 F	0442 6.4	1116 3.3	1712 6.4	
22 SA	0010 3.0	0615 6.6	1255 3.0	1837 6.7
23 SU	0137 2.6	0721 7.0	1411 2.5	1939 7.1
24 M	0244 2.0	0815 7.4	1513 1.9	2033 7.4
25 TU	0343 1.5	0904 7.8	1610 1.4	2123 7.9
26 W	0438 1.1	0951 8.1	1704 1.1	2211 8.1
27 TH	0529 0.9	1037 8.2	1753 0.9	2258 8.2
28 F	0616 0.8	1122 8.3	1839 0.8	2346 8.2
29 SA	0700 1.0	1207 8.2	1923 0.9	
30 SU	0032 8.0	0742 1.3	1251 7.9	2004 1.2
31 M	0119 7.7	0822 1.7	1336 7.6	2045 1.7

NOVEMBER

Day	Time m	Time m	Time m	Time m
1 TU	0208 7.3	0904 2.2	1424 7.2	2129 2.2
2 W	0302 6.9	0953 2.7	1521 6.8	2222 2.7
3 TH	0409 6.6	1057 3.1	1633 6.5	2331 2.9
4 F	0527 6.5	1212 3.2	1752 6.5	
5 SA	0045 2.9	0644 6.6	1323 3.0	1906 6.6
6 SU	0152 2.7	0746 6.8	1425 2.7	2003 6.9
7 M	0249 2.5	0831 7.1	1518 2.4	2047 7.1
8 TU	0338 2.2	0908 7.3	1603 2.1	2124 7.3
9 W	0421 2.0	0941 7.5	1644 1.9	2158 7.5
10 TH	0459 1.9	1013 7.6	1720 1.8	2231 7.5
11 F	0533 1.8	1045 7.6	1752 1.7	2305 7.6
12 SA	0604 1.8	1116 7.6	1823 1.7	2338 7.5
13 SU	0634 1.9	1148 7.6	1854 1.7	
14 M	0012 7.5	0707 2.0	1221 7.5	1927 1.8
15 TU	0048 7.4	0740 2.1	1258 7.4	2001 2.0
16 W	0128 7.2	0816 2.4	1340 7.2	2038 2.3
17 TH	0214 7.0	0856 2.6	1427 7.0	2121 2.5
18 F	0306 6.8	0947 2.9	1523 6.8	2219 2.7
19 SA	0413 6.7	1055 3.0	1634 6.7	2333 2.7
20 SU	0533 6.8	1213 2.8	1755 6.8	
21 M	0052 2.5	0642 7.1	1330 2.5	1903 7.1
22 TU	0206 2.1	0741 7.4	1440 2.0	2004 7.4
23 W	0311 1.7	0836 7.7	1542 1.6	2100 7.7
24 TH	0410 1.4	0927 7.9	1639 1.3	2153 7.9
25 F	0505 1.2	1016 8.1	1732 1.1	2243 8.0
26 SA	0555 1.2	1104 8.1	1821 1.0	2332 8.0
27 SU	0642 1.2	1150 8.1	1906 1.0	
28 M	0020 7.9	0726 1.4	1236 7.9	1950 1.2
29 TU	0106 7.7	0808 1.7	1320 7.7	2031 1.6
30 W	0152 7.4	0850 2.1	1405 7.4	2112 2.0

DECEMBER

Day	Time m	Time m	Time m	Time m
1 TH	0239 7.1	0933 2.5	1453 7.0	2155 2.4
2 F	0330 6.8	1020 2.8	1547 6.7	2244 2.7
3 SA	0429 6.6	1116 3.1	1651 6.5	2341 3.0
4 SU	0535 6.6	1218 3.2	1800 6.5	
5 M	0045 3.0	0643 6.6	1312 3.1	1908 6.6
6 TU	0151 2.9	0742 6.8	1424 2.8	2006 6.7
7 W	0252 2.7	0829 7.0	1524 2.5	2052 7.1
8 TH	0343 2.4	0909 7.2	1611 2.2	2132 7.2
9 F	0428 2.2	0946 7.4	1652 2.0	2210 7.3
10 SA	0507 2.0	1022 7.5	1729 1.8	2246 7.5
11 SU	0543 1.9	1057 7.6	1804 1.7	2322 7.5
12 M	0618 1.9	1131 7.6	1841 1.6	2358 7.5
13 TU	0655 1.9	1208 7.7	1918 1.6	
14 W	0037 7.5	0734 1.9	1247 7.6	1957 1.7
15 TH	0118 7.4	0813 2.0	1329 7.5	2036 1.8
16 F	0202 7.3	0854 2.2	1414 7.3	2118 2.0
17 SA	0249 7.1	0940 2.3	1503 7.2	2205 2.3
18 SU	0344 7.0	1033 2.5	1601 7.0	2302 2.4
19 M	0450 7.0	1136 2.6	1713 6.9	
20 TU	0010 2.5	0603 7.0	1249 2.6	1829 7.0
21 W	0127 2.4	0711 7.2	1408 2.3	1940 7.2
22 TH	0243 2.1	0813 7.5	1518 1.9	2045 7.4
23 F	0347 1.8	0911 7.7	1619 1.6	2142 7.7
24 SA	0445 1.6	1004 7.9	1716 1.3	2234 7.8
25 SU	0540 1.4	1052 8.0	1808 1.1	2322 7.9
26 M	0629 1.4	1138 8.0	1855 1.1	
27 TU	0007 7.9	0713 1.4	1221 7.9	1937 1.2
28 W	0050 7.8	0753 1.6	1302 7.9	2014 1.4
29 TH	0130 7.6	0830 1.8	1341 7.6	2049 1.7
30 F	0209 7.3	0905 2.1	1421 7.3	2121 2.1
31 SA	0248 7.1	0939 2.5	1501 7.0	2155 2.5

Chart Datum: 4·38 metres below IGN Datum
HAT is 8·4 metres above Chart Datum

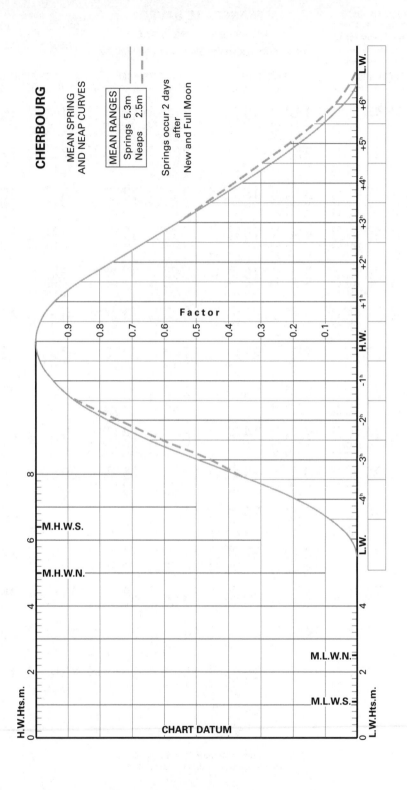

CHERBOURG

MEAN SPRING
AND NEAP CURVES

MEAN RANGES
Springs 5.3m
Neaps 2.5m

Springs occur 2 days
after
New and Full Moon

TIME ZONE -0100
(French Standard Time)
Subtract 1 hour for UT
For French Summer Time add
ONE hour in **non-shaded areas**

FRANCE – CHERBOURG

LAT 49°39′N   LONG 1°38′W

TIMES AND HEIGHTS OF HIGH AND LOW WATERS

Dates in amber are **SPRINGS**
Dates in yellow are **NEAPS**

2011

JANUARY

Day	Time m		Day	Time m
1 SA	0023 2.2 / 0605 5.6 / 1257 2.0 / 1837 5.5		**16** SU	0535 5.1 / 1232 2.5 / 1813 5.1
2 SU	0125 2.0 / 0703 5.8 / 1356 1.8 / 1936 5.7		**17** M	0052 2.4 / 0636 5.4 / 1329 2.1 / 1910 5.5
3 M	0219 1.8 / 0755 6.0 / 1446 1.6 / 2026 5.9		**18** TU	0148 2.0 / 0728 5.8 / 1420 1.6 / 1959 5.8
4 TU ●	0306 1.7 / 0839 6.2 / 1530 1.4 / 2108 6.0		**19** W ○	0238 1.6 / 0814 6.1 / 1508 1.3 / 2045 6.1
5 W	0348 1.6 / 0920 6.3 / 1610 1.3 / 2146 6.1		**20** TH	0326 1.3 / 0900 6.4 / 1554 0.9 / 2131 6.4
6 TH	0426 1.6 / 0957 6.3 / 1647 1.3 / 2222 6.0		**21** F	0411 1.1 / 0944 6.6 / 1638 0.7 / 2215 6.5
7 F	0503 1.6 / 1032 6.2 / 1722 1.4 / 2255 6.0		**22** SA	0455 1.0 / 1028 6.7 / 1721 0.6 / 2259 6.5
8 SA	0536 1.7 / 1106 6.1 / 1754 1.5 / 2327 5.8		**23** SU	0539 1.0 / 1112 6.7 / 1803 0.7 / 2341 6.4
9 SU	0608 1.8 / 1139 5.9 / 1826 1.7 / 2359 5.6		**24** M	0622 1.1 / 1154 6.5 / 1846 1.0
10 M	0641 2.0 / 1210 5.7 / 1858 1.9		**25** TU	0023 6.2 / 0706 1.4 / 1237 6.2 / 1930 1.4
11 TU	0030 5.4 / 0715 2.3 / 1244 5.4 / 1933 2.2		**26** W ☽	0106 5.8 / 0753 1.8 / 1323 5.8 / 2019 1.8
12 W ☽	0107 5.2 / 0755 2.5 / 1324 5.1 / 2014 2.5		**27** TH	0156 5.5 / 0849 2.2 / 1420 5.3 / 2119 2.3
13 TH	0153 5.0 / 0845 2.7 / 1419 4.9 / 2109 2.7		**28** F	0303 5.2 / 0959 2.5 / 1540 5.0 / 2239 2.6
14 F	0256 4.9 / 0954 2.9 / 1534 4.7 / 2223 2.8		**29** SA	0429 5.1 / 1127 2.6 / 1714 5.0
15 SA	0416 4.9 / 1116 2.8 / 1700 4.8 / 2344 2.7		**30** SU	0006 2.6 / 0550 5.2 / 1246 2.3 / 1834 5.2
			31 M	0117 2.3 / 0655 5.5 / 1349 2.0 / 1933 5.5

FEBRUARY

Day	Time m		Day	Time m
1 TU	0213 2.0 / 0747 5.8 / 1438 1.7 / 2018 5.8		**16** W	0127 2.0 / 0707 5.7 / 1400 1.6 / 1941 5.8
2 W	0258 1.8 / 0829 6.0 / 1519 1.4 / 2056 5.9		**17** TH	0221 1.6 / 0757 6.1 / 1450 1.1 / 2029 6.2
3 TH	0336 1.6 / 0907 6.2 / 1555 1.3 / 2130 6.1		**18** F ○	0309 1.1 / 0844 6.5 / 1537 0.7 / 2115 6.5
4 F ●	0410 1.4 / 0941 6.3 / 1629 1.2 / 2201 6.1		**19** SA	0355 0.8 / 0930 6.8 / 1621 0.5 / 2159 6.7
5 SA	0443 1.4 / 1013 6.3 / 1659 1.2 / 2231 6.1		**20** SU	0439 0.6 / 1014 6.9 / 1703 0.4 / 2241 6.7
6 SU	0513 1.4 / 1042 6.2 / 1728 1.3 / 2259 6.0		**21** M	0521 0.6 / 1056 6.9 / 1744 0.5 / 2321 6.6
7 M	0541 1.5 / 1110 6.1 / 1755 1.4 / 2325 5.9		**22** TU	0602 0.8 / 1136 6.6 / 1824 0.8 / 2359 6.3
8 TU	0609 1.7 / 1137 5.9 / 1823 1.6 / 2351 5.7		**23** W	0644 1.1 / 1216 6.2 / 1906 1.3
9 W	0639 1.9 / 1205 5.6 / 1852 1.9		**24** TH	0038 5.9 / 0728 1.6 / 1258 5.7 / 1951 1.9
10 TH	0020 5.4 / 0712 2.2 / 1321 5.3 / 1927 2.2		**25** F ☽	0122 5.5 / 0819 2.1 / 1351 5.2 / 2047 2.3
11 F ☽	0056 5.2 / 0753 2.5 / 1321 5.0 / 2013 2.6		**26** SA	0225 5.1 / 0928 2.5 / 1515 4.8 / 2212 2.8
12 SA	0148 4.9 / 0851 2.7 / 1429 4.7 / 2121 2.8		**27** SU	0401 4.8 / 1105 2.6 / 1706 4.7 / 2352 2.8
13 SU	0311 4.7 / 1017 2.8 / 1613 4.6 / 2256 2.8		**28** M	0535 5.0 / 1233 2.4 / 1828 5.0
14 M	0454 4.8 / 1151 2.6 / 1746 4.9			
15 TU	0023 2.5 / 0611 5.2 / 1304 2.1 / 1849 5.4			

MARCH

Day	Time m		Day	Time m
1 TU	0106 2.4 / 0642 5.3 / 1335 2.0 / 1920 5.4		**16** W	0542 5.1 / 1235 2.1 / 1825 5.3
2 W	0159 2.1 / 0731 5.7 / 1422 1.7 / 1959 5.7		**17** TH	0102 2.0 / 0642 5.7 / 1334 1.5 / 1918 5.8
3 TH	0241 1.8 / 0810 5.9 / 1500 1.4 / 2034 5.9		**18** F	0158 1.5 / 0734 6.2 / 1416 1.0 / 2006 6.3
4 F ●	0316 1.5 / 0846 6.1 / 1533 1.3 / 2105 6.1		**19** SA ○	0247 1.0 / 0823 6.6 / 1513 0.6 / 2052 6.6
5 SA	0348 1.4 / 0918 6.2 / 1603 1.2 / 2135 6.1		**20** SU	0334 0.7 / 0909 6.8 / 1559 0.4 / 2136 6.8
6 SU	0418 1.3 / 0948 6.3 / 1632 1.1 / 2203 6.1		**21** M	0418 0.5 / 0954 6.9 / 1641 0.4 / 2218 6.8
7 M	0446 1.3 / 1016 6.2 / 1659 1.2 / 2228 6.1		**22** TU	0500 0.5 / 1036 6.8 / 1722 0.6 / 2257 6.7
8 TU	0514 1.4 / 1042 6.1 / 1725 1.3 / 2253 6.0		**23** W	0541 0.7 / 1117 6.6 / 1802 1.0 / 2335 6.4
9 W	0541 1.5 / 1109 5.9 / 1752 1.5 / 2319 5.8		**24** TH	0623 1.1 / 1156 6.2 / 1842 1.5
10 TH	0609 1.7 / 1136 5.7 / 1821 1.8 / 2347 5.6		**25** F	0013 5.9 / 0706 1.6 / 1238 5.6 / 1927 2.1
11 F	0641 1.9 / 1207 5.4 / 1854 2.1		**26** SA ☽	0056 5.5 / 0755 2.1 / 1331 5.1 / 2022 2.6
12 SA	0020 5.3 / 0720 2.3 / 1247 5.0 / 1938 2.5		**27** SU	0157 5.0 / 0902 2.5 / 1454 4.7 / 2146 2.9
13 SU ☽	0107 5.0 / 0814 2.5 / 1351 4.7 / 2044 2.8		**28** M	0331 4.8 / 1035 2.7 / 1641 4.7 / 2323 2.8
14 M	0224 4.7 / 0936 2.7 / 1537 4.6 / 2220 2.8		**29** TU	0504 4.8 / 1201 2.5 / 1759 4.9
15 TU	0416 4.6 / 1115 2.5 / 1719 4.9 / 2354 2.5		**30** W	0037 2.5 / 0611 5.1 / 1303 2.1 / 1848 5.3
			31 TH	0129 2.2 / 0700 5.5 / 1349 1.8 / 1927 5.6

APRIL

Day	Time m		Day	Time m
1 F	0211 1.8 / 0740 5.8 / 1428 1.6 / 2002 5.8		**16** SA	0129 1.5 / 0706 6.1 / 1358 1.0 / 1938 6.3
2 SA	0247 1.6 / 0816 6.0 / 1501 1.4 / 2035 6.0		**17** SU	0222 1.0 / 0757 6.5 / 1447 0.7 / 2026 6.6
3 SU	0320 1.4 / 0850 6.1 / 1532 1.3 / 2105 6.1		**18** M ○	0310 0.8 / 0846 6.7 / 1534 0.6 / 2111 6.7
4 M	0350 1.3 / 0921 6.1 / 1601 1.3 / 2133 6.1		**19** TU	0356 0.6 / 0933 6.7 / 1618 0.6 / 2154 6.7
5 TU	0419 1.3 / 0949 6.1 / 1630 1.3 / 2159 6.1		**20** W	0440 0.6 / 1017 6.6 / 1700 0.6 / 2234 6.6
6 W	0448 1.3 / 1018 6.1 / 1658 1.4 / 2227 6.0		**21** TH	0522 0.8 / 1059 6.4 / 1741 0.9 / 2314 6.3
7 TH	0517 1.4 / 1047 5.9 / 1727 1.6 / 2256 5.9		**22** F	0604 1.1 / 1140 6.0 / 1823 1.6 / 2354 5.9
8 F	0547 1.6 / 1119 5.7 / 1758 1.8 / 2327 5.7		**23** SA	0648 1.6 / 1223 5.5 / 1908 2.1
9 SA	0621 1.8 / 1153 5.4 / 1834 2.1		**24** SU	0038 5.5 / 0736 2.0 / 1315 5.1 / 2002 2.5
10 SU	0004 5.4 / 0702 2.1 / 1237 5.1 / 1921 2.4		**25** M ☾	0135 5.1 / 0836 2.4 / 1425 4.8 / 2113 2.8
11 M	0052 5.1 / 0757 2.3 / 1339 4.8 / 2027 2.7		**26** TU	0252 4.8 / 0951 2.5 / 1550 4.7 / 2236 2.8
12 TU	0205 4.9 / 0913 2.5 / 1513 4.7 / 2156 2.7		**27** W	0413 4.8 / 1108 2.5 / 1704 4.9 / 2347 2.6
13 W	0342 4.9 / 1043 2.3 / 1647 5.0 / 2323 2.4		**28** TH	0521 5.0 / 1211 2.3 / 1800 5.1
14 TH	0507 5.2 / 1203 1.9 / 1754 5.4		**29** F	0044 2.3 / 0615 5.3 / 1303 2.0 / 1844 5.4
15 F	0032 1.9 / 0610 5.7 / 1304 1.5 / 1848 5.9		**30** SA	0131 2.0 / 0701 5.5 / 1346 1.8 / 1923 5.6

Chart Datum: 3·33 metres below IGN Datum
HAT is 7·0 metres above Chart Datum

TIDES

TIDES

TIME ZONE -0100
(French Standard Time)
Subtract 1 hour for UT
For French Summer Time add
ONE hour in **non-shaded areas**

FRANCE – CHERBOURG
LAT 49°39′N   LONG 1°38′W
TIMES AND HEIGHTS OF HIGH AND LOW WATERS

Dates in amber are **SPRINGS**
Dates in yellow are **NEAPS**

2011

MAY

Time	m	Time	m
1 SU 0211 1.8 / 0742 5.7 / 1424 1.6 / 2000 5.8		**16** M 0156 1.2 / 0733 6.2 / 1422 1.1 / 2001 6.4	
2 M 0246 1.6 / 0819 5.9 / 1458 1.5 / 2033 6.0		**17** TU 0248 1.0 / 0826 6.4 / 1511 1.0 / 2048 6.5	
3 TU 0320 1.5 / 0853 5.9 / 1531 1.5 / 2104 6.0		**18** W 0337 0.9 / 0915 6.4 / 1558 1.0 / 2133 6.5	
4 W 0353 1.4 / 0926 6.0 / 1603 1.4 / 2135 6.1		**19** TH 0423 0.9 / 1001 6.3 / 1642 1.2 / 2216 6.4	
5 TH 0425 1.3 / 0958 6.0 / 1636 1.5 / 2207 6.0		**20** F 0506 1.0 / 1044 6.1 / 1724 1.4 / 2257 6.2	
6 F 0459 1.4 / 1032 5.9 / 1709 1.6 / 2241 6.0		**21** SA 0549 1.2 / 1126 5.9 / 1807 1.7 / 2339 6.0	
7 SA 0533 1.5 / 1109 5.7 / 1745 1.8 / 2319 5.8		**22** SU 0632 1.5 / 1209 5.6 / 1851 2.0	
8 SU 0611 1.6 / 1150 5.5 / 1826 2.0		**23** M 0022 5.6 / 0716 1.8 / 1255 5.3 / 1938 2.3	
9 M 0001 5.6 / 0656 1.8 / 1237 5.3 / 1916 2.2		**24** TU 0111 5.3 / 0805 2.1 / 1347 5.0 / 2034 2.6	
10 TU 0051 5.2 / 0750 2.0 / 1335 5.1 / 2019 2.4		**25** W 0208 5.1 / 0902 2.3 / 1449 4.9 / 2139 2.7	
11 W 0154 5.2 / 0857 2.1 / 1450 5.0 / 2134 2.4		**26** TH 0313 4.9 / 1005 2.4 / 1556 4.9 / 2246 2.7	
12 TH 0312 5.1 / 1013 2.1 / 1611 5.0 / 2251 2.2		**27** F 0419 4.9 / 1109 2.4 / 1659 5.0 / 2348 2.5	
13 F 0429 5.3 / 1127 1.8 / 1719 5.5		**28** SA 0521 5.0 / 1208 2.3 / 1754 5.2	
14 SA 0000 1.9 / 0537 5.6 / 1232 1.5 / 1817 5.8		**29** SU 0043 2.3 / 0616 5.2 / 1259 2.1 / 1841 5.4	
15 SU 0101 1.6 / 0637 6.0 / 1329 1.3 / 1910 6.1		**30** M 0130 2.1 / 0705 5.4 / 1344 1.9 / 1924 5.6	
		31 TU 0213 1.8 / 0748 5.6 / 1425 1.8 / 2003 5.8	

JUNE

Time	m	Time	m
1 W 0252 1.6 / 0828 5.7 / 1503 1.7 / 2040 5.9		**16** TH 0323 1.1 / 0903 6.1 / 1542 1.3 / 2118 6.3	
2 TH 0330 1.5 / 0906 5.9 / 1541 1.6 / 2116 6.0		**17** F 0410 1.1 / 0949 6.1 / 1627 1.4 / 2202 6.3	
3 F 0407 1.4 / 0943 5.9 / 1619 1.5 / 2153 6.1		**18** SA 0453 1.1 / 1031 6.1 / 1710 1.5 / 2243 6.2	
4 SA 0446 1.3 / 1021 5.9 / 1658 1.5 / 2232 6.1		**19** SU 0534 1.2 / 1111 5.9 / 1750 1.6 / 2323 6.1	
5 SU 0525 1.3 / 1102 5.9 / 1739 1.6 / 2314 6.0		**20** M 0613 1.4 / 1149 5.7 / 1829 1.8	
6 M 0607 1.4 / 1146 5.8 / 1823 1.7 / 2358 5.9		**21** TU 0002 5.8 / 0651 1.6 / 1227 5.5 / 1909 2.1	
7 TU 0652 1.5 / 1233 5.6 / 1912 1.9		**22** W 0041 5.6 / 0730 1.9 / 1307 5.3 / 1951 2.3	
8 W 0046 5.7 / 0742 1.6 / 1324 5.4 / 2008 2.0		**23** TH 0123 5.3 / 0812 2.1 / 1351 5.1 / 2040 2.5	
9 TH 0140 5.5 / 0839 1.8 / 1425 5.3 / 2111 2.1		**24** F 0211 5.0 / 0901 2.4 / 1444 4.9 / 2138 2.7	
10 F 0243 5.4 / 0944 1.9 / 1534 5.3 / 2220 2.1		**25** SA 0309 4.8 / 1001 2.5 / 1547 4.9 / 2246 2.7	
11 SA 0354 5.4 / 1053 1.9 / 1644 5.4 / 2330 2.0		**26** SU 0418 4.8 / 1108 2.5 / 1656 5.0 / 2353 2.6	
12 SU 0506 5.5 / 1203 1.8 / 1748 5.7		**27** M 0529 4.9 / 1211 2.4 / 1759 5.2	
13 M 0036 1.8 / 0614 5.7 / 1305 1.6 / 1847 5.9		**28** TU 0051 2.3 / 0630 5.1 / 1307 2.2 / 1851 5.4	
14 TU 0137 1.5 / 0716 5.9 / 1402 1.5 / 1942 6.1		**29** W 0141 2.0 / 0721 5.4 / 1356 2.0 / 1937 5.7	
15 W 0232 1.3 / 0813 6.0 / 1454 1.4 / 2032 6.3		**30** TH 0227 1.8 / 0807 5.6 / 1441 1.8 / 2020 5.9	

JULY

Time	m	Time	m
1 F 0310 1.5 / 0849 5.8 / 1524 1.6 / 2100 6.1		**16** SA 0358 1.2 / 0937 6.0 / 1614 1.4 / 2148 6.3	
2 SA 0353 1.3 / 0930 6.0 / 1606 1.4 / 2141 6.2		**17** SU 0438 1.1 / 1015 6.1 / 1652 1.4 / 2226 6.3	
3 SU 0434 1.1 / 1012 6.1 / 1649 1.3 / 2223 6.3		**18** M 0514 1.2 / 1050 6.0 / 1729 1.5 / 2301 6.2	
4 M 0516 1.0 / 1054 6.1 / 1731 1.3 / 2305 6.3		**19** TU 0548 1.3 / 1123 5.9 / 1802 1.6 / 2335 6.0	
5 TU 0558 1.0 / 1137 6.1 / 1815 1.4 / 2349 6.2		**20** W 0620 1.5 / 1154 5.7 / 1835 1.8	
6 W 0641 1.1 / 1220 5.9 / 1900 1.5		**21** TH 0007 5.7 / 0652 1.7 / 1225 5.5 / 1908 2.1	
7 TH 0033 6.0 / 0726 1.3 / 1306 5.7 / 1949 1.7		**22** F 0039 5.4 / 0725 2.0 / 1258 5.3 / 1946 2.4	
8 F 0121 5.8 / 0817 1.6 / 1357 5.6 / 2045 2.0		**23** SA 0115 5.1 / 0804 2.3 / 1338 5.1 / 2034 2.6	
9 SA 0216 5.5 / 0915 1.9 / 1458 5.4 / 2151 2.1		**24** SU 0203 4.9 / 0854 2.6 / 1433 4.9 / 2138 2.8	
10 SU 0324 5.3 / 1024 2.1 / 1512 5.3 / 2305 2.2		**25** M 0311 4.7 / 1003 2.8 / 1550 4.8 / 2258 2.8	
11 M 0445 5.2 / 1140 2.1 / 1727 5.4		**26** TU 0440 4.7 / 1124 2.7 / 1716 4.9	
12 TU 0019 2.0 / 0603 5.3 / 1250 2.0 / 1834 5.7		**27** W 0014 2.5 / 0559 4.9 / 1234 2.5 / 1822 5.2	
13 W 0125 1.8 / 0710 5.6 / 1351 1.8 / 1932 5.9		**28** TH 0113 2.2 / 0657 5.2 / 1331 2.1 / 1914 5.6	
14 TH 0223 1.5 / 0807 5.8 / 1445 1.6 / 2023 6.1		**29** F 0204 1.8 / 0746 5.6 / 1420 1.8 / 2000 5.9	
15 F 0313 1.3 / 0856 6.0 / 1532 1.5 / 2108 6.2		**30** SA 0251 1.4 / 0831 5.9 / 1507 1.5 / 2044 6.2	
		31 SU 0336 1.1 / 0915 6.2 / 1551 1.2 / 2127 6.4	

AUGUST

Time	m	Time	m
1 M 0419 0.9 / 0957 6.3 / 1634 1.0 / 2209 6.6		**16** TU 0448 1.2 / 1022 6.1 / 1702 1.4 / 2234 6.3	
2 TU 0500 0.7 / 1039 6.4 / 1716 1.0 / 2252 6.6		**17** W 0518 1.2 / 1051 6.0 / 1731 1.5 / 2303 6.1	
3 W 0542 0.7 / 1121 6.4 / 1758 1.0 / 2334 6.5		**18** TH 0546 1.4 / 1118 5.9 / 1800 1.7 / 2331 5.9	
4 TH 0623 0.9 / 1201 6.2 / 1841 1.2		**19** F 0614 1.7 / 1144 5.7 / 1819 1.9 / 2358 5.6	
5 F 0015 6.3 / 0705 1.2 / 1242 6.0 / 1927 1.5		**20** SA 0643 2.0 / 1212 5.5 / 1901 2.0	
6 SA 0059 5.9 / 0752 1.6 / 1328 5.7 / 2019 1.9		**21** SU 0029 5.3 / 0716 2.3 / 1246 5.2 / 1940 2.5	
7 SU 0151 5.5 / 0847 2.1 / 1426 5.3 / 2125 2.3		**22** M 0110 4.9 / 0758 2.6 / 1333 4.9 / 2037 2.8	
8 M 0302 5.1 / 1000 2.4 / 1547 5.1 / 2249 2.4		**23** TU 0214 4.6 / 0903 2.9 / 1449 4.7 / 2202 2.9	
9 TU 0436 5.0 / 1128 2.5 / 1715 5.2		**24** W 0354 4.5 / 1038 2.9 / 1634 4.8 / 2338 2.7	
10 W 0012 2.2 / 0603 5.1 / 1244 2.3 / 1828 5.5		**25** TH 0531 4.8 / 1204 2.7 / 1754 5.1	
11 TH 0120 1.9 / 0709 5.4 / 1346 2.0 / 1925 5.8		**26** F 0046 2.3 / 0633 5.2 / 1307 2.2 / 1849 5.6	
12 F 0216 1.6 / 0800 5.7 / 1436 1.7 / 2012 6.1		**27** SA 0139 1.8 / 0723 5.7 / 1358 1.7 / 1937 6.0	
13 SA 0302 1.4 / 0842 6.0 / 1519 1.5 / 2053 6.2		**28** SU 0227 1.3 / 0809 6.1 / 1445 1.3 / 2022 6.4	
14 SU 0341 1.2 / 0918 6.1 / 1556 1.4 / 2129 6.3		**29** M 0313 0.9 / 0853 6.4 / 1530 1.0 / 2107 6.7	
15 M 0416 1.1 / 0951 6.1 / 1629 1.4 / 2203 6.3		**30** TU 0357 0.7 / 0936 6.6 / 1613 0.8 / 2150 6.8	
		31 W 0439 0.5 / 1018 6.7 / 1656 0.7 / 2232 6.8	

Chart Datum: 3·33 metres below IGN Datum
HAT is 7·0 metres above Chart Datum

TIME ZONE -0100
(French Standard Time)
Subtract 1 hour for UT
For French Summer Time add
ONE hour in **non-shaded areas**

FRANCE – CHERBOURG
LAT 49°39′N LONG 1°38′W
TIMES AND HEIGHTS OF HIGH AND LOW WATERS

Dates in amber are **SPRINGS**
Dates in yellow are **NEAPS**

2011

SEPTEMBER

Day	Time m	Day	Time m
1 TH	0520 0.6 / 1058 6.6 / 1737 0.8 / 2314 6.7	**16** F	0513 1.5 / 1041 6.0 / 1727 1.6 / 2256 5.9
2 F	0601 0.8 / 1138 6.4 / 1819 1.1 / 2355 6.5	**17** SA	0540 1.7 / 1106 5.8 / 1755 1.8 / 2324 5.7
3 SA	0642 1.3 / 1217 6.1 / 1904 1.5	**18** SU	0607 2.0 / 1134 5.6 / 1826 2.1 / 2354 5.4
4 SU ☽	0038 5.9 / 0728 1.8 / 1301 5.7 / 1956 2.0	**19** M	0639 2.3 / 1206 5.3 / 1903 2.4
5 M	0130 5.4 / 0823 2.3 / 1359 5.3 / 2104 2.4	**20** TU ☾	0034 5.0 / 0720 2.6 / 1252 5.0 / 1954 2.7
6 TU	0247 4.9 / 0942 2.7 / 1528 5.0 / 2237 2.6	**21** W	0135 4.7 / 0822 2.9 / 1404 4.8 / 2114 2.9
7 W	0434 4.8 / 1120 2.7 / 1705 5.1	**22** TH	0315 4.6 / 0957 3.0 / 1551 4.8 / 2256 2.7
8 TH	0004 2.4 / 0600 5.1 / 1236 2.4 / 1817 5.4	**23** F	0458 4.8 / 1131 2.7 / 1719 5.1
9 F	0109 2.0 / 0658 5.4 / 1334 2.1 / 1910 5.7	**24** SA	0014 2.3 / 0603 5.3 / 1238 2.2 / 1818 5.6
10 SA	0159 1.7 / 0741 5.8 / 1419 1.7 / 1952 6.0	**25** SU	0110 1.7 / 0654 5.8 / 1331 1.7 / 1908 6.1
11 SU	0240 1.5 / 0818 6.0 / 1457 1.6 / 2029 6.2	**26** M	0200 1.2 / 0740 6.2 / 1419 1.2 / 1955 6.5
12 M ○	0316 1.3 / 0851 6.2 / 1531 1.4 / 2103 6.3	**27** TU ●	0247 0.9 / 0826 6.5 / 1505 0.9 / 2041 6.8
13 TU	0348 1.2 / 0922 6.2 / 1602 1.4 / 2135 6.3	**28** W	0331 0.6 / 0909 6.8 / 1550 0.7 / 2126 6.9
14 W	0418 1.2 / 0951 6.2 / 1632 1.4 / 2204 6.3	**29** TH	0415 0.6 / 0952 6.8 / 1633 0.7 / 2210 6.9
15 TH	0446 1.3 / 1017 6.1 / 1700 1.5 / 2230 6.1	**30** F	0456 0.7 / 1033 6.7 / 1716 0.8 / 2253 6.7

OCTOBER

Day	Time m	Day	Time m
1 SA	0538 1.0 / 1113 6.5 / 1758 1.1 / 2335 6.3	**16** SU	0512 1.8 / 1038 5.9 / 1730 1.8 / 2300 5.7
2 SU	0621 1.5 / 1153 6.1 / 1844 1.6	**17** M	0542 2.0 / 1109 5.7 / 1802 2.0 / 2334 5.5
3 M	0020 5.8 / 0707 2.0 / 1238 5.7 / 1936 2.1	**18** TU	0615 2.3 / 1145 5.5 / 1840 2.3
4 TU ☾	0114 5.3 / 0804 2.5 / 1337 5.2 / 2044 2.5	**19** W	0016 5.2 / 0658 2.6 / 1231 5.2 / 1931 2.5
5 W	0232 4.9 / 0925 2.9 / 1504 5.0 / 2216 2.6	**20** TH ☾	0115 4.9 / 0759 2.8 / 1343 5.0 / 2042 2.7
6 TH	0415 4.8 / 1100 2.9 / 1639 5.1 / 2340 2.5	**21** F	0242 4.8 / 0923 2.9 / 1509 4.9 / 2214 2.6
7 F	0536 5.1 / 1212 2.6 / 1749 5.3	**22** SA	0417 4.9 / 1053 2.7 / 1636 5.2 / 2336 2.3
8 SA	0041 2.2 / 0629 5.4 / 1307 2.2 / 1840 5.6	**23** SU	0526 5.3 / 1203 2.2 / 1741 5.6
9 SU	0129 1.9 / 0709 5.7 / 1351 1.9 / 1922 5.9	**24** M	0037 1.8 / 0620 5.8 / 1300 1.7 / 1835 6.1
10 M	0209 1.6 / 0745 5.9 / 1428 1.7 / 1959 6.1	**25** TU	0129 1.3 / 0709 6.2 / 1352 1.3 / 1926 6.5
11 TU	0244 1.5 / 0819 6.1 / 1502 1.6 / 2033 6.2	**26** W ●	0219 1.0 / 0756 6.6 / 1440 1.0 / 2016 6.7
12 W ○	0316 1.4 / 0850 6.2 / 1533 1.5 / 2105 6.2	**27** TH	0306 0.8 / 0842 6.8 / 1527 0.8 / 2103 6.8
13 TH	0346 1.4 / 0918 6.2 / 1603 1.5 / 2134 6.2	**28** F	0351 0.8 / 0927 6.8 / 1612 0.7 / 2150 6.8
14 F	0415 1.5 / 0944 6.1 / 1632 1.5 / 2202 6.1	**29** SA	0435 0.9 / 1009 6.7 / 1657 0.9 / 2235 6.6
15 SA	0444 1.6 / 1010 6.1 / 1701 1.6 / 2230 5.9	**30** SU	0519 1.2 / 1051 6.5 / 1741 1.2 / 2319 6.2
		31 M	0603 1.6 / 1134 6.2 / 1827 1.6

NOVEMBER

Day	Time m	Day	Time m
1 TU	0005 5.8 / 0650 2.1 / 1220 5.8 / 1918 2.0	**16** W	0604 2.1 / 1136 5.7 / 1830 2.0
2 W ●	0058 5.4 / 0744 2.5 / 1315 5.4 / 2018 2.4	**17** TH	0009 5.4 / 0649 2.3 / 1222 5.5 / 1918 2.2
3 TH	0205 5.0 / 0854 2.8 / 1428 5.1 / 2134 2.6	**18** F	0103 5.1 / 0745 2.5 / 1319 5.3 / 2020 2.3
4 F	0327 4.9 / 1016 2.9 / 1549 5.0 / 2252 2.6	**19** SA	0212 5.1 / 0854 2.6 / 1431 5.2 / 2134 2.4
5 SA	0443 5.0 / 1128 2.7 / 1700 5.1 / 2355 2.4	**20** SU	0331 5.1 / 1012 2.5 / 1549 5.3 / 2251 2.2
6 SU	0542 5.2 / 1226 2.4 / 1757 5.4	**21** M	0443 5.4 / 1125 2.2 / 1701 5.6
7 M	0047 2.2 / 0628 5.5 / 1313 2.2 / 1844 5.6	**22** TU	0001 1.9 / 0544 5.8 / 1229 1.9 / 1803 5.9
8 TU	0131 1.7 / 0707 5.7 / 1355 1.9 / 1925 5.8	**23** W	0100 1.5 / 0639 6.1 / 1326 1.5 / 1901 6.2
9 W	0209 1.8 / 0744 5.9 / 1431 1.8 / 2003 6.0	**24** TH	0154 1.3 / 0730 6.4 / 1419 1.2 / 1955 6.5
10 TH ○	0244 1.7 / 0818 6.1 / 1505 1.6 / 2037 6.0	**25** F ●	0244 1.1 / 0819 6.6 / 1509 1.0 / 2046 6.6
11 F	0317 1.6 / 0849 6.1 / 1538 1.6 / 2109 6.1	**26** SA	0333 1.1 / 0906 6.7 / 1557 0.9 / 2135 6.6
12 SA	0349 1.6 / 0918 6.1 / 1609 1.5 / 2140 6.0	**27** SU	0419 1.1 / 0952 6.7 / 1643 1.0 / 2221 6.4
13 SU	0421 1.7 / 0948 6.1 / 1641 1.6 / 2212 6.0	**28** M	0504 1.3 / 1035 6.5 / 1728 1.2 / 2306 6.2
14 M	0453 1.8 / 1021 6.0 / 1714 1.7 / 2247 5.8	**29** TU	0548 1.6 / 1119 6.2 / 1812 1.5 / 2350 5.9
15 TU	0526 1.9 / 1057 5.9 / 1749 1.8 / 2325 5.6	**30** W	0633 2.0 / 1203 5.9 / 1857 1.8

DECEMBER

Day	Time m	Day	Time m
1 TH	0036 5.5 / 0720 2.3 / 1250 5.6 / 1945 2.1	**16** F	0001 5.7 / 0641 2.0 / 1213 5.8 / 1907 1.7
2 F ●	0126 5.2 / 0812 2.6 / 1344 5.3 / 2040 2.4	**17** SA	0048 5.5 / 0730 2.2 / 1301 5.6 / 1959 1.9
3 SA	0225 5.0 / 0914 2.8 / 1447 5.0 / 2143 2.6	**18** SU	0142 5.4 / 0827 2.3 / 1358 5.5 / 2059 2.1
4 SU	0331 5.0 / 1024 2.8 / 1555 5.0 / 2251 2.6	**19** M	0247 5.3 / 0934 2.3 / 1507 5.4 / 2209 2.1
5 M	0438 5.0 / 1131 2.7 / 1702 5.0 / 2353 2.5	**20** TU	0400 5.4 / 1048 2.3 / 1624 5.4 / 2324 2.1
6 TU	0537 5.2 / 1229 2.5 / 1800 5.2	**21** W	0511 5.6 / 1200 2.0 / 1738 5.6
7 W	0048 2.3 / 0627 5.4 / 1319 2.2 / 1850 5.5	**22** TH	0034 1.9 / 0615 5.9 / 1306 1.7 / 1844 5.9
8 TH	0134 2.1 / 0710 5.7 / 1401 2.0 / 1934 5.7	**23** F	0134 1.6 / 0712 6.1 / 1404 1.4 / 1943 6.1
9 F	0214 2.0 / 0750 5.9 / 1439 1.8 / 2013 5.8	**24** SA ●	0229 1.4 / 0805 6.4 / 1457 1.2 / 2036 6.3
10 SA ○	0252 1.8 / 0826 6.0 / 1516 1.6 / 2049 6.0	**25** SU	0319 1.3 / 0854 6.5 / 1546 1.0 / 2125 6.4
11 SU	0328 1.7 / 0900 6.1 / 1551 1.5 / 2124 6.0	**26** M	0407 1.3 / 0940 6.6 / 1632 1.0 / 2209 6.3
12 M	0404 1.7 / 0934 6.2 / 1628 1.4 / 2200 6.0	**27** TU	0451 1.3 / 1023 6.5 / 1715 1.1 / 2251 6.2
13 TU	0441 1.7 / 1010 6.2 / 1704 1.4 / 2238 6.0	**28** W	0533 1.5 / 1103 6.4 / 1754 1.3 / 2330 6.0
14 W	0518 1.7 / 1049 6.1 / 1742 1.5 / 2318 5.9	**29** TH	0612 1.7 / 1142 6.1 / 1832 1.5
15 TH	0558 1.8 / 1129 6.0 / 1823 1.6	**30** F	0008 5.8 / 0650 2.0 / 1220 5.8 / 1910 1.8
		31 SA	0045 5.5 / 0729 2.3 / 1300 5.5 / 1949 2.2

Chart Datum: 3·33 metres below IGN Datum
HAT is 7·0 metres above Chart Datum

TIDES

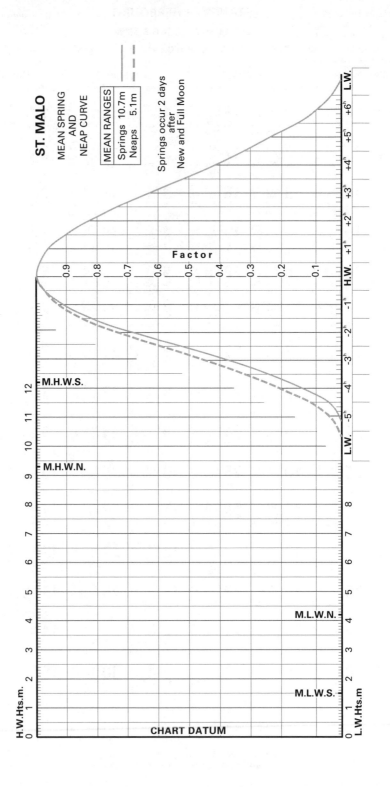

ST. MALO

MEAN SPRING
AND
NEAP CURVE

MEAN RANGES
Springs 10.7m
Neaps 5.1m

Springs occur 2 days
after
New and Full Moon

JANUARY

Time m	Time m
1 0421 10.1 / 1107 3.3 / SA 1651 10.2 / 2340 3.2	**16** 0345 9.1 / 1030 4.2 / SU 1622 9.3 / 2303 3.9
2 0522 10.6 / 1210 2.8 / SU 1750 10.6	**17** 0449 9.8 / 1136 3.5 / M 1722 10.0
3 0038 2.8 / 0614 11.1 / M 1304 2.4 / 1840 11.0	**18** 0004 3.2 / 0543 10.6 / TU 1234 2.7 / 1814 10.8
4 0127 2.5 / 0659 11.5 / TU 1351 2.1 / ● 1924 11.3	**19** 0059 2.5 / 0632 11.4 / W 1328 2.0 / ○ 1902 11.4
5 0210 2.3 / 0739 11.7 / W 1433 1.9 / 2003 11.4	**20** 0151 1.8 / 0719 12.0 / TH 1420 1.5 / 1948 11.9
6 0249 2.2 / 0816 11.7 / TH 1511 1.9 / 2038 11.4	**21** 0240 1.4 / 0804 12.5 / F 1509 1.0 / 2032 12.3
7 0325 2.2 / 0851 11.7 / F 1546 2.0 / 2112 11.3	**22** 0327 1.1 / 0847 12.8 / SA 1555 0.9 / 2115 12.4
8 0358 2.4 / 0924 11.4 / SA 1618 2.3 / 2143 11.0	**23** 0411 1.0 / 0930 12.7 / SU 1638 1.0 / 2156 12.2
9 0428 2.7 / 0955 11.0 / SU 1647 2.6 / 2213 10.6	**24** 0453 1.3 / 1012 12.4 / M 1718 1.4 / 2237 11.7
10 0456 3.1 / 1025 10.5 / M 1715 3.1 / 2243 10.2	**25** 0533 1.9 / 1054 11.7 / TU 1758 2.1 / 2319 11.0
11 0524 3.5 / 1055 10.0 / TU 1746 3.6 / 2315 9.7	**26** 0615 2.6 / 1138 10.9 / W 1840 3.0 / ◐
12 0558 4.0 / 1130 9.5 / W 1823 4.0 / ◑ 2355 9.2	**27** 0005 10.2 / 0702 3.4 / TH 1231 10.0 / 1930 3.7
13 0642 4.5 / 1219 8.9 / TH 1913 4.5	**28** 0106 9.5 / 0804 4.0 / F 1343 9.3 / 2040 4.3
14 0055 8.8 / 0743 4.8 / F 1336 8.6 / 2023 4.7	**29** 0233 9.2 / 0925 4.2 / SA 1519 9.1 / 2207 4.3
15 0223 8.7 / 0907 4.7 / SA 1508 8.7 / 2149 4.5	**30** 0405 9.4 / 1049 3.9 / SU 1643 9.5 / 2326 3.8
	31 0513 10.1 / 1158 3.2 / M 1743 10.1

FEBRUARY

Time m	Time m
1 0027 3.2 / 0604 10.7 / TU 1253 2.7 / 1831 10.7	**16** 0523 10.4 / 1214 2.7 / W 1757 10.7
2 0117 2.6 / 0647 11.2 / W 1339 2.2 / 1911 11.1	**17** 0041 2.4 / 0615 11.4 / TH 1313 1.8 / 1847 11.6
3 0158 2.2 / 0725 11.6 / TH 1419 1.9 / ● 1946 11.4	**18** 0137 1.5 / 0704 12.3 / F 1407 1.0 / ○ 1933 12.3
4 0235 2.0 / 0759 11.8 / F 1455 1.7 / 2019 11.5	**19** 0228 0.8 / 0749 12.9 / SA 1456 0.5 / 2016 12.7
5 0308 1.9 / 0831 11.8 / SA 1526 1.7 / 2049 11.6	**20** 0314 0.4 / 0832 13.2 / SU 1540 0.3 / 2058 12.9
6 0338 1.9 / 0901 11.7 / SU 1555 1.8 / 2118 11.4	**21** 0357 0.4 / 0914 13.2 / M 1621 0.5 / 2137 12.6
7 0405 2.1 / 0929 11.4 / M 1620 2.1 / 2144 11.1	**22** 0437 0.8 / 0953 12.7 / TU 1659 1.1 / 2215 12.1
8 0429 2.5 / 0955 11.0 / TU 1645 2.5 / 2209 10.7	**23** 0514 1.5 / 1032 11.9 / W 1734 2.0 / 2253 11.3
9 0453 2.9 / 1020 10.5 / W 1710 3.0 / 2235 10.2	**24** 0550 2.4 / 1112 10.9 / TH 1810 3.0 / 2334 10.3
10 0520 3.4 / 1047 9.9 / TH 1739 3.6 / 2306 9.6	**25** 0632 3.4 / 1159 9.8 / F 1855 4.0 / ◐
11 0554 4.0 / 1123 9.3 / F 1819 4.2 / ◑ 2348 9.0	**26** 0029 9.4 / 0729 4.2 / SA 1310 8.9 / 2004 4.7
12 0644 4.5 / 1219 8.6 / SA 1918 4.7	**27** 0202 8.8 / 0856 4.6 / SU 1502 8.6 / 2144 4.8
13 0103 8.5 / 0800 4.8 / SU 1409 8.3 / 2050 4.8	**28** 0348 9.0 / 1031 4.2 / M 1631 9.1 / 2311 4.2
14 0249 8.6 / 0945 4.5 / M 1551 8.8 / 2229 4.3	
15 0422 9.4 / 1109 3.7 / TU 1701 9.7 / 2341 3.3	

MARCH

Time m	Time m
1 0457 9.7 / 1143 3.5 / TU 1728 9.9	**16** 0351 9.4 / 1041 3.7 / W 1636 9.7 / 2315 3.4
2 0011 3.4 / 0546 10.5 / W 1235 2.8 / 1811 10.6	**17** 0457 10.4 / 1150 2.7 / TH 1733 10.8
3 0058 2.7 / 0627 11.1 / TH 1318 2.3 / 1848 11.1	**18** 0018 2.3 / 0552 11.5 / F 1251 1.7 / 1824 11.7
4 0137 2.2 / 0702 11.5 / F 1355 1.9 / ● 1921 11.4	**19** 0115 1.3 / 0642 12.4 / SA 1345 0.9 / ○ 1910 12.5
5 0212 1.9 / 0735 11.7 / SA 1429 1.7 / 1952 11.6	**20** 0207 0.7 / 0728 13.0 / SU 1434 0.4 / 1954 12.9
6 0243 1.8 / 0806 11.8 / SU 1459 1.6 / 2022 11.7	**21** 0254 0.3 / 0812 13.3 / M 1518 0.3 / 2035 13.1
7 0312 1.8 / 0835 11.8 / M 1526 1.7 / 2049 11.7	**22** 0336 0.3 / 0853 13.2 / TU 1558 0.5 / 2114 12.8
8 0337 1.9 / 0901 11.6 / TU 1551 1.9 / 2115 11.5	**23** 0415 0.7 / 0932 12.7 / W 1634 1.2 / 2151 12.2
9 0402 2.2 / 0926 11.3 / W 1615 2.3 / 2139 11.1	**24** 0451 1.5 / 1010 11.8 / TH 1708 2.1 / 2229 11.4
10 0426 2.6 / 0951 10.8 / TH 1640 2.8 / 2204 10.6	**25** 0526 2.4 / 1050 10.8 / F 1742 3.2 / 2309 10.4
11 0452 3.1 / 1017 10.2 / F 1708 3.4 / 2232 10.1	**26** 0605 3.4 / 1135 9.7 / SA 1824 4.2 / ◐
12 0524 3.7 / 1050 9.5 / SA 1744 4.0 / 2311 9.4	**27** 0002 9.4 / 0659 4.3 / SU 1244 8.8 / 1931 4.9
13 0609 4.3 / 1140 8.8 / SU 1839 4.6 / ◑	**28** 0131 8.8 / 0823 4.7 / M 1433 8.5 / 2113 5.0
14 0016 8.6 / 0718 4.7 / M 1321 8.4 / 2008 4.9	**29** 0317 8.9 / 1000 4.5 / TU 1601 9.0 / 2241 4.4
15 0217 8.6 / 0905 4.6 / TU 1521 8.8 / 2156 4.4	**30** 0426 9.5 / 1111 3.8 / W 1657 9.7 / 2339 3.6
	31 0515 10.2 / 1202 3.1 / TH 1740 10.4

APRIL

Time m	Time m
1 0024 3.0 / 0555 10.8 / F 1244 2.6 / 1816 10.9	**16** 0523 11.5 / 1222 1.8 / SA 1756 11.7
2 0104 2.5 / 0631 11.2 / SA 1321 2.2 / 1849 11.3	**17** 0047 1.5 / 0615 12.2 / SU 1317 1.1 / 1844 12.4
3 0139 2.2 / 0705 11.5 / SU 1355 1.9 / ● 1921 11.6	**18** 0141 0.9 / 0703 12.7 / M 1407 0.9 / ○ 1928 12.8
4 0212 2.0 / 0736 11.7 / M 1426 1.8 / 1951 11.7	**19** 0229 0.6 / 0749 12.9 / TU 1452 0.7 / 2011 12.9
5 0241 1.9 / 0806 11.7 / TU 1455 1.8 / 2019 11.8	**20** 0312 0.7 / 0831 12.8 / W 1533 1.0 / 2051 12.7
6 0309 1.9 / 0834 11.6 / W 1522 2.0 / 2046 11.6	**21** 0352 1.1 / 0912 12.3 / TH 1609 1.6 / 2129 12.1
7 0337 2.1 / 0901 11.4 / TH 1549 2.3 / 2113 11.4	**22** 0429 1.7 / 0951 11.6 / F 1644 2.4 / 2209 11.4
8 0405 2.4 / 0929 11.0 / F 1618 2.7 / 2142 11.0	**23** 0505 2.5 / 1032 10.7 / SA 1719 3.3 / 2250 10.5
9 0434 2.9 / 1000 10.4 / SA 1648 3.3 / 2215 10.4	**24** 0544 3.4 / 1118 9.8 / SU 1801 4.1 / 2342 9.7
10 0508 3.4 / 1037 9.8 / SU 1727 3.9 / 2258 9.8	**25** 0634 4.1 / 1218 9.1 / M 1900 4.8 / ◐
11 0554 4.0 / 1131 9.1 / M 1823 4.4 / ◑	**26** 0055 9.0 / 0743 4.6 / TU 1344 8.7 / 2025 5.0
12 0004 9.2 / 0700 4.4 / TU 1303 8.8 / 1947 4.6	**27** 0225 8.9 / 0907 4.6 / W 1509 8.9 / 2148 4.6
13 0146 9.1 / 0836 4.3 / W 1447 9.1 / 2126 4.2	**28** 0338 9.3 / 1018 4.1 / TH 1610 9.5 / 2249 4.0
14 0316 9.6 / 1009 3.6 / TH 1603 9.9 / 2244 3.3	**29** 0431 9.8 / 1113 3.6 / F 1657 10.1 / 2338 3.5
15 0425 10.5 / 1120 2.7 / F 1704 10.9 / 2349 2.3	**30** 0515 10.5 / 1159 3.1 / SA 1736 10.6

TIDES

Chart Datum: 6·29 metres below IGN Datum
HAT is 13·6 metres above Chart Datum

TIME ZONE -0100 (French Standard Time) **Subtract 1 hour for UT** For French Summer Time add ONE hour in **non-shaded areas**	**FRANCE – ST MALO** **LAT 48°38'N LONG 2°02'W** TIMES AND HEIGHTS OF HIGH AND LOW WATERS	Dates in amber are **SPRINGS** Dates in yellow are **NEAPS** **2011**

Chart Datum: 6·29 metres below IGN Datum
HAT is 13·6 metres above Chart Datum

MAY

Time m	Time m
1 0021 3.0 / 0554 10.8 / SU 1240 2.7 / 1813 11.1	**16** 0018 1.9 / 0549 11.8 / M 1248 1.7 / 1818 12.0
2 0100 2.6 / 0631 11.1 / M 1318 2.4 / 1847 11.4	**17** 0113 1.5 / 0640 12.1 / TU 1340 1.4 / ○ 1905 12.4
3 0136 2.4 / 0706 11.4 / TU 1352 2.2 / ● 1920 11.6	**18** 0204 1.2 / 0728 12.3 / W 1427 1.4 / 1949 12.5
4 0210 2.2 / 0739 11.5 / W 1425 2.1 / 1952 11.7	**19** 0250 1.2 / 0813 12.2 / TH 1509 1.6 / 2031 12.3
5 0243 2.1 / 0811 11.5 / TH 1458 2.2 / 2023 11.7	**20** 0331 1.4 / 0856 11.9 / F 1548 2.0 / 2112 12.0
6 0316 2.2 / 0843 11.4 / F 1530 2.3 / 2055 11.5	**21** 0410 1.9 / 0937 11.4 / SA 1625 2.5 / 2153 11.4
7 0350 2.3 / 0917 11.1 / SA 1604 2.7 / 2130 11.2	**22** 0448 2.5 / 1018 10.8 / SU 1702 3.1 / 2235 10.7
8 0425 2.7 / 0955 10.7 / SU 1641 3.1 / 2211 10.8	**23** 0527 3.1 / 1101 10.1 / M 1742 3.8 / 2320 10.1
9 0505 3.1 / 1039 10.2 / M 1725 3.6 / 2259 10.2	**24** 0609 3.7 / 1148 9.6 / TU 1830 4.3 / ◑
10 0553 3.5 / 1136 9.7 / TU 1821 4.0 / ◑	**25** 0014 9.5 / 0701 4.2 / W 1247 9.1 / 1930 4.6
11 0003 9.8 / 0655 3.8 / W 1250 9.4 / 1934 4.1	**26** 0119 9.1 / 0803 4.4 / TH 1357 9.0 / 2040 4.7
12 0122 9.7 / 0814 3.8 / TH 1413 9.5 / 2056 3.9	**27** 0231 9.1 / 0911 4.3 / F 1507 9.2 / 2147 4.4
13 0241 10.0 / 0935 3.4 / F 1527 10.1 / 2210 3.3	**28** 0334 9.4 / 1014 4.0 / SA 1604 9.6 / 2245 4.0
14 0351 10.6 / 1047 2.8 / SA 1631 10.8 / 2317 2.6	**29** 0427 9.8 / 1108 3.6 / SU 1652 10.1 / 2335 3.5
15 0453 11.2 / 1151 2.2 / SU 1727 11.5	**30** 0514 10.2 / 1157 3.2 / M 1735 10.6
	31 0021 3.1 / 0557 10.7 / TU 1241 2.8 / 1816 11.0

JUNE

Time m	Time m
1 0103 2.7 / 0638 11.0 / W 1322 2.6 / ● 1854 11.4	**16** 0144 1.8 / 0715 11.6 / TH 1407 2.0 / 1935 12.0
2 0144 2.4 / 0716 11.2 / TH 1401 2.4 / 1930 11.6	**17** 0232 1.7 / 0801 11.7 / F 1452 2.0 / 2018 12.0
3 0223 2.2 / 0754 11.4 / F 1440 2.3 / 2007 11.7	**18** 0315 1.7 / 0843 11.6 / SA 1532 2.1 / 2058 11.9
4 0302 2.1 / 0832 11.4 / SA 1519 2.3 / 2045 11.8	**19** 0355 1.9 / 0923 11.4 / SU 1610 2.4 / 2137 11.6
5 0343 2.1 / 0911 11.3 / SU 1559 2.4 / 2126 11.6	**20** 0432 2.2 / 1001 11.1 / M 1646 2.8 / 2215 11.1
6 0424 2.3 / 0954 11.1 / M 1641 2.6 / 2210 11.3	**21** 0507 2.7 / 1037 10.6 / TU 1720 3.3 / 2253 10.5
7 0507 2.6 / 1040 10.8 / TU 1727 3.0 / 2259 10.9	**22** 0542 3.2 / 1114 10.1 / W 1756 3.8 / 2332 10.0
8 0555 2.9 / 1131 10.4 / W 1818 3.3 / 2353 10.5	**23** 0619 3.7 / 1155 9.6 / TH 1838 4.2 / ◐
9 0648 3.2 / 1230 10.1 / TH 1918 3.6	**24** 0017 9.4 / 0704 4.1 / F 1246 9.2 / 1931 4.5
10 0056 10.3 / 0751 3.4 / F 1338 9.9 / 2027 3.6	**25** 0116 9.1 / 0801 4.4 / SA 1351 9.1 / 2037 4.6
11 0206 10.2 / 0902 3.4 / SA 1451 10.1 / 2139 3.4	**26** 0227 9.0 / 0909 4.4 / SU 1503 9.2 / 2148 4.5
12 0318 10.4 / 1014 3.1 / SU 1601 10.5 / 2248 2.9	**27** 0336 9.2 / 1017 4.2 / M 1607 9.6 / 2252 4.0
13 0427 10.7 / 1121 2.8 / M 1703 11.0 / 2352 2.5	**28** 0435 9.6 / 1117 3.7 / TU 1701 10.1 / 2346 3.5
14 0529 11.1 / 1223 2.4 / TU 1759 11.5	**29** 0527 10.2 / 1209 3.3 / W 1748 10.7
15 0051 2.1 / 0625 11.4 / W 1318 2.1 / ○ 1849 11.8	**30** 0036 3.0 / 0615 10.6 / TH 1257 2.8 / 1832 11.2

JULY

Time m	Time m
1 0123 2.5 / 0659 11.1 / F 1343 2.4 / ● 1915 11.6	**16** 0219 1.9 / 0749 11.5 / SA 1438 2.1 / 2004 12.0
2 0209 2.1 / 0742 11.4 / SA 1429 2.1 / 1956 11.9	**17** 0301 1.8 / 0828 11.6 / SU 1517 2.0 / 2042 12.0
3 0254 1.8 / 0824 11.7 / SU 1513 1.9 / 2038 12.1	**18** 0338 1.8 / 0903 11.6 / M 1553 2.1 / 2117 11.8
4 0339 1.7 / 0905 11.8 / M 1557 1.8 / 2120 12.2	**19** 0412 2.0 / 0937 11.4 / TU 1624 2.4 / 2150 11.4
5 0423 1.7 / 0948 11.7 / TU 1640 1.9 / 2203 12.0	**20** 0442 2.3 / 1008 11.0 / W 1652 2.8 / 2221 10.9
6 0506 1.9 / 1031 11.4 / W 1723 2.2 / 2248 11.6	**21** 0510 2.8 / 1038 10.6 / TH 1720 3.3 / 2251 10.3
7 0549 2.3 / 1115 10.9 / TH 1808 2.7 / 2336 11.1	**22** 0538 3.3 / 1109 10.1 / F 1751 3.8 / 2324 9.7
8 0634 2.8 / 1206 10.5 / F 1858 3.2	**23** 0612 3.8 / 1146 9.5 / SA 1830 4.3 / ◐
9 0029 10.5 / 0727 3.4 / SA 1305 10.1 / 1959 3.6	**24** 0008 9.2 / 0656 4.4 / SU 1239 9.0 / 1925 4.7
10 0135 10.1 / 0831 3.6 / SU 1418 9.9 / 2111 3.7	**25** 0116 8.7 / 0759 4.7 / M 1358 8.8 / 2044 4.9
11 0252 9.9 / 0946 3.7 / M 1538 10.0 / 2226 3.4	**26** 0245 8.7 / 0923 4.7 / TU 1523 9.0 / 2210 4.5
12 0411 10.1 / 1101 3.4 / TU 1650 10.5 / 2336 3.0	**27** 0401 9.1 / 1041 4.2 / W 1631 9.6 / 2317 3.8
13 0520 10.5 / 1207 3.0 / W 1749 11.0	**28** 0503 9.8 / 1143 3.6 / TH 1725 10.4
14 0038 2.5 / 0617 10.9 / TH 1305 2.6 / 1840 11.5	**29** 0013 3.1 / 0555 10.5 / F 1237 2.9 / 1814 11.1
15 0132 2.1 / 0706 11.3 / F 1355 2.2 / ○ 1924 11.8	**30** 0106 2.4 / 0643 11.1 / SA 1329 2.3 / ● 1859 11.8
	31 0157 1.8 / 0728 11.7 / SU 1418 1.7 / 1943 12.3

AUGUST

Time m	Time m
1 0245 1.4 / 0811 12.1 / M 1504 1.4 / 2026 12.7	**16** 0315 1.7 / 0837 11.7 / TU 1528 1.9 / 2050 11.9
2 0331 1.1 / 0853 12.3 / TU 1548 1.2 / 2108 12.8	**17** 0345 1.8 / 0907 11.6 / W 1556 2.2 / 2120 11.6
3 0414 1.1 / 0934 12.3 / W 1630 1.3 / 2149 12.6	**18** 0411 2.1 / 0935 11.3 / TH 1621 2.5 / 2146 11.2
4 0454 1.3 / 1014 12.0 / TH 1710 1.7 / 2230 12.1	**19** 0435 2.6 / 1001 10.9 / F 1645 3.0 / 2212 10.6
5 0533 1.9 / 1055 11.5 / F 1750 2.3 / 2313 11.4	**20** 0459 3.1 / 1027 10.4 / SA 1710 3.5 / 2239 10.0
6 0613 2.6 / 1140 10.8 / SA 1835 3.1 / ◑	**21** 0527 3.7 / 1056 9.8 / SU 1743 4.1 / ◑ 2312 9.3
7 0002 10.5 / 0700 3.4 / SU 1234 10.1 / 1932 3.8	**22** 0604 4.3 / 1136 9.2 / M 1828 4.7
8 0106 9.7 / 0803 4.1 / M 1351 9.5 / 2048 4.1	**23** 0006 8.7 / 0658 4.9 / TU 1247 8.6 / 1939 5.1
9 0235 9.3 / 0926 4.3 / TU 1525 9.6 / 2213 3.9	**24** 0152 8.4 / 0824 5.1 / W 1440 8.7 / 2125 4.9
10 0406 9.6 / 1051 3.9 / W 1643 10.1 / 2328 3.4	**25** 0331 8.8 / 1007 4.6 / TH 1601 9.3 / 2249 4.1
11 0515 10.2 / 1200 3.3 / TH 1741 10.8	**26** 0439 9.6 / 1118 3.8 / F 1701 10.3 / 2351 3.1
12 0029 2.7 / 0608 10.8 / F 1255 2.7 / 1828 11.4	**27** 0533 10.5 / 1216 2.8 / SA 1752 11.2
13 0120 2.2 / 0652 11.3 / SA 1341 2.3 / ○ 1909 11.8	**28** 0046 2.2 / 0622 11.4 / SU 1310 2.0 / 1839 12.1
14 0203 1.7 / 0731 11.6 / SU 1421 2.0 / 1945 12.0	**29** 0139 1.5 / 0708 12.0 / M 1400 1.3 / ● 1924 12.7
15 0241 1.7 / 0805 11.7 / M 1457 1.9 / 2019 12.0	**30** 0228 1.0 / 0751 12.6 / TU 1448 0.9 / 2007 13.1
	31 0314 0.7 / 0832 12.8 / W 1532 0.7 / 2049 13.2

TIME ZONE -0100
(French Standard Time)
Subtract 1 hour for UT
For French Summer Time add
ONE hour in **non-shaded areas**

FRANCE – ST MALO

LAT 48°38'N   LONG 2°02'W

TIMES AND HEIGHTS OF HIGH AND LOW WATERS

Dates in amber are **SPRINGS**
Dates in yellow are **NEAPS**

2011

SEPTEMBER

Day	Time m		Day	Time m
1 TH	0356 0.7 / 0913 12.8 / 1612 0.9 / 2129 12.9		**16** F	0337 2.1 / 0901 11.6 / 1549 2.4 / 2113 11.3
2 F	0434 1.1 / 0952 12.4 / 1651 1.5 / 2209 12.3		**17** SA	0401 2.5 / 0925 11.2 / 1613 2.9 / 2137 10.8
3 SA	0511 1.9 / 1031 11.7 / 1729 2.3 / 2250 11.4		**18** SU	0425 3.0 / 0950 10.7 / 1638 3.4 / 2203 10.2
4 SU ☽	0549 2.8 / 1113 10.8 / 1811 3.2 / 2337 10.3		**19** M	0452 3.6 / 1017 10.1 / 1708 4.0 / 2234 9.6
5 M	0632 3.8 / 1206 9.9 / 1906 4.1		**20** TU ☽	0526 4.3 / 1053 9.5 / 1750 4.5 / 2320 8.9
6 TU	0043 9.4 / 0736 4.6 / 1329 9.2 / 2027 4.5		**21** W	0616 4.9 / 1154 8.8 / 1854 5.0
7 W	0224 8.9 / 0911 4.8 / 1514 9.3 / 2203 4.3		**22** TH	0057 8.4 / 0738 5.2 / 1353 8.6 / 2038 5.0
8 TH	0359 9.3 / 1042 4.3 / 1630 9.9 / 2318 3.6		**23** F	0257 8.7 / 0929 4.8 / 1527 9.3 / 2217 4.2
9 F	0502 10.1 / 1147 3.5 / 1724 10.7		**24** SA	0409 9.6 / 1048 3.8 / 1631 10.3 / 2324 3.2
10 SA	0013 2.9 / 0549 10.8 / 1237 2.8 / 1808 11.3		**25** SU	0505 10.6 / 1149 2.8 / 1725 11.3
11 SU	0059 2.3 / 0629 11.3 / 1319 2.3 / 1845 11.7		**26** M	0021 2.2 / 0555 11.5 / 1244 1.9 / 1814 12.2
12 M ○	0138 2.0 / 0704 11.6 / 1356 2.1 / 1919 11.9		**27** TU ●	0114 1.4 / 0641 12.3 / 1337 1.2 / 1900 12.9
13 TU	0213 1.9 / 0736 11.8 / 1429 2.0 / 1951 12.0		**28** W	0204 0.8 / 0726 12.8 / 1425 0.7 / 1944 13.2
14 W	0244 1.8 / 0806 11.8 / 1459 2.0 / 2021 11.9		**29** TH	0250 0.6 / 0808 13.1 / 1510 0.7 / 2027 13.2
15 TH	0312 1.9 / 0835 11.8 / 1525 2.1 / 2048 11.7		**30** F	0332 0.8 / 0848 12.9 / 1551 0.9 / 2108 12.9

OCTOBER

Day	Time m		Day	Time m
1 SA	0411 1.3 / 0928 12.5 / 1630 1.5 / 2148 12.2		**16** SU	0332 2.6 / 0856 11.4 / 1548 2.8 / 2111 11.0
2 SU	0448 2.1 / 1007 11.7 / 1708 2.4 / 2229 11.2		**17** M	0359 3.0 / 0923 11.0 / 1616 3.2 / 2141 10.5
3 M	0525 3.1 / 1050 10.8 / 1749 3.4 / 2317 10.1		**18** TU	0429 3.5 / 0954 10.5 / 1648 3.7 / 2216 9.9
4 TU	0608 4.1 / 1143 9.9 / 1842 4.2		**19** W	0505 4.1 / 1033 9.8 / 1730 4.2 / 2303 9.2
5 W ☽	0022 9.2 / 0711 4.8 / 1306 9.2 / 2003 4.7		**20** TH ☽	0555 4.7 / 1132 9.2 / 1830 4.7
6 TH	0203 8.8 / 0848 5.0 / 1449 9.2 / 2139 4.5		**21** F	0025 8.7 / 0710 4.9 / 1309 9.0 / 2000 4.7
7 F	0335 9.2 / 1018 4.5 / 1604 9.7 / 2251 3.9		**22** SA	0214 8.9 / 0849 4.7 / 1444 9.4 / 2137 4.1
8 SA	0435 9.9 / 1119 3.7 / 1656 10.4 / 2343 3.2		**23** SU	0332 9.6 / 1012 3.8 / 1555 10.3 / 2249 3.2
9 SU	0520 10.6 / 1206 3.1 / 1738 11.0		**24** M	0432 10.6 / 1117 2.8 / 1653 11.2 / 2350 2.3
10 M	0027 2.7 / 0558 11.1 / 1247 2.6 / 1815 11.4		**25** TU	0525 11.5 / 1215 2.0 / 1745 12.1
11 TU	0105 2.3 / 0632 11.5 / 1323 2.3 / 1849 11.7		**26** W ●	0046 1.5 / 0614 12.3 / 1310 1.3 / 1835 12.7
12 W ○	0139 2.1 / 0704 11.7 / 1356 2.2 / 1921 11.8		**27** TH	0137 1.1 / 0700 12.8 / 1400 0.9 / 1921 13.0
13 TH	0210 2.1 / 0734 11.8 / 1426 2.2 / 1951 11.8		**28** F	0225 0.9 / 0744 13.0 / 1447 0.9 / 2006 12.9
14 F	0239 2.1 / 0803 11.8 / 1454 2.3 / 2018 11.6		**29** SA	0308 1.1 / 0826 12.6 / 1530 1.1 / 2049 12.6
15 SA	0306 2.3 / 0829 11.7 / 1521 2.5 / 2045 11.4		**30** SU	0349 1.6 / 0907 12.4 / 1610 1.7 / 2131 11.9
			31 M	0427 2.3 / 0949 11.7 / 1650 2.4 / 2214 11.1

NOVEMBER

Day	Time m		Day	Time m
1 TU	0505 3.2 / 1032 10.9 / 1731 3.3 / 2300 10.2		**16** W	0419 3.3 / 0946 10.9 / 1642 3.3 / 2211 10.2
2 W ☾	0548 4.0 / 1124 10.0 / 1820 4.1 / 2358 9.4		**17** TH	0459 3.7 / 1029 10.3 / 1725 3.7 / 2300 9.7
3 TH	0644 4.7 / 1232 9.3 / 1926 4.6		**18** F ☾	0548 4.1 / 1124 9.8 / 1820 4.1
4 F	0118 8.9 / 0803 5.0 / 1401 9.1 / 2048 4.7		**19** SA	0005 9.3 / 0653 4.4 / 1237 9.6 / 1932 4.2
5 SA	0246 9.0 / 0928 4.8 / 1518 9.4 / 2202 4.3		**20** SU	0129 9.3 / 0812 4.3 / 1400 9.7 / 2055 3.9
6 SU	0352 9.5 / 1033 4.2 / 1616 9.9 / 2258 3.7		**21** M	0249 9.7 / 0932 3.8 / 1515 10.2 / 2211 3.3
7 M	0441 10.1 / 1124 3.4 / 1701 10.4 / 2345 3.2		**22** TU	0357 10.4 / 1042 3.0 / 1620 10.9 / 2318 2.6
8 TU	0521 10.7 / 1208 3.1 / 1741 10.9		**23** W	0456 11.2 / 1145 2.3 / 1719 11.6
9 W	0026 2.8 / 0558 11.1 / 1247 2.8 / 1817 11.2		**24** TH	0017 2.0 / 0549 11.9 / 1244 1.7 / 1813 12.1
10 TH ○	0103 2.6 / 0632 11.4 / 1323 2.5 / 1852 11.4		**25** F ●	0112 1.6 / 0638 12.4 / 1338 1.3 / 1903 12.4
11 F	0138 2.4 / 0705 11.6 / 1356 2.4 / 1924 11.5		**26** SA	0202 1.4 / 0725 12.6 / 1427 1.2 / 1950 12.4
12 SA	0210 2.4 / 0736 11.7 / 1428 2.4 / 1955 11.5		**27** SU	0248 1.5 / 0810 12.6 / 1513 1.3 / 2035 12.2
13 SU	0241 2.4 / 0806 11.7 / 1459 2.4 / 2025 11.3		**28** M	0331 1.8 / 0853 12.3 / 1555 1.7 / 2118 11.8
14 M	0312 2.6 / 0836 11.5 / 1532 2.6 / 2057 11.1		**29** TU	0411 2.3 / 0935 11.8 / 1636 2.2 / 2200 11.2
15 TU	0345 2.9 / 0909 11.3 / 1605 2.9 / 2132 10.7		**30** W	0450 2.9 / 1017 11.1 / 1716 2.9 / 2243 10.5

DECEMBER

Day	Time m		Day	Time m
1 TH	0530 3.6 / 1102 10.4 / 1757 3.6 / 2328 9.8		**16** F	0459 3.0 / 1026 11.0 / 1724 2.9 / 2254 10.4
2 F ☾	0614 4.2 / 1152 9.7 / 1845 4.2		**17** SA	0544 3.3 / 1113 10.6 / 1812 3.3 / 2346 10.0
3 SA	0022 9.2 / 0708 4.6 / 1254 9.2 / 1943 4.5		**18** SU	0636 3.6 / 1210 10.2 / 1908 3.6
4 SU	0131 9.0 / 0816 4.8 / 1409 9.0 / 2051 4.6		**19** M	0049 9.7 / 0740 3.8 / 1319 9.8 / 2017 3.7
5 M	0246 9.0 / 0927 4.6 / 1520 9.2 / 2158 4.3		**20** TU	0205 9.7 / 0854 3.8 / 1436 10.0 / 2133 3.5
6 TU	0350 9.4 / 1031 4.2 / 1617 9.6 / 2256 3.9		**21** W	0322 10.0 / 1010 3.4 / 1552 10.3 / 2247 3.1
7 W	0440 10.0 / 1124 3.7 / 1705 10.1 / 2345 3.4		**22** TH	0432 10.6 / 1120 2.8 / 1700 10.8 / 2354 2.6
8 TH	0524 10.5 / 1210 3.3 / 1747 10.5		**23** F	0532 11.3 / 1224 2.2 / 1800 11.4
9 F	0029 3.0 / 0603 10.9 / 1252 2.9 / 1826 10.9		**24** SA	0053 2.1 / 0626 11.8 / 1321 1.7 / 1853 11.8
10 SA	0110 2.7 / 0641 11.3 / 1331 2.6 / 1904 11.2		**25** SU ○	0147 1.8 / 0714 12.2 / 1413 1.4 / 1941 12.0
11 SU	0147 2.5 / 0716 11.5 / 1409 2.4 / 1939 11.3		**26** M	0235 1.7 / 0759 12.3 / 1500 1.4 / 2025 12.0
12 M	0224 2.4 / 0751 11.7 / 1446 2.3 / 2015 11.4		**27** TU	0318 1.7 / 0841 12.2 / 1543 1.5 / 2106 11.8
13 TU	0301 2.4 / 0826 11.7 / 1524 2.3 / 2051 11.3		**28** W	0358 2.0 / 0921 11.9 / 1622 1.9 / 2144 11.4
14 W	0339 2.4 / 0903 11.6 / 1602 2.4 / 2129 11.1		**29** TH	0435 2.4 / 0959 11.5 / 1657 2.4 / 2220 10.9
15 TH	0418 2.6 / 0943 11.3 / 1642 2.6 / 2209 10.8		**30** F	0508 2.9 / 1035 10.9 / 1730 2.9 / 2256 10.3
			31 SA	0541 3.5 / 1112 10.2 / 1803 3.5 / 2332 9.8

Chart Datum: 6·29 metres below IGN Datum
HAT is 13·6 metres above Chart Datum

TIDES

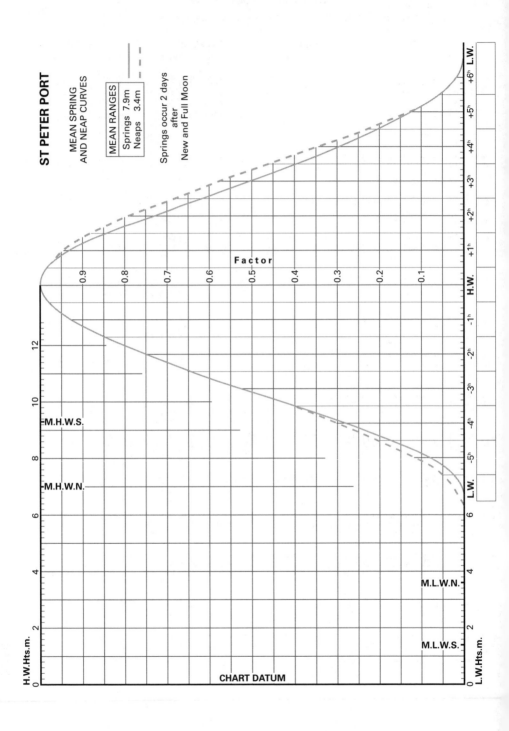

ST PETER PORT

MEAN SPRING
AND NEAP CURVES

MEAN RANGES	
Springs	7.9m
Neaps	3.4m

Springs occur 2 days
after
New and Full Moon

TIME ZONE (UT)
For Summer Time add ONE hour in **non-shaded areas**

CHANNEL ISLES – ST PETER PORT
LAT 49°27'N LONG 2°31'W
TIMES AND HEIGHTS OF HIGH AND LOW WATERS

Dates in amber are **SPRINGS**
Dates in yellow are **NEAPS**

2011

JANUARY

#	Time m	#	Time m
1 SA	0343 7.8 / 1012 2.9 / 1612 7.8 / 2241 2.8	**16** SU	0305 7.1 / 0933 3.5 / 1542 7.2 / 2200 3.3
2 SU	0443 8.2 / 1111 2.5 / 1710 8.1 / 2335 2.4	**17** M	0410 7.6 / 1037 2.9 / 1643 7.7 / 2300 3.0
3 M	0533 8.6 / 1202 2.1 / 1800 8.4	**18** TU	0505 8.2 / 1132 2.3 / 1736 8.2 / 2353 2.1
4 TU	0023 2.1 / 0619 8.9 / 1249 1.8 / ● 1844 8.6	**19** W	0555 8.8 / 1224 1.7 / 1825 8.7 ○
5 W	0106 1.9 / 0701 9.0 / 1331 1.6 / 1925 8.7	**20** TH	0042 1.6 / 0641 9.3 / 1312 1.2 / 1910 9.1
6 TH	0145 1.8 / 0740 9.1 / 1409 1.6 / 2002 8.7	**21** F	0129 1.2 / 0726 9.6 / 1357 0.9 / 1954 9.4
7 F	0221 1.9 / 0816 9.0 / 1444 1.7 / 2036 8.6	**22** SA	0212 1.0 / 0809 9.8 / 1440 0.7 / 2036 9.5
8 SA	0253 2.0 / 0848 8.8 / 1515 2.0 / 2107 8.4	**23** SU	0254 0.9 / 0851 9.8 / 1520 0.8 / 2116 9.4
9 SU	0322 2.3 / 0920 8.5 / 1545 2.3 / 2137 8.1	**24** M	0335 1.1 / 0932 9.5 / 1600 1.2 / 2157 9.0
10 M	0350 2.7 / 0951 8.1 / 1614 2.7 / 2207 7.8	**25** TU	0415 1.6 / 1015 9.0 / 1641 1.8 / 2239 8.5
11 TU	0420 3.0 / 1023 7.9 / 1645 3.0 / 2241 7.4	**26** W	0459 2.2 / 1100 8.3 / 1726 2.4 / ◐ 2327 7.9
12 W	0454 3.4 / 1101 7.3 / 1724 3.4 / ◐ 2323 7.1	**27** TH	0551 2.9 / 1155 7.6 / 1822 3.1
13 TH	0542 3.8 / 1151 7.0 / 1818 3.7	**28** F	0030 7.3 / 0701 3.4 / 1311 7.1 / 1940 3.6
14 F	0020 6.8 / 0653 4.0 / 1302 6.7 / 1933 3.8	**29** SA	0201 7.0 / 0836 3.6 / 1447 6.9 / 2118 3.6
15 SA	0142 6.8 / 0819 3.9 / 1428 6.8 / 2051 3.7	**30** SU	0329 7.2 / 1002 3.3 / 1605 7.2 / 2232 3.2
		31 M	0433 7.7 / 1103 2.8 / 1702 7.7 / 2326 2.7

FEBRUARY

#	Time m	#	Time m
1 TU	0523 8.2 / 1152 2.3 / 1749 8.1	**16** W	0446 8.1 / 1115 2.2 / 1720 8.2 / 2337 2.0
2 W	0011 2.3 / 0606 8.7 / 1235 1.9 / 1830 8.5	**17** TH	0538 8.8 / 1207 1.4 / 1809 8.9
3 TH	0052 1.9 / 0645 9.0 / 1314 1.6 / ● 1907 8.8	**18** F	0027 1.3 / 0625 9.5 / 1256 0.8 / ○ 1854 9.4
4 F	0128 1.7 / 0722 9.2 / 1349 1.4 / 1942 8.9	**19** SA	0113 0.7 / 0710 9.9 / 1340 0.4 / 1937 9.8
5 SA	0201 1.6 / 0755 9.2 / 1421 1.4 / 2013 8.9	**20** SU	0157 0.4 / 0753 10.2 / 1422 0.2 / 2017 9.9
6 SU	0230 1.6 / 0825 9.0 / 1449 1.6 / 2041 8.7	**21** M	0237 0.4 / 0833 10.1 / 1501 0.4 / 2056 9.8
7 M	0256 1.8 / 0854 8.8 / 1515 1.9 / 2107 8.5	**22** TU	0316 0.6 / 0913 9.8 / 1539 0.9 / 2134 9.3
8 TU	0321 2.2 / 0920 8.4 / 1539 2.3 / 2133 8.1	**23** W	0354 1.2 / 0952 9.1 / 1616 1.6 / 2212 8.6
9 W	0345 2.5 / 0947 8.0 / 1605 2.7 / 2201 7.8	**24** TH	0434 2.0 / 1034 8.3 / 1656 2.5 / ◑ 2255 7.9
10 TH	0412 3.0 / 1018 7.6 / 1635 3.1 / 2234 7.4	**25** F	0521 2.8 / 1123 7.4 / 1747 3.3 / 2351 7.1
11 F	0448 3.4 / 1058 7.1 / 1717 3.5 / ◐ 2321 7.0	**26** SA	0627 3.5 / 1239 6.7 / 1905 3.9
12 SA	0543 3.8 / 1159 6.7 / 1824 3.9	**27** SU	0129 6.7 / 0814 3.8 / 1434 6.6 / 2103 3.9
13 SU	0032 6.7 / 0719 4.0 / 1333 6.6 / 2004 3.9	**28** M	0313 6.9 / 0950 3.5 / 1554 7.0 / 2219 3.4
14 M	0216 6.8 / 0859 3.6 / 1514 6.9 / 2131 3.5		
15 TU	0343 7.3 / 1015 3.0 / 1624 7.5 / 2240 2.8		

MARCH

#	Time m	#	Time m
1 TU	0417 7.4 / 1048 2.9 / 1647 7.5 / 2309 2.8	**16** W	0314 7.3 / 0951 2.9 / 1601 7.5 / 2217 2.7
2 W	0505 8.0 / 1133 2.3 / 1729 8.0 / 2351 2.3	**17** TH	0421 8.1 / 1052 2.0 / 1657 8.3 / 2314 1.9
3 TH	0545 8.5 / 1212 1.9 / 1807 8.5	**18** F	0515 8.9 / 1144 1.2 / 1746 9.0
4 F	0029 1.8 / 0622 8.9 / 1249 1.5 / ● 1842 8.8	**19** SA	0005 1.1 / 0603 9.5 / 1232 0.6 / ○ 1831 9.6
5 SA	0104 1.5 / 0657 9.1 / 1322 1.3 / 1915 9.0	**20** SU	0052 0.5 / 0648 10.0 / 1317 0.2 / 1914 10.0
6 SU	0135 1.4 / 0729 9.2 / 1352 1.3 / 1945 9.0	**21** M	0135 0.2 / 0731 10.2 / 1359 0.1 / 1954 10.1
7 M	0203 1.4 / 0759 9.1 / 1420 1.4 / 2013 8.9	**22** TU	0217 0.2 / 0813 10.1 / 1438 0.4 / 2033 9.9
8 TU	0229 1.6 / 0826 8.9 / 1444 1.7 / 2038 8.7	**23** W	0256 0.5 / 0852 9.7 / 1516 0.9 / 2111 9.4
9 W	0253 1.9 / 0852 8.6 / 1508 2.1 / 2102 8.4	**24** TH	0334 1.1 / 0931 9.0 / 1553 1.7 / 2149 8.7
10 TH	0316 2.3 / 0918 8.2 / 1532 2.5 / 2129 8.0	**25** F	0414 1.9 / 1012 8.1 / 1633 2.6 / 2230 7.9
11 F	0342 2.7 / 0947 7.7 / 1601 2.9 / 2201 7.6	**26** SA	0459 2.8 / 1100 7.3 / 1721 3.4 / ◐ 2323 7.1
12 SA	0416 3.1 / 1026 7.3 / 1641 3.4 / ◐ 2245 7.2	**27** SU	0603 3.5 / 1214 6.6 / 1836 4.0
13 SU	0507 3.5 / 1125 6.8 / 1743 3.8 / 2354 6.8	**28** M	0054 6.6 / 0743 3.8 / 1407 6.5 / 2031 4.0
14 M	0635 3.8 / 1255 6.6 / 1925 3.9	**29** TU	0242 6.8 / 0920 3.5 / 1525 6.8 / 2149 3.6
15 TU	0134 6.8 / 0829 3.6 / 1445 6.8 / 2104 3.5	**30** W	0347 7.2 / 1017 3.0 / 1617 7.4 / 2239 3.0
		31 TH	0435 7.8 / 1101 2.5 / 1659 7.9 / 2320 2.5

APRIL

#	Time m	#	Time m
1 F	0515 8.3 / 1140 2.0 / 1736 8.4 / 2358 2.0	**16** SA	0446 8.8 / 1116 1.3 / 1717 9.0 / 2338 1.2
2 SA	0553 8.7 / 1216 1.7 / 1811 8.7	**17** SU	0537 9.4 / 1205 0.9 / 1805 9.5
3 SU	0032 1.7 / 0627 8.9 / 1249 1.5 / ● 1844 8.9	**18** M	0027 0.7 / 0624 9.7 / 1252 0.5 / ○ 1849 9.8
4 M	0104 1.5 / 0700 9.0 / 1320 1.5 / 1915 9.0	**19** TU	0113 0.4 / 0709 9.9 / 1336 0.5 / 1931 9.9
5 TU	0134 1.5 / 0731 9.0 / 1349 1.5 / 1943 8.9	**20** W	0156 0.4 / 0753 9.7 / 1417 0.7 / 2012 9.7
6 W	0201 1.6 / 0759 8.8 / 1416 1.7 / 2010 8.7	**21** TH	0237 0.7 / 0834 9.4 / 1456 1.2 / 2052 9.2
7 TH	0228 1.8 / 0827 8.5 / 1442 2.0 / 2037 8.5	**22** F	0318 1.3 / 0915 8.8 / 1535 1.9 / 2131 8.6
8 F	0254 2.1 / 0855 8.2 / 1509 2.4 / 2106 8.2	**23** SA	0359 2.0 / 0957 8.0 / 1615 2.6 / 2212 7.9
9 SA	0324 2.5 / 0928 7.8 / 1541 2.8 / 2141 7.8	**24** SU	0445 2.7 / 1044 7.3 / 1703 3.3 / 2303 7.3
10 SU	0401 2.9 / 1011 7.4 / 1624 3.2 / 2229 7.4	**25** M	0542 3.3 / 1147 6.8 / 1807 3.8 / ◐
11 M	0454 3.3 / 1111 7.0 / 1726 3.6 / ◐ 2337 7.1	**26** TU	0014 6.8 / 0658 3.6 / 1314 6.6 / 1932 4.0
12 TU	0616 3.5 / 1234 6.8 / 1859 3.7	**27** W	0145 6.8 / 0823 3.6 / 1435 6.9 / 2056 3.7
13 W	0106 7.1 / 0758 3.3 / 1412 7.1 / 2034 3.3	**28** TH	0259 7.0 / 0928 3.2 / 1532 7.2 / 2154 3.3
14 TH	0238 7.5 / 0919 2.7 / 1528 7.7 / 2147 2.6	**29** F	0352 7.5 / 1017 2.8 / 1618 7.6 / 2239 2.8
15 F	0349 8.1 / 1022 2.0 / 1627 8.4 / 2246 1.8	**30** SA	0436 7.9 / 1059 2.4 / 1658 8.1 / 2319 2.4

Chart Datum: 5·06 metres below Ordnance Datum (Local)
HAT is 10·3 metres above Chart Datum

TIDES

CHANNEL ISLES – ST PETER PORT
LAT 49°27'N   LONG 2°31'W
TIMES AND HEIGHTS OF HIGH AND LOW WATERS

TIME ZONE (UT)
For Summer Time add ONE hour in **non-shaded areas**

Dates in amber are **SPRINGS**
Dates in yellow are **NEAPS**

2011

MAY

Day	Time	m	Day	Time	m
1 SU	0516 / 1137 / 1735 / 2355	8.2 / 2.1 / 8.4 / 2.1	16 M	0511 / 1139 / 1739	9.0 / 1.3 / 9.2
2 M	0554 / 1212 / 1810	8.5 / 1.9 / 8.7	17 TU ○	0003 / 0602 / 1229 / 1826	1.1 / 9.2 / 1.1 / 9.4
3 TU ●	0030 / 0629 / 1247 / 1844	1.8 / 8.7 / 1.8 / 8.8	18 W	0052 / 0650 / 1315 / 1912	0.9 / 9.3 / 1.0 / 9.5
4 W	0104 / 0703 / 1319 / 1916	1.7 / 8.7 / 1.8 / 8.8	19 TH	0139 / 0736 / 1359 / 1955	0.9 / 9.3 / 1.2 / 9.4
5 TH	0136 / 0736 / 1351 / 1947	1.7 / 8.6 / 1.9 / 8.7	20 F	0222 / 0820 / 1441 / 2036	1.1 / 9.0 / 1.5 / 9.1
6 F	0208 / 0808 / 1423 / 2018	1.9 / 8.5 / 2.0 / 8.6	21 SA	0305 / 0902 / 1521 / 2116	1.4 / 8.6 / 2.0 / 8.7
7 SA	0240 / 0841 / 1456 / 2053	2.1 / 8.3 / 2.3 / 8.3	22 SU	0346 / 0943 / 1601 / 2157	1.9 / 8.1 / 2.5 / 8.1
8 SU	0316 / 0920 / 1533 / 2134	2.3 / 8.0 / 2.6 / 8.1	23 M	0429 / 1026 / 1643 / 2241	2.5 / 7.6 / 3.0 / 7.6
9 M	0358 / 1006 / 1619 / 2224	2.6 / 7.6 / 3.0 / 7.8	24 TU ◗	0516 / 1115 / 1733 / 2333	3.0 / 7.2 / 3.6 / 7.2
10 TU ◗	0452 / 1104 / 1719 / 2327	2.9 / 7.3 / 3.2 / 7.5	25 W	0611 / 1213 / 1833	3.3 / 6.9 / 3.7
11 W	0603 / 1216 / 1836	3.1 / 7.2 / 3.3	26 TH	0037 / 0712 / 1321 / 1940	6.9 / 3.5 / 6.8 / 3.8
12 TH	0042 / 0726 / 1336 / 1959	7.5 / 3.0 / 7.4 / 3.1	27 F	0148 / 0817 / 1427 / 2047	6.9 / 3.5 / 7.0 / 3.6
13 F	0202 / 0843 / 1451 / 2113	7.7 / 2.6 / 7.8 / 2.6	28 SA	0253 / 0916 / 1524 / 2144	7.1 / 3.2 / 7.3 / 3.2
14 SA	0314 / 0949 / 1553 / 2215	8.1 / 2.1 / 8.3 / 2.1	29 SU	0348 / 1008 / 1612 / 2232	7.4 / 2.9 / 7.7 / 2.9
15 SU	0416 / 1046 / 1648 / 2311	8.6 / 1.7 / 8.8 / 1.5	30 M	0435 / 1053 / 1656 / 2316	7.7 / 2.6 / 8.0 / 2.5
			31 TU	0519 / 1135 / 1737 / 2357	8.0 / 2.3 / 8.3 / 2.2

JUNE

Day	Time	m	Day	Time	m
1 W ●	0600 / 1215 / 1816	8.3 / 2.1 / 8.6	16 TH	0037 / 0637 / 1301 / 1857	1.4 / 8.8 / 1.5 / 9.2
2 TH	0037 / 0639 / 1255 / 1853	2.0 / 8.5 / 2.0 / 8.7	17 F	0126 / 0724 / 1346 / 1941	1.3 / 8.9 / 1.5 / 9.2
3 F	0116 / 0718 / 1333 / 1930	1.8 / 8.5 / 1.9 / 8.8	18 SA	0210 / 0808 / 1428 / 2022	1.3 / 8.8 / 1.7 / 9.1
4 SA	0155 / 0756 / 1411 / 2007	1.8 / 8.5 / 1.9 / 8.8	19 SU	0251 / 0848 / 1506 / 2100	1.5 / 8.6 / 1.9 / 8.8
5 SU	0234 / 0835 / 1450 / 2047	1.8 / 8.5 / 2.1 / 8.7	20 M	0329 / 0925 / 1542 / 2137	1.8 / 8.3 / 2.3 / 8.4
6 M	0314 / 0917 / 1531 / 2130	2.0 / 8.3 / 2.3 / 8.5	21 TU	0406 / 1001 / 1618 / 2213	2.2 / 8.0 / 2.7 / 8.0
7 TU	0358 / 1003 / 1617 / 2218	2.2 / 8.1 / 2.5 / 8.3	22 W	0443 / 1038 / 1655 / 2253	2.6 / 7.6 / 3.1 / 7.5
8 W	0448 / 1055 / 1710 / 2314	2.4 / 7.9 / 2.7 / 8.0	23 TH ◗	0523 / 1120 / 1738 / 2338	3.0 / 7.2 / 3.4 / 7.2
9 TH	0546 / 1154 / 1813	2.6 / 7.7 / 2.9	24 F ◗	0610 / 1210 / 1832	3.4 / 7.0 / 3.7
10 F	0017 / 0653 / 1302 / 1924	7.8 / 2.7 / 7.6 / 2.9	25 SA	0035 / 0707 / 1313 / 1936	6.9 / 3.6 / 6.9 / 3.8
11 SA	0128 / 0806 / 1414 / 2039	7.8 / 2.7 / 7.7 / 2.7	26 SU	0144 / 0810 / 1421 / 2043	6.8 / 3.6 / 7.0 / 3.6
12 SU	0242 / 0917 / 1523 / 2148	7.9 / 2.5 / 8.0 / 2.4	27 M	0253 / 0913 / 1524 / 2145	7.0 / 3.4 / 7.2 / 3.3
13 M	0350 / 1021 / 1624 / 2250	8.1 / 2.2 / 8.4 / 2.0	28 TU	0354 / 1021 / 1618 / 2239	7.3 / 3.1 / 7.6 / 2.9
14 TU	0451 / 1119 / 1719 / 2346	8.4 / 1.9 / 8.7 / 1.7	29 W	0447 / 1102 / 1707 / 2329	7.7 / 2.7 / 8.0 / 2.5
15 W ○	0547 / 1211 / 1810	8.7 / 1.7 / 9.0	30 TH	0535 / 1150 / 1752	8.0 / 2.3 / 8.4

JULY

Day	Time	m	Day	Time	m
1 F ●	0016 / 0620 / 1236 / 1835	2.1 / 8.4 / 2.0 / 8.7	16 SA	0113 / 0711 / 1332 / 1926	1.4 / 8.8 / 1.6 / 9.2
2 SA	0102 / 0704 / 1320 / 1918	1.7 / 8.6 / 1.8 / 9.0	17 SU	0155 / 0751 / 1411 / 2004	1.3 / 8.9 / 1.6 / 9.2
3 SU	0145 / 0746 / 1403 / 1959	1.5 / 8.8 / 1.6 / 9.1	18 M	0232 / 0827 / 1446 / 2039	1.4 / 8.8 / 1.7 / 9.0
4 M	0228 / 0828 / 1444 / 2040	1.4 / 8.9 / 1.6 / 9.2	19 TU	0306 / 0900 / 1518 / 2111	1.6 / 8.6 / 2.0 / 8.7
5 TU	0309 / 0909 / 1525 / 2122	1.4 / 8.8 / 1.7 / 9.0	20 W	0337 / 0930 / 1546 / 2141	1.9 / 8.3 / 2.3 / 8.3
6 W	0351 / 0952 / 1608 / 2207	1.6 / 8.7 / 1.9 / 8.8	21 TH	0406 / 1000 / 1615 / 2212	2.4 / 8.0 / 2.7 / 7.9
7 TH	0435 / 1037 / 1654 / 2255	1.9 / 8.4 / 2.2 / 8.4	22 F	0435 / 1032 / 1645 / 2247	2.8 / 7.6 / 3.2 / 7.4
8 F	0523 / 1128 / 1747 / 2350	2.3 / 8.0 / 2.6 / 8.0	23 SA	0510 / 1110 / 1725 / 2330	3.2 / 7.2 / 3.5 / 7.0
9 SA	0621 / 1229 / 1852	2.7 / 7.7 / 2.9	24 SU	0557 / 1200 / 1825	3.6 / 6.9 / 3.8
10 SU	0057 / 0731 / 1343 / 2010	7.6 / 3.0 / 7.5 / 3.1	25 M	0032 / 0707 / 1313 / 1946	6.7 / 3.8 / 6.8 / 3.9
11 M	0217 / 0851 / 1501 / 2130	7.4 / 3.0 / 7.6 / 2.9	26 TU	0158 / 0825 / 1436 / 2104	6.7 / 3.8 / 6.9 / 3.6
12 TU	0336 / 1006 / 1610 / 2239	7.6 / 2.8 / 7.9 / 2.5	27 W	0318 / 0935 / 1546 / 2211	6.9 / 3.5 / 7.3 / 3.2
13 W	0442 / 1113 / 1708 / 2336	7.9 / 2.3 / 8.4 / 2.1	28 TH	0422 / 1036 / 1643 / 2308	7.4 / 3.0 / 7.9 / 2.6
14 TH	0538 / 1201 / 1758	8.3 / 2.1 / 8.7	29 F	0516 / 1130 / 1733 / 2359	7.9 / 2.4 / 8.4 / 2.0
15 F ○	0027 / 0626 / 1249 / 1844	1.7 / 8.6 / 1.8 / 9.0	30 SA ●	0604 / 1220 / 1820	8.5 / 1.9 / 8.9
			31 SU	0047 / 0649 / 1307 / 1904	1.5 / 8.9 / 1.4 / 9.4

AUGUST

Day	Time	m	Day	Time	m
1 M	0133 / 0732 / 1350 / 1946	1.1 / 9.2 / 1.1 / 9.6	16 TU	0206 / 0800 / 1420 / 2012	1.3 / 9.0 / 1.5 / 9.2
2 TU	0215 / 0813 / 1432 / 2027	0.8 / 9.4 / 1.0 / 9.7	17 W	0236 / 0830 / 1448 / 2041	1.5 / 8.9 / 1.9 / 8.9
3 W	0255 / 0854 / 1512 / 2108	0.8 / 9.4 / 1.1 / 9.6	18 TH	0303 / 0857 / 1513 / 2108	1.8 / 8.6 / 2.1 / 8.5
4 TH	0335 / 0933 / 1551 / 2149	1.1 / 9.2 / 1.4 / 9.2	19 F	0328 / 0923 / 1537 / 2135	2.2 / 8.2 / 2.5 / 8.1
5 F	0415 / 1015 / 1633 / 2232	1.6 / 8.7 / 1.9 / 8.6	20 SA	0352 / 0950 / 1602 / 2203	2.7 / 7.8 / 3.0 / 7.6
6 SA ◗	0458 / 1101 / 1721 / 2323	2.2 / 8.2 / 2.5 / 7.9	21 SU ◗	0419 / 1021 / 1634 / 2239	3.1 / 7.4 / 3.4 / 7.2
7 SU	0551 / 1158 / 1823	2.9 / 7.6 / 3.1	22 M	0457 / 1104 / 1722 / 2333	3.6 / 7.0 / 3.8 / 6.7
8 M	0030 / 0702 / 1318 / 1949	7.3 / 3.4 / 7.2 / 3.5	23 TU	0600 / 1210 / 1848	4.0 / 6.7 / 4.1
9 TU	0204 / 0838 / 1450 / 2125	7.0 / 3.5 / 7.2 / 3.3	24 W	0101 / 0741 / 1349 / 2030	6.5 / 4.1 / 6.7 / 3.9
10 W	0333 / 1001 / 1603 / 2235	7.2 / 3.2 / 7.7 / 2.8	25 TH	0248 / 0907 / 1518 / 2148	6.8 / 3.7 / 7.2 / 3.3
11 TH	0437 / 1101 / 1658 / 2328	7.7 / 2.7 / 8.2 / 2.3	26 F	0401 / 1015 / 1621 / 2248	7.4 / 3.1 / 7.9 / 2.5
12 F	0528 / 1150 / 1745	8.2 / 2.2 / 8.7	27 SA	0456 / 1111 / 1713 / 2340	8.0 / 2.3 / 8.6 / 1.8
13 SA ○	0014 / 0611 / 1234 / 1827	1.8 / 8.6 / 1.8 / 9.0	28 SU	0544 / 1201 / 1800	8.7 / 1.7 / 9.2
14 SU	0055 / 0651 / 1313 / 1905	1.5 / 8.9 / 1.6 / 9.2	29 M ●	0028 / 0629 / 1248 / 1844	1.2 / 9.3 / 1.1 / 9.7
15 M	0133 / 0727 / 1348 / 1941	1.3 / 9.0 / 1.5 / 9.3	30 TU	0113 / 0711 / 1332 / 1927	0.7 / 9.7 / 0.7 / 10.0
			31 W	0155 / 0753 / 1413 / 2008	0.5 / 9.9 / 0.7 / 10.1

Chart Datum: 5·06 metres below Ordnance Datum (Local)
HAT is 10·3 metres above Chart Datum

TIME ZONE (UT)
For Summer Time add ONE hour in **non-shaded areas**

CHANNEL ISLES – ST PETER PORT

LAT 49°27'N   LONG 2°31'W

TIMES AND HEIGHTS OF HIGH AND LOW WATERS

Dates in amber are **SPRINGS**
Dates in yellow are **NEAPS**

2011

SEPTEMBER

Day	Time	m	Day	Time	m
1 TH	0235 / 0832 / 1453 / 2048	0.5 / 9.8 / 0.7 / 9.8	**16** F	0229 / 0824 / 1441 / 2037	1.8 / 8.8 / 2.0 / 8.6
2 F	0314 / 0911 / 1532 / 2128	0.9 / 9.5 / 1.2 / 9.3	**17** SA	0253 / 0849 / 1505 / 2103	2.2 / 8.4 / 2.4 / 8.2
3 SA	0352 / 0951 / 1612 / 2210	1.5 / 8.9 / 1.8 / 8.6	**18** SU	0317 / 0915 / 1529 / 2130	2.6 / 8.1 / 2.9 / 7.8
4 SU	0434 / 1035 / 1659 / 2259	2.3 / 8.2 / 2.6 / 7.7	**19** M	0343 / 0945 / 1600 / 2205	3.1 / 7.6 / 3.3 / 7.3
5 M	0525 / 1131 / 1801	3.1 / 7.5 / 3.4	**20** TU	0420 / 1026 / 1645 / 2258	3.6 / 7.2 / 3.7 / 6.9
6 TU	0008 / 0641 / 1300 / 1937	7.0 / 3.8 / 7.0 / 3.8	**21** W	0517 / 1131 / 1803	4.0 / 6.8 / 4.1
7 W	0159 / 0833 / 1441 / 2119	6.7 / 3.9 / 7.1 / 3.5	**22** TH	0022 / 0659 / 1308 / 1958	6.6 / 4.2 / 6.8 / 3.9
8 TH	0327 / 0953 / 1551 / 2223	7.1 / 3.4 / 7.6 / 3.0	**23** F	0216 / 0839 / 1446 / 2121	6.8 / 3.8 / 7.2 / 3.3
9 F	0424 / 1047 / 1642 / 2311	7.6 / 2.9 / 8.1 / 2.4	**24** SA	0334 / 0950 / 1553 / 2223	7.4 / 3.1 / 7.9 / 2.5
10 SA	0509 / 1131 / 1724 / 2352	8.2 / 2.3 / 8.6 / 1.9	**25** SU	0429 / 1047 / 1647 / 2316	8.2 / 2.3 / 8.7 / 1.7
11 SU	0548 / 1210 / 1803	8.6 / 1.9 / 9.0	**26** M	0518 / 1137 / 1735	8.9 / 1.5 / 9.4
12 M	0029 / 0624 / 1247 / 1839	1.6 / 8.9 / 1.6 / 9.2	**27** TU	0003 / 0603 / 1225 / 1821	1.1 / 9.5 / 0.9 / 9.9
13 TU	0104 / 0658 / 1320 / 1913	1.4 / 9.1 / 1.5 / 9.3	**28** W	0049 / 0647 / 1310 / 1905	0.6 / 9.9 / 0.6 / 10.2
14 W	0136 / 0729 / 1350 / 1943	1.4 / 9.1 / 1.5 / 9.2	**29** TH	0132 / 0729 / 1352 / 1947	0.4 / 10.1 / 0.5 / 10.1
15 TH	0204 / 0758 / 1417 / 2011	1.6 / 9.0 / 1.7 / 9.0	**30** F	0213 / 0810 / 1434 / 2028	0.6 / 10.0 / 0.7 / 9.8

OCTOBER

Day	Time	m	Day	Time	m
1 SA	0253 / 0850 / 1514 / 2109	1.0 / 9.6 / 1.2 / 9.3	**16** SU	0225 / 0821 / 1440 / 2038	2.3 / 8.6 / 2.4 / 8.3
2 SU	0332 / 0930 / 1555 / 2152	1.7 / 9.0 / 1.9 / 8.5	**17** M	0252 / 0849 / 1509 / 2109	2.6 / 8.2 / 2.8 / 7.9
3 M	0414 / 1015 / 1642 / 2241	2.5 / 8.2 / 2.7 / 7.6	**18** TU	0322 / 0922 / 1542 / 2147	3.0 / 7.9 / 3.2 / 7.5
4 TU	0505 / 1111 / 1745 / 2351	3.3 / 7.5 / 3.4 / 6.9	**19** W	0400 / 1006 / 1629 / 2240	3.5 / 7.5 / 3.6 / 7.1
5 W	0622 / 1238 / 1918	3.9 / 7.0 / 3.8	**20** TH	0457 / 1109 / 1740 / 2357	3.9 / 7.1 / 3.8 / 6.8
6 TH	0139 / 0811 / 1416 / 2054	6.7 / 4.0 / 7.0 / 3.6	**21** F	0625 / 1235 / 1922	4.0 / 7.1 / 3.7
7 F	0303 / 0928 / 1524 / 2156	7.0 / 3.6 / 7.5 / 3.1	**22** SA	0135 / 0804 / 1406 / 2047	7.0 / 3.7 / 7.4 / 3.2
8 SA	0357 / 1020 / 1614 / 2242	7.6 / 3.1 / 8.0 / 2.6	**23** SU	0257 / 0918 / 1518 / 2152	7.6 / 3.0 / 8.0 / 2.5
9 SU	0440 / 1102 / 1656 / 2321	8.1 / 2.6 / 8.4 / 2.2	**24** M	0357 / 1017 / 1616 / 2246	8.3 / 2.3 / 8.7 / 1.8
10 M	0518 / 1140 / 1734 / 2358	8.5 / 2.1 / 8.8 / 1.9	**25** TU	0449 / 1110 / 1708 / 2336	8.9 / 1.6 / 9.3 / 1.2
11 TU	0553 / 1216 / 1809	8.8 / 1.9 / 9.0	**26** W	0536 / 1200 / 1757	9.5 / 1.1 / 9.7
12 W	0031 / 0626 / 1249 / 1842	1.7 / 9.0 / 1.7 / 9.1	**27** TH	0024 / 0622 / 1247 / 1843	0.9 / 9.8 / 0.7 / 9.9
13 TH	0103 / 0657 / 1319 / 1914	1.7 / 9.1 / 1.7 / 9.1	**28** F	0110 / 0706 / 1333 / 1928	0.7 / 10.0 / 0.7 / 9.8
14 F	0132 / 0727 / 1347 / 1943	1.7 / 9.0 / 1.8 / 8.9	**29** SA	0153 / 0749 / 1417 / 2012	0.9 / 9.9 / 0.8 / 9.6
15 SA	0159 / 0755 / 1414 / 2011	2.0 / 8.8 / 2.1 / 8.6	**30** SU	0235 / 0832 / 1459 / 2055	1.2 / 9.5 / 1.3 / 9.1
			31 M	0316 / 0914 / 1543 / 2138	1.8 / 9.0 / 1.9 / 8.4

NOVEMBER

Day	Time	m	Day	Time	m
1 TU	0400 / 0959 / 1630 / 2227	2.5 / 8.3 / 2.6 / 7.7	**16** W	0312 / 0912 / 1537 / 2140	2.8 / 8.1 / 2.9 / 7.8
2 W	0449 / 1052 / 1727 / 2328	3.2 / 7.7 / 3.2 / 7.1	**17** TH	0353 / 0958 / 1624 / 2231	3.2 / 7.8 / 3.1 / 7.5
3 TH	0554 / 1202 / 1839	3.8 / 7.2 / 3.7	**18** F	0446 / 1056 / 1725 / 2336	3.5 / 7.6 / 3.3 / 7.3
4 F	0051 / 0720 / 1327 / 2002	6.8 / 4.0 / 7.0 / 3.7	**19** SA	0557 / 1206 / 1843	3.6 / 7.5 / 3.3
5 SA	0215 / 0842 / 1440 / 2110	7.0 / 3.8 / 7.2 / 3.4	**20** SU	0054 / 0722 / 1325 / 2004	7.3 / 3.5 / 7.6 / 3.1
6 SU	0316 / 0940 / 1535 / 2201	7.3 / 3.4 / 7.6 / 3.1	**21** M	0214 / 0841 / 1440 / 2115	7.6 / 3.1 / 8.0 / 2.6
7 M	0402 / 1026 / 1620 / 2244	7.8 / 3.0 / 8.0 / 2.7	**22** TU	0322 / 0946 / 1545 / 2216	8.1 / 2.5 / 8.4 / 2.1
8 TU	0442 / 1106 / 1700 / 2322	8.2 / 2.6 / 8.3 / 2.4	**23** W	0420 / 1044 / 1642 / 2311	8.7 / 1.9 / 8.9 / 1.7
9 W	0519 / 1142 / 1737 / 2357	8.5 / 2.3 / 8.6 / 2.1	**24** TH	0512 / 1138 / 1736	9.2 / 1.5 / 9.2
10 TH	0554 / 1217 / 1813	8.8 / 2.1 / 8.8	**25** F	0003 / 0601 / 1229 / 1826	1.3 / 9.5 / 1.1 / 9.4
11 F	0031 / 0628 / 1250 / 1847	2.0 / 8.9 / 2.0 / 8.8	**26** SA	0052 / 0649 / 1318 / 1914	1.2 / 9.7 / 1.0 / 9.5
12 SA	0103 / 0700 / 1322 / 1920	2.0 / 8.9 / 2.0 / 8.7	**27** SU	0138 / 0734 / 1404 / 1959	1.2 / 9.7 / 1.0 / 9.3
13 SU	0134 / 0731 / 1354 / 1952	2.1 / 8.8 / 2.1 / 8.6	**28** M	0222 / 0818 / 1448 / 2043	1.4 / 9.5 / 1.3 / 9.0
14 M	0205 / 0802 / 1426 / 2024	2.3 / 8.7 / 2.3 / 8.4	**29** TU	0304 / 0901 / 1532 / 2126	1.8 / 9.1 / 1.8 / 8.5
15 TU	0237 / 0835 / 1459 / 2059	2.5 / 8.4 / 2.6 / 8.1	**30** W	0346 / 0944 / 1615 / 2209	2.3 / 8.6 / 2.3 / 8.0

DECEMBER

Day	Time	m	Day	Time	m
1 TH	0429 / 1029 / 1701 / 2256	2.9 / 8.0 / 2.9 / 7.5	**16** F	0348 / 0951 / 1618 / 2220	2.6 / 8.4 / 2.5 / 8.0
2 F	0518 / 1120 / 1752 / 2351	3.4 / 7.5 / 3.3 / 7.1	**17** SA	0435 / 1041 / 1708 / 2313	2.8 / 8.1 / 2.8 / 7.7
3 SA	0616 / 1221 / 1852	3.8 / 7.2 / 3.6	**18** SU	0532 / 1139 / 1808	3.1 / 7.9 / 3.0
4 SU	0057 / 0725 / 1331 / 1957	6.9 / 3.9 / 7.0 / 3.7	**19** M	0017 / 0641 / 1248 / 1920	7.6 / 3.2 / 7.7 / 3.0
5 M	0210 / 0836 / 1438 / 2101	7.0 / 3.8 / 7.1 / 3.6	**20** TU	0132 / 0801 / 1404 / 2038	7.6 / 3.1 / 7.7 / 2.9
6 TU	0311 / 0936 / 1535 / 2156	7.3 / 3.5 / 7.4 / 3.3	**21** W	0249 / 0917 / 1518 / 2150	7.8 / 2.8 / 8.0 / 2.6
7 W	0401 / 1025 / 1623 / 2242	7.7 / 3.2 / 7.7 / 2.9	**22** TH	0356 / 1024 / 1624 / 2253	8.2 / 2.4 / 8.3 / 2.2
8 TH	0444 / 1108 / 1706 / 2323	8.1 / 2.8 / 8.1 / 2.6	**23** F	0455 / 1123 / 1722 / 2348	8.7 / 1.9 / 8.7 / 1.8
9 F	0524 / 1148 / 1747	8.4 / 2.5 / 8.3	**24** SA	0548 / 1217 / 1815	9.1 / 1.5 / 9.0
10 SA	0002 / 0602 / 1227 / 1826	2.3 / 8.7 / 2.2 / 8.5	**25** SU	0039 / 0637 / 1307 / 1904	1.5 / 9.4 / 1.2 / 9.2
11 SU	0040 / 0640 / 1304 / 1903	2.2 / 8.8 / 2.1 / 8.6	**26** M	0127 / 0723 / 1354 / 1949	1.4 / 9.6 / 1.1 / 9.2
12 M	0117 / 0716 / 1341 / 1940	2.1 / 8.9 / 2.0 / 8.6	**27** TU	0211 / 0806 / 1436 / 2031	1.4 / 9.5 / 1.2 / 9.1
13 TU	0154 / 0751 / 1418 / 2016	2.1 / 8.9 / 2.0 / 8.6	**28** W	0251 / 0846 / 1516 / 2109	1.6 / 9.3 / 1.5 / 8.8
14 W	0230 / 0828 / 1455 / 2054	2.2 / 8.8 / 2.1 / 8.4	**29** TH	0328 / 0924 / 1553 / 2145	1.9 / 8.9 / 1.9 / 8.4
15 TH	0307 / 0907 / 1535 / 2134	2.4 / 8.6 / 2.3 / 8.2	**30** F	0404 / 1000 / 1629 / 2220	2.4 / 8.4 / 2.4 / 7.9
			31 SA	0439 / 1038 / 1705 / 2257	2.9 / 7.9 / 2.9 / 7.5

Chart Datum: 5·06 metres below Ordnance Datum (Local)
HAT is 10·3 metres above Chart Datum

TIDES

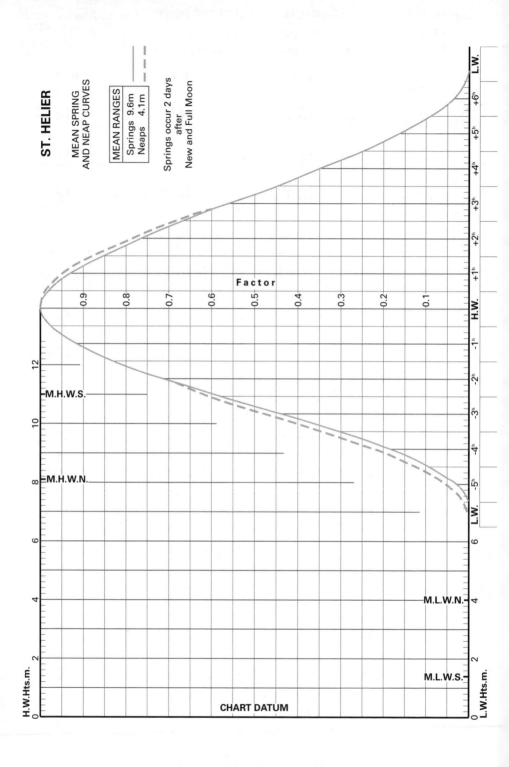

ST. HELIER

MEAN SPRING
AND NEAP CURVES

MEAN RANGES
Springs 9.6m
Neaps 4.1m

Springs occur 2 days
after
New and Full Moon

Factor

TIME ZONE (UT)
For Summer Time add ONE hour in **non-shaded areas**

Dates in amber are **SPRINGS**
Dates in yellow are **NEAPS**

JANUARY

Time m		Time m	
1 SA	0330 9.0 / 1010 3.1 / 1602 9.1 / 2243 3.0	**16** SU	0256 8.2 / 0941 3.9 / 1534 8.3 / 2211 3.6
2 SU	0434 9.5 / 1114 2.6 / 1703 9.5 / 2342 2.6	**17** M	0400 8.9 / 1045 3.2 / 1634 9.0 / 2310 2.9
3 M	0526 10.0 / 1210 2.2 / 1753 9.9	**18** TU	0455 9.6 / 1140 2.4 / 1727 9.8
4 TU	0032 2.3 / 0612 10.3 / 1258 2.0 / ● 1837 10.1	**19** W	0003 2.2 / 0544 10.3 / 1233 1.8 / ○ 1815 10.4
5 W	0116 2.1 / 0653 10.6 / 1339 1.8 / 1916 10.3	**20** TH	0053 1.7 / 0632 10.9 / 1322 1.3 / 1902 10.9
6 TH	0154 2.0 / 0731 10.6 / 1416 1.8 / 1952 10.3	**21** F	0140 1.3 / 0721 11.4 / 1408 0.9 / 1946 11.2
7 F	0228 2.1 / 0806 10.5 / 1448 1.9 / 2025 10.1	**22** SA	0224 1.0 / 0802 11.6 / 1451 0.8 / 2029 11.3
8 SA	0258 2.3 / 0838 10.3 / 1518 2.1 / 2056 9.9	**23** SU	0307 0.9 / 0844 11.6 / 1532 0.9 / 2110 11.1
9 SU	0327 2.6 / 0908 10.0 / 1547 2.5 / 2125 9.6	**24** M	0347 1.2 / 0926 11.3 / 1612 1.2 / 2151 10.7
10 M	0355 2.9 / 0938 9.6 / 1615 2.8 / 2156 9.2	**25** TU	0428 1.6 / 1007 10.6 / 1651 1.9 / 2232 10.0
11 TU	0425 3.3 / 1010 9.1 / 1647 3.3 / 2230 8.7	**26** W	0509 2.3 / 1049 9.8 / 1733 2.6 / ◑ 2317 9.3
12 W	0500 3.7 / 1047 8.6 / 1726 3.8 / ◑ 2312 8.2	**27** TH	0557 3.0 / 1140 9.0 / 1825 3.4
13 TH	0546 4.2 / 1136 8.2 / 1819 4.2	**28** F	0015 8.6 / 0701 3.7 / 1250 8.3 / 1941 3.9
14 F	0012 7.9 / 0652 4.5 / 1251 7.7 / 1934 4.4	**29** SA	0139 8.2 / 0829 3.9 / 1425 8.0 / 2113 3.9
15 SA	0135 7.8 / 0820 4.4 / 1421 7.8 / 2100 4.2	**30** SU	0312 8.4 / 0957 3.6 / 1553 8.4 / 2233 3.5
		31 M	0424 9.0 / 1107 3.0 / 1656 9.0 / 2334 2.9

FEBRUARY

Time m		Time m	
1 TU	0517 9.6 / 1201 2.4 / 1744 9.6	**16** W	0435 9.5 / 1121 2.4 / 1710 9.8 / 2345 2.1
2 W	0022 2.4 / 0600 10.1 / 1246 2.0 / 1824 10.0	**17** TH	0529 10.4 / 1216 1.5 / 1800 10.6
3 TH	0103 2.0 / 0639 10.5 / 1324 1.7 / ● 1900 10.3	**18** F	0037 1.3 / 0617 11.2 / 1307 0.9 / ○ 1846 11.2
4 F	0138 1.9 / 0714 10.7 / 1357 1.6 / 1932 10.4	**19** SA	0126 0.8 / 0702 11.8 / 1353 0.4 / 1929 11.7
5 SA	0208 1.8 / 0745 10.7 / 1426 1.6 / 2002 10.4	**20** SU	0210 0.5 / 0746 12.1 / 1435 0.3 / 2011 11.8
6 SU	0236 1.8 / 0814 10.6 / 1453 1.7 / 2029 10.3	**21** M	0251 0.4 / 0827 12.0 / 1515 0.4 / 2050 11.5
7 M	0302 2.0 / 0842 10.4 / 1519 2.0 / 2056 10.1	**22** TU	0330 0.7 / 0907 11.5 / 1552 0.9 / 2128 11.0
8 TU	0328 2.3 / 0908 10.0 / 1544 2.3 / 2121 9.7	**23** W	0408 1.3 / 0945 10.8 / 1627 1.8 / 2205 10.2
9 W	0353 2.7 / 0934 9.5 / 1611 2.9 / 2148 9.2	**24** TH	0445 2.1 / 1024 9.8 / 1704 2.7 / ◑ 2245 9.3
10 TH	0421 3.2 / 1001 8.9 / 1640 3.4 / 2218 8.6	**25** F	0528 3.1 / 1110 8.7 / 1751 3.4 / 2340 8.4
11 F	0455 3.8 / 1037 8.3 / 1719 4.0 / ◑ 2303 8.1	**26** SA	0629 3.9 / 1219 7.9 / 1907 4.3
12 SA	0547 4.3 / 1136 7.7 / 1824 4.4	**27** SU	0109 7.8 / 0805 4.2 / 1410 7.6 / 2056 4.3
13 SU	0020 7.7 / 0714 4.5 / 1320 7.5 / 2005 4.5	**28** M	0257 8.0 / 0944 3.8 / 1543 8.1 / 2221 3.7
14 M	0208 7.8 / 0859 4.1 / 1503 8.0 / 2139 3.8		
15 TU	0333 8.6 / 1018 3.3 / 1614 8.9 / 2248 3.0		

MARCH

Time m		Time m	
1 TU	0409 8.7 / 1052 3.1 / 1641 8.9 / 2318 3.0	**16** W	0305 8.5 / 0950 3.2 / 1551 8.9 / 2222 3.0
2 W	0459 9.5 / 1142 2.4 / 1725 9.5	**17** TH	0412 9.5 / 1056 2.2 / 1648 9.9 / 2321 2.0
3 TH	0002 2.4 / 0540 10.0 / 1224 2.0 / 1802 10.0	**18** F	0507 10.5 / 1152 1.4 / 1738 10.8
4 F	0041 2.0 / 0617 10.4 / 1300 1.7 / ● 1836 10.3	**19** SA	0014 1.2 / 0555 11.3 / 1244 0.7 / ○ 1824 11.4
5 SA	0114 1.8 / 0650 10.6 / 1331 1.6 / 1906 10.5	**20** SU	0104 0.6 / 0641 11.9 / 1331 0.3 / 1907 11.8
6 SU	0143 1.7 / 0720 10.7 / 1359 1.5 / 1934 10.6	**21** M	0149 0.3 / 0725 12.1 / 1413 0.2 / 1948 11.9
7 M	0210 1.6 / 0748 10.7 / 1426 1.6 / 2001 10.5	**22** TU	0231 0.3 / 0806 11.9 / 1453 0.5 / 2027 11.6
8 TU	0237 1.7 / 0815 10.5 / 1451 1.7 / 2026 10.3	**23** W	0310 0.6 / 0846 11.4 / 1530 1.1 / 2105 11.0
9 W	0302 2.0 / 0840 10.2 / 1517 2.1 / 2051 10.0	**24** TH	0348 1.3 / 0924 10.6 / 1605 1.9 / 2141 10.2
10 TH	0328 2.4 / 0904 9.7 / 1542 2.6 / 2115 9.5	**25** F	0425 2.2 / 1003 9.5 / 1641 2.9 / 2221 9.2
11 F	0354 2.9 / 0930 9.1 / 1609 3.2 / 2143 9.0	**26** SA	0507 3.1 / 1048 8.5 / 1726 3.8 / ◑ 2314 8.3
12 SA	0425 3.5 / 1003 8.5 / 1645 3.8 / ◑ 2224 8.4	**27** SU	0606 3.9 / 1157 7.7 / 1839 4.4
13 SU	0511 4.0 / 1057 7.9 / 1744 4.3 / 2335 7.8	**28** M	0043 7.8 / 0738 4.2 / 1346 7.5 / 2027 4.5
14 M	0632 4.3 / 1240 7.5 / 1924 4.4	**29** TU	0228 7.9 / 0913 3.9 / 1514 8.0 / 2150 3.9
15 TU	0129 7.8 / 0822 4.1 / 1435 8.0 / 2107 3.9	**30** W	0339 8.6 / 1020 3.3 / 1610 8.8 / 2246 3.2
		31 TH	0429 9.2 / 1108 2.6 / 1654 9.4 / 2330 2.6

APRIL

Time m		Time m	
1 F	0511 9.8 / 1149 2.2 / 1731 9.9	**16** SA	0439 10.5 / 1122 1.5 / 1711 10.7 / 2346 1.3
2 SA	0008 2.2 / 0547 10.2 / 1226 1.9 / 1804 10.2	**17** SU	0530 11.1 / 1215 0.9 / 1758 11.3
3 SU	0042 1.9 / 0620 10.4 / 1258 1.7 / ● 1835 10.4	**18** M	0037 0.8 / 0617 11.5 / 1304 0.7 / ○ 1842 11.6
4 M	0113 1.8 / 0651 10.5 / 1329 1.6 / 1904 10.5	**19** TU	0125 0.6 / 0702 11.7 / 1349 0.6 / 1925 11.6
5 TU	0143 1.7 / 0720 10.5 / 1358 1.7 / 1932 10.5	**20** W	0209 0.6 / 0746 11.5 / 1430 0.9 / 2005 11.4
6 W	0211 1.7 / 0748 10.4 / 1425 1.8 / 1959 10.4	**21** TH	0251 0.9 / 0827 11.0 / 1509 1.4 / 2044 10.8
7 TH	0239 1.9 / 0815 10.1 / 1453 2.1 / 2025 10.1	**22** F	0331 1.5 / 0907 10.3 / 1547 2.2 / 2123 10.1
8 F	0307 2.3 / 0843 9.7 / 1520 2.5 / 2053 9.7	**23** SA	0410 2.3 / 0947 9.4 / 1624 3.0 / 2204 9.3
9 SA	0336 2.7 / 0913 9.2 / 1551 3.1 / 2126 9.2	**24** SU	0452 3.1 / 1033 8.6 / 1709 3.7 / 2255 8.5
10 SU	0411 3.2 / 0951 8.7 / 1631 3.6 / 2210 8.7	**25** M	0545 3.7 / 1135 7.9 / 1811 4.3 / ◐
11 M	0500 3.7 / 1049 8.1 / 1730 4.0 / ◑ 2321 8.2	**26** TU	0009 8.0 / 0658 4.1 / 1301 7.7 / 1937 4.4
12 TU	0614 4.0 / 1223 7.8 / 1859 4.1	**27** W	0139 8.0 / 0820 4.0 / 1422 8.0 / 2057 4.0
13 W	0102 8.1 / 0751 3.7 / 1404 8.2 / 2035 3.7	**28** TH	0251 8.4 / 0927 3.5 / 1523 8.5 / 2158 3.5
14 TH	0233 8.7 / 0917 3.0 / 1520 9.0 / 2150 2.8	**29** F	0346 8.9 / 1020 3.1 / 1611 9.1 / 2245 3.0
15 F	0342 9.6 / 1024 2.2 / 1619 9.9 / 2251 2.0	**30** SA	0431 9.3 / 1105 2.6 / 1652 9.5 / 2327 2.6

Chart Datum: 5·88 metres below Ordnance Datum (Local)
HAT is 12·2 metres above Chart Datum

TIDES

TIME ZONE (UT)	CHANNEL ISLES – ST HELIER	Dates in amber are SPRINGS
For Summer Time add ONE hour in non-shaded areas	LAT 49°11′N LONG 2°07′W	Dates in yellow are NEAPS
	TIMES AND HEIGHTS OF HIGH AND LOW WATERS	**2011**

MAY

Day	Time m	Time m	Day	Time m	Time m
1 SU	0511 9.7	1145 2.3 / 1728 9.9	16 M	0504 10.6	1146 1.5 / 1732 10.8
2 M	0005 2.3 / 0547 10.0	1222 2.1 / 1801 10.1	17 TU ○	0012 1.3 / 0555 10.9	1239 1.3 / 1819 11.1
3 TU ●	0041 2.0 / 0620 10.1	1257 1.9 / 1833 10.3	18 W	0103 1.1 / 0643 11.0	1327 1.2 / 1904 11.2
4 W	0116 1.9 / 0653 10.2	1331 1.9 / 1905 10.4	19 TH	0151 1.1 / 0728 10.9	1411 1.4 / 1947 11.0
5 TH	0148 1.9 / 0725 10.2	1403 1.9 / 1936 10.4	20 F	0235 1.3 / 0812 10.6	1453 1.7 / 2028 10.7
6 F	0220 2.0 / 0758 10.1	1434 2.1 / 2009 10.2	21 SA	0317 1.7 / 0853 10.1	1532 2.3 / 2108 10.1
7 SA	0252 2.2 / 0832 9.8	1507 2.4 / 2043 9.9	22 SU	0356 2.2 / 0933 9.5	1610 2.8 / 2149 9.5
8 SU	0327 2.5 / 0910 9.4	1543 2.8 / 2123 9.5	23 M	0436 2.8 / 1015 8.9	1649 3.4 / 2233 8.9
9 M	0408 2.8 / 0955 9.0	1628 3.2 / 2212 9.1	24 TU ◑	0519 3.4 / 1103 8.4	1736 3.9 / 2327 8.4
10 TU ◑	0458 3.2 / 1053 8.6	1725 3.5 / 2317 8.7	25 W	0610 3.7 / 1203 8.1	1835 4.1
11 W	0604 3.4 / 1207 8.4	1840 3.6	26 TH	0035 8.1 / 0712 3.9	1314 8.0 / 1945 4.2
12 TH	0036 8.7 / 0723 3.3	1329 8.6 / 2001 3.4	27 F	0148 8.1 / 0819 3.8	1422 8.2 / 2054 3.9
13 F	0156 9.0 / 0841 2.9	1442 9.1 / 2115 2.8	28 SA	0251 8.4 / 0921 3.6	1519 8.6 / 2152 3.5
14 SA	0307 9.5 / 0949 2.4	1545 9.8 / 2219 2.2	29 SU	0344 8.8 / 1015 3.2	1607 9.0 / 2242 3.1
15 SU	0408 10.1 / 1050 1.9	1641 10.4 / 2317 1.7	30 M	0431 9.1 / 1102 2.8	1649 9.4 / 2327 2.7
			31 TU	0512 9.5 / 1146 2.5	1728 9.8

JUNE

Day	Time m	Time m	Day	Time m	Time m
1 W ●	0010 2.4 / 0551 9.8	1228 2.3 / 1806 10.1	16 TH	0048 1.6 / 0629 10.4	1311 1.7 / 1849 10.8
2 TH	0051 2.1 / 0630 10.0	1307 2.1 / 1843 10.3	17 F	0138 1.5 / 0715 10.5	1357 1.7 / 1933 10.8
3 F	0129 2.0 / 0708 10.1	1345 2.0 / 1920 10.4	18 SA	0222 1.5 / 0758 10.4	1438 1.9 / 2014 10.6
4 SA	0207 1.9 / 0747 10.2	1422 2.0 / 1959 10.4	19 SU	0302 1.7 / 0837 10.2	1516 2.1 / 2052 10.3
5 SU	0245 1.9 / 0827 10.1	1500 2.1 / 2040 10.3	20 M	0339 2.0 / 0914 9.8	1550 2.5 / 2128 9.9
6 M	0325 2.0 / 0910 9.9	1541 2.3 / 2124 10.1	21 TU	0412 2.5 / 0949 9.4	1623 3.0 / 2204 9.4
7 TU	0408 2.2 / 0956 9.6	1627 2.6 / 2212 9.8	22 W	0446 2.9 / 1026 8.9	1658 3.4 / 2243 8.9
8 W	0456 2.5 / 1047 9.3	1718 2.9 / 2306 9.4	23 TH ◑	0522 3.3 / 1108 8.5	1739 3.8 / 2331 8.4
9 TH	0551 2.8 / 1145 9.0	1819 3.1	24 F	0607 3.7 / 1202 8.2	1832 4.1
10 F	0009 9.2 / 0654 3.0	1252 8.9 / 1927 3.2	25 SA	0033 8.1 / 0704 4.0	1309 8.0 / 1939 4.2
11 SA	0119 9.1 / 0805 3.0	1404 9.0 / 2040 3.0	26 SU	0145 8.0 / 0814 4.0	1419 8.1 / 2052 4.0
12 SU	0232 9.2 / 0916 2.8	1513 9.4 / 2149 2.6	27 M	0253 8.2 / 0922 3.8	1520 8.5 / 2156 3.6
13 M	0341 9.5 / 1022 2.5	1615 9.8 / 2253 2.2	28 TU	0350 8.6 / 1022 3.3	1612 9.0 / 2252 3.1
14 TU	0443 9.9 / 1124 2.1	1712 10.3 / 2353 1.9	29 W	0441 9.0 / 1114 2.9	1659 9.5 / 2342 2.6
15 W ○	0539 10.2 / 1220 1.9	1803 10.6	30 TH	0527 9.6 / 1203 2.5	1743 10.0

JULY

Day	Time m	Time m	Day	Time m	Time m
1 F ●	0029 2.2 / 0611 9.9	1249 2.1 / 1826 10.4	16 SA	0126 1.6 / 0702 10.4	1343 1.8 / 1918 10.7
2 SA	0115 1.8 / 0655 10.3	1332 1.9 / 1909 10.7	17 SU	0207 1.5 / 0741 10.4	1421 1.8 / 1955 10.7
3 SU	0158 1.6 / 0737 10.5	1414 1.7 / 1952 10.9	18 M	0243 1.6 / 0816 10.4	1454 1.9 / 2029 10.5
4 M	0240 1.4 / 0820 10.6	1455 1.6 / 2034 10.9	19 TU	0314 1.8 / 0848 10.1	1524 2.2 / 2101 10.2
5 TU	0321 1.4 / 0903 10.6	1537 1.7 / 2118 10.8	20 W	0342 2.1 / 0918 9.8	1551 2.5 / 2131 9.8
6 W	0403 1.6 / 0946 10.3	1620 1.9 / 2201 10.4	21 TH	0410 2.5 / 0948 9.4	1620 3.0 / 2202 9.3
7 TH	0445 1.9 / 1030 9.9	1705 2.3 / 2248 9.9	22 F	0439 3.0 / 1020 9.0	1652 3.4 / 2236 8.7
8 F ◑	0531 2.4 / 1119 9.4	1755 2.8 / 2340 9.4	23 SA	0514 3.5 / 1058 8.4	1732 3.9 / 2320 8.1
9 SA	0625 2.9 / 1217 9.0	1856 3.2	24 SU	0559 4.0 / 1151 8.0	1830 4.3
10 SU	0044 8.9 / 0731 3.3	1328 8.8 / 2010 3.3	25 M	0027 7.7 / 0705 4.3	1309 7.8 / 1949 4.4
11 M	0202 8.7 / 0848 3.3	1447 8.9 / 2128 3.2	26 TU	0157 7.7 / 0829 4.3	1433 8.0 / 2113 4.1
12 TU	0323 8.9 / 1004 3.1	1559 9.3 / 2240 2.7	27 W	0315 8.1 / 0945 3.8	1540 8.6 / 2221 3.4
13 W	0433 9.3 / 1112 2.7	1700 9.8 / 2344 2.3	28 TH	0415 8.8 / 1047 3.1	1635 9.3 / 2318 2.7
14 TH	0530 9.7 / 1210 2.3	1752 10.3	29 F	0507 9.4 / 1141 2.5	1724 10.0
15 F ○	0038 1.9 / 0619 10.1	1300 2.0 / 1837 10.6	30 SA ●	0010 2.1 / 0554 10.1	1231 1.9 / 1810 10.6
			31 SU	0100 1.5 / 0640 10.6	1318 1.5 / 1855 11.1

AUGUST

Day	Time m	Time m	Day	Time m	Time m
1 M	0146 1.1 / 0724 11.0	1403 1.2 / 1939 11.4	16 TU	0216 1.6 / 0749 10.6	1426 1.8 / 2002 10.7
2 TU	0229 0.9 / 0806 11.2	1445 1.0 / 2021 11.6	17 W	0243 1.7 / 0817 10.4	1453 2.0 / 2031 10.5
3 W	0310 0.9 / 0847 11.2	1525 1.1 / 2103 11.4	18 TH	0309 1.9 / 0844 10.2	1519 2.2 / 2058 10.1
4 TH	0349 1.1 / 0928 10.9	1605 1.4 / 2144 10.9	19 F	0335 2.3 / 0910 9.8	1544 2.7 / 2124 9.6
5 F	0428 1.6 / 1008 10.3	1646 2.0 / 2225 10.1	20 SA	0401 2.8 / 0936 9.3	1612 3.2 / 2150 9.0
6 SA ◑	0508 2.3 / 1051 9.6	1731 2.7 / 2313 9.3	21 SU ◑	0430 3.4 / 1006 8.7	1645 3.8 / 2223 8.3
7 SU	0556 3.1 / 1144 8.9	1829 3.4	22 M	0507 4.0 / 1046 8.1	1734 4.3 / 2317 7.7
8 M	0015 8.5 / 0702 3.7	1259 8.4 / 1948 3.8	23 TU	0606 4.5 / 1157 7.7	1853 4.6
9 TU	0144 8.1 / 0831 3.9	1434 8.4 / 2118 3.6	24 W	0058 7.4 / 0738 4.6	1347 7.7 / 2033 4.3
10 W	0319 8.4 / 0958 3.5	1553 8.9 / 2236 3.0	25 TH	0244 7.8 / 0912 4.1	1512 8.4 / 2153 3.6
11 TH	0429 9.0 / 1106 2.9	1652 9.6 / 2336 2.4	26 F	0352 8.7 / 1022 3.3	1612 9.3 / 2255 2.7
12 F	0522 9.6 / 1159 2.4	1740 10.2	27 SA	0447 9.6 / 1119 2.4	1704 10.2 / 2349 1.8
13 SA ○	0025 1.9 / 0605 10.1	1245 2.0 / 1821 10.6	28 SU	0535 10.4 / 1210 1.7	1752 11.0
14 SU	0108 1.6 / 0643 10.4	1324 1.8 / 1858 10.8	29 M ●	0039 1.2 / 0620 11.0	1259 1.4 / 1837 11.5
15 M	0144 1.5 / 0717 10.6	1357 1.7 / 1931 10.8	30 TU	0127 0.8 / 0704 11.5	1344 0.8 / 1920 11.9
			31 W	0210 0.5 / 0746 11.7	1427 0.6 / 2002 11.9

Chart Datum: 5·88 metres below Ordnance Datum (Local)
HAT is 12·2 metres above Chart Datum

CHANNEL ISLES – ST HELIER

LAT 49°11′N   LONG 2°07′W

TIMES AND HEIGHTS OF HIGH AND LOW WATERS

Dates in amber are **SPRINGS**
Dates in yellow are **NEAPS**

2011

SEPTEMBER

Day	Time m	Day	Time m
1 TH	0251 0.6 / 0826 11.6 / 1507 0.8 / 2043 11.6	16 F	0236 1.9 / 0812 10.4 / 1448 2.1 / 2026 10.2
2 F	0329 1.0 / 0905 11.2 / 1546 1.3 / 2123 11.0	17 SA	0302 2.3 / 0836 10.1 / 1514 2.5 / 2051 9.7
3 SA	0407 1.6 / 0944 10.5 / 1626 2.0 / 2203 10.1	18 SU	0328 2.8 / 0901 9.6 / 1541 3.1 / 2116 9.1
4 SU	0446 2.5 / 1025 9.6 / 1710 2.9 / ☽ 2249 9.1	19 M	0356 3.4 / 0928 9.0 / 1612 3.7 / 2146 8.5
5 M	0532 3.4 / 1117 8.7 / 1808 3.7 / 2353 8.2	20 TU	0431 4.0 / 1004 8.4 / 1656 4.2 / ☾ 2234 7.9
6 TU	0642 4.1 / 1238 8.1 / 1936 4.1	21 W	0526 4.5 / 1108 7.8 / 1811 4.6
7 W	0136 7.8 / 0822 4.3 / 1426 8.2 / 2112 3.8	22 TH	0012 7.5 / 0657 4.7 / 1302 7.7 / 1955 4.4
8 TH	0314 8.2 / 0950 3.8 / 1543 8.8 / 2225 3.1	23 F	0212 7.8 / 0839 4.2 / 1441 8.4 / 2123 3.6
9 F	0417 9.0 / 1052 3.0 / 1637 9.6 / 2318 2.6	24 SA	0326 8.7 / 0954 3.3 / 1546 9.3 / 2227 2.6
10 SA	0504 9.6 / 1140 2.4 / 1720 10.2	25 SU	0421 9.7 / 1052 2.4 / 1639 10.3 / 2322 1.8
11 SU	0003 2.0 / 0542 10.2 / 1221 2.0 / 1758 10.6	26 M	0510 10.6 / 1144 1.6 / 1728 11.1
12 M	0041 1.7 / 0617 10.6 / 1257 1.8 / ○ 1832 10.8	27 TU	0013 1.1 / 0556 11.3 / 1234 1.0 / ● 1814 11.7
13 TU	0114 1.6 / 0649 10.6 / 1327 1.8 / 1904 10.8	28 W	0101 0.7 / 0640 11.7 / 1321 0.6 / 1858 12.0
14 W	0143 1.6 / 0718 10.7 / 1355 1.8 / 1933 10.8	29 TH	0146 0.5 / 0722 11.9 / 1405 0.6 / 1941 12.0
15 TH	0210 1.7 / 0746 10.6 / 1422 1.9 / 2000 10.6	30 F	0228 0.7 / 0803 11.7 / 1447 0.8 / 2022 11.6

OCTOBER

Day	Time m	Day	Time m
1 SA	0307 1.1 / 0843 11.2 / 1527 1.3 / 2103 10.8	16 SU	0235 2.3 / 0809 10.2 / 1450 2.5 / 2027 9.8
2 SU	0346 1.9 / 0922 10.5 / 1608 2.1 / 2144 9.9	17 M	0303 2.7 / 0836 9.6 / 1519 2.9 / 2055 9.3
3 M	0426 2.8 / 1004 9.5 / 1653 3.0 / 2231 8.9	18 TU	0334 3.2 / 0907 9.3 / 1552 3.4 / 2130 8.7
4 TU	0514 3.7 / 1056 8.7 / 1753 3.8 / ☽ 2337 8.1	19 W	0411 3.8 / 0946 8.7 / 1637 3.9 / 2220 8.2
5 W	0625 4.3 / 1218 8.0 / 1919 4.2	20 TH	0505 4.3 / 1048 8.2 / 1746 4.3 / ☾ 2345 7.8
6 TH	0118 7.8 / 0803 4.4 / 1403 8.1 / 2049 3.9	21 F	0627 4.4 / 1224 8.0 / 1919 4.4
7 F	0250 8.2 / 0925 3.9 / 1517 8.7 / 2156 3.3	22 SA	0131 8.0 / 0802 4.1 / 1401 8.5 / 2046 3.5
8 SA	0349 8.9 / 1024 3.2 / 1609 9.4 / 2247 2.7	23 SU	0250 8.8 / 0919 3.3 / 1512 9.4 / 2154 2.7
9 SU	0434 9.5 / 1109 2.6 / 1652 9.9 / 2329 2.3	24 M	0349 9.7 / 1021 2.4 / 1609 10.2 / 2251 1.9
10 M	0513 10.0 / 1149 2.3 / 1729 10.3	25 TU	0441 10.5 / 1115 1.7 / 1701 11.0 / 2344 1.3
11 TU	0006 2.0 / 0546 10.3 / 1224 2.0 / 1803 10.5	26 W	0530 11.2 / 1207 1.1 / 1750 11.5
12 W	0040 1.9 / 0618 10.5 / 1255 1.9 / ○ 1834 10.6	27 TH	0034 1.0 / 0615 11.6 / 1256 0.8 / 1836 11.7
13 TH	0110 1.8 / 0647 10.6 / 1324 1.9 / 1904 10.6	28 F	0121 0.8 / 0659 11.7 / 1343 0.8 / 1921 11.7
14 F	0139 1.9 / 0715 10.6 / 1353 2.0 / 1932 10.5	29 SA	0206 1.0 / 0742 11.6 / 1428 1.2 / 2005 11.3
15 SA	0207 2.0 / 0743 10.5 / 1421 2.2 / 2000 10.2	30 SU	0248 1.4 / 0824 11.2 / 1511 1.5 / 2047 10.6
		31 M	0330 2.1 / 0905 10.5 / 1554 2.2 / 2130 9.8

NOVEMBER

Day	Time m	Day	Time m
1 TU	0412 2.8 / 0948 9.7 / 1640 2.9 / 2217 9.0	16 W	0322 2.9 / 0900 9.7 / 1544 3.0 / 2129 9.1
2 W	0459 3.6 / 1039 8.9 / 1734 3.6 / ◐ 2315 8.3	17 TH	0402 3.3 / 0944 9.2 / 1630 3.4 / 2219 8.7
3 TH	0559 4.2 / 1146 8.3 / 1844 4.0	18 F	0454 3.7 / 1040 8.8 / 1729 3.7 / ◐ 2326 8.4
4 F	0034 7.9 / 0719 4.4 / 1314 8.1 / 2002 4.0	19 SA	0602 3.9 / 1153 8.6 / 1844 3.7
5 SA	0159 8.1 / 0838 4.1 / 1430 8.4 / 2109 3.7	20 SU	0046 8.4 / 0722 3.8 / 1316 8.7 / 2005 3.4
6 SU	0304 8.6 / 0940 3.6 / 1528 8.9 / 2203 3.2	21 M	0206 8.8 / 0840 3.3 / 1432 9.2 / 2117 2.9
7 M	0354 9.1 / 1029 3.1 / 1615 9.4 / 2248 2.8	22 TU	0313 9.5 / 0947 2.7 / 1537 9.9 / 2219 2.3
8 TU	0436 9.6 / 1111 2.7 / 1656 9.8 / 2328 2.5	23 W	0411 10.2 / 1047 2.0 / 1635 10.5 / 2316 1.8
9 W	0513 10.0 / 1148 2.4 / 1732 10.1	24 TH	0504 10.8 / 1143 1.5 / 1728 10.9
10 TH	0005 2.3 / 0547 10.2 / 1224 2.2 / ○ 1806 10.2	25 F	0010 1.4 / 0554 11.2 / 1236 1.2 / ○ 1818 11.2
11 F	0040 2.1 / 0619 10.4 / 1258 2.1 / 1838 10.3	26 SA	0101 1.3 / 0641 11.4 / 1327 1.1 / 1906 11.2
12 SA	0113 2.1 / 0650 10.5 / 1330 2.1 / 1910 10.3	27 SU	0149 1.3 / 0726 11.4 / 1414 1.2 / 1952 11.0
13 SU	0145 2.2 / 0720 10.4 / 1402 2.2 / 1941 10.1	28 M	0234 1.6 / 0810 11.1 / 1459 1.5 / 2035 10.6
14 M	0216 2.3 / 0751 10.3 / 1434 2.4 / 2014 9.9	29 TU	0317 2.0 / 0852 10.6 / 1542 2.0 / 2117 10.0
15 TU	0248 2.5 / 0824 10.0 / 1507 2.7 / 2049 9.5	30 W	0357 2.6 / 0933 10.0 / 1624 2.6 / 2159 9.3

DECEMBER

Day	Time m	Day	Time m
1 TH	0438 3.2 / 1016 9.3 / 1707 3.2 / 2244 8.7	16 F	0358 2.6 / 0941 9.9 / 1624 2.6 / 2212 9.4
2 F	0523 3.8 / 1105 8.7 / 1755 3.7 / ◐ 2338 8.3	17 SA	0444 3.0 / 1029 9.5 / 1713 3.0 / 2304 9.1
3 SA	0618 4.1 / 1208 8.3 / 1854 4.0	18 SU	0538 3.3 / 1126 9.2 / 1811 3.2 / ◐
4 SU	0046 8.1 / 0726 4.3 / 1323 8.2 / 2002 4.0	19 M	0006 8.8 / 0643 3.5 / 1234 8.9 / 1922 3.4
5 M	0159 8.2 / 0837 4.1 / 1433 8.3 / 2106 3.8	20 TU	0120 8.8 / 0800 3.4 / 1350 8.9 / 2039 3.2
6 TU	0303 8.5 / 0939 3.8 / 1531 8.7 / 2202 3.5	21 W	0236 9.1 / 0915 3.1 / 1506 9.3 / 2151 2.8
7 W	0355 9.0 / 1030 3.3 / 1620 9.1 / 2250 3.1	22 TH	0345 9.6 / 1024 2.6 / 1614 9.7 / 2256 2.4
8 TH	0439 9.4 / 1115 2.9 / 1702 9.4 / 2333 2.7	23 F	0446 10.1 / 1126 2.0 / 1714 10.2 / 2355 2.0
9 F	0518 9.8 / 1156 2.6 / 1741 9.8	24 SA	0540 10.7 / 1224 1.6 / 1808 10.6 / ●
10 SA	0013 2.4 / 0554 10.1 / 1236 2.3 / 1817 10.0	25 SU	0049 1.7 / 0629 11.0 / 1317 1.3 / 1856 10.8
11 SU	0052 2.2 / 0630 10.3 / 1314 2.1 / 1854 10.1	26 M	0138 1.5 / 0715 11.2 / 1404 1.2 / 1940 10.8
12 M	0128 2.2 / 0705 10.5 / 1350 2.1 / 1930 10.2	27 TU	0222 1.6 / 0757 11.1 / 1447 1.4 / 2021 10.6
13 TU	0204 2.1 / 0741 10.5 / 1425 2.1 / 2007 10.2	28 W	0302 1.8 / 0837 10.8 / 1526 1.7 / 2059 10.3
14 W	0239 2.2 / 0819 10.4 / 1502 2.2 / 2046 10.0	29 TH	0338 2.2 / 0914 10.4 / 1601 2.1 / 2134 9.8
15 TH	0317 2.4 / 0859 10.2 / 1541 2.4 / 2127 9.8	30 F	0411 2.7 / 0949 9.8 / 1633 2.7 / 2209 9.3
		31 SA	0443 3.2 / 1025 9.2 / 1706 3.2 / 2246 8.8

Chart Datum: 5·88 metres below Ordnance Datum (Local)
HAT is 12·2 metres above Chart Datum

TIDES

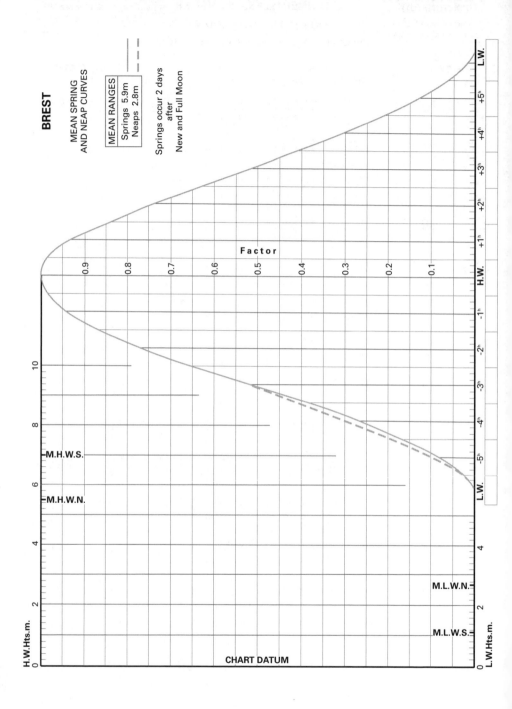

BREST

MEAN SPRING
AND NEAP CURVES

MEAN RANGES
Springs 5.9m
Neaps 2.8m

Springs occur 2 days
after
New and Full Moon

TIME ZONE -0100 (French Standard Time) Subtract 1 hour for UT
For French Summer Time add ONE hour in non-shaded areas

FRANCE – BREST

LAT 48°23'N   LONG 4°30'W

TIMES AND HEIGHTS OF HIGH AND LOW WATERS

Dates in amber are **SPRINGS**
Dates in yellow are **NEAPS**

2011

JANUARY

Time m   Time m

Days 1–15:

Day				
1 SA	0212 6.1	0835 2.2	1445 6.1	2104 2.1
2 SU	0311 6.4	0934 1.9	1540 6.3	2158 1.9
3 M	0402 6.6	1025 1.7	1627 6.5	2245 1.7
4 TU	0447 6.8	1110 1.5	1709 6.6	●2327 1.6
5 W	0528 6.9	1150 1.4	1748 6.7	
6 TH	0006 1.6	0605 6.9	1227 1.4	1823 6.6
7 F	0043 1.6	0640 6.9	1303 1.5	1856 6.5
8 SA	0118 1.7	0714 6.7	1337 1.7	1929 6.3
9 SU	0152 1.9	0746 6.5	1410 1.9	2001 6.1
10 M	0226 2.1	0820 6.2	1444 2.2	2035 5.9
11 TU	0302 2.4	0856 5.9	1522 2.5	2115 5.6
12 W	0342 2.7	0938 5.6	1607 2.8	◑2205 5.4
13 TH	0433 2.9	1036 5.4	1704 3.0	2312 5.2
14 F	0539 3.1	1150 5.2	1815 3.0	
15 SA	0028 5.3	0656 3.0	1309 5.3	1929 2.9

Days 16–31:

Day				
16 SU	0141 5.5	0809 2.7	1418 5.6	2034 2.5
17 M	0243 5.9	0909 2.3	1514 6.0	2128 2.1
18 TU	0335 6.3	1000 1.9	1603 6.4	2217 1.7
19 W	0422 6.7	1046 1.4	1648 6.8	○2303 1.4
20 TH	0507 7.1	1131 1.1	1732 7.1	2347 1.1
21 F	0551 7.4	1215 0.8	1815 7.2	
22 SA	0031 0.9	0634 7.5	1258 0.7	1858 7.2
23 SU	0116 0.9	0717 7.5	1342 0.8	1941 7.1
24 M	0200 1.0	0801 7.2	1428 1.1	2026 6.8
25 TU	0247 1.3	0847 6.8	1515 1.5	2114 6.4
26 W	0337 1.8	0936 6.4	1607 2.0	◑2208 6.0
27 TH	0433 2.2		1709 2.4	2315 5.7
28 F	0541 2.6	1153 5.5	1823 2.7	
29 SA	0037 5.6	0703 2.7	1322 5.5	1945 2.7
30 SU	0159 5.7	0824 2.5	1438 5.7	2055 2.4
31 M	0303 6.1	0927 2.1	1534 6.0	2149 2.1

FEBRUARY

Time m   Time m

Days 1–15:

Day				
1 TU	0353 6.4	1016 1.8	1618 6.3	2234 1.8
2 W	0436 6.7	1057 1.5	1656 6.5	2313 1.6
3 TH	0513 6.9	1134 1.4	1730 6.7	●2348 1.5
4 F	0546 7.0	1207 1.3	1801 6.7	
5 SA	0021 1.4	0617 7.0	1238 1.3	1830 6.7
6 SU	0052 1.5	0647 6.9	1308 1.5	1859 6.6
7 M	0122 1.6	0716 6.7	1337 1.6	1928 6.4
8 TU	0153 1.8	0745 6.5	1407 1.9	1957 6.2
9 W	0224 2.1	0814 6.2	1439 2.2	2030 5.9
10 TH	0259 2.4	0851 5.8	1517 2.5	2110 5.6
11 F	0342 2.7	0935 5.5	1607 2.9	◑2208 5.3
12 SA	0440 3.0	1045 5.2	1715 3.1	2329 5.2
13 SU	0559 3.1	1219 5.1	1841 3.0	
14 M	0058 5.3	0729 2.9	1347 5.4	2002 2.7
15 TU	0214 5.5	0843 2.4	1453 5.9	2105 2.2

Days 16–28:

Day				
16 W	0313 6.3	0939 1.8	1544 6.4	2157 1.6
17 TH	0404 6.8	1027 1.2	1630 6.9	2244 1.1
18 F	0450 7.3	1113 0.8	1714 7.3	○2330 0.7
19 SA	0534 7.6	1157 0.5	1757 7.5	
20 SU	0014 0.5	0617 7.8	1240 0.4	1838 7.6
21 M	0057 0.5	0659 7.7	1323 0.6	1920 7.4
22 TU	0141 0.7	0741 7.4	1406 0.9	2002 7.0
23 W	0226 1.1	0824 6.9	1450 1.5	2047 6.5
24 TH	0313 1.7	0910 6.3	1540 2.1	2139 6.0
25 F	0408 2.2	1007 5.7	1639 2.6	◑2246 5.6
26 SA	0516 2.7	1127 5.3	1758 2.9	
27 SU	0015 5.4	0643 2.8	1308 5.2	1929 2.9
28 M	0144 5.6	0812 2.5	1407 5.5	2041 2.5

MARCH

Time m   Time m

Days 1–15:

Day				
1 TU	0248 5.9	0912 2.2	1520 5.9	2134 2.1
2 W	0336 6.3	0958 1.9	1601 6.2	2216 1.8
3 TH	0416 6.6	1037 1.6	1636 6.5	2252 1.6
4 F	0450 6.8	1110 1.4	1706 6.7	●2325 1.4
5 SA	0521 6.9	1141 1.3	1735 6.8	2355 1.4
6 SU	0551 6.9	1210 1.3	1802 6.8	
7 M	0024 1.4	0619 6.9	1238 1.4	1830 6.7
8 TU	0054 1.5	0647 6.8	1306 1.5	1857 6.6
9 W	0123 1.7	0715 6.6	1335 1.8	1925 6.4
10 TH	0154 1.9	0744 6.3	1407 2.1	1957 6.1
11 F	0228 2.2	0818 5.9	1444 2.4	2036 5.8
12 SA	0310 2.5	0902 5.5	1532 2.7	2130 5.4
13 SU	0406 2.8	1009 5.2	1637 3.0	◑2249 5.2
14 M	0521 3.0	1143 5.1	1803 3.0	
15 TU	0022 5.3	0654 2.8	1317 5.4	1932 2.7

Days 16–31:

Day				
16 W	0145 5.7	0814 2.3	1427 5.9	2039 2.1
17 TH	0248 6.3	0913 1.7	1520 6.5	2133 1.5
18 F	0340 6.9	1004 1.1	1607 7.0	2222 1.0
19 SA	0427 7.4	1050 0.6	1651 7.4	○2308 0.6
20 SU	0512 7.7	1135 0.4	1734 7.7	2353 0.4
21 M	0555 7.8	1218 0.4	1816 7.7	
22 TU	0037 0.4	0638 7.7	1300 0.6	1857 7.4
23 W	0121 0.7	0720 7.3	1343 1.0	1939 7.1
24 TH	0205 1.1	0803 6.8	1427 1.6	2023 6.5
25 F	0253 1.7	0849 6.2	1516 2.2	2115 6.0
26 SA	0347 2.2	0945 5.6	1614 2.7	◑2222 5.5
27 SU	0453 2.7	1103 5.2	1731 3.0	2349 5.3
28 M	0617 2.8	1240 5.1	1902 2.9	
29 TU	0115 5.5	0741 2.7	1359 5.4	2014 2.6
30 W	0219 5.8	0842 2.3	1452 5.8	2106 2.3
31 TH	0307 6.1	0928 2.0	1532 6.1	2147 1.9

APRIL

Time m   Time m

Days 1–15:

Day				
1 F	0346 6.4	1006 1.8	1606 6.4	2223 1.7
2 SA	0420 6.6	1040 1.6	1637 6.6	2256 1.5
3 SU	0452 6.7	1110 1.5	1706 6.7	●2326 1.5
4 M	0522 6.8	1140 1.4	1734 6.8	2357 1.4
5 TU	0551 6.8	1210 1.4	1802 6.7	
6 W	0027 1.5	0621 6.7	1239 1.6	1831 6.7
7 TH	0058 1.6	0651 6.5	1310 1.7	1901 6.5
8 F	0131 1.8	0722 6.3	1343 2.0	1935 6.2
9 SA	0208 2.1	0800 6.0	1423 2.3	2016 5.9
10 SU	0252 2.4	0847 5.6	1512 2.6	2112 5.6
11 M	0347 2.6	0952 5.3	1615 2.8	◑2227 5.4
12 TU	0459 2.7	1119 5.3	1736 2.9	2353 5.5
13 W	0624 2.6	1245 5.5	1900 2.6	
14 TH	0112 5.8	0741 2.2	1355 6.0	2009 2.0
15 F	0217 6.3	0843 1.6	1451 6.5	2105 1.5

Days 16–30:

Day				
16 SA	0312 6.9	0936 1.1	1541 7.0	2157 1.0
17 SU	0402 7.3	1025 0.7	1627 7.4	2245 0.7
18 M	0449 7.5	1111 0.6	1711 7.5	○2331 0.5
19 TU	0534 7.5	1156 0.6	1754 7.5	
20 W	0017 0.6	0618 7.4	1239 0.8	1836 7.3
21 TH	0102 0.9	0701 7.0	1323 1.2	1919 7.0
22 F	0147 1.2	0745 6.6	1407 1.7	2005 6.5
23 SA	0235 1.7	0832 6.1	1455 2.2	2056 6.1
24 SU	0327 2.2	0925 5.6	1551 2.6	2157 5.7
25 M	0427 2.6	1033 5.3	1659 2.9	◑2311 5.4
26 TU	0538 2.8	1152 5.2	1817 2.9	
27 W	0026 5.4	0651 2.7	1308 5.3	1928 2.8
28 TH	0132 5.6	0755 2.5	1407 5.5	2024 2.5
29 F	0224 5.8	0845 2.2	1452 5.9	2109 2.2
30 SA	0307 6.1	0927 2.0	1530 6.1	2148 2.0

Chart Datum: 3·64 metres below IGN Datum
HAT is 7·9 metres above Chart Datum

TIDES

TIME ZONE -0100
(French Standard Time)
Subtract 1 hour for UT
For French Summer Time add
ONE hour in **non-shaded areas**

FRANCE – BREST

LAT 48°23'N   LONG 4°30'W

TIMES AND HEIGHTS OF HIGH AND LOW WATERS

Dates in amber are **SPRINGS**
Dates in yellow are **NEAPS**

2011

MAY

Date	Time	m	Time	m	Time	m	Time	m
1 SU	0344	6.3	1004	1.8	1603	6.4	2223	1.8
16 M	0338	6.9	1000	1.1	1603	7.1	2223	1.1
2 M	0419	6.5	1038	1.7	1636	6.5	2257	1.7
17 TU	0428	7.1	1049	1.0	1650	7.2	2312	0.9
3 TU	0453	6.6	1111	1.6	1707	6.6	2330	1.6
18 W	0515	7.1	1136	1.0	1736	7.2	2359	0.9
4 W	0526	6.6	1143	1.6	1739	6.7		
19 TH	0601	7.0	1221	1.2	1820	7.1		
5 TH	0004	1.6	0559	6.6	1216	1.6	1811	6.6
20 F	0045	1.1	0645	6.8	1305	1.4	1904	6.9
6 F	0038	1.6	0633	6.5	1251	1.7	1845	6.5
21 SA	0131	1.3	0729	6.5	1349	1.7	1948	6.6
7 SA	0115	1.7	0710	6.3	1328	1.9	1924	6.4
22 SU	0216	1.7	0813	6.1	1435	2.1	2034	6.2
8 SU	0155	1.9	0752	6.1	1411	2.1	2009	6.1
23 M	0303	2.1	0900	5.7	1523	2.4	2126	5.8
9 M	0242	2.1	0842	5.8	1501	2.4	2104	5.8
24 TU	0354	2.4	0953	5.5	1618	2.7	2223	5.6
10 TU	0337	2.3	0944	5.6	1601	2.5	2211	5.7
25 W	0450	2.6	1055	5.3	1720	2.9	2327	5.4
11 W	0442	2.4	1056	5.6	1712	2.6	2325	5.8
26 TH	0551	2.7	1201	5.3	1826	2.9		
12 TH	0555	2.3	1210	5.7	1828	2.4		
27 F	0030	5.4	0653	2.7	1305	5.4	1928	2.7
13 F	0038	6.0	0707	2.1	1320	6.0	1937	2.0
28 SA	0129	5.6	0750	2.6	1400	5.6	2022	2.5
14 SA	0145	6.3	0811	1.7	1420	6.4	2037	1.6
29 SU	0221	5.7	0841	2.4	1447	5.8	2108	2.3
15 SU	0244	6.6	0908	1.4	1514	6.8	2132	1.3
30 M	0306	6.0	0925	2.1	1528	6.1	2150	2.0
31 TU	0348	6.2	1005	2.0	1606	6.3	2229	1.9

JUNE

Date	Time	m	Time	m	Time	m	Time	m
1 W	0427	6.3	1043	1.8	1643	6.5	2307	1.2
16 TH	0501	6.7	1120	1.4	1722	7.0	2346	1.2
2 TH	0504	6.4	1121	1.7	1719	6.6	2345	1.4
17 F	0547	6.7	1206	1.4	1806	7.0		
3 F	0542	6.5	1158	1.7	1757	6.7		
18 SA	0030	1.2	0629	6.6	1248	1.5	1848	6.8
4 SA	0023	1.5	0621	6.5	1237	1.6	1835	6.7
19 SU	0112	1.4	0710	6.4	1329	1.7	1928	6.6
5 SU	0103	1.5	0702	6.4	1318	1.7	1917	6.6
20 M	0153	1.6	0750	6.2	1410	1.9	2007	6.4
6 M	0146	1.6	0746	6.3	1403	1.8	2003	6.4
21 TU	0233	1.9	0827	6.0	1451	2.2	2048	6.1
7 TU	0233	1.7	0835	6.1	1451	2.0	2054	6.3
22 W	0314	2.2	0908	5.7	1534	2.4	2132	5.8
8 W	0324	1.9	0929	6.0	1546	2.1	2152	6.1
23 TH	0359	2.4	0955	5.5	1623	2.7	2223	5.5
9 TH	0422	2.1	1030	5.9	1648	2.2	2256	6.0
24 F	0449	2.7	1051	5.3	1720	2.9	2323	5.3
10 F	0526	2.1	1136	5.8	1756	2.2		
25 SA	0547	2.8	1156	5.2	1824	2.9		
11 SA	0005	6.0	0634	2.1	1245	6.0	1905	2.1
26 SU	0028	5.3	0650	2.8	1301	5.3	1928	2.8
12 SU	0114	6.1	0741	2.0	1351	6.2	2012	1.9
27 M	0131	5.4	0751	2.7	1401	5.4	2027	2.6
13 M	0220	6.3	0844	1.8	1451	6.5	2112	1.6
28 TU	0229	5.6	0846	2.4	1453	5.8	2118	2.3
14 TU	0319	6.5	0940	1.6	1546	6.7	2208	1.4
29 W	0319	5.9	0935	2.2	1539	6.1	2204	2.0
15 W	0412	6.6	1032	1.4	1636	6.9	2258	1.2
30 TH	0404	6.1	1019	1.9	1622	6.4	2246	1.7

JULY

Date	Time	m	Time	m	Time	m	Time	m
1 F	0446	6.4	1101	1.7	1703	6.6	2328	1.5
16 SA	0532	6.6	1150	1.4	1750	6.9		
2 SA	0527	6.6	1142	1.5	1744	6.8		
17 SU	0013	1.3	0610	6.6	1229	1.4	1827	6.9
3 SU	0009	1.3	0609	6.7	1224	1.4	1825	6.9
18 M	0050	1.3	0645	6.5	1305	1.5	1902	6.8
4 M	0051	1.2	0651	6.7	1306	1.3	1907	6.9
19 TU	0125	1.5	0718	6.4	1340	1.7	1935	6.6
5 TU	0134	1.2	0734	6.7	1350	1.4	1951	6.9
20 W	0159	1.7	0750	6.2	1415	1.9	2008	6.3
6 W	0219	1.3	0820	6.5	1437	1.5	2038	6.6
21 TH	0233	2.0	0823	6.0	1450	2.2	2043	6.0
7 TH	0306	1.5	0908	6.3	1527	1.8	2129	6.4
22 F	0309	2.3	0900	5.7	1529	2.5	2123	5.6
8 F	0359	1.8	1002	6.1	1623	2.0	2227	6.1
23 SA	0350	2.6	0945	5.4	1616	2.8	2215	5.3
9 SA	0458	2.1	1104	5.9	1727	2.2	2334	5.9
24 SU	0441	2.8	1045	5.2	1717	3.0	2323	5.2
10 SU	0604	2.3	1214	5.8	1839	2.3		
25 M	0547	3.0	1200	5.2	1831	3.0		
11 M	0050	5.8	0717	2.3	1329	5.9	1953	2.2
26 TU	0041	5.2	0701	2.9	1310	5.3	1946	2.8
12 TU	0205	5.9	0827	2.2	1437	6.2	2101	1.9
27 W	0153	5.4	0810	2.7	1420	5.6	2048	2.5
13 W	0309	6.1	0928	1.9	1535	6.4	2158	1.7
28 TH	0253	5.7	0907	2.3	1514	6.0	2140	2.0
14 TH	0403	6.3	1021	1.7	1625	6.7	2248	1.4
29 F	0342	6.1	0956	1.9	1601	6.4	2226	1.6
15 F	0450	6.5	1108	1.5	1710	6.9	2332	1.3
30 SA	0427	6.5	1041	1.6	1645	6.8	2309	1.3
31 SU	0510	6.8	1124	1.2	1727	7.1	2352	1.0

AUGUST

Date	Time	m	Time	m	Time	m	Time	m
1 M	0551	7.0	1207	1.0	1809	7.3		
16 TU	0023	1.6	0616	6.7	1237	1.5	1832	6.9
2 TU	0034	0.8	0633	7.1	1250	0.9	1851	7.3
17 W	0053	1.4	0645	6.6	1308	1.6	1901	6.7
3 W	0116	0.8	0714	7.1	1333	1.0	1933	7.2
18 TH	0123	1.6	0714	6.4	1339	1.8	1931	6.4
4 TH	0159	1.0	0757	6.9	1418	1.2	2017	6.9
19 F	0153	1.8	0743	6.2	1410	2.1	2001	6.1
5 F	0245	1.3	0843	6.6	1506	1.6	2105	6.5
20 SA	0225	2.2	0814	5.9	1444	2.4	2035	5.8
6 SA	0334	1.8	0934	6.2	1559	2.0	2200	6.0
21 SU	0301	2.5	0853	5.6	1525	2.7	2118	5.4
7 SU	0431	2.2	1036	5.8	1703	2.3	2309	5.6
22 M	0347	2.8	0946	5.3	1620	3.0	2222	5.1
8 M	0540	2.5	1152	5.6	1820	2.5		
23 TU	0450	3.1	1103	5.1	1736	3.1	2353	5.0
9 TU	0035	5.5	0701	2.6	1318	5.7	1944	2.4
24 W	0613	3.1	1233	5.2	1905	3.0		
10 W	0159	5.6	0818	2.4	1430	6.0	2054	2.1
25 TH	0120	5.3	0736	2.8	1349	5.6	2019	2.5
11 TH	0304	5.9	0920	2.1	1526	6.3	2150	1.8
26 F	0227	5.7	0840	2.4	1448	6.1	2114	2.0
12 F	0354	6.2	1010	1.8	1613	6.6	2235	1.5
27 SA	0319	6.2	0932	1.8	1538	6.6	2202	1.5
13 SA	0436	6.5	1053	1.6	1653	6.8	2315	1.3
28 SU	0405	6.7	1018	1.4	1623	7.1	2247	1.0
14 SU	0513	6.6	1131	1.4	1729	6.9	2350	1.3
29 M	0448	7.1	1103	1.0	1706	7.4	2330	0.7
15 M	0546	6.7	1205	1.4	1801	6.9		
30 TU	0530	7.4	1146	0.7	1749	7.6		
31 W	0013	0.5	0611	7.5	1229	0.6	1830	7.6

Chart Datum: 3·64 metres below IGN Datum
HAT is 7·9 metres above Chart Datum

TIME ZONE -0100
(French Standard Time)
Subtract 1 hour for UT
For French Summer Time add
ONE hour in **non-shaded areas**

FRANCE – BREST

LAT 48°23′N   LONG 4°30′W

TIMES AND HEIGHTS OF HIGH AND LOW WATERS

Dates in amber are **SPRINGS**
Dates in yellow are **NEAPS**

2011

SEPTEMBER

Day	Time	m	Time	m		Day	Time	m	Time	m
1 TH	0055	0.6	0652	7.4		**16** F	0051	1.6	0641	6.6
	1313	0.7	1912	7.4			1307	1.8	1859	6.5
2 F	0138	0.9	0734	7.1		**17** SA	0120	1.8	0709	6.4
	1358	1.1	1956	7.0			1338	2.0	1927	6.2
3 SA	0222	1.3	0819	6.7		**18** SU	0151	2.1	0740	6.1
	1445	1.5	2043	6.5			1411	2.3	2001	5.9
4 SU	0311	1.9	0910	6.2		**19** M	0226	2.5	0817	5.8
◖	1539	2.0	2138	5.9			1452	2.6	2041	5.5
5 M	0408	2.4	1014	5.8		**20** TU	0311	2.8	0907	5.5
	1644	2.5	2252	5.4			1544	2.9	◗ 2146	5.2
6 TU	0521	2.8	1138	5.5		**21** W	0411	3.0	1022	5.2
	1807	2.7					1656	3.1	2316	5.1
7 W	0026	5.3	0649	2.8		**22** TH	0533	3.1	1155	5.3
	1308	5.6	1934	2.6			1827	3.0		
8 TH	0151	2.6	0808	5.6		**23** F	0047	5.3	0701	2.8
	1418	6.0	2042	2.2			1316	5.6	1946	2.5
9 F	0251	5.9	0906	2.2		**24** SA	0158	5.8	0810	2.3
	1510	6.3	2133	1.9			1419	6.2	2045	1.9
10 SA	0336	6.2	0952	1.8		**25** SU	0252	6.3	0905	1.8
	1553	6.6	2215	1.6			1511	6.7	2135	1.4
11 SU	0415	6.5	1032	1.6		**26** M	0339	6.9	0953	1.2
	1630	6.8	2251	1.4			1558	7.2	2222	0.9
12	0448	6.7	1106	1.6		**27** TU	0423	7.3	1039	0.8
	1702	6.9	○ 2323	1.4		●	1643	7.6	2306	0.6
13 TU	0518	6.8	1138	1.4		**28** W	0506	7.6	1124	0.6
	1732	6.9	2353	1.4			1726	7.8	2350	0.5
14 W	0546	6.8	1208	1.5		**29** TH	0548	7.7	1209	0.5
	1801	6.9					1809	7.7		
15 TH	0022	1.4	0614	6.7		**30** F	0033	0.6	0630	7.5
	1237	1.6	1830	6.7			1253	0.7	1853	7.4

OCTOBER

Day	Time	m	Time	m		Day	Time	m	Time	m
1 SA	0117	1.0	0713	7.2		**16** SU	0054	1.9	0645	6.5
	1339	1.1	1937	7.0			1314	2.0	1904	6.3
2 SU	0202	1.4	0759	6.8		**17** M	0126	2.1	0717	6.3
	1428	1.6	2025	6.4			1349	2.2	1940	6.0
3 M	0251	2.1	0851	6.3		**18** TU	0204	2.4	0756	6.0
	1522	2.1	2122	5.8			1431	2.5	2024	5.7
4 TU	0349	2.5	0956	5.8		**19** W	0249	2.7	0846	5.7
	1628	2.6	◖ 2236	5.4			1523	2.7	2125	5.4
5 W	0502	2.9	1119	5.5		**20** TH	0348	2.9	0956	5.5
	1748	2.8					1630	2.9	◗ 2247	5.3
6 TH	0007	5.3	0628	2.9		**21** F	0502	3.0	1121	5.5
	1244	5.6	1911	2.7			1752	2.8		
7 F	0127	5.5	0744	2.7		**22** SA	0011	5.5	0625	2.8
	1352	5.9	2015	2.3			1240	5.8	1910	2.4
8 SA	0225	5.8	0841	2.3		**23** SU	0123	5.9	0737	2.3
	1443	6.2	2105	2.0			1346	6.2	2013	1.9
9 SU	0309	6.2	0926	2.0		**24** M	0220	6.4	0835	1.8
	1525	6.5	2146	1.8			1442	6.8	2106	1.4
10 M	0346	6.4	1004	1.8		**25** TU	0311	6.9	0927	1.3
	1601	6.6	2221	1.6			1532	7.2	2155	1.0
11 TU	0419	6.6	1038	1.6		**26** W	0358	7.3	1016	0.9
	1633	6.8	2253	1.5			1620	7.5	● 2242	0.7
12 W	0449	6.7	1110	1.6		**27** TH	0443	7.6	1103	0.7
	1704	6.8	○ 2324	1.5			1706	7.6	2328	0.7
13 TH	0518	6.8	1140	1.6		**28** F	0528	7.6	1150	0.6
	1734	6.8	2353	1.6			1751	7.6		
14 F	0547	6.8	1211	1.6		**29** SA	0014	0.8	0612	7.5
	1804	6.7					1236	0.8	1836	7.3
15 SA	0023	1.7	0615	6.7		**30** SU	0059	1.1	0657	7.2
	1242	1.8	1834	6.5			1324	1.2	1922	6.9
						31 M	0145	1.6	0744	6.8
							1413	1.6	2011	6.4

NOVEMBER

Day	Time	m	Time	m		Day	Time	m	Time	m
1 TU	0234	2.0	0835	6.4		**16** W	0151	2.2	0746	6.2
	1506	2.1	2106	5.9			1418	2.2	2015	5.9
2 W	0329	2.5	0936	5.9		**17** TH	0236	2.4	0835	6.0
	1606	2.5	◖ 2211	5.5			1508	2.4	2112	5.7
3 TH	0435	2.8	1047	5.7		**18** F	0330	2.6	0936	5.8
	1715	2.7	2328	5.3			1608	2.6	◗ 2220	5.6
4 F	0550	2.9	1202	5.6		**19** SA	0435	2.7	1047	5.8
	1828	2.7					1718	2.6	2333	5.7
5 SA	0043	5.4	0703	2.8		**20** SU	0549	2.6	1202	5.9
	1310	5.7	1934	2.6			1832	2.4		
6 SU	0144	5.7	0803	2.5		**21** M	0044	5.9	0701	2.3
	1405	6.0	2027	2.3			1311	6.2	1938	2.0
7 M	0233	6.0	0851	2.3		**22** TU	0147	6.3	0805	1.9
	1450	6.2	2110	2.1			1413	6.6	2037	1.6
8 TU	0313	6.2	0932	2.0		**23** W	0244	6.7	0903	1.5
	1529	6.4	2149	1.9			1509	6.9	2131	1.3
9 W	0349	6.5	1009	1.9		**24** TH	0336	7.1	0956	1.1
	1605	6.6	2223	1.8			1601	7.2	2222	1.1
10 TH	0422	6.6	1044	1.8		**25** F	0425	7.4	1047	0.9
	1638	6.6	○ 2257	1.7		●	1650	7.3	2311	1.0
11 F	0454	6.7	1117	1.7		**26** SA	0513	7.5	1136	0.9
	1711	6.7	2329	1.7			1738	7.3	2358	1.0
12 SA	0525	6.7	1150	1.7		**27** SU	0559	7.4	1223	0.9
	1744	6.6					1824	7.1		
13 SU	0002	1.8	0557	6.7		**28** M	0044	1.2	0645	7.2
	1223	1.8	1817	6.5			1310	1.2	1909	6.8
14 M	0035	1.9	0630	6.6		**29** TU	0130	1.5	0730	6.9
	1258	1.9	1852	6.4			1357	1.5	1955	6.4
15 TU	0111	2.0	0705	6.5		**30** W	0217	1.9	0817	6.5
	1336	2.0	1930	6.1			1444	1.9	2042	6.0

DECEMBER

Day	Time	m	Time	m		Day	Time	m	Time	m
1 TH	0305	2.3	0906	6.2		**16** F	0225	2.0	0824	6.4
	1535	2.3	2134	5.7			1454	2.0	2056	6.1
2 F	0358	2.6	1002	5.8		**17** SA	0314	2.2	0915	6.2
	1630	2.6	◗ 2234	5.5			1546	2.2	2152	5.9
3 SA	0459	2.8	1105	5.6		**18** SU	0410	2.3	1015	6.0
	1732	2.8	2340	5.4		◗	1747	2.3	2256	5.8
4 SU	0605	2.9	1211	5.5		**19** M	0514	2.4	1124	6.0
	1836	2.8					1755	2.3		
5 M	0047	5.4	0710	2.8		**20** TU	0006	5.9	0626	2.4
	1314	5.6	1937	2.7			1237	6.0	1906	2.2
6 TU	0146	5.6	0809	2.7		**21** W	0116	6.1	0737	2.1
	1410	5.8	2030	2.5			1349	6.2	2013	2.0
7 W	0236	5.9	0858	2.4		**22** TH	0222	6.4	0843	1.8
	1457	6.0	2115	2.3			1453	6.5	2113	1.7
8 TH	0319	6.2	0941	2.2		**23** F	0321	6.8	0943	1.5
	1538	6.2	2155	2.1			1549	6.8	2208	1.4
9 F	0357	6.4	1020	2.0		**24** SA	0414	7.1	1036	1.2
	1617	6.4	2233	1.9		●	1640	7.0	2259	1.3
10 SA	0434	6.6	1057	1.8		**25** SU	0503	7.2	1125	1.0
	1653	6.5	2310	1.8			1727	7.0	2346	1.2
11 SU	0509	6.7	1133	1.7		**26** M	0549	7.3	1211	1.0
	1729	6.6	2346	1.7			1812	7.0		
12 M	0544	6.8	1210	1.6		**27** TU	0031	1.2	0632	7.2
	1806	6.6					1255	1.1	1854	6.8
13 TU	0022	1.7	0620	6.8		**28** W	0114	1.4	0713	7.0
	1247	1.6	1843	6.5			1337	1.4	1933	6.6
14 W	0100	1.7	0658	6.7		**29** TH	0155	1.7	0752	6.8
	1325	1.7	1923	6.4			1417	1.7	2012	6.3
15 TH	0141	1.8	0739	6.6		**30** F	0236	2.0	0832	6.6
	1408	1.8	2007	6.3			1458	2.0	2051	6.0
						31 SA	0318	2.3	0913	6.0
							1541	2.4	2136	5.6

Chart Datum: 3·64 metres below IGN Datum
HAT is 7·9 metres above Chart Datum

TIDES

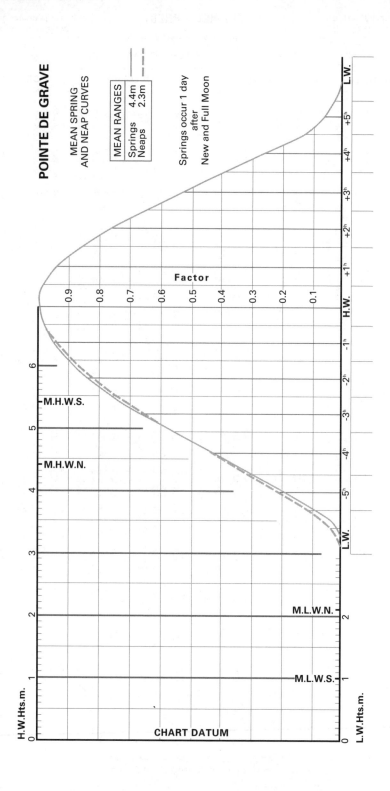

POINTE DE GRAVE

MEAN SPRING
AND NEAP CURVES

MEAN RANGES	
Springs	4.4m
Neaps	2.3m

Springs occur 1 day
after
New and Full Moon

Factor

TIME ZONE -0100
(French Standard Time)
Subtract 1 hour for UT
For French Summer Time add ONE hour in non-shaded areas

FRANCE – POINTE DE GRAVE

LAT 45°34'N   LONG 1°04'W

TIMES AND HEIGHTS OF HIGH AND LOW WATERS

Dates in amber are **SPRINGS**
Dates in yellow are **NEAPS**

2011

JANUARY

Time	m	Time	m
1 SA 0233	4.8	**16** SU 0207	4.4
0819	1.7	0757	2.1
1508	4.7	1439	4.4
2051	1.7	2022	2.0
2 SU 0326	4.9	**17** M 0301	4.6
0918	1.6	0855	1.9
1600	4.9	1530	4.7
2143	1.6	2115	1.7
3 M 0414	5.1	**18** TU 0348	4.9
1010	1.4	0947	1.6
1645	5.0	1616	4.9
2230	1.4	2204	1.5
4 TU 0457	5.2	**19** W 0432	5.2
1056	1.3	1035	1.3
1725	5.0	1700	5.2
● 2312	1.4	○ 2251	1.2
5 W 0537	5.3	**20** TH 0516	5.4
1137	1.3	1121	1.1
1802	5.0	1743	5.3
2352	1.3	2336	1.1
6 TH 0614	5.3	**21** F 0600	5.6
1215	1.3	1206	0.9
1836	5.0	1826	5.4
7 F 0028	1.4	**22** SA 0020	1.0
0649	5.2	0644	5.6
1250	1.3	1249	0.9
1907	4.9	1909	5.4
8 SA 0103	1.5	**23** SU 0103	0.9
0722	5.1	0729	5.6
1324	1.4	1331	1.0
1937	4.8	1954	5.3
9 SU 0138	1.6	**24** M 0146	1.0
0755	5.0	0815	5.4
1358	1.6	1414	1.1
2009	4.6	2040	5.1
10 M 0213	1.7	**25** TU 0231	1.2
0830	4.8	0903	5.1
1433	1.8	1459	1.3
2046	4.5	2131	4.8
11 TU 0250	1.9	**26** W 0320	1.4
0910	4.6	0959	4.8
1511	1.9	1551	1.6
2131	4.3	◐ 2234	4.6
12 W 0333	2.1	**27** TH 0418	1.7
0959	4.4	1109	4.5
1557	2.1	1654	1.9
◐ 2229	4.1	2352	4.4
13 TH 0427	2.3	**28** F 0529	1.9
1101	4.2	1236	4.3
1657	2.3	1812	2.1
2343	4.1		
14 F 0538	2.4	**29** SA 0113	4.4
1217	4.1	0652	2.0
1811	2.3	1359	4.3
		1933	2.1
15 SA 0100	4.2	**30** SU 0223	4.5
0652	2.3	0810	1.9
1335	4.2	1505	4.5
1921	2.2	2041	1.9
		31 M 0320	4.8
		0912	1.7
		1556	4.7
		2135	1.7

FEBRUARY

Time	m	Time	m
1 TU 0406	5.0	**16** W 0327	4.9
1002	1.5	0928	1.5
1636	4.8	1557	5.0
2220	1.5	2146	1.4
2 W 0445	5.1	**17** TH 0414	5.3
1044	1.3	1017	1.1
1711	4.9	1642	5.3
2300	1.3	2234	1.1
3 TH 0520	5.2	**18** F 0459	5.6
1122	1.3	1103	0.9
1742	5.0	1725	5.5
● 2336	1.3	○ 2319	0.8
4 F 0552	5.3	**19** SA 0543	5.7
1156	1.2	1148	0.7
1811	5.0	1807	5.6
5 SA 0009	1.2	**20** SU 0003	0.7
0623	5.2	0626	5.8
1227	1.2	1230	0.6
1838	5.0	1849	5.6
6 SU 0040	1.3	**21** M 0045	0.7
0652	5.2	0710	5.7
1257	1.3	1311	0.7
1904	4.9	1932	5.4
7 M 0110	1.4	**22** TU 0127	0.8
0721	5.1	0754	5.5
1326	1.4	1352	0.9
1932	4.8	2015	5.2
8 TU 0139	1.5	**23** W 0210	1.0
0752	4.9	0840	5.1
1355	1.5	1435	1.3
2003	4.7	2102	4.9
9 W 0210	1.7	**24** TH 0256	1.3
0825	4.7	0931	4.7
1427	1.7	1523	1.6
2038	4.5	2159	4.5
10 TH 0245	1.9	**25** F 0352	1.7
0903	4.4	1042	4.3
1504	1.9	1624	2.0
2123	4.3	◑ 2322	4.3
11 F 0329	2.1	**26** SA 0504	2.0
0957	4.2	1221	4.1
1552	2.2	1747	2.2
◐ 2230	4.1		
12 SA 0430	2.3	**27** SU 0056	4.3
1117	4.0	0636	2.1
1705	2.4	1351	4.2
		1917	2.2
13 SU 0000	4.0	**28** M 0211	4.4
0600	2.4	0758	2.0
1253	4.1	1456	4.4
1836	2.3	2027	2.0
14 M 0130	4.2		
0724	2.2		
1411	4.3		
1952	2.1		
15 TU 0235	4.5		
0832	1.9		
1508	4.6		
2053	1.8		

MARCH

Time	m	Time	m
1 TU 0307	4.6	**16** W 0206	4.6
0857	1.7	0804	1.8
1543	4.6	1442	4.7
2119	1.7	2026	1.7
2 W 0350	4.9	**17** TH 0302	5.0
0943	1.5	0902	1.4
1618	4.8	1533	5.0
2201	1.5	2122	1.4
3 TH 0426	5.0	**18** F 0351	5.3
1023	1.4	0953	1.1
1648	4.9	1618	5.3
2239	1.3	2211	1.0
4 F 0457	5.1	**19** SA 0437	5.6
1058	1.3	1040	0.8
1716	5.0	1702	5.5
● 2313	1.2	○ 2258	0.7
5 SA 0526	5.2	**20** SU 0522	5.8
1129	1.2	1125	0.6
1742	5.1	1745	5.6
2344	1.2	2342	0.6
6 SU 0554	5.2	**21** M 0606	5.8
1159	1.2	1207	0.6
1808	5.1	1827	5.6
7 M 0013	1.2	**22** TU 0025	0.6
0622	5.2	0650	5.7
1227	1.2	1248	0.7
1834	5.0	1910	5.5
8 TU 0041	1.3	**23** W 0106	0.7
0651	5.1	0734	5.4
1254	1.3	1329	1.0
1901	4.9	1953	5.2
9 W 0109	1.4	**24** TH 0149	1.0
0720	4.9	0819	5.0
1322	1.4	1411	1.3
1930	4.8	2039	4.9
10 TH 0139	1.5	**25** F 0235	1.3
0751	4.7	0911	4.6
1352	1.6	1458	1.7
2003	4.6	2134	4.6
11 F 0212	1.7	**26** SA 0329	1.7
0830	4.5	1021	4.2
1429	1.8	1558	2.0
2046	4.4	◑ 2253	4.3
12 SA 0254	1.9	**27** SU 0440	2.0
0922	4.2	1159	4.0
1515	2.1	1719	2.3
2147	4.2		
13 SU 0350	2.2	**28** M 0027	4.2
1040	4.0	0610	2.1
1621	2.3	1326	4.1
◑ 2315	4.1	1848	2.2
14 M 0517	2.3	**29** TU 0143	4.4
1218	4.1	0730	2.0
1756	2.3	1429	4.3
		1958	2.0
15 TU 0053	4.2	**30** W 0240	4.7
0651	2.1	0828	1.8
1342	4.3	1514	4.5
1920	2.1	2050	1.8
		31 TH 0322	4.7
		0914	1.6
		1549	4.7
		2133	1.6

APRIL

Time	m	Time	m
1 F 0357	4.9	**16** SA 0326	5.3
0952	1.4	0924	1.1
1618	4.8	1552	5.3
2210	1.4	2145	1.0
2 SA 0427	5.0	**17** SU 0414	5.5
1027	1.3	1013	0.8
1645	5.0	1638	5.5
2244	1.3	2233	0.8
3 SU 0457	5.1	**18** M 0501	5.6
1058	1.3	1059	0.7
1712	5.0	1722	5.6
● 2315	1.3	○ 2319	0.7
4 M 0526	5.1	**19** TU 0546	5.6
1127	1.3	1143	0.7
1740	5.1	1806	5.6
2345	1.2		
5 TU 0556	5.1	**20** W 0004	0.7
1156	1.3	0632	5.5
1808	5.1	1225	0.9
		1850	5.4
6 W 0014	1.3	**21** TH 0047	0.8
0626	5.0	0717	5.2
1225	1.3	1307	1.1
1837	5.0	1935	5.2
7 TH 0044	1.3	**22** F 0130	1.0
0658	4.9	0803	4.9
1255	1.4	1350	1.4
1908	4.9	2022	4.9
8 F 0116	1.4	**23** SA 0216	1.3
0732	4.7	0854	4.5
1328	1.6	1437	1.7
1944	4.7	2115	4.7
9 SA 0152	1.6	**24** SU 0307	1.7
0812	4.5	0957	4.2
1407	1.8	1533	2.0
2030	4.6	2221	4.4
10 SU 0235	1.8	**25** M 0411	1.9
0907	4.3	1117	4.1
1455	2.0	1644	2.2
2131	4.4	◑ 2339	4.3
11 M 0332	2.0	**26** TU 0527	2.1
1021	4.2	1237	4.1
1601	2.2	1803	2.2
◑ 2249	4.3		
12 TU 0451	2.1	**27** W 0052	4.3
1150	4.2	0642	2.1
1725	2.2	1342	4.2
		1913	2.1
13 W 0018	4.4	**28** TH 0153	4.4
0617	2.0	0744	1.9
1310	4.4	1431	4.4
1845	2.0	2009	1.9
14 TH 0133	4.7	**29** F 0241	4.6
0730	1.7	0831	1.8
1412	4.7	1509	4.6
1953	1.7	2055	1.7
15 F 0233	5.0	**30** SA 0320	4.7
0831	1.4	0914	1.6
1505	5.0	1541	4.7
2052	1.3	2134	1.6

Chart Datum: 2·83 metres below IGN Datum
HAT is 6·1 metres above Chart Datum

TIDES

FRANCE – POINTE DE GRAVE

LAT 45°34′N   LONG 1°04′W

TIMES AND HEIGHTS OF HIGH AND LOW WATERS

2011

TIME ZONE -0100
(French Standard Time)
Subtract 1 hour for UT
For French Summer Time add
ONE hour in **non-shaded areas**

Dates in amber are **SPRINGS**
Dates in yellow are **NEAPS**

MAY

Date	Time m	Time m	Time m	Time m
1 SU	0354 4.8	0950 1.5	1612 4.8	2210 1.5
2 M	0428 4.9	1024 1.4	1643 5.0	2244 1.4
3 TU ●	0501 5.0	1056 1.4	1715 5.0	2318 1.3
4 W	0535 5.0	1129 1.3	1747 5.0	2351 1.3
5 TH	0608 5.0	1202 1.4	1820 5.0	
6 F	0025 1.3	0643 4.9	1236 1.4	1855 4.9
7 SA	0102 1.4	0722 4.8	1313 1.5	1936 4.8
8 SU	0141 1.5	0807 4.6	1355 1.7	2025 4.6
9 M	0227 1.6	0901 4.5	1445 1.8	2122 4.6
10 TU ◐	0322 1.8	1006 4.4	1547 1.9	2230 4.5
11 W	0430 1.8	1122 4.4	1659 2.0	2347 4.6
12 TH	0543 1.8	1236 4.5	1811 1.8	
13 F	0100 4.7	0653 1.6	1340 4.7	1919 1.6
14 SA	0203 4.9	0757 1.4	1436 5.0	2021 1.4
15 SU	0300 5.1	0855 1.2	1527 5.2	2118 1.1
16 M	0353 5.3	0947 1.0	1615 5.3	2210 0.9
17 TU ○	0442 5.4	1035 1.0	1702 5.4	2259 0.9
18 W	0530 5.3	1121 1.0	1748 5.4	2345 0.8
19 TH	0617 5.2	1205 1.0	1834 5.3	
20 F	0030 0.9	0702 5.1	1248 1.2	1919 5.2
21 SA	0113 1.1	0748 4.8	1331 1.4	2005 5.0
22 SU	0158 1.3	0833 4.6	1416 1.6	2052 4.8
23 M	0244 1.6	0922 4.3	1506 1.8	2143 4.5
24 TU ◐	0336 1.8	1020 4.2	1603 2.0	2241 4.4
25 W	0435 2.0	1125 4.1	1708 2.1	2344 4.3
26 TH	0540 2.1	1231 4.1	1814 2.1	
27 F	0047 4.3	0644 2.0	1331 4.2	1914 2.1
28 SA	0145 4.3	0740 1.9	1420 4.4	2008 1.9
29 SU	0235 4.5	0829 1.8	1502 4.5	2054 1.8
30 M	0320 4.6	0912 1.7	1540 4.7	2136 1.6
31 TU	0400 4.7	0951 1.6	1616 4.8	2215 1.5

JUNE

Date	Time m	Time m	Time m	Time m
1 W ●	0439 4.8	1028 1.5	1653 4.9	2254 1.4
2 TH	0516 4.9	1106 1.4	1729 5.0	2332 1.3
3 F	0554 4.9	1144 1.3	1807 5.1	
4 SA	0012 1.3	0633 4.9	1223 1.3	1847 5.1
5 SU	0052 1.3	0714 4.9	1304 1.4	1930 5.0
6 M	0134 1.3	0759 4.8	1348 1.5	2018 4.9
7 TU	0219 1.4	0849 4.7	1436 1.7	2111 4.8
8 W	0309 1.5	0947 4.6	1531 1.8	2210 4.7
9 TH ◐	0407 1.6	1053 4.5	1633 1.7	2317 4.7
10 F	0511 1.6	1203 4.5	1740 1.7	
11 SA	0028 4.7	0619 1.6	1310 4.6	1848 1.6
12 SU	0137 4.7	0727 1.5	1411 4.8	1954 1.5
13 M	0239 4.8	0829 1.4	1506 5.0	2056 1.3
14 TU	0337 4.9	0926 1.3	1558 5.1	2152 1.2
15 W ○	0429 5.0	1017 1.2	1647 5.2	2244 1.1
16 TH	0518 5.1	1105 1.1	1734 5.3	2331 1.0
17 F	0603 5.0	1149 1.1	1819 5.3	
18 SA	0016 1.0	0646 5.0	1232 1.2	1901 5.2
19 SU	0057 1.1	0726 4.8	1312 1.3	1941 5.0
20 M	0137 1.3	0803 4.7	1353 1.5	2020 4.9
21 TU	0217 1.4	0840 4.5	1435 1.6	2100 4.7
22 W	0259 1.6	0921 4.3	1520 1.8	2146 4.5
23 TH ◐	0345 1.8	1012 4.2	1611 2.0	2238 4.3
24 F	0438 2.0	1114 4.1	1711 2.1	2339 4.2
25 SA	0539 2.1	1221 4.1	1815 2.2	
26 SU	0044 4.1	0642 2.1	1326 4.2	1917 2.1
27 M	0148 4.2	0741 2.0	1421 4.3	2013 2.0
28 TU	0245 4.4	0834 1.9	1509 4.5	2104 1.8
29 W	0333 4.5	0921 1.7	1551 4.7	2150 1.6
30 TH ○	0417 4.7	1005 1.5	1632 4.9	2234 1.4

JULY

Date	Time m	Time m	Time m	Time m
1 F ●	0458 4.9	1048 1.4	1712 5.1	2317 1.2
2 SA	0539 5.0	1130 1.2	1753 5.2	2359 1.1
3 SU	0620 5.0	1212 1.2	1835 5.2	
4 M	0041 1.1	0701 5.1	1254 1.1	1919 5.2
5 TU	0123 1.1	0745 5.0	1337 1.2	2004 5.2
6 W	0206 1.1	0832 4.9	1422 1.3	2053 5.0
7 TH	0251 1.2	0923 4.7	1511 1.4	2147 4.9
8 F ◐	0342 1.4	1022 4.6	1607 1.5	2249 4.7
9 SA	0441 1.6	1131 4.5	1712 1.7	
10 SU	0002 4.5	0549 1.7	1244 4.5	1824 1.7
11 M	0118 4.5	0703 1.7	1353 4.6	1937 1.7
12 TU	0228 4.6	0813 1.7	1454 4.8	2045 1.5
13 W	0328 4.7	0914 1.5	1547 5.0	2143 1.3
14 TH	0421 4.8	1006 1.3	1635 5.1	2234 1.2
15 F ○	0506 4.9	1053 1.2	1719 5.2	2319 1.1
16 SA	0547 4.9	1136 1.2	1759 5.2	
17 SU	0000 1.1	0623 4.9	1215 1.2	1836 5.2
18 M	0038 1.1	0656 4.9	1251 1.2	1910 5.1
19 TU	0112 1.2	0726 4.8	1326 1.4	1942 5.0
20 W	0146 1.4	0756 4.6	1401 1.5	2016 4.8
21 TH	0220 1.5	0830 4.5	1437 1.7	2054 4.6
22 F	0256 1.7	0910 4.3	1517 1.9	2140 4.3
23 SA ◐	0338 1.9	1003 4.1	1606 2.1	2236 4.1
24 SU	0431 2.1	1112 4.0	1713 2.3	2347 4.0
25 M	0541 2.2	1230 4.0	1829 2.3	
26 TU	0104 4.0	0655 2.2	1342 4.2	1937 2.1
27 W	0212 4.2	0800 2.0	1440 4.4	2036 1.9
28 TH	0307 4.4	0855 1.8	1527 4.7	2127 1.6
29 F	0354 4.7	0944 1.5	1611 5.0	2215 1.3
30 SA ●	0438 4.9	1030 1.3	1653 5.2	2300 1.1
31 SU	0519 5.1	1114 1.1	1735 5.4	2343 0.9

AUGUST

Date	Time m	Time m	Time m	Time m
1 M	0601 5.3	1157 1.0	1818 5.5	
2 TU	0025 0.8	0643 5.3	1239 0.9	1901 5.5
3 W	0106 0.8	0725 5.2	1320 0.9	1945 5.4
4 TH	0147 0.9	0809 5.1	1403 1.0	2032 5.2
5 F	0230 1.1	0857 4.9	1449 1.2	2123 4.9
6 SA ◐	0317 1.4	0953 4.6	1542 1.5	2225 4.6
7 SU	0414 1.7	1103 4.4	1648 1.8	2345 4.3
8 M	0525 1.9	1228 4.4	1807 1.9	
9 TU	0111 4.3	0647 2.0	1345 4.5	1930 1.8
10 W	0225 4.4	0804 1.9	1448 4.7	2040 1.6
11 TH	0325 4.6	0906 1.6	1539 4.9	2135 1.4
12 F	0411 4.7	0956 1.4	1622 5.1	2221 1.3
13 SA ○	0450 4.9	1039 1.3	1700 5.2	2302 1.2
14 SU	0524 4.9	1118 1.2	1734 5.2	2339 1.1
15 M	0554 5.0	1153 1.2	1806 5.2	
16 TU	0012 1.2	0622 5.1	1226 1.2	1836 5.2
17 W	0043 1.2	0649 4.9	1256 1.3	1905 5.0
18 TH	0113 1.5	0717 4.8	1326 1.4	1936 4.9
19 F	0142 1.5	0747 4.7	1357 1.6	2009 4.7
20 SA	0213 1.7	0821 4.5	1431 1.8	2048 4.4
21 SU ◐	0248 1.9	0903 4.3	1512 2.1	2140 4.2
22 M	0333 2.1	1005 4.1	1609 2.3	2255 4.0
23 TU	0438 2.3	1135 4.0	1738 2.4	
24 W	0024 4.0	0609 2.4	1304 4.2	1904 2.2
25 TH	0142 4.2	0727 2.2	1410 4.4	2009 1.9
26 F	0241 4.5	0828 1.9	1502 4.8	2103 1.6
27 SA	0329 4.8	0920 1.5	1547 5.1	2152 1.3
28 SU ○	0414 5.1	1008 1.2	1631 5.4	2237 1.0
29 M ●	0456 5.3	1053 1.0	1714 5.6	2321 0.8
30 TU	0538 5.5	1137 0.8	1756 5.7	
31 W	0004 0.7	0620 5.5	1219 0.7	1840 5.7

Chart Datum: 2·83 metres below IGN Datum
HAT is 6·1 metres above Chart Datum

TIME ZONE -0100
(French Standard Time)
Subtract 1 hour for UT
For French Summer Time add
ONE hour in **non-shaded areas**

FRANCE – POINTE DE GRAVE

LAT 45°34'N   LONG 1°04'W

TIMES AND HEIGHTS OF HIGH AND LOW WATERS

Dates in amber are **SPRINGS**
Dates in yellow are **NEAPS**

2011

SEPTEMBER		OCTOBER		NOVEMBER		DECEMBER	
Time m	Time m	Time m	Time m	Time m	Time m	Time m	Time m

SEPTEMBER

1 0045 0.8 / 0703 5.4 / TH 1301 0.8 / 1924 5.5	**16** 0039 1.4 / 0644 5.0 / F 1255 1.5 / 1902 4.9	**1** 0104 1.0 / 0727 5.4 / SA 1324 1.0 / 1954 5.2	**16** 0040 1.6 / 0650 4.9 / SU 1300 1.6 / 1913 4.8
2 0126 0.9 / 0747 5.3 / F 1343 1.0 / 2011 5.2	**17** 0108 1.5 / 0713 4.8 / SA 1324 1.6 / 1934 4.7	**2** 0147 1.3 / 0815 5.1 / SU 1410 1.3 / 2048 4.8	**17** 0112 1.7 / 0724 4.8 / M 1335 1.8 / 1951 4.6
3 0208 1.2 / 0833 5.0 / SA 1429 1.4 / 2103 4.8	**18** 0137 1.7 / 0745 4.7 / SU 1357 1.8 / 2011 4.5	**3** 0234 1.6 / 0912 4.8 / M 1504 1.7 / 2157 4.4	**18** 0149 1.9 / 0806 4.6 / TU 1416 2.0 / 2043 4.4
4 0255 1.5 / 0929 4.7 / SU 1521 1.6 / ◑ 2208 4.5	**19** 0212 1.9 / 0825 4.4 / M 1436 2.0 / 2101 4.3	**4** 0331 2.0 / 1029 4.5 / TU 1611 2.0 / ◑ 2330 4.2	**19** 0234 2.1 / 0904 4.4 / W 1508 2.2 / 2155 4.2
5 0351 1.8 / 1044 4.4 / M 1629 1.9 / 2339 4.2	**20** 0256 2.1 / 0923 4.2 / TU 1529 2.3 / ◑ 2218 4.1	**5** 0446 2.2 / 1200 4.4 / W 1737 2.2	**20** 0334 2.3 / 1021 4.4 / TH 1622 2.3 / ◑ 2320 4.2
6 0506 2.1 / 1218 4.4 / TU 1756 2.1	**21** 0356 2.4 / 1050 4.1 / W 1652 2.4 / 2351 4.1	**6** 0054 4.3 / 0613 2.3 / TH 1317 4.5 / 1900 2.1	**21** 0454 2.4 / 1148 4.4 / F 1748 2.2
7 0109 4.2 / 0635 2.2 / W 1337 4.5 / 1922 2.0	**22** 0527 2.4 / 1226 4.2 / TH 1828 2.3	**7** 0200 4.4 / 0728 2.1 / F 1416 4.7 / 2002 1.9	**22** 0039 4.4 / 0613 2.2 / SA 1303 4.7 / 1900 1.9
8 0220 4.4 / 0752 2.0 / TH 1438 4.7 / 2028 1.7	**23** 0112 4.3 / 0651 2.2 / F 1339 4.6 / 1937 2.0	**8** 0249 4.6 / 0825 1.8 / SA 1501 4.9 / 2051 1.7	**23** 0141 4.7 / 0720 1.9 / SU 1404 5.0 / 2000 1.6
9 0313 4.6 / 0851 1.7 / F 1525 4.9 / 2118 1.5	**24** 0212 4.6 / 0756 1.9 / SA 1434 4.9 / 2034 1.6	**9** 0327 4.8 / 0911 1.6 / SU 1538 5.0 / 2132 1.5	**24** 0234 5.1 / 0819 1.6 / M 1456 5.3 / 2053 1.3
10 0354 4.8 / 0937 1.5 / SA 1603 5.1 / 2200 1.4	**25** 0302 5.0 / 0852 1.5 / SU 1522 5.3 / 2124 1.2	**10** 0358 4.9 / 0950 1.5 / M 1609 5.1 / 2208 1.4	**25** 0322 5.3 / 0913 1.2 / TU 1544 5.6 / 2143 1.0
11 0427 4.9 / 1018 1.3 / SU 1636 5.2 / 2238 1.3	**26** 0348 5.3 / 0942 1.2 / M 1607 5.6 / 2211 1.0	**11** 0426 5.0 / 1026 1.4 / TU 1638 5.2 / 2240 1.4	**26** 0408 5.6 / 1004 1.0 / W 1631 5.7 / ○ 2230 0.9
12 0456 5.0 / 1054 1.3 / M 1706 5.1 / ○ 2311 1.2	**27** 0431 5.5 / 1029 0.9 / TU 1651 5.8 / ● 2256 0.8	**12** 0453 5.1 / 1051 1.3 / W 1708 5.2 / ○ 2311 1.4	**27** 0453 5.7 / 1051 0.8 / TH 1718 5.8 / 2316 0.9
13 0523 5.1 / 1127 1.2 / TU 1735 5.3 / 2342 1.2	**28** 0515 5.6 / 1114 0.8 / W 1736 5.8 / 2339 0.7	**13** 0522 5.1 / 1129 1.4 / TH 1738 5.2 / 2340 1.4	**28** 0538 5.7 / 1138 0.8 / F 1804 5.7
14 0549 5.1 / 1157 1.1 / W 1804 5.2	**29** 0558 5.7 / 1158 0.7 / TH 1820 5.7	**14** 0550 5.1 / 1159 1.4 / F 1808 5.1	**29** 0000 0.9 / 0625 5.6 / SA 1223 0.9 / 1852 5.5
15 0011 1.3 / 0616 5.0 / TH 1226 1.4 / 1833 5.1	**30** 0022 0.8 / 0642 5.6 / F 1241 0.8 / 1906 5.5	**15** 0010 1.5 / 0619 5.1 / SA 1229 1.5 / 1839 5.0	**30** 0044 1.1 / 0712 5.4 / SU 1308 1.1 / 1941 5.1
			31 0129 1.4 / 0802 5.2 / M 1355 1.4 / 2035 4.8

NOVEMBER / DECEMBER

1 0216 1.7 / 0858 4.9 / TU 1446 1.7 / 2140 4.5	**16** 0136 1.8 / 0800 4.8 / W 1405 1.8 / 2034 4.6	**1** 0247 1.8 / 0929 4.8 / TH 1518 1.8 / 2207 4.4	**16** 0211 1.7 / 0840 5.0 / F 1441 1.7 / 2113 4.7
2 0311 2.0 / 1005 4.6 / W 1548 2.0 / ◐ 2259 4.3	**17** 0222 2.0 / 0853 4.7 / TH 1455 2.0 / 2136 4.5	**2** 0342 2.0 / 1028 4.6 / F 1615 2.1 / ◐ 2312 4.3	**17** 0300 1.8 / 0934 4.8 / SA 1533 1.8 / 2215 4.6
3 0418 2.2 / 1123 4.5 / TH 1702 2.2	**18** 0317 2.1 / 0958 4.6 / F 1557 2.1 / ◐ 2248 4.4	**3** 0445 2.2 / 1132 4.4 / SA 1720 2.2	**18** 0356 1.9 / 1038 4.7 / SU 1634 1.8 / ◐ 2324 4.6
4 0017 4.3 / 0535 2.3 / F 1236 4.5 / 1818 2.2	**19** 0424 2.2 / 1112 4.6 / SA 1709 2.0	**4** 0020 4.2 / 0553 2.3 / SU 1238 4.4 / 1827 2.2	**19** 0501 1.9 / 1151 4.7 / M 1742 1.9
5 0122 4.4 / 0647 2.2 / SA 1338 4.6 / 1923 2.0	**20** 0003 4.5 / 0536 2.1 / SU 1226 4.7 / 1820 1.9	**5** 0122 4.3 / 0658 2.2 / M 1339 4.5 / 1928 2.1	**20** 0036 4.7 / 0611 1.9 / TU 1305 4.8 / 1852 1.8
6 0213 4.5 / 0748 2.0 / SU 1427 4.7 / 2015 1.9	**21** 0108 4.8 / 0644 1.9 / M 1333 5.0 / 1925 1.7	**6** 0212 4.5 / 0755 2.1 / TU 1430 4.6 / 2019 2.0	**21** 0141 4.8 / 0720 1.7 / W 1412 4.9 / 1959 1.6
7 0253 4.7 / 0837 1.9 / M 1506 4.9 / 2058 1.7	**22** 0206 5.0 / 0747 1.6 / TU 1432 5.2 / 2023 1.4	**7** 0254 4.6 / 0844 2.0 / W 1513 4.7 / 2102 1.8	**22** 0240 5.0 / 0826 1.5 / TH 1512 5.1 / 2059 1.4
8 0327 4.8 / 0919 1.7 / TU 1541 5.0 / 2135 1.6	**23** 0258 5.3 / 0846 1.4 / W 1525 5.4 / 2118 1.2	**8** 0332 4.8 / 0926 1.8 / TH 1552 4.8 / 2141 1.7	**23** 0334 5.2 / 0927 1.3 / F 1606 5.2 / 2154 1.3
9 0358 5.0 / 0956 1.6 / W 1614 5.1 / 2209 1.5	**24** 0348 5.5 / 0941 1.1 / TH 1616 5.5 / 2208 1.1	**9** 0408 4.9 / 1005 1.7 / F 1629 4.9 / 2217 1.6	**24** 0425 5.4 / 1021 1.1 / SA 1656 5.3 / ● 2244 1.2
10 0428 5.1 / 1030 1.5 / TH 1646 5.1 / ○ 2242 1.5	**25** 0436 5.6 / 1033 1.0 / F 1705 5.6 / ● 2257 1.0	**10** 0443 5.1 / 1043 1.6 / SA 1705 5.0 / ○ 2254 1.5	**25** 0513 5.5 / 1111 1.0 / SU 1744 5.3 / 2331 1.1
11 0500 5.1 / 1103 1.5 / F 1719 5.1 / 2314 1.5	**26** 0524 5.6 / 1122 0.9 / SA 1753 5.5 / 2343 1.1	**11** 0518 5.1 / 1120 1.5 / SU 1740 5.0 / 2330 1.5	**26** 0600 5.6 / 1158 1.0 / M 1828 5.3
12 0531 5.1 / 1137 1.5 / SA 1752 5.1 / 2347 1.5	**27** 0612 5.6 / 1209 1.0 / SU 1841 5.3	**12** 0553 5.2 / 1157 1.4 / M 1816 5.0	**27** 0015 1.2 / 0645 5.5 / TU 1241 1.1 / 1910 5.1
13 0604 5.1 / 1210 1.5 / SU 1826 5.0	**28** 0028 1.2 / 0659 5.5 / M 1254 1.1 / 1929 5.1	**13** 0008 1.5 / 0630 5.2 / TU 1235 1.4 / 1854 5.0	**28** 0057 1.3 / 0727 5.3 / W 1322 1.2 / 1950 4.9
14 0021 1.6 / 0638 5.0 / M 1246 1.6 / 1902 4.9	**29** 0113 1.4 / 0747 5.3 / TU 1340 1.3 / 2017 4.8	**14** 0047 1.5 / 0709 5.1 / W 1315 1.5 / 1935 4.9	**29** 0138 1.4 / 0806 5.1 / TH 1402 1.4 / 2027 4.7
15 0057 1.7 / 0715 4.9 / TU 1323 1.7 / 1944 4.7	**30** 0159 1.6 / 0836 5.0 / W 1427 1.6 / 2109 4.6	**15** 0127 1.6 / 0752 5.1 / TH 1356 1.6 / 2021 4.8	**30** 0220 1.6 / 0846 4.9 / F 1443 1.7 / 2107 4.5
			31 0303 1.8 / 0928 4.6 / SA 1528 1.9 / 2155 4.3

Chart Datum: 2·83 metres below IGN Datum
HAT is 6·1 metres above Chart Datum

TIDES

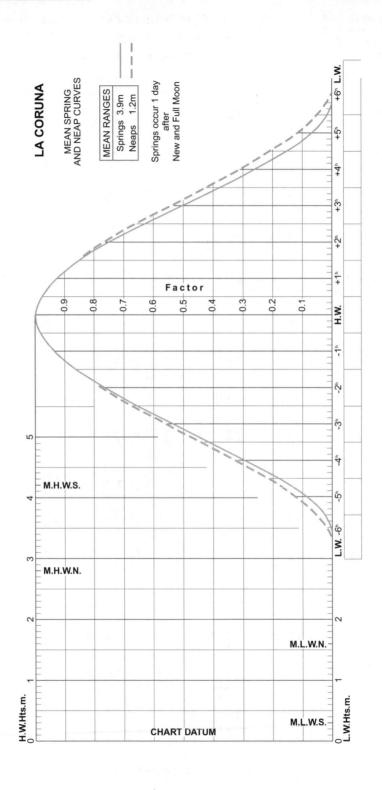

LA CORUNA

MEAN SPRING
AND NEAP CURVES

MEAN RANGES
Springs 3.9m
Neaps 1.2m

Springs occur 1 day
after
New and Full Moon

Factor

0.9
0.8
0.7
0.6
0.5
0.4
0.3
0.2
0.1

+6ʰ L.W.
+5ʰ
+4ʰ
+3ʰ
+2ʰ
+1ʰ
H.W.
-1ʰ
-2ʰ
-3ʰ
-4ʰ
-5ʰ
-6ʰ L.W.

M.H.W.S.
M.H.W.N.
M.L.W.N.
M.L.W.S.

CHART DATUM

H.W.Hts.m.
L.W.Hts.m.

TIME ZONE -0100
(Spanish Standard Time)
Subtract 1 hour for UT
For Spanish Summer Time add
ONE hour in **non-shaded areas**

SPAIN – CORUÑA

LAT 43°22′N LONG 8°24′W

TIMES AND HEIGHTS OF HIGH AND LOW WATERS

Dates in amber are **SPRINGS**
Dates in yellow are **NEAPS**

2011

JANUARY

Day	Time	m	Time	m
1 SA	0135 0744 1405 2010	3.4 1.2 3.4 1.1	16 SU	0109 0726 1337 1941	3.1 1.4 3.1 1.3
2 SU	0230 0842 1458 2059	3.6 1.0 3.5 1.0	17 M	0203 0820 1430 2031	3.3 1.2 3.3 1.1
3 M ●	0317 0931 1544 2143	3.8 0.9 3.5 0.9	18 TU	0250 0907 1516 2116	3.6 0.9 3.5 0.9
4 TU ●	0400 1014 1625 2223	3.9 0.8 3.6 0.8	19 W ○	0334 0950 1600 2159	3.8 0.7 3.7 0.6
5 W	0439 1053 1703 2300	3.9 0.7 3.6 0.8	20 TH	0417 1033 1642 2242	4.1 0.4 3.9 0.5
6 TH	0516 1130 1738 2336	3.9 0.7 3.6 0.8	21 F	0459 1115 1725 2324	4.2 0.3 4.0 0.4
7 F	0552 1204 1812	3.9 0.8 3.5	22 SA	0543 1157 1808	4.3 0.3 4.0
8 SA	0011 0627 1239 1845	0.9 3.8 0.9 3.4	23 SU	0007 0627 1241 1853	0.4 4.3 0.3 3.9
9 SU	0046 0702 1313 1920	1.0 3.6 1.0 3.3	24 M	0052 0714 1327 1940	0.5 4.1 0.5 3.7
10 M	0122 0739 1350 1957	1.1 3.5 1.2 3.1	25 TU	0140 0803 1416 2031	0.7 3.9 0.8 3.5
11 TU	0202 0818 1430 2041	1.3 3.3 1.3 3.0	26 W	0233 0857 1511 2132	0.9 3.5 1.1 3.3
12 W ◑	0248 0905 1519 2136	1.5 3.1 1.5 2.9	27 TH	0337 1003 1619 2246	1.2 3.2 1.3 3.1
13 TH	0346 1003 1621 2247	1.6 3.0 1.6 2.9	28 F	0456 1125 1740	1.4 3.0 1.6
14 F	0501 1116 1732	1.7 2.9 1.6	29 SA	0009 0625 1252 1859	3.1 1.4 3.0 1.4
15 SA	0003 0620 1232 1842	2.9 1.8 2.9 1.5	30 SU	0124 0742 1402 2002	3.2 1.3 3.1 1.2
			31 M	0222 0840 1454 2051	3.4 1.1 3.2 1.1

FEBRUARY

Day	Time	m	Time	m
1 TU	0308 0924 1536 2132	3.6 0.9 3.4 0.9	16 W	0229 0847 1458 2057	3.5 0.8 3.5 0.8
2 W	0348 1002 1611 2209	3.7 0.9 3.5 0.8	17 TH	0315 0931 1541 2141	3.9 0.5 3.8 0.5
3 TH ●	0423 1036 1644 2243	3.8 0.9 3.6 0.7	18 F ○	0358 1013 1623 2223	4.1 0.2 4.0 0.3
4 F	0457 1107 1714 2315	3.9 0.6 3.6 0.7	19 SA	0441 1055 1705 2306	4.3 0.1 4.1 0.1
5 SA	0528 1138 1744 2346	3.9 0.6 3.6 0.7	20 SU	0524 1136 1747 2348	4.4 0.1 4.1 0.2
6 SU	0559 1208 1814	3.8 0.7 3.5	21 M	0608 1218 1830	4.3 0.2 4.0
7 M	0017 0630 1237 1844	0.8 3.7 0.8 3.4	22 TU	0032 0653 1301 1915	0.3 4.1 0.4 3.8
8 TU	0048 0701 1308 1916	0.9 3.5 1.0 3.3	23 W	0118 0740 1348 2004	0.6 3.8 0.8 3.6
9 W	0121 0735 1342 1952	1.1 3.4 1.1 3.2	24 TH	0210 0832 1440 2102	0.9 3.4 1.1 3.3
10 TH	0159 0814 1421 2037	1.3 3.2 1.3 3.0	25 F	0313 0937 1547 2217	1.2 3.1 1.4 3.1
11 F ◑	0248 0904 1513 2137	1.5 3.0 1.5 2.9	26 SA ◐	0436 1106 1715 2348	1.4 2.8 1.5 3.0
12 SA	0356 1014 1627 2302	1.6 2.8 1.6 2.8	27 SU	0614 1243 1843	1.5 2.8 1.5
13 SU	0529 1148 1757	1.6 2.8 1.6	28 M	0109 0733 1352 1948	3.1 1.3 3.0 1.3
14 M	0030 0654 1310 1912	3.0 1.5 2.9 1.4			
15 TU	0137 0757 1410 2010	3.2 1.2 3.2 1.1			

MARCH

Day	Time	m	Time	m
1 TU	0207 0826 1440 2036	3.3 1.1 3.1 1.1	16 W	0106 0729 1344 1944	3.2 1.1 3.2 1.0
2 W	0251 0906 1517 2114	3.5 0.9 3.3 0.9	17 TH	0202 0820 1433 2033	3.6 0.7 3.6 0.7
3 TH	0328 0940 1549 2148	3.6 0.8 3.5 0.8	18 F	0250 0906 1518 2118	3.9 0.4 3.9 0.4
4 F ●	0401 1011 1619 2220	3.7 0.7 3.6 0.7	19 SA ○	0335 0949 1600 2202	4.2 0.2 4.1 0.2
5 SA	0432 1040 1647 2250	3.8 0.6 3.6 0.6	20 SU	0419 1031 1642 2245	4.4 0.0 4.2 0.1
6 SU	0502 1109 1715 2319	3.8 0.6 3.6 0.6	21 M	0503 1113 1725 2328	4.4 0.1 4.2 0.1
7 M	0530 1136 1743 2348	3.8 0.6 3.6 0.7	22 TU	0547 1155 1808	4.3 0.2 4.1
8 TU	0600 1204 1812	3.7 0.7 3.5	23 W	0013 0633 1238 1853	0.3 4.0 0.5 3.9
9 W	0018 0630 1233 1843	0.9 3.6 0.9 3.4	24 TH	0100 0720 1323 1942	0.6 3.7 0.8 3.6
10 TH	0050 0703 1305 1918	1.0 3.4 1.0 3.3	25 F	0152 0813 1414 2039	0.9 3.3 1.2 3.3
11 F	0127 0740 1342 1959	1.3 3.2 1.2 3.1	26 SA ◐	0255 0917 1520 2151	1.2 3.0 1.4 3.1
12 SA	0213 0828 1431 2055	1.3 3.0 1.4 3.0	27 SU	0416 1044 1647 2319	1.4 2.8 1.6 3.0
13 SU ◑	0318 0937 1543 2217	1.5 2.8 1.6 2.9	28 M	0548 1218 1815	1.5 2.8 1.5
14 M	0450 1114 1719 2352	1.6 2.8 1.6 3.0	29 TU	0038 0703 1325 1921	3.1 1.3 2.9 1.4
15 TU	0622 1242 1843	1.4 2.9 1.4	30 W	0138 0755 1412 2009	3.2 1.2 3.1 1.2
			31 TH	0223 0835 1448 2048	3.4 1.0 3.3 1.0

APRIL

Day	Time	m	Time	m
1 F	0300 0910 1520 2122	3.5 0.9 3.4 0.8	16 SA	0223 0838 1452 2054	3.9 0.4 3.9 0.4
2 SA	0333 0941 1550 2153	3.6 0.8 3.5 0.7	17 SU	0311 0923 1536 2140	4.1 0.3 4.1 0.3
3 SU ●	0404 1010 1618 2224	3.7 0.7 3.6 0.7	18 M ○	0357 1007 1620 2226	4.2 0.2 4.2 0.2
4 M	0433 1038 1647 2253	3.7 0.7 3.7 0.7	19 TU	0443 1050 1704 2311	4.2 0.2 4.2 0.2
5 TU	0503 1106 1716 2323	3.7 0.7 3.7 0.7	20 W	0529 1133 1748 2358	4.1 0.4 4.1 0.4
6 W	0533 1135 1746 2355	3.6 0.8 3.6 0.8	21 TH	0616 1217 1834	3.9 0.6 3.9
7 TH	0605 1206 1818	3.5 0.9 3.6	22 F	0046 0704 1303 1923	0.6 3.6 0.9 3.7
8 F	0029 0641 1239 1855	1.0 3.4 1.0 3.4	23 SA	0138 0756 1354 2018	0.9 3.3 1.2 3.4
9 SA	0109 0721 1319 1939	1.1 3.2 1.2 3.3	24 SU	0237 0856 1455 2122	1.2 3.0 1.4 3.2
10 SU	0157 0812 1411 2036	1.3 3.0 1.4 3.1	25 M ◑	0346 1009 1610 2237	1.4 2.8 1.5 3.1
11 M	0300 0920 1521 2152	1.4 2.9 1.5 3.0	26 TU	0503 1130 1730 2352	1.4 2.8 1.5 3.0
12 TU	0424 1048 1650 2318	1.4 2.9 1.5 3.1	27 W	0614 1239 1837	1.4 2.9 1.4
13 W	0548 1210 1810	1.3 3.0 1.3	28 TH	0054 0710 1330 1930	3.1 1.3 3.0 1.3
14 TH	0033 0655 1313 1913	3.3 1.0 3.3 1.0	29 F	0143 0755 1411 2013	3.2 1.1 3.2 1.1
15 F	0132 0750 1405 2006	3.6 0.7 3.6 0.7	30 SA	0224 0833 1446 2050	3.4 1.0 3.4 1.0

HAT is 4·5 metres above Chart Datum

TIDES

TIDES

TIME ZONE -0100
(Spanish Standard Time)
Subtract 1 hour for UT
For Spanish Summer Time add
ONE hour in **non-shaded areas**

SPAIN – CORUÑA
LAT 43°22'N   LONG 8°24'W
TIMES AND HEIGHTS OF HIGH AND LOW WATERS

Dates in amber are **SPRINGS**
Dates in yellow are **NEAPS**

2011

MAY

Day		m	Day		m
1 SU	0300	3.5	**16** M	0250	3.9
	0906	0.9		0900	0.5
	1518	3.5		1515	4.0
	2125	0.9		2122	0.5
2 M	0333	3.5	**17** TU	0340	4.0
	0938	0.8		0947	0.4
	1549	3.6	○	1602	4.1
	2158	0.8		2211	0.4
3 TU	0406	3.6	**18** W	0428	4.0
	1009	0.8		1032	0.5
	1620	3.7		1647	4.1
●	2230	0.8		2259	0.4
4 W	0438	3.6	**19** TH	0515	3.9
	1040	0.8		1116	0.6
	1652	3.7		1733	4.0
	2303	0.8		2346	0.5
5 TH	0512	3.6	**20** F	0602	3.7
	1112	0.8		1200	0.7
	1726	3.7		1819	3.9
	2338	0.8			
6 F	0548	3.5	**21** SA	0033	0.7
	1146	0.9		0648	3.5
	1802	3.7		1245	0.9
				1906	3.7
7 SA	0017	0.9	**22** SU	0121	0.9
	0628	3.4		0736	3.3
	1225	1.0		1333	1.1
	1843	3.6		1955	3.5
8 SU	0059	1.0	**23** M	0211	1.1
	0713	3.3		0827	3.1
	1309	1.1		1426	1.3
	1930	3.5		2048	3.3
9 M	0149	1.1	**24** TU	0306	1.3
	0805	3.2		0924	2.9
	1402	1.3		1526	1.4
	2027	3.3	◑	2148	3.1
10 TU	0250	1.2	**25** W	0408	1.4
	0908	3.1		1030	2.9
	1507	1.3		1634	1.5
◑	2134	3.3		2253	3.0
11 W	0400	1.2	**26** TH	0513	1.4
	1022	3.1		1137	2.9
	1622	1.3		1741	1.5
	2248	3.3		2357	3.0
12 TH	0514	1.1	**27** F	0613	1.4
	1136	3.2		1237	3.0
	1736	1.2		1841	1.4
	2359	3.4			
13 F	0620	1.0	**28** SA	0054	3.1
	1240	3.4		0706	1.3
	1841	1.0		1326	3.1
				1932	1.3
14 SA	0102	3.6	**29** SU	0142	3.2
	0719	0.8		0751	1.2
	1336	3.6		1408	3.2
	1939	0.8		2016	1.2
15 SU	0158	3.8	**30** M	0225	3.3
	0811	0.6		0830	1.1
	1427	3.8		1446	3.4
	2032	0.6		2056	1.1
			31 TU	0304	3.4
				0907	1.0
				1522	3.5
				2134	0.9

JUNE

Day		m	Day		m
1 W	0341	3.5	**16** TH	0418	3.7
	0942	0.9		1018	0.6
	1557	3.7		1635	4.0
●	2211	0.9		2249	0.5
2 TH	0418	3.5	**17** F	0503	3.7
	1018	0.8		1102	0.7
	1633	3.7		1719	4.0
	2248	0.8		2333	0.5
3 F	0456	3.6	**18** SA	0546	3.6
	1055	0.8		1144	0.7
	1711	3.8		1802	3.9
	2326	0.7			
4 SA	0536	3.6	**19** SU	0016	0.6
	1134	0.8		0628	3.5
	1751	3.8		1225	0.8
				1844	3.8
5 SU	0007	0.8	**20** M	0057	0.8
	0619	3.5		0709	3.4
	1215	0.9		1307	1.0
	1835	3.7		1926	3.6
6 M	0051	0.8	**21** TU	0139	1.0
	0704	3.4		0750	3.2
	1301	0.9		1351	1.1
	1922	3.7		2010	3.4
7 TU	0140	0.9	**22** W	0223	1.1
	0754	3.4		0835	3.1
	1352	1.0		1439	1.3
	2015	3.6		2057	3.2
8 W	0234	1.0	**23** TH	0311	1.3
	0850	3.3		0927	2.9
	1449	1.1		1534	1.4
	2113	3.5	◑	2151	3.1
9 TH	0335	1.0	**24** F	0407	1.4
	0954	3.2		1027	2.9
	1554	1.2		1637	1.5
◐	2218	3.4		2251	3.0
10 F	0441	1.1	**25** SA	0509	1.4
	1102	3.2		1134	2.9
	1704	1.2		1744	1.5
	2328	3.4		2356	2.9
11 SA	0548	1.0	**26** SU	0611	1.4
	1210	3.3		1236	3.0
	1813	1.1		1847	1.5
12 SU	0036	3.4	**27** M	0058	3.0
	0652	0.9		0707	1.4
	1312	3.5		1329	3.1
	1918	1.0		1942	1.3
13 M	0139	3.5	**28** TU	0151	3.1
	0750	0.8		0756	1.2
	1409	3.6		1415	3.3
	2017	0.8		2030	1.2
14 TU	0237	3.6	**29** W	0238	3.2
	0843	0.7		0840	1.1
	1500	3.8		1457	3.4
	2111	0.7		2113	1.0
15 W	0329	3.7	**30** TH	0320	3.4
	0932	0.7		0921	1.0
	1549	3.9		1537	3.6
○	2202	0.6		2153	0.8

JULY

Day		m	Day		m
1 F	0401	3.5	**16** SA	0448	3.6
	1000	0.8		1046	0.7
	1617	3.8		1702	3.9
●	2233	0.7		2315	0.5
2 SA	0441	3.6	**17** SU	0526	3.6
	1040	0.7		1124	0.7
	1657	3.9		1740	3.9
	2313	0.6		2352	0.6
3 SU	0522	3.7	**18** M	0601	3.5
	1121	0.7		1201	0.7
	1739	4.0		1817	3.8
	2354	0.5			
4 M	0605	3.7	**19** TU	0027	0.7
	1203	0.6		0636	3.4
	1822	4.0		1237	0.8
				1853	3.6
5 TU	0037	0.5	**20** W	0102	0.8
	0649	3.7		0711	3.3
	1247	0.7		1314	1.0
	1908	3.9		1930	3.5
6 W	0122	0.6	**21** TH	0139	1.0
	0736	3.6		0748	3.2
	1334	0.8		1353	1.2
	1957	3.8		2008	3.3
7 TH	0212	0.7	**22** F	0218	1.2
	0827	3.4		0829	3.0
	1427	0.9		1437	1.3
	2050	3.6		2052	3.1
8 F	0307	0.9	**23** SA	0304	1.3
	0925	3.3		0920	2.9
	1527	1.1		1532	1.5
◐	2152	3.4	◑	2146	2.9
9 SA	0410	1.1	**24** SU	0401	1.5
	1032	3.2		1025	2.8
	1637	1.2		1642	1.6
	2302	3.3		2255	2.8
10 SU	0520	1.1	**25** M	0510	1.5
	1145	3.2		1140	2.9
	1753	1.2		1800	1.6
11 M	0019	3.2	**26** TU	0013	2.8
	0632	1.1		0622	1.5
	1256	3.3		1250	3.0
	1907	1.1		1909	1.4
12 TU	0130	3.3	**27** W	0121	2.9
	0737	1.1		0724	1.4
	1359	3.5		1347	3.2
	2012	1.0		2005	1.2
13 W	0231	3.4	**28** TH	0214	3.1
	0834	0.9		0815	1.2
	1452	3.7		1434	3.4
	2107	0.8	○	2052	1.0
14 TH	0323	3.5	**29** F	0300	3.3
	0922	0.8		0900	0.9
	1540	3.8		1517	3.6
	2154	0.7		2133	0.7
15 F	0408	3.6	**30** SA	0342	3.5
	1006	0.7		0942	0.7
	1622	3.9		1558	3.9
○	2237	0.6	●	2214	0.5
			31 SU	0422	3.7
				1022	0.5
				1639	4.1
				2254	0.4

AUGUST

Day		m	Day		m
1 M	0503	3.9	**16** TU	0531	3.6
	1103	0.4		1133	0.6
	1720	4.2		1747	3.8
	2334	0.3		2354	0.7
2 TU	0545	3.9	**17** W	0601	3.5
	1144	0.4		1205	0.7
	1803	4.2		1818	3.7
3 W	0016	0.3	**18** TH	0025	0.8
	0628	3.9		0632	3.4
	1227	0.4		1249	0.9
	1848	4.1		1851	3.5
4 TH	0059	0.4	**19** F	0056	0.9
	0713	3.8		0705	3.3
	1313	0.6		1311	1.1
	1935	3.9		1925	3.3
5 F	0146	0.6	**20** SA	0130	1.1
	0802	3.6		0741	3.2
	1404	0.8		1350	1.2
	2027	3.6		2004	3.1
6 SA	0239	0.9	**21** SU	0209	1.3
	0858	3.4		0823	3.0
	1504	1.0		1437	1.5
◐	2129	3.3	◑	2052	2.9
7 SU	0342	1.2	**22** M	0259	1.5
	1007	3.2		0923	2.9
	1617	1.2		1544	1.6
	2245	3.1		2201	2.8
8 M	0459	1.3	**23** TU	0411	1.6
	1128	3.1		1045	2.8
	1744	1.3		1714	1.6
				2332	2.7
9 TU	0012	3.0	**24** W	0539	1.6
	0621	1.3		1211	2.9
	1248	3.2		1838	1.5
	1906	1.2			
10 W	0130	3.1	**25** TH	0052	2.9
	0731	1.2		0654	1.5
	1352	3.4		1317	3.1
	2010	1.0		1939	1.2
11 TH	0228	3.2	**26** F	0150	3.1
	0826	1.0		0750	1.2
	1444	3.6		1409	3.4
	2100	0.9		2027	0.9
12 F	0314	3.4	**27** SA	0237	3.4
	0911	0.9		0837	0.9
	1527	3.7		1453	3.7
	2141	0.7		2109	0.6
13 SA	0352	3.5	**28** SU	0319	3.7
	0950	0.7		0919	0.6
	1605	3.8		1535	4.0
○	2217	0.6		2149	0.4
14 SU	0427	3.6	**29** M	0359	3.9
	1026	0.6		1000	0.4
	1641	3.9		1616	4.2
	2251	0.5	●	2229	0.2
15 M	0500	3.6	**30** TU	0440	4.1
	1100	0.6		1041	0.2
	1714	3.9		1658	4.3
	2323	0.6		2310	0.1
			31 W	0521	4.1
				1123	0.2
				1741	4.3
				2352	0.2

HAT is 4·5 metres above Chart Datum

TIME ZONE -0100
(Spanish Standard Time)
Subtract 1 hour for UT
For Spanish Summer Time add ONE hour in **non-shaded areas**

LAT 43°22'N   LONG 8°24'W
TIMES AND HEIGHTS OF HIGH AND LOW WATERS

Dates in amber are **SPRINGS**
Dates in yellow are **NEAPS**

2011

SEPTEMBER

Day	Time m	Time m	Time m	Time m
1 TH	0604 4.1	1206 0.3	1826 4.2	
16 F	0558 3.6	1206 0.9	1816 3.6	
2 F	0035 0.4	0649 3.9	1253 0.5	1914 3.9
17 SA	0019 1.0	0629 3.5	1238 1.1	1849 3.4
3 SA	0121 0.7	0738 3.7	1344 0.8	2007 3.6
18 SU	0051 1.1	0704 3.3	1315 1.3	1927 3.2
4 SU	0213 1.0	0835 3.4	1446 1.1	2111 3.2
19 M	0127 1.3	0745 3.2	1400 1.4	2015 3.0
5 M	0319 1.3	0948 3.2	1605 1.3	2234 3.0
20 TU	0215 1.5	0840 3.0	1504 1.6	2122 2.8
6 TU	0443 1.5	1115 3.1	1740 1.4	
21 W	0325 1.7	0959 2.9	1634 1.6	2255 2.8
7 W	0009 2.9	0612 1.5	1237 3.2	1901 1.3
22 TH	0459 1.7	1131 3.0	1802 1.5	
8 TH	0123 3.0	0721 1.3	1340 3.4	1959 1.1
23 F	0021 2.9	0621 1.5	1244 3.2	1907 1.2
9 F	0215 3.2	0812 1.1	1428 3.6	2043 0.9
24 SA	0121 3.2	0721 1.2	1339 3.5	1956 0.9
10 SA	0256 3.4	0853 0.9	1507 3.7	2119 0.8
25 SU	0209 3.5	0809 0.9	1425 3.8	2040 0.6
11 SU	0330 3.5	0929 0.8	1543 3.8	2152 0.7
26 M	0252 3.8	0853 0.6	1509 4.1	2122 0.3
12 M	0401 3.6	1002 0.7	1615 3.8	2223 0.6
27 TU	0333 4.1	0935 0.3	1552 4.3	2204 0.2
13 TU	0431 3.7	1034 0.6	1646 3.8	2252 0.6
28 W	0415 4.2	1018 0.2	1635 4.4	2245 0.1
14 W	0500 3.7	1105 0.7	1716 3.8	2321 0.7
29 TH	0457 4.3	1102 0.2	1720 4.4	2328 0.3
15 TH	0529 3.7	1135 0.7	1745 3.7	2350 0.8
30 F	0541 4.2	1147 0.3	1806 4.2	

OCTOBER

Day	Time m	Time m	Time m	Time m
1 SA	0012 0.5	0628 4.0	1235 0.6	1855 3.9
16 SU	0602 3.6	1214 1.1	1824 3.4	
2 SU	0059 0.8	0718 3.8	1329 0.9	1950 3.5
17 M	0022 1.2	0638 3.5	1252 1.2	1904 3.3
3 M	0151 1.1	0816 3.5	1432 1.2	2055 3.2
18 TU	0101 1.3	0720 3.4	1338 1.4	1952 3.1
4 TU	0257 1.4	0928 3.3	1551 1.4	2220 3.0
19 W	0149 1.5	0815 3.2	1439 1.5	2057 2.9
5 W	0422 1.6	1053 3.2	1722 1.5	2351 2.9
20 TH	0256 1.6	0927 3.1	1559 1.6	2221 2.9
6 TH	0549 1.6	1213 3.2	1838 1.4	
21 F	0421 1.6	1051 3.1	1722 1.5	2343 3.0
7 F	0100 3.1	0657 1.4	1314 3.4	1933 1.2
22 SA	0542 1.5	1205 3.3	1829 1.2	
8 SA	0150 3.3	0747 1.2	1402 3.5	2015 1.1
23 SU	0047 3.3	0646 1.2	1305 3.6	1923 0.9
9 SU	0229 3.4	0828 1.0	1441 3.6	2051 0.9
24 M	0138 3.6	0739 0.9	1356 3.9	2011 0.6
10 M	0303 3.5	0904 0.9	1515 3.7	2123 0.8
25 TU	0225 3.9	0827 0.7	1443 4.1	2056 0.4
11 TU	0333 3.7	0937 0.8	1547 3.8	2153 0.8
26 W	0309 4.1	0913 0.4	1529 4.3	2140 0.3
12 W	0403 3.7	1008 0.8	1617 3.8	2222 0.8
27 TH	0353 4.3	0959 0.3	1616 4.3	2224 0.3
13 TH	0432 3.8	1039 0.8	1647 3.8	2251 0.8
28 F	0437 4.3	1045 0.3	1702 4.2	2308 0.4
14 F	0500 3.8	1109 0.9	1717 3.7	2319 0.9
29 SA	0523 4.3	1133 0.4	1750 4.1	2353 0.6
15 SA	0530 3.7	1141 1.0	1749 3.6	2350 1.0
30 SU	0611 4.1	1223 0.6	1840 3.8	
31 M	0040 0.9	0701 3.9	1316 0.9	1934 3.5

NOVEMBER

Day	Time m	Time m	Time m	Time m
1 TU	0132 1.2	0757 3.6	1415 1.2	2035 3.2
16 W	0046 1.2	0707 3.6	1325 1.2	1938 3.2
2 W	0233 1.4	0902 3.4	1524 1.4	2148 3.0
17 TH	0134 1.4	0758 3.4	1420 1.3	2036 3.1
3 TH	0347 1.6	1016 3.3	1641 1.5	2309 3.0
18 F	0234 1.5	0900 3.3	1526 1.4	2146 3.1
4 F	0507 1.6	1130 3.2	1754 1.5	
19 SA	0345 1.5	1012 3.3	1639 1.3	2301 3.2
5 SA	0019 3.0	0617 1.5	1235 3.3	1852 1.4
20 SU	0500 1.4	1124 3.4	1748 1.3	
6 SU	0113 3.2	0712 1.4	1326 3.4	1938 1.2
21 M	0009 3.3	0609 1.3	1230 3.6	1849 1.0
7 M	0156 3.3	0757 1.2	1409 3.5	2017 1.1
22 TU	0108 3.6	0709 1.0	1328 3.8	1943 0.8
8 TU	0232 3.5	0836 1.1	1446 3.6	2052 1.0
23 W	0200 3.8	0804 0.8	1422 3.9	2033 0.6
9 W	0305 3.6	0911 1.0	1519 3.6	2124 0.9
24 TH	0249 4.0	0856 0.6	1513 4.1	2121 0.5
10 TH	0337 3.7	0945 1.0	1552 3.7	2155 0.9
25 F	0336 4.2	0945 0.5	1602 4.1	2207 0.5
11 F	0407 3.8	1017 0.9	1624 3.7	2225 0.9
26 SA	0423 4.3	1034 0.4	1650 4.1	2253 0.6
12 SA	0438 3.8	1050 0.9	1657 3.7	2256 0.9
27 SU	0510 4.3	1123 0.5	1738 3.9	2338 0.7
13 SU	0510 3.8	1124 1.0	1731 3.6	2329 1.0
28 M	0557 4.2	1211 0.6	1826 3.7	
14 M	0545 3.8	1200 1.0	1808 3.5	
29 TU	0024 0.9	0645 4.0	1300 0.8	1915 3.5
15 TU	0005 1.1	0623 3.7	1239 1.1	1850 3.4
30 W	0111 1.1	0734 3.8	1350 1.1	2006 3.3

DECEMBER

Day	Time m	Time m	Time m	Time m
1 TH	0203 1.3	0828 3.5	1445 1.3	2102 3.1
16 F	0120 1.1	0742 3.7	1400 1.1	2014 3.3
2 F	0302 1.5	0927 3.3	1546 1.4	2207 3.0
17 SA	0212 1.2	0835 3.6	1455 1.1	2113 3.3
3 SA	0409 1.6	1032 3.2	1652 1.5	2318 3.0
18 SU	0312 1.3	0936 3.5	1559 1.2	2220 3.2
4 SU	0520 1.6	1138 3.1	1756 1.5	
19 M	0422 1.3	1046 3.4	1709 1.2	2332 3.3
5 M	0022 3.0	0625 1.5	1239 3.2	1852 1.4
20 TU	0535 1.3	1158 3.4	1817 1.1	
6 TU	0116 3.2	0720 1.4	1331 3.2	1940 1.3
21 W	0040 3.4	0645 1.2	1307 3.5	1921 1.0
7 W	0200 3.3	0806 1.3	1415 3.3	2020 1.2
22 TH	0141 3.6	0749 1.0	1409 3.7	2017 0.9
8 TH	0238 3.5	0847 1.2	1454 3.4	2057 1.1
23 F	0236 3.9	0847 0.8	1504 3.8	2109 0.7
9 F	0313 3.6	0925 1.1	1530 3.5	2132 1.0
24 SA	0326 4.0	0939 0.6	1555 3.9	2156 0.6
10 SA	0347 3.7	1000 1.0	1606 3.6	2206 0.9
25 SU	0414 4.2	1028 0.5	1642 3.9	2241 0.6
11 SU	0421 3.8	1035 0.9	1641 3.6	2240 0.9
26 M	0459 4.2	1113 0.5	1726 3.8	2324 0.6
12 M	0456 3.9	1111 0.9	1718 3.6	2316 0.9
27 TU	0542 4.1	1156 0.6	1808 3.7	
13 TU	0533 3.9	1148 0.9	1757 3.6	2354 0.9
28 W	0006 0.9	0625 4.0	1238 0.7	1849 3.6
14 W	0612 3.8	1228 0.9	1838 3.5	
29 TH	0047 0.9	0707 3.8	1319 0.9	1930 3.4
15 TH	0035 1.0	0655 3.8	1311 1.0	1923 3.4
30 F	0130 1.1	0750 3.6	1401 1.1	2013 3.2
31 SA	0215 1.3	0835 3.4	1448 1.3	2102 3.0

HAT is 4·5 metres above Chart Datum

TIDES

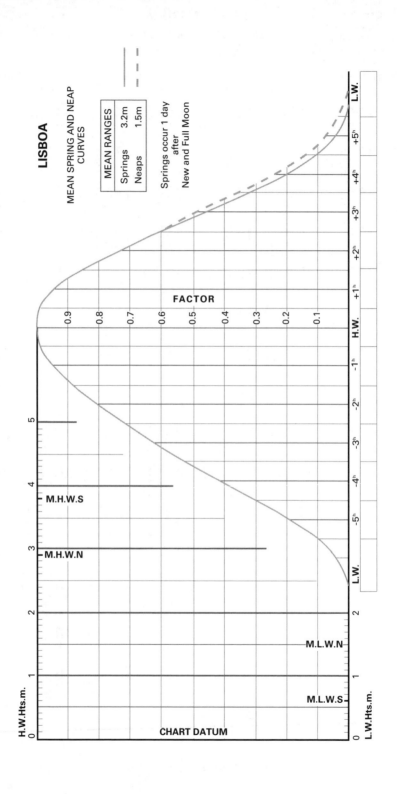

LISBOA

MEAN SPRING AND NEAP CURVES

MEAN RANGES	
Springs	3.2m
Neaps	1.5m

Springs occur 1 day after New and Full Moon

FACTOR

PORTUGAL – LISBOA
LAT 38°43'N   LONG 9°07'W
TIMES AND HEIGHTS OF HIGH AND LOW WATERS

Dates in amber are SPRINGS
Dates in yellow are NEAPS

2011

JANUARY

Day					Day				
1 SA	0029 3.3	0630 1.0	1302 3.3	1853 1.0	16 SU	0002 3.0	0608 1.3	1231 3.0	1826 1.1
2 SU	0126 3.3	0727 0.8	1357 3.3	1944 0.9	17 M	0058 3.2	0702 1.0	1326 3.1	1916 0.9
3 M	0217 3.6	0816 0.7	1446 3.4	2029 0.8	18 TU	0149 3.4	0749 0.8	1416 3.3	2003 0.7
4 TU ●	0302 3.7	0859 0.6	1529 3.4	2109 0.8	19 W ○	0236 3.7	0834 0.6	1503 3.5	2047 0.6
5 W	0344 3.7	0938 0.6	1608 3.4	2146 0.8	20 TH	0322 3.8	0918 0.4	1548 3.7	2130 0.4
6 TH	0421 3.7	1013 0.6	1643 3.4	2220 0.8	21 F	0407 4.0	1001 0.3	1632 3.8	2213 0.3
7 F	0454 3.6	1046 0.7	1715 3.3	2254 0.8	22 SA	0451 4.0	1043 0.2	1715 3.8	2256 0.3
8 SA	0526 3.5	1119 0.8	1745 3.3	2327 0.9	23 SU	0534 4.0	1126 0.3	1759 3.7	2340 0.4
9 SU	0557 3.4	1153 0.9	1817 3.2		24 M	0619 3.8	1210 0.5	1844 3.5	
10 M	0002 1.0	0630 3.3	1229 1.0	1853 3.0	25 TU	0026 0.6	0706 3.6	1257 0.7	1933 3.3
11 TU	0042 1.2	0709 3.1	1311 1.1	1937 2.9	26 W ☾	0118 0.8	0759 3.3	1351 0.9	2031 3.2
12 W ☾	0129 1.3	0757 2.9	1402 1.3	2033 2.8	27 TH	0220 1.1	0904 3.1	1457 1.2	2142 3.0
13 TH	0230 1.5	0858 2.8	1507 1.4	2143 2.7	28 F	0339 1.2	1024 2.9	1618 1.3	2303 3.0
14 F	0346 1.5	1012 2.8	1621 1.4	2257 2.8	29 SA	0509 1.2	1147 2.9	1740 1.3	
15 SA	0503 1.4	1127 2.8	1729 1.3		30 SU	0017 3.1	0627 1.1	1256 3.0	1846 1.1
					31 M	0117 3.3	0724 0.9	1350 3.2	1936 1.0

FEBRUARY

Day					Day				
1 TU	0207 3.5	0808 0.8	1435 3.3	2018 0.9	16 W	0129 3.5	0731 0.7	1359 3.4	1945 0.7
2 W	0249 3.6	0846 0.7	1513 3.4	2054 0.7	17 TH	0219 3.8	0816 0.5	1446 3.7	2031 0.4
3 TH ●	0326 3.7	0919 0.6	1547 3.4	2127 0.7	18 F ○	0305 4.0	0900 0.3	1530 3.9	2114 0.3
4 F	0359 3.7	0950 0.6	1618 3.5	2158 0.6	19 SA	0349 4.2	0942 0.1	1613 4.0	2156 0.2
5 SA	0429 3.7	1019 0.6	1647 3.5	2228 0.7	20 SU	0432 4.2	1023 0.1	1655 4.0	2237 0.2
6 SU	0458 3.6	1049 0.6	1715 3.4	2259 0.7	21 M	0515 4.1	1104 0.2	1736 3.9	2320 0.3
7 M	0527 3.5	1119 0.7	1744 3.3	2330 0.8	22 TU	0558 4.0	1146 0.4	1819 3.7	
8 TU	0558 3.4	1150 0.9	1816 3.2		23 W	0004 0.5	0643 3.7	1230 0.7	1906 3.5
9 W	0003 1.0	0632 3.2	1224 1.0	1852 3.0	24 TH ☽	0054 0.8	0734 3.3	1321 1.0	2001 3.2
10 TH	0041 1.2	0711 3.0	1304 1.2	1937 2.9	25 F	0156 1.1	0839 3.0	1426 1.3	2113 3.0
11 F ☾	0130 1.4	0802 2.8	1358 1.4	2038 2.8	26 SA	0320 1.3	1006 2.8	1557 1.5	2243 3.0
12 SA	0241 1.5	0914 2.7	1517 1.5	2159 2.8	27 SU	0501 1.4	1138 2.8	1730 1.5	
13 SU	0414 1.5	1044 2.7	1646 1.4	2324 2.9	28 M	0003 3.1	0619 1.2	1246 3.0	1835 1.3
14 M	0537 1.3	1205 2.9	1759 1.2						
15 TU	0033 3.2	0640 1.0	1307 3.1	1856 1.0					

MARCH

Day					Day				
1 TU	0103 3.3	0710 1.0	1335 3.2	1921 1.1	16 W	0008 3.3	0614 1.0	1245 3.3	1833 1.0
2 W	0149 3.4	0749 0.9	1415 3.3	1959 0.9	17 TH	0106 3.6	0707 0.7	1337 3.6	1923 0.7
3 TH	0227 3.6	0823 0.8	1449 3.5	2032 0.8	18 F	0156 3.9	0753 0.5	1423 3.8	2009 0.5
4 F ●	0301 3.7	0853 0.7	1520 3.5	2103 0.7	19 SA ○	0243 4.1	0837 0.3	1507 4.0	2052 0.3
5 SA	0332 3.7	0922 0.6	1550 3.6	2133 0.6	20 SU	0327 4.3	0918 0.2	1550 4.1	2135 0.2
6 SU	0402 3.7	0951 0.6	1618 3.6	2202 0.7	21 M	0411 4.3	1000 0.2	1632 4.1	2217 0.2
7 M	0431 3.7	1019 0.6	1646 3.6	2231 0.7	22 TU	0454 4.2	1041 0.3	1714 4.0	2301 0.4
8 TU	0500 3.6	1048 0.7	1715 3.5	2301 0.8	23 W	0538 3.9	1122 0.6	1757 3.8	2346 0.6
9 W	0530 3.5	1117 0.9	1746 3.4	2333 1.0	24 TH	0624 3.6	1206 0.9	1843 3.6	
10 TH	0602 3.3	1148 1.0	1820 3.2		25 F	0036 0.9	0715 3.3	1256 1.2	1937 3.3
11 F	0008 1.1	0640 3.1	1224 1.2	1901 3.1	26 SA ☽	0138 1.2	0819 3.0	1402 1.5	2048 3.1
12 SA ☾	0053 1.3	0727 2.9	1314 1.4	1956 2.9	27 SU	0302 1.4	0947 2.8	1534 1.6	2218 3.0
13 SU	0200 1.5	0836 2.8	1431 1.5	2117 2.9	28 M	0439 1.5	1117 2.8	1705 1.6	2337 3.1
14 M	0336 1.5	1012 2.8	1610 1.5	2251 3.0	29 TU	0551 1.3	1221 3.0	1808 1.4	
15 TU	0507 1.3	1141 3.0	1732 1.3		30 W	0035 3.3	0640 1.2	1307 3.2	1854 1.2
					31 TH	0120 3.4	0718 1.0	1345 3.4	1931 1.1

APRIL

Day					Day				
1 F	0157 3.5	0751 0.9	1418 3.5	2004 0.9	16 SA	0130 3.9	0726 0.6	1357 3.9	1944 0.5
2 SA	0231 3.7	0822 0.8	1450 3.6	2036 0.8	17 SU	0218 4.1	0811 0.4	1442 4.1	2030 0.4
3 SU ●	0303 3.7	0852 0.7	1520 3.6	2106 0.8	18 M ○	0304 4.2	0854 0.3	1526 4.2	2115 0.3
4 M	0334 3.7	0922 0.7	1549 3.7	2136 0.8	19 TU	0350 4.2	0937 0.4	1610 4.1	2159 0.3
5 TU	0404 3.7	0951 0.8	1619 3.7	2207 0.8	20 W	0435 4.0	1019 0.5	1654 4.0	2244 0.5
6 W	0435 3.6	1020 0.8	1650 3.6	2238 0.9	21 TH	0521 3.8	1102 0.8	1739 3.9	2331 0.7
7 TH	0507 3.5	1050 0.9	1722 3.5	2311 1.0	22 F	0608 3.5	1147 1.0	1825 3.6	
8 F	0542 3.3	1122 1.1	1758 3.4	2349 1.1	23 SA	0022 1.0	0658 3.2	1236 1.3	1917 3.4
9 SA	0621 3.2	1201 1.2	1840 3.3		24 SU	0121 1.3	0758 3.0	1338 1.5	2020 3.2
10 SU	0036 1.3	0711 3.0	1253 1.4	1936 3.1	25 M ☽	0232 1.4	0913 2.8	1456 1.7	2136 3.0
11 M	0142 1.4	0819 2.9	1408 1.5	2052 3.0	26 TU	0352 1.5	1033 2.9	1617 1.6	2251 3.1
12 TU ☾	0310 1.4	0950 2.9	1541 1.5	2222 3.1	27 W	0501 1.4	1137 3.0	1723 1.5	2351 3.2
13 W	0436 1.3	1113 3.1	1701 1.3	2338 3.4	28 TH	0554 1.3	1226 3.2	1813 1.4	
14 TH	0543 1.0	1217 3.4	1804 1.1		29 F	0039 3.3	0637 1.2	1307 3.3	1855 1.2
15 F	0038 3.6	0638 0.8	1309 3.7	1857 0.8	30 SA	0120 3.4	0715 1.0	1343 3.5	1932 1.1

HAT is 4·3 metres above Chart Datum

TIDES

TIME ZONE (UT)	PORTUGAL – LISBOA	Dates in amber are **SPRINGS**
For Summer Time add ONE hour in **non-shaded areas**	**LAT 38°43'N LONG 9°07'W** TIMES AND HEIGHTS OF HIGH AND LOW WATERS	Dates in yellow are **NEAPS** **2011**

MAY

Day	Time m	Time m	Time m	Time m
1 SU	0156 3.5	0749 0.9	1417 3.6	2006 1.0
16 M	0155 3.9	0746 0.6	1419 4.0	2011 0.5
2 M	0231 3.6	0821 0.9	1450 3.6	2040 0.9
17 TU ○	0245 3.9	0832 0.6	1506 4.0	2058 0.5
3 TU ●	0305 3.6	0853 0.9	1522 3.7	2113 0.9
18 W	0333 3.9	0917 0.6	1553 4.0	2145 0.5
4 W	0339 3.6	0924 0.9	1555 3.7	2146 0.9
19 TH	0421 3.8	1001 0.7	1638 4.0	2232 0.6
5 TH	0414 3.5	0956 0.9	1630 3.7	2220 0.9
20 F	0507 3.6	1045 0.9	1723 3.8	2318 0.8
6 F	0450 3.5	1030 1.0	1706 3.6	2258 1.0
21 SA	0553 3.4	1129 1.0	1808 3.6	
7 SA	0529 3.4	1107 1.1	1746 3.5	2340 1.1
22 SU	0005 1.0	0639 3.2	1215 1.2	1853 3.4
8 SU	0613 3.3	1151 1.2	1831 3.4	
23 M	0054 1.1	0728 3.0	1306 1.4	1942 3.2
9 M	0030 1.2	0705 3.1	1245 1.3	1927 3.4
24 TU ◐	0149 1.3	0823 2.9	1406 1.5	2040 3.1
10 TU ◐	0132 1.3	0809 3.0	1353 1.4	2035 3.2
25 W	0250 1.4	0929 2.9	1514 1.6	2146 3.0
11 W	0245 1.3	0926 3.1	1511 1.4	2152 3.3
26 TH	0355 1.4	1035 2.9	1622 1.5	2251 3.0
12 TH	0401 1.2	1040 3.2	1627 1.3	2305 3.4
27 F	0456 1.4	1133 3.0	1722 1.5	2348 3.1
13 F	0508 1.0	1144 3.4	1732 1.1	
28 SA	0549 1.3	1222 3.2	1814 1.3	
14 SA	0007 3.6	0606 0.9	1240 3.6	1829 0.9
29 SU	0037 3.2	0634 1.2	1304 3.3	1858 1.2
15 SU	0103 3.8	0658 0.7	1331 3.8	1921 0.7
30 M	0120 3.3	0714 1.1	1343 3.4	1938 1.1
31 TU	0200 3.4	0751 1.0	1420 3.5	2015 1.0

JUNE

Day	Time m	Time m	Time m	Time m
1 W ●	0239 3.4	0826 0.9	1457 3.6	2052 0.9
16 TH	0321 3.6	0903 0.7	1540 3.9	2135 0.6
2 TH	0318 3.4	0902 0.9	1535 3.6	2130 0.8
17 F	0408 3.6	0947 0.8	1624 3.8	2219 0.6
3 F	0358 3.5	0939 0.9	1615 3.7	2208 0.8
18 SA	0452 3.5	1029 0.8	1706 3.7	2300 0.7
4 SA	0439 3.5	1017 0.9	1656 3.7	2249 0.8
19 SU	0533 3.4	1109 0.9	1745 3.6	2340 0.9
5 SU	0522 3.4	1059 0.9	1740 3.6	2333 0.9
20 M	0611 3.3	1148 1.0	1823 3.5	
6 M	0607 3.3	1144 1.0	1825 3.6	
21 TU	0020 1.0	0649 3.1	1229 1.2	1901 3.3
7 TU	0022 0.9	0657 3.3	1235 1.1	1917 3.5
22 W	0102 1.1	0730 3.0	1315 1.3	1944 3.1
8 W	0116 1.0	0753 3.2	1334 1.2	2015 3.4
23 TH ◐	0150 1.3	0819 2.9	1410 1.4	2036 3.0
9 TH	0218 1.1	0857 3.2	1440 1.2	2122 3.3
24 F	0247 1.4	0920 2.8	1514 1.5	2139 2.9
10 F	0325 1.1	1005 3.2	1551 1.2	2231 3.3
25 SA	0351 1.4	1027 2.9	1624 1.5	2247 2.9
11 SA	0432 1.0	1111 3.3	1701 1.1	2338 3.4
26 SU	0455 1.4	1129 3.0	1728 1.4	2349 3.0
12 SU	0536 0.9	1212 3.5	1805 0.9	
27 M	0551 1.3	1222 3.1	1823 1.3	
13 M	0040 3.5	0634 0.9	1309 3.6	1904 0.8
28 TU	0043 3.0	0639 1.2	1309 3.2	1910 1.1
14 TU	0137 3.6	0727 0.8	1402 3.8	1958 0.7
29 W	0131 3.2	0723 1.1	1353 3.4	1953 1.0
15 W ○	0231 3.6	0817 0.7	1452 3.8	2048 0.6
30 TH	0217 3.3	0803 0.9	1436 3.5	2034 0.8

JULY

Day	Time m	Time m	Time m	Time m
1 F ●	0301 3.4	0844 0.8	1519 3.7	2115 0.7
16 SA	0353 3.5	0931 0.7	1607 3.8	2200 0.6
2 SA	0344 3.5	0925 0.7	1602 3.8	2156 0.6
17 SU	0431 3.5	1008 0.8	1644 3.7	2235 0.7
3 SU	0427 3.5	1006 0.7	1645 3.8	2238 0.6
18 M	0506 3.4	1043 0.8	1718 3.7	2309 0.7
4 M	0510 3.6	1049 0.7	1728 3.8	2321 0.6
19 TU	0538 3.4	1117 0.9	1749 3.5	2342 0.8
5 TU	0554 3.5	1133 0.7	1813 3.8	
20 W	0609 3.3	1152 1.0	1821 3.4	
6 W	0006 0.7	0640 3.5	1219 0.8	1900 3.6
21 TH	0017 1.0	0643 3.1	1230 1.1	1857 3.2
7 TH	0054 0.8	0730 3.4	1311 0.9	1952 3.5
22 F	0056 1.1	0722 3.0	1313 1.3	1939 3.0
8 F ◐	0148 0.9	0826 3.3	1411 1.0	2052 3.3
23 SA ◐	0143 1.3	0812 2.9	1409 1.5	2034 2.9
9 SA	0250 1.0	0932 3.2	1520 1.1	2202 3.2
24 SU	0243 1.4	0917 2.8	1521 1.6	2144 2.8
10 SU	0400 1.1	1042 3.2	1637 1.0	2317 3.2
25 M	0356 1.5	1031 2.8	1641 1.5	2301 2.8
11 M	0512 1.1	1152 3.3	1752 1.1	
26 TU	0507 1.4	1140 3.0	1750 1.4	
12 TU	0027 3.2	0619 1.0	1255 3.5	1857 0.9
27 W	0010 2.9	0607 1.3	1239 3.1	1846 1.2
13 W	0129 3.3	0717 0.9	1351 3.6	1952 0.8
28 TH	0107 3.1	0658 1.1	1330 3.4	1933 1.0
14 TH	0223 3.4	0807 0.8	1441 3.7	2040 0.7
29 F	0157 3.3	0744 0.9	1417 3.6	2016 0.7
15 F ○	0310 3.5	0851 0.8	1526 3.8	2122 0.6
30 SA ●	0243 3.5	0827 0.7	1502 3.8	2058 0.6
31 SU	0327 3.6	0909 0.6	1546 3.9	2139 0.4

AUGUST

Day	Time m	Time m	Time m	Time m
1 M	0410 3.7	0951 0.5	1628 4.0	2220 0.4
16 TU	0434 3.6	1015 0.7	1647 3.8	2235 0.7
2 TU	0452 3.8	1032 0.4	1711 4.0	2302 0.4
17 W	0503 3.5	1046 0.8	1716 3.6	2306 0.8
3 W	0534 3.8	1115 0.5	1754 4.0	2344 0.5
18 TH	0532 3.4	1117 0.9	1745 3.5	2337 0.9
4 TH	0618 3.7	1159 0.6	1839 3.8	
19 F	0603 3.3	1150 1.1	1818 3.3	
5 F	0029 0.7	0705 3.5	1248 0.8	1928 3.5
20 SA	0010 1.1	0638 3.2	1227 1.3	1856 3.1
6 SA ◐	0119 0.9	0758 3.3	1345 1.0	2027 3.3
21 SU ◐	0049 1.3	0721 3.0	1314 1.5	1944 2.9
7 SU	0220 1.1	0903 3.2	1458 1.2	2142 3.1
22 M	0140 1.5	0818 2.9	1422 1.6	2051 2.8
8 M	0336 1.3	1021 3.1	1626 1.3	2307 3.0
23 TU	0256 1.6	0936 2.8	1555 1.6	2219 2.7
9 TU	0501 1.3	1140 3.2	1750 1.2	
24 W	0425 1.6	1101 2.8	1719 1.5	2342 2.9
10 W	0023 3.1	0614 1.2	1247 3.4	1855 1.0
25 TH	0539 1.4	1211 3.2	1821 1.2	
11 TH	0123 3.2	0710 1.1	1342 3.6	1945 0.9
26 F	0045 3.1	0635 1.2	1307 3.5	1910 0.9
12 F	0212 3.4	0756 0.9	1428 3.7	2026 0.7
27 SA	0136 3.4	0723 0.9	1355 3.7	1954 0.7
13 SA ○	0254 3.5	0835 0.8	1508 3.8	2102 0.7
28 SU	0222 3.7	0807 0.6	1441 4.0	2036 0.5
14 SU	0330 3.6	0911 0.7	1544 3.8	2134 0.6
29 M ●	0305 3.9	0849 0.5	1524 4.2	2117 0.3
15 M	0404 3.6	0943 0.7	1616 3.8	2205 0.6
30 TU	0347 4.0	0930 0.3	1607 4.2	2157 0.3
31 W	0429 4.0	1012 0.3	1649 4.2	2238 0.3

HAT is 4·3 metres above Chart Datum

PORTUGAL – LISBOA
LAT 38°43'N   LONG 9°07'W
TIMES AND HEIGHTS OF HIGH AND LOW WATERS

Dates in amber are **SPRINGS**
Dates in yellow are **NEAPS**

2011

SEPTEMBER

Day	Time m	Day	Time m
1 TH	0511 4.0 / 1054 0.4 / 1733 4.1 / 2320 0.5	**16** F	0500 3.6 / 1046 0.9 / 1714 3.5 / 2301 1.0
2 F	0554 3.9 / 1138 0.6 / 1818 3.8	**17** SA	0530 3.5 / 1118 1.1 / 1746 3.4 / 2332 1.2
3 SA	0004 0.7 / 0640 3.7 / 1227 0.8 / 1908 3.5	**18** SU	0603 3.3 / 1153 1.3 / 1823 3.2
4 SU	0054 1.0 / 0734 3.4 / 1326 1.1 / ☽ 2009 3.2	**19** M	0008 1.4 / 0643 3.2 / 1237 1.5 / 1909 3.0
5 M	0156 1.3 / 0842 3.2 / 1445 1.3 / 2130 3.0	**20** TU	0054 1.5 / 0737 3.0 / 1340 1.6 / ☽ 2014 2.8
6 TU	0321 1.5 / 1007 3.1 / 1623 1.4 / 2302 3.0	**21** W	0208 1.7 / 0853 2.9 / 1515 1.7 / 2146 2.8
7 W	0455 1.5 / 1130 3.2 / 1747 1.3	**22** TH	0347 1.7 / 1026 3.0 / 1646 1.5 / 2316 3.0
8 TH	0016 3.1 / 0606 1.4 / 1235 3.4 / 1844 1.1	**23** F	0509 1.5 / 1142 3.3 / 1751 1.3
9 F	0110 3.3 / 0657 1.2 / 1325 3.6 / 1927 1.0	**24** SA	0019 3.3 / 0609 1.2 / 1240 3.6 / 1843 0.9
10 SA	0152 3.5 / 0738 1.0 / 1406 3.7 / 2003 0.8	**25** SU	0110 3.6 / 0658 0.9 / 1330 3.9 / 1928 0.7
11 SU	0229 3.6 / 0813 0.9 / 1443 3.8 / 2035 0.8	**26** M	0156 3.8 / 0743 0.6 / 1416 4.1 / 2010 0.5
12 M	0303 3.7 / 0845 0.8 / 1516 3.8 / ○ 2105 0.7	**27** TU	0240 4.0 / 0826 0.4 / ● 1500 4.3 / 2052 0.3
13 TU	0333 3.7 / 0916 0.8 / 1546 3.8 / 2134 0.7	**28** W	0323 4.2 / 0908 0.3 / 1544 4.3 / 2133 0.3
14 W	0403 3.7 / 0946 0.8 / 1616 3.8 / 2203 0.8	**29** TH	0405 4.2 / 0951 0.3 / 1628 4.3 / 2215 0.4
15 TH	0431 3.7 / 1016 0.9 / 1645 3.7 / 2232 0.9	**30** F	0448 4.1 / 1035 0.4 / 1713 4.1 / 2257 0.6

OCTOBER

Day	Time m	Day	Time m
1 SA	0533 4.0 / 1121 0.6 / 1800 3.8 / 2342 0.9	**16** SU	0504 3.5 / 1054 1.1 / 1723 3.4 / 2304 1.2
2 SU	0620 3.8 / 1212 0.9 / 1852 3.5	**17** M	0539 3.4 / 1131 1.2 / 1802 3.2 / 2341 1.4
3 M	0033 1.2 / 0715 3.5 / 1313 1.2 / 1955 3.2	**18** TU	0620 3.3 / 1215 1.4 / 1849 3.0
4 TU	0137 1.5 / 0823 3.3 / 1433 1.4 / ☽ 2117 3.0	**19** W	0029 1.5 / 0712 3.2 / 1316 1.5 / 1952 2.9
5 W	0304 1.6 / 0948 3.2 / 1608 1.5 / 2245 3.0	**20** TH	0138 1.6 / 0824 3.1 / 1441 1.6 / ☽ 2118 2.9
6 TH	0436 1.6 / 1109 3.2 / 1724 1.4 / 2354 3.1	**21** F	0310 1.6 / 0951 3.1 / 1607 1.5 / 2243 3.1
7 F	0543 1.5 / 1210 3.4 / 1817 1.2	**22** SA	0432 1.5 / 1108 3.3 / 1715 1.2 / 2348 3.3
8 SA	0044 3.3 / 0632 1.3 / 1258 3.5 / 1858 1.1	**23** SU	0536 1.2 / 1209 3.6 / 1810 1.0
9 SU	0124 3.6 / 0711 1.1 / 1338 3.7 / 1933 1.0	**24** M	0041 3.6 / 0629 0.9 / 1301 3.9 / 1858 0.7
10 M	0159 3.6 / 0746 1.0 / 1413 3.7 / 2004 0.9	**25** TU	0128 3.9 / 0717 0.7 / 1350 4.1 / 1944 0.5
11 TU	0232 3.7 / 0818 0.9 / 1446 3.8 / 2035 0.8	**26** W	0214 4.1 / 0803 0.5 / ● 1436 4.2 / 2027 0.4
12 W	0303 3.7 / 0850 0.9 / 1517 3.8 / ○ 2105 0.8	**27** TH	0259 4.2 / 0848 0.4 / 1523 4.2 / 2111 0.4
13 TH	0333 3.7 / 0920 0.9 / 1547 3.7 / 2134 0.9	**28** F	0344 4.2 / 0933 0.4 / 1609 4.1 / 2154 0.5
14 F	0402 3.7 / 0951 1.0 / 1618 3.6 / 2203 0.9	**29** SA	0429 4.2 / 1020 0.5 / 1657 4.0 / 2239 0.7
15 SA	0432 3.6 / 1022 1.0 / 1649 3.5 / 2233 1.0	**30** SU	0516 4.0 / 1108 0.7 / 1745 3.7 / 2325 0.9
		31 M	0604 3.8 / 1159 0.9 / 1838 3.4

NOVEMBER

Day	Time m	Day	Time m
1 TU	0016 1.2 / 0657 3.5 / 1258 1.2 / 1937 3.2	**16** W	0608 3.4 / 1205 1.2 / 1838 3.1
2 W	0116 1.5 / 0759 3.3 / 1407 1.4 / ● 2048 3.0	**17** TH	0017 1.3 / 0659 3.3 / 1300 1.3 / 1936 3.0
3 TH	0230 1.6 / 0912 3.2 / 1525 1.5 / 2206 3.0	**18** F	0118 1.4 / 0801 3.2 / 1409 1.4 / ☽ 2047 3.0
4 F	0351 1.6 / 1027 3.2 / 1637 1.4 / 2313 3.1	**19** SA	0233 1.5 / 0915 3.2 / 1524 1.3 / 2203 3.1
5 SA	0500 1.5 / 1130 3.2 / 1734 1.3	**20** SU	0350 1.4 / 1029 3.3 / 1634 1.2 / 2311 3.3
6 SU	0006 3.2 / 0554 1.4 / 1221 3.3 / 1820 1.2	**21** M	0459 1.2 / 1135 3.5 / 1735 1.0
7 M	0049 3.4 / 0638 1.2 / 1303 3.5 / 1858 1.1	**22** TU	0009 3.5 / 0558 1.0 / 1233 3.7 / 1829 0.8
8 TU	0127 3.5 / 0717 1.1 / 1341 3.5 / 1933 1.0	**23** W	0101 3.7 / 0653 0.7 / 1326 3.8 / 1919 0.6
9 W	0201 3.6 / 0752 1.0 / 1416 3.6 / 2006 0.9	**24** TH	0151 3.9 / 0744 0.6 / 1417 3.9 / 2007 0.5
10 TH	0234 3.6 / 0825 0.9 / 1450 3.6 / ○ 2038 0.9	**25** F	0240 4.0 / 0833 0.4 / 1507 3.9 / 2054 0.5
11 F	0307 3.7 / 0858 0.9 / 1523 3.6 / 2109 0.9	**26** SA	0328 4.1 / 0921 0.4 / 1557 3.9 / 2139 0.6
12 SA	0339 3.7 / 0931 0.9 / 1557 3.5 / 2140 1.0	**27** SU	0415 4.1 / 1009 0.5 / 1645 3.8 / 2225 0.7
13 SU	0412 3.6 / 1005 1.0 / 1632 3.4 / 2213 1.0	**28** M	0502 3.9 / 1057 0.6 / 1732 3.6 / 2310 0.9
14 M	0447 3.6 / 1040 1.0 / 1709 3.4 / 2248 1.1	**29** TU	0549 3.8 / 1144 0.8 / 1820 3.4 / 2356 1.1
15 TU	0525 3.5 / 1119 1.1 / 1750 3.3 / 2328 1.2	**30** W	0636 3.6 / 1233 1.0 / 1908 3.2

DECEMBER

Day	Time m	Day	Time m
1 TH	0046 1.3 / 0725 3.3 / 1326 1.2 / 2002 3.0	**16** F	0005 1.0 / 0646 3.5 / 1242 1.0 / 1917 3.2
2 F	0143 1.4 / 0821 3.2 / 1425 1.4 / ● 2104 2.9	**17** SA	0057 1.1 / 0738 3.3 / 1338 1.0 / 2015 3.1
3 SA	0248 1.5 / 0925 3.0 / 1530 1.4 / 2211 2.9	**18** SU	0158 1.2 / 0840 3.3 / 1442 1.1 / ☽ 2122 3.1
4 SU	0358 1.5 / 1032 3.0 / 1635 1.4 / 2314 3.0	**19** M	0308 1.2 / 0950 3.2 / 1552 1.1 / 2232 3.2
5 M	0504 1.5 / 1132 3.0 / 1732 1.3	**20** TU	0422 1.1 / 1102 3.3 / 1701 1.0 / 2339 3.3
6 TU	0006 3.1 / 0559 1.4 / 1223 3.1 / 1821 1.2	**21** W	0532 1.0 / 1208 3.4 / 1804 0.9
7 W	0051 3.2 / 0646 1.2 / 1308 3.2 / 1902 1.1	**22** TH	0039 3.5 / 0635 0.8 / 1310 3.5 / 1902 0.8
8 TH	0131 3.3 / 0727 1.1 / 1349 3.3 / 1940 1.0	**23** F	0135 3.7 / 0733 0.6 / 1406 3.6 / 1954 0.7
9 F	0208 3.5 / 0805 1.0 / 1427 3.3 / 2015 1.0	**24** SA	0228 3.8 / 0825 0.5 / 1458 3.7 / ● 2043 0.6
10 SA	0245 3.5 / 0841 0.9 / 1505 3.4 / ○ 2049 0.9	**25** SU	0318 3.9 / 0914 0.4 / 1547 3.7 / 2128 0.6
11 SU	0321 3.6 / 0916 0.8 / 1542 3.4 / 2124 0.9	**26** M	0404 3.9 / 0959 0.4 / 1632 3.6 / 2211 0.6
12 M	0358 3.6 / 0953 0.8 / 1621 3.4 / 2201 0.9	**27** TU	0448 3.9 / 1042 0.5 / 1715 3.5 / 2252 0.7
13 TU	0437 3.6 / 1030 0.8 / 1700 3.4 / 2239 0.9	**28** W	0529 3.7 / 1122 0.6 / 1754 3.4 / 2332 0.9
14 W	0517 3.6 / 1110 0.8 / 1742 3.3 / 2320 0.9	**29** TH	0608 3.6 / 1201 0.8 / 1832 3.2
15 TH	0559 3.5 / 1154 0.9 / 1827 3.3	**30** F	0012 1.0 / 0646 3.4 / 1241 1.0 / 1911 3.1
		31 SA	0054 1.2 / 0726 3.2 / 1325 1.1 / 1955 2.9

HAT is 4·3 metres above Chart Datum

TIDES

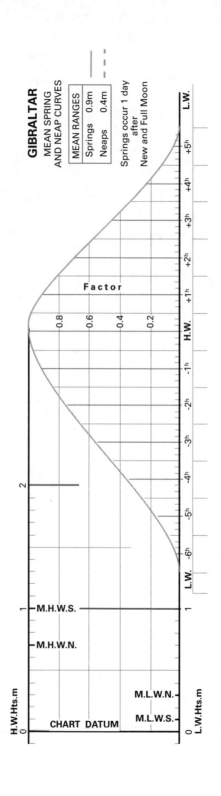

GIBRALTAR
MEAN SPRING
AND NEAP CURVES

MEAN RANGES	
Springs	0.9m
Neaps	0.4m

Springs occur 1 day
after
New and Full Moon

TIME ZONE -0100
(Gibraltar Standard Time)
Subtract 1 hour for UT
For Gibraltar Summer Time add
ONE hour in **non-shaded areas**

GIBRALTAR

LAT 36°08'N   LONG 5°21'W

TIMES AND HEIGHTS OF HIGH AND LOW WATERS

Dates in amber are **SPRINGS**
Dates in yellow are **NEAPS**

2011

	JANUARY				FEBRUARY				MARCH				APRIL		
	Time	m	Time	m	Time	m	Time	m	Time	m	Time	m	Time	m	Time	m

JANUARY

Day	Time m	Time m	Time m	Time m	Day	Time m	Time m	Time m	Time m
1 SA	0033 0.8	0624 0.2	1254 0.9	1900 0.1	16 SU	0013 0.7	0608 0.3	1223 0.8	1837 0.2
2 SU	0128 0.8	0713 0.2	1345 0.9	1946 0.1	17 M	0108 0.8	0653 0.1	1316 0.8	1920 0.1
3 M	0217 0.9	0756 0.1	1433 0.9	2028 0.1	18 TU	0154 0.8	0734 0.1	1405 0.9	2001 0.1
4 TU	0301 0.9	0837 0.1	1517 0.9	● 2106 0.1	19 W	0238 0.9	0816 0.1	1452 0.9	○ 2042 0.0
5 W	0342 0.9	0916 0.1	1559 0.9	2143 0.1	20 TH	0321 1.0	0859 0.0	1537 1.0	2123 0.0
6 TH	0419 0.9	0953 0.2	1638 0.9	2217 0.1	21 F	0404 1.0	0943 0.0	1622 1.0	2204 0.0
7 F	0455 0.9	1029 0.1	1715 0.9	2251 0.1	22 SA	0446 1.0	1027 0.0	1706 1.0	2245 0.0
8 SA	0529 0.9	1104 0.1	1751 0.8	2323 0.1	23 SU	0529 1.0	1111 0.0	1751 1.0	2326 0.0
9 SU	0603 0.8	1139 0.2	1827 0.8	2357 0.2	24 M	0615 1.0	1158 0.1	1838 0.9	
10 M	0639 0.8	1217 0.2	1905 0.7		25 TU	0010 0.1	0704 0.9	1250 0.1	1930 0.8
11 TU	0034 0.2	0719 0.8	1301 0.3	1947 0.7	26 W	0101 0.2	0759 0.9	1351 0.2	☽ 2028 0.8
12 W	0118 0.3	0806 0.7	1355 0.3	☽ 2038 0.6	27 TH	0204 0.2	0903 0.8	1508 0.2	2137 0.7
13 TH	0219 0.3	0901 0.7	1505 0.3	2140 0.6	28 F	0331 0.3	1020 0.7	1647 0.2	2305 0.7
14 F	0346 0.3	1007 0.7	1634 0.3	2300 0.6	29 SA	0516 0.3	1143 0.7	1806 0.2	
15 SA	0511 0.3	1120 0.7	1747 0.2		30 SU	0027 0.7	0624 0.2	1251 0.8	1900 0.1
					31 M	0128 0.8	0712 0.2	1344 0.8	1942 0.1

FEBRUARY

Day	Time m	Time m	Time m	Time m	Day	Time m	Time m	Time m	Time m
1 TU	0214 0.8	0752 0.1	1429 0.8	2020 0.1	16 W	0136 0.8	0721 0.1	1350 0.9	1947 0.0
2 W	0254 0.8	0829 0.1	1509 0.9	2055 0.0	17 TH	0221 0.9	0804 0.0	1438 0.9	2028 0.0
3 TH	0330 0.9	0904 0.1	1545 0.9	● 2128 0.0	18 F	0304 1.0	0847 0.0	1523 1.0	○ 2108 -0.1
4 F	0402 0.9	0937 0.1	1620 0.9	2159 0.0	19 SA	0347 1.0	0930 -0.1	1607 1.0	2149 -0.1
5 SA	0432 0.9	1009 0.1	1652 0.9	2228 0.0	20 SU	0429 1.1	1013 -0.1	1651 1.0	2228 -0.1
6 SU	0501 0.9	1040 0.1	1723 0.8	2257 0.1	21 M	0512 1.0	1055 0.0	1735 1.0	2308 0.0
7 M	0530 0.8	1109 0.1	1754 0.8	2325 0.1	22 TU	0556 1.0	1138 0.0	1821 0.9	2349 0.1
8 TU	0601 0.8	1140 0.1	1826 0.8	2353 0.2	23 W	0643 0.9	1224 0.1	1912 0.8	
9 W	0636 0.8	1213 0.2	1904 0.7		24 TH	0034 0.1	0736 0.8	1320 0.2	2007 0.8
10 TH	0026 0.2	0717 0.7	1254 0.2	1950 0.6	25 F	0132 0.2	0839 0.7	1438 0.3	◑ 2115 0.7
11 F	0110 0.3	0810 0.7	1354 0.3	◑ 2049 0.6	26 SA	0302 0.3	0959 0.7	1633 0.3	2245 0.6
12 SA	0224 0.3	0916 0.6	1537 0.3	2208 0.6	27 SU	0511 0.3	1134 0.7	1758 0.2	
13 SU	0429 0.3	1039 0.6	1724 0.3	2339 0.6	28 M	0017 0.7	0620 0.2	1245 0.7	1847 0.2
14 M	0548 0.3	1159 0.7	1822 0.2						
15 TU	0045 0.7	0638 0.2	1300 0.8	1906 0.1					

MARCH

Day	Time m	Time m	Time m	Time m	Day	Time m	Time m	Time m	Time m
1 TU	0116 0.7	0704 0.2	1335 0.8	1926 0.1	16 W	0018 0.7	0617 0.2	1240 0.8	1842 0.1
2 W	0158 0.8	0739 0.1	1415 0.8	2000 0.1	17 TH	0111 0.8	0703 0.1	1331 0.9	1924 0.0
3 TH	0234 0.9	0812 0.1	1451 0.8	2032 0.1	18 F	0157 0.9	0746 0.0	1418 0.9	2005 0.0
4 F	0306 0.9	0843 0.1	1524 0.9	● 2103 0.0	19 SA	0241 1.0	0829 -0.1	1503 1.0	○ 2046 0.0
5 SA	0336 0.9	0914 0.0	1555 0.9	2133 0.0	20 SU	0325 1.0	0912 -0.1	1548 1.0	2127 -0.1
6 SU	0404 0.9	0944 0.0	1625 0.9	2201 0.0	21 M	0408 1.1	0954 -0.1	1632 1.0	2207 0.0
7 M	0432 0.9	1013 0.1	1655 0.9	2229 0.1	22 TU	0452 1.0	1036 0.0	1717 1.0	2247 0.0
8 TU	0500 0.9	1041 0.1	1724 0.8	2255 0.1	23 W	0536 1.0	1117 0.0	1804 0.9	2328 0.1
9 W	0529 0.9	1109 0.1	1756 0.8	2323 0.1	24 TH	0623 0.9	1201 0.1	1854 0.9	
10 TH	0603 0.8	1139 0.2	1833 0.7	2354 0.2	25 F	0012 0.2	0716 0.8	1251 0.2	1950 0.8
11 F	0643 0.7	1215 0.2	1920 0.7		26 SA	0109 0.3	0819 0.7	1410 0.3	◑ 2055 0.7
12 SA	0034 0.3	0734 0.7	1309 0.3	2018 0.6	27 SU	0237 0.3	0936 0.7	1559 0.3	2217 0.7
13 SU	0142 0.3	0841 0.6	1450 0.3	◑ 2133 0.6	28 M	0446 0.3	1109 0.7	1725 0.3	2344 0.7
14 M	0350 0.3	1005 0.6	1653 0.3	2305 0.6	29 TU	0558 0.3	1221 0.7	1816 0.2	
15 TU	0523 0.3	1135 0.7	1757 0.2		30 W	0043 0.7	0638 0.2	1310 0.8	1853 0.2
					31 TH	0125 0.8	0712 0.2	1348 0.8	1927 0.1

APRIL

Day	Time m	Time m	Time m	Time m	Day	Time m	Time m	Time m	Time m
1 F	0200 0.8	0744 0.1	1423 0.8	1959 0.1	16 SA	0128 0.9	0723 0.0	1353 0.9	1937 0.0
2 SA	0232 0.9	0816 0.1	1455 0.9	2031 0.1	17 SU	0214 1.0	0808 0.0	1440 1.0	2020 0.0
3 SU	0302 0.9	0847 0.1	1527 0.9	● 2102 0.1	18 M	0300 1.0	0852 -0.1	1526 1.0	○ 2103 0.0
4 M	0332 0.9	0917 0.1	1558 0.9	2132 0.1	19 TU	0345 1.0	0935 0.0	1612 1.0	2145 0.0
5 TU	0402 0.9	0947 0.1	1628 0.9	2201 0.1	20 W	0431 1.0	1017 0.0	1658 1.0	2227 0.1
6 W	0432 0.9	1016 0.1	1659 0.9	2230 0.1	21 TH	0517 0.9	1059 0.0	1746 0.9	2309 0.1
7 TH	0504 0.8	1045 0.1	1733 0.8	2300 0.2	22 F	0605 0.9	1142 0.1	1837 0.8	2355 0.2
8 F	0539 0.8	1116 0.2	1813 0.8	2334 0.2	23 SA	0659 0.8	1233 0.2	1932 0.8	
9 SA	0620 0.8	1154 0.2	1900 0.7		24 SU	0050 0.3	0759 0.7	1340 0.3	2032 0.7
10 SU	0019 0.3	0712 0.7	1248 0.3	1958 0.7	25 M	0206 0.3	0907 0.7	1505 0.3	◑ 2139 0.7
11 M	0128 0.3	0818 0.7	1421 0.3	◑ 2108 0.7	26 TU	0342 0.3	1024 0.7	1625 0.3	2251 0.7
12 TU	0315 0.3	0937 0.7	1609 0.3	2229 0.7	27 W	0505 0.3	1136 0.7	1725 0.3	2353 0.7
13 W	0447 0.3	1104 0.7	1719 0.3	2343 0.8	28 TH	0557 0.2	1229 0.7	1810 0.2	
14 TH	0549 0.2	1212 0.8	1810 0.1		29 F	0039 0.8	0636 0.2	1312 0.8	1848 0.2
15 F	0040 0.8	0638 0.1	1305 0.9	1855 0.1	30 SA	0118 0.8	0711 0.2	1348 0.8	1923 0.2

Chart Datum: 0·25 metres below Alicante Datum (Mean Sea Level, Alicante)
HAT is 1·2 metres above Chart Datum

TIDES

GIBRALTAR

LAT 36°08'N   LONG 5°21'W

TIMES AND HEIGHTS OF HIGH AND LOW WATERS

2011

TIME ZONE -0100
(Gibraltar Standard Time)
Subtract 1 hour for UT
For Gibraltar Summer Time add
ONE hour in **non-shaded areas**

Dates in amber are **SPRINGS**
Dates in yellow are **NEAPS**

MAY

Day	Time m	Time m	Time m	Time m
1 SU	0152 0.8	0745 0.1	1423 0.8	1957 0.2
16 M	0148 1.0	0748 0.0	1418 0.9	1957 0.1
2 M	0226 0.9	0818 0.1	1457 0.9	2030 0.2
17 TU	0237 1.0	0834 0.0	1506 0.9	2042 0.1
3 TU	0259 0.9	0851 0.1	1530 0.9	2103 0.2
18 W	0325 1.0	0919 0.0	1554 0.9	2127 0.1
4 W	0333 0.9	0923 0.1	1604 0.9	2136 0.2
19 TH	0413 1.0	1002 0.0	1642 0.9	2211 0.1
5 TH	0408 0.9	0954 0.1	1639 0.9	2209 0.2
20 F	0500 0.9	1044 0.1	1729 0.9	2254 0.1
6 F	0444 0.9	1027 0.1	1716 0.9	2244 0.2
21 SA	0548 0.9	1126 0.1	1818 0.9	2339 0.2
7 SA	0523 0.8	1102 0.2	1757 0.8	2323 0.2
22 SU	0639 0.8	1212 0.2	1909 0.8	
8 SU	0606 0.8	1143 0.2	1845 0.8	
23 M	0029 0.2	0732 0.8	1306 0.2	2001 0.8
9 M	0012 0.3	0657 0.8	1238 0.2	1940 0.8
24 TU	0128 0.3	0829 0.7	1408 0.3	2055 0.8
10 TU	0119 0.3	0759 0.7	1355 0.3	2044 0.8
25 W	0236 0.3	0930 0.7	1515 0.3	2152 0.7
11 W	0241 0.3	0910 0.7	1520 0.3	2154 0.8
26 TH	0348 0.3	1035 0.7	1621 0.3	2251 0.7
12 TH	0403 0.2	1029 0.7	1633 0.2	2306 0.8
27 F	0458 0.3	1138 0.7	1719 0.3	2345 0.8
13 F	0514 0.2	1140 0.8	1734 0.2	
28 SA	0553 0.3	1228 0.7	1807 0.3	
14 SA	0007 0.9	0611 0.1	1238 0.8	1825 0.1
29 SU	0031 0.8	0636 0.2	1311 0.8	1847 0.2
15 SU	0059 0.9	0701 0.1	1329 0.9	1912 0.1
30 M	0111 0.9	0715 0.2	1350 0.8	1925 0.2
31 TU	0150 0.9	0751 0.2	1427 0.8	2001 0.3

JUNE

Day	Time m	Time m	Time m	Time m
1 W	0229 0.9	0826 0.2	1505 0.9	2037 0.2
16 TH	0310 0.9	0907 0.0	1541 0.9	2114 0.1
2 TH	0309 0.9	0902 0.1	1542 0.9	2114 0.2
17 F	0358 0.9	0949 0.0	1626 0.9	2157 0.1
3 F	0348 0.9	0937 0.1	1621 0.9	2152 0.2
18 SA	0444 0.9	1028 0.1	1710 0.9	2238 0.1
4 SA	0429 0.9	1013 0.1	1700 0.9	2232 0.2
19 SU	0529 0.9	1106 0.1	1753 0.9	2319 0.2
5 SU	0510 0.9	1052 0.1	1742 0.9	2315 0.2
20 M	0613 0.8	1145 0.1	1837 0.9	
6 M	0555 0.9	1134 0.2	1829 0.9	
21 TU	0001 0.2	0659 0.8	1227 0.2	1920 0.8
7 TU	0003 0.2	0644 0.8	1225 0.2	1920 0.9
22 W	0046 0.2	0746 0.7	1313 0.2	2005 0.8
8 W	0102 0.2	0741 0.8	1326 0.2	2018 0.8
23 TH	0137 0.3	0836 0.7	1407 0.3	2052 0.8
9 TH	0209 0.2	0844 0.8	1436 0.2	2121 0.8
24 F	0234 0.3	0930 0.7	1509 0.3	2143 0.7
10 F	0322 0.2	0955 0.8	1548 0.2	2229 0.8
25 SA	0342 0.3	1033 0.7	1618 0.3	2241 0.7
11 SA	0439 0.2	1108 0.8	1700 0.2	2336 0.9
26 SU	0459 0.3	1139 0.7	1723 0.3	2340 0.8
12 SU	0548 0.2	1214 0.8	1802 0.2	
27 M	0601 0.3	1233 0.7	1815 0.3	
13 M	0035 0.9	0645 0.1	1310 0.9	1855 0.1
28 TU	0032 0.8	0647 0.2	1319 0.8	1857 0.3
14 TU	0129 0.9	0736 0.1	1402 0.9	1943 0.1
29 W	0119 0.9	0726 0.2	1401 0.8	1937 0.2
15 W	0220 0.9	0823 0.1	1453 0.9	2029 0.1
30 TH	0204 0.9	0804 0.2	1442 0.9	2016 0.2

JULY

Day	Time m	Time m	Time m	Time m
1 F	0248 0.9	0842 0.1	1522 0.9	2056 0.2
16 SA	0344 0.9	0931 0.1	1608 0.9	2141 0.1
2 SA	0331 0.9	0920 0.1	1603 1.0	2137 0.1
17 SU	0425 0.9	1006 0.1	1646 0.9	2218 0.1
3 SU	0414 1.0	0959 0.1	1643 1.0	2219 0.1
18 M	0504 0.9	1040 0.1	1722 0.9	2253 0.1
4 M	0457 1.0	1038 0.1	1725 1.0	2303 0.1
19 TU	0541 0.9	1112 0.1	1757 0.9	2328 0.2
5 TU	0541 1.0	1120 0.1	1809 1.0	2349 0.1
20 W	0619 0.8	1145 0.2	1832 0.9	
6 W	0628 0.9	1205 0.1	1858 1.0	
21 TH	0004 0.2	0657 0.8	1221 0.2	1909 0.8
7 TH	0040 0.2	0721 0.9	1257 0.2	1951 0.9
22 F	0043 0.2	0740 0.7	1302 0.3	1951 0.8
8 F	0140 0.2	0820 0.8	1358 0.2	2051 0.9
23 SA	0129 0.3	0828 0.7	1355 0.3	2038 0.7
9 SA	0248 0.2	0926 0.8	1511 0.3	2158 0.8
24 SU	0228 0.3	0926 0.7	1508 0.4	2136 0.7
10 SU	0410 0.2	1043 0.8	1635 0.3	2312 0.8
25 M	0353 0.3	1040 0.7	1637 0.4	2245 0.7
11 M	0535 0.2	1158 0.8	1751 0.2	
26 TU	0525 0.3	1154 0.7	1745 0.3	2355 0.8
12 TU	0020 0.8	0638 0.2	1301 0.8	1848 0.2
27 W	0621 0.3	1250 0.8	1834 0.3	
13 W	0119 0.9	0729 0.1	1355 0.9	1936 0.2
28 TH	0052 0.8	0703 0.2	1337 0.8	1916 0.2
14 TH	0211 0.9	0813 0.1	1443 0.9	2020 0.1
29 F	0142 0.9	0742 0.1	1419 0.9	1957 0.2
15 F	0259 0.9	0854 0.1	1528 0.9	2102 0.1
30 SA	0228 0.9	0821 0.1	1501 1.0	2038 0.1
31 SU	0313 1.0	0900 0.1	1542 1.0	2120 0.1

AUGUST

Day	Time m	Time m	Time m	Time m
1 M	0357 1.0	0939 0.0	1623 1.1	2203 0.1
16 TU	0433 0.9	1008 0.1	1646 1.0	2222 0.1
2 TU	0440 1.0	1019 0.0	1705 1.1	2246 0.1
17 W	0505 0.9	1037 0.1	1716 1.0	2253 0.1
3 W	0524 1.0	1059 0.1	1748 1.1	2329 0.1
18 TH	0537 0.9	1107 0.2	1745 1.0	2324 0.2
4 TH	0610 1.0	1141 0.1	1834 1.0	
19 F	0609 0.9	1137 0.2	1817 0.9	2356 0.2
5 F	0016 0.1	0700 0.9	1229 0.2	1925 1.0
20 SA	0646 0.8	1210 0.3	1855 0.9	
6 SA	0111 0.2	0757 0.9	1325 0.3	2023 0.9
21 SU	0033 0.3	0733 0.7	1253 0.3	1943 0.8
7 SU	0218 0.3	0903 0.8	1440 0.3	2132 0.8
22 M	0125 0.3	0832 0.7	1402 0.4	2042 0.7
8 M	0351 0.3	1024 0.8	1621 0.3	2256 0.8
23 TU	0252 0.4	0946 0.7	1552 0.4	2157 0.7
9 TU	0530 0.3	1150 0.8	1748 0.3	
24 W	0450 0.3	1114 0.7	1718 0.4	2322 0.8
10 W	0014 0.8	0633 0.2	1256 0.8	1844 0.3
25 TH	0555 0.3	1221 0.8	1811 0.3	
11 TH	0115 0.8	0718 0.2	1347 0.9	1927 0.2
26 F	0029 0.8	0639 0.2	1311 0.9	1854 0.2
12 F	0203 0.9	0757 0.1	1430 0.9	2006 0.2
27 SA	0121 0.9	0718 0.1	1354 0.9	1936 0.1
13 SA	0246 0.9	0832 0.1	1508 1.0	2043 0.1
28 SU	0208 1.0	0756 0.1	1436 1.1	2017 0.1
14 SU	0324 0.9	0906 0.1	1543 1.0	2117 0.1
29 M	0252 1.1	0835 0.1	1519 1.1	2100 0.0
15 M	0400 0.9	0937 0.1	1616 1.0	2151 0.1
30 TU	0336 1.1	0915 0.0	1600 1.1	2142 0.0
31 W	0420 1.1	0955 0.0	1642 1.1	2224 0.0

Chart Datum: 0·25 metres below Alicante Datum (Mean Sea Level, Alicante)
HAT is 1·2 metres above Chart Datum

TIME ZONE -0100 (Gibraltar Standard Time) **Subtract 1 hour for UT** For Gibraltar Summer Time add ONE hour in **non-shaded areas**	**GIBRALTAR** LAT 36°08'N LONG 5°21'W TIMES AND HEIGHTS OF HIGH AND LOW WATERS	Dates in amber are **SPRINGS** Dates in yellow are **NEAPS** **2011**

SEPTEMBER

Day	Time	m	Time	m	Day	Time	m	Time	m
1 TH	0504	1.1	1036	0.1	**16** F	0458	0.9	1032	0.2
	1725	1.1	2307	0.1		1706	0.9	2249	0.2
2 F	0549	1.0	1117	0.1	**17** SA	0529	0.9	1102	0.2
	1811	1.0	2351	0.1		1738	0.9	2319	0.2
3 SA	0639	1.0	1202	0.2	**18** SU	0605	0.8	1133	0.3
	1901	1.0				1815	0.9	2353	0.3
4 SU	0042	0.2	0735	0.9	**19** M	0651	0.8	1213	0.4
	1257	0.3	☽ 2000	0.9		1903	0.8		
5 M	0151	0.3	0843	0.8	**20** TU	0039	0.4	0751	0.7
	1417	0.4	2112	0.8		1317	0.4	☽ 2004	0.8
6 TU	0335	0.4	1007	0.8	**21** W	0203	0.4	0905	0.7
	1612	0.4	2245	0.8		1513	0.4	2120	0.7
7 W	0518	0.3	1139	0.8	**22** TH	0413	0.4	1032	0.8
	1740	0.4				1646	0.4	2250	0.8
8 TH	0009	0.8	0616	0.3	**23** F	0524	0.3	1147	0.8
	1243	0.9	1830	0.3		1744	0.3		
9 F	0105	0.9	0657	0.2	**24** SA	0003	0.9	0610	0.2
	1329	0.9	1909	0.2		1241	0.9	1829	0.2
10 SA	0147	0.9	0731	0.2	**25** SU	0057	0.9	0651	0.2
	1406	1.0	1943	0.2		1326	1.0	1912	0.1
11 SU	0224	0.9	0803	0.2	**26** M	0144	1.0	0729	0.1
	1440	1.0	2016	0.2		1409	1.1	1954	0.1
12 M	0258	1.0	0834	0.1	**27** TU	0229	1.1	0809	0.1
	○ 1511	1.0	2048	0.1		● 1453	1.2	2036	0.0
13 TU	0330	1.0	0905	0.1	**28** W	0313	1.0	0850	0.1
	1541	1.0	2120	0.1		1536	1.2	2119	0.0
14 W	0400	1.0	0934	0.1	**29** TH	0358	1.1	0931	0.1
	1609	1.0	2150	0.1		1619	1.2	2201	0.0
15 TH	0429	1.0	1004	0.2	**30** F	0442	1.1	1012	0.1
	1637	1.0	2220	0.2		1703	1.1	2244	0.1

OCTOBER

Day	Time	m	Time	m	Day	Time	m	Time	m
1 SA	0528	1.0	1054	0.2	**16** SU	0500	0.9	1035	0.3
	1749	1.0	2327	0.2		1711	0.9	2251	0.3
2 SU	0617	1.0	1140	0.3	**17** M	0538	0.9	1109	0.3
	1840	1.0				1750	0.9	2325	0.3
3 M	0016	0.3	0714	0.9	**18** TU	0623	0.8	1150	0.4
	1235	0.3	1940	0.9		1838	0.8		
4 TU	0124	0.4	0821	0.8	**19** W	0010	0.4	0720	0.8
	1356	0.4	☽ 2053	0.8		1253	0.4	1938	0.8
5 W	0306	0.4	0943	0.8	**20** TH	0126	0.4	0830	0.8
	1548	0.4	2224	0.8		1436	0.4	☽ 2051	0.8
6 TH	0445	0.4	1110	0.8	**21** F	0325	0.4	0950	0.8
	1714	0.4	2348	0.8		1608	0.4	2215	0.8
7 F	0545	0.3	1213	0.9	**22** SA	0445	0.3	1108	0.9
	1803	0.3				1711	0.3	2332	0.9
8 SA	0041	0.8	0625	0.3	**23** SU	0538	0.3	1207	0.9
	1258	0.9	1840	0.3		1802	0.2		
9 SU	0122	0.9	0659	0.2	**24** M	0030	0.9	0622	0.2
	1334	1.0	1913	0.2		1257	1.0	1847	0.1
10 M	0156	0.9	0731	0.2	**25** TU	0119	1.0	0703	0.1
	1406	1.0	1945	0.2		1342	1.1	1930	0.1
11 TU	0228	1.0	0802	0.2	**26** W	0205	1.1	0745	0.1
	1436	1.0	2018	0.2		1427	1.1	● 2014	0.0
12 W	0258	1.0	0833	0.2	**27** TH	0251	1.1	0827	0.1
	1506	1.0	○ 2049	0.2		1512	1.1	2058	0.1
13 TH	0328	1.0	0904	0.2	**28** F	0337	1.1	0910	0.2
	1536	1.0	2120	0.2		1558	1.1	2141	0.1
14 F	0357	1.0	0934	0.2	**29** SA	0422	1.1	0953	0.2
	1606	1.0	2150	0.2		1644	1.1	2224	0.1
15 SA	0428	1.0	1004	0.2	**30** SU	0509	1.0	1037	0.2
	1637	1.0	2220	0.2		1732	1.0	2308	0.2
					31 M	0558	1.0	1124	0.3
						1823	0.9	2356	0.3

NOVEMBER

Day	Time	m	Time	m	Day	Time	m	Time	m
1 TU	0654	0.9	1218	0.3	**16** W	0605	0.9	1139	0.3
	1922	0.9				1822	0.9	2355	0.3
2 W	0057	0.3	0756	0.8	**17** TH	0658	0.8	1238	0.4
	1331	0.4	○ 2028	0.8		1918	0.8		
3 TH	0221	0.4	0907	0.8	**18** F	0059	0.3	0800	0.8
	1502	0.4	2145	0.8		1400	0.4	☽ 2023	0.8
4 F	0349	0.4	1022	0.8	**19** SA	0230	0.3	0911	0.8
	1623	0.4	2304	0.8		1523	0.3	2138	0.8
5 SA	0457	0.4	1128	0.8	**20** SU	0355	0.3	1025	0.9
	1722	0.3	2256	0.8		1635	0.3	2256	0.8
6 SU	0005	0.8	0546	0.3	**21** M	0502	0.3	1132	0.9
	1218	0.9	1805	0.3		1734	0.2		
7 M	0050	0.9	0625	0.2	**22** TU	0002	0.9	0555	0.2
	1257	0.9	1842	0.2		1228	1.0	1825	0.1
8 TU	0126	0.9	0701	0.2	**23** W	0057	0.9	0642	0.2
	1331	1.0	1917	0.2		1318	1.0	1913	0.1
9 W	0159	0.9	0734	0.2	**24** TH	0146	1.0	0727	0.1
	1404	1.0	1951	0.2		1406	1.1	1959	0.0
10 TH	0231	1.0	0807	0.2	**25** F	0234	1.0	0811	0.1
	1436	1.0	○ 2024	0.2		1454	1.1	● 2044	0.0
11 F	0303	1.0	0839	0.2	**26** SA	0321	1.0	0856	0.1
	1510	1.0	2057	0.2		1542	1.0	2129	0.1
12 SA	0334	1.0	0912	0.2	**27** SU	0408	1.0	0941	0.1
	1544	1.0	2129	0.2		1630	1.0	2212	0.1
13 SU	0407	1.0	0944	0.2	**28** M	0455	1.0	1026	0.2
	1619	1.0	2201	0.2		1718	1.0	2255	0.1
14 M	0443	0.9	1018	0.3	**29** TU	0542	1.0	1112	0.2
	1655	0.9	2234	0.2		1807	0.9	2340	0.2
15 TU	0521	0.9	1055	0.3	**30** W	0632	0.9	1202	0.3
	1736	0.9	2311	0.3		1900	0.8		

DECEMBER

Day	Time	m	Time	m	Day	Time	m	Time	m
1 TH	0030	0.3	0726	0.9	**16** F	0639	0.9	1223	0.2
	1300	0.3	1956	0.8		1901	0.8		
2 F	0132	0.3	0824	0.8	**17** SA	0037	0.3	0734	0.9
	1408	0.3	2056	0.8		1328	0.3	1959	0.8
3 SA	0243	0.4	0925	0.8	**18** SU	0145	0.3	0837	0.8
	1520	0.4	2203	0.7		1442	0.3	☽ 2105	0.8
4 SU	0355	0.4	1028	0.8	**19** M	0304	0.3	0947	0.8
	1629	0.3	2313	0.7		1559	0.3	2221	0.8
5 M	0500	0.3	1128	0.8	**20** TU	0425	0.3	1100	0.9
	1728	0.3	2337	0.8		1712	0.2	2337	0.8
6 TU	0011	0.8	0552	0.3	**21** W	0534	0.2	1206	0.9
	1217	0.8	1814	0.3		1813	0.1		
7 W	0057	0.8	0634	0.3	**22** TH	0040	0.8	0630	0.2
	1258	0.9	1854	0.2		1302	0.9	1906	0.1
8 TH	0135	0.8	0711	0.2	**23** F	0135	0.8	0719	0.2
	1336	0.9	1931	0.2		1354	1.0	1954	0.0
9 F	0210	0.9	0747	0.2	**24** SA	0225	0.9	0806	0.2
	1414	0.9	2006	0.2		1445	1.0	● 2039	0.0
10 SA	0245	0.9	0821	0.2	**25** SU	0313	0.9	0851	0.1
	1451	0.9	○ 2041	0.2		1533	1.0	2123	0.0
11 SU	0319	0.9	0855	0.2	**26** M	0359	1.0	0935	0.1
	1529	0.9	2115	0.2		1620	1.0	2204	0.0
12 M	0355	0.9	0931	0.2	**27** TU	0443	1.0	1017	0.1
	1607	0.9	2150	0.2		1705	0.9	2243	0.1
13 TU	0431	0.9	1007	0.2	**28** W	0525	0.9	1059	0.1
	1646	0.9	2225	0.2		1749	0.9	2322	0.1
14 W	0510	0.9	1047	0.2	**29** TH	0608	0.9	1140	0.2
	1726	0.9	2303	0.2		1834	0.8		
15 TH	0552	0.9	1130	0.2	**30** F	0002	0.2	0652	0.8
	1811	0.9	2345	0.2		1225	0.2	1919	0.8
					31 SA	0046	0.2	0739	0.8
						1315	0.3	2008	0.7

Chart Datum: 0·25 metres below Alicante Datum (Mean Sea Level, Alicante)
HAT is 1·2 metres above Chart Datum

INDEX